Prentice Hall

LITERATURE
Timeless Voices, Timeless Themes

Copper

Bronze

Silver

Gold

Platinum

The American Experience

The British Tradition

PROGRAM ADVISORS

The program advisors provided ongoing input throughout the development of Prentice Hall Literature: Timeless Voices, Timeless Themes. *Their valuable insights ensure that the perspectives of the teachers throughout the country are represented within this literature series.*

Diane Cappillo
Language Arts Department Chair
Barbara Goleman Senior High School
Miami, Florida
Facilitator at the University of Miami/Dade County Public Schools Summer Writing Institute. Past president of the Dade County Council of Teachers of English.

Anita Clay
English Instructor
Gateway Institute of Technology
St. Louis, Missouri
Former supervisory positions: Middle School Team Leader Chairman, High School English Department; Coordinator, Effective and Efficient School; Coordinator, Writing Across the Curriculum Project.

Nancy M. Fahner
Language Arts Instructor
Charlotte High School
Charlotte, Michigan
Recipient of Charlotte Teacher of the Year Award 1992. Currently working on School-to-Work Curriculum Development.

Terri Fields
Language Arts and Communication Arts Teacher,
Author
Sunnyslope High School
Phoenix, Arizona
Recipient of both Arizona Teacher of the Year and U.S. WEST Outstanding Arizona Teacher

awards. Member of the Northern Arizona University Center for Excellence in Education Advisory Council. First place award for educational writing from National Federation of Press Women.

Argelia Arizpe Guadarrama
Secondary Curriculum Coordinator
Phar–San Juan–Alamo Independent School District
San Juan, Texas
Recognized by Texas Education Agency for work on Texas Assessment of Academic Skills. Recipient of National Recognition of Positive Avenues for Student Success Program.

V. Pauline Hodges, Ph.D.
Teacher and Educational Consultant
Forgan High School
Forgan, Oklahoma
Formerly Language Arts Coordinator
Jefferson County, Colorado
Denver Professor in English Education/Reading, Colorado State University. President-elect of the National Rural Education Association. Recipient of Oklahoma Foundation for Excellence Award for Secondary Teaching 1993 and Outstanding Educator Award from the Colorado Language Arts Society.

Jennifer Huntress
Secondary Language Arts Coordinator
Putnam City Schools
Oklahoma City, Oklahoma
National trainer for writing evaluation, curriculum integration, and alternative assessment strategies. Instructor of language arts methods classes at Oklahoma City University.

Angelique McMath Jordan
English Teacher
Dunwoody High School
Dunwoody, Georgia
*Teacher of the Year at Dunwoody
High School, 1991.*

Nancy L. Monroe
English and Speed Reading Teacher
Bolton High School
Alexandria, Louisiana
*Past president of the Rapides Council of Teachers
of English and the Louisiana Council
of Teachers. National Advanced Placement
Consultant.*

Rosemary A. Naab
English Chairperson
Ryan High School
Archdiocese of Philadelphia
Philadelphia, Pennsylvania
*English Curriculum Committee.
Awarded Curriculum Quill Award by the Archdiocese
of Philadelphia for the development of effective strate-
gies for the teaching of writing and the integration of
technology and writing.*

Ann Okamura
English Teacher
Laguna Creek High School
Elk Grove, California
*Participant of the College Board Pacesetters Program.
Formerly K–12 District Resource Specialist in Writing,
Foreign Languages, Lay Readers, District Writing,
Competency Assessment, and the Elk Grove Writing
Project. A fellow in the San Joaquin Valley Writing
Project and California Literature Project.*

Jonathan L. Schatz
English Teacher/Team Leader
Tappan Zee High School
Orangeburg, New York
*Creator of a literacy program to assist students
with reading in all content areas.*

John Scott
English Teacher
Hampton High School
Hampton, Virginia
*Recipient of the Folger Shakespeare Library
Renaissance Forum Award. Master Teacher
in Shakespeare who produces workshops for
professional development at the local, state,
and national levels. Selected to participate in four
National Endowment for the Humanities teacher
programs.*

Ken Spurlock
Assistant Principal
Boone County High School
Florence, Kentucky
*Former English Teacher at Holmes High School
and district writing supervisor. Past president of
Kentucky Council of Teachers of English.*

Prentice Hall
LITERATURE
Timeless Voices, Timeless Themes

THE AMERICAN EXPERIENCE

PRENTICE HALL
Upper Saddle River, New Jersey
Needham, Massachusetts

ISBN 0-13-434059-0

3 4 5 6 7 8 9 10   02 01 00 99 98

PRENTICE HALL
Simon & Schuster Education Group

STAFF CREDITS FOR PRENTICE HALL LITERATURE

(in alphabetical order)

Advertising and Promotion: Judy Goldstein, Carol Leslie, Rip Odell, Rob Richman, Ann Shea

Business Office: Emily Heins

Design: Laura Jane Bird, Sarah Carroll, Annemarie Franklin, Monduane Harris, Jim O'Shea, AnnMarie Roselli, Gerry Schrenk

Director of Language Arts: Douglas McCollum

Editorial: Ellen Bowler, Pam Cardiff, Megan Chill, Barbara W. Coe, Donna C. DiCuffa, Elisa Mui Eiger, Amy E. Fleming, Philip Fried, Rebecca Z. Graziano, James S. Jeglikowski, Jacqueline M. Regan

Electronic Publishing: Gregory Myers, Cleasta Wilburn

Manufacturing: Katherine Clarke, Rhett Conklin

Market Research: Eileen Friend, Joan McCulley

Marketing: Glenn E. Bell, Jean Faillace, Belinda Loh

Media Resources: Martha Conway, Libby Forsyth, Melanie Jones, Vickie Menanteaux, Maureen Raymond, Melissa Shustyk, Keirsten Wallace

National Language Arts Consultants: Linda Alexander, Kelly Ford, Karen Massey, Gail Witt

Permissions: Doris Robinson

PrePress Production: Kathryn Dix, William J. Hanna

Production: Christina Burghard, Holly Gordon, Elizabeth Torjussen

Technology: Rick Hickox

Art/Photograph Credits begin on p. 1226.

ACKNOWLEDGMENTS

Grateful acknowledgment is made to the following for permission to reprint copyrighted material:

Addison-Wesley Longman Inc.
"Gardening" from *Mama Makes Up Her Mind* by Bailey White. Copyright © 1993 by Bailey White. Reprinted by permission of Addison-Wesley Longman Inc.

American Demographics Inc.
"Most Immigrants Find the Dream" by Brad Edmondson from *Forecast*, May 1997. © 1997 Cowles Business Media. Reprinted with permission of American Demographics Inc.

(Acknowledgments continue on p. 1220)

Beginnings–1750

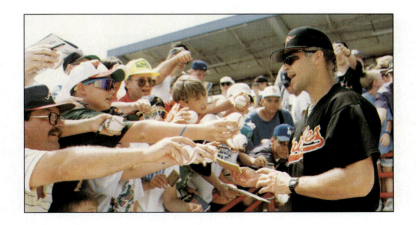

A Nation Is Born (1750–1800)

PART 3   THE EMERGING AMERICAN IDENTITY: DEFINING AN AMERICAN

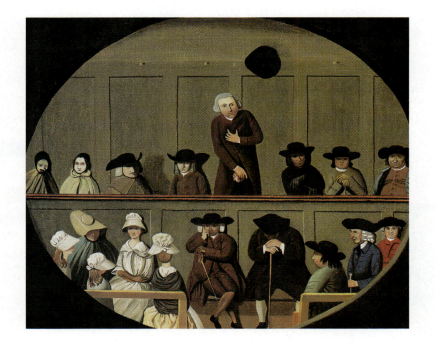

A Growing Nation (1800–1870)

Unit 3

Division, Reconciliation, and Expansion (1850–1914)

PART I   THE EMERGING AMERICAN IDENTITY: A NATION DIVIDED

PART 2   FOCUS ON LITERARY FORMS: DIARIES, JOURNALS, AND LETTERS

Unit 4

Disillusion, Defiance, and Discontent (1914–1946)

Unit 5

The Harlem Renaissance

Prosperity and Protest (1946–Present)

PART 1   LITERATURE CONFRONTS THE EVERYDAY

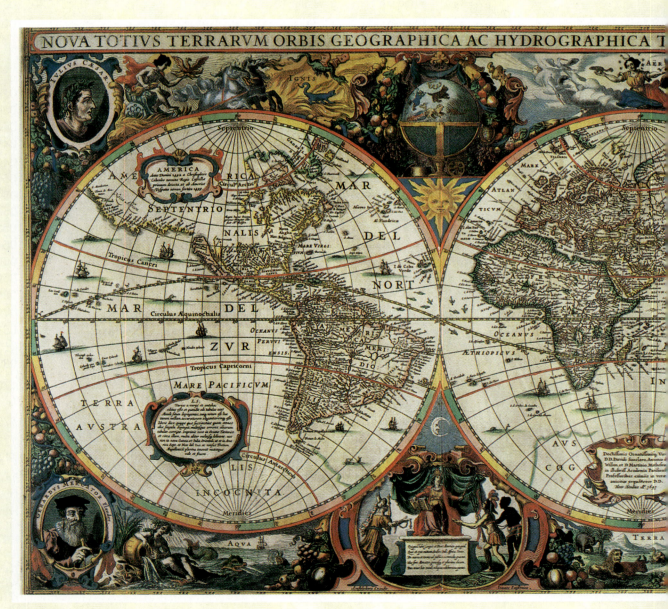

World Map, 1630, The Huntington Library, Art Collections and Botanical Gardens, San Marino, CA

Beginnings – 1750

"We shall be as a City upon a Hill, the eyes of all people are upon us; so that if we shall deal falsely with our God in this work we have undertaken and so cause him to withdraw his present help from us, we shall be made a story and a by-word through the world."

—John Winthrop, Governor of the Massachusetts Bay Colony

Timeline
1490–1750

American Events

- **1492** Native American groups first encounter European explorers.
  - **1492** Christopher Columbus lands in the Bahamas. ◄
  - **1515** Juan Ponce de Léon lands on the Florida peninsula.
  - **1515** Vasco Núñez de Balboa reaches the Pacific Ocean.
  - **1540** Francisco Vázquez de Coronado explores the Southwest.

IR FIRST PRINTING PRESS BROUGHT TO AMERICA.

- **1565** St. Augustine, Florida, first permanent settlement in U.S., founded by Pedro Menendez.
- **1586** English colony at Roanoke Island disappears; known as the Lost Colony.
- **1590** Iroquois Confederacy established to stop warfare among the Five Nations.

- **1607** First permanent English settlement at Jamestown, Virginia.
- **1608** Captain John Smith writes *A True Relation . . . of Virginia.* ◄
  - **1619** House of Burgesses established in Virginia; first legislature in the Western Hemisphere.
  - **1620** Pilgrims land at Plymouth, Massachusetts. ►

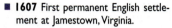

- **1620** William Bradford begins writing *Of Plymouth Plantation;* completed in 1651.
- **1636** Harvard College founded in Massachusetts.
- **1640** First printing press in English-speaking North America arrives in Massachusetts. ◄
- **1640** *Bay Psalm Book* published; first book printed in the colonies.

World Events

- **1499** England: 20,000 die in London plague.
- **1503** Italy: Leonardo da Vinci paints the *Mona Lisa.*
- **1508** Italy: Michelangelo paints ceiling of Sistine Chapel. ▲
- **1518** Africa: Barbarossa drives the Spanish from Algiers and most of Algeria.
  - **1519** Spain: Chocolate introduced to Europe.
  - **1520** Magellan sails around the world. ◄
  - **1520** Mexico: Cortez conquers Aztecs.
  - **1531** Peru: Pizarro conquers Incas.

- **1558** England: Elizabeth I inherits throne. ►
- **1560** Brazil: Smallpox epidemic kills millions.
- **1566** Belgium: Bruegel paints *The Wedding Dance.*
- **1580** France: Montaigne's *Essays* published.

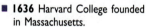

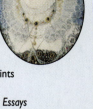

- **1595** England: Shakespeare completes *A Midsummer Night's Dream.*
- **1605** Spain: Cervantes publishes Part I of *Don Quixote.*
- **1609** Italy: Galileo builds first telescope. ▲
- **1630** Japan: All Europeans expelled.
- **1633** England: John Donne publishes *Poems.*
- **1640** India: English establish settlement at Madras.
- **1642** Holland: Rembrandt paints *Night Watch.*
- **1643** England: Civil War begins.
- **1644** China: Ming Dynasty ends. ◄

1646	1698	1750

- **1647** Massachusetts establishes free public schools.
- **1650** London publication of Anne Bradstreet's *The Tenth Muse . . .*, a collection of poems.
- **1674** John Eliot, Apostle to the Indians, publishes *The Indian Primer.*

- **1675** King Philip, chief of the Wampanoags, begins raiding New England frontier towns. ▲
- **1676** Nat Bacon's ill-fated rebellion launched against Virginia's governor Berkeley. ▶
- **1692** Salem witchcraft trials result in the execution of twenty people.

- **1710** Smallpox epidemic breaks out in Boston; Cotton Mather argues for inoculation.
- **1735** John Peter Zenger acquitted of libel, furthering freedom of the press.
- **1741** Great Awakening, a series of religious revivals, begins to sweep the colonies. ▶
- **1741** Jonathan Edwards first delivers his sermon *Sinners in the Hands of an Angry God.*

- **1652** South Africa: First Dutch settlers arrive.
- **1664** France: Molière's *Tartuffe* first performed.
- **1667** England: Milton publishes *Paradise Lost.*
- **1680** China: All ports opened to foreign trade.
- **1691** India: Calcutta founded by British.

- **1702** England: First daily newspaper begins publication.
- **1720** England: Daniel Defoe publishes *Robinson Crusoe.*
- **1721** Germany: Bach composes *Brandenburg Concertos.* ▶
- **1726** England: Jonathan Swift publishes *Gulliver's Travels.*
- **1727** Brazil: First coffee planted. ◀
- **1748** France: Montesquieu publishes *The Spirit of Laws.*

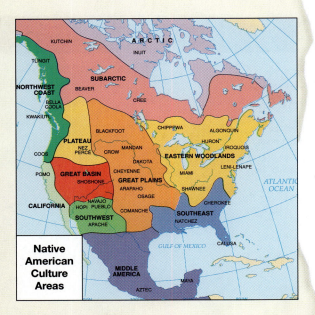

Native American Culture Areas

▲ **Read a Map** As Native Americans spread out to populate North America, they developed varied cultures. (a) Name two tribes in the Southwest culture area. (b) With which area are the Cherokees associated? (c) What geographic features might have led to the development of different ways of life?

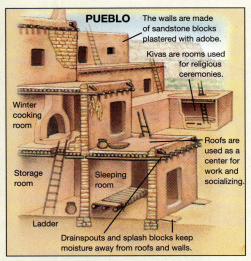

PUEBLO The walls are made of sandstone blocks plastered with adobe.

Kivas are rooms used for religious ceremonies.

Winter cooking room

Roofs are used as a center for work and socializing.

Storage room

Sleeping room

Ladder

Drainspouts and splash blocks keep moisture away from roofs and walls.

▲ **Connect** How does this pueblo dwelling reflect the southwestern environment in which it was built?

The Story of the Times
Beginnings to 1750

More than a century after European explorers first landed in North America, there were still no permanent settlements in the Western Hemisphere north of St. Augustine, Florida. By 1607, however, a small group of English settlers was struggling to survive on a marshy island in the James River in the present state of Virginia. In 1611, Thomas Dale, governor of the colony, wrote a report to the king expressing the colonists' determination to succeed. Despite disease and starvation, Jamestown did survive.

The first settlers were entranced by the native inhabitants they met. They did not at first realize that these earlier Americans, like Europeans, had cultural values and literary traditions of their own. Their literature was entirely oral, for the tribes of North America had not yet developed writing systems. This extensive oral literature, along with the first written works of the colonists, forms the beginning of the American literary heritage.

Historical Background

When Christopher Columbus reached North America in 1492, the continent was already populated, though sparsely, by several hundred Native American tribes. Europeans did not encounter these tribes all at one time. Explorers from different nations came into contact with them at different times. As we now know, these widely dispersed tribes of Native Americans differed greatly from one another in language, government, social organization, customs, housing, and methods of survival.

The Native Americans No one knows for certain when or how the first Americans arrived in what is now the United States. It may have been as recently as 12,000 years ago or as long ago as 70,000 years. Even if the shorter estimate is correct, Native Americans have been on the continent thirty times longer than the Europeans.

Colonists from Europe did not begin arriving on the east coast of North America until the late 1500's.

What were the earliest Americans doing for those many centuries? To a great extent, the answer is shrouded in mystery. No written story of the Native Americans exists. Archaeologists have deduced a great deal from artifacts, however, and folklorists have recorded a rich variety of songs, legends, and myths.

What we do know is that the Native Americans usually, but by no means always, greeted the earliest European settlers as friends. They instructed the newcomers in their agriculture and woodcraft, introduced them to maize, beans, squash, maple sugar, snowshoes, toboggans, and birch bark canoes. Indeed, many more of the European settlers would have succumbed to the bitter northeastern winters had it not been for the help of these first Americans.

Pilgrims and Puritans A small group of Europeans sailed from England on the *Mayflower* in 1620. The passengers were religious reformers—Puritans who were critical of the Church of England. Having given up hope of "purifying" the Church from within, they chose instead to withdraw from the Church. This action earned them the name Separatists. We know them as the Pilgrims. They landed in North America and established a settlement at what is now Plymouth, Massachusetts. With help from friendly tribes of Native Americans, the Plymouth settlement managed to survive the rigors of North America. The colony never grew very large, however. Eventually, it was engulfed by the Massachusetts Bay Colony, the much larger settlement to the north.

Like the Plymouth Colony, the Massachusetts Bay Colony was also founded by religious reformers. These reformers, however, did not withdraw from the Church of England. Unlike the Separatists, they were Puritans who intended instead to reform the Church from within. In America, the Puritans hoped to establish what John Winthrop, governor of the Colony, called a "city upon a hill," a model community guided in all aspects by the Bible. Their form of government would be a theocracy, a state under the immediate guidance of God.

▲ **Make an Inference** What Puritan values does this painting illustrate?

▲ **Analyze Art** These Puritan children posed for a portrait about 1670. Like other Puritans, they could expect to live twice as long as children in other colonies, where life was harder. What evidence of prosperity do you see in this painting?

▲ **Draw a Conclusion** John White, a colonist at Roanoke, made these vivid drawings and others that gave many Europeans the first glimpse of the plants and animals of the Americas. Why would White's drawings be of value to Europeans who planned to settle in North America?

Among the Puritans' central beliefs were the ideas that human beings exist for the glory of God and that the Bible is the sole expression of God's will. They also believed in predestination—John Calvin's doctrine that God has already decided who will achieve salvation and who will not. The elect, or saints, who are to be saved cannot take election for granted, however. Because of that, all devout Puritans searched their souls with great rigor and frequency for signs of grace. The Puritans felt that they could accomplish good only through continual hard work and self-discipline. When people today speak of the "Puritan ethic," that is what they mean.

Puritanism was in decline throughout New England by the early 1700's, as more liberal Protestant congregations attracted followers. A reaction against this new freedom, however, set in around 1720. The Great Awakening, a series of religious revivals led by such eloquent ministers as the famous Jonathan Edwards and George Whitefield, swept through the colonies. The Great Awakening attracted thousands of converts to many Protestant groups, but it did little to revive old-fashioned Puritanism. Nevertheless, Puritan ideals of hard work, frugality, self-improvement, and self-reliance are still regarded as basic American virtues.

The Southern Planters The Southern Colonies differed from New England in climate, crops, social organization, and religion. Prosperous coastal cities grew up in the South, just as in the North, but beyond the southern cities lay large plantations, not small farms. Despite its romantic image, the plantation was in fact a large-scale agricultural enterprise and a center of commerce. Up to a thousand people, many of them enslaved, might live and work on a single plantation.

The first black slaves were brought to Virginia in 1619, a year before the Pilgrims landed at Plymouth. The plantation system and the institution of slavery were closely connected from the very beginning, although slavery existed in every colony, including Massachusetts.

Most of the plantation owners were Church of England members who regarded themselves as aristocrats. The first generation of owners, the men who established the great plantations, were ambitious, energetic, self-disciplined, and resourceful, just as the Puritans were. The way of life on most plantations, however, was more sociable and elegant than that of any Puritan. By 1750, Puritanism was in decline everywhere, and the plantation system in the South was just reaching its peak.

Literature of the Period

It was an oddly assorted group that established the foundations of American literature: the Native Americans with their oral traditions, the Puritans with their preoccupation with sin and salvation, and the southern planters with their busy social lives. Indeed, much of the literature that the colonists read was not produced in the colonies—it came from England. Yet, by 1750, there were the clear beginnings of a native literature that would one day be honored throughout the English-speaking world.

Native American Tradition For a long time, Native American literature was viewed mainly as folklore. The consequence was that song lyrics, hero tales, migration legends, and accounts of the creation were studied more for their content than for their literary qualities. In an oral tradition, the telling of the tale may change with each speaker, and the words are almost sure to change over time. Thus, no fixed versions of such literary works exist. Still, in cases where the words of Native American lyrics or narratives have been captured in writing, the language is often poetic and moving. As might be expected in an oral setting, oratory was much prized among Native Americans. The names of certain orators, such as Logan and Red Jacket, were widely known.

The samples of Native American literature in this unit reveal the depth and power of those original American voices.

"In Adam's Fall/We Sinned All" Just as religion dominated the lives of the Puritans, it also dominated their writings—most of which would not be considered literary works by modern standards. Typically, the Puritans wrote theological studies, hymns, histories, biographies, and autobiographies. The purpose of such writing was to provide spiritual insight and instruction. When Puritans wrote for themselves in journals

▲ **Make an Inference** Like native artists throughout Central America, Mexican artists crafted elaborate works of gold. Their designs were rich in symbolism and natural references. How do you think the fine quality of gold ornaments like this one reinforced the European desire to conquer the Western Hemisphere?

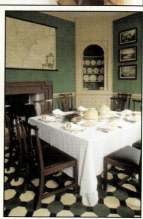

▲ **Compare and Contrast** These rooms from Colonial Williamsburg illustrate the living quarters of white landowners and African slaves. (a) What do these rooms have in common? (b) What are the major differences?

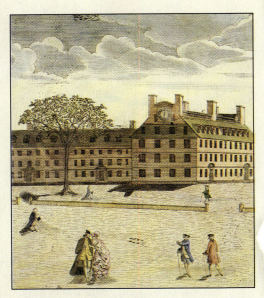

▲ Interpret Place Names The Puritans founded Harvard College at Newtowne in 1636. Three years later, they renamed the city Cambridge to honor the British city where many of the colonists had studied. What does this fact reveal about the group who fled England?

▲ Link Past to Present Many of the books printed in the colonies were religious publications. Compare this 1640 hymnal cover with covers of modern magazines and printed material.

or diaries, their aim was the serious kind of self-examination they practiced in other aspects of their lives. The Puritans produced neither fiction nor drama because they regarded both as sinful. The Puritans did write poetry, however, as a vehicle of spiritual enlightenment. Although they were less concerned with a poem's literary form than with its message, some writers were naturally more gifted than others. A few excellent Puritan poets emerged in the 1600's, among them Anne Bradstreet and Edward Taylor. Anne Bradstreet's moving, personal voice and Edward Taylor's devotional intensity shine through the conventional Puritanism of their themes.

The Puritans had a strong belief in education for both men and women. In 1636, they founded Harvard College to ensure a well-educated ministry. Two years later, they set up the first printing press in the colonies. In 1647, free public schools were established in Massachusetts. *The New England Primer*, first published around 1690, combined instruction in spelling and reading with moralistic teachings, such as "In Adam's fall/We sinned all."

One of the first books printed in the colonies was the *Bay Psalm Book*, the standard hymnal of the time. Increase Mather, one of the book's three authors, served for many years as pastor of the North Church in Boston. He was also the author of some 130 books. *Cases of Conscience Concerning Evil Spirits*, published in 1693, was a discourse on the Salem witchcraft trials of the previous year. The trials, conducted in an atmosphere of hysteria, resulted in the hanging of twenty people as witches.

Increase's eldest son, Cotton Mather, far exceeded his father's literary output, publishing at least 400 works in his lifetime. Cotton Mather, like his father, is remembered in part because of his connection with the Salem witchcraft trials. Although he did not actually take part in the trials, his works on witchcraft had helped to stir up some of the hysteria. Still, Cotton Mather was one of the most learned men of his time, a power in the state and a notable author. His theory of writing was simple (although his writing was not): The more information a work contains, the better its style.

In fact, the Puritans in general had a theory of literary style. They believed in a plain style of writing—one in which clear statement is the highest goal. An ornate or clever style would be a sign of vanity and, as such, would not be in accordance with God's will. Despite the restrictions built into their life and literature, the Puritans succeeded in producing a small body of excellent writing.

Southern Voices Considering the number of brilliantly literate statesmen who would later emerge in the South, especially in Virginia, it seems surprising that only a few notable southern writers appeared prior to 1750. As in Puritan New England, those who were educated produced a substantial amount of writing, but it was mostly of a practical nature. For example, John Smith, the leader of the settlement at Jamestown, Virginia, wrote *The General History of Virginia* to describe his experiences for Europeans. In addition to accounts like Smith's, letters written by southern planters also provide insight into this time period. Unlike the Puritans, southerners did not oppose fiction or drama, and the first theater in America opened in Williamsburg, Virginia, in 1716.

The Planter From Westover The important literature of the pre-Revolutionary South can be summed up in one name—William Byrd. Byrd lived at Westover, a magnificent plantation on the James River bequeathed to him by his wealthy father. Commissioned in 1728 to survey the boundary line between Virginia and North Carolina, Byrd kept a journal of his experiences. That journal served as the basis for his book, *The History of the Dividing Line,* which was circulated in manuscript form among Byrd's friends in England. Published nearly a century after Byrd's death, the book was immediately recognized as a minor humorous masterpiece. More of Byrd's papers were published later, establishing his reputation as the finest writer in the pre-Revolutionary South.

The writers whose work appears in this unit are not the great names in American literature. They are the founders, the men and women who laid the groundwork for the towering achievements that followed. The modest awakening of American literature seen in this unit had repercussions that echoed down the years.

▲ **Make an Inference** John Smith was the leader of the Jamestown settlement at Virginia. What does the clothing in this portrait reveal about his social stature or rank?

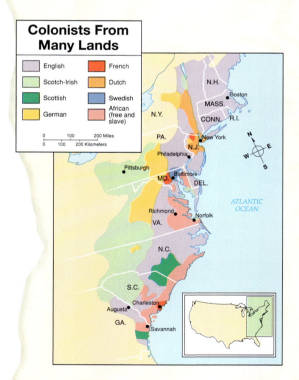

Colonists From Many Lands

- English
- Scotch-Irish
- Scottish
- German
- French
- Dutch
- Swedish
- African (free and slave)

▲ **Draw a Conclusion** New immigrants from Europe, as well as enslaved Africans, carried their own cultures to the American colonies. (a) Which group settled in all the colonies? (b) What would explain this?

The Development of American English

OUR NATIVE AMERICAN HERITAGE

by Richard Lederer

If you had been one of the early explorers or settlers of North America, you would have found many things in your new environment unknown to you. The handiest way of filling voids in your vocabulary would have been to ask local Native Americans what words they used. The early colonists began borrowing words from friendly Native Americans almost from the moment of their first contact, and many of those shared words have remained in our everyday language.

Anglicizing Pronouncing many of the Native American words was difficult for the early explorers and settlers. In many instances, they shortened and simplified the names. For example, *otchock* became "woodchuck," *rahaugcum* turned to "raccoon," and the smelly *segankw* transformed into a "skunk." The North American menagerie brought more new words into the English language including caribou (Micmac), chipmunk (Ojibwa), moose (Algonquian), muskrat (Abenaki), and porgy (Algonquian).

The Poetry of Place Names
William Penn said he did not know "a language spoken in Europe that hath words of more sweetness and greatness." To Walt Whitman, *Monongahela* "rolls with venison richness upon the palate." Some of our loveliest place names—*Susquehanna, Shenandoah, Rappahannock*—began life as Native American words. Such names are the stuff of poetry.

If you look at a map of the United States, you will realize how freely settlers used words of Indian origin to name our states, cities, towns, mountains, lakes, rivers, and ponds. Five of our six Great Lakes and exactly half of our states have names that were borrowed from Native American words. Many other bodies of water and land have taken on names we have come to know as part of the American language.

Activities

1. Brainstorm for a list of the states that have Native American names. Research the origin of each name.

2. With help from an encyclopedia or other source, find out what Native American tribes live or once lived in your part of the country. Do their languages survive in many place names? Pick out ten names of places in your state—cities, towns, mountains, or bodies of water—that have Native American names. Try to find their exact origins. What can you find out about the history of your state that will help explain why these names were chosen?

Food

squash (Natick)	pecan (Algonquian)
hominy (Algonquian)	pone (Algonquian)
pemmican (Cree)	succotash (Narraganset)

People

sachem (Narraganset)	papoose (Narraganset)
squaw (Massachuset)	mugwump (Natick)

Native American life

moccasin (Chippewa)	toboggan (Algonquian)
tomahawk (Algonquian)	wigwam (Abenaki)
tepee (Dakota)	caucus (Algonquian)
pow-wow (Narraganset)	wampum (Massachuset)
bayou (Choctaw)	potlatch (Chinook)
hogan (Navajo)	hickory (Algonquian)
kayak (Inuit)	totem (Ojibwa)

PART 1 Meeting of Cultures

Oneida Chieftain Shikellamy
Unknown American Artist
Philadelphia Museum of Art

Guide for Interpreting

Christopher Columbus
(1451–1506)

Not much is known about the early life of Christopher Columbus, one of history's most famous explorers. Evidently, he left his home in Genoa, Italy, and went to sea at a young age. At age 25, he was shipwrecked off the coast of Portugal. Once back on land, Columbus studied mapmaking and navigation. He also learned Latin and read Marco Polo's account of the riches of Asia.

Between 1480 and 1482, Columbus sailed to the Azores and to the Canary Islands off Africa. He then began to dream of more challenging voyages.

One goal became the focus of Columbus's life: reaching the fabled cities of Asia by sailing westward around the world.

First, Columbus tried to convince King John II of Portugal to fund a westward voyage. When his requests were rejected there, Columbus sought funding from other European rulers. After a series of unsuccessful attempts, Columbus won the support of Queen Isabella of Spain.

A Hard Bargain Queen Isabella and her husband, King Ferdinand, agreed to finance Columbus's first voyage in 1492. In forging the agreements, the explorer had negotiated favorable terms. In addition to funding, he asked for and received the right to rule any lands he conquered. He would also be entitled to 10 percent of all wealth from those lands.

The Famous Voyage Columbus set sail on August 3. On October 12, he reached one of the Bahama islands, which he mistook for an island off India. Columbus named the island San Salvador. Then he continued to explore the Caribbean. Over the next twelve years, he made three more transatlantic voyages, ever convinced that he had reached Asia and always hopeful of finding Marco Polo's fabled cities.

◆ Background for Understanding

HISTORY: THE ERA OF EXPLORATION

In the 1450's, the only known way to India from Europe involved traveling through Turkey. When the Turks announced a new tax on Europe's profitable overland trade with India in 1453, Portugal and Spain began to look for an alternate sea route to India. Their search brought Europe into contact with North and South America. Within a century, much of these two vast continents would come under European control. It was not until 1498 that Vasco da Gama found the all-sea route to India—around the horn of Africa.

As this map shows, Columbus's voyages took him from Lisbon, Portugal, to Palos, Spain, and the Canary Islands before crossing the Atlantic. He landed first on the island of San Salvador, where this account begins.

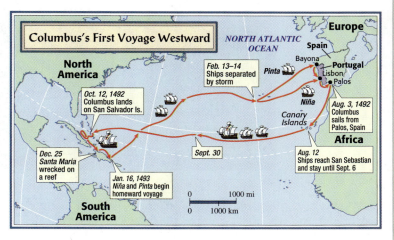

Columbus's First Voyage Westward

from Journal of the First Voyage to America

◆ *Literature and Your Life*

CONNECT YOUR EXPERIENCE

"If you can dream it, you can do it," one motivational motto asserts. However, to fulfill the desire to circle the globe in a boat or discover the cure for a deadly disease takes much more than sheer will. A dreamer needs financial resources. Even Christopher Columbus had to secure and retain backers for his voyages. Many of his journal entries stressed the rich potential of the new lands, so that, upon reading them, Queen Isabella would decide to continue her sponsorship.

Journal Writing How would you have sold the idea of traveling around the globe to people who believed it would not be worth the expense? Write a convincing argument in your journal.

THEMATIC FOCUS: MEETING OF CULTURES

The earliest days of European exploration of North America brought native peoples into contact with curious newcomers. What kind of things can happen when cultures first meet?

◆ Build Vocabulary

WORD ROOTS: *-flict-*

Columbus calls his ignorance of botany an *affliction*. Words like *afflict, conflict,* and *inflict* contain the root *-flict-,* meaning "to strike." An *affliction* is anything causing pain or misery.

WORD BANK

Before you read, preview this list of words from the journal.

> indications
> abundance
> exquisite
> affliction

◆ Grammar and Style

ACTION VERBS AND LINKING VERBS

Action verbs—like *anchored, found,* and *saw*—express physical or mental action. **Linking verbs**—such as *be, become,* and *look*—express a state of being. Linking verbs are followed by a noun or pronoun that renames the subject or by an adjective that describes it.

Action Verb: We <u>arrived</u> at a cape off the island.

Linking Verb: Groves of trees <u>are</u> abundant.

Action verbs make writing more lively. Notice that Columbus often relies on action verbs to describe his experience.

◆ Literary Focus

JOURNALS

The European encounters with and conquest of the Americas are recorded in the journals of the explorers. A **journal** is an individual's day-by-day account of events. It provides valuable details that can be supplied only by a participant or an eyewitness. As a record of personal reactions, a journal reveals much about the writer.

While offering insight into the life of the writer, a journal is not necessarily a reliable record of facts. The writer's impressions may color the telling of events, particularly when he or she is a participant. Journals written for publication rather than private use are even less likely to be objective. As you read Columbus's journal, look for evidence that the explorer was writing for an audience.

Reading for Success

Literal Comprehension Strategies

Before you can begin to analyze or critique a piece of literature, you must be certain that you understand what the writer is saying. Some writing you'll encounter is easy to understand—it is written plainly and uses language familiar to you. However, if a writer uses long, complex sentences, a word order you don't recognize, or language that is archaic, you may run into difficulty. These strategies will offer you pathways to understanding complex writing.

Recognize the historical context of the literature.

Knowing about the historical period in which a work was written will help you comprehend the writer's words and ideas. The introduction to this unit provides background on the period. Read the selections in the context of this information.

Reread or read ahead.

▶ Reread a sentence or a paragraph to find the connections among the words, or connect the ideas in several sentences to get the sense of a passage.
▶ Read ahead. A detail you don't understand may become clear further on.

Break down long or confusing sentences.

▶ Read sentences in meaningful sections, not word by word.
▶ Figure out the subject (what the sentence is about). Then determine what the sentence is saying about the subject. Sometimes you may need to rearrange the parts of a sentence or to take other groups of words out of the way to do this.

Use context clues.

Context refers to the words, phrases, and sentences that surround a word. You can often use clues in the context to figure out the meaning of a word. Look, for example, at this passage from Columbus's journal:

After having *dispatched* a meal, I went ashore . . .

The word *dispatched* may be unfamiliar to you, but the word *meal* provides a clue that *dispatch* probably deals in this case with eating or finishing.

Restate for understanding.

▶ Paraphrase or restate a sentence or paragraph in your own words.
▶ Summarize at appropriate points—reviewing the main points of what has happened. Notice story details that seem to be important.

Look for signal words.

Signal words indicate time order and importance or other relationships between ideas.

As you read the following passage from the journal of Columbus, notice the notes along the side. The notes demonstrate how to apply these strategies to your reading.

from # Journal of the First Voyage to America

Christopher Columbus

This account begins nine days after Columbus landed on San Salvador.

SUNDAY, OCT. 21ST [1492]. At 10 o'clock, we arrived at a cape of the island,[1] and anchored, the other vessels in company. After having dispatched a meal, I went ashore, and found no habitation save a single house, and that without an occupant; we had no doubt that the people had fled in terror at our approach, as the house was completely furnished. I suffered nothing to be touched, and went with my captains and some of the crew to view the country. This island even exceeds the others in beauty and fertility. Groves of lofty and flourishing trees are abundant, as also large lakes, surrounded and overhung by the foliage, in a most enchanting manner. Everything looked as green as in April in Andalusia.[2] The melody of the birds was so <u>exquisite</u> that

> **Read ahead** to see whether Columbus retains this level of respect for the island natives.

---

1. **the island:** San Salvador.
2. **Andalusia** (an´ də lōō´ zhə): A region of Spain.

◆ **Build Vocabulary**

exquisite (eks´ kwi zit) *adj.*: Very beautiful; delicate; carefully wrought

▲ **Critical Viewing** The astrolabe was an invention that made the age of exploration possible. What features of this one suggest that it is an instrument of navigation? **[Support]**

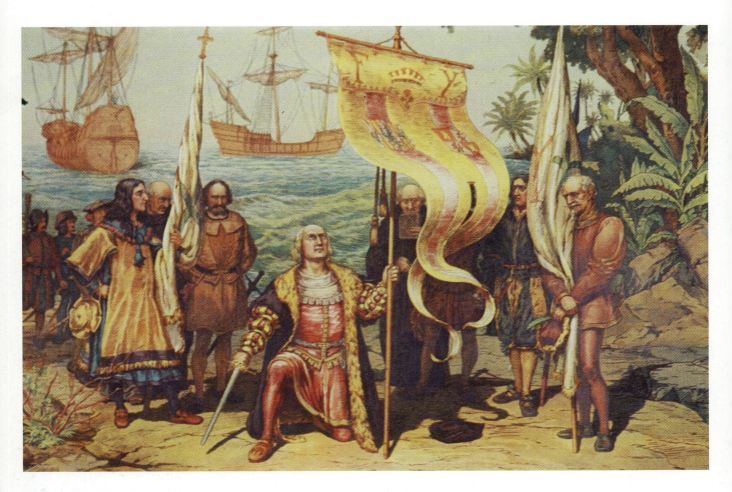

▲ **Critical Viewing** Evaluate the artist's interpretation of Columbus's landing in the Western Hemisphere. What aspects of the moment does he emphasize? **[Evaluate; Support]**

one was never willing to part from the spot, and the flocks of parrots obscured the heavens. The diversity in the appearance of the feathered tribe from those of our country is extremely curious. A thousand different sorts of trees, with their fruit were to be met with, and of a wonderfully delicious odor. It was a great <u>affliction</u> to me to be ignorant of their natures, for I am very certain they are all valuable; specimens of them and of the plants I have preserved. Going round one of these lakes, I saw a snake, which we killed, and I have kept the skin for your Highnesses; upon being discovered he took to the water,

whither[3] we followed him, as it was not deep, and dispatched him with our lances; he was seven spans[4] in length; I think there are many more such about here. I discovered also the aloe tree, and am determined to take on board the ship tomorrow, ten quintals[5] of it, as I am told it is valuable. While we were in search of some good water we came upon a village of the natives about half a league from the place where the ships lay; the

> **Reconnect** to the historical context. Columbus may want to flatter his financial backers in order to get future funding.

> Use **context clues** to discover that *dispatched* used this way means "to finish off" or "kill."

> Columbus uses the **signal words** "While we were in search of some good water" to show that the group is not just touring, but is looking with a purpose.

---

3. **whither:** To which place.
4. **spans** *n.*: Units of measure, each equal to about nine inches.
5. **quintals** (kwint´əlz) *n.*: Units of weight, each equal to 100 kilograms, or 220.46 pounds.

Reread this sentence to conclude that Columbus is maintaining his level of respect for the property of others.

inhabitants on discovering us abandoned their houses, and took to flight, carrying off their goods to the mountain. I ordered that nothing which they had left should be taken, not even the value of a pin. Presently we saw several of the natives advancing towards our party, and one of them came up to us, to whom we gave some hawk's bells and glass beads, with which he was delighted. We asked him in return, for water, and after I had gone on board the ship, the natives came down to the shore with their calabashes[6] full, and showed great pleasure in presenting us with it. I ordered more glass beads to be given them, and they promised to return the next day. It is my wish to fill all the water

Break down this long sentence by separating clauses and deleting descriptive details. You will be left with this: I want to fill the water tanks and leave. I'll sail around the island to meet the king. I want the gold he has.

casks of the ships at this place, which being executed, I shall depart immediately, if the weather serve, and sail round the island, till I succeed in meeting with the king, in order to see if I can acquire any of the gold, which I hear he possesses. Afterwards I shall set sail for another very large island which I believe to be *Cipango*,[7] according to the indications I receive from the Indians on board. They call the Island *Colba*,[8] and say there are many large ships, and sailors there. This other island they name *Bosio* [9] and inform me that it is very large; the others which lie in our course, I shall examine on the passage, and according as I find gold or spices in abundance, I shall determine what to do; at all events I am determined to proceed on to the continent, and visit the city of Guisay[10] where I shall deliver the letters of your Highnesses to the *Great Can*,[11] and demand an answer, with which I shall return.

Paraphrase this sentence this way: On my travels, I will look for riches. My main goal is to get to the continent. At Guisay, I will meet with the Great Can and act as a diplomat for the king and queen.

---

10. **Guisay** (gē sā´): The City of Heaven, the name given by Marco Polo to the residence of Kublai Khan (kōō´ blī kän), the ruler of China from A.D. 1260–1294.
11. **Great Can** (kän): Kublai Khan.

---

6. **calabashes** (kal´ ə bash´ əz) n.: Dried, hollow shells of gourds used as cups or bowls.
7. **Cipango** (si paŋ´gō): Old name for a group of islands east of Asia, probably what is now Japan.
8. **Colba** (kôl´ bə): Cuba.
9. **Bosio** (bō´ sē ō): Probably the island on which the Dominican Republic and Haiti are now located.

◆ **Build Vocabulary**

affliction (ə flik´ shən) n.: Something causing pain or suffering

indications (in´ di kā´ shənz) n.: Signs; things that point out or signify

abundance (ə bun´ dəns) n.: A great supply; more than enough

Guide for Responding

◆ *Literature and Your Life*

Reader's Response If you had sponsored Columbus's voyage, how would you feel upon reading this account of his experience?

Thematic Focus Columbus's journals record one of the earliest meetings of Europeans and native North Americans. What kind of interaction did the two groups have? What evidence does the journal offer to help you decide?

Leadership Poll With a group of classmates, list qualities that make a good leader. Then use this list to determine whether Columbus was a good leader. Share your results with the class.

☑ **Check Your Comprehension**

1. What is Columbus's reaction to the landscape?
2. According to Columbus, why are the houses empty when he and his crew arrive?
3. How long does Columbus plan to spend on this island?

Guide for Responding (continued)

◆ Critical Thinking

INTERPRET

1. How can you tell that Columbus was struck by the beauty of the island? **[Support]**
2. What appears to have been Columbus's primary consideration in choosing "specimens" to send back to Spain? **[Analyze]**
3. According to Columbus, how did the first meeting with the natives go? **[Generalize]**

EVALUATE

4. If Columbus was writing to generate further support, how well did he justify the value of his explorations? **[Make a Judgment]**

APPLY

5. How would this account be different if it had been written by a crew member? **[Hypothesize]**
6. How would this account be different if it had been written by a Native American observing the acts of the crew members? **[Hypothesize]**

◆ Reading for Success

LITERAL COMPREHENSION STRATEGIES

Review the reading strategies and the notes showing how to comprehend a writer's words and intention. Then apply them to answer the following:

1. Using context clues, identify the meaning of *habitation* on p. 15.
2. Based on the the signal word *Afterwards* on p. 17, list the four things Columbus plans to do when he leaves the island.
3. Apply historical context to explain why Columbus hoped to find "gold or spices in abundance."

◆ Literary Focus

JOURNALS

A **journal** is an individual's day-by-day account of events and personal reactions. Although most journals are kept solely as personal records, Columbus chronicled his voyage to the Americas for his investors, the king and queen of Spain.

1. Why do you think Columbus often refers to the monetary value of things he has seen?
2. What impression of the Americas does Columbus seem to be trying to convey?

◆ Build Vocabulary

USING THE WORD ROOT *-flict-*

The following words contain the root *-flict-*, which means "to strike." Look at the definitions provided. Explain how the root contributes to the meaning of each word. Then write a sentence for each.

1. conflicting: fighting; battling
2. inflict: to give or cause pain
3. affliction: the condition of pain and suffering

USING THE WORD BANK

In your notebook, write the letter of the word that is closest in meaning to the first word.

1. indication: (a) delight, (b) sign, (c) value
2. abundance: (a) overflow, (b) dearth, (c) preservation
3. exquisite: (a) shocking, (b) beautiful, (c) sorrowful
4. affliction: (a) extension, (b) gift, (c) trouble

◆ Grammar and Style

ACTION AND LINKING VERBS

Action verbs show physical or mental action and tell what the subject is doing. **Linking verbs** express a state of being and connect the subject to a word that renames or describes the subject.

Practice On your paper, indicate whether each italicized word is an action verb or a linking verb.

1. I *am* very certain that they *are* all valuable.
2. Presently, we *saw* several of the natives advancing toward our party.
3. The diversity in the appearance of the feathered tribe from those of our country *is* extremely curious.
4. I *ordered* more glass beads to be given them and they *promised* to return the next day.
5. Everything *looked* as green as in April in Andalusia.

Writing Application Write two descriptive paragraphs—one using only linking verbs and the other using only action verbs. Contrast the two paragraphs to draw a conclusion about how these verb types produce different effects. Share your conclusion with your classmates.

Build Your Portfolio

Idea Bank

Writing

1. **Crew Member's Journal** Imagine that you are one of Columbus's crew members, and rewrite this account from your point of view.

2. **Continuation** Pick up where Columbus left off. Write a journal entry in which you describe your thoughts as you explore the Caribbean. Use the map on page 12, along with your imagination, to come up with details.

3. **Comparing Journals** Columbus went on to make many more voyages, but never achieved his goal of reaching Asia. Use library sources to locate journals from one of Columbus's later voyages. Write an essay comparing the mood of the later journal entry with this one. Offer an explanation of the differences. **[Social Studies Link]**

Speaking and Listening

4. **Informative Speech** Native Americans inhabited the Americas centuries before the arrival of the European explorers. Some historians have begun to rethink Columbus's legacy. Research this issue and present a brief speech on your findings. **[Social Studies Link]**

5. **Formal Remarks at a Renaming Ceremony** Imagine that your town has decided to rename a school in honor of Columbus. Prepare the comments you would deliver at the festivities. **[Community Link]**

Projects

6. **Map** Draw a map of the island, showing where Columbus landed and the areas he explored.

7. **Columbus Collection** Demonstrate Columbus's presence in today's world. Find prominent public places named for him (parks and cities, for example) and learn how Columbus Day is celebrated in different parts of the country. Present your findings in a scrapbook.

Writing Mini-Lesson

Oral Report on the Voyage

Columbus's funding depended on his ability to sell his experiences to an audience who hadn't seen the lands he explored. As Columbus, write and present an oral report you would give to the king and queen of Spain upon your return to Europe.

Writing Skills Focus: Elaboration for Vividness

To help you listeners share your experiences, **elaborate** by providing in-depth, detailed descriptions. Include sensory details, which tell what can be seen, heard, felt, touched, or smelled. In this model, Columbus helps readers imagine what they have never experienced.

Model From the Journal

Groves of lofty and flourishing trees are abundant, as also large lakes, surrounded and overhung by the foliage in a most enchanting manner. Everything looked as green as in April in Andalusia. The melody of the birds was so exquisite that one was never willing to part from the spot, and the flocks of parrots obscured the heavens.

By using sensory details to describe the island, Columbus elaborates on his idea that the fertile landscape was beautiful.

Prewriting Imagine the landscape of the island Columbus visited. List the tropical sights, sounds, textures, smells, and tastes that he may have encountered.

Drafting As your describe the island, include as many sensory details as you can. Instead of telling your audience how lovely the island was, include details to show the lushness of the region.

Revising Add details to strengthen each image you've described. Add smells to descriptions that appeal only to sight and sound; consider adding details about texture or taste where appropriate.

Guide for Interpreting

Onondaga

As one of the original five member nations, the Onondaga were an influential force in the Iroquois Confederation, a league of Iroquoian-speaking Native Americans. The Onondaga live in what is now central New York State, in villages of wood and bark longhouses occupied by related families. Following the breakup of the Iroquois Confederation after the American Revolution, factions of Onondaga scattered to various parts of the country, but the majority returned to their ancestral valley in New York, where the Onondaga reservation now exists.

Modoc

The Modoc once lived in villages in the area of Oregon and northern California, where they farmed, fished, and hunted. Though each village was independent and had its own leaders, in times of war they would band together. In the mid-nineteenth century, the Modoc were forced onto a reservation in Oregon. A band of Modoc, under the leadership of a subchief known as Captain Jack, later fled the reservation. The result was several years of hostilities with United States troops and the eventual relocation of Captain Jack's followers to Oklahoma. They were later allowed to return to the Oregon reservation, which was dissolved in the mid-1950's.

Navajo

Today, the Navajo nation is the largest Native American nation in the United States, with more than 100,000 members. Many live on the Navajo reservation, which covers 24,000 square miles of Arizona, Utah, and New Mexico. Fierce warriors and hunters, the ancient Navajo settled in the Southwest about 1,000 years ago and eventually intermarried with the peaceful Pueblo people, who taught them to weave and raise crops. In 1864, after decades of fighting off encroaching American settlers, the Navajo were driven from their territory by the United States Army. They were eventually allowed to return to a reservation on Navajo land. Many Navajo still carry on traditional customs, living in earth-and-log structures and practicing the tribal religion.

Iroquois

The powerful Iroquois nation lived in what is now the northeastern United States. During the fourteenth century, an Iroquoian mystic and prophet named Dekanawidah traveled from village to village urging the Iroquois-speaking people to stop fighting and band together in peace and brotherhood. Dekanawidah's efforts led to the formation of the Iroquois Confederation of the Five Nations, a league of five Iroquois tribes: Mohawk, Oneida, Seneca, Cayuga, and Onondaga.

◆ Background for Understanding

CULTURE: HUMANS AND THE NATURAL WORLD

Native Americans have great respect for the natural world. They believe that each creature has its own power by which it maintains itself and affects others. Each Native American culture has its own name for this power, but early white settlers learned the Algonquian term *manito*. Manitos come in all shapes and sizes, but many Native American cultures recognize a chief manito, or Great Spirit—an invisible power that is the source of life and good for humans.

Many of the animals that helped feed and clothe the early Native Americans are revered as powerful manitos. Native American folklore and art, much of which portrays animals, reflect this great respect.

Journal Writing Look closely at the images of the moose and bear on this piece of Native American pottery. Given what you now know about Native American beliefs, explain what the arrows might symbolize.

The Earth on Turtle's Back ◆ When Grizzlies Walked Upright
from The Navajo Origin Legend ◆ from The Iroquois Constitution

◆ Literature and Your Life

CONNECT YOUR EXPERIENCE
"What was I like when I was born?" "What do you remember about my great-grandparents?" You ask questions like these for the same reason we all ask them. We share a fundamental desire to understand our origins—where we come from, our place in the world. Just as you collect stories of your family history, cultures create stories to explain the world as they know it.

THEMATIC FOCUS: MEETING OF CULTURES
Think of these origin stories as Native American responses to the universal questions of how and why we came to be. Notice as you read them that all four works are filled with images from nature.

What role does nature play in explaining—and maintaining—Native American life?

◆ Build Vocabulary

SUFFIXES: -tion
The word *deliberation* contains the frequently used suffix *-tion*, which forms a noun from the verb to which it is added. The literal meaning of *deliberation*, then, is "the act of deliberating." In *The Iroquois Constitution,* Dekanawidah tells the lords not to take actions without carefully considering them.

WORD BANK
As you read these four works, you will encounter the words on this list. Each word is defined on the page where it first appears. Preview the list before you read.

> ablutions
> protruded
> confederate
> disposition
> deliberation

◆ Grammar and Style

COMPOUND SENTENCES
In oral, as well as in written, language, compound sentences provide a natural way to link ideas. A **compound sentence** has two or more main clauses linked by a coordinating conjunction—*and, or,* or *but*—or by a semicolon. A main clause is a complete thought that contains a subject (which tells who or what the sentence is about) and a predicate (which tells what the subject is or does).

    subj.   pred.   subj.   pred.
The snow melted in his footsteps, and the water ran down in rivers.

◆ Literary Focus

ORIGIN MYTHS
The need to explain how life began gave birth to **myths**, traditional stories, often about immortal beings, that are passed down from generation to generation. When these stories recount the origins of earthly life, we call them **origin myths.** Myths often explain many other phenomena, including customs, institutions, or religious rites; natural landmarks, such as a great mountain; or events beyond people's control. As you read each myth, note who or what is responsible for the start of life on Earth, and look for explanations of natural phenomena.

◆ Reading Strategy

RECOGNIZE CULTURAL DETAILS
The Navajo Origin Legend excerpt opens with an image of the spirit men and women drying themselves with cornmeal. The gods they call appear carrying ears of corn. The myth's repeated references to corn reflect its importance to the Navajo way of life.

Literature mirrors the culture that produced it. As you read, **recognize cultural details** by noticing references to objects, animals, or practices that signal how the people of a culture live, think, or worship.

The Earth on Turtle's Back

Onondaga

Retold by Michael J. Caduto and Joseph Bruchac

Before this Earth existed, there was only water. It stretched as far as one could see, and in that water there were birds and animals swimming around. Far above, in the clouds, there was a Skyland. In that Skyland there was a great and beautiful tree. It had four white roots which stretched to each of the sacred directions,[1] and from its branches all kinds of fruits and flowers grew.

There was an ancient chief in the Skyland. His young wife was expecting a child, and one night she dreamed that she saw the Great Tree uprooted. The next day she told her husband the story.

◆ **Reading Strategy**

What do the Chief's words to his wife tell you about the beliefs of the Onondaga?

He nodded as she finished telling her dream. "My wife," he said, "I am sad that you had this dream. It is clearly a dream of great power and, as is our way, when one has such a powerful dream we must do all we can to make it true. The Great Tree must be uprooted."

Then the Ancient Chief called the young men together and told them that they must pull up the tree. But the roots of the tree were so deep, so strong, that they could not budge it. At last the Ancient Chief himself came to the tree. He wrapped his arms around it, bent his knees and strained. At last, with one great effort, he uprooted the tree and placed it on its side. Where the tree's roots had gone deep into the Skyland there was now a big hole. The wife of the chief came close and leaned over to look down, grasping the tip of one of the Great Tree's branches to steady her. It seemed as if she saw something down there, far below, glittering like water. She leaned out further to look and, as she leaned, she lost her balance and fell into the hole. Her grasp slipped off the tip of the branch, leaving her with only a handful of seeds as she fell, down, down, down, down.

Far below, in the waters, some of the birds and animals looked up.

"Someone is falling toward us from the sky," said one of the birds.

"We must do something to help her," said another. Then two Swans flew up. They caught the Woman From The Sky between their wide wings. Slowly, they began to bring her down toward the water, where the birds and animals were watching.

"She is not like us," said one of the animals. "Look, she doesn't have webbed feet. I don't think she can live in the water."

"What shall we do then?" said another of the water animals.

"I know," said one of the water birds. "I have heard that there is Earth far below the waters. If we dive down and bring up Earth, then she will have a place to stand."

So the birds and animal decided that someone would have to bring up Earth. One by one they tried.

The Duck dove first, some say. He swam down and down, far beneath the surface, but could not reach the bottom and floated back up. Then the Beaver tried. He went even deeper, so deep that all was dark, but he could not reach the bottom either. The Loon tried, swimming with his strong wings. He was gone a long, long time, but he, too, failed to bring up Earth. Soon it seemed that all had tried and all had failed. Then a small voice spoke.

---

1. **the sacred directions:** North, South, East, and West.

"I will bring up Earth or die trying."

They looked to see who it was. It was the Tiny Muskrat. She dove down and swam and swam. She was not as strong or as swift as the others, but she was determined. She went so deep that it was all dark, and still she swam deeper. She swam so deep that her lungs felt ready to burst, but she swam deeper still. At last, just as she was becoming unconscious, she reached out one small paw and grasped at the bottom, barely touching it before she floated up, almost dead.

When the other animals saw her break the surface they thought she had failed. Then they saw her right paw was held tightly shut.

"She has the Earth," they said. "Now where can we put it?"

"Place it on my back," said a deep voice. It was the Great Turtle, who had come up from the depths.

They brought the Muskrat over to the Great Turtle and placed her paw against his back. To this day there are marks at the back of the Turtle's shell which were made by the Muskrat's paw. The tiny bit of Earth fell on the back of the Turtle. Almost immediately, it began to grow larger and larger and larger until it became the whole world.

Then the two Swans brought the Sky Woman down. She stepped onto the new Earth and opened her hand, letting the seeds fall onto the bare soil. From those seeds the trees and the grass sprang up. Life on Earth had begun.

▲ **Critical Viewing** What characteristics of this turtle are explained in this origin myth? **[Connect]**

Guide for Responding

◆ Literature and Your Life

Reader's Response If you had been the Ancient Chief, would you have pulled up the Great Tree? Explain your answer.

Thematic Focus How do the animals portrayed in this myth embody the best aspects of human nature?

Informal Debate Work with a group of classmates to stage an informal debate on whether Muskrat or Turtle deserves more credit for the creation of the Earth.

☑ Check Your Comprehension

1. According to the myth, what existed before this Earth?
2. What starts the chain of events that eventually leads to Earth's creation?
3. What does the Sky Woman bring with her from Skyland, and how does it affect the Earth?

◆ Critical Thinking

INTERPRET

1. Name at least two things that are lost or sacrificed in the Skyland so there would be life on Earth. **[Analyze]**
2. How do the animals in this myth exhibit human virtues? **[Interpret]**
3. Whom do you think the Onondaga ultimately credit with bringing Earth into existence? **[Infer]**
4. What can you conclude from this myth about the relationship between the Onondaga and their natural environment? Explain your answer. **[Draw Conclusions]**

EXTEND

5. Muskrat was willing to give up her life to save the Sky Woman. Describe someone you know from literature or real life who has also acted selflessly. **[Synthesize]**

When Grizzlies Walked Upright

Modoc

Retold by Richard Erdoes and Alfonso Ortiz

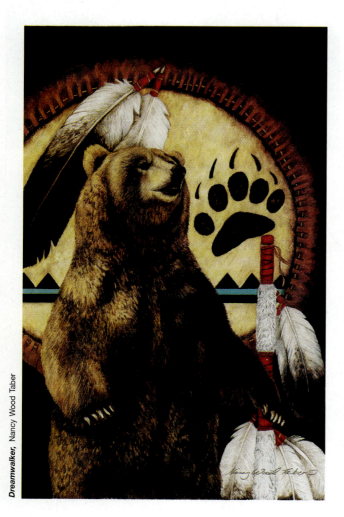

Dreamwalker, Nancy Wood Taber

▲ **Critical Viewing** Which elements of the natural world are included in this image? Which elements represent the human world? What is the effect of the presentation of both together? **[Assess]**

Before there were people on earth, the Chief of the Sky Spirits grew tired of his home in the Above World, because the air was always brittle with an icy cold. So he carved a hole in the sky with a stone and pushed all the snow and ice down below until he made a great mound that reached from the earth almost to the sky. Today it is known as Mount Shasta.

Then the Sky Spirit took his walking stick, stepped from a cloud to the peak, and walked down to the mountain. When he was about halfway to the valley below, he began to put his finger to the ground here and there, here and there. Wherever his finger touched, a tree grew. The snow melted in his footsteps, and the water ran down in rivers.

The Sky Spirit broke off the small end of his giant stick and threw the pieces into the rivers. The longer pieces turned into beaver and otter; the smaller pieces became fish. When the leaves dropped from the trees, he picked them up, blew upon them, and so made the birds. Then he took the big end of his giant stick and made all the animals that walked on the earth, the biggest of which were the grizzly bears.

Now when they were first made, the bears were covered with hair and had sharp claws, just as they do today, but they walked on two feet and could talk like people. They looked so fierce that the Sky Spirit sent them away from him to live in the forest at the base of the mountain.

Pleased with what he'd done, the Chief of the Sky Spirits decided to bring his family down and live on earth himself. The mountains of snow and ice became their lodge. He made a big fire in the center of the mountain and a hole in the top so that the smoke and sparks could fly out. When he put a big log on the fire, sparks would fly up and the earth would tremble.

Late one spring while the Sky Spirit and his family were sitting round the fire, the Wind Spirit sent a great storm that shook the top of the mountain. It blew and blew and roared and roared. Smoke blown back into the lodge hurt their eyes, and finally the Sky Spirit said to his youngest daughter, "Climb up to the smoke hole and ask the Wind Spirit to blow more gently. Tell him I'm afraid he will blow the mountain over."

As his daughter started up, her father said, "But be careful not to stick your head out at the top. If you do, the wind may catch you by the hair and blow you away."

The girl hurried to the top of the mountain and stayed well inside the smoke hole as she spoke to the Wind Spirit. As she was about to climb back down, she remembered that her father had once said you could see the ocean from the top of their lodge. His daughter wondered what the ocean looked like, and her curiosity got the better of her. She poked her head out of the hole and turned toward the west, but before she could see anything, the Wind Spirit caught her long hair, pulled her out of the mountain, and blew her down over the snow and ice. She landed among the scrubby fir trees at the edge of the timber and snow line, her long red hair trailing over the snow.

◆ **Reading Strategy**
What detail about the way Native American women wear their hair is revealed here?

There a grizzly bear found the little girl when he was out hunting food for his family. He carried her home with him, and his wife brought her up with their family of cubs. The little red-haired girl and the cubs ate together, played together, and grew up together.

When she became a young woman, she and the eldest son of the grizzly bears were married. In the years that followed they had many children, who were not as hairy as the grizzlies, yet did not look exactly like their spirit mother, either.

All the grizzly bears throughout the forests were so proud of these new creatures that they made a lodge for the red-haired mother and her children. They placed the lodge near Mount Shasta—it is called Little Mount Shasta today.

After many years had passed, the mother grizzly bear knew that she would soon die. Fearing that she should ask of the Chief of the Sky Spirits to forgive her for keeping his daughter, she gathered all the grizzlies at the lodge they had built. Then she sent her eldest grandson in a cloud to the top of Mount Shasta, to tell the Spirit Chief where he could find his long-lost daughter.

When the father got this news he was so glad that he came down the mountainside in giant strides, melting the snow and tearing up the land under his feet. Even today his tracks can be seen in the rocky path on the south side of Mount Shasta.

As he neared the lodge, he called out, "Is this where my little daughter lives?"

He expected his child to look exactly as she had when he saw her last. When he found a grown woman instead, and learned that the strange creatures she was taking care of were his grandchildren, he became very angry. A new race had been created that was not of his making! He frowned on the old grandmother so sternly that she promptly fell dead. Then he cursed all the grizzlies:

"Get down on your hands and knees. You have wronged me, and from this moment all of you will walk on four feet and never talk again."

He drove his grandchildren out of the lodge, put his daughter over his shoulder, and climbed back up the mountain. Never again did he come to the forest. Some say that he put out the fire in the center of his lodge and took his daughter back up to the sky to live.

Those strange creatures, his grandchildren, scattered and wandered over the earth. They were the first Indians, the ancestors of all the Indian tribes.

That's why the Indians living around Mount Shasta would never kill a grizzly bear. Whenever a grizzly killed an Indian, his body was burned on the spot. And for many years all who passed that way cast a stone there until a great pile of stones marked the place of his death.

from The Navajo Origin Legend

Navajo

Retold by Washington Matthews

On the morning of the twelfth day the people washed themselves well. The women dried themselves with yellow cornmeal; the men with white cornmeal. Soon after the <u>ablutions</u> were completed they heard the distant call of the approaching gods.[1] It was shouted, as before, four times—nearer and louder at each repetition—and, after the fourth call, the gods appeared. Blue Body and Black Body each carried a sacred buckskin. White Body carried two ears of corn, one yellow, one white, each covered at the end completely with grains.

---

1. **the approaching gods:** The four Navajo gods: White Body, Blue Body, Yellow Body, and Black Body.

▼ **Critical Viewing** This painting depicts the Blessingway chant, which is based on another Navajo legend. Compare the ceremony depicted in the painting with the one described in this excerpt of *The Navajo Origin Legend*. Which elements are common to both? **[Compare]**

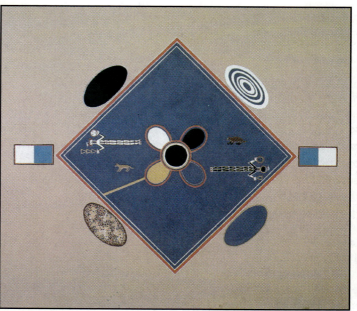

The Place of Emergence and the Four Worlds, 1938, Navajo, Wheelwright Museum of the American Indian

The gods laid one buckskin on the ground with the head to the west: on this they placed the two ears of corn, with their tips to the east, and over the corn they spread the other buckskin with its head to the east; under the white ear they put the feather of a white eagle, under the yellow ear the feather of a yellow eagle. Then they told the people to stand at a distance and allow the wind to enter. The white wind blew from the east, and the yellow wind blew from the west, between the skins. While the wind was blowing, eight of the Mirage People[2] came and walked around the objects on the ground four times, and as they walked the eagle feathers, whose tips protruded from between the buckskins, were seen to move. When the Mirage People had finished their walk the upper buckskin was lifted; the ears of corn had disappeared, a man and a woman lay there in their stead.

The white ear of corn had been changed into a man, the yellow ear into a woman. It was the

---

2. **Mirage People:** Mirages personified.

wind that gave them life. It is the wind that comes out of our mouths now that gives us life. When this ceases to blow we die. In the skin at the tips of our fingers we see the trail of the wind; it shows us where the wind blew when our ancestors were created.

The pair thus created were First Man and First Woman (Atsé Hastin and Atsé Estsán). The gods directed the people to build an enclosure of brushwood for the pair. When the enclosure was finished, First Man and First Woman entered it, and the gods said to them: "Live together now as husband and wife."

◆ **Literary Focus**

Why might the Navajo have viewed the wind as the source of life?

◆ **Build Vocabulary**

ablutions (ab loo´ shənz) *n.*: Washing or cleansing the body as part of a religious rite

protruded (prō trood´ id) *v.*: Jutted out

Guide for Responding

◆ *Literature and Your Life*

Reader's Response What words would you use to describe the images in these tales and the impression they made on you?

Thematic Focus What happens when the spirit and natural worlds meet?

Group Activity *The Navajo Origin Legend* describes a ritual performed by the gods and the Mirage People. What formal and informal rituals are part of our lives today? Consider social, religious, educational, and even sports-related rituals, such as tossing a coin to start a game. List suggestions on the chalkboard.

☑ **Check Your Comprehension**

1. According to the Modoc myth, how are the landscape and creatures of the Earth formed?
2. Summarize the Navajo creation ceremony.

◆ **Critical Thinking**

INTERPRET

1. (a) In the eyes of the Modoc Sky Spirit, what was the true crime of the grizzly bears? (b) What does his reaction reveal about him? **[Analyze]**
2. What is the meaning of the Modoc custom of marking the site where an Indian was killed by a grizzly? **[Interpret]**
3. Why do the Navajo associate the tips of the fingers with the trail of the wind? **[Interpret]**
4. Find evidence in the passage that suggests that four is a sacred number for the Navajo. **[Analyze]**

APPLY

5. In what ways do these tales differ from each other? **[Contrast]**

from The Iroquois Constitution

Iroquois

Translated by Arthur C. Parker

Red Jacket, George Catlin, The Thomas Gilcrease Institute of American History and Art, Tulsa, Oklahoma

▲ **Critical Viewing** How does this portrait reflect a belief in the dignity and nobility of the Native Americans? **[Analyze]**

I am Dekanawidah and with the Five Nations[1] confederate lords I plant the Tree of the Great Peace. I name the tree the Tree of the Great Long Leaves. Under the shade of this Tree of the Great Peace we spread the soft white feathery down of the globe thistle as seats for you, Adodarhoh, and your cousin lords.

We place you upon those seats, spread soft with the feathery down of the globe thistle, there beneath the shade of the spreading branches of the Tree of Peace. There shall you sit and watch the council fire of the confederacy of the Five Nations, and all the affairs of the Five Nations shall be transacted at this place before you.

Roots have spread out from the Tree of the Great Peace, one to the north, one to the east, one to the south and one to the west. The name of these roots is the Great White Roots and their nature is peace and strength.

If any man or any nation outside the Five Nations shall obey the laws of the Great Peace and make known their disposition to the lords of the confederacy, they may trace the roots to the tree and if their minds are clean and they are obedient and promise to obey the wishes of the confederate council, they shall be welcomed to take shelter beneath the Tree of the Long Leaves.

We place at the top of the Tree of the Long Leaves an eagle who is able to see afar. If he sees in the distance any evil approaching or any danger threatening he will at once warn the people of the confederacy.

The smoke of the confederate council fire shall ever ascend and pierce the sky so that other nations who may be allies may see the council fire of the Great Peace . . .

Whenever the confederate lords shall assemble for the purpose of holding a council, the Onondaga lords shall open it by expressing their gratitude to their cousin lords and greeting them, and they shall make an address and offer thanks to the earth where men dwell, to the streams of water, the pools, the springs and the lakes, to the maize and the fruits, to the medicinal herbs and trees, to the forest trees for their usefulness, to the animals that serve as food and give their pelts for clothing, to the great winds and the lesser winds, to the thunderers, to the sun, the mighty warrior, to the moon, to the messengers of the Creator who reveal his wishes and to the Great Creator who dwells in the heavens above, who gives all the things useful to men, and who is the source and the ruler of health and life.

Then shall the Onondaga lords declare the council open . . .

◆ **Reading Strategy**
What can you learn about the Iroquois culture from the items on this list?

---

1. **Five Nations:** The Mohawk, Oneida, Onondaga, Cayuga, and Seneca tribes. Together, these tribes formed the Iroquois Confederation.

All lords of the Five Nations' Confederacy must be honest in all things . . . It shall be a serious wrong for anyone to lead a lord into trivial affairs, for the people must ever hold their lords high in estimation out of respect to their honorable positions.

When a candidate lord is to be installed he shall furnish four strings of shells (or wampum)[2] one span in length bound together at one end. Such will constitute the evidence of his pledge to the confederate lords that he will live according to the constitution of the Great Peace and exercise justice in all affairs.

When the pledge is furnished the speaker of the council must hold the shell strings in his hand and address the opposite side of the council fire and he shall commence his address saying: "Now behold him. He has now become a confederate lord. See how splendid he looks." An address may then follow. At the end of it he shall send the bunch of shell strings to the opposite side and they shall be received as evidence of the pledge. Then shall the opposite side say:

"We now do crown you with the sacred emblem of the deer's antlers, the emblem of your lordship. You shall now become a mentor of the people of the Five Nations. The thickness of your skin shall be seven spans—which is to say that you shall be proof against anger, offensive actions and criticism. Your heart shall be filled with peace and good will and your mind filled with a yearning for the welfare of the people of the confederacy. With endless patience you shall carry out your duty and your firmness shall be tempered with tenderness for your people. Neither anger nor fury shall find lodgement in your mind and all your words and actions shall be marked with calm deliberation. In all of your deliberations in the confederate council, in your efforts at law making, in all your official acts, self-interest shall be cast into oblivion. Cast not over your shoulder behind you the warnings of the nephews and nieces should they chide you for any error or wrong you may do, but return to the way of the Great Law which is just and right. Look and listen for the welfare of the whole people and have always in view not only the present but also the coming generations, even those whose faces are yet beneath the surface of the ground—the unborn of the future nation."

---

2. **wampum** (wäm´ pəm) n.: Small beads made of shells.

◆ **Build Vocabulary**

confederate (kən fed´ ər it) adj.: United with others for a common purpose

disposition (dis´ pə zish´ ən) n.: An inclination or tendency

deliberation (di lib´ ə rā´ shən) n.: Careful consideration

Guide for Responding

◆ Literature and Your Life

Reader's Response If you were the chief of a Native American nation, would this speech persuade you to join the confederation? Explain.

Thematic Focus How does Dekanawidah use images from nature in the Iroquois Constitution? What do these references tell you about the Iroquois?

☑ **Check Your Comprehension**

1. What three natural images does Dekanawidah use in association with the Great Peace?
2. Summarize the qualities and conduct required of council lords by the Iroquois Constitution.

◆ **Critical Thinking**

INTERPRET

1. The constitution tells the lords to "offer thanks to the earth where men dwell." What does this decree suggest about the Iroquois? **[Infer]**
2. What do you learn about Dekanawidah from the constitution he created? **[Infer]**

EVALUATE

3. Explain whether you believe a tree can effectively represent peace. **[Evaluate]**

APPLY

4. The constitution outlines Iroquois leadership qualities. What qualities do you think modern leaders should possess? Explain. **[Synthesize]**

Guide for Responding (continued)

◆ Reading Strategy

RECOGNIZE CULTURAL DETAILS

Cultural details—those that reflect aspects of daily life or prevalent attitudes—can provide insight into the culture behind the literature. Drawing on the details you noted while reading, write two or three sentences describing what each selection reveals about the culture that created it.

◆ Literary Focus

ORIGIN MYTHS

Ears of corn transform into people. Immortal beings and mystical events like this are typical of **origin myths**—stories passed from generation to generation to explain the creation of the world and all it holds.

1. Describe the natural phenomena, customs, and creatures (other than humans) explained in "When Grizzlies Walked Upright."
2. List those who share in the process of bringing about human life on Earth in (a) "When Grizzlies Walked Upright," (b) "The Earth on Turtle's Back," and (c) *The Navajo Origin Legend*.

Beyond Literature

History Connection

The United States Constitution

From the fourteenth-century Iroquois Constitution to the Pilgrim's 1620 Mayflower Compact to the 1787 United States Constitution, legal documents governing societies have flourished on North American soil.

In more than two centuries, the original United States Constitution has been amended only twenty-seven times. The first ten amendments, known as the Bill of Rights, outline the relationship of government and citizen rights.

Read a copy of the United States Constitution. In what ways is it similar to the Iroquois document? In what ways is it different?

◆ Build Vocabulary

USING THE SUFFIX -tion

Change each of the following verbs to a noun by adding the suffix *-tion*. Make any other necessary spelling changes (check a dictionary if you're not sure). Then use each new word in a sentence.

1. constitute: to set up in a legal form; establish
2. estimate: to form an opinion or judgment
3. dispose: to tend or incline

USING THE WORD BANK

For each grouping, write the letter of the word whose meaning does not match the other two:

1. (a) cleansings, (b) imaginings, (c) ablutions
2. (a) deliberation, (b) consideration, (c) commotion
3. (a) protruded, (b) dangled, (c) jutted
4. (a) disposition, (b) inclination, (c) assumption
5. (a) varied, (b) confederate, (c) united

◆ Grammar and Style

COMPOUND SENTENCES

Closely related main clauses are often joined to form **compound sentences.** Each clause of a compound sentence contains its own subject and predicate and can stand alone as a complete thought.

> A **compound sentence** has two or more main clauses linked by a coordinating conjunction—*and, or,* and *but*—or by a semicolon.

Writing Application On your paper, rewrite the following paragraph so that it contains at least three compound sentences. You may need to add or change some words. Then underline the subject and predicate in each clause.

> Then the Beaver tried. He went deeper into the darkness. He could not reach the bottom. Next, the loon dove into the water. Even he could not reach the bottom. He floated back up. Then a voice spoke, "I will bring up Earth or die trying."

Build Your Portfolio

 ## Idea Bank

Writing

1. New Ending According to "The Earth on Turtle's Back," Muskrat was responsible for creating the "new Earth." Draft a new ending for the myth that includes an explanation of how the Sky Spirits reward her.

2. Origin Myth Write a myth that explains the origin of a local natural landmark, such as a nearby lake, valley, or cliff.

3. Essay The Iroquois Constitution had to hold the listener's attention. In an essay, analyze how this document uses imagery and phrasing to create a memorable impression.

Speaking and Listening

4. Native American Chant Locate information about and recordings of Native American chants. Then present a brief oral report on Native American music and play a chant for your class. **[Music Link]**

5. Dramatic Reenactment Reenact a council meeting at which a new Iroquois lord is to be installed. Create the roles of the Onondaga lords, the candidate lord, the speaker of the council, and the gathering of council lords. Perform the scene for your class. **[Performing Arts Link]**

Projects

6. Totem Pole Research the Native American practice of carving vertical logs decorated with images. On a totem you research or create, identify each image on the totem with a label and caption explaining its significance.

7. Logo Using the images contained in the Iroquois Constitution for inspiration, design a logo representing the Iroquois Confederation. **[Art Link]**

 ## Writing Mini-Lesson

Retelling of a Myth

Myths are oral forms of communication, repeated over the years by storytellers, all of whom added something of their own to the retelling. Select a myth with which you're familiar and retell it to a friend. Keep the structure and sequence of events, but rewrite the tale to appeal to your audience. For example, you might update the setting.

Writing Skills Focus: Effective Repetition

Effective repetition—the practice of repeating actions, phrases, or words to produce a desired effect—can make an oral tale more memorable and create drama and heighten suspense.

Repetition of the boldfaced and italicized words in this passage from "The Earth on Turtle's Back" creates both rhythm and drama.

Model From the Story

[Muskrat] dove down and **swam and swam**. *She was not as strong* or as swift as the others, but *she was determined*. She went so **deep** that it was all dark, and **still she swam deeper**.

As you formulate your retelling, look for ways to use repetition to captivate your audience.

Prewriting Create a rough plot outline based on what you remember about the myth. Then make a list of elements of the myth that you will retain and elements that you will adapt.

Drafting Following your plot outline, create a rough draft. Look for places where you can use repetition to create drama and establish rhythm.

Revising Read your tale aloud and decide whether it is dramatic and memorable. Does your use of repetition succeed in creating the sound you hoped for? Polish your writing to get the effect you want.

Alvar Núñez Cabeza de Vaca
(1490?–1557?)

In 1528, Pánfilo de Narváez and 400 Spanish soldiers landed near Tampa Bay and set out to explore Florida's west coast. Alvar Núñez Cabeza de Vaca (äl´ bär nōōn´ yes kä bā´ sä dä bä´ kä) was second in command. Beset by illness and the prospect of starvation, Narváez and his men set sail for Mexico in five flimsy boats. He and most of the men drowned. Cabeza de Vaca and a party of about sixty reached the Texas shore.

Only fifteen of the group lived through the winter. In the end, Cabeza de Vaca and three others survived. They were captured by Indians and spent the next several years as captives. Cabeza de Vaca gained a reputation as a medicine man and trader. The four Spaniards finally escaped and wandered for eighteen months across the Texas plains. In 1536, the survivors finally reached Mexico City.

Cabeza de Vaca's adventures and his reports on the richness of Texas sparked exploration of the region. In this passage, he speaks of Estevanico, the first African to set foot in Texas.

García López de Cárdenas
(c. 1540)

García López de Cárdenas (gär sē´ ä lō´ pes dä kär´ dä näs) is best remembered as the first European to visit the Grand Canyon. As a leader of Francisco Vásquez de Coronado's expedition to New Mexico (1540–1542), Cárdenas was dispatched from Cibola (Zuni) in western New Mexico to see a river that the Moqui Native Americans of northeastern Arizona had described to one of Coronado's captains. The river was the Colorado. López de Cárdenas departed on August 25, 1540, and reached the Grand Canyon after a westward jaunt of about twenty days. He became the first explorer to view the canyon and its river, which from the vantage of the canyon's rim they believed to be a stream merely six feet across! Unable to descend to the river, they brought back descriptions that attempted to record the magnitude of the great sight.

Route of Cabeza de Vaca

◆ Background for Understanding

HISTORY: EXPEDITIONS IN THE SOUTHWEST

In March of 1536, Cabeza de Vaca and the three remaining members of his party stumbled out of the desert and into history as the first Europeans to have crossed North America from Florida to Mexico. The party of Spaniards who came across a raving, half-naked white man (Cabeza de Vaca) on Mexico's northern frontier did not at first understand who he was. Once Cabeza de Vaca told his tale, however, the Spanish viceroy ordered that it be recorded.

Cabeza de Vaca's account gave rise to rumors of cities of great wealth north of the Rio Grande. In response, conquistador Francisco Vásquez de Coronado, in 1540, led a two-year expedition to what is now New Mexico.

◆ *Literature and Your Life*

CONNECT YOUR EXPERIENCE

If you ever traveled to a new place, the first thing you probably did upon your return was tell your friends what you saw. Just imagine the tales you would have told if, like the authors of these two selections, you were among the first Europeans to travel the southwestern region of North America and meet the native inhabitants.

THEMATIC FOCUS: MEETING OF CULTURES

Often people have difficulty appreciating a culture radically different from their own. How do the Spaniards respond to the native inhabitants of the Southwest?

Journal Writing Write about the knowledge you gained from meeting someone from a different culture.

◆ Literary Focus

EXPLORATION NARRATIVE

The European men who trail-blazed the Americas recounted their experiences in **exploration narratives**—firsthand accounts that tell the story of their experiences. The purpose of these accounts was to provide information to the people back home in Europe, so the explorers were careful to record in detail what they observed during their travels. Exploration narratives generally are factual, although the viewpoints expressed in them are sometimes distinctly personal. The writers often described the difficulties and discoveries of their explorations to impress others and perhaps to inspire readers to follow in their footsteps.

◆ Grammar and Style

PAST AND PAST PERFECT VERB TENSES

The **past tense** shows an action or condition that began and ended at a given time in the past. The **past perfect tense** shows a past action or condition that ended before another past action began. Verbs in the past perfect consist of *had*, followed by the past participle. Look at these examples:

past perfect   past

After five days they <u>had</u> not <u>returned</u> and the Indians <u>explained</u>

past perfect

that it might be because they <u>had</u> not <u>found</u> anybody.

◆ Reading Strategy

SIGNAL WORDS

When you read a detailed narrative account, it's easy to lose track of the order of events. One way to avoid having this happen, however, is to pay close attention to **signal words**—words that point out relationships among ideas and events. Often signal words show time relationships. They can also indicate level of importance, cause-and-effect relationships, or contrasts. Look at these examples:

Words signaling

   time: *After five days*, they had not *yet* returned.

   contrast: . . . *although* this was the warm season, no one could live in this canyon because of the cold.

◆ Build Vocabulary

WORD ROOTS: -mort-

The word *mortality* has as its root the Latin -*mort*-, meaning "death." You may already know the word *mortal*, a term commonly used to distinguish humans, who are subject to death, from the *immortal* gods of mythology.

WORD BANK

Before you read, preview this list of words from the narratives.

entreated
feigned
mortality
subsisted
traversed
dispatched

A Journey Through Texas

Alvar Núñez Cabeza de Vaca

▲ **Critical Viewing** How would a landscape like this one pose difficulty for the expeditions that explored it? **[Speculate]**

Alvar Núñez Cabeza de Vaca and his three countrymen wandered for months through Texas as they journeyed toward the Spanish settlement in Mexico City. In the course of his travels, Cabeza de Vaca healed a Native American by performing the first recorded surgery in Texas. His resulting fame attracted so many followers that Cabeza de Vaca noted in his journal, "the number of our companions became so large that we could no longer control them." As they continued traveling westward, the group was well received by the Native Americans they encountered.

The same Indians led us to a plain beyond the chain of mountains, where people came to meet us from a long distance. By those we were treated in the same manner as before, and they made so many presents to the Indians who came with us that, unable to carry all, they left half of it. . . . We told these people our route was towards sunset, and they replied that in that direction people lived very far away. So we ordered them to send there and inform the inhabitants that we were coming and how. From this they begged to be excused, because the others were their enemies, and they did not want us to go to them. Yet they did not venture to disobey in the end, and sent two women, one of their own and the other a captive. They selected women because these can trade everywhere, even if there be war.

We followed the women to a place where it had been agreed we should wait for them. After five days they had not yet returned, and the Indians explained that it might be because they had not found anybody. So we told them to take us north, and they repeated that there were no people, except very far away, and neither food nor water. Nevertheless we insisted, saying that we wanted to go there, and they still excused themselves as best they could, until at last we became angry.

One night I went away to sleep out in the field apart from them; but they soon came to where I was, and remained awake all night in great alarm, talking to me, saying how frightened they were. They <u>entreated</u> us not to be angry any longer, because, even if it was their death, they would take us where we chose. We <u>feigned</u> to be angry still, so as to keep them in suspense, and then a singular[1] thing happened.

On that same day many fell sick, and on the next day eight of them died! All over the country, where it was known, they became so afraid that it seemed as if the mere sight of us would kill them. They besought[2] us not to be angry nor to procure the death of any more of their number, for they were convinced that we killed them by merely thinking of it. In truth, we were very much concerned about it, for, seeing the great <u>mortality</u>, we dreaded that all of them might die or forsake us in their terror, while those further on, upon learning of it, would get out of our way hereafter. We prayed to God our Lord to assist us, and the sick began to get well. Then we saw something that astonished us very much, and it was that, while the parents, brothers and wives of the dead had shown deep grief at their illness, from the moment they died the survivors made no demonstration whatsoever, and showed not the slightest feeling; nor did they dare to go near the bodies until we ordered their burial. . . .

The sick being on the way of recovery, when we had been there already three days, the women whom we had sent out returned, saying that they had met very few people, nearly all having gone after the cows, as it was the season. So we ordered those who had been sick to remain, and those who were well to accompany us, and that, two days' travel from there, the same women should go with us and get people to come to meet us on the trail for our reception.

The next morning all those who were strong enough came along, and at the end of three journeys we halted. Alonso del Castillo and Estevanico,[3] the negro, left with the women as guides, and the woman who was a captive took them to a river that flows between mountains, where there was a village, in which her father lived, and these were the first abodes we saw that were like unto real houses. Castillo and Estevanico went to these and, after holding parley[4] with the Indians, at the end of three days Castillo returned to where he had left us, bringing with him five or six of the Indians. He told how he had found permanent houses, inhabited, the people of which ate beans and squashes, and that he had also seen maize.

Of all things upon earth this caused us the greatest pleasure, and we gave endless thanks to our Lord for this news. Castillo also said that the negro was coming to meet us on the way, near by, with all the people of the houses. For that reason we started, and after going a league and a half met the negro and the people that came to receive us, who gave us beans and many squashes to eat, gourds to carry water in, robes of cowhide, and other things. As those people and the Indians of our company were enemies, and did not understand each other, we took leave of the latter, leaving them all that had been given to us, while we went on with the former and, six leagues beyond, when night was already approaching, reached their houses, where they received us with great ceremonies. Here we remained one day, and left on the next, taking them with us to other permanent

---

3. **Estevanico** (es´ tä vä nē´ kō): Of Moorish extraction, Estevanico was the first African man to set foot in Texas.
4. **holding parley** (pär´ lē): Conferring.

◆ **Build Vocabulary**

entreated (en trēt´ id) *v.*: Begged; pleaded

feigned (fānd) *v.*: Pretended; faked

mortality (môr tal´ ə tē) *n.*: Death on a large scale, as from disease or war

---

1. **singular:** Strange.
2. **besought:** (bē sôt´) Pleaded with.

A Journey Through Texas ◆ 35

houses, where they subsisted on the same food also, and thence on we found a new custom.

The people who heard of our approach did not, as before, come out to meet us on the way, but we found them at their homes, and they had other houses ready for us. . . . There was nothing they would not give us. They are the best formed people we have seen, the liveliest and most capable; who best understood us and answered our questions. We called them "of the cows," because most of the cows die near there, and because for more than fifty leagues up that stream they go to kill many of them. Those people go completely naked, after the manner of the first we met. The women are covered with deerskins, also some men, especially the old ones, who are of no use any more in war.

The country is well settled. We asked them why they did not raise maize, and they replied that they were afraid of losing the crops, since for two successive years it had not rained, and the seasons were so dry that the moles had eaten the corn, so that they did not dare to plant any more until it should have rained very hard. And they also begged us to ask Heaven for rain, which we promised to do. We also wanted to know from where they brought their maize, and they said it came from where the sun sets, and that it was found all over that country, and the shortest way to it was in that direction. We asked them to tell us how to go, as they did not want to go themselves, to tell us about the way.

▲ **Critical Viewing** This stamp was issued in Spain to commemorate the four-hundredth anniversary of the discovery of Florida. What does the portrait suggest about Cabeza de Vaca's character? **[Analyze]**

They said we should travel up the river towards the north, on which trail for seventeen days we would not find a thing to eat, except a fruit called *chacan*, which they grind between stones; but even then it cannot be eaten, being so coarse and dry; and so it was, for they showed it to us and we could not eat it. But they also said that, going upstream, we could always travel among people who were their enemies, although speaking the

▼ **Critical Viewing** What does this painting suggest about the relationship between Cabeza de Vaca and the Native Americans? Why? **[Infer]**

Painting of Cabeza de Vaca, Esteban, and their companions among various Texas Indian tribes, Tom Mirrat, The Institute of Texan Cultures, San Antonio, Texas

same language, and who could give us no food, but would receive us very willingly, and give us many cotton blankets, hides and other things; but that it seemed to them that we ought not to take that road.

In doubt as to what should be done, and which was the best and most advantageous road to take, we remained with them for two days. They gave us beans, squashes, and calabashes.[5] Their way of cooking them is so new and strange that I felt like describing it here, in order to show how different and queer are the devices and industries of human beings. They have no pots. In order to cook their food they fill a middle-sized gourd with water, and place into a fire such stones as easily become heated, and when they are hot to scorch they take them out with wooden tongs, thrusting them into the water of the gourd, until it boils. As soon as it boils they put into it what they want to cook, always taking out the stones as they cool off and throwing in hot ones to keep the water steadily boiling. This is their way of cooking.

◆ **Literary Focus**
Why does the author include these cooking customs in his exploration narrative?

After two days were past we determined to go in search of maize, and not to follow the road to the cows, since the latter carried us to the north, which meant a very great circuit, as we

---

5. **calabashes** (kal´ ə bash´ əz) *n.*: Dried, hollow shells of gourds used to hold food or beverages.

held it always certain that by going towards sunset we should reach the goal of our wishes.

So we went on our way and traversed the whole country to the South Sea,[6] and our resolution was not shaken by the fear of great starvation, which the Indians said we should suffer (and indeed suffered) during the first seventeen days of travel. All along the river, and in the course of these seventeen days we received plenty of cowhides, and did not eat of their famous fruit (*chacan*), but our food consisted (for each day) of a handful of deer-tallow, which for that purpose we always sought to keep, and so endured these seventeen days, at the end of which we crossed the river and marched for seventeen days more. At sunset, on a plain between very high mountains, we met people who, for one-third of the year, eat but powdered straw, and as we went by just at that time, had to eat it also, until, at the end of that journey we found some permanent houses, with plenty of harvested maize, of which and of its meal they gave us great quantities, also squashes and beans, and blankets of cotton. . . .

---

6. **the South Sea:** The Gulf of Mexico.

◆ **Build Vocabulary**

subsisted (səb sist´ id) *v.*: Remained alive; were sustained

traversed (trə vʉrst´) *v.*: Moved over, across, or through

Guide for Responding

◆ *Literature and Your Life*

Reader's Response Would you find the many stops in the journey through Texas to be frustrating or fascinating? Explain your answer.

Thematic Focus How might Cabeza de Vaca's experiences with Native American cultures have changed him as a person?

☑ Check Your Comprehension

1. Why do the Spaniards order the Native Americans to travel with them?
2. Why do the Spaniards become fearful when Native Americans in their company die?

◆ Critical Thinking

INTERPRET

1. Why do the Native Americans obey the orders of the Spaniards? **[Infer]**
2. (a) What do the Native Americans believe was the cause of the sickness that struck them on the journey? (b) What are some of the more likely explanations for the illness? **[Draw Conclusions]**

EXTEND

3. Do you think the Native Americans would have extended a warm welcome to Cabeza de Vaca if he had been the hundredth Spaniard to journey through their lands? Explain. **[Social Studies Link]**

Boulders Taller Than the Great Tower of Seville

From an account by García López de Cárdenas
Retold by Pedro de Castañeda

Information was obtained of a large river and that several days down the river there were people with very large bodies.

As Don Pedro de Tovar had no other commission, he returned from Tusayán and gave his report to the general. The latter at once dispatched Don García López de Cárdenas there with about twelve men to explore this river. When he reached Tusayán he was well received and lodged by the natives. They provided him with guides to proceed on his journey. They set out from there laden with provisions, because they had to travel over some uninhabited land before coming to settlements, which the Indians said were more than twenty days away. Accordingly when they had marched for twenty days they came to gorges of the river, from the edge of which it looked as if the opposite side must have been more than three or four leagues[1] away by air. This region was high and covered with low and twisted pine trees; it was extremely cold, being open to the north, so that, although this was the warm season, no one could live in this canyon because of the cold.

The men spent three days looking for a way down to the river; from the top it looked as if the water were a fathom[2] across. But, according to the information supplied by the Indians, it must have been half a league wide. The descent was almost impossible, but, after these three days, at a place which seemed less difficult, Captain Melgosa, a certain Juan Galeras, and another companion, being the most agile, began to go down. They continued descending within view of those on top until they lost sight of them, as they could not be seen from the top. They returned about four o'clock in the afternoon, as they could not reach the bottom because of the many obstacles they met, for what from the top seemed easy, was not so, on the contrary, it was rough and difficult. They said that they had gone down one-third of the distance and that, from the point they had reached, the river seemed very large, and that, from what they saw, the width given by the Indians was correct. From the top they could make out, apart from the canyon, some small boulders which seemed to be as high as a man. Those who

---

1. **leagues** (lēgz) *n.*: Units of measurement of approximately 3 miles.

2. **fathom** (fath´ əm): A unit of measurement of six feet, used for the depth of water or the length of a rope or cable.

◆ **Build Vocabulary**

dispatched (dis pacht´) *v.*: Sent off on a specific assignment

went down and who reached them swore that they were taller than the great tower of Seville.[3]

The party did not continue farther up the canyon of the river because of the lack of water. Up to that time they had gone one or two leagues inland in search of water every afternoon.

◆ **Reading Strategy**

How do the words "Up to that time" alert you to a change in the action?

3. **great tower of Seville:** One of the largest cathedrals in the world, the Cathedral of Seville in Spain, was built between 1403 and 1506. The Giralda (hē räl´ dä), the tower, rises above the cathedral, more than twice its height.

When they had traveled four additional days the guides said that it was impossible to go on because no water would be found for three or four days, that when they themselves traveled through that land they took along women who brought water in gourds, that in those trips they buried the gourds of water for the return trip, and that they traveled in one day a distance that took us two days.

This was the Tizón river, much closer to its source than where Melchior Díaz and his men had crossed it. These Indians were of the same type, as it appeared later. From there Cárdenas and his men turned back, as that trip brought no other results.

Guide for Responding

◆ Literature and Your Life

Reader's Response How does this description compare with your knowledge of the Grand Canyon?

Thematic Focus How does the help provided by Native Americans make it possible for the explorers to experience the wonders of the Grand Canyon?

☑ Check Your Comprehension

1. What factual details do you learn about the canyon from this account?
2. What two factors prevent the group from finding their way down to the river?

◆ Critical Thinking

INTERPRET

1. How do the author's experiences with the rough terrain affect which details he chooses to include in this account? **[Analyze]**

APPLY

2. The explorers are searching for a river. How does their mission affect the way they perceive the Grand Canyon? Explain your answer. **[Apply]**

EXTEND

3. How might this account have been different if it had been written to secure future funding? **[Social Studies Link]**

Guide for Responding (continued)

◆ Reading Strategy

SIGNAL WORDS

Staying alert to **signal words** that indicate the relationships between events in these narratives helped you better understand when and why actions took place. On your paper, write the type of relationship (time, reason, or contrast) signaled by the italicized words in each of these passages:

1. *Nevertheless* we insisted, saying that we wanted to go there, and they still excused themselves as best they could, *until* at last we became angry.
2. We feigned to be angry still, *so as* to keep them in suspense, and *then* a singular thing happened.
3. The party did not continue farther up the canyon of the river *because* of the lack of water.

◆ Literary Focus

EXPLORATION NARRATIVE

New sights, new people, uncharted lands— these are the basic ingredients of **exploration narratives** like those of Cabeza de Vaca and López de Cárdenas. These narratives recount the experiences of the first Europeans to set foot in unexplored regions of North America.

Though it may have been years or even centuries before their work was published (the account of the Coronado expedition wasn't printed until 1896), these narratives offer readers insight into these explorers' achievements.

1. Why do the men who descend into the Grand Canyon use the image of the great tower of Seville to convey the size of the boulders they see?
2. What do you think motivated each explorer to record the things he saw?
3. What impression of the Americas does each writer convey?
4. Compare and contrast the two writers' reactions to the Native Americans they encounter in their explorations.
5. Both writers documented territories previously unknown to the Spaniards. What other searches have led to settlement of specific areas of what is now the United States?

◆ Build Vocabulary

USING THE WORD ROOT -mort-

In your notebook, write about a firefighter who dies while trying to rescue people from a burning building. Use the words *mortally, mortuary, mortician,* and *immortalized* in your description.

USING THE WORD BANK

Choose the word from the Word Bank that best completes each of the following sentences.

1. The soldier was ___?___ by the expedition leader to find the river they had heard so much about.
2. The Spaniards ___?___ their guides to continue leading the way to their destination.
3. When pleading didn't work, they ___?___ anger in order to intimidate their guides.
4. In the course of their seventeen-day march, they ___?___ a barren stretch of land.
5. The starving travelers ___?___ on mouthfuls of deer tallow.
6. The conquistadors were alarmed by the ___?___ that befell the natives.

◆ Grammar and Style

PAST TENSES OF VERBS

The **past tense** of a verb shows an action that began and ended at a given time in the past. The **past perfect tense** indicates an action that ended before another past action began. It is formed with the helping verb *had* and the past participle of the verb.

Practice In your notebook, write the tense of the italicized verb.

1. We *followed* the women to a place where it *had been agreed* we should wait for them.
2. Many *fell* sick.
3. On the next day eight of them *died*!
4. They *had gone* down one third of the distance.
5. Until then, they *had gone* one or two leagues inland in search of water.

Writing Application Write a description of an activity you recently completed that you'd worked on for some time. Use both the past and past perfect tenses.

Build Your Portfolio

 ## Idea Bank

Writing

1. **Journal Entry** After years of wanderings in the wilderness, what would you feel upon finally gaining sight of a town? In a journal entry, describe the experience of rejoining "civilization."

2. **Creative Description** Select an awe-inspiring natural wonder such as Niagara Falls or a towering mountain. Write a description conveying its majesty to someone who has never seen it.

3. **Comparison-and-Contrast Essay** Each writer had a unique purpose for relating his experiences. In an essay, compare and contrast the circumstances and attitudes revealed in each account.

Speaking and Listening

4. **Persuasive Speech** As a member of the small party that explored the Grand Canyon with López de Cárdenas, give a speech to convince the general that the view of the canyon is well worth a trip by the entire Coronado expedition.

5. **Television Interview** Stage an interview with Cabeza de Vaca upon his arrival in the Spanish settlement. Imagine that your broadcast will be beamed to Spain, where millions will hear about Cabeza de Vaca's experiences. **[Media Link]**

Projects

6. **"America the Beautiful" Presentation** Create a multimedia presentation using photographs or videos that capture the beauty of our country's varied terrain. Set the presentation to music, and provide narration. **[Media Link]**

7. **Television Series** Create a concept for a television series rooted in exploration. Describe the premise of the series, along with its setting and characters. **[Media Link]**

 ## Writing Mini-Lesson

Explorer's Journal

Imagine that like Cabeza de Vaca and López de Cárdenas, you have begun to explore a territory where no one has gone before. Write a journal that details what you discover. Be as descriptive as possible so that others may follow in your footsteps.

Writing Skills Focus: Precise Details

To make your explorer's journal useful to others who may want to study your experiences, use **precise details** in your account. For example, instead of vaguely reporting that the trees flowered in a *variety of bright hues*, identify the colors by name.

To introduce readers to a completely unfamiliar fruit, notice how Cabeza de Vaca uses specific details:

Model From the Journal

. . . except a fruit called chacan, which they grind between stones; but even then it cannot be eaten, being so coarse and dry . . .

This factual—almost scientific—description would be more informative than an empty notation that called the fruit "strangely exotic."

Prewriting First, choose the location that you will explore. It can be a place you've visited or one you've only read about or seen on television. Gather details to include in your journal. If you've never been to the place, you'll need to do some research.

Drafting Limit your journal entry to a specific day or moment. Focus on a few objects to describe in full. Keep in mind that you're writing for an audience unfamiliar with these objects.

Revising Ask a partner to read your first draft and comment on the level of detail you provide. If your reader can't "see" an item you've described, add more information to flesh out the image.

Guide for Interpreting

Olaudah Equiano (1745–1797)

When published in 1789, the autobiography of Olaudah Equiano (ō lä o͞o´ dä ek´ wē än´ ō) created a sensation.

The Interesting Narrative made society face the cruelties of slavery and contributed to the banning of the slave trade in both the United States and England.

The son of a tribal elder in the powerful kingdom of Benin, Equiano might have followed in his father's footsteps had he not been sold into slavery. When Equiano was eleven years old, he and his sister were kidnapped from their home in West Africa and sold to British slave traders. Separated from his sister, Equiano was taken first to the West Indies, then to Virginia, where he was purchased by a British captain and employed at sea.

Saving to Buy Liberty Renamed Gustavus Vassa, Equiano was enslaved for nearly ten years. After managing his Philadelphia master's finances and making his own money in the process, Equiano amassed enough to buy his freedom. In later years, he settled in England and devoted himself to the abolition of slavery. To publicize the plight of slaves, he wrote his two-volume autobiography, *The Interesting Narrative*. Although Equiano's writing raised concern about the less than humane conditions inherent in slavery, the slave trade in the United States was not abolished by law until 1808, nearly twenty years after its publication.

◆ Background for Understanding

HISTORY: THE SLAVE TRADE

The slave trade Equiano describes was in full operation during the colonization of the Western Hemisphere. While many people came to the new world in search of wealth or riches, many others were brought against their will.

Between 1500 and 1800, about 15 million Africans were captured and shipped to the Western Hemisphere. As Equiano attests, the conditions of the Atlantic crossing, known as "the middle passage," were atrocious. For six to ten weeks, Africans were crammed below deck in spaces sometimes less than five feet high. Families were torn apart; men and women placed in separate holds. During the voyage, men were often shackled together in pairs. Overcrowding, disease, and despair claimed many lives. Some Africans mutinied, and others tried to starve themselves or jump overboard. His-torians estimate that nearly 2 million slaves died before reaching their destination. This map shows the most common routes of the middle passage.

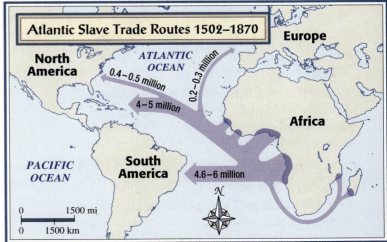

Atlantic Slave Trade Routes 1502–1870

from The Interesting Narrative of the Life of Olaudah Equiano

◆ *Literature and Your Life*

CONNECT YOUR EXPERIENCE

Imagine knowing that members of your community were valuable merchandise and that your family could be shipped away to a distant land to perform forced labor! Living in a world where slavery existed, you might develop a new attitude about the sweetness of freedom and the value of life.

Journal Writing How would you feel if you were sent to another country against your will? Jot down your thoughts.

THEMATIC FOCUS: MEETING OF CULTURES

European traditions and ideas often came into conflict with Native American customs. However, these were not the only cultures clashing on this continent. Equiano, an African brought against his will, represents another culture to be absorbed into the American scene.

◆ Literary Focus

SLAVE NARRATIVES

Equiano's account of the middle passage is an early example of a slave narrative. A uniquely American literary genre, a **slave narrative** is an autobiographical account of life as a slave. Often written to expose the horrors of human bondage, it documents a slave's experiences from his or her own point of view.

Encouraged by abolitionists, many freed or escaped slaves published narratives in the years before the Civil War.

◆ Grammar and Style

ACTIVE AND PASSIVE VOICE

A verb is in the **active voice** when the subject of the sentence performs the action. A verb is in the **passive voice** when the action is performed on the subject. When the performer of an action is not known or is not important, the writer uses the passive voice.

Active Voice: . . . <u>they</u> <u>tossed</u> the remaining fish into the sea . . .
(The subject, *they*, performs the action of the verb *tossed*.)

Passive Voice: This <u>situation</u> <u>was</u> <u>aggravated</u> by the galling of the chains . . .
(The subject *situation* receives the action of the verb.)
What is the effect of Equiano's use of the passive voice?

◆ Reading Strategy

SUMMARIZE

As you read material published in another time period or written in an unfamiliar style, it is often helpful to summarize the main points. When you **summarize**, you state briefly in your own words the main ideas and key details of the text. You might pause to summarize each page, each event, or even each paragraph. For example, you might summarize Equiano's first paragraph in this way:

> The slaves were kept below deck in tight confinement. The conditions were unbearable. People were chained in pairs and disease ran rampant. Many died. Equiano himself, although allowed to stay on deck, often wished to die.

◆ Build Vocabulary

WORD ROOTS: *-vid-*

Equiano calls his captors *improvident*. The root *-vid-*, which comes from the Latin *videre*, means "to see." The word *provident* means "to have foresight." *Improvident* describes someone who lacks foresight.

WORD BANK

Before you read, preview this list of words from the selection.

loathsome
pestilential
copious
improvident
avarice
pacify

from

The Interesting Narrative of the Life of Olaudah Equiano

Olaudah Equiano

In the first several chapters, Equiano describes how he and his sister were kidnapped from their home in West Africa by slave traders and transported to the African coast. During this six- or seven-month journey, Equiano was separated from his sister and held at a series of way stations. After reaching the coast, Equiano was shipped with other slaves to this continent. The following account describes this horrifying journey.

At last when the ship we were in, had got in all her cargo, they made ready with many fearful noises, and we were all put under deck, so that we could not see how they managed the vessel. But this disappointment was the least of my sorrow. The stench of the hold while we were on the coast was so intolerably loathsome, that it was dangerous to remain there for any time, and some of us had been permitted to stay on the deck for the fresh air; but now that the whole ship's cargo were confined together, it became absolutely pestilential. The closeness of the place, and the heat of the climate, added to the number in the ship, which was so crowded that each had scarcely room to turn himself, almost suffocated us. This produced copious perspirations, so that the air soon became unfit for respiration, from a variety of loathsome smells, and brought on a sickness among the slaves, of which many died—thus falling victims to the improvident avarice, as I may call it, of their purchasers. This wretched situation was again aggravated by the galling of the chains, now become insupportable, and the

Slaves Below Deck (detail), Lt. Francis Meynell, National Maritime Museum, Greenwich

▲ **Critical Viewing** The artist portrays conditions on a slave ship. Compare and contrast this image with the one that Equiano describes. [**Compare and Contrast**]

filth of the necessary tubs, into which the children often fell, and were almost suffocated. The shrieks of the women, and the groans of the dying, rendered the whole a scene of horror almost inconceivable. Happily perhaps, for myself, I was soon reduced so low here that it was thought necessary to keep me almost always on deck; and from my extreme youth I was not put in fetters.[1] In this situation I expected every hour to share the fate of my companions, some of whom were almost daily brought upon deck at the point of death, which I began to hope would soon put an end to my miseries. Often did I think many of the inhabitants of the deep much more happy than myself. I envied them the freedom they enjoyed, and as often wished I could change my condition for theirs. Every circumstance I met with, served only to render my state more painful, and heightened my apprehensions, and my opinion of the cruelty of the whites.

One day they had taken a number of fishes; and when they had killed and satisfied themselves with as many as they thought fit, to our astonishment who were on deck, rather than give any of them to us to eat, as we expected, they tossed the remaining fish into the sea again, although we begged and prayed for some as well as we could, but in vain; and some of my countrymen, being pressed by hunger, took an opportunity, when they thought no one saw them, of trying to get a little privately; but they were discovered, and the attempt procured them some very severe floggings. One day, when we had a smooth sea and moderate wind, two of my wearied countrymen who were chained together

◆ Reading Strategy
Summarize the conditions on the ship.

1. **fetters** (fet´ ərz) *n*.: Chains.

from *The Interesting Narrative of the Life of Olaudah Equiano* ◆ 45

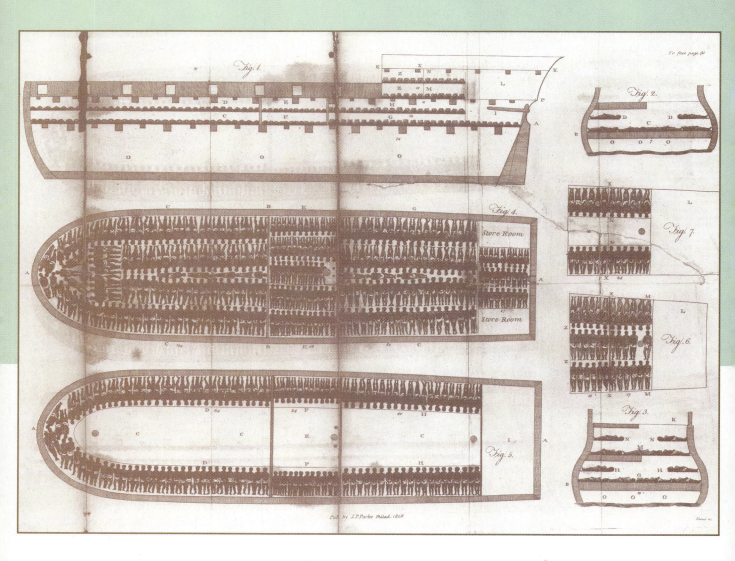

▲ **Critical Viewing** Estimate the number of slaves that this ship can carry. What do the drawings suggest about the ship designer's attitude toward slavery? [Draw Conclusions]

(I was near them at the time), preferring death to such a life of misery, somehow made through the nettings and jumped into the sea; immediately, another quite dejected fellow, who, on account of his illness, was suffered to be out of irons, also followed their example; and I believe many more would very soon have done the same, if they had not been prevented by the ship's crew, who were instantly alarmed. Those of us that were the most active, were in a moment put down under the deck; and there was such a noise and confusion amongst the people of the ship as I never heard before, to stop her, and get the boat out to go after the slaves. However, two of the wretches were drowned, but they got the other, and afterwards flogged him unmercifully, for thus attempting to prefer death to slavery.

◆ **Literary Focus**
What does this detail reveal about the captors' attitude?

In this manner we continued to undergo more hardships than I can now relate, hardships which are inseparable from this accursed trade. Many a time we were near suffocation from the want of fresh air, which we were often without for whole days together. This, and the stench of the necessary tubs, carried off many.

During our passage, I first saw flying fishes, which surprised me very much; they used frequently to fly across the ship, and many of them fell on the deck. I also now first saw the use of the quadrant;[2] I had often with astonishment seen the mariners make observations with it, and I could not think what it meant. They at last took notice of my surprise; and one of them, willing to increase it, as well as to gratify my curiosity, made me one day look through it. The clouds appeared to me to be land, which disappeared as they passed along. This heightened my wonder; and I was now more persuaded than ever, that I was in another world, and that every thing about me was magic. At last, we came in sight of the island of Barbados, at which the whites on board gave a great shout, and made many signs of joy to us. We did not know what to think of this; but as the vessel drew nearer, we plainly saw the harbor, and other ships of different kinds and sizes, and we soon anchored amongst them, off Bridgetown.[3] Many merchants and planters now came on board, though it was in the evening. They put us in separate parcels,[4] and examined us attentively. They also made us jump, and pointed to the land, signifying we were to go there. We thought by this, we should be eaten by these ugly men, as they appeared to us; and, when soon after we were all put down under the deck again, there was much dread and trembling among us, and nothing but bitter cries to be heard all the night from these apprehensions, insomuch, that at last the white people got some old slaves from the land to pacify us. They told us we were not to be eaten, but to work, and were soon to go on land, where we should see many of our country people. This report eased us much. And sure enough, soon after we were landed, there came to us Africans of all languages.

We were conducted immediately to the merchant's yard, where we were all pent up together, like so many sheep in a fold, without regard to sex or age. . . . We were not many days in the merchant's custody, before we were sold after their usual manner, which is this: On a signal given (as the beat of a drum), the buyers rush at once into the yard where the slaves are confined, and make choice of that parcel they like best. . . .

---

2. **quadrant** (kwä´ drənt) *n.*: An instrument used by navigators to determine the position of a ship.
3. **Bridgetown** *n.*: The capital of Barbados.
4. **parcels** (pär´ səlz) *n.*: Groups.

◆ **Build Vocabulary**
pacify (pas´ ə fī´) *v.*: Calm; soothe

Guide for Responding

◆ Literature and Your Life

Reader's Response Based on his narrative, what is your impression of Equiano?

Thematic Focus When one culture dominates another, what troubles might a society face?

Journal Writing Jot down your reactions to Equiano's account. What emotions did it stir up?

☑ Check Your Comprehension

1. How did Equiano's age affect his experiences during the voyage?
2. (a) For what crimes were slaves punished? (b) What was the punishment?
3. Summarize the conditions for the slaves on board the ship.

Guide for Responding (continued)

◆ Critical Thinking

INTERPRET

1. Why does Equiano blame the illness aboard the ship on the "improvident avarice" of the traders? **[Support]**
2. How can you tell that Equiano has a great zest for life despite his assertion that he wanted to die? Provide examples from the story. **[Support]**

APPLY

3. Equiano's narrative was instrumental in the fight to ban the slave trade in America. What persuasive evidence does his description of the middle passage offer? **[Defend]**

EXTEND

4. How does Equiano's voyage compare with those of explorers and colonists? **[Social Studies Link]**

◆ Reading Strategy

SUMMARIZE

When you **summarize** a piece of writing, you state the main points and key details of a selection.

Write a summary of Equiano's narrative, identifying at least three main ideas the author conveys about the voyage.

◆ Literary Focus

SLAVE NARRATIVE

A **slave narrative** is an autobiographical account of life as a slave. In describing significant events in his or her life, the writer often documents the horrors of slavery. This selection from Equiano's narrative provides a grim description of the middle passage and the operation of the slave trade.

1. What aspect of the conditions aboard ship does Equiano stress in this account?
2. What was the general feeling of the slaves toward their situation?
3. Cite two examples of the slave traders' cruelty to the slaves.
4. Cite two examples that show the traders' concern for the slaves' well-being.
5. What might have motivated the traders' behavior toward their human cargo? Explain.

◆ Build Vocabulary

USING THE WORD ROOT -vid-

Considering the meaning of the root -vid-, "to see," answer these questions:

1. Why is *evidence* useful in establishing guilt?
2. How would *video* technology change telephone habits?

USING THE WORD BANK

Decide whether the words in each of the following pairs are synonyms or antonyms. On your paper, write A for *Antonym* or S for *Synonym*.

1. loathsome/hateful
2. pestilential/sanitary
3. copious/sparse
4. improvident/cautious
5. avarice/greed
6. pacify/torment

◆ Grammar and Style

ACTIVE AND PASSIVE VOICE

When Equiano explains, ". . . they were discovered," he uses the **passive voice** to emphasize the slaves rather than their captors. The use of the passive voice was common when Equiano wrote, but today, most writers choose the **active voice** whenever possible to make their writing more forceful and effective.

> A verb is in the **active voice** when the subject of the sentence performs the action. A verb is in the **passive voice** when the action is performed on the subject.

Practice Rewrite the following sentences using the active voice. You may need to add words to indicate who performed the action.

1. Some of us had been permitted to stay on the deck for the fresh air.
2. We thought we should be eaten by these ugly men.
3. I was soon reduced low here.
4. It was thought necessary to keep me almost always on deck.

Build Your Portfolio

Idea Bank

Writing

1. **Activist List** Equiano's autobiography contributed to the end of the slave trade. Create a list of problems facing today's society, and offer suggestions for how people could be educated about each problem.

2. **Editorial** Imagine that you are an American newspaper publisher in 1789 when Equiano's *The Interesting Narrative* was released. As an abolitionist who would like to ban slavery, write the editorial you might have printed in response to the book.

3. **Character Sketch** As a director staging a production of *The Interesting Narrative*, write a description of the character of Equiano. Include Equiano's strengths and weaknesses in order to enable an actor to portray him.

Speaking and Listening

4. **Debate** Is it possible for slavery to exist in today's society? With a group of classmates, debate this question. **[Social Studies Link]**

5. **Antislavery Speech** Prepare and deliver a speech arguing against slavery in the newly formed Union to present to the 1789 Congress. Use Equiano's narrative to bolster your argument. **[Social Studies Link]**

Projects

6. **Internet Research** Organizations such as Amnesty International work to increase awareness of injustices around the world. Use the Internet or the library to learn about Amnesty International and the causes it publicizes. Report your findings to the class. **[Technology Link]**

7. **Movie Poster** Design a poster to advertise a Hollywood version of Equiano's narrative. You may want to retitle the work for film audiences.

Writing Mini-Lesson

Museum Placard

To educate today's audiences, institutions like Detroit's Museum of African American History have been developing exhibits that document the slave trade of the 1800's. Imagine that you've been asked to write the introductory material that will appear on a large placard at the beginning of such an exhibit. Explain the sequence of events of the slave trade, beginning with the capture of Africans on their native continent, and conclude with the auctioning of enslaved Africans in the Americas. Use this tip to help you develop your placard.

Writing Skills Focus: Sequence of Events

A chronological **sequence** leads readers clearly from the first step to the next in the order in which events took place. Outline the sequence you'll be describing. Follow these suggestions:
- Begin with what happens first and continue in time order.
- Use words like *next, then,* and *finally* to make the sequence as clear to readers as possible.
- Avoid shifts in time sequence.

Prewriting Use library sources to gather facts about the slave trade. Organize your information, perhaps by drawing a map on which you can indicate the routes of the slave trade, dates, and other key details.

Drafting Refer to your notes as you begin writing. Keep events in chronological order and use transition words—such as *at first, next, while, then, finally,* and *after*—to ensure that the order is clear.

Revising Reread your work to confirm that the placard will highlight the important stages of the slave trade. Eliminate any nonessential details, and add transitions to sharpen the sequence of events.

CONNECTIONS TO TODAY'S WORLD

Diamond Island: Alcatraz
Darryl Babe Wilson

Big Yellow Taxi
Joni Mitchell

Thematic Connection

MEETING OF CULTURES

Though quite different, the works in Part 1 share one thing in common: they record impressions of the world, of new experiences, of new people seen through the filter of the writer's experiences and culture. The Native Americans saw nature as the source of earthly life. The conquistadors viewed new lands and people within the framework of European values. Olaudah Equiano vividly portrayed the consequences of one culture's belief in its right to dominate another. Each of their stories contributes uniquely to our understanding of the country that would become the United States of America.

Today, the distinct lines that separated these cultures have blurred into a shared "American experience." America is still celebrated as a melting pot of cultures from around the world, but there are those who feel that some of the values that once shaped the nation are in danger of being left behind.

O BEAUTIFUL FOR SPACIOUS SKIES . . .

The Native Americans who saw the Earth as the handiwork of gods, enchanted animals, and magical winds could not have foreseen a world paved over with parking lots, such as folk singer Joni Mitchell describes in "Big Yellow Taxi." The early Native Americans, who lived in harmony with their environment, would have been shocked to discover how much of the American wilderness has given way to development. Today, the wide open spaces and awe-inspiring sights that greeted the explorers still exist, but they are fewer and farther between.

KEEPING THE FLAME ALIVE

The last two centuries have also seen the gradual disappearance of many of the cultures and customs of Native American peoples. Darryl Babe Wilson preserves in writing the memories of Native American elders. Wilson confronts the elders' fear that the younger generation of Native Americans are unenlightened about their ancestral heritage. Wilson strives to bring about a "meeting of cultures" *within* his Native American nation, as well as from without.

DARRYL BABE WILSON (1939–)

Darryl Babe Wilson is a Native American poet and short-story writer. He lives in California's San

Francisco Bay area and teaches writing at two local colleges. Before moving to California in 1997, Wilson taught Native American studies at the University of Arizona, where he earned his Ph.D. in Comparative Culture and Literary Studies. Wilson often writes about the struggles of his people. For his book *Voices from the Earth*, he interviewed Native Americans from Barrow, Alaska, to the Mayan Peninsula of Mexico and Guatemala.

JONI MITCHELL (1943–)

Joni Mitchell is a well-loved and influential folk singer-songwriter. Born in Ft. MacLeod, Alberta, Canada, she began performing while in her twenties at local coffeehouses. After cutting her first album in 1968, she produced a title almost every year through 1982. Her album

Clouds won a Grammy award for best folk performance.

Diamond Island: Alcatraz

Allisti Ti-Tanin-Miji
(Rock Rainbow)

Darryl Babe Wilson

San Francisco, 1849, Attributed to Joshua Pierce

There was a single letter in the mailbox. Somehow it seemed urgent. The address, although it was labored over, could hardly be deciphered—square childlike print that did not complete the almost individual letters. Inside, five pages written on both sides. Blunt figures. Each word pressed

▲ **Critical Viewing** This painting shows Alcatraz as seen from a San Francisco hilltop at twilight. What is the mood created by this depiction of the island? **[Describe]**

heavily into the paper. I could not read it but I could feel the message. "Al traz" was in the first paragraph, broken and scattered, but there. At the very bottom of the final page—running out of space—he scrawled his name. It curved down just past the right-hand corner. The last letter of his name, *n*, did not fit: *Gibso*. It was winter, 1971. I hurried to his home.

Grandfather lived at Atwam, 100 miles east of Redding, California, in a little shack out on the flat land. His house was old and crooked just like in a fairy tale. His belongings were few and they, too, were old and worn. I always wanted to know his age and often asked some of the older of our people if they could recall when Grandfather was born. After silences that sometimes seemed more than a year, they always shook their silver-gray heads and answered: "I dunno. He was old and wrinkled with white hair for as long as I can remember. Since I was just a child." He must have been born between 1850 and 1870.

Thanksgiving weekend, 1989. It is this time of the year when I think about Grandfather and his ordeal. I keep promising myself that I will write his story down because it is time to give the island of Alcatraz a proper identity and a "real" history. It is easy for modern people to think that the history of Alcatraz began when a foreign ship sailed into the bay and a stranger named Don Juan Manuel de Ayala[1] observed the "rock" and recorded "Alcatraz" in a log book in 1775. That episode, that sailing and that recording was only moments ago.

Grandfather said that long ago the Sacramento Valley was a huge freshwater lake, that it was "as long as the land" (from the northern part of California to the southern), and that a great shaking of an angry spirit within the earth caused part of the coastal range to crumble into the outer-ocean. When the huge lake finally drained and the waves from the earthquake finally settled, there was the San Francisco Bay, and there, in isolation and containing a "truth," was Diamond Island (Alcatraz).

He told me the story one winter in his little one-room house in Atwam. It is bitter cold there during winters. I arrived late in the evening, tires of my truck spinning up his driveway. The driveway was a series of frozen, broken mudholes in a general direction across a field to his home. The headlights bounced out of control.

My old 1948 Chevy pickup was as cold inside as it was outside. The old truck kept going, but it was a fight to make it go in the winter. It was such a struggle that we called it "Mr. Miserable." Mr. Miserable and I came to a jolting halt against a snowbank that was the result of someone shoveling a walk in the front yard. We expended our momentum. The engine died with a sputtering cough. Lights flopped out.

It was black outside but the crusted snow lay like a ghost upon the earth and faded away in every direction. The night sky trembled with the fluttering of a million stars—all diamond blue. Wind whipped broken tumbleweeds across his neglected yard. The snow could not conceal the yard's chaos.

The light in the window promised warmth. Steam puffing from every breath, I hurried to his door. The snow crunched underfoot, sounding like a horse eating a crisp apple. The old door lurched open with a complaint. Grandfather's fatigued, centenarian[2] body a black silhouette against the brightness—bright although he had but a single shadeless lamp to light the entire house. I saw a skinned bear once. It looked just like Grandfather. Short, stout arms and bowed legs. Compact physique. Muscular—not fat. Thick chest. Powerful. Natural.

Old powder-blue eyes strained to see who was out there in the dark. "Hallo. You're just the man I'm lookin' for." Coffee aroma exploded from the open door. Coffee. Warmth!

Grandfather stood back and I entered the comfort of his jumbled little bungalow. It was cozy in there. He was burning juniper wood. Juniper, cured for a summer, has a clean, delicate aroma—a perfume. After a healthy handshake we huddled over steaming cups of coffee. Grandfather looked long at me. I think that he was not totally convinced that I was there. The hot coffee was good. It was not a fancy Colombian, aromatic blend, but it was so good!

---

1. **Don Juan Manuel de Ayala** (dän hwän män welʹ dä ä yäʹ lä): An eighteenth-century Spanish explorer who was the first European to enter San Francisco Bay.

---

2. **centenarian** (senʹ tə nerʹ ē ən) *adj*.: At least one hundred years old.

We were surrounded by years of Grandfather's collections. It was like a museum. Everything was very old and worn. It seemed that every part of the clutter had a history—sometimes a history that remembered the origin of the earth, like the bent pail filled with obsidian[3] that he had collected from Glass Mountain many summers before, "just in case."

He also had a radio that he was talked into purchasing when he was a young working man in the 1920's. The radio cost $124. I think he got conned by that merchant and the episode magnified in mystery when he recalled that it was not until 1948 before he got the electric company to put a line to his home. By that time he forgot about the radio and he did not remember to turn it on until 1958. It worked. There was an odor of oldness—like a mouse that died then dried to a stiffness through the years—a redolence of old neglected newspapers.

The old person in the old house under the old moon began to tell the story of his escape from "the rock" long ago. He gathered himself together and reached back into a painful past. The silence was long and I thought that he might be crying silently. Then, with a quiver in his voice, he started telling the story that he wanted me to know:

"Alcatraz Island. Where the Pit River runs into the sea is where I was born, long ago. *Alcatraz*, that's the white man's name for it. To our people, in our legends, we always knew it as *Allisti Ti-tanin-miji* [Rock Rainbow], Diamond Island. In our legends, that's where the Mouse Brothers, the twins, were told to go when they searched for a healing treasure for our troubled people long, long ago. They were to go search at the end of *It A-juma* [Pit River]. They found it. They brought it back. But it is lost now. It is said, the 'diamond' was to bring goodness to all our people, everywhere.

"We always heard that there was a 'diamond' on an island near the great salt water. We were always told that the 'diamond' was a thought, or a truth. Something worth very much. It was not a jewelry. It sparkled and it shined, but it was not a jewelry. It was more. Colored lights came from inside it with every movement. That is why we always called it [Alcatraz] *Allisti Ti-Tanin-miji.*" With a wave of an ancient hand and words filled with enduring knowledge, Grandfather spoke of a time long past.

In one of the many raids upon our people of the Pit River country, his pregnant mother was taken captive and forced, with other Indians, to make the long and painful march to Alcatraz in the winter. At that same time, the military was "sweeping" California. Some of our people were "removed" to the Round Valley Reservation at Covelo; others were taken east by train in open cattle cars during the winter to Quapa, Oklahoma. Still others were taken out into the ocean at Eureka and thrown overboard into icy waters.

Descendants of those that were taken in chains to Quapa are still there. Some of those cast into the winter ocean at Eureka made it back to land and returned to Pit River country. A few of those defying confinement, the threat of being shot by "thunder sticks," and dark winter nights of a cold Alcatraz-made-deadly by churning, freezing currents, made it back to Pit River country, too.

Grandfather said, "I was very small, too small to remember, but my grandmother remembered it all. The guards allowed us to swim around the rock. Every day, my mother swam. Every day, the people swam. We were not just swimming. We were gaining strength. We were learning the currents. We had to get home.

"When it was time, we were ready. We left at darkness. Grandmother said that I was a baby and rode my mother's back, clinging as she swam from Alcatraz to solid ground in night. My Grandmother remembered that I pulled so hard holding on that I broke my mother's necklace. It is still there in the water . . . somewhere." With a pointing of a stout finger southward, Grandfather indicated where "there" was.

Quivering with emotion, he hesitated. He trembled. "I do not remember if I was scared,"

---

3. **obsidian** (əb sid′ ē ən) *n*.: Hard, dark-colored or black volcanic glass.

◆ Build Vocabulary

expended (ek spend′ id) *v*.: To have spent or used by consuming

redolence (red′ əl əns) *n*.: Scent; smell

Grandfather said, crooked, thick fingers rubbing a creased and wrinkled chin covered with white stubble. "I must have been."

When those old, cloudy eyes dripped tears down a leathery, crevassed[4] face, and long silences were between his sentences, often I trembled too. He softly spoke of his memory.

Our cups were long empty; *maliss* (fire) needed attention. The moon was suspended in the frozen winter night—round, bright, scratched and scarred—when Grandfather finally paused in his thinking. The old castiron heater grumbled and screamed when I slid open the top to drop in a fresh log. Sparks flew up into the darkness then disappeared. I slammed the top closed. Silence, again.

Grandfather continued, "There was not real diamonds on the island. At least I don't think so. I always thought the diamonds were not diamonds but some kind of understanding, some kind of good thought—or something." He shook a white, shaggy head and looked off into the distance into a time that was so long ago that the mountains barely remembered. For long moments he reflected, he gathered his thoughts. He knew that I "wrote things down on paper."

The night was thick. To the north a coyote howled. Far to the west an old coyote rasped a call to the black wilderness, a supreme presence beneath starry skies with icy freedom all around.

"When first I heard about the 'diamond,' I thought it might be a story of how we escaped. But after I heard that story so many times, I don't think so. I think there was a truth there that the Mouse Brothers were instructed to get and bring back long ago to help our people. I don't think that I know where that truth is now. Where can it be? It must be deep *inside Axo-Yet* [Mount Shasta][5] or *Sa Titt* [Medicine Lake]. It

Photo of a Native American male (Wailaki tribe), Edward S. Curtis, Southwest Museum, Los Angeles

▲ **Critical Viewing** How does this portrait convey the wisdom of the grandfather in the story? [**Connect**]

hides from our people. The truth hides from us. It must not like us. It denies us."

The One-as-Old-as-the-Mountains made me wonder about this story. It seems incredible that there was such an escape from Alcatraz. Through American propaganda I have been trained to believe that it was impossible to escape from that isolated rock because of the currents and because of the freezing temperature as the powerful ocean and the surging rivers merged in chaos. I was convinced—until I heard Grandfather's story and until I realized that he dwelled within a different "time," a different "element." He dwelled within a spirituality of a natural source. In his world, I was only a foreign infant. It is true today that when I talk with the old people I feel like *nilladuwi*—(a white man). I feel like some domesticated creature addressing original royalty—knowing that the old ones were pure savage, born into the wild, free.

In his calm manner, Grandfather proceeded. "We wandered for many nights. We hid during the day. It is said that we had to go south for three nights before we could turn north. [My people landed at San Francisco and had to sneak to what is now San Jose, traveling at night with no food until they could turn northward.] They [the U.S. Army] were after us. They were after us all. We had to be careful. We had to be careful and not make mistakes. We headed north for two nights.

"We came to a huge river. We could not cross it. It was swift. My mother walked far upstream then jumped in. Everybody followed. The river washed us to the other shore [possibly the Benicia Straits]. We rested for two days eating dead fish that we found along the river. We could not build a fire because they would see the smoke and catch us so we must eat it [fish] raw. At night we traveled again. Again we traveled, this time for two nights also.

"There is a small island of mountains in the

_____

4. **crevassed** (krə vast´) *adj.*: Deeply cracked.
5. **Mount Shasta** (shas´ tə): A volcanic mountain in northern California.

great valley [Sutter Buttes]. When we reached that place one of the young men climbed the highest peak. He was brave. We were all brave. It was during the sunlight. We waited for him to holler as was the plan. We waited a long, long time. Then we heard: *'Axo-Yet! Axo-Yet! To-ho-ja-toki! To-ho-ja-toki Tanjan'* [Mount Shasta! Mount Shasta! North direction!]. Our hearts were happy. We were close to home. My mother squeezed me to her. We cried. I know we cried. I was there. So was my mother and grandmother."

Grandfather has been within the earth for many snows now. The volumes of knowledge that were buried with him are lost to my generation, a generation that needs original knowledge now more than ever, if we are to survive as a distinct and <u>autonomous</u> people. Perhaps a generation approaching will be more aware, more excited with tradition and custom and less satisfied to being off balance somewhere between the world of the "white man" and the world of the "Indian," and will seek this knowledge.

It is nearing winter, 1989. Snows upon *Axo-Yet* (Mount Shasta) are deep. The glaring white makes Grandfather's hair nearly yellow—now that I better recall the coarse strands that I often identified as "silver." That beautiful mountain. The landmark that caused the hunted warrior 140 years ago to forget the tragic episode that could have been the termination of our nation, and, standing with the sun shining full upon him, hollered to a frightened people waiting below: *"Axo-Yet! Axo-Yet! To-ho-ja-toki Tanjan!"*

Perhaps the approaching generation will seek and locate *Allisti Ti-tanin-miji* within the mountains. Possibly that generation will reveal many truths to this world society that is immense and confused in its immensity. An old chief of the Pit River country, "Charlie Buck," said often: "Truth. It is truth that will set us free." Along with Grandfather, I think that it was a "truth" that the Mouse Brothers brought to our land from Diamond Island long ago. A truth that needs to be understood, appreciated, and acknowledged. A truth that needs desperately to be found and known for its value.

Grandfather's letter is still in my files. I still can't read it, but if I could, I am sure that the message would be the same as this story that he gave to me as the moon listened and the winds whispered across a frozen Atwam, during a sparkling winter night long ago.

◆ **Build Vocabulary**

autonomous (ô tän′ ə məs) *adj.*: Independent

Guide for Responding

◆ *Literature and Your Life*

Reader's Response If you could ask Grandfather a question about his story, what would you ask? Why?

Thematic Focus Wilson implies that the existence of Native American culture is endangered today just as it was more than one hundred years ago when his ancestors were persecuted by those who didn't understand or value their culture. What is the source of the modern threat to the survival of his people's heritage?

☑ **Check Your Comprehension**

1. How did Grandfather learn the story of his family's escape from Alcatraz—an event that took place when he was a small boy?
2. According to the story, what does the "diamond" of Diamond Island represent?
3. What does Grandfather believe has become of the "diamond"?

("Critical Thinking" questions appear on p. 57.)

BIG YELLOW TAXI

Words and Music by *Joni Mitchell*

They paved paradise, put up a parking lot,
With a pink hotel, a boutique
And a swinging hot spot.

Don't it always seem to go
5   That you don't know what you've got till it's gone,
They paved paradise, put up a parking lot.

They took all the trees, put 'em in a tree museum,
And they charged the people
A dollar and a half just to see 'em.

10   Don't it always seem to go
That you don't know what you've got till it's gone,
They paved paradise, put up a parking lot.

Hey, farmer, farmer put away that D.D.T. now,
Give me spots on the apples,
15   But leave me the birds and the bees, please.

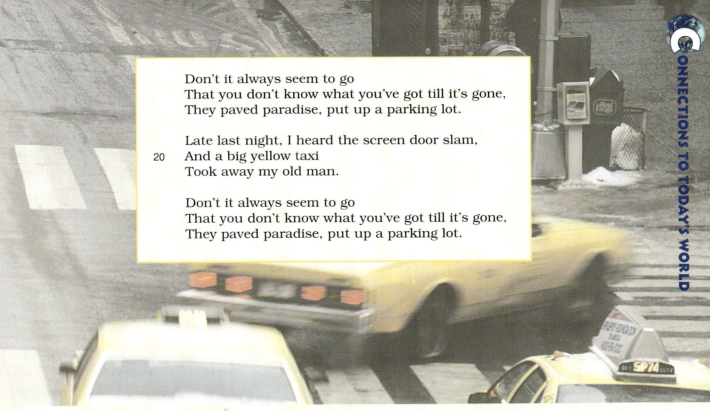

Don't it always seem to go
That you don't know what you've got till it's gone,
They paved paradise, put up a parking lot.

Late last night, I heard the screen door slam,
20 And a big yellow taxi
Took away my old man.

Don't it always seem to go
That you don't know what you've got till it's gone,
They paved paradise, put up a parking lot.

Guide for Responding

◆ Literature and Your Life

Reader's Response Give an example of someone or something you didn't fully appreciate until it was too late.

Thematic Focus What are the two "cultures" represented in "Big Yellow Taxi"? How would Mitchell describe the interaction of these cultures?

☑ Check Your Comprehension

1. What human creations replace nature in "Big Yellow Taxi"?
2. What happens to the trees?
3. What examples does Mitchell provide to prove "you don't know what you've got till it's gone"?

◆ Critical Thinking

INTERPRET

1. Why does Grandfather ask the narrator to visit in "Diamond Island: Alcatraz"?
2. Explain why Darryl Babe Wilson's generation needs "original knowledge" in order to survive. **[Infer]**
3. What do the apples with spots symbolize in this song? **[Interpret]**

EVALUATE

4. How do you think the Native American creators of the origin myths would feel about the world Mitchell describes in "Big Yellow Taxi"? Explain. **[Speculate]**

EXTEND

5. Wilson writes about preserving a heritage. What do people in your culture do to preserve their identity as a culture? **[Community Link]**.
6. How can the phrase "you don't know what you've got till it's gone" be applied to Darryl Babe Wilson's efforts as a writer? **[Literature Link]**

Thematic Connection

MEETING OF CULTURES

Though Cabeza de Vaca's experiences with Native Americans he encountered while traveling through Texas are a classic example of the meeting of two very different cultures, this theme can take many different forms. Sometimes, as illustrated in "Big Yellow Taxi" and "Diamond Island: Alcatraz," there can be a conflict between different aspects of the same culture or a clash between opposing values of different cultures.

1. Wilson says that he feels like a domesticated creature or "white man" when he talks to the elders of his people. In what ways does the relationship between younger and more elderly Native Americans reflect a "meeting of cultures"?
2. Explain how the saying "Paradise once lost can never be regained" relates to "Big Yellow Taxi." (a) What does "paradise" symbolize, and to what is it lost? (b) Why can it never be regained?
3. Describe a situation from your own life or observations that you feel represents a "meeting of cultures." What are the "cultures" involved? Is the meeting characterized by friendly exchange, or is it more a clash of cultures?

Idea Bank

Writing

1. **Cultural Story** Think of a story that you believe represents your culture or deserves to be handed down to future generations. Then preserve it in writing. The story may be about an incident from your own life or that of a relative or family friend.

2. **Museum Brochure** "Big Yellow Taxi" paints a picture of a world so far removed from its natural state that trees are a rarity seen only in a "tree museum." In such a world, what else might be found only in museums? Create a brochure for a museum of the future that exhibits endangered objects. Include an overview of the museum's collection and background information on where or how several important display items were obtained.

3. **Persuasive Essay** Though often dominated by colonists who did not understand or respect their cultures, both Native Americans and enslaved Africans clung tightly to the unifying strength of their respective heritage. Thanks to that determination, many Native and African Americans still practice the customs and religions of their ancestors. Write an essay in which you persuade your readers to explore and preserve their own cultural heritage for themselves and for future generations. Use the selections you have read to argue the need for greater awareness and understanding of the richness of the many cultures that form the American mosaic. **[Social Studies Link]**

Speaking and Listening

4. **Television Interview** Work with a classmate to stage an interview with Grandfather for a television program called "Native American Focus." Begin by developing a set of interview questions about Grandfather's memories of his childhood escape from Alcatraz. Then outline Grandfather's answers using information from the selection. Use your prepared notes to stage the interview for your class. **[Media Link]**

Projects

5. **Time Capsule** How would you represent modern American culture to future generations or a different culture? Work in a small group to create a time capsule of items that you believe capture the time in which you live. Choose a range of items that reflect current events, popular culture, trends, and attitudes. Once you have gathered at least a half dozen items, create identifying labels for each. Present your finished time capsule to your class, and explain the rationale for selecting each item. **[Social Studies Link]**

Writing Process Workshop

When Europeans stepped onto North American soil, they opened the door for more settlements and the eventual creation of a new nation. They set off a chain of events that changed the world. The European settlement of North America is an ideal topic for a **cause-and-effect essay**—an essay that examines the reasons behind an event or phenomenon and explains the effects of that event. Write a cause-and-effect essay explaining an event or phenomenon that interests you. The following skills, introduced in this section's Writing Mini-Lessons, will help you write your essay.

Writing Skills Focus

▶ **Use precise details** to support your explanations. (See p. 41.)

▶ **Use effective repetition** to emphasize your main points. (See p. 31.)

▶ **Outline the sequence of events** to make it easy for readers to follow the causes and effects. (See p. 49.)

Note that in this example, Olaudah Equiano gives several causes for a single effect—his awe and amazement at the unfamiliar things he observes while on a slave ship.

MODEL FROM LITERATURE
---

from *The Interesting Narrative of the Life of Olaudah Equiano*
by Olaudah Equiano

During our passage, I first saw flying fishes, which surprised me very much; they used frequently to fly across the ship, and many of them fell on the deck. ① I also now first saw the use of the quadrant; I had often with astonishment seen mariners make observations with it, and I could not think what it meant. They at last took notice of my surprise; and one of them, willing to increase it, as well as to gratify my curiosity, made me one day look through it. The clouds appeared to me to be land, which disappeared as they passed along. This heightened my wonder; ② and I was now more persuaded than ever that I was in another world, and that every thing about me was magic . . . ③

① This precise detail about flying fish helps the reader see why this sight inspired awe in Equiano.

② Equiano emphasizes his amazement through repeated references to his feelings.

③ Equiano provides a list of causes—from flying fish to unusual clouds—that contribute to his amazement.

APPLYING LANGUAGE SKILLS:
Correct Run-on Sentences

A run-on sentence has two or more main clauses incorrectly punctuated as a single sentence.

Run-on Sentence:

The strike hurt baseball, fans lost interest.

To correct a run-on sentence, divide the main clauses into separate sentences, add a semicolon, or use a comma and a conjunction between main clauses.

Revised Sentences:

The strike hurt baseball. Fans lost interest in the game.

or

The strike hurt baseball; fans lost interest in the game.

or

The strike hurt baseball, and fans lost interest in the game.

Practice Revise this sentence three ways.

Ticket prices went up, fans stayed away.

Writing Application Revise your essay to eliminate any run-on sentences.

Writer's Solution Connection
Language Lab

For more practice correcting run-on sentences, complete the Language Lab lesson on Fragments and Run-on Sentences.

Prewriting

Choose a Topic Your essay can explain the cause of a current effect (for example, why the stock market is surging or sagging) or predict the future effects of current causes (where the stock market will be next year). You can also choose one of the topic ideas listed here.

> ### Topic Ideas
> - The causes of rush-hour traffic jams on local roadways
> - The effects of expansion on a professional sport
> - The effects of a certain school rule on student behavior

Gather Details Conduct research to learn more about causes and effects related to your topic. Use questions like these to guide your research. To direct your exploration toward the most relevant points, address these key questions about your subject:

▶ Who are the people involved?
▶ How are they affected?
▶ What are the causes?
▶ What can be done to change the situation?

Outline the Sequence of Events Once you've finished gathering information, use a flowchart like this one to outline the sequence of causes and effects. Keep in mind that the cause of a subsequent event may itself be the effect of a preceding cause.

> Baseball strike results in the cancellation of 1994 World Series.
>
> ↕
>
> Attendance remains low.
>
> ↕
>
> Owners introduce limited regular season interleague play.
>
> ↕
>
> Temporary surge in attendance.

Drafting

Organize Your Material Into an Introduction, Body, and Conclusion To arrange your material in the most readable and understandable way, introduce your topic clearly, develop it fully in the body of your essay, and restate it persuasively in your conclusion.

Note Places for Further Development If your first draft has passages that could use more specific details, don't stop to fill them in. Complete your draft, but mark those sections for further development.

Revising

Use a Checklist Refer to the Writing Skills Focus on p. 59, and use the items as a checklist to evaluate and revise your essay.

▶ Have I used precise details?
   Replace vague or abstract details with more precise language and images. Fill in any spots that you marked for later development.

▶ Have I used repetition effectively?
   Look for places where you can reinforce key points through repetition.

▶ Have I clearly outlined the sequence of events?
   Ask a peer reviewer to restate the chain of causes and effects. If the relationships are unclear, refer to your outline and add transitions to strengthen connections between ideas.

REVISION MODEL

The dramatic impact of interleague play was especially

visible in New York in 1997, when the New York

Yankees met the New York Mets ①[*at Yankee Stadium*] before a ②[*capacity*] crowd [*of 56,000. The roaring enthusiasm of the huge crowd left no doubt that the temporary experiment had a long future.*] ~~that was much larger than usual.~~ ③

① The writer fills in missing details.
② The writer replaces a long phrase with a single precise word.
③ The writer adds a prediction about the future.

Publishing

▶ **Informative Speech** Present your essay in a speech to classmates. Use charts, graphs, or diagrams to clarify the cause-and-effect relationships you describe.

Strategies for Success

When you think of a map, the first thing that comes to mind may be an atlas or a history textbook. Maps are also common in newspapers, news magazines, and many other written texts. By offering a visual representation of a place, a map can help give you a clearer picture of a scene that an author describes using words.

Read Between the Lines Like a book, a map must be read carefully to be properly understood. Most maps have a legend that provides distance scales and explains any symbols included on the map.

Connect the Dots The map on this page shows fighting that took place in and around the city of Sarajevo in a one-week period during the civil war in Bosnia. If you look closely, you'll see symbols representing Serb troop movement in the direction of the city of Sarajevo. Judging by the direction of the arrows, you can conclude that the Serbs' goal was to capture the city. By connecting the symbols in this way, you can gather important information from the map.

Apply the Strategy

Using the map on the left, answer the following questions.

1. Where was the fighting most intense during the week of June 14–21, 1995?
2. Why do you think the fighting was most intense in this area?
3. What can you infer about the priorities of the Bosnian government, judging by where it placed its troops?
4. What features would hinder an invasion of the city of Sarajevo?
5. How might this map have been of use to Bosnian government leaders?

> ✔ *Here are other situations in which you can apply map-reading skills:*
> ▶ Reading news magazines
> ▶ Reading historical novels
> ▶ Traveling

PART 2 _Focus on Literary Forms:_
Narrative Accounts

Building the Fort, Julien Binford,
The Jamestown/Yorktown Educational Trust

The settlers who journeyed across a hostile ocean and forged homes in a new land were generally far too busy just surviving to create poems and other types of literature that matched those of other areas of the world. The early settlers did succeed, however, in writing vivid narrative accounts—a literary form that has remained popular to this day.

Guide for Interpreting

John Smith (1580–1631)

If John Smith were alive today, he'd be starring opposite Arnold Schwarzenegger in blockbuster adventure films—at least, that's probably where he'd see himself. Adventurer, poet, mapmaker, and egotist are just a few of the labels that apply to Smith, who earned a reputation as one of England's most famous explorers by helping to lead the first successful English colony in America. Stories of his adventures, often embellished by his own pen, fascinated readers of his day and continue to provide details about early exploration of the Americas.

Following a ten-year career as a soldier, Smith led a group of colonists to this continent, where they landed in Virginia in 1607 and founded Jamestown. As president of the colony from 1608 to 1609, Smith helped to obtain food, enforce discipline, and deal with the local Native Americans.

Though Smith returned to England in 1609, he made two more voyages to America to explore the New England coast. He published several works in the course of his life, including *The General History of Virginia, New England, and the Summer Isles* (1624).

William Bradford (1590–1657)

Survival in North America was a matter of endurance, intelligence, and courage. William Bradford had all three. Thirteen years after the founding of Jamestown, Bradford helped lead the Pilgrims to what is now Massachusetts.

Bradford, who was born in Yorkshire, England, joined a group of Puritan extremists who believed the Church of England was corrupt and wished to separate from it. In the face of stiff persecution, they eventually fled to Holland and from there sailed to North America.

After the death of the colony's first leader, the Pilgrims elected William Bradford governor. He was re-elected thirty times. During his tenure, he organized the repayment of debts to financial backers, encouraged new immigration, and established good relations with the Native Americans, without whose help the colony never would have survived.

In 1630, Bradford began writing *Of Plymouth Plantation,* a firsthand account of the Pilgrims' struggle to endure, sustained only by courage and unbending faith. The work, written in the simple language known as Puritan Plain Style, was not published until 1856.

◆ Background for Understanding

HISTORY: THE COLONIAL EXPERIENCE

The trading company that financed the Jamestown expedition mistakenly believed that there was much money to be made in North America. John Smith was nearly sent to prison for not meeting his backers' financial expectations. It is not surprising, then, that Smith sometimes exaggerated the exploits of the settlers as they struggled to survive in the new land.

The Jamestown settlers weren't the only ones struggling. In 1620, after a difficult voyage aboard the tiny *Mayflower,* the Pilgrims landed not in Virginia, as intended, but much farther north near Cape Cod, Massachusetts. It was mid-December before they could build shelters and move ashore. During those dreary weeks of waiting on the ship, William Bradford's wife, Dorothy, fell overboard and was drowned.

Once ashore, the Pilgrims found the hardships of settling in a strange land worsened by a harsh winter and disputes over the validity of their charter, which had been for Virginia. The conflict led the settlers to create the "Mayflower Compact," the first agreement for self-government made by the colonists and a model for later settlements.

from The General History of Virginia
◆ from Of Plymouth Plantation ◆

◆ *Literature and Your Life*

CONNECT YOUR EXPERIENCE

You can probably remember a point in your life when everything seemed to be going against you. Consider what the early American colonists faced: starvation, exhaustion, illness, and the terror of the unknown. As the narratives show, determination pushed them on.

Journal Writing Write down your thoughts about what you imagine it was like to be an early settler.

THEMATIC FOCUS: MEETING OF CULTURES

The settlers faced many terrible risks for a chance at a new life. Would they have survived without the help of the Native Americans?

◆ Reading Strategy

BREAK DOWN SENTENCES

Break down the meaning of complex sentences by considering one section at a time. Separate the essential parts of the sentence (the *who* and *what*) from difficult language. Mentally bracket any descriptions that aren't essential. Below, John Smith explains why establishing a colony at Jamestown was so difficult.

Such actions have [ever since the world's beginning] been subject to such accidents, [and everything of worth is found full of difficulties,] but nothing so difficult as to establish a commonwealth so far remote from men and means.

When you ignore the passages in brackets, you can easily get at the central point: *Actions like these have resulted in accidents before, but nothing as hard as establishing a commonwealth so far away from people and resources.*

◆ Grammar and Style

PLURAL AND POSSESSIVE NOUNS

In their narratives, Smith and Bradford use **possessive** nouns to show kinship and ownership. Notice that they follow these rules:

• Add an apostrophe and -*s* to show the possessive case of most singular nouns: the King's dearest daughter
• Add an apostrophe to show the possessive of plural nouns ending in -*s* or -*es*: in two or three months' time
• Add an apostrophe and -*s* to show the possessive of plural nouns that do not end in -*s* or -*es*: where men's minds are so untoward

◆ Literary Focus

NARRATIVE ACCOUNTS

Narrative accounts tell the story of real-life events. The selections that follow are **historical narratives,** narrative accounts that record significant historical events. Some historical narratives, including these, are firsthand accounts by people who lived through the events. Others are secondhand, or secondary, accounts by people who researched, but did not live through, the events. As you read, keep in mind that firsthand accounts are sometimes subjective because of the writer's personal involvement in the events.

◆ Build Vocabulary

RELATED WORDS: FORMS OF *PERIL*

In *Of Plymouth Plantation*, the Pilgrims found themselves in *peril*, or danger. You could describe their journey as *perilous*, an adjective meaning "full of danger." You could also say that undertaking such a risky voyage could *imperil* their lives. Now you've learned a verb that means "to place in danger."

WORD BANK

Preview this list of words from the selections.

pilfer
palisades
conceits
mollified
peril
loath
sundry
recompense

from The General History of Virginia

John Smith

What Happened Till the First Supply

Founding of the First Permanent English Settlement in America, A. C. Warren, New York Public Library

▲ **Critical Viewing** What can you infer about the artist's attitude toward Native Americans from the way he depicts them? **[Infer]**

Being thus left to our fortunes, it fortuned[1] that within ten days, scarce ten amongst us could either go[2] or well stand, such extreme weakness and sickness oppressed us. And thereat none need marvel if they consider the cause and reason, which was this: While the ships stayed, our allowance was somewhat bettered by a daily proportion of biscuit which the sailors would pilfer to sell, give, or exchange with us for money, sassafras,[3] or furs. But when they departed, there remained neither tavern, beer house, nor place of relief but the common kettle.[4] Had we been as free from all sins as gluttony and drunkenness we might have been canonized for saints, but our President[5] would never have been admitted for engrossing to his private,[6] oatmeal, sack,[7] oil, aqua vitae,[8] beef, eggs, or what not but the kettle; that indeed he allowed equally to be distributed, and that was half a pint of wheat and as much barley boiled with water for a man a day, and this, having fried some twenty-six weeks in the ship's hold, contained as many worms as grains so that we might truly call it rather so much bran than corn; our drink was water, our lodgings castles in the air.

With this lodging and diet, our extreme toil in bearing and planting palisades so strained and bruised us and our continual labor in the extremity of the heat had so weakened us, as were cause sufficient to have made us as miserable in our native country or any other place in the world.

From May to September, those that escaped lived upon sturgeon and sea crabs. Fifty in this time we buried; the rest seeing the President's projects to escape these miseries in our pinnace[9] by flight (who all this time had neither felt want nor sickness) so moved our dead spirits as we deposed him and established Ratcliffe in his place . . .

But now was all our provision spent, the sturgeon gone, all helps abandoned, each hour expecting the fury of the savages; when God, the patron of all good endeavors, in that desperate extremity so changed the hearts of the savages that they brought such plenty of their fruits and provision as no man wanted.

◆ **Reading Strategy**
"Buried" in this long sentence is an important turn of events for the colonists. Break the sentence down to understand its meaning.

And now where some affirmed it was ill done of the Council[10] to send forth men so badly provided, this incontradictable reason will show them plainly they are too ill advised to nourish such ill conceits: First, the fault of our going was our own; what could be thought fitting or necessary we had, but what we should find, or want, or where we should be, we were all ignorant and supposing to make our passage in two months, with victual to live and the advantage of the spring to work; we were at sea five months where we both spent our victual and lost the opportunity of the time and season to plant, by the unskillful presumption of our ignorant transporters that understood not at all what they undertook.

Such actions have ever since the world's beginning been subject to such accidents, and everything of worth is found full of difficulties, but nothing so difficult as to

---

9. **pinnace** (pin´ is) *n.*: Small sailing ship.
10. **Council:** The seven persons in charge of the expedition.

◆ **Build Vocabulary**

pilfer (pil´ fər) *v.*: Steal

palisades (pal´ə sādz´) *n.*: Large, pointed stakes set in the ground to form a fence used for defense

conceits (kən sēts´) *n.*: Strange or fanciful ideas

---

1. **fortuned** *v.*: Happened.
2. **go** *v.*: Be active.
3. **sassafras** (sas´ ə fras´) *n.*: A tree, the root of which was valued for its supposed medicinal qualities.
4. **common kettle:** Communal cooking pot.
5. **President:** Wingfield, the leader of the colony.
6. **engrossing to his private:** Taking for his own use.
7. **sack** *n.*: Type of white wine.
8. **aqua vitae** (ak´ wə vīt´ ē): Brandy.

establish a commonwealth so far remote from men and means and where men's minds are so untoward[11] as neither do well themselves nor suffer others. But to proceed.

The new President and Martin, being little beloved, of weak judgment in dangers, and less industry in peace, committed the managing of all things abroad[12] to Captain Smith, who, by his own example, good words, and fair promises, set some to mow, others to bind thatch, some to build houses, others to thatch them, himself always bearing the greatest task for his own share, so that in short time he provided most of them lodgings, neglecting any for himself. . . .

Leading an expedition on the Chickahominy River, Captain Smith and his men are attacked by Indians, and Smith is taken prisoner.

When this news came to Jamestown, much was their sorrow for his loss, few expecting what ensued.

◆ **Literary Focus**
How does this paragraph alert you to the fact that Smith's account is not completely objective?

Six or seven weeks those barbarians kept him prisoner, many strange triumphs and conjurations they made of him, yet he so demeaned himself amongst them, as he not only diverted them from surprising the fort, but procured his own liberty, and got himself and his company such estimation amongst them, that those savages admired him.

The manner how they used and delivered him is as followeth:

The savages having drawn from George Cassen whither Captain Smith was gone, prosecuting that opportunity they followed him with three hundred bowmen, conducted by the King of Pamunkee,[13] who in divisions searching the turnings of the river found Robinson and Emry by the fireside; those they shot full of arrows and slew. Then finding the Captain, as is said, that used the savage that was his guide as his shield (three of them being slain and divers[14] others so galled),[15] all the rest would not come near him. Thinking thus to have returned to his boat, regarding them, as he marched, more than his way, slipped up to the middle in an oozy creek and his savage with him; yet dared they not come to him till being near dead with cold he threw away his arms. Then according to their compositions[16] they drew him forth and led him to the fire where his men were slain. Diligently they chafed his benumbed limbs.

He demanding for their captain, they showed him Opechancanough, King of Pamunkee, to whom he gave a round ivory double compass dial. Much they marveled at the playing of the fly and needle,[17] which they could see so plainly and yet not touch it because of the glass that covered them. But when he demonstrated by that globe-like jewel the roundness of the earth and skies, the sphere of the sun, moon, and stars, and how the sun did chase the night round about the world continually, the greatness of the land and sea, the diversity of nations, variety of complexions, and how we were to them antipodes[18] and many other such like matters, they all stood as amazed with admiration.

Nothwithstanding, within an hour after, they tied him to a tree, and as many as could stand about him prepared to shoot him, but the King holding up the compass in his hand, they all laid down their bows

---

11. **untoward** *adj.*: Stubborn.
12. **abroad** *adv.*: Outside the palisades.

13. **Pamunkee:** Pamunkee River.
14. **divers** (dī′ vərz) *adj.*: Several.
15. **galled** *v.*: Wounded.
16. **composition** *n.*: Ways.
17. **fly and needle** *n.*: Parts of a compass.
18. **antipodes** (an tip′ ə dēz′) *n.*: Two places on opposite sides of the Earth.

and arrows and in a triumphant manner led him to Orapaks where he was after their manner kindly feasted and well used. . . .

At last they brought him to Werowocomoco, where was Powhatan, their Emperor. Here more than two hundred of those grim courtiers stood wondering at him, as he had been a monster, till Powhatan and his train had put themselves in their greatest braveries. Before a fire upon a seat like a bedstead, he sat covered with a great robe made of raccoon skins and all the tails hanging by. On either hand did sit a young wench of sixteen or eighteen years and along on each side the house, two rows of men and behind them as many women, with all their heads and shoulders painted red, many of their heads bedecked with the white down of birds, but every one with something, and a great chain of white beads about their necks.

At his entrance before the King, all the people gave a great shout. The queen of Appomattoc was appointed to bring him water to wash his hands, and another brought him a bunch of feathers, instead of a towel, to dry them; having feasted him after their best barbarous manner they

◆ **Reading Strategy**
Break down this long sentence to clarify the sequence of events.

could, a long consultation was held, but the conclusion was, two great stones were brought before Powhatan: then as many as could, laid hands on him, dragged him to them, and thereon laid his head and being ready with their clubs to beat out his brains, Pocahontas, the King's dearest daughter, when no entreaty could prevail, got his head in her arms and laid her own upon his to save him from death; whereat the Emperor was contented he should live to make him hatchets, and her bells, beads, and copper, for they thought him as well of all occupations as themselves.[19] For the King himself will make his own robes, shoes, bows, arrows, pots; plant, hunt, or do anything so well as the rest.

Two days after, Powhatan, having disguised himself in the most fearfulest manner he could, caused Captain Smith to be brought forth to a great house in the woods and there upon a mat by the fire to be left alone. Not long after, from behind a mat that divided the house, was made the most dolefulest noise he ever heard; then Powhatan more like a devil than a man, with some two hundred more as black as himself, came unto him and told him now they were friends, and presently he should go to Jamestown to send him two great guns and a grindstone for which he would give him the country of Capahowasic and forever esteem him as his son Nantaquond.

So to Jamestown with twelve guides Powhatan sent him. That night they quartered in the woods, he still expecting (as he had done all this long time of his imprisonment) every hour to be put to one death or other, for all their feasting. But almighty God (by His divine providence) had <u>mollified</u> the hearts of those stern barbarians with compassion. The next morning betimes they came to the fort, where Smith having used the savages with what kindness he could, he showed Rawhunt, Powhatan's trusty servant, two demiculverins[20] and a millstone to carry Powhatan; they found them somewhat too heavy, but when they did see him discharge them, being loaded with stones, among the boughs of a great tree loaded with icicles, the ice and branches came so tumbling down that the poor savages ran away half dead with fear. But at last we regained some conference with them and gave them such toys and sent to Powhatan, his women, and children such presents as gave them in general full content.

---

19. **as well . . . themselves:** Capable of making them just as well as they could themselves.

20. **demiculverins** (dem′ ē kul′ vər inz): Large cannons.

◆ **Build Vocabulary**
mollified (mäl′ ə fīd′) v.: Soothed; calmed

Now in Jamestown they were all in combustion,[21] the strongest preparing once more to run away with the pinnace; which, with the hazard of his life, with saker falcon[22] and musket shot, Smith forced now the third time to stay or sink.

Some, no better than they should be, had plotted with the President the next day to have him put to death by the Levitical law,[23] for the lives of Robinson and Emry; pretending the fault was his that had led them to their ends: but he quickly took such order with such lawyers that he laid them by their heels till he sent some of them prisoners for England.

---

21. **combustion** (kəm bəs´ chən) *n.*: Tumult.
22. **saker falcon**: Small cannon.
23. **Levitical law**: "He that killeth man shall surely be put to death" (Leviticus 24:17).

Now every once in four or five days, Pocahontas with her attendants brought him so much provision that saved many of their lives, that else for all this had starved with hunger.

His relation of the plenty he had seen, especially at Werowocomoco, and of the state and bounty of Powhatan (which till that time was unknown), so revived their dead spirits (especially the love of Pocahontas) as all men's fear was abandoned.

Thus you may see what difficulties still crossed any good endeavor; and the good success of the business being thus oft brought to the very period of destruction; yet you see by what strange means God hath still delivered it.

> ◆ **Literary Focus**
> What does this last paragraph reveal about Smith's purpose in creating his narrative account?

Guide for Responding

◆ *Literature and Your Life*

Reader's Response Would you have returned to England at the earliest opportunity or stayed on at Jamestown? Why?

Thematic Focus What might have prompted colonists to leave England and start new lives in America?

☑ Check Your Comprehension

1. What hardships do the colonists face during their first several months in this country?
2. What assistance do the colonists receive?
3. What criticisms does Smith make of the new president and colonist Martin?
4. Who or what does Smith praise in this account?

◆ Critical Thinking

INTERPRET

1. What impression of Smith do you get from this account? **[Infer]**
2. Describe Smith's attitude toward the Native Americans. **[Analyze]**
3. Why do you think Smith writes in the third person, referring to himself as "he" instead of "I"? **[Draw Conclusions]**

EVALUATE

4. Do you think that Smith's account is accurate down to the last detail? Why or why not? **[Evaluate]**

EXTEND

5. If Smith were alive today, what career might he have? Explain. **[Career Link]**

from Of Plymouth Plantation

William Bradford

The Coming of the Mayflower, N. C. Wyeth, from the Collection of the Metropolitan Life Insurance Company, New York City

▲ **Critical Viewing** Is this an idealized or a realistic depiction of the *Mayflower's* Atlantic crossing? Explain your decision. **[Judge; Support]**

Of Their Voyage and How They Passed the Sea; and of Their Safe Arrival at Cape Cod

After they had enjoyed fair winds and weather for a season, they were encountered many times with cross winds and met with many fierce storms with which the ship was shroudly[1] shaken, and her upper works made very leaky; and one of the main beams in the midships was bowed and cracked, which put them in some fear that the ship

---

1. **shroudly** (shro͞od´ lē) *adv.*: Wickedly.

could not be able to perform the voyage. So some of the chief of the company, perceiving the mariners to fear the sufficiency of the ship as appeared by their mutterings, they entered into serious consultation with the master and other officers of the ship, to consider in time of the danger, and rather to return than to cast themselves into a desperate and inevitable peril. And truly there was great distraction and difference of opinion amongst the mariners themselves: fain would they do what could be done for their wages' sake (being now near half the seas over) and on the other hand they were loath to hazard their lives too desperately. But in examining of all opinions, the master and others affirmed they knew the ship to be strong and firm under water; and for the buckling of the main beam, there was a great iron screw the passengers brought out of Holland, which would raise the beam into his place; the which being done, the carpenter and master affirmed that with a post put under it, set firm in the lower deck and otherways bound, he would make it sufficient. And as for the decks and upper works, they would caulk them as well as they could, and though with the working of the ship they would not long keep staunch, yet there would otherwise be no great danger, if they did not overpress her with sails. So they committed themselves to the will of God and resolved to proceed.

In sundry of these storms the winds were so fierce and the seas so high, as they could not bear a knot of sail, but were forced to hull[2] for divers days together. And in one of them, as they thus lay at hull in a mighty storm, a lusty[3] young man called John Howland, coming upon some occasion above the gratings was, with a seel[4] of the ship, thrown into sea; but it pleased God that he caught hold of the topsail halyards[5] which hung overboard and ran out at length. Yet he held his hold (though he was sundry fathoms under water) till he was hauled up by the same rope to the brim of the water, and then with a boat hook and other means got into the ship again and his life saved. And though he was something ill with it, yet he lived many years after and became a profitable member both in church and commonwealth. In all this voyage there died but one of the passengers, which was William Butten, a youth, servant to Samuel Fuller, when they drew near the coast.

But to omit other things (that I may be brief) after long beating at sea they fell with that land which is called Cape Cod; the which being made and certainly known to be it, they were not a little joyful. After some deliberation had amongst themselves and with the master of the ship, they tacked about and resolved to stand for the southward (the wind and weather being fair) to find some place about Hudson's River for their habitation. But after they had sailed that course about half the day, they fell amongst dangerous shoals and roaring breakers, and they were so far entangled therewith as they conceived themselves in great danger; and the wind shrinking upon them withal,[6] they resolved to bear up again for the Cape and thought themselves happy to get out of those dangers before night overtook them, as by God's good providence they did. And the next day they got into the Cape Harbor[7] where they rid in safety.

Being thus arrived in a good harbor, and brought safe to land, they fell upon their knees and blessed the God of Heaven who had brought them over the vast and furious ocean, and delivered them from all the perils and miseries thereof, again to set their feet on the firm and stable earth, their proper element.

◆ **Reading Strategy**

Many ideas and actions are expressed in this lengthy sentence. To better comprehend its meaning, break the passage down into shorter sentences.

---

6. **withal** (with´ ôl) *adv.*: Also.
7. **Cape Harbor:** Now Provincetown Harbor.

---

2. **hull** *v.*: Drift with the wind.
3. **lusty** *adj.*: Strong; hearty.
4. **seel** *n.*: Rolling.
5. **halyards** (hal´ yərdz) *n.*: Ropes for raising or lowering sails.

◆ **Build Vocabulary**

peril (per´ əl) *n.*: Danger
loath (lōth) *adj.*: Reluctant; unwilling
sundry (sun´ drē) *adj.*: Various; different

▲ **Critical Viewing** What can you learn about the lifestyle at Plymouth Plantation from this photograph of an authentic re-creation of the settlement? **[Infer]**

The Starving Time

But that which was most sad and lamentable was, that in two or three months' time half of their company died, especially in January and February, being the depth of winter, and wanting houses and other comforts: being infected with the scurvy[8] and other diseases which this long voyage and their inaccommodate[9] condition had brought upon them. So as there died sometimes two or three of a day in the foresaid time, that of one hundred and odd persons, scarce fifty remained. And of these, in the time of most distress, there was but six or seven sound persons who to their great commendations, be it spoken, spared no pains night or day, but with abundance of toil and hazard of their own health, fetched them wood, made them fires, dressed them meat, made their beds, washed their loathsome clothes, clothed and unclothed them. In a word, did all the homely[10] and necessary offices for them which dainty and queasy stomachs cannot endure to hear named; and all this willingly and cheerfully, without any grudging in the least, showing herein their true love unto their friends and brethren; a rare example and worthy to be remembered. Two of these seven were Mr. William Brewster, their reverend Elder, and Myles Standish, their

8. **scurvy** (skʉr′ vē) *n*.: Disease caused by vitamin C deficiency.
9. **inaccommodate** (in′ ə käm′ ə dət) *adj*.: Unfit.

10. **homely** (hōm′ lē) *adj*.: Domestic.

Captain and military commander, unto whom myself and many others were much beholden in our low and sick condition. And yet the Lord so upheld these persons as in this general calamity they were not at all infected either with sickness or lameness. And what I have said of these I may say of many others who died in this general visitation,[11] and others yet living: that whilst they had health, yea, or any strength continuing, they were not wanting to any that had need of them. And I doubt not but their <u>recompense</u> is with the Lord.

But I may not here pass by another remarkable passage not to be forgotten. As this calamity fell among the passengers that were to be left here to plant, and were hasted ashore and made to drink water that the seamen might have the more beer, and one[12] in his sickness desiring but a small can of beer, it was answered that if he were their own father he should have none. The disease began to fall amongst them also, so as almost half of their company died before they went away, and many of their officers and lustiest men, as the boatswain, gunner, three quartermasters, the cook and others. At which the Master was something strucken and sent to the sick ashore and told the Governor he should send for beer for them that had need of it, though he drunk water homeward bound.

But now amongst his company there was far another kind of carriage[13] in this misery than amongst the passengers. For they that before had been boon[14] companions in drinking and jollity in the time of their health and welfare, began now to desert one another in this calamity, saying they would not hazard their lives for them, they should be infected by coming to help them in their cabins; and so, after they came to lie by it, would do little or nothing for them but, "if they died, let them die." But such of the passengers as were yet aboard showed them what mercy they could which made some of their hearts relent, as the boatswain (and some others) who was a proud young man and would often curse and scoff at the passengers. But when he grew weak, they had compassion on him and helped him; then he confessed he did not deserve it at their hands, he had abused them in word and deed. "Oh!" (saith he) "you, I now see, show your love like Christians indeed one to another, but we let one another lie and die like dogs." Another lay cursing his wife, saying if it had not been for her he had never come this unlucky voyage, and anon cursing his fellows, saying he had done this and that for some of them; he had spent so much and so much amongst them, and they were now weary of him and did not help him, having need. Another gave his companion all he had, if he died, to help him in his weakness; he went and got a little spice and made him a mess[15] of meat once or twice. And because he died not so soon as he expected, he went amongst his fellows and swore the rogue would cozen[16] him, he would see him choked before he made him any more meat; and yet the poor fellow died before morning.

Indian Relations

All this while the Indians came skulking about them, and would sometimes show themselves aloof off, but when any approached near them, they would run away; and once they stole away their tools where they had been at work and were gone to dinner. But about the sixteenth of March, a certain Indian came boldly amongst them and spoke to them in broken English, which they could well understand but marveled at it. At length they understood by discourse with him, that he was not of these parts, but

---

11. **visitation** *n.*: Affliction.
12. **one:** William Bradford.
13. **carriage** *n.*: Behavior.
14. **boon** *adj.*: Close.

♦ **Build Vocabulary**

recompense (rek´ əm pens´) *n.*: Reward; repayment

---

15. **mess** *n.*: Meal.
16. **cozen** (kuz´ ən) *v.*: Cheat.

belonged to the eastern parts where some English ships came to fish, with whom he was acquainted and could name sundry of them by their names, amongst whom he had got his language. He became profitable to them in acquainting them with many things concerning the state of the country in the east parts where he lived, which was afterwards profitable unto them; as also of the people here, of their names, number and strength, of their situation and distance from this place, and who was chief amongst them. His name was Samoset. He told them also of another Indian whose name was Squanto, a native of this place, who had been in England and could speak better English than himself.

Being, after some time of entertainment and gifts dismissed, a while after he came again, and five more with him, and they brought again all the tools that were stolen away before, and made way for the coming of their great Sachem,[17] called Massasoit. Who, about four or five days after, came with the chief of his friends and other attendance, with the aforesaid Squanto. With whom, after friendly entertainment and some gifts given him, they made a peace with him (which hath now continued this twenty-four years) in these terms:

17. **Sachem** (sā´ chəm): Chief.

1. That neither he nor any of his should injure or do hurt to any of their people.
2. That if any of his did hurt to any of theirs, he should send the offender, that they might punish him.
3. That if anything were taken away from any of theirs, he should cause it to be restored; and they should do the like to his.
4. If any did unjustly war against him, they would aid him; if any did war against them, he should aid them.
5. He should send to his neighbors confederates to certify them of this, that they might not wrong them, but might be likewise comprised in the conditions of peace.
6. That when their men came to them, they should leave their bows and arrows behind them.

After these things he returned to his place called Sowams, some 40 miles from this place, but Squanto continued with them and was their interpreter and was a special instrument sent of God for their good beyond their expectation. He directed them how to set their corn, where to take fish, and to procure other commodities, and was also their pilot to bring them to unknown places for their profit, and never left them till he died.

Guide for Responding

◆ *Literature and Your Life*

Reader's Response If you had been making the journey on the *Mayflower*, what would you have done differently to better prepare for life in America?

Thematic Focus How has this account changed your impression of the Pilgrims?

☑ Check Your Comprehension

1. What hardships do the Pilgrims endure during their trip across the Atlantic?
2. What hardships do they encounter during their first winter at Plymouth?
3. (a) In what ways does Samoset help the Pilgrims? (b) What does Squanto do for them?

◆ Critical Thinking

INTERPRET

1. How would you characterize the Pilgrims' reactions to the hardships they encountered during their first winter in Plymouth? [Classify]
2. Find two statements that convey the Pilgrims' belief that they were being guided and protected by God. [Analyze]

APPLY

3. Do you feel that the changing attitudes of the settlers and the Native Americans reflect typical experiences with newcomers? Why or why not? [Synthesize]

Guide for Responding (continued)

◆ Reading Strategy

BREAK DOWN SENTENCES

When you **break down sentences** into simpler parts, you can get at the meaning of even lengthy or difficult sentences. Scan the narratives for a sentence that you found particularly challenging. Write the sentence on your paper, then do the following:

1. Use brackets or slashes to show how you broke the sentence down.
2. Write the meaning of the sentence as you understand it.

◆ Literary Focus

NARRATIVE ACCOUNTS

These selections are both **narrative accounts**, stories about real-life experiences. Both are also firsthand **historical narratives**, written about key events by people who experienced them. Firsthand accounts capture the flavor of the time and what it was like to participate in the event. The information presented is not always accurate, however, since the writer often tries to persuade or entertain readers.

1. Find two examples in which Smith exaggerates or displays subjectivity in recounting events.
2. (a) What do you think Smith's purpose was in writing this narrative? (b) How was Bradford's purpose different?

Beyond Literature

History Connection

Archaeologists Unearth the Jamestown Fort In 1996, a team of archaeologists located the remains of a fort built by John Smith and Jamestown's original inhabitants. It was long believed that the fort had been washed away by the James River. When archaeologist William Kelso found a shard of pottery that he believed dated back to 1545, however, he kept digging and found more than 100,000 artifacts—armor, coins, musket balls—from the seventeenth-century colony.

What can artifacts reveal about a colony that might be missing from a written account?

◆ Build Vocabulary

USING RELATED WORDS

Use the definitions you have learned to understand the meaning of other forms of the words in the Word Bank. On your paper, write the letter of the word that best answers each question.

a. mollification   b. pilferer   c. conceited

1. Which word describes people who are full of fanciful dreams of themselves?
2. Which word refers to the act of soothing or calming someone?
3. Which word describes someone who steals?

USING THE WORD BANK

Decide whether the words in each of the following pairs are antonyms or synonyms. On your paper, write A for *Antonymn* or S for *Synonym*.

1. pilfer, donate
2. palisades, fences
3. conceits, fantasies
4. mollified, angered
5. peril, safety
6. loath, willing
7. sundry, single
8. recompense, reward

◆ Grammar and Style

PLURAL AND POSSESSIVE NOUNS

The **possessive** form of nouns indicates kinship and ownership. Add an apostrophe and -s to form the possessive singular of most nouns. Add an apostrophe to form the possessive of plural nouns that end in -s or -es.

Incorrect: All the passenger's spirits were flagging.

Correct: All the passengers' spirits were flagging.

Use the apostrophe *only* for the possessive form; do *not* use it to form simple plurals.

Writing Application Rewrite this paragraph, correcting any mistakes in plurals or possessives.

Much to *Bradfords* amazement, Samoset spoke to the *Pilgrims* in broken English. Samoset convinced his fellow *Indians'* to return the *settler's* tools. He persuaded Massasoit to pay his *respects* to the *Pilgrims*, and introduced them to one of his *friend's*, Squanto.

Build Your Portfolio

Idea Bank

Writing

1. **Memorial Speech** As a Jamestown settler, you have been asked to speak at a memorial service for John Smith. Write a speech in which you describe Smith's adventures and accomplishments.

2. **Dramatic Scene** Write a scene that captures Samoset's first meeting with the Plymouth settlers. Include dialogue and stage directions. **[Performing Arts Link]**

3. **News Article** Pocahontas married a Jamestown settler and traveled to England. As a reporter for *The London Times,* research Pocahontas's life. Write an article about her visit to England.

Speaking and Listening

4. **Persuasive Speech** Imagine that you are Samoset. Deliver a persuasive speech in which you make the case for fostering peace between the settlers and your tribe. **[Social Studies Link]**

5. **Mock Trial** The company that backed Smith's expedition wanted him jailed for failing to provide a return on their investment. Stage a mock trial with students taking the roles of the judge, Smith, his defense lawyer, and the trading company representative. **[Social Studies Link]**

Projects

6. **Advertisement** Create a poster advertising life at Plymouth Plantation. Encourage others to journey to America to join the Pilgrim settlers.

7. **Menu** Many Pilgrims suffered from scurvy, a disease caused by a diet lacking in vitamin C. Learn more about the foods the colonists ate and the crops they planted. Then create a historically accurate menu for a typical day in the life of an early colonist. **[Health Link]**

Writing Mini-Lesson

Comparison of Narratives

These narratives leave the reader with the impression that Smith and Bradford were very different people with distinctly different outlooks on life. Write a comparison of these firsthand accounts.

Writing Skills Focus: Clear Organization

When you are comparing and contrasting, use a **clear organization**—one that will help to define the similarities and differences between your subjects. Two basic types of comparison-and-contrast organization are point by point and subject by subject:

- In a point-by-point organization, discuss each aspect of your subject in turn. For example, discuss one aspect of Smith's tone and immediately contrast it with an aspect of Bradford's tone.
- In a subject-by-subject organization, discuss all the qualities of one subject—say, the tone *and* content of Smith's narrative—and then the qualities of the other.

Prewriting Review the two narratives, noting each author's style, purpose, and objectivity. To help you gather and organize details, use a Venn diagram like this one.

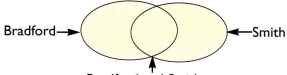

Drafting Focus each paragraph on a single author or point of comparison. To connect paragraphs and keep the relationships of ideas clear, use transitions such as *similarly, also, likewise, equally, in contrast, but, although, however, instead, on the other hand.*

Revising Revise your paper, reordering information to make the organization clearer and adding details when appropriate to strengthen your points.

CONNECTIONS TO TODAY'S WORLD

The Right Stuff
Tom Wolfe

Thematic Connection

THE PIONEER SPIRIT

The early American settlers struggled through rough seas, sickness, and starvation to carve out a home in a new land. They would have offered many different reasons to explain why—religious freedom, economic opportunity, political autonomy. At heart, it was a hunger for uncharted territory that drove the settlers to sail across the wide ocean and set foot on a forbidding continent. That spirit kept Americans going for three more centuries, setting their feet ever westward, blazing trails across the continent.

On the brink of a new millennium, the frontier has given way to a network of highways, airports, and shopping malls. When the frontier disappeared, the pioneer spirit had nowhere to go but up. In the twentieth century, this spirit pushed Americans into tiny, cramped capsules. The new pioneers have defied gravity itself and leaped upward into space. Tom Wolfe's book *The Right Stuff* documents this new American exploration.

Literary Connection

NARRATIVE ACCOUNTS

John Smith, William Bradford, and Tom Wolfe all wrote historical **narrative accounts**—factual reports of notable events. You will notice big differences between Wolfe's twentieth-century account of John Glenn's brief zooms around the planet and Smith's and Bradford's seventeenth-century chronicles of the colonists' struggles to survive. One obvious difference is in the style, the shift from the formal vocabulary of seventeenth-century men of authority to the more casual, slang-filled language of a twentieth-century journalist.

Wolfe's account represents a great departure from the nonfiction writing of his own day. Just as the astronauts pushed the limits of human experience, stretching it beyond the Earth, Wolfe's writing broke out of the tradition of narrative nonfiction to incorporate the more imaginative techniques of fiction writing. Wolfe and other practitioners of the "New Journalism" of the 1960's highlight vivid details of character and setting and call attention to the way the observer feels about what is being observed.

TOM WOLFE
(1930–   )

Born in a Virginia far different from the one that John Smith knew, Tom Wolfe began his career working as a reporter and Latin America correspondent for the *Washington Post*. He then turned to magazine writing and eventually published essays, articles, and, later, full-length books that focused on various aspects of the contemporary American scene. He described elements of popular culture in *The Kandy-Kolored Tangerine Flake Streamline Baby* and dissected the art world in *The Painted Word*. Many critics regard *The Right Stuff*, an account of the Mercury space program, as Wolfe's best work.

from
The Right Stuff

Tom Wolfe

▲ **Critical Viewing** How do you imagine the astronauts' impressions of a liftoff differ from the views of spectators? [**Hypothesize**]

H ere he is!—within twenty seconds of lift-off, and the only strange thing is how little adrenaline[1] is pumping when the moment comes . . . He can hear the rumble of the Atlas engines building up down there below his back. All the same, it isn't terribly loud. The huge squat rocket shakes a bit and struggles to overcome its own weight. It all happens very slowly in the first few seconds, like an extremely heavy elevator rising. They've lit the candle and there's no turning

---

1. adrenaline (ə dren´ ə lin´) *n*.: Stress-related hormone secreted by the adrenal gland. When released, it increases heartbeat and raises blood pressure.

back, and yet there's no surge inside him. His pulse rises only to 110, no more than the minimum rate you should have if you have to deal with a sudden emergency. How strange that it should be this way! He has been more wound up for a takeoff in an F-102.[2]

"The clock is operating," he said, "We're underway."

It was all very smooth, much smoother than the centrifuge[3] . . . just as Shepard and Grissom said it would be. He had gone through the same g-forces[4] so many times . . . he hardly noticed them as they built up. It would have bothered him much more if they had been less. Nothing novel! No excitement, please! It took thirteen seconds for the huge rocket to reach transonic speed. The vibrations started. It was just as Shepard and Grissom said: it was much gentler than the centrifuge. He was still lying flat on his back, and the g-forces drove him deeper and deeper into the seat, but it all felt so familiar. He barely noticed it. He kept his eyes on the instrument panel the whole time . . . All quite normal, every little needle and switch in the right place . . . No <u>malevolent</u> instructor feeding *Abort* problems into the loop . . . As the rocket entered the transonic zone, the vibration became intense. The vibrations all but <u>obliterated</u> the roar of the engines. He was entering the area of "max q," maximum aerodynamic pressure, in which the pressure of the shaft of the Atlas forcing its way through the atmosphere at supersonic speed would reach almost a thousand pounds per square foot. Through the cockpit window he could see the sky turning black. Almost 5 g's were driving him back into his seat. And yet . . . *easier than the centrifuge* . . . All at once he was through *max q*, as if through a turbulent strait, and the <u>trajectory</u> was smooth and he was supersonic and the rumble of the rocket engines was more muffled than ever and he could hear all the little fans and recorders and the busy little kitchen, the humming little shop . . . . The pressure on his chest reached 6 g's. The rocket pitched down. For the first time he could see clouds and the horizon. In a moment—*there it was*—the Atlas rocket's two booster engines shut down and were <u>jettisoned</u> from the side of the shaft and his body was slammed forward, as if he were screeching to a halt, and the g-forces suddenly dropped to 1.25, almost as if he were on earth and not accelerating at all, but the central sustainer engine and two smaller engines were still driving him up through the atmosphere . . . A flash of white smoke went up past the window . . . . *No! The escape tower was firing early—but the* JETTISON TOWER *light wasn't on!* . . . He didn't see the tower go . . . Wait a minute . . . There went the tower, on schedule . . . The JETTISON TOWER light came on green . . . The smoke must have been from the booster rockets as they left the shaft . . . The rocket pitched back up . . . going straight up . . . The sky was very black now . . . The g-forces began pushing him back into his seat again . . . 3 g's . . . 4 g's . . . 5 g's . . . Soon he would be forty miles up . . . the last critical moment of powered flight, as the capsule separated from the rocket and went into its orbital trajectory . . . or didn't . . . *Hey!* . . . All at once the whole capsule was whipping up and down, as if it were tied to the end of a diving board, a springboard. The g-forces built up and the capsule whipped up and down. Yet no sooner had it begun than Glenn knew what it was. The weight of the rocket on the launch pad had been 260,000 pounds, practically all of it rocket fuel, the liquid oxygen. This was being consumed at such a furious rate, about one ton per second, that the rocket was becoming merely a skeleton with a thin skin of metal stretched over it, a tube so long and light that it was flexing. The g-forces reached six and

---

2. **F-102:** U.S. Air Force fighter plane.
3. **centrifuge** (sen´ trə fyo͞oj´) *n.*: A machine using force to pull a rotating object outward from a center. This type of machine was used to train the astronauts for the effects of spaceflight.
4. **g-forces** *n.*: Units measuring inertial pressure on a body during rapid acceleration. Units represent multiples of the acceleration of gravity.

◆ Build Vocabulary

malevolent (mə lev´ ə lənt) *adj.*: Mean-spirited; showing ill will

obliterated (ə blit´ ər āt´ id) *v.*: Blotted out; destroyed

trajectory (trə jek´ tə rē) *n.*: The curved path of an object hurtling through space

jettisoned (jet´ ə sənd) *v.*: Thrown overboard to lighten the weight of a ship

then he was weightless, just like that. The sudden release made him feel as if he were tumbling head over heels, as if he had been catapulted off the end of that same springboard and was falling through the air doing forward rolls. But he had felt this same thing on the centrifuge when they ran the g-forces up to seven and then suddenly cut the speed. At the same moment, right on schedule . . . a loud report . . . the posigrade rockets fired, throwing the capsule free of the rocket shaft . . . the capsule began its automatic turnabout, and all the proper green lights went on in front of him, and he knew he was "through the gate," as they said.

"Zero-g and I feel fine," he said. "Capsule is turning around . . ."

Glenn knew he was weightless. From the instrument readings and through sheer logic he knew it, but he couldn't feel it, just as Shepard and Grissom had never felt it. The turnaround brought him up to a sitting position, vertical to the earth, and that was the way he felt. He was sitting in a chair, upright, in a very tiny cramped quiet little cubicle 125 miles above the earth, a little metal closet, silent except for the humming of its electrical system, the inverters, the gyros, the cameras, the radio . . . *the radio* . . . He had

been specifically instructed to violate the Fighter Jock code of No Chatter. He was supposed to radio back every sight, every sensation, and otherwise give the taxpayers the juicy stuff they wanted to hear. Glenn, more than any of the others, was fully capable of doing the job. Yet it was an awkward thing. It seemed unnatural.

"Oh!" he said. "That view is tremendous!"

Well, it was a start. In fact, the view was not particularly extraordinary. It was extraordinary that he was up here in orbit about the earth. He could see the exhausted Atlas rocket following him. It was tumbling end over end from the force of the small rockets throwing the capsule free of it.

He could hear Alan Shepard, who was serving as capcom[5] in the Mercury Control Center at the Cape. His voice came in very clearly. He was saying, "You have a go, at least seven orbits."

"Roger," said Glenn. "Understand Go for at least seven orbits . . . This is *Friendship 7*. Can see clear back, a big cloud pattern way back across toward the Cape. Beautiful sight."

---

5. **capcom** (kap´ käm) *n. jargon*: Capsule communicator; person speaking directly to astronaut.

Guide for Responding

◆ Literature and Your Life

Reader's Response How would you have felt if you had been in that space capsule instead of John Glenn? What struck you as the most exciting part of his first few minutes in space?

Thematic Focus What takes more courage: riding in a capsule into space like the astronauts or making a new life in an uncharted land like the early settlers? Why?

☑ Check Your Comprehension

1. What does Glenn find so strange about his physical reactions on liftoff?
2. What had Shepard and Grissom told Glenn about their own experiences in space?
3. Why does Glenn radio the comment, "That view is tremendous"? How does he actually feel about the view?

◆ Critical Thinking

INTERPRET

1. What would you say are John Glenn's principal attributes, as shown in this excerpt? **[Analyze]**
2. Why do you think Glenn keeps comparing his training experiences in the centrifuge with his experiences during the actual spaceflight? **[Infer]**
3. Why is Glenn supposed to "radio back every sight . . . and otherwise give taxpayers the juicy stuff they wanted to hear"? **[Interpret]**

APPLY

4. Imagine that Glenn was heading to Mars to start the first human settlement. How might his thoughts have been different? What kind of "right stuff" would be necessary for such a venture? **[Synthesize]**

Thematic Connection

THE PIONEER SPIRIT

In the early 1960's, when the space age was just dawning, President Kennedy referred to space as our "new ocean," likening the advances in the space program to the discovery, exploration, and settlement of America by Europeans centuries before.

1. In what ways is John Glenn's experience similar to that of the Europeans who crossed the Atlantic Ocean and settled in America?

2. How do twentieth-century advances make Glenn's experience different from that of the colonists? Do you think these advances enhance his experience or diminish it? Why?

3. Tom Wolfe's title, *The Right Stuff,* refers to the qualities test pilots needed to fly higher, faster, and farther than anyone had ever done before. What personal qualities give John Glenn "the right stuff"? How do you think John Smith or William Bradford would have defined "the right stuff" needed to make a home in the American wilderness?

Literary Connection

NARRATIVE ACCOUNTS

Narrative accounts, like other types of writing, reflect their times. As you consider Tom Wolfe's account of the spaceflight, think of the specific differences between it and either John Smith's or William Bradford's chronicle of life in an early American colony.

1. List three words to describe each narrative account you read. Defend your choices.

2. Explain what each narrative tells you about the frame of mind of the people who lived during that time.

 Idea Bank

Writing

1. **Dialogue** Write a dialogue between John Glenn and William Bradford, in which Glenn argues why it is important for humans to explore space and Bradford argues why such exploration is wrong.

2. **News Article** Write the lead for a contemporary news article about the New England colonists' early struggles. Be sure to cover the *who? what? when? where? why?* and *how?* of their experiences.

3. **Sci-Fi Story** Recent discoveries suggest that life may have existed on Mars at some time. Write a science-fiction story set in the twenty-first century, in which John Smith is heading toward Mars with a group of colonists to set up the first station on that planet.

Speaking and Listening

4. **Debriefing Speech** This excerpt continually refers to the pre-flight practice Glenn and the other astronauts endured. Write the debriefing comments Glenn may have given after his flight. Include the details future astronauts would find useful in preparation for flight. **[Science Link]**

Projects

5. **Diagram** Do some research about Glenn's vehicle, then draw a diagram showing the rocket with the space capsule. Label the various parts of the diagram. Then read about the *Mayflower* (or similar ships), and draw a diagram of the kind of boat that took the Pilgrims across the ocean. Use a similar scale for your two diagrams to show how small *Friendship 7* is compared with the *Mayflower.* **[Science Link; Art Link]**

Writing Process Workshop

Since no one has yet invented a time machine, the selections in this unit are as close as you are likely to come to knowing the texture and feel of the life of our forebears in early America. Historians often use such accounts—along with other kinds of sources—to reconstruct the past. For students and scholars, one invaluable resource is on **annotated bibliography**—a list of materials on a certain topic. Beyond source information such as titles, authors, and publication dates, an annotated bibliography includes summaries or reviews of the material.

The following skills will help you to create an annotated bibliography.

Writing Skills Focus

▶ **Use clear organization** in summarizing the major elements of the book. (See p. 77.)

▶ **Communicate the main ideas** briefly and clearly.

▶ **Present publishing information** accurately so that readers can find the sources you include.

The following is a sample item from an annotated bibliography covering historical novels about pre-1750 America. Note how the writer clearly organizes the material into distinct areas.

MODEL

Rinaldi, Ann. *A Break With Charity: A Story About the Salem Witch Trials.* New York: Harcourt Brace Jovanovich/Gulliver Books, 1992. Fiction.

    The 1692 witchcraft trials caused mass hysteria in the once tranquil Massachusetts town of Salem. Susanna English, the fictional heroine of this novel, her family, and her friends find their lives sucked into the controversy. ① Susanna's determined character springs to life as she grapples with this tragedy and sets out to stop the madness in her community. ② The issues of individual conscience and the pressures of social conformity emerge with compelling clarity. ③ The author's meticulous research is evident in the historically authentic details of character and setting that embellish this excellent novel. ④

① The author immediately states the basic plot and setting.

② The entry provides a strong sense of the protagonist's character.

③ The entry includes a brief statement of theme.

④ The writer offers an overall evaluation of the work.

APPLYING LANGUAGE SKILLS: Citing Sources

Any bibliography should list source information thoroughly and accurately and in alphabetical order. Note the title, author, publication date, and publisher of each source you cite.

Book With One Author:

Myerhoff, Barbara. *Number Our Days*. New York: Touchstone, 1978.

Book With More Than One Author:

Jaffe, Nina, and Steve Zeitlin. *While Standing on One Foot*. New York: Henry Holt, 1993.

Magazine Article:

Squires, Sally. "The Heart Is a Hungry Hunter." *Cooking Light*, May 1996: 50–56.

If you cannot use italicized type, underline titles of full works.

Writing Application As you finalize your annotated bibliography, be sure the order and punctuation of each entry are correct.

Writer's Solution Connection
Writing Lab

For more information about citing and crediting sources, use the Drafting section of the Writing Lab Research tutorial.

Prewriting

Choose a Topic American history provides an almost endless store of fascinating ideas for research. Think about an aspect of the American past that especially interests you, or choose one of the topic ideas listed here.

> **Topic Ideas**
> - Political biographies
> - Nutrition advice for adolescents
> - Detective stories
> - College guides

Gathering Information When preparing an annotated bibliography, it is helpful to consider the widest possible array of resources.

▶ Consult the library's card or computer catalog using key words related to your subject.

▶ Look in fiction, poetry, drama, social science, and general nonfiction sections of the library.

▶ Use the *Readers' Guide* to locate articles in magazines, newspapers, and journals. To find sources on the Internet, use search networks, such as AltaVista.

Record the Information When You Find It As you find and review material, note the publishing information accurately. Doing so will save you time in the drafting, revising, and proofreading stages.

Plan a Clear Organization Make a list of the key areas you wish to cover in your comments about each source—for nonfiction: topic, time period, scope; and for fiction: plot, character, and theme—and then take notes on each item.

Drafting

Organize Your Entries Whether you organize your bibliography in a "best" to "worst" order or list the entries alphabetically by title, implement that plan as you draft. Within each entry, follow a logical order that provides both factual summaries and your critical evaluation.

Use Correct Format Your teacher might ask you to use the MLA (Modern Language Association) style for proper bibliographic form. Follow that format or use the information in the Apply Language Skills lesson on this page to make sure your entries consistently follow an appropriate format.

Revising

Cut Out Unnecessary Information To keep your annotations brief, delete any information that wouldn't be essential to someone researching your topic.

Proofread Your Work Any errors a writer makes in grammar or mechanics can distract or confuse a reader. Proofread your work carefully to eliminate errors. Use this checklist:

▶ Are all your sentences complete?

▶ Does every verb agree with its subject?

▶ Is your punctuation correct?

▶ Does your bibliographic entry follow the standard form specified in a reliable style guide?

REVISION MODEL

The son of a Scottish earl, James Gour is only fifteen ① *years* ~~yaers~~

old when he is kidnapped and sent to prerevolutionary

② *He eventually joins the revolutionary*
North Carolina under a new name, John Scot. ~~He has~~

struggle for independence from the British.
~~exciting adventures. . . .~~

① The writer corrects a typographical error.

② This sentence offers more information than the vague one it replaces.

Publishing

▶ **Create a Class Collection of Annotated Bibliographies** Publish your own anthology of annotated bibliographies. Make this resource available to other students in the library.

▶ **Go On-line** Find the appropriate Web site for your topic, and share your annotated bibliography with a wider audience. You might even update your work with input from Web browsers.

APPLYING LANGUAGE SKILLS: Avoiding Vague Statements

Make your sentences as clear and informative as possible by eliminating any vague statements.

Vague Sentence:

This biography of a Houston mayor is interesting.

Revision:

Because it reveals the obstacles he overcame while in office, this biography of a Houston mayor is an inspiration to readers.

Notice how the added details provide specific reasons why the biography is being praised.

Practice Revise the following sentences to make them less vague.

1. The library's collection of biographies is large.

2. The author creates a good setting.

Writing Application As you revise your annotated bibliography, add details as necessary to eliminate any vague sentences.

Writer's Solution Connection
Language Lab

For more information about revising vague sentences, complete the Language Lab lesson on Writing With Nouns and Verbs.

Real-World Reading Skills Workshop

Strategies for Success

Whenever you want to find information about something—whether it's a rumor about your best friend or a statistic about a favorite sports team—it's always best to go to the source. Going to the source will assure you that the information will be as accurate as possible. When you want to learn something about the past, you should also get as much of your information as possible from people who lived during the time.

Why Do We Read Historical Texts?

Historical texts—the diaries, letters, and other writings of those who lived long ago—offer us a vivid window into everyday life in the distant past. These texts are often challenging to read, however, because the spelling, vocabulary, and grammar can differ greatly from modern English.

Malden March 23, 1691

I make bold to spread before you these following considerations, which possibly may help to clear up your way before you return an answer unto the motion I have made to you. I hope you will take them in good part, and ponder them seriously.

1st. I have a great persuasion that the motion is of God, for diverse reasons: [such] as, first, that I should get a little acquaintance with you by a short and transient visit, having been altogether a stranger to you before, and that so little acquaintance should leave such an impression behind it as neither length of time, distance of place, nor any other objects could wear off, but that my thoughts and heart have been toward you ever since.

2ly. That upon serious, earnest, and frequent seeking of God for guidance and direction in so weighty a matter, my thoughts have still been determined unto and fixed upon yourself as the most suitable person for me . . .

3ly. Be pleased to consider, that although you may [possibly] have offers made you by persons more eligible, yet you can hardly meet with one that can love you better, or whose love is built on a surer foundation, or that may be capable of doing more for you in some respects than myself. But let this be spoken with all humility, and without ostentation. I can never think meanly enough of myself . . .

Don't Panic Use these strategies for deciphering difficult texts:

- ► Read historical texts more slowly than you would a modern text.
- ► Don't be frightened by different spellings and grammar. Identify the present-day equivalent of any words with unusual spellings. Rearrange sentences with an inverted word order.
- ► Reread a piece that is incomprehensible at first. It will become clearer each time you reread it.
- ► Break down long sentences into parts. Identify the core—the subject, verb, and predicate—of each long sentence.

Apply the Strategy

Use the strategies above to answer these questions about the text on the left, a marriage proposal from a Massachusetts man named Michael Wigglesworth.

1. In your opinion, what words or ideas in the proposal would still be relevant today? Which are outdated? Explain.

2. Explain the advantages and disadvantages of a written marriage proposal as compared with a spoken one.

3. What does this proposal tell you about Mr. Wigglesworth personally? What does it tell you about the society in which he lived?

4. Would you accept a marriage proposal like this one? Why or why not?

> ✔ *Here are other situations in which you can apply skills for breaking down difficult texts:*
> - ► **Reading technical publications**
> - ► **Reading legal documents, such as contracts**

PART **3**

The Puritan Influence

Pilgrims Going to Church (detail)
George Henry Boughton
© Collection of The New York Historical Society

The Puritans—who came to America in the 1600's for religious freedom—were characterized by a strict moral code and a strong work ethic. Although Puritanism eventually died out, many Puritan values, including a belief in the importance of hard work and an unbending faith in the face of adversity, have remained an important part of the American identity.

Guide for Interpreting

Anne Bradstreet (1612–1672)

Anne Bradstreet and her husband, Simon, arrived in the Massachusetts Bay Colony in 1630, when she was only eighteen. Armed with the strength of her Puritan upbringing, she left behind her hometown of Northampton, England, to start afresh in America. It was not an easy life for Bradstreet, who raised eight children and faced many hardships.

Despite the hardships she faced, Bradstreet was able to devote her spare moments to the very "unladylike" occupation of writing. In 1650, a collection of her scholarly poems, *The Tenth Muse Lately Sprung Up in America, By a Gentlewoman of Those Parts*, was published in England. Bradstreet's later poems, such as "To My Dear and Loving Husband," are more personal, expressing her feelings about the joys and difficulties of everyday Puritan life.

Bradstreet's poetry reflects the Puritans' knowledge of the stories and language of the Bible, as well as their awareness of the relationship between earthly and heavenly life. Her work also exhibits some of the characteristics of the French and English poetry of her day.

Edward Taylor (1642–1729)

Before the English government's lack of tolerance for his Puritan beliefs prompted him to emigrate to America, Edward Taylor worked as a teacher in England. Upon arriving in Boston in 1668, Taylor entered Harvard College, graduating in 1671. He accepted the position of minister and physician in the small farming community of Westfield, Massachusetts, then walked more than one hundred miles, much of it through snow, to his new home.

Life in Westfield was filled with hardships. Fierce battles between the Native Americans and the colonists left the community in constant fear. Taylor also experienced many personal tragedies. Five of his eight children died in infancy; then his wife died while still a young woman. He remarried and had five or six more children. (Biographers differ on the exact number.)

Edward Taylor is now generally regarded as the best of the colonial poets. Yet, because Taylor thought of his poetry as a form of personal worship, he allowed only two stanzas to be published while he was alive. Few people knew about his work until his poems were published more than two centuries after his death.

◆ Background for Understanding

LITERATURE: PURITAN WRITING

For the Puritans, the sole purpose of literature was moral instruction. They were aware of the emotional power of poetry but approved of it only if, like the Psalms, it "moved hearts to righteousness." There were many writers of verse in Puritan times, but few were women. Bradstreet was aware that writing was considered unacceptable behavior for women, but she persevered nonetheless.

Taylor's work was generally unknown during his lifetime. Some believe that he chose not to publish his poems because their joyousness and delight in sensory experience ran counter to New England attitudes. The discovery of a stash of Taylor's poetry in the 1930's is considered one of the major literary finds of the twentieth century.

◆ *Literature and Your Life*

CONNECT YOUR EXPERIENCE

If preserved, your belongings would convey a sense of your individuality to people born centuries from now. Puritans had few possessions, dressed somberly and uniformly, and didn't believe in expressing themselves creatively. Because they have left so little behind, they remain a mystery in many ways.

Journal Writing List the five personal possessions that best express your individuality. What would they tell future generations about your lifestyle and personality?

THEMATIC FOCUS: THE PURITAN INFLUENCE

These poems are like a glimpse behind the thick curtain of Puritanism at the thoughts and feelings of real people. How do the beliefs they express make these poems distinctly Puritan?

◆ Build Vocabulary

SUFFIXES: -fold

Although you may not know the word *manifold,* you've heard references to returning good wishes *tenfold* or increasing an investment *fourfold.* These words describe actions performed *ten* ways and *four* times. Applying this pattern, you can determine that *manifold* describes an action performed "many ways or times." The suffix *-fold*, meaning "a specific number of times or ways," is used to form both adjectives and adverbs.

WORD BANK

Preview this list of words from the poems.

> recompense
> manifold
> persevere

◆ Grammar and Style

DIRECT ADDRESS

In the opening line, the speaker in "Huswifery" calls upon God with the words, "Make me, O Lord, Thy spinning wheel complete." The phrase "O Lord," which is set off by commas, signals that the speaker is addressing God directly. As used here, "O Lord" is a term of **direct address**—a name or phrase used when speaking directly to someone or something. As you read, think about the reasons why the poets use terms of direct address in their poems.

◆ Literary Focus

THE PURITAN PLAIN STYLE

The writing style of the Puritans reflected the plain style of their lives—spare, simple, and straightforward. The **Puritan Plain Style** is characterized by short words, direct statements, and references to ordinary, everyday objects. Puritans believed that poetry should serve God by clearly expressing only useful or religious ideas. Poetry appealing to the senses or emotions was viewed as dangerous.

◆ Reading Strategy

PARAPHRASE

While these poems truly capture the essence of Puritan life, they can also present a challenge to the reader. To help you better absorb the meaning of each poem, take time to **paraphrase**, or restate ideas expressed by the poets in your own words.

Bradstreet's Version

My love is such that rivers
    cannot quench,
Nor ought but love from
    thee, give recompense.

Paraphrased

My love is so strong that rivers can't drown it; only your love can repay it.

Use the information in the footnotes to help you paraphrase unfamiliar references.

To My Dear and Loving Husband

Anne Bradstreet

Eighteenth-century pastoral scene in needlework, Mary Whitehead, c. 1750, Lyman Allyn Art Museum, New London, Connecticut, USA

▲ **Critical Viewing** Anne Bradstreet embroidered silk and linen samplers like this one. Which Puritan values are reflected in this scene? **[Analyze]**

If ever two were one, then surely we.
If ever man were lov'd by wife, then thee;
If ever wife was happy in a man,
Compare with me ye women if you can.

5   I prize thy love more than whole mines of gold,
Or all the riches that the East doth hold.
My love is such that rivers cannot quench,
Nor ought[1] but love from thee, give recompense.
Thy love is such I can no way repay,

10   The heavens reward thee manifold, I pray.
Then while we live, in love let's so persevere,[2]
That when we live no more, we may live ever.

---

1. **ought** (ôt) *n.*: Anything whatever.
2. **persevere**: Pronounced *per se´ ver* in the seventeenth century, and thus rhymed with the word *ever*.

◆ **Build Vocabulary**

recompense (rek´ əm pens´) *n.*: Repayment; something given
or done in return for something else

manifold (man´ ə fōld´) *adv.*: In many ways

persevere (pʉr sə vir´) *v.*: Persist; be steadfast in purpose

Guide for Responding

◆ Literature and Your Life

Reader's Response What is your image of Anne Bradstreet after reading this poem? Does she fit your concept of a Puritan? Why or why not?

Thematic Focus How does this poem express emotions that are distinctly Puritan yet universally human?

Group Discussion With a group of classmates, discuss the advice on how to make a marriage work that the Bradstreets might give modern couples.

☑ Check Your Comprehension

1. In the first four lines of the poem, what is Bradstreet saying about her relationship with her husband?
2. According to Bradstreet, what is the only thing that can match or reward her unquenchable love for her husband?

◆ Critical Thinking

INTERPRET
1. What does Bradstreet mean by the apparent paradox, or contradiction, in the last two lines: "... let's so persevere, / That when we live no more, we may live ever"? **[Interpret]**
2. How do Bradstreet's repetition and images help to convey the strength of the emotion being expressed? **[Analyze]**
3. Why might some of Bradstreet's Puritan contemporaries have considered this poem inappropriate? **[Infer]**

APPLY
4. Do you think personal devotion is as much esteemed today as it was in Anne Bradstreet's day? Support your answer. **[Apply]**

Huswifery

Edward Taylor

▲ **Critical Viewing** What makes this sampler an effective illustration to accompany Taylor's poem? **[Make a Judgment]**

Make me, O Lord, Thy spinning wheel complete.
Thy holy word my distaff[1] make for me.
Make mine affections[2] Thy swift flyers[3] neat
And make my soul Thy holy spoole to be.
5   My conversation make to be Thy reel
And reel the yarn thereon spun of Thy wheel.

Make me Thy loom then, knit therein this twine:
And make Thy holy spirit, Lord, wind quills:[4]
Then weave the web Thyself. The yarn is fine.
10   Thine ordinances[5] make my fulling mills.[6]
Then dye the same in heavenly colors choice.
All pinked[7] with varnished flowers of paradise.

Then clothe therewith mine understanding, will,
Affections, judgment, conscience, memory
15   My words, and actions, that their shine may fill
My ways with glory and Thee glorify.
Then mine apparel shall display before Ye
That I am clothed in holy robes for glory.

---

1. **distaff** (dis´ taf) *n.*: Staff on which flax or wool is wound for use in spinning.
2. **affections** (ə fek´ shenz) *n.*: Emotions.
3. **flyers** *n.*: Part of a spinning wheel that twists fibers into yarn.
4. **quills** *n.*: Weaver's spindles or bobbins.
5. **ordinances** (ôrd´ ən əns əz) *n.*: Sacraments or religious rites.
6. **fulling mills** *n.*: Machines that shrink and thicken cloth to the texture of felt.
7. **pinked** *v.*: Decorated.

Guide for Responding

◆ Literature and Your Life

Reader's Response *Huswifery* means "housekeeping." Given the title, were you surprised by the content of this poem? Explain.

Thematic Focus How did Puritans find opportunities for worship even in everyday tasks and objects?

Class Poll Conduct a quick poll to determine whether your classmates feel "Huswifery" should be considered a prayer or a poem.

☑ Check Your Comprehension

1. To what household task does the speaker liken the granting of salvation?
2. What does the speaker want to do with God's handiwork?

◆ Critical Thinking

INTERPRET

1. What does the poem suggest about the speaker's attitude toward God? **[Infer]**
2. How do the final two lines convey Taylor's belief that religious grace comes as a gift from God, rather than as a result of a person's efforts? **[Analyze]**
3. What does Taylor's comparison of a household task with the granting of grace suggest about his perception of God's relationship to the earthly world? **[Infer]**

APPLY

4. What process might Taylor describe if he were writing this poem today? **[Synthesize]**

Guide for Responding (continued)

◆ Reading Strategy

PARAPHRASE

When you **paraphrase** by restating important ideas in your own words as you read, you better absorb the meaning of difficult or old-fashioned language, such as you encountered in these poems.

In your notebook, paraphrase these passages from the poems as though you were explaining their meaning to a friend. Wherever applicable, use the information in the poems' footnotes to help you.

1. Thy love is such I can no way repay,
   The heavens reward thee manifold, I pray.

2. Then weave the web Thyself. The yarn is fine.
   Thine ordinances make my fulling mills.
   Then dye the same in heavenly colors choice,
   All pinked with varnished flowers of paradise.

◆ Build Vocabulary

USING THE SUFFIX -fold

Replace the italicized phrase with a word with the same meaning that contains the suffix -fold.

1. The savvy investor watched the value of his stock increase *to three times its size.*
2. Since having quadruplets last spring, Sandy claims her laundry has grown *in four ways.*

USING THE WORD BANK

Identify the letter of the situation that best demonstrates the meaning of the first phrase.

1. well-deserved recompense: (a) getting a flat tire while taking your grandmother to the doctor, (b) getting a day off after working long hours, (c) cleaning a messy room after a tiring day
2. to increase manifold: (a) to receive a 15 percent salary increase, (b) to add a drop of water to an overflowing bucket, (c) to get a 300 percent return on an investment
3. persevere: (a) quit when you get tired of playing, (b) practice until you improve your average, (c) argue with a referee

◆ Literary Focus

PURITAN PLAIN STYLE

In "To My Dear and Loving Husband," Bradstreet expresses her deep love for her husband as well as her own spiritual convictions in the simple and direct **Puritan Plain Style.** This style of poetry is characterized by the use of short, easily understood words, common to seventeenth-century conversation. Although "Huswifery" is written in a more ornate style, with unusual metaphors and decorative language, it also reflects a strict Puritan view of the world.

1. (a) Identify three aspects of the Puritan Plain Style reflected in "To My Dear and Loving Husband." Support your answer with examples from the poem. (b) Which aspects of the poem are not typical of the Puritan Plain Style?

2. (a) Identify three aspects of the Puritan Plain Style reflected in "Huswifery." Support your answer with examples from the poem. (b) In what ways is the poem not typical of the Puritan Plain Style?

◆ Grammar and Style

DIRECT ADDRESS

Use commas to separate a word or phrase of **direct address** from the rest of the sentence.

Middle: Make me, O Lord, Thy spinning wheel complete.

End: May you be rewarded for your love, dear husband.

Practice On your paper, rewrite the following passages, adding punctuation where needed. Underline the word or phrase of direct address in each.

1. Baa, baa, Black Sheep have you any wool?
2. Swing low sweet chariot / Coming for to carry me home. . . .
3. I could not love thee dear so much, / Loved I not honor more.
4. Are you sleeping Brother John?

Looking at Style Explain why you think the two writers used direct address in their poems.

Build Your Portfolio

Idea Bank

Writing

1. **Letter** Choose a character from literature or life who loved with an intensity equal to Bradstreet's. Writing as that character, compose a letter to your loved one, using comparisons to express the depth of your feelings.

2. **Magazine Article** People today could learn a lot about personal devotion from these poems. Write a magazine article stressing the need for people to show such devotion to their loved ones and to the values in which they believe.

3. **Poem** Create a modern version of "Huswifery," replacing the spinning wheel with a contemporary image that is equally appropriate to the theme of personal religious devotion.

Speaking and Listening

4. **Informal Debate** Foremost among the Puritan values were their strong work ethic and devotion to God and family. Stage a debate to argue whether the Puritan ethic is still alive.

5. **Love Song** Create a love song based on Bradstreet's poem. Set your lyrics to music and perform the song for your class. **[Music Link]**

Projects

6. **Bradstreet Sampler** On paper, design a sampler like the one on p. 90 for the Bradstreet home. Include a motto that expresses Bradstreet's beliefs and concerns as reflected in her poetry. **[Art Link]**

7. **Process Poster** Research the process of spinning yarn and weaving cloth as it was practiced in the colonial era. Create a poster that identifies the steps and tools referenced in "Huswifery," and write the corresponding line(s) of verse next to each. **[Social Studies Link]**

Writing Mini-Lesson

Editorial: Men and Housework

We do not generally associate men with tasks such as spinning and weaving—chores normally delegated to colonial women. Today, however, men are taking on more of what was once classified as "women's work." In a newspaper editorial, address the need for men to do their share of housework.

Writing Skills Focus: Anticipation of Opposing Arguments

You can expect that some readers might disagree with your proposals. **Anticipate opposing arguments** by considering objections your readers might raise and addressing them up front in your editorial. For example, to answer an argument that a man who works all day should not have to scrub floors when he comes home, you might observe that many women who work away from home face those tasks when they return from work. Build your case by addressing each of the opposing arguments you anticipate.

Prewriting In order to anticipate opposing arguments, use a problem-and-solution chart. List tasks to be completed in the average household. For each task, list objections or obstacles in the "problem" column; in the "solution" column, identify ways to get them done by both the men and women of the household.

Drafting Clearly state your position in the opening paragraph, then support your reasoning in the body of the editorial. Use the ideas you developed in your problem-and-solution chart to deflate opposing arguments by confronting them head on.

Revising Ask a classmate to critique your editorial and strengthen any weak spots he or she identifies. Was the editorial persuasive? Were there any points you omitted that could leave you open to objections?

Guide for Interpreting

Jonathan Edwards (1703–1758)

Jonathan Edwards is so synonymous with "fire and brimstone"—a phrase symbolizing the torments of hell endured by sinners—that his name alone was enough to make many eighteenth-century Puritans shake in their shoes.

This great American theologian and powerful Puritan preacher was born in East Windsor, Connecticut, where he grew up in an

> *As a young boy, Edwards is said to have preached sermons to his playmates from a makeshift pulpit he built behind his home.*

atmosphere of devout discipline.

A brilliant academic, he learned Latin, Greek, and Hebrew by the age of twelve, entered Yale at thirteen, and graduated four years later as class valedictorian. He went on to earn his master's degree in theology.

A Preacher Born and Raised Edwards began his preaching career in 1727 as assistant to his grandfather, Solomon Stoddard, pastor of the church at Northampton, Massachusetts, one of the largest and wealthiest congregations in the Puritan world. Edwards also preached as a visiting minister throughout New England. Strongly desiring a return to the orthodoxy and fervent faith of the Puritan past, he became a leader of the Great Awakening, a religious revival that swept the colonies in the 1730's and 1740's.

Changing Attitudes The Great Awakening did not last, however, and in 1750 Edwards was dismissed from his position after his extreme conservatism alienated much of the congregation. He continued to preach and write until his death in 1758, shortly after becoming president of the College of New Jersey (now Princeton University).

Edwards's highly emotional sermon "Sinners in the Hands of an Angry God" is by far his most famous work. It was delivered to a congregation in Enfield, Connecticut, in 1741, and it is said to have caused listeners to rise from their seats in a state of hysteria.

◆ Background for Understanding

HISTORY: EDWARDS IN THE PULPIT

You would never guess from looking at the intimidating cover of this contemporary reprint that Edwards preached this "fire and brimstone" sermon in a speaking style that was quiet and restrained. According to one account, he read the six-hour sermon in a level voice, staring over the heads of his congregation at the bell rope that

hung against the back wall "as if he would stare it in two." In spite of his calm demeanor, his listeners are said to have groaned and screamed in terror. Edwards reportedly had to stop several times and ask for silence. Without once resorting to dramatic techniques, he was able to build religious emotion to a fever pitch through effective use of vivid imagery and repetition of his main points.

Journal Activity Think about why Edwards might have chosen to use a quiet, level tone rather than a more dramatic or emotional delivery. Explain why you think listeners might find a quiet style even more terrifying than an overly dramatic one.

from Sinners in the Hands of an Angry God

◆ *Literature and Your Life*

CONNECT YOUR EXPERIENCE

Suppose your younger brother is involved with the "wrong crowd." Perhaps all you can do to get him back on track is paint a bleak picture of the awful future that may await him if he doesn't turn himself around. Jonathan Edwards had the same concerns about his fellow worshipers. He believed many were walking a path of certain destruction, and he desperately wanted to turn them toward repentance and heaven. Edwards achieved his goal by filling his sermons with terrifying descriptions of the horrors that awaited those who did not mend their ways.

THEMATIC FOCUS: THE PURITAN INFLUENCE

Is "scaring them straight" an effective way to change people's behavior for the better?

◆ Build Vocabulary

PREFIXES: *omni-*

Edwards describes how the wrath of God could rush down with *omnipotent* power upon sinners. The adjective *potent* means "strong or powerful." The addition of the prefix *omni-*, meaning "all or everywhere," creates a new word, *omnipotent*, which literally means "all powerful."

WORD BANK

Preview this list of words from the sermon.

| omnipotent |
| ineffable |
| dolorous |

◆ Grammar and Style

FORMS OF ADJECTIVES AND ADVERBS

The power of Edwards's sermon is largely a result of his use of vivid modifiers. Most adjectives and adverbs have three forms. The **basic,** or **positive**, **form** is used when a comparison is *not* being made. The **comparative form** shows two things being compared. The **superlative form** identifies one or more of the members of a group as having the most or least of a certain characteristic.

Positive: holy, mercifully, good/well
Comparative: holier, more/less mercifully, better
Superlative: holiest, most/least mercifully, best

Most one-syllable and some two-syllable adjectives and adverbs use -er to form the comparative and -est to form the superlative. For all other adjectives and adverbs, use *more* or *less* to form the comparative and *most* or *least* to form the superlative.

◆ Literary Focus

SERMON

Though often associated with stern lectures or "fire and brimstone" speeches like this one, sermons can also be instructional or inspiring. A **sermon** is broadly defined as a speech given from a pulpit in a house of worship, usually as part of a religious service. Like its written counterpart, the essay, a sermon expresses the message or point of view its author wishes to convey to his or her audience, called a congregation. The sermon flourished as a popular literary form in colonial America.

◆ Reading Strategy

CONTEXT CLUES

Searching the **context**—the surrounding words, phrases, and sentences—for clues can help you come up with the meaning of unfamiliar words as you read. Look at the word *abominable* in this passage:

> . . . you are ten thousand times more *abominable* in his [God's] eyes, than the most hateful venomous serpent is in ours. . . .

The context clue comes in the form of a comparison: Edwards likens the way the sinner appears in God's eye with our view of "the most hateful venomous serpent." From this clue, you can determine that *abominable* must be close in meaning to *disgusting* or *horrible*—words evoked by the image of a deadly snake.

from Sinners in the Hands of an Angry God

Jonathan Edwards

This is the case of every one of you that are out of Christ:[1] That world of misery, that lake of burning brimstone, is extended abroad under you. There is the dreadful pit of the glowing flames of the wrath of God; there is Hell's wide gaping mouth open; and you have nothing to stand upon, nor anything to take hold of; there is nothing between you and Hell but the air; it is only the power and mere pleasure of God that holds you up.

You probably are not sensible of this; you find you are kept out of Hell, but do not see the hand of God in it; but look at other things, as the good state of your bodily constitution, your care of your own life, and the means you use for your own preservation. But indeed these things are nothing; if God should withdraw his hand, they would avail no more to keep you from falling than the thin air to hold up a person that is suspended in it.

Your wickedness makes you as it were heavy as lead, and to tend downwards with great weight and pressure towards Hell; and if God should let you go, you would immediately sink and swiftly descend and plunge into the bottomless gulf, and your healthy constitution, and your own care and prudence, and best contrivance, and all your righteousness, would have no more influence to uphold you and keep you out of Hell, than a spider's web would have to stop a fallen rock. Were it not for the sovereign pleasure of God, the earth would not bear you one moment . . . The world would spew you out, were it not for the sovereign hand of Him who hath subjected it in hope. There are black clouds of God's wrath now hanging directly over your heads, full of the dreadful storm, and big with thunder; and were it not for the restraining hand of God, it would immediately burst forth upon you. The sovereign pleasure of God, for the present, stays[2] his rough wind; otherwise it would come with fury, and your destruction would come like a whirlwind, and you would be like the chaff of the summer threshing floor.

The wrath of God is like great waters that are dammed for the present; they increase more and more, and rise higher and higher, till an outlet is given; and the longer the stream is stopped, the more rapid and mighty is its course, when once it is let loose. It is true, that

---

1. **out of Christ:** Not in God's grace.

2. **stays:** Restrains.

judgment against your evil works has not been executed hitherto; the Hoods of God's vengeance have been withheld; but your guilt in the meantime is constantly increasing, and you are every day treasuring up more wrath; the waters are constantly rising, and waxing more and more mighty; and there is nothing but the mere pleasure of God, that holds the waters back, that are unwilling to be stopped, and press hard to go forward. If God should only withdraw his hand from the floodgate, it would immediately fly open, and the fiery floods of the fierceness and wrath of God, would rush forth with inconceivable fury, and would come upon you with <u>omnipotent</u> power; and if your strength were ten thousand times greater than it is, yea, ten thousand times greater than the strength of the stoutest, sturdiest devil in Hell, it would be nothing to withstand or endure it.

The bow of God's wrath is bent, and the arrow made ready on the string, and justice bends the arrow at your heart, and strains the bow, and it is nothing but the mere pleasure of God, and that of an angry God, without any promise or obligation at all, that keeps the arrow one moment from being made drunk with your blood. Thus all you that never passed under a great change of heart, by the mighty power of the spirit of God upon your souls; all you that were never born again, and made new creatures, and raised from being dead in sin, to a state of

The Puritan, 1898, Frank E. Schoonover, Collection of the Brandywine River Museum

▲ **Critical Viewing** What words from the text would you apply to describe the mood of this painting? **[Analyze]**

◆ **Build Vocabulary**

omnipotent (äm nip′ ə tənt) *adj.*: All-powerful

new, and before altogether unexperienced light and life, are in the hands of an angry God. However you may have reformed your life in many things, and may have had religious affections, and may keep up a form of religion in your families and closets,[3] and in the house of God, it is nothing but His mere pleasure that keeps you from being this moment swallowed up in everlasting destruction. However unconvinced you may now be of the truth of what you hear, by and by you will be fully convinced of it.

Those that are gone from being in the like circumstances with you, see that it was so with them; for destruction came suddenly upon most of them; when they expected nothing of it, and while they were saying, peace and safety: now they see, that those things on which they depended for peace and safety, were nothing but thin air and empty shadows.

The God that holds you over the pit of Hell, much as one holds a spider, or some loathsome insect over the fire, abhors you, and is dreadfully provoked: his wrath towards you burns like fire; he looks upon you as worthy of nothing else, but to be cast into the fire; he is of purer eyes than to bear to have you in his sight; you are ten thousand times more abominable in his eyes, than the most hateful venomous serpent is in ours. . . .

O sinner! Consider the fearful danger you are in: it is a great furnace of wrath, a wide and bottomless pit, full of the fire of wrath, that you are held over in the hand of that God, whose wrath is provoked and incensed as much against you, as against many of the damned in Hell. You hang by a slender thread, with the flames of divine wrath flashing about it, and ready every moment to singe it, and burn it asunder; and you have no interest in any mediator, and nothing to lay hold of to save yourself, nothing to keep off the flames of wrath, nothing of your own, nothing that you ever have done, nothing that you can do, to induce God to spare you one moment. . . .

When God beholds the <u>ineffable</u> extremity of your case, and sees your torment to be so vastly disproportioned to your strength, and sees how your poor soul is crushed, and sinks down, as it were, into an infinite gloom; he will have no compassion upon you, he will not forbear the executions of his wrath, or in the least lighten his hand; there shall be no moderation or mercy, nor will God then at all stay his rough wind; he will have no regard to your welfare, nor be at all careful lest you should suffer too much in any other sense, than only that you shall *not suffer beyond what strict justice requires.* . . .

God stands ready to pity you; this is a day of mercy; you may cry now with some encouragement of obtaining mercy. But once the day of mercy is past, your most lamentable and <u>dolorous</u> cries and shrieks will be in vain; you will be wholly lost and thrown away of God, as to any regard to your welfare. God will have no other use to put you to, but to suffer misery; you shall be continued in being to no other end; for you will be a vessel of wrath fitted to destruction; and there will be no other use of this vessel, but to be filled full of wrath. . . .

Thus it will be with you that are in an unconverted state, if you continue in it; the infinite might, and majesty, and terribleness of the omnipotent God shall be magnified upon you, in the ineffable strength of your torments. You shall be tormented in the presence of the holy angels, and in the presence of the Lamb,[4] and when you shall be in this state of suffering, the glorious inhabitants of Heaven shall go forth and look on the awful spectacle, that they may see what the wrath and fierceness of the Almighty is; and when they have seen it, they will fall down and adore that great power and majesty. . . .

It would be dreadful to suffer this fierceness and wrath of Almighty God one moment; but you must suffer it to all eternity. There will be no end to this exquisite horrible misery. When you look forward, you shall see a long forever, a boundless duration before you, which will swallow up your thoughts and amaze your soul; and you will absolutely despair of ever having any deliverance, any end, any mitigation, any rest at all. . . .

How dreadful is the state of those that are daily and hourly in the danger of this great

◆ **Reading Strategy**
Use the reference to "furnace of wrath" as a clue to the meaning of *provoked* and *incensed.*

---

3. **closets** *n.*: Small, private rooms for meditation.

4. **the Lamb:** Jesus.

wrath and infinite misery! But this is the dismal case of every soul in this congregation that has not been born again, however moral and strict, sober and religious, they may otherwise be. Oh that you would consider it, whether you be young or old! . . . Those of you that finally continue in a natural condition, that shall keep you out of Hell longest will be there in a little time! Your damnation does not slumber; it will come swiftly, and, in all probability, very suddenly upon many of you. You have reason to wonder that you are not already in Hell. It is doubtless the case of some whom you have seen and known, that never deserved Hell more than you, and that heretofore appeared as likely to have been now alive as you. Their case is past all hope; they are crying in extreme misery and perfect despair; but here you are in the land of the living and in the house of God, and have an opportunity to obtain salvation. What would not those poor damned hopeless souls give for one day's opportunity such as you now enjoy!

And now you have an extraordinary opportunity, a day wherein Christ has thrown the door of mercy wide open, and stands in calling and crying with a loud voice to poor sinners; a day wherein many are flocking to him, and pressing into the kingdom of God. Many are daily coming from the east, west, north and south; many that were very lately in the same miserable condition that you are in, are now in a happy state, with their hearts filled with love to him who has loved them, and washed them from their sins in his own blood, and rejoicing in hope of the glory of God. How awful is it to be left behind at such a day! To see so many others feasting, while you are pining and perishing! To see so many rejoicing and singing for joy of heart, while you have cause to mourn for sorrow of heart, and howl for vexation of spirit! . . .

Therefore, let everyone that is out of Christ now awake and fly from the wrath to come. The wrath of Almighty God is now undoubtedly hanging over a great part of this congregation: let everyone fly out of Sodom.[5] "Haste and escape for your lives, look not behind you, escape to the mountain, lest you be consumed."[6]

---

5. **Sodom** (säd′ əm): In the Bible, a city destroyed by fire because of the sinfulness of its people.
6. **"Haste . . . consumed"**: From Genesis 19:17, the angels' warning to Lot, the only virtuous man in Sodom, to flee the city before they destroy it.

◆ *Literature and Your Life*

What does the image of a door that's "wide open" mean to you?

Guide for Responding

◆ *Literature and Your Life*

Reader's Response How do you think you would have reacted if you had heard Edwards deliver this sermon?

Thematic Focus In the fifteen years of the Great Awakening, Edwards succeeded in converting thousands to Puritanism before his congregation rebelled against his conservative beliefs and dismissed him from his position. Do you think Edwards's message and tactics would be well received today?

Journal Activity Do you think scare tactics like those of Edwards are an effective way of changing people's behavior? Think about the impact Edwards made on his congregation as you answer this question in your journal.

☑ Check Your Comprehension

1. According to the opening paragraph, what keeps sinners from falling into Hell?
2. Describe at least two images Edwards uses to depict the wrath of God.
3. (a) Toward the end of the sermon, what does Edwards say that sinners can obtain? (b) What must they do to obtain it?

Guide for Responding (continued)

◆ Critical Thinking

INTERPRET

1. Why do you think Edwards opens this portion of his sermon with a description of Hell? **[Infer]**
2. (a) What impact is created by the repeated use of the word *wrath*? (b) How do the many symbols and images of God's wrath add to the impact? **[Analyze]**

EVALUATE

3. Would Edwards's sermon and style of delivery be as effective on a modern congregation? Why or why not? **[Evaluate; Support]**

APPLY

4. In which situations, if any, is it justifiable to use fear to get a person to improve his or her behavior? Explain your answer. **[Synthesize]**

◆ Reading Strategy

CONTEXT CLUES

Using the **context**—the surrounding words or sentences—can be an effective way to unlock the meaning of an unfamiliar word. Use the context in the passages below to define the italicized words.

1. . . . you are every day treasuring up more wrath; the waters are constantly rising, and *waxing* more and more mighty . . .
2. The God that holds you over the pit of Hell, much as one holds a spider, or some loathsome insect over the fire, *abhors* you, and is dreadfully provoked . . .

◆ Literary Focus

SERMON

Jonathan Edwards fought his crusade for salvation with words that often took the form of a **sermon**—a speech that has a definite point of view and is delivered from the pulpit during a worship service.

1. What point of view or message is Edwards conveying in this sermon?
2. (a) To what emotion does he appeal in his effort to motivate the congregation? (b) Considering Edwards's purpose, why is this an appropriate choice? Explain your answer.

◆ Build Vocabulary

USING THE PREFIX *omni-*

Each of these adjectives contains the prefix *omni-*, meaning "all" or "every." Use the information in parentheses to match each adjective with the situation to which it best applies.

1. omnipotent (*potent* = powerful)
2. omniscient (*sciens* = knowing)
3. omnivorous (*vor* = to eat)

a. how a student might describe a smart teacher
b. how a prisoner might describe his powerful jailer
c. how a zoologist might describe an animal that eats both meat and plants

USING THE WORD BANK

Write this sentence in your notebook, filling each blank with the appropriate word from the Word Bank:

The citizens of Oz sighed with a ____?____ air, indicating their ____?____ sadness at learning that the Wizard they considered ____?____ was just an ordinary man, hiding behind a curtain.

◆ Grammar and Style

FORMS OF ADJECTIVES AND ADVERBS

The **comparative** form of adjectives and adverbs is used to compare two things or ideas; the **superlative** form is used when comparing more than two things or ideas.

Writing Application Rewrite the following paragraph in your notebook, correcting all errors in comparisons:

> When we think of great preachers, Edwards is the name that quickliest comes to mind. Of the many Puritan sermonizers who rose to fame during the Great Awakening, Edwards is still considered the more influential. Most of his writing appealed to reason and logic; "Sinners in the Hands of an Angry God" is his most emotional and more famous work.

Looking at Style Review the sermon and find an adjective and an adverb in each form that you feel is especially vivid. Explain how Edwards uses each one you've chosen to create a powerful image.

Build Your Portfolio

 ## Idea Bank

Writing

1. **Diary Entry** You are a devout member of the Enfield, Connecticut, congregation. In a diary entry, describe your feelings after listening to all six hours of Edwards's sermon.

2. **Newscast** Edwards was dismissed as pastor of the Northampton congregation after he publicly named members who he believed had lapsed in their devotion. Write a newscast announcing the dismissal and the reasons for it. **[Media Link]**

3. **Public Letter** As Edwards, write an open letter defending the actions that led to your dismissal. Explain why you publicly denounced members of the congregation.

Speaking and Listening

4. **Oral Interpretation** Read an excerpt from the sermon in your choice of dramatic style. Invite your classmates to critique the impact of your delivery. **[Performing Arts Link]**

5. **Oral Report** Sermons like those of Dr. Martin Luther King, Jr., still have the power to inspire us. Research Dr. King's sermons and their role in the civil rights movement. Give a brief oral report on your findings. **[Social Studies Link]**

Projects

6. **Television Commercial** Create a commercial to persuade people to adopt a healthier lifestyle. Include music or sound effects as you share your commercial with your class. **[Media Link]**

7. **Puritan Handbook** Gather information about Puritan beliefs and the famous "work ethic." Create a handbook that includes guidelines and rules for living and worshiping as a proper Puritan.

 ## Writing Mini-Lesson

Evaluation of Persuasion

A speaker's choice of persuasive techniques should depend on the audience and the occasion. At Enfield, Edwards decided to appeal to the congregation's emotions. Was it the best choice? Write an evaluation of the persuasive techniques Edwards used. Discuss the response he evoked in his listeners and the ways in which he achieved it. Are his techniques an appropriate and effective means of persuading the audience? Why or why not? Your evaluation will have greater clarity and strength if its elements work together to create a unified effect.

Writing Skills Focus: Unity

Unity refers to a singleness of effect. A piece of writing is unified when its elements or paragraphs express one main idea; a paragraph has unity when each sentence relates to a single topic.

Note how this paragraph conveys a single idea that supports the overall theme of the sermon.

Model From the Sermon

Therefore, let everyone that is out of Christ, now awake and fly from the wrath to come. The wrath of Almighty God is now undoubtedly hanging over a great part of this congregation: let everyone fly out of Sodom. "Haste and escape for your lives, look not behind you, escape to the mountains, lest you be consumed."

Prewriting To help focus your writing, summarize Edwards's techniques and your evaluation of their effectiveness in a clearly defined statement.

Drafting Use the statement you created as the basis for a strong, focused opening paragraph. Support your main point in the paragraphs that follow.

Revising Read your evaluation as though you were seeing it for the first time. Eliminate any information that's unrelated to the main idea.

CONNECTIONS TO TODAY'S WORLD

Iron Bird: Cal Ripken's Work Ethic
Steve Wulf

Thematic Connection

THE PURITAN INFLUENCE

Stand tall, speak plainly, work hard, and put all you've got into the game—every game, year in and year out. While it may not exactly qualify as a Puritan credo, Cal Ripken Jr.'s approach to playing baseball is firmly rooted in the Puritan ethic. Though it's doubtful the Puritans would have endorsed professional sports, they almost certainly would have approved of Ripken, the Baltimore Orioles shortstop known for his unwavering work ethic, modesty, and dedication to his fans.

ONE FOR THE RECORD BOOKS

On September 6, 1995, Ripken shattered Lou Gehrig's famous streak by playing his 2,131st consecutive game. Ripken's streak was a long time in the making; in the process, he won the admiration of fans, colleagues, and the sports media. He's been hailed as a true sports hero, an increasingly rare accolade in an age where salaries and endorsements, rather than love of the game, seem to come first in the hearts of many professional athletes.

Ripken, however, does not consider himself a hero, just a hard worker, a trait he claims to have learned from his father. When Cal Ripken Sr. became manager of the Orioles' Double A team in 1972, Cal Jr. was old enough to help out—and to notice how his dad dedicated himself to his team. "I think that's when I first picked up my work ethic," says Cal Jr. "My dad did everything. He was not only the manager but also the pitching coach, the batting coach, the batting-practice pitcher, the groundkeeper."

PURITAN AND PROUD OF IT

Hard work and heroism are closely linked in the American mind, due largely to the influence of the Puritans. The self-discipline and steadfastness that characterize Ripken have their roots in the Puritans' simple code of faithful endurance. Life for the Puritans was not easy, but they believed in meeting the challenge with perseverance and fidelity. Today, we still respect people like Ripken who approach their personal and professional lives in the same way. Whether the game is life or simply baseball, we continue to admire those who embody the principles prized by the Puritans centuries ago.

STEVE WULF
(1950–)

Steve Wulf loves baseball. Not that baseball is the only subject he covers: as a senior writer, Wulf has written for every section of *Time* since joining the newsweekly in 1995. His *Time* cover story on the assassination of Israeli President Yitzhak Rabin even won one of the Overseas Press Club's highest honors in 1996. Wulf had plenty of opportunities to write about baseball during his seventeen years as a reporter, writer, and editor with *Sports Illustrated*. He's also authored several popular books, including *Baseball Anecdotes*. Most recently, he co-authored *I Was Right on Time*, the autobiography of the Negro Leagues' legend Buck O'Neil. Wulf, who was also a consultant for Ken Burns's acclaimed documentary *Baseball*, has appeared on numerous national television programs and networks.

Iron Bird: Cal Ripken's Work Ethic

Steve Wulf

In early September 1995, baseball fans everywhere waited in anticipation for Cal Ripken to break the record set by baseball great Lou Gehrig for most consecutive games played. As the big day drew closer, the self-effacing Ripken found himself at the center of a whirlwind of national media attention. This article appeared in Time magazine shortly before Ripken earned his place in the record books.

The streak is such an inadequate description for something that began 2,127 games, 29 different double-play partners and 13¼ years ago. If you pitch 59 consecutive shutout innings or hit in 56 straight games, you are on a streak. But if you play so long that 3,695 other major leaguers have gone on the disabled list since the last time you spent an entire game on the bench, so continuously that more than 50 million fans have seen nobody but you start the game at your position, you are not on a streak. You are on a river, a long, meandering river like, say, the Susquehanna, which begins its 444-mile journey in Cooperstown, New York,[1] the purported cradle of baseball. From there the Susquehanna finds its way to Oneonta, the home of 1950 National League MVP Jim Konstanty; dips down into Pennsylvania before re-crossing the border near Binghamton, where Wee Willie Keeler and Whitey Ford cut their professional teeth; winds back down south toward Wilkes-Barre,

---

1. **Cooperstown, New York:** Site of the National Baseball Hall of Fame and considered by some to be the place where baseball was invented in 1839.

◆ **Build Vocabulary**

purported (pər pôrt′ id) *adj*.: Supposed

▶ **Critical Viewing** Decide whether Cal Ripken appears comfortable in the spotlight as he accepts the crowd's applause for setting the record for most consecutive games played. Explain your answer. **[Assess]**

Pennsylvania, where Joe McCarthy managed his first team; meets up with the West Branch, which flows past Williamsport, the birthplace of Little League Baseball, and Lewisburg, home of Christy Mathewson's alma mater, Bucknell University; bisects Harrisburg, where Hall of Fame pitcher Vic Willis got his start; rushes past York, which once knew Brooks Robinson as a second baseman; crosses the border into Maryland and—at long last—enters the Chesapeake Bay at Havre de Grace, which happens to be the birthplace of Calvin Edwin Ripken Jr.

Unless something unforeseen or unthinkable happens, Cal Ripken, the 35-year-old shortstop for the Baltimore Orioles, will play in his 2,131st straight game on Sept. 6, against the California Angels in Oriole Park at Camden Yards. That will break the record set by Lou Gehrig, the first baseman for the New York Yankees from 1925 until 1939. The "Streak," as it has come to be called, officially began on May 30, 1982, when Orioles manager Earl Weaver started Ripken at third base, which was then his position, against the Toronto Blue Jays. The previous day, Weaver had rested the 21-year-old rookie in the second game of a doubleheader.

Unofficially, the Streak probably began in the late '60s in the basement of the Ripken household, by then in Aberdeen, Maryland. Says Vi Ripken, the matriarch of the Ripken clan (daughter Ellen, sons Cal Jr., Fred and Billy): "I wish I had a nickel for every time I heard 'Just one more game, Mom.' The kids would be playing Ping Pong in the basement, and it was always a struggle to get them to come upstairs for dinner, and even more of a struggle to get them to go to bed. Nobody liked to end the night on a loss, especially Junior. 'Just one more game, Mom.' "

Just one more game. Therein lies the true beauty of the Streak. Ripken never set out to eclipse the "Iron Horse," who he modestly and somewhat mistakenly believes was a much better ballplayer than himself. "I'm not even in Gehrig's league," says Ripken. Offensively speaking, Ripken may be right, although he has had two MVP, Gehrigian seasons (1983 and 1991). But defensively Ripken plays a much tougher position than Gehrig did, and he does a much better job of it at that. As durable as Lou was, he played every inning of every game for only one season; Ripken played every inning of 904 straight games from 1982 to '87—only his father, then the manager of the Orioles, could sit him down. While Gehrig occasionally resorted to artifice to extend his streak, Ripken has never done anything untoward to keep *his* alive, or played anything less than hard. Gehrig was literally afraid of leaving the lineup; Ripken is in it for the fun. "There's a joy to Cal's game that never ceases to amaze me," says Mike Flanagan, the Orioles' pitching coach who has played for Cal Sr. and played with Cal Jr. "People who think he's out for glory just don't get it." Indeed, fans who think that Ripken will sit down shortly after No. 2,131 are mistaken. Barring injury or sudden ineptitude, Ripken will play in Nos. 2,132, 2,133, 2,134 . . . The Iron Bird.

Occasionally given to slumps, Ripken is approaching the Streak in something of a hitting malaise that has dropped his average into the .260s. But he still plays his position with amazing grace; at 6 ft. 4 in. he is not only the tallest shortstop in history but also one of the smoothest. And rather than go into a shell to protect his privacy this season, he has been making a concerted effort to meet the needs of the media and the wants of the fans. At the All-Star Game in Arlington, Texas, he worked his way from dugout to dugout in 100°F heat, signing everything put in his way. In Baltimore this summer, he has been conducting after-the-game autograph sessions to make up for lost time and repair the wounds of the baseball strike.[2]

There are times in which Ripken seems not just a throwback but the last true sports hero. He carries the requisite superstar salary— $6 million annually for two more years—but almost none of the other baggage that has come to be associated with the modern-day profes-

2. **the baseball strike:** A Major League Baseball Players Association strike put an early end to the 1994 baseball season and resulted in a delayed start to the 1995 season.

◆ Build Vocabulary

artifice (ärt´ ə fis) *n*.: Artful trickery

untoward (un tō´ ərd) *adj*.: Inappropriate or improper

malaise (ma lāz´) *n*.: Decline or slump

malingered (mə liŋ´ gərd) *v*.: Escaped work or duty by pretending to be ill

immersed (im mʉrst´) *v*.: Plunged or completely submerged

sional athlete. He has never sulked, <u>malingered</u>, strutted, whined, wheedled or referred to himself in the third person. He has turned down several opportunities to become a free agent, preferring to remain an Oriole and a Baltimorean. He has endorsements, to be sure, but his most famous one is for milk.

America never stops moaning about the absence of heroes—"Where have you gone, Joe DiMaggio?"—yet when it has someone who daily displays grit, generosity, spirit and skill, not to mention incredibly blue eyes, what does it do? It looks this generation's gift horse in the mouth. Robert Lipsyte, the respected New York *Times* columnist, recently suggested that Ripken take a seat rather than sully Gehrig's memory. And the hate mail that Ripken has received this summer has been of such volume and venom that Major League Baseball has had to beef up the security around him.

Opponents and teammates alike hold Ripken in the same awe in which he holds Gehrig. Says the Toronto Blue Jays' veteran designated hitter Paul Molitor: "As someone who has spent a few years of my life on the disabled list, I can tell you that what Cal has done and is still doing is beyond my comprehension. He plays the second toughest position on the field every day, often on artificial turf, sometimes in day games after night games, sometimes after flying all night. He's still a dangerous hitter, still the most reliable shortstop out there, and he is the essence of class on and off the field. He's enough to make you sick."

The Streak has had two close calls. The first came during game No. 444 in April 1985, when Ripken sprained his ankle on a pick-off play in the third inning. Although he continued playing, his ankle was badly swollen and discolored after the game. Fortunately, the Orioles had scheduled an exhibition game against the Naval Academy the next day. The second near-miss came as a result of a bench-clearing mêlée[3] with the

▲ **Critical Viewing** From this photograph, what can you learn about Ripken's relationship with his fans? **[Infer]**

Seattle Mariners during game No. 1,790 in June of '93. Ripken twisted his knee, and when he woke up the next morning, he couldn't put his weight on it. He told his wife Kelly he might not be able to play that night. According to Kelly, "Just before he left for the ball park, I said, 'Maybe you could just play one inning and then come out.' He snapped, 'No! Either I play the whole game or I don't play at all.' I told him, 'Just checking, dear.' "

Ripken did play the full nine innings that night. In fact, he has played in 99.2% of every Orioles game since the Streak began. The percentage would be even higher had Ripken not been ejected from two games in the first inning. . . .

If Ripken does have a flaw, it is his temper. He doesn't tolerate incompetence on the part of umpires or teammates. "I'm also stubborn," he says. "I think that's one trait I share with Gehrig." But by and large he conducts himself with consideration and intelligence and good humor. His parents have something to do with that, but so does the Orioles' organization, which has a unique tradition of encouraging players to become active in the community. Ripken is particularly involved in an adult-literacy program in Baltimore.

It's not easy being Ripken, especially these days. Before a recent 7:30 P.M. game with the Cleveland Indians, he arrived at the ball park at 12:30 for a two-hour discussion with Oriole officials on the plans for "Streak Week." At 2:45 he had a photo shoot with the Rawlings Sporting Goods company. At 3 he did a CNN interview; at 3:30 two local TV interviews; at 4:05 an ESPN interview. After that he <u>immersed</u> himself in his pregame routine, stretching and laughing with Brady Anderson, taking his cuts in batting practice, prancing around his shortstop territory in infield practice—how can any man find so much enjoyment in a ground ball, much less his 100,000,000th ground ball? Then he went off to work on his swing on the indoor batting tee for 15 minutes, and then he went over scouting reports on the Indians. Once the game started,

---

3. mêlée (mā´ lā´) *n.*: Noisy, confused fight.

he went hitless and drew a walk, but played his position flawlessly. (A shortstop has some special responsibility on every play that's not a strikeout.) And when the 3-hr. 16-min. 8-5 defeat was over, Ripken didn't just dress and go home. He went back out onto the field for one of his post game autograph sessions, signing for and kibitzing[4] with 2,000 fans. "Cal Ripken personifies everything that is right with baseball," said Bob Seal, 33, an engineer for the Norfolk Southern Railroad who came up to the game from Chattanooga, Tennessee.

A Ripken autograph session is illuminating because he doesn't just sign, sign, sign in the joyless way that many other ballplayers do. He engages people in conversation, talking to them as one baseball fan would to another. ("Man, did you see the stuff Mussina had tonight?" says Ripken, the fan.) If he sees a child with a rival's hat on, he'll kid him or her and maybe even exchange the cap for one of his own.

Actually, Ripken's easy way with the fans had something to do with the way he met his wife. Kelly Geer's mother chatted him up at a restaurant signing one night in 1983, telling him about her eligible daughter, and Cal signed the ball to Kelly, "If you look like your mother, I'm sorry I missed you. Cal Ripken." As Kelly recalls, "My reaction was, 'Who's Cal Ripken?' But a couple of months later, I was in a restaurant where he was signing, and when I thanked him for being so nice to my mom, he said, 'You must be Kelly. You're 6 ft. tall, blond, you have green eyes, you went to the University of Maryland, and you work for the airlines.' The next day he called."

---

4. **kibitzing** (kib´ its in) v.: Giving advice or making observations.

Kelly and Cal were married four years later. They now have two children: Rachel, who was born in November 1989, and Ryan, who was born in July 1993 on—somebody up there likes Cal—an off day.

Both the Orioles and Ripken feared that this season might be overwhelming for him, but it has become quite the opposite. "This is the most relaxed I've seen Cal in years," says Kelly. "He's at peace with himself. He realizes that even though the Streak will always be a part of his identity, it's a positive thing."

When Ripken is asked how he's changed during the Streak, he responds, "Less and grayer hair." But then he gives a more thoughtful answer: "I'm much better with people, kids particularly. When I was young and fans would give me their babies to hold for a picture, the babies always ended up crying. But now that I have kids of my own, I find it easier not only to hold them, but to talk to them. And they ask—no offense—the best questions. Like 'How come you're not crying? How come you're not mad you lost the game?' And I tell them, 'I am mad, but I've learned not to show it.' Or they'll ask, 'What's it like to hit a home run to win the game? Is it the best feeling in the world?' And I tell them, 'It is the best feeling.' The kids reduce the game to its most basic level, and they remind me why it is I love baseball so much."

Travel upriver from Havre de Grace all the way to Cooperstown, and right there on Main Street is a statue of a boy called *The Sandlot Kid*. He's barefoot, and he's wearing a straw hat. But he holds his bat over his shoulder a little like Cal Ripken. Just one more game.

Guide for Responding

◆ Literature and Your Life

Reader's Response If you were Ripken, would you have risked playing with injuries rather than miss a game and end your streak? Explain.

☑ Check Your Comprehension

Why is Cal Ripken's 2,131st game such an important one?

◆ Critical Thinking

INTERPRET
1. What impression does the writer convey with the complete account of Ripken's schedule on the day of the Cleveland Indians game? **[Analyze]**

EVALUATE
2. Do you believe that Ripken has earned the right to be called a hero? Explain. **[Evaluate]**

Thematic Connection

THE PURITAN INFLUENCE: ALIVE AND WELL AND LIVING IN THE UNITED STATES?

At first glance, modern American lifestyles and values might seem to have little in common with those of the Puritans. Scratch the surface, however, and you'd be surprised at what you find. At the heart of our culture, for instance, is an enduring belief in the "American dream," the promise that anyone who works hard enough will succeed in life. Though the media are filled with stories and statistics that suggest that the American dream is in danger of becoming just that—a dream—the United States still has a special place in its collective heart for those who "pull themselves up by their bootstraps." Self-made individuals who succeed through merit and honest hard work will always be among our most respected heroes.

Puritan ethics have also left their mark on much of what is considered uniquely American culture. The Puritans' belief in simplicity is evident in everything from the simple lines of traditional American furniture and architecture to the value we place on traits like forthright speech: "Mean what you say and say what you mean" are still words to live by for many. Though life in the United States seems to grow increasingly complicated, the renewed emphasis on "family values" shows that our nation still cherishes simple Puritan virtues—honesty, hard work, and devotion to religion, family, and neighbor.

1. How does Ripken's involvement in an adult-literacy program reflect Puritan virtues?
2. What might Jonathan Edwards and his Puritan followers have admired about Cal Ripken's character?

 Idea Bank

Writing

1. **Newspaper Editorial** As the editor of *The Puritan Plain Speaker,* you have decided to write an editorial celebrating Cal Ripken's new record for most consecutive games played. Explain in your editorial why you believe the achievement is worthy of the attention of the Puritan community.

2. **Character Defense** Imagine that Jonathan Edwards has just condemned Cal Ripken for "wasting his life in the idle pursuit of a child's game." Write an open letter to the Puritan community in which you defend Ripken's character. Explain how Ripken's career embodies so many of the traits that Puritans value most.

3. **Baseball Poem** Compose a poem in the Puritan Plain Style that praises Ripken's baseball skill, dedication, and hard work. List words or phrases that describe Ripken's virtues as both a person and a player. Use each word or phrase as the basis for one or two lines of your poem.

Speaking and Listening

4. **Group Debate** Work with a group of classmates to stage a debate. The topic of your debate is the Puritan influence: Making a comeback or gone for good? Group members should work in two teams to develop and outline the main points of their arguments before staging the debate for the class.

Projects

5. **Reference Guide** "A place for everything and everything in its place." "Silence is golden." "A penny saved is a penny earned." These and many more of the sayings we still repeat have their roots in Puritan values and virtues. Work with a partner to gather famous quotations that reflect a Puritan influence. Ask a librarian to help you locate potential sources, such as Benjamin Franklin's *Poor Richard's Almanack* (an excerpt of the *Almanack* begins on p. 188 of this book). Compile your collection into a reference guide. Annotate each saying with a brief explanation of how it relates to Puritanism.

Writing Process Workshop

There are various levels of persuasion: for example, a teenager trying to coax the car keys from Dad, grass-roots volunteers encouraging voter registration, or Puritan minister Jonathan Edwards warning his awestruck congregants to save their souls from eternal damnation.

You can polish your powers to sway and convince by writing a **persuasive essay**—a short piece of writing that tries to influence readers to take an action or accept a position on a particular issue. The following skills, introduced in this section's Writing Mini-Lessons, will help you write a persuasive essay.

Writing Skills Focus

▶ **Anticipate opposing arguments** so that you can address likely objections to your position in the course of your essay. (See p. 95.)

▶ **Evaluate persuasive techniques** to decide how best to appeal to your audience: through logic, shared experience, humor, emotion, or some combination of these. (See p. 103.)

Jonathan Edwards, for example, churns up a powerful emotional whirlwind in his famous sermon.

① Edwards paints a frightening picture, playing on his audience's fear.

② Edwards anticipates his listeners' possible descriptions of themselves and turns their ideas against them.

MODEL FROM LITERATURE

from "Sinners in the Hands of an Angry God"
by Jonathan Edwards

How dreadful ① is the state of those that are daily and hourly in the danger of this great wrath and infinite misery! But this is the dismal case of every soul in this congregation that has not been born again, however moral and strict, sober and religious, ② they may otherwise be. Oh that you would consider it, whether you be young or old! . . .

Prewriting

Choose a Topic Have a friend or classmate conduct an interview with you about local or national issues. Review your responses, and choose the issue that's most important to you. As an alternative, you may want to choose to take a stand on one of the following issues.

> ### Topic Ideas
> - HDTV: bright future or sales gimmick?
> - Business downsizing: problem or solution?
> - Television rating system: helpful guide or form of censorship?

Clarify Your Position Although many issues entail more than two perspectives, it will help you organize your thoughts if you start out with the two major poles of the controversy and decide where you stand.

Gather and Evaluate Evidence To make your viewpoint convincing, you have to back it up with **facts**—statements that can be verified or proved—and not just pile up more **opinions**—personal beliefs that cannot be proved true or false. Unless you are already an expert on your topic, you will need to do research at the library, on the Internet, or through your own interviews, surveys, and experiments.

Use Pro-and-Con Organization You won't convince anybody by ignoring opposing ideas; the best strategy is to anticipate them, meet them head-on, and knock them down through use of the pro-and-con structure. Here's an example:

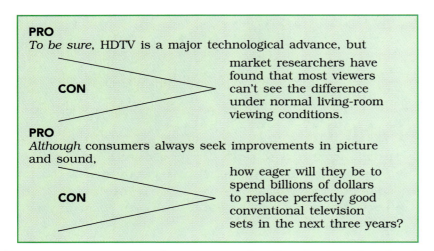

PRO
To be sure, HDTV is a major technological advance, but

CON market researchers have found that most viewers can't see the difference under normal living-room viewing conditions.

PRO
Although consumers always seek improvements in picture and sound,

CON how eager will they be to spend billions of dollars to replace perfectly good conventional television sets in the next three years?

APPLYING LANGUAGE SKILLS: Comparative and Superlative Forms

Most adjectives have a **positive form**, a **comparative form** for comparing two items, and a **superlative form** for comparing more than two items.

Positive	Comparative	Superlative
slow	slower	slowest
arid	more arid	most arid

When in doubt about how to form the comparative or superlative, check a dictionary. If no acceptable *-er* or *-est* forms are listed, use *more* and *most*.

Practice Choose the appropriate form for each example.

1. Of all the new technology, HDTV offers the (clearer, clearest) reception.

2. I'd prefer the (less, least) costly of the two models.

Writing Application Look for places in your essay in which you compare items. Revise any incorrect comparative and superlative forms.

Writer's Solution Connection Writing Lab

For more topic ideas for your essay, use the Inspirations in the Writing Lab tutorial on Persuasion.

Applying Language Skills: Complex Sentences

A **complex sentence** has one main clause and one or more subordinate clauses. A **subordinate clause,** underlined here, has a subject and a predicate but cannot stand alone as a sentence.

Although truer colors would improve the picture, we can still appreciate the movie this way.

Use conjunctions such as *after, as, before, although,* and *unless* to create subordinate clauses.

Practice Combine clauses to make complex sentences. Use the conjunctions provided.

1. We watch hours of television. We would benefit from the sharpest images. (because)
2. The first models proved to be the most expensive. Later ones were more affordable. (although)

Writing Application To add variety to your essay, replace short, choppy sentences with complex sentences.

Writer's Solution Connection
Language Lab

For more practice, complete the Language Lab lesson on Varying Sentence Structure.

Drafting

Evaluate Persuasive Techniques As you begin writing, consider whether you should appeal to your audience's emotions, sense of reason, or both.

Organize Into Introduction, Body, and Conclusion Begin with an introduction that grabs your readers and states your viewpoint clearly. In the body, develop your supporting evidence as you address opposing ideas. Conclude by reinforcing your argument with a decisive restatement of your main point.

Revising

Use a Peer Reviewer Have a friend or classmate read your draft to see whether he or she is convinced by your argument. Note any holes or weak spots the reviewer brings to your attention.

Self-Evaluation Use the following criteria for a good persuasive essay to guide your revisions.

► Is your viewpoint clearly stated in the introduction?
► Have you presented enough supporting facts and evidence?
► Have you anticipated and addressed opposing arguments?
► Is there a suitable balance of logic and emotion that will sway your intended audience?

REVISION MODEL

① Maybe the sound quality of the new technology is slightly improved, but spend hundreds to ②
∧ How many times are we going to ∧ revamp our entire

entertainment library?

① The writer anticipates an objection by noting the benefits of the technology.
② This reference to money provides a financial reason to persuade readers.

Publishing

Here are some ways to reach a larger audience:

► **Speak Out** Deliver your essay as a speech to your class or to a local civic group.
► **Local News** Send your piece to the op-ed editor of your daily newspaper.

Real-World Reading Skills Workshop

Strategies for Success

Whether you're reading a national newspaper, your favorite magazine, or the town information letter, identifying key points in an article will help you read efficiently and productively. Key points are the main ideas that the author of an article wants to communicate.

Orient Yourself Read the article title and any subheads or pull-out quotations. Scan any visual images. What is the article's topic? What existing knowledge do you have of this topic?

Identify Key Points in the Article Start by reading the entire article. Then return to the opening paragraph and study it. What is its main focus? How does it set the stage for the text that follows?

Check the first and last sentences in each paragraph as a starting place when looking for key ideas. Then look for ideas that tie the text together. These are usually key points.

Synthesize All the Information Review the titles and visuals. How do they support the key points stated in the article? Checking these elements can help you verify key ideas.

Apply the Strategy

The "Science Club Newsletter" contains this article about the Mars space program. Before discussing it at the next club meeting, you want to identify its key points.

1. What is the overall topic of this article?
2. What is the article's most significant point?
3. Identify another key point in the article.
4. How do the article's title and subtitle support its overall point?

✔ *Here are other situations in which identifying key points in an article is useful:*
▶ College brochures
▶ Magazine features
▶ Movie reviews

NASA Says Faster Isn't Necessarily Better

You might be surprised to learn that the computer used in the 1997 Pathfinder mission to Mars was a dinosaur in its own time. Its 20 megahertz microprocessor could never compete with the average 100 megahertz home computer. Still, the RAD6000 guided Pathfinder more than 300 million miles to the red planet. Why didn't NASA use a more advanced computer?

Reliability Is Priority #1

Supported by complex computers at NASA's Earth stations, Pathfinder doesn't need lightning-speed processing. What it demands, however, is reliability. After all, it's a long way to a repair shop. On-board computers must also be lighter, more energy efficient, and tolerant of radiation and vacuum. RAD6000 does have some bells and whistles—128 megabites of memory and an operating system that understands the importance of precision timing when opening the air bags. As NASA's Brian Schneider said, "Your computer may be faster and more powerful than ours, but it wouldn't get the job done in space."

Speaking and Listening Workshop

Strategies for Success

Imagine trying to explain a blizzard to an audience of Florida natives. With some topics, it's not enough to describe or explain—the audience has to *see* or *hear* for themselves. In such situations, visual aids can be as important as your words. Use these strategies to help you prepare for a presentation in which you use visuals.

Gather a Variety of Material Thoroughly research your topic. Look for photographs, slides, audio and video recordings, fine art, letters, and other primary source materials. If possible, gather materials appealing to more than one sense. As with any research, document sources thoroughly.

Blend Visual and Audio Cues Into Your Presentation Weave the visual and audio components you've gathered into a spoken presentation. Use lines like, "As this picture demonstrates," or simple gestures, like a turn of your head, to direct the audience toward multimedia features.

✔ Tips for Giving an Oral Presentation With Visuals

▶ *Choose high-interest visuals to grab viewers' attention.*

▶ Interact with the audience, directing their attention to multiple media.

▶ Take advantage of Internet resources by downloading video, audio, and text materials.

▶ Make sure all your technology works. Check before your presentation begins.

▶ Rehearse the presentation. Correct awkward transitions, and adjust those sections that overload viewers with too much media.

Apply the Strategies

Explore the possibilities for impact through oral, visual, and audio materials as you complete one or more of these activities.

1. Brainstorm for possible sources of visual material. List these with an example or two from each source.

2. In a group, plan a multimedia presentation about the lives of early residents of your community. Create a script and storyboard that indicate where you might include visual or audio materials.

3. With a partner, exchange stories and photographs of a recent special occasion. Discuss ways to use visuals to build an oral presentation around your memories and pictures.

Extended Reading Opportunities

The literature of this period reflects the birth of a new culture and the rich heritage of an ancient one. Here are suggestions for extending your exploration of the people who inhabited the land during the colonial period and the centuries preceding it.

Suggested Titles

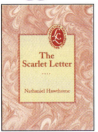

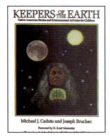

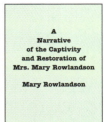

The Scarlet Letter
Nathaniel Hawthorne

They were very few in number, but their courage, hard work, and intense perseverance enabled the Puritans who landed at Plymouth in 1620 to establish a colony. Though *The Scarlet Letter* was published in 1850, Nathaniel Hawthorne chose this setting—a world in which people lived simple lives and followed a strict moral code—for his masterpiece. The novel tells the story of Hester Prynne, who is branded as an outcast and struggles to create her own redemption.

Keepers of the Earth
Joseph Bruchac

In an effort to preserve the culture of his people—he is descended from the Abenaki—Joseph Bruchac has published many volumes of Native American tales and literature—both ancient and contemporary. In this collection, Bruchac presents a sampling of traditional tales. With each, Bruchac provides environmentally focused activities that highlight the relationship between Native American cultures and the natural world.

A Narrative of the Captivity and Restoration of Mrs. Mary Rowlandson
Mary Rowlandson

At sunrise on a February day in 1676, during King Philip's War, a frontier village in Massachusetts was attacked by Native Americans. Among the survivors taken hostage was Mary Rowlandson, who in her own words recounts the story of her captivity. Her tale was among the first of the colonial frontier adventure thrillers that captured the imagination of seventeenth-century readers.

Other Possibilities

The Journal of John Winthrop   John Winthrop
The History of the Dividing Line   William Byrd

Washington Crossing the Delaware, Emanuel Gottlieb Leutze, Metropolitan Museum of Art

UNIT 2

A Nation Is Born (1750–1800)

"The time is now near at hand which must probably determine whether Americans are to be freemen or slaves; whether they are to have any property they can call their own; whether their houses and farms are to be pillaged and destroyed and themselves consigned to a state of wretchedness from which no human efforts will deliver them. The fate of unborn millions will now depend, under God, on the courage and conduct of this army. Our cruel and unrelenting enemy leaves us only the choice of brave resistance, or the most abject submission. We have, therefore, to resolve to conquer or die."

—George Washington,
addressing the Continental Army
before the battle of Long Island, August 27, 1776.

Timeline
1750–1800

1750	1760	1770

American Events

- **1748** *Poor Richard's Almanack* sold to new owner after 25 years under Benjamin Franklin. ▶

- **1752** Benjamin Franklin conducts his kite and key experiment with lightning. ▼

- **1753** Benjamin Banneker constructs the first striking clock with all parts made in America. The clock keeps perfect time for the next 40 years.

- **1754** French and Indian War begins.

- **1759–63** France gives up claims to North American territory.
- **1765** Stamp Act passed by British Parliament; colonists protest bitterly.
- **1767** Townshend Acts impose new taxes, angering colonists further.

- **1771** Benjamin Franklin begins his *Autobiography*.
- **1773** Parliament's Tea Act prompts Boston Tea Party. ▲
- **1773** Phillis Wheatley's *Poems on Various Subjects* published in England.
- **1774** First Continental Congress meets in Philadelphia.
- **1775** Patrick Henry gives his "liberty or death" speech.
- **1775** The American Revolution begins.
- **1776** Second Continental Congress adopts Declaration of Independence. ▼
- **1776** Congress approves the enlistment of African American men.
- **1778** France recognizes U.S. independence and signs treaty of alliance.

World Events

- **1755** France: School for deaf opens in Paris. ▼
- **1755** England: Samuel Johnson publishes *Dictionary of the English Language*.
- **1757** England: Robert Clive defeats native army at Plassey, India.
- **1759** France: Voltaire publishes *Candide*, satirizing optimism of Rousseau.

- **1762** France: Jean Jacques Rousseau states his political philosophy in *The Social Contract*.
- **1763** Seven Years War ends.
- **1769** Scotland: James Watt invents an improved steam engine.
- **1769** England: Richard Arkwright invents a frame for spinning; helps bring about factory system.

- **1770** Germany: Ludwig von Beethoven is born. ▶
- **1772** Poland: First of three partitions of Poland gives land to Russia, Prussia, and Austria.
- **1774** England: Joseph Priestley discovers oxygen, named later by Lavoisier.
- **1779** England: Captain James Cook becomes first European to see Hawaii.
- **1779** South Africa: First of Kaffir wars between blacks and whites breaks out.

| 1780 | 1790 | 1800 |

- **1780** James Derham becomes the first black man licensed to practice medicine in the U.S.
- **1781** General Cornwallis surrenders British army to George Washington at Yorktown. ▲
- **1782** Michel-Guillaume Jean de Crève-coeur's *Letters From an American Farmer* published in London.
- **1783** Noah Webster's *Spelling Book* first appears; 60 million copies would be sold.
- **1783** Revolutionary War ends.
- **1787** Constitutional Convention meets in Philadelphia to draft Constitution.
- **1789** George Washington elected first President of United States. ▼

- **1790** First federal U.S. census shows approximately 757,208 blacks in the U.S., nearly 20% of the total population. 59,557 are free.
- **1793** Eli Whitney invents cotton gin. ▶
- **1795** University of North Carolina opens as America's first state university.

- **1801** Thomas Jefferson, principal author of Declaration of Independence, elected President.

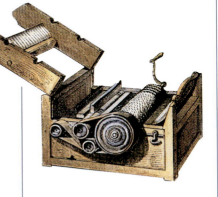

- **1781** England: William Herschel discovers planet Uranus. ▼
- **1782** Germany: Goethe begins 50 years of work on the poem *Faust*.
- **1785** France: Jean-Pierre Blanchard makes first balloon crossing of English Channel.
- **1786** Scotland: Robert Burns is widely acclaimed for his first book of poems.
- **1786** Austria: Wolfgang Amadeus Mozart creates the comic opera *The Marriage of Figaro*.
- **1789** France: Storming of Bastille in Paris sets off French Revolution.

- **1791** England: James Boswell publishes *The Life of Samuel Johnson*. ▲
- **1793** France: King Louis XVI and Marie Antoinette executed.
- **1796** England: Edward Jenner develops smallpox vaccine.
- **1796** France: Napoleon Bonaparte comes to power in France. ▶
- **1797** Spain: Goya creates *Los Caprichos* etchings.
- **1798** England: William Wordsworth and Samuel Taylor Coleridge publish *Lyrical Ballads*.

- **1800** Germany: Ludwig von Beethoven composes *First Symphony*.

The Story of the Times

1750–1800

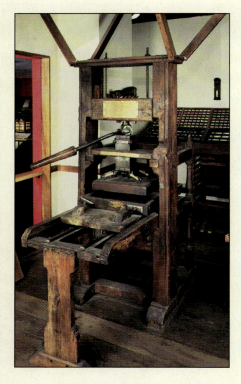

▲ **Assess Technology** Colonial printers played an important role in uniting colonists against the British. Why are newspapers, letters, and pamphlets critical to inspiring revolution?

▼ **Make an Inference** Almost from its founding in 1682, Philadelphia was a thriving port. This painting shows the busy Philadelphia waterfront in 1720. Why did ports become the major cities of the colonies?

Historical Background

It is easy to forget how long the thirteen original states had been colonies. By 1750, there were fourth- and fifth-generation Americans of European descent living in Virginia and New England. These people were English subjects, and, on the whole, they were well satisfied with that status. In fact, as late as the early 1760's, few Americans had given much thought to the prospect of independence.

Between the mid-1760's and the mid-1770's, however, attitudes changed dramatically. King George III and Parliament imposed a number of regulations that threatened the liberties of the colonists. With each succeeding measure, the outrage in America grew, finally erupting into war.

The Age of Reason Great upheavals in history occur when circumstances are ripe. The American Revolution was such an upheaval, and the groundwork for it had been laid by European writers and thinkers as well as by the English king and Parliament. The eighteenth century is often characterized as the Enlightenment, or the Age of Reason. Spurred by the work of many seventeenth-century thinkers—such as scientists Galileo and Sir Isaac Newton, philosophers Voltaire and Jean Jacques Rousseau, and political theorist John Locke, the writers and thinkers of the Enlightenment valued reason over faith. Unlike the Puritans, they had little interest in the

hereafter, believing instead in the power of reason and science to further human progress. They spoke of a social contract that forms the basis of government. Above all, they believed that people are by nature good, not evil. A perfect society seemed to them to be more than just an idle dream.

The American statesmen of the Revolutionary period were themselves figures of the Enlightenment. No history of the period would be complete without mention of the ideas and writings of Benjamin Franklin, Thomas Paine, and Thomas Jefferson. These Americans not only expressed the ideas of the Age of Reason, but they also helped to put them spectacularly into practice.

Toward a Clash of Arms The American Revolution was preceded by the French and Indian War, a struggle between England and France for control of North America. The conflict broke out in 1754 and continued for nearly a decade. When the war officially ended in 1763, defeated France gave up its claims to North American territory. There was general jubilation in the thirteen English colonies.

The good feelings were short-lived, however. The British government, wanting to raise revenue in the colonies to pay its war debt, passed the Stamp Act in 1765. Colonial reaction to the Stamp Act, which required the buying and affixing of stamps to each of 54 ordinary items, was swift and bitter. Stamps were burned. Stamp distributors were beaten and their shops destroyed. Eventually, the Stamp Act was repealed.

Other acts and reactions followed. The Townshend Acts of 1767 taxed paper, paint, glass, lead, and tea. When the colonists organized a boycott, the British dissolved the Massachusetts legislature and sent two regiments of British troops to Boston. In 1770, these Redcoats fired into a taunting mob, causing five fatalities. This so-called Boston Massacre further inflamed colonial passions. Parliament repealed the Townshend duties except for the tax on tea, but a separate Tea Act giving an English company a virtual monopoly soon greeted the colonists. Furious, a group of Bostonians dressed as Mohawks dumped a shipment of tea

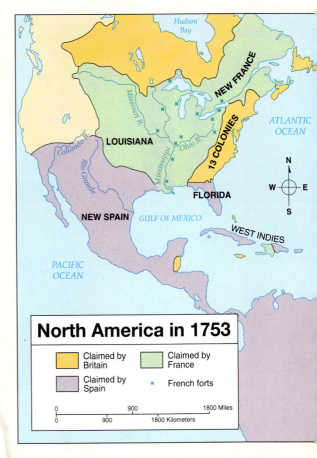

North America in 1753

| Claimed by Britain | Claimed by France |
| Claimed by Spain | ■ French forts |

0   900   1800 Miles
0   900   1800 Kilometers

▲ **Interpret a Map** On the eve of the French and Indian War, France still had claim to a majority of the interior of North America. What strategic advantage did the thirteen colonies enjoy because of their geographic location?

▲ **Assess** Many critical battles of the American Revolution were fought in New York, New Jersey, and Pennsylvania during the fall and winter of 1776 to 1777. What challenges would the weather pose for the soldiers?

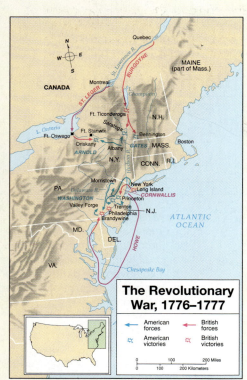

The Revolutionary War, 1776–1777

American forces
American victories
British forces
British victories

0   100   200 Miles
0   100   200 Kilometers

▲ **Identify Cause and Effect** Based on this map, why do you think many Patriots left Philadelphia in 1777?

into Boston harbor. As punishment for this Boston Tea Party, the English Parliament passed the Coercive Acts. Because they shut down the port of Boston, forbade meetings other than annual town meetings, and insisted that British troops could be housed in colonists' homes, colonists immediately dubbed these laws the Intolerable Acts.

In September 1774, colonial leaders, although not speaking openly of independence, met in Philadelphia for the First Continental Congress. The British, their authority slipping away, appointed General Thomas Gage governor of Massachusetts. The stage was set for war.

"The Shot Heard Round the World" On April 19, 1775, 700 British troops met some 70 colonial minutemen on the Lexington green. A musket shot was fired (from which side, no one knows), and before the shooting that followed was over, eight Americans lay dead. The British marched west to Concord, where another skirmish took place. The encounters at Lexington and Concord, a landmark in American history, have been referred to as "the shot heard round the world." The American Revolution had begun, and there would be no turning back.

More than a year would pass before the colonies declared their independence. After six years of fighting, the war finally came to an end at Yorktown, Virginia, on October 19, 1781. Aided by the French army and the French navy, and enlisting the service of black soldiers, General Washington's army bottled up the 8,000-man British force under General Cornwallis. Seeing that escape was impossible, General Cornwallis surrendered.

The New Nation The path to self-government was not always smooth, however. After the Revolution, the Articles of Confederation established a "league of friendship" among the new states. This arrangement did not work well. The federal Constitution that replaced the Articles required many compromises and was ratified only after a long fight. Even then, a Bill of Rights had to be added to placate those who feared the centralized power that the Constitution conferred.

The old revolutionaries, by and large, remained true to their principles and continued their public duties. George Washington became the nation's first president. John Adams, a signer of the Declaration of Independence, succeeded him in that office. Then, in 1800, Americans elected as their president the brilliant statesman who had drafted the Declaration, one of the heroes of the Enlightenment, Thomas Jefferson.

Literature of the Period

A Time of Crisis In contrast to the private soul-searching of the Puritans of New England, much of what was produced during the Revolutionary period was public writing. By the time of the War for Independence, nearly fifty newspapers had been established in the coastal cities. At the time of Washington's inauguration, there were nearly forty magazines. Almanacs were popular from Massachusetts to Georgia.

The mind of the nation was on politics. Journalists and printers provided a forum for the expression of ideas. After 1763, those ideas were increasingly focused on relations with Great Britain and, more broadly, on the nature of government. As the literature presented in this unit testifies, the writing of permanent importance from the Revolutionary era is mostly political writing.

Politics as Literature The public writing and speaking of American statesmen in two tumultuous decades, the 1770's and 1780's, helped to reshape not only the nation but also the world.

Patrick Henry was a spellbinding orator whose speech against the Stamp Act in the Virginia House of Burgesses brought cries of "Treason!" Ten years later, his electrifying speech to the Virginia Convention expressed the rising sentiment for independence.

Thomas Paine was perhaps more influential than any other in swaying public opinion in favor of independence. His 1776 pamphlet *Common Sense* swept the colonies, selling 100,000 copies in three months.

The Declaration of Independence was first drafted by Thomas Jefferson in June 1776. The finished document is largely his work, although

New-York Historical Society

▲ **Hypothesize** This cotton handkerchief, probably made in 1777, honors General George Washington. Why might a new country glorify its wartime heroes?

▲ **Draw a Conclusion** When Patrick Henry railed against the Stamp Act, Virginia became the first colony officially to protest the new tax law. Based on this painting, what type of citizen do you think was generally elected to serve in the Virginia House of Burgesses?

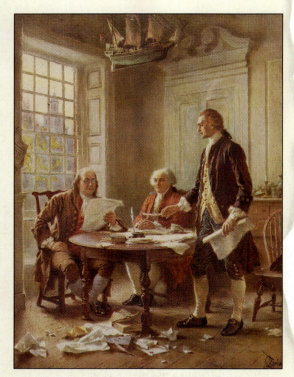

▲ **Make an Inference** This painting captures the writing of the Declaration of Independence. What do the many papers on the floor of the room suggest about the writing of the Declaration?

▲ **Analyze Bias** Paul Revere's engraving of the Boston Massacre played a major role in whipping up colonial fury against the British. Revere purposefully distorted the events. For example, notice that Revere shows the British general giving orders to shoot. Eyewitnesses have said this never happened. What other details suggest the artist was pro-colonist?

a committee of five statesmen, including Benjamin Franklin, was involved in its creation. The Declaration, despite some exaggerated charges against King George III, is one of the most influential political statements ever made.

Another Revolutionary period document written by committee that has stood the test of time is the Constitution of the United States, drafted in 1787. The framers, whose new nation boasted about four million people, hoped that the Constitution would last at least a generation. It still survives, amended only 27 times, as the political foundation of a superpower of 50 states and more than 250 million people.

The Cultural Scene While politics dominated the literature of the Revolutionary period, not every writer of note was a statesman. Verse appeared in most of the newspapers, and numerous broadside ballads were published. (A broadside ballad is a single sheet of paper, printed on one or both sides, dealing with a current topic.) One of the most popular broadside ballads was called "The Dying Redcoat," supposedly written by a British sergeant mortally wounded in the Revolution.

Two other poets of the day whose works were more sophisticated than the broadside ballads were Joel Barlow and Phillis Wheatley. Barlow, a 1778 Yale graduate, is best remembered for "The Hasty Pudding," a mock-heroic tribute to corn-meal mush. Phillis Wheatley, born in Africa and brought to Boston in childhood as a slave, showed early signs of literary genius. A collection of her poems was published in England while she was still a young woman.

Another writer of the Revolutionary period recorded his impressions of everyday American life. Born into an aristocratic French family, Michel-Guillaume Crèvecoeur became a soldier of fortune, a world traveler, and a farmer. For fifteen years, he owned a plantation in Orange County, New York, and his impressions of life there were published in London in 1782 as *Letters From an American Farmer*.

Perhaps the best-known writing of the period outside the field of politics was done by Benjamin Franklin. His *Poor Richard's Almanack* became familiar to most households in the colonies. A statesman, printer, author, inventor, and scientist, Franklin was a true son of the Enlightenment. His *Autobiography,* covering only his early years, is regarded as one of the finest autobiographies in any language.

Culture and Art During the Revolutionary period, America began to establish a cultural identity of its own. Theaters were built from New York to Charleston. A number of new colleges were established after the war, especially in the South. Several outstanding painters were at work in the colonies and the young republic. Among them were John Singleton Copley, Gilbert Stuart, John Trumbull, and Charles Willson Peale. Patience Wright, famous in the colonies as a sculptor of wax portraits, moved to London before the war. While there, she acted as a Revolutionary spy. In music, William Billings produced *The New England Psalm-Singer* and a number of patriotic hymns. This was a turbulent time—a time of action—and its legacy was cultural as well as political.

American Literature at Daybreak By the early 1800's, America could boast a small body of national literature. The Native Americans had contributed haunting poetry and legends through their oral traditions. The Puritans had written a number of powerful, inward-looking works. The statesmen of the Revolutionary period had produced political documents for the ages. A few poets and essayists had made a permanent mark on the literature of the young republic. There were, however, no American novels or plays of importance, and the modern short story had yet to be invented.

As the eighteenth century came to a close, however, the raw materials for a great national literature were at hand, waiting to be used. The nation stood on the threshold of a territorial and population explosion unique in the history of the world. It would take almost exactly a century to close the frontier on the vast and varied continent beyond the Appalachians. During that century, American literature would burst forth with a vitality that might have surprised even the farsighted founders of the nation. The colonial age ended with a narrow volume of memorable literature. The nineteenth century would close with a library of works that form a major part of America's literary heritage.

▲ **Identify Problems** These bills were issued by Rhode Island and South Carolina after the war. What problems would thirteen separate currencies cause the new nation?

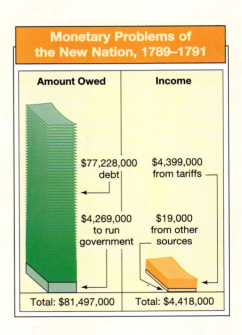

Monetary Problems of the New Nation, 1789–1791

Amount Owed	Income
$77,228,000 debt	$4,399,000 from tariffs
$4,269,000 to run government	$19,000 from other sources
Total: $81,497,000	Total: $4,418,000

▲ **Read a Chart** As the first secretary of the treasury, Alexander Hamilton had to develop a financial plan for the government. What was the government's income in 1789? How much did it owe?

The Development of American English

NOAH WEBSTER AND THE AMERICAN LANGUAGE

by Richard Lederer

Travel back in time to May 1787 to the city of Philadelphia. It is thronged with important visitors, including Benjamin Franklin, Alexander Hamilton, James Madison, and the brightest of these luminaries—George Washington. They have come to attend the Constitutional Convention "in order to form a more perfect Union" of states that have recently won a surprising military victory.

On the evening of May 26, 1787, General Washington pays a visit to talk about education with a 28-year-old New Englander who is teaching school in Philadelphia. His name is Noah Webster.

America's Schoolmaster Why did Washington call on a young man scarcely half his age who was neither a Revolutionary War hero nor a Convention delegate? One reason was that Noah Webster was the author, publisher, and salesman of *The Blue-Backed Speller*, a book that was then more widely read in the United States than any other except the Bible.

Webster and the American Dictionary On top of such an amazing achievement, Webster devoted thirty years to creating the first great American dictionaries. The fact that the name *Webster* and the word *dictionary* are practically synonymous indicates the enduring brightness of Webster's reputation.

Throughout his life, Noah Webster was afire with the conviction that the United States should have its own version of the English language. In 1789, he wrote:

> As an independent nation, our honor requires us to have a system of our own, in language as well as government. Great Britain, whose children we are and whose language we speak, should no longer be our standard.

In putting this theory into practice, Noah Webster traveled throughout the East and South, listening to the speech of American people, and taking endless notes. He included in his dictionaries an array of shiny new American words, among them *applesauce, bullfrog, chowder, handy, hickory, succotash, tomahawk*—and *skunk*: "a quadruped remarkable for its smell."

In shaping the American language, Noah Webster also taught a new nation a new way to spell.

British spelling	Webster's spelling
honour, humour	honor, humor
musick, publick	music, public
centre, theatre	center, theater
plough	plow

Activities

1. Dictionary-makers are the biographers of words. Pick a word from the *Oxford English Dictionary* and write its "biography"—when the word was born and how it acquired new meanings over the course of its life.
2. Give the American equivalent of each of the following British words: (a) braces, (b) lift, (c) lorry, (d) petrol, (e) telly. Identify additional words that distinguish Americans from British citizens.

PART 1

Voices for Freedom

Miss Liberty, Abby Aldrich
Rockefeller Folk Art Center,
Williamsburg, Virginia

Guide for Interpreting

Benjamin Franklin (1706–1790)

No other colonial American more closely embodied the promise of America than Benjamin Franklin. Through hard work, dedication, and ingenuity, Franklin was able to rise out of poverty to become a wealthy, famous, and influential person. Although he never received a formal education, Franklin made important contributions in a variety of fields, including literature, journalism, science, diplomacy, education, and philosophy.

Early Years Franklin, one of seventeen children, was born in Boston. After leaving school at the age of ten, he spent two years working for his father before becoming an apprentice to his older brother, who was a printer. When he was seventeen, Franklin left Boston and traveled to Philadelphia, hoping to open his own print shop. Once he established himself as a printer, Franklin began producing a newspaper and an annual publication called *Poor Richard's Almanack,* which contained information, observations, and advice. The *Almanack,* published from 1732 through 1757, was very popular and earned Franklin a reputation as a talented writer.

Man of Science When Franklin was forty-two, he retired from the printing business to devote himself to science. He proved to be as successful a scientist as he had been a printer. Over the course of his lifetime,

Franklin was responsible for inventing the lightning rod, bifocals, and a new type of stove; confirming the laws of electricity; and contributing to the scientific understanding of earthquakes and ocean currents. In spite of all these achievements, Franklin is best remembered for his career in politics.

Statesman and Diplomat Franklin played an important role in drafting the Declaration of Independence, enlisting French support during the Revolutionary War, negotiating a peace treaty with Britain, and drafting the United States Constitution. In his later years, he was ambassador first to England and then to France.

Even before Washington, Franklin was considered "the father of his country."

The Story Behind the Story

Franklin wrote the first section of *The Autobiography* in 1771 at the age of sixty-five. At the urging of friends, he wrote three more sections—the last shortly before his death—but succeeded only in bringing the account of his life to the years 1757 to 1759. Though never completed, his *Autobiography,* filled with his opinions and suggestions, provides not only a record of his achievements but also an understanding of his character. (For more on Franklin, see pp.166 and 186.)

◆ Background for Understanding

HISTORY: FRANKLIN IN PHILADELPHIA

Benjamin Franklin greatly influenced daily life in colonial Philadelphia. He helped establish the city's public library and fire department, as well as its first college. In addition, through his efforts Philadelphia became the first city in the colonies to have street lights.

Philadelphia was an important center of activity during the period leading up to the American Revolution. It was here that the Declaration of

Independence, establishing the United States as an independent nation, was written and signed.

In Philadelphia today, you can still walk down cobblestone streets and visit historic sites. Independence Hall, where the Declaration of Independence was signed, the Liberty Bell, and the home of Betsy Ross are within walking distance for tourists and history enthusiasts.

from The Autobiography

◆ *Literature and Your Life*

CONNECT YOUR EXPERIENCE

Real-life stories can provide as much excitement as any fictional drama. It's not surprising, then, that bestseller lists frequently include the autobiographies of celebrities; we want to know how people have achieved fame and dealt with adversity. Autobiographies of historical figures, such as Franklin, can be equally gripping, allowing us a firsthand look at events that have helped shape our world.

Journal Writing List the experiences you would choose to write about if you were preparing an autobiography.

THEMATIC FOCUS: VOICES FOR FREEDOM

Beyond throwing out the British government, people living at the time of the American Revolution wanted to create a uniquely American way of life. In many ways, Franklin represents that new American. *The Autobiography* describes his desire to improve himself. He writes of this ambition to help others follow in his path.

◆ Build Vocabulary

WORD ROOTS: -*vigil*-

The word *vigilance,* used in *The Autobiography,* contains the word root -*vigil*-, which means, "the act or period of remaining awake so as to guard or observe something." The meaning of -*vigil*- can help you define *vigilance* as "watchfulness."

> arduous
> avarice
> vigilance
> disposition
> foppery
> felicity

WORD BANK

Preview this list of words from *The Autobiography*.

◆ Grammar and Style

PRONOUN CASE

Pronouns are words that replace nouns. **Pronoun case** refers to the form that a pronoun takes to indicate its function in a sentence. **Subjective case** pronouns—such as *I, we, you, he, she, it,* and *they*— are used when the pronoun is the subject of the sentence. **Objective case** pronouns—such as *me, us, him, her, it* and *them*—are used when the pronoun receives the action of the verb (direct object) or serves as the object of a preposition. Look at this example:

subj.   obj. of prep.
I always carried my little book with *me.*

◆ Literary Focus

AUTOBIOGRAPHY

Benjamin Franklin's *Autobiography* set the standard for what was then a new genre. An **autobiography** is a person's account of his or her life. Generally written in the first person, with the author speaking as "I," autobiographies present life events as the writer views them. In addition to providing inside details about the writer's life, autobiographies offer insights into the beliefs and perceptions of the author. Autobiographies also offer a glimpse of what it was like to live in the author's time period. Autobiographies often provide a view of historical events that you won't find in history books.

As you read, use an organizer like this one to note what the selection reveals about Franklin's life, his attitudes, and the period in which he lived.

| Details of Franklin's Life |
| Franklin's Attitudes |
| Details of the Time |

Reading for Success

Strategies for Constructing Meaning

When you read a work of literature, you look for what it means. Why did the author write it? What does he or she want to convey? What does the work mean to you? In looking for answers to questions like these, you construct the meaning that the work has for you.

Constructing meaning from a work of literature is a process in which you examine the author's ideas in the light of what you already know. There are many ways that you can construct meaning from a text. Here are a few strategies to direct you through the process:

Make inferences.

Writers don't always tell you everything. You need to "read between the lines" to arrive at ideas writers suggest but don't say. Often writers provide details and actions of a character from which you infer information about the author's message.

Draw conclusions.

A conclusion is a general statement that you can make based on details in the text. A series of inferences can lead you to a conclusion.

Recognize the writer's purpose or bias.

Be aware of the writer's views on an issue. A writer who is strongly inclined toward one position or another may not present an issue impartially. Consider the writer's purpose. Does the writer want you to believe as he or she does? This factor can affect the meaning that you take from a work.

Distinguish fact from opinion.

A fact is a statement that can be proved. An opinion is someone's belief, not necessarily supported by proof. An opinion carries more weight if it is supported by facts. Take care not to think that an opinion is a fact, and look to see whether a writer has supported his or her opinions.

Interpret the information.

▶ Explain to yourself the meaning or the significance of what the author is saying.
▶ Restate the author's message.

Use your knowledge of the historical time period.

The political climate and the intellectual trends of a specific time period are reflected in the writing that comes out of it. Apply the information from the introduction to this unit as you read the selections.

As you read the following excerpt from Benjamin Franklin's *Autobiography,* look at the notes along the sides. These notes demonstrate how to apply these strategies to a work of literature.

from The Autobiography

Benjamin Franklin

It was about this time I conceived the bold and <u>arduous</u> project of arriving at moral perfection. I wished to live without committing any fault at any time; I would conquer all that either natural inclination, custom, or company might lead me into. As I knew, or thought I knew, what was right and wrong, I did not see why I might not always do the one and avoid the other. But I soon found I had undertaken a task of more difficulty than I had imagined. While my care was employed in guarding against one fault, I was often surprised by another; habit took the advantage of inattention; inclination was sometimes too strong for reason. I concluded, at length, that the mere speculative conviction that it was our interest to be completely virtuous was not sufficient to prevent our slipping; and that the contrary habits must be broken, and good ones acquired and established, before we can have any dependence on a steady, uniform rectitude of conduct. For this purpose I therefore contrived the following method.

> Franklin's **purpose** seems to be to impress readers with his good intentions and his diligent efforts.

> Franklin begins this paragraph by stating **factually** how he planned to achieve moral perfection. He concludes the paragraph with his **opinion** that virtue is not inborn but must be steadily worked at.

In the various enumerations of the moral virtues I had met with in my reading, I found the catalog more or less numerous, as different writers included more or fewer ideas under the same name. Temperance, for example, was by some confined to eating and drinking, while by others it was extended to mean the moderating every other pleasure, appetite, inclination, or passion, bodily or mental, even to our <u>avarice</u> and ambition. I proposed to myself, for the sake of clearness, to use rather more names, with fewer ideas annexed to each, than a few names with more ideas; and I included under thirteen names of virtues all that at that time occurred to me as necessary or desirable, and annexed to each a short precept, which fully expressed the extent I gave to its meaning.

Benjamin Franklin as a Young Printer in Philadelphia, The Granger Collection, New York

◀ **Critical Viewing** What does the expression on Franklin's face suggest about his personality? **[Infer]**

◆ **Build Vocabulary**
arduous (är′ jōō wəs) *adj*.: Difficult
avarice (av′ ər is) *n.*: Greed

These names of virtues, with their precepts, were:

1. TEMPERANCE Eat not to dullness; drink not to elevation.
2. SILENCE Speak not but what may benefit others or yourself; avoid trifling conversation.
3. ORDER Let all your things have their places; let each part of your business have its time.
4. RESOLUTION Resolve to perform what you ought; perform without fail what you resolve.
5. FRUGALITY Make no expense but to do good to others or yourself; i.e., waste nothing.
6. INDUSTRY Lose no time; be always employed in something useful; cut off all unnecessary actions.
7. SINCERITY Use no hurtful deceit; think innocently and justly, and, if you speak, speak accordingly.
8. JUSTICE Wrong none by doing injuries, or omitting the benefits that are your duty.
9. MODERATION Avoid extremes; forebear resenting injuries so much as you think they deserve.
10. CLEANLINESS Tolerate no uncleanliness in body, clothes, or habitation.
11. TRANQUILLITY Be not disturbed at trifles, or at accidents common or unavoidable.
12. CHASTITY
13. HUMILITY Imitate Jesus and Socrates.[1]

> From this list, you can **infer** that Franklin is organized and diligent.

My intention being to acquire the *habitude* of all these virtues, I judged it would be well not to distract my attention by attempting the whole at once but to fix it on one of them at a time; and, when I should be master of that, then to proceed to another, and so on, till I should have gone through the thirteen; and, as the previous acquisition of some might facilitate the acquisition of certain others, I arranged them with that view, as they stand above. *Temperance* first, as it tends to procure that coolness and clearness of head, which is so necessary where constant vigilance was to be kept up, and guard maintained against the unremitting attraction of ancient habits and the force of perpetual temptations. This being acquired and established, *Silence* would be more easy; and my desire being to gain knowledge at the same time that I improved in virtue, and considering that in conversation it was obtained rather by the use of the ears than of the tongue, and therefore wishing to break a habit I was getting into of prattling, punning, and joking, which only made me acceptable to trifling company, I gave *Silence* the second place. This and the next, *Order,* I expected would allow me more time for attending to my project and my studies. *Resolution,* once become habitual, would keep me firm in my endeavors to obtain all the subsequent virtues; *Frugality* and *Industry* freeing me from my remaining debt and producing affluence and independence, would make more easy the practice of *Sincerity* and *Justice,* etc., etc. Conceiving then, that, agreeably to the advice of Pythagoras[2] in his *Golden Verses,* daily examination would be necessary, I contrived the following method for conducting that examination.

I made a little book, in which I allotted a page for each of the virtues. I ruled each page with red ink, so as to have seven columns, one for each day of the week, marking each column with a letter for the day. I crossed these columns with thirteen red lines, marking the beginning of each line with the first letter of one of the virtues, on which line and in its proper column I might mark, by a little black spot, every fault I found upon examination to have been committed respecting that virtue upon that day.

> The details of Franklin's methodical approach lead you to **infer** that Franklin is seriously dedicated to his goal.

I determined to give a week's strict attention to each of the virtues successively. Thus, in the

---

1. **Socrates** (säk´ rə tēz´): Greek philosopher and teacher (470?–399 B.C.).

◆ **Build Vocabulary**

vigilance (vij´ ə ləns) *n.*: Watchfulness
disposition (dis´ pə zish´ ən) *n.*: Management

---

2. **Pythagoras** (pi thag´ ə rəs): Greek philosopher and mathematician who lived in the sixth century B.C.

first week, my great guard was to avoid every[3] the least offense against *Temperance*, leaving the other virtues to their ordinary chance, only marking every evening the faults of the day. Thus, if in the first week I could keep my first line, marked *T.* clear of spots, I supposed the habit of that virtue so much strengthened, and its opposite weakened, that I might venture extending my attention to include the next, and for the following week keep both lines clear of spots. Proceeding thus to the last, I could go through a course complete in thirteen weeks, and four courses in a year. And like him who, having a garden to weed, does not attempt to eradicate all the bad herbs at once, which would exceed his reach and his strength, but works on one of the beds at a time, and, having accomplished the first, proceeds to a second, so I should have, I hoped, the encouraging pleasure of seeing on my pages the progress I made in virtue, by clearing successively my lines of their spots, till in the end, by a number of courses, I should be happy in viewing a clean book, after a thirteen weeks' daily examination. . . .

The precept of *Order* requiring that *every part of my business should have its allotted time,* one page in my little book contained the following scheme of employment for the twenty-four hours of a natural day.

THE MORNING.		
Question. What good shall I do this day?	5	Rise, wash, and
	6	address *Powerful Goodness!* Contrive day's business, and take the resolution of the
	7	day; prosecute the present study, and breakfast.
	8	
	9	Work.
	10	
	11	
NOON.	12	Read, or overlook
	1	my accounts, and dine.
	2	

	3	Work.
	4	
EVENING.	6	Put things in
Question. What good have I done today?	7	their places. Supper. Music or
	8	per. Music or
	9	diversion, or conversation. Examination of the day.
	10	
	11	
	12	
NIGHT.	1	Sleep.
	2	
	3	
	4	

I entered upon the execution of this plan for self-examination, and continued it with occasional intermissions for some time. I was surprised to find myself so much fuller of faults than I had imagined; but I had the satisfaction of seeing them diminish. To avoid the trouble of renewing now and then my little book, which, by scraping out the marks on the paper of old faults to make room for new ones in a new course, became full of holes, I transferred my tables and precepts to the ivory leaves of a memorandum book, on which the lines were drawn with red ink that made a durable stain, and on those lines I marked my faults with a black-lead pencil, which marks I could easily wipe out with a wet sponge. After a while I went through one course only in a year, and afterward only one in several years, till at length I omitted them entirely, being employed in voyages and business abroad, with a multiplicity of affairs that interfered; but I always carried my little book with me.

My scheme of *Order* gave me the most trouble; and I found that, though it might be practicable where a man's business was such as to leave him the disposition of his time, that of a journeyman printer, for instance, it was not possible to be exactly observed by a master, who must mix with the world and often receive people of business at their own hours. *Order,* too, with regard to places for things,

> **Interpret** this passage to mean that Franklin expects that he will eventually achieve the perfection he seeks.

---

3. **every:** Even.

Quaker Meeting, British, fourth quarter 18th century or first quarter 19th century, Museum of Fine Arts, Boston

papers, etc., I found extremely difficult to acquire. I had not been early accustomed to it, and, having an exceeding good memory, I was not so sensible of the inconvenience attending want of method. This article, therefore, cost me so much painful attention, and my faults in it vexed me so much, and I made so little progress in amendment, and had such frequent relapses, that I was almost ready to give up the attempt, and content myself with a faulty character in that respect, like the man who, in buying an ax of a smith, my neighbor, desired to have the whole of its surface as bright as the edge. The smith consented to

> From this information and your previous inferences, **draw the conclusion** that despite his efforts, Franklin failed to achieve perfection.

▲ **Critical Viewing** Relate this picture to *The Autobiography*. What does each suggest about discipline and order? [**Draw Conclusions**]

grind it bright for him if he would turn the wheel; he turned, while the smith pressed the broad face of the ax hard and heavily on the stone, which made the turning of it very fatiguing. The man came every now and then from the wheel to see how the work went on, and at length would take his ax as it was, without farther grinding. "No," said the smith, "turn on, turn on; we shall have it bright by and by; as yet, it is only speckled." "Yes," says the man, *"but I think I like a speckled ax best."* And I believe this may have been the case with many, who, having, for want of some such means as I employed, found the difficulty of obtaining good

> The **historical context** makes this anecdote about the ax appropriate. Axes were in common use at that time.

◆ **Build Vocabulary**

foppery (fäp´ ər ē) *n.*: Foolishness
felicity (fə lis´ ə tē) *n.*: Happiness; bliss

and breaking bad habits in other points of vice and virtue, have given up the struggle, and concluded that *"a speckled ax was best"*; for something, that pretended to be reason, was every now and then suggesting to me that

Recognize Franklin's **opinion** that people detest success in others. He uses this belief as an excuse for not becoming "perfect."

such extreme nicety as I exacted of myself might be a kind of foppery in morals, which, if it were known, would make me ridiculous; that a perfect character might be attended with the inconvenience of being envied and hated; and that a benevolent man should allow a few faults in himself, to keep his friends in countenance.

Interpret this passage to mean that Franklin doesn't regret that he never achieved perfection, but he is a better person for trying.

In truth, I found myself incorrigible with respect to *Order;* and now I am grown old, and my memory bad, I feel very sensibly the want of it. But, on the whole, though I never arrived at the perfection I had been so ambitious of obtaining, but fell far short of it, yet I was, by the endeavor, a better and a happier man than I otherwise should have been if I had not attempted it; as those who aim at perfect writing by imitating the engraved copies, though they never reached the wished-for excellence of those copies, their hand is mended by the endeavor, and is tolerable while it continues fair and legible.

It may be well my posterity should be informed that to this little artifice, with the blessing of God, their ancestor owed the constant felicity of his life, down to his seventy-ninth year in which this is written. What reverses may attend the remainder is in the hand of Providence; but, if they arrive, the reflection on past happiness enjoyed ought to help his bearing them with more resignation. To *Temperance* he ascribes his long-continued health, and what is still left to him of a good constitution; to *Industry* and *Frugality,* the early easiness of his circumstances and acquisition of his fortune, with all that knowledge that enabled him to be a useful citizen, and obtained for him some degree of reputation among the learned; to *Sincerity* and *Justice,* the confidence of his country, and the honorable employs it conferred upon him; and to the joint influence of the whole mass of the virtues, even in the imperfect state he was able to acquire them, all that evenness of temper, and that cheerfulness in conversation, which makes his company still sought for, and agreeable even to

Franklin admits to the **purpose** of wanting to look good in the eyes of his descendants. He also wants to show he produced some positive results in his life.

his younger acquaintance. I hope, therefore, that some of my descendants may follow the example and reap the benefit.

Guide for Responding

◆ Literature and Your Life

Reader's Response What do you think of Franklin's plan? Why?

Thematic Focus Autobiographies reflect the time period in which they are written. What elements of Franklin's *Autobiography* suggest that it was written at the dawn of American independence?

Group Activity In a small group, devise a self-improvement plan for Americans today. What "virtues" would you include? Compare the virtues chosen by Franklin with your group's decisions.

☑ Check Your Comprehension

1. In your own words, outline Franklin's plan to achieve moral perfection.
2. Explain why Franklin included *Silence* among his list of virtues.
3. Under the virtue of *Order,* Franklin lays out a basic daily schedule. What are the activities for which he provides time each day?
4. What aspects of Franklin's plan did not go as he expected?

Guide for Responding (continued)

◆ Critical Thinking

INTERPRET

1. Why does Franklin include the story about the man with the speckled ax? **[Analyze]**
2. How does Franklin's perspective about the importance of achieving moral perfection change over time? **[Compare and Contrast]**
3. What does Franklin see as the long-term benefits of his efforts to achieve moral perfection? **[Analyze Cause and Effect]**

APPLY

4. How can analyzing behavior contribute to personal growth? **[Synthesize]**

EXTEND

5. Many people use daily planners organized like Franklin's daily activity sheet. What are the benefits of such a system? **[Career Link]**

◆ Reading for Success

STRATEGIES FOR CONSTRUCTING MEANING

Review the reading strategies and the notes showing how to construct meaning. Then apply them to answer the following:

1. Identify an opinion of Franklin's that he presents as a fact.
2. Draw a conclusion about Franklin from this segment of *The Autobiography*.
3. Explain in terms of the historical context why Franklin was interested in sharing his plan with future generations.

◆ Literary Focus

AUTOBIOGRAPHY

An **autobiography** is the story of a person's life written by that person. Because the author's attitudes, thoughts, and feelings color the self-portrayal, the autobiography is subjective. For example, Franklin's sense of morality is revealed in this excerpt from *The Autobiography*.

1. What does Franklin convey about his character?
2. How would this selection be different if it were written *about* Frankin rather than by him?

◆ Build Vocabulary

USING THE WORD ROOT -*vigil*-

The word root -*vigil*- means "the act or period of remaining awake so as to guard or observe something." Use the definition of -*vigil*-, as well as the context, to write a definition of the italicized word in each sentence.

1. His mother said that she would be *vigilant* in her efforts to make sure he did his homework.
2. To restore safety, members of a *vigilante* group began patroling the neighborhood at night.

USING THE WORD BANK

In your notebook, complete each of these analogies with a word from the Word Bank.

1. *Permission* is to *authorization* as _____?_____ is to *greed*.
2. *Danger* is to *peril* as _____?_____ is to *silliness*.
3. *Tragedy* is to *comedy* as _____?_____ is to *negligence*.
4. *Order* is to *chaos* as _____?_____ is to *sadness*.
5. *Exceptional* is to *common* as _____?_____ is to *easy*.
6. *Error* is to *mistake* as _____?_____ is to *arrangement*.

◆ Grammar and Style

PRONOUN CASE

The **subjective case** is used when the pronoun is the subject of the sentence or renames the subject after a linking verb. The **objective case** is used when the pronoun is a direct or indirect object of the verb or the object of a preposition.

Practice Choose the correct pronoun to complete each sentence.

1. At length a fresh difference arose between my brother and (I, me).
2. It was time for (we, us) to leave that place.
3. Though I did not give them any dissatisfaction, (they, them) dismissed me from my position.
4. (We, Us) two undertook to move to Boston.
5. Wilson and (he, him) took care to prevent my getting employment anywhere else.

Build Your Portfolio

Idea Bank

Writing

1. **Advertisement** Write an advertisement for Franklin's book, designed to appear in a Philadelphia newspaper of Franklin's time.

2. **Personal Improvement Plan** Think of a few areas in which you'd like to improve. Then consider what you can do to improve in these areas. Present your ideas in a written plan. **[Health Link]**

3. **Report** *The Autobiography* shows the world a certain side of Franklin's life. Find out about his political achievements. Compare what you learn from *The Autobiography* with Franklin's career as a statesman. Share your findings in a short paper. **[Social Studies Link]**

Speaking and Listening

4. **Oral Interpretation** Choose a short portion of the selection to read out loud. Practice it until you feel comfortable with the old-fashioned way it is written, then perform it for the class. **[Performing Arts Link]**

5. **Interview** Ask an older relative to tell you about his or her own life. Summarize the interview for your class, identifying the lessons someone else's life has taught you.

Projects

6. **Poster** Find out more about Franklin's accomplishments in the field of science. Create a poster that highlights some of his inventions. **[Science Link]**

7. **Travel Brochure** Create a brochure for tourists visiting Philadelphia. Highlight Franklin's accomplishments and include pictures of some of the relevant historic sites.

Writing Mini-Lesson

Autobiographical Account

Anyone can write an autobiography. With your activities, friendships, family and school events, successes, and failures, you have a vast amount of material from which to choose. Choose an important experience in your life and write an autobiographical account of the experience. Tell what made this moment memorable and what you've learned from it.

**Writing Skills Focus:
Show Cause and Effect**

In your account, clearly show the effects of an experience on your life. Notice how Franklin deliberately anticipates the effect of each virtue:

Model From the Autobiography

Resolution, once become habitual, would keep me firm in my endeavors to obtain all the subsequent virtues; *Frugality* and *Industry,* freeing me from my remaining debt and producing affluence and independence, would make more easy the practice of *Sincerity* and *Justice,* etc. . . .

Prewriting Brainstorm for a list of details from the experience you want to describe. Note what happened, what you felt, and what you may have learned. Include as many specific details as you can.

Drafting Write your autobiographical account, incorporating those details that will make the event and its significance clear to readers. Remember to show the cause-and-effect relationship between the event or experience and your life. Use transition words such as *since, if/then,* and *consequently* to highlight the relationship for readers.

Revising When you revise, pay attention to cause-and-effect relationships. Whenever a transition would make cause and effect more obvious, add one.

Guide for Interpreting

Thomas Jefferson
(1743–1826)

When you look at all the things Thomas Jefferson accomplished in his lifetime, it seems there was virtually nothing that Jefferson couldn't do. Not only did he help our nation win its independence and serve as its third president, but he also founded the University of Virginia, helped establish the public school system, designed his own home, invented a type of elevator for sending food from floor to floor, and created the decimal system for American money. He was also a skilled violinist, an art enthusiast, and a brilliant writer.

Born into a wealthy Virginia family, Jefferson attended the College of William and Mary and went on to earn a law degree. While serving in the Virginia House of Burgesses, he became an outspoken defender of American rights. When conflict between the colonists and the British erupted into a revolution, Jefferson emerged as a leader in the effort to win independence.

When the war ended, Jefferson served as the American minister to France for several years. He then served as the nation's first secretary of state and second vice president before becoming president in 1801. While in office, Jefferson nearly doubled the size of the nation by authorizing the purchase of the Louisiana Territory from France.

Thomas Paine
(1737–1809)

Thomas Paine met Benjamin Franklin in London, and the introduction changed his life—and American history. Paine emigrated to the colonies from England in 1774. With a letter of introduction from Franklin, Paine began a career as a journalist. In January 1776, he published *Common Sense*, in which he argued that Americans must fight for independence. The pamphlet created a national mood for revolution.

Paine enlisted in the American army toward the end of 1776. At that time, the army had just suffered a crushing defeat by the British in New Jersey and had retreated into Pennsylvania. They were suffering from freezing weather, a shortage of provisions, and low morale. Paine was writing the first of a series of essays entitled *The American Crisis*. Washington ordered Paine's essay read to his troops before they crossed the Delaware to defeat the Hessians at the Battle of Trenton.

Paine's later works supported the French Revolution (*The Rights of Man*, 1792). His attack on organized religion (*The Age of Reason*, 1794) turned American public opinion against him, and when he died in 1809, he was a broken man. Years later, however, he was once again recognized as a hero of the Revolution.

◆ Background for Understanding

HISTORY: JEFFERSON AND THE DECLARATION

In 1776, Jefferson was chosen (with Franklin, Adams, and others) to write a declaration of the colonies' independence. The draft presented to the Second Continental Congress was largely Jefferson's work. To his disappointment, however, Congress made changes before approving the document. They dropped Jefferson's condemnation of the British for tolerating a corrupt Parliament, and they struck out a strong statement against slavery.

Despite these changes, what remained was plainly treasonous, and the penalty for treason was death. Considering that the odds were heavily stacked against the colonists at the time, it took tremendous bravery for members of Congress to sign the document and send it off to King George III. Had the colonists failed to win the war, all who had signed the Declaration would most likely have been executed.

The Declaration of Independence
◆ *from* The Crisis, Number 1 ◆

◆ *Literature and Your Life*

CONNECT YOUR EXPERIENCE

When shouts for freedom are transformed into military force, we recognize the signs of revolution. Today, we experience revolutions through images and reports in the news media. The best way to experience what our own Revolution was like, however, is to read documents that capture the spirit that enabled the colonists to win their independence.

Journal Writing Write about the concept of freedom. Are there different types of freedom?

THEMATIC FOCUS: VOICES FOR FREEDOM

Jefferson and Paine were eloquent speakers for American freedom. How are their voices similar, and how are they distinct?

◆ Build Vocabulary

WORD ROOTS: *-fid-*

Paine and Jefferson use two related words— *infidel* and *perfidy*—in the selections that follow. These words contain the Latin root *-fid-*, which means "faith" or "trust." An *infidel* is a person without faith, and *perfidy* is a betrayal of trust.

WORD BANK

Preview this list of words from the selections.

unalienable
usurpations
perfidy
redress
magnanimity
consanguinity
acquiesce
impious
infidel

◆ Grammar and Style

PARALLELISM

Parallelism refers to the repeated use of phrases, clauses, or sentences that are similar in structure or meaning. Writers use this technique to emphasize important ideas and create rhythm. Jefferson uses parallelism to list the reasons that Americans declared their independence. Note Jefferson's rhythmic use of parallel verbs and direct objects in the following sentence:

He has *plundered our seas, ravaged our coasts, burned our towns,* and *destroyed the lives* of our people.

◆ Literary Focus

PERSUASION

Persuasion is writing meant to convince readers to think or act in a certain way. A persuasive writer appeals to emotions or reason, offers opinions, and urges action.

Jefferson wrote to persuade the king that the colonists were justified in declaring their independence. Paine wrote to convince American citizens of the justness of revolution and to lift the spirits of American soldiers on the battlefield. Notice the techniques each writer uses to persuade readers to share his views.

◆ Reading Strategy

RECOGNIZING CHARGED WORDS

As you read these documents, be sensitive to each writer's use of **charged words**—words with strong connotations likely to produce an emotional response. For example, Paine uses *tyranny*, a word meaning "oppressive power." The word may evoke feelings of fear or outrage, as well as images of cruel political leaders.

It's important to avoid being swayed by charged words. Look for thorough support—facts, statistics, quotations from authorities—to back up the words.

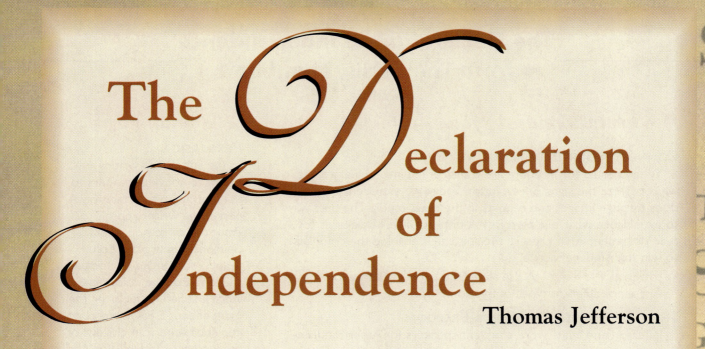

The Declaration of Independence

Thomas Jefferson

When in the course of human events, it becomes necessary for one people to dissolve the political bands which have connected them with another, and to assume among the powers of the earth, the separate and equal station to which the laws of nature and of nature's God entitle them, a decent respect to the opinions of mankind requires that they should declare the causes which impel them to the separation.

We hold these truths to be self-evident: that all men are created equal; that they are endowed by their Creator with certain <u>unalienable</u> rights; that among these are life, liberty and the pursuit of happiness; that to secure these rights, governments are instituted among men, deriving their just powers from the consent of the governed; that whenever any form of government becomes destructive of these ends, it is the right of the people to alter or to abolish it, and to institute new government, laying its foundation on such principles and organizing its powers in such form, as to them shall seem most likely to effect their safety and happiness. Prudence, indeed, will dictate that governments long established should not be changed for light and transient causes; and accordingly all experience hath shown, that mankind are more disposed to suffer while evils are sufferable than to right themselves by abolishing the forms to which they are accustomed. But when a long train of abuses and <u>usurpations</u>, pursuing invariably the same object, evinces a design to reduce them under absolute despotism,[1] it is their right, it is their duty, to throw off such government, and to provide new guards for their future security. Such has been the patient sufferance of these colonies; and such is now the necessity which constrains[2] them to alter their former systems of government. The history of the present king of Great Britain is a history of repeated injuries and usurpations, all having in direct object the establishment of an

---

1. **despotism** (des´ pə tiz əm) *n*.: Tyranny.
2. **constrains** *v*.: Forces.

♦ **Build Vocabulary**

unalienable (un āl´ yən ə bəl) *adj*.: Not to be taken away

usurpations (yoo͞´ sər pā´ shənz) *n*.: Unlawful seizures of rights or privileges

The Declaration of Independence, John Trumbull, Yale University Art Gallery

▲ **Critical Viewing** What is the mood of this painting? How does the mood suit the occasion? **[Relate]**

absolute tyranny over these states. To prove this, let facts be submitted to a candid world.

He has refused his assent to laws the most wholesome and necessary for the public good.

He has forbidden his governors to pass laws of immediate and pressing importance, unless suspended in their operation till his assent should be obtained; and when so suspended, he has utterly neglected to attend to them.

He has refused to pass other laws for the accommodation of large districts of people, unless those people would relinquish the right of representation in the legislature, a right inestimable to them and formidable to tyrants only.

He has called together legislative bodies at places unusual, uncomfortable, and distant from the depository of their public records, for the sole purpose of fatiguing them into compliance with his measures.

He has dissolved representative houses repeatedly, for opposing with manly firmness his invasions on the rights of the people.

He has refused for a long time after such dissolutions to cause others to be elected, whereby the legislative powers, incapable of annihilation, have returned to the people at large for their exercise, the state remaining in the mean time exposed to all the dangers of invasion from without, and convulsions within.

He has endeavored to prevent the population of these states; for that purpose obstructing the laws for naturalization of foreigners, refusing to pass others to encourage their migration hither, and raising the conditions of new appropriations of lands.

He has obstructed the administration of justice, by refusing his assent to laws for establishing judiciary powers.

He has made judges dependent on his will alone, for the tenure of their offices, and the

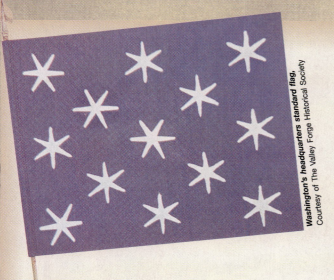

Washington's **headquarters standard flag.**
Courtesy of The Valley Forge Historical Society

▲ **Critical Viewing** Contrast this 1781 flag with today's American flag. What do the stars on this one and the current one represent? How does today's flag reflect the importance of the thirteen stars shown here? [Contrast]

amount and payment of their salaries.

He has erected a multitude of new offices, and sent hither swarms of officers to harass our people and eat out their substance.

He has kept among us in times of peace standing armies without the consent of our legislatures.

He has affected to render the military independent of, and superior to, the civil power.

He has combined with others to subject us to a jurisdiction foreign to our constitution and unacknowledged by our laws, giving his assent to their acts of pretended legislation: for quartering large bodies of armed troops among us; for protecting them by a mock trial from punishment for any murders which they should commit on the inhabitants of these states; for cutting off our trade with all parts of the world; for imposing taxes on us without our consent; for depriving us, in many cases, of the benefits of trial by jury; for transporting us beyond seas to be tried for pretended offenses; for abolishing the free system of English laws in a neighboring province,[3] establishing therein an arbitrary government, and enlarging its boundaries, so

as to render it at once an example and fit instrument for introducing the same absolute rule into these colonies; for taking away our charters, abolishing our most valuable laws, and altering fundamentally the forms of our governments; for suspending our own legislatures, and declaring themselves invested with power to legislate for us in all cases whatsoever.

He has abdicated government here, by declaring us out of his protection and waging war against us.

He has plundered our seas, ravaged our coasts, burned our towns, and destroyed the lives of our people.

He is at this time transporting large armies of foreign mercenaries to complete the works of death, desolation, and tyranny, already begun with circumstances of cruelty and <u>perfidy</u> scarcely paralleled in the most barbarous ages, and totally unworthy the head of a civilized nation.

He has constrained our fellow citizens taken captive on the high seas to bear arms against their country, to become the executioners of their friends and brethren, or to fall themselves by their hands.

He has excited domestic insurrections amongst us, and has endeavored to bring on the inhabitants of our frontiers, the merciless Indian savages, whose known rule of warfare is an undistinguished destruction of all ages, sexes, and conditions.

In every stage of these oppressions we have petitioned for <u>redress</u> in the most humble terms. Our repeated petitions have been answered only by repeated injury.

◆ **Literary Focus**
How does this catalog of offenses support Jefferson's argument?

◆ **Build Vocabulary**

perfidy (pʉr′ fə dē) *n.*: Betrayal of trust

redress (ri dres′) *n.*: Compensation for a wrong done

magnanimity (mag′ nə nim′ ə tē) *n.*: Ability to rise above pettiness or meanness

consanguinity (kän′ saŋ gwin′ ə tē) *n.*: Kinship

acquiesce (ak′ wē es′) *v.*: Agree without protest

---

3. **neighboring province:** Quebec.

A prince whose character is thus marked by every act which may define a tyrant is unfit to be the ruler of a free people.

Nor have we been wanting in attentions to our British brethren. We have warned them from time to time of attempts by their legislature to extend an unwarrantable jurisdiction over us. We have reminded them of the circumstances of our emigration and settlement here. We have appealed to their native justice and magnanimity and we have conjured[4] them by the ties of our common kindred to disavow these usurpations which would inevitably interrupt our connections and correspondence. They too have been deaf to the voice of justice and of consanguinity. We must therefore acquiesce in the necessity which denounces[5] our separation and hold them, as we hold the rest of mankind, enemies in war, in peace friends.

We, therefore, the representatives of the United States of America in general congress assembled, appealing to the Supreme Judge of the world for the rectitude of our intentions, do in the name and by authority of the good people of these colonies, solemnly publish and declare that these united colonies are and of right ought to be free and independent states; that they are absolved from all allegiance to the British Crown, and that all political connection between them and the state of Great Britain is and ought to be totally dissolved; and that as free and independent states, they have full power to levy war, conclude peace, contract alliances, establish commerce, and to do all other acts and things which independent states may of right do.

And for the support of this declaration, with a firm reliance on the protection of divine providence, we mutually pledge to each other our lives, our fortunes and our sacred honor.

---

4. **conjured** v.: Solemnly appealed to.
5. **denounces** v.: Here, announces.

Guide for Responding

◆ Literature and Your Life

Reader's Response What feelings does this document evoke? Why?

Thematic Focus What do you think is the difference between a "voice for freedom" and a "voice of treason"? Explain.

☑ Check Your Comprehension

1. What are the three "unalienable rights" listed in the second paragraph?
2. According to Jefferson, when should a government be abolished?
3. List three statements presented to support his claim that the king's objective is "the establishment of an absolute tyranny over these states."
4. (a) What does Jefferson claim the colonists have done at "every stage of these oppressions"? (b) How has the king responded to the colonists' actions?

◆ Critical Thinking

INTERPRET

1. What effect does Jefferson's list of grievances have on his argument? **[Analyze]**
2. Why does Jefferson focus his attack on King George III rather than on the British Parliament or people? **[Deduce]**
3. How is the eighteenth-century faith in reason reflected in the Declaration? **[Connect]**

APPLY

4. Considering Jefferson's views concerning the purpose of a government, which governments in today's world might he find objectionable? Why? **[Hypothesize]**

EXTEND

5. Could the Declaration of Independence be delivered effectively as a speech? Why or why not? **[Performing Arts Link]**

from The Crisis, Number 1

Thomas Paine

▲ **Critical Viewing** How does this image capture the patriotic fervor of Paine's essay? **[Connect]**

These are the times that try men's souls. The summer soldier and the sunshine patriot will in this crisis, shrink from the service of his country; but he that stands it NOW, deserves the love and thanks of man and woman. Tyranny, like hell, is not easily conquered; yet we have this consolation with us, that the harder the conflict, the more glorious the triumph. What we obtain too cheap, we esteem too lightly; 'tis dearness only that gives everything its value. Heaven knows how to put a proper price upon its goods; and it would be strange indeed, if so celestial an article as FREEDOM should not be highly rated. Britain, with an army to enforce her tyranny, has declared that she has a right (*not only to* TAX) but "to BIND *us in* ALL CASES WHATSOEVER," and if being *bound in that manner,* is not slavery, then is there not such a thing as slavery upon earth. Even the expression is impious, for so unlimited a power can belong only to God . . .

I have as little superstition in me as any man living, but my secret opinion has ever been, and still is, that God Almighty will not give up a people to military destruction, or leave them unsupportedly to perish, who have so earnestly and so repeatedly sought to avoid the calamities of war, by every decent method which wisdom could invent. Neither have I so much of the infidel in me, as to suppose that he has relinquished the government of the world, and given us up to the care of devils; and as I do not, I cannot see on what grounds the king of Britain can look up to heaven for help against us: a common murderer, a highwayman, or a housebreaker, has as good a pretense as he . . .

I once felt all that kind of anger, which a man ought to feel, against the mean[1] principles that are held by the Tories:[2] a noted one, who kept a tavern at Amboy, was standing at his door, with as pretty a child in his hand, about eight or nine years old, as I ever saw, and after speaking his mind as freely as he thought was prudent, finished with this unfatherly expression, *"Well! give me peace in my day."* Not a man lives on the continent but fully believes that a separation must some time or other finally take place, and a generous parent should have said, *"If there must be trouble let it be in my day, that my child may have peace";* and this single reflection, well applied, is sufficient to awaken every man to duty. Not a place upon earth might be so happy as America. Her situation is remote from all the wrangling world, and she has nothing to do but to trade with them. A man can distinguish himself between temper and principle, and I am as confident, as I am that God governs the world, that America will never be happy till she gets clear of foreign dominion. Wars, without ceasing, will

---

1. **mean** *adj.*: Here, small-minded.
2. **Tories:** Colonists who remained loyal to Great Britain.

break out till that period arrives, and the continent must in the end be conqueror; for though the flame of liberty may sometimes cease to shine, the coal can never expire . . .

I turn with the warm ardor of a friend to those who have nobly stood, and are yet determined to stand the matter out: I call not upon a few, but upon all; not on *this* state or *that* state, but on *every* state; up and help us; lay your shoulders to the wheel; better have too much force than too little, when so great an object is at stake. Let it be told to the future world, that in the depth of winter, when nothing but hope and virtue could survive, that the city and the country, alarmed at one common danger, came forth to meet and to repulse it. Say not that thousands are gone, turn out your tens of thousands; throw not the burden of the day upon Providence, but "*show your faith by your works*," that God may bless you. It matters not where you live, or what rank of life you hold, the evil or the blessing will reach you all. The far and the near, the home counties and the back, the rich and the poor, will suffer or rejoice alike. The heart that feels not now, is dead: the blood of his children will curse his cowardice, who shrinks back at a time when a little might have saved the whole, and made *them* happy. (I love the man that can smile at trouble; that can gather strength from distress, and grow brave by reflection.) 'Tis the business of little minds to shrink; but he whose heart is firm, and whose conscience approves his conduct, will pursue his principles unto death. My own line of reasoning is to myself as straight and clear as a ray of light. Not all the treasures of the world, so far as I believe, could have induced me to support an offensive war, for I think it murder; but if a thief breaks into my house, burns and destroys my property, and kills or threatens to kill me, or those that are in it, and to "*bind me in all cases whatsoever*," to his absolute will, am I to suffer it? What signifies it to me, whether he who does it is a king or a common man: my countryman, or not my countryman; whether it be done by an individual villain or an army of them? If we reason to the root of things we shall find no difference; neither can any just cause be assigned why we should punish in the one case and pardon in the other.

◆ Build Vocabulary

impious (im´ pē əs) *adj.*: Lacking reverence for God

infidel (in´ fə dəl) *n.*: A person who holds no religious belief

Guide for Responding

◆ *Literature and Your Life*

Reader's Response Which of Thomas Paine's images of the American Revolution do you find most stirring or memorable? Why?

Thematic Focus Do you find Paine's voice compelling? Do you think Paine is trustworthy as a reporter? Explain.

☑ Check Your Comprehension

1. Of what is Paine confident in the third paragraph?
2. What opinion of offensive wars does Paine express in the final paragraph?

◆ Critical Thinking

INTERPRET
1. Name two emotions to which the author appeals in this essay. **[Classify]**
2. (a) What is the main idea of the essay? (b) How does Paine develop his main idea? **[Support]**

APPLY
3. In your opinion, how persuasive is Paine's essay? Support your answer. **[Evaluate]**
4. How might a colonist who had remained loyal to the British react to Paine's argument? **[Hypothesize]**

Guide for Responding (continued)

◆ Reading Strategy

RECOGNIZING CHARGED WORDS

These two political works are filled with **charged words**—words chosen to evoke emotional responses. In "The Crisis," for example, Paine uses the charged word *thief* to characterize the colonists' British caretakers. Had Paine used a kinder word, such as *custodian* or *supporters*, he would have tapped a different response in his audience.

1. What responses are evoked by these words from the Declaration of Independence?

    a. liberty **b.** justice **c.** honor **d.** barbarous

2. Cite two other charged words in these selections and identify the connotations of each.

◆ Build Vocabulary

USING THE WORD ROOT -fid-

Use the root *-fid-,* meaning "faith" or "trust," to help you define each of the following words:

1. confident **2.** fidelity **3.** confidential

USING THE WORD BANK

Indicate which of the following statements are true and which are false. Explain the reasoning behind each answer.

1. If a child *acquiesces* about being put to bed, she accepts her bedtime.
2. *Magnanimity* is a desirable trait in elected officials.
3. There is no need for *redress* if no wrong has been committed.
4. American citizens would not be within their rights to protest *usurpations* of their property.
5. Enemies at war feel *consanguinity* toward one another.
6. The woman felt grateful for the *perfidy* I had demonstrated toward her.
7. *Unalienable* rights must be agreed upon annually.
8. *Infidels* observe certain religious holidays.
9. A pastor's *impious* behavior would be celebrated by his parishioners.

◆ Literary Focus

PERSUASION

Both the Declaration of Independence and "The Crisis, Number 1" are examples of **persuasion**—writing that attempts to convince an audience to think or act in a certain way. In the Declaration of Independence, Jefferson presents a long list of grievances to support his argument. Paine, on the other hand, presents a variety of types of information—anecdotes, opinions, facts, and examples—to persuade his audience that fighting the British is just.

1. Do the charges in the Declaration of Independence get more serious as the list of grievances continues? What is the effect of this kind of organization?
2. Give two examples of Paine's use of opinions in "The Crisis."
3. In your opinion, does Paine appeal more to readers' emotions or reason in this essay? Explain.
4. Which selection do you find more persuasive? Why?

◆ Grammar and Style

PARALLELISM

Parallelism—like Lincoln's "Gettysburg Address" lines "*of the people, by the people, for the people*"—emphasizes ideas, creates rhythm, and makes writing forceful.

> **Parallelism** is the use of the same grammatical structure to present several ideas of equal importance.

Practice Rewrite each sentence to correct errors in parallel structure.

1. Thomas Jefferson was patriotic, intelligent, imaginative, and he had courage.
2. Jefferson wrote the Declaration, designed his home at Monticello, and was one of the people who founded the University of Virginia.
3. Patrick Henry was a brilliant speaker; Thomas Jefferson was a gifted writer; and the talented military leader was George Washington.

Writing Application Write one or two paragraphs presenting your opinion on an issue about which you have strong feelings. Use parallelism to emphasize your key points.

Build Your Portfolio

Idea Bank

Writing

1. **Letter** In a December 1776 letter, George Washington wrote, "I am wearied to death. I think the game is pretty near up." As Washington, write a letter conveying your thoughts after hearing Paine's essay.

2. **Précis** A précis is a concise summary of essential points or statements. Write a précis of Jefferson's Declaration. **[Social Studies Link]**

3. **Newspaper Stories** As a colonial journalist, write an article recounting the signing of the Declaration. Then write the version of the story that might have appeared in a London paper following the receipt of the document.

Speaking and Listening

4. **Oral Presentation** The song "Yankee Doodle Dandy" helped spur American troops on to victory. Investigate the surprising origin of the song. Share your findings in an oral presentation.

5. **Dramatic Reading** With a small group of classmates, rehearse and prepare a dramatic reading of the Declaration of Independence. **[Performing Arts Link]**

Projects

6. **Poster** Design a Revolutionary War recruitment poster based on Paine's ideas. Like Paine, you might also deride "the summer soldier and the sunshine patriot." **[Art Link]**

7. **Class Discussion on Paine** Research Paine's early years. Prepare notes to help you lead a class discussion on Paine's contributions to the Revolutionary cause. **[Social Studies Link]**

Writing Mini-Lesson

A Proposal to the Principal

With a group of classmates, choose a problem or situation in your school that you think should be changed. Then draft a proposal to the principal explaining why the situation needs attention and how you think it should be corrected.

Writing Skills Focus: Use Forceful Language

Forceful words can make your argument more effective. Use language with positive connotations to present ideas you want your audience to accept; use language with negative connotations to present ideas you wish your audience to reject. Notice how Paine uses the negative power of words:

Model From the Essay

. . . I cannot see on what grounds the king of Britain can look up to heaven for help against us: a common murderer, a highwayman, or a housebreaker, has as good a pretense as he . . .

Paine compares royalty to an average criminal—a comparison that would elicit a strong response. In your proposal, use words that can have such a powerful impact.

Prewriting List the reasons that the situation in your school should be changed. Write details—including facts, examples, explanations—supporting each reason.

Drafting Use terms such as *superior* and *wise* to reinforce the soundness of your proposal. Where appropriate, use words with negative connotations to present opposing points. Keep in mind, however, that you are writing for your principal.

Revising Carefully review your proposal and revise any statements that seem unreasonable. Check that you have offered evidence to support your argument.

Guide for Interpreting

Phillis Wheatley (1753?–1784)

Phillis Wheatley, an African slave known in Boston for her poetic gift, attracted great attention at an early age.

Wheatley was one of the finest American poets of her day—an amazing feat, considering that few women in the colonies and even fewer slaves could read or write.

Brought to America from West Africa on a slave ship when she was about eight years old, Phillis Wheatley was purchased by a Boston merchant named John Wheatley in 1761. The Wheatleys recognized the girl's high intelligence and taught her to read and write. She avidly read the Bible, Latin and Greek classics, and works by contemporary English poets. At age thirteen, she saw her first poem published.

Fame Abroad at an Early Age

In 1772, Wheatley met several British aristocrats who admired her poetry and helped her to publish *Poems on Various Subjects: Religious and Moral* in London in 1773. This text was probably the first book published by an African.

The Story Behind the Poem

During the Revolutionary War, Wheatley wrote a poem addressed to the commander of the American forces, George Washington. In October 1775, Wheatley sent the poem to Washington. He responded:

I thank you most sincerely for your polite notice of me in the elegant lines you enclosed; and however undeserving I may be of such encomium [high praise] and panegyric [tribute], the style and manner exhibit a striking proof of your poetical talents; in honor of which, and as a tribute justly due you, I would have published the poem, had I not been apprehensive that, while I only meant to give the world this new instance of your genius, I might have incurred the imputation of vanity. . . .

Slide From Glory

Despite being freed by John Wheatley in 1773, Phillis Wheatley lived with hardship and sorrow as the years went on. Two of her children died in infancy, her husband was jailed for debt, and she fell into obscurity as a poet. After she died in poverty around the age of thirty, her *Poems on Various Subjects: Religious and Moral* finally found an American publisher.

◆ Background for Understanding

HISTORY: PHILLIS WHEATLEY'S EXAM

Getting a volume of verse published in 1773 was difficult for Phillis Wheatley: Publishers were skeptical that an African girl of eighteen was capable of writing such sophisticated poems. Consequently, Boston's leading political and intellectual lights—led by Governor Thomas Hutchinson—administered an oral examination to her. Apparently, Wheatley made impressive responses to each question, for her inquisitors eventually drafted a two-paragraph letter to the public stating, in part:

We . . . assure the World, that the POEMS specified in the following Page, were (as we verily believe) written by PHILLIS, a young Negro Girl, who was but a few Years since, brought . . . from *Africa*.

This judgment was crucial in getting *Poems on Various Subjects: Religious and Moral* published in England. However, Boston publishers refused to print the work for thirteen years.

◆ *Literature and Your Life*

CONNECT YOUR EXPERIENCE

A movie, a haircut, a suggestion—you may informally praise several things or people every day. You probably find colorful ways to explain why you admire a subject. At times you may express praise in a more formal way—in a song, essay, or poem—as Phillis Wheatley does in these poems.

Journal Writing Write a paragraph praising an unusual subject. Vividly convey why you find the subject praiseworthy.

THEMATIC FOCUS: VOICES FOR FREEDOM

As the spirit of revolution spread, General Washington became a symbol of freedom. His image graced flags, teacups, and other items. Wheatley helped to forge Washington's fame.

George Washington on a Horse,
New York State Historical Association, Cooperstown

◆ Build Vocabulary

PREFIXES: *re-*

In Phillis Wheatley's poetry, you will find the words *refulgent* and *refluent*. The prefix *re-*, which means "again" or "back," can help you define these words. Coming from the Latin word *refulgere* meaning "to flash back," *refulgent* has come to mean "brilliant." The Latin word *fluere* means "to flow," and *refluent* can be defined as "flowing back."

> celestial
> refulgent
> propitious
> refluent
> pensive
> placid
> scepter

WORD BANK

Before you read, preview this list of words from the poems.

◆ Grammar and Style

SUBJECT AND VERB AGREEMENT

Even in poetry, the rules of **subject-verb agreement** apply. Verbs become either singular or plural to agree with their subject in number. Singular subjects take singular verb forms; plural subjects take plural verb forms. Look at these lines from Wheatley's poems:

        s   v

Singular: <u>She</u> <u>flashes</u> dreadful in refulgent arms.

        s   v

Plural: And <u>nations</u> <u>gaze</u> at scenes before unknown!

◆ Literary Focus

PERSONIFICATION

When writers attribute human powers and characteristics to something that is not human, such as an object, an aspect of nature, or an idea, they're using **personification.**

For instance, in the line "Astonish'd ocean feels the wild uproar," the sea is personified with a human emotion (astonishment) and sensibility (feeling the wild uproar).

Eighteenth-century English poets often personified concepts as gods or goddesses. Similarly, Wheatley personifies America, England, and the west wind as gods or goddesses in these poems.

◆ Reading Strategy

CLARIFY MEANING

You may need to **clarify** the meaning of passages of complex prose or poetry, such as these poems, by figuring out grammatical structures and checking the definition of every word.

For example, this line from "To His Excellency, General Washington" may pose some difficulty:

> See mother earth her offspring's fate bemoan . . .

By reordering the words and defining *offspring* and *bemoan,* you may unlock the meaning:

> See mother earth weep over the fate of her children.

To His Excellency, General Washington

Phillis Wheatley

Liberty and Washington, New York State Historical Association, Cooperstown

▲ **Critical Viewing** Noting the symbols of the Revolutionary conflict, explain the action of the painting. **[Interpret]**

Celestial choir! enthron'd in realms of light,
   Columbia's[1] scenes of glorious toils I write.
While freedom's cause her anxious breast alarms,
She flashes dreadful in refulgent arms.
5   See mother earth her offspring's fate bemoan,
And nations gaze at scenes before unknown!
See the bright beams of heaven's revolving light
Involved in sorrows and the veil of night!
   The goddess comes, she moves divinely fair,
10 Olive and laurel binds her golden hair:
Wherever shines this native of the skies,
Unnumber'd charms and recent graces rise.
   Muse![2] bow propitious while my pen relates
How pour her armies through a thousand gates,
15 As when Eolus[3] heaven's fair face deforms,
Enwrapp'd in tempest and a night of storms;
Astonish'd ocean feels the wild uproar,
The refluent surges beat the sounding shore;
Or thick as leaves in Autumn's golden reign,
20 Such, and so many, moves the warrior's train.
In bright array they seek the work of war,

---

1. **Columbia:** America personified as a goddess.
2. **Muse:** A Greek goddess, in this case Erato, who is thought to inspire poets. She is one of nine muses presiding over literature, the arts, and the sciences.
3. **Eolus** (ē′ ə ləs): The Greek god of the winds.

Where high unfurl'd the ensign[4] waves in air.
Shall I to Washington their praise recite?
Enough thou know'st them in the fields of fight.
25 Thee, first in peace and honors,—we demand
The grace and glory of thy martial band.
Fam'd for thy valor, for thy virtues more,
Hear every tongue thy guardian aid implore!
    One century scarce perform'd its destined round,
30 When Gallic[5] powers Columbia's fury found;
And so may you, whoever dares disgrace
The land of freedom's heaven-defended race!
Fix'd are the eyes of nations on the scales,
For in their hopes Columbia's arm prevails.
35 Anon Britannia[6] droops the pensive head,
While round increase the rising hills of dead.
Ah! cruel blindness to Columbia's state!
Lament thy thirst of boundless power too late.
    Proceed, great Chief, with virtue on thy side,
40 Thy ev'ry action let the goddess guide.
A crown, a mansion, and a throne that shine,
With gold unfading, WASHINGTON! be thine.

---

4. **ensign** (en´ sin): Flag.
5. **Gallic** (gal´ ik): French. The colonists, led by Washington,
defeated the French in the French and Indian War (1754–1763).
6. **Britannia:** England.

◆ **Build Vocabulary**

celestial (sə les´ chəl) *adj.*: Of
the heavens

refulgent (ri ful´ jənt) *adj.*: Radiant; shining

propitious (prō pish´ əs) *adj.*:
Favorably inclined or disposed

refluent (ref´ lo͞o ənt) *adj.*: Flowing back

pensive (pen´ siv) *adj.*: Thinking
deeply or seriously

Guide for Responding

◆ *Literature and Your Life*

Reader's Response Do you think that Columbia and General Washington are worthy subjects of the poet's praise? Why or why not?

Thematic Focus In your opinion, is there a contradiction between freedom and war? Explain your answer.

☑ **Check Your Comprehension**

1. To whom is the poem addressed?
2. Whom does the speaker praise?
3. Which two nations does the speaker describe as being in military opposition to America?

◆ **Critical Thinking**

INTERPRET

1. According to the poet, what is the nature of the relationship between God and the American cause? **[Analyze]**
2. What do the comparisons in lines 13–20 suggest? **[Interpret]**

EVALUATE

3. How successful is Wheatley in conveying the power and righteousness of American military forces? **[Assess]**

EXTEND

4. How might a historian's treatment of the British-American conflict differ from Wheatley's treatment of the same subject? **[Social Studies Link]**

An Hymn to

Phillis Wheatley

Soon as the sun forsook the eastern main
The pealing thunder shook the heav'nly plain;
Majestic grandeur! From the zephyr's[1] wing,
Exhales the incense of the blooming spring.
5   Soft purl[2] the streams, the birds renew their notes,
And through the air their mingled music floats.

   Through all the heav'ns what beauteous dyes are spread!
But the west glories in the deepest red:
So may our breasts with ev'ry virtue glow,
10   The living temples of our God below!

---

1. **zephyr's** (zef´ ərz) *n*.: Belonging to the west wind.
2. **purl** (pʉrl) *v*.: To move in ripples or with a murmuring sound.

◆ Build Vocabulary

placid (plas´ id) *adj*.: Tranquil; calm; quiet

scepter (sep´ tər) *n*.: A rod or staff held by rulers as a symbol of sovereignty

the Evening

Filled with the praise of him who gives the light;
And draws the sable curtains of the night,
Let placid slumbers soothe each weary mind,
At morn to wake more heav'nly, more refined;
15   So shall the labours of the day begin
More pure, more guarded from the snares of sin.

Night's leaden scepter seals my drowsy eyes,
Then cease, my song, till far *Aurora* rise.

Guide for Responding

◆ Literature and Your Life

Reader's Response Did you find this poem inspiring? Why or why not?

Thematic Focus How does this poem relate to the concept of freedom?

Group Discussion Phillis Wheatley's poem in praise of evening contains many descriptive details about the natural world. Would it be possible to praise evening in a poem containing descriptions of an urban setting? Why or why not?

☑ Check Your Comprehension

1. What happens in the first stanza?
2. According to the poet, what are "living temples of our God below"?
3. When are human beings "more pure"?

◆ Critical Thinking

INTERPRET
1. What does the poet find praiseworthy about the evening? **[Analyze]**
2. Given her comments in lines 14 and 16, why do you think Wheatley focuses her praise on evening rather than on morning? **[Infer]**

EVALUATE
3. In your view, how accurate is Wheatley's contrast of a person's state of mind at night and in the morning? **[Evaluate]**

EXTEND
4. How might a physician, psychologist, or sleep researcher add insight to Wheatley's description of night's healing powers? **[Science Link]**

Guide for Responding (continued)

◆ Reading Strategy

CLARIFYING MEANING

Poetry often requires close reading. It's necessary to look at each passage very carefully and **clarify the meaning** of any sections that seem confusing or unclear. To do so, check the definition of any unfamiliar words, and rephrase passages that are written in unusual word orders. In these poems, Wheatley frequently inverts common sentence order by placing a verb before its subject. Rephrase the wording to interpret the meaning.

1. Clarify lines 11–14 of "To His Excellency, General Washington" by explaining the meaning of *unnumber'd* and *graces* and reordering the sentence parts.
2. Find two more examples of inverted subject and verb order in these poems and restate the poet's meaning.
3. What is the effect of inverted subject and verb order on the style of the poetry?

◆ Literary Focus

PERSONIFICATION

Personification is the attribution of human powers or qualities to something that is not human, such as an inanimate object, an aspect of nature, or an abstract idea. For centuries, writers have used personification to satisfy a desire to understand the world in human terms. For example, the ocean was personified as the god Poseidon by ancient Greeks and as the god Neptune by ancient Romans. Today, phrases like "a raging fire" are so common that we rarely think of them as personifications. In "To His Excellency, General Washington," Phillis Wheatley personifies America as the goddess Columbia.

1. In "To His Excellency, General Washington," how does the poet characterize Columbia?
2. (a) What details does she use in describing Columbia's physical appearance? (b) How do these details contribute to an overall impression of Columbia?
3. What does the god Eolus (line 15) personify?
4. How does Wheatley personify Britain?
5. In "An Hymn to the Evening," what nonhuman subjects does Wheatley personify?

◆ Build Vocabulary

USING THE PREFIX *re-*

The common prefix *re-* means "back" or "again." In your notebook, match each word in the left column with its definition in the right column.

1. revolve   **a.** repeat from memory
2. relate   **b.** make new again
3. recite   **c.** turn or roll again and again
4. renew   **d.** link back to; connect

USING THE WORD BANK

On your paper, write the word whose meaning is most nearly opposite that of the first word:

1. celestial: (a) heavenly, (b) earthbound, (c) windy
2. refulgent: (a) tarnished, (b) sparkling, (c) colorful
3. propitious: (a) evil, (b) lucky, (c) inopportune
4. refluent: (a) surging, (b) stagnant, (c) ebbing
5. pensive: (a) reflective, (b) mournful, (c) carefree
6. placid: (a) unfettered, (b) agitated, (c) generous
7. scepter: (a) trinket, (b) emblem, (c) wand

◆ Grammar and Style

SUBJECT AND VERB AGREEMENT

A verb must agree in number with its subject. Singular subjects take **singular verbs**; plural subjects take **plural verbs.** In this example, the subject and verb are separated by other parts of the sentence:

Shall I to Washington their praise recite?

Practice In your notebook, copy the following lines. Underline the subject, and then choose the correct form of the verb in parentheses.

1. The thunder (shake, shakes) the heavenly plain.
2. When Gallic powers Columbia's fury (find, finds).
3. So may our breasts with every virtue (glow, glows).
4. Slumbers (soothe, soothes) each weary mind.
5. While round (increase, increases) the rising hills of dead.

Build Your Portfolio

 ## Idea Bank

Writing

1. Letter Imagine that Phillis Wheatley is still alive. Write a letter to her, asking questions about her work, giving your reactions to it, and praising her accomplishments.

2. Diary Entry Write the diary entry that Wheatley might have composed the night before her oral examination in the Boston courthouse.

3. Poem or Essay Develop a list of traits that express the ideals of today's society. In a poem or essay, describe the appearance and behavior of someone who personifies these traits.

Speaking and Listening

4. Dramatic Reading When read aloud, poems gain richness because sound devices—rhyme, meter, alliteration, assonance—become fully animated. Rehearse one of Wheatley's poems and present a dramatic reading for your classmates. **[Performing Arts Link]**

5. Paraphrasing Paraphrase, or restate in your own words, "To His Excellency, General Washington." Begin with reading aloud the poem's first complete thought; then you can restate the ideas in your own words. Write your version as you go along. Then read it to the class.

Projects

6. Report on Washington Research George Washington's military career, political life, or youth. Prepare a report on your findings. **[Social Studies Link]**

7. Portrait Draw an image depicting today's America as a person. Compare and contrast your work with the illustration of Columbia. **[Art Link]**

 ## Writing Mini-Lesson

Inscription for a Monument

Washington is one of the most revered men in American history. Choose a figure from history whom you admire. Imagine that you have been hired to write an inscription for a monument or statue honoring this individual. Speak volumes in very few words and convey the heroic qualities of this historical figure.

Writing Skills Focus: Persuasive Tone

To write an inscription that is honest and accurate, you'll need to choose language that emphasizes the subject's greatness. Use a **persuasive tone** and words with positive connotations. Look at this celebration of George Washington:

Model of Persuasive Tone

A man of supreme courage and skill, George Washington was an inspiring general, a true patriot, and a fearless leader—a conqueror who not only risked his life, but left a legacy of liberty for generations to savor.

By using positive adjectives such as *supreme* and *fearless*, as well as charged words like *conqueror* and *liberty*, the writer emphasizes qualities that communicate Washington's heroism.

Prewriting You may wish to research your chosen historical subject. Make a list of specific accomplishments and notable qualities—both personal and professional.

Drafting Use forceful nouns and adjectives that have positive connotations. For example, use *trailblazer* instead of *worker,* or *tireless* in place of *good.*

Revising Reread your inscription, looking for opportunities to be more economical and precise with your word choices. Check that you've included the figure's most important accomplishments.

CONNECTIONS TO TODAY'S WORLD

from Letter From Birmingham City Jail
Martin Luther King, Jr.

Thematic Connection

VOICES FOR FREEDOM

The voices who cried out for freedom during the Revolutionary period began a tradition that has carried on to this day. In recent years, a wide spectrum of Americans have raised insistent voices in the name of personal, social, and political freedoms. We have lobbied for women's rights, protested against wars, petitioned for election reform, and championed causes as varied as reduced taxes and illiteracy. Among the most eloquent of these voices for freedom was Martin Luther King, Jr.

TWENTIETH-CENTURY CALLS FOR FREEDOM

Martin Luther King, Jr., and other American civil rights leaders of the 1950's and 1960's shared similar ideas of freedom expressed by early Americans such as Paine, Jefferson, and Wheatley. In his sermons and speeches, King addressed some of the same themes as his Revolutionary forebears did—freedom, the fundamental importance of justice, and strategies for fighting oppression. Like Paine's, King's language was vivid; like Wheatley's, his words alluded to deities and heroes; and like Jefferson's, his voice called for boldness, wisdom, and morality.

Arrested in 1963 for protesting racial segregation in Birmingham, Alabama, King sat in jail and read a newspaper article in which eight white clergymen chastised him for "unwise and untimely" demonstrations. Without proper writing paper, King drafted a response—the "Letter From Birmingham City Jail"— in the cramped margins of that newspaper. King's impassioned words focus both protest and hope on his small audience of white peers. A few months later, King would lead the March on Washington. On this occasion, more than 200,000 Americans of all races would gather around the Lincoln Memorial and hear his voice ring out again for the causes of racial justice and freedom.

MARTIN LUTHER KING, JR. (1929–1968)

A charismatic Baptist minister and civil rights leader, Martin Luther King, Jr., struggled to bring African Americans into the political and economic mainstream of American life in the 1950's and 1960's. King drew inspiration from the Christian ideals of his father and grandfather, both of whom were also Baptist ministers.

Armed with the philosophy of Mohandas K. Gandhi, the Indian leader, Dr. King insisted that political and social freedoms were attainable through nonviolent actions. Starting in his native Atlanta and moving to Montgomery and Birmingham, Alabama, King led boycotts, marches, and sit-ins to protest segregation. He became a national figure, organizing the March on Washington and speaking out against discrimination. King stressed nonviolence; however, he became an American martyr for freedom when he was assassinated at the age of 39. His widow, Coretta Scott King, works to keep King's message and achievements alive.

from

Letter From Birmingham City Jail

Dr. Martin Luther King, Jr.

I hope the church as a whole will meet the challenge of this decisive hour. But even if the church does not come to the aid of justice, I have no despair about the future. I have no fear about the outcome of our struggle in Birmingham, even if our <u>motives</u> are presently misunderstood. We will reach the goal of freedom in

◆ Build Vocabulary

motives (mōt´ ivz) *n.*: Reasons for action; inner drives

◀ **Critical Viewing** To prevent others from joining this African American sitting at a "whites only" lunch counter, the other seats were piled with linen supplies. Basing your response on their posture and activity, what might the customer and the waitress be feeling? **[Hypothesize]**

Birmingham and all over the nation, because the goal of America is freedom. Abused and scorned though we may be, our destiny is tied up with the destiny of America. Before the Pilgrims landed at Plymouth we were here. Before the pen of Jefferson etched across the pages of history the majestic words of the Declaration of Independence, we were here. For more than two centuries our foreparents labored in this country without wages; they made cotton king; and they built the homes of their masters in the midst of brutal injustice and shameful humiliation—and yet out of a bottomless vitality they continued to thrive and develop. If the inexpressible cruelties of slavery could not stop us, the opposition we now face will surely fail. We will win our freedom because the sacred heritage of our nation and the eternal will of God are embodied in our echoing demands.

I must close now. But before closing I am impelled to mention one other point in your statement that troubled me profoundly. You warmly commended the Birmingham police force for keeping "order" and "preventing violence." I don't believe you would have so warmly commended the police force if you had seen its angry violent dogs literally biting six unarmed, nonviolent Negroes. I don't believe you would so quickly commend the policemen if you would observe their ugly and inhuman treatment of Negroes here in the city jail; if you would watch them push and curse old Negro women and young Negro girls; if you would see them slap and kick old Negro men and young Negro boys; if you will observe them, as they did on two occasions, refuse to give us food because we wanted to sing our grace together. I'm sorry that I can't join you in your praise for the police department.

It is true that they have been rather disciplined in their public handling of the demonstrators. In this sense they have been rather publicly "nonviolent." But for what purpose? To preserve the evil system of segregation. Over the last few years I have consistently preached that nonviolence demands that the means we use must be as pure as the ends we seek. So I have tried to make it clear that it is wrong to use immoral means to attain moral ends. But now I must affirm that it is just as wrong, or even more so, to use moral means to preserve immoral ends. Maybe Mr. Connor and his policemen have been rather publicly nonviolent, as Chief Pritchett was in Albany, Georgia, but they have used the moral means of nonviolence to maintain the immoral end of flagrant racial injustice. T. S. Eliot has said that there is no greater treason than to do the right deed for the wrong reason.

I wish you had commended the Negro sit-inners and demonstrators of Birmingham for their sublime courage, their willingness to suffer and their amazing discipline in the midst of the most inhuman provocation. One day the South will recognize its real heroes. They will be the James Merediths, courageously and with a majestic sense of purpose facing jeering and hostile mobs and the agonizing loneliness that characterizes the life of the pioneer. They will be old, oppressed, battered Negro women, symbolized in a seventy-two-year-old woman of Montgomery, Alabama, who rose up with a sense of dignity and with her people decided not to

> **Before the pen of Jefferson etched across the pages of history the majestic words of the Declaration of Independence, we were here.**

◆ Build Vocabulary

vitality (vī talʹ ə tē) *n*.: Power to endure or survive; life force

impelled (im peldʹ) *v*.: Moved; forced

flagrant (flāʹ grənt) *adj*.: Glaring, outrageous

profundity (prō funʹ də tē) *n*.: Intellectual depth

monotony (mə nätʹ ən ē) *n*.: Tiresome, unchanging sameness; lack of variety

scintillating (sintʹ əl ātʹ iŋ) *adj*.: Sparkling

ride the segregated buses, and responded to one who inquired about her tiredness with ungrammatical profundity: "My feet is tired, but my soul is rested." They will be the young high school and college students, young ministers of the gospel and a host of their elders courageously and nonviolently sitting-in at lunch counters and willingly going to jail for conscience's sake. One day the South will know that when these disinherited children of God sat down at lunch counters they were in reality standing up for the best in the American dream and the most sacred values in our Judeo-Christian heritage, and thusly, carrying our whole nation back to those great wells of democracy which were dug deep by the Founding Fathers in the formulation of the Constitution and the Declaration of Independence.

Never before have I written a letter this long (or should I say a book?). I'm afraid that it is much too long to take your precious time. I can assure you that it would have been much shorter if I had been writing from a comfortable desk, but what else is there to do when you are alone for days in the dull monotony of a narrow jail cell other than write long letters, think strange thoughts, and pray long prayers?

If I have said anything in this letter that is an overstatement of the truth and is indicative of an unreasonable impatience, I beg you to forgive me. If I have said anything in this letter that is an understatement of the truth and is indicative of my having a patience that makes me patient with anything less than brotherhood, I beg God to forgive me.

I hope this letter finds you strong in the faith. I also hope that circumstances will soon make it possible for me to meet each of you, not as an integrationist or a civil rights leader, but as a fellow clergyman and a Christian brother. Let us all hope that the dark clouds of racial prejudice will soon pass away and the deep fog of misunderstanding will be lifted from our fear-drenched communities and in some not too distant tomorrow the radiant stars of love and brotherhood will shine over our great nation with all of their scintillating beauty.

Yours for the cause of Peace
and Brotherhood,
Martin Luther King, Jr.

Guide for Responding

◆ Literature and Your Life

Reader's Response What are your thoughts about King's ideas of justice, freedom, and heroism?

Thematic Focus How does King's reference to Jefferson add to his argument?

Journal Writing King notes the importance of making means and ends equally "pure." In your mind, how does a specific goal direct the way you achieve it? Discuss your ideas in a journal entry.

☑ Check Your Comprehension

1. What is the author's opinion of the Birmingham police officers' behavior?
2. Which people does the author identify as unsung heroes of the South?

◆ Critical Thinking

INTERPRET

1. What does the author mean by the statement, "the goal of America is freedom"? **[Interpret]**
2. Why do you think King finds the comment "My feet is tired, but my soul is rested" heroic and profound? **[Infer]**

APPLY

3. How might the effect of this letter have been different if it had been written from "a comfortable desk" rather than "a narrow jail cell"? **[Hypothesize]**

EXTEND

4. Explain how Martin Luther King's letter can be seen as an echo of Thomas Jefferson's Declaration. **[Literature Link]**

Thematic Connection

VOICES FOR FREEDOM

Paine, Jefferson, and Wheatley did not merely record a momentous period of history; their voices resounded on battlefields and in palaces and helped bring freedom to the citizens of the new United States of America. Similarly, Martin Luther King's calls for freedom and justice were heard not only by his immediate audience, but also eventually by millions of people across America.

1. How is King's imprisonment related to "those great wells of democracy which were dug deep by the Founding Fathers in the formulation of the Constitution and the Declaration of Independence"?

2. Both "Letter From Birmingham City Jail" and "To His Excellency, General Washington" glorify freedom. What similarities and differences can you identify between the war for independence and the struggle for civil rights?

Idea Bank

Writing

1. **Poem for a Prisoner** If Phillis Wheatley had known Martin Luther King, Jr., she might have written poetry to celebrate his courage and beliefs. Use your knowledge of Wheatley and King to write a poem she might have written in tribute to him. **[Literature Link]**

2. **Essay** In "Letter From Birmingham City Jail," Martin Luther King makes a brief comparison between "the inexpressible cruelties of slavery" and "the opposition we now face." Write an essay in which you compare and contrast more extensively the situation of slaves and the situation of segregated blacks in the early 1960's.

3. **Editorial** Write an editorial to bring King's imprisonment to light. Use Paine's emotional persuasive style or Jefferson's logical persuasive style to argue against the actions of the Birmingham police force.

Speaking and Listening

4. **Oration** Use a portion of "Letter From Birmingham City Jail" as a springboard for a speech about leadership, freedom, or devotion to a cause. Carefully analyze the text to discover stylistic or rhetorical techniques—such as repetition, parallelism, alliteration, and so on—that could contribute to a stirring oral performance. **[Performing Arts Link]**

5. **Freedom Survey** Spending time in jail might teach a prisoner about a loss of freedom. However, the presence of freedom may be more difficult to observe. Ask a variety of people to share their definitions of freedom. Then compile their responses into a report. **[Career Link]**

Projects

6. **Voices of Freedom Booklet** Create a booklet that celebrates the American tradition of fighting for freedom. Include the colonists and also more contemporary citizens who have worked to earn rights and fight injustice. Briefly identify and highlight the causes and achievements of the voices you have chosen. Include copies of photographs, drawings, news headlines and articles, and other images. **[Art Link]**

7. **Report on Dr. King** Using primary sources such as newspaper accounts, letters or speeches, prepare an oral or written report on an important moment in Dr. King's eventful life. Consider the 1955 Montgomery bus boycott, the 1965 march from Selma to Montgomery, the 1960 sit-ins at lunch counters, or the 1963 March on Washington.

Writing Process Workshop

An **editorial**—essentially a brief persuasive essay—is the form in which the management of a newspaper, magazine, or radio or television station airs its views on major political and social issues. *The Crisis, Number 1,* Thomas Paine's stirring summons to revolution, departs from this definition in two respects: It is longer than a typical editorial, and it wasn't just part of a publication—it *was* the publication, a pamphlet published by Paine himself. Its urgency and powerful impact, however, have made *The Crisis* a model for editorial writers for more than two hundred years.

The following skills, introduced in this section's Writing Mini-Lessons, will help you write an effective editorial of your own:

Writing Skills Focus

▶ **Show causes and effects** to help readers see the implications of decisions or courses of action. (See p. 137.)

▶ **Use forceful language** to command your readers' attention and bolster the impact of your arguments. (See p. 147.)

▶ **Adopt a persuasive tone** by using positive, emotionally charged words. (See p. 155.)

Notice how this excerpt from an editorial illustrates these skills.

Recruiting for the Continental Army, (detail), William T. Ranney, Munson-Williams-Proctor Institute, Museum of Art, Utica, New York

---

WRITING MODEL

Introduction to an editorial arguing against congressional term limits

Because Franklin Delano Roosevelt had been elected to unprecedented third and fourth terms during World War II, Congress subsequently enacted a two-term limit for the presidency in order to discourage dictatorial ambitions in the chief of state. ① The recent movement to dose the sluggish House and Senate with the same two-term medicine is a misguided attack on the very core of the democracy it claims to bolster. ②

① Terms such as "because" and "in order to" establish a clear cause-and-effect relationship between issues and events.

② Forceful language such as "dose," "sluggish" and "misguided attack" creates a compelling argument.

APPLYING LANGUAGE SKILLS: Prepositional Phrases

A **prepositional phrase** is a group of words that includes a preposition—such as *for, in, because, throughout*—and a noun or pronoun. The noun or pronoun that generally follows the preposition is the object of the preposition.

Prepositional Phrases

Prepositions	Objects of Prepositions
for	her
through	the years
because of	his inspiring patriotism

Practice Write each prepositional phrase from the passage below on your paper. Then underline each preposition and circle each object.

In difficult times, people are often capable of great things. Without sufficient provisions or fuel, the ragged army of volunteers under General Washington managed to beat back well-trained British troops.

Writer's Solution Connection Writing Lab

To help you develop a balanced argument, use the Pros and Cons organizer in the Tutorial on Persuasion.

Prewriting

Choose a Topic Because editorials focus on issues of current concern, you might brainstorm with classmates to learn the issues that concern or involve them. You can get additional ideas by scanning a newspaper or watching television news programs. You might also choose one of these topic suggestions.

Topic Ideas

- Term limits
- Local environmental concerns
- Television content ratings
- Rap lyrics
- School uniforms
- Volunteerism

Gather Evidence Consider your topic and point of view. Do you know everything you need to know in order to make a persuasive argument? To help build your case, conduct research in the library or on the Internet to find relevant magazine articles or reference works.

Brainstorm for "Forceful Language" If you don't feel strongly about your topic, neither will your readers. That's why it's important to use forceful language to convey your views. Notice the difference between the impact of the weak "opinion" words and their more forceful alternatives in the chart below. Jot down a list of forceful words that you can use to make your argument persuasive and effective.

Weak	Forceful
disapprove	deplore
support	applaud
should	must
ask	implore

Drafting

Use a Condensed Essay Structure Use the basic structure of introduction-body-conclusion to organize and present your thoughts. Begin with an introduction that grabs your readers' attention and states your argument clearly. Develop and support your main points in the body, showing logical cause-and-effect relationships between ideas. In the conclusion, restate your point of view and any call to action on the readers' part.

Maintain a Positive Tone Readers can be turned off by an overly negative approach. If you have a criticism to make, state it concisely and fairly. Then devote at least as much space to explaining and defending a constructive alternative, using positive, persuasive language.

Revising

Work With a Peer Reviewer Ask a classmate to read and evaluate your editorial, using the following checklist.

- ► Does the editorial successfully communicate the writer's views on the issue?
- ► Is it coherent and organized, with a clear introduction, body, and conclusion?
- ► Are ideas developed and supported with clear cause-and-effect statements?
- ► Is the language forceful and compelling? Does it succeed in persuading you to adopt the writer's point of view?

Use your reviewer's responses to these questions to help you improve your editorial.

REVISION MODEL

① *congressional gridlock has stalled*

Americans know that ~~there has been no real~~ action on key

issues, such as national health care, campaign financing,

education reform, poverty, and so on. The answer to our
② *Term limits for Congress would infringe on our freedom of choice by automatically eliminating two-term incumbents from the election race.*
problems, however, is more democracy, not less. Let the

voters, not the legislators, decide if and when they want to

"throw the bums out"; and even more to the point, let's

③ *preserve*   ④ *dedicated public servants who have earned our trust.*
~~not give up~~ our right not to throw out the ~~people we want.~~

① *The writer uses more forceful language.*
② *This addition of a clear cause-and-effect relationship strengthens the writer's case.*
③–④ *These revisions adopt a more persuasive tone by substituting positive, emotionally charged language.*

Publishing

Consider sharing your editorial with others:

- ► **Newspapers** Submit your editorial to the school newspaper or to the op-ed page of your town's newspaper.
- ► **Send to Appropriate Recipients** Send your editorial, with a brief cover letter, to an appropriate civic leader or elected official.

APPLYING LANGUAGE SKILLS: Varying Sentence Beginnings

To avoid monotony and enhance your writing, use a variety of sentence openers. Below are just a few of the structures you can use to begin a sentence.

Examples:

Subject first: *British troops were sent to destroy colonial munitions at Concord.*

Adjective first: *Enraged, colonial minutemen challenged them on the Lexington green.*

Prepositional phrase first: *From out of nowhere, a shot rang out.*

Adverb first: *Immediately, the firing became widespread, leaving eight Americans dead.*

Practice Write a five-sentence paragraph about a work from this section. Begin each sentence with a different structure.

Writing Application Use a variety of sentence openers to enliven your editorial.

Writer's Solution Connection Writing Lab

To ensure variety in your sentences, use the revision checker for sentence openers in the Revising and Editing section of the tutorial on Persuasion.

Real-World Reading Skills Workshop

Strategies for Success

Just because a piece of writing has been published doesn't mean it's accurate and reliable. Often, the writer has a particular agenda or point of view and may slant the piece in one direction. A writer may even include incorrect information. That's why it's critical to evaluate carefully the source you use when you gather information on a topic.

Examine the Source Ask questions like these when considering each source:

▶ What are the author's qualifications? Are they appropriate to the topic?

▶ If the source is a periodical, what is its reputation for accuracy and thoroughness? Who is its intended audience?

▶ What, if any, evidence of bias appears in the information? Might the source have an interest in slanting the information to support a specific point of view?

▶ Is the information supported with verifiable facts?

Apply the Strategy

You want to gather information about contemporary African life before applying to a cultural exchange program. The poster at left advertises a lecture and book about Africa. As you consider attending the lecture, evaluate the poster, lecture, and book as information sources.

1. What credentials does Dr. Matho have for writing about Africa?

2. How reliable do you think Dr. Matho's information about Africa will be? Explain.

3. Do you think *Traveling My Homeland* will present an objective or a subjective view of Africa?

4. What is the purpose of the poster? How might that purpose result in a biased presentation of information?

✔ Here are other situations in which it's important to evaluate information sources:

▶ Research reports
▶ Political campaigns
▶ Product packaging claims

MEET THE AUTHOR!

Well-known travel writer and Professor of African Studies Alice Matho shares the experiences that inspired her latest book about Africa

Traveling My Homeland:
My personal observations of changing life in today's Africa

Slide show * Lecture * Discussion
8:00 P.M. Monday—Rolly Hall Auditorium

Copies of Dr. Matho's earlier books on Africa will also be available at the lecture.

PART 2 *Focus on Literary Forms:*
Speeches

George Washington Standing on the Platform,
Pennsylvania State Capitol, Harrisburg

The colonial period of American history witnessed speeches and oratory powerful enough to start the Revolution. In speeches that rang through the halls of government, speakers such as Patrick Henry and Benjamin Franklin turned away from colonial loyalty toward a spirit of independence.

Guide for Interpreting

Patrick Henry (1736–1799)

It was said that Patrick Henry could move his listeners to anger, fear, or laughter more easily than the most talented actor. Remembered most for his fiery battle cry "Give me liberty or give me death," Henry is considered the most powerful orator of the American Revolution. He helped to inspire colonists to unite in an effort to win their independence. Shortly after his 1765 election to the Virginia House of Burgesses, Henry delivered one of his most powerful speeches, declaring his opposition to the Stamp Act. Over the protests of some of the most influential members, the Virginia House adopted Henry's resolutions.

Voice of Protest In 1775, Henry delivered his most famous speech at the Virginia Provincial Convention. While most of the speakers that day argued that the colony should seek a compromise with the British, Henry boldly urged armed resistance to England. His speech had a powerful impact on the audience, feeding the Revolutionary spirit that led to the signing of the Declaration of Independence.

In the years that followed, Henry continued to be an important political leader, serving as governor of Virginia and member of the Virginia General Assembly.

Benjamin Franklin (1706–1790)

Although his achievements spanned a wide range of areas—including science, literature, journalism, and education—Benjamin Franklin is most remembered as a statesman. He is the only American to sign the four documents that established the nation: the Declaration of Independence, the treaty of alliance with France, the peace treaty with England, and the Constitution.

A Persuasive Diplomat Franklin was a leader in the movement for independence. In 1776, Congress sent him to France to enlist desperately needed aid for the American Revolution. Franklin's persuasive powers proved effective, as he was able to achieve his goal—a pivotal breakthrough that may have been the deciding factor in the war.

Helping Forge a Nation In 1783, Franklin signed the peace treaty that ended the war and established the new nation. He returned home to serve as a delegate to the Constitutional Convention in Philadelphia. There, as politicians clashed over plans for the new government, Franklin worked to resolve conflicts and ensure ratification of the Constitution. (For more on Franklin, see pp. 128 and 186.)

◆ Background for Understanding

HISTORY: PATRICK HENRY'S BRAVERY

Today, it's hard for us to imagine the bravery it took for speakers like Patrick Henry to publicly denounce the British king. England was the most powerful country in the world, and the odds were overwhelmingly against the colonies' winning their freedom. By criticizing the king, Patrick Henry and other colonial leaders were putting their lives on the line. If the colonies' efforts to win their independence had failed, Henry could have been executed for treason.

Henry was quite aware of this. In fact, he had openly been accused of treason when he delivered his speech in opposition to the Stamp Act in 1765. On that occasion, Henry had referred to two leaders who had been killed for political reasons and declared that King George III of Britain might "profit by their example." This shocked the members of the audience so much that they screamed out, accusing him of treason. Henry is reported to have replied, "If this be treason, make the most of it!"

◆ *Literature and Your Life*

CONNECT YOUR EXPERIENCE

You're probably already familiar with lines from many famous speeches— even though you may not be aware of it. Lines like Martin Luther King's "I have a dream" and John F. Kennedy's "Ask not what your country can do for you" have become a part of most Americans' vocabularies. The reason why those lines have become so famous is that they come from speeches—like the two you're about to read—that have shaped our nation's history.

Journal Writing What slogans or mottoes capture the attention of your generation? Choose one—from politics, music, or advertisements—and explain why it works.

THEMATIC FOCUS: A NATION IS BORN

What ideas about "life, liberty, and the pursuit of happiness" that the Constitution promises are planted in the speeches of Henry and Franklin?

◆ Build Vocabulary

SUFFIXES: *-ity*

Benjamin Franklin warns colleagues not to be overconfident of their infallibility. The suffix *-ity* turns adjectives into nouns. Added to the adjective *infallible,* meaning "incapable of error," it creates the noun *infallibility,* meaning "the state of being infallible."

WORD BANK

Preview this list of words from the speeches.

> arduous
> insidious
> subjugation
> vigilant
> infallibility
> despotism
> salutary
> unanimity
> posterity
> manifest

◆ Grammar and Style

DOUBLE NEGATIVES

Today, it is not acceptable to use **double negatives**—two negative words where only one is needed. In previous centuries, however, double negatives were sometimes used to emphasize an idea. For example, Benjamin Franklin uses this sentence in his speech:

I am *not* sure I shall *never* approve it.

Franklin was stressing a possibility. The context of his statement suggests that Franklin might approve at a later date.

As you read these speeches, look for double negatives. Evaluate whether they effectively emphasize an idea.

◆ Literary Focus

SPEECHES

Speeches have played an important role in American politics—from the Revolutionary period to the present. An effective speaker uses a variety of techniques to emphasize important points:

- *Restatement:* repeating an idea in a variety of ways
- *Repetition:* restating an idea using the same words
- *Parallelism:* repeating grammatical structures
- *Rhetorical question:* asking a question whose answer is self-evident; intended to stir emotions.

◆ Reading Strategy

EVALUATING PERSUASIVE APPEALS

To stir an audience, speakers often appeal to people's emotions—their hopes, fears, likes, and dislikes. Speakers can also appeal to their audience's sense of reason. When you read a persuasive speech, it's important to recognize and evaluate the types of appeals that the speaker makes. Ask yourself: What is the speaker's purpose in evoking these emotions? What arguments and evidence does the speaker offer to back up his or her emotional appeals? How well do the appeals suit the audience and occasion?

Patrick Henry Before the Virginia House of Burgesses, Peter F. Rothermel, Red Hill, The Patrick Henry National Memorial

▲ **Critical Viewing** Patrick Henry's dramatic speeches swayed sentiment away from loyalty to the British crown and toward armed resistance. How effectively does the artist convey the power of Henry's oratory? **[Evaluate]**

SPEECH IN THE VIRGINIA CONVENTION

Patrick Henry

Mr. President: No man thinks more highly than I do of the patriotism, as well as abilities, of the very worthy gentlemen who have just addressed the house. But different men often see the same subject in different lights; and, therefore, I hope it will not be thought disrespectful to those gentlemen, if, entertaining, as I do, opinions of a character very opposite to theirs, I shall speak forth my sentiments freely and without reserve. This is no time for ceremony. The question before the house is one of awful moment[1] to this country. For my own part, I consider it as nothing less than a question of freedom or slavery. And in proportion to the magnitude of the subject ought to be the freedom of the debate. It is only in this way that we can hope to arrive at truth, and fulfill the great responsibility which we hold to God and our country. Should I keep back my opinions at such a time, through fear of giving offense, I should consider myself as guilty of treason toward my country, and of an act of disloyalty toward the Majesty of Heaven, which I revere above all earthly kings.

Mr. President, it is natural to man to indulge in the illusions of hope. We are apt to shut our eyes against a painful truth, and listen to the song of that siren till she transforms us into beasts.[2] Is this the part of wise men, engaged in a great and <u>arduous</u> struggle for liberty? Are we disposed to be of the

---

1. **moment:** Importance.

2. **listen . . . beasts:** In Homer's *Odyssey,* the enchantress Circe transforms men into swine after charming them with her singing.

◆ Build Vocabulary

arduous (är´ jōo wəs) *adj.*: Difficult

number of those who having eyes see not, and having ears hear not,[3] the things which so nearly concern their temporal salvation? For my part, whatever anguish of spirit it may cost, I am willing to know the whole truth; to know the worst and to provide for it.

I have but one lamp by which my feet are guided, and that is the lamp of experience. I know of no way of judging of the future but by the past. And judging by the past, I wish to know what there has been in the conduct of the British ministry for the last ten years to justify those hopes with which gentlemen have been pleased to solace themselves and the house? Is it that <u>insidious</u> smile with which our petition has been lately received? Trust it not, sir; it will prove a snare to your feet. Suffer not yourselves to be betrayed with a kiss.[4] Ask yourselves how this gracious reception of our petition comports with those warlike preparations which cover our waters and darken our land. Are fleets and armies necessary to a work of love and reconciliation? Have we shown ourselves so unwilling to be reconciled that force must be called in to win back our love? Let us not deceive ourselves, sir. These are the implements of war and <u>subjugation</u>—the last arguments to which kings resort.

I ask gentlemen, sir, what means this martial array, if its purpose be not to force us to submission? Can gentlemen assign any other possible motive for it? Has Great Britain any enemy in this quarter of the world, to call for all this accumulation of navies and armies? No, sir, she has none. They are meant for us: they can be meant for no other. They are sent over to bind and rivet upon us those chains which the British ministry have been so long forging.

And what have we to oppose to them? Shall we try argument? Sir, we have been trying that for the last ten years. Have we anything new to offer upon the subject? Nothing. We have held the subject up in every light of which it is capable; but it has been all in vain. Shall we resort to entreaty and humble supplication? What terms shall we find which have not been already exhausted? Let us not, I beseech you, sir, deceive ourselves longer. Sir, we have done everything that could be done to avert the storm which is now coming on. We have petitioned; we have remonstrated; we have supplicated; we have prostrated ourselves before the throne, and have implored its interposition[5] to arrest the tyrannical hands of the ministry and Parliament. Our petitions have been slighted; our remonstrances have produced additional violence and insult; our supplications have been disregarded; and we have been spurned with contempt from the foot of the throne! In vain, after these things, may we indulge the fond[6] hope of peace and reconciliation. There is no longer any room for hope. If we wish to be free, if we mean to preserve inviolate those inestimable privileges for which we have been so long contending, if we mean not basely to abandon the noble struggle in which we have been so long engaged, and which we have pledged ourselves never to abandon until the glorious object of our contest shall be obtained—we must fight! I repeat it, sir, we must fight! An appeal to arms and to the God of Hosts is all that is left us!

They tell us, sir, that we are weak—unable to cope with so formidable an adversary. But when shall we be stronger? Will it be the next week, or the next year? Will it be when we are totally disarmed, and when a British guard shall be stationed in every house? Shall we gather strength by irresolution and inaction? Shall we acquire the means of effectual

3. **having eyes . . . hear not:** In Ezekiel 12:2, those "who have eyes to see, but see not, who have ears to hear, but hear not" are addressed.
4. **betrayed with a kiss:** In Luke 22:47–48, Jesus is betrayed with a kiss.

5. **interposition:** Intervention.
6. **fond:** Foolish.

♦ **Build Vocabulary**

insidious (in sid´ ē əs) *adj.*: Deceitful; treacherous
subjugation (sub´ jə gā´ shən) *n.*: The act of conquering
vigilant (vij´ ə lənt) *adj.*: Alert to danger

resistance by lying supinely on our backs and hugging the delusive phantom of hope until our enemies shall have bound us hand and foot? Sir, we are not weak, if we make a proper use of those means which the God of nature hath placed in our power. Three millions of people, armed in the holy cause of liberty, and in such a country as that which we possess, are invincible by any force which our enemy can send against us. Besides, sir, we shall not fight our battles alone. There is a just God

◆ Reading Strategy
How does Henry appeal to emotions in this passage?

who presides over the destinies of nations and who will raise up friends to fight our battles for us. The battle, sir, is not to the strong alone;[7] it is to the vigilant, the active, the brave. Besides, sir, we have no election;[8] if we were base

enough to desire it, it is now too late to retire from the contest. There is no retreat but in submission and slavery! Our chains are forged! Their clanging may be heard on the plains of Boston! The war is inevitable—and let it come! I repeat it, sir, let it come!

It is in vain, sir, to extenuate the matter. Gentlemen may cry, "Peace, peace"—but there is no peace. The war is actually begun! The next gale that sweeps from the north[9] will bring to our ears the clash of resounding arms! Our brethren are already in the field! Why stand we here idle? What is it that gentlemen wish? What would they have? Is life so dear, or peace so sweet, as to be purchased at the price of chains and slavery? Forbid it, Almighty God! I know not what course others may take; but as for me, give me liberty or give me death!

---

7. **The battle . . . alone:** "The race is not to the swift, nor the battle to the strong." (Ecclesiastes 9:11)
8. **election:** Choice.

9. **The next gale . . . north:** In Massachusetts, some colonists had already shown open resistance to the British.

Guide for Responding

◆ *Literature and Your Life*

Reader's Response What is your impression of Patrick Henry? Based on this speech, do you think his reputation as a powerful orator was deserved? Explain.

Thematic Focus How important of a role can a political speech like Henry's play in a time of crisis? Explain.

Classroom Poll Henry implies that death is preferable to life without liberty. Take a poll to determine whether your classmates agree.

☑ Check Your Comprehension

1. How does Henry say that he judges the future?
2. (a) What does Henry say is the reason for the British military buildup in America? (b) What course of action must the colonists take?
3. What does Henry say "the next gale that sweeps from the north" will bring?

◆ Critical Thinking

INTERPRET

1. Why do you think Henry begins by stating his opinions of the previous speakers? **[Infer]**
2. Why does Henry believe that compromise with the British is not a workable solution? **[Support]**
3. How does Henry answer the objection that the colonists are not ready to fight? **[Analyze]**
4. To what does Henry compare the colonists' situation? **[Analyze]**

APPLY

5. What occasion or situation might prompt a statesman to deliver such a formal, dramatic speech today? **[Relate]**

EXTEND

6. Compare Henry's speech with political speeches today. What speakers, if any, measure up to his power? **[Social Studies Link]**

Speech in the Convention

Benjamin Franklin

Mr. President,

I confess, that I do not entirely approve of this Constitution at present; but, Sir, I am not sure I shall never approve it; for, having lived long, I have experienced many instances of being obliged, by better information or fuller consideration, to change my opinions even on important subjects, which I once thought right, but found to be otherwise. It is therefore that, the older I grow, the more apt I am to doubt my own judgment of others. Most men, indeed, as well as most sects in religion, think themselves in possession of all truth, and that wherever others differ from them, it is so far error. . . . Though many private Persons think almost as highly of their own infallibility as of that of their Sect, few express it so naturally as a certain French Lady, who, in a little dispute with her sister, said, "But I meet with nobody but myself that is *always* in the right." *"Je ne trouve que moi qui aie toujours raison."*

In these sentiments, Sir, I agree to this Constitution, with all its faults,—if they are such; because I think a general Government necessary for us, and there is no form of government but what may be a blessing to the people, if well administered; and I believe, farther, that this is likely to be well administered for a course of years, and can only end in despotism, as other forms have done before it, when the people shall become so corrupted as to need despotic government, being incapable of any other. I doubt, too, whether any other Convention we can obtain, may be able to make a better constitution; for, when you assemble a number of men, to have the advantage of their joint wisdom, you inevitably assemble with those men all their prejudices, their passions, their errors of opinion, their local interests, and their selfish views. From such an assembly can a *perfect* production be expected? It therefore astonishes me, Sir, to find this system approaching so near to perfection as it does; and I think it will astonish our enemies, who are waiting with confidence to hear, that our councils are confounded like those of the builders of Babel, and that our States are on the point of separation, only to meet hereafter for the purpose of cutting one another's throats. Thus I consent, Sir, to this Constitution, because I expect no better, and because I am not sure that it is not the best. The opinions I have had of its *errors* I sacrifice to the public good. I have never whispered a syllable of them abroad. Within these walls they were born, and here they shall die. If every one of us, in returning to our Constituents, were to report the objections he has had to it, and endeavour to gain Partisans in support of them, we might prevent its being generally received, and thereby lose all the salutary effects and great advantages resulting naturally in our favour among foreign nations, as well as among ourselves, from our real or apparent unanimity. Much of the strength and efficiency of any government, in procuring and securing happiness to the people, depends on *opinion,* on the general opinion of the goodness of that government, as well as of the wisdom and integrity of its governors. I hope, therefore, for our own sakes,

as a part of the people, and for the sake of our posterity, that we shall act heartily and unanimously in recommending this Constitution, wherever our Influence may extend, and turn our future thoughts and endeavors to the means of having it *well administered.*

On the whole, Sir, I cannot help expressing a wish, that every member of the Convention who may still have objections to it, would with me on this occasion doubt a little of his own infallibility, and, to make *manifest* our *unanimity,* put his name to this Instrument.

◆ Build Vocabulary

infallibility (in fal′ ə bil′ ə tē) *n.:* Inability to be wrong; reliability

despotism (des′ pət iz′ əm) *n.:* Government by absolute rule; tyranny

salutary (sal′ yōō ter′ ē) *adj.:* Beneficial; promoting a good purpose

unanimity (yōō′ nə nim′ ə tē) *n.:* Complete agreement

posterity (päs ter′ ə tē) *n.:* All succeeding generations

manifest (man′ ə fest′) *adj.:* Evident; obvious; clear

Guide for Responding

◆ Literature and Your Life

Reader's Response Based on Franklin's argument, would you have ratified the Constitution? Why or why not?

Thematic Focus How does Franklin use his experience as a diplomat to persuade his audience?

✓ Check Your Comprehension

1. What three reasons does Franklin give for agreeing to the Constitution?
2. Of what has Franklin "never whispered a syllable . . . abroad"?
3. What advantage does Franklin see in the unanimity of the delegates?

◆ Critical Thinking

INTERPRET

1. What effect does Franklin achieve by his "confession" in the first paragraph? **[Interpret]**
2. Why does Franklin acknowledge the "faults" of the Constitution? **[Infer]**
3. What is Franklin's purpose in suppressing his "opinions" for "the public good"? **[Analyze]**

EVALUATE

4. How effective is the overall organization of Franklin's speech? Explain. **[Evaluate]**

EXTEND

5. In the excerpt from his *Autobiography* on p. 131, Franklin details his attempt to achieve moral perfection. Compare and contrast the younger Franklin described there with the one who delivered this speech. **[Literature Link]**

Guide for Responding (continued)

◆ Reading Strategy

EVALUATING PERSUASIVE APPEALS

An effective speaker uses a variety of **persuasive appeals.** Patrick Henry uses a blend of appeals to reason and to emotion in his speech.

1. Considering the purpose of Henry's speech, why are these two techniques appropriate?
2. Why do you think Henry chose to end his speech with an emotional appeal?

◆ Literary Focus

SPEECHES

In these **speeches**, Henry and Franklin use a variety of devices, including rhetorical questions, restatement, repetition, and parallelism (see definitions on p. 167) to emphasize their points.

1. (a) Find an instance where Henry uses a series of rhetorical questions. (b) What purpose does this series of questions serve?
2. Find an instance where Henry uses repetition.
3. (a) List three examples of restatement from Franklin's speech. (b) What is the effect of this restatement?
4. Find an example of parallelism in Franklin's speech. What effect does this have?

Beyond Literature

Media Connection

Political Conventions in the Age of Television In the United States, the major political parties meet every four years to draft their platforms and nominate presidential candidates. These conventions have been part of the political landscape since 1830. However, in recent decades, live television broadcasts have turned the conventions into extravaganzas and made them more commercial than ever before. What do you imagine conventions were like before television? What are the benefits and drawbacks of televising conventions?

◆ Build Vocabulary

USING THE SUFFIX -ity

The suffix -ity creates nouns that mean "the state of [the original adjective]." Write a definition for each of the following words:

1. complexity 　　2. flexibility 　　3. unanimity

USING THE WORD BANK

On your paper, match the word from the Word Bank with its definition.

1. arduous 　　 a. beneficial
2. insidious 　　 b. evident; clear
3. subjugation 　 c. deceitful; treacherous
4. vigilant 　　　 d. complete agreement
5. infallibility 　 e. succeeding generations
6. despotism 　　 f. the act of conquering
7. salutary 　　　 g. alert to danger
8. unanimity 　　 h. difficult
9. posterity 　　　 i. reliability
10. manifest 　　　 j. tyranny

◆ Grammar and Style

DOUBLE NEGATIVES

Although orators in the Revolutionary period sometimes used **double negatives** to stress their opinions, it is no longer considered acceptable to use double negatives in speaking or in writing.

Incorrect: I d*on't hardly* know where to begin. Here, the negatives are *n't* (*not*) and *hardly.* Use only one to make a negative sentence.

Correct: I don't know where to begin.

Practice On your paper, revise each sentence below that contains a double negative. If a sentence is correct, write "correct."

1. Don't sign nothing until you hear from me.
2. You don't have enough information.
3. I don't think you'll want hardly anything from me.
4. I didn't have any idea that he wouldn't show up.
5. It wouldn't make no difference to me if they cancelled the meeting.

Build Your Portfolio

Idea Bank

Writing

1. **Diary Entry** As a member of the Virginia House of Burgesses, you have just heard Henry's powerful speech. Write a diary entry in which you record your feelings.

2. **Speech** Imagine that you are a speaker in the Virginia Provincial Convention and that you do not agree with Patrick Henry. Write a speech in which you rebut each of Henry's points.

3. **Critique** According to critic Richard Beeman, Henry had a remarkable "ability to comprehend the essential meaning and import of the political issues [of the day. He was] one of the most powerful, effective, and generally constructive local politicians that America had ever produced." Using evidence from the speech, write a brief essay in which you respond to Beeman's assessment.

Speaking and Listening

4. **Dramatic Delivery** Present a dramatic reading of Henry's speech. Use appropriate hand gestures and vary the pitch and loudness of your voice.

5. **Debate** Use either speech as the subject of a debate. With a group, present arguments for and against independence or the ratification of the Constitution. **[Social Studies Link]**

Projects

6. **Display of Famous Speeches** Collect speeches from different periods of history, along with photographs or illustrations. Create a display highlighting key passages from the speeches.

7. **Multimedia Presentation** Use illustrations, maps, and music to create a multimedia presentation that brings the American Revolution to life for your class. **[Technology Link]**

Writing Mini-Lesson

Commentary on a Speech

Patrick Henry had the ability to deliver a moving speech at a moment's notice. Choose a speech by a skilled modern orator—such as Mario Cuomo, Ronald Reagan, or Jesse Jackson—and write a commentary that evaluates the way in which the speaker leads an audience to agree with his or her ideas.

Writing Skills Focus: Anticipating Questions

If you think about the questions or objections your audience may have, you can address those issues and eliminate the questions from readers' minds. Notice how Henry uses these rhetorical questions to **anticipate objections** from his audience:

Model From the Speech

And what have we to oppose to them? Shall we try argument? Sir, we have been trying that for the last ten years. Have we anything new to offer upon the subject? Nothing.

By summing up and responding to possible objections before they are voiced, Henry controls the direction his argument takes.

Prewriting Review the speech you've chosen several times to outline the speaker's key points or note the persuasive techniques the writer uses. Then critically analyze how well the speaker has supported his or her key points and how effectively he or she has used persuasive techniques.

Drafting Focus each of your paragraphs on a single point. For example, one paragraph might focus on the speaker's appeals to emotions.

Revising Anticipate your critics' questions. Review your essay as you would if someone disagreed with it. Note the points you might refute or the questions you might ask. Then go back and respond to those potential objections.

CONNECTIONS TO TODAY'S WORLD

Inaugural Address
John F. Kennedy

Thematic Connection

AMERICAN SPEECHMAKING

"Give me liberty or give me death!" "Four score and seven years ago ..." "We have nothing to fear but fear itself." "Ask not what your country can do for you, ask what you can do for your country." "I have a dream ..." All these lines from famous speeches cry out from the pages of American history, forming an important part of our nation's identity. Public speaking has been an important American tradition from the Revolutionary period to the present. Speeches provide a valuable record of the events and issues that have been pivotal in shaping our nation.

Many of our nation's most memorable speeches were delivered in difficult or troubled times. Patrick Henry's speech was delivered at a time when the colonies were on the brink of war with England. Benjamin Franklin's speech was presented during the heated struggle to forge our Constitution.

When John F. Kennedy took office in 1961, the United States was locked in a potentially explosive stalemate with the Soviet Union and its allies. Fierce adversaries, the United States and the Soviet Union were stockpiling nuclear weapons, creating the possibility of a disastrous war that could destroy the Earth. In his now-famous inaugural address, Kennedy addressed our nation's fears and reached out to our adversaries, while reaffirming our nation's strength.

Literary Connection

SPEECHES

The issues that Kennedy addresses in his speech are very different from those presented in Henry's and Franklin's speeches. However, Kennedy uses many of the same techniques as his predecessors. That's because while the world has changed tremendously since America won its independence, effective speakers still use many of the same persuasive techniques. These include rhetorical questions, or questions asked only for effect; repetition, the presentation of the same idea using the same language; the restatement of the same idea in different ways; and parallelism, the use of a repeated grammatical structure.

JOHN F. KENNEDY
(1917–1963)

Elected thirty-fifth president of the United States, John Fitzgerald Kennedy was the youngest person ever to serve in that office. The era over which Kennedy presided during his brief presidency witnessed events as diverse as the launch of the first communication satellite, Telstar, and the signing of the first nuclear non-proliferation treaty with the Soviet Union. The United States teetered on the brink of nuclear war during the Cuban missile crisis and put its first astronaut into orbit around the Earth. Tragically, Kennedy was assassinated on November 22, 1963, after serving only two years and ten months in office.

Inaugural Address

John F. Kennedy

Vice President Johnson, Mr. Speaker, Mr. Chief Justice, President Eisenhower, Vice President Nixon, President Truman,[1] *reverend clergy, fellow citizens,* we observe today not a victory of party, but a celebration of freedom—symbolizing an end, as well as a beginning—signifying renewal, as well as change. For I have sworn before you and Almighty God the same solemn oath our forebears prescribed nearly a century and three quarters ago.

The world is very different now. For man holds in his mortal hands the power to abolish all forms of human poverty and all forms of human life. And yet the same revolutionary beliefs for which our forebears fought are still at issue around the globe—the belief that the rights of man come not from the generosity of the state, but from the hand of God.

We dare not forget today that we are the <u>heirs</u> of that first revolution. Let the word go forth from this time and place, to friend and foe alike, that the torch has been passed to a new generation of Americans—born in this century, tempered by war, disciplined by a hard and bitter peace, proud of our ancient heritage—and unwilling to witness or permit the slow undoing of those human rights to which this Nation has always been committed, and to which we are committed today at home and around the world.

Let every nation know, whether it wishes us well or ill, that we shall pay any price, bear any burden, meet any hardship, support any friend, oppose any foe, in order to assure the survival and the success of liberty.

This much we pledge—and more.

To those old allies whose cultural and spiritual origins we share, we pledge the loyalty of faithful friends. United, there is little we cannot do in a host of cooperative ventures. Divided, there is little we can do—for we dare not meet a powerful challenge at odds and split asunder.[2]

Retroactive I, Robert Rauschenberg, 1964, Wadsworth Atheneum, Hartford, Connecticut
© Robert Rauschenberg/Licensed by VAGA, New York, N.Y.

▲ **Critical Viewing** What do the images in this montage—and the unfinished quality of the upper right corner—suggest about Kennedy? **[Infer]**

---

1. **Vice President . . . Truman:** Present at Kennedy's inauguration were Lyndon B. Johnson, Kennedy's vice president; 34th president Dwight D. Eisenhower and his vice president, Richard M. Nixon; and 33rd president Harry S. Truman.
2. **United . . . Divided . . . split asunder:** Kennedy echoes the famous lines from Abraham Lincoln's second inaugural address: "United we stand . . . divided we fall."

◆ **Build Vocabulary**

heirs (erz) *n*.: People who carry on the tradition of predecessors

To those new States whom we welcome to the ranks of the free, we pledge our word that one form of colonial control shall not have passed away merely to be replaced by a far more iron tyranny. We shall not always expect to find them supporting our view. But we shall always hope to find them strongly supporting their own freedom—and to remember that, in the past, those who foolishly sought power by riding the back of the tiger ended up inside.

To those peoples in the huts and villages across the globe struggling to break the bonds of mass misery, we pledge our best efforts to help them help themselves, for whatever period is required—not because the Communists may be doing it, not because we seek their votes, but because it is right. If a free society cannot help the many who are poor, it cannot save the few who are rich.

To our sister republics south of our border, we offer a special pledge—to convert our good words into good deeds—in a new alliance for progress—to assist free men and free governments in casting off the chains of poverty. But this peaceful revolution of hope cannot become the prey of hostile powers. Let all our neighbors know that we shall join with them to oppose aggression or subversion anywhere in the Americas. And let every other power know that this Hemisphere intends to remain the master of its own house.

To that world assembly of sovereign states, the United Nations, our last best hope in an age where the instruments of war have far outpaced the instruments of peace, we renew our pledge of support—to prevent it from becoming merely a forum for invective—to strengthen its shield of the new and the weak—and to enlarge the area in which its writ may run.

Finally, to those nations who would make themselves our adversary, we offer not a pledge but a request: that both sides begin anew the quest for peace, before the dark powers of destruction[3] unleashed by science engulf all humanity in planned or accidental self-destruction.

We dare not tempt them with weakness. For only when our arms are sufficient beyond doubt can be we certain beyond doubt that they will never be employed.

But neither can two great and powerful groups of nations take comfort from our present course—both sides overburdened by the cost of modern weapons, both rightly alarmed by the steady spread of the deadly atom, yet both racing to alter that uncertain balance of terror that stays the hand of mankind's final war.

So let us begin anew—remembering on both sides that civility is not a sign of weakness, and sincerity is always subject to proof. Let us never negotiate out of fear. But let us never fear to negotiate.

Let both sides explore what problems unite us instead of belaboring those problems which divide us.

Let both sides, for the first time, formulate serious and precise proposals for the inspection and control of arms—and bring the absolute power to destroy other nations under the absolute control of all nations.

Let both sides seek to invoke the wonders of science instead of its terrors. Together let us explore the stars, conquer the deserts, eradicate disease, tap the ocean depths, and encourage the arts and commerce.

Let both sides unite to heed in all corners of the earth the command of Isaiah—to "undo the heavy burdens . . . and to let the oppressed go free."[4]

> My fellow citizens of the world: Ask not what America will do for you, but what together we can do for the freedom of man.

◆ Build Vocabulary

tyranny (tir´ ə nē) *n.*: Oppressive and unjust government

alliance (ə lī´əns) *n.*: Union of nations for a specific purpose

invective (in vek´ tiv) *n.*: Verbal attack; strong criticism

adversary (ad´ vər ser´ ē) *n.*: Opponent; enemy

invoke (in vōk´) *v.*: Call on for help, inspiration, or support

eradicate (e rad´ i kāt´) *v.*: Get rid of; wipe out; destroy

---

3. **dark powers of destruction:** Nuclear war.
4. **Isaiah:** The quotation refers to the passage in Isaiah 58:6.

And if a beachhead of cooperation may push back the jungle of suspicion, let both sides join in creating a new endeavor, not a new balance of power, but a new world of law, where the strong are just and the weak secure and the peace preserved.

All this will not be finished in the first 100 days. Nor will it be finished in the first 1,000 days, nor in the life of this Administration, nor even perhaps in our lifetime on this planet. But let us begin.

In your hands, my fellow citizens, more than in mine, will rest the final success or failure of our course. Since this country was founded, each generation of Americans has been summoned to give testimony to its national loyalty. The graves of young Americans who answered the call to service surround the globe.

Now the trumpet summons us again—not as a call to bear arms, though arms we need; not as a call to battle, though embattled we are— but a call to bear the burden of a long twilight struggle, year in and year out, "rejoicing in hope, patient in tribulation"[5]—a struggle against the common enemies of man: tyranny,

poverty, disease, and war itself.

Can we forge against these enemies a grand and global alliance, North and South, East and West, that can assure a more fruitful life for all mankind? Will you join in that historic effort?

In the long history of the world, only a few generations have been granted the role of defending freedom in its hour of maximum danger. I do not shrink from this responsibility—I welcome it. I do not believe that any of us would exchange places with any other people or any other generation. The energy, the faith, the devotion which we bring to this endeavor will light our country and all who serve it—and the glow from that fire can truly light the world.

And so, my fellow Americans: Ask not what your country can do for you—ask what you can do for your country.

My fellow citizens of the world: Ask not what America will do for you, but what together we can do for the freedom of man.

Finally, whether you are citizens of America or citizens of the world, ask of us the same high standards of strength and sacrifice which we ask of you. With a good conscience our only sure reward, with history the final judge of our deeds, let us go forth to lead the land we love, asking His blessing and His help, but knowing that here on earth God's work must truly be our own.

---

5. **"rejoicing . . . tribulation":** From Romans 12:12. In Paul's letter to the Romans, he enjoins people to work together in love and mutual respect.

Guide for Responding

◆ Literature and Your Life

Reader's Response Which lines or phrases from Kennedy's speech do you find most memorable? Why? Which have you heard quoted elsewhere?

Thematic Focus What does Kennedy's speech reveal about the time in which it was delivered?

☑ Check Your Comprehension

1. What is the "end, as well as a beginning" to which Kennedy refers?
2. List two specific pledges Kennedy makes.

◆ Critical Thinking

INTERPRET
1. Why does Kennedy make reference to the founders of the country? **[Infer]**
2. What do the "new generation of Americans" have in common with the Revolutionary colonists? **[Compare]**
3. What strategy does Kennedy defend with "We dare not tempt . . . with weakness"? **[Interpret]**
4. What do you think Kennedy saw as the country's greatest challenge? **[Draw Conclusions]**

EXTEND
5. Locate evidence in this speech to prove that Kennedy believed in volunteerism. **[Social Studies Link]**

Thematic Connection

AMERICAN SPEECHMAKING

You may not consider yourself an audience for speechmakers, but modern media, especially television, has put speakers and audiences in closer contact today than ever before in history. Even the most casual channel surfer will encounter news clips from speeches at fund-raisers or political gatherings or the floor of the legislature. In fact, in this age of instant news, some speakers anticipate a reporter's need for brief quotations and include succinct phrases for the "sound bites" that will appear in newscasts.

1. (a) What expectations do you have when listening to a political speaker? (b) How does Kennedy's speech fulfill those expectations?

2. (a) How does setting—the Oval Office, the steps of the Capitol, or the halls of Congress—affect the way a speech is received? (b) How would Kennedy's speech be different if it were presented as a radio address?

3. How does Kennedy's speech compare with other political speeches you've heard or seen?

Literary Connection

SPEECHES

American leaders have delivered speeches to announce new beginnings, calm a worried public, or set a firm stance against our enemies. For some speakers, the style of the message is just as important as the message itself. A carefully turned phrase, a memorable line, or the slightest hint of poetry can make a speech more moving. Other persuasive techniques include parallelism, the repeated use of a grammatical structure; repetition, the presentation of the same idea using the same language; and the restatement of an idea in different ways.

1. For each of the following lines from Kennedy's speech, identify the technique used.
   a. If a free society cannot help the many who are poor, it cannot save the few who are rich.
   b. Let us never negotiate out of fear. But let us never fear to negotiate.

2. Choose one of the two preceding passages. Then write two sentences of your own that follow the pattern Kennedy used in that passage.

 Idea Bank

Writing

1. **Summation** Recall an effective speech that you have heard. Write an essay that sums up the main ideas the speaker expressed.

2. **Research Writing** Use the Internet to find the transcript, audio, or video of another president's inaugural speech. Read or listen carefully and compare the one you choose with the speeches of Kennedy, Franklin, and Henry. Sum up your findings in a brief essay. **[Technology Link]**

3. **Comparative Essay** Compare Kennedy's oratorical skills with those of either Franklin or Henry. Decide what elements are unique to each speaker's style and clarify points of contrast. End by offering your opinion on which man was the better speech writer. Back up your opinion with details from the two speeches.

Speaking and Listening

4. **Volunteerism Survey** Kennedy's belief in humanity's ability to help one another was the driving force behind the founding of the Peace Corps. Find out about volunteer opportunities in your community. To learn what attracts people to their work, interview people who volunteer. Collate their responses and share your findings with your class. **[Community Link]**

Projects

5. **Video Record** Put together a videotape of a program of student speakers or a local community meeting. Edit the recording to illustrate effective speechmaking techniques the speakers have used. Present your edited video to the class and invite their critiques. **[Technology Link]**

Writing Process Workshop

What comes to mind when you hear the word **speech**? The science talk on black holes that fired your imagination? Martin Luther King at the Washington Monument, searing the conscience of a nation? Or, Patrick Henry changing the course of history? These are examples of oratory at its best: combining the power of the word and the drama of the human voice to inform, entertain, persuade, inspire.

Most of the speeches you are likely to encounter—television sales pitches, campaign talks, or Patrick Henry's address to the Virginia legislature—seek to persuade. Speeches can be just as effective in educating and informing, however. The following skills will help you to deliver an effective informative speech.

Writing Skills Focus

▶ **Anticipate questions** by considering your likely audience and listing the questions that your listeners are likely to have. Try to answer as many of these questions as possible. (See p. 175.)

▶ **Use transitional words and phrases** to make clear connections among your ideas.

▶ **Check the accuracy** of the facts you are reporting.

Patrick Henry Before the Virginia House of Burgesses, (detail), Peter F. Rothermel, Red Hill, the Patrick Henry National Memorial

WRITING MODEL

Imagine learning that your only hope for survival is a heart transplant! ① In the United States, your chances of finding a heart for transplant are the best in the world. Yet ② you have no guarantees: Last year 52,000 people waited for organ transplants, but only 19,410 were actually performed. Consider your quandary, then, if you lived in Japan, where a stricter definition of the moment of death has led to a shortage of donated organs. The result: ③ Each year, hundreds of Japanese lives are lost.

④ What exactly is the difference in the way Japan and the Western countries define the end of life?

① The writer immediately grabs the listeners, using their imaginations to place them in a suspenseful situation.

② The speaker leads into a statistic with a transitional word.

③ The speaker maintains a conversational tone by varying the length of sentences.

④ The speaker anticipates listeners' questions and thereby fastens on the main topic.

Applying LANGUAGE SKILLS: Misplaced or Dangling Modifiers

A modifying word or phrase should be placed as close as possible to the modified words in order to avoid confusing or even unintentionally comical results.

Misplaced Modifier:

Entering the main exhibition hall, the dinosaur display was breath-taking. (dangling participle)

Corrected:

Entering the main exhibition hall, we found the dinosaur display breathtaking.

Notice that the participle "entering," which absurdly seems to modify "dinosaur display" in the first sentence, correctly modifies "we" in the corrected version.

Practice On your paper, correct the following misplaced modifiers.

1. Careening down the ski slope, a tree suddenly appeared directly in my path.

2. The mechanic said that he only works on weekdays.

3. Yesterday we heard a fascinating lecture about quasars in the auditorium.

Writing Application Review your informative speech for any misplaced or dangling modifiers, and correct them by placing them as close as possible to the word or words they modify.

Prewriting

Choose a Topic You can't fake interest or enthusiasm: If you're not genuinely interested in your topic, you will likely have an audience of squirmy clock-watchers. Make a list of topics that really interest you, that you'd like to know more about, and that you would enjoy sharing with others. Keep in mind that your informative speech is really an expository essay adapted to the spoken word, so a wide array of topical categories are suitable: comparison and contrast, problem and solution, cause and effect, consumer report, or summary.

> ## Topic Ideas
> - Dog-training techniques
> - The history of women's professional basketball
> - Skiing: pleasures and dangers
> - The effect of pollution on global warming
> - Summary of a favorite novel or movie
> - Personal guide to local hiking trails

Research Your Topic Unless your topic is something in which you already possess considerable expertise (say, skiing or hiking), you will have to gather enough material to make your presentation truly informative to your listeners. Don't stint on research: Be sure your listeners will really learn something from your talk.

Drafting

Organize Your Ideas Decide whether it's best to develop your ideas chronologically or in order of importance.

Decide Between Note Cards and Writing Out the Text Speeches that are read verbatim from a text often have a stiff, inexpressive quality. Consider the possibility of jotting down your key ideas on note cards and expanding on your notes informally as you give your talk.

Think of a Snappy Opening Most often you will either win or lose your audience in the first few minutes of your speech. A snappy, lively opening is crucial in "hooking" your audience. If appropriate to the topic, a time-tested way to engage your listeners is to open with a joke or humorous anecdote.

Use a Varied Rhythm and Structure Avoid a monotonous, sing-song delivery that will lull your listeners into dreamland. It's equally important to vary sentence length, although shorter sentences, even the occasional fragment, work best in oral presentations.

Practice Tape yourself, stand in front of a mirror, or ask someone to listen to your speech.

Revising

As you revise your speech following your rehearsal, ask yourself these questions:

- ▶ Are my ideas presented clearly and logically?
- ▶ Did I "hook" my listeners with a lively opening?
- ▶ Did I use transitional words and phrases?
- ▶ Did I vary the length of my sentences?
- ▶ Have I anticipated my listeners' questions?

REVISION MODEL

Many Japanese believe that death occurs when the heart

stops beating, whereas Western medicine defines death as ① . In contrast,

the moment when the brain stops functioning, even if the

heart is still beating with the help of a respirator, an outlook ② . This

that makes it easier to obtain healthy, functioning organs for

transplant to others. ③ other patients whose lives hang in the balance.

① ② The speaker breaks up two longer sentences into shorter ones with transitional phrases to make the speech easier to follow.

③ This insertion of punchier, more emotive language enlivens the presentation.

Publishing

Deliver Your Speech As you deliver your speech, vary the volume and tone of your voice to emphasize key ideas. In addition, use hand gestures as a means of reinforcing your ideas. Try to avoid focusing your eyes on a single person. Instead, scan your audience, trying to meet as many eyes as possible.

APPLYING LANGUAGE SKILLS: Using Transitions

Transitional words or phrases can help you make your writing more coherent by clarifying various kinds of relationships among ideas: in time, space, order of importance, cause and effect, comparison and contrast, or example.

No Transition: Flying is the fastest way of getting there. Taking the train allows you to see the country close up.

Transition: Flying is the fastest way of getting there, but taking the train allows you to see the country close up.

The addition of "but" drives home the contrast between the two forms of travel.

Practice On your paper, join the following ideas with the appropriate transitional word or phrase.

1. Vicky is a talented singer. Yolanda is a more versatile performer.
2. The frost was severe. The orange crop is in danger.
3. A serious hobby can be very satisfying. Marco enjoys building furniture in his workshop.

Writing Application As you draft your informative speech, look for relationships between ideas that could be clarified through the use of transitional words or phrases.

Strategies for Success

From presidential elections to a proposition funding skateboard parks, political candidates and political issues surround you. Messages seeking your support appear in magazines, on television and billboards, or on radio. It's important to evaluate these messages before taking action.

Recognize the Purpose Understand that political messages are persuasive—writers want you to agree with the message and perhaps take action supporting it. Keep this knowledge in mind as you read.

Evaluate the Message Thoroughly review the facts and the positions stated in the message. Use strategies like these to guide your evaluation:

- ▶ Find the facts and the opinions in the message.
- ▶ Look for evidence supporting persuasive statements.
- ▶ Stay alert for mud-slinging, which makes unsupported or biased claims about the opposing candidate or view, especially about a candidate's personal life.
- ▶ Identify emotional appeals contained in the message.

Implementing Your Evaluation Decide whether or not you believe the claims in the message. You can do research to verify or disprove any claims that seem questionable. Consider your judgment about the political message as you choose to support or oppose the candidate or issue.

Apply the Strategy

It's voting time again! Whom should you support in the school election? The hallways are plastered with posters for the two major candidates. Evaluate the message of this one.

1. What is the purpose of the poster at left? Explain.

2. List examples of facts and opinions in the poster.

3. How is the overall message supported by evidence?

4. How is the message negatively biased against the candidate's opponent? Cite at least one example of mud-slinging.

One Good Year Deserves Another!

Reelect

Jennifer Morales

STUDENT BODY PRESIDENT

Choose the best-qualified candidate for a better future for your school:

✓**Progress:**
- Expanded student role in school policy decisions

✓**Concern:**
- Established monthly student government open house to hear student concerns

✓**Honesty:**
- Provided to students a written record of all student government sessions and votes

✓**Achievements:**
- Honor student for the third straight year
- Editor of the school newspaper
- Tutor for students with special needs

Unlike her opponent, Morales knows how to do more than just talk about accomplishing things—she know's how to get them done!

If you don't want a slacker as your student body president, remember to

VOTE MORALES ON ELECTION DAY!!

✔ *Here are other situations in which it's important to evaluate political messages:*
- ▶ *Community elections*
- ▶ *National political campaigns*

PART **3**

Defining an American

Eighteenth-century New England needlework
Colonial Williamsburg Foundation

The colonial victory in the Revolutionary War brought
about the creation of a nation unlike any other. While the
young nation was busy devising a new government and
designing new currency, writers, including those in this
section, tackled the task of defining what it means to be
an American. The definitions that emerged include many
of the characteristics that Americans still use in defining
themselves today.

Guide for Interpreting

Benjamin Franklin (1706–1790)

From his teen years until his retirement at forty-two, Benjamin Franklin worked as a printer. Franklin got his start as an apprentice to his brother, a Boston printer. By the time he was sixteen, he was not only printing, but writing parts of his brother's newspaper. Using the name "Silence Dogood," Franklin satirized daily life and politics in Boston. His printing career gave birth to one of Franklin's most popular and enduring contributions to American culture, *Poor Richard's Almanack*. This annual publication, which Franklin published from 1732 through 1757, contained information, observations, and advice that was very popular with readers of his day.

The "Write" Reputation

Just as he had signed "Silence Dogood" to the letters he wrote for his brother's paper, Franklin created for the *Almanack* a fictitious author/editor, the chatty Richard Saunders (and his wife, Bridget). It was, however, well known that Franklin was the author. Despite the fact that he published under a pseudonym, the *Almanack* earned him a reputation as a talented writer.

Secret to Success

Like most almanacs, Franklin's contained practical information about the calendar, the sun and moon, and the weather.

Poor Richard's Almanack also featured a wealth of homespun sayings and observations, many of which are still quoted today.

It was these aphorisms, with their characteristic moral overtones, that made the *Almanack* a bestseller. Franklin put an aphorism at the top or bottom of most pages of his almanacs. The wit and brevity of these sayings allowed Franklin to include many moral messages in very little space, while also entertaining his readers.

Franklin sold the almanac in 1758, and it continued publication under a different name until 1796. While *Poor Richard's Almanack* is no longer with us, the aphorisms that enlivened its pages under Franklin live on as classic bits of Americana. (For more on Benjamin Franklin, see pp. 128 and 166.)

◆ Background for Understanding

SOCIAL STUDIES: THE PROVERB TRADITION

Most of Benjamin Franklin's aphorisms are adapted from anonymous traditional or folk sayings, known as **proverbs.** Franklin, who believed that clarity and brevity were two of the most important characteristics of good prose, rewrote many proverbs, crafting short, direct, witty sayings that taught a lesson.

Proverbs are nearly as old as language itself. They have many different purposes and are used in different types of situations—to amuse, to educate, to sanction, to shame, to make a point, or to add color to a conversation.

As expressions of basic principles of folk wisdom drawn from the daily experiences of a group of people, proverbs exist in all societies. They reflect a particular culture's view of the world and convey feelings about fate, the seasons, the natural world, work and effort, love, death, and other universal experiences. These memorable bits of wisdom have survived centuries, perhaps because they reflect unchanging truths about human nature.

from Poor Richard's Almanack

◆ Literature and Your Life

CONNECT YOUR EXPERIENCE

"No pain, no gain." "Garbage In, Garbage Out." You see sayings like these on bumper stickers, T-shirts, and billboards. Though such snippets of pop-wisdom are more likely to originate in entertainment media than an almanac, they mirror modern social values, just as Franklin's aphorisms reflect the values of colonial America.

Journal Writing Think of at least three contemporary aphorisms. What do they say about our culture? Write your answers in your journal.

THEMATIC FOCUS: DEFINING AN AMERICAN

Franklin's aphorisms were so influential that even this early United States coin was stamped "mind your business," a motto supposedly suggested by Franklin. His sayings helped shape the nation's image as a country of people who prized hard work and common sense.

◆ Grammar and Style

IRREGULAR COMPARISON OF ADJECTIVES AND ADVERBS

While most adjectives and adverbs use -er or more/less to form the comparative, and -est or most/least to form the superlative, some have **irregular** forms. Notice the comparative form of well in this sentence:

Well done is better than well said. . .

Better is the irregular comparative of the adverb well. If the aphorism compared a third item, the irregular superlative best would have been used:

. . . but best of all is well fed.

◆ Build Vocabulary

WORDS WITH MULTIPLE MEANINGS

The Almanack says, "He that lives upon hope will die fasting." In this context, fasting has little to do with speed. Fasting is the gerund formed from the verb fast, which means "to eat little or nothing." The adverb fast can also mean "firmly" or "thoroughly," as in "fast asleep."

WORD BANK

Preview this list of words from the Almanack.

| fasting |
| squander |

◆ Literary Focus

APHORISMS

You may find that you are already familiar with many of the witty sayings, or aphorisms, from *Poor Richard's Almanack*. An **aphorism** is a short, concise statement expressing a wise or clever observation or a general truth. A variety of devices make aphorisms easy to remember. Some contain rhymes or repeated words or sounds; others use parallel structure to present contrasting ideas. The aphorism "no pain, no gain," for instance, uses rhyme, repetition, and parallel structure.

◆ Reading Strategy

RELATE TO YOUR EXPERIENCES

Though these eighteenth-century aphorisms may at first appear to have little relevance to your world, careful reading reveals meanings that you can **relate to your own experiences**. By definition, aphorisms—like most literature—contain observations about human nature that are just as true today as they were centuries ago. Increase your understanding of what you read by asking yourself how the meaning of each aphorism applies to experiences you've had.

from Poor Richard's Almanack

Benjamin Franklin

Poor Richard's Almanack, The Granger Collection, New York

Poor Richard, 1733.

AN

Almanack

For the Year of Christ

1733,

Being the First after LEAP YEAR:

And makes since the Creation — Years

By the Account of the Eastern *Greeks* — 7241
By the Latin Church, when ☉ ent. ♈ — 6932
By the Computation of *W.W.* — 5742
By the *Roman* Chronology — 5682
By the *Jewish* Rabbies — 5494

Wherein is contained

The Lunations, Eclipses, Judgment of the Weather, Spring Tides, Planets Motions & mutual Aspects, Sun and Moon's Rising and Setting, Length of Days, Time of High Water, Fairs, Courts, and observable Days. Fitted to the Latitude of Forty Degrees, and a Meridian of Five Hours West from *London,* but may without sensible Error, serve all the adjacent Places, even from *Newfoundland* to South-Carolina.

By *RICHARD SAUNDERS,* Philom.

PHILADELPHIA:

Printed and sold by *B. FRANKLIN,* at the New Printing-Office near the Market.

▲ **Critical Viewing** In the byline, after Benjamin Franklin's pseudonym, Richard Saunders, is the title "Philom.," short for philomath. Use your knowledge of word roots to infer the meaning of the word philomath. [Speculate]

Fools make feasts, and wise men eat them.

⋙

Be slow in choosing a friend, slower in changing.

⋙

Keep thy shop, and thy shop will keep thee.

⋙

Early to bed, early to rise, makes a man healthy, wealthy, and wise.

⋙

Three may keep a secret if two of them are dead.

⋙

God helps them that help themselves.

⋙

The rotten apple spoils his companions.

⋙

An open foe may prove a curse; but a pretended friend is worse.

⋙⋙

Have you somewhat to do tomorrow, do it today.

⋙

A true friend is the best possession.

⋙

A small leak will sink a great ship.

⋙

No gains without pains.

⋙

'Tis easier to prevent bad habits than to break them.

⋙

Well done is better than well said.

Dost thou love life? Then do not squander time; for
    that's the stuff life is made of.

※

Write injuries in dust, benefits in marble.

※

A slip of the foot you may soon recover, but a
    slip of the tongue you may never get over.

※

If your head is wax, don't walk in the sun.

※

A good example is the best sermon.

※

Hunger is the best pickle.

※

Genius without education is like silver in the mine.

※

For want of a nail the shoe is lost; for want of
    a shoe the horse is lost; for want of a horse
    the rider is lost.

※

Haste makes waste.

※

The doors of wisdom are never shut.

※

Love your neighbor; yet don't pull down your hedge.

※

He that lives upon hope will die fasting.

Guide for Responding

◆ Literature and Your Life

Reader's Response Which of Franklin's
aphorisms have friends or family members quoted?

Thematic Focus Which of Franklin's aphorisms
express values that are still widely held in America?

Group Activity Ask your classmates to share
ethnic or cultural proverbs they may have learned
from family members or friends. Write them on the
chalkboard and label the country of origin for each.
Do any reflect the same values as Franklin's?

☑ Check Your Comprehension

1. What does Ben Franklin say is "the best possession"?
2. Identify two aphorisms that address education.
3. What advice does Franklin offer about breaking
bad habits?
4. Paraphrase three of the aphorisms presented
here.

Guide for Responding (continued)

◆ Critical Thinking

INTERPRET

1. Explain the connection between the aphorisms "Be slow in choosing a friend, slower in changing" and "Write injuries in dust, benefits in marble." **[Connect]**
2. In your own words, state at least two recurring themes apparent in Franklin's aphorisms. **[Analyze]**
3. Based on these aphorisms, how would you describe Franklin's approach to life? **[Infer]**

APPLY

4. If you had to select one aphorism from *Poor Richard's Almanack* as a motto for your life, which would you choose and why? **[Relate]**

◆ Literary Focus

APHORISMS

Franklin uses repetition, parallelism, and rhyme to make the observations expressed in these **aphorisms** more memorable.

1. For each of the following aphorisms, identify Franklin's technique(s), then state the meaning of the aphorism:
   a. "A slip of the foot you may soon recover, but a slip of the tongue you may never get over."
   b. "Early to bed and early to rise, makes a man healthy, wealthy, and wise."
2. Explain why an aphorism has more of an impact than the simple statement of its meaning.
3. Using Franklin's techniques, write an aphorism for contemporary life.

◆ Reading Strategy

RELATE TO YOUR EXPERIENCES

If reading the aphorism "A good example is the best sermon" made you think of how your aunt's charity work inspired you to volunteer as a tutor, you were **relating to your experiences** as you read. Select an aphorism from *Poor Richard's Almanack* that struck a chord with you and explain how it relates to a situation or observation from your own life.

◆ Build Vocabulary

USING WORDS WITH MULTIPLE MEANINGS

Fast, wax, and *hedge* are three words from *Poor Richard's Almanack* that have more than one meaning.

Wax: a substance used in candles; *or* to grow larger gradually

Hedge: a fence of greenery; *or* to avoid answering directly; *or* to try to minimize loss by making counterbalancing bets or investments

In your notebook, write the synonym for the italicized word(s) in each sentence.

1. If the moon continues to *wax* in size, we will be able to read by moonlight in two days.
   (a) remain, (b) shrink, (c) grow
2. He was about to *avoid answering* when he changed his mind and replied truthfully.
   (a) fast, (b) hedge, (c) wax

USING THE WORD BANK

1. If your little brother regularly *squanders* his allowance, would he have much money saved?
2. Would a person who has been *fasting* for several days be saving money on meals?

◆ Grammar and Style

IRREGULAR COMPARISON OF ADJECTIVES AND ADVERBS

Since there are no rules for comparison of **irregular modifiers,** it's best to learn the most common ones:

good/well, better, best   little, less, least
bad, worse, worst   much/many, more, most

Writing Application Rewrite the following paragraph, substituting the appropriate adjective or adverb for the phrase in parentheses.

Benjamin Franklin, one of America's (superlative of well)-loved founding fathers, has left us with aphorisms that are far (comparative of well) known than the almanac in which they appeared. While Franklin satirized the (superlative of bad) in human nature, he also saw the (comparative of good) aspects of humankind.

Build Your Portfolio

Idea Bank

Writing

1. Personal Narrative Write an account of an episode or situation from your life that relates to one of Franklin's aphorisms. Summarize what you learned from the experience.

2. Magazine Article Write a how-to article on successful friendships. Include suggestions for keeping good friends. Use at least four of Franklin's aphorisms to support your points.

3. Folk Tale Write an original folk tale or fable illustrating an aphorism from the *Almanack*.

Speaking and Listening

4. Rap Write and perform a rap using one or more of Franklin's aphorisms. Your lyrics should illustrate the message behind the aphorism(s) you choose. **[Performing Arts Link]**

5. Oral Presentation Locate proverbs from around the world. Ask friends familiar with their heritage to share proverbs native to their cultures. Do you notice similar themes recurring in different cultures? Share your findings in an oral presentation. **[Social Studies Link]**

Projects

6. Instruction Manual Create a manual called "Poor Richard's Guide to Living Well." Refer to a complete collection of *Almanack* aphorisms. Group related aphorisms under headings, such as "Words on Running a Business" and "Making the Most of Each Day." Introduce each section with a summary of Poor Richard's advice on the topic.

7. Board Game Create a game based on the *Almanack*. Design game rules and a playing board. One possible approach: Make game cards labeled by subject, such as Friendship and Education.

Writing Mini-Lesson

Internet Page for Aphorisms

Imagine that you have been assigned to develop an aphorisms Web page geared to teens. Write an engaging introduction to the *Almanack* aphorisms, then create two or three links, such as "Poor Richard on Friendship," that a user could click on to view aphorisms related to a subject.

Writing Skills Focus: Style Appropriate to Medium

To write for the Internet, select a writing **style appropriate to the medium** by considering how people get information from various media. The way in which a medium delivers news—or any information—to its audience determines its style:
- *Radio:* key facts communicated quickly in concise, vivid language
- *Television:* copy explains or supplements visual images and video footage
- *News magazine:* in-depth coverage examines many aspects of a story

As you draft your Web page, remember that the *people* getting the information and *how* they get it should determine your style.

Prewriting Use your knowledge of your audience to determine how best to present Franklin's aphorisms. Review the aphorisms, decide which links to include, name the links, then choose aphorisms to list under each.

Drafting Consider how people use the Internet—they scan quickly to decide whether a page interests them. Create an interesting and informative page.

Revising Make sure that every aspect of your writing style is geared to the fast pace of the Internet. Would you be tempted to click on these links? Rework any weak spots you identify.

Guide for Interpreting

Abigail Smith Adams
(1744–1818)

Wife, mother, writer, first lady, revolutionary, women's rights pioneer—Abigail Smith Adams was all these and more. As the intelligent, outspoken wife of John Adams, the second president of the United States, and the mother of John Quincy Adams, the sixth president, Abigail Adams was one of the most influential American women of her time.

John Adams's political duties during and after the Revolution kept him from home for the better part of ten years. Abigail, therefore, became an avid correspondent, penning hundreds of letters to her husband and relatives, discussing everything from women's rights to her opposition to slavery. During the war, she even kept her husband posted on the movements of British troops.

When John Adams was elected president of the United States, he and Abigail became the first couple to live in the White House. This letter to her daughter, which describes their temporary home, captures the essence of life in the new nation.

Twenty-two years after Abigail Adams's death, her letters were published. Today, she is widely recognized as a pioneer of the American women's movement.

Michel-Guillaume Jean de Crèvecoeur
(1735–1813)

The first writer to compare America to a melting pot, French aristocrat Michel-Guillaume Jean de Crèvecoeur (mē shel′ gē yôm zhän də krev koer′) chronicled his experiences as a European immigrant in America. His idealistic descriptions confirmed many people's vision of America as a land of great promise.

After spending ten years traveling the colonies, Crèvecoeur married and settled on a farm in Orange County, New York, where he began writing about his experiences in America. In 1780, he sailed to London, where his *Letters From an American Farmer* was published two years later. This book, which was translated into several languages, made Crèvecoeur famous.

After visiting France, he returned to America in 1783 as a French Consul to find his farm burned, his wife killed, and his children sent to live with foster parents. When the French Revolution began in 1789, he was obliged to return to Paris. He later fled to Normandy, where he continued to write about the adoptive country he would never again see.

◆ Background for Understanding

HISTORY: CRÈVECOEUR'S AMERICA IDEALIZED

When Michel-Guillaume Jean de Crèvecoeur published *Letters From an American Farmer*, he captured the imagination of downtrodden Europeans hungry for a better life. Life in America, however, was far from idyllic, but that was not what Europeans wanted to hear.

Because the country needed hard workers, not those seeking an easy life, it is no wonder that some American leaders worried about the effects of Crèvecoeur's glowing descriptions. George Washington called the *Letters* "rather too flattering," and the wise and witty Ben Franklin responded by writing and publishing (first in France) *Advice to Such as Would Remove to America* in 1784. Franklin begins by warning that even though "there are in that country few people so miserable as the poor of Europe," neither are there many rich. "America is a land of labor," he continues, and what it needs are dedicated, skilled workers. Those interested in a life of leisure need not apply.

Letter to Her Daughter From the New White House
◆ *from* Letters From an American Farmer ◆

◆ *Literature and Your Life*

CONNECT YOUR EXPERIENCE

When you want to get in touch with a friend, you probably pick up the phone or send an e-mail. In our high-tech world, fewer and fewer people reach for pen and paper. Not too long ago, however, letters were the only means of communicating over distances.

Journal Writing How might your life change if letter writing were the only communication option available to you?

THEMATIC FOCUS: DEFINING AN AMERICAN

Letters were the lifeline through which early Americans sent and received personal, professional, and political information. In a country founded on free thought, letters were an important means of sharing ideas and opinions with both private and public readers. What do the letters of Crèvecoeur and Adams tell us about what it meant to be an American during our nation's early years?

◆ Build Vocabulary

WORD ORIGINS: ETYMOLOGIES

The word *extricate* comes from the Latin *extricare* meaning "disentangle"—a definition closely related to the meaning of *extricate*: set free or disengage. You can learn how words evolved by using a dictionary that shows etymologies, or word histories.

WORD BANK

Before you read, preview this list of words from the letters.

> extricate
> agues
> asylum
> penury
> despotic
> subsistence

◆ Grammar and Style

SEMICOLONS

The **semicolon (;)** joins independent clauses that have a close relationship to each other and are not already joined by a conjunction (*and, but, for, nor, or, so,* or *yet*). Both Adams and Crèvecoeur make frequent use of semicolons—with and without conjunctions:

> The American is a new man, who acts upon new principles; he must therefore entertain new ideas, and form new opinions.

◆ Literary Focus

PRIVATE AND PUBLIC LETTERS (EPISTLES)

Personal or **private letters,** like Adams's, tend to be conversational and intended only for the reader(s) to whom they are addressed. Crèvecoeur's *Letters*, on the other hand, while supposedly written by an American farmer named James to his friend Mr. F. B., are actually public letters intended for a wide audience. Called **epistles,** these works of literature are created for general publication but written in the form of personal letters.

◆ Reading Strategy

DISTINGUISH BETWEEN FACT AND OPINION

Crèvecoeur had an idealistic view of life in America, and his writing is colored by this opinion. To avoid being too easily swayed by writers, distinguish **facts**—statements that can be proven—from **opinions**—personal beliefs that cannot be proven. Look at these examples:

> *Fact:* Upstairs there is the oval room, which is designed for the drawing room . . .

> *Opinion:* It is a very handsome room now; but, when complete, it will be beautiful.

A good persuasive writer uses facts to provide support for his or her opinions.

BUILDING THE FIRST WHITE HOUSE

WASHINGTON D.C. 1798

Building the First White House, N. C. Wyeth, White House Historical Association

▲ **Critical Viewing** How might Abigail Adams have reacted to this scene? **[Speculate]**

Letter to Her Daughter From the New White House

Abigail Adams

Washington, 21 November, 1800

My Dear Child:

I arrived here on Sunday last, and without meeting with any accident worth noticing, except losing ourselves when we left Baltimore and going eight or nine miles on the Frederick road, by which means we were obliged to go the other eight through woods, where we wandered two hours without finding a guide or the path. Fortunately, a straggling black came up with us, and we engaged him as a guide to extricate us out of our difficulty; but woods are all you see from Baltimore until you reach *the city,* which is only so in name. Here and there is a small cot, without a glass window, interspersed amongst the forests, through which you travel miles without seeing any human being. In the city there are buildings enough, if they were compact and finished, to accommodate Congress and those attached to it; but as they are, and scattered as they are, I see no great comfort for them. The river, which runs up to Alexandria,[1] is in full view of my window, and I see the vessels as they pass and repass. The house is upon a grand and superb scale, requiring about thirty servants to attend and keep the apartments in proper order, and perform the ordinary business of the house and stables; an establishment very well proportioned to the President's salary. The lighting of the apartments, from the kitchen to parlors and chambers, is a tax indeed; and the fires we are obliged to keep to secure us from daily agues is another very cheering comfort. To assist us in this great castle, and render less attendance necessary, bells are wholly wanting, not one single one being hung through the whole house, and promises are all you can obtain. This is so great an inconvenience, that I know not what to do, or how to do. The ladies from Georgetown[2] and in the city have many of them visited me. Yesterday I returned fifteen visits—but such a place as Georgetown appears—why, our Milton is beautiful.

But no comparisons—if they will put me up some bells and let me have wood enough to keep fires, I design to be pleased. I could content myself almost anywhere three months; but, surrounded with forests, can you believe that wood is not to be had because people cannot be found to cut and cart it? Briesler entered into a contract with a man to supply him with wood. A small part, a

---

1. **Alexandria:** City in northeastern Virginia.

2. **Georgetown:** Section of Washington, D.C.

◆ **Build Vocabulary**

extricate (eks´ trə kāt´) *v.*: Set free

agues (ā´ gyo̅o̅z) *n.*: Fits of shivering

few cords only, has he been able to get. Most of that was expended to dry the walls of the house before we came in, and yesterday the man told him it was impossible for him to procure it to be cut and carted. He has had recourse to coals; but we cannot get grates made and set. We have, indeed, come into a *new country.*

You must keep all this to yourself, and, when asked how I like it, say that I write you the situation is beautiful, which is true. The house is made habitable, but there is not a single apartment finished, and all withinside, except the plastering, has been done since Briesler came. We have not the least fence, yard, or other convenience without and the great unfinished audience room I make a drying-room of, to hang up the clothes in. The principal stairs are not up, and will not be this winter. Six chambers are made comfortable; two are occupied by the President and Mr. Shaw; two lower rooms, one for a common parlor, and one for a levee room. Upstairs there is the oval room, which is designed for the drawing room, and has the crimson furniture in it. It is a very handsome room now; but, when completed, it will be beautiful. If the twelve years, in which this place has been considered as the future seat of government had been improved, as they would have been if in New England, very many of the present inconveniences would have been removed. It is a beautiful spot, capable of every improvement, and, the more I view it, the more I am delighted with it.

Since I sat down to write, I have been called down to a servant from Mount Vernon,[3] with a billet[4] from Major Custis, and a haunch of venison, and a kind, congratulatory letter from Mrs. Lewis, upon my arrival in the city, with Mrs. Washington's love, inviting me to Mount Vernon, where, health permitting, I will go before I leave this place.

Affectionately, your mother,
Abigail Adams

---

3. **Mount Vernon:** Home of George Washington, located in northern Virginia.
4. **billet** (bil′ it) *n.*: Brief letter.

Guide for Responding

◆ Literature and Your Life

Reader's Response What, if anything, surprised you about Adams's description of the White House and the area around Washington, D.C.?

Thematic Focus How does Adams's letter help us appreciate the challenges that faced our nation's first leaders as they strove to establish a centralized national government?

☑ Check Your Comprehension

1. How does Adams describe the city of Washington and its surroundings?
2. Describe the state of the living quarters in the White House.

◆ Critical Thinking

INTERPRET

1. Why do you think Adams tells her daughter not to share her complaints with anyone? **[Infer]**
2. How would you characterize Adams's feelings about her new home? **[Classify]**

EVALUATE

3. Adams lived in an age when the ability to write an entertaining, informative letter was highly prized. Would you describe Adams as a good letter writer? Explain your answer. **[Evaluate; Support]**

from

Letters From an American Farmer

Michel-Guillaume Jean de Crèvecoeur

Independence (Squire Jack Porter), 1858, Frank Blackwell Mayer, National Museum of American Art, Smithsonian Institution

▲ **Critical Viewing** How does this painting relate to Crèvecoeur's *Letters From an American Farmer*? **[Connect]**

In this great American asylum, the poor of Europe have by some means met together, and in consequence of various causes; to what purpose should they ask one another what countrymen they are? Alas, two thirds of them had no country. Can a wretch who wanders about, who works and starves, whose life is a continual scene of sore affliction or pinching penury, can that man call England or any other kingdom his country? A country that had no bread for him, whose fields procured him no harvest, who met with nothing but the frowns of the rich, the severity of the laws, with jails and punishments; who owned not a single foot of the extensive surface of this planet? No! Urged by a variety of motives, here they came. Everything has tended to regenerate them; new laws, a new mode of living, a new social system; here they are become men: in Europe they were as so many useless plants, wanting vegetative mold[1] and refreshing showers; they withered, and were mowed down by want, hunger, and war; but now by the power of transplantation, like all other plants they have taken root and flourished!

Formerly they were not numbered in any civil lists[2] of their country, except in those of the poor; here they rank as citizens. By what invisible power has this surprising metamorphosis been performed? By that of the laws and that of their industry. The laws, the indulgent laws, protect them as they arrive, stamping on them the symbol of adoption; they receive ample rewards for their labors; these accumulated rewards procure them lands; those lands confer on them the title of freemen, and to that title every benefit is affixed which men can possibly require. This is the great operation daily performed by our laws. From whence proceed these laws? From our government. Whence the government? It is derived from the original genius and strong desire of the people ratified and confirmed by the crown. . . .

What attachment can a poor European emigrant have for a country where he had nothing? The knowledge of the language, the love of a few kindred as poor as himself, were the only cords that tied him: his country is now that which gives him land, bread, protection, and consequence: *Ubi panis ibi patria*[3] is the motto of all emigrants. What then is the American, this new man? He is either a European, or the descendant of a European, hence that strange mixture of blood, which you will find in no other country. I could point out to you a family whose grandfather was an Englishman, whose wife was Dutch, whose son married a French woman, and whose present four sons have now four wives of different nations. *He* is an American, who, leaving behind him all his ancient prejudices and manners, receives new ones from the new mode of life he has embraced, the new government he obeys, and the new rank he holds. He becomes an American by being received in the broad lap of our great *Alma Mater*.[4] Here individuals of all nations are melted into a new race of men, whose labors and posterity will one day cause great changes in the world. Americans are the west-

---

1. **vegetative mold:** Enriched soil.
2. **civil lists:** Lists of distinguished persons.
3. *Ubi . . . patria:* (ü´ bē pä nis ib´ ē pä´ trē ə) "Where there is bread, there is one's fatherland" (Latin).
4. **Alma Mater** (al´ mə mä´ tər): "Fostering mother." Here, referring to America; usually used in reference to a school or college.

ern pilgrims, who are carrying along with them that great mass of arts, sciences, vigor, and industry which began long since in the east; they will finish the great circle. The Americans were once scattered all over Europe: here they are incorporated into one of the finest systems of population which has ever appeared, and which will hereafter become distinct by the power of the different climates they inhabit. The American ought therefore to love this country much better than that wherein either he or his forefathers were born. Here the rewards of his industry follow with equal steps the progress of his labor; his labor is founded on the basis of nature, *self-interest;* can it want a stronger allurement? Wives and children, who before in vain demanded of him a morsel of bread, now, fat and frolicsome, gladly help their father to clear those fields whence exuberant crops are to arise to feed and to clothe them all; without any part being claimed, either by a despotic prince, a rich abbot,[5] or a mighty lord. Here religion demands but little of him; a small voluntary salary to the minister, and gratitude to God; can he refuse these? The American is a new man, who acts upon new principles; he must therefore entertain new ideas, and form new opinions. From involuntary idleness, servile dependence, penury, and useless labor, he has passed to toils of a very different nature, rewarded by ample subsistence—This is an American.

5. **abbot** *n*.: The head of a monastery.

◆ Build Vocabulary

asylum (ə sī′ ləm) *n*.: Place of refuge

penury (pen′ yə rē) *n*.: Lack of money, property, or necessities

despotic (de spät′ ik) *adj*.: Harsh; cruel; unjust

subsistence (səb sis′ təns) *n*.: Means of support

Guide for Responding

◆ *Literature and Your Life*

Reader's Response If you were an eighteenth-century European, would this passage motivate you to relocate to the United States? Why or why not?

Thematic Focus Can Crèvecoeur's views be applied to America today? Why or why not?

☑ Check Your Comprehension

1. To what does Crèvecoeur compare impoverished Europeans before their emigration to America?
2. What are the sources of the "invisible power" responsible for transforming humble European peasants into esteemed American citizens?

◆ Critical Thinking

INTERPRET
1. To what theme does Crèvecoeur return again and again when describing life in America? **[Analyze]**
2. How would you summarize Crèvecoeur's definition of an American? **[Draw Conclusions]**

EVALUATE
3. Crèvecoeur implies that self-interest is a valuable quality because it motivates people to work harder. Does modern society commonly regard self-interest as a desirable quality? Explain your answer. **[Assess]**

Guide for Responding (continued)

◆ Reading Strategy

DISTINGUISH BETWEEN FACT AND OPINION

While the **opinions,** or personal beliefs, Adams and Crèvecoeur express in these letters help us appreciate their points of view, it is important to distinguish their beliefs from verifiable, historical **facts.**

1. Identify the following statement as fact or opinion. Explain your reasoning. "The house is made habitable, but there is not a single apartment finished, and all withinside, except the plastering, has been done since Briesler came."
2. Identify at least one fact Crèvecoeur uses to support the following opinion. ". . . here they are become men: in Europe they were as so many useless plants . . ."

◆ Literary Focus

PRIVATE AND PUBLIC LETTERS (EPISTLES)

The **private letters** of Abigail Adams provide an interesting view of life in a new nation. These letters were originally intended for her family's eyes alone. Crèvecoeur, on the other hand, reached a broad readership through **epistles**—public letters often addressed to a fictional person.

1. Name at least two ways Adams's letter would be different if written for a general audience.
2. How does the epistle form help Crèvecoeur persuade his readers to accept his ideas? Explain.

◆ Grammar and Style

USING SEMICOLONS

The **semicolon (;)** is used in place of a conjunction to join closely related independent clauses in a compound sentence.

Practice Rewrite the following sentences, adding semicolons where they are needed:

1. The travelers sought help finding Baltimore the woods blocked their view of the city.
2. Six rooms were completed two were not.
3. Adams thought she could be happy anywhere for three months however, the wood shortage caused her distress.

◆ Build Vocabulary

USING ETYMOLOGIES

Following is an *etymology*—a word history—for the word *interspersed.* Use the etymology to answer in your notebook the questions that follow.

> < L *interspersus,* pp. of *interspegere* < *inter-,* among + *spargere,* to scatter

1. *Interspersed* can ultimately be traced back to what two words or word parts?
2. Based on its etymology, what is the probable meaning of *interspersed*?

USING THE WORD BANK

Review the Word Bank. Then, on your paper, write the word that best describes each situation.

1. a steady income
2. what people who live in drafty houses suffer from
3. how you might describe an evil dictator
4. the quiet privacy of your room
5. to work your way out of an argument
6. the condition in which most homeless people live

Beyond Literature

Media Connection

Signal Flags, Morse Codes, Telegrams, e-mail New technologies continue to improve communication, and a variety of methods—both hi-tech and low-tech—is still in use today. Sailors use signal flags for short-range communication. Ham radio operators tap out messages in Morse code. Fax machines energize the flow of ideas in business. In the 1990's the information superhighway—the Internet—has revolutionized the way we connect even more. E-mail, once meant as a link for scientists, facilitates communication worldwide.

Activity Telephone, fax, e-mail, or letter? Poll your class to discover how most students communicate.

Build Your Portfolio

 ## Idea Bank

Writing

1. **Descriptive Letter** In a letter, describe your home to a friend who has never seen it. Create a picture of your home in the reader's mind.

2. **Reflective Essay** Crèvecoeur saw the United States as a land of great promise. How do you see this nation? In a brief essay, reflect on what the United States means to you.

3. **"Melting Pot" Epistle** In an epistle, celebrate the ethnic diversity found in American cities. Write with the intention of convincing the general public that cultural diversity is beneficial.

Speaking and Listening

4. **Letter Reading** Abigail Adams's letters provide vivid firsthand accounts of history. In a library, find a letter that captures a period of history. Read it aloud to the class and discuss what it reveals about the time in which it was written. **[Social Studies Link]**

5. **Immigrant Interview** Interview a recent immigrant to find out why and how he or she came to this country. Record your interview, then share it with your class. **[Social Studies Link]**

Projects

6. **American Interpretation** What is an American? Respond to Crèvecoeur's question in a form of your choice. Consider a poem or a photo montage to communicate your response.

7. **Advertising Campaign** Produce an advertising campaign to attract immigrants in the late eighteenth century. Draw upon the descriptions that Crèvecoeur presents in his letter. **[Media Link]**

 ## Writing Mini-Lesson

Personal Letter

If you could write to someone from the past, what would you tell that person about modern life? Select a figure from American history who intrigues you. In a personal letter, provide an update on how an area of interest to the recipient has changed since his or her lifetime. Like a foreign pen pal, your reader lives in a different country—the country of the past—and will need help understanding your world.

Writing Skills Focus: Necessary Context/Background

When writing for an audience whose culture is different from your own, provide **necessary context and background**—the information a reader needs in order to make sense of the references you make. Don't assume that words such as *work* and *school* mean to the reader what they mean to you.

For example, Abigail Adams, a champion of women's rights, would be fascinated by advances in women's issues, such as paid maternity leave, but would need information about the changing roles of women in the family and the workplace in order to appreciate the concept.

Prewriting Decide on an appropriate subject for your letter. Outline the developments you will cover. Then decide what background information your reader will need to understand your points.

Drafting Keep in mind the person to whom you are writing as you draft your letter. Remember that this is a personal letter intended as a one-on-one form of communication between the two of you.

Revising Reread your letter and ask yourself whether the recipient would be able to understand the references you make. Have you provided context and background information necessary to someone unfamiliar with twentieth-century America?

CONNECTIONS TO TODAY'S WORLD

from Roots
Alex Haley

Thematic Connection

THE EMERGING AMERICAN IDENTITY: DEFINING AN AMERICAN

What is an American? The works in Part 3 offer a telling look at a young nation consciously struggling with this question. At the time, neither Abigail Adams, Michel-Guillaume Jean de Crèvecoeur, nor Benjamin Franklin could have foreseen the impact that descendants of enslaved Africans would one day have on America's answer. Those writers could not have known that a book written by an African American would influence the way in which millions of Americans defined their identities.

That book, *Roots*, published in 1976, and the television mini-series of the same name, changed the nation's perception of itself as only very powerful events can. A fictionalized tale of the author Alex Haley's search for his African ancestors and the story of his family's history from their beginnings in Africa to emancipation, the book focused America's attention on the richness of the African cultural heritage. Civil rights leader Vernon Jordan called the television mini-series based on Haley's book "the single most spectacular educational experience in race relations in America."

African Americans everywhere followed Haley's example by renewing ties with their African ancestry. Thanks to a single book, the identities of millions of Americans expanded to include a new awareness of rich roots firmly planted in another time and place.

ALEX HALEY
(1921–1992)

Alex Haley spent twenty years in the Coast Guard as a journalist before deciding to become a freelance writer. His first big success came with his highly praised *The Autobiography of Malcolm X*. His greatest and best-known accomplishment, however, is *Roots: The Saga of an American Family*. The book was an immediate bestseller and within two years had won 271 awards. The television mini-series based on the book was viewed by 130 million people. About *Roots'* success, Haley said, "when you start talking about family, about lineage and ancestry, you are talking about every person on earth. We all have it; it's a great equalizer. . . . I think the book has touched a strong, subliminal chord."

from Roots

Alex Haley

Alex Haley's search for his African roots takes him to the small village of Juffure, located in the country in western Africa now known as The Gambia. The elderly village historian honors the American visitor by relating for him the ancestral history of the Kinte clan.

T he old *griot*[1] had talked for nearly two hours up to then, and perhaps fifty times the narrative had included some detail about someone whom he had named. Now after he had just named those four sons, again he appended a detail, and the interpreter translated—

1. **griot** (grē´ ō) *n.*: The village oral historian, generally an elderly man who recites histories of famous heroes and families on special occasions.

"About the time the King's soldiers came"—another of the *griot's* time-fixing references—"the oldest of these four sons, Kunta, went away from his village to chop wood . . . and he was never seen again. . . ." And the *griot* went on with his narrative.

I sat as if I were carved of stone. My blood seemed to have congealed. This man whose lifetime had been in this back-country African village had no way in the world to know that he had just echoed what I had heard all through my boyhood years on my grandma's front porch in Henning, Tennessee . . . of an African who always had insisted that his name was "Kin-tay"; who had called a guitar a *"ko,"* and a river within the state of Virginia, "Kamby Bolongo";[2] and who had been kidnaped into slavery while not far from his village, chopping wood, to make himself a drum.

I managed to fumble from my duffelbag my basic notebook, whose first pages containing grandma's story I showed to an interpreter. After briefly reading, clearly astounded, he spoke rapidly while showing it to the old *griot,* who became agitated; he got up, exclaiming to the people, gesturing at my notebook in the interpreter's hands, and *they* all got agitated.

I don't remember hearing anyone giving an order, I only recall becoming aware that those seventy-odd people had formed a wide human ring around me, moving counterclockwise, chanting softly, loudly, softly; their bodies close together, they were lifting their knees high, stamping up reddish puffs of the dust. . . .

The woman who broke from the moving circle was one of about a dozen whose infant children were within cloth slings across their backs. Her jet-black face deeply contorting, the woman came charging toward me, her bare feet slapping the earth, and snatching her baby free, she thrust it at me almost roughly, the gesture saying "Take it!" . . . and I did, clasping the baby to me. Then she snatched away her baby; and another woman was thrusting her baby, then another, and another . . . until I had embraced probably a dozen babies. I wouldn't learn until maybe a year later, from a Harvard University professor, Dr. Jerome Bruner, a scholar of such matters, "You didn't know you were participating in one of the oldest ceremonies of humankind, called 'The laying on of hands'! In their way, they were telling you 'Through this flesh, which is us, we are you, and you are us!'"

Later the men of Juffure[3] took me into their mosque[4] built of bamboo and thatch, and they prayed around me in Arabic. I remember thinking, down on my knees, "After I've found out where I came from, I can't understand a word they're saying." Later the crux of their prayer was translated for me: "Praise be to Allah for one long lost from us whom Allah has returned."

Since we had come by the river, I wanted to return by land. As I sat beside the wiry young Mandingo driver who was leaving dust pluming behind us on the hot, rough, pitted, back-country road toward Banjul, there came from somewhere into my head a staggering awareness . . . that *if* any black American could be so blessed as I had been to know only a few ancestral clues—could he or she know *who* was either the paternal or maternal African ancestor or ancestors, and about *where* that ancestor lived when taken, and finally about *when* the ancestor was taken—then only those few clues might well see that black American able to locate some wizened old black *griot* whose narrative could reveal the black American's ancestral clan, perhaps even the very village.

In my mind's eye, rather as if it were mistily being projected on a screen, I began envisioning descriptions I had read of how collectively millions of our ancestors had been enslaved. Many thousands were individually kidnaped, as my own forebear Kunta had been, but into the millions had come awake screaming in the night, dashing out into the bedlam of raided villages, which were often in flames. The captured able survivors were linked neck-by-neck with thongs into processions called "coffles," which were sometimes as much as a mile in length. I envisioned the many dying, or left to

---

2. **"Kamby Bolongo"** (käm´ bē bō lôŋ´ gō): "Gambia River" in the Mandinka language of western Africa.

3. **Juffure** (jōō´ fōō rā)

4. **mosque** (mäsk) *n*.: Muslim temple or place of worship.

◆ **Build Vocabulary**

congealed (kən jēld´) *v*.: Thickened or solidified

crux (kruks) *n*.: Essential point

Dance Africa, Synthia Saint James, Third World Art Exchange

▲ **Critical Viewing** How does the artist convey the vibrancy of African dance without depicting movement? Does Haley's description of Africa convey the same feeling? **[Relate]**

die when they were too weak to continue the torturous march toward the coast, and those who made it to the beach were greased, shaved, probed in every orifice, often branded with sizzling irons; I envisioned them being lashed and dragged toward the longboats; their spasms of screaming and clawing with their hands into the beach, biting up great choking mouthfuls of the sand in their desperation efforts for one last hold on the Africa that had been their home; I envisioned them shoved, beaten, jerked down into slave ships' stinking holds and chained onto shelves, often packed so tightly that they had to lie on their sides like spoons in a drawer. . . .

My mind reeled with it all as we approached another, much larger village. Staring ahead, I realized that word of what had happened in

Juffure must have left there well before I did. The driver slowing down, I could see this village's people thronging the road ahead; they were weaving, amid their cacophony of crying out something; I stood up in the Land-Rover, waving back as they seemed grudging to open a path for the Land-Rover.

I guess we had moved a third of the way through the village when it suddenly registered in my brain what they were all crying out . . . the wizened, robed elders and younger men, the mothers and the naked tar-black children, they were all waving up at me; their expressions buoyant, beaming, all were crying out together, *"Meester Kinte! Meester Kinte!"*

Let me tell you something: I am a man. A sob hit me somewhere around my ankles; it came surging upward, and flinging my hands over my face, I was just bawling, as I hadn't since I was a baby. *"Meester Kinte!"* I just felt like I was weeping for all of history's incredible atrocities against fellowmen, which seems to be mankind's greatest flaw. . . .

Flying homeward from Dakar, I decided to write a book. My own ancestors would automatically also be a symbolic saga of all African-descent people—who are without exception the seeds of someone like Kunta who was born and grew up in some black African village, someone who was captured and chained down in one of those slave ships that sailed them across the same ocean, into some succession of plantations, and since then a struggle for freedom.

◆ **Build Vocabulary**

cacophony (kə käf′ ə nē) *n.*: Harsh, jarring sound

Guide for Responding

◆ *Literature and Your Life*

Reader's Response If you had the opportunity to learn about your own ancestors, what would you want to discover or see for yourself?

Thematic Focus How does *Roots* expand our understanding of what it means to be an American?

Journal Writing What do you already know about your ancestry, and what would you like to learn? Jot down facts about your heritage, along with questions you would like to have answered. Then list possible sources of information about your family's history, including relatives, old family photographs, and so on.

☑ **Check Your Comprehension**

1. Before Haley visited Juffure, what information did he have about his ancestor?
2. Which detail of the *griot's* tale convinced Haley that Kunta was the same ancestor his grandmother had described?
3. (a) Why did the African mothers hand their babies to Haley? (b) What were the villagers telling Haley through this gesture?
4. What is the "staggering awareness" that comes to Haley while traveling toward Banjul?

◆ **Critical Thinking**

INTERPRET

1. What does being addressed as "Meester Kinte" represent to Haley? **[Interpret]**
2. (a) Contrast Haley's portrayal of enslaved Africans with his descriptions of the Africans who greet him as he travels through Juffure and Banjul. (b) How do his descriptions of the Africans he meets in his travels make the plight of enslaved Africans seem even more tragic? **[Compare and Contrast]**
3. What does Haley mean when he writes, "My own ancestors would automatically also be a symbolic saga of all African-descent people"? **[Interpret]**

APPLY

4. If the villagers had treated Haley as an outsider rather than as a kinsman, how might his search for his heritage have been affected? **[Speculate]**

EVALUATE

5. Critics have suggested that *Roots* blurs the lines between fact and fiction, and that Haley may have presented fictional segments of the story as fact. Do you think that this blurring detracts from the book's value? Explain. **[Make a Judgment]**

Thematic Connection

THE EMERGING AMERICAN IDENTITY: DEFINING AN AMERICAN

Today, thanks in part to the awareness generated by *Roots*, Americans tend to be more sensitive to the value of our many ethnic and cultural heritages. Though we can proudly trace our ancestry to hundreds of nations, Americans are unified by a belief in many of the same values that Crèvecoeur and Franklin professed centuries ago; we still trust in hard work, self-reliance, and democracy. We even struggle with many of the same problems Abigail Adams addressed in her lifetime of correspondence, including such national issues as education and equal rights for women and such personal challenges as keeping families united over long distances. Alex Haley has earned a place in this celebrated tradition of writers whose works help us answer the question, What is an American?

1. How do you think Alex Haley might answer the question, What is an American? Why?

2. Which of the beliefs expressed by other writers in this section do you think Haley might share? Why?

Idea Bank

Writing

1. **Journal Entry** Alex Haley describes the moment in which he realizes that he has "found" his ancestry in the village of Juffure. Imagine that you are Haley, reflecting on the events of this emotional day in your journal. Use both the excerpt and your own imagination to describe your thoughts and feelings in a journal entry.

2. **Director's Notes** As a director filming the scene in which Haley discovers his ancestral clan in Juffure, how would you want the actors to speak, move, and gesture as they recite their lines? What expressions should they wear? Write a series of notes that explain how you would like the characters to look, act, and sound at each point in the scene. **[Career Link]**

3. **Book Jacket** *Roots: The Saga of an American Family* is the fictionalized account of Haley's family history and his search for his African ancestors. The book and television mini-series raised awareness of black heritage in the 1970's. How would you convince a new generation of potential readers to buy the book? Convey the excitement and historic significance of *Roots* in a book-jacket summary that would make people want to read the book.

Speaking and Listening

4. **Informal Debate** Michel-Guillaume Jean de Crèvecoeur says that true Americans ought to cut their ties to their country of origin. Would Haley have shared that philosophy? Work with a small group to stage an informal debate between Haley and Crèvecoeur on the question of whether Americans should retain their ties to the lands from which their ancestors came.

Projects

5. **Multimedia *Roots* Presentation** Research the media coverage surrounding the influential 1977 *Roots* mini-series. How was it received? How did it impact the way Americans viewed their heritage? Present your findings in a narrated multimedia presentation. You might make a montage of articles about the series, play a recording of the *Roots* theme music, or show a series excerpt or interview with Haley. **[Media Link]**

6. **Cultural Heritage Display** Celebrate your own cultural heritage by creating a display. Pull together objects that capture important elements of your culture or cultures of origin. Write a paragraph explaining each of the objects. Then assemble the objects and the accompanying descriptions into an appealing visual display.

Multimedia Presentation

Writing Process Workshop

The word **media** is the plural of *medium*—in this case, a medium of communication, a way of conveying human thoughts and feelings. Poetic writing is the original multimedia spectacle. It uses language to simulate or evoke sight, sound, touch, feeling, and thought, just as Crèvecoeur does with his captivating metaphors and images in his letter featured in this unit.

With the media of modern technology at your fingertips, you can offer more than mere verbal simulations of sights and sounds. You can dazzle your audience with the real thing: stunning full-color videos, slides, and paintings or spectacular surround-sound.

The following skills will help you produce an effective multimedia presentation.

Writing Skills Focus

▶ **Select a writing style appropriate** to a multimedia presentation. Your spoken text should be briefer than it would be in an entirely verbal context. (See p. 191.)

▶ **Provide the necessary context and background** if your listeners are unfamiliar with your topic. (See p. 201.)

▶ **Show, don't tell.** Since you have a variety of media at your disposal, rely more on direct sensory appeal and less on words.

This script for a multimedia presentation uses these skills.

① The directions are set off in capital letters and brackets.

② The writer uses both the visual and auditory possibilities of the video to convey important background details.

③ By using a handout of sheet music, the writer uses still another medium—print— to enhance the presentation by showing, not merely telling.

WRITING MODEL

[VIDEOTAPE: SCENE OF CHARLIE PARKER AND DIZZY GILLESPIE] ① What you see and hear on this video is a kinescope of a TV broadcast from 1951—the heydey of bebop, a revolutionary movement in jazz. Charlie Parker on alto sax and Dizzy Gillespie on trumpet lead a quartet on the tune "Koko." ② The chordal and harmonic complexity of bebop were a challenge for talented musicians, and Parker's blizzards of improvisation astonish even now. Imagine yourself playing what you see on this sheet music, a transcription of one of Parker's solos. [HANDOUT] ③

Prewriting

Choose a Topic Start by coming up with a topic that interests you and for which there is multimedia material available. You might consider these topics.

> ### Topic Ideas
> - The national parks
> - Joys of owning a pet
> - The election process
> - Skiing, scuba diving, or hiking
> - Your favorite pop musicians
> - New York City's theater district

Consider Possible Media Gather material through research. Your ingenuity and imagination are the only limits. You might want to consider these types of media:

- ▶ Audiotapes of music or interviews
- ▶ Videotaped interviews, films, or television programs
- ▶ Printed articles, graphs, charts, and maps
- ▶ Scale models
- ▶ Foods and plants

Drafting

Use an Outline and Flowchart Outline the information you want to include in your presentation. Next to the headings, name your multimedia resources. You might also want to create a flowchart that shows what you or another student will be saying, doing, playing, or showing at each point during your presentation. Generate a script from your flowchart, relying as little as possible on words and as much as possible on your multimedia resources. Provide the context necessary for the background of your audience.

Treat Your Presentation as a Performance Rehearse with all your items, equipment, and any co-presenters, to make sure everything works and runs smoothly. Practice making eye contact with your listeners.

APPLYING LANGUAGE SKILLS: Vague or Ambiguous Pronoun References

The antecedents of a pronoun should be clear; there should be no possibility that the pronoun refers to more than one antecedent.

Vague Pronoun Reference:
Call of the Wild is very suspenseful, which most readers enjoy.

Clear Pronoun Reference:
Call of the Wild is filled with suspense, which most readers enjoy.

Practice Revise these examples of vague pronoun references.

1. Carla is hunched over her stamp collection because it is a fascinating hobby.
2. He is an inspiring coach, and this was evident from the team's winning record.
3. The gardeners used the noisy leaf blowers early in the morning, which the neighbors disapproved of.

Writing Application Review your multimedia presentation, and eliminate any vague or confusing pronoun references.

Writer's Solution Connection
Writing Lab

For information on using on-line media sources, use the Prewriting section of the Research Writing tutorial.

APPLYING LANGUAGE SKILLS: Adverb or Adjective?

Some adjectives that end in *-ly* can easily be mistaken for adverbs. Keep in mind that adjectives modify nouns and adverbs modify verbs, adjectives, or other adverbs.

Adverb:

We arrived early. (Here early modifies the verb arrived.)

Adjective:

We caught the early train. (Here early modifies the noun train.)

Practice Identify the italicized word in each of the following items as an adjective or an adverb.

1. My sister thought that the stray dog was *homely*, but I thought he was cute.
2. The new student seemed *friendly*.
3. I devoured the book *eagerly*.

Writing Application As you draft your multimedia presentation, be sure that you have used all your *-ly* words correctly.

Writer's Solution Connection
Language Lab

For more practice, complete the Problems with Modifiers lesson.

Revising

Strike a Balance Be sure you have successfully integrated multimedia elements into your script. For example, if you rely on one slide for a long part of your presentation and then flash several more images in quick succession, you may want to rework the pacing of your presentation.

Use a Checklist After your rehearsal, go over the following points to be sure your presentation will be successful:

▶ Is all my equipment in proper working order?
▶ Have I presented the necessary background and context?
▶ Have I written in a concise style that does not compete with my audiovisual tools—that is, have I spent enough time showing rather than telling?

REVISION MODEL

Many of Dizzy Gillespie's compositions have become classics.

① As you listen to
② notice the unique rhythm and harmonies

This recording of "A Night in Tunisia," ~~show the qualities~~ that made bebop famous.

① The writer makes better use of the music by directing the audience's attention.
② The writer adds more specific information about the qualities of bebop

Presenting

Deliver Your Presentation Once you've finished polishing your presentation, present it to a live audience. Be sure to allow time to answer questions.

Think Big Do you think that your show is good enough to take on the road? You might start thinking bigger by moving from your classroom to a school assembly program. The next step might be a nearby school or a local club or organization that seeks out speakers on your topic. Ask the librarian at your school or in your community to help you in locating such groups.

Real-World Reading Skills Workshop

Strategies for Success

Reading a news article is a very different experience from laughing through a humor column—even if the topic is the same! Why? The main reason is that the writers have very different goals: one to inform and the other to entertain. Judging a writer's purpose helps you respond to your reading.

Be Aware of Possible Purposes Most writing seeks to entertain, inform, persuade, or describe. Often, these goals overlap—a travel brochure describes a place, informs readers about its features, and persuades readers to visit. Familiarize yourself with these main writing purposes by listing some examples of each from your own recent reading.

Recognize a Writer's Purpose To evaluate a writer's purpose, examine the topic, style, and focus of the writing. Questions like these can help:

▶ Who is the intended audience?
▶ How does the writer hope to affect or change the audience?
▶ What is the topic? Which writing purposes best fit it?
▶ What type of language does the writer use, and what does it suggest about the writer's attitude toward the subject?

Now What? Once you recognize the writer's purpose, you can read more critically—alert to biased statements in persuasion, looking carefully for details in informative material, or relaxing to enjoy reading meant only for entertainment.

Apply the Strategy

Your brother left his newspaper on the kitchen table, open to this article. Read it and determine its writer's purpose.

1. What is the writer's purpose? How do you know?
2. Choose another purpose, but keep the same topic. Rewrite the article to reflect the new purpose, adding information from your imagination if you wish.

✔ Here are other situations in which it's important to recognize the writer's purpose:
▶ Advertisements and promotional literature
▶ Political statements
▶ News articles

Food for Thought
by Dave Barry

It's getting late on a school night, but I'm not letting my son go to bed yet, because there's serious work to be done.

"Robert!" I'm saying, in a firm voice. "Come to the kitchen right now and blow-dry the ant!"

We have a large ant, about the size of a mature raccoon, standing on our kitchen counter. In fact, it looks kind of like a raccoon, or possibly even a mutant lobster. We made the ant out of papier-mâché, a substance you create by mixing flour and water and newspapers together into a slimy goop that drips down and gets licked up by your dogs, who operate on the wise survival principle that you should immediately eat everything that falls onto the kitchen floor, because if it turns out not to be food, you can always throw it up later.

The ant, needless to say, is part of a Science Fair project. . . .

As a young adult with original ideas, you can make an important impact on the world around you. One way you can make your feelings known or influence others is by giving a persuasive speech. Use these strategies to help you:

Take a Stand First, whenever possible, address issues about which you feel strongly. You will be more persuasive if you truly believe the arguments you are presenting. Stay objective, however, in preparing your speech—verify all facts in respected sources and support all arguments with evidence.

Get Organized Introduce yourself and tell listeners why you are addressing them. State your main position early, before moving on to supporting evidence and ideas. Outline actions or positions you want the audience to take. Remember—your goal is to persuade them to act or think a certain way!

Control Counts Go ahead, let your feelings show. Use gestures and tone of voice to add impact to your words. Come out from behind the podium or stand to emphasize important points, but stay in control. Listeners will be put off by overly emotional behavior.

Tips for Delivering a Persuasive Speech

✔ *If you want listeners to respond to your persuasive speech—or any speech—try these strategies:*

▶ Speak slowly, clearly, and loud enough to be heard at the back of the room.

▶ Look at the audience as much as possible. This means memorizing the main points of your speech.

▶ Emphasize charged words to underscore the emotional impact of your message and to sway listeners to your point of view.

▶ Pause during any applause. Ignore any negative comments or gestures.

▶ End your speech by restating your position and the actions, positions, or changes you seek from the audience.

Apply the Strategies

Complete one or more of these activities to gain experience and practice in delivering persuasive speeches.

1. View videotapes of speakers such as Martin Luther King or observe congressional leaders on C-Span. Identify and discuss how these speakers employ persuasive speaking techniques.

2. Working in a small group, develop an outline for a new speech about a contemporary issue. Take turns rehearsing and delivering the speech. Critique one another's presentations.

3. As a class, attend a public meeting at school or elsewhere in the community. During the question-and-answer period, express your views about the issues being discussed. Alternatively, you may role-play such a meeting in class.

Extended Reading Opportunities

To learn more about the fiery personalities that helped shape our nation during the Revolutionary War period, consider these suggestions for extending your reading.

Suggested Titles

The Autobiography
Benjamin Franklin

Meet one of the greatest minds and sharpest wits in American history as Benjamin Franklin shares the story of his life in *The Autobiography.* This "rags to riches" tale recounts his rise from humble beginnings to a prosperous Renaissance man—a printer, scientist, inventor, and witty commentator on human nature. Though Franklin died before he could complete *The Autobiography,* the book provides a fascinating look at the life and character of one of the greatest diplomats in our nation's history.

1776
Peter Stone and Sherman Edwards

Thomas Jefferson, John and Abigail Adams, Benjamin Franklin—these famous names from the pages of history come alive in this drama about the people and events surrounding the birth of our nation. The events leading to the signing of the Declaration of Independence unfold in a sometimes humorous, sometimes touching portrayal of the personal and political conflicts behind the fight for independence.

Citizen Tom Paine
Howard Fast

Less then two years after setting foot in the American colonies, English-born Thomas Paine published *Common Sense,* the pamphlet that fueled the colonies' fight for independence. After enlisting in the colonial army, Paine continued to inspire his adopted country with his fiery writings. Why would an Englishman incite revolt against his homeland? How could such a famous hero of the American Revolution die unappreciated and misunderstood? You'll find the answers in this classic portrait of the life and times of a fascinating American.

Other Possibilities

Common Sense	Thomas Paine
Letters From an American Farmer	Michel-Guillaume Jean de Crèvecoeur
The Federalist Papers	James Madison
Travels Through North and South Carolina	William Bartram

Niagara Falls, Thomas Chambers, Wadsworth Atheneum, Hartford, Connecticut

A Growing Nation
(1800–1870)

"America is a land of wonders, in which everything is in constant motion and every change seems an improvement. . . . No natural boundary seems to be set to the efforts of man; and in his eyes what is not yet done is only what he has not yet attempted to do."

—Alexis de Tocqueville

Timeline
1800—1870

1800 **1810** **1820**

American Events

- **1803** Louisiana Purchase extends nation's territory to the Rocky Mountains.
- **1804** Lewis and Clark begin expedition exploring and mapping vast region of the West. ◄
- **1807** Robert Fulton's steamboat makes first trip from New York City to Albany.
- **1809** *A History of New York . . .* by Diedrich Knickerbocker brings recognition to Washington Irving.

- **1812** U.S. declares war on Great Britain; early battles in War of 1812 are at sea.
- **1814** Bombardment of Fort McHenry inspires Francis Scott Key to write "The Star-Spangled Banner." ▼
- **1817** William Cullen Bryant publishes early draft of "Thanatopsis" in a Boston magazine.
- **1819** Spain relinquishes claims to Florida for $5 million.

- **1820** Missouri Compromise bans slavery in parts of new territories.
- **1825** Completion and success of Erie Canal spurs canal building throughout the nation. ▶
- **1827** Edgar Allan Poe publishes *Tamerlane,* his first collection of poems.

World Events

- **1800** England: Samuel Taylor Coleridge finishes writing "Kubla Khan."
- **1804** France: Napoleon Bonaparte proclaims himself emperor. ◄
- **1804** England: William Wordsworth completes "Ode on Intimations of Immortality."
- **1805** Germany: Ludwig von Beethoven breaks formal musical conventions with Third Symphony.

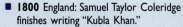

- **1813** England: Jane Austen publishes *Pride and Prejudice.* ◄
- **1815** Belgium: French army under Napoleon routed at Waterloo.
- **1815** Austria: Congress of Vienna redraws map of Europe following Napoleon's downfall.
- **1818** England: Mary Wollstonecraft Shelley creates a legend with *Frankenstein.*
- **1819** England: John Keats writes "Ode to a Nightingale" and "Ode on a Grecian Urn."
- **1819** France: René Läennec invents the stethoscope. ◄

- **1821** Mexico: Mexico gains independence from Spain.
- **1824** Hawaii: King Kamehameha III, who favors U.S. interests, ascends the throne. ▲
- **1829** England: George Stephenson perfects a steam locomotive for Liverpool-Manchester Railway. ◄

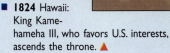

1830   1840   1850

- **1830** Tom Thumb, America's first steam-driven locomotive, begins service on Baltimore and Ohio railroad. ▲
- **1831** Cyrus McCormick invents mechanical reaper. ▶
- **1836** Battles at the Alamo and San Jacinto fought while Texas is a republic.
- **1837** Mount Holyoke, first women's college in United States, founded.

- **1837** Samuel F. B. Morse patents electromagnetic telegraph. ◀
- **1838** U.S. Army marches Cherokees of Georgia on long "Trail of Tears" to Oklahoma. ▶
- **1839** Edgar Allan Poe's "The Fall of the House of Usher" first appears in print.

- **1840** The Transcendentalist magazine, *The Dial*, begins publication.
- **1841** Ralph Waldo Emerson publishes *Essays*.
- **1842** Anesthesia first used for medical purposes.
- **1843** John Greenleaf Whittier publishes *Lays of My Home and Other Poems*.
- **1844** First telegraph message sent.
- **1845** Texas admitted to the Union. ▲
- **1846** Mexican War begins.
- **1846** Abraham Lincoln first elected to Congress.
- **1848** Mexican War ends; United States expands borders.
- **1848** California gold rush begins.
- **1848** Women's Rights Convention held in Seneca Falls, New York.

- **1850** Nathaniel Hawthorne publishes *The Scarlet Letter*.
- **1850** California admitted to the Union. ▶
- **1851** Herman Melville publishes *Moby-Dick*.
- **1851** Nathaniel Hawthorne publishes *The House of the Seven Gables*.
- **1851** *The New York Times* begins publication.

- **1852** Harriet Beecher Stowe publishes *Uncle Tom's Cabin*. ▲
- **1853** Arizona and New Mexico purchased from Mexico.
- **1854** Henry David Thoreau publishes *Walden*.
- **1854** Republican Party organized.

- **1831** France: Victor Hugo publishes *Notre Dame de Paris*, popularly called *The Hunchback of Notre Dame*. ▲
- **1832** England: Alfred, Lord Tennyson completes "The Lady of Shalott," a poem.
- **1835** Denmark: Hans Christian Andersen publishes his first book of fairy tales. ◀
- **1837** England: Charles Dickens achieves great success with *Oliver Twist*.

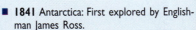

- **1841** Antarctica: First explored by Englishman James Ross.
- **1842** Asia: Hong Kong becomes a British colony.
- **1844** Germany: Heinrich Heine publishes *Germany: A Winter's Tale*.
- **1845** Ireland: Famine results from failure of potato crop.
- **1847** Italy: Verdi's opera *Macbeth* first performed.
- **1847** England: Emily Brontë publishes *Wuthering Heights*.
- **1848** Belgium: Karl Marx and Friedrich Engels publish *The Communist Manifesto*.
- **1848** England: Queen's College for Women opens.

- **1850** France: Life insurance introduced.
- **1850** England: Elizabeth Barrett Browning publishes *Sonnets From the Portuguese*.
- **1850** China: Taiping Rebellion begins.
- **1851** Australia: Gold discovered in New South Wales.
- **1853** Europe: Crimean War begins.
- **1853** Japan: Ports open to trade.

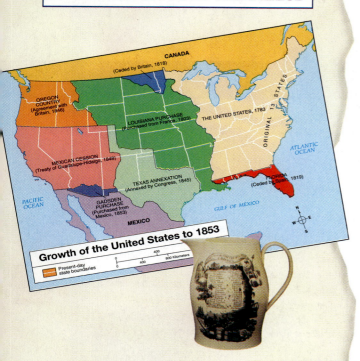

Growth of the United States to 1853

▲ **Read a Map** By 1848, the United States stretched from the Atlantic Ocean to the Pacific Ocean. As the pitcher showing state populations suggests, the growth of the country was a source of great pride. What region of the map was the last to be added to the United States?

◀ **Analyze an Artifact** Lewis and Clark led an expedition to explore the territory of the Louisiana Purchase. During the expedition, they gave friendship medals like this one to Native American chiefs. What message do the inscriptions—and the medals themselves—send about President Jefferson's hopes for the relationship between the United States and Native American groups?

The Story of the Times
1800–1870

In 1831, the Frenchman Alexis de Tocqueville, sent to report on America's prisons, ultimately wrote about something far more interesting: a bustling new nation full of individuals optimistically pursuing their destinies. His *Democracy in America* observed that Americans had "a lively faith in the perfectibility of man," believing "what appears to them today to be good may be superseded by something better tomorrow."

The bustling spirit that had enchanted De Tocqueville in 1831 would make for a turbulent "tomorrow" in the decades to come: By 1870, industrialism, explosive population and economic growth, and the Civil War had all aged the nation's spirit. American literature also matured during this time. In 1831, De Tocqueville wrote, "America has produced very few writers of distinction . . . . [The literature of England] still darts its rays into the forests of the New World." By 1870, America had produced many "writers of distinction": Irving, Cooper, Bryant, Poe, Emerson, Thoreau, Hawthorne, Melville, Dickinson, and Whitman—all of whom eventually shone their unmistakably American light into and far beyond "the forests of the New World."

Historical Background

In 1800, the United States consisted of sixteen states clustered near the east coast. In 1803, Thomas Jefferson doubled the nation's size by signing the Louisiana Purchase. The rapid growth of the nation inspired an upsurge in national pride and self-awareness.

The Growth of Democracy at Home: 1800–1840
As the nation expanded, Americans began to take more direct control of their government. The 1828 election of Andrew Jackson, "the People's President," ushered in the era of the common man, as property requirements for voting began to be eliminated. The democratic advances of the time, however, were confined

to white males. Scant political attention was paid to women, and most African Americans remained enslaved. One of the most tragic policies of this period was "Indian removal," the forced westward migration of Native Americans from confiscated tribal lands—as in the 1838 "Trail of Tears," in which 4,000 of 15,000 Cherokee perished on the trek from Georgia to Oklahoma.

Young Nation on the World Stage The War of 1812 convinced Europeans that the United States was on the world stage to stay. In the Monroe Doctrine of 1823, President James Monroe warned Europe not to intervene in the new Latin American nations. In the 1830's, the U.S. became embroiled in a conflict over the secession of Texas from Mexico; in 1836, the Mexican Army made its famous assault on the Alamo, in which every Texan defender was killed. When Texas was admitted to the Union in 1845, the resulting war with Mexico (1846–1848) ended in a U.S. victory, which added more territory to the nation, including California. Soon after, the Gold Rush of 1849 drew hundreds of thousands to this new land of promise.

The Way West and Economic Growth In a sense, the entire course of American history can be seen as a pageant rolling ever westward, as new territories opened up and transportation improved. The Erie Canal, completed in New York in 1825, set off a wave of canal building. In the 1850's, the "iron horse"—the railroad—began to dominate long-distance American travel; by 1869, rail lines linked east and west coasts.

Advances in technology spurred social change. Factories sprang up all over the Northeast. The steel plow and reaper encouraged frontier settlement by making farming practical on the vast, sod-covered grasslands. The telegraph facilitated almost instant communication across great distances. Inventor Samuel F. B. Morse's message from Washington to Baltimore in 1844 could serve as the motto for this era: "What hath God wrought!"

Winds of Change It was evident to even the most cheerful observer that the United States at mid-century faced trouble as well as bright promise. The new prosperity unleashed fierce competition, leading to the creation of factories

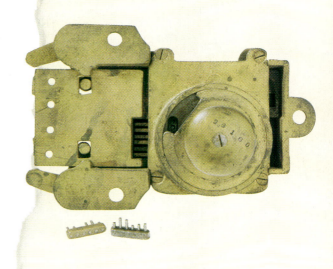

▲ **Analyze Technology** The Industrial Revolution brought change to many aspects of life in the United States. How would factory-made, mass-produced items like this lock and this adjustable wrench improve daily life?

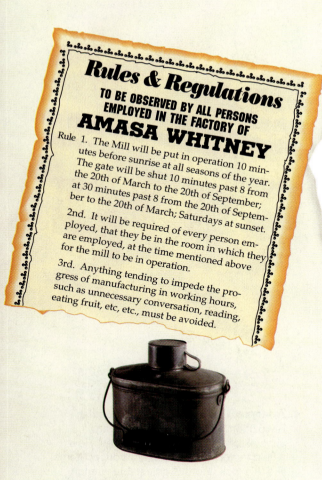

Rules & Regulations

TO BE OBSERVED BY ALL PERSONS EMPLOYED IN THE FACTORY OF

AMASA WHITNEY

Rule 1. The Mill will be put in operation 10 minutes before sunrise at all seasons of the year. The gate will be shut 10 minutes past 8 from the 20th of March to the 20th of September; at 30 minutes past 8 from the 20th of September to the 20th of March; Saturdays at sunset.

2nd. It will be required of every person employed, that they be in the room in which they are employed, at the time mentioned above for the mill to be in operation.

3rd. Anything tending to impede the progress of manufacturing in working hours, such as unnecessary conversation, reading, eating fruit, etc, etc., must be avoided.

▲ **Evaluate Information** A great number of factory and mill towns sprang up in the Northeast. Francis C. Lowell, the inventor of the power loom, hired young women from nearby farms to work in his Massachusetts textile mills. These "Lowell factory girls" lived in supervised boarding houses, attended a company-built church, followed strict rules, and worked from 5:00 A.M. to 7:30 P.M. They were allowed two half-hour breaks to eat the meals that they carried in lunch pails like this one. The rules and regulations shown above establish the working conditions in another factory. What does this information show about life for factory workers in the mid-1800's?

scarred by child labor and unsafe working conditions. In 1840, most women could not vote or file a lawsuit. The 1840's and 1850's saw an outburst of efforts promoting women's rights, notably the 1848 Seneca Falls Convention. Above all, the centuries-old institution of slavery bitterly divided the nation. The conflict between abolitionists, who opposed slavery, and the advocates of states' rights, who argued that the federal government could not bend states to its will, sharpened in the 1850's. The gathering storm finally burst into war in 1861, but it was a storm that had been building for 250 years, ever since the first slave was brought in chains to this continent.

Literature of the Period

American Literature Comes of Age Before 1800, American writers were not widely read—not even in America, but that situation soon began to change. The writers of this period would define the American voice—personal, idiosyncratic, bold—and its primary theme: the quest of the individual to define him or herself.

Romanticism Despite their unmistakable differences, the writers of the early nineteenth century—Washington Irving, James Fenimore Cooper, William Cullen Bryant, and Edgar Allan Poe—can all be described as Romantics. Romanticism is an artistic movement that dominated Europe and America during the nineteenth century. Romantic writers elevated the imagination over reason and intuition over fact. Washington Irving, the first American to be read widely overseas, made his mark with his *History of New York* (1809), which is not a dry historical record but a rollicking narrative that alters facts at will.

The Romantics reveled in nature. William Cullen Bryant is best known for his lyric poems rejoicing in the healing powers of nature. Irving's "Rip Van Winkle" and "The Legend of Sleepy Hollow" sparked an interest in his beloved Hudson River Valley. James Fenimore Cooper's four *Leatherstocking Tales* feature the exploits of Natty Bumppo in the frontier forests of upstate New York. A man of absolute moral integrity, Natty Bumppo preferred nature over civilization, establishing the pattern for countless American heroes to come.

Romantic writing often accented the fantastic aspects of human experience. The tortured genius Edgar Allan Poe remains popular to this day for his haunting poems and suspenseful stories whose characters, as one biographer has said, "are either grotesques or the inhabitants of another world than this."

New England Renaissance: 1840–1855 In 1837, Ralph Waldo Emerson, a former Boston minister, delivered his famous oration "The American Scholar," calling for American intellectual independence from Europe. Emerson believed that American writers should begin to interpret their own culture in new ways. As if in response to Emerson's call, an impressive burst of literary activity took place in and around Boston between 1840 and 1855. This "flowering of New England" would produce an array of great writers and enduring literature.

Transcendentalism Most, if not all, of these writers were influenced by the Transcendental philosophy originally expressed by the German Immanuel Kant. In his *Critique of Practical Reason* (1788), Kant defines the transcendental as the understanding a person gains intuitively. Closely associated with Emerson, American Transcendentalism drew on other thinkers as well: the Greek philosopher Plato, the French mathematician Pascal, the Swedish mystic and scientist Swedenborg, and the anti-materialism of Buddhist thought. The Transcendentalists believed that the most fundamental truths lie outside the experience of the senses, residing instead, as Emerson put it, in the "Over-Soul . . . a universal and benign omnipresence."

Walden The most influential expression of Transcendental philosophy came from Emerson and his younger friend and protégé, Henry David Thoreau, who withdrew from society to live by himself on the shores of Walden Pond. Thoreau begins *Walden*, his account of this experience, by writing, "When I wrote the following pages . . . I lived alone, in the woods, a mile from any neighbor, in a house which I had built myself, on the shore of Walden Pond, in Concord, Massachusetts, and earned my living by the labor of my hands only." Published in 1854, *Walden* consists

▲ **Make an Inference** Abolitionist newspapers like *The Liberator* stirred strong emotions about the issue of slavery. These broadsides, for example, announce meetings to garner support for both sides. Why would some citizens oppose slavery? Why would others oppose abolition?

of eighteen essays about matters ranging from a battle between red and black ants to the individual's relation to society. Thoreau's observations of nature reveal his philosophy of individualism, simplicity, and passive resistance to injustice.

The Possibility of Evil Not everyone shared the Transcendentalists' optimistic views. Nathaniel Hawthorne and Herman Melville expressed the darker vision of those who, in Hawthorne's words, "burrowed into the depths of our common nature" and found the area not always shimmering, but often "dusky." Hawthorne's Puritan heritage was never far from his consciousness. His masterpiece, *The Scarlet Letter* (1850), set in Boston in the seventeenth century, deals with sin, concealed guilt, hypocrisy, and humility. In *The House of the Seven Gables*, he delves into seventeenth-century witchcraft, insanity, and a legendary curse.

Hawthorne became a kind of mentor to Melville. Depressed about the negative critical response to his novel *Moby-Dick* (1851), Melville befriended the older, more successful writer. Both men saw human life in grim terms, but their personalities were quite different. Hawthorne, despite a tendency toward solitude, was stable and self-possessed, a shrewd man without illusions. Melville, by contrast, was a man at odds with the world, a tortured and cryptic personality. For a large part of his career, he raged against his fate, much as Captain Ahab in *Moby-Dick* unleashed his fury against the white whale that had maimed him.

At Home in Amherst While Thoreau was planting beans next to Walden Pond, Emily Dickinson was growing up in the nearby town of Amherst, Massachusetts. Her startling, intensely focused poetry catapulted her into the company of the greatest American poets—although not in her lifetime. A recluse for the second half of her life, Dickinson did not write for publication, or even for her family, but rather from a personal need to wrestle with questions about death, immortality, and the soul—questions unresolved by conventional religion.

▲ **Connect** Hoping that Americans would
▼ expand their minds as they expanded the nation, in 1839 the American Society for the Diffusion of Useful Knowledge published a traveling library, like the one above, for settlers in the West. Below is a ticket to Charles Willson Peale's museum, which he ran to teach Americans how to learn by observing nature. How do these efforts reflect Transcendentalist beliefs?

Beyond New England Meanwhile, the quintessential American poet was tramping about the countryside, laboring at odd jobs to finance his poetry. In 1855, New Yorker Walt Whitman published his groundbreaking series of poems, *Leaves of Grass*, proudly broadcasting his "barbaric yawp" from Brooklyn to the universe. Most American readers ignored the irregular forms and frank language of this revolutionary poet, but Emerson knew an American original when he saw one and praised Whitman's work. Of all the poets of the period between 1800 and 1870, Whitman would have the most lasting effect on American literature—despite the fact that the first edition of *Leaves* sold fewer than twenty copies.

Fireside Poets Those were the literary giants of the period, as singled out by twentieth-century scholars. In 1850, however, the American reading public would probably have pointed instead to four other New England writers, known as the Fireside Poets: Henry Wadsworth Longfellow, a Harvard professor and tremendously popular poet; John Greenleaf Whittier, from a hardworking Quaker farm family; James Russell Lowell, born to wealth and position; and Oliver Wendell Holmes, a poet-physician and the unofficial laureate of the group.

After the Flowering As the war clouds gathered, the great burst of creativity in the Northeast began to subside. Antislavery writers, such as Emerson, Melville, Whittier, and Lowell, strongly supported the northern effort in the Civil War. Thoreau and Hawthorne died before the war ended. Whitman worked as a nurse in the war and incorporated war poems in his later editions of *Leaves of Grass*. Dickinson ignored the war in her poetry. Oliver Wendell Holmes, energetic and cheerful, outlasted the rest of his renowned generation. He became "the last leaf upon the tree," to quote words he himself had written about Melville's grandfather, an old Revolutionary War veteran, in a poem published in 1831, when the poet and his country were still young.

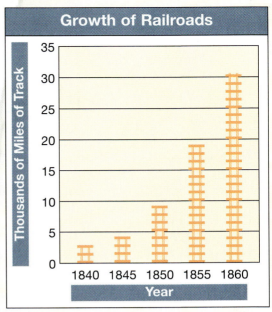

Growth of Railroads

▲ **Read a Graph** Railroads expanded rapidly after 1840. Most new railroad track was laid in the North and the Midwest. According to this graph, what five-year period saw the greatest growth in railroads?

▲ **Form a Hypothesis** The railroad was a key to the growth of industry in the North. In this image, a freight train delivers ore to a foundry where it will be turned into steel. What other effects do you think the growth of the railroads had on northern life?

The Development of American English

THE TRUTH ABOUT O.K.

by Richard Lederer

We Americans seem to have a passion for stringing initial letters together. We use *a.m.* and *p.m.* to separate light from darkness and B.C. and A.D. to identify vast stretches of time. We may listen to a deejay or veejay on *ABC, CBS, NBC,* or *MTV* or a crusading *DA* on *CNN, NPR,* or *PBS.*

Perhaps the most widely understood American word in the world is O.K. The explanations for its origin have been as imaginative as they have been various. Some have claimed that O.K. is a version of the Chocktaw affirmative *okeh.* Others have asserted that it is short for the Greek *olla kalla* ("all good") or *Orrin Kendall* crackers or *Aux Kayes* rum, or the name of chief *Old Keokuk.*

The truth is more politically correct than any of these theories.

In the 1830's in New England, there was a craze for initialisms, in the manner of the currently popular *T.G.I.F.* and *F.Y.I.* The fad went so far as to generate letter combinations of intentional misspellings: *K.G.* for "know go," *K.Y.* for "know use," and *O.W.* for "oll wright." *O.K.* for "oll korrect" naturally followed.

Of all the loopy initialisms and misspellings of the time, *O.K.* alone survived. That's because of a presidential

Martin Van Buren

nickname that consolidated the letters in the national memory.

Martin Van Buren, elected our eighth president in 1836, was born in Kinderhook, New York, and, early in his political career, was dubbed "Old Kinderhook." Echoing the "Oll Korrect" initialism, *O.K.* became the rallying cry of the Old Kinderhook Club, a political organization supporting Van Buren during the 1840 campaign.

The coinage did Van Buren no good, and he was defeated in his bid for reelection. But the word honoring his name today remains what H. L. Mencken identified as "the most shining and successful Americanism ever invented."

Activities

1. What do each of these initialisms stand for?
   - (a) A.D./B.C.
   - (b) aka
   - (c) GOP
   - (d) A.M./F.M.
   - (e) CD
   - (f) ERA
   - (g) a.m./p.m.
   - (h) IQ
   - (i) PS
   - (j) RIP
   - (k) RSVP
   - (l) UFO
2. Identify ten additional initialisms and the words each represents.

PART 1 *Fireside and Campfire*

Gettysburg National Military Museum

Guide for Interpreting

Margaret Fuller *(1810–1850)*

A strong individual, Margaret Fuller scorned the inferior lot of most women and urged women to develop their talents. She envisioned an equal partnership for men and women that would extend from married life to the highest ranks of government and business. She wrote, "We would have every path laid open to woman as to man."

An Influential Intellectual Fuller began her career as a teacher, first in Boston and later in Providence. She gave up teaching to conduct a series of public discussion groups for women on intellectual topics. She developed an association with Ralph Waldo Emerson and other New England writers and thinkers who were involved in a philosophical and literary movement, known as Transcendentalism, that emphasized humanity's connection to nature. When they launched their magazine *The Dial*, Fuller both edited and contributed to the publication.

Her activities attracted the attention of Horace Greeley, the editor of the New York *Tribune*, who invited her to be a columnist for his paper. Her critical pieces for the *Tribune* and her book *Woman in the Nineteenth Century* (1845) established her reputation as a social critic.

A Tragic End Fulfilling a lifelong wish, she traveled to Europe in 1846. Returning in 1850, she drowned, with her husband and son, in a shipwreck off Fire Island, New York.

Ralph Waldo Emerson *(1803–1882)*

Ralph Waldo Emerson was one of the most influential writers and philosophers of his time. The publication in 1836 of his essay "Nature" marks the beginning of Transcendentalism. Emerson, Fuller, Henry David Thoreau, and others associated with the movement formed a discussion circle known as the Transcendental Club. The group met regularly at Emerson's house in Concord, Massachusetts, to discuss their ideas related to nature, individuality, and the human spirit. (For more on Ralph Waldo Emerson, see p. 362.)

◆ Background for Understanding

LITERATURE: MARGARET FULLER AND *THE DIAL*

In the 1830's in New England, the literary and philosophical movement known as Transcendentalism took hold, with Ralph Waldo Emerson as its main spokesperson. As the movement grew, those involved in it sought a wider audience for their ideas. They decided to publish a journal, which they called *The Dial*, and chose Margaret Fuller and Ralph Waldo Emerson to be co-editors. Their choice of Fuller was both remarkable and wise—remarkable because a woman editor was unheard of, but wise because it was only through Fuller's practicality, organization, and drive that the magazine succeeded.

The Dial was to be published four times a year. After numerous delays in getting started, Fuller herself wrote several articles necessary to fill the first issue, which appeared in July 1840. In the four years that it was published, *The Dial* was instrumental in establishing the reputations of a number of authors, including Henry David Thoreau. Much of the work was done by Fuller, and after two years, she gave up the editorship because of the strain. Beset with funding problems, and without Fuller's organized leadership, the magazine lasted another two years.

The Announcement of *The Dial*

◆ *Literature and Your Life*

CONNECT YOUR EXPERIENCE

Have you ever collaborated with a group of friends on a project intended for a wider audience? Maybe you produced a play, created a newsletter, or painted a mural. Whatever your purpose, you probably got caught up in the excitement of sharing ideas and working toward a common goal. This was the spirit that produced *The Dial* in 1840.

Journal Writing Record your thoughts about the topic you'd choose if you were to produce a newsletter.

THEMATIC FOCUS: FIRESIDE AND CAMPFIRE

As adventurous pioneers moved west in the mid-nineteenth century, intellectual pioneers, such as the Transcendentalists, were exploring ideas in philosophy and literature. The Transcendentalists hoped to encourage others to change their attitudes, values, and behaviors. How can a magazine make such an impact on a nation's identity?

◆ Literary Focus

ANNOUNCEMENT

Politicians and writers depend on announcements to publicize events or books they want to make known to the public. An **announcement** is a public notice, an official and formal declaration. The main purpose of announcements is to attract interest, but they can also serve various other goals. For example, in "The Announcement of *The Dial*," Emerson and Fuller wanted to win over their audience, build expectations about the publication, and solicit articles from writers. They also outlined the philosophy of the journal.

◆ Build Vocabulary

WORD ROOTS: *-spect-*

The word *circumspect*, which you will encounter in "The Announcement of *The Dial*," contains the root *-spect-*, which means "to look or see." When you combine *-spect-* with *circum-*, meaning "around," you have a word that means "to look around something." In looking around something, you are acting with circumspection; that is, you are being cautious—examining all related circumstances before making a decision or judgment.

You will recognize the root in other familiar words, such as *spectacle*, *spectator*, and *inspection*.

WORD BANK

Before you read, preview this list of words from the selection.

compunctions
privations
rudiments
pittance
contingent
superseding
circumspection
reiterate
inappeasable
polemics

◆ Grammar and Style

COMMONLY CONFUSED WORDS: *PRINCIPAL* AND *PRINCIPLE*

Principal and *principle* are words that sound alike but are spelled differently and have different meanings. ***Principal*** can be a noun or an adjective and means "first in rank, authority, or importance." ***Principle*** is always a noun and means "a basic rule or truth." Look at these sample sentences:

The *principal* cause was never discovered.

I believe in the *principle* of integrity in the face of adversity.

Look for the use of *principle* in this announcement.

Reading for Success

Strategies for Reading Critically

When you read a work that presents a writer's perspective or ideas on a subject, it is a good idea to read the work critically. When you read critically, you examine the writer's ideas, especially in light of his or her purpose. You also evaluate the information the writer includes (or doesn't include) as support, and you form a judgment about the validity of the work. Here are specific strategies that will help you read critically.

Make inferences.

Writers don't always say everything they mean. Often they suggest, or imply, ideas they want their readers to grasp. You need to infer the author's larger point or message by looking beyond the details and information provided.

Recognize the author's purpose or bias.

▶ The author's purpose may be to persuade you, to inform you, or just to entertain you. Be aware that the writer's purpose can influence what he or she includes and how he or she chooses to present material.

▶ Writers often, deliberately or not, present an issue through their own bias—their point of view on a subject. Look for factors that might bias a writer's opinion. For example, the belief of Fuller and Emerson in Transcendental philosophy influenced their attitude about *The Dial*.

Evaluate the writer's points or statements.

Evaluating involves making a critical judgment. You should weigh the evidence a writer brings to bear on a subject. Consider whether the examples, reasons, or illustrations used to support points are sound and effective.

Challenge the text.

You need not always accept what a writer says at face value. Question the author's assertions, points, portrayals, and presentation. Are characters and situations true to life? Has the writer left out information that should be considered? Is the writer's evidence appropriate and relevant?

Judge the writer's work.

Apply your critical judgment to the work as a whole. As you look at the work in its totality, consider questions like these: Do the statements or points follow logically? Is the material clearly organized? Are the writer's points interesting and well supported?

As you read the announcement of the publication of *The Dial*, look at the notes along the sides. These notes demonstrate how to apply the strategies to a piece of nonfiction writing.

THE ANNOUNCEMENT OF
THE DIAL

Margaret Fuller and Ralph Waldo Emerson

We invite the attention of our countrymen to a new design. Probably not quite unexpected or unannounced will our Journal appear, though small pains have been taken to secure its welcome. Those, who have immediately acted in editing the present Number, cannot accuse themselves of any unbecoming forwardness in their undertaking, but rather of a backwardness, when they remember how often in many private circles the work was projected, how eagerly desired, and only postponed because no individual volunteered to combine and concentrate the freewill offerings of many cooperators. With some reluctance the present conductors of this work have yielded themselves to the wishes of their friends, finding something sacred and not to be withstood in the importunity which urged the production of a Journal in a new spirit.

As they have not proposed themselves to the work, neither can they lay any the least claim to an option or determination of the spirit in which it is conceived, or to what is peculiar in the design. In that respect, they have obeyed, though with great joy, the strong current of thought and feeling, which, for a few years past, has led many sincere persons in New England to make new demands on literature, and to reprobate[1] that rigor of our conventions of religion and education which is turning us to stone, which renounces hope, which looks only backward, which asks only such a future as the past, which suspects improvement, and holds nothing so much in horror as new views and the dreams of youth.

With these terrors the conductors of the present Journal have nothing to do,—not even so much as a word of reproach to waste. They know that there is a portion of the youth and of the adult population of this country, who have not shared them; who have in secret or in public paid their vows to truth and freedom; who love reality too well to care for names, and who live by a Faith too earnest and profound to suffer them to doubt the eternity of its object, or to shake themselves free from its authority. Under the fictions and customs which occupied others, these have explored the Necessary, the Plain, the True, the Human,—and so gained a vantage ground, which commands the history of the past and the present.

No one can converse much with different classes of society in New England, without remarking the progress of a revolution. Those who share in it have no external organization, no badge, no creed, no name. They do not vote, or print, or even meet together. They do not know each other's faces or names. They are united only in a common love of truth, and love of its work. They are of all conditions and constitutions. Of these acolytes,[2] if some are happily born and well bred, many are no doubt ill dressed, ill placed, ill made—with as many

---

Infer from this reference to "private circles" that there is an audience for the journal.

Challenge this statement by noting the significant literature being written during this time period.

Recognize authors' purpose: These are the people the writers wish to reach.

From the details presented, you can **infer** that this audience is large.

---

1. **reprobate** (rep´ rə bāt) v.: To reject; disapprove of; censure strongly.

2. **acolytes** (ak´ ə līts´) n.: Followers of a creed or belief system; also assistants to a religious order.

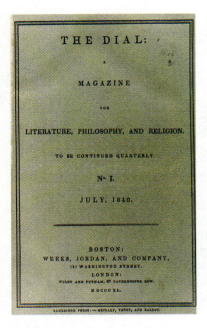

◀ **Critical Viewing** How do the language of the announcement and the cover of the magazine reflect the time period in which they were written? How might the cover be designed for today's audience? **[Connect]**

scars of hereditary vice as other men. Without pomp, without trumpet, in lonely and obscure places, in solitude, in servitude, in compunctions and privations, trudging beside the team in a dusty road, or drudging a hireling in other men's cornfields, schoolmasters, who teach a few children rudiments for a pittance, ministers of small parishes of the obscurer sects, lone women in dependent condition, matrons and young maidens, rich and poor, beautiful and hard-favored, without concert or proclamation of any kind, they have silently given in their several adherence to a new hope, and in all companies do signify a greater trust in the nature and resources of man, than the laws or the popular opinions will well allow.

This spirit of the time is felt by every individual with some difference,—to each one casting its light upon the objects nearest to his temper and habits of thought;—to one, coming in the shape of special reforms in the state; to another, in modifications of the various callings of men, and the customs of business; to a third, opening a new scope for literature and art; to a fourth, in philosophical insight; to a fifth, in the vast solitudes of prayer. It is in every form a protest against usage, and a search for principles. In all its movements, it is peaceable, and in the very lowest marked with a triumphant success. Of course, it rouses the opposition of all which it judges and condemns, but it is too confident in its tone to comprehend an objection, and so builds no outworks for possible defense against contingent enemies. It has the step of Fate, and goes on existing like an oak or a river, because it must.

> This passage reveals the **authors' bias** in support of the new philosophy.

In literature, this influence appears not yet in new books so much as in the higher tone of criticism. The antidote to all narrowness is the comparison of the record with nature, which at once shames the record and stimulates to new attempts. Whilst we look at this, we wonder how any book has been thought worthy to be preserved. There is somewhat in all life untranslatable into language. He who keeps his eye on that will write better than others, and think less of his writing, and of all writing. Every thought has a certain imprisoning as well as uplifting quality, and, in proportion to its energy on the will, refuses to become an object of intellectual contemplation. Thus what is great usually slips through our fingers, and it seems wonderful how a lifelike word ever comes to be written. If our Journal share the impulses of the time, it cannot now prescribe its own course. It cannot foretell in orderly propositions what it shall attempt. All criticism should be poetic; unpredictable; superseding, as every new thought does, all foregone thoughts, and making a new light on the whole world. Its brow is not wrinkled with circumspection, but serene, cheerful, adoring. It has all things to say, and no less than all the world for its final audience.

> **Challenge** this statement. Do you believe that some earlier literature was worth preserving?

Our plan embraces much more than criticism; were it not so, our criticism would be naught. Everything noble is directed on life, and this is. We do not wish to say pretty or curious things, or to reiterate a few propositions in varied forms, but, if we can, to give expression to that spirit which lifts men to a higher platform, restores to them the religious sentiment, brings them worthy aims and pure pleasures, purges the inward eye, makes life less desultory,[3] and, through raising men to the level of nature, takes away its melancholy

> **Evaluate** the support for the statement that this, like everything noble, is directed on life.

---

3. **desultory** (des´ əl tôr´ ē) *adj.*: Random; wandering.

from the landscape, and reconciles the practical with the speculative powers.

But perhaps we are telling our little story too gravely. There are always great arguments at hand for a true action, even for the writing of a few pages. There is nothing but seems near it and prompts it,—the sphere in the ecliptic,[4] the sap in the apple tree,—every fact, every appearance seem to persuade to it.

Our means correspond with the ends we have indicated. As we wish not to multiply books, but to report life, our resources are therefore not so much the pens of practiced writers, as the discourse of the living, and the portfolios which friendship has opened to us. From the beautiful recesses of private thought; from the experience and hope of spirits which are withdrawing from all old forms, and seeking in all that is new somewhat to meet their inappeasable longings; from the secret confession of genius afraid to trust itself to aught[5] but sympathy; from the conversations of fervid and mystical pietists; from tear-stained diaries of sorrow and passion; from the manuscripts of young poets; and from the records of youthful taste commenting on old works of art; we hope to draw thoughts and feelings, which being alive can impart life.

And so with diligent hands and good intent we set down our Dial on the

> Judge this statement. Do you believe that thoughts can impart life?

earth. We wish it may resemble that instrument in its celebrated happiness, that of measuring no hours but those of sunshine. Let it be one cheerful rational voice amidst the din of mourners and polemics. Or to abide by our chosen image, let it be such a Dial, not as the dead face of a clock, hardly even such as the Gnomon[6] in a garden, but rather such a Dial as in the Garden itself, in whose leaves and flowers and fruits the suddenly awakened sleeper is instantly apprised not what part of dead time, but what state of life and growth is now arrived and arriving.

---

4. **sphere in the ecliptic** (i klip′ tik): Sun's path among the stars.
5. **aught** (ôt) n. (archaic): Any least part; anything whatsoever.

6. **Gnomon** (nō′ män) n.: A sundial; an indicator of the hour by the shadow cast by an object.

◆ Build Vocabulary

compunctions (kəm puŋk′ shənz) n.: Anxieties; regrets

privations (prī vā′ shənz) n.: Loss of things previously possessed

rudiments (roo′ də məntz) n.: Fundamental skills

pittance (pit′ əns) n.: Meager wage or remuneration

contingent (kən tin′ jənt) adj.: Unpredictable; accidental; dependent on

superseding (soo′ pər sēd′ iŋ) v.: Overriding; making outmoded

circumspection (sʉr′ kəm spekt′ shən) n.: Cautiousness; prudence

reiterate (rē it′ ə rāt′) v.: Repeat or state over again

inappeasable (in′ ə pē′ zə bəl) adj.: Unable to be quieted or calmed

polemics (pō lem′ iks) n.: Controversial arguments; branch of theology devoted to refuting errors

---

Guide for Responding

◆ *Literature and Your Life*

Reader's Response Would you want to read the articles announced as forthcoming in *The Dial?* Why or why not?

Thematic Focus How do the writers characterize the period in which they live? Are they hopeful or discouraged about the future of the country?

☑ Check Your Comprehension

1. Where did the idea for this journal originate? Explain.
2. Who are the participants in the "revolution" in progress? What unites them?
3. Who will write for *The Dial?* What should they write about?

Guide for Responding (continued)

◆ Critical Thinking

INTERPRET

1. What characterizes the "spirit" of the launchers of *The Dial*? **[Infer]**
2. How appropriate is the word *acolytes* (see footnote on p. 229)to describe the intended audience of *The Dial*? **[Analyze]**
3. (a) What distinction do the writers make between "a garden" and "the Garden"? (b) Why is *The Dial* an appropriate name for the new journal? **[Distinguish; Support]**

APPLY

4. Which techniques in "The Announcement of *The Dial*" would be most effective in appealing to an audience today? **[Apply]**

EXTEND

5. Compare a commercial announcing a new product or a trailer for a new film with "The Announcement of *The Dial*." What similarities and differences do you find? **[Media Link]**

◆ Reading for Success

STRATEGIES FOR READING CRITICALLY

Review the strategies for critical reading and the notes showing how to apply them. Then answer the following questions.

1. What can you infer from the announcement about the writers' belief in the individual?
2. What claim for the publication would you challenge as most unrealistic?
3. Which phrase or sentence from the announcement do you think states the purpose of *The Dial* most clearly?

◆ Literary Focus

ANNOUNCEMENT

An **announcement** informs the public about a forthcoming event. When Fuller and Emerson announce the first issue of *The Dial*, they present this information in a way that encourages potential readers to eagerly anticipate the magazine.

1. How do the writers create a sense of eager anticipation for *The Dial*?
2. List two examples that show "The Announcement of *The Dial*" flatters its audience.

◆ Build Vocabulary

USING THE WORD ROOT -*spect*-

Knowing that -*spect*- means "to see" can help you to decode words with this root. Explain the meaning of the following italicized words. Consult a dictionary, if necessary, to confirm your definition.

1. In *retrospect*, history is understandable as a series of causes and effects.
2. Have you *inspected* your essay for errors?
3. A conscientious effort earns the *respect* of others.
4. Don't make a *spectacle* of yourself.

USING THE WORD BANK

Complete the following sentences, filling in the blanks with appropriate words from the Word Bank.

1. He had few ___?___ about deciding to work for a ___?___.
2. As she easily learned the ___?___ of the job, supervisors found no need to ___?___ basic instructions.
3. Accustomed to ___?___, he approached dubious employment offers with ___?___ .
4. Fuller was ___?___ in her rejection of ___?___.
5. She received several tempting offers. ___?___ all other offers was a bid from the *Tribune*, but her acceptance was ___?___ on Emerson's approval.

◆ Grammar and Style

COMMONLY CONFUSED WORDS: *PRINCIPAL* AND *PRINCIPLE*

In "The Announcement of *The Dial*" the writers refer to the **principles,** or ideals, upon which their journal is founded. Don't confuse that word with **principal,** meaning "most important."

Practice On your paper, write the following sentences, completing them with the words *principal* and *principle*.

1. Our ___?___ follows strict ___?___ in running our school.
2. The ___?___ result was increased sales.
3. Which ___?___ apply to the decision to cancel that account?

Writing Application Write a paragraph about something in which you believe. Use both *principle* and *principal* correctly.

Build Your Portfolio

Idea Bank

Writing

1. Announcement Letter Write a letter to a friend announcing a project or event. Design your letter to make the friend feel as if the project were planned especially for him or her.

2. Persuasive Credo Take a stand on an issue in which you believe strongly, and write an article that both expresses your credo, or belief, and convinces others to accept your view.

3. Persuasive Essay Like Emerson and Fuller, do you feel that reading philosophical writings can change your behavior or improve your life? In an essay, argue for or against this assertion.

Speaking and Listening

4. Literary Reading Prepare a reading of selections from your school's literary magazine. Organize the selections in meaningful groupings and choose classmates to read whose voices will enhance the selections. **[Performing Arts Link]**

5. Panel Discussion Research influential publications in American history, such as William Lloyd Garrison's journal *The Liberator* or Upton Sinclair's novel *The Jungle*. In a panel discussion, evaluate the extent to which such works can be credited with bringing about significant changes.

Projects

6. Journal Review Make a study of the publications at other schools. Collect samples and compare them with your school's publications. Present your report to the school's administration.

7. Articles Display Collect articles that express exciting and well-presented ideas. Group the articles in subject areas, and arrange them into a display for your classmates.

Writing Mini-Lesson

Proposal for a Student Magazine

A proposal addresses an audience for a specific purpose—to win their support for a project. Suppose you and a group of classmates want to start a student magazine at your school. Write a proposal to convince school administrators to allow you to start publishing this magazine.

Writing Skills Focus: A Clear and Consistent Purpose

In order to persuade school administrators to allocate funds or supervision, present your case **clearly and consistently**. Notice how Fuller and Emerson present the goals for *The Dial*:

Model From the Announcement

We do not wish to say pretty or curious things, or to reiterate a few propositions in varied forms, but, if we can, to give expression to that spirit which lifts men to a higher platform . . . and, through raising men to the level of nature, takes away its melancholy from the landscape, and reconciles the practical with the speculative powers.

Prewriting Brainstorm to identify a focus for your magazine. Write your goal in one concise statement of purpose. Research the costs involved in obtaining the resources you will need. This information will demonstrate that you have thought out your proposal carefully.

Drafting State the purpose of your magazine, and support it with a philosophy. Then itemize the costs. Emphasize the need for the magazine in order to justify the expenses needed to produce it.

Revising Every fact you supply should relate to your main purpose. If necessary, add details that make the connection explicit. Ask a classmate whether your plan seems clear, consistent, and reasonable. Make changes based on feedback from your reviewer.

Guide for Interpreting

Washington Irving *(1783–1859)*

Named after the first American president, Washington Irving became the first American writer to achieve an international reputation.

An American Youth Born into a wealthy family, Irving began studying law at the age of sixteen. Though he had planned to be a lawyer, he found he was more interested in travel and writing. He spent much time traveling throughout Europe and New York's Hudson Valley and reading European literature. Irving also wrote satirical essays using the pen name Jonathan Oldstyle. When Irving was twenty-four, he and his brother began publishing a magazine anonymously, *Salmagundi* (the name of a spicy appetizer), which carried humorous sketches and essays about New York society.

In 1809, he published his first major work, *A History of New York From the Beginning of the World to the End of the Dutch Dynasty,* using the pseudonym Diedrich Knickerbocker. The book, a humorous examination of New York during colonial times, was well received and made Irving famous.

Tour of Europe From 1815 to 1832, Irving lived in Europe. There he traveled extensively and learned about European customs, traditions, and folklore. Inspired by the European folk heritage, Irving created two of his most famous stories, "The Legend of Sleepy Hollow" and "Rip Van Winkle," transforming two traditional German tales into distinctly American stories set in the Hudson Valley. When Irving published these two stories in the *Sketchbook* (1820), under the pseudonymn Geoffrey Crayon, writers and critics throughout Europe and the United States responded enthusiastically.

The international success of Irving's stories marked the beginning of a distinctly American literary heritage.

A Devoted American While in Europe, Irving completed three other books, including *Tales of a Traveller*, which contains "The Devil and Tom Walker." When his patriotism was questioned because of his time abroad, Irving responded: "I am endeavoring to serve my country. Whatever I have written has been written with the feelings and published as the writing of an American. Is that renouncing my country? How else am I to serve my country—by coming home and begging an office of it: which I should not have the kind of talent or the business habits requisite to fill?—If I can do any good in this world it is with my pen." Although Irving continued to publish after returning to the United States, he is remembered mainly for a few characters he created while in Europe.

◆ Background for Understanding

LITERATURE: THE LEGEND OF FAUST

"The Devil and Tom Walker" is a variation of the Faust legend—a tale about a man who sells his soul to the Devil for earthly benefits. The legend was inspired by a real person, a wandering scholar and conjurer named Faust, who lived in early sixteenth-century Germany. *Faustbach,* the first printed version of a Faust legend, was published in 1587. That story proposed that Faust had made a pact with the Devil for knowledge and power on Earth.

Over the years, many variations of the Faust legend have appeared, including a 1604 play by English dramatist Christopher Marlowe, a two-part dramatic poem (1808, 1832) by Johann Goethe, an 1859 opera by Charles Gounod, and a 1947 novel by Thomas Mann. Each retelling involves a person who trades his soul for experience, knowledge, or treasure. Adaptations do not share the same ending—in some, the protagonist is doomed; in others, he is redeemed.

The Devil and Tom Walker

◆ *Literature and Your Life*

CONNECT YOUR EXPERIENCE

In our society, it's not uncommon to see political candidates who fight to win at any cost, business executives who make money in a dishonest way, and Olympic athletes who bend the rules to get the gold. The main character in this story goes to even greater extremes to achieve his goal of great wealth: He makes a pact with the Devil—even though he knows that he will eventually have to pay for this decision.

Journal Writing Give examples of people in today's news who are driven by their need for money, power, or fame.

THEMATIC FOCUS: FIRESIDE AND CAMPFIRE

What details make this story, based on a German legend, a distinctly American tale that reflects the characteristics of its time?

◆ Reading Strategy

INFER CULTURAL ATTITUDES

This story reveals many of the **cultural attitudes** of the people living in New England in the 1720's. Irving doesn't tell you these attitudes directly; he suggests them through the details of the story. It's left up to you to **make inferences**, or draw conclusions, about cultural attitudes based on the details Irving provides. Look, for example, at this description of the old Indian fort:

> . . . the common people had a bad opinion of it, from the stories handed down from the time of the Indian wars; when it was asserted that the savages held incantations here, and made sacrifices to the evil spirit.

From these details, you can infer that the colonists had a suspicious attitude toward the Native Americans and a belief in the Devil.

◆ Grammar and Style

ADJECTIVE CLAUSES

An **adjective clause**, also known as a relative clause, is a subordinate clause (a clause that cannot stand alone as a sentence) that modifies a noun or pronoun. Look at this example from the story:

> A miserable horse, *whose ribs were as articulate as the bars of a gridiron,* stalked about a field . . .

The words in italics are an adjective clause that modifies *horse*.

◆ Literary Focus

OMNISCIENT NARRATOR

"The Devil and Tom Walker" is told not by a participant in the story but by an **omniscient** (all-knowing) **narrator** who stands outside the action and relates the thoughts and feelings of all the characters. When a story is told by an omniscient narrator, the reader is not limited to the thoughts and perspective of a single character but may know the thoughts and feelings of any character. The narrator may even comment on the events of the story.

◆ Build Vocabulary

PREFIXES: *ex-*

Tom Walker *extorts* money from people; that is, he obtains it by threat or force. The prefix *ex-* means "out." The word *extort* literally means "to twist something out of someone."

WORD BANK

Before you read, preview this list of words.

| avarice |
| usurers |
| extort |
| ostentation |
| parsimony |

The Devil and Tom Walker

Washington Irving

A few miles from Boston in Massachusetts, there is a deep inlet, winding several miles into the interior of the country from Charles Bay, and terminating in a thickly wooded swamp or morass. On one side of this inlet is a beautiful dark grove; on the opposite side the land rises abruptly from the water's edge into a high ridge, on which grow a few scattered oaks of great age and immense size. Under one of these gigantic trees, according to old stories, there was a great amount of treasure buried by Kidd the pirate.[1] The inlet allowed a facility to bring the money in a boat secretly and at night to the very foot of the hill; the elevation of the place permitted a good look-out to be kept that no one was at hand; while the remarkable trees formed good landmarks by which the place might easily be found again. The old stories add, moreover, that the Devil presided at the hiding of the money, and took it under his guardianship; but this it is well known he always does with buried treasure, particularly when it has been ill-gotten.

---

1. **Kidd the pirate:** Captain William Kidd (1645–1701).

The Devil and Tom Walker, 1856, John Quidor, The Cleveland Museum of Art

▲ **Critical Viewing** This painting is called *The Devil and Tom Walker*. Explain how the lighting and other elements reflect the mood of Irving's story. **[Analyze]**

Be that as it may, Kidd never returned to recover his wealth; being shortly after seized at Boston, sent out to England, and there hanged for a pirate.

About the year 1727, just at the time that earthquakes were prevalent in New England, and shook many tall sinners down upon their knees, there lived near this place a meager, miserly fellow, of the name of Tom Walker. He had a wife as miserly as himself: they were so miserly that they even conspired to cheat each other. Whatever the woman could lay hands on, she hid away;

a hen could not cackle but she was on the alert to secure the new-laid egg. Her husband was continually prying about to detect her secret hoards, and many and fierce were the conflicts that took place about what ought to have been common property. They lived in a forlorn-looking house that stood alone, and had an air of starvation. A few straggling savin trees, emblems of sterility, grew near it; no smoke ever curled from its chimney; no traveler stopped at its door. A miserable horse, whose ribs were as articulate as the bars of a gridiron, stalked about a field, where a thin carpet of moss, scarcely covering the ragged beds of puddingstone, tantalized and balked his hunger; and sometimes he would lean his head over the fence, look piteously at the passerby, and seem to petition deliverance from this land of famine.

The house and its inmates had altogether a bad name. Tom's wife was a tall termagant,[2] fierce of temper, loud of tongue, and strong of arm. Her voice was often heard in wordy warfare with her husband; and his face sometimes showed signs that their conflicts were not confined to words. No one ventured, however, to interfere between them. The lonely wayfarer shrunk within himself at the horrid clamor and clapperclawing;[3] eyed the den of discord askance; and hurried on his way, rejoicing, if a bachelor, in his celibacy.

One day that Tom Walker had been to a distant part of the neighborhood, he took what he considered a shortcut homeward, through the swamp. Like most shortcuts, it was an ill-chosen route. The swamp was thickly grown with great gloomy pines and hemlocks, some of them ninety feet high, which made it dark at noonday, and a retreat for all the owls of the neighborhood. It was full of pits and quagmires, partly covered with weeds and mosses, where the green surface often betrayed the traveler into a gulf of black, smothering mud; there were also dark and stagnant pools, the abodes of the tadpole, the bullfrog, and the watersnake; where the trunks of pines and hemlocks lay half-drowned, half-rotting, looking like alligators sleeping in the mire.

Tom had long been picking his way cautiously through this treacherous forest; stepping from tuft to tuft of rushes and roots, which afforded precarious footholds among deep sloughs; or pacing carefully, like a cat, along the prostrate trunks of trees; startled now and then by the sudden screaming of the bittern, or the quacking of a wild duck, rising on the wing from some solitary pool.

---

2. **termagant** (tŭr′ mə gənt) n.: Quarrelsome woman.
3. **clapperclawing** (klap′ ər klô′ iŋ) n.: Clawing or scratching.

At length he arrived at a piece of firm ground, which ran out like a peninsula into the deep bosom of the swamp. It had been one of the strongholds of the Indians during their wars with the first colonists. Here they had thrown up a kind of fort, which they had looked upon as almost impregnable, and had used as a place of refuge for their squaws and children. Nothing remained of the old Indian fort but a few embankments, gradually sinking to the level of the surrounding earth, and already overgrown in part by oaks and other forest trees, the foliage of which formed a contrast to the dark pines and hemlocks of the swamp.

It was late in the dusk of evening when Tom Walker reached the old fort, and he paused there awhile to rest himself. Anyone but he would have felt unwilling to linger in this lonely, melancholy place, for the common people had a bad opinion of it, from the stories handed down from the time of the Indian wars; when it was asserted that the savages held incantations here, and made sacrifices to the evil spirit.

Tom Walker, however, was not a man to be troubled with any fears of the kind. He reposed himself for some time on the trunk of a fallen hemlock, listening to the boding cry of the tree toad, and delving with his walking staff into a mound of black mold at his feet. As he turned up the soil unconsciously, his staff struck against something hard. He raked it out of the vegetable mold, and lo! a cloven skull, with an Indian tomahawk buried deep in it, lay before him. The rust on the weapon showed the time that had elapsed since this deathblow had been given. It was a dreary memento of the fierce struggle that had taken place in this last foothold of the Indian warriors.

◆ **Reading Strategy**
What do these sentences tell you about the **colonists' attitude** toward Native Americans?

"Humph!" said Tom Walker, as he gave it a kick to shake the dirt from it.

"Let that skull alone!" said a gruff voice. Tom lifted up his eyes, and beheld a great black man seated directly opposite him, on the stump of a tree. He was exceedingly surprised, having neither heard nor seen anyone approach; and he was still more perplexed on observing, as well as the gathering gloom would permit, that the stranger was neither Negro nor Indian. It is true he was dressed in a rude half-Indian garb, and had a red belt or sash swathed round his body; but his face was neither black nor copper color, but swarthy and dingy, and begrimed with soot, as if he had been accustomed to toil among fires and forges. He had a shock of coarse black hair, that stood out from his head in all directions, and bore an ax on his shoulder.

He scowled for a moment at Tom with a pair of great red eyes.

"What are you doing on my grounds?" said the black man, with a hoarse growling voice.

"Your grounds!" said Tom with a sneer, "no more your grounds than mine; they belong to Deacon Peabody."

"Deacon Peabody be d—d," said the stranger, "as I flatter myself he will be, if he does not look more to his own sins and less to those of his neighbors. Look yonder, and see how Deacon Peabody is faring."

Tom looked in the direction that the stranger pointed, and beheld one of the great trees, fair and flourishing without, but rotten at the core, and saw that it had been nearly hewn through, so that the first high wind was likely to blow it down. On the bark of the tree was scored the name of Deacon Peabody, an eminent man, who had waxed wealthy by driving shrewd bargains with the Indians. He now looked round, and found most of the tall trees marked with the name of some great man of the colony, and all more or less scored by the ax. The one on which he had been seated, and which had evidently just been hewn down, bore the name of Crowninshield: and he recollected a mighty rich man of that name, who made a vulgar display of wealth, which it was whispered he had acquired by buccaneering.

"He's just ready for burning!" said the black man, with a growl of triumph. "You see I am likely to have a good stock of firewood for winter."

"But what right have you," said Tom, "to cut down Deacon Peabody's timber?"

"The right of a prior claim," said the other. "This woodland belonged to me long before one of your white-faced race put foot upon the soil."

"And pray, who are you, if I may be so bold?" said Tom.

"Oh, I go by various names. I am the wild huntsman in some countries; the black miner in others. In this neighborhood I am known by the name of the black woodsman. I am he to whom the red men consecrated this spot, and in honor of whom they now and then roasted a white man, by way of sweet-smelling sacrifice. Since the red men have been exterminated by you white savages, I amuse myself by presiding at the persecutions of Quakers and Anabaptists;[4] I am the great patron and prompter of slave dealers, and the grandmaster of the Salem witches."

"The upshot of all which is, that, if I mistake not," said Tom, sturdily, "you are he commonly called Old Scratch."

"The same, at your service!" replied the black man, with a half-civil nod.

Such was the opening of this interview, according to the old story; though it has almost too familiar an air to be credited. One would think that to meet with such a singular personage, in this wild, lonely place, would have shaken any man's nerves; but Tom was a hard-minded fellow, not easily daunted, and he had lived so long with a termagant wife, that he did not even fear the Devil.

It is said that after this commencement they had a long and earnest conversation together, as Tom returned homeward. The black man told him of great sums of money buried by Kidd the pirate, under the oak trees on the high ridge, not far from the morass. All

---

4. **Quakers and Anabaptists:** Two religious groups that were persecuted for their beliefs.

Walking stick, King Georges County, Virginia, 1846, Abby Aldrich Rockefeller Folk Art Center, Williamsburg, Virginia

these were under his command, and protected by his power, so that none could find them but such as propitiated his favor. These he offered to place within Tom Walker's reach, having conceived an especial kindness for him; but they were to be had only on certain conditions. What these conditions were may easily be surmised, though Tom never disclosed them publicly. They must have been very hard, for he required time to think of them, and he was not a man to stick at trifles where money was in view. When they had reached the edge of the swamp, the stranger paused—"What proof have I that all you have been telling me is true?" said Tom. "There is my signature," said the black man, pressing his finger on Tom's forehead. So saying, he turned off among the thickets of the swamp, and seemed, as Tom said, to go down, down, down, into the earth, until nothing but his head and shoulders could be seen, and so on, until he totally disappeared.

When Tom reached home, he found the black print of a finger, burnt, as it were, into his forehead, which nothing could obliterate.

The first news his wife had to tell him was the sudden death of Absalom Crowninshield, the rich buccaneer. It was announced in the papers with the usual flourish, that "A great man had fallen in Israel."[5]

Tom recollected the tree which his black friend had just hewn down, and which was ready for burning, "Let the freebooter roast,"

▲ **Critical Viewing** On page 241, Tom Walker's wife packs up her valuables to take into the forest. Why might a teapot like this one be considered valuable? **[Support]**

Teapot, Yale University Art Gallery, New Haven

said Tom, "who cares!" He now felt convinced that all he had heard and seen was no illusion.

He was not prone to let his wife into his confidence; but as this was an uneasy secret, he willingly shared it with her. All her avarice was awakened at the mention of hidden gold, and she urged her husband to comply with the black man's terms and secure what would make them wealthy for life. However Tom might have felt disposed to sell himself to the Devil, he was determined not to do so to oblige his wife; so he flatly refused, out of the mere spirit of contradiction. Many and bitter were the quarrels they had on the subject, but the more she talked, the more resolute was Tom not to be damned to please her.

At length she determined to drive the bargain on her own account, and if she succeeded, to keep all the gain to herself. Being of the same fearless temper as her husband, she set off for the old Indian fort towards the close of a summer's day. She was many hours absent. When she came back, she was reserved and sullen in her replies. She spoke something of a black man, whom she had met about twilight, hewing at

◆ **Literary Focus**
What does the narrator reveal about Tom's wife here?

◆ **Build Vocabulary**
avarice (av´ ər is) *n.*: Greed

5. **A . . . Israel:** A reference to II Samuel 3:38 in the Bible. The Puritans often called New England "Israel."

the root of a tall tree. He was sulky, however, and would not come to terms: she was to go again with a propitiatory offering, but what it was she forbore to say.

The next evening she set off again for the swamp, with her apron heavily laden. Tom waited and waited for her, but in vain; midnight came, but she did not make her appearance: morning, noon, night returned, but still she did not come. Tom now grew uneasy for her safety, especially as he found she had carried off in her apron the silver teapot and spoons, and every portable article of value. Another night elapsed, another morning came; but no wife. In a word, she was never heard of more.

What was her real fate nobody knows, in consequence of so many pretending to know. It is one of those facts which have become confounded by a variety of historians. Some asserted that she lost her way among the tangled mazes of the swamp, and sank into some pit or slough; others, more uncharitable, hinted that she had eloped with the household booty, and made off to some other province; while others surmised that the tempter had decoyed her into a dismal quagmire, on the top of which her hat was found lying. In confirmation of this, it was said a great black man, with an ax on his shoulder, was seen late that very evening coming out of the swamp, carrying a bundle tied in a checked apron, with an air of surly triumph.

The most current and probable story, however, observes that Tom Walker grew so anxious about the fate of his wife and his property, that he set out at length to seek them both at the Indian fort. During a long summer's afternoon he searched about the gloomy place, but no wife was to be

seen. He called her name repeatedly, but she was nowhere to be heard. The bittern alone responded to his voice, as he flew screaming by; or the bullfrog croaked dolefully from a neighboring pool. At length, it is said, just in the brown hour of twilight, when the owls began to hoot, and the bats to flit about, his attention was attracted by the clamor of carrion crows hovering about a cypress tree. He looked up, and beheld a bundle tied in a checked apron, and hanging in the branches of the tree, with a great vulture perched hard by, as if keeping watch upon it. He leaped with joy; for he recognized his wife's apron, and supposed it to contain the household valuables.

"Let us get hold of the property," said he, consolingly to himself, "and we will

▶ **Critical Viewing** The narrator describes "a great vulture perched hard by" and a checked apron hanging in the tree. What do you think happened to Tom Walker's wife? **[Infer]**

endeavor to do without the woman."

As he scrambled up the tree, the vulture spread its wide wings, and sailed off screaming into the deep shadows of the forest. Tom seized the checked apron, but woeful sight! found nothing but a heart and liver tied up in it!

Such, according to the most authentic old story, was all that was to be found of Tom's wife. She had probably attempted to deal with the black man as she had been accustomed to deal with her husband; but though a female scold is generally considered a match for the Devil, yet in this instance she appears to have had the worst of it. She must have died game, however; for it is said Tom noticed many prints of cloven feet deeply stamped about the tree, and found handfuls of hair, that looked as if they had been plucked from the coarse black shock of the woodsman. Tom knew his wife's prowess by experience. He shrugged his shoulders, as he looked at the signs of a fierce clapperclawing. "Egad," said he to himself, "Old Scratch must had had a tough time of it!"

Tom consoled himself for the loss of his property, with the loss of his wife, for he was a man of fortitude. He even felt something like gratitude towards the black woodsman, who, he considered, had done him a kindness. He sought, therefore, to cultivate a further acquaintance with him, but for some time without success; the old black-legs played shy, for whatever people may think, he is not always to be had for calling for: he knows how to play his cards when pretty sure of his game.

◆ **Literary Focus**
What does the narrator reveal about Tom's feelings here?

At length, it is said, when delay had whetted Tom's eagerness to the quick, and prepared him to agree to anything rather than not gain the promised treasure, he met the black man one evening in his usual woodsman's dress, with his ax on his shoulder, sauntering along the swamp, and humming a tune. He affected to receive Tom's advances with great indifference, made brief replies, and went on humming his tune.

By degrees, however, Tom brought him to business, and they began to haggle about the terms on which the former was to have the pirate's treasure. There was one condition which need not be mentioned, being generally understood in all cases where the Devil grants favors; but there were others about which, though of less importance, he was inflexibly obstinate. He insisted that the money found through his means should be employed in his service. He proposed, therefore, that Tom should employ it in the black traffic; that is to say, that he should fit out a slave ship. This, however, Tom resolutely refused: he was bad enough in all conscience, but the Devil himself could not tempt him to turn slave-trader.

Finding Tom so squeamish on this point, he did not insist upon it, but proposed, instead, that he should turn usurer; the Devil being extremely anxious for the increase of usurers, looking upon them as his peculiar[6] people.

To this no objections were made, for it was just to Tom's taste.

"You shall open a broker's shop in Boston next month," said the black man.

"I'll do it tomorrow, if you wish," said Tom Walker.

"You shall lend money at two per cent a month."

"Egad, I'll charge four!" replied Tom Walker.

"You shall extort bonds, foreclose mortgages, drive the merchant to bankruptcy—"

---

6. **peculiar:** Particular; special.

"I'll drive him to the D——l," cried Tom Walker.

"You are the usurer for my money!" said the blacklegs with delight. "When will you want the rhino?"[7]

"This very night."

"Done!" said the Devil.

"Done!" said Tom Walker. So they shook hands and struck a bargain.

A few days' time saw Tom Walker seated behind his desk in a countinghouse in Boston.

His reputation for a ready-moneyed man, who would lend money out for a good consideration, soon spread abroad. Everybody remembers the time of Governor Belcher,[8] when money was particularly scarce. It was a time of paper credit. The country had been deluged with government bills; the famous Land Bank[9] had been established; there had been a rage for speculating; the people had run mad with schemes for new settlements, for building cities in the wilderness; land jobbers[10] went about with maps of grants, and townships, and El Dorados,[11] lying nobody knew where, but which everybody was ready to purchase. In a word, the great speculating fever which breaks out every now and then in the country, had raged to an alarming degree, and everybody was dreaming of making sudden fortunes from nothing. As usual the fever had subsided; the dream had gone off, and the imaginary fortunes with it; the patients were left in doleful plight, and the whole country resounded with the consequent cry of "hard times."

At this propitious time of public distress did Tom Walker set up as usurer in Boston. His door was soon thronged by customers. The needy and adventurous, the gambling speculator, the dreaming land jobber, the thriftless tradesman, the merchant with cracked credit, in short, everyone driven to raise money by desperate means and desperate sacrifices, hurried to Tom Walker.

Thus Tom was the universal friend of the needy, and acted like a "friend in need"; that is to say, he always exacted good pay and good security. In proportion to the distress of the applicant was the hardness of his terms. He accumulated bonds and mortgages; gradually squeezed his customers closer and closer, and sent them at length, dry as a sponge, from his door.

In this way he made money hand over hand, became a rich and mighty man, and exalted his cocked hat upon 'Change.[12] He built himself, as usual, a vast house, out of <u>ostentation</u>; but left the greater part of it unfinished and unfurnished, out of <u>parsimony</u>. He even set up a carriage in the fullness of his vainglory, though he nearly starved the horses which drew it; and as the ungreased wheels groaned and screeched on the axletrees, you would have thought you heard the souls of the poor debtors he was squeezing.

As Tom waxed old, however, he grew thoughtful. Having secured the good things of this world, he began to feel anxious about those of the next. He thought with regret on the bargain he had made with his black friend, and set his wits to work to cheat him out of the conditions. He became, therefore, all of a sudden, a violent churchgoer. He prayed loudly and strenuously, as if heaven

◆ **Reading Strategy**
What can you infer about the attitudes of the day toward money?

---

7. **rhino** (rī′nō): Slang term for money.
8. **Governor Belcher:** Jonathan Belcher, the governor of Massachusetts Bay Colony from 1730 through 1741.
9. **Land Bank:** A bank that financed transactions in real estate.
10. **land jobbers:** People who bought and sold undeveloped land.
11. **El Dorados** (el də rä′ dōz) n.: Places that are rich in gold or opportunity. El Dorado was a legendary country in South America sought by early Spanish explorers for its gold and precious stones.

12. **'Change:** Exchange where bankers and merchants did business.

◆ **Build Vocabulary**

usurers (yōō′ zhōō rərz) n.: Moneylenders who charge very high interest

extort (eks tôrt′) v.: To obtain by threat or violence

ostentation (äs′ tən tā′ shən) n.: Boastful display

parsimony (pär′ sə mō′ nē) n.: Stinginess

were to be taken by force of lungs. Indeed, one might always tell when he had sinned most during the week, by the clamor of his Sunday devotion. The quiet Christians who had been modestly and steadfastly traveling Zionward,[13] were struck with self-reproach at seeing themselves so suddenly outstripped in their career by this new-made convert. Tom was as rigid in religious as in money matters; he was a stern supervisor and censurer of his neighbors, and seemed to think every sin entered up to their account became a credit on his own side of the page. He even talked of the expediency of reviving the persecution of Quakers and Anabaptists. In a word, Tom's zeal became as notorious as his riches.

Still, in spite of all this strenuous attention to forms, Tom had a lurking dread that the Devil, after all, would have his due. That he might not be taken unawares, therefore, it is said he always carried a small Bible in his coat pocket. He had also a great folio Bible on his countinghouse desk, and would frequently be found reading it when people called on business; on such occasions he would lay his green spectacles in the book, to mark the place, while he turned round to drive some usurious bargain.

Some say that Tom grew a little crack-brained in his old days, and that fancying his end approaching, he had his horse newly shod, saddled and bridled, and buried with his feet uppermost; because he supposed that at the last day the world would be turned upside down, in which case he should find his horse standing ready for mounting, and he was determined at the worst to give his old friend a run for it. This, however, is probably a mere old wives' fable. If he really did take such a precaution, it was totally superfluous; at least so says the authentic old legend, which closes his story in the following manner.

One hot summer afternoon in the dog days, just as a terrible black thunder-gust was com-

◆ **Literary Focus**
How does the word *legend* distance the narrator from the story?

ing up, Tom sat in his countinghouse in his white linen cap and India silk morning gown. He was on the point of foreclosing a mortgage, by which he would complete the ruin of an unlucky land speculator for whom he had professed the greatest friendship. The poor land jobber begged him to grant a few months' indulgence. Tom had grown testy and irritated, and refused another day.

"My family will be ruined and brought upon the parish," said the land jobber. "Charity begins at home," replied Tom; "I must take care of myself in these hard times."

"You have made so much money out of me," said the speculator.

Tom lost his patience and his piety— "The Devil take me," said he, "if I have made a farthing!"

Just then there were three loud knocks at the street door. He stepped out to see who was there. A black man was holding a black horse, which neighed and stamped with impatience.

"Tom, you're come for," said the black fellow, gruffly. Tom shrunk back, but too late. He had left his little Bible at the bottom of his coat pocket, and his big Bible on the desk buried under the mortgage he was about to foreclose: never was sinner taken more unawares. The black man whisked him like a child into the saddle, gave the horse the lash, and away he galloped, with Tom on his back, in the midst of the thunderstorm. The clerks stuck their pens behind their ears, and stared after him from the windows. Away went Tom Walker, dashing down the streets, his white cap bobbing up and down, his morning gown fluttering in the wind, and his steed striking fire out of the pavement at every bound. When the clerks turned to look for the black man he had disappeared.

Tom Walker never returned to foreclose the mortgage. A countryman who lived on the border of the swamp, reported that in the height of the thunder-gust he had heard a great clattering of hoofs and a howling along the road, and running to the window caught sight of a figure, such as I have described, on a horse that galloped like mad across the fields, over the hills and down into the black

---

13. **Zionward** (zī´ ən wôrd): Toward heaven.

hemlock swamp towards the old Indian fort; and that shortly after a thunderbolt falling in that direction seemed to set the whole forest in a blaze.

The good people of Boston shook their heads and shrugged their shoulders, but had been so much accustomed to witches and goblins and tricks of the Devil, in all kind of shapes from the first settlement of the colony, that they were not so much horror struck as might have been expected. Trustees were appointed to take charge of Tom's effects. There was nothing, however, to administer upon. On searching his coffers all his bonds and mortgages were found reduced to cinders. In place of gold and silver his iron chest was filled with chips and shavings; two skeletons lay in his stable instead of his half-starved horses, and the very next day his great house took fire and was burned to the ground.

Such was the end of Tom Walker and his ill-gotten wealth. Let all griping money brokers lay this story to heart. The truth of it is not to be doubted. The very hole under the oak trees, whence he dug Kidd's money, is to be seen to this day; and the neighboring swamp and old Indian fort are often haunted in stormy nights by a figure on horseback, in morning gown and white cap, which is doubtless the troubled spirit of the usurer. In fact, the story has resolved itself into a proverb, and is the origin of that popular saying, so prevalent throughout New England, of "The Devil and Tom Walker."

Guide for Responding

◆ *Literature and Your Life*

Reader's Response Do you feel that Tom Walker deserves his fate? Why or why not?

Thematic Focus In what ways is this tale distinctly American?

Group Activity Stories abound in which the main character learns that an agreement he makes comes with an unexpectedly high price. With a small group, brainstorm for three other examples of characters in films who learn a similar lesson. Then contrast your choices with those of Tom Walker.

☑ Check Your Comprehension

1. Describe Tom Walker's first encounter with the Devil.
2. Explain why Tom does not, at first, agree to make a bargain with the Devil.
3. Describe Tom's reaction to the loss of his wife.
4. (a) What is the agreement that Tom Walker ultimately makes with the Devil? (b) What does he do when he begins to regret his agreement?

◆ Critical Thinking

INTERPRET
1. What does the description of their house and horse indicate about the Walkers? **[Infer]**
2. What details in the story indicate that Tom's nature remains the same although his condition changes? **[Support]**
3. (a) What does Irving mean when he says that Tom became a "*violent* churchgoer"? (b) How is Tom's approach to religion similar to his approach to financial dealings? **[Interpret]**
4. What is the lesson Irving wants his readers to learn from this story? **[Draw Conclusions]**

EVALUATE
5. Tom Walker sells his soul for money. Would he have been a more sympathetic character if he had sold his soul for knowledge? **[Evaluate]**

EXTEND
6. How might a banker respond to Irving's implication that moneylenders are greedy? What would prevent Tom Walker from having a successful moneylending business today? **[Career Link]**

Guide for Responding (continued)

◆ Literary Focus

OMNISCIENT NARRATOR

Using an **omniscient** (all-knowing) **narrator** allows a writer to reveal the thoughts and feelings of many characters, thereby presenting events from more than one point of view. In this tale, Irving uses the voice of an informed storyteller who seems to be weaving the story from various reports he has gathered over time.

1. Give three examples of Tom Walker's thoughts or perspective on a situation in the story.
2. Find one place in the story where the narrator reveals the thoughts or unspoken plans of Tom Walker's wife.

◆ Build Vocabulary

USING THE PREFIX ex-

Knowing that the prefix ex- means "out" can help you determine the meaning of words with this prefix. For example, *extort* means "to squeeze out." On a separate sheet of paper, match words on the left from the story with their definitions on the right.

1. exceed	a.	elevate; glorify
2. exact	b.	go beyond normal limits
3. exalt	c.	look out; look forward
4. expedite	d.	wring; pry out
5. expect	e.	speed up; hasten

USING THE WORD BANK

On a separate sheet of paper, write the word from the Word Bank that best completes each sentence.

1. We had borrowed money from _____?_____ who charged an excessive rate of interest.
2. He would _____?_____ money by threatening to harm victims if they did not pay.
3. Her _____?_____ led her to refuse to send for a doctor when she was ill.
4. The house was such a model of _____?_____ that visitors guessed about its excessive cost.
5. A main characteristic of Mrs. Walker's personality was _____?_____; she always wanted more than she had.

◆ Reading Strategy

INFER CULTURAL ATTITUDES

From the dialogue, the narrator's comments about the characters, and the outcome of events, you can **make inferences,** or draw conclusions, about some of the **cultural attitudes** of the people in New England in the 1720's. What inferences about cultural attitudes can you make from each of the following passages?

1. . . . the great speculating fever which breaks out every now and then in the country, had raged to an alarming degree, and everybody was dreaming of making sudden fortunes from nothing.
2. The quiet Christians who had been modestly and steadfastly traveling Zionward, were struck with self-reproach at seeing themselves so suddenly outstripped in their career by this new-made convert.

◆ Grammar and Style

ADJECTIVE CLAUSES

Adjective clauses are introduced with relative pronouns: *who* or *whom, whose, which,* or *that.*

> An **adjective clause** is a subordinate clause that modifies a noun or pronoun.

Practice On your paper, write the adjective clause and the word it modifies in each of these sentences.

1. At length he arrived at a piece of firm ground, which ran out like a peninsula into the . . . deep bosom of the swamp.
2. His reputation for a ready-moneyed man, who would lend money out for a good consideration, soon spread abroad.
3. She spoke something of a black man, whom she had met about twilight, hewing at the root of a tall tree.
4. He had a shock of coarse black hair, that stood out from his head in all directions, and bore an ax on his shoulder.

Build Your Portfolio

 ## Idea Bank

Writing

1. Correspondence As Tom Walker, write a letter to your niece shortly before the Devil comes to take you away. In it, warn your niece about the dangers of making a pact with the Devil.

2. Revised Ending What if Tom Walker's wife had also made a bargain with the Devil? Write a new ending to the story based on this idea.

3. Analysis A critic has said, "One of Washington Irving's great gifts to prose is his ability to find humor even in the most grotesque circumstances." In an essay, identify and discuss the effect of humorous elements in this story.

Speaking and Listening

4. Missing Scene Speculate about what happens when Mrs. Walker meets the Devil. Write and perform the scenes that might have taken place between the two. **[Performing Arts Link]**

5. Impromptu Speech Deliver an unrehearsed speech about the dangers of greed. Prepare by jotting down notes on your topic. Present your speech. Avoid reading directly from your notes. After finishing, discuss the experience of extemporaneous, or ad-libbed, speaking. **[Career Link]**

Projects

6. Board Game Create a board game to teach younger students about the consequences of greed and rash decisions. Present your game to classmates. **[Art Link]**

7. Exhibition The Faust legend has inspired plays, operas, and even a Broadway musical. Research these works, and create an exhibit about what you have learned. If possible, include tape recordings, CDs, and video excerpts of some of the performances. **[Media Link]**

 ## Writing Mini-Lesson

Updating a Story

The message of Irving's story continues to be relevant. Create an updated version of the story, set in today's world with new plot events and character details, that conveys the story's message in a way that will appeal to a contemporary audience.

Writing Skills Focus: Appropriateness for Audience

As you develop your story, focus on using language and details that today's readers will find familiar and engaging. Notice that the vocabulary and syntax in this example from "The Devil and Tom Walker," which would have appealed to readers in Irving's day, now seems dated.

Model From the Story

"And pray, who are you, if I may be so bold?" said Tom.

In your updated version of the story, you'll probably want to have Tom Walker speak in a way that will appeal more to a contemporary audience. In addition, you'll want to keep your audience's interests and background in mind as you develop details of plot and setting.

Prewriting Outline the plot of the original story. Consider the best way to update each plot event you list. For example, instead of meeting in a forest, Tom Walker might run into the Devil at the mall.

Drafting Write your story. Have your characters speak, dress, and act in a way that makes it clear the story is set in modern times. Include references to food, clothes, and shows that are currently popular.

Revising Confirm that your draft balances the original elements and new details that update it. Check to see that the conflict and the message are the same, but that you have brought the language and setting into today's world.

Guide for Interpreting

Henry Wadsworth Longfellow *(1807–1882)*

Henry Wadsworth Longfellow once wrote, "Music is the universal language of mankind—poetry their universal pastime and delight." During the latter half of the nineteenth century, Longfellow's poetry certainly was a "universal pastime and delight"; his work was translated into two dozen languages and read by millions.

The Teaching Years Longfellow was born and reared in Portland, Maine. He attended Bowdoin College, where one of his classmates was Nathaniel Hawthorne. After graduating in 1825, Longfellow spent three years in Europe before returning to Bowdoin as a professor of modern languages. He left the college after five years to spend another year in Europe before accepting a position at Harvard University, where he taught for eighteen years.

Tragedy Strikes Longfellow suffered the tragic deaths of two wives. His first wife, Mary, died in Europe in 1835 from an infection following a miscarriage. Eight years later, after a long courtship, Longfellow married Frances Appleton of Boston. Their happy marriage ended tragically when Frances was fatally burned in a household accident. Longfellow's attempts to beat out the flames left him badly burned. The resulting scars prevented him from shaving, and he grew the long, flowing beard so familiar to generations of his readers.

Poet to the People Longfellow enjoyed a long and successful career as a poet, publishing his first collection of poems, *Voices in the Night*, in 1839.

> *By writing poetry that soothed and encouraged readers, Longfellow became the first American poet to reach a wide audience and create a national interest in poetry.*

He experimented with adapting traditional European verse forms and themes to American subjects. Many of his narrative poems, such as *Evangeline* (1847), *The Song of Hiawatha* (1855), *The Courtship of Miles Standish* (1858), and "Paul Revere's Ride" (1860), gave a romanticized view of America's early history and democratic ideals.

Longfellow's poetry has been criticized for being overly optimistic and sentimental. Yet it was Longfellow's optimism and sentimentality that made him the most popular poet of his time. He became known as one of the "fireside poets," whose works were read by families gathered around the fireplace. Just as many of today's families are likely to gather around the television set to watch a favorite program, families of Longfellow's time would have spent evenings reading and discussing their favorite poems by Longfellow.

◆ Background for Understanding

LITERATURE: THE STORY BEHIND THESE POEMS

Longfellow wrote "A Psalm of Life" in 1838, after suffering through the tragic death of his first wife, Mary, coupled with the loss of the child the couple was expecting. Longfellow intended the poem as an inspiration to himself and others to overcome the misfortunes of the past and to live productively in the present.

"The Tide Rises, The Tide Falls" was penned when Longfellow was in his early seventies. The poem reveals the poet's acceptance of the inevitability of death. Gone are the youthful optimism and spirited desire to deny the power of the grave that characterize "A Psalm of Life"; the later poem is the work of a man whose life is nearing its end.

◆ A Psalm of Life ◆
The Tide Rises, The Tide Falls

◆ *Literature and Your Life*

CONNECT YOUR EXPERIENCE

In each stage of our lives, we want to leave a mark that will make others remember us. It could be by breaking a school scoring record in basketball, by committing acts of charity, or simply by establishing relationships that others won't soon forget. In these poems, Longfellow explores the passage of time, the fleeting nature of life, and the human desire to leave a mark on the world.

Journal Writing How would you like to be remembered?

THEMATIC FOCUS: FIRESIDE AND CAMPFIRE

As you read, think about why families of Longfellow's time might have chosen to recite poems such as these around the fireplace.

◆ Reading Strategy

ASSOCIATE IMAGES WITH LIFE

Writers often use images that take on greater meaning when we consider them as symbols of larger ideas and principles. Many of the images in these poems deal with journeys. To discover their deeper meaning, **associate the images with life** by thinking about what they mean in the broader context of the journey of life. Look, for example, at the line "The twilight darkens, the curlew calls" from "The Tide Rises, The Tide Falls." The darkening sky and evening bird signal the close of the day. In terms of life's "big picture," however, Longfellow is also foreshadowing the end of a lifetime.

◆ Grammar and Style

INVERTED WORD ORDER

To achieve a rhyme or maintain a certain rhythm, poets sometimes change the normal English sentence order of subject-verb-complement. For example, Longfellow sometimes uses **inverted word order,** reversing the subject and verb of a sentence:

> …nevermore / Returns the traveler to the shore,

The complement—the word or group of words that completes the meaning of the predicate—can also be placed at the start of a sentence or line of poetry to achieve emphasis.

> Dust thou art …

◆ Literary Focus

STANZA FORMS

Like most traditional poets, Longfellow organized his poetry in **stanzas**—units of two or more lines arranged in a pattern of rhythm (or meter) and rhyme. Like a prose paragraph, each stanza develops a single main idea. Unlike paragraphs, however, stanzas are often a fixed length and share the same rhythm. Stanzas are commonly named according to the number of lines they contain. A two-line stanza is a **couplet;** a four-line stanza is a **quatrain;** and a five-line stanza is a **cinquain.**

As you read "A Psalm of Life" and "The Tide Rises, The Tide Falls," note which form of stanza Longfellow uses in each.

◆ Build Vocabulary

WORD ROOTS: *-face-*

In "The Tide Rises, The Tide Falls," the waves "Efface the footprints in the sands." The word *efface* contains the prefix *e-*, a form of *ex-*, meaning "out" or "without," and the root *-face-*, meaning "appearance or outward aspect." To efface a footprint, then, is to remove any trace of its appearance.

WORD BANK

Preview this list of words from the poems.

> bivouac
> sublime
> efface

A Psalm of Life

Henry Wadsworth Longfellow

Tell me not, in mournful numbers,[1]
　　Life is but an empty dream!—
For the soul is dead that slumbers,
　　And things are not what they seem.

5　Life is real! Life is earnest!
　　And the grave is not its goal:
Dust thou art, to dust returnest,
　　Was not spoken of the soul.

　Not enjoyment, and not sorrow,
10　　Is our destined end or way;
But to act, that each tomorrow
　　Find us farther than today.

　Art is long, and Time is fleeting,
　　And our hearts, though stout and brave,
15　Still, like muffled drums, are beating
　　Funeral marches to the grave.

　In the world's broad field of battle,
　　In the <u>bivouac</u> of Life,
Be not like dumb, driven cattle!
20　　Be a hero in the strife!

---

1. numbers: Verses.

▲ **Critical Viewing** What do you associate with the image of footprints in the sand? **[Respond]**

Trust no Future, howe'er pleasant!
   Let the dead Past bury its dead!
Act—act in the living Present!
   Heart within, and God o'erhead!

25 Lives of great men all remind us
   We can make our lives <u>sublime</u>,
And, departing, leave behind us
   Footprints on the sands of time;

Footprints, that perhaps another,
30   Sailing o'er life's solemn main,[2]
A forlorn and shipwrecked brother,
   Seeing, shall take heart again.

Let us, then, be up and doing,
   With a heart for any fate;
35 Still achieving, still pursuing,
   Learn to labor and to wait.

---

2. **main:** Open sea.

◆ **Build Vocabulary**

bivouac (biv′ wak) *n.*: Temporary encampment
sublime (sə blīm′) *adj.*: Noble; inspiring

Guide for Responding

◆ Literature and Your Life

Reader's Response What "footprints" would you like to leave "on the sands of time"?

Thematic Focus What is Longfellow's idea of how a person should live?

Group Discussion The phrase "Art is long, and Time is fleeting" is a translation of a Latin motto echoed in the works of many great English poets. How do you interpret its meaning?

☑ Check Your Comprehension

1. What attitude or idea does the speaker challenge in the first two stanzas?
2. What can we learn from the "Lives of great men"?

◆ Critical Thinking

INTERPRET

1. Describe the speaker's attitude concerning individuality and self-reliance. **[Infer]**
2. According to the poem, how can our lives influence future generations? **[Interpret]**
3. Summarize the speaker's view of life. **[Draw Conclusions]**

EVALUATE

4. This poem has been criticized as trite and overly sentimental. Explain why you agree or disagree with this opinion. **[Evaluate]**

APPLY

5. What advice might the speaker give to someone suffering a personal misfortune? **[Relate]**

The Tide Rises, The Tide Falls

Henry Wadsworth Longfellow

Breakers at Floodtide, 1909, Frederick J. Waugh, Butler Institute of American Art, Youngstown, Ohio

▲ **Critical Viewing** Which lines of the poem does this painting suggest to you? **[Connect]**

The tide rises, the tide falls.
The twilight darkens, the curlew[1] calls;
Along the sea sands damp and brown
The traveler hastens toward the town,
5   And the tide rises, the tide falls.

Darkness settles on roofs and walls,
But the sea, the sea in the darkness calls:
The little waves, with their soft, white hands,
<u>Efface</u> the footprints in the sands,
10   And the tide rises, the tide falls.

The morning breaks; the steeds in their stalls
Stamp and neigh, as the hostler[2] calls:
The day returns, but nevermore
Returns the traveler to the shore,
15   And the tide rises, the tide falls.

_____

1. **curlew** (kʉr′ lo͞o) *n*.: Large, long-legged wading bird whose call is associated with the evening.
2. **hostler** (häs′ lər) *n*.: Person who tends horses at an inn or stable.

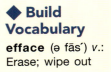

◆ **Build Vocabulary**

efface (ə fās′) *v*.: Erase; wipe out

Guide for Responding

◆ Literature and Your Life

Reader's Response What did you see and hear in your mind as you read this poem?

Thematic Focus What remains when we are gone from this world?

Journal Writing What associations do you have with the rising and falling of the tide? Explore your thoughts in a journal entry.

☑ Check Your Comprehension

1. Summarize the action of the poem.
2. What is the implied fate of the traveler?

◆ Critical Thinking

INTERPRET

1. (a) What details in the first stanza suggest that the traveler is nearing death? (b) What details in the second stanza suggest that he has died? **[Support]**
2. (a) What is the effect of the refrain, or repeated line? (b) How does the rhythm of the refrain reinforce its meaning? **[Analyze]**
3. What does the poem suggest about the relationship between humanity and nature? **[Draw Conclusions]**

EVALUATE

4. What do you think Longfellow's outlook on life and death was when he wrote "The Tide Rises, The Tide Falls"? Explain. **[Evaluate]**

EXTEND

5. How does the philosophy of life expressed in this poem differ from that of "A Psalm of Life"? **[Literature Link]**

Guide for Responding (continued)

◆ Reading Strategy

ASSOCIATE IMAGES WITH LIFE

Associating Longfellow's images, or word pictures, **with broader life** events can help you find greater meaning in these poems. Copy the chart below into your notebook. Complete it by filling in the possible meaning of each italicized image as it relates to life's journey. Feel free to offer more than one possible meaning for a particular image.

When you're finished, get together with a group of classmates and share and discuss your interpretations of the various images. How do the images contribute to the overall meaning of the two poems?

Image	How It Relates to Life
1. *Footprints* on the sands of time	
2. Sailing o'er life's *solemn main*	
3. A forlorn and *shipwrecked* brother	
4. . . . the *sea sands* damp and brown	
5. . . . *the sea*, the sea in the darkness calls	
6. Returns the *traveler* to the shore	

◆ Build Vocabulary

USING THE WORD ROOT -face-

Use your knowledge of the root *-face-*, meaning "appearance or outward aspect," to match each word with its definition. Write your answers in your notebook. Then use a dictionary to check your answers.

1. facade   a. to ruin the appearance of
2. interface   b. the front of a building
3. deface   c. the exterior of an object
4. surface   d. to encounter or come in contact with

USING THE WORD BANK

Complete each analogy using a word from the Word Bank. Write your answers on a separate sheet of paper.

1. *Raise* is to *lower* as *inscribe* is to ____?____.
2. *Hut* is to *shack* as *campsite* is to ____?____.
3. *Aggravated* is to *calm* as *humble* is to ____?____.

◆ Literary Focus

STANZA FORMS

Longfellow uses a different **stanza form**—a unit of poetry containing a specific number of lines—in each of these poems. Consider how his choice of the number, length, and rhythm of the stanzas contributes to each poem's overall impact.

1. Describe the stanza form and rhyme pattern of (a) "A Psalm of Life" (b) "The Tide Rises, The Tide Falls."
2. With only one exception, every stanza in "A Psalm of Life" develops a separate idea and is capable of standing alone. Which stanza is dependent on the one before for its meaning?
3. How does Longfellow's choice of stanza form in "The Tide Rises, The Tide Falls" allow him to emphasize the repetition of nature's cycles?

◆ Grammar and Style

INVERTED WORD ORDER

Poetry is not the only form of writing that permits inverted word order. You can also change the structure of a prose sentence in order to emphasize a particular word or idea.

> **Inverted word order** is a change in the normal English word order of subject-verb-complement.

Writing Application Write a paragraph, a series of stanzas, or a song describing how you'd like to leave your mark on the world. Include at least two examples of inverted word order.

Looking at Style In your notebook, answer these questions about lines 9 and 10 of "A Psalm of Life."

> Not enjoyment, and not sorrow,
> Is our destined end or way;

1. What word order is shown in these lines?
2. What effect does this word order have on the meaning of the lines? Explain.
3. Rewrite the lines in conventional subject-verb-complement word order.
4. What do you notice about the rhythm of these new lines when they are read aloud?

Build Your Portfolio

Idea Bank

Writing

1. **Epitaph** Write a brief epitaph, or tribute, for Longfellow's tomb to reflect the philosophy expressed in one of the two poems you just read. Include one or two lines from the poem.

2. **Personal Response** Do we leave "Footprints on the sands of time" or does death erase all traces of our lives? In a brief paper, contrast the views presented in the two poems. With which viewpoint do you agree? Why?

3. **Essay** A German motto says: "Look not mournfully into the Past. It comes not back again. Wisely improve the Present. It is thine. Go forth to meet the shadowy Future, without fear, and with a manly heart." Write an essay explaining how "A Psalm of Life" reflects these sentiments.

Speaking and Listening

4. **Audio Presentation/Discussion** Play a recording of ocean sounds for the class. Then present the ideas and emotions you associate with the sea. Follow by having classmates share their associations with the ocean.

5. **Commencement Address** As Longfellow, deliver an inspirational commencement speech on how to live a worthwhile life. Base your comments on the ideas expressed in "A Psalm of Life."

Projects

6. **Performance** Listen to the beat of "The Tide Rises, The Tide Falls" as you read it aloud. Then create a piece of music or choreograph a dance to accompany the poem. **[Performing Arts Link]**

7. **Poster** Create a poster displaying "A Psalm of Life" and one or more photographs or illustrations that capture the ideas expressed in the poem. **[Media Link]**

Writing Mini-Lesson

Credo

Longfellow's personal beliefs about the meaning of life and death are expressed in his poetry. Summarize your approach to life in a credo—a statement of principles or beliefs that guides your conduct. Write your credo with the goal of persuading others to adopt the same principles.

Writing Skills Focus: Persuasive Tone

A writer's tone conveys his or her attitude toward a subject. Only when it is clear that you believe in what you are saying (or writing!) can you convince others to share those beliefs. Communicate your convictions with a **persuasive tone** that is forceful and to the point. Consider the difference tone makes in these two sentences:

Neutral: Living each day to the fullest can be a worthwhile approach to life.

Persuasive: A life lived to the fullest is the only kind worth living.

Though both sentences have the same basic message, the second is more likely to influence a reader to accept the ideas being presented.

Prewriting You can't persuade others of your beliefs until they're clear in your own mind. Jot down as many of your personal beliefs as you can. Then go through the list to identify which ideas are most important. Finally, state in a sentence or two the overall outlook that ties together your various beliefs.

Drafting Start by stating your overall outlook. Then explain each of the individual beliefs that fit into this outlook. Provide examples of personal experiences that support your ideas.

Revising As you revise your credo, focus on replacing vague or weak words with more persuasive ones that will strengthen your tone.

Guide for Interpreting

William Cullen Bryant *(1794–1878)*

As a journalist and political activist, William Cullen Bryant fought to ensure that industrialization and rapid growth did not obscure America's democratic values and principles. As a poet, Bryant helped to establish an American literary tradition by producing poems that were a match for the work of the best European poets of his day.

Bryant learned Greek and Latin from his father, a country doctor. He began writing poetry at the age of nine and wrote the first version of "Thanatopsis," his most famous poem, when he was only nineteen.

To support himself, Bryant practiced law for ten years while continuing to write poetry in his spare time. In 1825, he moved to New York City and became a journalist; by 1829, he had become editor-in-chief and part owner of the New York *Evening Post,* a newspaper. Bryant used his position to defend human rights and personal freedoms, and he was an outspoken advocate of women's rights and the abolition of slavery.

Bryant was the first American poet to win worldwide critical acclaim. His work helped establish the Romantic Movement in this country and influenced the next generation of American poets.

Oliver Wendell Holmes *(1809–1894)*

A man of many talents and interests, Oliver Wendell Holmes made important contributions to both literature and medicine. Holmes, a descendant of seventeenth-century poet Anne Bradstreet (p. 88), graduated from Harvard University, briefly studied law, then moved on to the study of medicine. After studying in Paris, he completed a medical degree at Harvard University in 1836, the same year his first collection of poetry, *Poems*, was published.

Holmes went on to have a long teaching career at Harvard, during which time he became a leading medical researcher and continued his literary pursuits. Along with James Russell Lowell, Holmes founded *The Atlantic Monthly*, in which many of his best-known poems and essays were published. His love of humorous exaggeration, colorful expressions, and quotable quotes made his essays popular with readers.

While still studying law at Harvard in 1830, Holmes wrote "Old Ironsides" to protest the planned destruction of the battleship *Constitution*, nicknamed "Old Ironsides" for its ability to withstand British attacks during the War of 1812. The poem saved the ship and earned Holmes national recognition as a poet.

James Russell Lowell *(1819–1891)*

James Russell Lowell may have been the most talented of the Fireside Poets (see Background for Understanding, p. 257). His literary career, however, was disrupted by personal tragedies, including the infant deaths of three of his four children. Following the death of his wife in 1853, the young writer lost much of his focus and was never able to match his earlier work.

Still, Lowell made many important literary contributions as a poet, editor, and critic. He published his first book of poetry, *A Year's Life,* in 1841. His literary career reached its peak in 1848 with the publication of three highly successful works—*A Fable for Critics, The Bigelow Papers,* and *The Vision of Sir Launfal*—that gained him international fame.

During the second half of his life, Lowell turned toward other interests. He wrote editorials supporting the abolition of slavery. He succeeded Longfellow as professor of languages at Harvard, and he helped found and served as the first editor of *The Atlantic Monthly.* In later years, he served as an American ambassador to Spain, then to Great Britain.

John Greenleaf Whittier *(1807–1892)*

Unlike the other Fireside Poets (see Background for Understanding), John Greenleaf Whittier was born in poverty and received virtually no formal education. He was more deeply involved in the social issues of his day than were his fellow poets, and, because of his devotion to the abolitionist cause, he did not gain national prominence until after the Civil War. The son of Quakers who taught him to believe in hard work, simplicity, pacifism, religious devotion, and social justice, Whittier spent his youth working on his family's debt-ridden farm near Haverhill, Massachusetts.

As a young man, Whittier worked for antislavery newspapers, wrote a large number of antislavery poems, and became active in politics. When the Civil War ended, he focused on writing poetry. He earned national fame with the 1866 publication of *Snowbound,* which depicts the simple warmth of rural New England life.

As the way of life captured in his poetry disappeared, the popularity of Whittier's poems grew. Despite his tremendous success as a poet, he remained faithful at all times to his social and spiritual convictions.

◆ Background for Understanding

LITERATURE: THE FIRESIDE POETS—AMERICA'S FIRST GENERATION OF WRITERS

Until the third decade of the nineteenth century, America had little real literature to call its own. The Fireside Poets—Henry Wadsworth Longfellow, Oliver Wendell Holmes, James Russell Lowell, and John Greenleaf Whittier—represented a literary coming of age for the young country. This first generation of acclaimed American poets took their name from the popularity of their works, which were widely read both as fireside family entertainment and in the schoolroom, where generations of children memorized them.

The four poets—all New England born and bred—chose uniquely American settings and subjects. Their themes, meter, and imagery, however, borrowed heavily from the English tradition. Though their reliance on conservative literary styles prevented them from being truly innovative, the Fireside Poets were literary giants of their day. In their own time, and for decades afterward, they ranked as America's most read and best-loved poets.

The Four Seasons of Life, Currier & Ives

Guide for Interpreting *(continued)*

◆ Literature and Your Life

CONNECT YOUR EXPERIENCE

Do you find that the lyrics, approach to life, or attitudes of your favorite musical artists reflect *your* feelings, *your* concerns, and *your* views? Memorable musicians do more than strike a chord with listeners; they give voice to a generation.

Journal Writing Think about song lyrics that you find particularly meaningful, and relate them to something you've felt in your own life.

THEMATIC FOCUS: FIRESIDE AND CAMPFIRE

The works of the Fireside Poets are the early nineteenth-century equivalent of today's popular music, enjoyed by people from all walks of life. What do the themes reflected in these poems tell you about the values of the public who popularized them?

◆ Build Vocabulary

WORD ROOTS: *-patr-*

The root *-patr-*, found in the word *patriarch*, comes from the Latin word *pater,* meaning "father." In *Snowbound,* "hornèd *patriarch* of the sheep" refers to the father sheep that leads the flock.

WORD BANK

Before you read, preview this list of words from the poems.

sepulcher
pensive
venerable
gloaming
ominous
querulous
patriarch

◆ Grammar and Style

PARTICIPLES AS ADJECTIVES

A **participle** is a verb form that can act as an adjective. There are two kinds of participles: **present participles,** which end in *-ing,* and **past participles,** which often end in *-ed, -d, -t,* or *-en.*

In *Snowbound,* John Greenleaf Whittier describes "A tunnel *walled* and *overlaid* / With *dazzling* crystal . . ." In these lines, *walled* and *overlaid* are past participles; *dazzling* is a present participle. All three modify "tunnel." Notice that, like adjectives, participles answer the question *what kind?* or *which one?* about the nouns and pronouns they modify.

◆ Literary Focus

METER

In poetry, a systematic arrangement of stressed (´) and unstressed (˘) syllables is called **meter.** The basic unit of meter is the **foot,** which usually consists of one stressed syllable and one or more unstressed syllables. The most frequently used foot in American and English verse is the *iamb,* which consists of one unstressed syllable followed by a stressed syllable. The type and number of feet in the lines of a poem determine its meter. A pattern of four iambs per line, as in this example from *Snowbound,* is known as **iambic tetrameter.**

> Thĕ sún thăt bríef
> Dĕcémbĕr dáy

> Rŏse cheérlĕss óvĕr hílls
> ŏf gráy

◆ Reading Strategy

SUMMARIZE

To check your understanding of what you've read, it's a good idea to **summarize** the work or parts of the work by briefly stating the main points and key details in your own words.

As you read these poems, summarize each stanza on paper or in your head. With lengthy verses, like those in "Thanatopsis" and *Snowbound,* you may find it easier to summarize after every four to six lines.

Thanatopsis

William Cullen Bryant

Kindred Spirits, Asher B. Durand, New York Public Library

▶ **Critical Viewing**
This painting pays tribute to the friendship between Bryant and land-scape painter Thomas Cole. What does the painting suggest about the two men's shared interests? [Infer]

To him who in the love of Nature holds
Communion with her visible forms, she speaks
A various language; for his gayer hours
She has a voice of gladness, and a smile
5   And eloquence of beauty, and she glides

Into his darker musings, with a mild
And healing sympathy, that steals away
Their sharpness, ere[1] he is aware. When thoughts
Of the last bitter hour come like a blight
10   Over thy spirit, and sad images
Of the stern agony, and shroud, and pall,
And breathless darkness, and the narrow house,[2]
Make thee to shudder, and grow sick at heart—
Go forth, under the open sky, and list
15   To Nature's teachings, while from all around—
Earth and her waters, and the depths of air—
Comes a still voice—Yet a few days, and thee
The all-beholding sun shall see no more
In all his course; nor yet in the cold ground,
20   Where thy pale form was laid, with many tears,
Nor in the embrace of ocean, shall exist
Thy image. Earth, that nourished thee, shall claim
Thy growth, to be resolved to earth again,
And, lost each human trace, surrendering up
25   Thine individual being, shalt thou go
To mix forever with the elements,
To be a brother to the insensible rock
And to the sluggish clod, which the rude swain[3]
Turns with his share,[4] and treads upon. The oak
30   Shall send his roots abroad, and pierce thy mold.

     Yet not to thine eternal resting place
Shalt thou retire alone, nor couldst thou wish
Couch[5] more magnificent. Thou shalt lie down
With patriarchs of the infant world—with kings,
35   The powerful of the earth—the wise, the good,
Fair forms, and hoary seers of ages past,
All in one mighty sepulcher. The hills
Rock-ribbed and ancient as the sun—the vales
Stretching in pensive quietness between;
40   The venerable woods—rivers that move
In majesty, and the complaining brooks
That make the meadows green; and, poured round all,
Old Ocean's gray and melancholy waste—
Are but the solemn decorations all
45   Of the great tomb of man. The golden sun,
The planets, all the infinite host of heaven,
Are shining on the sad abodes of death,
Through the still lapse of ages. All that tread
The globe are but a handful to the tribes
50   That slumber in its bosom. Take the wings
Of morning,[6] pierce the Barcan[7] wilderness,
Or lose thyself in the continuous woods
Where rolls the Oregon,[8] and hears no sound,
Save his own dashings—yet the dead are there:
55   And millions in those solitudes, since first
The flight of years began, have laid them down

1. **ere:** Before.

2. **narrow house:** Coffin.

3. **swain:** Country youth.
4. **share:** Plowshare.

5. **couch:** Bed.

6. **Take . . . morning:** Allusion to Psalm 139:9.
7. **Barcan** (bär´ kən): Referring to Barca, a desert region in North Africa.
8. **Oregon:** River flowing between Oregon and Washington, now known as the Columbia River.

In their last sleep—the dead reign there alone.
So shalt thou rest, and what if thou withdraw
In silence from the living, and no friend
60 Take note of thy departure? All that breathe
Will share thy destiny. The gay will laugh
When thou art gone, the solemn brood of care
Plod on, and each one as before will chase
His favorite phantom; yet all these shall leave
65 Their mirth and their employments, and shall come
And make their bed with thee. As the long train
Of ages glide away, the sons of men,
The youth in life's green spring, and he who goes
In the full strength of years, matron and maid,
70 The speechless babe, and the gray-headed man—
Shall one by one be gathered to thy side,
By those, who in their turn shall follow them.

    So live, that when thy summons comes to join
The innumerable caravan, which moves
75 To that mysterious realm, where each shall take
His chamber in the silent halls of death,
Thou go not, like the quarry-slave at night,
Scourged to his dungeon, but, sustained and soothed
By an unfaltering trust, approach thy grave,
80 Like one who wraps the drapery of his couch
About him, and lies down to pleasant dreams.

◆ **Build Vocabulary**

sepulcher (sep´əl kər) *n*.: Grave; tomb

pensive (pen´ siv) *adj*.: Expressing deep thoughtfulness

venerable (ven´ ər ə bəl) *adj*.: Worthy of respect

Guide for Responding

◆ *Literature and Your Life*

Reader's Response Did this poem make you think of nature in a new way? Explain.

Thematic Focus How does nature provide a sense of meaning to the mysteries of life and death?

☑ Check Your Comprehension

1. How does the speaker find comfort in Nature's "various language"?
2. What is the fate of the individual being?
3. In the end, who shares the individual's destiny?

◆ Critical Thinking

INTERPRET

1. The title is a composite of the Greek words *thanatos* (death) and *opsis* (a vision). Explain how the title applies to the poem. **[Connect]**
2. How would you summarize the poet's attitude toward life and death? **[Draw Conclusions]**

APPLY

3. Do you think this poem has the same impact on modern readers as it had on nineteenth-century readers? Why or why not? **[Apply]**

EXTEND

4. What belief about death characterizes both "Thanatopsis" and "The Tide Rises, The Tide Falls" by Henry Wadsworth Longfellow? **[Literature Link]**

Old Ironsides

Oliver Wendell Holmes

▲ **Critical Viewing** The U.S.S. *Constitution* had not sailed on her own power in more than 116 years. To celebrate her two-hundredth birthday in July 1997, the ship sailed in Marblehead, Massachusetts. What lines from the poem still apply? **[Analyze]**

Ay, tear her tattered ensign down!
    Long has it waved on high,
And many an eye has danced to see
    That banner in the sky;
5 Beneath it rung the battle shout,
    And burst the cannons roar;—
The meteor of the ocean air
    Shall sweep the clouds no more.

Her deck, once red with heroes' blood,
10   Where knelt the vanquished foe,
When winds were hurrying o'er the flood,
      And waves were white below,
No more shall feel the victor's tread,
      Or know the conquered knee;—
15 The harpies[1] of the shore shall pluck
      The eagle of the sea!

Oh, better that her shattered hulk
      Should sink beneath the wave;
Her thunders shook the mighty deep,
20   And there should be her grave;
Nail to the mast her holy flag.
      Set every threadbare sail,
And give her to the god of storms,
      The lightning and the gale!

1. **harpies** (här´ pēz): In Greek mythology, hideous, filthy winged monsters with the head and trunk of a woman and the tail, legs, and talons of a bird. Here, the word refers to relentless, greedy, or grasping people.

Guide for Responding

◆ Literature and Your Life

Reader's Response If you had been alive in 1830, would this poem have inspired you to protest the demolition of *Old Ironsides*? Explain.

Thematic Focus What value do historical monuments have to American society?

☑ Check Your Comprehension

1. In the opening stanza, is the speaker agreeing that the government should "tear [the battleship *Constitution's*] tattered ensign down"? Explain.
2. What does the speaker suggest might be a more fitting end for the ship?

◆ Critical Thinking

INTERPRET
1. What did *Old Ironsides*, which Holmes calls "The eagle of the sea," represent to the poet? **[Interpret]**
2. How does the poet appeal to the American sense of patriotism? **[Analyze]**

EVALUATE
3. Is the ship or its historic role more important to the speaker? Explain. **[Make a Judgment]**

EXTEND
4. This poem aroused such protest that the ship was saved. Could a poem have such a powerful effect on the American public today? Why or why not? **[Social Studies Link]**

The First Snowfall

James Russell Lowell

The snow had begun in the gloaming,
  And busily all the night
Had been heaping field and highway
  With a silence deep and white.

5   Every pine and fir and hemlock
  Wore ermine too dear for an earl
And the poorest twig on the elm tree
  Was ridged inch deep with pearl.

From sheds new-roofed with Carrara[1]
10   Came Chanticleer's[2] muffled crow
The stiff rails softened to swan's-down,
  And still fluttered down the snow.

I stood and watched by the window
  The noiseless work of the sky,
15 And the sudden flurries of snowbirds.
  Like brown leaves whirling by.

I thought of a mound in sweet Auburn[3]
  Where a little headstone stood;

---

1. **Carrara** (kə rä′ rə) *n.*: Fine, white marble.
2. **Chanticleer's** (chan′ tə klirz′): Referring to a rooster.
3. **Auburn:** Mt. Auburn Cemetery in Cambridge, Massachusetts.

◀ **Critical Viewing** What words from the poem can describe both death and the snow in this photograph? **[Connect]**

How the flakes were folding it gently,
20   As did robins the babes in the wood.

Up spoke our own little Mabel,
    Saying, "Father, who makes it snow?"
And I told of the good All-Father
    Who cares for us here below.

25   Again I looked at the snowfall,
    And thought of the leaden sky
That arched o'er our first great sorrow,
    When that mound was heaped so high.

I remembered the gradual patience
30   That fell from that cloud like snow,
Flake by flake, healing and hiding
    The scar that renewed our woe.

And again to the child I whispered,
    "The snow that husheth all,
35   Darling, the merciful Father
    Alone can make it fall!"

Then, with eyes that saw not, I kissed her:
    And she, kissing back, could not know
That my kiss was given to her sister,
40   Folded close under deepening snow.

◆ **Build Vocabulary**

gloaming (glō′ miŋ) *n.*:
Evening dusk; twilight

Guide for Responding

◆ *Literature and Your Life*

Reader's Response What natural events trigger personal memories for you?
Thematic Focus How do personal experiences affect the way in which we perceive natural events?

☑ Check Your Comprehension

1. Of what does the snowstorm make the speaker think?
2. (a) How does the speaker first respond to his daughter's question about the snow? (b) What does he later add to this response?
3. What does the speaker's daughter not know when he kisses her?

◆ Critical Thinking

INTERPRET
1. (a) How does the speaker imply that "our first great sorrow" is the death of his daughter? (b) Why does the snowfall remind him of her death? **[Analyze]**
2. In lines 29–36, what process is likened to the snowfall? **[Interpret]**
3. What do lines 34–36 suggest about the source of emotional healing? **[Infer]**

EXTEND
4. In the nineteenth century, infant deaths were far more common than they are today. How might the high infant mortality rate have affected the attitudes and values of the day? **[Social Studies Link]**

Old Holley House, Cos Cob, John Henry Twachtman, Cincinnati Art Museum

266 ◆ A Growing Nation (1800–1870)

from

Snowbound

John Greenleaf Whittier

A Winter Idyll

The sun that brief December day
Rose cheerless over hills of gray,
And, darkly circled, gave at noon
A sadder light than waning moon.
5   Slow tracing down the thickening sky
Its mute and <u>ominous</u> prophecy,

◆ **Build Vocabulary**
ominous (äm´ ə nəs) *adj*.: Threatening

◄ **Critical Viewing** At the end of this poem, the speaker describes the inside of his home. Contrast that interior with the exterior of the house in this painting. **[Contrast]**

A portent seeming less than threat,
It sank from sight before it set.
A chill no coat, however stout,

10 Of homespun stuff could quite shut out,
A hard, dull bitterness of cold,
That checked, mid-vein, the circling race
Of lifeblood in the sharpened face,
The coming of the snowstorm told.

15 The wind blew east; we heard the roar
Of Ocean on his wintry shore,
And felt the strong pulse throbbing there
Beat with low rhythm our inland air.

Meanwhile we did our nightly chores—

20 Brought in the wood from out of doors,
Littered the stalls, and from the mows
Raked down the herd's-grass for the cows:
Heard the horse whinnying for his corn;
And, sharply clashing horn on horn,

25 Impatient down the stanchion[1] rows
The cattle shake their walnut bows;
While, peering from his early perch
Upon the scaffold's pole of birch,
The cock his crested helmet bent

30 And down his querulous challenge sent.

Unwarmed by any sunset light
The gray day darkened into night,
A night made hoary with the swarm
And whirl-dance of the blinding storm,

35 As zigzag, wavering to and fro,
Crossed and recrossed the winged snow:
And ere the early bedtime came
The white drift piled the window frame,
And through the glass the clothesline posts

40 Looked in like tall and sheeted ghosts.

So all night long the storm roared on:
The morning broke without a sun;
In tiny spherule[2] traced with lines
Of Nature's geometric signs,

45 In starry flake, and pellicle,[3]
All day the hoary meteor fell;
And, when the second morning shone,
We looked upon a world unknown,
On nothing we could call our own.

1. stanchion
(stan´ chən):
Restraining device
fitted around the
neck of a cow to
confine it to its
stall.

2. spherule (sfer´ ool):
Small sphere.

3. pellicle (pel´ i kəl):
Thin film of crystals.

◆ **Build Vocabulary**

querulous (kwer´ ə ləs) *adj*.: Complaining

patriarch (pā´ trē ärk´) *n*.: The father and ruler
of a family or tribe

50   Around the glistening wonder bent
      The blue walls of the firmament,
      No cloud above, no earth below—
      A universe of sky and snow!
      The old familiar sights of ours
55   Took marvelous shapes; strange domes and towers
      Rose up where sty or corncrib stood,
      Or garden wall, or belt of wood;
      A smooth white mound the brush pile showed,
      A fenceless drift what once was road;
60   The bridle post an old man sat
      With loose-flung coat and high cocked hat;
      The wellcurb had a Chinese roof;
      And even the long sweep,[4] high aloof,
      In its slant splendor, seemed to tell
65   Of Pisa's leaning miracle.[5]

      A prompt, decisive man, no breath
      Our father wasted: "Boys, a path!"
      Well pleased (for when did farmer boy
      Count such a summons less than joy?)
70   Our buskins[6] on our feet we drew;
      With mittened hands, and caps drawn low,
      To guard our necks and ears from snow,
      We cut the solid whiteness through.
      And, where the drift was deepest, made
75   A tunnel walled and overlaid
      With dazzling crystal: we had read
      Of rare Aladdin's[7] wondrous cave,
      And to our own his name we gave,
      With many a wish the luck were ours
80   To test his lamp's supernal powers.
      We reached the barn with merry din,
      And roused the prisoned brutes within,
      The old horse thrust his long head out,
      And grave with wonder gazed about;
85   The cock his lusty greeting said,
      And forth his speckled harem led;
      The oxen lashed their tails, and hooked,
      And mild reproach of hunger looked;
      The hornèd patriarch of the sheep,
90   Like Egypt's Amun[8] roused from sleep,
      Shook his sage head with gesture mute,
      And emphasized with stamp of foot.

      All day the gusty north wind bore
      The loosening drift its breath before:
95   Low circling round its southern zone,
      The sun through dazzling snow-mist shone.
      No church bell lent its Christian tone
      To the savage air, no social smoke
      Curled over woods of snow-hung oak

4. sweep: Pole with a bucket at one end, used for raising water from a well.

5. Pisa's leaning miracle: Famous leaning tower of Pisa in Italy.

6. buskins: High-cut leather shoes or boots.

7. Aladdin's: Referring to Aladdin, a boy in *The Arabian Nights* who found a magic lamp and through its powers discovered a treasure in a cave.

8. Amun: Egyptian god with a ram's head.

100 A solitude made more intense
By dreary-voicèd elements,
The shrieking of the mindless wind,
The moaning tree boughs swaying blind,
And on the glass the unmeaning beat
105 Of ghostly fingertips of sleet.
Beyond the circle of our hearth
No welcome sound of toil or mirth
Unbound the spell, and testified
Of human life and thought outside.
110 We minded that the sharpest ear
The buried brooklet could not hear,
The music of whose liquid lip
Had been to us companionship,
And, in our lonely life, had grown
115 To have an almost human tone.

As night drew on, and, from the crest
Of wooded knolls that ridged the west,
The sun, a snow-blown traveler, sank
From sight beneath the smothering bank,
120 We piled, with care, our nightly stack
Of wood against the chimney back—
The oaken log, green, huge, and thick,
And on its top the stout backstick;
The knotty forestick laid apart,
125 And filled between with curious art
The ragged brush; then, hovering near,
We watched the first red blaze appear,
Heard the sharp crackle, caught the gleam
On whitewashed wall and sagging beam,
130 Until the old, rude-furnished room
Burst, flowerlike, into rosy bloom;
While radiant with a mimic flame
Outside the sparkling drift became,
And through the bare-boughed lilac tree
135 Our own warm hearth seemed blazing free.
The crane and pendent trammels[9] showed,
The Turks' heads[10] on the andirons glowed;
While childish fancy, prompt to tell
The meaning of the miracle,
140 Whispered the old rhyme: *"Under the tree,*
When fire outdoors burns merrily,
There the witches are making tea."

The moon above the eastern wood
Shone at its full; the hill range stood
145 Transfigured in the silver flood,
Its blown snows flashing cold and keen,
Dead white, save where some sharp ravine
Took shadow, or the somber green

9. trammels (tram´ əlz)
n.: Adjustable pothooks hanging from the movable arm, or crane, attached to the hearth.
10. Turks' heads: Turbanlike knots at the top of the andirons.

Of hemlocks turned to pitchy black
150 Against the whiteness at their back.
For such a world and such a night
Most fitting that unwarming light,
Which only seemed where'er it fell
To make the coldness visible.

155 Shut in from all the world without,
We sat the clean-winged hearth[11] about,
Content to let the north wind roar
In baffled rage at pane and door,
While the red logs before us beat
160 The frost line back with tropic heat;
And ever, when a louder blast
Shook beam and rafter as it passed,
The merrier up its roaring draft
The great throat of the chimney laughed;
165 The house dog on his paws outspread
Laid to the fire his drowsy head.
The cat's dark silhouette on the wall
A couchant tiger's seemed to fall:
And, for the winter fireside meet,
170 Between the andirons' straddling feet.
The mug of cider simmered slow.
The apples sputtered in a row.
And, close at hand, the basket stood
With nuts from brown October's wood.

11. **clean-winged
hearth:** A turkey wing
was used for the hearth
broom.

Guide for Responding

◆ *Literature and Your Life*

Reader's Response Would you find it pleasant to be isolated, like the narrator and his family, by a powerful snowstorm? Why or why not?

Thematic Focus What effect does this strong natural event have on the residents of a rural New England farm?

☑ Check Your Comprehension

1. What weather conditions forewarn the narrator of the approaching snowstorm?
2. How long does the storm last?
3. (a) After the storm has ended, what does the narrator's father tell the boys to do? (b) How do the boys respond to the request?

◆ Critical Thinking

INTERPRET
1. What does the family's response to the storm suggest about their relationship with nature? **[Draw Conclusions]**
2. What descriptive details in lines 47–80 convey the narrator's sense of wonder upon viewing the snow-covered landscape? **[Analyze]**
3. What details in the final stanza convey a sense of warmth and security? **[Analyze]**

APPLY
4. (a) How do you think most people today would respond to the prospect of being isolated by a major snowstorm? (b) How does this response reflect the ways in which life has changed since *Snowbound* was written in 1865? **[Apply; Analyze]**

Guide for Responding (continued)

◆ Reading Strategy

SUMMARIZE

Whenever you tell friends about the plot of the television show they missed the night before, you are using your **summarizing** skills. Imagine that, for reasons of space, the first two stanzas of "A Winter Idyll" from *Snowbound* had to be omitted from a reprinting. Write a summary of the first and second stanzas that would enable a reader to understand everything that happened before "the gray day darkened into night" at the start of the third stanza. Include the main ideas in each stanza, as well as key supporting details.

Then use a graphic organizer like this one to help you summarize "The First Snowfall." In the middle column, jot down the key details from each stanza. Review all the details you've noted. Use them to write a complete summary in the third column.

Stanza	Key Details	Summary
1		
2		

◆ Literary Focus

METER

The poems in this group have a regular pattern of stressed and unstressed syllables known as **meter.** "Thanatopsis" is written in **iambic pentameter**—a pattern of five iambs per line—whereas "Old Ironsides" alternates lines of iambic tetrameter with lines of **iambic trimeter**—three iambs per line.

1. Copy these lines from "Thanatopsis," and mark the stressed and unstressed syllables:

   So shalt thou rest, and what if thou withdraw
   In silence from the living, and no friend

2. Mark the stressed and unstressed syllables in these lines from "Old Ironsides":

   Her deck, once red with heroes' blood,
   Where knelt the vanquished foe,

◆ Build Vocabulary

USING THE WORD ROOT -patr-

The Latin root *-patr-*, meaning "father," can be found in many familiar words. Complete each of these sentences with one of the following words: *patrimony, patriots, paternal.*

1. People who love and loyally support their fatherland are called _____?_____.
2. My father's mother is my _____?_____ grandmother.
3. He knew the family business would come to him as part of his _____?_____.

USING THE WORD BANK

Decide whether the words in each of the following pairs are antonyms or synonyms. On your paper, write *A* for *antonyms* and *S* for *synonyms*.

1. sepulcher, tomb
2. pensive, frivolous
3. venerable, contemptible
4. melancholy, merry
5. gloaming, sunlight
6. ominous, forbidding
7. querulous, content
8. patriarch, father

◆ Grammar and Style

PARTICIPLES AS ADJECTIVES

Like adjectives, participles modify nouns or pronouns and answer the question *what kind?* or *which one?*

> A **participle** is a verb form that can be used as an adjective.

Practice Identify the participle(s) in each item, along with the noun each participle modifies.

1. The sun that brief December day / Rose cheerless over hills of gray, / And, darkly circled, gave at noon / A sadder light than waning moon.
2. Yet not to thine eternal resting place / Shalt thou retire alone, . . .
3. Into his darker musings, with a mild / And healing sympathy, . . .
4. . . . Yet a few days, and thee / The all-beholding sun shall see no more / In all his course; . . .

Writing Application In your notebook, write two or three sentences describing a snow-covered landscape. Use participial forms of the following verbs as adjectives: *dazzle, coat, crust, drift, chill.*

Build Your Portfolio

 ## Idea Bank

Writing

1. Letter Imagine that you are a guest in Whittier's home during the snowstorm described in *Snowbound.* Write a letter to a friend telling about your experience. Use details from the poem to enliven your account.

2. Poem Write a poem that expresses your position on a political issue, just as Oliver Wendell Holmes expresses his views on preserving the *Constitution.* **[Social Studies Link]**

3. Analytical Essay In a brief essay, explain the symbolic role of snow and the tide as they relate to the deaths described in Lowell's "The First Snowfall" and Longfellow's "The Tide Rises, The Tide Falls" (p. 253). **[Literature Link]**

Speaking and Listening

4. Dramatic Reading Convey Holmes's patriotic fervor in a dramatic reading of "Old Ironsides." Afterward, ask your classmates to critique your reading. Did they find it moving or persuasive? **[Performing Arts Link]**

5. Poetry Critique Read aloud a poem by one of the Fireside Poets. Then lead a class discussion about the work. What is its theme? Is it a poem to which modern readers can relate?

Projects

6. Oral Presentation The painting on p. 259 depicts William Cullen Bryant and Thomas Cole. Prepare an oral presentation on Cole and the Hudson River School. In what sense can he claim kinship with Bryant? **[Art Link]**

7. Art Exhibit Create a classroom display by mounting two or more of these poems and illustrating them with appropriate images from magazines or your own snapshots. **[Art Link]**

 ## Writing Mini-Lesson

Précis

Put your summarizing skills to the test by writing a **précis** (prā´ sē)—a concise abridgment or brief summary of a longer work—of the selection from *Snowbound.* Include all the main ideas and key details a reader would need in order to understand what happened in the poem. Like the poem itself, your summary should have a clear beginning, middle, and end.

Writing Skills Focus: Clear Beginning, Middle, and End

Have you ever told a friend the plot of a book and started with the middle of the story? It probably wasn't the clearest summary your friend ever heard. Whether you are listening or reading, you expect information to be presented in a logical sequence. A **clear beginning, middle, and end** are especially important to a précis, which should reflect the structure or progression of the original work.

Prewriting Review *Snowbound.* For each stanza, list the main ideas and key details you will include in your précis. Select enough details to convey the feel of the poem, but not so many that your writing becomes cluttered. Can you convey a whole series of details with a single phrase or sentence?

Drafting Set the mood for the coming storm by opening your précis with a summary of the poem's opening stanza. Refer to your prewriting notes to avoid confusing the sequence of events as you draft the middle and end.

Revising Read your précis as though you were seeing it for the first time. Does it accurately reflect the phases of the storm as the narrator relates them? Have you included enough details to convey the wonder of the snowy landscape and the coziness of the farmhouse hearth?

Guide for Interpreting

Meriwether Lewis *(1774-1809)*

Along with William Clark and a team of hearty former soldiers, Meriwether Lewis completed a two-year, 8,000-mile expedition across the uncharted territory that the United States acquired in the Louisiana Purchase. Between 1804 and 1806, Lewis and Clark traveled from St. Louis up the Missouri River to its source, then across the Rocky Mountains to the Pacific coast. When they returned to St. Louis, they brought back valuable information about the Pacific Northwest.

Lewis's efforts were sponsored by President Thomas Jefferson, who gave him and his team a rigorous assignment—map a passage to the Pacific Ocean, collect scientific information about the regions they traveled, trace the boundaries of the Louisiana territory, and claim the Oregon territory for the United States.

In preparation for his journey, Lewis spent time in Philadelphia learning about scientific classification. These skills served him well as he documented the plants, animals, and minerals he encountered during his journey. To complement Lewis's naturalist interests, Clark provided strong map skills and created detailed sketches of the regions they crossed. The men also encountered a variety of Indian nations, trading gifts and information with these natives of the frontier.

John Wesley Powell *(1834–1902)*

As a Union soldier fighting in the Civil War, John Wesley Powell lost an arm at the Battle of Shiloh. Despite this injury, Powell was the first to navigate and chart the Colorado River and the Grand Canyon.

Powell was a geologist who conducted a daring and dangerous three-month journey on the Colorado River in 1869. Financed by the Smithsonian Institution and Congress, Powell led a party of ten men and four boats. In a reflective moment before he entered the canyon, Powell described the experience ahead of him as "an unknown distance yet to run; an unknown river yet to explore." Entering the Grand Canyon by boat, the members of the expedition party faced raging rapids, towering waterfalls, and dangerously sharp rock formations. Once in the canyon, Powell's expedition party split. Those that became terrified of the river went overland at "Separation Rapids" and perished. Powell, and the others who remained on the river, survived and completed the expedition.

Powell later conducted other expeditions surveying the Rocky Mountains and the canyons of the Green River. In the 1870's, he directed a federal geographic survey of western lands in the public domain, urging the government to develop plans for using the land.

◆ Background for Understanding

HISTORY: THE LOUISIANA PURCHASE

In 1803, the United States doubled the amount of territory it controlled with a single purchase of land from the French. Looking for money to finance its wars against other European nations, France sold the land shown in red on the map to the United States for a total price of $15 million—less than three cents an acre. Known as the Louisiana Purchase, the acquisition began an era of westward expansion that lasted nearly a century.

The Louisiana Purchase

Crossing the Great Divide
◆ The Most Sublime Spectacle on Earth ◆

◆ *Literature and Your Life*

CONNECT YOUR EXPERIENCE

If you've ever had an outdoor adventure—like backpacking, mountain climbing, or white-water rafting—you know how exciting it can be to gain firsthand experiences with the beauty and power of nature. Just imagine what it would have been like to chart new territory like Meriwether Lewis and John Wesley Powell and the other adventurers who blazed a trail across the western frontier.

THEMATIC FOCUS: FIRESIDE AND CAMPFIRE

These accounts provide a firsthand view of the joys, terrors, and hardships that adventurers like Lewis and Powell experienced during their travels. How would you have reacted in their place?

◆ Literary Focus

DESCRIPTION

Travel writing can either be fascinating or dry as a bone. Often, description makes the difference. **Description** is writing that captures sights, sounds, smells, tastes, and physical sensations. For example, Powell vividly captures the sound of the river when he writes that "the river *thunders* in perpetual *roar*." Through descriptions, a writer can bring a scene to life in readers' minds.

As you read, use a graphic organizer like this one to record descriptive details appealing to each sense.

Sights	Sounds	Smells	Physical Sensations	Tastes

Journal Writing Picture a beautiful place. Then write a short description of it using language that captures what you see, hear, feel, or smell.

◆ Reading Strategy

NOTING SPATIAL RELATIONSHIPS

When descriptions are very detailed, you can get caught up in the language and lose sight of the actual object or scene. **Noting spatial relationships** as you read can help. Pay attention to sizes, distances, and locations in space of the features being described. Use this information to form an accurate mental picture of the subject.

◆ Build Vocabulary

PREFIXES: *multi-*

Multi- is a common prefix that means "many" or "much." For example, a *multivitamin* contains many different vitamins. Powell's selection includes the word *multitudinous,* which means "the state of being numerous."

WORD BANK

Preview this list of words from the narratives.

conspicuous
sublime
labyrinth
excavated
demarcation
multifarious
multitudinous

◆ Grammar and Style

PARTICIPIAL PHRASES

In "The Most Sublime Spectacle," Powell makes frequent use of participial phrases. A **participial phrase** is a group of words that includes a participle—a verb form that modifies a noun or pronoun—and its modifiers and complements. Powell uses mostly participial phrases beginning with past participles, which usually end in *-d* or *-ed.* The participial phrase in this example modifies the noun *canyon.*

The Grand Canyon of the Colorado is a canyon *composed of many canyons.*

Crossing the

August 17–20, 1805
Meriwether Lewis

Saturday, August 17th, 1805

This morning I arose very early and dispatched Drewyer and the Indian down the river. Sent Shields to hunt. I made McNeal cook the remainder of our meat which afforded a slight breakfast for ourselves and the Chief. Drewyer had been gone about 2 hours when an Indian who had straggled some little distance down the river returned and reported that the white men were coming, that he had seen them just below. They all appeared transported with joy, and the chief repeated his fraternal hug. I felt quite as much gratified at this information as the Indians appeared to be. Shortly after Capt. Clark arrived with the Interpreter Charbono, and the Indian woman, who proved to be a sister of the Chief Cameahwait. The meeting of those was really affecting, particularly between Sah-ca-ga-we-ah and an Indian woman, who had been taken prisoner at the same time with her, and who had afterwards escaped from the Minnetares and rejoined her nation. At noon the canoes arrived, and we had the satisfaction once more to find ourselves all together, with a flattering prospect of being able to obtain as many horses shortly as would enable us to prosecute our voyage by land should that by water be deemed unadvisable.

We now formed our camp just below the junction of the forks on the Lard. side[1] in a level smooth bottom covered with a fine turf

▲ ▶ **Critical Viewing** What do visuals like maps and illustrations add to the narrative of exploration accounts? **[Interpret]**

---

1. **Lard. side:** Abbreviation for larboard, the port side of a ship. From their perspective, they camped on the left side of the river.

Great Divide

of greensward. Here we unloaded our canoes and arranged our baggage on shore; formed a canopy of one of our large sails and planted some willow brush in the ground to form a shade for the Indians to sit under while we spoke to them, which we thought it best to do this evening. Accordingly about 4 P.M. we called them together and through the medium of Labuish, Charbono and Sah-ca-ga-we-ah, we communicated to them fully the objects which had brought us into this distant part of the country, in which we took care to make them a <u>conspicuous</u> object of our own good wishes and the care of our government. We made them sensible of their dependence on the will of our government for every species of merchandise as well for their defense and comfort; and apprised them of the strength of our government and its friendly dispositions towards them. We also gave them as a reason why we wished to penetrate the country as far as the ocean to the west of them was to examine and find out a more direct way to bring merchandise to them. That as no trade could be carried on with them before our

Lewis and Clark With Sacagawea at the Great Falls of the Missouri, Olaf Seltzer, The Thomas Gilcrease Institute of Art, Tulsa, Oklahoma

▲ **Critical Viewing:** What does this picture suggest about the relationship among the people in it? Does the text support the suggestion? **[Infer; Support]**

return to our homes that it was mutually advantageous to them as well as to ourselves that they should render us such aids as they had it in their power to furnish in order to hasten our voyage and of course our return home.

◆ **Build Vocabulary**

conspicuous (kən spik′ yoo əs) *adj.*: Obvious; easy to see or perceive

Guide for Responding

◆ *Literature and Your Life*

Reader's Response What did you think of the way Lewis negotiated with the Indians? Explain.

Thematic Focus Lewis knew that one day his journal might be made public. How might this have affected his writing?

☑ Check Your Comprehension

1. Summarize the first paragraph of Lewis's account.
2. Why is Lewis so pleased at being reunited with the rest of his party?

◆ Critical Thinking

INTERPRET

1. Is Lewis being candid when he tells the Indians why the expedition is there? Explain. **[Infer]**
2. Lewis distributed gifts after negotiating with the Indians. Why might he have done this? **[Analyze]**
3. Is obtaining their help Lewis's sole interest in the Indians? Explain. **[Draw Conclusions]**

EVALUATE

4. How would you rate Lewis as a negotiator? Explain. **[Assess]**

The Most Sublime Spectacle on Earth

John Wesley Powell

The Grand Canyon of the Colorado is a canyon composed of many canyons. It is a composite of thousands, of tens of thousands, of gorges. In like manner, each wall of the canyon is a composite structure, a wall composed of many walls, but never a repetition. Every one of these almost innumerable gorges is a world of beauty in itself. In the Grand Canyon there are thousands of gorges like that below Niagara Falls, and there are a thousand Yosemites. Yet all these canyons unite to form one grand canyon, the most <u>sublime</u> spectacle on the earth. Pluck up Mt. Washington by the roots to the level of the sea and drop it headfirst into the Grand Canyon, and the dam will not force its waters over the walls. Pluck up the Blue Ridge and hurl it into the Grand Canyon, and it will not fill it.

The carving of the Grand Canyon is the work of rains and rivers. The vast <u>labyrinth</u> of canyon by which the plateau region drained by the Colorado is dissected is also the work of waters. Every river has <u>excavated</u> its own gorge and every creek has excavated its gorge. When a shower comes in this land, the rills carve canyons—but a little at each storm; and though storms are far apart and the heavens above are cloudless for most of the days of the year, still, years are plenty in the ages, and an intermittent rill called to life by a shower can do much work in centuries of centuries.

The erosion represented in the canyons, although vast, is but a small part of the great erosion of the region, for between the cliffs blocks have been carried away far superior in magnitude to those necessary to fill the canyons. Probably there is no portion of the whole region from which there have not been more than a thousand feet degraded, and there are districts from which more than 30,000 feet of rock have been carried away. Altogether, there is a district of country more than 200,000 square miles in extent from which on the average more than 6,000 feet have been eroded. Consider a rock 200,000 square miles in extent and a mile in thickness, against which the clouds have hurled their storms and beat it into sands and the rills have carried the sands into the creeks and the creeks have carried them into the rivers and the Colorado has carried them into the sea. We think of the mountains as forming clouds about their brows, but the clouds have formed the mountains. Great continental blocks are upheaved from beneath the sea by internal geologic forces that fashion the earth. Then the wander-

ing clouds, the tempest-bearing clouds, the rainbow-decked clouds, with mighty power and with wonderful skill, carve out valleys and canyons and fashion hills and cliffs and mountains. The clouds are the artists sublime.

In winter some of the characteristics of the Grand Canyon are emphasized. The black gneiss[1] below, the variegated quartzite, and the green or alcove sandstone form the foundation for the mighty red wall. The banded sandstone entablature is crowned by the tower limestone. In winter this is covered with snow. Seen from below, these changing elements seem to graduate into the heavens, and no plane of <u>demarcation</u> between wall and blue firmament[2] can be seen. The heavens constitute a portion of the facade and mount into a vast dome from wall to wall, spanning the Grand Canyon with empyrean blue. So the earth and the heavens are blended in one vast structure.

When the clouds play in the canyon, as they often do in the rainy season, another set of

effects is produced. Clouds creep out of canyons and wind into other canyons. The heavens seem to be alive, not moving as move the heavens over a plain, in one direction with the wind, but following the multiplied courses of these gorges. In this manner the little clouds seem to be individualized, to have wills and souls of their own, and to be going on diverse errands—a vast assemblage of self-willed clouds, faring here and there, intent upon purposes hidden in their own breasts. In the imagination the clouds belong to the sky, and when they are in the canyon the skies come down into the gorges and cling to the cliffs and lift them up to immeasurable heights, for the sky must still be far away. Thus they lend infinity to the walls.

---

1. **gneiss** (nīs) *n.*: Coarse-grained metamorphic rock resembling granite, consisting of alternating layers of minerals such as feldspar, quartz, and mica and having a banded appearance.
2. **firmament** (fʉrm´ ə mənt) *n.*: Sky.

◆ **Build Vocabulary**

sublime (sə blīm´) *adj.*: Inspiring awe or admiration through grandeur or beauty

labyrinth (lab´ə rin*th*´) *n.*: Intricate network of winding passages; maze

excavated (eks´ kə vā tid) *v.*: Dug out; made a hole

demarcation (dē´ mär kā´ shən) *n.*: Separation

Grand Canyon With Rainbow, 1912 (detail), Thomas Moran, Fine Arts Museum of San Francisco

The wonders of the Grand Canyon cannot be adequately represented in symbols of speech, nor by speech itself. The resources of the graphic art are taxed beyond their powers in attempting to portray its features. Language and illustration combined must fail. The elements that unite to make the Grand Canyon the most sublime spectacle in nature are <u>multifarious</u> and exceedingly diverse. The Cyclopean forms which result from the sculpture of tempests through ages too long for man to compute, are wrought into endless details, to describe which would be a task equal in magnitude to that of describing the stars of the heavens or the <u>multitudinous</u> beauties of the forest with its traceries of foliage presented by oak and pine and poplar, by beech and linden and hawthorn, by tulip and lily and rose, by fern and moss and

▲ **Critical Viewing** Compare Powell's description with the painter's interpretation of the same natural wonder. **[Compare]**

lichen. Besides the elements of form, there are elements of color, for here the colors of the heavens are rivaled by the colors of the rocks. The rainbow is not more replete with hues. But form and color do not exhaust all the divine qualities of the Grand Canyon. It is the land of music. The river thunders in perpetual roar, swelling in floors of music when the storm gods play upon the rocks and fading away in soft and low murmurs when the infinite blue of heaven is unveiled. With the melody of the great tide rising and falling, swelling and vanishing forever, other melodies are heard in the gorges of the lateral[3] canyons, while the waters plunge in the rapids among the rocks or leap in great cataracts. Thus the Grand Canyon is a land of song. Mountains of music swell in the rivers, hills of music billow in the creeks, and meadows of music murmur in the rills that ripple over the rocks. Altogether it is a symphony of multitudinous melodies. All this is the music of waters. The adamant foundations of the earth have been wrought into a sublime harp, upon which the clouds of the heavens play with mighty tempests or with gentle showers.

The glories and the beauties of form, color, and sound unite in the Grand Canyon—forms unrivaled even by the mountains, colors that vie with sunsets, and sounds that span the diapason[4] from tempest to tinkling raindrop, from cataract to bubbling fountain. But more: it is a vast district of country. Were it a

valley plain it would make a state. It can be seen only in parts from hour to hour and from day to day and from week to week and from month to month. A year scarcely suffices to see it all. It has infinite variety, and no part is ever duplicated. Its colors, though many and complex at any instant, change with the ascending and declining sun; lights and shadows appear and vanish with the passing clouds, and the changing seasons mark their passage in changing colors. You cannot see the Grand Canyon in one view, as if it were a changeless spectacle from which a curtain might be lifted, but to see it you have to toil from month to month through its labyrinths. It is a region more difficult to traverse than the Alps or the Himalayas, but if strength and courage are sufficient for the task, by a year's toil a concept of sublimity can be obtained never again to be equaled on the hither side of Paradise.

---

3. **lateral** (lat´ ər əl) *adj.*: Of, from, or at the sides.
4. **diapason** (dī´ə pā´zən) *n.*: Entire range of a musical instrument.

◆ **Build Vocabulary**

multifarious (mul´ tə far´ ē əs) *adj.*: Having many parts or elements; diverse

multitudinous (mul´ tə tōōd´ ən əs) *adj.*: Numerous

Guide for Responding

◆ *Literature and Your Life*

Reader's Response Did you enjoy reading this piece? Why or why not?

Thematic Focus Powell says much about the Grand Canyon but almost nothing about his journey. What do you think this says about him?

☑ **Check Your Comprehension**

1. List four aspects of the Grand Canyon that Powell describes at length.
2. Powell describes two special visual effects that are produced seasonally. What are they?
3. To what sense besides sight does Powell appeal?

◆ **Critical Thinking**

INTERPRET
1. What point is Powell making when he writes that in portraying the Grand Canyon, "Language and illustration combined must fail"? **[Interpret]**
2. What do you think it meant to Powell to explore the Grand Canyon? **[Draw Conclusions]**

EVALUATE
3. How effective is Powell's description? Support your answer. **[Criticize]**

EXTEND
4. What might a painting of the Grand Canyon show that a description cannot? What can a description include that a painting cannot? **[Fine Art Link]**

Guide for Responding (continued)

◆ Reading Strategy

NOTING SPATIAL RELATIONSHIPS

Powell's poetic yet dense descriptions in "The Most Sublime Spectacle on Earth" call for readers to carefully note **spatial relationships.** By tracking where things are and comparing them with other objects, you can see a clear, precise picture of the immense canyon that Powell describes.

1. Reread Powell's description of erosion in the Grand Canyon, noting relationships of space and size as you read. (a) Which is greater—the erosion of the canyons or the erosion of the region? (b) How do you know?
2. Describe in your own words the phenomenon of "the earth and the heavens are blended in one vast structure," which Powell describes when he talks about the walls of the Grand Canyon in winter. Include details indicating size and spatial relationships.

◆ Literary Focus

DESCRIPTION

The detailed writings of Meriwether Lewis and John Wesley Powell are both products of expeditions into uncharted western territory, but there the similarity ends. **Description**—the portrayal in words of something that can be perceived by the senses—is what sets them apart. Through his use of vivid description, Powell enables us to see and hear the Grand Canyon in all its "infinite variety." For example, Powell compares the colors of the canyon to the rainbow and the sound of the river to a melody. In contrast, while Lewis conveys much information, he doesn't create a picture that we can see.

1. Find three descriptive passages in the Powell piece. Explain what makes each effective.
2. Lewis is not as descriptive as Powell, but he does include some descriptive elements in his writing. Identify a passage in Lewis's writing that helps readers to see his camp.
3. Based on the amount of description each writer includes, what would you guess is the purpose of each piece? Why?
4. Which account did you find more effective? Why?
5. Which account did you enjoy more? Explain.

◆ Build Vocabulary

USING THE PREFIX *multi-*

Knowing that the prefix *multi-* means "many" or "much," write definitions for each of the following words.

1. multimillionaire   2. multicultural   3. multimedia

USING THE WORD BANK

Using your knowledge of the Word Bank, answer the following questions. Explain each answer.

1. Are *conspicuous* omissions easy to find?
2. Is a graduation day rainstorm a *sublime* experience?
3. Would you enter an unexplored *labyrinth*?
4. What tools are used to *excavate* a sandbox?
5. Is a fence a sign of *demarcation*?
6. Is your wardrobe *multifarious*?
7. Are the inhabitants of an anthill *multitudinous*?

◆ Grammar and Style

PARTICIPIAL PHRASES

A **participial phrase** is a group of words that consists of a participle—a verb form that modifies a noun or pronoun—and its complements and modifiers. Participial phrases provide an effective way to add details to descriptions.

Practice Copy the following sentences into your notebook. Underline each participial phrase, and identify the word each modifies.

1. Sights described by Powell can be seen today.
2. Lewis's expedition would not have succeeded without the woman known as Sacagawea.
3. Begun in 1804, the expedition took two years.
4. Deeply moved by what he saw, Powell produced a description both poetic and accurate.
5. Powell's description of the Grand Canyon, published years after his visit, set off a wave of tourism.

Writing Application Write a short paragraph describing something you recently witnessed. Include at least three participial phrases.

Build Your Portfolio

Idea Bank

Writing

1. **Abstract** Stripped of descriptive language, what are Powell's essential points? Write a brief summary capturing the essential details in "The Most Sublime Spectacle on Earth."

2. **Travel Advertisement** Write an advertisement for a sightseeing tour of the Grand Canyon. Create a headline and text that will entice readers to spend their next vacation exploring "the most sublime spectacle on earth." **[Career Link]**

3. **Newspaper Article** Imagine that you are a reporter on the scene with Meriwether Lewis on August 17, 1805. Write a newspaper article reporting the events of the day. **[Media Link]**

Speaking and Listening

4. **Speech** President Jefferson instructed Lewis to treat the Native Americans he encountered in a "friendly and conciliatory manner." Assuming the role of Lewis, deliver a speech to Native Americans that would have pleased Jefferson.

5. **Television Documentary** Make "The Most Sublime Spectacle on Earth" into a television documentary. Condense and rewrite the text into a script. Choose photographs, artwork, or music to accompany the reading of the script.

Projects

6. **Expedition Map** Lewis and Clark left St. Louis, Missouri, in April 1804. Make a map showing the route of their expedition, with important places and dates labeled. **[Social Studies Link]**

7. **Research Report** The Grand Canyon is the product of geologic forces at work over the course of eons. Write a brief research report on the canyon's geologic history. **[Science Link]**

Writing Mini-Lesson

Description of a Natural Wonder

John Wesley Powell's object of inspiration—the Grand Canyon—is one of the great natural wonders of the world. Have you ever seen a natural wonder—something so amazing that it leaves you searching for words to describe it? Choose a natural wonder that you have either observed yourself, learned about through research, or seen on film. For example, you might choose Old Faithful, a giant redwood tree, or an erupting volcano. Write a brief description of it. Keep the following tip in mind as you develop your description.

Writing Skills Focus: Use Transitions to Show Place

When writing a description, use **transitions** to show the relationship of the details you include. Following are some transitions that show relationships in space:

behind, next to, in front of, at the bottom, behind, above, below, to the right, on the left, in the north, toward the west, inside, outside, near, between.

Use such words and phrases as signposts to keep your reader oriented in space.

Prewriting Picture the natural wonder you are going to describe. Create a rough sketch of your subject, and jot down some details—sights, sounds, scents—you can use to describe it.

Drafting Decide which feature you will describe first, and continue logically—and spatially—from that point. Use your sketch to help orient yourself.

Revising Review your description to see whether it conveys a precise picture of your subject. Add or change your sensory details to make your description clearer. Also, look for places where you can add transitions to make the spatial relationships easier to follow.

CONNECTIONS TO TODAY'S WORLD

from Seeing
Annie Dillard

Thematic Connection

FIRESIDE AND CAMPFIRE: VIEWS OF NATURE

The world of nature takes on a different meaning for just about every person. Henry Wadsworth Longfellow looked at the eternal flow of the ocean's tides and saw a reminder of our mortality. William Cullen Bryant found comfort in nature's never-ending cycle of life and death. For James Russell Lowell, snow symbolized emotional healing, while Whittier saw a force with the power to transform the landscape. John Wesley Powell encountered awesome majesty. What do you see?

A NEW PERSPECTIVE

In an effort to find new ways of viewing nature, contemporary writer and naturalist Annie Dillard lived for a year in a small cabin next to Tinker Creek in the Blue Ridge Mountains of Virginia, with her only companion—a goldfish named Ellery Channing. She described her life and thoughts there in the award-winning book *Pilgrim at Tinker Creek*, published in 1974, from which this excerpt is taken. As "Seeing" reveals, Dillard's experiences in the Virginia wilderness reshaped her way of viewing nature and led her to find underlying meaning in her observations of trees, water, animals, and the changing seasons.

As you read, use a Venn diagram like the one below to compare and contrast Dillard's views of nature with those of one of the other writers in this section.

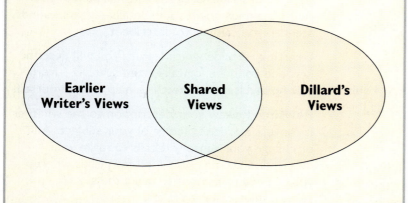

Earlier Writer's Views · Shared Views · Dillard's Views

ANNIE DILLARD
(1945–   )

As a child in Pittsburgh, Pennsylvania, Annie Dillard loved reading, drawing, and observing the natural world. She attended Hollins College in Roanoke, Virginia, and graduated with a B.A. and later an M.A. in English. Her exploration of a Virginia valley during her years at Hollins led to the publication of *Pilgrim at Tinker Creek* (1974), which won the Pulitzer Prize for Nonfiction in 1975. A few years later, on an island in the Puget Sound, she wrote *Holy the Firm* (1978), a meditation on the ultimate meaning of life.

In her essays, poetry, and fiction, Dillard accurately and vividly records the natural world, seeking its spiritual meanings. Her books include *An American Childhood* (1987), *The Writing Life* (1989), *Living by Fiction* (1982), *Teaching a Stone to Talk* (1982), and a novel, *The Living* (1992).

from

Pilgrim *at* Tinker Creek

Annie Dillard

Seeing

When I was six or seven years old, growing up in Pittsburgh, I used to take a precious penny of my own and hide it for someone else to find. It was a curious compulsion; sadly, I've never been seized by it since. For some reason I always "hid" the penny along the same stretch of sidewalk up the street. I would cradle it at the roots of a sycamore, say, or in a hole left by a chipped-off piece of sidewalk. Then I would take a piece of chalk and, starting at either end of the block, draw huge arrows leading up to the penny from both directions. After I learned to write I labeled the arrows: SURPRISE AHEAD or MONEY THIS WAY. I was greatly excited, during all this arrow drawing, at the thought of the first lucky passerby who would receive in this way, regardless of merit, a free gift from the universe. But I never lurked about, I would go straight home and not give the matter another thought until, some months later, I would be gripped by the impulse to hide another penny.

It is still the first week in January, and I've got great plans. I've been thinking about seeing. There are lots of things to see, unwrapped gifts and free surprises. The world is fairly studded and strewn with pennies cast broadside from a generous hand. But—and this is the point—who gets excited by a mere penny? If you follow one arrow, if you crouch motionless on a bank to watch a tremulous ripple thrill on the water and are rewarded by the sight of a muskrat kit paddling from its den, will you count that sight a chip of copper only, and go your rueful way? It is dire poverty indeed when a man is so malnourished and fatigued that he won't stoop to pick up a penny. But if you cultivate a healthy poverty and simplicity, so that finding a penny will literally make your day, then, since the world is in fact planted in pennies, you have with your poverty bought a lifetime of days. It is that simple. What you see is what you get.

I used to be able to see flying insects in the air. I'd look ahead and see, not the row of hemlocks across the road, but the air in front of it. My eyes would focus along that column of air, picking out flying insects. But I lost interest, I guess, for I dropped the habit. Now I can see birds. Probably some people can look at the grass at their feet and discover all the crawling creatures. I would like to know grasses and sedges—and care. Then my least journey into the world would be a field trip, a series of happy recognitions. Thoreau, in an expansive mood, exulted, "What a rich book might be made about buds, including, perhaps, sprouts!" It would be nice to think so. I cherish mental images of three perfectly happy people. One collects stones. Another—an Englishman, say—watches clouds. The third lives on a coast and collects drops of seawater, which he examines microscopically and mounts. But I don't see what the specialist sees, and so I cut myself off, not only from the total picture, but from the various forms of happiness.

Unfortunately, nature is very much a now-you-see-it, now-you-don't affair. A fish flashes, then dissolves in the water, before my eyes like so much salt. Deer apparently ascend bodily into heaven; the brightest oriole fades into leaves. These disappearances stun me into stillness and concentration; they say of nature that it conceals with a grand nonchalance, and they say of vision that it is a deliberate gift, the revelation of a dancer who for my eyes only flings away her seven veils. For nature does reveal as well as conceal: now you don't see it, now you do. For a week last September, migrating red-winged blackbirds were feeding heavily down by the creek at the back of the house. One day I went out to investigate the racket; I walked up to a tree, an Osage orange, and a hundred birds flew away. They simply materialized out of the tree. I saw a tree, then a whisk of color, then a tree again. I walked closer, and another hundred blackbirds took flight. Not a branch, not a twig budged: the birds were apparently weightless as well as invisible. Or it was as if the leaves of the Osage orange had been freed from a spell in the form of red-winged blackbirds: they flew from the tree, caught my eye in the sky, and vanished. When I looked again at the tree, the leaves had reassembled as if nothing had happened. Finally I walked directly to the trunk of the tree, and a final hundred, the real diehards, appeared, spread, and vanished. How could so many hide in the tree without my seeing them? The Osage orange, unruffled, looked just as it had looked from the house, when three hundred red-winged blackbirds cried from its crown. I looked downstream where they flew, and they were gone. Searching, I couldn't spot one. I wandered downstream to force them to play their hand, but they'd crossed the creek and scattered. One show to a customer. These appearances catch at my throat; they are the free gifts, the bright coppers at the roots of trees.

It's all a matter of keeping my eyes open. Nature is like one of those line drawings of a tree that are puzzles for children: Can you find hidden in the leaves a duck, a house, a boy, a bucket, a zebra, and a boot? Specialists can find the most incredibly well-hidden things. A book I read when I was young recommended an easy way to find caterpillars to rear: you simply find some fresh caterpillar droppings, look up, and there's your caterpillar. Most recently an author advised me to set my mind at ease about those piles of cut stems on the ground in grassy fields. Field mice make them; they cut the grass down by degrees to reach the seeds at the head. It seems that when the grass is tightly packed, as in a field of ripe grain, the blade won't topple at a single cut through the stem; instead the cut

stem simply drops vertically, held in the crush of grain. The mouse severs the bottom again and again, the stem keeps dropping an inch at a time, and finally the head is low enough for the mouse to reach the seeds. Meanwhile, the mouse is positively littering the field with its little piles of cut stems, into which, presumably, the author of the book is constantly stumbling.

If I can't see these minutiae,[1] I still try to keep my eyes open. I'm always on the lookout for ant lion traps in sandy soil, monarch pupae near milkweed, skipper larvae in locust leaves. These things are utterly common, and I've not seen one. I bang on hollow trees near water, but so far no flying squirrels have appeared. In flat country I watch every sunset in hopes of seeing the green ray. The green ray is a seldom-seen streak of light that rises from the sun like a spurting fountain at the moment of sunset; it throbs into the sky for two seconds and disappears. One more reason to keep my eyes open. A photography professor at the University of Florida just happened to see a bird die in mid-flight; it jerked, died, dropped, and smashed on the ground. I squint at the wind because I read Stewart Edward White: "I have always maintained that if you looked closely enough you could *see* the wind—the dim, hardly-made-out, fine débris fleeing high in the air." White was an excellent observer, and devoted an entire chapter of *The Mountains* to the subject of seeing deer: "As soon as you can forget the naturally obvious and construct an artificial obvious, then you too will see deer."

But the artificial obvious is hard to see. My eyes account for less than one percent of the weight of my head; I'm bony and dense; I *see* what I expect. I once spent a full three minutes looking at a bullfrog that was so unexpectedly large I couldn't see it even though a dozen enthusiastic campers were shouting directions. Finally I asked, "What color am I looking for?" and a fellow said, "Green." When at last I picked out the frog, I saw what painters are up against: the thing wasn't green at all, but the color of wet hickory bark.

The lover can see, and the knowledgeable. I visited an aunt and uncle at a quarter-horse ranch in Cody, Wyoming. I couldn't do much of

---

1. **minutiae** (mi noo´ shē ĭ) *n.*: Small or relatively unimportant details.

anything useful, but I could, I thought, draw. So as we all sat around the kitchen table after supper, I produced a sheet of paper and drew a horse. "That's one lame horse," my aunt volunteered. The rest of the family joined in: "Only place to saddle that one is his neck"; "Looks like we better shoot the poor thing, on account of those terrible growths." Meekly, I slid the pencil and paper down the table. Everyone in that family, including my three cousins, could draw a horse. Beautifully. When the paper came back, it looked as though five shining, real quarter horses had been corraled by mistake with a papier-mâché moose; the real horses seemed to gaze at the monster with a steady, puzzled air. I stay away from horses now, but I can do a creditable goldfish. The point is that I just don't know what the lover knows; I just can't see the artificial obvious that those in the know construct. The herpetologist[2] asks the native, "Are there snakes in the ravine?" "Nosir." And the herpetologist comes home with, yessir, three bags full. Are there butterflies on that mountain? Are the bluets in bloom, are there arrowheads here, or fossil shells in the shale?

Peeping through my keyhole, I see within the range of only about 30 percent of the light that comes from the sun; the rest is infrared and some little ultraviolet, perfectly apparent to many animals, but invisible to me. A nightmare network of ganglia,[3] charged and firing without my knowledge, cuts and splices what I do see, editing it for my brain. Donald E. Carr points out that the sense impressions of one-celled animals are not edited for the brain: "This is philosophically interesting in a rather mournful way, since it means that only the simplest animals perceive the universe as it is."

A fog that won't burn away drifts and flows across my field of vision. When you see fog move against a backdrop of deep pines, you see not the fog itself but streaks of clearness floating across the air in dark shreds. So I see only tatters of clearness through a pervading obscurity. I can't distinguish the fog from the overcast sky; I can't be sure if the light is direct or reflected. Everywhere darkness and the presence of the unseen appalls. We estimate now that only one atom dances alone in every cubic meter of intergalactic space. I blink and squint. What planet or power yanks Halley's Comet out of orbit? We haven't seen that force yet; it's a question of distance, density, and the pallor of reflected light. We rock, cradled in the swaddling band of darkness. Even the simple darkness of night whispers suggestions to the mind.

2. **herpetologist** (hur′ pə täl′ ə jəst): One who practices the study of reptiles and amphibians.

3. **ganglia** (gaŋ′ glē ə): Masses of nerve cells that serve as centers from which nerve impulses are transmitted.

Guide for Responding

◆ Literature and Your Life

Reader's Response What "unwrapped gifts and free surprises" have you received from nature?

Thematic Focus Why do we overlook the "bright coppers" in a world "planted with pennies"?

Journal Writing Take a few moments to observe something you see every day—your own hand, your bookbag, the bracelet on your wrist. Then write a detailed description of it. What do you really see? What have you never noticed before?

☑ Check Your Comprehension

1. Why did Dillard "hide" pennies as a child?
2. What does the author mean when she comments that she would "like to know grasses and sedges—and care"?
3. Why couldn't Dillard see the bullfrog that campers were pointing out to her?

◆ Critical Thinking

INTERPRET

1. Why does Dillard tell a story of her cousins' ability to draw horses? **[Connect]**
2. Explain how the image of "streaks of clearness" in a fog symbolizes, or represents, our vision of the world in which we live. **[Support]**
3. (a) How might Dillard advise someone to improve his or her ability to see? (b) What is beyond our power to change? **[Draw Conclusions]**

EVALUATE

4. Could this passage influence the way a reader sees and appreciates the world? Explain. **[Assess]**

APPLY

5. Apply the idea "The lover can see, and the knowledgeable" to your own life. How do you see and experience differently those things in which you take a special interest? **[Apply]**

Thematic Connection

WHAT DO WE SEE IN NATURE?

After reading "Seeing," you may have been struck by how much you've probably missed in the world around you. Dillard shows us that, for those who are willing to educate their minds and eyes, there is always more to see and appreciate in nature than in any manufactured form of entertainment. The more attention we give to our natural surroundings, the greater the rewards for our efforts.

1. What does Dillard see when she looks at nature?
2. According to "Seeing," why are we unable to see much of what surrounds us in nature?
3. What enables some people to see things in nature that go unnoticed by others?
4. Name two poems in Part 1 in which the speakers share the appreciation of nature expressed in "Seeing." Explain your choices.

Idea Bank

Writing

1. **Folk Ballad** Write the lyrics to a folk ballad that commemorates the year that Dillard spent communing with nature in the mountains of Virginia. Your ballad should include a refrain, or group of repeated lines. **[Music Link]**

2. **Description** Have you ever received an "unwrapped gift" from nature? Describe in detail what you saw and why it was special to you. Include an explanation of the emotional impact of the experience.

3. **Compare-and-Contrast Essay** How is Annie Dillard connected to the literary tradition of the nineteenth-century writers featured in this section? Compare and contrast Dillard's view of the natural world with that of the Part 1 writer with whom you feel she has the most in common. Support your ideas with examples from the selections.

Speaking and Listening

4. **Music Critique** Most of us hear the way we see; we miss the details. Select a familiar song or piece of music and listen to it repeatedly until you begin to hear its subtleties. For instance, you might distinguish the bass line from the melody, gain new insight into the lyrics, or detect a change in rhythm that you never noticed before. Play the music for the class, share your insights, and then play the music again. Were your classmates able to hear what you did? **[Music Link]**

Projects

5. **Nature Journal** Spend five minutes sitting quietly and observing nature. What do you see? What small changes and movements do you notice? Record your detailed impressions in a journal entry. Continue recording your observations over the course of three or four days. Then write a paragraph summarizing what you learned from the experience. You may wish to illustrate your journal entries. **[Science Link; Art Link]**

Writing Process Workshop

The foreign, the strange, and the exotic have always exerted a powerful pull on the human imagination. Reading about the adventurous wanderings of John Wesley Powell and Meriwether Lewis, do you find yourself yearning to explore some unknown part of the world or wanting to share your observations of a place you've visited? Choose a place that you've visited or would like to explore, and create a travel brochure filled with vivid descriptions to entice your audience to visit that place.

The following skills, introduced in this section's Writing Mini-Lessons will help you create your travel brochure.

Writing Skills Focus

▶ **Use language that is appropriate for your audience** to communicate your message effectively. (See p. 247.)

▶ **Adopt a persuasive tone** that will entice your readers to visit the destination. (See p. 255.)

▶ **A clear beginning, middle, and end** are crucial in conveying an accurate picture to your readers. (See p. 273.)

▶ **Use transitional words** to connect your details. (See p. 283.)

Notice how John Wesley Powell uses these skills in his description of the Grand Canyon.

MODEL FROM LITERATURE

from *The Most Sublime Spectacle on Earth*
by John Wesley Powell

The glories and the beauties of form, color, and sound unite in the Grand Canyon ① —forms unrivaled even by the mountains, colors that vie with sunsets, and sounds that span the diapason from tempest to tinkling raindrop, from cataract to bubbling fountain. But more: ② it is a vast district of country. Were it a valley plain it would make a state.

① Powell's soaring prose carries great conviction, persuading the reader of the greatness of what he is describing.

② Words like "span," "from," "to," and "more" show a shift in place and carry the reader from image to image.

Applying Language Skills: Appositives

An **appositive** is a noun or a noun phrase that generally follows another noun or pronoun to identify or provide extra information about it. The appositives below are underlined:

Grier and Ericka, <u>my new friends</u>, speak fluent Japanese.

Their band, <u>Ichi Ban</u>, played at the last school dance.

Because they can be used to combine sentences that contain related information, appositives are a cure for a dull style.

Practice On your paper, combine each set of sentences using appositives.

1. (a) Take a scenic evening boat ride through Paris.
   (b) Paris is "the City of Lights."
2. (a) Chocolate crepes are sold on the street.
   (b) Crepes are Parisian fast-food.

Writing Application Revise your travel brochure, using appositives to combine choppy sentences.

Writer's Solution Connection
Writing Lab

To help you gather sensory details, use the Sensory Word Bin in this tutorial on Descriptions.

Prewriting

Choose a Topic Consider the places that have captured your imagination—places you've read about, seen in the movies, or actually visited. Make a list of those that interest you most. Then choose one as the subject for your travel brochure. If you choose a place you haven't visited, you'll need to conduct research to gather details about it.

Topic Ideas

- Paris, London, Venice, Moscow, Nairobi, or another foreign city
- The fictional city where your favorite television drama is set
- Your hometown

Use a Sensory Language Chart To make your brochure as persuasive as possible, use vivid language that appeals to the reader's senses. To help you do so, create a chart with five columns. Then brainstorm for words that appeal to each of the five senses. The following chart lists a few words that might help you get started.

Sounds	Sights	Smells	Tastes	Physical Sensations
roaring	glowing	aromatic	savory	smooth
blaring	mountainous	spicy	buttery	warm
buzzing	panoramic	fresh	fruity	pillow soft
pounding	colorful	flowery	zesty	balmy

Drafting

Organize Your Brochure A travel brochure presents details relating to culture, architecture, music, food, and scenic features. Focus on the most appealing aspects of your locale, and decide on a clear organization. You might want to use a spatial order, describing the place in the form of a walking or driving tour.

Use Transitional Words Make use of key transitional words to show shifts in spatial order as you move from place to place in your brochure. Words like *behind, next to, on top of, below, left, north, in the center, background,* and *within* will keep your description clear.

Include Visuals to Bring a Place to Life Whenever possible, let a location sell itself. If a map, photograph, or a piece of fine art will convey the "feel" of a city, be sure to include it.

Revising

Sharpen Your Language Read over your brochure as if you were seeing it for the first time. Focus on finding any parts that could be made more clear. Look for unnecessary details to eliminate, and find places where you might need to add details to enhance your descriptions.

Polish Your Organization Ask a classmate to read your brochure. If your writing confuses a peer reviewer, it will probably confuse others. You may want to add subheads to help make your organizational plan more appealing.

REVISION MODEL

Robert's Grove in Belize offers every modern

① , yet

convenience. You'll feel transported to another

② by the beautiful Spanish colonial decor featuring carved colonial furniture, Mexican tile floors, ceiling fans,

time and place. Guatemalan fabrics and rugs, and fine art from around the world.

① The use of the transitional word "yet" makes the contrast more effective.

② The addition of vivid, specific language makes the description far more persuasive.

Publishing

Create a Multimedia Anthology Working with other students, select travel brochures that have visual appeal. Gather photographs, art, illustrations, and musical accompaniment for each piece. If possible, videotape the visuals with an audio voice-over. Make the recordings available in your classroom, computer lab, or school library for others to share.

Hold a Travel Fair Get together with classmates to present a "Fantastic Destinations" travel fair. Using your travel brochures as the centerpiece, create booths that advertise each location you've described. To make the fair entertaining as well as educational, you might want to provide traditional music and food at each booth.

APPLYING LANGUAGE SKILLS: Figurative Language

Figurative language is writing or speech not meant to be taken literally. Writers use figurative language to express ideas in vivid and imaginative ways. Two of the most common figures of speech are metaphors (implied comparisons of unlike things without using *like* or *as*) and similes (direct comparisons of unlike things using *like* or *as*).

Simile:
He had biceps like iron.

Metaphor:
He flexed his iron biceps.

Practice On your paper, use the suggested comparisons to revise these sentences:

1. Crowds filled the arena. [compare crowds to swarms of bees]

2. The airport was confusing. [compare airport to a maze]

Writing Application Look for places in your travel brochure where metaphors or similes would bring life to your description.

Writer's Solution Connection Writing Lab

For more practice with figurative language, see the Prewriting section of the tutorial on Description.

Strategies for Success

Behind every text you read is a writer with real opinions. Even if a piece of writing looks factual and objective, a writer's opinions can filter into the text. Recognizing bias—an author's personal beliefs—helps you separate these opinions from the facts.

Consider the Writer's Purpose

Some written forms—such as advertisements—are openly biased. Ads present a product in only a positive light and omit any negative information. Other types of writing, such as front page news articles, are supposed to be objective accounts of events. Determining the writer's purpose in the text will help alert you to the likelihood of bias.

Recognize Bias To identify bias, examine the text carefully. Watch for signals such as these:

- ▶ **Loaded language**: charged words with strong negative or positive connotations
- ▶ **Unsupported statements**: claims about an issue or product with little factual basis
- ▶ **Hidden assumptions:** descriptions or other language that suggests the writer has already reached a conclusion
- ▶ **Missing information:** facts that should logically be included but are omitted

Reach a Conclusion Once you've noted evidence of bias, you'll want to use your awareness to interpret the reading. If the writing is essentially sound, you might research to find missing information or to compare others' accounts. If its bias obscures the facts, you may want to reject the source altogether.

Wildcats Lose Again!
by Bo Stans

Are you one of the lucky ones who missed Saturday's disaster? The Wildcats were soundly clobbered by Newtown's High. Our guys gave it their all, but with referees who were surely wearing blinders and with sneaky Pete at quarterback for Newtown, they never had a chance.

The opening kickoff set the tone for the game. Jonah Sorensen's kick soared high over Newtown's receivers. They struggled pathetically to field it, and our guys pounced on the ball. However, the play was called back because of an off-side call—even though the refs were clearly wrong.

Apply the Strategy

Review the above article from a school newspaper. Then answer the questions that follow.

1. What is the writer's purpose? How might this influence his objectivity?

2. How does the statement that the "referees . . . were surely wearing blinders" reveal the writer's bias? Find two other examples of language that indicates the writer's bias.

3. Respond to the writer's complaints with an unbiased account of the game, adding information from your imagination.

✔ **Here are other situations in which it's important to recognize bias:**
- ▶ Sales messages
- ▶ First-person historical accounts
- ▶ Political reporting

PART 2 Shadows of the Imagination

Mysterious Night, ca. 1895, Daingerfield, Morris Museum of Art, Georgia

Guide for Interpreting

Edgar Allan Poe (1809–1849)

When Edgar Allan Poe died, Rufus Griswold wrote a slanderous obituary of the eccentric writer. He claimed that Poe had been expelled from college, that he had neither good friends nor good qualities, and that he committed unparalleled plagiarism. Suspicious of this unconventional obituary, some have speculated that Poe orchestrated the death notice himself to keep his name alive.

Poe's own life was almost as dark and dismal as the fiction he produced.

A Troubled Childhood
Poe was born in Boston in 1809, the son of impoverished traveling actors. Shortly after Poe's birth, his father deserted the family; a year later, his mother died. Young Edgar was taken in—though never formally adopted—by the family of John Allan, a wealthy Virginia merchant. The Allans provided for Poe's education; however, when his stepfather refused to pay Poe's large gambling debts at the University of Virginia, the young man was forced to leave the school.

Building a Literary Career
In 1827, after joining the army under an assumed name, Poe published his first volume of poetry, *Tamerlane and Other Poems*. Two years later, he published a second volume, *Al Aaraaf*. In 1830, John Allan helped Poe win an appointment to the Military Academy at West Point. Within a year, Poe was expelled for academic violations, and his dismissal resulted in an irreparable break with his stepfather.

An Unhappy Ending
During the second half of his short life, Poe pursued a literary career in New York, Richmond, Philadelphia, and Baltimore, barely supporting himself by writing and working as an editor for several magazines. After a third volume of poetry, *Poems* (1831), failed to bring him money or acclaim, he turned to fiction and literary criticism. Five of his short stories were published in newspapers in 1832, and in 1838 he published his only novel, *The Narrative of Arthur Gordon Pym*. Though his short stories gained him some recognition and his poem "The Raven" (1845) was greeted with enthusiasm, he could never escape from poverty. In 1849, two years after the death of his beloved wife, Virginia, Poe died in Baltimore alone and unhappy.

A Legacy
In the years since his death, Poe's work has been a magnet for attention. Poe is widely known as the inventor of the detective story, and his psychological thrillers have been imitated by scores of modern writers. Some scholars have harshly criticized Poe's writing; others have celebrated his use of vivid imagery and sound effects and his tireless exploration of altered mental states and the dark side of human nature. Despite Poe's uncertain status among critics, however, his work has remained extremely popular among generations of American readers.

◆ Background for Understanding

LITERATURE: POE AS AN EDITOR

In 1839, Poe lived in Philadelphia and became co-editor of *Burton's Gentleman's Magazine*, a journal that published essays, fiction, reviews, and poems, as well as various articles on sailing, hunting, and cricket. Poe's articles ran the gamut of topics.

He explained the parallel bars, mused about the mysteries of Stonehenge, and reviewed more than eighty books on a variety of topics.

It was in this magazine that Poe first published "The Fall of the House of Usher" in 1839.

The Fall of the House of Usher
◆ The Raven ◆

◆ *Literature and Your Life*

CONNECT YOUR EXPERIENCE

It's natural to feel anxiety. We're all familiar with the trembling hand or the fluttering stomach that can accompany a dreaded event. In extreme circumstances, however, "nerves" can become a destructive part of a person's personality. Stress can even lead to emotional breakdowns, as is the case for characters in both the poem and the story that follow.

Journal Writing Write a paragraph about some event or situation that makes you feel nervous. In your opinion, is there any difference between nervousness and fear?

THEMATIC FOCUS: SHADOWS OF THE IMAGINATION

Edgar Allan Poe was fascinated by the dark reaches the imagination can inhabit when a person is under great stress. How do shadows of the *reader's* imagination contribute to the atmosphere of terror in the following story and poem?

◆ Literary Focus

SINGLE EFFECT

Poe was the first writer to define the short story as a distinct literary genre and to argue that it deserved the same status as a poem or novel. In Poe's definition (which appeared in his review of Hawthorne's *Twice-Told Tales*), he asserted that a story should be constructed to achieve "a certain unique or **single effect**." He believed that every character, incident, and detail in a story should contribute to this effect. Poe said that if a writer's "very initial sentence tend not to the outbringing of this effect, then he has failed in his first step."

◆ Grammar and Style

COORDINATE ADJECTIVES

Poe uses adjectives to infuse his writing with mood and atmosphere. When two or more adjectives precede a noun, they may be either coordinate or not coordinate. **Coordinate adjectives** modify the same noun to an equal degree and are separated by commas. Adjectives that are not coordinate do not need a comma between them.

Coordinate: a *dull*, *dark*, and *soundless* day

Not Coordinate: a *gloomy young* man (*gloomy* modifies *young man*)

◆ Reading Strategy

BREAK DOWN LONG SENTENCES

Long, complicated sentences can challenge a reader's understanding. By **breaking down a long sentence** into logical parts and analyzing the relationship of these parts, a reader can clarify the author's meaning. Look for a sentence's core: its subject and its predicate. You can find further clues to the structure of a sentence in punctuation, conjunctions, and modifying words. Pare away Poe's decorative language. While descriptive details can intensify mood, they may not be central to the meaning of the sentence.

◆ Build Vocabulary

WORD ROOTS: -*voc*-

Poe uses the word *equivocal* to describe the naming of the "House of Usher." This word contains the root -*voc*-, meaning "voice." In *equivocal*, the root is joined by the word form -*equi*-, meaning "equal." *Equivocal* can be defined as "equal voices" or "having two or more interpretations."

WORD BANK

Before you read, preview this list of words from the selections.

importunate
munificent
equivocal
appellation
specious
anomalous
sentience
obeisance
craven

" *I at length...*" Edgar Allan Poe's *Tales of Mystery and Imagination*, Arthur Rackham, The New York Public Library

▲ **Critical Viewing** How do the shapes and colors contribute to the mood of this painting? What details of the story's opening paragraph does the painter convey? [Analyze]

The Fall of the House of Usher

Edgar Allan Poe

Son Coeur est un luth suspendu:
Sitôt qu'on le touche il résonne.[1]

During the whole of a dull dark, and soundless day in the autumn of the year, when the clouds hung oppressively low in the heavens, I had been passing alone, on horseback, through a singularly dreary tract of country, and at length found myself, as the shades of evening drew on, within view of the melancholy House of Usher. I know not how it was—but, with the first glimpse of the building, a sense of insufferable gloom pervaded my spirit. I say insufferable; for the feeling was unrelieved by any of that half-pleasurable, because poetic, sentiment, with which the mind usually receives even the sternest natural images of the desolate or terrible. I looked upon the scene before me—upon the mere house, and the simple landscape features of the domain—upon the bleak walls—upon the vacant eyelike windows—upon a few rank sedges[2]—and upon a few white trunks of decayed trees—with an utter depression of soul, which I can compare to no earthly sensation more properly than to the afterdream of the reveler upon opium—the bitter lapse into everyday life—the hideous dropping off of the veil. There was an iciness, a sinking, a sickening of the heart—an unredeemed dreariness of thought which no goading of the imagination could torture into aught[3] of the sublime. What was it—I paused to think—what was it that so unnerved me in the contemplation of the House of Usher? It was a mystery all insoluble; nor could I grapple with the shadowy fancies that crowded upon me as I pondered. I was forced to fall back upon the unsatisfactory conclusion, that while, beyond doubt, there *are* combinations of very simple natural objects which have the power of thus affecting us, still the analysis of this power lies among considerations beyond our depth. It was possible, I reflected, that a mere different arrangement of the particulars of the scene, of the details of the picture, would be sufficient to modify, or perhaps to annihilate its capacity for sorrowful impression; and, acting upon this idea, I reined my horse to the precipitous brink of a black and lurid tarn[4] that lay in unruffled luster by the dwelling, and gazed down—but with a shudder even more thrilling than before—upon the remodeled and inverted images of the gray sedge, and the ghastly tree stems, and the vacant and eyelike windows.

Nevertheless, in this mansion of gloom I now proposed to myself a sojourn of some weeks. Its proprietor, Roderick Usher, had been one of my boon companions in boyhood; but many years had elapsed since our last meeting. A letter, however, had lately reached me in a distant part of the country—a letter from him—which,

◆ **Literary Focus**
What "single effect" does Poe create in the first sentence?

---

1. **Son . . . résonne:** "His heart is a suspended lute: as one touches it, it resounds." From "Le Rufus" by Pierre Jean de Béranger (1780–1857).
2. **sedges** (sej′ iz) *n.*: Grasslike plants.
3. **aught** (ôt): Anything.
4. **tarn** (tärn) *n.*: Small lake.

in its wildly importunate nature, had admitted of no other than a personal reply. The MS[5] gave evidence of nervous agitation. The writer spoke of acute bodily illness—of a mental disorder which oppressed him—and of an earnest desire to see me, as his best and indeed his only personal friend, with a view of attempting, by the cheerfulness of my society, some alleviation of his malady. It was the manner in which all this, and much more, was said—it was the apparent *heart* that went with his request—which allowed me no room for hesitation; and I accordingly obeyed forthwith what I still considered a very singular summons.

Although, as boys, we had been even intimate associates, yet I really knew little of my friend. His reserve had been always excessive and habitual. I was aware, however, that his very ancient family had been noted, time out of mind, for a peculiar sensibility of temperament, displaying itself, through long ages, in many works of exalted art, and manifested, of late, in repeated deeds of munificent yet unobtrusive charity, as well as in a passionate devotion to the intricacies, perhaps even more than to the orthodox and easily recognizable beauties, of musical science. I had learned, too, the very remarkable fact, that the stem of the Usher race, all time-honored as it was, had put forth, at no period, any enduring branch: in other words, that the entire family lay in the direct line of descent, and had always, with very trifling and very temporary variations, so lain. It was this deficiency, I considered, while running over in thought the perfect keeping of the character of the premises with the accredited character of the people, and while speculating upon the possible influence which the one, in the long lapse of centuries, might have exercised upon the other—it was this deficiency, perhaps of collateral issue,[6] and the consequent undeviating transmission, from sire to son, of the patrimony[7] with the name, which had, at length, so identified the two as to merge the original title of the estate in the

5. **MS.** *abbr.*: Manuscript.
6. **collateral issue** (kə lat′ ər əl): Descended from the same ancestors but in a different line.
7. **patrimony** (pat′ rə mō′ nē) *n.*: Property inherited from one's father.

quaint and equivocal appellation of the "House of Usher"—an appellation which seemed to include, in the minds of the peasantry who used it, both the family and the family mansion.

I have said that the sole effect of my somewhat childish experiment—that of looking down within the tarn—had been to deepen the first singular impression. There can be no doubt that the consciousness of the rapid increase of my superstition—for why should I not so term it?—served mainly to accelerate the increase itself. Such, I have long known, is the paradoxical law of all sentiments having terror as a basis. And it might have been for this reason only, that, when I again uplifted my eyes to the house itself, from its image in the pool, there grew in my mind a strange fancy—a fancy so ridiculous, indeed, that I but mention it to show the vivid force of the sensations which oppressed me. I had so worked upon my imagination as really to believe that about the whole mansion and domain there hung an atmosphere peculiar to themselves and their immediate vicinity—an atmosphere which had no affinity with the air of heaven, but which had reeked up from the decayed trees, and the gray wall, and the silent tarn—a pestilent and mystic vapor, dull, sluggish, faintly discernible and leaden-hued.

Shaking off from my spirit what *must* have been a dream, I scanned more narrowly the real aspect of the building. Its principal feature seemed to be that of an excessive antiquity. The discoloration of ages had been great. Minute fungi overspread the whole exterior, hanging in a fine tangled web-work from the eaves. Yet all this was apart from any extraordinary dilapidation. No portion of the masonry had fallen; and there appeared to be a wild inconsistency between its still perfect adaptation of parts, and the crumbling condition of the individual

---

♦ **Reading Strategy**

What is the core of this sentence?

♦ **Build Vocabulary**

importunate (im pôr′ chə nit) *adj.*: Insistent

munificent (myoo nif′ ə sənt) *adj*: Generous

equivocal (i kwiv′ ə kəl) *adj*: Having more than one possible interpretation; uncertain

appellation (ap′ ə lā′ shən) *n.*: Name or title

specious (spē′ shəs) *adj.*: Seeming to be good or sound without actually being so

stones. In this there was much that reminded me of the specious totality of old woodwork which has rotted for long years in some neglected vault, with no disturbance from the breath of the external air. Beyond this indication of extensive decay, however, the fabric gave little token of instability. Perhaps the eye of a scrutinizing observer might have discovered a barely perceptible fissure, which, extending from the roof of the building in front, made its way down the wall in a zigzag direction, until it became lost in the sullen waters of the tarn.

Noticing these things, I rode over a short causeway to the house. A servant in waiting took my horse, and I entered the Gothic[8] archway of the hall. A valet, of stealthy step, then conducted me, in silence, through many dark and intricate passages in my progress to the *studio* of his master. Much that I encountered on the way contributed, I know not how, to heighten the vague sentiments of which I have already spoken. While the objects around me— while the carvings of the ceilings, the somber tapestries of the walls, the ebon blackness of the floors, and the phantasmagoric[9] armorial trophies which rattled as I strode, were but matters to which, or to such as which, I had been accustomed from my infancy—while I hesitated not to acknowledge how familiar was all this—I still wondered to find how unfamiliar were the fancies which ordinary images were stirring up. On one of the staircases, I met the physician of the family. His countenance, I thought, wore a mingled expression of low cunning and perplexity. He accosted me with trepidation and passed on. The valet now threw open a door and ushered me into the presence of his master.

The room in which I found myself was very large and lofty. The windows were long, narrow, and pointed, and at so vast a distance from the black oaken floor as to be altogether inaccessible from within. Feeble gleams of encrimsoned light made their way through the trellised panes, and served to render sufficiently distinct the more prominent objects around; the eye, however, struggled in vain to reach the remoter angles of the chamber, or the recesses of the vaulted and fretted[10] ceiling. Dark draperies hung upon the walls. The general furniture was profuse, comfortless, antique, and tattered. Many books and musical instruments lay scattered about, but failed to give any vitality to the scene. I felt that I breathed an atmosphere of sorrow. An air of stern, deep, and irredeemable gloom hung over and pervaded all.

Upon my entrance, Usher arose from a sofa on which he had been lying at full length, and greeted me with a vivacious warmth which had much in it, I at first thought, of an overdone cordiality—of the constrained effort of the *ennuyé*[11] man of the world. A glance, however, at his countenance convinced me of his perfect sincerity. We sat down; and for some moments, while he spoke not, I gazed upon him with a feeling half of pity, half of awe. Surely, man had never before so terribly altered, in so brief a period, as had Roderick Usher! It was with difficulty that I could bring myself to admit the identity of the wan being before me with the companion of my early boyhood. Yet the character of his face had been at all times remarkable. A cadaverousness of complexion; an eye large, liquid, and luminous beyond comparison; lips somewhat thin and very pallid, but of a surpassingly beautiful curve; a nose of a delicate Hebrew model, but with a breadth of nostril unusual in similar formations; a finely molded chin, speaking, in its want of prominence, of a want of moral energy; hair of a more than weblike softness and tenuity—these features, with an inordinate expansion above the regions of the temple, made up altogether a countenance not easily to be forgotten. And now in the mere exaggeration of the prevailing character of these features, and of the expression they were wont to convey, lay so much of change that I doubted to whom I spoke. The now ghastly pallor of the skin, and the now miraculous luster of the eye, above all things startled and even awed me. The silken hair, too, had been suffered to grow all unheeded, and as, in its wild gossamer texture, it floated rather than fell about the face, I could

---

8. **Gothic:** High and ornate.
9. **phantasmagoric** (fan taz′ mə gôr′ ik) adj.: Fantastic or dreamlike.

10. **fretted** (fret′ id) v.: Ornamented with a pattern of small straight intersecting bars.
11. **ennuyé** (än′ wē ā′) adj.: Bored (French).

not, even with effort, connect its Arabesque[12] expression with any idea of simple humanity.

In the manner of my friend I was at once struck with an incoherence—an inconsistency; and I soon found this to arise from a series of feeble and futile struggles to overcome an habitual trepidancy—an excessive nervous agitation. For something of this nature I had indeed been prepared, no less by his letter than by reminiscences of certain boyish traits, and by conclusions deduced from his peculiar physical conformation and temperament. His action was alternately vivacious and sullen. His voice varied rapidly from a tremulous indecision (when the animal spirits seemed utterly in abeyance) to that species of energetic concision—that abrupt, weighty, unhurried, and hollow-sounding enunciation—that leaden, self-balanced, and perfectly modulated guttural utterance, which may be observed in the lost drunkard, or the irreclaimable eater of opium, during the periods of his most intense excitement.

It was thus that he spoke of the object of my visit, of his earnest desire to see me, and of the solace he expected me to afford him. He entered, at some length, into what he conceived to be the nature of his malady. It was, he said, a constitutional and a family evil and one for which he despaired to find a remedy—a mere nervous affection,[13] he immediately added, which would undoubtedly soon pass off. It displayed itself in a host of unnatural sensations. Some of these, as he detailed them, interested and bewildered me; although, perhaps, the terms and the general manner of their narration had their weight. He suffered much from a morbid acuteness of the senses; the most insipid food was alone endurable; he could wear only garments of certain texture; the odors of all flowers were oppressive; his eyes were tortured by even a faint light; and there were but peculiar sounds, and these from stringed instruments, which did not inspire him with horror.

To an <u>anomalous</u> species of terror I found him a bounden slave. "I shall perish," said he, "I *must* perish in this deplorable folly. Thus, thus, and not otherwise, shall I be lost. I dread the events of the future, not in themselves, but in their results. I shudder at the thought of any, even the most trivial, incident, which may operate upon this intolerable agitation of soul. I have, indeed, no abhorrence of danger, except in its absolute effect—in terror. In this unnerved, in this pitiable, condition I feel that the period will sooner or later arrive when I must abandon life and reason together, in some struggle with the grim phantasm, FEAR."

I learned, moreover, at intervals, and through broken and equivocal hints, another singular feature of his mental condition. He was enchained by certain superstitious impressions in regard to the dwelling which he tenanted, and whence, for many years, he had never ventured forth—in regard to an influence whose supposititious[14] force was conveyed in terms too shadowy here to be restated—an influence which some peculiarities in the mere form and substance of his family mansion had, by dint of long sufferance, he said, obtained over his spirit—an effect which the physique of the gray walls and turrets, and of the dim tarn into which they all looked down, had at length, brought about upon the morale of his existence.

He admitted, however, although with hesitation, that much of the peculiar gloom which thus afflicted him could be traced to a more natural and far more palpable origin—to the severe and long-continued illness—indeed to the evidently approaching dissolution—of a tenderly beloved sister, his sole companion for long years, his last and only relative on earth. "Her decease," he said, with a bitterness which I can never forget, "would leave him (him, the hopeless and the frail) the last of the ancient race of the Ushers." While he spoke, the lady Madeline (for so was she called) passed through a remote portion of the apartment, and, without having noticed my presence, disappeared. I regarded her with an utter astonishment not unmingled with dread; and yet I found it impossible to account for such feelings. A sensation of stupor oppressed me as my eyes

---

12. **Arabesque** (ar´ ə besk´) *adj.*: Of complex and elaborate design.
13. **affection**: Affliction.

---

14. **supposititious** (sə päz´ ə tish´ əs) *adj.*: Supposed.

◆ **Build Vocabulary**
anomalous (ə näm´ ə ləs) *adj*: Abnormal

followed her retreating steps. When a door, at length, closed upon her, my glance sought instinctively and eagerly the countenance of the brother; but he had buried his face in his hands, and I could only perceive that a far more than ordinary wanness had overspread the emaciated fingers through which trickled many passionate tears.

The disease of the lady Madeline had long baffled the skill of her physicians. A settled apathy, a gradual wasting away of the person, and frequent although transient affections of a partially cataleptical[15] character were the unusual diagnosis. Hitherto she had steadily borne up against the pressure of her malady, and had not betaken herself finally to bed; but on the closing in of the evening of my arrival at the house, she succumbed (as her brother told me at night with inexpressible agitation) to the prostrating power of the destroyer; and I learned that the glimpse I had obtained of her person would thus probably be the last I should obtain— that the lady, at least while living, would be seen by me no more.

◆ **Literary Focus**
How does Madeline's surrender on this night contribute to a single effect?

For several days ensuing, her name was unmentioned by either Usher or myself; and during this period I was busied in earnest endeavors to alleviate the melancholy of my friend. We painted and read together, or I listened, as if in a dream, to the wild improvisations of his speaking guitar. And thus, as a closer and still closer intimacy admitted me more unreservedly into the recesses of his spirit, the more bitterly did I perceive the futility of all attempt at cheering a mind from which darkness, as if an inherent positive quality, poured forth upon all objects of the moral and physical universe in one unceasing radiation of gloom.

I shall ever bear about me a memory of the many solemn hours I thus spent alone with the master of the House of Usher. Yet I should fail in any attempt to convey an idea of the exact character of the studies, or of the occupations, in which he involved me, or led me the way. An excited and highly distempered ideality[16] threw a sulfureous[17] luster over all. His long improvised dirges will ring forever in my ears. Among other things, I hold painfully in mind a certain singular perversion and amplification of the wild air of the last waltz of von Weber.[18] From the paintings over which his elaborate fancy brooded, and which grew, touch by touch, into vaguenesses at which I shuddered the more thrillingly, because I shuddered knowing not why—from these paintings (vivid as their images now are before me) I would in vain endeavor to educe more than a small portion which should lie within the compass of merely written words. By the utter simplicity, by the nakedness of his designs, he arrested and overawed attention. If ever mortal painted an idea, that mortal was Roderick Usher. For me at least, in the circumstances then surrounding me, there arose out of the pure abstractions which the hypochondriac contrived to throw upon his canvas, an intensity of intolerable awe, no shadow of which felt I ever yet in the contemplation of the certainly glowing yet too concrete reveries of Fuseli.[19]

One of the phantasmagoric conceptions of my friend, partaking not so rigidly of the spirit of abstraction, may be shadowed forth, although feebly, in words. A small picture presented the interior of an immensely long and rectangular vault or tunnel, with low walls, smooth, white and without interruption or device. Certain accessory points of the design served well to convey the idea that this excavation lay at an exceeding depth below the surface of the earth. No outlet was observed in any portion of its vast extent, and no torch or other artificial source of light was discernible; yet a flood of intense rays rolled throughout, and bathed the whole in a ghastly and inappropriate splendor.

I have just spoken of that morbid condition of the auditory nerve which rendered all music intolerable to the sufferer, with the exception of

---

15. cataleptical (kat´ əl ep´ tik əl) *adj.*: In a state in which consciousness and feeling are suddenly and temporarily lost and the muscles become rigid.

16. ideality (ī dē al´ i tē) *n.*: Something that is ideal and has no reality.

17. sulfureous (sul fyo͞or´ ē əs) *adj.*: Greenish-yellow.

18. von Weber (fôn vā´ bər): Karl Maria von Weber (1786–1826), a German Romantic composer.

19. Fuseli (fo͞o ze´ lē): Johann Hinrich Fuseli (1742–1825), Swiss-born painter who lived in England and was noted for his work in the supernatural.

certain effects of stringed instruments. It was, perhaps, the narrow limits to which he thus confined himself upon the guitar which gave birth, in great measure, to the fantastic character of his performances. But the fervid facility of his impromptus could not be so accounted for. They must have been, and were, in the notes, as well as in the words of his wild fantasias (for he not unfrequently accompanied himself with rhymed verbal improvisations), the result of that intense mental collectedness and concentration to which I have previously alluded as observable only in particular moments of the highest artificial excitement. The words of one of these rhapsodies I have easily remembered. I was, perhaps, the more forcibly impressed with it as he gave it because, in the under or mystic current of its meaning, I fancied that I perceived, and for the first time, a full consciousness on the part of Usher of the tottering of his lofty reason upon her throne. The verses, which were entitled "The Haunted Palace," ran very nearly, if not accurately, thus:

I

In the greenest of our valleys,
  By good angels tenanted,
Once a fair and stately palace—
  Radiant palace—reared its head.
In the monarch Thought's dominion—
  It stood there!
Never seraph[20] spread a pinion
  Over fabric half so fair.

II

Banners yellow, glorious, golden,
  On its roof did float and flow
(This—all this—was in the olden
  Time long ago)
And every gentle air that dallied,
  In that sweet day,
Along the ramparts plumed and pallid,
  A winged odor went away.

III

Wanderers in that happy valley
  Through two luminous windows saw
Spirits moving musically
  To a lute's well-tunéd law;
Round about a throne, where sitting
  (Porphyrogene!)[21]
In state his glory well befitting,
  The ruler of the realm was seen.

IV

And all with pearl and ruby glowing
  Was the fair palace door,
Through which came flowing, flowing, flowing
  And sparkling evermore,
A troop of Echoes whose sweet duty
  Was but to sing,
In voices of surpassing beauty,
  The wit and wisdom of their king.

V

But evil things, in robes of sorrow,
  Assailed the monarch's high estate;
(Ah, let us mourn, for never morrow
  Shall dawn upon him, desolate!)
And, round about his home, the glory
  That blushed and bloomed
Is but a dim-remembered story
  Of the old time entombed.

VI

And travelers now within that valley,
  Through the red-litten[22] windows see
Vast forms that move fantastically
  To a discordant melody;
While, like a rapid ghastly river,
  Through the pale door,
A hideous throng rush out forever,
  And laugh—but smile no more.

I well remember that suggestions arising from this ballad led us into a train of thought wherein there became manifest an opinion of

---

20. **seraph** (ser´ əf): Angel.

21. **Porphyrogene** (pôr fər ō jēn´): Born to royalty or "the purple."
22. *litten*: Lighted.

Usher's which I mention not so much on account of its novelty (for other men have thought thus), as on account of the pertinacity with which he maintained it. This opinion, in its general form, was that of the <u>sentience</u> of all vegetable things. But, in his disordered fancy the idea had assumed a more daring character, and trespassed, under certain conditions, upon the kingdom of inorganization.[23] I lack words to express the full extent, or the earnest abandon of his persuasion. The belief, however, was connected (as I have previously hinted) with the gray stones of the home of his forefathers. The conditions of the sentience had been here, he imagined, fulfilled in the method of collocation of these stones—in the order of their arrangement, as well as in that of the many fungi which overspread them, and of the decayed trees which stood around—above all, in the long undisturbed endurance of this arrangement, and in its reduplication in the still waters of the tarn. Its evidence—the evidence of the sentience—was to be seen, he said (and I here started as he spoke), in the gradual yet certain condensation of an atmosphere of their own about the waters and the walls. The result was discoverable, he added, in that silent yet importunate and terrible influence which for centuries had molded the destinies of his family, and which made him what I now saw him— what he was. Such opinions need no comment, and I will make none.

Our books—the books which, for years, had formed no small portion of the mental existence of the invalid—were, as might be supposed, in strict keeping with this character of phantasm. We pored together over such works as the *Ververt et Chartreuse*[24] of Gresset; the *Belphegor* of Machiavelli; the *Heaven and Hell* of Swedenborg; the *Subterranean Voyage of Nicholas Klimm* by Holberg; the *Chiromancy* of Robert Flud, of Jean D'Indaginé and of De la Chambre; the *Journey into the Blue Distance* of Tieck; and the *City of the Sun* of Campanella. One favorite volume was a small octavo edition of the *Directorium Inquisitorium*, by the Dominican Eymeric de Gironne; and there were passages in Pomponius Mela, about the old African Stayrs and Œgipans, over which Usher would sit dreaming for hours. His chief delight, however, was found in the perusal of an exceedingly rare and curious book in quarto Gothic—the manual of a forgotten church—the *Vigilae Mortuorum secundum Chorum Ecclesiae Maguntinae*.

I could not help thinking of the wild ritual of this work, and of its probable influence upon the hypochondriac, when, one evening, having informed me abruptly that the lady Madeline was no more, he stated his intention of preserving her corpse for a fortnight (previously to its final interment), in one of the numerous vaults within the main walls of the building. The worldly reason, however, assigned for this singular proceeding, was one which I did not feel at liberty to dispute. The brother had been led to his resolution (so he told me) by consideration of the unusual character of the malady of the deceased, of certain obtrusive and eager inquiries on the part of her medical men, and of the remote and exposed situation of the burial ground of the family. I will not deny that when I called to mind the sinister countenance of the person whom I met upon the staircase, on the day of my arrival at the house, I had no desire to oppose what I regarded as at best but a harmless, and by no means an unnatural precaution.

At the request of Usher, I personally aided him in the arrangements for the temporary entombment. The body having been encoffined, we two alone bore it to its rest. The vault in which we placed it (and which had been so long unopened that our torches, half smothered in its oppressive atmosphere, gave us little opportunity for investigation) was small, damp, and entirely without means of admission for light; lying, at great depth, immediately beneath that portion of the building in which was my own sleeping apartment. It had been used, apparently, in remote feudal times, for the worst purposes of a donjon-keep, and, in later days, as a place of deposit for powder, or some other highly combustible substance, as a portion of

---

23. **inorganization** (in′ ôr gə ni zā′ shən) *n.*: Inanimate objects.
24. ***Ververt et Chartreuse*, etc.:** All the books listed deal with magic or mysticism.

◆ **Build Vocabulary**
sentience (sen′ shəns) *n.*: Capacity of feeling

its floor, and the whole interior of a long arch-way through which we reached it, were carefully sheathed with copper. The door, of massive iron, had been, also, similarly protected. Its immense weight caused an unusually sharp, grating sound, as it moved upon its hinges.

Having deposited our mournful burden upon trestles within this region of horror, we partially turned aside the yet unscrewed lid of the coffin, and looked upon the face of the tenant. A strik-ing similitude between the brother and sister now first arrested my attention; and Usher, divining, perhaps, my thoughts, murmured out some few words from which I learned that the deceased and himself had been twins, and that sympathies of a scarcely intelligible nature had always existed between them. Our glances, however, rested not long upon the dead—for we could not regard her unawed. The disease which had thus entombed the lady in the maturity of youth, had left, as usual in all maladies of a strictly cataleptical character, the mockery of a faint blush upon the bosom and the face, and that suspiciously lingering smile upon the lip which is so terrible in death. We replaced and screwed down the lid, and, having secured the door of iron, made our way, with toil, into the scarcely less gloomy apartments of the upper portion of the house.

And now, some days of bitter grief having elapsed, an observable change came over the features of the mental disorder of my friend. His ordinary manner had vanished. His ordinary occupations were neglected or forgotten. He roamed from chamber to chamber with hurried, unequal, and object-less step. The pallor of his countenance had assumed, if possible, a more ghastly hue—but the luminousness of his eye had utterly gone out. The once occasional husk-iness of his tone was heard no more; and a tremulous quaver, as if of extreme terror, habit-ually characterized his utterance. There were times, indeed, when I thought his unceasingly agitated mind was laboring with some oppres-sive secret, to divulge which he struggled for the necessary courage. At times, again, I was obliged to resolve all into the mere inexplicable vagaries[25] of madness, for I beheld him gazing

upon vacancy for long hours, in an attitude of the profoundest attention, as if listening to some imaginary sound. It was no wonder that his con-dition terrified—that it infected me. I felt creep-ing upon me, by slow yet uncertain degrees, the wild influences of his own fantastic yet impressive superstitions.

It was, especially, upon retiring to bed late in the night of the seventh or eighth day after the placing of the lady Madeline within the donjon, that I experienced the full power of such feel-ings. Sleep came not near my couch—while the hours waned and waned away. I struggled to reason off the nervousness which had domin-ion over me. I endeavored to believe that much, if not all of what I felt, was due to the bewilder-ing influence of the gloomy furniture of the room—of the dark and tattered draperies, which, tortured into motion by the breath of a rising tempest, swayed fitfully to and fro upon the walls, and rustled uneasily about the deco-rations of the bed. But my efforts were fruit-less. An irrepressible tremor gradually pervaded my frame; and, at length, there sat upon my very heart an incubus[26] of utterly causeless alarm. Shaking this off with a gasp and a struggle, I uplifted myself upon the pil-lows, and, peering earnestly within the intense darkness of the chamber, hearkened—I know not why, except that an instinctive spirit prompted me—to certain low and indefinite sounds which came, through the pauses of the storm, at long intervals, I knew not whence. Overpowered by an intense sentiment of horror, unaccountable yet unendurable, I threw on my clothes with haste (for I felt that I should sleep no more during the night), and endeavored to arouse myself from the pitiable condition into which I had fallen by pacing rapidly to and fro through the apartment.

I had taken but few turns in this manner, when a light step on an adjoining staircase ar-rested my attention. I presently recognized it as that of Usher. In an instant afterward he rapped, with a gentle touch, at my door, and entered, bearing a lamp. His countenance was, as usual, cadaverously wan—but, moreover, there was a species of mad hilarity in his eyes—an evidently

---

25. vagaries (vā gerˊ ēz) *n.*: Odd, unexpected actions or notions.

26. incubus (inˊ kyə bəs) *n.*: Something nightmarishly burdensome.

restrained hysteria in his whole demeanor. His air appalled me—but anything was preferable to the solitude which I had so long endured, and I even welcomed his presence as a relief.

"And you have not seen it?" he said abruptly, after having stared about him for some moments in silence—"you have not then seen it?—but, stay! you shall." Thus speaking, and having carefully shaded his lamp, he hurried to one of the casements, and threw it freely open to the storm.

The impetuous fury of the entering gust nearly lifted us from our feet. It was, indeed, a tempestuous yet sternly beautiful night, and one wildly singular in its terror and its beauty. A whirlwind had apparently collected its force in our vicinity; for there were frequent and violent alterations in the direction of the wind; and the exceeding density of the clouds (which hung so low as to press upon the turrets of the house) did not prevent our perceiving the lifelike velocity with which they flew careering from all points against each other, without passing away into the distance. I say that even their exceeding density did not prevent our perceiving this—yet we had no glimpse of the moon or stars, nor was there any flashing forth of the lightning. But the under surfaces of the huge masses of agitated vapor, as well as all terrestrial objects immediately around us, were glowing in the unnatural light of a faintly luminous and distinctly visible gaseous exhalation which hung about and enshrouded the mansion.

> ◆ **Literary Focus**
> How does the description of the storm contribute to the growing sense of terror?

"You must not—you shall not behold this!" said I, shuddering, to Usher, as I led him, with a gentle violence, from the window to a seat. "These appearances, which bewilder you, are merely electrical phenomena not uncommon— or it may be that they have their ghastly origin in the rank miasma²⁷ of the tarn. Let us close this casement:—the air is chilling and danger- ous to your frame. Here is one of your favorite romances. I will read, and you shall listen:—and so we will pass away this terrible night together."

The antique volume which I had taken up was the *Mad Trist* of Sir Launcelot Canning;²⁸ but I had called it a favorite of Usher's more in sad jest than in earnest; for, in truth, there is little in its uncouth and unimaginative prolixity which could have had interest for the lofty and spiritual ideality of my friend. It was, however, the only book immediately at hand; and I indulged a vague hope that the excitement which now agi- tated the hypochondriac, might find relief (for the history of mental disorder is full of similar anom- alies) even in the extremeness of the folly which I should read. Could I have judged, indeed, by the wild overstrained air of vivacity with which he hearkened, or apparently hearkened, to the words of the tale, I might well have congratulated myself upon the success of my design.

I had arrived at that well-known portion of the story where Ethelred, the hero of the Trist, hav- ing sought in vain for peaceable admission into the dwelling of the hermit, proceeds to make good an entrance by force. Here, it will be re- membered, the words of the narrative run thus:

"And Ethelred, who was by nature of a doughty heart, and who was now mighty withal, on account of the powerfulness of the wine which he had drunken, waited no longer to hold parley with the hermit, who, in sooth, was of an obstinate and maliceful turn, but feeling the rain upon his shoulders, and fearing the rising of the tempest, uplifted his mace outright, and, with blows, made quickly room in the plankings of the door for his gauntleted hand; and now pulling therewith sturdily, he so cracked, and ripped, and tore all asunder, that the noise of the dry and hollow-sounding wood alarumed and reverberated throughout the forest."

At the termination of this sentence I started and, for a moment, paused; for it appeared to me (although I at once concluded that my ex- cited fancy had deceived me)—it appeared to me that, from some very remote portion of the mansion, there came, indistinctly to my ears, which might have been, in its exact similarity of character, the echo (but a stifled and dull one certainly) of the very cracking and ripping sound which Sir Launcelot had so particularly described. It was, beyond doubt, the coincidence alone which had arrested my attention; for, amid

---

27. **miasma** (mī az′ mə) *n*.: Unwholesome atmosphere.

28. *Mad Trist* **of Sir Launcelot Canning:** Fictional book and author.

the rattling of the sashes of the casements, and the ordinary commingled noises of the still increasing storm, the sound, itself, had nothing, surely, which should have interested or disturbed me. I continued the story:

"But the good champion Ethelred, now entering within the door, was sore enraged and amazed to perceive no signal of the maliceful hermit; but, in the stead thereof, a dragon of a scaly and prodigious demeanor, and of a fiery tongue, which sate in guard before a palace of gold, with a floor of silver; and upon the wall there hung a shield of shining brass with this legend enwritten—

> Who entereth herein, a conqueror
>   hath bin;
> Who slayeth the dragon, the shield
>   he shall win.

And Ethelred uplifted his mace, and struck upon the head of the dragon, which fell before him, and gave up his pasty breath, with a shriek so horrid and harsh, and withal so piercing, that Ethelred had fain to close his ears with his hands against the dreadful noise of it, the like whereof was never before heard."

Here again I paused abruptly, and now with a feeling of wild amazement—for there could be no doubt whatever that, in this instance, I did actually hear (although from what direction it proceeded I found it impossible to say) a low and apparently distant, but harsh, protracted, and most unusual screaming or grating sound—the exact counterpart of what my fancy had already conjured up for the dragon's unnatural shriek as described by the romancer.

Oppressed, as I certainly was, upon the extraordinary coincidence, by a thousand conflicting sensations, in which wonder and extreme terror were predominant, I still retained sufficient presence of mind to avoid exciting, by an observation, the sensitive nervousness of my companion. I was by no means certain that he had noticed the sounds in question; although, assuredly, a strange alteration had, during the last few minutes, taken place in his demeanor. From a position fronting my own, he had gradually

brought round his chair; so as to sit with his face to the door of the chamber; and thus I could but partially perceive his features, although I saw that his lips trembled as if he were murmuring inaudibly. His head had dropped upon his breast— yet I knew that he was not asleep, from the wide and rigid opening of the eye as I caught a glance of it in profile. The motion of his body, too, was at variance with this idea—for he rocked from side to side with a gentle yet constant and uniform sway. Having rapidly taken notice of all this, I resumed the narrative of Sir Launcelot, which thus proceeded:

"And now, the champion, having escaped from the terrible fury of the dragon, bethinking himself of the brazen shield, and of the breaking up of the enchantment which was upon it, removed the carcass from out of the way before him, and approached valorously over the silver pavement of the castle to where the shield was upon the wall; which in sooth tarried not for his full coming, but fell down at his feet upon the silver floor, with a mighty great and terrible ringing sound."

No sooner had these syllables passed my lips, than—as if a shield of brass had indeed, at the moment, fallen heavily upon a floor of silver—I became aware of a distinct, hollow, metallic, and clangorous, yet apparently muffled, reverberation. Completely unnerved, I leaped to my feet; but the measured rocking movement of Usher was undisturbed. I rushed to the chair in which he sat. His eyes were bent fixedly before him, and throughout his whole countenance there reigned a stony rigidity. But, as I placed my hand upon his shoulder, there came a strong shudder over his whole person; a sickly smile quivered about his lips; and I saw that he spoke in a low, hurried, and gibbering murmur, as if unconscious of my presence. Bending closely over him I at length drank in the hideous import of his words.

◆ **Literary Focus**
Which words and details from this description add to the single effect?

Separation, 1896, Edvard Munch, Munch Museet, Oslo, Norway

▲ **Critical Viewing** How does the painting convey the same unnatural sense of terror Poe creates in the story? **[Analyze]**

"Not hear it?—yes, I hear it, and have heard it. Long—long—long—many minutes, many hours, many days, have I heard it—yet I dared not—oh, pity me, miserable wretch that I am!—I dared not—I *dared* not speak! *We have put her living in the tomb!* Said I not that my senses were acute? I *now* tell you that I heard her first feeble movement in the hollow coffin. I heard them—many, many days ago—yet I dared not—*I dared not speak!* and now—tonight—Ethelred—ha! ha!—the breaking of the hermit's door, and the death

cry of the dragon, and the clangor of the shield— say, rather, the rending of her coffin, and the grating of the iron hinges of her prison, and her struggles within the coppered archway of the vault! Oh! wither shall I fly? Will she not be here anon? Is she not hurrying to upbraid me for my haste? Have I not heard her footstep on the stair? Do I not distinguish that heavy and horrible beating of her heart? Madman!"—here he sprang furiously to his feet, and shrieked out his syllables, as if in the effort he were giving up his soul—"*Madman! I tell you that she now stands without the door!*"

As if in the superhuman energy of his utterance there had been found the potency of a spell, the huge antique panels to which the speaker pointed threw slowly back, upon the instant, their ponderous and ebony jaws. It was the work of the rushing gust—but then without those doors there *did* stand the lofty and enshrouded figure of the lady Madeline of Usher. There was blood upon her white robes, and the evidence of some bitter struggle upon every portion of her emaciated frame. For a moment she remained trembling and reeling to and fro upon the threshold—then, with a low moaning cry, fell heavily inward upon the person of her brother, and in her violent and now final death agonies, bore him to the floor a corpse, and a victim to the terrors he had anticipated.

From that chamber, and from that mansion, I fled aghast. The storm was still abroad in all its wrath as I found myself crossing the old causeway. Suddenly there shot along the path a wild light, and I turned to see whence a gleam so unusual could have issued; for the vast house and its shadows were alone behind me. The radiance was that of the full, setting, and blood-red moon, which now shone vividly through that once barely discernible fissure, of which I have before spoken as extending from the roof of the building, in a zigzag direction, to the base. While I gazed, this fissure rapidly widened—there came a fierce breath of the whirlwind—the entire orb of the satellite burst at once upon my sight—my brain reeled as I saw the mighty walls rushing asunder—there was a long tumultuous shouting sound like the voice of a thousand waters—and the deep and dank tarn at my feet closed sullenly and silently over the fragments of the "*House of Usher.*"

Guide for Responding

◆ Literature and Your Life

Reader's Response What images from the story linger in your mind? Why?

Thematic Focus In this story, the narrator barely escapes being drawn into Roderick's fantasy world. Were you drawn into the fantasy world of the story? What was the effect of the story upon your imagination? Explain.

☑ Check Your Comprehension

1. Why has the narrator come to the Usher house?
2. When the narrator meets Usher, what startles him most about Usher's appearance and behavior?
3. To what is Usher a "bounden slave"?
4. What opinion does Usher offer following his performance of "The Haunted Palace"?
5. What does the narrator find striking about Madeline's dead body?
6. (a) What noises does the narrator hear in the midst of reading the *Mad Tryst*? (b) How does Usher explain these noises? (c) What happens immediately after Usher finishes his explanation?

◆ Critical Thinking

INTERPRET
1. How is the appearance of the interior of the house of Usher related to Usher's appearance and to the condition of his mind? **[Connect]**
2. Critics have argued that Madeline and Roderick are actually physical and mental components of the same being. What evidence is there in the story to support this claim? **[Support]**
3. What is the significance of the fact that, rather than helping Usher, the narrator finds himself infected by Usher's condition? **[Analyze]**
4. What message does this story convey about the importance of maintaining contact with the outside world? Support your answer. **[Draw Conclusions]**

EVALUATE
5. Poe's story may suggest that the human imagination is capable of producing false perceptions of reality. Do you agree with this suggestion? Why or why not? **[Evaluate]**

EXTEND
6. Compare this story with Irving's "The Devil and Tom Walker." (p. 236) How does each address the dark side of human experience? **[Literature Link]**

the Raven

Edgar Allan Poe

Once upon a midnight dreary, while I pondered, weak and weary,
Over many a quaint and curious volume of forgotten lore—
While I nodded, nearly napping, suddenly there came a tapping,
As of some one gently rapping, rapping at my chamber door.
5   "'Tis some visitor," I muttered, "tapping at my chamber door—
                    Only this, and nothing more."

Ah, distinctly I remember it was in the bleak December;
And each separate dying ember wrought its ghost upon the floor.
Eagerly I wished the morrow;—vainly I had sought to borrow
10 From my books surcease[1] of sorrow—sorrow for the lost Lenore—
For the rare and radiant maiden whom the angels name Lenore—
                              Nameless *here* for evermore.

And the silken, sad, uncertain rustling of each purple curtain
Thrilled me—filled me with fantastic terrors never felt before;
15 So that now, to still the beating of my heart, I stood repeating
"'Tis some visitor entreating entrance at my chamber door—
Some late visitor entreating entrance at my chamber door;—
                              This it is and nothing more."

Presently my soul grew stronger; hesitating then no longer,
20 "Sir," said I, "or Madam, truly your forgiveness I implore;
But the fact is I was napping, and so gently you came rapping,
And so faintly you came tapping, tapping at my chamber door,
That I scarce was sure I heard you"—here I opened wide the door;—
                              Darkness there and nothing more.

25 Deep into that darkness peering, long I stood there wondering, fearing,
Doubting, dreaming dreams no mortal ever dared to dream before;
But the silence was unbroken, and the stillness gave no token,
And the only word there spoken was the whispered word, "Lenore?"
This I whispered, and an echo murmured back the word, "Lenore!"
30   Merely this and nothing more.

Back then into the chamber turning, all my soul within me burning,
Soon again I heard a tapping somewhat louder than before.
"Surely," said I, "surely that is something at my window lattice;
Let me see, then, what thereat is, and this mystery explore—
35 Let my heart be still a moment and this mystery explore;—
                              'Tis the wind and nothing more!"

Open here I flung the shutter, when, with many a flirt and flutter,
In there stepped a stately Raven of the saintly days of yore;
Not the least <u>obeisance</u> made he; not a minute stopped or stayed he;
40 But, with mien of lord or lady, perched above my chamber door—
Perched upon a bust of Pallas[2] just above my chamber door—
                              Perched, and sat, and nothing more.

---

1. **surcease** (sʉr sēs´): End.
2. **Pallas** (pal´ əs): Pallas Athena, the ancient
Greek goddess of wisdom.

◆ Build Vocabulary

obeisance (ō bā´ səns) *n.*: Gesture of respect
craven (krā´ vən) *adj.*: Very cowardly

The Raven, Edmund Dulac

▲ **Critical Viewing** Explain the effect produced by the lines and shading of this drawing. Does the mood of the illustration match that of the poem? Explain. **[Assess]**

Then this ebony bird beguiling[3] my sad fancy into smiling,
By the grave and stern decorum of the countenance[4] it wore,
45 "Though thy crest be shorn and shaven, thou," I said, "art sure no <u>craven</u>,
Ghastly grim and ancient Raven wandering from the Nightly shore—
Tell me what thy lordly name is on the Night's Plutonian[5] shore!"
              Quoth the Raven, "Nevermore."

Much I marveled this ungainly fowl to hear discourse so plainly,
50 Though its answer little meaning—little relevancy bore;
For we cannot help agreeing that no living human being
Ever yet was blessed with seeing bird above his chamber door—
Bird or beast upon the sculptured bust above his chamber door,
              With such name as "Nevermore."

---

3. beguiling (bi gīl´ iŋ) *part*.: Charming.
4. countenance (koun´ tə nəns) *n*.: Facial expression.
5. Plutonian (plōō tō´ nē ən) *adj*.: Like the underworld or infernal regions.
Refers to Pluto, Greek and Roman god of the underworld.

55   But the Raven, sitting lonely on the placid bust, spoke only
      That one word, as if his soul in that one word he did outpour.
      Nothing farther than he uttered—not a feather then he fluttered—
      Till I scarcely more than muttered, "Other friends have flown before—
      On the morrow *he* will leave me, as my Hopes have flown before."
60   Then the bird said, "Nevermore."

      Startled at the stillness broken by reply so aptly spoken,
      "Doubtless," said I, "what it utters is its only stock and store
      Caught from some unhappy master whom unmerciful Disaster
      Followed fast and followed faster till his songs one burden bore—
65   Till the dirges of his Hope that melancholy burden bore
                                            Of 'Never—nevermore.'"

      But the Raven still beguiling my sad fancy into smiling,
      Straight I wheeled a cushioned seat in front of bird, and bust and door;
      Then, upon the velvet sinking, I betook myself to linking
70   Fancy unto fancy, thinking what this ominous[6] bird of yore—
      What this grim, ungainly, ghastly, gaunt, and ominous bird of yore
                                            Meant in croaking "Nevermore."

      This I sat engaged in guessing, but no syllable expressing
      To the fowl whose fiery eyes now burned into my bosom's core;
75   This and more I sat divining, with my head at ease reclining
      On the cushion's velvet lining that the lamp-light gloated o'er,
      But whose velvet-violet lining with the lamp-light gloating o'er,
                                            She shall press, ah, nevermore!

      Then, methought, the air grew denser, perfumed from an unseen censer
80   Swung by seraphim whose foot-falls tinkled on the tufted floor.
      "Wretch," I cried, "thy God hath lent thee—by these angels he hath sent thee
      Respite—respite and nepenthe[7] from thy memories of Lenore;
      Quaff, oh quaff this kind nepenthe and forget this lost Lenore!"
                                            Quoth the Raven, "Nevermore."

85   "Prophet!" said I, "thing of evil!—prophet still, if bird or devil!—
      Whether Tempter sent, or whether tempest tossed thee here ashore,
      Desolate yet all undaunted, on this desert land enchanted—
      On this home by Horror haunted—tell me truly, I implore—
      Is there—*is* there balm in Gilead?[8]—tell me—tell me, I implore!"
90   Quoth the Raven, "Nevermore."

---

6. ominous (äm´ ə nəs) *adj.*: Threatening; sinister.
7. nepenthe (ni pen´ thē) *n.*: Drug that the ancient Greeks believed could relieve sorrow.
8. balm in Gilead (gil´ ē əd): In the Bible, a healing ointment made in Gilead, a region of ancient Palestine.

"Prophet!" said I, "thing of evil!—prophet still, if bird or devil!
By that Heaven that bends above us—by that God we both adore—
Tell this soul with sorrow laden if, within the distant Aidenn,[9]
It shall clasp a sainted maiden whom the angels name Lenore—
95   Clasp a rare and radiant maiden whom the angels name Lenore."
                              Quoth the Raven, "Nevermore."

"Be that word our sign of parting, bird or fiend!" I shrieked, upstarting—
"Get thee back into the tempest and the Night's Plutonian shore!
Leave no black plume as a token of that lie thy soul hath spoken!
100 Leave my loneliness unbroken!—quit the bust above my door!
Take thy beak from out my heart, and take thy form from off my door!"
                              Quoth the Raven, "Nevermore."

And the Raven, never flitting, still is sitting, *still* is sitting
On the pallid bust of Pallas just above my chamber door;
105 And his eyes have all the seeming of a demon's that is dreaming;
And the lamp-light o'er him streaming throws his shadow on the floor;
And my soul from out that shadow that lies floating on the floor
                              Shall be lifted—nevermore!

---

9. **Aidenn** (āʹ den): Arabic for Eden or heaven.

Guide for Responding

◆ Literature and Your Life

Reader's Response What are your impressions of the poem's speaker? Explain.

Thematic Focus What does the poem say about the dark power of the imagination?

Class Discussion "The Raven" has been popular for well over one hundred years. Explain why you think the poem does or does not merit this continued attention.

☑ Check Your Comprehension

1. How does the speaker respond to the noise he hears?
2. What does the speaker of "The Raven" want to forget?
3. (a) What does the speaker ask the raven? (b) What is the response? (c) What does the speaker order the raven to do?

◆ Critical Thinking

INTERPRET

1. (a) During the course of "The Raven," what changes occur in the speaker's attitude toward the bird? (b) What brings about each change? (c) What does the raven finally come to represent? **[Analyze]**
2. How does the speaker's emotional state change during the poem? (b) How are these changes related to the changes in his attitude toward the raven? **[Connect]**
3. How is the word *nevermore* related to the speaker's emotional state at the end of the poem? **[Interpret]**

APPLY

4. How might a psychologist explain the speaker's experience? **[Synthesize]**

Guide for Responding (continued)

◆ Reading Strategy

BREAK DOWN LONG SENTENCES

By **breaking down a long sentence** into logical parts, you can unlock the meaning at its core.

1. Identify the subject(s) and predicate(s) in the sentence below. Then restate it in your own words.

   At times, again, I was obliged to resolve all into the mere inexplicable vagaries of madness, for I beheld him gazing upon vacancy for long hours, in an attitude of the profoundest attention, as if listening to some imaginary sound.

2. Find another long sentence in Poe's story. Identify its subject(s) and predicate(s), and restate it in your own words.

◆ Build Vocabulary

USING THE WORD ROOT -voc-

The root -voc- derives from the Latin word vox, meaning "voice." Explain how the root influences each of the following words.

1. vocal 2. equivocate 3. vociferous 4. vocation

USING THE WORD BANK

Identify each pair as synonyms or antonyms.

1. anomalous, normal
2. appellation, title
3. craven, weak
4. equivocal, ambiguous
5. importunate, yielding
6. munificent, charitable
7. obeisance, reverence
8. specious, sound

Beyond Literature

Media Connection

Hitchcock and the Gothic Tradition

"At sixteen I discovered the work of Edgar Allan Poe," recalled Alfred Hitchcock (1899–1980), the great director of horror and suspense films. Hitchcock won fame for thrillers as eerie and frightening as Poe's tales. Borrowing from the Gothic tradition and adding film techniques of lighting and sound, Hitchcock created suspense classics such as *Rebecca* (1940) and *Psycho* (1960). What cinematic elements can help create a movie that is scarier than the written story that inspired it?

◆ Literary Focus

SINGLE EFFECT

In his definition of a short story, Poe asserted that a story should be constructed to achieve a **single effect,** to which every word, detail, character, and incident in a story should contribute. While the theory was originally developed for stories, Poe also applied it to poetry.

1. Explain how the following events or details contribute to the effect of a growing sense of terror in "The Fall of the House of Usher."
   a. the description of the house of Usher
   b. storms and other natural phenomena
   c. Madeline's appearance at the end of the story
2. Explain how the following details contribute to the sense of a deteriorating emotional state in "The Raven."
   a. the growing loudness of a tapping (line 32)
   b. a raven is a bird of ill omen (line 70)
   c. the raven's fiery eyes (line 74)

◆ Grammar and Style

COORDINATE ADJECTIVES

To determine whether adjectives are coordinate, switch their order. If the sentence still makes sense, the adjectives are coordinate. **Coordinate adjectives** should always be separated by commas.

> **Coordinate adjectives** are adjectives of equal rank that separately modify the noun they precede.

Practice On your paper, insert commas where they are necessary in the following sentences. If a sentence needs no commas, write *Correct*.

1. I was his only personal friend.
2. He gazed longingly at the clear placid lake.
3. She marveled at the low smooth white walls of the tunnel.
4. The guests noticed her wild theatrical manner.
5. As the dry hollow-sounding wood splintered and crashed, the horrible noise reverberated throughout the forest.

Build Your Portfolio

Idea Bank

Writing

1. **Letter** Write a letter to a film student explaining why you think he or she would benefit from analyzing the suspenseful works of Poe.

2. **Obituary** Elaborate on details from the story to write an obituary of Roderick Usher. Include the circumstances of his death, a brief biography, and information about the funeral arrangements.

3. **Essay** Poe stated, "A poem, in my opinion, is opposed to a work of science by having, for its *immediate* object, pleasure, not truth. . . ." Using "The Raven" as evidence, write a response to this provocative statement.

Speaking and Listening

4. **Dramatic Reading** Present a dramatic reading of "The Raven" that captures the poem's building tension and brings to life its unique rhymes and rhythms. Rehearse before delivering your reading. **[Performing Arts Link]**

5. **Movie Analysis** Watch a contemporary horror film, and note the techniques the film employs to create fear. Write a brief report comparing and contrasting Poe's methods of creating horror with those of the film. **[Media Link]**

Projects

6. **Report** Research the Gothic novel in Europe and America, and write a report in which you summarize the important works in this genre.

7. **Set Design** Design the set for a local stage production of "The Fall of the House of Usher." Reread Poe's description of the "mansion of doom"; then draw a picture, create a model, or describe in detail the set you would use. **[Performing Arts Link]**

Writing Mini-Lesson

Introduction to a Radio Show

The works of Edgar Allan Poe are remarkable for their vivid dramatic effects. Choose "The Raven" or "The Fall of the House of Usher," and think about how you would introduce a dramatic reading of it on the radio. Your goal is to set the stage for listeners who are far removed from the worlds of Poe's work. Your introduction should both capture the interest of listeners and provide any background information they might need.

> **Writing Skills Focus: Appropriateness for Medium**
>
> In preparing an effective introduction to a radio presentation, keep in mind that your writing must be **appropriate for the medium**. Follow these tips:
> - Use sound effects to establish the atmosphere you desire for your *listeners*, who are unable to see characters, actions, settings, or lighting.
> - Write sentences that are clear and to the point for a radio audience, which has no "second chance" to understand your words and ideas.

Prewriting Begin by rereading the Poe selection you've chosen to introduce. Jot down words or phrases that might help to prepare a listener for the work. Add your own explanatory notes and possible sound effects. Finally, organize your notes in a way that will lead to an effective introduction.

Drafting Orient listeners by identifying or clarifying obscure or difficult elements of the work, such as a theme or setting. Don't reveal important plot details or ruin the suspense that so delights an audience. Refer to your prewriting notes as you draft.

Revising Read aloud your introduction, listening to how it sounds. Where appropriate, simplify sentences to make them clearer. Change long, winding sentences to shorter ones.

Guide for Interpreting

Nathaniel Hawthorne
(1804–1864)

Although he lived in a time when many intellectuals embraced the power of the human spirit, Nathaniel Hawthorne found it impossible to adopt an optimistic world view. He believed that evil was a dominant force in the world, and his fiction expresses a gloomy vision of human affairs.

Inherited Guilt Born in Salem, Massachusetts, Hawthorne was descended from a prominent Puritan family. One of Hawthorne's ancestors was a Puritan judge who played a key role in the Salem witchcraft trials. Another ancestor was a judge known for his persecution of Quakers.

Both Hawthorne's character and his focus as a writer were shaped by a sense of inherited guilt.

Hawthorne was haunted by the intolerance and cruelty of these ancestors, even though he wasn't a Puritan and was born 112 years after the Salem witchcraft trials.

The Long Seclusion After graduation from Maine's Bowdoin College in 1825, Hawthorne secluded himself at his mother's house in Salem and wrote a novel, *Fanshawe.* Soon after the book's anonymous publication in 1828, the young author was seized by shame and abruptly burned most available copies of it. During the nine years that followed, Hawthorne single-mindedly honed his writing skills, while remaining in seclusion at his mother's house for a period of twelve years. In 1837, he published *Twice-Told Tales,* a story collection. At that point, he ended what he termed his self-imposed isolation and moved out of his mother's house. In 1842, Hawthorne married Sophia Peabody and moved to Concord, Massachusetts, where Ralph Waldo Emerson lived. During his years in Concord, Hawthorne befriended both Emerson and Henry David Thoreau—two men whose upbeat spiritual philosophy drastically opposed his. Hawthorne published a second collection of stories, *Mosses From an Old Manse* (1846), and saw the birth of his first daughter, Una.

Man of Letters When he was appointed surveyor at the Salem customhouse, Hawthorne moved with his family back to his birthplace. In 1850, he published his masterpiece, *The Scarlet Letter,* a powerful novel about sin and guilt among early Puritans. The book earned him international fame. He soon wrote two more novels, *The House of the Seven Gables* (1851) and *The Blithedale Romance* (1852).

When his college friend Franklin Pierce became president, Hawthorne was made the American consul at Liverpool, England. He spent several years in England and traveled through Italy before returning to Massachusetts. He used his Italian experiences in the novel *The Marble Faun* (1860). Hawthorne died four years later, leaving four unfinished novels among his belongings.

◆ Background for Understanding

HISTORY: THE WORLD OF HAWTHORNE'S PURITAN ANCESTORS

This story reflects Hawthorne's deep awareness of his Puritan ancestry. The story is set in the 1600's, a time when the Puritans dominated New England. The Puritans lived stern, simple lives and emphasized hard work and religious devotion. They believed that only certain people were predestined by God to go to heaven. This belief led Puritans to search their souls continually for signs of grace.

The Puritans were intolerant of those who lived lives that didn't conform to their ways. People who behaved unusually were often believed to be controlled by evil forces. This attitude contributed to the Salem witchcraft trials of 1692, when at least twenty accused witches were executed.

The Minister's Black Veil

◆ *Literature and Your Life*

CONNECT YOUR EXPERIENCE

When kept over a period of time, a secret can grow increasingly mysterious, important, or even menacing. People can become consumed by a desire to learn the secret and will draw their own conclusions if the secret isn't revealed. In "The Minister's Black Veil," a Puritan parson keeps a secret from an entire village for many years.

Journal Writing Recall a time when you or someone you know kept an important secret. Write about how others reacted and the time it took before the secret was revealed.

THEMATIC FOCUS: SHADOWS OF THE IMAGINATION

This story takes place in a gloomy world inhabited by people haunted by guilt. What role does imagination play in the story?

◆ Build Vocabulary

WORD ROOTS: -equi-

The root -*equi*- means "equal" or "plain." The spelling of the root changes slightly in the word *iniquity*, which Hawthorne uses to describe the evil thoughts of parishioners. The word's meaning—"sin or gross injustice"—comes from the combination of the root -*equi*- and the prefix *in*- ("not").

WORD BANK

Preview this list of words from the story.

> venerable
> iniquity
> indecorous
> ostentatious
> sagacious
> vagary
> tremulous
> waggery
> impertinent
> obstinacy

◆ Grammar and Style

VARYING SENTENCE OPENERS

In Hawthorne's story, each sentence flows smoothly into the next sentence. This chart shows just a few of the **varied sentence openers** that he uses.

Sentence Openers	
Article/Subject/Verb	The old people . . . came stooping along the street.
Participial Phrase	Swathed about his forehead, . . . Mr. Hooper had on a black veil.
Transitional Phrase	At the close of the services, the people hurried out . . .

◆ Literary Focus

ALLEGORY

An **allegory** is a work of literature in which events, characters, and details of setting have a symbolic meaning. For example, a character in an allegory may personify a single human trait, such as jealousy, greed, or compassion. Allegories are used to teach or explain moral principles and universal truths.

◆ Reading Strategy

JUDGE THE AUTHOR'S MESSAGES

A good piece of literature not only can entertain us but can also challenge us to consider new points of view or outlooks on life. Through the portrayal of characters, settings, and events, writers often convey a message about life that reflects their view of the world. In "The Minister's Black Veil," for example, Hawthorne conveys a message closely tied to his dark view of human nature.

Use the details in the story to interpret Hawthorne's message. Then **judge the author's message** by weighing it against your own experiences and beliefs. Ask yourself: In what ways do I agree with the points Hawthorne is making? In what ways do I disagree?

The Minister's Black Veil

NATHANIEL HAWTHORNE

A PARABLE

The sexton[1] stood in the porch of Milford meetinghouse, pulling busily at the bell rope. The old people of the village came stooping along the street. Children, with bright faces, tripped merrily beside their parents, or mimicked a graver gait, in the conscious dignity of their Sunday clothes. Spruce bachelors looked sidelong at the pretty maidens, and fancied that the Sabbath sunshine made them prettier than on weekdays. When the throng had mostly streamed into the porch, the sexton began to toll the bell, keeping his eye on the Reverend Mr. Hooper's door. The first glimpse of the clergyman's figure was the signal for the bell to cease its summons.

"But what has good Parson Hooper got upon his face?" cried the sexton in astonishment.

All within hearing immediately turned about, and beheld the semblance of Mr. Hooper, pacing slowly his meditative way towards the meetinghouse. With one accord they started, expressing more wonder than if some strange minister were coming to dust the cushions of Mr. Hooper's pulpit.

"Are you sure it is our parson?" inquired Goodman[2] Gray of the sexton.

"Of a certainty it is good Mr. Hooper," replied the sexton. "He was to have exchanged pulpits with Parson Shute, of Westbury; but Parson Shute sent to excuse himself yesterday, being to preach a funeral sermon."

The cause of so much amazement may appear sufficiently slight. Mr. Hooper, a gentlemanly person, of about thirty, though still a bachelor, was dressed with due clerical neatness, as if a careful wife had starched his band, and brushed the weekly dust from his Sunday's garb. There was but one thing remarkable in his appearance. Swathed about his forehead, and hanging down over his face, so low as to be shaken by his breath, Mr. Hooper had on a black veil. On a nearer view it seemed to consist of two folds of crape,[3] which entirely concealed his features, except the mouth and chin, but probably did not intercept his sight, further than to give a darkened aspect to all living and inanimate things. With this gloomy shade before him, good Mr. Hooper walked onward, at a slow and quiet pace, stooping somewhat, and looking on the ground, as is customary with abstracted men, yet nodding kindly to those of his parishioners who still waited on the

---

1. **sexton** (seks´ tən) n.: Person in charge of the maintenance of a church.
2. **Goodman:** Title of respect similar to "Mister."

---

3. **crape** (krāp) n.: Piece of black cloth worn as a sign of mourning.

▲ **Critical Viewing** Identify the elements or details of this painting that correspond to those in Hawthorne's story. **[Connect]**

meetinghouse steps. But so wonderstruck were they that his greeting hardly met with a return.

"I can't really feel as if good Mr. Hooper's face was behind that piece of crape," said the sexton.

"I don't like it," muttered an old woman, as she hobbled into the meetinghouse. "He has changed himself into something awful, only by hiding his face."

"Our parson has gone mad!" cried Goodman Gray, following him across the threshold.

A rumor of some unaccountable phenomenon had preceded Mr. Hooper into the meeting-house, and set all the congregation astir. Few could refrain from twisting their heads towards the door; many stood upright, and turned directly about; while several little boys clambered upon the seats, and came down again with a terrible racket. There was a general bustle, a rustling of the women's gowns and shuffling of the men's feet, greatly at variance with that hushed repose which should attend the entrance of the minister. But Mr. Hooper appeared not to notice the perturbation of his people. He entered with an almost noiseless step, bent his head mildly to the pews on each side, and bowed as he passed his oldest parishioner, a white-haired great-grandsire, who occupied an armchair in the center of the aisle. It was strange to observe how slowly this venerable man became conscious of something singular in the appearance of his pastor. He seemed not fully to partake of the prevailing wonder, till Mr. Hooper had ascended the stairs, and showed himself in the pulpit, face to face with his congregation, except for the black veil. That mysterious emblem was never once withdrawn. It shook with his measured breath, as he gave out the psalm; it threw its obscurity between him and the holy page, as he read the Scriptures; and while he prayed, the veil lay heavily on his uplifted countenance. Did he seek to hide it from the dread Being whom he was addressing?

◆ **Literary Focus**
Here is the first suggestion that the veil is a symbol. What might the veil symbolize?

Such was the effect of this simple piece of crape, that more than one woman of delicate nerves was forced to leave the meetinghouse. Yet perhaps the palefaced congregation was almost as fearful a sight to the minister, as his black veil to them.

Mr. Hooper had the reputation of a good preacher, but not an energetic one: he strove to win his people heavenward by mild, persuasive influences, rather than to drive them thither by the thunders of the Word. The sermon which he now delivered was marked by the same characteristics of style and manner as the general series of his pulpit oratory. But there was something, either in the sentiment of the discourse itself, or in the imagination of the auditors, which made it greatly the most powerful effort that they had ever heard from their pastor's lips. It was tinged, rather more darkly than usual, with the gentle gloom of Mr. Hooper's temperament. The subject had reference to secret sin, and those sad mysteries which we hide from our nearest and dearest, and would fain conceal from our own consciousness, even forgetting that the Omniscient[4] can detect them. A subtle power was breathed into his words. Each member of the congregation, the most innocent girl, and the man of hardened breast, felt as if the preacher had crept upon them, behind his awful veil,

---

4. **Omniscient** (äm nish′ ənt): All-knowing God.

and discovered their hoarded iniquity of deed or thought. Many spread their clasped hands on their bosoms. There was nothing terrible in what Mr. Hooper said, at least, no violence; and yet, with every tremor of his melancholy voice, the hearers quaked. An unsought pathos came hand in hand with awe. So sensible were the audience of some unwonted attribute in their minister, that they longed for a breath of wind to blow aside the veil, almost believing that a stranger's visage would be discovered, though the form, gesture, and voice were those of Mr. Hooper.

At the close of the services, the people hurried out with indecorous confusion, eager to communicate their pent-up amazement, and conscious of lighter spirits the moment they lost sight of the black veil. Some gathered in little circles, huddled closely together, with their mouths all whispering in the center; some went homeward alone, wrapt in silent meditation; some talked loudly, and profaned the Sabbath day with ostentatious laughter. A few shook their sagacious heads, intimating that they could penetrate the mystery; while one or two affirmed that there was no mystery at all, but only that Mr. Hooper's eyes were so weakened by the midnight lamp, as to require a shade. After a brief interval, forth came good Mr. Hooper also, in the rear of his flock. Turning his veiled face from one group to another, he paid due reverence to the hoary heads, saluted the middle-aged with kind dignity as their friend and spiritual guide, greeted the young with mingled authority and love, and laid his hands on the little children's heads to bless them. Such was always his custom on the Sabbath day. Strange and bewildered looks repaid him for his courtesy. None, as on former occasions, aspired to the honor of walking by their pastor's side. Old Squire Saunders, doubtless by an accidental lapse of memory, neglected to invite Mr. Hooper to his table, where the good clergyman had been wont to bless the food, almost every Sunday since his settlement. He returned, therefore, to the parsonage, and, at the moment of closing the door, was observed to look back upon the people, all of whom had their eyes fixed upon the minister. A sad smile gleamed faintly from beneath the black veil, and flickered about his mouth, glimmering as he disappeared.

"How strange," said a lady, "that a simple black veil, such as any woman might wear on her bonnet, should become such a terrible thing on Mr. Hooper's face!"

"Something must surely be amiss with Mr. Hooper's intellects," observed her husband, the physician of the village. "But the strangest part of the affair is the effect of this vagary, even on a sober-minded man like myself. The black veil, though it covers only our pastor's face, throws its influence over his whole person, and makes him ghostlike from head to foot. Do you not feel it so?"

"Truly do I," replied the lady; "and I would not be alone with him for the world. I wonder he is not afraid to be alone with himself!"

"Men sometimes are so," said her husband.

The afternoon service was attended with similar circumstances. At its conclusion, the bell tolled for the funeral of a young lady. The relatives and friends were assembled in the house, and the more distant acquaintances stood about the door, speaking of the good qualities of the deceased, when their talk was interrupted by the appearance of Mr. Hooper, still covered with his black veil. It was now an appropriate emblem. The clergyman stepped into the room where the corpse was laid, and bent over the coffin, to take a last farewell of his deceased parishioner. As he stooped, the veil hung straight down from his forehead, so that, if her eyelids had not been closed forever, the dead maiden might have seen his face. Could Mr. Hooper be fearful of her glance, that he so hastily caught back the black veil? A person who watched the interview between the dead and living, scrupled not to affirm, that, at the instant when the clergyman's features were disclosed, the corpse had slightly shuddered, rustling the shroud and muslin cap, though the countenance retained the composure of death. A superstitious old woman was the only witness of this prodigy. From the coffin Mr. Hooper passed into the chamber of the mourners, and thence to the head of the staircase; to make the funeral prayer. It was a tender and heart-dissolving prayer, full of sorrow, yet so imbued with celestial hopes, that the music of a heavenly harp, swept by the fingers of the dead, seemed faintly to be heard among the saddest accents of the minister. The people trembled, though they but darkly understood him when he prayed that they, and himself, and all of mortal race, might be ready, as he trusted this young maiden had been, for the dreadful hour that should snatch the veil from their faces. The bearers went heavily forth, and the mourners followed, saddening all the street, with the dead before them, and Mr. Hooper in his black veil behind.

"Why do you look back?" said one in the procession to his partner.

"I had a fancy," replied she, "that the minister and the maiden's spirit were walking hand in hand."

"And so had I, at the same moment," said the other.

That night, the handsomest couple in Milford village were to be joined in wedlock. Though reckoned a melancholy man, Mr. Hooper had a placid cheerfulness for such occasions, which often excited a sympathetic smile where livelier merriment would have been thrown away. There was no quality of his disposition which made him more beloved than this. The company at the wedding awaited his arrival with impatience, trusting that the strange awe, which had gathered over him throughout the day, would now be dispelled. But such was not the result. When Mr. Hooper came, the first thing that their eyes rested on was the same horrible black veil, which had added deeper gloom to the funeral, and could portend nothing but evil to the wedding. Such

◆ **Build Vocabulary**

venerable (ven´ ər ə bəl) *adj*.: Commanding respect

iniquity (in ik´ wə tē) *n*.: Sin

indecorous (in dek´ ər əs) *adj*.: Improper

ostentatious (äs´ tən tā´ shəs) *adj*: Intended to attract notice

sagacious (sə gā´ shəs) *adj*.: Shrewd

vagary (və ger´ ē) *n*.: Unpredictable occurrence

was its immediate effect on the guests that a cloud seemed to have rolled duskily from beneath the black crape, and dimmed the light of the candles. The bridal pair stood up before the minister. But the bride's cold fingers quivered in the <u>tremulous</u> hand of the bridegroom, and her deathlike paleness caused a whisper that the maiden who had been buried a few hours before was come from her grave to be married. If ever another wedding were so dismal, it was that famous one where they tolled the wedding knell.[5] After performing the ceremony, Mr. Hooper raised a glass of wine to his lips, wishing happiness to the new-married couple in a strain of mild pleasantry that ought to have brightened the features of the guests, like a cheerful gleam from the hearth. At that instant, catching a glimpse of his figure in the looking glass, the black veil involved his own spirit in the horror with which it overwhelmed all others. His frame shuddered, his lips grew white, he spilt the untasted wine upon the carpet, and rushed forth into the darkness. For the Earth, too, had on her Black Veil.

The next day, the whole village of Milford talked of little else than Parson Hooper's black veil. That, and the mystery concealed behind it, supplied a topic for discussion between acquaintances meeting in the street, and good women gossiping at their open windows. It was the first item of news that the tavernkeeper told to his guests. The children babbled of it on their way to school. One imitative little imp covered his face with an old black handkerchief, thereby so affrighting his playmates that the panic seized himself, and he well nigh lost his wits by his own <u>waggery</u>.

It was remarkable that of all the busybodies and <u>impertinent</u> people in the parish, not one ventured to put the plain question to Mr. Hooper, wherefore he did this thing. Hitherto, whenever there appeared the slightest call for such interference, he had never lacked advisers, nor shown himself averse to be guided by their judgment. If he erred at all, it was by so

painful a degree of self-distrust that even the mildest censure would lead him to consider an indifferent action as a crime. Yet, though so well acquainted with this amiable weakness, no individual among his parishioners chose to make the black veil a subject of friendly remonstrance. There was a feeling of dread, neither plainly confessed nor carefully concealed, which caused each to shift the responsibility upon another, till at length it was found expedient to send a deputation of the church, in order to deal with Mr. Hooper about the mystery, before it should grow into a scandal. Never did an embassy so ill discharge its duties. The minister received them with friendly courtesy, but became silent, after they were seated, leaving to his visitors the whole burden of introducing their important business. The topic, it might be supposed, was obvious enough. There was the black veil swathed round Mr. Hooper's forehead, and concealing every feature above his placid mouth, on which, at times, they could perceive the glimmering of a melancholy smile. But that piece of crape, to their imagination, seemed to hang down before his heart, the symbol of a fearful secret between him and them. Were the veil but cast aside, they might speak freely of it, but not till then. Thus they sat a considerable time, speechless, confused, and shrinking uneasily from Mr. Hooper's eye, which they felt to be fixed upon them with an invisible glance. Finally, the deputies returned abashed to their constituents, pronouncing the matter too weighty to be handled, except by a council of the churches, if, indeed, it might not require a general synod.[6]

But there was one person in the village unappalled by the awe with which the black veil had impressed all beside herself. When the deputies returned without an explanation, or even venturing to demand one, she, with the calm energy of her character, determined to chase away the strange cloud that appeared to be settling round Mr. Hooper, every moment more darkly than before. As his plighted wife,[7]

---

5. If . . . knell: Reference to Hawthorne's short story "The Wedding Knell." A knell is the slow ringing of a bell, as at a funeral.

6. synod (sin′ əd) *n.*: High governing body in certain Christian churches.
7. plighted wife: Fiancée.

it should be her privilege to know what the black veil concealed. At the minister's first visit, therefore, she entered upon the subject with a direct simplicity, which made the task easier both for him and her. After he had seated himself, she fixed her eyes steadfastly upon the veil, but could discern nothing of the dreadful gloom that had so overawed the multitude: it was but a double fold of crape, hanging down from his forehead to his mouth, and slightly stirring with his breath.

"No," said she aloud, and smiling, "there is nothing terrible in this piece of crape, except that it hides a face which I am always glad to look upon. Come, good sir, let the sun shine from behind the cloud. First lay aside your black veil; then tell me why you put it on."

Mr. Hooper's smile glimmered faintly.

"There is an hour to come," said he, "when all of us shall cast aside our veils. Take it not amiss, beloved friend, if I wear this piece of crape till then."

"Your words are a mystery, too," returned the young lady. "Take away the veil from them, at least."

"Elizabeth, I will," said he, "so far as my vow may suffer me. Know, then, this veil is a type and a symbol, and I am bound to wear it ever, both in light and darkness, in solitude and before the gaze of multitudes, and as with strangers, so with my familiar friends. No mortal eye will see it withdrawn. This dismal shade must separate me from the world: even you, Elizabeth, can never come behind it!"

"What grievous affliction hath befallen you," she earnestly inquired, "that you should thus darken your eyes forever?"

"If it be a sign of mourning," replied Mr. Hooper, "I, perhaps, like most other mortals, have sorrows dark enough to be typified by a black veil."

"But what if the world will not believe that it is the type of an innocent sorrow?" urged Elizabeth. "Beloved and respected as you are, there may be whispers that you hide your face under the consciousness of secret sin. For the sake of your holy office, do away this scandal!"

The color rose into her cheeks as she intimated the nature of the rumors that were already abroad in the village. But Mr. Hooper's mildness did not forsake him. He even smiled again—that same sad smile, which always appeared like a faint glimmering of light, proceeding from the obscurity beneath the veil.

"If I hide my face for sorrow, there is cause enough," he merely replied; "and if I cover it for secret sin, what mortal might not do the same?"

And with this gentle, but unconquerable obstinacy did he resist all her entreaties. At length Elizabeth sat silent. For a few moments she appeared lost in thought, considering, probably, what new methods might be tried to withdraw her lover from so dark a fantasy, which, if it had no other meaning, was perhaps a symptom of mental disease. Though of a firmer character than his own, the tears rolled down her cheeks. But in an instant, as it were, a new feeling took the place of sorrow: her eyes were fixed insensibly on the black veil, when, like a sudden twilight in the air, its terrors fell around her. She arose, and stood trembling before him.

"And do you feel it then, at last?" said he mournfully.

She made no reply, but covered her eyes with her hand, and turned to leave the room. He rushed forward and caught her arm.

"Have patience with me, Elizabeth!" cried he, passionately. "Do not desert me, though this veil must be between us here on earth. Be mine, and hereafter there shall be no veil over my face, no darkness between our souls! It is but a mortal veil—it is not for eternity! O! you know not how lonely I am, and how frightened, to be alone behind my black veil. Do not leave me in this miserable obscurity forever!"

"Lift the veil but once, and look me in the face," said she.

"Never! It cannot be!" replied Mr. Hooper. "Then farewell!" said Elizabeth.

She withdrew her arm from his grasp, and slowly departed, pausing at the door, to give one long shuddering gaze, that seemed almost to penetrate the mystery of the black veil. But, even amid his grief, Mr. Hooper smiled to think that only a material emblem had separated him from happiness, though the horrors, which it shadowed forth, must be drawn darkly between the fondest of lovers.

◆ **Reading Strategy**
How might this passage relate to Hawthorne's message?

From that time no attempts were made to remove Mr. Hooper's black veil, or, by a direct appeal, to discover the secret which it was supposed to hide. By persons who claimed a superiority to popular prejudice, it was reckoned merely an eccentric whim, such as often mingles with the sober actions of men otherwise rational, and tinges them all with its own semblance of insanity. But with the multitude, good Mr. Hooper was irreparably a bugbear.[8] He could not walk the street with any peace of mind, so conscious was he that the gentle and timid would turn aside to avoid him, and that others would make it a point of hardihood to throw themselves in his way. The impertinence of the latter class compelled him to give up his customary walk at sunset to the burial ground; for when he leaned pensively over the gate, there would always be faces behind the gravestones, peeping at his black veil. A fable went the rounds that the stare of the dead people drove him thence. It grieved him, to the very depth of his kind heart, to observe how the children fled from his approach, breaking up their merriest sports, while his melancholy figure was yet afar off. Their instinctive dread caused him to feel more strongly than aught else, that a preternatural[9] horror was interwoven with the threads of the black crape. In truth, his own antipathy to the veil was known to be so great that he never willingly passed before a mirror, nor stooped to drink at a still fountain, lest, in its peaceful bosom, he should be affrighted by himself. This was what gave plausibility to the whispers, that Mr. Hooper's conscience tortured him for some great crime too horrible to be entirely concealed, or otherwise than so obscurely intimated. Thus, from beneath the black veil, there rolled a cloud into the sunshine, an ambiguity of sin or sorrow, which enveloped the poor minister, so that love or sympathy could never reach him. It was said that ghost and fiend consorted with him there. With self-shudderings and outward terrors, he walked continually in its shadow, groping darkly within his own soul or gazing through a medium that saddened the whole world. Even the lawless wind, it was believed, respected his dreadful secret, and never blew aside the veil. But still good Mr. Hooper sadly smiled at the pale visages of the worldly throng as he passed by.

◆ **Literary Focus**
Why is it significant that nature respects his veil?

Among all its bad influences, the black veil had the one desirable effect, of making its wearer a very efficient clergyman. By the aid of his mysterious emblem—for there was no other apparent cause—he became a man of awful power over souls that were in agony for sin. His converts always regarded him with a dread peculiar to themselves, affirming, though but figuratively, that, before he brought them to celestial light, they had been with him behind the black veil. Its gloom, indeed, enabled him to sympathize with all dark affections. Dying sinners cried aloud for Mr. Hooper, and would not yield their breath till he appeared; though ever, as he stooped to whisper consolation, they shuddered at the veiled face so near their own. Such were the terrors of the black veil, even when Death had bared his visage! Strangers came long distances to attend service at his church, with the mere idle purpose of gazing at his figure, because it was forbidden them to behold his face. But many were made to quake ere they departed! Once, during Governor Belcher's[10] administration, Mr. Hooper was appointed to preach the election sermon. Covered

---

8. **bugbear** n.: Something causing needless fear.
9. **preternatural** (prēt′ ər nāch′ ər əl) adj.: Supernatural.

10. **Governor Belcher:** Jonathan Belcher (1682–1757), the royal governor of the Massachusetts Bay Colony, from 1730 to 1741.

Cemetery, Peter McIntyre, Courtesy of the artist

▲ **Critical Viewing** Describe the atmosphere in this painting. What has the artist done to create this atmosphere? **[Identify; Support]**

with his black veil, he stood before the chief magistrate, the council, and the representatives, and wrought so deep an impression that the legislative measures of that year were characterized by all the gloom and piety of our earliest ancestral sway.

In this manner Mr. Hooper spent a long life, irreproachable in outward act, yet shrouded in dismal suspicions; kind and loving, though unloved, and dimly feared; a man apart from men, shunned in their health and joy, but ever summoned to their aid in mortal anguish. As years wore on, shedding their snows above his sable veil, he acquired a name throughout the New England churches, and they called him Father Hooper. Nearly all his parishioners, who were of mature age when he was settled, had been borne away by many a funeral: he had one congregation in the church, and a more crowded one in the churchyard; and having wrought so late into the evening, and done his work so well, it was now good Father Hooper's turn to rest.

Several persons were visible by the shaded candlelight, in the death chamber of the old clergyman. Natural connections[11] he had none. But there was the decorously grave, though unmoved physician, seeking only to mitigate the last pangs of the patient whom he could not save. There were the deacons, and other eminently pious members of his church. There, also, was the Reverend Mr. Clark, of Westbury, a young and zealous divine, who had ridden in haste to pray by the bedside of the expiring minister. There was the nurse, no hired hand-maiden of death, but one whose calm affection had endured thus long in secrecy, in solitude, amid the chill of age, and would not perish, even at the dying hour. Who, but Elizabeth! And there lay the hoary head of good Father Hooper upon the death pillow, with the black veil still swathed about his brow, and reaching down over his face, so that each more difficult gasp of his faint breath caused it to stir. All through life that piece of crape had hung be-tween him and the world: it had separated him from cheerful brotherhood and woman's love, and kept him in that saddest of all prisons, his own heart; and still it lay upon his face, as if to deepen the gloom of his darksome chamber, and shade him from the sunshine of eternity.

For some time previous, his mind had been confused, wavering doubtfully between the past and the present, and hovering forward, as it were, at intervals, into the indistinctness of the world to come. There had been feverish turns, which tossed him from side to side, and wore

away what little strength he had. But in his most convulsive struggles, and in the wildest vagaries of his intellect, when no other thought retained its sober influence, he still showed an awful solicitude lest the black veil should slip aside. Even if his bewildered soul could have forgotten, there was a faithful woman at his pillow, who, with averted eyes, would have covered that aged face, which she had last beheld in the comeliness of manhood. At length the death-stricken old man lay quietly in the torpor of mental and bodily exhaustion, with an imperceptible pulse, and breath that grew fainter and fainter, except when a long, deep, and irregular inspiration seemed to prelude the flight of his spirit.

The minister of Westbury approached the bedside.

"Venerable Father Hooper," said he, "the moment of your release is at hand. Are you ready for the lifting of the veil that shuts in time from eternity?"

Father Hooper at first replied merely by a feeble motion of his head; then, apprehensive, perhaps, that his meaning might be doubtful, he exerted himself to speak.

"Yea," said he, in faint accents, "my soul hath a patient weariness until that veil be lifted."

"And is it fitting," resumed the Reverend Mr. Clark, "that a man so given to prayer, of such a blameless example, holy in deed and thought, so far as mortal judgment may pronounce; is it fitting that a father in the church should leave a shadow on his memory, that may seem to blacken a life so pure? I pray you, my venerable brother, let not this thing be! Suffer us to be gladdened by your triumphant aspect as you go to your reward. Before the veil of eternity be lifted, let me cast aside this black veil from your face!"

And thus speaking, the Reverend Mr. Clark bent forward to reveal the mystery of so many years. But, exerting a sudden energy, that made all the beholders stand aghast, Father Hooper snatched both his hands from beneath the bedclothes, and pressed them strongly on the black veil, resolute to struggle, if the minister of Westbury would contend with a dying man.

---

11. **natural connections:** Relatives.

"Never!" cried the veiled clergyman. "On earth, never!"

"Dark old man!" exclaimed the affrighted minister, "with what horrible crime upon your soul are you now passing to the judgment?"

Father Hooper's breath heaved; it rattled in his throat; but, with a mighty effort, grasping forward with his hands, he caught hold of life, and held it back till he should speak. He even raised himself in bed; and there he sat, shivering with the arms of death around him, while the black veil hung down, awful, at that last moment, in the gathered terrors of a lifetime. And yet the faint, sad smile, so often there, now seemed to glimmer from its obscurity, and linger on Father Hooper's lips.

"Why do you tremble at me alone?" cried he, turning his veiled face round the circle of pale spectators. "Tremble also at each other! Have men avoided me, and women shown no pity, and children screamed and fled, only for my black veil? What, but the mystery which it obscurely typifies, has made this piece of crape so awful? When the friend shows his inmost heart to his friend; the lover to his best beloved; when man does not vainly shrink from the eye of his Creator, loathsomely treasuring up the secret of his sin; then deem me a monster, for the symbol beneath which I have lived, and die! I look around me, and, lo! on every visage a Black Veil!"

While his auditors shrank from one another, in mutual affright, Father Hooper fell back upon his pillow, a veiled corpse, with a faint smile lingering on the lips. Still veiled, they laid him in his coffin, and a veiled corpse they bore him to the grave. The grass of many years has sprung up and withered on that grave, the burial stone is moss-grown, and good Mr. Hooper's face is dust; but awful is still the thought that it moldered beneath the Black Veil!

Guide for Responding

◆ Literature and Your Life

Reader's Response If you were a member of the congregation, how would you have reacted to the black veil?

Thematic Focus How does Parson Hooper use the imaginations of his parishioners to convey a religious message?

✓ Check Your Comprehension

1. How do the parishioners first react to the minister's veil?
2. (a) What is different about Parson Hooper's sermon on the first day he wears the veil? (b) What is the sermon's subject?
3. What is the veil's "one desirable effect"?
4. (a) What happens when Reverend Clark tries to remove the veil? (b) What does Parson Hooper suggest that makes the veil so awful?

◆ Critical Thinking

INTERPRET

1. (a) Explain how the veil affects Parson Hooper's perception of the world. (b) In what way does it isolate him? (c) Why does it make him a more effective minister? **[Analyze]**
2. What does Parson Hooper mean when he tells Elizabeth, "There is an hour to come . . . when all of us shall cast aside our veils"? **[Interpret]**
3. Why does the veil have such a powerful effect on people? **[Analyze]**
4. Why do you think Hawthorne does not reveal the reason Parson Hooper begins wearing the veil? **[Draw Conclusion]**

APPLY

5. This story involves characters who live very differently from the way we live today. What messages does the story convey that can be applied to today's world? **[Apply]**

Guide for Responding (continued)

◆ Literary Focus

ALLEGORY

An **allegory** is a literary work in which characters, events, details of setting, and other story elements have a symbolic meaning. For example, the minister's veil in Hawthorne's story is a symbol of the secret sins of all humanity.

1. Find three details or events in the story that hint at the veil's symbolic meaning. Explain the meaning of each of these symbols.
2. Through the use of symbols such as the minister's veil, allegories teach a moral lesson. What is the moral lesson that Hawthorne's story teaches? Support your answer.

◆ Build Vocabulary

USING THE WORD ROOT -*equi*-

The root -*equi*- means "equal." Using your knowledge of this root, complete the following sentences using the words below.

    equidistant   equivalent
    equate   equilibrium

1. The rest area was ____?____ between the towns of Bath and Brunswick.
2. Clearly the dog had begun to ____?____ the small kitchen cupboard with a tasty reward.
3. Despite gale-force winds, the sailor never lost her ____?____.
4. I handed over a $20 bill and asked for the ____?____ in Japanese currency.

USING THE WORD BANK

On a separate sheet of paper, write the letter of the best synonym for each numbered word.

1. venerable	a. perceptive
2. iniquity	b. agitated
3. indecorous	c. wickedness
4. ostentatious	d. inflexibility
5. sagacious	e. oddity
6. vagary	f. respected
7. tremulous	g. showy
8. waggery	h. discourteous
9. impertinent	i. vulgar
10. obstinacy	j. jocularity

◆ Reading Strategy

JUDGE THE AUTHOR'S MESSAGES

In stories such as "The Minister's Black Veil," Hawthorne conveys messages that reflect his dark view of the world. By drawing on your own experiences, you can **judge the messages** he conveys and decide whether or not you agree with the messages and consider what, if anything, you can learn from the stories.

1. (a) What does the way the other characters react to Parson Hooper suggest about human nature? (b) Based on your own experience, do you agree with this suggestion about human nature? Explain.
2. (a) What message is conveyed through the parishioners' inability to grasp the meaning of the veil? Support your answer. (b) Do you agree with this message? Why or why not?

◆ Grammar and Style

VARYING SENTENCE OPENERS

By **varying the sentence openers** he uses, Hawthorne helps readers flow from detail to detail and event to event. For example, some sentences begin with an article followed by the subject and verb; others begin with transitions. Look at this example from the story:

> *That night*, the handsomest couple in Milford village were to be joined in wedlock. *Though reckoned a melancholy man*, Mr. Hooper had a placid cheerfulness for such occasions, which often excited a sympathetic smile where livelier merriment would have been thrown away. *There was* no quality of his disposition which made him more beloved than this.

Looking at Style Review the story, and find two paragraphs that contain at least three types of sentence openers. Copy the paragraphs into your notebook. Using the Grammar and Mechanics Handbook on page 1197 for help, identify the type of opener used in each sentence. Then rewrite the two paragraphs so that all of the sentences have the same type of opener. Finally, explain why the rewritten paragraphs are less effective than the original ones.

*B*uild *Y*our *P*ortfolio

 ## Idea Bank

Writing

1. **Letter** As Elizabeth, write a personal letter in which you appeal to your fiancé to remove his black veil. Capture Elizabeth's directness, as well as her deep love for her fiancé.

2. **Memo to New Ministers** The narrator comments, "perhaps the palefaced congregation was almost as fearful a sight to the minister, as his black veil to them." As Parson Hooper, write a memo to future ministers, telling what to expect and giving advice about how to prepare to face a congregation for the first time. **[Career Link]**

3. **Essay** Did Hawthorne have a negative attitude toward the Puritans? Explore your response in an essay, using examples from the story.

Speaking and Listening

4. **Debate** Parson Hooper is a religious leader commanding the utmost respect. His action throws the village into confusion and anxiety. Stage a debate on whether a leader has the right to take such an action. **[Social Studies Link]**

5. **Soundtrack** Select an excerpt of this story for an oral reading. Choose an appropriate piece of music to accompany your reading. Present your reading with the music to the class. **[Music Link]**

Projects

6. **Reading Report** Read "The Wedding Knell"— another story in *Twice-Told Tales*. Compare and contrast it with "The Minister's Black Veil." Then prepare and deliver an oral presentation in which you discuss the two stories.

7. **Illustrations** Create a series of drawings or paintings to illustrate the story. Focus on capturing the mood of each scene. **[Art Link]**

 ## Writing Mini-Lesson

Response to a Short Story

Some aspect of this odd and ambiguous story probably made a distinct impression on you. Perhaps you were fascinated by the spectacle of the veil or upset by Parson Hooper's (or the villagers') behavior. Write a short paper in which you present your response to an element of the story that made an especially strong impression on you. Support your response with specific details from the story.

Writing Skills Focus: Precise Details

Often, the most effective way to cite **details** from a literary work is to use brief or extended word-for-word quotations. For example, if you wanted to capture the parishioners' reaction to Parson Hooper, you might include this quotation:

> In this manner, Mr. Hooper spent a long life, irreproachable in outward act, yet shrouded in dismal suspicions; . . .

If you wanted to include a description of the veil, on the other hand, you might simply quote a couple of words from the story:

> The Parson's veil, which Hawthorne describes as a "gloomy shade," conceals his entire face except for his chin and mouth.

Prewriting Review the story, and jot down your thoughts and feelings about the characters, setting, plot, and symbols. Choose one element to which you have an especially strong reaction. Then find passages and other details that you can use to help you explain your reactions.

Drafting In an introductory paragraph, identify the element of the story on which you're focusing and explain your reaction to it. Then provide an explanation of the role of this element in the story, citing the passage and other details for support. Follow with a more detailed description of your reactions.

Revising Is your reaction to the story clear? Do you include enough passages and details from the story? Make revisions to strengthen your response.

Guide for Interpreting

Herman Melville (1819–1891)

Deemed by his father to be "backward in speech and somewhat slow in comprehension" as a youth, Herman Melville is now widely considered one of America's greatest novelists.

Melville was born in New York City, the son of a wealthy merchant. His family's financial situation changed drastically in 1830, however, when his father's import business failed. Two years later his father died, leaving the family in debt. Forced to leave school, Melville spent the rest of his childhood working as a clerk, a farmhand, and a teacher to help support his family.

Whaling in the South Pacific

Melville became a sailor at the age of nineteen and spent several years working on whaling ships and exploring the South Pacific. After returning to the United States in 1844, he began his career as a writer, using his adventures in the South Seas as material for his fiction. He quickly produced two popular and financially successful novels, *Typee* (1846) and *Omoo* (1847), both set in the Pacific islands. His third novel, *Mardi* (1849), was considerably more abstract and symbolic. When readers rejected the book and his fame began to fade, Melville grew increasingly melancholy. He continued writing, however, turning out two more novels, *Redburn* (1849) and *White-Jacket* (1850), over the next two years.

Writing in the Berkshires

Using the profits from his popular novels, Melville bought a farm in Massachusetts, where he befriended Nathaniel Hawthorne, who lived nearby. Encouraged by Hawthorne's interest and influenced by his reading of Shakespeare, Melville began producing deeper and more sophisticated works. In 1851, he published his masterpiece, *Moby-Dick*, under the title *The Whale*. *Moby-Dick* is a novel with several layers of meaning. On the surface, it is the story of the fateful voyage of a whaling ship. On another level, it is the story of a bitter man's quest for vengeance and truth. On still another level, it is a philosophical examination of humanity's relationship to the natural world.

Unable to appreciate the novel's depth, nineteenth-century readers responded unfavorably to *Moby-Dick*. Audiences also rejected his next two novels, *Pierre* (1852) and *The Confidence Man* (1857). As a result, Melville fell into debt and was forced to accept a job as an inspector at a New York customshouse.

Disillusioned and bitter, Melville turned away from writing fiction during the latter part of his life. He produced only a handful of short stories and the powerful novella *Billy Budd*. Melville died unappreciated and unnoticed in 1891. In the 1920's, however, his novels and tales were rediscovered and hailed by scholars. Today, *Moby-Dick* is widely regarded as one of the finest novels in all of American literature.

◆ Background for Understanding

LITERATURE: MELVILLE'S SOUTH PACIFIC INSPIRATION

Melville's whaling career in the South Pacific provided him with rich material for his writing. While working aboard the whaling ship *Acushnet*, he often heard stories about an elusive, monstrous white whale known as "Mocha Dick," or "Moby Dick." Melville expanded this legend—adding his knowledge of the day-to-day workings of a whaling vessel—into his best-known work, *Moby-Dick*.

When the *Acushnet* rounded Cape Horn and crossed the Pacific to the Marquesas Islands in 1842, Melville deserted the ship and headed inland. There, he encountered the Typees, an island tribe rumored to be cannibals. To Melville's surprise, the people were peaceful and generous. He was to use this experience later as the basis for his 1846 novel *Typee*.

from Moby-Dick

◆ Literature and Your Life

CONNECT YOUR EXPERIENCE

You may remember a time when you needed to focus all your attention on some complicated or daunting task. Some situations demand intense concentration. However, as this selection illustrates, it is possible to focus *too* much on a problem, an idea, or a goal. Such an obsession can produce a sense of isolation and anxiety.

Journal Writing List some of the warning signs indicating that a personal interest may be turning into an obsession.

THEMATIC FOCUS: SHADOWS OF THE IMAGINATION

Melville focuses on the grim, shadowy imagination of Captain Ahab. What is Melville saying about nature, humanity, and life?

◆ Literary Focus

SYMBOL

A **symbol** is a person, place, or thing that has a meaning in itself and also represents something larger. For example, a flag symbolizes the character and values of a country. The white whale of Melville's *Moby-Dick* is an extremely complex symbol. Only by examining every meaning suggested by its appearance and behavior does one understand that ultimately the whale represents everything contradictory, inexplicable, and uncontrollable in nature. Like nature, Moby-Dick is massive, threatening, and awe-inspiring, yet beautiful; and though it seems unpredictable and mindless, the whale is controlled by natural laws. Like nature itself, Moby-Dick seems immortal and indifferent to human mortality.

◆ Grammar and Style

AGREEMENT WITH COLLECTIVE NOUNS

Collective nouns—such as *class, team*, or *flock*—refer to a group of people or things. They can be either singular or plural depending on the meaning you wish them to have. Verbs must agree in number with the meaning of the collective noun. In the first example, *company* refers to each group member; thus, the plural verb *were* is necessary. In the second example, *company* refers to a unit and takes the singular verb *consists*.

> When the entire ship's *company were* assembled, ...
> The *company consists* of 150 sailors.

◆ Reading Strategy

RECOGNIZE SYMBOLS

To **recognize symbols,** look for characters, places, or objects that are stressed, mentioned repeatedly, or connected by the narrator or characters to larger concepts or idea. For example, Ahab's description of Moby-Dick in this passage makes it clear that the whale has a symbolic meaning: "All visible objects, man, are but as pasteboard masks. . . . If man will strike, strike through the mask! How can the prisoner reach outside except by thrusting through the wall? To me, the white whale is that wall, shoved near to me. Sometimes I think there's naught beyond." From Ahab's description, you might guess that Moby-Dick symbolizes things that are beyond our reach or control.

◆ Build Vocabulary

PREFIXES: *mal-*

Melville's narrator speaks of "maledictions against the white whale." The word *malediction* contains the prefix *mal-*, which means "bad" or "badly." Based on this prefix and the way the word is used, what do you think *malediction* means?

WORD BANK

Preview these words from the story.

| inscrutable |
| maledictions |
| prescient |
| pertinaciously |

from

MOBY-DICK

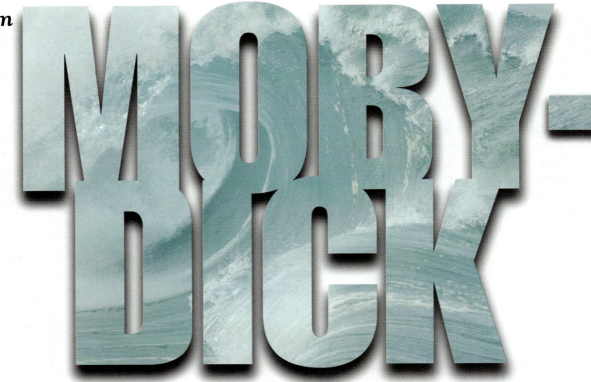

Herman Melville

Moby-Dick *is the story of a man's obsession with the dangerous and mysterious white whale that years before had taken off one of his legs. The man, Captain Ahab, guides the* Pequod, *a whaling ship, and its crew in relentless pursuit of this whale, Moby-Dick. Among the more important members of the crew are Starbuck, the first mate; Stubb, the second mate; Flask, the third mate;* Queequeg, Tashtego, and Daggoo, the harpooners; and Ishmael, the young sailor who narrates the book.

When the crew signed aboard the Pequod, *the voyage was to be nothing more than a business venture. However, in the following excerpt early in the voyage, Ahab makes clear to the crew that his purpose is to seek revenge against Moby-Dick.*

from The Quarter-Deck

One morning shortly after breakfast, Ahab, as was his wont, ascended the cabin gangway to the deck. There most sea captains usually walk at that hour, as country gentlemen, after the same meal, take a few turns in the garden.

Soon his steady, ivory stride was heard, as to and fro he paced his old rounds, upon planks so familiar to his tread, that they were all over dented, like geological stones, with the peculiar mark of his walk. Did you fixedly gaze, too, upon that ribbed and dented brow; there also, you would see still stranger footprints—the footprints of his one unsleeping, ever-pacing thought.

But on the occasion in question, those dents looked deeper, even as his nervous step that morning left a deeper mark. And, so full of his thought was Ahab, that at every uniform turn that he made, now at the mainmast and now at the binnacle,[1] you could almost see that thought turn in him as he turned, and pace in

---

1. **binnacle** (bin´ ə kəl) *n.:* Case enclosing a ship's compass.

him as he paced; so completely possessing him, indeed, that it all but seemed the inward mold of every outer movement.

"D'ye mark him, Flask?" whispered Stubb; "the chick that's in him pecks the shell. 'Twill soon be out."

The hours wore on—Ahab now shut up within his cabin; anon, pacing the deck, with the same intense bigotry of purpose[2] in his aspect.

It drew near the close of day. Suddenly he came to a halt by the bulwarks, and inserting his bone leg into the auger hole there, and with one hand grasping a shroud, he ordered Starbuck to send everybody aft.

"Sir!" said the mate, astonished at an order seldom or never given on shipboard except in some extraordinary case.

"Send everybody aft," repeated Ahab. "Mastheads, there! come down!"

When the entire ship's company were assembled, and with curious and not wholly unapprehensive faces, were eyeing him, for he looked not unlike the weather horizon when a storm is coming up, Ahab, after rapidly glancing over the bulwarks, and then darting his eyes among the crew, started from his standpoint; and as though not a soul were nigh him resumed his heavy turns upon the deck. With bent head and half-slouched hat he continued to pace, unmindful of the wondering whispering among the men; till Stubb cautiously whispered to Flask, that Ahab must have summoned them there for the purpose of witnessing a pedestrian feat. But this did not last long. Vehemently pausing, he cried:

"What do ye do when ye see a whale, men?"

"Sing out for him!" was the impulsive rejoinder from a score of clubbed voices.

"Good!" cried Ahab, with a wild approval in his tones; observing the hearty animation into which his unexpected question had so magnetically thrown them.

"And what do ye next, men?"

"Lower away, and after him!"

"And what tune is it ye pull to, men?"

"A dead whale or a stove[3] boat!"

More and more strangely and fiercely glad and approving, grew the countenance of the old man at every shout; while the mariners began to gaze curiously at each other, as if marveling how it was that they themselves became so excited at such seemingly purposeless questions.

But, they were all eagerness again, as Ahab, now half-revolving in his pivot hole, with one hand reaching high up a shroud,[4] and tightly, almost convulsively grasping it, addressed them thus:

"All ye mastheaders have before now heard me give orders about a white whale. Look ye! d'ye see this Spanish ounce of gold?"—holding up a broad bright coin to the sun—"it is a sixteen-dollar piece, men. D'ye see it? Mr. Starbuck, hand me yon topmaul."

While the mate was getting the hammer, Ahab, without speaking, was slowly rubbing the gold piece against the skirts of his jacket, as if to heighten its luster, and without using any words was meanwhile lowly humming to himself, producing a sound so strangely muffled and inarticulate that it seemed the mechanical humming of the wheels of his vitality in him.

Receiving the topmaul from Starbuck, he advanced towards the mainmast with the hammer uplifted in one hand, exhibiting the gold with the other, and with a high raised voice exclaiming: "Whosoever of ye raises me a white-headed whale with a wrinkled brow and a crooked jaw; whosoever of ye raises me that white-headed whale, with three holes punctured in his starboard fluke[5]—look ye, whosoever of ye raises me that same white whale, he shall have this gold ounce, my boys!"

"Huzza! huzza!" cried the seamen, as with swinging tarpaulins they hailed the act of nailing the gold to the mast.

"It's a white whale, I say," resumed Ahab, as he threw down the topmaul: "a white whale. Skin your eyes for him, men; look sharp for white water; if ye see but a bubble, sing out."

All this while Tashtego, Daggoo, and Queequeg had looked on with even more intense interest and surprise than the rest, and at the mention of the wrinkled brow and crooked jaw they had started as if each was separately touched by some specific recollection.

"Captain Ahab," said Tashtego, "that white whale must be the same that some call

---

2. **bigotry of purpose:** Complete single-mindedness.
3. **stove** *v.*: Broken; smashed.

4. **shroud** *n.*: Set of ropes from a ship's side to the masthead.
5. **starboard fluke** (flook) *n.*: Right half of a whale's tail.

Captain Ahab on the Deck of the Pequod, Rockwell Kent

"Corkscrew!" cried Ahab, "aye, Queequeg, the harpoons lie all twisted and wrenched in him; aye, Daggoo, his spout is a big one, like a whole shock of wheat, and white as a pile of our Nantucket wool after the great annual sheepshearing; aye, Tashtego, and he fantails like a split jib in a squall. Death and devils! men, it is Moby-Dick ye have seen—Moby-Dick—Moby-Dick!"

"Captain Ahab," said Starbuck, who, with Stubb and Flask, had thus far been eyeing his superior with increasing surprise, but at last seemed struck with a thought which somewhat explained all the wonder. "Captain Ahab, I have heard of Moby-Dick—but it was not Moby-Dick that took off thy leg?"

"Who told thee that?" cried Ahab; then pausing, "Aye, Starbuck; aye, my hearties all round; it was Moby-Dick that dismasted me; Moby-Dick that brought me to this dead stump I stand on now. Aye, aye," he shouted with a terrific, loud, animal sob, like that of a heart-stricken moose; "Aye, aye! it was that accursed white whale that razeed me; made a poor pegging lubber[8] for me forever and a day!" Then tossing both arms, with measureless imprecations he shouted out: "Aye, aye! and I'll chase him round Good Hope, and round the Horn, and round the Norway Maelstrom, and round perdition's flames before I give him up. And this is what ye have shipped for, men! to chase that white whale on both sides of land, and over all sides of earth, till he spouts black blood and rolls fin out. What say ye, men, will ye splice hands on it, now? I think ye do look brave."

"Aye, aye!" shouted the harpooneers and seamen, running closer to the excited old man: "A sharp eye for the white whale; a sharp lance for Moby-Dick!"

"God bless ye," he seemed to half sob and half shout. "God bless ye, men. Steward! go

Moby-Dick."

"Moby-Dick?" shouted Ahab. "Do ye know the white whale then, Tash?"

"Does he fantail[6] a little curious, sir, before he goes down?" said the Gay-Header deliberately.

"And has he a curious spout, too," said Daggoo, "very bushy, even for a parmacetty,[7] and mighty quick, Captain Ahab?"

"And he have one, two, tree—oh! good many iron in him hide, too, Captain," cried Queequeg disjointedly, "all twiske-tee betwisk, like him—him—" faltering hard for a word, and screwing his hand round and round as though uncorking a bottle—"like him—him—"

---

6. fantail *v.:* To spread the tail like a fan.
7. parmacetty (pär′ mə set′ ē) *n.:* Dialect for spermaceti, a waxy substance taken from a sperm whale's head and used to make candles.

---

8. lubber (lub′ ər) *n.:* Slow, clumsy person.

draw the great measure of grog. But what's this long face about, Mr. Starbuck; wilt thou not chase the white whale? art not game for Moby-Dick?"

"I am game for his crooked jaw, and for the jaws of Death too, Captain Ahab, if it fairly comes in the way of the business we follow; but I came here to hunt whales, not my commander's vengeance. How many barrels will thy vengeance yield thee even if thou gettest it, Captain Ahab? it will not fetch thee much in our Nantucket market."

"Nantucket market! Hoot! But come closer, Starbuck; thou requirest a little lower layer. If money's to be the measurer, man, and the accountants have computed their great counting-house the globe, by girdling it with guineas, one to every three parts of an inch; then, let me tell thee, that my vengeance will fetch a great premium *here!*"

"He smites his chest," whispered Stubb, "what's that for? methinks it rings most vast, but hollow."

"Vengeance on a dumb brute!" cried Starbuck, "that simply smote thee from blindest instinct! Madness! To be enraged with a dumb thing, Captain Ahab, seems blasphemous."

"Hark ye yet again—the little lower layer. All visible objects, man, are but as pasteboard masks. But in each event—in the living act, the undoubted deed—there, some unknown but still reasoning thing puts forth the moldings of its features from behind the unreasoning mask. If man will strike, strike through the mask! How can the prisoner reach outside except by thrusting through the wall? To me, the white whale is that wall, shoved near to me. Sometimes I think there's naught beyond. But 'tis enough. He tasks me; he heaps me; I see in him outrageous strength, with an <u>inscrutable</u> malice sinewing it. That inscrutable thing is chiefly what I hate; and be the white whale agent, or be the white whale principal,

I will wreak that hate upon him. Talk not to me of blasphemy, man; I'd strike the sun if it insulted me. For could the sun do that, then could I do the other; since there is ever a sort of fair play herein, jealousy presiding over all creations. But not my master, man, is even that fair play. Who's over me? Truth hath no confines. Take off thine eye! more intolerable than fiends' glarings is a doltish stare! So, so; thou reddenest and palest; my heat has melted thee to anger-glow. But look ye, Starbuck, what is said in heat, that thing unsays itself. There are men from whom warm words are small indignity. I meant not to incense thee. Let it go. Look! see yonder Turkish cheeks of spotted tawn—living, breathing pictures painted by the sun. The pagan leopards—the unrecking and unworshiping things, that live, and seek, and give no reasons for the torrid life they feel! The crew, man, the crew! Are they not one and all with Ahab, in this matter of the whale? See Stubb! he laughs! See yonder Chilean! he snorts to think of it. Stand up amid the general hurricane, thy one tossed sapling cannot, Starbuck! And what is it? Reckon it. 'Tis but to help strike a fin; no wondrous feat for Starbuck. What is it more? From this one poor hunt, then, the best lance out of all Nantucket, surely he will not hang back, when every foremasthand has clutched a whetstone. Ah! constrainings seize thee; I see! the billow lifts thee! Speak, but speak!—Aye, aye! thy silence, then, *that* voices thee. (*Aside*) Something shot from my dilated nostrils, he has inhaled it in his lungs. Starbuck now is mine; cannot oppose me now, without rebellion."

"God keep me!—keep us all!" murmured Starbuck, lowly.

But in his joy at the enchanted, tacit acquiescence of the mate, Ahab did not hear his foreboding invocation; nor yet the low laugh from the hold; nor yet the presaging vibrations of the winds in the cordage; nor yet the hollow flap of the sails against the masts, as for a moment their hearts sank in. For again Starbuck's downcast eyes lighted up with the stubbornness of life; the subterranean laugh died away; the winds blew on; the sails filled out; the ship heaved and rolled as before. Ah, ye admonitions and warnings! why stay ye not when ye come? But rather are ye predictions than warnings, ye shadows! Yet not so much predictions from without, as verifications of the foregoing things within. For with little external to constrain us, the innermost necessities in our being, these still drive us on.

"The measure! the measure!" cried Ahab.

Receiving the brimming pewter, and turning to the harpooneers, he ordered them to produce their weapons. Then ranging them before him near the capstan,[9] with their harpoons in their hands, while his three mates stood at his side with their lances, and the rest of the ship's company formed a circle round the group; he stood for an instant searchingly eyeing every man of his crew. But those wild eyes met his, as the bloodshot eyes of the prairie wolves meet the eye of their leader, ere he rushes on at their head in the trail of the bison; but, alas! only to fall into the hidden snare of the Indian.

"Drink and pass!" he cried, handing the heavy charged flagon to the nearest seamen. "The crew alone now drink. Round with it, round! Short drafts—long swallows, men; 'tis hot as Satan's hoof. So, so; it goes round excellently. It spiralizes in ye; forks out at the serpent-snapping eye. Well done; almost drained. That way it went, this way it comes. Hand it me—here's a hollow! Men, ye seem the years; so brimming life is gulped and gone. Steward, refill!

"Attend now, my braves. I have mustered ye all round this capstan; and ye mates, flank me with your lances; and ye harpooneers, stand there with your irons; and ye, stout mariners, ring me in, that I may in some sort revive a noble custom of my fishermen fathers before me. O men, you will yet see that—Ha! boy, come back? bad pennies come not sooner. Hand it me. Why, now, this pewter had run brimming again, wer't not thou St. Vitus' imp[10]—away, thou ague![11]

"Advance, ye mates! cross your lances full before me. Well done! Let me touch the axis." So saying, with extended arm, he grasped the three level, radiating lances at their crossed center; while so doing, suddenly and nervously twitched them; meanwhile glancing intently from Starbuck to Stubb; from Stubb to Flask. It seemed as though, by some nameless, interior volition, he would fain have shocked into them the same fiery emotion accumulated within the Leyden jar[12] of his own magnetic life. The three mates quailed before his strong, sustained, and mystic aspect. Stubb and Flask looked sideways from him; the honest eye of Starbuck fell downright.

"In vain!" cried Ahab; "but, maybe, 'tis well. For did ye three but once take the full-forced shock, then mine own electric thing, *that* had perhaps expired from out me. Perchance, too, it would have dropped ye dead. Perchance ye need it not. Down lances! And now, ye mates, I do appoint ye three cupbearers to my three pagan kinsmen there—yon three most honorable gentlemen and noblemen, my valiant harpooneers. Disdain the task? What, when the great Pope washes the feet of beggars, using his tiara for ewer? Oh, my sweet cardinals! your own condescension, that shall bend ye to it. I do not order ye; ye will it. Cut your seizings and draw the poles, ye harpooneers!"

Silently obeying the order, the three harpooneers now stood with the detached iron part of their harpoons, some three feet long, held, barbs up, before him.

"Stab me not with that keen steel! Cant them; cant them over! know ye not the goblet end? Turn up the socket! So, so; now, ye cupbearers, advance. The irons! take them; hold them while I fill!" Forthwith, slowly going from one officer to the other, he brimmed the harpoon sockets with the fiery waters from the pewter.

◆ **Literary Focus**
How do these details suggest that the harpooners' actions have a symbolic meaning?

"Now, three to three, ye stand. Commend the murderous chalices! Bestow them, ye who are now made parties to this indissoluble league. Ha! Starbuck! but the deed is done! Yon ratifying sun now waits to sit upon it. Drink, ye harpooneers! drink and swear, ye men that man the deathful whaleboat's bow—Death to Moby-Dick! God hunt us all, if we do not hunt Moby-

---

9. **capstan** (kap´ stən) n.: Large cylinder, turned by hand, around which cables are wound.

10. **St. Vitus' imp:** Offspring of St. Vitus, the patron saint of people stricken with the nervous disorder chorea, which is characterized by irregular, jerking movements.

11. **ague** (ā´ gyōō) n.: A chill or fit of shivering.

12. **Leyden** (līd´ən) **jar** n.: Glass jar coated inside and out with tinfoil and having a metal rod connected to the inner lining; used to condense static electricity.

Dick to his death!" The long, barbed steel goblets were lifted; and to cries and <u>maledictions</u> against the white whale, the spirits were simultaneously quaffed down with a hiss. Starbuck paled, and turned, and shivered. Once more, and finally, the replenished pewter went the rounds among the frantic crew; when, waving his free hand to them, they all dispersed; and Ahab retired within his cabin.

After Moby-Dick has been sighted in the Pacific Ocean, the Pequod's *boats pursue the whale for two days. One of the boats has been sunk, and Ahab's ivory leg has been broken off. However, as the next day dawns, the chase continues.*

The Chase—Third Day

The morning of the third day dawned fair and fresh, and once more the solitary night man at the foremasthead was relieved by crowds of the daylight lookouts, who dotted every mast and almost every spar.

"D'ye see him?" cried Ahab; but the whale was not yet in sight.

"In his infallible wake, though; but follow that wake, that's all. Helm there; steady, as thou goest, and hast been going. What a lovely day again! were it a new-made world, and made for a summerhouse to the angels, and this morning the first of its throwing open to them, a fairer day could not dawn upon that world. Here's food for thought, had Ahab time to think; but Ahab never thinks; he only feels, feels, feels; that's tingling enough for mortal man! to think's audacity. God only has that right and privilege. Thinking is, or ought to be, a coolness and a calmness; and our poor hearts throb, and our poor brains beat too much for that. And yet, I've sometimes thought my brain was very calm—frozen calm, this old skull cracks so, like a glass in which the contents turned to ice, and shiver it. And still this

hair is growing now; this moment growing, and heat must breed it; but no, it's like that sort of common grass that will grow anywhere, between the earthy clefts of Greenland ice or in Vesuvius lava. How the wild winds blow it; they whip it about me as the torn shreds of split sails lash the tossed ship they cling to. A vile wind that has no doubt blown ere this through prison corridors and cells, and wards of hospitals, and ventilated them, and now comes blowing hither as innocent as fleeces.[13] Out upon it!—it's tainted. Were I the wind, I'd blow no more on such a wicked, miserable world. I'd crawl somewhere to a cave, and slink there. And yet, 'tis a noble and heroic thing, the wind! who ever conquered it? In every fight it has the last and bitterest blow. Run tilting at it, and you but run through it. Ha! a coward wind that strikes stark-naked men, but will not stand to receive a single blow. Even Ahab is a braver thing—a nobler thing than *that.* Would now the wind but had a body but all the things that most exasperate and outrage mortal man, all these things are bodiless, but only bodiless as objects, not as agents. There's a most special, a most cunning, oh, a most malicious difference! And yet, I say again, and swear it now, that there's something all glorious and gracious in the wind. These warm trade winds, at least, that in the clear heavens blow straight on, in strong and steadfast, vigorous mildness; and veer not from their mark, however the baser currents of the sea may turn and tack, and mightiest Mississippis of the land swift and swerve about, uncertain where to go at last. And by the eternal poles! these same trades that so directly blow my good ship on; these trades, or something like them—something so unchangeable, and full as strong, blow my keeled soul along! To it! Aloft there! What d'ye see?"

"Nothing, sir."

"Nothing! and noon at hand! The doubloon[14] goes a-begging! See the sun! Aye, aye, it must be so. I've oversailed him. How, got the start? Aye, he's chasing me now; not I, him—that's bad; I might have known it, too. Fool! the lines—the harpoons he's towing.

Build Vocabulary

maledictions (mal´ ə dik´ shənz) *n.:* Curses

---

13. fleeces (flēs´ əz) *n.:* Sheep.
14. doubloon (du blōōn´) *n.:* Old Spanish gold coin. (Ahab offered it as a reward to the first man to spot the whale.)

Moby-Dick, Rockwell Kent

▲ **Critical Viewing** Draw an inference about the size of the whale pictured. On what details do you base your inference? **[Infer]**

Aye, aye, I have run him by last night. About! about! Come down, all of ye, but the regular lookouts! Man the braces!"

Steering as she had done, the wind had been somewhat on the Pequod's quarter, so that now being pointed in the reverse direction, the braced ship sailed hard upon the breeze as she rechurned the cream in her own white wake.

"Against the wind he now steers for the open jaw," murmured Starbuck to himself, as he coiled the new-hauled main brace upon the rail. "God keep us, but already my bones feel damp within me, and from the inside wet my flesh. I misdoubt me that I disobey my God in obeying him!"

"Stand by to sway me up!" cried Ahab, advancing to the hempen basket.[15] "We should meet him soon."

"Aye, aye, sir," and straightway Starbuck did Ahab's bidding, and once more Ahab swung on high.

A whole hour now passed; gold-beaten out to ages. Time itself now held long breaths with keen suspense. But at last, some three points off the weather bow, Ahab descried the spout again, and instantly from the three mastheads three shrieks went up as if the tongues of fire had voiced it.

"Forehead to forehead I meet thee, this third time, Moby-Dick! On deck there!—brace sharper up; crowd her into the wind's eye. He's too far off to lower yet, Mr. Starbuck. The sails shake! Stand over that helmsman with a topmaul! So, so; he travels fast, and I must down. But let me have one more good round look aloft here at the sea; there's time for that. An old, old sight, and yet somehow so young; aye, and not changed a wink since I first saw it, a boy, from the sand hills of Nantucket! The same!—the same!—the same to Noah as to me. There's a soft shower to leeward. Such lovely leewardings! They must lead somewhere—to something else than common land, more palmy than the palms. Leeward! the white whale goes that way; look to windward, then; the better if the bitterer quarter. But good-bye, good-bye, old masthead! What's this?—green? aye, tiny mosses in these warped cracks. No such green

weather stains on Ahab's head! There's the difference now between man's old age and matter's. But aye, old mast, we both grow old together; sound in our hulls, though, are we not, my ship? Aye, minus a leg, that's all. By heaven this dead wood has the better of my live flesh every way. I can't compare with it; and I've known some ships made of dead trees outlast the lives of men made of the most vital stuff of vital fathers. What's that he said? he should still go before me, my pilot; and yet to be seen again? But where? Will I have eyes at the bottom of the sea, supposing I descend those endless stairs? and all night I've been sailing from him, wherever he did sink to. Aye, aye, like many more thou told'st direful truth as touching thyself, O Parsee; but, Ahab, there thy shot fell short. Good-bye, masthead—keep a good eye upon the whale, the while I'm gone. We'll talk tomorrow, nay, tonight, when the white whale lies down there, tied by head and tail."

He gave the word; and still gazing round him, was steadily lowered through the cloven blue air to the deck.

In due time the boats were lowered; but as standing in his shallop's stern, Ahab just hovered upon the point of the descent, he waved to the mate—who held one of the tackle ropes on deck—and bade him pause.

"Starbuck!"

"Sir?"

"For the third time my soul's ship starts upon this voyage, Starbuck."

"Aye, sir, thou wilt have it so."

"Some ships sail from their ports, and ever afterwards are missing, Starbuck!"

"Truth, sir: saddest truth."

"Some men die at ebb tide; some at low water; some at the full of the flood—and I feel now like a billow that's all one crested comb, Starbuck. I am old—shake hands with me, man."

Their hands met; their eyes fastened; Starbuck's tears the glue.

"Oh, my captain, my captain!—noble heart—go not—go not!—see, it's a brave man that weeps; how great the agony of the persuasion then!"

◆ Literary Focus
What symbolic meaning can you detect in the comparison between Ahab and the mast?

---

15. **hempen basket:** Rope basket. (The basket was constructed earlier by Ahab, so that he could be raised, by means of a pulley device, to the top of the mainmast.)

"Lower away!"—cried Ahab, tossing the mate's arm from him. "Stand by the crew!"

In an instant the boat was pulling round close under the stern.

"The sharks! the sharks!" cried a voice from the low cabin window there; "O master, my master, come back!"

But Ahab heard nothing; for his own voice was high-lifted then; and the boat leaped on.

Yet the voice spake true; for scarce had he pushed from the ship, when numbers of sharks, seemingly rising from out the dark waters beneath the hull, maliciously snapped at the blades of the oars, every time they dipped in the water; and in this way accompanied the boat with their bites. It is a thing not uncommonly happening to the whaleboats in those swarming seas; the sharks at times apparently following them in the same prescient way that vultures hover over the banners of marching regiments in the east. But these were the first sharks that had been observed by the *Pequod* since the White Whale had been first descried; and whether it was that Ahab's crew were all such tiger-yellow barbarians, and therefore their flesh more musky to the senses of the sharks—a matter sometimes well known to affect them—however it was, they seemed to follow that one boat without molesting the others.

"Heart of wrought steel!" murmured Starbuck gazing over the side, and following with his eyes the receding boat—"canst thou yet ring boldly to that sight?—lowering thy keel among ravening sharks, and followed by them, open-mouthed to the chase; and this the critical third day?—For when three days flow together in one continuous intense pursuit; be sure the first is the morning, the second the noon, and the third the evening and the end of that thing—be that end what it may. Oh! my God! what is this that shoots through me, and leaves me so deadly calm, yet expectant—fixed at the top of a shudder! Future things swim before me, as in empty outlines and skeletons; all the past is somehow grown dim. Mary, girl; thou fadest in

pale glories behind me; boy! I seem to see but thy eyes grown wondrous blue.[16] Strangest problems of life seem clearing; but clouds sweep between—Is my journey's end coming? My legs feel faint; like his who has footed it all day. Feel thy heart—beats it yet? Stir thyself, Starbuck!—stave it off—move, move! speak aloud!—Masthead there! See ye my boy's hand on the hill?—Crazed—aloft there!—keep thy keenest eye upon the boats—mark well the whale!—Ho! again!—drive off that hawk! see! he pecks—he tears the vane"—pointing to the red flag flying at the maintruck—"Ha, he soars away with it!—Where's the old man now? see'st thou that sight, oh Ahab!—shudder, shudder!"

The boats had not gone very far, when by a signal from the mastheads—a downward pointed arm, Ahab knew that the whale had sounded; but intending to be near him at the next rising, he held on his way a little sideways from the vessel; the becharmed crew maintaining the profoundest silence, as the head-beat waves hammered and hammered against the opposing bow.

"Drive, drive in your nails, oh ye waves! to their uttermost heads drive them in! ye but strike a thing without a lid; and no coffin and no hearse can be mine:—and hemp only can kill me! Ha! ha!"

Suddenly the waters around them slowly swelled in broad circles; then quickly upheaved, as if sideways sliding from a submerged berg of ice, swiftly rising to the surface. A low rumbling sound was heard; a subterraneous hum; and then all held their breaths; as bedraggled with trailing ropes, and harpoons, and lances, a vast form shot lengthwise, but obliquely from the sea. Shrouded in a thin drooping veil of mist, it hovered for a moment in the rainbowed air; and then fell swamping back into the deep. Crushed thirty feet upwards, the waters flashed for an instant like heaps of fountains, then brokenly sank in a shower of flakes, leaving the circling surface creamed like new milk round the marble trunk of the whale.

"Give way!" cried Ahab to the oarsmen, and the boats darted forward to the attack; but maddened by yesterday's fresh irons that corroded in him, Moby-Dick seemed combinedly

♦ **Build Vocabulary**

prescient (presh´ ent) *adj.*: Having foreknowledge

---

16. **Mary . . . blue:** Reference to Starbuck's wife and son.

Moby-Dick, Rockwell Kent

◀ **Critical Viewing** What details from *Moby-Dick* did the artist probably use to create this illustration? [Hypothesize]

round to the fish's back; pinioned in the turns upon turns in which, during the past night, the whale had reeled the involutions of the lines around him, the half-torn body of the Parsee was seen; his sable raiment frayed to shreds; his distended eyes turned full upon old Ahab.

The harpoon dropped from his hand.

"Befooled, befooled!"—drawing in a long lean breath—"Aye, Parsee! I see thee again—Aye, and thou goest before; and this, this then is the hearse that thou didst promise. But I hold thee to the last letter of thy word. Where is the second hearse? Away, mates, to the ship! those boats are useless now; repair them if ye can in time, and return to me; if not, Ahab is enough to die—Down, men! the first thing that but offers to jump from this boat I stand in, that thing I harpoon. Ye are not other men, but my arms and my legs; and so obey me—Where's the whale? gone down again?"

But he looked too nigh the boat; for as if bent upon escaping with the corpse he bore, and as if the particular place of the last encounter had been but a stage in his leeward voyage, Moby-Dick was now again steadily swimming forward; and had almost passed the ship—which thus far had been sailing in the contrary direction to him, though for the present her headway had been stopped. He seemed swimming with his utmost velocity, and now only intent upon pursuing his own straight path in the sea.

"Oh! Ahab," cried Starbuck, "not too late is

◆ *Literature and Your Life*

Have you ever pursued a goal with Ahab's desperate persistence?

possessed by all the angels that fell from heaven. The wide tiers of welded tendons overspreading his broad white forehead, beneath the transparent skin, looked knitted together; as head on, he came churning his tail among the boats; and once more flailed them apart; spilling out the irons and lances from the two mates' boats, and dashing in one side of the upper part of their bows, but leaving Ahab's almost without a scar.

While Daggoo and Queequeg were stopping the strained planks; and as the whale swimming out from them, turned, and showed one entire flank as he shot by them again; at that moment a quick cry went up. Lashed round and

it, even now, the third day, to desist. See! Moby-Dick seeks thee not. It is thou, thou, that madly seekest him!"

Setting sail to the rising wind, the lonely boat was swiftly impelled to leeward, by both oars and canvas. And at last when Ahab was sliding by the vessel, so near as plainly to distinguish Starbuck's face as he leaned over the rail, he hailed him to turn the vessel about, and follow him, not too swiftly, at a judicious interval. Glancing upwards he saw Tashtego, Queequeg, and Daggoo, eagerly mounting to the three mastheads; while the oarsmen were rocking in the two staved boats which had just been hoisted to the side, and were busily at work in repairing them, one after the other, through the portholes, as he sped, he also caught flying glimpses of Stubb and Flask, busying themselves on deck among bundles of new irons and lances. As he saw all this; as he heard the hammers in the broken boats; far other hammers seemed driving a nail into his heart. But he rallied. And now marking that the vane or flag was gone from the main masthead, he shouted to Tashtego, who had just gained that perch, to descend again for another flag, and a hammer and nails, and so nail it to the mast.

Whether fagged by the three days' running chase, and the resistance to his swimming in the knotted hamper he bore; or whether it was some latent deceitfulness and malice in him: whichever was true, the White Whale's way now began to abate, as it seemed, from the boat so rapidly nearing him once more; though indeed the whale's last start had not been so long a one as before. And still as Ahab glided over the waves the unpitying sharks accompanied him; and so pertinaciously stuck to the boat; and so continually bit at the plying oars, that the blades became jagged and crunched, and left small splinters in the sea, at almost every dip.

"Heed them not! those teeth but give new rowlocks to your oars. Pull on! 'tis the better rest, the sharks' jaw than the yielding water."

"But at every bite, sir, the thin blades grow smaller and smaller!"

"They will last long enough! pull on!—But who can tell"—he muttered—"whether these sharks swim to feast on the whale or on Ahab?—But pull on! Aye, all alive, now—we

near him. The helm! take the helm! let me pass"—and so saying, two of the oarsmen helped him forward to the bows of the still flying boat.

At length as the craft was cast to one side, and ran ranging along with the White Whale's flank, he seemed strangely oblivious of its advance—as the whale sometimes will—and Ahab was fairly within the smoky mountain mist, which, thrown off from the whale's spout, curled round his great Monadnock[17] hump; he was even thus close to him; when, with body arched back, and both arms lengthwise highlifted to the poise, he darted his fierce iron, and his far fiercer curse into the hated whale. As both steel and curse sank to the socket, as if sucked into a morass, Moby-Dick sidewise writhed; spasmodically rolled his nigh flank against the bow, and, without staving a hole in it, so suddenly canted the boat over, that had it not been for the elevated part of the gunwale to which he then clung, Ahab would once more have been tossed into the sea. As it was, three of the oarsmen—who foreknew not the precise instant of the dart, and were therefore unprepared for its effects—these were flung out; but so fell, that, in an instant two of them clutched the gunwale again, and rising to its level on a combing wave, hurled themselves bodily inboard again; the third man helplessly dropping astern, but still afloat and swimming.

Almost simultaneously, with a mighty volition of ungraduated, instantaneous swiftness, the White Whale darted through the weltering sea. But when Ahab cried out to the steersman to take new turns with the line, and hold it so; and commanded the crew to turn round on their seats, and tow the boat up to the mark; the moment the treacherous line felt that double strain and tug, it snapped in the empty air!

"What breaks in me? Some sinew cracks!—'tis whole again; oars! oars! Burst in upon him!"

Hearing the tremendous rush of the sea-

---

17. **Monadnock** (mə nad′ näk): Mountain in New Hampshire.

◆ **Build Vocabulary**

pertinaciously (pʉr′ tə nā′ shəs lē) *adv.*: Holding firmly to some purpose

crashing boat, the whale wheeled round to present his blank forehead at bay; but in that evolution, catching sight of the nearing black hull of the ship; seemingly seeing in it the source of all his persecutions; bethinking it—it may be—a larger and nobler foe; of a sudden, he bore down upon its advancing prow, smiting his jaws amid fiery showers of foam.

Ahab staggered; his hand smote his forehead. "I grow blind; hands! stretch out before me that I may yet grope my way. Is't night?"

"The whale! The ship!" cried the cringing oarsmen.

"Oars! oars! Slope downwards to thy depths. O sea that ere it be forever too late, Ahab may slide this last, last time upon his mark! I see: the ship! the ship! Dash on, my men! will ye not save my ship?"

But as the oarsmen violently forced their boat through the sledge-hammering seas, the before whale-smitten bow-ends of two planks burst through, and in an instant almost, the temporarily disabled boat lay nearly level with the waves; its half-wading, splashing crew, trying hard to stop the gap and bale out the pouring water.

Meantime, for that one beholding instant, Tashtego's masthead hammer remained suspended in his hand; and the red flag, half wrapping him as with a plaid, then streamed itself straight out from him, as his own forward-flowing heart; while Starbuck and Stubb, standing upon the bowsprit beneath, caught sight of the down-coming monster just as soon as he.

"The whale, the whale! Up helm, up helm! Oh, all ye sweet powers of air, now hug me close! Let not Starbuck die, if die he must, in a woman's fainting fit. Up helm I say—ye fools, the jaw! the jaw! Is this the end of all my bursting prayers? all my lifelong fidelities? Oh, Ahab, Ahab, lo, thy work. Steady! helmsman, steady. Nay, nay! Up helm again! He turns to meet us! Oh, his unappeasable brow drives on towards one, whose duty tells him he cannot depart. My God, stand by me now!"

"Stand not by me, but stand under me, whoever you are that will now help Stubb; for Stubb, too, sticks here. I grin at thee, thou grinning whale! Who ever helped Stubb, or kept Stubb awake, but Stubb's own unwinking eye? And now poor Stubb goes to bed upon a mattress that is all too soft; would it were stuffed with brushwood! I grin at thee, thou grinning whale! Look ye, sun, moon, and stars! I call ye assassins of as good a fellow as ever spouted up his ghost. For all that, I would yet ring glasses with thee, would ye but hand the cup! Oh, oh! oh, oh! thou grinning whale, but there'll be plenty of gulping soon! Why fly ye not, O Ahab! For me, off shoes and jacket to it; let Stubb die in his drawers! A most moldy and oversalted death, though—cherries! cherries! cherries! Oh, Flask, for one red cherry ere we die!"

"Cherries? I only wish that we were where they grow. Oh, Stubb, I hope my poor mother's drawn my part-pay ere this; if not, few coppers will now come to her, for the voyage is up."

From the ship's bows, nearly all the seamen now hung inactive; hammers, bits of plank, lances, and harpoons, mechanically retained in their hands, just as they had darted from their various employments; all their enchanted eyes intent upon the whale, which from side to side strangely vibrating his predestinating head, sent a broad band of overspreading semicircular foam before him as he rushed. Retribution, swift vengeance, eternal malice were in his whole aspect, and spite of all that mortal man could do, the solid white buttress of his forehead smote the ship's starboard bow, till men and timbers reeled. Some fell flat upon their faces. Like dislodged trucks, the heads of the harpooneers aloft shook on their bull-like necks. Through the breach, they heard the waters pour, as mountain torrents down a flume.

"The ship! The hearse!—the second hearse!" cried Ahab from the boat; "its wood could only be American!"

Diving beneath the settling ship, the whale ran quivering along its keel; but turning under water, swiftly shot to the surface again, far off the other bow, but within a few yards of Ahab's boat, where, for a time, he lay quiescent.

"I turn my body from the sun. What ho, Tashtego! let me hear thy hammer. Oh! ye three unsurrendered spires of mine; thou uncracked keel; and only god-bullied hull; thou firm deck, and haughty helm, and Polepointed prow—death-glorious ship! must ye then perish, and without me? Am I cut off from the last fond pride of meanest shipwrecked captains? Oh, lonely death on lonely life! Oh, now I feel my topmost greatness lies in my topmost grief. Ho, ho! from all your furthest bounds, pour ye now in, ye bold billows of my whole foregone life, and top this one piled comber of my death! Towards thee I roll, thou all-destroying but unconquering whale; to the last I grapple with thee; from hell's heart I stab at thee; for hate's sake I spit my last breath at thee. Sink all coffins and all hearses to one common pool! and since neither can be mine, let me then tow to pieces, while still chasing thee, though tied to thee, thou damned whale! *Thus*, I give up the spear!"

The harpoon was darted; the stricken whale flew forward; with igniting velocity the line ran through the groove;—ran foul. Ahab stooped to clear it; he did clear it; but the flying turn caught him round the neck, and voicelessly as Turkish mutes bowstring their victim, he was shot out of the boat, ere the crew knew he was gone. Next instant, the heavy eye splice in the rope's final end flew out of the stark-empty tub, knocked down an oarsman, and smiting the sea, disappeared in its depths.

For an instant, the tranced boat's crew stood still; then turned. "The ship? Great God, where is the ship?" Soon they through dim, bewildering mediums saw her sidelong fading phantom, as in the gaseous fata morgana,[18] only the uppermost masts out of water: while fixed by infatuation, or fidelity, or fate, to their once lofty perches, the pagan harpooneers still maintained their sinking lookouts on the sea. And now, concentric circles seized the lone boat itself, and all its crew, and each floating oar, and every lance pole, and spinning, animate and inanimate, all round and round in one vortex, carried the smallest chip of the *Pequod* out of sight.

---

18. **fata morgana** (fät´ ə môr gän´ ə) *n*.: Mirage seen at sea.

◆ **Literary Focus**
What details in this paragraph suggest that the whale has become a symbol of retribution?

But as the last whelmings intermixingly poured themselves over the sunken head of the Indian at the mainmast, leaving a few inches of the erect spar yet visible, together with long streaming yards of the flag, which calmly undulated, with ironical coincidings, over the destroying billows they almost touched—at that instant, a red arm and a hammer hovered backwardly uplifted in the open air, in the act of nailing the flag faster and yet faster to the subsiding spar. A sky hawk that tauntingly had followed the main-truck downwards from its natural home among the stars, pecking at the flag, and incommoding Tashtego there: this bird now chanced to intercept its broad fluttering wing between the hammer and the wood: and simultaneously feeling that ethereal thrill, the submerged savage beneath, in his deathgasp, kept his hammer frozen there: and so the bird of heaven, with archangelic shrieks, and his imperial beak thrust upwards, and his whole captive form folded in the flag of Ahab, went down with his ship, which, like Satan, would not sink to hell till she had dragged a living part of heaven along with her, and helmeted herself with it.

Now small fowls flew screaming over the yet yawning gulf; a sullen white surf beat against its steep sides; then all collapsed, and the great shroud of the sea rolled on as it rolled five thousand years ago.

Guide for Responding

◆ *Literature and Your Life*

Reader's Response How do you feel about the fate of Ahab and his crew? Explain.

Thematic Focus Do you admire, despise, or pity Captain Ahab? What role does the imagination play in Ahab's quest for Moby-Dick? Explain.

Journal Writing Review Melville's last paragraph to discover his attitude about the relationship between humanity and nature. In a journal entry, state the writer's view and your own feelings.

☑ Check Your Comprehension

1. What does Ahab offer to the man who spots Moby-Dick?
2. (a) Why is Ahab obsessed with killing Moby-Dick? (b) How does Starbuck interpret Ahab's obsession?
3. (a) Just before his whaleboat is lowered into the water, what does Ahab tell Starbuck? (b) What follows Ahab's boat as it pulls away from the ship?
4. What happens to Ahab, Moby-Dick, and the *Pequod* at the end?

◆ Critical Thinking

INTERPRET

1. (a) What does Ahab's obsession with Moby-Dick reveal about his character? (b) In what ways is Starbuck different from Ahab? **[Infer; Contrast]**
2. (a) Why does Starbuck obey Ahab though he disagrees with him? (b) Why does the crew join Ahab's quest without hesitation? **[Interpret]**
3. What do Ahab's comments about the wind at the start of "The Chase—Third Day" suggest about his attitude toward nature? **[Interpret]**
4. (a) What omens appear as Ahab's whaleboat pulls away from the ship and when Moby-Dick surfaces? (b) How does Ahab respond to these omens? **[Analyze]**
5. What is the significance of the fact that Moby-Dick seems "strangely oblivious" to the advance of Ahab's boat? **[Interpret]**

EVALUATE

6. Ahab believes people are guided by instinct and intuition rather than by reason. Explain why you believe his view is valid or flawed. **[Evaluate]**

EXTEND

7. (a) How can obsession with a goal affect a person's ability to reach that goal? (b) What goals are people obsessed with today? **[Health Link]**

Guide for Responding (continued)

◆ Literary Focus

SYMBOL

A **symbol** is a person, place, or thing that has a meaning in itself and also represents something larger than itself. For instance, the fact that the crew of the *Pequod* includes representatives from many of the world's races and cultures indicates that the crew is more than just a collection of people. It may symbolize humanity itself.

1. Explain the possible symbolic meaning of Ishmael in *Moby-Dick*.
2. Given the fact that the crew of the *Pequod* symbolizes humanity and that Moby-Dick symbolizes everything in nature that is paradoxical, unexplainable, and uncontrollable, what do you think the ship's voyage symbolizes?
3. Considering the journey's symbolic meaning and outcome, speculate about the novel's theme, or central idea.

◆ Grammar and Style

AGREEMENT WITH COLLECTIVE NOUNS

A collective noun may be either singular or plural, depending on whether the group it names is seen as a unit or as a collection of individuals. The verb must agree with the intended meaning.

> A **collective noun** names a group of persons or things.

Practice Identify the collective noun in each sentence. Then choose the verb form that agrees with each collective noun.

1. The crew (lines, line) up along the railing of the ship.
2. A team of horses (draws, draw) the carriage.
3. The crew (is, are) composed of fine, upstanding men and women.
4. A flock of gulls (glide, glides) over the ship.
5. A crowd (gathers, gather) near the site of the accident.

◆ Reading Strategy

RECOGNIZE SYMBOLS

You can **recognize symbols** by noticing an author's effort to connect a place, thing, or character with some larger concept or value. Melville's elaborate description of Moby-Dick suggests that the whale has many facets of symbolic meaning. Find events or descriptions in the text of *Moby-Dick* that demonstrate each of the following aspects of the whale's symbolism.

1. nature's beauty
2. nature's power and destructiveness
3. nature's immortality

◆ Build Vocabulary

USING THE PREFIX *mal-*

The prefix *mal-* means "bad" or "badly." Each of the words in the left column contains this prefix. In your notebook, write the letter of the definition that matches each of these words. Refer to a dictionary if you need help.

1. malcontent   a   active ill will
2. malevolent   b. causing or likely to cause death
3. malign   c. wishing harm to others
4. malignant   d. dissatisfied
5. malice   e. to slander

USING THE WORD BANK

On your paper, write the word that best completes each sentence.

inscrutable   maledictions   prescient   pertinaciously

1. They ___?___ continued to believe in my innocence of the crime.
2. We marveled at the child's ___?___ comment; the rain poured down on us just as she said it would.
3. The woman's behavior was odd, and her intentions were ___?___.
4. The deposed dictator was greeted with ___?___ from the crowd.

Build Your Portfolio

 ## Idea Bank

Writing

1. **Eulogy** Write the eulogy that Ishmael might have delivered at a memorial service for his shipmates.

2. **Character Sketch** Ahab, the protagonist of *Moby-Dick*, has become one of the most famous characters in all of American literature. Write a character sketch in which you concisely describe Ahab's personality and behavior.

3. **Essay** Write an essay in which you discuss how the theme of *Moby-Dick* is revealed through Melville's symbolism. Discuss two or three symbols, defining each symbol in your own words.

Speaking and Listening

4. **Monologue** Take the part of Ishmael and retell the tale of his experience aboard the doomed *Pequod* to a crowd of whalemen. Use the selection to help you duplicate Ishmael's unique tone and outlook. **[Performing Arts Link]**

5. **Reader's Theater** With a group of your classmates, take the parts of Ahab, Stubb, Starbuck, Flask, Tashtego, Daggoo, Queequeg, other sailors, and a narrator, and dramatize the scene in which Ahab exhorts his crew to hunt Moby-Dick. **[Performing Arts Link]**

Projects

6. **Model** Research the harpoon, the special tool the crew used to hunt Moby-Dick. Then make a scale model of a whaling harpoon, using wood, wire, or clay. **[Art Link]**

7. **Report** Find out which species of whales face possible extinction today and what efforts are being made to save them. Present your findings in a brief oral or written report. **[Science Link]**

 ## Writing Mini-Lesson

A Dramatic Scene

Because they are meant to be seen and not read, dramas must convey character, establish and resolve conflict, and develop plot through dialogue and physical actions. Choose a scene from *Moby-Dick,* and adapt it as a dramatic scene for the stage. As you develop your scene, use dialogue that sounds natural.

Writing Skills Focus: Realistic Dialogue

One of the keys to an effective drama is **realistic dialogue**—dialogue that sounds like natural speech. People often use contractions and speak in incomplete sentences. In addition, many people use slang expressions or speak in a way that is grammatically incorrect. As you write dialogue, check to see that it sounds natural by pausing to read it aloud. Revise passages that seem stiff or unnatural. In addition, make sure that the dialogue you've written is appropriate for each character's background and level of education.

Prewriting Choose a scene that would be effective in a stage setting. Make some notes about the characters' behavior and the conflict in the scene. Outline the scene's natural beginning, middle, and end; pinpoint any physical actions that occur.

Drafting Use some of Melville's dialogue in your scene, but modernize the language for a contemporary audience. You may also transform important descriptive passages into speeches for one or more characters. Remember to include written stage directions (in parentheses) that clarify characters' actions, tone of voice, and position on stage.

Revising Perform your scene with a classmate. Listen carefully to the dialogue. Notice places where it seems unnatural. Revise these sections. Then look for places where you need to add stage directions.

Where *Is* Here?
Joyce Carol Oates

Thematic Connection

SHADOWS OF THE IMAGINATION

Edgar Allan Poe, Nathaniel Hawthorne, and Herman Melville are towering figures in American literature. They were fascinated by the ways in which human beings behave in extreme situations, and each often portrayed characters acting in disturbing or extraordinary ways because of an internal conflict or a crisis. Using their powerful imaginations, these writers transformed realistic details of daily human life into ambiguous, shadowy, and precarious worlds.

In Edgar Allan Poe's work, for instance, gloomy heroes like Roderick Usher languish as their mental equilibrium teeters and the outside world—which once seemed orderly and healthful—collapses. Many of Nathaniel Hawthorne's characters have some secret, shadowy knowledge that leads them to behave in unsettling and unaccountable ways; often Hawthorne focuses on the odd ways human beings think and act when they are struggling with dark emotions such as guilt. One of Herman Melville's finest fictional creations, Captain Ahab, is a man who suffers an episode of violence and then proves unable to stop chasing the shadows of his own diseased imagination.

MODERN GOTHIC

In the twentieth century, only a few American writers have been inclined to embrace or evoke the dusky themes, characters, and atmospheres that stamped the work of their Romantic forebears. One of these writers is Joyce Carol Oates.

Many of Oates's novels and stories concern individuals whose ordinary lives are suddenly upset by mysterious forces beyond their control. Much of the suspense and emotional power in Oates's fiction can be traced to her depiction of common people who seem powerless to save their identities from alteration or destruction by some shadowy force.

JOYCE CAROL OATES (1938–)

In her short stories, novels, poems, and plays, Joyce Carol Oates delves into the human mind. Her work often focuses on characters who are disturbed or who are searching anxiously for their identities.

Oates grew up in a tiny town on the Erie Canal, and her earliest stories and first novel are accounts of life in Erie County. Oates's fictional Eden County is elaborately conceived and populated with inhabitants who turn up in various ways from story to story. Eden County is not the paradise its name implies; in fact, it can be insufferable to its inhabitants. It has been suggested that Oates may have chosen the name to remind readers just how much human beings have lost.

Where *Is* Here?

Joyce Carol Oates

For years they had lived without incident in their house in a quiet residential neighborhood when, one November evening at dusk, the doorbell rang, and the father went to answer it, and there on his doorstep stood a man he had never seen before. The stranger apologized for disturbing him at what was probably the dinner hour and explained that he'd once lived in the house— "I mean, I was a child in this house"—and since he was in the city on business he thought he would drop by. He had not seen the house since January 1949 when he'd been eleven years old and his widowed mother had sold it and moved away but, he said, he thought of it often, dreamt of it often, and never more powerfully than in recent months. The father said, "Would you like to come inside for a few minutes and look around?" The stranger hesitated, then said firmly, "I think I'll just poke around outside for a while, if you don't mind. That might be sufficient." He was in his late forties, the father's approximate age. He wore a dark suit, conservatively cut; he was hatless, with thin silver-tipped neatly combed hair; a plain, sober, intelligent face and frowning eyes. The father, reserved by nature, but genial and even gregarious when taken unaware, said amiably, "Of course we

don't mind. But I'm afraid many things have changed since 1949."

So, in the chill, damp, deepening dusk, the stranger wandered around the property while the mother set the dining room table and the father peered covertly out the window. The children were upstairs in their rooms. "Where is he now?" the mother asked. "He just went into the garage," the father said. "The garage! What does he want in there!" the mother said uneasily. "Maybe you'd better go out there with him." "He wouldn't want anyone with him," the father said. He moved stealthily to another window, peering through the curtains. A moment passed in silence. The mother, paused in the act of setting down plates, neatly folded paper napkins, and stainless-steel cutlery, said impatiently, "And where is he now? I don't like this." The father said, "Now he's coming out of the garage," and stepped back hastily from the window. "Is he going now?" the mother asked. "I wish I'd answered the door." The father watched for a moment in silence then said,

◆ Build Vocabulary

genial (jēn´ yəl) *adj*.: Cheerful; friendly
gregarious (grə ger´ ē əs) *adj*.: Sociable
covertly (kō vərt´ lē) *adv*.: Secretly; surreptitiously

▶ **Critical Viewing**
How does this photograph lend an air of mystery — even menace — to an ordinary house? **[Analyze]**

Summer Nights, #18, 1985, Robert Adams, Museum of Modern Art

"He's headed into the backyard." "Doing what?" the mother asked. "Not *doing* anything, just walking," the father said. "He seems to have a slight limp." "Is he an older man?" the mother asked. "I didn't notice," the father confessed. "Isn't that just like you!" the mother said.

She went on worriedly, "He could be anyone, after all. Any kind of thief, or mentally disturbed person, or even a murderer. Ringing our doorbell like that with no warning and you don't even know what he looks like!"

The father had moved to another window and stood quietly watching, his cheek pressed against the glass. "He's gone down to the old swings. I hope he won't sit in one of them, for memory's sake, and try to swing—the posts are rotted almost through." The mother drew breath to speak but sighed instead, as if a powerful current of feeling had surged through her. The father was saying, "Is it possible he remembers those swings from his childhood? I can't believe they're actually that old." The mother said vaguely, "They were old when we bought the house." The father said, "But we're talking about forty years or more, and that's a long time." The mother sighed again, involuntarily. "Poor man!" she murmured. She was standing before her table but no longer seeing it. In her hand were objects—forks, knives, spoons—she could not have named. She said, "We can't bar the door against him. That would be cruel." The father said, "What? No one has barred any door against anyone." "Put yourself in his place," the mother said. "He told me he didn't *want* to come inside," the father said. "Oh—isn't that just like you!" the mother said in exasperation.

Without a further word she went to the back door and called out for the stranger to come inside, if he wanted, when he had finished looking around outside.

They introduced themselves rather shyly, giving names, and forgetting names, in the confusion of the moment. The stranger's handshake was cool and damp and tentative. He was smiling hard, blinking moisture from his eyes; it was clear that entering his childhood home was enormously exciting yet intimidating to him.

Repeatedly he said, "It's so nice of you to invite me in—I truly hate to disturb you—I'm really so grateful, and so—" But the perfect word eluded him. As he spoke his eyes darted about the kitchen almost like eyes out of control. He stood in an odd stiff posture, hands gripping the lapels of his suit as if he meant to crush them. The mother, meaning to break the awkward silence, spoke warmly of their satisfaction with the house and with the neighborhood, and the father concurred, but the stranger listened only politely, and continued to stare, and stare hard. Finally he said that the kitchen had been so changed—"so modernized"—he almost didn't recognize it. The floor tile, the size of the windows, something about the position of the cupboards—all were different. But the sink was in the same place, of course; and the refrigerator and stove; and the door leading down to the basement—"That *is* the door leading down to the basement, isn't it?" He spoke strangely, staring at the door. For a moment it appeared he might ask to be shown the basement but the moment passed, fortunately—this was not a part of their house the father and mother would have been comfortable showing to a stranger.

Finally, making an effort to smile, the stranger said, "Your kitchen is so—pleasant." He paused. For a moment it seemed he had nothing further to say. Then, "A—controlled sort of place. My mother—When we lived here—" His words trailed off into a dreamy silence and the mother and father glanced at each other with carefully neutral expressions.

On the windowsill above the sink were several lushly blooming African violet plants in ceramic pots and these the stranger made a show of admiring. Impulsively he leaned over to sniff the flowers— "Lovely!"—though African violets have no smell. As if embarrassed he said, "Mother too had plants on this windowsill but I don't recall them ever blooming."

The mother said tactfully, "Oh they were probably the kind that don't bloom—like ivy."

In the next room, the dining room, the stranger appeared to be even more deeply moved. For some time he stood staring, wordless. With fastidious slowness he turned on his heel, blinking, and frowning, and tugging at his lower lip in a rough gesture that must have hurt. Finally, as if remembering the presence of his hosts, and the necessity for some display of civility, the stranger expressed his admiration for the attractiveness of the room, and its coziness. He'd remembered it as cavernous, with a ceiling twice as high. "And dark most of the time," he said wonderingly. "Dark by day, dark by night." The mother turned the lights of the little brass chandelier to their fullest: shadows were dispersed like ragged ghosts and the cut-glass fruit bowl at the center of the table glowed like an exquisite multifaceted jewel. The stranger exclaimed in surprise. He'd extracted a handkerchief from his pocket and was dabbing carefully at his face, where beads of perspiration shone. He said, as if thinking aloud, still wonderingly, "My father was a unique man. Everyone who knew him admired him. He sat *here*," he said, gingerly touching the chair that was in fact the father's chair, at one end of the table. "And Mother sat *there*," he said, merely pointing. "I don't recall my own place or my sister's but I suppose it doesn't matter. . . . I see you have four place settings, Mrs. . . .? Two children, I suppose?" "A boy eleven, and a girl thirteen," the mother said. The stranger stared not at her but at the table, smiling. "And so too *we* were—I mean, there were two of us: my sister and me."

The mother said, as if not knowing what else to say, "Are you—close?"

The stranger shrugged, distractedly rather than rudely, and moved on to the living room.

This room, cozily lit as well, was the most carefully furnished room in the house. Deep-piled wall-to-wall carpeting in hunter green, cheerful chintz drapes, a sofa and matching chairs in nubby heather green, framed reproductions of classic works of art, a gleaming gilt-framed mirror over the fireplace: wasn't the living room impressive as a display in a furniture store? But the stranger said nothing at first. Indeed, his eyes narrowed sharply as if he were confronted with a disagreeable spectacle. He whispered, "Here too! Here too!"

He went to the fireplace, walking, now, with a decided limp; he drew his fingers with excruciating slowness along the mantel as if testing its materiality. For some time he merely stood, and stared, and listened. He tapped a section of wall with his knuckles—"There used to be a large water stain here, like a shadow."

"Was there?" murmured the father out of politeness, and "Was there!" murmured the mother. Of course, neither had ever seen a water stain there.

Then, noticing the window seat, the stranger uttered a soft surprised cry, and went to sit in it. He appeared delighted: hugging his knees like a child trying to make himself smaller. "This was one of my happy places! At least when Father wasn't home. I'd hide away here for hours, reading, daydreaming, staring out the window! Sometimes Mother would join me, if she was in the mood, and we'd plot to-gether—oh, all sorts of fantastical things!" The stranger remained sitting in the window seat for so long, tears shining in his eyes, that the father and mother almost feared he'd forgotten them. He was stroking the velvet fabric of the cushioned seat, gropingly touching the leaded windowpanes. Wordlessly, the father and mother exchanged a glance: who was this man, and how could they tactfully get rid of him? The father made a face signaling impatience and the mother shook her head without seem-ing to move it. For they couldn't be rude to a guest in their house.

The stranger was saying in a slow, dazed voice, "It all comes back to me now. How could I have forgotten! Mother used to read to me, and tell me stories, and ask me riddles I couldn't answer. 'What creature walks on four legs in the morning, two legs at midday, three legs in the evening?' 'What is round, and flat, measuring mere inches in one direction, and infinity in the other?' 'Out of what does our life arise? Out of what does our consciousness arise? Why are we here? Where *is* here?' "

The father and mother were perplexed by these strange words and hardly knew how to respond. The mother said uncertainly, "Our daughter used to like to sit here too, when she was younger. It *is* a lovely place." The father said with surprising passion, "I hate riddles—they're moronic some of the time and obscure the rest of the time." He spoke with such un-characteristic rudeness, the mother looked at him in surprise.

Hurriedly she said, "Is your mother still living, Mr. . . . ?" "Oh no. Not at all," the stranger said, rising abruptly from the window seat, and looking at the mother as if she had said something mildly preposterous. "I'm sorry," the mother said. "Please don't be," the stranger said. "We've all been dead—*they've* all been dead—a long time."

The stranger's cheeks were deeply flushed as if with anger and his breath was quickened and audible.

The visit might have ended at this point but so clearly did the stranger expect to continue on upstairs, so purposefully, indeed almost defiantly, did he limp his way to the stairs, neither the father nor the mother knew how to dissuade him. It was as if a force of nature, benign at the outset, now uncontrollable, had swept its way into their house! The mother fol-lowed after him saying nervously, "I'm not sure what condition the rooms are in, upstairs. The children's rooms especially—" The stranger muttered that he did not care in the slightest about the condition of the household and con-tinued on up without a backward glance.

The father, his face burning with resentment and his heart accelerating as if in preparation for combat, had no choice but to follow the stranger and the mother up the stairs. He was flexing and unflexing his fingers as if to rid them of stiffness.

On the landing, the stranger halted abruptly to examine a stained-glass fanlight—"My God, I haven't thought of this in years!" He spoke ex-citedly of how, on tiptoe, he used to stand and peek out through the diamonds of colored glass, red, blue, green, golden yellow: seeing with amazement the world outside so *altered*. "After such a lesson it's hard to take the world on its own terms, isn't it?" he asked. The father asked, annoyed, "On what terms should it be taken, then?" The stranger replied, regarding him levelly, with a just perceptible degree of disdain, "Why, none at all."

It was the son's room—by coincidence, the stranger's old room—the stranger most wanted to see. Other rooms on the second floor, the "master" bedroom in particular, he decidedly did not want to see. As he spoke of it, his mouth twisted as if he had been offered some-thing repulsive to eat.

The mother hurried on ahead to warn the boy and to straighten up his room a bit. No one had expected a visitor this evening! "So you have two children," the stranger murmured, looking at the father with a small quizzical smile. "Why?" The father stared at him as if he hadn't heard correctly. "'Why'? " he asked. "Yes. *Why*?" the stranger repeated. They looked at each other for a long strained moment, then the stranger said quickly, "But you love them—of course." The father controlled his temper and said, biting off his words, "Of course."

"Of course, of course," the stranger murmured, tugging at his necktie and loosening his collar, "otherwise it would all come to an end." The two men were of approximately the same height but the father was heavier in the shoulders and torso; his hair had thinned more severely so that the scalp of the crown was exposed, flushed, damp with perspiration, sullenly alight.

With a stiff <u>avuncular</u> formality the stranger shook the son's hand. "So this is your room, now! So you live here, now!" he murmured, as if the fact were an astonishment. Not used to shaking hands, the boy was stricken with shyness and cast his eyes down. The stranger limped past him, staring. "The same!—the same!—walls, ceiling, floor—window—" He drew his fingers slowly along the windowsill; around the frame; rapped the glass, as if, again, testing materiality; stooped to look outside—but it was night, and nothing but his reflection bobbed in the glass, ghostly and insubstantial. He groped against the walls, he opened the closet door before the mother could protest, he sat heavily on the boy's bed, the springs creaking beneath him. He was panting, red-faced, dazed. "And the ceiling overhead," he whispered. He nodded slowly and repeatedly, smiling. "And the floor beneath. That is what *is*."

He took out his handkerchief again and fastidiously wiped his face. He made a visible effort to compose himself.

The father, in the doorway, cleared his throat and said, "I'm afraid it's getting late—it's almost six."

The mother said, "Oh yes I'm afraid— I'm afraid it *is* getting late. There's dinner, and the children have their homework—"

The stranger got to his feet. At his full height he stood for a precarious moment swaying, as if the blood had drained from his head and he was in danger of fainting. But he steadied himself with a hand against the slanted dormer ceiling. He said, "Oh yes!—I know!—I've disturbed you terribly!—you've been so *kind*." It seemed, surely, as if the stranger *must* leave now, but, as chance had it, he happened to spy, on the boy's desk, an opened mathematics textbook and several smudged sheets of paper, and impulsively offered to show the boy a mathematical riddle—"You can take it to school tomorrow and surprise your teacher!"

So, out of dutiful politeness, the son sat down at his desk and the stranger leaned familiarly over him, demonstrating adroitly with a ruler and a pencil how "what we call 'infinity' " can be contained within a small geometrical figure on a sheet of paper. "First you draw a square; then you draw a triangle to fit inside the square; then you draw a second triangle, and a third, and a fourth, each to fit inside the square, but without their points coinciding, and as you continue—here, son, I'll show you—give me your hand, and I'll show you—the border of the triangles' common outline gets more complex and measures larger, and larger, and larger—and soon you'll need a magnifying glass to see the details, and then you'll need a microscope, and so on and so forth, forever, laying triangles neatly down to fit inside the original square *without their points coinciding*—!" The stranger spoke with increasing fervor; spittle gleamed in the corners of his mouth. The son stared at the geometrical shapes rapidly materializing on the sheet of paper before him with no seeming comprehension but with a rapt staring fascination as if he dared not look away.

After several minutes of this the father came abruptly forward and dropped his hand on the stranger's shoulder. "The visit is over," he said calmly. It was the first time since they'd shaken hands that the two men had touched, and the touch had a <u>galvanic</u> effect upon the stranger: he dropped ruler and pencil at once, froze in his stooped posture, burst into frightened tears.

Now the visit truly was over; the stranger, at last, *was* leaving, having wiped away his tears and made a stoical effort to compose himself; but on the doorstep, to the father's astonishment, he made a final, preposterous appeal—he wanted to see the basement. "Just to sit on the stairs?

◆ Build Vocabulary

avuncular (ə vuŋ´ kyo͞o lər) *adj*.: Having traits considered typical of uncles: jolly, indulgent, stodgy

galvanic (gal van´ ik) *adj*.: Startling; stimulating as if by electric current

In the dark? For a few quiet minutes? And you could close the door and forget me, you and your family could have your dinner and—"

The stranger was begging but the father was resolute. Without raising his voice he said, "No. *The visit is over.*"

He shut the door, and locked it.

Locked it! His hands were shaking and his heart beat angrily.

He watched the stranger walk away—out to the sidewalk, out to the street, disappearing in the darkness. Had the streetlights gone out?

Behind the father the mother stood apologetic and defensive, wringing her hands in a classic stance. "Wasn't that sad! Wasn't that—*sad!* But we had no choice but to let him in, it was the only decent thing to do." The father pushed past her without comment. In the living room he saw that the lights were flickering as if on the brink of going out; the patterned wallpaper seemed drained of color; a shadow lay upon it shaped like a bulbous cloud or growth. Even the robust green of the carpeting looked faded. Or was it an optical illusion? Everywhere the father looked, a pulse beat mute with rage. "*I* wasn't the one who opened the door to that man in the first place," the mother said, coming up behind the father and touching his arm. Without seeming to know what he did the father violently jerked his arm and thrust her away.

"Shut up. We'll forget it," he said.

"But—"

"*We'll forget it.*"

The mother entered the kitchen walking slowly as if she'd been struck a blow. In fact, a bruise the size of a pear would materialize on her forearm by morning. When she reached out to steady herself she misjudged the distance of the door frame—or did the door frame recede an inch or two—and nearly lost her balance.

In the kitchen the lights were dim and an odor of sourish smoke, subtle but unmistakable, made her nostrils pinch.

She slammed open the oven door. Grabbed a pair of pot holders with insulated linings. "*I* wasn't the one, . . ." she cried, panting, "and you know it."

Guide for Responding

◆ Literature and Your Life

Reader's Response Would you have reacted or behaved differently from the father and mother in the story? Why or why not?

Thematic Focus In what sense does this story explore the shadows of the imagination?

Movie Adaptation With a small group, consider whether this story would be a suspenseful movie. What parts or scenes would you emphasize? What might you add?

☑ Check Your Comprehension

1. According to the stranger, when was the last time he saw the house?
2. How does the stranger react when the father tells him, "The visit is over"?
3. How do the rooms of the house seem changed after the stranger's visit?

◆ Critical Thinking

INTERPRET

1. How would you describe the characters of the father and mother in the story? **[Infer]**
2. What does the stranger do that makes the family uncomfortable or anxious? **[Analyze]**
3. How does the mother's attitude toward the stranger change? **[Connect]**
4. What details in the story suggest that the stranger's visit is some kind of bizarre, unnatural event? **[Interpret]**

EVALUATE

5. How well does Oates maintain suspense in the story? Explain. **[Evaluate]**

EXTEND

6. What advice might a police officer provide the couple after their experience? **[Career Link]**

Thematic Connection

SHADOWS OF THE IMAGINATION

The fiction of Poe, Hawthorne, and Melville is filled with shadowy characters, gloomy settings, and often tragic events. Similarly, Oates's story centers on a mysterious character whose actions and appearance contribute to the story's gloomy mood, or atmosphere.

1. Mystery plays an important role in the works of Poe, Hawthorne, and Melville. What is the role of mystery in Oates's story?
2. Compare Parson Hooper in "The Minister's Black Veil" and the stranger in "Where *Is* Here?" In what sense are they the most powerful figures in their respective stories? What role does imagination play in their power?

Idea Bank

Writing

1. **Diary Entry** How would either the husband or the wife describe the experience with the mysterious stranger? Assuming the role of one of the two characters, write a diary entry describing the stranger's visit and presenting your reactions to it.

2. **Comparison and Contrast** Both the villagers of Hawthorne's Milford in "The Minister's Black Veil" and the mother and father in Oates's "quiet residential neighborhood" are unnerved by the sudden appearance of something strange and mysterious. Write a short paper comparing and contrasting the reactions of the husband and wife with those of the townspeople.

3. **Essay** In "The Minister's Black Veil," Hawthorne uses many unnamed characters—*the sexton*, *the physician,* and *the bridegroom*—who are less developed than the central character, Parson Hooper. Similarly, Oates calls her characters *the father, the mother,* and *the stranger.* In an essay, discuss why Hawthorne and Oates may have chosen to leave these characters nameless.

Speaking and Listening

4. **Radio Presentation** Both "Where *Is* Here?" and "The Raven" contain elements of mystery and suspense—qualities that make both works good candidates for chilling dramatic readings. With a small group of classmates, prepare dramatic readings of these two works, as if they were being paired on a radio broadcast. Discuss whether you wish to use sound effects or music in either work. Then rehearse the readings and record them for your classmates. **[Performing Arts Link]**

Project

5. **Floor Plans** The houses that figure centrally in "The Fall of the House of Usher" and "Where *Is* Here?" are radically different from each other. Review the two stories and jot down facts, details, and descriptions of these two structures. Then make labeled architect's diagrams of the floor plans of each house. **[Art Link; Math Link]**

Writing Process Workshop

All day long, our eyes are awash in images from the mass media—from computer screens to the movies to television to advertising billboards. With all these polished images, it is easy to forget that the final product is only the tip of an iceberg: Hidden from the eye is a long process of careful planning and scripting.

Holding and pointing a video camera is easy, but did you ever try to craft a video script complete with story, dialogue, stage directions, and technical actions? Here's your chance to plan and create a video script for a drama, comedy, or documentary. Strive for visual images as sharp and memorable as the verbal ones you found in this unit in the works of Poe and Melville. The following skills, introduced in this section's Writing Mini-Lessons, will help you to create your video script.

Writing Skills Focus

▶ **Use a style that is appropriate for your medium** and your type of project—depending on whether it is a drama, comedy, or documentary. You'll probably want to rely as much on visual images as dialogue. (See p. 315.)

▶ **Use precise details,** both visual and verbal, to create a vivid impression of the characters, setting, and events. (See p. 329.)

▶ **Use realistic dialogue** to enhance the impact of a fictional drama or comedy. (See p. 347.)

The following scene from Melville's *Moby-Dick* has been adapted as a video script.

MODEL

[CLOSEUP of Ahab on deck addressing the sailors] ①
  AHAB: "What do ye do when ye see a whale, men?"
[WIDE SHOT of sailors on deck]
  SAILORS: Sing out for him! [the sailors cry out enthusiastically, some raising harpoons above their heads] ②
[SHOT behind Ahab facing sailors]
  AHAB: "Good!" [with a wild approval in his tones; observing the hearty animation into which his unexpected question had so magnetically thrown the men] ③

① The explicit camera directions indicate the visual images to be presented.

② The dialogue is realistic for the time when it takes place.

③ Precise details in these stage directions vividly capture the sailors' attitudes.

APPLYING LANGUAGE SKILLS: Eliminating Unnecessary Words

Students sometimes overwrite, using too many words or an unnecessarily flowery tone. The most impressive prose, however, is simple and direct. Eliminate overwriting by condensing clauses to phrases and phrases to single words.

Wordy:
My father, who is a surgeon, has nerves of steel.

Better:
My father, a surgeon, has nerves of steel.

Practice Revise these wordy sentences.

1. On our walk, we reveled in a flurry of leaves that were falling.
2. Jorge, who is my friend, excels in soccer.

Writing Application Review your script, and pare down any bloated sentences.

Writer's Solution Connection
Language Lab

For more practice with editing unnecessary words, see the Writing Style lesson in the Language Lab.

Prewriting

Choose a Topic Your video script can be a work of fiction that springs from a combination of imagination and experience or a documentary based on an issue that concerns you. The key to finding a topic is choosing one that has meaning to you. Consider the topic ideas listed here or choose one of your own:

> ### Topic Ideas
> - Music video script
> - Hiking in the wilderness
> - A threat to the local environment (factory waste, an incinerator, overdevelopment)
> - Contemporary styles in dress and fashion
> - A fictional drama about conflict—betrayal by a friend, facing disease or natural disaster, a battle with conscience
> - A courtroom drama

Use Specific Details Specific details are critical in bringing your script to life. If your script involves a fictional character, for example, don't scrimp on specifics of speech patterns, dress, outward mannerisms, or tone of voice. Likewise, a documentary achieves its impact by *showing*, not merely *telling*: a polluted river, the features of Thoreau's cabin, a personal interview with a role model, and so on.

Drafting

Create Realistic Dialogue Realistic dialogue is essential to making a teleplay come alive for your audience. Remember that people often speak in incomplete sentences and use contractions and slang expressions. As you write your dialogue, pause after each exchange and ask yourself: Can I imagine two people I know saying these things or do their words seem stilted and contrived? Here's one case where everyday speech, even slang, might be a more reliable guide than standard English.

Indicate Stage and/or Camera Directions Technical instructions are critical to a drama or documentary. Use clear and concise language in this portion of the text. You can recommend the actors' delivery, settings, costumes, and stage movements, as well as indicating camera angles. Be specific: This is your chance to communicate your vision.

Revising

Use a Checklist Go back to the Writing Skills Focus on the first page of the lesson and use the items as part of a checklist to evaluate and revise your script.

- ▶ Is my language appropriate to the video medium and to my project?
- ▶ Have I provided enough precise details, both visual and verbal, to make the script come alive for the viewer?
- ▶ If my project is a fictional drama, have I checked the dialogue to make sure that it sounds natural?

Add to Stage and/or Camera Direction Sometimes adding a few words to your camera or stage directions can make all the difference. Look at this example:

REVISION MODEL

TASHTEGO: Captain Ahab, that white whale must be the

same that some call Moby-Dick.

① [shouting]

AHAB: Moby-Dick? Do ye know the white whale, then, Tash?

① By adding this direction, the writer makes Ahab's emotions clear to both the reader and the actor.

Publishing

Videotape Your Script Share your work with an audience by capturing it on videotape. Follow these suggestions to successfully record your production:

- ▶ Use the stage directions to direct actors, set designers, and camera operators.
- ▶ Rehearse each scene in your script. Plan and practice where actors will stand, how they will move, and where the camera will be in each scene. Run through the action a few times before filming.
- ▶ Take advantage of the portability of the video camera, but don't take the technology for granted. Make sure that the audio and video are being recorded correctly.

APPLYING LANGUAGE SKILLS: Spoken vs. Written Language

In your script, be sensitive to the differences between written English and spoken English. Spoken language allows a wider range of informal expressions and may contradict the rules of grammar. Here's an example:

Written:
Jamie, whom I met at the theater, wishes to be an actor.

Spoken:
Jamie, who I met at the theater, wants to be an actor.

Although grammatically correct, "whom" is so rare in everyday speech that it makes the dialogue sound stilted.

Practice Rewrite these sentences in less formal spoken English.

1. I grew utterly exasperated at his obstinacy.
2. The quality of which I speak is self-esteem.

Writing Application Check that the dialogue in your script sounds natural and believable.

Writer's Solution Connection
Writing Lab

To help you write your video script, use the instruction and activities in the tutorial on Creative Writing.

Strategies for Success

Whether you are researching a topic for a school report or looking up your favorite television show, you need to adjust your reading rate to suit the difficulty of the material and your reading goals.

Identify Your Reading Goals Determine why you are reading this particular material. Are you searching for a quotation to support a persuasive argument? Do you want to evaluate products before making a purchase? Are you studying for an important exam? Identifying your reading purpose is a key step in selecting an appropriate reading rate.

Evaluate the Content Estimate how difficult it is likely to be to read this particular material. For example, some people find poetry very difficult to read, while others struggle with sequential directions. Consider:

- ▶ density of the text
- ▶ vocabulary difficulty
- ▶ level of detail
- ▶ your familiarity with topic and format

Adjust Your Reading Rate Review your conclusions about your reading goal and the difficulty of the text. The harder the material, the more slowly you need to read. However, if you're looking only for a particular piece of data—such as a quotation, specific statistics, or a geographic location—you may be able to skim quickly through even very difficult material.

Apply the Strategy

Imagine you were assigned to read the items on this list during an upcoming school break. Review the list, and then answer the following questions:

1. How will your reading goals differ for each of the three categories? Explain.

Spring Reading List

For Science Research Report:
- Theories of Basic Chemistry
- "Jill Sanders Wins Nobel Prize in Chemistry" **Chemistry Profiles Magazine**

For Summer Job Hunting:
- Newsletter from a job fair
- Job description letter from potential employer

For Entertainment:
- **The Case of Dr. Diamond's Death**
- **Sports Illustrated**, March issue

---

2. How would you read to find a quotation by the prize-winning chemist?

3. What reading rate suits the mystery? Explain.

4. At what rate would you read the job description letter? Why?

5. Which text on the list would you expect to read most carefully? Why?

✔ *Here are other situations in which adjusting reading rate can be helpful:*
- ▶ Preparing for a debate
- ▶ Locating your responsibilities on a chart
- ▶ Planning study and leisure reading time
- ▶ Reading consumer reports before a major purchase

PART 3

The Human Spirit and the Natural World

Early Morning at Cold Spring, 1850,
Asher B. Durand, Montclair Art Museum,
Montclair, New Jersey

By the mid-1800's, The United States had firmly established itself as a nation. Inspired by the words and actions of writers in this section, the nation embraced a belief in individuality and an awareness of the vastness and beauty of nature.

Guide for Interpreting

Ralph Waldo Emerson
(1803–1882)

Individuality, independence, and an appreciation for the wonders of nature—these are just a few of the principles that Ralph Waldo Emerson helped to ingrain in our nation's identity. Although his ideas were sometimes considered controversial, he had a tremendous influence on the young people of his time, and his beliefs have continued to inspire people to this day.

Throughout his life, Emerson's mind was constantly in motion, generating new ideas and defining and redefining his view of the world. His natural eloquence in expressing these ideas—in essays, lectures, and poetry—makes him one of the most quoted writers in American literature.

A New England Childhood The son of a Unitarian minister, Emerson was born in Boston. When Emerson was eight, his father died. The boy turned to a brilliant and eccentric aunt, Mary Moody Emerson, who encouraged his independent thinking. At fourteen, Emerson entered Harvard, where he began the journal he was to keep all his life. After postgraduate studies at Harvard Divinity School, he became pastor of the Second Church of Boston.

Finding His Niche Emerson's career as a minister was short-lived. Grief-stricken at the death of his young wife, and dissatisfied with what he saw as the spiritual restrictions in Unitarianism, Emerson resigned after three years. He then went to Europe, where he met the English writers Thomas Carlyle, Samuel Taylor Coleridge, and William Wordsworth. On his return to the United States, Emerson settled in Concord, Massachusetts. He married again and began his life-long career of writing and lecturing.

An Independent Thinker Emerson was a soft-spoken man, given to neither physical nor emotional excess.

> *Beneath Emerson's calm, sober demeanor existed a restless, highly individualistic mind that resisted conformity.*

"Good men," he once wrote, "must not obey the laws too well."

Emerson first achieved national fame in 1841, when he published *Essays,* a collection based on material from his journals and lectures. He went on to publish several more volumes of essays, including *Essays, Second Volume* (1844), *Representative Men* (1849), and *The Conduct of Life* (1860).

Though Emerson was known mostly for his essays and lectures, he considered himself primarily a poet. "I am born a poet," he once wrote, "of a low class without doubt, yet a poet. That is my nature and my vocation." He published two successful volumes of poetry, *Poems* (1847) and *May-Day and Other Pieces* (1867). Like his essays, Emerson's poems express his beliefs in individuality and in humanity's spiritual connection to nature.

◆ Background for Understanding

PHILOSOPHY: EMERSON AND THE TRANSCENDENTAL CLUB

During the 1830's and 1840's, Emerson and a small group of like-minded intellectual friends gathered regularly in his study to discuss philosophy, religion, and literature. Among them were Emerson's protégé, Henry David Thoreau, as well as educator Bronson Alcott, feminist writer Margaret Fuller, and ex-clergyman and author George Ripley. The group, known as the Transcendental Club, developed a philosophical system that stressed intuition, individuality, and self-reliance.

In 1836, Emerson published "Nature," a lengthy essay that became the Transcendental Club's unofficial statement of belief. (For more on the Transcendentalists, see p. 221.)

◆ *Literature and Your Life*

CONNECT YOUR EXPERIENCE

"Be true to yourself." "Follow your dream." Do these words sound familiar? Most of us have faced the choices these sentiments address: whether to conform to what's expected or to step out of the crowd and follow our own judgment. In "Self-Reliance," Emerson states his views on the matter in uncompromising terms, coming down squarely in favor of nonconformity.

Journal Writing Describe a time when you had to choose whether to follow others or to blaze your own trail.

THEMATIC FOCUS: THE HUMAN SPIRIT AND THE NATURAL WORLD

Emerson found spirituality and profound meaning in nature. How can a study of the natural world reveal the human spirit?

◆ Literary Focus

TRANSCENDENTALISM

Transcendentalism was an intellectual movement founded by Emerson that affected most of the writers of his day. The Transcendentalists believed that the human senses can know only physical reality. To the Transcendentalists, the fundamental truths of existence lay outside the reach of the senses and could be grasped only through intuition. As a result, the Transcendentalists focused their attention on the human spirit. They also had a deep interest in the natural world and its relationship to humanity. Through the careful observation of nature, they believed that the human spirit is reflected in the natural world. This led them to the conclusion that formed the heart of their beliefs: All forms of being—God, nature, and humanity—are spiritually united through a shared universal soul, or Over-Soul.

◆ Build Vocabulary

WORD ROOTS: -radi-

The word root -radi- means "spoke" or "ray." This root contributes to the meaning of *radiant*—"shining brightly" or "giving off rays of light"—a word that you'll find in "The Snowstorm." What other words can you think of that contain the root -radi-?

WORD BANK

Before you read, preview this list of words.

blithe
connate
chaos
aversion
suffrage
divines
radiant
tumultuous
bastions

◆ Reading Strategy

CHALLENGE THE TEXT

When you read a work that presents an individual's ideas, don't simply accept the ideas, challenge them. To **challenge a text** simply means to question the author's assertions and reasoning. In "Self-Reliance," for example, Emerson states: "Whoso would be a man must be a nonconformist." Look for how he backs up this statement. Compare the evidence he offers with what you already know through personal experience or other reading. Then decide whether you agree with Emerson.

◆ Grammar and Style

VARY SENTENCE LENGTH

Good writers vary the length of their sentences to help sustain the reader's interest and to establish rhythm. Notice in this passage from "Nature" how Emerson follows a long sentence with a short one:

> Crossing a bare common, in snow puddles, at twilight, under a clouded sky, without having in my thoughts any occurrence of special good fortune, I have enjoyed a perfect exhilaration. I am glad to the brink of fear.

from
Nature

Ralph Waldo Emerson

Nature is a setting that fits equally well a comic or a mourning piece. In good health, the air is a cordial of incredible virtue. Crossing a bare common,[1] in snow puddles, at twilight, under a clouded sky, without having in my thoughts any occurrence of special good fortune, I have enjoyed a perfect exhilaration. I am glad to the brink of fear. In the woods, too, a man casts off his years, as the snake his slough, and at what period soever of life is always a child. In the woods is perpetual youth. Within these plantations of God, a decorum and sanctity reign, a perennial festival is dressed, and the guest sees not how he should tire of them in a thousand years. In the woods, we return to reason and faith. There I feel that nothing can befall me in life—no disgrace, no calamity (leaving me my eyes), which nature cannot repair. Standing on the bare ground—my head bathed by the <u>blithe</u> air and uplifted into infinite space—all mean egotism vanishes. I become a transparent eyeball; I am nothing; I see all; the currents of the Universal Being circulate through me; I am part or parcel of God. The name of the nearest friend sounds then foreign and ac- cidental: to be brothers, to be acquain- tances, master or servant, is then a trifle and a disturbance. I am the lover of uncon- tained and immortal beauty. In the wilder- ness, I find something more dear and <u>connate</u> than in the streets or villages. In the tranquil landscape, and especially in the distant line of the horizon, man beholds somewhat as beautiful as his own nature.

The greatest delight which the fields and woods minister is the suggestion of an occult relation between man and the veg- etable. I am not alone and unacknowledged. They nod to me, and I to them. The waving of the boughs in the storm is new to me and old. It takes me by surprise, and yet is not unknown. Its effect is like that of a higher thought or a better emotion coming over me, when I deemed I was thinking justly or doing right.

Yet it is certain that the power to produce this delight does not reside in nature, but in man, or in a harmony of both. It is neces- sary to use these pleasures with great tem- perance. For nature is not always tricked[2] in holiday attire, but the same scene which yesterday breathed perfume and glittered as for the frolic of the nymphs is overspread with melancholy today. Nature always wears the colors of the spirit. To a man laboring under calamity, the heat of his

---

1. **common** *n.*: Piece of open public land.

2. **tricked** *v.*: Dressed.

◆ Build Vocabulary

blithe (blīth) *adj.*: Carefree

connate (kän´ āt) *adj.*: Existing naturally; innate

Sunset, Frederick E. Church, Munson-Williams-Proctor Institute Museum of Art, Utica, New York

own fire hath sadness in it. Then there is a kind of contempt of the landscape felt by him who has just lost by death a dear friend. The sky is less grand as it shuts down over less worth in the population.

▲ **Critical Viewing** Emerson says that nature often allows us to become transparent eyeballs, seeing all, but detaching from the business of the world. How does this image reinforce his statement? **[Support]**

Guide for Responding

◆ *Literature and Your Life*

Reader's Response Which of your experiences have made you "glad to the brink of fear"?

Thematic Focus Do you find any evidence of Emerson's reverence for nature in American culture today? Explain.

☑ Check Your Comprehension

1. According to Emerson, where can we "return to reason and faith"?
2. What happens to Emerson when he stands with his head "uplifted into infinite space"?
3. What is the "greatest delight which the fields and woods minister"?

◆ Critical Thinking

INTERPRET

1. What does Emerson mean when he says that in the woods "a man casts off his years"? **[Analyze]**
2. What does Emerson mean when he describes himself as a "transparent eyeball"? **[Interpret]**
3. Find evidence in this essay to support the Transcendentalist belief in the unity of the human spirit and the natural world. **[Support]**

EVALUATE

4. How persuasive is Emerson? Explain why you do or do not accept his ideas about nature. **[Assess]**

EXTEND

5. In what ways is Emerson's attitude toward nature different from that of a scientist? **[Science Link]**

from Self-Reliance

Ralph Waldo Emerson

There is a time in every man's education when he arrives at the conviction that envy is ignorance; that imitation is suicide; that he must take himself for better, for worse, as his portion; that though the wide universe is full of good, no kernel of nourishing corn can come to him but through his toil bestowed on that plot of ground which is given to him to till. The power which resides in him is new in nature, and none but he knows what that is which he can do, nor does he know until he has tried. Not for nothing one face, one character, one fact makes much impression on him, and another none. This sculpture in the memory is not without preestablished harmony. The eye was placed where one ray should fall, that it might testify of that particular ray. We but half express ourselves, and are ashamed of that divine idea which each of us represents. It may be safely trusted as proportionate and of good issues, so it be faithfully imparted, but God will not have his work made manifest by cowards. A man is relieved and gay when he has put his heart into his work and done his best; but what he has said or done otherwise, shall give him no peace. It is a deliverance which does not deliver. In the attempt his genius deserts him; no muse befriends; no invention, no hope.

Trust thyself: every heart vibrates to that iron string. Accept the place the divine providence has found for you; the society of your contemporaries, the connection of events. Great men have always done so and confided themselves childlike to the genius of their age, betraying their perception that the absolutely trustworthy was stirring at their heart, working through their hands, predominating in all their being. And we are now men, and must accept in the highest mind the same transcendent destiny; and not minors and invalids in a protected corner, but guides, redeemers, and benefactors. Obeying the Almighty effort and advancing on <u>Chaos</u> and the Dark. . . .

Society everywhere is in conspiracy against the manhood of every one of its members. Society is a joint-stock company in which the members agree for the better securing of his bread to each shareholder, to surrender the liberty and culture of the eater. The virtue in most request is conformity. Self-reliance is its <u>aversion</u>. It loves not realities and creators, but names and customs.

Whoso would be a man must be a nonconformist. He who would gather immortal

> ◆ **Reading Strategy**
> **Challenge** this statement. Do you agree with Emerson?

palms must not be hindered by the name of goodness, but must explore if it be goodness. Nothing is at last sacred but the integrity of your own mind. Absolve you to yourself, and you shall have the suffrage of the world. . . .

A foolish consistency is the hobgoblin of little minds, adored by little statesmen and philosophers and divines. With consistency a great soul has simply nothing to do. He may as well concern himself with his shadow on the wall. Speak what you think now in hard words and tomorrow speak what tomorrow thinks in hard words again, though it contradict everything you said today. "Ah, so you shall be sure to be misunderstood?"— is it so bad, then, to be misunderstood? Pythagoras was misunderstood, and Socrates, and Jesus, and Luther, and Copernicus, and Galileo, and Newton,[1] and every pure and wise spirit that ever took flesh. To be great is to be misunderstood. . . .

---

1. **Pythagoras . . . Newton:** Individuals who made major contributions to scientific, philosophical, or religious thinking.

◆ Build Vocabulary

Chaos (kā´ äs) *n.*: Disorder of formless matter and infinite space, supposed to have existed before the ordered universe

aversion (ə vur´ zhən) *n.*: Object arousing an intense or definite dislike

suffrage (suf´ rij) *n.*: Vote or voting

divines (də vīnz´) *n.*: Clergy

Guide for Responding

◆ Literature and Your Life

Reader's Response Which of Emerson's statements, if any, would you choose as a guideline for personal conduct? Explain.

Thematic Focus Transcendentalism is a uniquely American philosophy. What aspects of today's American culture reflect Emerson's belief in self-reliance?

Group Discussion Conforming to society's expectations can have its advantages and disadvantages, as can nonconformity. In small groups, discuss and list the pros and cons of each.

☑ Check Your Comprehension

1. According to the first paragraph, what conviction does every person eventually adopt?
2. How does Emerson describe society?
3. What is Emerson's view of consistency?

◆ Critical Thinking

INTERPRET

1. According to Emerson, why should people trust themselves? **[Analyze]**
2. How does Emerson believe people should be affected by the way others perceive them? **[Interpret]**
3. How does Emerson support his claim that "to be great is to be misunderstood"? **[Support]**

EVALUATE

4. Based on this essay, what is your assessment of Emerson's character? **[Assess]**

EXTEND

5. Do you think Benjamin Franklin would agree or disagree with Emerson's message? Explain. **[Literature Link]**

The Snowstorm

Ralph Waldo Emerson

Announced by all the trumpets of the sky,
Arrives the snow, and, driving o'er the fields,
Seems nowhere to alight: the whited air
Hides hills and woods, the river, and the heaven,
5   And veils the farmhouse at the garden's end.
The sled and traveler stopped, the courier's feet
Delayed, all friends shut out, the house mates sit
Around the <u>radiant</u> fireplace, enclosed
In a <u>tumultuous</u> privacy of storm.

10   Come see the north wind's masonry.
Out of an unseen quarry evermore
Furnished with tile, the fierce artificer
Curves his white <u>bastions</u> with projected roof
Round every windward stake, or tree, or door.
15   Speeding, the myriad-handed, his wild work
So fanciful, so savage, nought cares he
For number or proportion. Mockingly,
On coop or kennel he hangs Parian[1] wreaths;
A swan-like form invests the hidden thorn;
20   Fills up the farmer's lane from wall to wall.

Maugre[2] the farmer's sighs; and at the gate
A tapering turret overtops the work.
And when his hours are numbered, and the world
Is all his own, retiring, as he were not,
25   Leaves, when the sun appears, astonished Art
To mimic in slow structures, stone by stone,
Built in an age, the mad wind's nightwork,
The frolic architecture of the snow.

---

1. **Parian** (per´ ē ən) *adj.*: Referring to a fine, white marble of the Greek city Paros.
2. **Maugre** (mô´ gər) *prep.*: In spite of.

◆ **Build Vocabulary**
radiant (rā´ dē ənt) *adj.*: Shining brightly
tumultuous (too mult´ choo wəs) *adj.*: Rough; stormy
bastions (bas´ chənz) *n.*: Fortifications

Concord Hymn

Sung at the Completion of the Battle Monument, April 19, 1836

Ralph Waldo Emerson

By the rude[1] bridge that arched the flood,
   Their flag to April's breeze unfurled,
Here once the embattled farmers stood,
   And fired the shot heard round the world.

5 The foe long since in silence slept;
   Alike the conqueror silent sleeps;
And Time the ruined bridge has swept
   Down the dark stream which seaward creeps.

On this green bank, by this soft stream,
10   We set today a votive[2] stone;
That memory may their deed redeem,
   When, like our sires, our sons are gone.

Spirit, that made those heroes dare
   To die, and leave their children free,
15 Bid Time and Nature gently spare
   The shaft we raise to them and thee.

---

1. **rude** (ro͞od) *adj.*: Crude or rough in form or workmanship.
2. **votive** (vōt´iv) *adj.*: Dedicated in fulfillment of a vow or pledge.

▲ **Critical Viewing** This poem was written for the unveiling of this monument commemorating the minutemen, who fought the British at Lexington and Concord, Massachusetts, in April 1775. How does the sculpture communicate the emotions of the poem? **[Connect]**

Guide for Responding

♦ Literature and Your Life

Reader's Response Do you think it is important to build war monuments? Why or why not?

Thematic Focus What beliefs and values does the poet convey in these poems?

✓ Check Your Comprehension

1. Summarize the action of "The Snowstorm."
2. (a) In "Concord Hymn," what event took place by the "rude bridge"? (b) What has since happened to the bridge?
3. According to "Concord Hymn," what may redeem the farmers' deeds?

♦ Critical Thinking

INTERPRET

1. In "The Snowstorm," Emerson compares the storm and an artist at work. How does he develop this comparison in the poem? **[Analyze]**
2. What element in "The Snowstorm" expresses Emerson's belief in a spiritual unity betwen humanity and nature? Explain. **[Support]**
3. In "Concord Hymn," what is Emerson's attitude toward the minutemen? Explain. **[Infer]**

EXTEND

4. Having read both his essays and his poetry, where do you think Emerson's greater talent lies? Explain. **[Literature Link]**

Guide for Responding (continued)

◆ Reading Strategy

CHALLENGE THE TEXT

In "Nature" and "Self-Reliance," you encountered the opinions of one of the most individualistic men of nineteenth-century letters. By **challenging the text,** or questioning his assertions, you can reach an informed decision about whether or not you agree with the ideas he presents.

Look at this assertion from "Self-Reliance": "A foolish consistency is the hobgoblin of little minds. . . ." Challenge the assertion by answering these questons.

1. What evidence does Emerson provide to support his position?
2. Offer two arguments against this statement.
3. After weighing both sides of this controversial statement, explain whether you agree with it. Support your answer.

◆ Literary Focus

TRANSCENDENTALISM

Emerson's writings introduce readers to **Transcendentalism,** the intellectual movement that asserted that knowledge of fundamental reality was beyond the reach of a person's limited senses and was derived through intuition rather than sensory experience. Transcendentalists focused on the human spirit, the spiritual relationship between humanity and nature, and an optimistic belief in human potential. At the core of their philosophy was the belief that all forms of being are spiritually united through a shared universal soul, or Over-Soul.

1. What does "Nature" reveal about the Transcendentalists' attitude toward nature? Support your answers with specific examples from the text.
2. Find two passages in "Nature" that express the Transcendentalists' belief in the Over-Soul.
3. Toward the end of "Self-Reliance," Emerson writes: "Speak what you think now in hard words and tomorrow speak what tomorrow thinks in hard words again, though it contradict everything you said today." Explain how this statement reflects the Transcendentalist belief in the importance of intuition.

◆ Build Vocabulary

USING THE WORD ROOT *-radi-*

The word root *-radi-* means "spoke" or "ray." Knowing this, write a definition for each of these words.

1. radiator   3. radical   5. radio
2. radiation   4. radiology

USING THE WORD BANK

Read the following word pairs. In your notebook, label each pair *A* for *antonyms,* or *S* for *synonyms.*

1. chaos, order
2. aversion, repugnance
3. suffrage, vote
4. divines, ministers
5. blithe, anxious
6. connate, acquired
7. radiant, luminous
8. tumultuous, serene
9. bastions, bulwarks

◆ Grammar and Style

VARYING SENTENCE LENGTH

In "Nature" and "Self-Reliance," Emerson often follows a very long sentence with one or more short ones. If he had relied entirely on long sentences, he could easily have lost the reader's interest or made his writing difficult to follow. On the other hand, if he'd relied mainly on short sentences, his writing would have been choppy. By varying the length of his sentences, he makes his writing lively and engaging. In addition, you may notice that he often uses a short sentence to clarify or emphasize ideas he's expressed in the longer sentence preceding it.

Looking at Style Find three passages from Emerson's essays in which he varies the length of his sentences. Explain the effect of the sentence variation in each passage.

Writing Application Rewrite the following passage to create more sentence variety.

Like Emerson, I love nature. I enjoy taking long walks. Most often, I walk in a forest near my house. The ground is covered with pine needles. I usually take a path that leads to a waterfall. When I reach the waterfall, I take time to reflect on events in my life.

Build Your Portfolio

 ## Idea Bank

Writing

1. **Poem About Nature** Write a poem that expresses experiences, sensations, or emotions you have had in connection with nature.

2. **Advertisement** Suppose you wanted to form a group similar to the Transcendentalist Club. How would you attract members? In an advertisement, inform and persuade people to join.

3. **Critical Evaluation** Write an essay summarizing "Self-Reliance" and stating your opinion of its ideas and the way in which these ideas are expressed. Back up your opinion with examples.

Speaking and Listening

4. **Public Service Announcement** Drawing from Emerson's words and ideas, create a public service announcement encouraging people to resist conformity. Record your announcement and share it with the class. **[Media Link]**

5. **Debate** Forging a unique path may suit certain individuals, but there are also benefits to conformity. Stage a debate on this issue. Ask the audience to decide which side is more persuasive.

Projects

6. **Art** Illustrate a vivid phrase from "Nature" in any way you choose. Draw a picture, find a piece of music, or create and perform a dance. **[Art Link; Music Link; Performing Arts Link]**

7. **Research** According to Emerson, the misunderstood individual joins the ranks of Pythagoras, Socrates, Jesus, Joan of Arc, Martin Luther, Copernicus, Galileo, and Newton. Research one of these "great souls" to learn how or why the person was misunderstood. Share your findings with your classmates. **[Social Studies Link]**

 ## Writing Mini-Lesson

Letter to the Editor

If Emerson were alive today, he would probably be a dedicated conservationist. Choose a current environmental issue, and decide where you stand on it. Write a letter to the editor of a local newspaper expressing your opinion and defending it with reasons, facts, or examples. The more personal your examples are, the more persuasive your letter will be.

Writing Skills Focus: Elaboration to Make Writing Personal

One way to **elaborate** on, or develop, the ideas in a piece of writing is to share personal experiences or observations. For example, if you're writing about pollution in a local lake, you might describe how you used to swim at the lake as a child, and point out that on a recent visit you noticed that no one swims there anymore. Sharing such experiences not only helps make your writing convincing by demonstrating your firsthand knowledge, but it also helps to establish a personal connection to your readers.

Prewriting Make a list of the main points you want to make. Jot down personal experiences and obserations you can use to support each point. In addition, you may want to gather other facts and statistics you can use for support.

Drafting Start your letter by stating your main points up front. Then support your points by presenting your experiences and observations, along with any facts and statistics you've gathered. Throughout your letter, be as direct and to the point as possible.

Revising Have a classmate read your letter and suggest ways to make it more personal, direct, and convincing.

Guide for Interpreting

Henry David Thoreau
(1817–1862)

From the time he was a child, Henry David Thoreau was known by his Concord, Massachusetts, neighbors as an eccentric. He rarely followed rules. He was independent, strong willed, and not very dedicated to his studies, but his mother's love of nature and her own drive convinced him to pursue an education. Thoreau went to Concord Academy, a college preparatory school, and five years later he enrolled at Harvard, where he pursued his studies in his own unique style.

Although Harvard University's code called for students to wear black, Thoreau wore green.

Questioning Authority Thoreau always questioned the rules that were presented to him. When his objection to corporal punishment forced him to quit his first teaching job, Thoreau and his older brother John opened their own school in Concord. The school was quite successful, but they had to close it when John became ill.

In 1842, Thoreau moved into the house of another famous Concord resident, Ralph Waldo Emerson. He lived there for two years, performing odd jobs to pay for his room and board. While there, Thoreau was fascinated by Emerson's Transcendentalist beliefs, and soon Thoreau became Emerson's close friend and devoted disciple.

Deciding not to go back to teaching and refusing to pursue another career, Thoreau dedicated himself to testing the Transcendentalist philosophy through experience. By simplifying his needs, Thoreau was able to devote the rest of his life to exploring and writing about the spiritual relationship between humanity and nature and supporting his political and social beliefs.

On Walden Pond For two years (1845–1847) Thoreau lived alone in a cabin he built himself at Walden Pond outside of Concord. Thoreau's experiences during this period provided him with the material for his masterwork, *Walden* (1854). Condensing his experiences at Walden Pond into one year, Thoreau used the four seasons as a structural framework for the book. A unique blend of natural observation, social criticism, and philosophical insight, *Walden* is now generally regarded as the supreme work of Transcendentalist literature.

Carefully and deliberately crafted, Thoreau's work reflects the economy for which he strove throughout his life and about which he wrote in *Walden*.

When Henry David Thoreau died of tuberculosis at the age of forty-four, his work had received little recognition. However, his reputation has steadily grown since his death. His work has inspired writers, environmentalists, and social and political leaders. It has made generations of readers aware of the possibilities of the human spirit and the limitations of society.

◆ Background for Understanding

HISTORY: THOREAU AND THE MEXICAN WAR

The Mexican War was a conflict between Mexico and the United States that took place from 1846 to 1848. The war was caused by a dispute over the boundary between Texas and Mexico, as well as Mexico's refusal to discuss selling California and New Mexico to the United States. Believing that President Polk had intentionally provoked the conflict before having congressional approval,

Thoreau and many other Americans strongly objected to the war. To demonstrate his disapproval, Thoreau refused to pay his taxes and was forced to spend a night in jail for his convictions. After that experience, Thoreau wrote "Civil Disobedience," urging people to resist governmental policies with which they disagree.

from Walden ◆ from Civil Disobedience

◆ *Literature and Your Life*

CONNECT YOUR EXPERIENCE

In today's world, we rely on countless modern conveniences—cellular phones, computers, televisions. Not long ago, all of these things existed only in the imagination. Although most of us don't ever think about it, some people wonder whether technological advances have really made life better—or just more complicated.

THEMATIC FOCUS: THE HUMAN SPIRIT AND THE NATURAL WORLD

The time in which Thoreau lived was also an age in which modernization was bringing about rapid change. As the experiences described in *Walden* reveal, Thoreau believed that people needed to simplify their lives and rekindle their connection with nature.

Journal Writing Explain what you think it would be like to live in the woods without modern conveniences.

◆ Literary Focus

STYLE

Style refers to the manner in which a writer puts his or her thoughts into words. In *Walden*, Thoreau's style is closely related to his purpose, which is to encourage us to examine the way we live and think. To achieve his purpose, Thoreau constructs paragraphs so that the sentences build to a climax.

Like Emerson, who admired Thoreau's style, most contemporary readers and critics are struck by the strength and vigor of Thoreau's writing. Within his most effective paragraphs, the sentences build to create an effect that can be compared to a hammer driving a nail into wood.

◆ Grammar and Style

INFINITIVES AND INFINITIVE PHRASES

Infinitive phrases combine an **infinitive** (the basic form of the verb preceded by the word *to*) and its complements and modifiers. Infinitive phrases function as nouns, adjectives, or adverbs.

Noun: I dearly love *to talk.* [functions as object of the verb *love*]

Adjective: It seemed to me that I had several more lives *to live.* [modifies the noun *lives*]

Adverb: This was an airy . . . cabin, fit *to entertain a traveling god.* [modifies the participle *fit*]

◆ Reading Strategy

EVALUATE THE WRITER'S STATEMENT OF PHILOSOPHY

Thoreau wrote to educate himself and his audience. He outlined a philosophy, a system of beliefs and values, that guided his life and actions. As a reader, you are not bound to accept everything you see in print. In fact, when reading essays like those of philosophers, you should **evaluate the writer's philosophy.** To do this, pay special attention to the proof or support the writer provides to back up his or her outlook. Weigh the writer's ideas and supporting details against your own experiences.

◆ Build Vocabulary

WORD ROOTS: *-flu-*

Thoreau uses the word *superfluous* to describe things that are unnecessary. The Latin root *-flu-*, found in words like *fluid, fluent,* and *influence*, means "flow." The word *superfluous* means "overflowing" or "exceeding what is sufficient."

WORD BANK

Before you read, preview this list of words from the selections.

dilapidated
sublime
superfluous
evitable
magnanimity
expedient
posterity
alacrity

from Walden

Henry David Thoreau

from Where I Lived, and What I Lived For

At a certain season of our life we are accustomed to consider every spot as the possible site of a house. I have thus surveyed the country on every side within a dozen miles of where I live. In imagination I have bought all the farms in succession, for all were to be bought, and I knew their price. I walked over each farmer's premises, tasted his wild apples, discoursed on husbandry[1] with him, took his farm at his price, at any price, mortgaging it to him in my mind; even put a higher price on it—took everything but a deed of it—took his word for his deed, for I dearly love to talk—cultivated it, and him too to some extent, I trust, and withdrew when I had enjoyed it long enough, leaving him to carry it on. This experience entitled me to be regarded as a sort of real-estate broker by my friends. Wherever I sat, there I might live, and the landscape radiated from me accordingly. What is a house but a *sedes*, a seat?—better if a country seat. I discovered many a site for a house not likely to be soon improved, which some might have thought too far from the village, but to my eyes the village was too far from it. Well, there might I live, I said; and there I did live, for an hour, a summer and a winter life; saw how I could let the years run off, buffet the winter through, and see the spring come in. The future inhabitants of this region, wherever they may place their houses, may be sure that they have been anticipated. An afternoon sufficed to lay out the land into orchard woodlot and pasture, and to decide what fine oaks or pines should be left to stand before the door, and whence each blasted tree could be seen to the best advantage; and then I let it lie, fallow[2] perchance, for a man is rich in proportion to the number of things which he can afford to let alone.

My imagination carried me so far that I even had the refusal of several farms—the refusal was all I wanted—but I never got my fingers burned by actual possession. The nearest that I came to actual possession was when I bought the Hollowell Place, and had begun to sort my seeds, and collected materials with which to make a wheelbarrow to carry it on or off with; but before the owner gave me a deed of it, his wife—every man has such a wife—changed her mind and wished to keep it, and he offered me ten dollars to release him. Now, to speak the truth, I had but ten cents in the world, and it surpassed my arithmetic to tell, if I was that

---

1. **husbandry** (huz´ bən drē) *n*.: Farming.

2. **fallow** (fal´ ō) *adj*.: Left uncultivated or unplanted.

From J. Lyndon Shanley, ed., *Walden: The Writings of Henry D. Thoreau.* Copyright © 1971 by Princeton University Press. Excerpts, pp. 81–98 and 320–333, reprinted with permission of Princeton University Press.

◀ **Critical Viewing** Based on this picture, what do you think it would be like to live at Walden Pond? **[Speculate]**

man who had ten cents, or who had a farm, or ten dollars, or all together. However, I let him keep the ten dollars and the farm too, for I had carried it far enough; or rather, to be generous, I sold him the farm for just what I gave for it, and, as he was not a rich man, made him a present of ten dollars, and still had my ten cents, and seeds, and materials for a wheelbarrow left. I found thus that I had been a rich man without any damage to my poverty. But I retained the landscape, and I have since annually carried off what it yielded without a wheelbarrow. With respect to landscapes:

> "I am monarch of all I *survey,*
> My right there is none to dispute."[3]

I have frequently seen a poet withdraw, having enjoyed the most valuable part of a farm, while the crusty farmer supposed that he had got a few wild apples only. Why, the owner does not know it for many years when a poet has put his farm in rhyme, the most admirable kind of invisible fence, has fairly impounded it, milked it, skimmed it, and got all the cream, and left the farmer only the skimmed milk.

The real attractions of the Hollowell farm, to me, were: its complete retirement, being about two miles from the village, half a mile from the nearest neighbor, and separated from the highway by a broad field; its bounding on the river, which the owner said protected it by its fogs from frosts in the spring, though that was nothing to me; the gray color and ruinous state of the house and barn, and the <u>dilapidated</u> fences, which put such an interval between me and the last occupant; the hollow and lichen-covered apple trees, gnawed by rabbits, showing what kind of neighbors I should have; but above all, the recollection I had of it from my earliest voyages up the river, when the house was concealed behind a dense grove of red maples, through which I heard the house-dog bark. I was in haste to buy it, before the proprietor finished getting out some rocks, cutting down the hollow apple trees, and grubbing up some young birches which had sprung up in the pasture, or, in short, had made any more of his improvements. To enjoy these advantages I was ready to carry it on; like Atlas,[4] to take the world on my shoulders—I never heard what compensation he received for that—and do all those things which had no other motive or excuse but that I might pay for it and be unmolested in my possession of it; for I knew all the while that it would yield the most abundant crop of the kind I wanted if I could only afford to let it alone. But it turned out as I have said.

All that I could say, then, with respect to farming on a large scale (I have always cultivated a garden) was that I had had my seeds ready. Many think that seeds improve with age. I have no doubt that time discriminates between the good and the bad; and when at last I shall plant, I shall be less likely to be disappointed. But I would say to my fellows, once for all, As long as possible live free and uncommitted. It makes but little difference whether you are committed to a farm or the county jail.

---

3. **"I . . . dispute":** From William Cowper's *Verses Supposed to Be Written by Alexander Selkirk.*

---

4. **Atlas** (at´ ləs): From Greek mythology, a Titan who supported the heavens on his shoulders.

◆ **Build Vocabulary**

dilapidated (di lap´ ə dā tid) *adj.*: In disrepair

Old Cato,[5] whose "De Re Rustica" is my "Cultivator," says, and the only translation I have seen makes sheer nonsense of the passage, "When you think of getting a farm, turn it thus in your mind, not to buy greedily; nor spare your pains to look at it, and do not think it enough to go round it once. The oftener you go there the more it will please you, if it is good." I think I shall not buy greedily, but go round and round it as long as I live, and be buried in it first, that it may please me the more at last. . . .

I do not propose to write an ode to dejection, but to brag as lustily as chanticleer[6] in the morning, standing on his roost, if only to wake my neighbors up.

When first I took up my abode in the woods, that is, began to spend my nights as well as days there, which, by accident, was on Independence Day, or the fourth of July, 1845, my house was not finished for winter, but was merely a defense against the rain, without plastering or chimney, the walls being of rough weatherstained boards, with wide chinks, which made it cool at night. The upright white hewn studs and freshly planed door and window casings gave it a clean and airy look, especially in the morning, when its timbers were saturated with dew, so that I fancied that by noon some sweet gum would exude from them. To my imagination it retained throughout the day more or less of this auroral[7] character, reminding me of a certain house on a mountain which I had visited the year before. This was an airy and unplastered cabin, fit to entertain a traveling god, and where a goddess might trail her garments. The winds which passed over my dwelling were such as sweep over the ridges of mountains, bearing the broken strains, or celestial parts only, of terrestrial music. The morning wind forever blows, the poem of creation is uninterrupted; but few are the ears that hear it. Olympus[8] is but the outside of the earth everywhere. . . .

I went to the woods because I wished to live deliberately, to front only the essential facts of life, and see if I could not learn what it had to teach, and not, when I came to die, discover that I had not lived. I did not wish to live what was not life, living is so dear; nor did I wish to practice resignation, unless it was quite necessary. I wanted to live deep and suck out all the marrow of life, to live so sturdily and Spartanlike[9] as to put to rout all that was not life, to cut a broad swath and shave close, to drive life into a corner, and reduce it to its lowest terms, and, if it proved to be mean, why then to get the whole and genuine meanness of it, and publish its meanness to the world; or if it were sublime, to know it by experience, and be able to give a true account of it in my next excursion. For most men, it appears to me, are in a strange uncertainty about it, whether it is of the devil or of God, and have *somewhat hastily* concluded that it is the chief end of man here to "glorify God and enjoy him forever."[10]

Still we live meanly, like ants; though the fable tells us that we were long ago changed into men; like pygmies we fight with cranes:[11] it is error upon error, and clout upon clout, and our best virtue has for its occasion a superfluous and evitable wretchedness. Our life is frittered away by detail. An honest man has hardly need to count more than his ten fingers, or in extreme cases he may add his ten toes, and lump the rest. Simplicity, simplicity, simplicity! I say, let your affairs be as two or three, and not a hundred or a thousand; instead of a million count half a dozen, and keep your accounts on your thumbnail. In the midst of this chopping sea of civilized life, such are the clouds and storms and quicksands and thousand-and-one items to be

---

5. Old Cato: Roman statesman (234–149 B.C.). "De Re Rustica" is Latin for "Of Things Rustic."
6. Chanticleer (chan´ tə klir´) *n.*: Rooster.
7. auroral (ô rôr´ əl) *adj.*: Resembling the dawn.

8. Olympus (ō lim´ pəs): In Greek mythology, the home of the gods.
9. Spartanlike: Like the people of Sparta, an ancient Greek state whose citizens were known to be hardy, stoical, simple, and highly disciplined.
10. "glorify . . . forever": The answer to the question "What is the chief end of man?" in the Westminster catechism.
11. like . . . cranes: In the *Iliad*, the Trojans are compared to cranes fighting against pygmies.

allowed for, that a man has to live, if he would not founder and go to the bottom and not make his port at all, by dead reckoning,[12] and he must be a great calculator indeed who succeeds. Simplify, simplify. Instead of three meals a day, if it be necessary eat but one; instead of a hundred dishes, five; and reduce other things in proportion. Our life is like a German Confederacy,[13] made up of petty states, with its boundary forever fluctuating,so that even a German cannot tell you how it is bounded at any moment. The nation itself, with all its so-called internal improvements, which, by the way, are all external and superficial, is just such an unwieldy and overgrown establishment, cluttered with furniture and tripped up by its own traps, ruined by luxury and heedless expense, by want of calculation and a worthy aim, as the million households in the land; and the only cure for it as for them is in a rigid economy, a stern and more than Spartan simplicity of life and elevation of purpose. It lives too fast. Men think that it is essential that the *Nation* have commerce, and export ice, and talk through a telegraph, and ride thirty miles an hour, without a doubt, whether *they* do or not; but whether we should live like baboons or like men, is a little uncertain. If we do not get out sleepers,[14] and forge rails, and devote days and nights to the work, but go to tinkering upon our *lives* to improve *them*, who will build railroads? And if railroads are not built, how shall we get to heaven in season? But if we stay at home and mind our business, who will want railroads? We do not ride on the railroad; it rides upon us. . . .

Time is but the stream I go a-fishing in. I drink at it; but while I drink I see the sandy bottom and detect how shallow it is. Its thin current slides away, but eternity remains. I would drink deeper; fish in the sky, whose bottom is pebbly with stars. I cannot count one. I know not the first letter of the alphabet. I have always been regretting that I was not as wise as the day I was born. The intellect is a cleaver; it discerns and rifts its way into the secret of things. I do not wish to be any more busy with my hands than is necessary. My head is hands and feet. I feel all my best faculties concentrated in it. My instinct tells me that my head is an organ for burrowing, as some creatures use their snout and forepaws, and with it I would mine and burrow my way through these hills. I think that the richest vein is somewhere hereabouts; so by the divining rod[15] and thin rising vapors I judge; and here I will begin to mine. . . .

from The Conclusion

I left the woods for as good a reason as I went there. Perhaps it seemed to me that I had several more lives to live, and could not spare any more time for that one. It is remarkable how easily and insensibly we fall into a particular route, and make a beaten track for ourselves. I had not lived there a week before my feet wore a path from my door to the pondside; and though it is five or six years since I trod it, it is still quite distinct. It is true, I fear that others may have fallen into it, and so helped to keep it open. The surface of the earth is soft and impressible by the feet of men; and so with the paths which the mind travels. How worn and dusty, then, must be the highways of the world, how deep the ruts of tradition and conformity! I did not wish to take a cabin passage, but rather to go before the mast and on the deck of the world, for there I could best see the moonlight amid the mountains. I do not wish to go below now.

I learned this, at least, by my experiment; that if one advances confidently in the direction

---

12. **dead reckoning:** Navigating without the assistance of stars.

13. **German Confederacy:** At the time, Germany was a loose union of thirty-eight independent states, with no common government.

14. **sleepers** (slē´ pərz) *n*.: Ties supporting railroad tracks.

◆ **Build Vocabulary**

sublime (sə blīm´) *adj*.: Noble; majestic

superfluous (sʊ pʉr´ flʊ wəs) *adj*.: Excessive; not necessary

evitable (ev´ ə tə bəl) *adj*.: Avoidable

---

15. **divining rod:** A forked branch or stick alleged to reveal underground water or minerals.

of his dreams, and endeavors to live the life which he has imagined, he will meet with a success unexpected in common hours. He will put some things behind, will pass an invisible boundary; new, universal, and more liberal laws will begin to establish themselves around and within him; or the old laws be expanded, and interpreted in his favor in a more liberal sense, and he will live with the license of a higher order of beings. In proportion as he simplifies his life, the laws of the universe will appear less complex, and solitude will not be solitude, nor poverty poverty, nor weakness weakness. If you have built castles in the air, your work need not be lost; that is where they should be. Now put the foundations under them. . . .

Why should we be in such desperate haste to succeed, and in such desperate enterprises? If a man does not keep pace with his companions, perhaps it is because he hears a different drummer. Let him step to the music which he hears, however measured or far away. It is not important that he should mature as soon as an apple tree or an oak. Shall he turn his spring into summer? If the condition of things which we were made for is not yet, what were any reality which we can substitute? We will not be shipwrecked on a vain reality. Shall we with pains erect a heaven of blue glass over ourselves, though when it is done we shall be sure to gaze still at the true ethereal heaven far above, as if the former were not? . . .

However mean your life is, meet it and live it; do not shun it and call it hard names. It is not so bad as you are. It looks poorest when you are richest. The faultfinder will find faults even in paradise. Love your life, poor as it is. You may perhaps have some pleasant, thrilling, glorious hours, even in a poorhouse. The setting sun is reflected from the windows of the almshouse[16] as brightly as from the rich man's abode; the snow melts before its door as early in the spring. I do not see but a quiet mind may live as contentedly there, and have as cheering thoughts, as in a palace. The town's poor seem to me often to live the most independent lives

of any. Maybe they are simply great enough to receive without misgiving. Most think that they are above being supported by the town; but it oftener happens that they are not above supporting themselves by dishonest means, which should be more disreputable. Cultivate poverty like a garden herb, like sage. Do not trouble yourself much to get new things, whether clothes or friends. Turn the old; return to them. Things do not change; we change. Sell your clothes and keep your thoughts. God will see that you do not want society. If I were confined to a corner of a garret[17] all my days, like a spider, the world would be just as large to me while I had my thoughts about me. The philosopher said: "From an army of three divisions one can take away its general, and put it in disorder; from the man the most abject and vulgar one cannot take away his thought." Do not seek so anxiously to be developed, to subject yourself to many influences to be played on; it is all dissipation. Humility like darkness reveals the heavenly lights. The shadows of poverty and meanness gather around us, "and lo! creation widens to our view."[18] We are often reminded that if there were bestowed on us the wealth of Croesus,[19] our aims must still be the same, and our means essentially the same. Moreover, if you are restricted in your range by poverty, if you cannot buy books and newspapers, for instance, you are but confined to the most significant and vital experiences; you are compelled to deal with the material which yields the most sugar and the most starch. It is life near the bone where it is sweetest. You are defended from being a trifler. No man loses ever on a lower level by magnanimity on a higher. Superfluous wealth can buy superfluities only. Money is not required to buy one necessary of the soul. . . .

---

16. **almshouse** *n*.: Home for people too poor to support themselves.

17. **garret** (gar´ it) *n*.: Attic.
18. **"and . . . view":** From the sonnet "To Night" by British poet Joseph Blanco White (1775–1841).
19. **Croesus** (krē´ səs): King of Lydia (d. 546 B.C.), believed to be the wealthiest person of his time.

The life in us is like the water in the river. It may rise this year higher than man has ever known it, and flood the parched uplands; even this may be the eventful year, which will drown out all our muskrats. It was not always dry land where we dwell. I see far inland the banks which the stream anciently washed, before science began to record its freshets. Everyone has heard the story which has gone the rounds of New England, of a strong and beautiful bug which came out of the dry leaf of an old table of apple-tree wood, which had stood in a farmer's kitchen for sixty years, first in Connecticut, and afterward in Massachusetts—from an egg deposited in the living tree many years earlier still, as appeared by counting the annual layers beyond it; which was heard gnawing out for several weeks, hatched perchance by the heat of an urn. Who does not feel his faith in a resurrection and immortality strengthened by hearing of this? Who knows what beautiful and winged life, whose egg has been buried for ages under many concentric layers of woodenness in the dead dry life of society, deposited at first in the alburnum[20] of the green and living tree, which has been gradually converted into the semblance of its well-seasoned tomb—heard perchance gnawing out now for years by the astonished family of man, as they sat round the festive board—may unexpectedly come forth from amidst society's most trivial and handselled furniture, to enjoy its perfect summer life at last!

I do not say that John or Jonathan[21] will realize all this; but such is the character of that morrow which mere lapse of time can never make to dawn. The light which puts out our eyes is darkness to us. Only that day dawns to which we are awake. There is more day to dawn. The sun is but a morning star.

---

20. **alburnum** (al bur´ nəm) n.: Soft wood between the bark and the heartwood, where water is conducted.
21. **John or Jonathan:** Average person.

◆ **Build Vocabulary**

magnanimity (mag´ nə nim´ ə tē) n.: Generosity

Guide for Responding

◆ Literature and Your Life

Reader's Response From your point of view, what would be the advantages and disadvantages of spending two solitary years in a natural setting?

Thematic Focus What might Thoreau think of today's fast-paced society? What specific things in your life might especially concern him?

☑ Check Your Comprehension

1. What does Thoreau imagine doing?
2. (a) Why does Thoreau go to live in the woods? (b) Why does he eventually leave?
3. What does he learn from his "experiment"?
4. What advice does Thoreau offer to those who live in poverty?

◆ Critical Thinking

INTERPRET

1. What does Thoreau mean by his comment: "It makes but little difference whether you are committed to a farm or the county jail"? **[Analyze]**
2. In your own words, describe Thoreau's attitude toward individuality and conformity. **[Interpret]**
3. Why, according to Thoreau, are people better off being poor than wealthy? **[Support]**

APPLY

4. Explain why you either do or do not believe that it would be possible for Thoreau to conduct his "experiment" in today's society. **[Hypothesize]**

EXTEND

5. Today's travel agencies and vacation planners design vacations for people who want to get back to nature. Why is such a trip appealing? **[Career Link]**

from CIVIL DISOBEDIENCE

Henry David Thoreau

▲ **Critical Viewing** This flag, which dates back to 1775, displays the motto adopted by the American colonies. What makes the flag an appropriate illustration for this work? **[Support]**

I heartily accept the motto, "That government is best which governs least";[1] and I should like to see it acted up to more rapidly and systematically. Carried out, it finally amounts to this, which also I believe: "That government is best which governs not at all"; and when men are prepared for it, that will be the kind of government which they will have. Government is at best but an <u>expedient</u>; but most governments are usually, and all governments are sometimes, inexpedient. The objections which have

been brought against a standing army, and they are many and weighty, and deserve to prevail, may also at last be brought against a standing government. The standing army is only an arm of the standing government. The government itself, which is only the mode which the people have chosen to execute their will, is equally liable to be abused and perverted before the people can act through it. Witness the present Mexican war, the work of comparatively a few individuals using the standing government as their tool; for in the outset, the people would not have consented to this measure.

This American government—what is it but

---

1. **"That . . . least":** The motto of the *United States Magazine and Democratic Review*, a literary-political journal.

a tradition, though a recent one, endeavoring to transmit itself unimpaired to posterity, but each instant losing some of its integrity? It has not the vitality and force of a single living man; for a single man can bend it to his will. It is a sort of wooden gun to the people themselves; and, if ever they should use it in earnest as a real one against each other, it will surely split. But it is not the less necessary for this; for the people must have some complicated machinery or other, and hear its din, to satisfy that idea of government which they have. Governments show thus how successfully men can be imposed on, even impose on themselves, for their own advantage. It is excellent, we must all allow; yet this government never of itself furthered any enterprise, but by the alacrity with which it got out of its way. *It* does not keep the country free. *It* does not settle the West. *It* does not educate. The character inherent in the American people has done all that has been accomplished; and it would have done somewhat more, if the government had not sometimes got in its way. For government is an expedient by which men would fain succeed in letting one another alone; and, as has been said, when it is most expedient, the governed are most let alone by it. Trade and commerce, if they were not made of India rubber,[2] would never manage to bounce over the obstacles which legislators are continually putting in their way; and, if one were to judge these men wholly by the effects of their actions, and not partly by their intentions, they would deserve to be classed and punished with those mischievous persons who put obstructions on the railroads.

But, to speak practically and as a citizen, unlike those who call themselves no government men, I ask for, not at once no government, but *at once* a better government. Let every man make known what kind of government would command his respect, and that will be one step toward obtaining it. . . .

---

2. **India rubber:** A form of crude rubber.

◆ **Build Vocabulary**

expedient (ik spē′ dē ənt) *n*.: Resource
posterity (päs ter′ ə tē) *n*.: All succeeding generations
alacrity (ə lak′ rə tē) *n*.: Speed

Guide for Responding

◆ *Literature and Your Life*

Reader's Response What kind of government commands your respect? Why?

Thematic Focus Does Thoreau's philosophy of government agree or conflict with the Transcendentalist belief in the human spirit and the natural world? Explain.

Group Discussion Discuss Thoreau's ideas about the role of government. Then list five things he would think government should do and five things he would think a government should not do.

☑ Check Your Comprehension

1. What motto does Thoreau heartily accept?
2. How does Thoreau suggest people can contribute to improving the government?

◆ Critical Thinking

INTERPRET
1. Whom does Thoreau suggest is responsible for the Mexican War? **[Infer]**
2. Why does Thoreau think that a small handful of individuals can get away with perverting the government? **[Analyze]**
3. According to Thoreau, when will Americans get the best possible kind of government? **[Draw Conclusions]**

EVALUATE
4. Does Thoreau present a convincing argument for opposing a government policy of which one does not approve? **[Evaluate]**

APPLY
5. Thoreau says "if ever [the people] should use [the government] in earnest as a real [gun] against each other, it will surely split." Use your knowledge of history to judge this statement. **[Social Studies Link]**

Guide for Responding (continued)

◆ Reading Strategy

EVALUATE THE WRITER'S STATEMENT OF PHILOSOPHY

Evaluate a writer's ideas and arguments by weighing them against your own knowledge.

1. Thoreau writes that people should simplify their lives. (a) What support for this belief does he provide? (b) How could you argue against this idea? (c) Is his argument convincing? Explain.

2. (a) How does Thoreau support his contention that "That government is best which governs not at all"? (b) Do you agree with Thoreau? Explain.

◆ Literary Focus

STYLE

The way a writer puts thoughts into words is called **style**. Thoreau's style is characterized by his continual reinforcement of his ideas. Some critics argue that Thoreau overstates his points. Thoreau, however, felt that it was impossible to overstate the truth about human potential. He deliberately repeated his main ideas to reinforce his message.

1. (a) How does the paragraph in *Walden* on simplicity demonstrate Thoreau's tendency to make sentences build to a climax? (b) Find one other paragraph that is structured in this manner.

2. Thoreau often starts a paragraph by discussing specific incidents or examples. He then applies them to a larger truth. Find one such paragraph.

Beyond Literature

History Connection

Civil Disobedience in the 1960's

Thoreau's concept of civil disobedience greatly influenced the civil rights movement in the 1960's. Martin Luther King, Jr., one of the major leaders of the movement, was committed to the concept of civil disobedience and helped to organize boycotts, marches, and sit-ins, which brought about important social changes. Debate the pros and cons of this type of protest with your classmates.

◆ Build Vocabulary

USING THE WORD ROOT -flu-

The root -flu-, found in *fluency* and *influence*, means "flow." Match each of the following words containing the root -flu- with its definition. Check your answers in a dictionary.

a. affluence   **b.** confluence   **c.** fluent

1. a flowing together; for example, the flowing together of two or more streams
2. wealth; an abundant flow; prosperity
3. effortlessly smooth; flowing

USING THE WORD BANK

On your paper, write the word or phrase whose meaning is closer to that of the first word.

1. dilapidated: (a) depressed, (b) in disrepair
2. sublime: (a) majestic, (b) filthy
3. superfluous: (a) superb, (b) unnecessary
4. evitable: (a) avoidable, (b) evident
5. magnanimity: (a) spontaneity, (b) kindness
6. expedient: (a) resource, (b) expense
7. posterity: (a) succeeding generations, (b) previous generations
8. alacrity: (a) awareness, (b) readiness

◆ Grammar and Style

INFINITIVES AND INFINITIVE PHRASES

Thoreau makes frequent use of infinitives and infinitive phrases to explain his beliefs and the motives for his actions.

Practice Find at least six infinitives or infinitive phrases in the paragraph on p. 376 that begins "I went to the woods . . ." Identify the function of the infinitive in each.

> An **infinitive** is a form of a verb that generally appears with the word *to* and acts as a noun, adjective, or adverb. **Infinitive phrases** contain an infinitive and its complements.

Writing Application
Complete these sentences by adding infinitive phrases.

1. Thoreau went to Walden Pond hoping __?__ .
2. Thoreau wants us __?__ .
3. Thoreau says that time is merely a stream __?__ .

Build Your Portfolio

Idea Bank

Writing

1. **Letter to the Editor** How well do Thoreau's philosophies apply today? Write a letter to the editor of a newspaper, promoting the idea that people should simplify their lives.

2. **Report** Thoreau spent a night in jail to protest the Mexican War. In a report, explain the causes and results of the war and the response by United States citizens. **[Social Studies Link]**

3. **Compare-and-Contrast Essay** Write an essay in which you compare and contrast the beliefs of Emerson and Thoreau, using passages and details from their writings for support.

Speaking and Listening

4. **Television Script** It is said that when Thoreau was in jail, Emerson came to see him and asked, "Henry, what are you doing in there?" to which Thoreau replied, "Waldo, what are you doing out there?" Using ideas from the essays, write a script for a scene depicting this famous meeting. **[Media Link]**

5. **Debate** Stage a debate to argue the pros and cons of civil disobedience as a form of protest. **[Social Studies Link]**

Projects

6. **Walden Pond Today** Conduct research to find out what Walden Pond is like today. If possible, gather photographs of the area. Share your findings with the class. Follow with a discussion of how Walden Pond has changed since Thoreau's day.

7. **Nature Journal** Make several visits to an area close to you—a park, forest, or seashore— where you can observe nature. Record your observations in a nature journal to share with classmates. **[Science Link]**

Writing Mini-Lesson

Persuasive Essay

Thoreau writes persuasively on subjects about which he has strong feelings. Choose an issue of importance to you. Then write an essay persuading others to accept your position and take an action. Use a cause-and-effect organization to show your audience the consequences of action—or inaction.

Writing Skills Focus: Cause-and-Effect Organization

To argue why or how something happened or will happen, connect ideas by using a **cause-and-effect organization**. Follow either of these two approaches:

- State a cause—evidence that something has happened or will happen—followed by the effects that have resulted or will result from that cause.
- Alternatively, state a series of related effects, and then state the cause that shows your evidence is or will be responsible for those effects.

Prewriting Think about the main idea you want to convey and the kinds of evidence you will need to support it. To help you gather evidence of causes and effects, use a chart like the following:

Topic: _____

Causes	Effects

Drafting State your position clearly in an introduction. Develop each point you wish to make in a separate paragraph, and organize your points in a logical order. Refer to your list of causes and effects to help you develop your argument.

Revising Reread your draft, adding details as necessary to sharpen your argument and clarify all cause-and-effect relationships.

Gardening
Bailey White

Hammer and a Nail
Emily Saliers

Thematic Connection

THE HUMAN SPIRIT AND THE NATURAL WORLD

When was the last time you strolled through a meadow or hiked in a forest? The untouched natural landscapes that gave so much joy and meaning to the lives of Emerson and Thoreau are not as accessible today as they were in the nineteenth century. Even if they were, most Americans don't have the leisure time to commune with nature on the shores of a pond as did Thoreau or take the twilight rambles that Emerson describes in "Nature."

So how do we make the universal connection that these writers found in the unspoiled wilderness? Where do we turn to find the greater meaning that Emerson and Thoreau saw reflected in the wonder of a snowstorm or the beauty of a sunset?

SIMPLICITY, SIMPLICITY, SIMPLICITY!

"Getting back to nature" and "getting back to basics" have become catch phrases for everything from weekend camping trips to the decision to trade big-city life for small-town living. The implication is that nature, or something of unifying and enduring value, has been lost or left behind, and we must find our way back to it.

This need to return to "the simpler things in life" drives millions to spend their weekends working in the garden or puttering with tools. This kind of work can become a pleasure in and of itself. In her humorous essay "Gardening," Bailey White discovers the satisfaction that comes from working the land. In the song "Hammer and a Nail," Emily Saliers, of the modern folk duo Indigo Girls, writes of the liberating effect of taking shovel and hammer in hand—both literally and figuratively. These contemporary works celebrate a sense of well-being that closely resembles the simple pleasures that Emerson and Thoreau found in nature.

BAILEY WHITE
(1950–   )

Until the summer of 1993, Bailey White was little known outside her hometown of Thomasville, Georgia, where she taught first grade at the local elementary school. As a commentator for National Public Radio, White had earned a loyal audience with her sketches about rural southern life. With the publication of her first book, however, White became, to her own surprise, a best-selling author. The success of *Mama Makes Up Her Mind* hasn't changed White at all; she's still a homebody who appreciates life's simple pleasures.

EMILY SALIERS
(1963–   )

Emily Saliers was in the sixth grade when her family moved from New Haven, Connecticut, to Decatur, Georgia, where she met musical partner Amy Ray. Today, this duo, which records under the name the Indigo Girls, is known for its gutsy yet spiritual brand of contemporary folk music. Saliers and Ray—both singers, songwriters, and guitarists—began performing while still in high school. In 1989, the Indigo Girls released their first recording with a major label. The album, also called "Indigo Girls," won a Grammy Award. The duo has been recording and performing ever since.

Gardening

BAILEY WHITE

About six years ago, like so many romantic gardening fools, I fell for it: the wildflower meadow. I don't know whether it was the pictures on the seed packets, or the vision I had of myself, dressed all in white, strolling through an endless vista of poppies and daisies.

"A garden in a can," the seed catalogs said. The pictures showed a scene of rolling hills and dales, an area about the size of Georgia and Alabama combined, covered solid as far as the eye could see with billowing drifts of lupine and phlox.

But I wasn't born yesterday. I had been tricked by those pictures before. I come from down south, where vegetation does not know its place. Honeysuckle can work through cracks in your walls and strangle you while you sleep. Kudzu can completely shroud a house and a car parked in the yard in one growing season. Wisteria can lift a building off its foundation, and certain terrifying mints spread so rapidly that just the thought of them on a summer night can make your hair stand on end.

I knew what Lady Bird Johnson[1] was talking about when she gave the wildflower romantics a look and said, "You can't just scatter the seeds around as if you were feeding chickens." Even the more responsible plant catalogs, in their offer of wildflower seed mixes for the various regions of the country admitted, "We have not been able to develop a mixture suitable for Zone 9." So I knew it wouldn't be easy.

---

1. **Lady Bird Johnson:** First Lady and wife of Lyndon Baines Johnson, 36th president of the United States.

But it's hard to squash a romantic. I made a plan. I would prepare my ground, about a half acre, and plant the wildflowers in rows. I would keep the weeds out for five years, by cultivating between the rows with a push plow and a hoe, and weeding by hand within each row. By the end of those five years, I figured I would have eliminated any perennial weeds and weed seeds. Then the garden would be on its own. The wildflowers would spread, eventually taking up the spaces between the rows, and I would get out my white dress and begin my leisurely strolls.

My garden's first spring: the seeds arrived. I planted by hand. The rows, neatly set out with stakes and string, seemed endless. I crawled up and down and up and down every afternoon examining each seedling as it sprouted. Was this spotted spurge or sweet Annie? Red-root pigweed or showy primrose? I recognized most of our common weeds and tweaked them out.

After every rain I hoed between the rows. My hands got hard and callused. They took on the curve of the hoe handle so that everywhere I went, I looked as if I were gripping a ghostly hoe.

The first summer, my annual plants bloomed. The *Coreopsis tinctoria* was spectacular, a glowing red, and the cosmos was shoulder high. Its lavender petals brushed my face as I scritched and scritched up and down each row. I loved the sight of the clean brown earth stretching away from the blade of my hoe. On my hands and knees I weeded between plants. My knees ached, but the smell down there was nice, damp ground and bruised artemisia. I developed a gardener's stoop and a horticulturist's[2] squint.

That first winter, I could relax only a little. Bermuda grass can establish itself during a winter and get away from you the following spring. So every evening at dusk, I would stalk up and down my garden like a demented wraith, peering at the ground for each loathed blue-green blade, my cloak billowing in the wind and my scarf snagging on the bare gray branches of last summer's sunflowers.

At night, I would lie in my bed under the quilt listening to the wind outside and pinching and sniffing the little bunches of sweet Annie I had harvested and dried in July. I dreamed of that summer, only four years away now, when the garden would be finished. My white dress would be linen, I decided.

The second summer was very fine. Some of the annuals had reseeded, and the perennials and biennials bloomed for the first time. But I had a real problem with something called Old Horrible Snakeroot, one of the terrifying mints, creeping in around the edges. Every afternoon, dressed in a wide straw hat, big boots, and little else, and pouring sweat, I violently hoed the perimeter of my garden. I wore out my first hoe that year with sharpening the blade, and the handles of my Little Gem cultivator became as smooth as ivory.

During the third and fourth years the rows began to close in. There were great irregular patches of gaillardia spanning several rows, with Queen Anne's lace and moss verbena weaving themselves among clumps of black-eyed Susans. When I stood up to ease my back and looked across the garden, I could see that it was truly as beautiful as the picture in the Park's seed catalog. I wiped the sweat out of my eyes and washed my face in the watering can. My white linen dress would have lace.

The fifth summer, I had to go to the doctor about my knees. "You've got to quit squatting down," he told me.

"I can't quit squatting down," I said. "I've got

a garden." He sighed and gave me a pair of elastic bandages.

I had a problem with thistles that year. The seeds must have blown in from somewhere. I wore gloves to pull them out, and every time I took out a thistle, I would transplant a wildflower in its place. Every one of the transplants thrived and multiplied, and by the end of that summer, there was not a spot of bare ground for a weed seed to settle in. My garden was complete.

That winter I bought the linen and the lace and sewed my white dress.

In March I went out to the garden. The linaria was the first thing to bloom. I knew it would be. I knew that a week later the verbena would show up, then the shasta daisies and the gaillardia—a clump here, here, and here. In midsummer the Queen Anne's lace would begin to bloom. I knew exactly how it would be. I knew the name of every plant. I could recognize each one even before it got its true leaves.

I sighted down the length of the garden. There was no trace of the neat rows I had worked and worked for all those years. The garden had taken over itself, just as I had planned.

I walked back to the house. I looked at my soft, limp hands. I looked at my white linen dress, with lace. It seemed like the stupidest thing I had ever thought up. "The fact is," I said to myself, "I want something to hoe."

I've started reading about intensive gardening. It involves double digging and raised beds. Every season you pull out the old plants and put in new ones. It's a garden that never gets finished.

I gave the white dress to my sister, Louise. Sometimes she comes for a visit and strolls in the wildflower meadow. She ooohs and aaahs and brings her friends to see it. They pick armloads of flowers. I sit on the edge and draw diagrams of my next season's garden in the raised beds. I'm learning about companion planting.

In the wildflower meadow, the Queen Anne's lace waves its filigree heads over the marsh pinks, and the sweet alyssum tucks up neatly around the clumps of painted daisies. But I hardly notice. I've got a new garden now.

---

2. horticulturist's: Belonging or pertaining to someone who practices the art and science of growing flowers, fruits, vegetables, and shrubs.

◆ **Build Vocabulary**

filigree (fil′ i grē′) *adj.*: Resembling delicate, lacelike ornamental work of intertwined gold or silver wires

HAMMER AND A NAIL

Words and Music by Emily Saliers

Clearing webs from the <u>hovel</u>
A blistered hand on the handle of a shovel
I've been diggin too deep, I always do.
I see my face on the surface
5 I look a lot like Narcissus[1]
A dark <u>abyss</u> of an emptiness
Standing on the edge of a drowning blue

I look behind my ears for the green
Even my sweat smells clean
10 Glare off the white hurts my eyes
Gotta get out of bed get a hammer and a nail
Learn how to use my hands not just my head
I think myself into jail
Now I know a refuge never grows
15 From a chin in a hand in a thoughtful pose
Gotta tend the earth if you want a rose

I had a lot of good intentions
Sit around for fifty years and then collect a
    pension
Started seeing the road to hell and just where it
    starts
20 But my life is more than a vision
The sweetest part is acting after making a decision
Started seeing the whole as a sum of its parts.

My life is part of the global life
I'd found myself becoming more immobile
25 When I'd think a little girl in the world can't do
    anything
A distant nation my community
A street person my responsibility
If I have a care in the world I have a gift to bring

---

1. **Narcissus** (när sis´ əs): In Greek mythology, a beautiful youth who pines away for love of his own reflection in the pool of a spring and is changed into a flower.

◆ Build Vocabulary

hovel (huv´ əl) *n.:* Low, open storage shed; hut

abyss (ə bis´) *n.:* Bottomless gulf; immeasurable depth

Guide for Responding

◆ Literature and Your Life

Reader's Response Which ideas in these selections reflect ideas with which you agree? Explain.

Thematic Focus How does taking action or "making things happen" give you a sense of purpose in life?

☑ Check Your Comprehension

1. (a) At the end of "Gardening," how does White feel about her garden? (b) On what is she focused?
2. What does the singer in "Hammer" want to learn?
3. What do the lyrics refer to as the "sweetest part" of life?

◆ Critical Thinking

INTERPRET

1. In "Gardening," how do the writer's feelings about the white dress reflect her changing ideas about what she expects to receive from her garden? **[Connect]**
2. In "Hammer and a Nail," why is the speaker seized with the need to work with her hands? **[Infer]**
3. Explain values expressed in both "Gardening" and "Hammer and a Nail."

APPLY

4. How might White or Saliers define a "meaningful life"? **[Generalize]**

EXTEND

5. What activities in your hometown might both White and Saliers suggest to people who feel "out of touch" with nature? **[Community Link]**

Thematic Connection

THE HUMAN SPIRIT AND THE NATURAL WORLD

Spending time out of doors on a beautiful summer day, walking through a rolling park or picturesque garden, even doing yard work—activities like these lift our spirits in a unique way. This kind of day-to-day contact with nature was once a way of life in this country.

Today, these experiences are fewer and farther between for millions of Americans who spend their days confined in offices and factories—often without so much as a glimpse of blue sky or green grass. This enforced separation may increase nature's power to affect and restore the human spirit.

1. How does White's approach to nature differ from that of Emerson and Thoreau?
2. What details from "Hammer and a Nail" express the idea that working with one's hands can inspire the human spirit to better things?

Idea Bank

Writing

1. **Personal Anecdote** Have you ever made something with your own hands? Perhaps you baked a cake or built something in woodworking shop. Write an anecdote, or story, about such an experience. What part of the experience was most satisfying? What did you learn?

2. **Grant Proposal** Imagine that a group from your school is applying for a grant to develop a community garden. Write a proposal that explains your plans for an empty lot and why you feel it is important. Base your argument on the ideas expressed in the works of Emerson, Thoreau, White, and Saliers. **[Community Link]**

3. **Critique** In *Walden,* Thoreau writes, "I do not wish to be any more busy with my hands than is necessary." What might Thoreau have thought of the years White worked at creating something that was meant to look as though it had occurred naturally? From the viewpoint of Thoreau, write a critique of "Gardening" or "Hammer and a Nail."

Speaking and Listening

4. **Music Analysis** Listen to a recording of the song "Hammer and a Nail" from the album *nomads. indians. saints.* by the Indigo Girls. Did anything strike you that you hadn't noticed from reading the lyrics? Was the emotional tone what you expected? Jot down your answers in your journal. **[Music Link]**

Project

5. **Drawing** Reread the passages in which White describes herself at work in her garden. Then, using charcoals or watercolors, draw or paint a scene depicting White in her wildflower meadow. **[Art Link]**

Writing Process Workshop

What does thought add to an experience? Reflecting on an event can help you realize its importance or uncover attitudes and values you may not have known you had. Emerson and Thoreau spent a great deal of time analyzing and reflecting on their experiences; this helped them develop and refine their philosophies.

In a **reflective essay**, a writer describes personal experiences or pivotal events and conveys his or her feelings about these events or experiences. Often, the writer reflects on the meaning or significance of the experience being described, as Emerson and Thoreau do in the pieces you have read in this section. Think about a meaningful event in your own life, and write a reflective essay that describes the event and explains its significance to you.

The following skills will help you write your reflective essay:

Writing Skills Focus

▶ **Use specific examples** when describing the experience and explaining its impact. Be as specific as possible so your readers will be able to share your experience.

▶ **Write with a personal tone** to give your essay an authentic, heartfelt quality. (See p. 371.)

Thoreau uses these skills as he reflects on the busy lives he sees in nineteenth-century America.

MODEL FROM LITERATURE

from *Walden* by Henry David Thoreau

. . . Our life is frittered away by detail. An honest man has hardly need to count more than his ten fingers, or in extreme cases he may add his ten toes, and lump the rest. Simplicity, simplicity, simplicity! I say, ① let your affairs be as two or three, and not a hundred or a thousand; instead of a million count half a dozen, and keep your accounts on your thumbnail. ②

① Thoreau's use of the first-person pronoun helps to give his reflection a personal tone.

② Thoreau clearly expresses his position regarding how people should approach life.

Applying Language Skills: Precise Nouns

Good writers avoid general, abstract nouns and instead choose specific, precise nouns to make their writing clearer and more interesting. These sentences demonstrate the difference:

General:

I drove my car to a restaurant.

Precise:

I drove my convertible to the pizza parlor.

Practice Make the general nouns in these sentences more precise.

1. The trees on the road were bending during the storm.
2. The surface was wet after I spilled the liquid.
3. I saw the book at a store.

Writing Application As you draft your reflective essay, be sure that your nouns are as specific and precise as possible.

Writer's Solution Connection Writing Lab

To help you gather precise nouns for your reflective essay, use the Sensory Word Bin activities in the Writing Lab tutorial on Description.

Prewriting

Choose a Topic Look through your possessions to find objects that relate to specific memories or important periods from your childhood: perhaps an old collection of dolls or a shoebox of baseball cards. Jot down your thoughts in a notebook, and then review the notes to find a topic. You might also consider one of the following topics:

Topic Ideas

- Nature (a favorite place or an occurrence like a thunderstorm)
- Being a teenager
- Dance
- The importance of the telephone or e-mail in your life
- A work of art—music, theater, film, painting—that influenced you

Consider Your Audience and Purpose For whom are your reflections intended, and what is your purpose? Your choice of words and details will be shaped to a large extent by who is reading your work and what you want to convey to them. Look at these examples:

Topic: The Uncertainties of Adolescence		
Audience:	**Purpose:**	**Language:**
Peers	Share feelings	Informal
Adults	Plea for greater understanding	More formal
Children	Offer cautionary advice	Simple

Drafting

Organize Your Reflections When you write your essay, take the time to develop a clear organization. Most likely, you'll want to organize your details either in the order in which they happened or by order of importance.

Revising

Replace Vague Words Don't view your revision as a chore; greet it as an opportunity or a challenge. Focus on finding parts of your reflection that could be clearer; see where you might add clarifying details or vivid verbs to strengthen weak or vague words. For example, replace "good" with stronger words, such as "exciting," "critical," and "revealing."

Make Your Writing More Personal Look for places in your essay that could benefit from a personal touch. Make stiff words informal, and make your opening and closing paragraphs friendly in tone.

REVISION MODEL

① *a chorus of discouragement*

When I signed up for acting class, I heard ~~the usual~~ ~~objections~~ from friends and family. But then I remembered Thoreau's inspiring advice to advance "confidently in the

② *It was time, I realized, to step to the music that I hear.*

direction of one's dreams."

① *The writer enlivens the sentence with more vivid, concrete language.*
② *The added sentence creates a more urgent, personal tone.*

Publishing

Prepare a Bulletin Board Display A classroom, hall, or library bulletin board offers an excellent place to display your writing.

▶ Choose illustrations from magazines or prepare artwork to accompany your piece.

▶ Choose attractive background colors and designs, and arrange the illustrations dramatically. It might be helpful to design the arrangement on paper before setting up the actual display.

Stage a Round Table Discussion With a group of classmates, hold a meeting to share your reflective essays. Read each essay aloud, and then offer each student feedback. To conclude the discussion, look for similarities among all essays.

APPLYING LANGUAGE SKILLS: Pronoun Case

Personal pronouns have different subject and object forms, or cases, that reflect how they are used in the sentence.

Subjective Case:

She is delighted.

The first-prize winner is *she*.

Objective Case:

Tyrone handed the letter to *him*.

Tyrone handed *him* the letter.

The letter mentioned *him*.

Practice On your paper, circle the correct choice in each item.

1. My friend and (me/I) made the wrong turn.
2. Antonio gave a lift to (he/him) and Terry.
3. The ending was too intense for Olivia and (she/her) to watch.

Writing Application Review your reflective essay, and be sure that all your personal pronouns are in the correct case.

Writer's Solution Connection Language Lab

For more practice, complete the Language Lab lesson on Pronoun Case.

Real-World Reading Skills Workshop

Strategies for Success

Whether you're traveling to a new friend's house or changing a vacuum cleaner bag, following directions is important. Directions explain the necessary steps in a process and tell you the correct sequence in which to perform those steps. Followed accurately, directions can make even the most complicated procedure simple. When directions are followed poorly or ignored, however, the results can be disastrous, expensive, or embarrassing.

Orient Yourself Whenever you are doing something for the first time, read the directions through completely. Note any necessary tools or materials, and estimate the amount of time the process should take. Before you try to follow the directions, define any unfamiliar terms.

Study the Sequence Examine the sequence of the steps. What should you do first? How will each step prepare you for the next? Then mentally complete each step, referring to visual material, such as street maps or diagrams. On travel directions, locate the places where turns are needed. With diagrams, read captions that indicate sequence. When possible, do a rehearsal or a "dry run."

Follow the Directions Proceed slowly and carefully through the directions. Check off each completed step before continuing. If you get stuck, retrace the sequence from the last step you *do* understand.

Apply the Strategy

You're submitting an application letter for a camp counselor job. The camp has asked you to e-mail the application letter with a written essay about your goals for the job. Refer to the directions for sending an e-mail with attachments and then answer the questions.

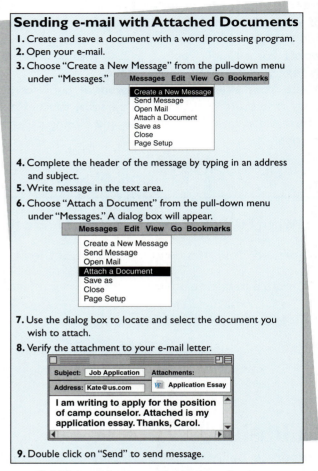

Sending e-mail with Attached Documents

1. Create and save a document with a word processing program.
2. Open your e-mail.
3. Choose "Create a New Message" from the pull-down menu under "Messages."

   Messages Edit View Go Bookmarks
   - Create a New Message
   - Send Message
   - Open Mail
   - Attach a Document
   - Save as
   - Close
   - Page Setup

4. Complete the header of the message by typing in an address and subject.
5. Write message in the text area.
6. Choose "Attach a Document" from the pull-down menu under "Messages." A dialog box will appear.

   Messages Edit View Go Bookmarks
   - Create a New Message
   - Send Message
   - Open Mail
   - Attach a Document
   - Save as
   - Close
   - Page Setup

7. Use the dialog box to locate and select the document you wish to attach.
8. Verify the attachment to your e-mail letter.

   Subject: Job Application   Attachments:
   Address: Kate@us.com   Application Essay

   I am writing to apply for the position of camp counselor. Attached is my application essay. Thanks, Carol.

9. Double click on "Send" to send message.

1. What software will you need to complete this task?
2. (a) What is the first step in the process? (b) What is the last step?
3. Should you write your essay before or after opening a new message page? Explain.
4. How long do you estimate the process should take?

✔ *Here are other situations in which following directions can be helpful:*
   - ▶ Getting to a new movie theater
   - ▶ Programing an alarm clock

Looking at Literary Forms:
Poetry

Walden Pond Revisited, 1942, N.C. Wyeth, Brandywine River Museum

As the nation's boundaries pushed west in the nineteenth century, writers were pioneering new styles of poetry. Walt Whitman abandoned traditional poetic forms in favor of free verse. Emily Dickinson combined striking languages and a highly imaginative view of the world. Together, these two influential poets set the stage for a new American poetry.

Guide for Interpreting

Emily Dickinson (1830–1886)

Of the 1,775 poems Emily Dickinson wrote during her lifetime, only seven were published before her death—and these few appeared anonymously. Dickinson was a private person who was extremely reluctant to reveal herself (or her work) to the world. As a result, few people outside her family and a few friends knew of her poetic genius. Today, however, she is widely regarded as one of the greatest American poets.

A Life Apart Dickinson was born in Amherst, Massachusetts, the daughter of a prominent lawyer. As a child, she was energetic and enjoyed the tasks of daily life—cooking, sewing, playing with friends, winter sports, even studying at a boarding school. Her childhood seemed normal in many respects. However, as an adult she became increasingly isolated. Though she traveled as a young woman to Boston, Washington, D.C., and Philadelphia to visit friends, she rarely left her small valley town as she grew older. In fact, during the last ten years of her life, she refused to leave even her house and garden.

> *Dickinson's circle of friends grew smaller and smaller, and she communicated with the few that remained mainly through notes and fragments of poems.*

Her Talent Is Recognized Though she chose to live most of her life in virtual isolation, Emily Dickinson was a remarkably energetic, intense person. She possessed a clear sense of purpose and devoted most of her time to writing poetry. Yet because she shared her work with few people, she sometimes doubted her abilities. In 1862, she sent four poems to Thomas Wentworth Higginson, an influential literary critic, and asked him to tell her whether her verse was "alive."

Like the editors who first published her work after her death, Higginson sought to change her unconventional style—her eccentric use of punctuation and irregular meter and rhyme. He did not understand that she had crafted her poetry with great precision and that her unique style was an important element of it. Still, he did recognize her talent and encouraged her to keep writing.

Her Final Years In the last several years of her life, Dickinson dressed only in white and would not allow neighbors or strangers to see her. Her reluctance to interact with people grew so extreme that, despite failing health, she permitted her doctor to examine her only from a distance.

In 1886, after fighting illness for two years, she died in the same house in which she had been born. After her death, her sister Lavinia discovered packets of poems in the drawers of Emily's dresser. Her first books of verse were published four years later.

◆ Background for Understanding

LITERATURE: DICKINSON'S TALENT IS DISCOVERED

The extent of Emily Dickinson's gift was not generally recognized until 1955, when a complete, unedited edition of her poems was published under the guidance of Thomas H. Johnson. Viewing her work in its original form, writers and critics could see that Dickinson was utterly unlike other poets of her era. For the first time, her poetry was appreciated for its unique style, concrete imagery, and simple but forceful language. Dickinson's work is often compared with that of the modern poets, and she is now acknowledged as a visionary who was far ahead of her time.

Emily Dickinson's Poetry

◆ *Literature and Your Life*

CONNECT YOUR EXPERIENCE

Although you may not often speak your most private thoughts about life's "big topics," you probably have many ideas and feelings about them. In the following poems, Emily Dickinson shines light on shadowy "private" thoughts and ideas about several vast or abstract topics—society, death, solitude, consciousness, and the soul.

Journal Writing Choose one of these abstract topics and quickly write your immediate thoughts about it. Use your initial reaction to help you approach Dickinson's poetry.

THEMATIC FOCUS: THE HUMAN SPIRIT AND THE NATURAL WORLD

As a truly American literature emerged, some of it reflected the nation's vitality and open spaces. A few writers, however, chose to examine details of personal, domestic, or spiritual life in the young nation. How does Dickinson illuminate her own inner landscape?

◆ Literary Focus

SLANT RHYME

Poets use rhyme to create pleasant musical sounds and to unify groups of lines or stanzas. **Exact rhyme** occurs when two words have identical sounds in their final accented syllables. However, in a **slant rhyme,** the final sounds are similar but not identical. *Glove-above* is an exact rhyme, but *glove-prove* is a slant rhyme.

Dickinson uses both exact and slant rhyme in her poetry. Her independence from strict rhyme keeps her verses surprising.

◆ Reading Strategy

ANALYZE IMAGES

Poets often link abstract concepts such as love, life, death, and spirituality to concrete images, or word pictures. In "Because I could not stop for Death—" Dickinson uses an image of a carriage ride to capture the experience of death. It is important to **analyze** what the author is conveying through the choice of each **image**.

Complete a chart like this one to help you.

Image	Abstract Idea
Carriage, slow journey	Death
Schoolchildren, grain, sunset	Life
House, roof below ground	Eternity

◆ Build Vocabulary

WORD ROOTS: *-finis-*

In "There is a solitude of space," you'll find the words *finite* and *infinity,* both of which contain the Latin root *-finis-,* meaning "end" or "limit." A finite entity is limited in time or space; infinity is limitless.

WORD BANK

As you read these selections, you will encounter the words on this list. Preview the list before you read.

cornice
surmised
oppresses
finite
infinity

◆ Grammar and Style

GERUNDS

A **gerund** is a verb form that ends in *-ing* and is used as a noun. Like nouns, they function in sentences as subjects, complements (such as direct objects and subject complements), and objects of prepositions. In the following passage, Dickinson uses the gerund *meanings:*

> We can find no scar,
> But internal difference,
> Where the Meanings,
>   are—

I heard a Fly buzz—when I died—

Emily Dickinson

Room With a Balcony, Adolph von Menzel, Staatliche Museen Preußischer Kulturbesitz Nationgalerie, Berlin

◀ **Critical Viewing**
Why is this an appropriate illustration for Dickinson's poem? **[Support]**

I heard a Fly buzz—when I died—
The Stillness in the Room
Was like the Stillness in the Air—
Between the Heaves of Storm—

5   The Eyes around—had wrung them dry—
And Breaths were gathering firm
For that last Onset—when the King
Be witnessed—in the Room—

I willed my Keepsakes—Signed away
10   What portion of me be
Assignable—and then it was
There interposed a Fly—

With Blue—uncertain stumbling Buzz—
Between the light—and me—
15   And then the Windows failed—and then
I could not see to see—

Because I could not stop for Death—

Emily Dickinson

Because I could not stop for Death—
He kindly stopped for me—
The Carriage held but just Ourselves—
And Immortality.

5   We slowly drove—He knew no haste
And I had put away
My labor and my leisure too,
For his Civility—

We passed the School, where Children strove
10   At Recess—in the Ring—
We passed the Fields of Gazing Grain—
We passed the Setting Sun—

Or rather—He passed Us—
The Dews drew quivering and chill—
15   For only Gossamer,[1] my Gown—
My Tippet[2]—only Tulle[3]—

We paused before a House that seemed
A Swelling of the Ground—
The Roof was scarcely visible—
20   The Cornice—in the Ground—

Since then—'tis Centuries—and yet
Feels shorter than the Day
I first surmised the Horses Heads
Were toward Eternity—

---

1. Gossamer: Very thin, soft, filmy cloth.
2. Tippet: Scarflike garment worn over the shoulders and hanging down in front.
3. Tulle (tool) *n.*: Thin, fine netting used for scarves.

◆ Build Vocabulary

Cornice (kôr′ nis) *n.*: Projecting decorative molding along the top of a building
surmised (sər mīzd′) *v.*: Guessed

Guide for Responding

◆ Literature and Your Life

Reader's Response How did the images and ideas in these poems make you feel?
Thematic Focus In "Because I could not stop for Death—" how does Dickinson use images of nature to convey her speaker's inner landscape?

☑ Check Your Comprehension

1. In "I heard a Fly buzz—when I died—" what three sounds does the speaker note?
2. (a) Why does Death stop for the speaker of "Because I could not stop for Death—"? (b) What is in the carriage?
3. How much time has passed since Death stopped for the speaker?

◆ Critical Thinking

INTERPRET

1. (a) How can you tell that the speaker of "I heard a Fly buzz—when I died—" has prepared herself for death? (b) What happens in the poem's last moment? **[Support; Analyze]**
2. What statement about dying do you think Dickinson makes in this poem? **[Draw Conclusions]**
3. (a) How is Death characterized in the first two stanzas of "Because I could not stop for Death—"? (b) In what sense is this characterization ironic? **[Analyze]**
4. (a) What is the significance of the carriage's passing "the School," "the Fields," and "the Setting Sun"? (b) What does the "House" in stanza five represent? **[Interpret]**

APPLY

5. Why do you think Emily Dickinson is so interested in death? **[Hypothesize]**

My life closed twice before its close—

Emily Dickinson

My life closed twice before its close—
It yet remains to see
If Immortality unveil
A third event to me.

5   So huge, so hopeless to conceive
As these that twice befell.
Parting is all we know of heaven.
And all we need of hell.

The Soul selects her own Society—

Emily Dickinson

The Soul selects her own Society—
Then—shuts the Door—
To her divine Majority—
Present no more—

5   Unmoved—she notes the Chariots—pausing—
At her low Gate—
Unmoved—an Emperor be kneeling
Upon her Mat—

I've known her—from an ample nation—
10   Choose One—
Then—close the Valves of her attention—
Like Stone—

There's a certain Slant of light,

Emily Dickinson

There's a certain Slant of light,
Winter Afternoons—
That oppresses, like the Heft
Of Cathedral Tunes—

5   Heavenly Hurt, it gives us—
We can find no scar,
But internal difference,
Where the Meanings, are—

None may teach it—Any—
10   'Tis the Seal Despair—
An imperial affliction
Sent us of the Air—

When it comes, the Landscape listens—
Shadows—hold their breath—
15   When it goes, 'tis like the Distance
On the look of Death—

◆ **Build Vocabulary**

oppresses (ə pres′ əz) *v.*: Weighs heavily on the mind

Guide for Responding

◆ Literature and Your Life

Reader's Response Which do you prefer—the light of the morning, afternoon, or evening? Why?

Thematic Focus How does "My life closed twice before its close—" relate details of personal history to ideas about eternity?

☑ Check Your Comprehension

1. According to the speaker of "My life closed twice before its close—" what were "huge" and "hopeless to conceive"?
2. In "The Soul selects her own Society—" what leaves the soul "unmoved"?
3. According to the speaker of "There's a certain Slant of light," how does "a certain Slant of light" affect people?

◆ Critical Thinking

INTERPRET

1. (a) In "My life closed twice before its close—" what event could have caused the speaker's life to close "twice before its close"? (b) Which line holds a clue to the nature of the events "that twice befell"? (c) What is the third event to which the speaker refers? (d) How are the three events related? **[Analyze; Interpret; Connect]**
2. (a) In "The Soul selects her own Society —" what is the soul's "divine Majority"? (b) How many people make up the soul's "Society"? **[Interpret]**
3. (a) What mood is created by the "Slant of light"? (b) What does this light seem to represent to the speaker? **[Analyze; Interpret]**

APPLY

4. You probably don't limit your companions to a "society" of one; you might choose a variety of different "societies." What do these variations indicate about your nature? **[Apply]**

Twilight in the Wilderness, Frederick E. Church, The Cleveland Museum of Art

▲ **Critical Viewing** What feelings are evoked by the sweep of sky, mountains, and water in this painting? **[Respond]**

There is a solitude of space

Emily Dickinson

There is a solitude of space
A solitude of sea
A solitude of death, but these
Society shall be
5   Compared with that profounder site
That polar privacy
A soul admitted to itself—
Finite Infinity.

◆ **Build Vocabulary**

Finite (fī′ nīt) *adj*.: Having measurable or definable limits

Infinity (in fin′ i tē) *n*.: Endless or unlimited space, time, or distance

The Brain—is wider than the Sky—

Emily Dickinson

The Brain—is wider than the Sky—
For—put them side by side—
The one the other will contain
With ease—and You—beside—

5   The Brain is deeper than the sea—
For—hold them—Blue to Blue—
The one the other will absorb—
As Sponges—Buckets—do—

The Brain is just the weight of God—
10 For—Heft them—Pound for Pound—
And they will differ—if they do—
As Syllable from Sound—

Water, is taught by thirst.

Emily Dickinson

Water, is taught by thirst.
Land—by the Oceans passed.
Transport[1]—by throe[2]—
Peace—by its battles told—
5 Love, by Memorial Mold[3]—
Birds, by the Snow.

---

1. **Transport:** Ecstasy; rapture.
2. **throe:** Spasm or pang of pain.
3. **Memorial Mold:** Memorial grounds or cemetery.

Guide for Responding

◆ *Literature and Your Life*

Reader's Response Do you think it is a good idea for people to seek solitude? Why or why not?

Thematic Focus In "The Brain—is wider than the Sky—" what meaning does the speaker deduce from the comparison between an outer and inner landscape?

☑ **Check Your Comprehension**

1. In "There is a solitude of space," what three things does the speaker compare to "polar privacy"?
2. In "The Brain—is wider than the Sky—" what three things does the speaker compare or contrast to the human brain?
3. In "Water, is taught by thirst," what is the relationship between each line's first word and the following words?

◆ **Critical Thinking**

INTERPRET

1. In "There is a solitude of space," how does the solitude of a "soul admitted to itself" differ from the solitude of space, sea, and death? **[Contrast]**
2. In "The Brain—is wider than the Sky—" Dickinson makes three figurative comparisons. Explain in your own words how the human brain can "contain with ease" both the sky and one's self.
3. How would you state the theme or message of "Water, is taught by thirst." in a single sentence? **[Interpret]**

APPLY

4. Identify two or three situations or examples from everyday life that demonstrate the theme of "Water, is taught by thirst." **[Relate]**

Guide for Responding (continued)

◆ Reading Strategy

ANALYZE IMAGES

The ability to **analyze images** allows you to understand and appreciate poetry and other types of literature more deeply. When you come across each image, look to see if it is connected to a larger idea. Analyze the meaning conveyed through the image and the associated idea.

For example, in "Because I could not stop for Death—" Dickinson describes the speaker riding with Death and Immortality in a carriage drawn by horses headed toward "Eternity." This image suggests that the speaker is describing her own death.

1. What does Dickinson use to describe a grave site in "Because I could not stop for Death—"?

2. In "I heard a Fly buzz—when I died—" what does the image of a fly in a still room suggest about the moment of death?

3. (a) Identify two images in "Water, is taught by thirst." (b) Identify two images in "The Brain—is wider than the Sky—." (c) How do these images help the speaker communicate an idea?

◆ Build Vocabulary

USING THE WORD ROOT -finis-

The words *finite* and *infinity* derive from the Latin root *-finis-*, meaning "end" or "limit." Explain how the meaning of the root *-finis-* relates to the meaning of each of the following words.

1. finish   2. confine   3. final

USING THE WORD BANK

Identify the word whose meaning is most nearly the same as that of the first word in each item.

1. cornice: (a) ledge, (b) corner, (c) spire

2. surmised: (a) explained, (b) determined, (c) reduced

3. oppresses: (a) inhibits, (b) obliges, (c) judges

4. finite: (a) heavenly, (b) endless, (c) limited

5. infinity: (a) mystery, (b) multitude, (c) endlessness

◆ Literary Focus

SLANT RHYME

A **slant rhyme** occurs when two or more words have similar (but not identical) vowel sounds. For instance, in "The Soul selects her own Society—" Emily Dickinson uses the slant rhyme *one-stone*.

1. What two other slant rhymes appear in "The Soul selects her own Society—"?

2. In "Because I could not stop for Death—," what three words does Dickinson use to create slant rhymes for *immortality, civility,* and *eternity*?

3. In "I heard a Fly buzz—" Dickinson rhymes the words *room* and *storm, be* and *fly,* and *me* and *see.* Which are slant rhymes, and why?

◆ Grammar and Style

GERUNDS

Because gerunds function as nouns, they can appear in sentences as subjects, direct objects, predicate nominatives, and objects of prepositions.

> **Gerunds** are verb forms that end in *-ing* and are used as nouns.

Subject: *Writing* requires discipline.
Direct Object: Dickinson left her *writing* in her dresser.
Object of Preposition: She learned about *writing* by *practicing.*

Practice   Each of these sentences contains at least one gerund. Write each gerund on your paper. Tell how it is used in its sentence.

1. We paused before a House that seemed / A Swelling of the Ground—.

2. Writing was Emily Dickinson's greatest passion.

3. Parting is all we know of heaven. / And all we need of hell.

4. Among Dickinson's favorite activities were cooking and reading.

5. Dickinson avoided traveling great distances.

Writing Application   Write a paragraph to describe an interest or hobby—skiing or painting, for example. Include at least three gerunds.

Build Your Portfolio

Idea Bank

Writing

1. **Poem** Emily Dickinson wrote poetry that addressed timeless themes. Write a poem using images that convey your thoughts about a universal theme, such as happiness, time, or family.

2. **Editor's Letter** Imagine that you are an editor of a nineteenth-century literary journal. In a letter to Dickinson, comment on two or three of her poems and ask questions about the work.

3. **Critical Response** A critic has stated that Dickinson's poetry "is exploration on a variety of levels of the ultimate meaning of life itself and equally important of the depths and heights of her own inner nature." Write an essay supporting this statement with evidence from the poems.

Speaking and Listening

4. **Oral Interpretation** Choose three Dickinson poems to read aloud. Consider the meaning of each idea, image, and punctuation mark. Convey your understanding of the works in a reading for the class. **[Performing Arts Link]**

5. **Musical Interpretation** Set a Dickinson poem to music. Consider the poem's use of rhythm and its overall tone, and choose or write music that suits the mood. **[Music Link]**

Projects

6. **Painting** Dickinson communicates her ideas through strong images and comparison. Depict one of Dickinson's literary images in a drawing or painting. Try to capture or convey the content of Dickinson's imagery. **[Art Link]**

7. **Report** Dickinson was close to her brother Austin. Research him and their relationship. Present your findings in a written report.

Writing Mini-Lesson

Letter to an Author

Dickinson's poetry may have stirred your emotions, challenged you to think about an idea or aspect of existence, or helped you better understand yourself. Imagine that Dickinson is still alive. Write a letter to the poet in which you express your reactions to her verses. Be sure to use a clear organization in presenting your ideas.

Writing Skills Focus: Clear and Logical Organization

An effective letter—whether it is addressed to a friend, an author, or a business associate—contains ideas that are not only well expressed, but also **organized clearly and logically**.

Open your letter with an explanation of your reason for writing.

- Develop each important idea in a separate paragraph, and support it with examples.
- Use transitions to carry the reader from one paragraph to the next.
- Summarize your ideas or reactions in a conclusion that leaves the reader with some memorable reflection, opinion, or piece of information.

Prewriting Select a single poem or group of two or three on which to focus. Jot down some thoughts and feelings about the poetry and how it affected you. Boil down your reactions to three or four important points; then consider how your notes support each idea.

Drafting Open your letter with an explanation of why you are writing. Then develop and support each important idea in a separate paragraph.

Revising Ask yourself how Dickinson might react to your letter. Are your tone and word choice appropriate? Make sure that your thoughts are conveyed in a clear and logical way, with appropriate transitions between each paragraph.

Guide for Interpreting

Walt Whitman (1819–1892)

Walt Whitman was harshly denounced for his first volume of poetry. Yet in the following decades, his poems gained popularity, and he became famous as "the Good Gray Poet" and "the Bard of Democracy." In his later years, Whitman was admired by writers and intellectuals on both sides of the Atlantic. Today, he is widely recognized as one of the greatest and most influential poets the United States has ever produced.

The Poet at Work
Whitman was born on Long Island and raised in Brooklyn, New York. He trained to be a printer and spent his early years alternating between printing jobs and newspaper writing. At age twenty-seven, he became the editor of the Brooklyn *Eagle*, a respected newspaper. After the newspaper's ownership dismissed him in 1848 because of his opposition to slavery, Whitman traveled across the country to New Orleans, observing the diversity of America's landscapes and people.

Whitman soon returned to New York City, however, and in 1850 quit journalism to devote his energy to writing poetry. Five years later, when the first edition of *Leaves of Grass* was published, critics attacked Whitman's subject matter and abandonment of traditional poetic devices such as rhyme and meter. Noted poet John Greenleaf Whittier hated Whitman's poems so much that he hurled his copy of *Leaves of Grass* into the fireplace. Ralph Waldo Emerson, on the other hand, responded with great enthusiasm, remarking that the collection was "the most extraordinary piece of wit and wisdom that America has yet contributed."

The Bard of Democracy
Though Whitman did publish other works in the course of his career, his life's work proved to be *Leaves of Grass*, which he continually revised, reshaped, and expanded until his death in 1892. He viewed the volume as a single long poem that expressed his evolving vision of the world. Using his poetry to convey his passionate belief in democracy, equality, and the spiritual unity of all forms of life, he celebrated the potential of the human spirit. Though Whitman's philosophy grew out of the ideas of the Transcendentalists, his poetry was mainly shaped by his ability to absorb and comprehend everything he observed. From its first appearance as twelve unsigned and untitled poems in 1855, *Leaves of Grass* grew to include 383 poems in its final, "death-bed" edition (1892). The collection captures the diversity of the American people and conveys the energy and intensity of all forms of life. In the century since Whitman's death, *Leaves of Grass* has become one of the most highly regarded collections of poetry ever written.

◆ Background for Understanding

LITERATURE: PRAISE FOR WHITMAN'S WORK

In his lifetime, Whitman's poetry provoked both glowing reviews and fiercely negative reactions. After receiving his complimentary copy of *Leaves of Grass*, Ralph Waldo Emerson had abundant praise for the poet. In a letter to Whitman, he said:

. . . I give you joy of your free and brave thought. I have great joy in it. I find incomparable things said incomparably well, as they must be. I find the courage of treatment, which so delights me, and which large perception only can inspire. I greet you at the beginning of a great career. . . .

Walt Whitman's Poetry

◆ *Literature and Your Life*

CONNECT YOUR EXPERIENCE

You probably learn something new about yourself, your world, or life in general almost every day. You may not even be aware of all you're learning. As you'll discover in these poems, Walt Whitman devoted his life to making new discoveries and reaching new understandings.

Journal Writing Write a brief journal entry in which you describe an important exploration you have made.

THEMATIC FOCUS: THE HUMAN SPIRIT AND THE NATURAL WORLD

Like many writers of his day, Whitman's self-exploration led him to look at his relationship to the natural world. In what ways, if any, does the world of nature shape your view of yourself?

◆ Literary Focus

FREE VERSE

In contrast to verse written in iambic pentameter or other fixed patterns, **free verse** is poetry that has irregular meter and line length. Free verse is designed to re-create the rising and falling cadences of natural speech. A writer of free verse uses whatever rhythms and line lengths are appropriate to what he or she is saying.

Though free verse is as old as the Psalms in the Bible, it was not widely used until the twentieth century. Whitman was the first American poet to write free verse—the perfect form for this individualist: It allowed him to express himself without formal restraints.

◆ Reading Strategy

INFER THE POET'S ATTITUDE

You can **infer a poet's attitude** toward a subject by examining his or her choice of words and details. Look at this passage from Whitman's "Song of Myself":

I am there, I help, I came stretch'd atop of the load, / I felt its soft jolts, one leg reclined on the other, / I jump from the crossbeams and seize the clover and timothy, / And roll head over heels . . .

From these words and images—*reclined, jump, seize,* and *roll head over heels*—you can infer that he is invigorated by rural life.

As you read, note key words and images and the attitudes they suggest.

◆ Build Vocabulary

WORD ROOTS: *-fus-*

In "Song of Myself," Whitman writes, "I effuse my flesh in eddies, and drift it in lacy jags." The word *effuse* is based on the root *-fus-*, meaning "pour." The prefix *e-* means "out" or "away." By combining the meanings, you can see how *effuse* has come to mean "pour" or "spread out."

WORD BANK

Before you read, preview these words from Whitman's works.

| abeyance |
| effuse |

◆ Grammar and Style

PRONOUN AND ANTECEDENT AGREEMENT

A **pronoun** must **agree** in number (singular or plural) and gender (masculine, feminine, or neuter) with its **antecedent**—the word to which it refers. In the following line from "I Hear America Singing," the pronouns *he* and *his* (masculine, singular) agree with the antecedent *shoemaker* (also masculine, singular):

The *shoemaker* singing as *he* sits on *his* bench.

from Preface to the 1855 Edition of

Leaves of Grass

Walt Whitman

America does not repel the past or what it has produced under its forms or amid other politics or the idea of castes or the old religions . . . . accepts the lesson with calmness . . . is not so impatient as has been supposed that the slough still sticks to opinions and manners and literature while the life which served its requirements has passed into the new life of the new forms . . . perceives that the corpse is slowly borne from the eating and sleeping rooms of the house . . . perceives that it waits a little while in the door . . . that it was fittest for its days . . . that its action has descended to the stalwart and well-shaped heir who approaches . . . and that he shall be fittest for his days.

The Americans of all nations at any time upon the earth have probably the fullest poetical nature. The United States themselves are essentially the greatest poem. In the history of the earth hitherto the largest and most stirring appear tame and orderly to their ampler largeness and stir. Here at last is something in the doings of man that corresponds with the broadcast doings of the day and night. Here is not merely a nation but a teeming nation of nations. Here is action untied from strings necessarily blind to particulars and details magnificently moving in vast masses. Here is the hospitality which forever indicates heroes. . . . Here are the roughs and beards and space and ruggedness and nonchalance that the soul loves. Here the performance disdaining the trivial unapproached in the tremendous audacity of its crowds and groupings and the push of its perspective spreads with crampless and flowing breadth and showers its prolific and splendid extravagance. One sees it must indeed own the riches of the summer and winter, and need never be bankrupt while corn grows from the ground or the orchards drop apples or the bays contain fish or men beget children upon women. . . .

Guide for Responding

◆ *Literature and Your Life*

Reader's Response Do you think that Whitman's characterization of the United States is still accurate? Why or why not?

Thematic Focus What is unusual or original about the idea of the United States as a poem?

Group Discussion With a small group, develop your definition of America. Provide examples to clarify your definition.

☑ Check Your Comprehension

1. What theme or subject does the speaker address in the first paragraph?
2. According to the speaker, what is the greatest of all poems?

◆ Critical Thinking

INTERPRET
1. What is Whitman's view of the past? **[Interpret]**
2. What is the meaning of Whitman's notion that the United States "is not merely a nation but a teeming nation of nations"? **[Interpret]**
3. In your own words, describe the poet's attitude toward the United States. **[Interpret]**

EXTEND
4. What parallels can you draw between Whitman's ideas about the United States and those expressed by Michel-Guillaume Jean de Crèvecoeur in *Letters From an American Farmer* on p. 197? **[Literature Link]**

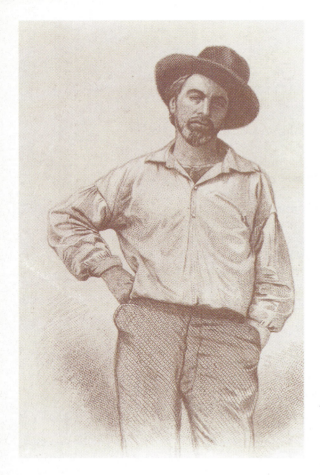

from

Song of Myself

Walt Whitman

◀ **Critical Viewing** This illustration depicts Walt Whitman as a young man. What can you conclude about his attitudes and personality from this picture? How are they reflected in this poem? **[Infer; Support]**

1

I celebrate myself, and sing myself,
And what I assume you shall assume,
For every atom belonging to me as good belongs to you.

I loaf and invite my soul,
5   I lean and loaf at my ease observing a spear of summer grass.

My tongue, every atom of my blood, formed from this soil, this air,
Born here of parents born here from parents the same, and their
   parents the same,
I, now thirty-seven years old in perfect health begin,
Hoping to cease not till death.

10   Creeds and schools in abeyance,
Retiring back a while sufficed at what they are, but never forgotten,
I harbor for good or bad, I permit to speak at every hazard,
Nature without check with original energy.

<h1 style="text-align:center">6</h1>

A child said *What is the grass?* fetching it to me with full hands,
How could I answer the child? I do not know what it is any more
 than he.

I guess it must be the flag of my disposition, out of hopeful green
 stuff woven.

Or I guess it is the handkerchief of the Lord,
5 A scented gift and remembrancer[1] designedly dropped,
Bearing the owner's name someway in the corners, that we may
 see and remark, and say *Whose?*
    . . .
What do you think has become of the young and old men?
And what do you think has become of the women and children?

They are alive and well somewhere,
10 The smallest sprout shows there is really no death,
And if ever there was it led forward life, and does not wait at the
 end to arrest it,
And ceas'd the moment life appear'd.
All goes onward and outward, nothing collapses,
And to die is different from what anyone supposed, and luckier.

<h1 style="text-align:center">9</h1>

The big doors of the country barn stand open and ready,
The dried grass of the harvest-time loads the slow-drawn wagon.
The clear light plays on the brown gray and green intertinged,
The armfuls are pack'd to the sagging mow.

5 I am there, I help, I came stretch'd atop of the load,
I felt its soft jolts, one leg reclined on the other,
I jump from the crossbeams and seize the clover and timothy,
And roll head over heels and tangle my hair full of wisps.

<h1 style="text-align:center">14</h1>

The wild gander leads his flock through the cool night,
Ya-honk he says, and sounds it down to me like an invitation,
The pert may suppose it meaningless, but I listening close,
Find its purpose and place up there toward the wintry sky.

---

1. remembrancer: Reminder.

◆ **Build Vocabulary**

abeyance (ə bā′ əns) *n.*: Temporary suspension

5 The sharp-hoof'd moose of the north, the cat on the house-sill,
    the chickadee, the prairie dog,
The litter of the grunting sow as they tug at her teats,
The brood of the turkey hen and she with her half-spread wings,
I see in them and myself the same old law.

The press of my foot to the earth springs a hundred affections,
10 They scorn the best I can do to relate them.

I am enamor'd of growing outdoors,
Of men that live among cattle or taste of the ocean or woods,
Of the builders and steerers of ships and the wielders of axes and
    mauls, and the drivers of horses,
I can eat and sleep with them week in and week out.

15 What is commonest, cheapest, nearest, easiest, is Me,
Me going in for my chances, spending for vast returns,
Adorning myself to bestow myself on the first that will take me,
Not asking the sky to come down to my good will,
Scattering it freely forever.

17

These are really the thoughts of all men in all ages and lands,
    they are not original with me,
If they are not yours as much as mine they are nothing, or next
    to nothing,
If they are not the riddle and the untying of the riddle they are
    nothing,
If they are not just as close as they are distant they are nothing.
5 This is the grass that grows wherever the land is and the water is,
This is the common air that bathes the globe.

51

The past and present wilt—I have fill'd them, emptied them,
And proceed to fill my next fold of the future.

Listener up there! what have you to confide to me?
Look in my face while I snuff the sidle of evening,[2]
5 (Talk honestly, no one else hears you, and I stay only a minute
    longer.)

Do I contradict myself?
Very well then I contradict myself,
(I am large, I contain multitudes.)

---

2. snuff . . . evening: Put out the hesitant last light of day, which is moving
sideways across the sky.

I concentrate toward them that are nigh,[3] I wait on the
   door-slab.

10 Who has done his day's work? who will soonest be through with
      his supper?
    Who wishes to walk with me?

    Will you speak before I am gone? will you prove already too late?

52

    The spotted hawk swoops by and accuses me, he complains
      of my gab and my loitering.

    I too am not a bit tamed, I too am untranslatable,
    I sound my barbaric yawp over the roofs of the world.

    The last scud[4] of day holds back for me,
5   It flings my likeness after the rest and true as any on the
      shadow'd wilds,
    It coaxes me to the vapor and the dusk.

    I depart as air, I shake my white locks at the runaway sun,
    I effuse my flesh in eddies, and drift it in lacy jags.

    I bequeath myself to the dirt to grow from the grass I love,
10 If you want me again look for me under your boot soles.

    You will hardly know who I am or what I mean,
    But I shall be good health to you nevertheless,
    And filter and fiber your blood.

    Failing to fetch me at first keep encouraged,
15 Missing me one place search another,
    I stop somewhere waiting for you.

---

3. nigh: Near.
4. scud: Low, dark, wind-driven clouds.

◆ **Build Vocabulary**
effuse (e fyoōz´) v.: Spread out; diffuse

Guide for Responding

◆ Literature and Your Life

Reader's Response Which of the ideas expressed in "Song of Myself" do you find most—and least—appealing?

Thematic Focus Which images in "Song of Myself" show that the United States was expanding and maturing?

Journal Writing If you were to celebrate yourself in a poem, what qualities and self-realizations would you include? Jot down your ideas in your journal.

☑ Check Your Comprehension

1. According to the speaker, where do the dead reside?
2. In which lines of section 14 does the speaker distinguish himself from people with less sensitivity to the natural world?
3. In section 52, what does the speaker suggest will happen to his spirit and message when he is gone?

◆ Critical Thinking

INTERPRET

1. (a) In section 1, what is the speaker's conception of his relationship with nature? (b) How does he view the relationship between himself and other people? **[Analyze]**
2. What do lines 6–14 of section 6 reveal about the speaker's attitude toward death? **[Infer]**
3. How do the images of grass and air in section 17 convey a belief in the spiritual unity of all natural forms? **[Support]**
4. In section 51, whom do you think the speaker is addressing? **[Infer]**

EVALUATE

5. In section 52, Whitman proudly characterizes his poetry as "barbaric yawp." How would you describe and evaluate his work? **[Assess]**

APPLY

6. In what ways is your own attitude toward nature similar to or different from the attitude conveyed in "Song of Myself"? **[Relate]**

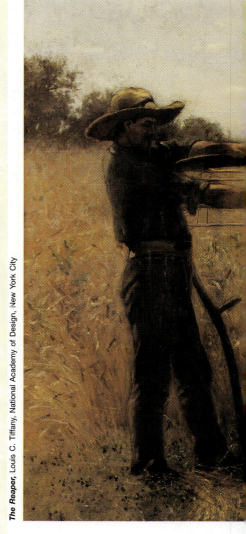

The Reaper, Louis C. Tiffany, National Academy of Design, New York City

▲ **Critical Viewing** What might Whitman say about the work of this farmer? **[Speculate]**

I Hear America Singing

Walt Whitman

I hear America singing, the varied carols I hear,
    Those of mechanics, each one singing his as it should be blithe
      and strong,
    The carpenter singing his as he measures his plank or beam,
    The mason singing his as he makes ready for work, or leaves
      off work,
5   The boatman singing what belongs to him in his boat, the
      deckhand singing on the steamboat deck,
    The shoemaker singing as he sits on his bench, the hatter[1]
      singing as he stands,
    The wood-cutter's song, the ploughboy's on his way in the
      morning, or at noon intermission or at sundown,
    The delicious singing of the mother, or of the young wife at
      work, or of the girl sewing or washing,
    Each singing what belongs to him or her and to none else,
10   The day what belongs to the day—at night the party of young
      fellows, robust, friendly,
    Singing with open mouths their strong melodious songs.

---

1. **hatter:** Person who makes, sells, or cleans hats.

Guide for Responding

◆ Literature and Your Life

Reader's Response If Whitman were to write this poem today, how might he change it? Do you think his message would be the same?

Thematic Focus How does Whitman celebrate the originality of American laborers?

☑ Check Your Comprehension

1. What "belongs to" each worker?
2. What are the speaker's associations with daytime and with night?

◆ Critical Thinking

INTERPRET

1. (a) How would you characterize this poem's mood? (b) In what way is this mood apt for a poem written in the mid-1800's? **[Analyze]**
2. How does the poem's form—free verse and parallel structures—support Whitman's ideas about work? Explain. **[Assess]**

EXTEND

3. Which voices (or careers) would you add to this poem to reflect modern society? **[Career Link]**

A Noiseless Patient Spider

Walt Whitman

A noiseless patient spider,
I mark'd where on a little promontory it
    stood isolated,
Mark'd how to explore the vacant vast
    surrounding,
It launch'd forth filament, filament, filament,
    out of itself,
5 Ever unreeling them, ever tirelessly
    speeding them.

And you O my soul where you stand,
Surrounded, detached, in measureless
    oceans of space,
Ceaselessly musing, venturing, throwing,
    seeking the spheres to connect them,
Till the bridge you will need be form'd,
    till the ductile anchor hold,
10 Till the gossamer thread you fling catch
    somewhere, O my soul.

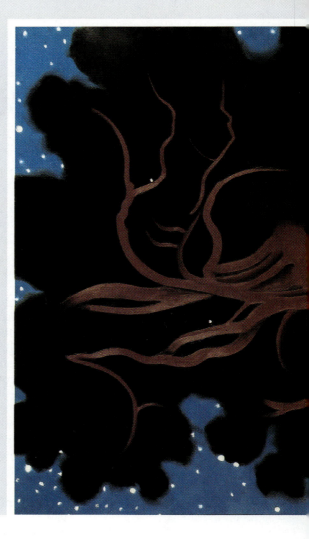

By the Bivouac's Fitful Flame

Walt Whitman

By the bivouac's[1] fitful flame,
A procession winding around me, solemn and sweet
    and slow—but first I note,
The tents of the sleeping army, the fields' and woods'
    dim outline,
The darkness lit by spots of kindled fire, the silence,
5 Like a phantom far or near an occasional figure moving,
The shrubs and trees, (as I lift my eyes they seem to
    be stealthily watching me,)
While wind in procession thoughts, O tender and
    wondrous thoughts,
Of life and death, of home and the past and loved,
    and of those that are far away;
A solemn and slow procession there as I sit on the
    ground,
10 By the bivouac's fitful flame.

---

1. bivouac (biv′ wak′) *n*.: Night guard to prevent surprise attacks.

The Lawrence Tree, 1929, Georgia O'Keeffe, Wadsworth Atheneum, Hartford

WHEN I HEARD THE LEARN'D ASTRONOMER

Walt Whitman

When I heard the learn'd astronomer,
When the proofs, the figures, were ranged
    in columns before me,
When I was shown the charts and
    diagrams, to add, divide and measure
    them,
When I sitting heard the astronomer where
    he lectured with much applause in the
    lecture room,
5   How soon unaccountable I became tired
    and sick,
Till rising and gliding out I wander'd off
    by myself,
In the mystical moist night air, and from
    time to time,
Look'd up in perfect silence at the stars.

◀ Critical Viewing How does the artist's viewpoint in this painting compare with Whitman's in "When I Heard the Learn'd Astronomer"? **[Connect]**

Guide for Responding

◆ *Literature and Your Life*

Reader's Response To which of these poems do you relate most strongly? Why?

Thematic Focus How do the speakers of these poems demonstrate individuality or originality?

☑ Check Your Comprehension

1. In "A Noiseless Patient Spider," why does the spider "tirelessly" spin out filament?
2. What actions are performed by the speaker of "When I Heard the Learn'd Astronomer"?

◆ Critical Thinking

INTERPRET

1. (a) In "A Noiseless Patient Spider," how is the speaker's soul similar to the spider? (b) In what sense is his soul's "venturing" different from the spider's exploration? **[Support; Analyze]**
2. (a) In "Astronomer," how are the speaker's and the astronomer's attitudes toward the stars different? (b) How would you express the poem's theme? **[Compare and Contrast; Interpret]**
3. (a) Where is the speaker in "By the Bivouac's Fitful Flame"? (b) Explain the procession to which he refers. **[Infer; Interpret]**

Guide for Responding (continued)

◆ Reading Strategy

INFER THE POET'S ATTITUDE

By making **inferences,** you can gain insight into Whitman's feelings and beliefs about his subjects. To help you do this, carefully consider the writers subjects, details, and word choice.

1. In "When I Heard the Learn'd Astronomer," how would you describe Whitman's attitude toward (a) the astronomer and (b) the stars themselves?
2. Name at least five descriptive words or phrases in "When I Heard the Learn'd Astronomer" that help you infer the contrast between Whitman's attitude toward the science of astronomy and his feelings about the stars.
3. Use the catalog, or list, of workers in "I Hear America Singing" to determine Whitman's attitude toward labor.
4. Find a passage from another Whitman poem that conveys his attitude or belief about something. Explain what the passage reveals.

◆ Literary Focus

FREE VERSE

At the beginning of "A Noiseless Patient Spider," Walt Whitman uses lines of different lengths and meters:

A noiseless patient spider,
I mark'd where on a little promontory
  it stood isolated, . . .

This is an example of **free verse**—poetry that has irregular meter and line length. Whitman's use of free verse reflects his belief in freedom, democracy, and individuality.

1. "Song of Myself" is an exploration of the speaker's relationship with the world that surrounds him. How does free verse allow the poet to express these ideas more freely?
2. Whitman rebels against a scientific interpretation of the wonders of nature in "When I Heard the Learn'd Astronomer." Why is free verse an appropriate form for the poem?
3. How does "I Hear America Singing" represent a perfect marriage of form and theme?

◆ Build Vocabulary

USING THE WORD ROOT -FUS-

The root *-fus-* means "pour." Each of the words in the left column is based on this root. On your paper, match each word with its definition in the right column.

1. profusion	**a.** rich or lavish supply
2. infuse	**b.** dispersed
3. effusive	**c.** gushing
4. diffuse	**d.** fill

USING THE WORD BANK

Answer the following questions on your paper. Be prepared to explain your answer.

1. If a judge hands down a ruling in *abeyance* of a particular law, is she enforcing that law?
2. Does light that *effuses* from a lamp spread softly through a room or shine in a sharply focused beam?

◆ Grammar and Style

PRONOUN AND ANTECEDENT AGREEMENT

When the word to which a pronoun refers is a singular indefinite pronoun—a word like *each* or *someone*—a writer must refer to it with singular pronouns. Notice that Whitman uses *him* or *her* (singular)—not *their* (plural)—to refer to *each* in the following line: "*Each* singing what belongs to *him* or *her* and to none else."

> A **pronoun** must agree in number and gender with its antecedent.

Practice In your notebook, write the correct pronoun for each sentence. Then write the antecedent to which the pronoun refers.

1. The turkey hen awoke, and then (she, it) stepped toward the door of the cage.
2. The woman and child opened (his, their) books and began to sing.
3. Life has (its, their) challenges and gratifications.
4. The shoemaker went on (their, his) lunch break.
5. All of the laborers received a pay increase after (he, they) made requests to the company boss.

Build Your Portfolio

Idea Bank

Writing

1. **Inscription** It is 1892 and you are attending a book-signing for the final edition of *Leaves of Grass*. What might the poet write in your copy? Write an inscription that he addresses to you.

2. **Poem** Write a poem in free verse expressing your connection with an element of nature, such as the ocean, the sun, or the moon. Choose and arrange words to approximate natural speech.

3. **Speculative Essay** Whitman revised *Leaves of Grass* many times. He called it an attempt to put a human being on record. Why did he choose to revise this "attempt" rather than write brand-new books? Explore this question in an essay.

Speaking and Listening

4. **Persuasive Speech** Whitman's poems capture America at the dawning of the Industrial Age. Do you think his attitude toward his country would be different if he were alive today? Explain your ideas on this topic in a five-minute speech.

5. **Oral Interpretation** Rehearse and make an oral presentation of two or three of Whitman's lyrics. Use voice tone and volume, as well as your sense of rhythm, to achieve musicality in your delivery. **[Performing Arts Link]**

Projects

6. **Mural** Work with a group to create a mural illustrating all twelve of the workers described in "I Hear America Singing." **[Art Link]**

7. **Report** Whitman's poems have much in common with Eastern thought. Research the Chinese religion of Taoism. In a report, examine the similarities between Taoist philosophy and poetry and Whitman's ideas. **[Social Studies Link]**

Writing Mini-Lesson

Imitation of an Author's Style

Walt Whitman is acclaimed not only for the ideas in his poems, but also for his original style. Write a poem in which you imitate Whitman's typical way of writing. Choose several elements of Whitman's style —his word choice, tone, degree of formality, figurative language, rhythm, use of lists, and organization— and use them throughout your poem.

Writing Skills Focus: Consistent Style

Whenever you write, make sure that the style in which you write remains the same from start to finish. For example, if you begin in a very informal style, don't switch to more formal language and structures; maintain a **consistent style** from start to finish.

Prewriting Reread Whitman's poems and note which elements of his style you will imitate. Decide on a "Whitmanesque" topic, and review the characteristics of free verse. Make a list or cluster diagram of sensory details to record images or details related to your topic.

Drafting As you write, maintain a consistent style and tone—whether it is exuberant, reflective, or full of wonder—and let the meaning of what you are saying determine the lengths of lines and stanzas.

Revising Read your poem aloud many times as you revise it. Do you hear the natural rhythm of speech in Whitman's poems, or do you hear unnatural rhythms or formal grammatical structures?

I, Too
Langston Hughes

To Walt Whitman
Angela de Hoyos

Thematic Connection

THE EMERGENCE OF AN AMERICAN VOICE

Walt Whitman and Emily Dickinson were two of the poets most responsible for establishing a distinctly American poetic voice. The American poets who preceded them were all heavily influenced by the styles and themes of British poets of the time. Whitman and Dickinson, on the other hand, produced poetry that was fresh and original. Different in style and content from the work of any earlier poet, Whitman's poetry embodies the freedom that characterizes the American spirit and captures the immensity of the American landscape. Dickinson's poetry is filled with stylistic innovations and has a highly personal quality that parallels the American emphasis on individuality.

The America that Walt Whitman celebrated in his poetry has grown increasingly diverse. The growing diversity has once again expanded the boundaries of American literature, introducing readers to the traditions and issues of the myriad of cultures represented in our population. Like Whitman and Dickinson, Langston Hughes helped establish a new American literature. He and a group of other African American poets associated with an artistic movement known as the Harlem Renaissance (see page 838) produced musical verse that captured the African American experience during the first half of this century. More recently, Angela de Hoyos and a growing number of Hispanic American poets have brought the rhythms of the Spanish language to American literature and captured the experiences of people descended from various Latin American cultures. In the two poems that follow, Hughes and de Hoyos offer their modifications to Walt Whitman's vision of what it means to be an American.

Literary Connection

POETRY

Dickinson and Whitman started the movement toward a uniquely American poetry, but they certainly were not the last innovative American poets. Twentieth-century poets such as Langston Hughes and Angela de Hoyos continue to experiment with poetic form. These poems by Hughes and de Hoyos—written in free verse—reflect the influence of Whitman and Dickinson.

LANGSTON HUGHES (1902–1967)

Langston Hughes emerged from the Harlem Renaissance as the most prolific and successful African American writer. Hughes published several volumes of poetry. In these works he experimented with a variety of forms and techniques and often tried to re-create the rhythms of contemporary jazz. (For more information on Hughes, see page 838.)

ANGELA DE HOYOS (1945–)

Angela de Hoyos has emerged as a voice of her times, celebrating her heritage and knowledge of what it means to live in a world of diversity. De Hoyos first published poetry in high school, and by her early twenties, she had published poetry in literary journals. Between 1969 and 1975, de Hoyos studied, wrote,

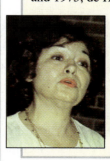

and established her reputation through readings at Chicano gatherings in the Southwest. She has published five collections of poetry.

I, Too

Langston Hughes

I, too, sing America.

I am the darker brother.
They send me to eat in the kitchen
When company comes,
5 But I laugh,
And eat well,
And grow strong.

Tomorrow,
I'll be at the table
10 When company comes.
Nobody'll dare
Say to me,
"Eat in the kitchen,"
Then.

15 Besides,
They'll see how beautiful I am
And be ashamed—

I, too, am America.

▲ **Critical Viewing** Which image in this painting better illustrates the sentiments of this poem—the man or the lion? Explain. **[Make a Decision]**

To Walt Whitman

Angela de Hoyos

hey man, my brother
world-poet
prophet democratic
here's a guitar
5   for you
—a chicana guitar—
so you can spill out a song
for the open road
big enough for my people
10   —my Native Amerindian race
that I can't seem to find
in your poems

Mandolin, Rosa Ibarra

▶ **Critical Viewing**
How does the mood of this painting compare with that of the poem? Explain. **[Assess]**

Guide for Responding

◆ Literature and Your Life

Reader's Response To which poem do you have a stronger response? Why?

Thematic Focus How do these two poems reflect the idea of emerging American voices?

☑ Check Your Comprehension

1. (a) What causes the speaker in "I, Too" to be banished to the kitchen? (b) According to the speaker, what changes will occur in the future?
2. Why does the speaker of "To Walt Whitman" offer a gift to the famous poet?

◆ Critical Thinking

INTERPRET

1. (a) To what or whom does the first line of "I, Too" allude? (b) To whom does *they* refer? **[Interpret]**
2. What is the significance of the actions the speaker names in lines 5–7 of "I, Too"? **[Infer]**
3. Summarize the attitude of the speaker of "To Walt Whitman" toward Whitman. **[Analyze]**

EXTEND

4. How do "I, Too" and "To Walt Whitman" expand the message about America that Whitman conveys in his poetry? **[Literature Link]**

Thematic Connection

THE EMERGENCE OF AN AMERICAN VOICE

Since the nineteenth century, writers with new vantage points have continued to change the face of American literature. Poets such as Langston Hughes and Angela de Hoyos, for example, have sought to challenge conventional notions about which topics (and which people) are appropriate for serious poetry.

1. Compare the speaker's declaration of his own beauty in Hughes's "I, Too" with the opening verses of Walt Whitman's "Song of Myself." How are the two speakers alike? How are their circumstances different?

2. Angela de Hoyos's speaker in "To Walt Whitman" offers a challenge or reproach to Whitman. What would de Hoyos like to have added to or changed about Whitman's portrayal of America?

Literary Connection

POETRY

The unique sensibilities of Walt Whitman and Emily Dickinson—as well as their arresting ideas about poetic form—signaled that America was developing a literary culture distinct from Europe's.

1. How might the effect of either of the poems presented here be different if the writer had used rhyming stanzas?

2. How do "To Walt Whitman" and "I, Too" reflect the changes in the American literary voice since the time of Dickinson and Whitman?

Idea Bank

Writing

1. **Letter** Both Langston Hughes and Angela de Hoyos chose to "answer" Walt Whitman in their own poems. Imagine that the "Good Gray Poet" was able to read these responses to his work. As Whitman, write a letter to either Hughes or de Hoyos in which you respond to his or her poem.

2. **Compare-and-Contrast Essay** Write a short essay comparing these two poems. Point out similarities and differences in subject matter, theme, style, and word choice.

3. **Poetic Response** Both these poems are direct responses to specific Whitman poems and echo lines from the original poetry. Follow this example by writing your own poetic response to one of Dickinson's or Whitman's poems. Your poem should be similar in style to the original poem and should echo one or more of its lines.

Speaking and Listening

4. **Group Discussion** Both Dickinson and Whitman were stylistic innovators. Whitman's use of free verse led the way for innumerable twentieth-century poets to express their views of the world. Analyze the writing styles of Dickinson, Whitman, Hughes, and de Hoyos. Then select a poem from each writer's work that you believe represents his or her style. Read the four poems aloud for the class; then lead a discussion comparing these poets' use of language.

Projects

5. **Diptych** The word *diptych* (dip´ tik´) comes from an ancient Greek word for a writing tablet made of two hinged pieces. Today the term refers to a picture painted on two hinged canvases or pages. Paint or draw a diptych that evokes or conveys the connection between two poems—one by Whitman and one by Hughes or de Hoyos. **[Art Link]**

Writing Process Workshop

Without even realizing it, you probably evaluate each piece of literature that you read. You might decide whether a novel you've just read is worth recommending to friends or whether a poem has a special meaning that makes you want to read other works by that poet. When you write your own **critical evaluation,** you simply capture your opinion of a literary work on paper. Your evaluation doesn't have to be positive, but you do have to back up your opinions with passages and details from the piece.

Choose an author or poem that interests you, and write a critical evaluation of the work. The following skills will help you write your critical evaluation:

Writing Skills Focus

▶ **Follow a clear and logical organization.** Discuss one aspect of the work in each paragraph, and arrange the paragraphs in an order that makes sense. (See p. 403.)

▶ **Use specific examples** from the work to thoroughly back up your opinion.

▶ **Use a consistent style**. For example, if you begin with a serious tone and formal language, stick with it. (See p. 417.)

This model uses these skills to create an effective and clear evaluation of Walt Whitman's style.

---

① The writer begins with a clear statement of her point of view regarding Whitman's poem.

② The writer follows with specific examples to support her opinion.

WRITING MODEL

Walt Whitman's poem "I Hear America Singing" is an inspirational catalog of the many workers who bring life and pride to their jobs. ① Through his signature listings, Whitman celebrates the usually unsung. Whitman starts with the carpenter, "singing as he measures his plank or beam."② In this poem, he names mechanics, masons, and other working class laborers, calling out and acknowledging the importance of the contribution each one makes.

Prewriting

Choose a Topic Because they're fresh in your mind, you may want to write an evaluation of one of the poems you've just read in this section. As an alternative, you can search your memory to recall other literary works that have evoked an especially strong reaction—either positive or negative—in you.

Use Your Journal to Get Started Once you've chosen a literary work to write about, quickly write down your thoughts and impressions about that work. This process will help you sort through your feelings about the work and pinpoint what it was about the work that evoked these feelings.

Review the Work In a critical evaluation, it isn't enough to simply state your opinion about a work—you have to back up your opinion. As a result, it's essential to review the work you've chosen to refresh your memory and to gather details to back up your opinion. You might want to use note cards to record passages and details you identify. Look at this example:

Opinion: Whitman vividly captures the unique importance of work to each person.

Support: "Each singing what belongs to him or her and to none else," I Hear America Singing, line 9

Organize Your Ideas Arrange your note cards into groups, with each group focusing on one of your opinions or on a single aspect of the work.

Drafting

Follow a Clear Organization The best way to organize your evaluation is to follow the classic sequence of thesis-body-conclusion: stating your main idea clearly in your introduction, developing it with specific examples in the body, and clinching it with a persuasive restatement in your conclusion. Focus each of your body paragraphs on a single main point.

APPLYING LANGUAGE SKILLS: Quotations and Quotation Marks

Use quotation marks to set off direct quotations from literary works. Commas and periods go inside the final quotation marks, colons and semicolons go outside.

Poe opens his poem, "Once upon a midnight dreary."

"I celebrate myself, and sing myself": surely this is among the most famous lines in American poetry.

When a question mark or exclamation point is part of the quotation, place it inside the final closing quotation marks; otherwise, place it outside:

The poet asks, "Was it a dream?"

Why does the poet ask if it was "a dream"?

Writing Application As you revise your critical evaluation, check that you are using quotation marks correctly.

Writer's Solution Connection
Language Lab

For more practice with quotation marks, see the Language Lab lesson on Semicolons, Colons, and Quotation Marks in the Punctuation unit.

APPLYING LANGUAGE SKILLS: Indirect and Direct Quotations

When you use a **direct quotation**, you repeat someone else's words exactly. When you use an **indirect quotation**, you paraphrase, or restate, someone else's words.

Indirect:

The critic wrote that Emily Dickinson was the greatest American poet.

Direct:

The critic wrote, "Emily Dickinson was the greatest American poet."

Practice Decide whether each sentence makes a direct or indirect quotation. Then add quotation marks as needed.

1. The writer said that citizens should be concerned.

2. Pascal wrote Man is a reed, but a thinking reed.

Writing Application Check that you have used proper punctuation for direct and indirect quotations.

Writer's Solution Connection Writing Lab

For additional instruction and support in all stages of the writing process, use the models and activities in the tutorial on Response to Literature.

Back Up Your Opinions Throughout your evaluation, cite details and passages from the literary work to support your opinions. For example, if you say that a poem has musical qualities, quote passages that contain sound devices such as rhyme and alliteration.

Revising

Use a Checklist Go back to the Writing Skills Focus on page 422, and use the items as a checklist to evaluate and revise your evaluation.

▶ Have I followed a clear and logical organization throughout the evaluation? What can I do to improve the organization?

▶ Are my key ideas thoroughly supported with specific examples from the text? What additional support can I include?

▶ Have I maintained a consistent writing style that is appropriate to my topic? How can I refine my style?

REVISION MODEL

① the "varied carols" of

By outlining ⌄the American working landscape, Whitman

creates poetry that inspires.

① The writer strengthens the conclusion with a quotation to illustrate the point.

Publishing

Create a Class Literary Magazine As a group project, gather the critical evaluations of several class members into a class literary magazine. Include a cover, title, and table of contents; artistically talented students might also create illustrations to accompany the pieces.

Publish On-line To reach a wide audience, consider publishing your response on-line. You might post your work to an on-line bulletin board, a student magazine, or a Web site devoted to the writer you discuss.

Real-World Reading Skills Workshop

Strategies for Success

Before you buy or use products—food, games, computer software, clothing, and so on—it is important to read and understand the information printed on the packaging.

Identify the Type of Data Identify the kind of information you are reading—ingredients, care instructions, safety warnings, nutritional information, or directions for use. Classifying the information within a familiar category will help focus your reading.

Read Carefully To gain useful information from a product label, read carefully, applying these strategies:

▶ Study the order of ingredients listed on food products—it appears in order of greatest volume.

▶ Use headings and labels to understand chart data.

▶ Consider how required care—"dry clean only," for example—might influence your use of this product.

▶ Note addresses or phone numbers for assistance or questions.

▶ Check for warnings about who should not use the product. The label might offer important information about side effects as well. For example, many cold medications warn about drowsiness or slowed reaction times.

Apply the Strategy

You're at the market buying cereal for the family. You want to find a cereal everyone will like—even your eight-year-old sister—without sacrificing nutrition. Look at this product label, and decide whether this cereal meets your criteria.

1. What is the most significant ingredient in this cereal?

2. For how many vitamins or minerals does this cereal provide at least 100 percent of the daily values?

3. Where can you write for more information?

✔ *Here are other situations in which it's important to read product labels:*

▶ *Care labels for clothing*

▶ *Safety warnings on sports equipment*

▶ *Allergy notations on health and beauty aids*

CRISPY CORN

Nutrition Facts

Serving Size: 1 1/3 Cup (30g)
Servings Per Container: About 9

Amount Per Serving	CRISPY CORN	With 1/4 cup skim milk
Calories	110	150
Calories from fat	5	5

	% Daily Value **	
Total Fat 0.5g*	1%	1%
Saturated Fat 0g	0%	0%
Cholesterol 0mg	0%	1%
Sodium 21mg	9%	11%
Potassium 30mg	1%	7%
Total Carbohydrate 25g	8%	10%
Sugars 3g		
Other Carbohydrates 22g		
Protein 2g		

Vitamin A	25%	30%
Vitamin C	100%	100%
Calcium	20%	35%
Iron	100%	100%
Vitamin D	10%	25%
Vitamin E	100%	100%
Thiamin	100%	100%
Riboflavin	100%	110%
Niacin	100%	100%
Vitamin B$_2$	100%	100%
Folic Acid	100%	100%
Vitamin B$_{12}$	100%	110%
Pantothenic Acid	100%	100%
Phosphorus	10%	25%
Magnesium	0%	4%
Zinc	100%	100%

Not a significant source of dietary fiber

* Amount in cereal. A serving of cereal plus skim milk provides 0.5g fat, less than 5mg cholesterol, 270mg sodium, 230mg potassium, 31mg carbohydrate (9g sugars), and 6g protein.

** Percentage of Daily Values are based on a 2,000 calorie diet. Your daily values may be higher or lower, depending on your calorie needs:

	Calories:	2,000	2,500
Total Fat	Less than	65g	80g
Sat Fat	Less than	20g	25g
Cholesterol	Less than	300mg	300mg
Sodium	Less than	2,400mg	2,400mg
Potassium		3,500mg	3,500mg
Total Carbohydrate		300g	375g
Dietary Fiber		25g	30g

INGREDIENTS: CORN MEAL, SUGAR, WHEAT STARCH, TRICALICUM PHOSPHATE, SALT, BROWN SUGAR SYRUP, MALT EXTRACT, CORN SYRUP, HIGH MALTOSE CORN SYRUP, CALCIUM CARBONATE, VITAMIN C (SODIUM ASCORBATE), TRISODIUM PHOSPHATE, ZINC AND IRON (MINERAL NUTRIENTS), VITAMIN E (TOCOPHERYL ACETATE), B VITAMIN (NIACIN), B VITAMIN (CALCIUM PANTOTHENATE), VITAMIN B$_6$ (PYRIDOXINE HYDRO-CHLORIDE), VITAMIN B$_2$ (RIBOFLAVIN), VITAMIN B$_1$ (THIAMIN MONONITRATE), VITAMIN A (PALMITATE), B VITAMIN (FOLIC ACID), VITAMIN B$_{12}$, VITAMIN D, FRESHNESS PRESERVED BY BHT

MFR'D FOR **CEREAL CORPORATION, INC.**
CENTRAL OFFICES
OVERLAND, KANSAS 10101
© 1998 CEREAL CORP., INC.

Speaking and Listening Workshop

An interview is just an informal chat, a chance to say hello, right? Think again. Sometimes your interview is the deciding factor in getting a job or securing college admission.

Do Some Homework Both you and the interviewer have certain goals for your conversation. If possible, learn about your interviewer's focus—and any biases he or she may have—before the interview. Identify your own goals as well. What do you want to know about this job or college? Make a list of key questions.

Listen . . . and Respond Answer the questions you are asked—even if they are different from those you expected. If you can't answer, try to address the question topic from another angle. Present your own inquiries at the appropriate time, and listen thoughtfully for the information you seek.

Value the Interviewer's Time Give concise answers, and stay on the subject. Always thank your interviewer for his or her time, in person at the close of the interview and later with a note.

Tips for Handling College or Job Interviews

✔ *If you want to secure your success with a great interview, follow these strategies:*
- ▶ Make eye contact with the interviewer.
- ▶ Be courteous and respectful.
- ▶ Develop replies as you did questions—avoid giving yes or no answers in favor of greater depth.
- ▶ Focus on what you can offer the school or business.
- ▶ Relax. It's okay to make a small joke or express your enthusiasm appropriately.

Apply the Strategies

You're at a college or job interview. Consider carefully, and respond to each of the following situations.

1. The interviewer asks you to describe your experience with a skill you have never tried. What might you say?
2. After introducing herself, the interviewer sits back and waits for you to speak. Develop some questions to jump-start the interview.
3. As the meeting progresses, your interest in the job or school increases. How might you express your enthusiasm appropriately to the interviewer? Role-play some ideas with a partner.

Extended Reading Opportunities

This unit focuses on a time of rapid growth character-ized by faith in the human spirit and appreciation for nature. The following are a few possibilities for extend-ing your exploration of the literature of the period.

Suggested Titles

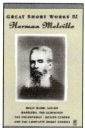

Great Short Works of Herman Melville
Herman Melville

A young sailor held captive in the Marquesas Islands makes a daring escape to Tahiti, where he lives on the beach before joining the crew of a ship bound for Hawaii. No, this is not the plot of an adventure story—it's the story of Herman Melville's life. In his day, the author was best known not for the symbolic richness of *Moby-Dick,* but for exotic tales of South Sea adven-tures. This collection includes a number of these works, which were drawn from Melville's ex-periences aboard whaling ships in the South Pacific.

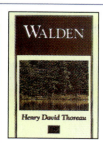

Walden
Henry David Thoreau

To read *Walden* is to under-stand why Henry David Thoreau still has the power to influence and inspire today's leaders, writers, and environ-mentalists. One of only two Thoreau books published in his lifetime, *Walden* received little attention when it appeared in 1845. Since then, it has been recognized as a literary master-piece. It describes Thoreau's two-year experiment in self-sufficiency, in which he built and lived in a small wooden hut on the shores of Walden Pond, near Concord, Massachusetts.

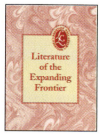

Literature of the Expanding Frontier

As our nation grew, the frontier was pushed farther and farther west as pioneers, lured by the promise of wide-open spaces, journeyed into untamed lands. This collection of stories, folk tales, songs, and poems captures the spirit of these courageous people who lived life on the edge of an expanding frontier. Their litera-ture conveys the excitement of a time when both land and opportunities seemed limitless.

Other Possibilities

The House of the Seven Gables   Nathaniel Hawthorne
The Legend of Sleepy Hollow   Washington Irving
The Deerslayer   James Fenimore Cooper

Detail of Battle of Cedar Creek (partial study for larger painting), Julian Scott, Historical Society of Plainfield, New Jersey

Division, Reconciliation, and Expansion (1850–1914)

"If we do not make common cause to save the good old ship of the Union on this voyage, nobody will have a chance to pilot her on another voyage."

—Abraham Lincoln, President of the United States of America, February 15, 1861

"I worked night and day for twelve years to prevent the war, but I could not. The North was mad and blind, would not let us govern ourselves, and so the war came. Now it must go on until the last man of this generation falls in his tracks and his children seize his musket and fight our battles."

—Jefferson Davis, President of the Confederate States of America, July 17, 1864

Timeline
1850 – 1914

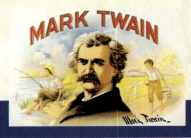

1850	1860	1870

American Events

- **1852** Harriet Beecher Stowe's *Uncle Tom's Cabin* becomes an instant bestseller.
- **1855** Walt Whitman publishes first edition of *Leaves of Grass.*
- **1855** *My Bondage and My Freedom*, Frederick Douglass's second autobiography makes its appearance. ▶

- **1858** Oliver Wendell Holmes publishes *The Autocrat of the Breakfast-Table.*
- **1858** Lincoln-Douglas debates help make Abraham Lincoln a national figure.
- **1859** John Brown, an abolitionist, leads a raid on federal arsenal at Harpers Ferry, Virginia; he is hanged for treason. ▲
- **1859** The Supreme Court supports slave owners in the Dred Scott decision.

- **1860** Essays by Ralph Waldo Emerson published as *The Conduct of Life.*
  - **1860** Republican Abraham Lincoln is elected United States president.
  - **1860** South Carolina secedes from the Union.
  - **1860** Civil War begins in April with firing on Fort Sumter.
  - **1861** Lincoln inaugurated in March.
  - **1862** Julia Ward Howe writes "The Battle Hymn of the Republic."
- **1862** Major battles are fought at Shiloh, Antietam, and Fredericksburg.
- **1863** After Antietam, Lincoln issues the Emancipation Proclamation.
- **1863** Union forces lose at Chancellorsville but win at Gettysburg and Vicksburg.
- **1864** Lincoln wins reelection. ▶
- **1865** President Lincoln is assassinated.
- **1865** The 13th Amendment abolishes slavery.
- **1865** General Robert E. Lee surrenders to General Ulysses S. Grant at Appomattox. ▶
- **1869** The Wyoming and Utah territories grant women the right to vote.

- **1870** Bret Harte publishes *The Luck of Roaring Camp and Other Stories.*
- **1876** Baseball's National League founded.
- **1876** Republican Rutherford B. Hayes wins the presidential election despite losing the popular vote.
- **1876** Mark Twain publishes *The Adventures of Tom Sawyer.* ▲
- **1877** The Compromise of 1877 ends military occupation of the South.
  - **1877** Thomas Edison patents the phonograph.

World Events

- **1855** England: Alfred, Lord Tennyson publishes his long poem *Maud.*
- **1857** France: Gustave Flaubert completes *Madame Bovary*, a classic novel of realism.
  - **1859** England: Charles Dickens adds to his fame with *A Tale of Two Cities.*
  - **1859** England: Charles Darwin introduces theory of evolution in *The Origin of Species.* ◀

- **1861** England: George Eliot (Mary Ann Evans) publishes her popular novel *Silas Marner.*
- **1862** France: Louis Pasteur proposes modern germ theory of disease.
- **1863** Mexico: French occupy Mexico City and establish Maximilian as emperor of Mexico.
- **1864** England: *Dramatis Personae* by Robert Browning appears.
- **1865** England: Lewis Carroll completes *Alice's Adventures in Wonderland.*
- **1865** Germany: Karl Benz builds first automobile powered by the internal-combustion engine.

- **1869** France: Jules Verne publishes *Twenty Thousand Leagues Under the Sea.*
- **1872** Russia: Leo Tolstoy publishes *War and Peace.*
- **1874** France: Claude Monet gathers Impressionist painters for first exhibition.
- **1877** England: First tennis championship held at Wimbledon. ▼
- **1879** Norway: Henrick Ibsen writes *A Doll's House.*

1880   **1890**   **1900**

American Events

- **1883** Railroads adopt standard time zones.
- **1883** The Brooklyn Bridge is opened.
- **1884** Mark Twain publishes *The Adventures of Huckleberry Finn.*

- **1886** Statue of Liberty dedicated in New York Harbor. ▲

- **1888** Great mid-March blizzard in eastern United States piles 30-foot drifts in New York's Herald Square. ◄

- **1890** Last major battle between U.S. troops and Native Americans fought at Wounded Knee, South Dakota.
- **1890** Daughters of the American Revolution founded in Washington.
- **1893** Boston and Chicago are linked by long-distance telephone.
- **1893** Ambrose Bierce publishes *Can Such Things Be?*
- **1894** Kate Chopin's *Bayou Folk* published.
- **1895** Stephen Crane publishes *The Red Badge of Courage.*
- **1895** First professional football game played in Latrobe, Pennsylvania.
- **1896** Paul Laurence Dunbar publishes *Lyrics of Lowly Life.*
- **1896** *The Country of the Pointed Firs,* Sarah Orne Jewett's masterpiece, appears.

- **1901** President William McKinley shot in Buffalo; succeeded by Theodore Roosevelt.
- **1903** Jack London publishes *The Call of the Wild.*
- **1903** Boston Red Sox and Pittsburgh Pirates play in first World Series.
- **1903** Wright Brothers stay aloft for 582 feet in their airplane at Kitty Hawk, North Carolina. ▲
- **1905** Willa Cather publishes *The Troll Garden.*
- **1905** Edith Wharton's *The House of Mirth* appears.
- **1908** Henry Ford builds his first car. ▼

- **1909** National Association for the Advancement of Colored People (NAACP) founded.

World Events

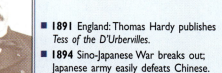

- **1881** French scientist Louis Pasteur administers the first successful rabies vaccination. ▶
- **1884** Russia: Leo Tolstoy completes *The Death of Ivan Ilyich.*
- **1886** England: Thomas Hardy publishes *The Mayor of Casterbridge.*

- **1891** England: Thomas Hardy publishes *Tess of the D'Urbervilles.*
- **1894** Sino-Japanese War breaks out; Japanese army easily defeats Chinese.
- **1895** Germany: Wilhelm Roentgen discovers X-rays.
- **1898** France: Pierre and Marie Curie discover radium and polonium.

- **1901** Italy: First transatlantic radio telegraphic message is achieved by Marconi.
- **1903** Spain: Pablo Picasso paints *The Old Guitarist.*

- **1904** Russo-Japanese War begins.
- **1905** Germany: Albert Einstein proposes his relativity theory. ◄
- **1908** Italy: Earthquake in Calabria and Sicily: 150,000 killed.

CHARLESTON

MERCURY

EXTRA:

Passed unanimously at 1.15 o'clock, P. M., December 20th, 1860.

AN ORDINANCE

To dissolve the Union between the State of South Carolina and other States united with her under the compact entitled "The Constitution of the United States of America."

We, the People of the State of South Carolina, in Convention assembled, do declare and ordain, and it is hereby declared and ordained,

That the Ordinance adopted by us in Convention, on the twenty-third day of May, in the year of our Lord one thousand seven hundred and eighty-eight, whereby the Constitution of the United States of America was ratified, and also, all Acts and parts of Acts of the General Assembly of this State, ratifying amendments of the said Constitution, are hereby repealed; and that the union now subsisting between South Carolina and other States, under the name of "The United States of America," is hereby dissolved.

THE

UNION

IS

DISSOLVED!

▲ **Analyze a Primary Source** This broadside announced the news of South Carolina's decision to secede from the Union. How might you have reacted to this poster if you were a citizen of this state? What questions would you have asked? Why?

▲ **Support a Hypothesis** What evidence is there to suggest that this Pennsylvania soldier and his family tried to continue normal life even while encamped?

The Story of the Times
1850 – 1914

The years between 1850 and 1914 witnessed a transformation of the United States. During those years, America changed from a decentralized, mostly agricultural nation to the modern industrial nation that we know today. This transformation began with the Civil War. The Civil War era was a time of intense conflict. Americans took up arms against other Americans to determine which should prevail: North or South? freedom or slavery? the federal Union or states' rights? The North won, the Union held, and slavery was abolished, but at a devastating cost to the nation.

Historical Background

Prelude to War Disagreements over slavery were nothing new, but the controversy was rekindled in 1850 by passage of the Fugitive Slave Act. It required all citizens—of free states as well as slave states—to help catch runaway slaves. Southerners saw the law as just; northerners, as an outrage.

The expansion of slavery into the West was hotly contested. When, in 1854, the Kansas-Nebraska Act opened up a vast area of previously free western land to slavery, the argument became a fight. "We will engage in competition for the virgin soil of Kansas," a senator from New York insisted. The "competition" turned Kansas into a bloody battleground.

Just as it dominated politics and preoccupied the nation, the controversy over slavery influenced the literature of the day—and in one classic case, literature fueled the controversy. Harriet Beecher Stowe's novel *Uncle Tom's Cabin*, published in 1852, vividly depicted the cruelty of slavery. The book became a powerful antislavery weapon, selling more than 300,000 copies within a year. Its impact was such that within three years no fewer than thirty southern novels came out attempting to counter its influence.

The deep national division intensified in 1859 when a group of antislavery extremists raided a federal arsenal. Led by John Brown, the group had intended to provoke an armed slave revolt. The attempt failed, and Brown was executed for treason, but this only fed the controversy which now threatened to escalate out of control.

The Union Is Dissolved The conflict between North and South came to a head when Abraham Lincoln was elected in 1860. Lincoln represented the newly formed Republican party, which had dedicated itself to halting the spread of slavery. South Carolina had threatened to secede if Lincoln was elected, and in December it did so. Six states followed South Carolina out of the Union. In February 1861, the secessionist states established the Confederate States of America.

Fighting began on April 11, 1861, when Confederate artillery fired on Union troops holding Fort Sumter, in Charleston Harbor. Many on both sides anticipated a short war ending in victory. No one could know what lay ahead—the carnage of Antietam, where 23,000 men fell in a single day; the deprivation of the seige of Vicksburg, where people survived by eating dogs and rats; the wholesale destruction of Georgia, when Union general William T. Sherman's troops marched to the sea. In fact, the devastating war would last four long years.

By the time Confederate general Robert E. Lee surrendered to Union general Ulysses S. Grant in the spring of 1865, more than 620,000 soldiers had lost their lives. Nearly that number had been wounded. The South lay in ruins, its cities razed, its farms and plantations destroyed.

An Expanding America If conflict characterized the Civil War years, change—on an astonishing scale—characterized the period that followed. Over the next fifty years, physical expansion and industrialization transformed our landscape, economy, society, and identity.

The Homestead Act of 1862 promised 160 acres of land to anyone who would farm it for five years. This shifted the westward movement into high gear. Half a million farmers, including tens of thousands of emancipated African Americans, staked claims on the Great Plains. Miners went west by the thousands, lured by the prospect of striking it rich in gold. Still others moved west to become cattle ranchers. Westward expansion was

▲ **Compare and Contrast** Robert E. Lee (left) and Ulysses S. Grant (right) were the military leaders of the Confederacy and the Union, respectively. What can you infer about their different personalities and backgrounds by comparing and contrasting their posture and dress?

▲ **Link Past to Present** This picture shows a young Confederate soldier, Private Edwin Jennison. Most of the soldiers in both armies were between the ages of 18 and 21. Some were even younger. What problems do you think a 16-year-old would face? Could a 16-year-old serve in the army today? Explain.

▲ **Respond to a Photograph** This 1865 photograph shows the effects of the war on southern cities. What adjectives would you use to describe the destruction?

▼ **Analyze a Situation** For African Americans, the West offered the hope of freedom. Here the Shores family poses in front of their Nebraska sod house. What opportunities might the West offer African Americans that the East did not?

boosted by completion of the first transcontinental railroad in 1868. As the national railroads grew, the covered wagon—symbol of the American pioneer—was replaced by the railroad as the main means of transportation.

The Disappearing Frontier By 1890, the frontier as Americans had known it for centuries had ceased to exist. The steady influx of settlers, the burgeoning railroads, the growth of mining and cattle ranching—all had combined to transform the West. Gone were the great herds of buffalo. Gone was the expanse of open range. In its place was an enormous patchwork of plowed fields and grazing lands, separated by miles of barbed wire fencing.

Gone, too, were the Indian nations, many of which had depended on the buffalo for survival. By 1890, virtually all the Native Americans in the West had been forced from their land. Decades of fierce and bloody resistance had ultimately proved futile. "I am tired of fighting," Chief Joseph of the Nez Percé reportedly said after being hunted down by the United States Army in 1877. Like others before them, Chief Joseph and his people were sent to live in Indian Territory, in what is now Oklahoma. However, even Indian Territory, which Congress had set aside in 1834, was not safe from white encroachment. In 1889, unassigned land in Indian Territory was opened up to settlers.

The frontier may have disappeared, but its legacy lived on in a rich western folk tradition. Larger-than-life folk heros like Pecos Bill were celebrated in tall tales and legends. The frontier survived, too, in the songs of the sod busters and railroad workers, cowpokes, and miners.

A Changing American Society With the introduction of electricity in the 1880's, the second Industrial Revolution began in earnest. Electricity replaced steam power in many manufacturing industries. The now familiar trappings of modern life began to make their appearance: the electric light, telephone, automobile, motion picture, phonograph. The mass production of consumer goods sparked the rise of an important new medium: advertising. Skyscrapers, department stores, and mass transportation became part of city life—as did noise, traffic jams, air pollution, crime, and slums.

The country's industrial and urban growth were both fueled by immigration. Between 1865 and 1915, 25 million people came to the United States seeking freedom and economic opportunity. (By comparison, the population of the entire nation at the end of the Civil War was 31.5 million.) Most, though not all, of the newcomers settled in cities. In the same period, millions of Americans left farms and small towns and moved to the cities seeking work. This influx swelled urban populations and provided an inexhaustible supply of cheap labor for industry.

The industrial boom of the late nineteenth century created new extremes of wealth and poverty. The wages of industrial workers were so low that a single worker, or even two, often could not support a family. Child labor became the norm among the poor working class. Immigrant families often lived in small, dark, unventilated apartments with no toilet. In these conditions, disease was rampant.

Meanwhile, a relative handful of men—the owners of big industrial corporations—made fortunes and lived like royalty. Their ostentatious displays of wealth led Mark Twain to dub this period "The Gilded Age," implying a thin veneer of glitter over something of poor quality.

Indeed, just beneath the nation's prosperity, discontentment grew. Women, African Americans, and workers agitated for changes in their social, economic, and political status. Women still did not have the vote; most African Americans, despite emancipation, were hardly better off in 1914 than they had been in 1850; labor reform was desperately needed. Bitter struggles erupted between emerging workers' unions and management.

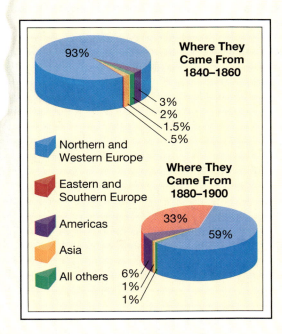

▲ **Interpret a Pattern** Most new immigrants settled in cities. Use these charts to summarize the changing pattern of immigration in the late 1800's. Where did most immigrants come from between 1840 and 1860? 1880 and 1900?

▼ **Read a Graph** The ups and downs of the economy were felt more sharply as the nation industrialized and more people worked for wages. Which years were the most prosperous? In which years did severe depression strike?

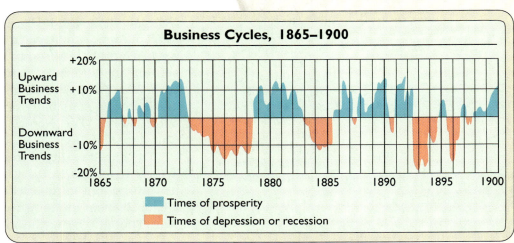

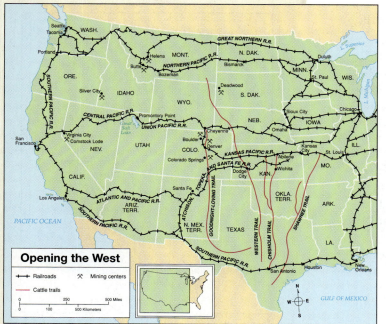

Opening the West

+‒+	Railroads	✕	Mining centers
—	Cattle trails		

0　　　250　　　500 Miles
0　　100　　500 Kilometers

▲ **Read a Map** Railroads, mining, and cattle grazing helped open the Great Plains for later settlement, as indicated on this map. Which cattle trail ended in Abilene? In Cheyenne? What relationships do you see between railroads and cattle trails? Railroads and mining centers?

◄ **Analyze a Primary Source** Barbed wire fencing was introduced in the 1870's. Barbed wire was used to separate privately owned land. How might Native Americans react to this physical and symbolic addition to the landscape? Explain.

Literature of the Period

Wartime Voices Thousands of diaries, letters, journals, and speeches were produced during the war, providing a richly detailed and moving record of what Americans—from the lowliest private to General Lee himself experienced. The 400,000-word diary of Mary Chesnut, the wife of a high-ranking Confederate officer, is a notable example of the extraordinary literary output of the Civil War years.

One of the greatest masters of the language at mid-century was President Lincoln. His speeches and letters are models of clarity and eloquence. His Gettysburg Address, a mere ten sentences in length, has become a classic expression of the meaning of American democracy.

Lincoln guided the nation through the worst crisis in its history. At the end, however, he did not have the chance to reconstruct the Union. Just days after Lee's surrender, Lincoln was assassinated. He died on April 15, 1865. The nation, war-torn and weary, would have to face the daunting tasks of reconciliation and reconstruction without him.

Frontier Voices As America expanded westward, so, too, did America's literature. In this period, for the first time, a number of writers represented the Midwest and the Far West. Some, like Bret Harte and Willa Cather, were born in the East or South but later moved West. As a young man, Harte moved from New York to California. Cather moved from Virginia to Nebraska as a child. One of the greatest writers in all of American literature—Mark Twain—grew up in Hannibal, Missouri, but traveled widely, settling in a Nevada mining town during the Civil War. Twain drew on the colorful language and outsized sensibility of the West for his first short story, "The Notorious Jumping Frog of Calaveras County."

The harsh reality of frontier life coupled with artists' reactions to the Civil War gave rise to a new movement in American literature called Realism. Realism in literature began after the Civil War. Though the war's outcome had given the nation a hard-won sense of unity, the war's enormous cost in human life had shattered the nation's idealism. Young writers turned away from the Romanticism that was popular before the war. Instead, writers began to focus on portraying "real life" as ordinary people lived it and attempted to show characters and events in an honest, objective, almost factual way. Willa Cather, for example, was a Realist noted for her unflinching portrayal of the loneliness and cultural isolation of life on the prairie. In "A Wagner Matinée," she contrasts this isolation with the cultural richness of an eastern city.

An important literary offshoot of Realism was Naturalism. Naturalist writers also depicted real people in real situations, but they believed that forces larger than the individual—nature, fate, heredity—shaped individual destiny. Jack London, for example, set much of his fiction in Alaska, where the environment was cruel and unforgiving. The theme of human endurance in the face of overwhelming natural forces pervades his fiction, including "To Build a Fire."

If the reality these writers depicted seemed always to be a harsh one, it was because hardship influenced their artistic vision. It was a vision rooted in war, in the frontier, and, increasingly, in America's growing cities.

Literature of Discontent The social ills that grew out of industrialization came under the sharp eye and pen of many talented writers of the day. Kate Chopin's writing, for example, explored women's desire for equality and independence. The Naturalists saw industrialization as a force against which individuals were powerless. Stephen Crane, a leader of the Naturalist movement, took this view in his first novel, *Maggie: A Girl of the Streets,* a realistic depiction of life in New York City's slums. Poets, too, captured a growing sense of dissatisfaction. Paul Laurence Dunbar's "We Wear the Mask" revealed the alienation of African Americans who smile in white society to mask despair.

By 1914, America had grown up; in a sense, American literature had, too. The Civil War, the closing of the frontier, and industrialization had brought about a loss of innocence, a shift from idealism to pragmatism in the American character. In their rejection of Romanticism and embrace of Realism, American writers reflected this change.

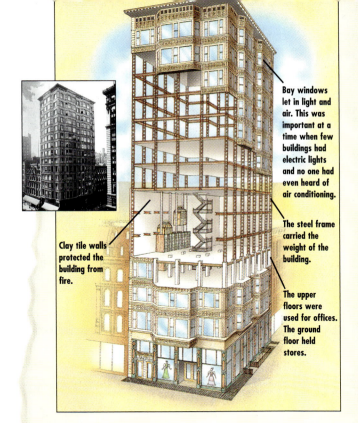

Bay windows let in light and air. This was important at a time when few buildings had electric lights and no one had even heard of air conditioning.

The steel frame carried the weight of the building.

Clay tile walls protected the building from fire.

The upper floors were used for offices. The ground floor held stores.

▲ **Interpret an Illustration** As people crowded into American cities, architects began building up instead of out. When the Reliance Building in Chicago was built in the 1890's, its sixteen stories made it a "skyscraper." According to this illustration, what new technology of the period made buildings of more than six stories possible?

United States Patents Issued 1861–1900	
Five-Year Periods	**Number of Patents**
1861–1865	20,725
1866–1870	58,734
1871–1875	60,976
1876–1880	64,462
1881–1885	97,156
1886–1890	110,358
1891–1895	108,420
1896–1900	112,188

▲ **Draw a Conclusion** What does this chart suggest about the relationship between new inventions and the growth of the country?

The Development of American English

MARK TWAIN AND THE AMERICAN LANGUAGE

by Richard Lederer

American literature comes of age

On February 18, 1885, thirty thousand copies of Mark Twain's *The Adventures of Huckleberry Finn* were released in the United States. The novel turned out to be Twain's masterpiece, and it changed the direction of American letters. Twain captured the everyday speech of characters, instead of the more formal, standard English that writers before him used. In *The Adventures of Huckleberry Finn*, Twain used seven distinct dialects to reflect the speech patterns of various characters, and he also became the first important author to show the freshness and vitality of the new American idiom in narrative as well as in dialogue. Just as Geoffrey Chaucer's *The Canterbury Tales* is the first significant work written in English, *Huckleberry Finn* is the first novel of world rank to be written entirely in American.

Readin', Writin', and Twain

Twain held strong opinions about a passel of subjects, and he possessed the gift of being able to state these views in memorable ways: "It's better to keep your mouth shut and appear stupid than to open it and remove all doubt"; "Be careful about reading health books. You may die of a misprint."

Twain also had a lot to say about style, literature, and the American language that he, more than any other writer, helped to shape:

▶ *On American English, compared with British English:* The property has gone into the hands of a joint stock company, and we own the bulk of the shares.

▶ *On dialects:* I have traveled more than anyone else, and I have noticed that even the angels speak English with an accent.

▶ *On choosing words:* The difference between the almost right word and the right word is really a large matter—'tis the difference between the lightning-bug and the lightning.

▶ *On style* (in a letter to a twelve-year-old boy): I notice that you use plain, simple language, short words, and brief sentences. That is the way to write English—it is the modern way and the best way. Stick to it; and don't let fluff and flowers and verbosity creep in.

▶ *On being concise:* A successful book is not made of what is in it, but what is left out of it.

▶ *On using short words:* I never write metropolis for seven cents when I can get the same for city. I never write

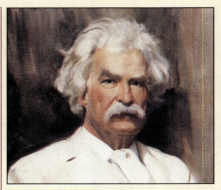

policeman because I can get the same for cop.

▶ *On reading:* The man who does not read good books has no advantage over the man who can't read them.

Activities

1. With a group, discuss Twain's statement on dialects, above. In your discussion, include some of the outstanding characteristics of the dialect that you speak.

2. Use one of Mark Twain's statements about writing or language, above, as the thesis for an essay or discussion on the subject.

3. In 1885, Twain wrote in his notebook, "My works are like water. The works of the great masters are like wine. But everyone drinks water." Choose a passage from one of Twain's stories or essays, and show how that passage exemplifies the author's philosophy of style.

PART **1**   *A Nation Divided*

Fight for the Standard, Wadsworth
Atheneum, Hartford, Connecticut

Possibly the most painful chapter in our nation's history, the Civil War era left a lasting imprint on our nation's identity. Although at the time, the war tore our nation apart, the legacy that it left behind is the country's ability to survive in the face of tremendous adversity.

Guide for Interpreting

Stephen Crane (1871–1900)

Stephen Crane hadn't even been born when the last battle of the American Civil War was fought, yet he is best remembered for his compelling depiction of the conflict. During his tragically brief life, Crane established himself as both a leader of the Naturalist movement and one of the greatest writers of his time.

Early in his career, Crane worked as a newspaper writer in New York City. His experiences there inspired his first novel, *Maggie: A Girl of the Streets* (1893). Its grimly realistic portrayal of life in the city's slums was so frank and shocking that Crane was unable to find a publisher, so he printed the book at his own expense.

His second novel, published in 1895, was *The Red Badge of Courage: An Episode of the American Civil War*. A psychological exploration of a young soldier's mental and emotional reactions under enemy fire, the wildly successful novel earned international acclaim for the twenty-four-year-old. Though Crane had never experienced military combat, he interviewed Civil War veterans and studied photographs, battle plans, and biographical accounts before writing the realistic battle scenes.

Crane later viewed war firsthand when he served as a newspaper correspondent during the Greco-Turkish War in 1897 and the Spanish-American War in 1898. His war experiences provided material for a collection of poetry, *War Is Kind* (1899), but they took their toll on his health. He died of tuberculosis at the age of twenty-eight.

Stephen Foster (1826–1864)

The popular minstrel songs and sentimental ballads written by Stephen Foster earned him an honored place in American music. He composed about 200 works in his rather short lifetime, including such classics as "The Old Folks at Home" (popularly known as "Way Down Upon the Swanee River"), "Camptown Races," "Oh! Susanna," and "My Old Kentucky Home." Foster wrote the words as well as the music to most of his songs, though he collaborated with lyricist George Cooper on the Civil War ballad "Willie Has Gone to the War."

◆ Background for Understanding

HISTORY: THE BLOODY LEGACY OF THE AMERICAN CIVIL WAR

Both this short story and this song were inspired by the American Civil War, the bloodiest war in American history. The conflict claimed the lives of 600,000 soldiers—more American casualties than the total of all other wars in which the United States has fought. Hundreds of thousands more were left maimed by battle wounds and crude medical care.

© Museum of the Confederacy, Richmond, Virginia

As you read "An Episode of War," keep in mind that amputation was routine treatment for injured limbs. A wounded soldier knew that he risked losing his injured arm or leg to a surgeon's saw, like those in this Civil War medical kit.

When the war began, neither side was prepared to care for the wounded. There were no ambulances to transport them from the battlefield, no medical corps to treat them, no medicines, no nursing staff. Barns, warehouses, and schools were converted into makeshift hospitals, like the one described in this story. The conditions were terrible. Even a minor injury was liable to result in death, most often from disease; twice as many Civil War soldiers died of infections than of combat wounds.

◆ An Episode of War ◆
Willie Has Gone to the War

◆ *Literature and Your Life*

CONNECT YOUR EXPERIENCE

Being "in control" of a situation and making responsible decisions help to make you feel in command of your life. Often, however, you don't have control over the situations—good and bad—that life presents. Do you imagine that the soldiers who fought in the Civil War felt as if they were in control of their destinies?

Journal Writing Has a chance event ever had an effect on your life? Write about the experience and its impact.

THEMATIC FOCUS: A NATION DIVIDED

Stephen Crane was a proponent of Naturalism, which holds that all humanity is driven by the winds of chance, with human suffering the only certainty. Stephen Foster was a popular musician. As you read the two selections, ask yourself: How do these works reflect a difference in attitude toward the "glories" of war?

◆ Build Vocabulary

WORD ROOTS: *-greg-*

Crane describes a group of men and horses pulling cannons as an "aggregation of wheels, levers, and motors." The word *aggregation* contains the root *-greg-*, meaning "herd" or "flock." An *aggregation* is a group of people or things considered as a whole.

precipitate
aggregation
inscrutable
disdainfully
glade

WORD BANK

Preview these words from the selections.

◆ Grammar and Style

CORRECT USE OF *LIKE* AND *AS*

Although *like* and *as, as if*, and *as though* are often used interchangeably, they actually serve different purposes. **As, as if**, and **as though** are subordinating conjunctions that introduce subordinating—or less important—ideas. **Like** is a preposition; it takes a noun or pronoun as its object and introduces a prepositional phrase. Notice the difference between these examples from "An Episode of War":

[The lieutenant] looked quickly at a man near him *as if he suspected it was a case of personal assault.*

He had winced *like a man stung* ...

◆ Literary Focus

REALISM AND NATURALISM

"An Episode of War" is a harsh tale of how a chance event forever changes the life of a Civil War officer. The story is characteristic of two new literary movements that sprang up in reaction to Romanticism—an earlier nineteenth-century literary movement that stressed emotion, imagination, and an appreciation of nature. The first movement, **Realism**, sought to portray real life as faithfully and accurately as possible. Realists focused on ordinary people faced with the harsh realities of everyday life—a far cry from the improbable situations and optimistic vision of the world typical of Romanticism.

From the Realism movement grew **Naturalism**, which also focused on truthfully portraying the lives of ordinary people. Naturalists, however, believed that a person's fate is determined by environment, heredity, and chance. As a result, they often depicted characters whose lives were shaped by forces they could neither understand nor control, but endured with strength and dignity, thereby affirming the significance of their existence.

Reading for Success

Interactive Reading Strategies

Interactive is a term that applies to more than video games and computer technology. It also describes a way to approach your reading. Your experiences and knowledge actively affect the way you understand a piece of literature. The more you bring to your reading, the more you'll get from it. Use these strategies to help you.

Use prior knowledge.

As you read, keep in mind what you already know about the subject—in this case, the Civil War. Use that knowledge to make connections with what the author is saying.

Question.

Ask questions about important ideas in the text. List ideas you'd like to clarify or topics about which you would like to learn. Then search the text for answers to your questions.

Predict.

Using information from the text—details, dialogue, facts—make predictions about what will happen. Confirm or revise predictions as you gain new information or understanding from your reading.

Clarify details and information.

Focus on sections that seem confusing or unclear, and use questioning to identify the source of your confusion.
- ▶ Draw on prior knowledge to place information in context.
- ▶ Reread an earlier passage for information you may have missed.
- ▶ Organize information visually. Setting details, for example, may be clearer if you draw them, and relationships among characters might be understood if you represented them in a visual organizer.
- ▶ Read ahead. Your confusion may be clarified by text read later on.

Use your knowledge of the historical time period.

Consider the social and political climate surrounding a piece of writing as part of its setting and context. Determine how the attitudes of both writer and characters reflect the ideas of their day.

Respond to the work.

Reflect on what you have read. Do you agree with the characters' ideas or actions? How might you behave in the same situation?

As you read "An Episode of War," look at the notes along the sides. They demonstrate how to apply these strategies to your reading.

An Episode of War

Stephen Crane

The lieutenant's rubber blanket lay on the ground, and upon it he had poured the company's supply of coffee. Corporals and other representatives of the grimy and hot-throated men who lined the breast-work[1] had come for each squad's portion.

The lieutenant was frowning and serious at this task of division. His lips pursed as he drew with his sword various crevices in the heap, until brown squares of coffee, astoundingly equal in size, appeared on the blanket. He was on the verge of a great triumph in mathematics, and the corporals were thronging forward, each to reap a little square, when suddenly the lieutenant cried out and looked quickly at a man near him as if he suspected it was a case of personal assault. The others cried out also when they saw blood upon the lieutenant's sleeve.

He had winced like a man stung, swayed dangerously, and then straightened. The sound of his hoarse breathing was plainly audible. He looked sadly, mystically, over the breast-work at the green face of a wood, where now were many little puffs of white smoke. During this moment the men about him gazed statuelike and silent, astonished and awed by this catastrophe which happened when catastrophes were not expected—when they had leisure to observe it.

As the lieutenant stared at the wood, they too swung their heads, so that for another instant all hands, still silent, contemplated the distant forest as if their minds were fixed upon the mystery of a bullet's journey.

---

1. **breast-work:** Low wall put up quickly as a defense in battle.

▼ **Critical Viewing** This is an actual photograph of a temporary Civil War hospital. Do you think that soldiers received quality treatment there? On what details do you base your answer? **[Assess]**

◀ **Critical Viewing**
How does this photograph correspond with Crane's description of the wounded lieutenant being helped by his men? [**Connect**]

The officer had, of course, been compelled to take his sword into his left hand. He did not hold it by the hilt. He gripped it at the middle of the blade, awkwardly. Turning his eyes from the hostile wood, he looked at the sword as he held it there, and seemed puzzled as to what to do with it, where to put it. In short, this weapon had of a sudden become a strange thing to him. He looked at it in a kind of stupefaction, as if he had been endowed with a trident, a sceptre,[2] or a spade.

> **Use prior knowledge** about the military to understand the soldier's dilemma: Many weapons are held in the right hand.

Finally he tried to sheathe it. To sheathe a sword held by the left hand, at the middle of the blade, in a scabbard hung at the left hip, is a feat worthy of a sawdust ring.[3] This wounded officer engaged in a desperate struggle with the sword and the wobbling scabbard, and during the time of it breathed like a wrestler.

> **Clarify** this awkward movement by "seeing" it in your mind.

2. **a trident, a sceptre** (trīd´ ənt; sep´ tər): Three-pronged spear; decorated ornamental rod or staff symbolizing royal authority.
3. **sawdust ring:** Ring in which circus acts are performed.

But at this instant the men, the spectators, awoke from their stone-like poses and crowded forward sympathetically. The orderly-sergeant took the sword and tenderly placed it in the scabbard. At the time, he leaned nervously backward, and did not allow even his finger to brush the body of the lieutenant. A wound gives strange dignity to him who bears it. Well men shy from his new and terrible majesty. It is as if the wounded man's hand is upon the curtain which hangs before the revelations of all existence—the meaning of ants, potentates,[4] wars, cities, sunshine, snow, a feather dropped from a bird's wing; and the power of it sheds radiance upon a bloody form, and makes the other men understand sometimes that they are little. His comrades look at him with large eyes thoughtfully. Moreover, they fear vaguely that the weight

4. **potentates** (pōt´ ən tāts): *n.*: Rulers; powerful people.

◆ **Build Vocabulary**

precipitate (prē sip´ ə tāt´) *v.*: Cause to happen before expected or desired

aggregation (ag´ grə gā´ shən) *n.*: Group or mass of distinct objects or individuals

inscrutable (in skro͞ot´ ə bəl) *adj.*: Impossible to see; completely obscure or mysterious

Question the men's fearful reaction. The soldier's wound may remind them of the life-threatening dangers of the war.

of a finger upon him might send him headlong, precipitate the tragedy, hurl him at once into the dim, grey unknown. And so the orderly-sergeant, while sheathing the sword, leaned nervously backward.

There were others who proffered assistance. One timidly presented his shoulder and asked the lieutenant if he cared to lean upon it, but the latter waved him away mournfully. He wore the look of one who knows he is the victim of a terrible disease and understands his helplessness. He again stared over the breast-work at the forest, and then, turning, went slowly rearward. He held his right wrist tenderly in his left hand as if the wounded arm was made of very brittle glass.

Use your knowledge of the historical period to realize the potential outcomes of injury during the Civil War—among them, death and amputation.

And the men in silence stared at the wood, then at the departing lieutenant; then at the wood, then at the lieutenant.

As the wounded officer passed from the line of battle, he was enabled to see many things which as a participant in the fight were unknown to him. He saw a general on a black horse gazing over the lines of blue infantry at the green woods which veiled his problems. An aide galloped furiously, dragged his horse suddenly to a halt, saluted, and presented a paper. It was, for a wonder, precisely like a historical painting.

To the rear of the general and his staff a group, composed of a bugler, two or three orderlies, and the bearer of the corps standard,[5] all upon maniacal horses, were working like slaves to hold their ground, preserve their respectful interval, while the shells boomed in the air about them, and caused their chargers to make furious quivering leaps.

A battery, a tumultuous and shining mass, was swirling toward the right. The wild thud of hoofs, the cries of the riders shouting blame and praise, menace and encouragement, and, last, the roar of the wheels, the slant of the glistening guns, brought the lieutenant to an intent pause. The battery swept in curves that stirred the heart; it made halts as dramatic as the crash of a wave on the rocks, and when it fled onward this aggregation of wheels, levers, motors had a beautiful unity, as if it were a missile. The sound of it was a war-chorus that reached into the depths of man's emotion.

The lieutenant, still holding his arm as if it were of glass, stood watching this battery until all detail of it was lost, save the figures of the riders, which rose and fell and waved lashes over the black mass.

Later, he turned his eyes toward the battle, where the shooting sometimes crackled like bush-fires, sometimes sputtered with exasperating irregularity, and sometimes reverberated like the thunder. He saw the smoke rolling upward and saw crowds of men who ran and cheered, or stood and blazed away at the inscrutable distance.

Note the soldier's detachment from the rest of the battle scene. Read ahead to find details about his thoughts and feelings.

He came upon some stragglers, and they told him how to find the field hospital. They described its exact location. In fact, these men, no longer having part in the battle, knew more of it than others. They told the performance of every corps, every division, the opinion of every general. The lieutenant, carrying his wounded arm rearward, looked upon them with wonder.

At the roadside a brigade was making coffee and buzzing with talk like a girls' boarding-school. Several officers came out to him and inquired concerning things of which he knew nothing. One, seeing his arm, began to scold. "Why, man, that's no way to do. You want to fix that thing." He appropriated the lieutenant and the lieutenant's wound. He cut the sleeve and laid bare the arm, every nerve of which softly fluttered under his touch. He bound his handkerchief over the wound, scolding away in the meantime. His tone allowed one to think that he was in the habit of being wounded every day.

Use the vivid details of this sentence to respond to the soldier's situation. You may find you understand the pain he must be feeling.

The lieutenant hung his head, feeling, in this presence, that he did not know how to be correctly wounded.

---

5. **corps standard** (kôr): Flag or banner representing a military unit.

The low white tents of the hospital were grouped around an old schoolhouse. There was here a singular commotion. In the foreground two ambulances interlocked wheels in the deep mud. The drivers were tossing the blame of it back and forth, gesticulating and berating, while from the ambulances, both crammed with wounded, there came an occasional groan. An interminable crowd of bandaged men were coming and going. Great numbers sat under the trees nursing heads or arms or legs. There was a dispute of some kind raging on the steps of the schoolhouse. Sitting with his back against a tree a man with a face as grey as a new army blanket was serenely smoking a corncob pipe. The lieutenant wished to rush forward and inform him that he was dying.

A busy surgeon was passing near the lieutenant. "Good-morning," he said, with a friendly smile. Then he caught sight of the lieutenant's arm, and his face at once changed. "Well, let's have a look at it." He seemed possessed suddenly of a great contempt for the lieutenant. This wound evidently placed the latter on a very low social plane. The doctor cried out impatiently, "What mutton-head had tied it up that way anyhow?" The lieutenant answered, "Oh, a man."

When the wound was disclosed the doctor fingered it disdainfully. "Humph," he said. "You come along with me and I'll 'tend to you." His voice contained the same scorn as if he were saying: "You will have to go to jail."

The lieutenant had been very meek, but now his face flushed, and he looked into the doctor's eyes. "I guess I won't have it amputated," he said.

"Nonsense, man! Nonsense! Nonsense!" cried the doctor. "Come along, now. I won't amputate it. Come along. Don't be a baby."

"Let go of me," said the lieutenant, holding back wrathfully, his glance fixed upon the door of the old schoolhouse, as sinister to him as the portals of death.

And this is the story of how the lieutenant lost his arm. When he reached home, his sisters, his mother, his wife, sobbed for a long time at the sight of the flat sleeve. "Oh, well," he said, standing shamefaced amid these tears, "I don't suppose it matters so much as all that."

> Do you believe the doctor? **Predict** what will happen to the lieutenant.

◆ Build Vocabulary

disdainfully (dis dān′ fəl ē) *adv*.: Showing scorn or contempt

Young Soldier: Separate Study of a Soldier Giving Water to a Wounded Companion, 1861,
Winslow Homer, Cooper-Hewitt, National Museum of Design, Smithsonian Institution

▲ **Critical Viewing** This teenaged Union soldier may have enlisted in the army in hopes of finding glory on the battlefield. How does "An Episode of War" contrast with this sentiment? **[Contrast]**

Willie Has Gone to the War

Words by George Cooper   Music by Stephen Foster

The blue bird is singing his lay,[1]
To all the sweet flow'rs of the dale,
The wild bee is roaming at play,
And soft is the sigh of the gale;
5 I stray by the brookside alone,
Where oft we have wander'd before,
And weep for my lov'd one, my own,
My Willie has gone to the war!

Willie has gone to the war, Willie,
10 Willie my lov'd one, my own;
Willie has gone to the war, Willie,
Willie my lov'd one is gone!

'Twas here, where the lily bells grow,
I last saw his noble young face,
15 And now while he's gone to the foe,
Oh! dearly I love the old place;
The whispering waters repeat
The name that I love o'er and o'er,
And daisies that nod at my feet,
20 Say Willie has gone to the war!

Willie has gone to the war, Willie,
Willie my lov'd one, my own;
Willie has gone to the war, Willie,
Willie my lov'd one is gone!

25 The leaves of the forest will fade,
The roses will wither and die,
But spring to our home in the glade,
On fairy like pinions[2] will fly;
And still I will hopefully wait
30 The day when these battles are o'er,
And pine like a bird for its mate,
Till Willie comes home from the war!

Willie has gone to the war, Willie,
Willie my lov'd one, my own;
35 Willie has gone to the war, Willie,
Willie my lov'd one is gone!

---

1. **lay** *n.*: Song or melody.
2. **pinions** (pin´ yənz) *n.*: Antiquated term meaning "wings."

◆ Build Vocabulary

glade (glād) *n.*: Open space in a wood or forest

Guide for Responding

◆ *Literature and Your Life*

Reader's Response Which aspects of "An Episode of War" did you find particularly tragic or unsettling? Explain.

Thematic Focus How does the portrayal of the Civil War in the story differ in perspective or point of view from the song?

☑ Check Your Comprehension

1. Give two reasons that the lieutenant's comrades "look at him with large eyes thoughtfully" but will not touch him in "An Episode of War."
2. In "An Episode of War," what treatment does the doctor ultimately administer to the lieutenant's wounded arm?
3. Why is the brook special to the speaker in "Willie Has Gone to the War"?

◆ Critical Thinking

INTERPRET
1. How does the way in which the lieutenant is wounded in "An Episode of War" make him a sympathetic character? **[Analyze]**
2. In "An Episode of War," the lieutenant walks with the detached air of a man watching someone else's nightmare unfold. What accounts for his numb state? **[Infer]**
3. Name three ways in which "An Episode of War" suggests that the lieutenant is seen by both himself and others as separate from, and somehow less a human being than, the uninjured people he encounters. **[Support]**
4. How does "Willie Has Gone to the War" romanticize the monotony and anguish of waiting for a soldier to return from war? **[Analyze]**

APPLY
5. According to the Naturalists, humans are weak and ineffectual beings at the mercy of deterministic forces. Defend this statement using examples from "An Episode of War." **[Defend]**

Guide for Responding (continued)

◆ Reading for Success

INTERACTIVE READING STRATEGIES

As you read, you used a series of interactive strategies that rely on your personal involvement, experiences, and knowledge to help you get the most from your reading. Consider the doctor's promise not to amputate, and answer these questions.

1. Using your knowledge of Civil War medical practices, why do you think the doctor made such a promise?
2. What was your response to this promise?
3. How does the final paragraph of the story help you to clarify the doctor's actual intent?

◆ Grammar and Style

CORRECT USE OF *LIKE* AND *AS*

The subordinating conjunction *as* sometimes introduces elliptical clauses in which all or part of the verb is omitted but understood. The omitted part of the verb is shown in brackets:

> **Like** is a preposition. **As, as if**, and **as though** are subordinating conjunctions used to introduce a subordinate clause.

He hesitated to follow the doctor, as any soldier would [hesitate].

DO NOT USE *LIKE* IN PLACE OF *AS.*

Practice On your paper, write the following sentences, correcting any errors in the use of *like, as, as if,* or *as though.* If a sentence contains no errors, write "correct."

1. The lieutenant divided the coffee evenly, just like he promised he would.
2. He staggered as though weak with fatigue.
3. The men stood as stones, frightened like they had never seen a man wounded in battle.
4. The lieutenant stumbled toward the field hospital as if a man in a trance.
5. Like any wounded man, he dwelled on the possibility of amputation.

◆ Literary Focus

REALISM AND NATURALISM

"An Episode of War" includes elements of both **Realism,** a literary movement that emphasized the faithful and accurate portrayal of ordinary life, and **Naturalism,** which generally portrayed people as being manipulated by forces beyond their control.

1. How does the fact that the lieutenant is rationing coffee at the time of his shooting contribute to the realistic quality of "An Episode of War"?
2. How can the same situation be used to support the assertion that this story is distinctly Naturalistic?
3. Give two examples of how the lieutenant exhibits the quiet, courageous endurance typical of characters in Naturalist works.
4. How would you refute the statement that "Willie Has Gone to the War" reflects Realism? Cite examples from the lyrics to support your argument.

◆ Build Vocabulary

USING THE WORD ROOT *-greg-*

Knowing that *-greg-* means "herd" or "flock" will help you remember that a *congregation* is a "group" and a *gregarious* person enjoys being part of a crowd.

Copy the paragraph below, filling in the blanks with the appropriate words from the following list.

aggregate   gregarious   congregated

The wounded soldiers ____?____ on the steps, waiting to see the doctor. They were silent, except for one ____?____ private who described his injury to everyone. In the ____?____, a nearby orderly reflected, wounded men are a quiet bunch, but there is always an exception.

USING THE WORD BANK

Copy these analogies, and complete each one with the appropriate word from the Word Bank.

1. *Quickly* is to *rapidly* as ____?____ is to *scornfully.*
2. *Hidden* is to *revealed* as ____?____ is to *obvious.*
3. *Brook* is to *stream* as ____?____ is to *meadow.*
4. *Laugh* is to *cry* as ____?____ is to *delay.*
5. *Sum* is to *parts* as ____?____ is to *individual.*

Build Your Portfolio

Idea Bank

Writing

1. **Letter** As the lieutenant, write a letter to your wife explaining how you lost your arm.

2. **Editorial** During the Civil War, infections spread by a lack of basic sanitary procedures killed more soldiers than combat wounds did. Write a newspaper editorial exposing disease and poor sanitary conditions as the biggest killers of the war.

3. **Definition Essay** What events in this story reflect the belief that humankind is helpless in the face of events it cannot control? In an essay, use "An Episode of War" to define Naturalism.

Speaking and Listening

4. **Dramatic Improvisation** Imagine what took place when the doctor informed the lieutenant that his arm was about to be amputated. Work with a small group to dramatize your interpretation of the scene. **[Performing Arts Link]**

5. **Music Performance** The Civil War inspired hundreds of songs. Among the most familiar are "Battle Hymn of the Republic" and "Dixie." Select one such Civil War song, give some background on its origins, then perform or play a recording of the song for the class. **[Music Link]**

Projects

6. **Soldier's Scrapbook** Create a scrapbook documenting the experiences of an imaginary Civil War soldier. Include photocopied photographs from history and Civil War books, and write brief captions for each. **[Social Studies Link; Art Link]**

7. **Oral Presentation on Civil War Heroines** Research Dorothea Dix, Dr. Elizabeth Blackwell, Clara Barton, or another Civil War heroine. Share your findings in an oral presentation.

Writing Mini-Lesson

Field Report on Hospital Conditions

Imagine that the lieutenant serves under a colonel who wants to know why so many of his soldiers are dying from minor wounds. Writing as the lieutenant, provide the colonel with a report on the treatment you received and the problems you observed during your stay at the army hospital.

Writing Skills Focus: Precise Details

To make your report—or any piece of writing—more vivid and complete, **include precise details** to support your ideas and opinions. Simply stating that the wounded soldiers are neglected, for example, wouldn't give the colonel enough information to solve problems. Adding precise details provides a more complete picture of hospital conditions.

Model

The wounded often lie on filthy beds and floors for hours and even days at a time without being fed, bathed or treated.

Prewriting Scan the Background for Understanding on p. 440 and the photograph on p. 443 to help you develop a list of issues for your report. Jot down the precise details you will use to support each issue. Consult a Civil War reference book if you feel that you need more information.

Drafting After an introduction in which you state the purpose of your report, present each issue and supporting details in a separate paragraph. Then, summarize the main points of your report in the conclusion. Remember to use formal language.

Revising Reread your report, checking to see that you have presented your points in a logical order and with sufficient supporting details. Ask yourself what you can do to improve your organization and what information might strengthen or clarify your writing.

Guide for Interpreting

Spirituals

Spirituals are folk songs that originated among enslaved African Americans. The songs served as an important means of communication and a way of expressing the desire for freedom and religious salvation. At the same time, the songs helped to replace lost African religious traditions and allowed men and women to maintain a connection to their musical heritage.

Plantation owners, fearing discontent among their slaves, encouraged field hands to sing while they picked cotton or sugar, reasoning that people who were busy singing could not plot escape or rebellion. The slaves, however, found ways to benefit from singing. Their songs provided an outlet for the grief and frustration they often kept bottled up inside. Spirituals also fostered a sense of personal self-worth by portraying slaves as innocents of a mighty God, deserving of a heavenly reward for their earthly labors. By grafting African styles and rhythms onto Christian hymns, enslaved Africans managed to hold on to part of their heritage. In addition, the language in some songs provided a means to communicate forbidden thoughts and feelings.

A Double Message Many spirituals had a double meaning. References to figures and events in the Bible were a kind of code for the slaves' own experience. Slaves identified with the ancient Israelites, who had once been the slaves of the Egyptians. Singing about the Israelites was a safe way to voice their own yearning for liberty. One work song did more than just express discontent; it gave directions for escape: In "Follow the Drinking Gourd," fugitive slaves were advised to follow the Big Dipper north to freedom.

◆ Background for Understanding

HISTORY: HARRIET TUBMAN AND THE UNDERGROUND RAILROAD

Africans first came to this country as slaves in 1619. After 1808, the slave trade was banned, but slavery remained legal. In response to slave rebellions in the 1820's and 1830's, many southern states enacted tough new laws. In the years before the Civil War, deprived of nearly all their rights under these laws, many enslaved Africans ran away. They were hidden and transported by the Underground Railroad, a secret network of activists dedicated to helping fugitives reach freedom in the northern states and in Canada.

One of those activists was Harriet Tubman, called the Moses of her people. In the Old Testament, Moses led the Israelites out of their captivity in Egypt. Harriet Tubman followed his example in the years before the Civil War. Born a slave around 1820, she eventually escaped to the North along the Underground Railroad. She then risked her life to go back and rescue her family. Driven by the desire to help others still oppressed, this quick-witted and courageous woman returned to the South again and again to rescue other enslaved Africans who were desperate for a life of liberty. Tubman, standing at the left, posed for this photograph with just a few of the more than 300 people she led to freedom. The spiritual "Go Down, Moses" most likely refers to Tubman as well as to the Moses of the Bible.

Swing Low, Sweet Chariot
◆ Go Down, Moses ◆

◆ *Literature and Your Life*

CONNECT YOUR EXPERIENCE
Songs have an amazing power to sway our emotions. They can soothe us when we're feeling sad, or bring back memories or special people or places. As is the case with the two songs you're about to read, songs can even help people endure great hardships.

Journal Writing Discuss one or two songs that have an especially strong emotional impact on you.

THEMATIC FOCUS: A NATION DIVIDED
In these two spirituals, you will hear the singers' pain, their yearning for freedom, and their rage against slavery. These songs bring to life the emotional impact of an issue that divided our nation for decades and played a key role in causing the Civil War.

◆ Build Vocabulary

WORD ROOTS: -press-
In "Go Down, Moses," the people of Israel are described as *oppressed*. The root *-press-* means "push." If you weren't sure of the meaning of *oppressed* but knew the root *-press-*, you might still determine that the Israelites were pushed or kept down in some way.

WORD BANK
Preview these words from the spirituals.

| oppressed |
| smite |

◆ Grammar and Style

DIRECT ADDRESS
In both spirituals, the speaker creates a dramatic effect by using **direct address** in the opening lines. When a speaker directly addresses someone or something by name, the name is set off by one or more commas, depending on its position in the sentence. Look at these examples.

> Swing low, sweet chariot,
> Coming for to carry me home.
>
> Go down, Moses,
> Way down in Egypt land.

The use of direct address adds to the emotional intensity of these songs.

◆ Literary Focus

REFRAIN
If you're searching for the meaning of a song or poem, you'll often find it in the **refrain**—a word, phrase, line, or group of lines repeated at regular intervals throughout the work. Most spirituals, including these, contain at least one refrain. It emphasizes the most important ideas and helps establish the rhythm of the song. A chorus usually sang the refrain of a spiritual, with a soloist singing the other words. This back-and-forth pattern resembles the African tradition known as "call and response." Soloists often improvised, creating new lyrics as they sang. Refrains, however, seldom changed.

◆ Reading Strategy

LISTEN
Since songs are created for the ear, not the eye, **listening** is an especially important skill for appreciating lyrics. Read each spiritual aloud, listening to its rhythm. Also pay attention to rhymes and other repeated sounds. For example, the opening line in "Go Down, Moses" contains three stressed syllables in a row. Often, the rhythms and sounds of a song suggest a mood. What mood do these three strong consecutive sounds create? What mood do you sense as you listen to these spirituals?

Swing Low, Sweet Chariot

Spiritual

Swing low, sweet chariot,
Coming for to carry me home,
Swing low, sweet chariot,
Coming for to carry me home.

5   I looked over Jordan[1] and what did I see
Coming for to carry me home,
A band of angels coming after me,
Coming for to carry me home.

If you get there before I do,
10 Coming for to carry me home,
Tell all my friends I'm coming too,
Coming for to carry me home.

Swing low, sweet chariot,
Coming for to carry me home,
15 Swing low, sweet chariot,
Coming for to carry me home.

▲ **Critical Viewing**
Looking at the clothing of the escaped slaves in this photograph, what can you infer about their lives as fugitives?
[Infer]

---

1. Jordan: River of the Near East that flows from the Lebanon Mountains through the Sea of Galilee to the Dead Sea. Many spirituals use the phrase "crossing over Jordan" as a metaphor for crossing the Ohio River to freedom or going to heaven.

GO DOWN, MOSES

Spiritual

Go down, Moses,
Way down in Egypt land
Tell old Pharaoh
To let my people go.

5   When Israel was in Egypt land
Let my people go
<u>Oppressed</u> so hard they could not stand
Let my people go.

Go down, Moses,
10 Way down in Egypt land
Tell old Pharaoh
"Let my people go."

"Thus saith the Lord," bold Moses said,
"Let my people go;
15 If not I'll <u>smite</u> your first-born dead
Let my people go."

Go down, Moses,
Way down in Egypt land,
Tell old Pharaoh,
20 "Let my people go!"

◆ **Build Vocabulary**

oppressed (ə prest′) *v.*: Kept down by cruel or unjust power or authority

smite (smīt) *v.*: To kill by a powerful blow

Guide for Responding

◆ Literature and Your Life

Reader's Response Think about the spirituals you just read. If you were a slave, which do you think would better express your feelings? Why?

Thematic Response How do spirituals soothe the feelings of longing, sadness, and injustice they express?

☑ Check Your Comprehension

1. In "Swing Low, Sweet Chariot," who is coming over Jordan to carry the speaker home?
2. According to Moses, with what punishment does the Lord threaten the Egyptians if they refuse to free the Israelites?

◆ Critical Thinking

INTERPRET

1. If "Swing Low..." is an expression of the slaves' desire for escape, explain what each of these represents: (a) chariot, (b) home, (c) band of angels. **[Interpret]**
2. In the comparison of America with ancient Egypt in "Go Down, Moses," whom does the old Pharaoh represent? **[Interpret]**
3. Compare the mood of "Go Down, Moses," with that of "Swing Low, Sweet Chariot." **[Compare]**

EVALUATE

4. Explain the effectiveness of the mix of formal and informal language in "Go Down, Moses." **[Evaluate]**

Guide for Responding (continued)

◆ Reading Strategy

LISTEN

Listening to the sounds and rhythms of "Swing Low, Sweet Chariot" and "Go Down, Moses" as you read helps you to gain more insight into the songs.

1. Explain how each of the songs uses rhythm, rhyme, and repetition to reinforce meaning.
2. In each song, which lines might have been sung by a soloist and which by the chorus? Why?

◆ Literary Focus

REFRAIN

Both "Swing Low, Sweet Chariot" and "Go Down, Moses" use **refrains** to express the speaker's deepest yearnings. Sometimes the refrain is a single repeated line; at other times, the refrain is an entire stanza. Each time the refrain is repeated, the image or emotion it contains gathers force.

1. List all the refrains, both lines and entire stanzas, in (a) "Swing Low ..." and (b) "Go Down ..."
2. What idea or message is emphasized through the single-line refrain in "Go Down, Moses"?

◆ Build Vocabulary

USING THE WORD ROOT -press-

Copy the following sentences into your notebook, filling in the blanks with an appropriate word consisting of the root -press-, meaning "push," and one of the prefixes defined below.

    com- ("together")   re- ("back")
    de- ("down")   im- ("into")

1. ____?____ the metal seal on the hot wax to make your mark.
2. Watch as I ____?____ the paper into a tight ball.
3. If you ____?____ that button, a buzzer will go off.
4. The enthusiastic fans weren't able to ____?____ their squeals.

USING THE WORD BANK

On your paper, write the word that is the closest antonym, or opposite, of the first word.

1. oppressed: (a) crushed, (b) assisted, (c) punished, (d) ignored
2. smite: (a) hit, (b) question, (c) criticize, (d) caress

◆ Grammar and Style

DIRECT ADDRESS

When you use direct address, put a comma after the name if it comes first in the sentence, before the name if it comes at the end of the sentence, and both before and after the name if it comes in the middle of the sentence.

> In **direct address**, commas are used to set off the name of the person or thing being addressed by the speaker.

Practice On your paper, copy the following sentences. Underline the noun or noun phrase of direct address, and add punctuation where necessary.

1. Selena, sing slowly and with great feeling.
2. The choir performed beautifully Ms. Phipps.
3. I think, choir members that you need to stand straighter.
4. Everyone agrees Joe that you have a great voice.

Writing Application Rewrite each sentence, inserting the noun of direct address in the part of the sentence indicated. Insert commas where necessary.

1. Sing the refrain as if you really mean it. (sopranos—beginning of sentence)
2. Do you plan to join the senior choir? (Nathan—end of sentence)
3. Before you begin the first verse take a deep breath. (students—middle of sentence)

Beyond Literature

Music Connection

Spirituals and Modern Music Spirituals may be nearly two hundred years old, but they are still alive and well. Many of today's gospel singers still perform spirituals. Spirituals have also influenced or inspired many other types of contemporary music, including gospel, blues, rock 'n' roll, jazz, and rhythm and blues. The origins of jazz music can be directly linked to the African rhythms and musical traditions that characterize spirituals. Can you hear a connection to spirituals in any of the music you enjoy? [Music Connection]

Build Your Portfolio

 Idea Bank

Writing

1. Letter Think of a contemporary performer (from country, rap, rock, or jazz) with the potential to perform spirituals in an interesting new way. Write to the artist, proposing that he or she record this type of music, and explain why.

2. Original Spiritual Write your own spiritual, using refrains to emphasize an important idea.

3. Reflective Essay Imagine that you are a free person living in the South before the Civil War. You hear these spirituals and, for the first time, really pay attention to the lyrics. In a reflective essay, analyze what the songs have taught you about the realities of slavery.

Speaking and Listening

4. Choral Reading With a small group, read a spiritual aloud in call-and-response format, with one student calling out the verses and the rest answering with the refrains. Each "soloist" should create at least one new verse. **[Performing Arts Link]**

5. Music Appreciation Find contemporary recordings of spirituals in a library's gospel music collection. Play several for the class; then compare the songs' messages and images with the spirituals you just studied. **[Music Link]**

Projects

6. Map In an on-line or printed historical atlas, find a map showing ancient Palestine, the river Jordan, and ancient Egypt. Make a copy of the map; then label each location with a caption that explains how it relates to these spirituals. **[Social Studies Link]**

7. Logo Design a logo for the Underground Railroad. Use words or images from the spirituals to symbolize the organization's mission. **[Art Link]**

 Writing Mini-Lesson

Song to Support a Cause

"Go Down, Moses" is a plea for freedom from slavery based on the Old Testament story of Moses' demand of freedom for the Israelites. Over the years, songwriters have written lyrics urging everything from an end to war to a cure for world hunger. Write a song in support of a cause about which you feel strongly. Use repetition to emphasize your most important ideas.

Writing Skills Focus: Effective Repetition

The use of the same word, phrase, or sound more than once to create an effect or emphasize a point is known as **effective repetition.** Don't repeat just any word or phrase; rather, repeat images or statements that communicate your main idea. In "Swing Low, Sweet Chariot," for example, the speaker uses the word *home*—a word with deep emotional connotations—a total of eight times in sixteen lines.

Prewriting Choose a cause in which you believe. Jot down several good reasons for supporting the cause, then select one or two that appeal directly to the emotions. Brainstorm for words and images that capture these ideas and feelings.

Drafting Write at least two verses and a refrain.

> **Verses:** State your cause and build support for it.
> **Refrain:** Use emotional words and/or powerful images to get to the heart of the issue.

Build the intensity of your message by repeating the key words and phrases you identified while brainstorming in the prewriting phase.

Revising Read your song aloud as though seeing it for the first time. Is your message strong and clear? Does your use of repetition emphasize the main idea?

Guide for Interpreting

Frederick Douglass
(1818–1895)

Frederick Douglass rose out of slavery to become one of the most gifted writers and orators of his time. Using these talents, he dedicated his life to fighting for the abolition of slavery and for civil rights. Douglass's life served as an inspiration and example for both blacks and whites throughout the country.

Early Years Douglass was born on a Maryland plantation. It is believed that his name at birth was Frederick Augustus Bailey. At the age of eight, he was sent as a slave to the Baltimore home of the Auld family, where he learned to read and write, at first with the encouragement of Mrs. Auld and later despite her objections. Learning soon became an unquenchable thirst for the boy.

> *Douglass often traded biscuits for reading lessons with his playmates.*

His reading fueled a quest for freedom. At age twenty-one he escaped to Massachusetts, a free state, and took the surname Douglass to avoid arrest as a fugitive.

A Public Life Despite his fear of being arrested, Douglass delivered a tremendously powerful and moving debut speech at the 1841 convention of an abolitionist organization. He then spent the next four years lecturing against slavery and arguing for the need for civil rights for all people.

Rumors spread that a man of such eloquence could not possibly have been a slave. In response, Douglass published his first autobiography, *Narrative of the Life of Frederick Douglass, an American Slave, Written By Himself* (1845). He then fled to England, where he spent years trying to gain British support for the abolitionist movement. After English friends raised money to buy his freedom, Douglass returned to the United States, established a newspaper for African Americans, and resumed lecturing. In 1855, he published *My Bondage and My Freedom,* an updated version of his autobiography.

During the Civil War, Douglass helped recruit African American soldiers for the Union army. After slavery was abolished, he fought vigorously for civil rights for African Americans. He became a consultant to President Lincoln and held several government positions, including United States minister to Haiti.

◆ Background for Understanding

CULTURE: THE INFLUENCE OF FREDERICK DOUGLASS

Frederick Douglass was perhaps the most prominent African American leader of the nineteenth century, and his influence is still felt. As a crusader for human rights, Douglass served as a role model for African American leaders such as Booker T. Washington and W.E.B. DuBois. In our own era, the civil rights movement has drawn inspiration from Douglass, who opposed segregation decades before other voices of objection were raised. As a young man, he protested segregated seating on trains by sitting in cars reserved for whites until the authorities forcibly removed him.

Later, he fought job discrimination against African Americans and protested segregation in schools.

Douglass did not limit himself to fighting for the civil rights of African Americans. He also helped women in their battle to win the vote. Because he did not segregate his causes, Douglass is a model for all those who struggle against injustice.

Many American writers have paid tribute to Douglass in their works. Two of those works are included in this book: Paul Laurence Dunbar's poem "Douglass" on p. 600 and Robert Hayden's poem "Frederick Douglass" on p. 1053.

from My Bondage and My Freedom

◆ *Literature and Your Life*

CONNECT YOUR EXPERIENCE

Can you remember your pride and excitement as you learned to read by yourself? Imagine another person denying your right to read just as you were discovering what it meant to learn. If you were enslaved like Frederick Douglass, you would have no choice but to submit (or at least appear to submit) to your owner's wishes.

Journal Writing Briefly discuss whether you believe that education is a privilege or an undeniable right.

THEMATIC FOCUS: A NATION DIVIDED

Douglass's autobiography presents a powerful argument against slavery—a major cause of the Civil War. Few issues have more dramatically torn apart our nation. As you read, consider both the political and personal divisions caused by this issue.

◆ Literary Focus

AUTOBIOGRAPHY

An **autobiography** is a person's written account of his or her own life, focusing on the events the author considers most significant. Because the writer's life is presented as he or she views it, the portrayal of people and events is colored by the author's feelings and beliefs. In fact, some of the writer's attitudes and beliefs may be directly stated. Usually, the writers of autobiographies believe that their lives are interesting or important or can in some way serve as examples for others. Frederick Douglass, for instance, wrote his autobiography because he believed that his life proved that blacks were no less perceptive, intelligent, and capable than whites.

◆ Grammar and Style

CORRELATIVE CONJUNCTIONS

Douglass writes of Mrs. Auld that "the good lady had *not only* ceased to instruct me, herself, *but* had set her face as a flint against my learning to read by any means." The italicized words in the passage are **correlative conjunctions**—pairs of connecting words that link ideas. The words *not only* and *but* show the relationship between the two actions in the sentence. Here are some common correlative conjunctions, which are usually used in pairs.

either . . . or	neither . . . nor	whether . . . or
not only . . . but (also)	just as . . . so	

◆ Reading Strategy

SET A PURPOSE

Setting a purpose for reading helps you get more from a work by giving you an idea or concept on which to focus. Read this section from Douglass's autobiography with the purpose of learning about the author's special qualities and expanding your understanding of what it was like to be a slave. Record appropriate details in a chart like this one.

Douglass's Character Traits	Details About Slavery

◆ Build Vocabulary

WORD ROOTS: *-bene-*

Frederick Douglass describes his owner, Mrs. Auld, as a *benevolent* woman. The root *-bene-* means "well" or "good." Other words containing this root—*benefit, benediction,* and *benefactor*—all relate in some way to the concept of goodness.

WORD BANK

Preview this list of words from *My Bondage and My Freedom.*

congenial
benevolent
stringency
depravity
consternation
redolent

from My Bondage and My Freedom

Frederick Douglass

▶ **Critical Viewing**
What is symbolized by
the light shining on
the reader? **[Interpret]**

I lived in the family of Master Hugh, at Baltimore, seven years, during which time—as the almanac makers say of the weather—my condition
was variable. The most interesting feature of my
history here, was my learning to read and write,
under somewhat marked disadvantages. In at-
taining this knowledge, I was compelled to resort

to indirections by no means congenial to my nature, and which were really humiliating to me. My mistress—who had begun to teach me—was suddenly checked in her benevolent design, by the strong advice of her husband. In faithful compliance with this advice, the good lady had not only ceased to instruct me, herself, but had set her face as a flint against my learning to read by any means. It is due, however, to my mistress to say, that she did not adopt this course in all its stringency at the first. She either thought it unnecessary, or she lacked the depravity indispensable to shutting me up in mental darkness. It was, at least, necessary for her to have some training, and some hardening, in the exercise of the slaveholder's prerogative, to make her equal to forgetting my human nature and character, and to treating me as a thing destitute of a moral or an intellectual nature. Mrs. Auld—my mistress—was, as I have said, a most kind and tenderhearted woman; and, in the humanity of her heart, and the simplicity of her mind, she set out, when I first went to live with her, to treat me as she supposed one human being ought to treat another.

It is easy to see, that, in entering upon the duties of a slaveholder, some little experience is needed. Nature has done almost nothing to prepare men and women to be either slaves or slaveholders. Nothing but rigid training, long persisted in, can perfect the character of the one or the other. One cannot easily forget to love freedom; and it is as hard to cease to respect that natural love in our fellow creatures. On entering upon the career of a slaveholding mistress, Mrs. Auld was singularly deficient; nature, which fits nobody for such an office, had done less for her than any lady I had known. It was no easy matter to induce her to think and to feel that the curly-headed boy, who stood by her side, and even leaned on her lap; who was loved by little Tommy, and who loved little Tommy in turn; sustained to her only the relation of a chattel. I was *more* than that, and she felt me to be more than that. I could talk and sing; I could laugh and weep; I could reason and remember; I could love and hate. I was human, and she, dear lady, knew and felt me to be so. How could she, then, treat me as a brute, without a mighty struggle with all the noble powers of her own soul. That struggle came, and the will and power of the husband was victorious. Her noble soul was overthrown; but, he that overthrew it did not, himself, escape the consequences. He, not less than the other parties, was injured in his domestic peace by the fall.

When I went into their family, it was the abode of happiness and contentment. The mistress of the house was a model of affection and tenderness. Her fervent piety and watchful uprightness made it impossible to see her without thinking and feeling—"that woman is a Christian." There was no sorrow nor suffering for which she had not a tear, and there was no innocent joy for which she did not a smile. She had bread for the hungry, clothes for the naked, and comfort for every mourner that came within her reach. Slavery soon proved its ability to divest her of these excellent qualities, and her home of its early happiness. Conscience cannot stand

◆ **Literary Focus**
Douglass blames slavery, rather than Mrs. Auld, for the changes that take place in the household. What does this tell you about him?

◆ **Build Vocabulary**
congenial (kən jēn′ yəl) *adj.*: Agreeable
benevolent (bə nev′ ə lənt) *adj.*: Kindly; charitable
stringency (strin′ jən sē) *n.*: Strictness; severity
depravity (di prav′ ə tē) *n.*: Corruption; wickedness

A Home on the Mississippi, Currier & Ives, The Museum of the City of New York

▲ **Critical Viewing** How does this idealized picture of plantation life contrast with Douglass's experiences as an enslaved African American? **[Contrast]**

much violence. Once thoroughly broken down, *who* is he that can repair the damage? It may be broken toward the slave, on Sunday, and toward the master on Monday. It cannot endure such shocks. It must stand entire, or it does not stand at all. If my condition waxed bad, that of the family waxed not better. The first step, in the wrong direction, was the violence done to nature and to conscience, in arresting the benevolence that would have enlightened my young mind. In ceasing to instruct me, she must begin to justify herself *to* herself; and, once consenting to take sides in such a debate, she was riveted to her position. One needs very

little knowledge of moral philosophy, to see *where* my mistress now landed. She finally became even more violent in her opposition to my learning to read, than was her husband himself. She was not satisfied with simply doing as *well* as her husband had commanded her, but seemed resolved to better his instruction. Nothing appeared to make my poor mistress—after her turning toward the downward path—more angry, than seeing me, seated in some nook or corner, quietly reading a book or a newspaper. I have had her rush at me, with the utmost fury, and snatch from my hand such newspaper or book, with something of the wrath and <u>consternation</u> which a traitor might be supposed to feel on being discovered in a plot by some dangerous spy.

Mrs. Auld was an apt woman, and the advice of her husband, and her own experience, soon demonstrated, to her entire satisfaction, that education and slavery are incompatible with each other. When this conviction was thoroughly established, I was most narrowly watched in all my movements. If I remained in a separate room from the family for any considerable length of time, I was sure to be suspected of having a book, and was at once called upon to give an account of myself. All this, however, was entirely *too late*. The first, and never to be retraced, step had been taken. In teaching me the alphabet, in the days of her simplicity and kindness, my mistress had given me the "inch," and now, no ordinary precaution could prevent me from taking the "ell."[1]

Seized with a determination to learn to read, at any cost, I hit upon many expedients to accomplish the desired end. The plea which I mainly adopted, and the one by which I was most successful, was that of using my young white playmates, with whom I met in the street, as teachers. I used to carry, almost constantly, a copy of Webster's spelling book in my pocket; and, when sent on errands, or when play time was allowed me, I would step, with my young friends, aside, and take a lesson in spelling. I generally paid my *tuition fee* to the boys, with bread, which I also carried in my pocket. For a single biscuit, any of my hungry little comrades would give me a lesson more valuable to me than bread. Not everyone, however, demanded this consideration, for there were those who took pleasure in teaching me, whenever I had a

chance to be taught by them. I am strongly tempted to give the names of two or three of those little boys, as a slight testimonial of the gratitude and affection

I bear them, but prudence forbids; not that it would injure me, but it might, possibly, embarrass them; for it is almost an unpardonable offense to do anything, directly or indirectly, to promote a slave's freedom, in a slave state. It is enough to say, of my warm-hearted little play fellows, that they lived on Philpot Street, very near Durgin & Bailey's shipyard.

Although slavery was a delicate subject, and very cautiously talked about among grownup people in Maryland, I frequently talked about it—and that very freely—with the white boys. I would, sometimes, say to them, while seated on a curbstone or a cellar door, "I wish I could be free, as you will be when you get to be men." "You will be free, you know, as soon as you are twenty-one, and can go where you like, but I am a slave for life. Have I not as good a right to be free as you have?" Words like these, I observed, always troubled them; and I had no small satisfaction in wringing from the boys, occasionally, that fresh and bitter condemnation of slavery, that springs from nature, unseared and unperverted.[2] Of all consciences let me have those to deal with which have not been bewildered by the cares of life. I do not remember ever to have met with a *boy*, while I was in slavery, who defended the slave system; but I have often had boys to console me, with the hope that something would yet occur, by

---

1. **ell** *n.*: Former English measure of length, equal to forty-five inches.

2. **unperverted** (un′ pər vʉrt′ id) *adj.*: Uncorrupted; pure.

◆ **Build Vocabulary**

consternation (kän′ stər nā′ shən) *n.*: Great fear or shock that makes one feel helpless or bewildered

which I might be made free. Over and over again, they have told me, that "they believed *I* had as good a right to be free as *they* had"; and that "they did not believe God ever made anyone to be a slave." The reader will easily see, that such little conversations with my play fellows, had no tendency to weaken my love of liberty, nor to render me contented with my condition as a slave.

When I was about thirteen years old, and had succeeded in learning to read, every increase of knowledge, especially respecting the free states, added something to the almost intolerable burden of the thought—"I am a slave for life." To my bondage I saw no end. It was a terrible reality, and I shall never be able to tell how sadly that thought chafed my young spirit. Fortunately, or unfortunately, about this time in my life, I had made enough money to buy what was then a very popular schoolbook, the *Columbian Orator*. I bought this addition to my library, of Mr. Knight, on Thames street, Fell's Point, Baltimore, and paid him fifty cents for it. I was first led to buy this book, by hearing some little boys say they were going to learn some little pieces out of it for the Exhibition. This volume was, indeed, a rich treasure, and every opportunity afforded me, for a time, was spent in diligently perusing it . . . The dialogue and the speeches were all <u>redolent</u> of the principles of liberty, and poured floods of light on the nature and character of slavery. As I read, behold! the very discontent so graphically predicted by Master Hugh, had already come upon me. I was no longer the light-hearted, gleesome boy, full of

mirth and play, as when I landed first at Baltimore. Knowledge had come . . . This knowledge opened my eyes to the horrible pit, and revealed the teeth of the frightful dragon that was ready to pounce upon me, but it opened no way for my escape. I have often wished myself a beast, or a bird—anything, rather than a slave. I was wretched and gloomy, beyond my ability to describe. I was too thoughtful to be happy. It was this everlasting thinking which distressed and tormented me; and yet there was no getting rid of the subject of my thoughts. All nature was redolent of it. Once awakened by the silver trump[3] of knowledge, my spirit was roused to eternal wakefulness. Liberty! the inestimable birthright of every man, had, for me, converted every object into an asserter of this great right. It was heard in every sound, and beheld in every object. It was ever present, to torment me with a sense of my wretched condition. The more beautiful and charming were the smiles of nature, the more horrible and desolate was my condition. I saw nothing without seeing it, and I heard nothing without hearing it. I do not exaggerate, when I say, that it looked from every star, smiled in every calm, breathed in every wind, and moved in every storm.

I have no doubt that my state of mind had something to do with the change in the treatment adopted, by my once kind mistress toward me. I can easily believe, that my leaden, downcast, and discontented look, was very offensive to her. Poor lady! She did not know my

◆ **Literary Focus**
How does reading this book become a turning point in Douglass's life?

◆ Build Vocabulary
redolent (red´ əl ənt) *adj.*: Suggestive

---

3. **trump:** Trumpet.

trouble, and I dared not tell her. Could I have freely made her acquainted with the real state of my mind, and given her the reasons therefor, it might have been well for both of us. Her abuse of me fell upon me like the blows of the false prophet upon his ass; she did not know that an *angel* stood in the way;[4] and—such is the relation of master and slave—I could not tell her. Nature had made us *friends*; slavery made us *enemies*. My interests were in a direction opposite to hers, and we both had our private thoughts and plans. She aimed to keep me ignorant; and I resolved to know, although knowledge only increased my discontent. My feelings were not the result of any marked cruelty in the treatment I received; they sprung

from the consideration of my being a slave at all. It was *slavery*—not its mere *incidents*—that I hated. I had been cheated. I saw through the attempt to keep me in ignorance . . . The feeding and clothing me well, could not atone for taking my liberty from me. The smiles of my mistress could not remove the deep sorrow that dwelt in my young bosom. Indeed, these, in time, came only to deepen my sorrow. She had changed; and the reader will see that I had changed, too. We were both victims to the same overshadowing evil—*she*, as mistress, *I*, as slave. I will not censure her harshly; she cannot censure me, for she knows I speak but the truth, and have acted in my opposition to slavery, just as she herself would have acted, in a reverse of circumstances.

---

4. **blows . . . the way:** Allusion to a biblical tale (Numbers 22: 21–35) about an ass that cannot move, though she is beaten by her master, because her path is blocked by an angel.

◆ **Reading Strategy**
Reread this final paragraph and explain why Douglass doesn't blame Mrs. Auld for the way she treated him.

Guide for Responding

◆ *Literature and Your Life*

Reader's Response Do you think it is possible to be a benevolent slaveholder? Why or why not?

Thematic Focus How does slavery make victims of both slaves and slaveholders?

Group Poll Conduct a quick poll to determine whether fellow students agree or disagree that slavery and education are incompatible. Prompt respondents with opposing viewpoints to explain their reasoning.

☑ **Check Your Comprehension**

1. Why does Douglass live with the Auld family?
2. How does he learn to read?
3. Describe the changes in Mrs. Auld's behavior toward young Douglass.
4. What is responsible for his transformation from a "light-hearted" boy to a "wretched and gloomy" one?
5. What is it that Douglass says "looked from every star, smiled in every calm, breathed in every wind, and moved in every storm"?

Guide for Responding (continued)

◆ Critical Thinking

INTERPRET

1. How does Douglass's experience prove his mistress's belief that education and slavery are incompatible? **[Support]**
2. Why do you think that the white children's attitude toward slavery is different from that of their parents? **[Analyze]**

EVALUATE

3. How effectively does Douglass support his view that slaveholders, as well as slaves, are victims of slavery? Explain. **[Assess]**

APPLY

4. Mahatma Gandhi wrote, "The moment the slave resolves that he will no longer be a slave, his fetters fall." Based on the selection, explain whether or not you feel Douglass was free even while in bondage. **[Apply]**

◆ Reading Strategy

SET A PURPOSE

Before you read from *My Bondage and My Freedom*, you **set a purpose** of learning more about Douglass's special qualities and expanding your understanding of slavery.

1. Which of Douglass's special qualities are conveyed through this section of his autobiography? Explain.
2. How did reading this section add to your understanding of the effects of slavery?

◆ Literary Focus

AUTOBIOGRAPHY

The portrayal of people and events in an **autobiography** is colored by the author's personal feelings, views, and purpose in writing. Douglass intended that his autobiography be both an inspiration to others and a condemnation of slavery.

1. How do the tone and style of this selection support Douglass's desire to serve as a model?
2. Douglass is well cared for as a slave. How, then, does he go about making his case against slavery?
3. How do you think this account would be different if it had been written by Mrs. Auld?

◆ Build Vocabulary

USING THE WORD ROOT -bene-

Define each of the following words, incorporating the meaning of the root -bene- ("well" or "good") into your definition. If necessary, use a dictionary for help.

1. benefit   2. benefactor   3. benediction

USING THE WORD BANK

Copy this passage into your notebook, filling the blanks with appropriate Word Bank words.

I could see my neighbor scowling with a look of ____?____. Usually she wore a ____?____ expression, so I knew something was wrong. Her yard was usually ____?____ with the fragrance of roses, which she was ____?____ enough to share with me. The bushes were cut down to the ground! I was stunned at the ____?____ of the deed. I could understand the ____?____ of her message as she tacked up a KEEP OUT sign.

◆ Grammar and Style

CORRELATIVE CONJUNCTIONS

Correlative conjunctions are used to connect similar kinds of words and word groups that are grammatically alike, such as the underlined words in this example.

*Not only **my body,** but also **my soul** was bound by slavery.*

Practice For each item, add a pair of correlative conjunctions from the italicized list to create a logical sentence.

either. . .or; neither. . .nor; whether. . .or;
not only. . .but (also); just as. . .so

1. ____?____ slave ____?____ mistress was truly free.
2. ____?____ Maryland ____?____ Mississippi and Tennessee were slave states.
3. ____?____ a slave ____?____ a slaveholder, all people are harmed by slavery.
4. ____?____ Douglass worked to abolish slavery, ____?____ did the Grimké sisters and Sojourner Truth.

Writing Application Write an original sentence using each of the five pairs of correlative conjunctions listed in the previous activity.

Build Your Portfolio

 ## Idea Bank

Writing

1. **Diary Entry** Once Mrs. Auld was persuaded to prevent Douglass from reading, she took her position to extremes. Write a diary entry in which she justifies "herself *to* herself."

2. **New Version** Imagine that one of the boys who helped teach Douglass to read were to write his own life story. Tell the story of the reading lessons as they might appear in his autobiography.

3. **Essay** Slavery not only divided the nation; Douglass suggests that it also divided people from one another and from the better aspects of their own natures. Explore this idea in an essay, supported with examples from the selection.

Speaking and Listening

4. **Dramatic Dialogue** Imagine that one of the boys who helped teach Douglass to read were to meet him again years later. With a partner, prepare and perform a dialogue between the two men. **[Performing Arts Link]**

5. **Oral Interpretation** Select a passage from this selection or another of Douglass's writings and speeches. Present the excerpt as Douglass might have read it to an audience of abolitionist sympathizers. **[Social Studies Link]**

Projects

6. **Interpretive Dance** Create an interpretive dance that conveys Douglass's feelings about slavery. Select background music to accompany your dance. **[Performing Arts Link; Music Link]**

7. **Literacy Collage** Using words and pictures from magazines, newspapers, photographs, and other sources, make a collage that expresses the importance of literacy. **[Art Link]**

 ## Writing Mini-Lesson

College Admissions Essay

A college application often requires you to write about an experience that helped to make you the person you are today. Think about a key event from your life, and write an essay describing it and explaining how it affected you. Keep the following in mind as you develop your essay.

Writing Skills Focus: Clear and Logical Organization

A **clear and logical organization** will make your essay easy for your audience to follow. Start with a paragraph in which you introduce the experience you plan to describe, and explain why you're writing about it. Then write a series of body paragraphs describing the details of the experience in chronological order. Conclude with a paragraph that sums up the impact that the experience has had on you.

Prewriting Outline the details of the event, and describe how it affected you. You might use a chart similar to the following to organize your details.

Event:				
Who	What	Where	When	Effect It Had on Me

Drafting Using the details you've gathered, write a draft of your essay. Focus on using precise words that capture your experience as vividly as possible. Use transition words to connect your ideas.

Revising Ask a friend to read your essay aloud as you listen. Are your ideas related? Do they flow logically from one paragraph to the next? Is it clear how this event made you the person you are today?

Guide for Interpreting

Ambrose Bierce (1842–1914?)

Ambrose Bierce's writing and philosophy of life were shaped by his career as a Union officer in the Civil War. The poverty in which he was raised fostered Bierce's unsentimental, pessimistic view of the world; the brutality he saw during the war cemented his cynicism.

Writing that harped on themes of cruelty and death earned Ambrose Bierce the nickname "Bitter Bierce."

A Civil War Soldier Bierce was born in Ohio and raised on a farm in Indiana. Having educated himself by reading his father's books, he left the farm while in his teens to attend a military academy in Kentucky. When the Civil War broke out, he enlisted in the Union army. He fought in several important battles, rose from private to major, and won many awards for bravery. Toward the end of the war, he was seriously wounded, but he returned to battle a few months later.

Poisoned Pen After the war, Bierce settled in San Francisco as a journalist. His column, the "Prattler," which appeared in *The Argonaut* (1877–1879), the *Wasp* (1880–1886), and the *San Francisco Sunday Examiner* (1887–1896), mixed political and social satire, literary reviews, and gossip. The broodingly handsome writer was dubbed "the wickedest man in San Francisco" for his cynical and often malicious commentary. Though his journalistic barbs angered many key political and business figures, Bierce's dark reputation only added to his personal popularity. He was a magnetic figure who charmed those around him despite the malice of his words.

Though Bierce published many of his finest stories in his column, he decided in the early 1890's to publish his collected short stories in two volumes, entitled *Tales of Soldiers and Civilians* (1891) and *Can Such Things Be?* (1893). The concise, carefully plotted stories in these collections, set for the most part during the Civil War, capture the cruelty and futility of war and the indifference of death. His pessimism is also reflected in *The Devil's Dictionary* (1906), a book of humorous and cynical definitions.

The Perfect Cynic Writer George Sterling wrote of Bierce, his longtime friend, that he "never troubled to conceal his justifiable contempt of humanity. . . . Bierce was a 'perfectionist,' a quality that in his case led to an intolerance involving merciless cruelty. He demanded in all others, men or women, the same ethical virtues that he found essential to his own manner of life. . . . To deviate from his point of view, indeed, to disagree with him even in slight particulars, was the unpardonable sin."

Though professionally successful, Bierce found little happiness in a world where so few people met his expectations. His marriage ended in divorce, and both of his sons died at an early age. In 1913, at age 71, the lonely writer traveled to Mexico, a country in the midst of a bloody civil war. To this day, his fate is unknown.

◆ Background for Understanding

HISTORY: THE CIVIL WAR

The senseless violence, death, and destruction Ambrose Bierce witnessed during the American Civil War (1861–1865) convinced him that war was terrible and futile. He set much of his best fiction, including this story, against the backdrop of this divisive war in which the agricultural South, whose economy was based on slavery, battled the more industrialized North. Fought mostly in the South, the war caused hundreds of thousands of casualties on both sides. Yet because the North had more than twice the amount of railroad track, more than twice the population, and five times as many factories, many have argued that the North's victory was assured from the beginning.

An Occurrence at Owl Creek Bridge

◆ Literature and Your Life

CONNECT YOUR EXPERIENCE

"All's fair in love and war." This phrase has been used to excuse everything from trivial lies to wide-scale atrocities. Though you've heard the words countless times, you've probably never given them much thought. Do you think that there are times when the rules of the game are no rules at all? How do you define those times?

Journal Writing In a journal entry, write about an experience from literature or your own life where the phrase "all's fair in love and war" might explain or justify certain actions.

THEMATIC FOCUS: A NATION DIVIDED

In "An Occurrence at Owl Creek Bridge," a civilian who believes that all's fair in love and war finds himself in a life-threatening situation. Does war justify actions that would be deemed unfair in times of peace?

◆ Build Vocabulary

WORD ROOTS: -sum-

You may not know what it means to be "*summarily* hanged." You do know, however, that *summary* suggests a brief, general idea. Likewise, *summarily* describes an action taken hastily or promptly, without attention to detail. These words derive from the Latin root -*sum*- or -*summ*-, meaning "highest," as in a *summary* of high points or the *summit*, or peak, of a mountain.

WORD BANK

Preview this list of words from the story.

> etiquette
> deference
> imperious
> dictum
> summarily
> effaced
> oscillation
> apprised
> malign
> ineffable

◆ Grammar and Style

SEMICOLONS IN COMPOUND SENTENCES

Bierce frequently forms **compound sentences** by linking independent clauses—clauses that can stand alone as sentences—with a **semicolon** rather than a conjunction. This style emphasizes the connection between the ideas in the clauses. Look at this example:

> They hurt his ear like the thrust of a knife; he feared he would shriek.

The pattern of short clauses creates a rhythm of gunfire, shooting out facts and eliminating excess descriptions.

◆ Literary Focus

POINT OF VIEW

In "An Occurrence at Owl Creek Bridge," Bierce uses his main character's warped perception of time to distort reality. The way that you perceive time in a story may depend on the **point of view**—or vantage point from which it is told. In stories told from an objective point of view, you follow the action without understanding each character's thoughts about the events. In stories told from the third-person limited point of view, the narrator relates the inner thoughts and feelings of one character. In this story, Bierce uses both an objective and a third-person limited point of view. As he shifts from one to the other, the emotional tone and sense of time may change as well.

◆ Reading Strategy

SEQUENCE OF EVENTS

In many stories, including Bierce's, events are not presented in the order in which they occurred. Instead, the action jumps backward or forward in time. As you read, you have to reorder events. This process will help you see the true **sequence of events.** Pay attention to the order and time duration of events in this story. To help you, create a timeline of story events, and note the amount of time you estimate each event takes.

An Occurrence at Owl Creek Bridge

Ambrose Bierce

I

A man stood upon a railroad bridge in northern Alabama, looking down into the swift water twenty feet below. The man's hands were behind his back, the wrists bound with a cord. A rope closely encircled his neck. It was attached to a stout cross timber above his head and the slack fell to the level of his knees. Some loose boards laid upon the sleepers supporting the metals of the railway supplied a footing for him and his executioners—two private soldiers of the Federal army, directed by a sergeant who in civil life may have been a deputy sheriff. At a short remove upon the same temporary platform was an officer in the uniform of his rank, armed. He was a captain. A sentinel at each end of the bridge stood with his rifle in the position known as "support," that is to say, vertical in front of the left shoulder, the hammer resting on the forearm thrown straight across the chest—a formal and unnatural position, enforcing an erect carriage of the body. It did not appear to be the duty of these two men to know what was occurring at the center of the bridge; they merely blockaded the two ends of the foot planking that traversed it.

Beyond one of the sentinels nobody was in sight; the railroad ran straight away into a forest for a hundred yards, then, curving, was lost to view. Doubtless there was an outpost farther along. The other bank of the stream was open ground—a gentle acclivity[1] topped with a stockade of vertical tree trunks, loopholed for rifles, with a single embrasure through which protruded the muzzle of a brass cannon commanding the bridge. Midway of the slope between bridge and fort were the spectators—a single company of infantry in line, at "parade rest," the butts of the rifles on the ground, the barrels inclining slightly backward against the right shoulder, the hands crossed upon the stock. A lieutenant stood at the right of the line, the point of his sword upon the ground, his left hand resting upon his right. Excepting the

---

1. **acclivity** (ə klivˊ ə tē) *n.*: Upward slope.

group of four at the center of the bridge, not a man moved. The company faced the bridge, staring stonily, motionless. The sentinels, facing the banks of the stream, might have been statues to adorn the bridge. The captain stood with folded arms, silent, observing the work of his subordinates, but making no sign. Death is a dignitary who when he comes announced is to be received with formal manifestations of respect, even by those most familiar with him. In the code of military etiquette silence and fixity are forms of deference.

The man who was engaged in being hanged was apparently about thirty-five years of age. He was a civilian, if one might judge from his habit, which was that of a planter. His features were good—a straight nose, firm mouth, broad forehead, from which his long, dark hair was combed straight back, falling behind his ears to the collar of his well-fitting frock coat. He wore a mustache and pointed beard, but no whiskers; his eyes were large and dark gray, and had a kindly expression which one would hardly have expected in one whose neck was in the hemp. Evidently this was no vulgar assassin. The liberal military code makes provision for hanging many kinds of persons, and gentlemen are not excluded.

The preparations being complete, the two private soldiers stepped aside and each drew away the plank upon which he had been standing. The sergeant turned to the captain, saluted and placed himself immediately behind that officer, who in turn moved apart one pace. These movements left the condemned man and the sergeant standing on the two ends of the same plank, which spanned three of the crossties of the bridge. The end upon which the civilian stood almost, but not quite, reached a fourth. This plank had been held in place by the weight of the captain; it was now held by that of the sergeant. At a signal from the former the latter would step aside, the plank would tilt and the condemned man go down between two ties. The arrangement commended itself to his judgment as simple and effective. His face had not been covered nor his eyes bandaged. He looked a moment at his "unsteadfast footing," then let his gaze wander to the swirling water of the stream racing madly beneath his feet. A piece of dancing driftwood caught his attention and his eyes followed it down the current. How slowly it appeared to move! What a sluggish stream!

He closed his eyes in order to fix his last thoughts upon his wife and children. The water, touched to gold by the early sun, the brooding mists under the banks at some distance down the stream, the fort, the soldiers, the piece of drift—all had distracted him. And now he became conscious of a new

disturbance. Striking through the thought of his dear ones was a sound which he could neither ignore nor understand, a sharp, distinct, metallic percussion like the stroke of a blacksmith's hammer upon the anvil; it had the same ringing quality. He wondered what it was, and whether immeasurably distant or near by—it seemed both. Its recurrence was regular, but as slow as the tolling of a death knell. He awaited each stroke with impatience and—he knew not why—apprehension. The intervals of silence grew progressively longer; the delays became maddening. With their greater infrequency the sounds increased in strength and sharpness. They hurt his ear like the thrust of a knife; he feared he would shriek. What he heard was the ticking of his watch.

He unclosed his eyes and saw again the water below him. "If I could free my hands," he thought, "I might throw off the noose and spring into the stream. By diving I could evade the bullets and, swimming vigorously, reach the bank, take to the woods and get away home. My home, thank God, is as yet outside their lines; my wife and little ones are still beyond the invader's farthest advance."

As these thoughts, which have here to be set down in words, were flashed into the doomed man's brain rather than evolved from it the captain nodded to the sergeant. The sergeant stepped aside.

II

Peyton Farquhar was a well-to-do planter, of an old and highly respected Alabama family. Being a slave owner and like other slave owners a politician he was naturally an original secessionist and ardently devoted to the Southern cause. Circumstances of an imperious nature, which it is unnecessary to relate here, had prevented him from taking service with the gallant army that had fought the disastrous campaigns ending with the fall of Corinth,[2]

---

2. **Corinth:** Mississippi town that was the site of an 1862 Civil War battle.

and he chafed under the inglorious restraint, longing for the release of his energies, the larger life of the soldier, the opportunity for distinction. That opportunity, he felt, would come, as it comes to all in war time. Meanwhile he did what he could. No service was too humble for him to perform in aid of the South, no adventure too perilous for him to undertake if consistent with the character of a civilian who was at heart a soldier, and who in good faith and without too much qualification assented to at least a part of the frankly villainous dictum that all is fair in love and war.

One evening while Farquhar and his wife were sitting on a rustic bench near the entrance to his grounds, a gray-clad soldier rode up to the gate and asked for a drink of water. Mrs. Farquhar was only too happy to serve him with her own white hands. While she was fetching the water her husband approached the dusty horseman and inquired eagerly for news from the front.

"The Yanks are repairing the railroads," said the man, "and are getting ready for another advance. They have reached the Owl Creek bridge, put it in order and built a stockade on the north bank. The commandant has issued an order, which is posted everywhere, declaring that any civilian caught interfering with the railroad, its bridges, tunnels or trains will be summarily hanged. I saw the order."

"How far is it to the Owl Creek bridge?" Farquhar asked.

"About thirty miles."

"Is there no force on this side the creek?"

"Only a picket post[3] half a mile out, on the railroad, and a single sentinel at this end of the bridge."

"Suppose a man—a civilian and student of hanging—should elude the picket post and

---

3. **picket post:** Troops sent ahead with news of a surprise attack.

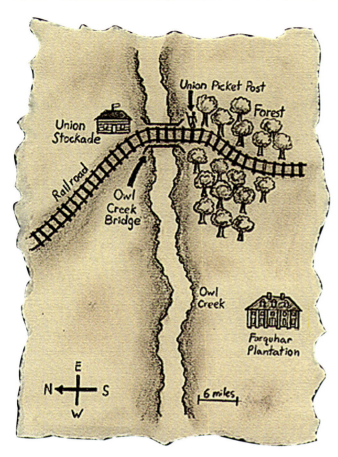

▲ **Critical Viewing** How does the map reveal why the bridge was so important to the Union army? **[Interpret]**

husband and rode away. An hour later, after nightfall, he repassed the plantation, going northward in the direction from which he had come. He was a Federal scout.

III

As Peyton Farquhar fell straight downward through the bridge he lost consciousness and was as one already dead. From this state he was awakened—ages later, it seemed to him— by the pain of a sharp pressure upon his throat, followed by a sense of suffocation. Keen, poignant agonies seemed to shoot from his neck downward through every fiber of his body and limbs. These pains appeared to flash along well-defined lines of ramification[5] and to beat with an inconceivably rapid periodicity. They seemed like streams of pulsating fire heating him to an intolerable temperature. As to his head, he was conscious of nothing but a feeling of fullness—of congestion. These sensations were unaccompanied by thought. The intellectual part of his nature was already <u>effaced</u>: he had power only to feel, and feeling was torment. He was conscious of motion. Encompassed in a luminous cloud, of which he was now merely the fiery heart, without material substance, he swung through unthinkable arcs of <u>oscillation</u>, like a vast pendulum. Then all at once, with terrible suddenness, the light about him shot upward with the noise of a loud plash; a frightful roaring was in his ears, and all was cold and dark. The power of thought was restored; he knew that the rope

perhaps get the better of the sentinel," said Farquhar, smiling, "what could he accomplish?"

The soldier reflected. "I was there a month ago," he replied. "I observed that the flood of last winter had lodged a great quantity of driftwood against the wooden pier at this end of the bridge. It is now dry and would burn like tow."[4]

The lady had now brought the water, which the soldier drank. He thanked her ceremoniously, bowed to her

---

4. **tow** (tō) *n.:* Coarse, broken fibers of hemp or flax before spinning.

---

5. **flash along well-defined lines of ramification:** Spread out quickly along branches from a central point.

◆ **Build Vocabulary**
effaced (ə fāsd´) *adj.:* Erased; wiped out
oscillation (äs´ ə lā´ shən) *n.:* Act of swinging or moving regularly back and forth

had broken and he had fallen into the stream. There was no additional strangulation; the noose about his neck was already suffocating him and kept the water from his lungs. To die of hanging at the bottom of a river!—the idea seemed to him ludicrous. He opened his eyes in the darkness and saw above him a gleam of light, but how distant, how inaccessible! He was still sinking, for the light became fainter and fainter until it was a mere glimmer. Then it began to grow and brighten, and he knew that he was rising toward the surface— knew it with reluctance, for he was now very comfortable. "To be hanged and drowned," he thought, "that is not so bad; but I do not wish to be shot. No; I will not be shot; that is not fair."

He was not conscious of an effort, but a sharp pain in his wrist apprised him that he was trying to free his hands. He gave the struggle his attention, as an idler might observe the feat of a juggler, without interest in the outcome. What splendid effort!—what magnificent, what superhuman strength! Ah, that was a fine endeavor! Bravo! The cord fell away; his arms parted and floated upward, the hands dimly seen on each side in the growing light. He watched them with a new interest as first one and then the other pounced upon the noose at his neck. They tore it away and thrust it fiercely aside, its undulations resembling those of a watersnake. "Put it back, put it back!" He thought he shouted these words to his hands, for the undoing of the noose had been succeeded by the direst pang that he had yet experienced. His neck ached horribly; his brain was on fire; his heart, which had been fluttering faintly, gave a great leap, trying to force itself out at his mouth. His whole body was racked and wrenched with an insupportable anguish! But his disobedient hands gave no heed to the command. They beat the water vigorously with quick, downward strokes, forcing him to the surface. He felt his head emerge; his eyes were blinded by the sunlight; his chest expanded convulsively, and with a supreme and crowning agony his lungs en-gulfed a great draft of air, which instantly he expelled in a shriek!

He was now in full possession of his physical senses. They were, indeed, preternaturally[6] keen and alert. Something in the awful disturbance of his organic system had so exalted and refined them that they made record of things never before perceived. He felt the ripples upon his face and heard their separate sounds as they struck. He looked at the forest on the bank of the stream, saw the individual trees, the leaves and the veining of each leaf— saw the very insects upon them: the locusts, the brilliant-bodied flies, the gray spiders stretching their webs from twig to twig. He noted the prismatic colors in all the dewdrops upon a million blades of grass. The humming of the gnats that danced above the eddies of the stream, the beating of the dragonflies' wings, the strokes of the water spiders' legs, like oars which had lifted their boat—all these made audible music. A fish slid along beneath his eyes and he heard the rush of its body parting the water.

He had come to the surface facing down the stream; in a moment the visible world seemed to wheel slowly round, himself the pivotal point, and he saw the bridge, the fort, the soldiers upon the bridge, the captain, the sergeant, the two privates, his executioners. They were in silhouette against the blue sky. They shouted and gesticulated, pointing at him. The captain had drawn his pistol, but did not fire; the others were unarmed. Their movements were grotesque and horrible, their forms gigantic.

Suddenly he heard a sharp report and something struck the water smartly within a few inches of his head, spattering his face with spray. He heard a second report, and saw one of the sentinels with his rifle at his shoulder, a light cloud of blue smoke rising from the muzzle. The man in the water saw the eye of the man on the bridge gazing into his own through the sights of the rifle. He observed that it was a gray eye and remembered having read that gray eyes were keenest, and that all famous marksmen had them. Nevertheless,

◆ **Build Vocabulary**

apprised (ə prīzd´) *v.:* Informed; notified

6. **preternaturally** (prēt´ ər nach´ ər əl ē) *adv.:* Abnormally; extraordinarily.

this one had missed.

A counterswirl had caught Farquhar and turned him half round; he was again looking into the forest on the bank opposite the fort. The sound of a clear, high voice in a monotonous singsong now rang out behind him and came across the water with a distinctness that pierced and subdued all other sounds, even the beating of the ripples in his ears. Although no soldier, he had frequented camps enough to know the dread significance of that deliberate, drawling, aspirated chant; the lieutenant on shore was taking a part in the morning's work. How coldly and pitilessly—with what an even, calm intonation, presaging,[7] and enforcing tranquillity in the men—with what accurately measured intervals fell those cruel words:

"Attention, company! . . . Shoulder arms!

---

7. **presaging** (prē sāj´ iŋ): Predicting; warning.

. . . Ready! . . . Aim! . . . Fire!"

Farquhar dived—dived as deeply as he could. The water roared in his ears like the voice of Niagara, yet he heard the dulled thunder of the volley and, rising again toward the surface, met shining bits of metal, singularly flattened, oscillating slowly downward. Some of them touched him on the face and hands, then fell away, continuing their descent. One lodged between his collar and neck; it was uncomfortably warm and he snatched it out.

As he rose to the surface, gasping for breath, he saw that he had been a long time under water; he was perceptibly farther down stream—nearer to safety. The soldiers had almost finished reloading; the metal ramrods flashed all at once in the sunshine as they were drawn from the barrels, turned in the air, and thrust into their sockets. The two sentinels fired again, independently and ineffectually.

▼ **Critical Viewing** What potential obstacles to Farquhar's escape are presented by the stream bank? [Analyze]

The hunted man saw all this over his shoulder; he was now swimming vigorously with the current. His brain was as energetic as his arms and legs; he thought with the rapidity of lightning.

"The officer," he reasoned, "will not make that martinet's[8] error a second time. It is as easy to dodge a volley as a single shot. He has probably already given the command to fire at will. God help me, I cannot dodge them all!"

An appalling plash within two yards of him was followed by a loud, rushing sound, *diminuendo*,[9] which seemed to travel back through the air to the fort and died in an explosion which stirred the very river to its deeps! A rising sheet of water curved over him, fell down upon him, blinded him, strangled him! The cannon had taken a hand in the game. As he shook his head free from the commotion of the smitten water he heard the deflected shot humming through the air ahead, and in an instant it was cracking and smashing the branches in the forest beyond.

"They will not do that again," he thought; "the next time they will use a charge of grape[10]. I must keep my eye upon the gun; the smoke will apprise me—the report arrives too late; it lags behind the missile. That is a good gun."

Suddenly he felt himself whirled round and round—spinning like a top. The water, the banks, the forests, the now distant bridge, fort and men—all were commingled and blurred. Objects were represented by their colors only; circular horizontal streaks of color—that was all he saw. He had been caught in a vortex and was being whirled on with a velocity of advance and gyration that made him giddy and sick. In a few moments he was flung upon the gravel at the foot of the left bank of the stream—the southern bank—and behind a projecting point which concealed him from his enemies. The sudden arrest of his motion, the abrasion of one of his hands on the gravel, restored him, and he wept with delight. He dug his fingers into the sand, threw it over himself

in handfuls and audibly blessed it. It looked like diamonds, rubies, emeralds; he could think of nothing beautiful which it did not resemble. The trees upon the bank were giant garden plants; he noted a definite order in their arrangement, inhaled the fragrance of their blooms. A strange, roseate[11] light shone through the spaces among their trunks and the wind made in their branches the music of aeolian harps.[12] He had no wish to perfect his escape—was content to remain in that enchanting spot until retaken.

A whiz and rattle of grapeshot among the branches high above his head roused him from his dream. The baffled cannoneer had fired him a random farewell. He sprang to his feet, rushed up the sloping bank, and plunged into the forest.

All that day he traveled, laying his course by the rounding sun. The forest seemed interminable; nowhere did he discover a break in it, not even a woodman's road. He had not known that he lived in so wild a region. There was something uncanny in the revelation.

By night fall he was fatigued, footsore, famishing. The thought of his wife and children urged him on. At last he found a road which led him in what he knew to be the right direction. It was as wide and straight as a city street, yet it seemed untraveled. No fields bordered it, no dwelling anywhere. Not so much as the barking of a dog suggested human habitation. The black bodies of the trees formed a straight wall on both sides, terminating on the horizon in a point, like a diagram in a lesson in perspective. Overhead, as he looked up through this rift in the wood, shone great golden stars looking unfamiliar and grouped in strange constellations. He was sure they were arranged in some order which had a secret and malign significance. The wood on either side was full of singular noises, among which—once, twice, and again, he distinctly heard whispers in an unknown tongue.

His neck was in pain and lifting his hand to it he found it horribly swollen. He knew that it

---

8. **martinet** (märt´ən et´): Strict military disciplinarian.
9. *diminuendo* (də min´ yo͞o en´ do): Musical term used to describe a gradual reduction in volume.
10. **charge of grape:** Cluster of small iron balls— "grape shot"—that disperse once fired from a cannon.

---

11. **roseate** (ro͞´ zē it) *adj.*: Rose-colored.
12. **aeolian** (ē o͞´ lē ən) **harps:** Stringed instruments that produce music when played by the wind. In Greek mythology, Aeolus is the god of the winds.

had a circle of black where the rope had bruised it. His eyes felt congested: he could no longer close them. His tongue was swollen with thirst; he relieved its fever by thrusting it forward from between his teeth into the cold air. How softly the turf had carpeted the un-traveled avenue—he could no longer feel the roadway beneath his feet!

Doubtless, despite his suffering, he had fallen asleep while walking, for now he sees another scene—perhaps he has merely recov-ered from a delirium. He stands at the gate of his own home. All is as he left it, and all bright and beautiful in the morning sunshine. He must have traveled the entire night. As he pushes open the gate and passes up the wide white walk, he sees a flutter of female garments: his wife, looking fresh and cool and sweet, steps down from the veranda to meet him. At the bot-tom of the steps she stands waiting, with a smile of ineffable joy, an attitude of matchless grace and dignity. Ah, how beautiful she is! He springs forward with extended arms. As he is about to clasp her he feels a stunning blow upon the back of the neck; a blinding white light blazes all about him with a sound like the shock of a cannon—then all is darkness and silence!

Peyton Farquhar was dead; his body, with a bro-ken neck, swung gently from side to side beneath the timbers of the Owl Creek bridge.

◆ **Reading Strategy**
How much time has passed from the opening scene until this last paragraph? How do you know?

◆ **Build Vocabulary**

malign (mə līn´) adj.: Malicious; very harmful

ineffable (in ef´ə bəl) adj.: Too overwhelming to be described in words

Guide for Responding

◆ Literature and Your Life

Reader's Response What emotions did the story's ending evoke? Why?

Thematic Focus Is Farquhar's death a fair one? Why or why not?

Class Poll Farquhar knew in advance that death was the penalty for tampering with the bridge. Is his fate therefore justified? Using this question, conduct a quick poll of classmates.

☑ Check Your Comprehension

1. Which pieces of information about Farquhar's background explain why he would risk his life on such a dangerous mission?
2. (a) What do Farquhar and his wife learn from the visitor? (b) What do you learn about the visitor after he leaves the couple?
3. What is Farquhar's fate?

◆ Critical Thinking

INTERPRET

1. In Part I, Bierce reveals little about the con-demned man and the reason for his hanging. How do these omissions create suspense? **[Analyze]**
2. (a) In what ways are Farquhar's perceptions of time and motion distorted as he waits to be hanged? (b) What causes this distortion? **[Support; Interpret]**
3. Bierce creates contrasts between reality and fan-tasy in this story. What details suggest that Far-quhar's escape occurs in his mind? **[Distinguish]**
4. How does the contrast between real and imag-ined time help prepare you for the ending of the story? **[Compare and Contrast]**

EVALUATE

5. Explain whether you think that the portrayal of Farquhar's final thoughts is realistic. **[Evaluate]**

EXTEND

6. Why were railroad bridges like the one at Owl Creek such an important target during the Civil War? **[Social Studies Link]**

Guide for Responding (continued)

◆ Reading Strategy

SEQUENCE OF EVENTS

Because the events in this story aren't presented in chronological order, you have to piece together the **sequence of events** in order to follow the action.

1. Which takes place first: Farquhar's encounter with the Federal scout or his preoccupation with the ticking of his watch?
2. How much real time do you estimate elapses from the opening to the closing scene of the story?
3. How did the story's ending change your initial perception of the sequence and duration of the story's events?

◆ Build Vocabulary

USING THE WORD ROOT -*sum*-

The root -*sum*- means "highest" and denotes authority. Use your understanding of this root to decide whether each of the following statements is true or false. Write your answers in your notebook.

1. A painter of *consummate* artistry is among the most skilled at his or her craft.
2. Dialing 911 is a fast way to *summon* the police.
3. A *summation* covers every detail of an argument.
4. A *summons* is a casual invitation to visit a courtroom.

USING THE WORD BANK

Review the vocabulary words in the Word Bank; then use them to answer these questions in your notebook.

1. Which four words best relate to a book entitled *Lady Windmere's Authoritative Guide to Manners for Servants*?
2. Which two words best relate to an unspeakably vicious comment?
3. Which three words best relate to a court clerk who hastily interrupts a judge to inform her that audiotaped evidence had been accidentally erased?
4. Which word relates to a table fan that revolves to cool an entire room?

◆ Literary Focus

POINT OF VIEW

The **point of view,** or vantage point from which this story is narrated, changes several times. An objective point of view provides a detached description of the opening scene at Owl Creek bridge. Then, a shift to the third-person limited point of view allows readers to share Farquhar's thoughts and emotions.

1. How is the limited point of view effective where it is used?
2. (a) In which parts of the story does Bierce use the objective point of view? (b) What effect does it create?
3. What is the effect of the shift in point of view in the last paragraph of the story?

◆ Grammar and Style

SEMICOLONS IN COMPOUND SENTENCES

Compound sentences can be formed by joining two closely related independent clauses with a **semicolon**.

The pattern of short clauses connected by semicolons in this story often creates a rapid-fire rhythm. Notice how Bierce makes greater use of this style in parts of the story that are cold and objective but abandons it in other parts.

> **Compound sentences** can be formed by joining two closely related independent clauses with a **semicolon**.

Writing Application Choose from among the following clauses to create three compound sentences. Use semicolons to join clauses that make meaningful, powerful sentences.

1. Thoughts of escape rushed through his mind.
2. Peyton Farquhar dropped from the bridge to the stream below.
3. The silent, interminable moment finally ended.
4. The shock of the cold water jolted his senses.
5. A thunderous roar shattered the calm.
6. Peyton Farquhar desperately surveyed the landscape.

Build Your Portfolio

Idea Bank

Writing

1. **Farewell Letter** Imagine that Farquhar has been allowed to communicate his fate to his wife. Compose his message to her. Be true to Farquhar's character as a loyal southern gentleman.

2. **Prequel** How was Farquhar captured? Did the soldiers dread or anticipate his hanging? Write a narrative of the events leading up to the hanging.

3. **Critical Essay** Bierce was one of the first writers to use stream of consciousness—a style that imitates the natural flow of thoughts, images, and feelings. In an essay, explain how this technique makes the story more dramatic. Use details from the narrative to support your ideas.

Speaking and Listening

4. **Spoken Review** Imagine that you are the host of a radio talk show on literature. Prepare and present a review of this story in which you explain why you did or did not find the story engaging, and explain what you learned from it.

5. **Oral Presentation** Ask a librarian to help you find a science article about the perception of time. Summarize it—and its connection to this story—for your classmates. **[Science Link]**

Projects

6. **Chart** Use the map on p. 471 to estimate how long it would have taken Farquhar to reach the bridge, destroy it, and return. Include key information, such as Farquhar's mode of travel (on horse or foot) and rate of speed. **[Mathematics Link]**

7. **Museum Exhibit** Gather photographs and visuals related to the Civil War. Write captions for the images. Then put everything together to create a museum exhibit about the war.

Writing Mini-Lesson

Fictional News Article

Bierce's story underscores the horrible way in which war can impact individuals. Write a news article that reports the effects of a contemporary civil war on civilians. Remember that news writing must be impartial; use a tone like the one in the opening and closing paragraphs of Bierce's story.

Writing Skills Focus: Objective Tone

An objective tone can be described as the lack of any detectable attitude. Writing in the objective tone is unbiased and reveals no hint of the writer's value judgments toward the subject. For example, Bierce's initial description of Farquhar betrays neither sympathy nor contempt for the character.

Model From the Story

The man who was engaged in being hanged was apparently about thirty-five years of age. He was a civilian, if one might judge from his habit, which was that of a planter. His features were good. . . . He wore a mustache and pointed beard, but no whiskers. . . .

News reporting should maintain an objective tone, even if the subject is emotionally charged.

Prewriting Scan newspapers or magazines or listen to television news reports to find a civil war you can use as your topic. Gather information to provide a balanced, factual background on the conflict.

Drafting Open with a statement that answers as many of the *who, what, where, when, why,* and *how* questions as possible. Without injecting your own judgments, describe the events and their effects on civilians. Remain objective; include facts other than those that favor your own opinion.

Revising How does your article compare with reports you might find in the international news pages of a newspaper? Is your reporting as unbiased?

Guide for Interpreting

Abraham Lincoln (1809–1865)

Serving as president during one of the most tragic periods in American history, Abraham Lincoln fought to reunite a nation torn apart by war. His courage, strength, and dedication in the face of an overwhelming national crisis have made him one of the most admired and respected American presidents.

A man of humble origins, Lincoln developed an early interest in politics. He served in the Illinois state legislature and the United States Congress, where he earned a reputation as a champion of emancipation. In 1858, he ran for the United States Senate against Stephen Douglas. Lincoln lost the election, but his heated debates with Douglas brought him national recognition and helped him win the presidency in 1860.

Shortly after his election, the Civil War erupted. Throughout the war, Lincoln showed great strength and courage. He also demonstrated his gift for oratory. He was invited to make "a few appropriate remarks" in November 1863 for a dedication of the Gettysburg battlefield as a national cemetery. The world has long remembered what he said there.

Robert E. Lee (1807–1870)

The job of commanding the Confederate army during the Civil War wasn't one that Robert E. Lee wanted. As the dispute over slavery grew, Lee was torn. He believed in the Union, he opposed both slavery and secession, and he was regarded as one of the finest military leaders in the United States Army. When President Lincoln offered him command of the Union forces, however, Lee refused to lead an army against his native state and resigned from the army, vowing to fight only in defense of Virginia.

Unlike many Confederate leaders, Lee had no illusions about the South's power. Serving initially as commander of the army of northern Virginia and later of all the Confederate armies, he expected the widespread bloodshed and destruction caused by the war. He was an extraordinary military leader whose accomplishments and personal integrity in the face of overwhelming odds inspired great loyalty in both soldiers and civilians.

On the eve of resigning his U.S. Army commission, Lee explored his divided loyalties in "Letter to His Son."

◆ Background for Understanding

HISTORY: LINCOLN PREPARES TO SPEAK AT GETTYSBURG

The battle of Gettysburg, Pennsylvania, fought in July 1863, was an important Union victory and marked a turning point in the war. More than 51,000 soldiers were injured in the battle. On November 19, 1863, a military cemetery on the battlefield was dedicated. Unsure of President Lincoln's availability, the dedication organizers slated him as a secondary speaker, asking him to make only "a few appropriate remarks." In drafting that brief address, Lincoln wanted to lead the 15,000 American citizens at the cemetery dedication through an emotional final rite of passage. He also needed to gain continuing support for a bloody conflict that was far from won.

Stories abound regarding Lincoln's drafting of the speech: He wrote it the week before; he wrote it the night before; he wrote it on the train; he wrote it on a piece of scrap paper. Certainly, he was still revising even as he spoke, adding the phrase "under God" to describe the nation. An experienced speaker, Lincoln probably anticipated the positive effect this suggestion of divine approval of the United States and its goals of freedom would have on the audience.

The Gettysburg Address ◆ Second Inaugural Address ◆ Letter to His Son ◆

◆ *Literature and Your Life*

CONNECT YOUR EXPERIENCE

Divided loyalties like Robert E. Lee's were common in a time when many felt more closely tied to their home state than to the nation. Divided loyalties are still common, though the choices are different. Friends with opposing priorities, commitments at school and work—all can become forces in a tug of war for your loyalty.

Journal Writing Describe a situation—in your life, a film or book, or recent public events—where divided loyalties required a difficult choice. Explore how the decision was made.

THEMATIC FOCUS: A NATION DIVIDED

The right words can often overcome division. In the "Second Inaugural Address," President Lincoln sought to heal a torn nation. How can a moving description of common beliefs and goals encourage enemies to set aside their differences?

◆ Build Vocabulary

WORD ROOTS: -archy-

The word *anarchy* in "Letter to His Son" derives from the root *-archy-,* meaning "rule" or "government." In combination with the prefix *an-,* meaning "without," you can guess that *anarchy* means "without government."

WORD BANK

Preview this list of words from the selections.

> consecrate
> hallow
> deprecated
> insurgents
> discern
> scourge
> malice
> anarchy
> redress

◆ Grammar and Style

PARALLEL STRUCTURE

Lincoln uses **parallel structure**—the expression of similar ideas in similar form—to emphasize his important ideas. For example, these phrases from his "Second Inaugural Address" make such an impression that the words remain among Lincoln's most memorable:

> With malice toward none; with charity for all;
> with firmness in the right . . .

Each phrase is an introductory prepositional phrase containing the preposition "with." You will find many other examples of parallel structure in Lincoln's two speeches. Note how they linger in your memory.

◆ Literary Focus

DICTION

You'll notice that Lee's **diction**—or word choice—in writing to his son was more informal than that of President Lincoln in drafting a public speech. Word choice—formal or informal, concrete or abstract—gives a writer's voice its unique quality. For example, Lee's phrase, *"I see that four states have declared themselves out of the Union . . ."* is more personal and informal than Lincoln's statement, *"insurgent agents were . . . seeking to dissol[v]e the Union, and divide effects, by negotiation."* Notice how each writer's diction reflects his audience and purpose.

◆ Reading Strategy

USE PRIOR KNOWLEDGE

Reading a historical document without understanding its historical context is like viewing a sequel before the original film: You may grasp the basic story, but you'll miss much of the underlying meaning. As you read, **use prior knowledge** of the Civil War to help you analyze ideas, actions, and decisions in context. For example, you already know that Lee felt more closely allied to his home state than to the nation. Use this knowledge to understand the decisions he presents in his letter.

The Gettysburg Address

Abraham Lincoln

Abraham Lincoln's Address at the Dedication of the Gettysburg National Cemetery, 19 November 1863

◄ **Critical Viewing**
What personal qualities of President Lincoln are conveyed through this illustration of his delivery of "The Gettysburg Address"? **[Analyze]**

Four score and seven years ago our fathers brought forth on this continent a new nation, conceived in Liberty, and dedicated to the proposition that all men are created equal.

Now we are engaged in a great civil war, testing whether that nation, or any nation so conceived and so dedicated, can long endure. We are met on a great battle-field of that war. We have come to dedicate a portion of that field, as a final resting place for those who here gave their lives that that nation might live. It is altogether fitting and proper that we should do this.

But, in a larger sense, we cannot dedicate—we cannot <u>consecrate</u>—we cannot <u>hallow</u>—this ground. The brave men, living and dead, who struggled here, have consecrated it, far above our poor power to add or detract. The world will little note, nor long remember what we say here, but it can never forget what they did here. It is for us the living, rather, to be dedicated here to the unfinished work which they who fought here have thus far so nobly advanced. It is rather for us to be here dedicated to the great task remaining before us—that from these honored dead we take increased devotion to that cause for which they gave the last full measure of devotion—that we here highly resolve that these dead shall not have died in vain—that this nation, under God, shall have a new birth of freedom—and that government of the people, by the people, for the people, shall not perish from the earth.

◆ **Build Vocabulary**
consecrate (kän′ sə krāt′) *v.*: Cause to be revered or honored
hallow (hal′ ō) *v.*: Honor as sacred

Second Inaugural Address

Abraham Lincoln March 4, 1865

At this second appearing to take the oath of the presidential office, there is less occasion for an extended address than there was at the first. Then a statement, somewhat in detail, of a course to be pursued, seemed fitting and proper. Now, at the expiration of four years, during which public declarations have been constantly called forth on every point and phase of the great contest which still absorbs the attention, and engrosses the energies of the nation, little that is new could be presented. The progress of our arms, upon which all else chiefly depends, is as well known to the public as to myself; and it is, I trust, reasonably satisfactory and encouraging to all. With high hope for the future, no prediction in regard to it is ventured.

On the occasion corresponding to this four years ago, all thoughts were anxiously directed to an impending civil war. All dreaded it—all sought to avert it. While the inaugural address was being delivered from this place, devoted altogether to *saving* the Union without war, insurgent agents were in the city seeking to *destroy* it without war—seeking to dissol[v]e the Union, and divide effects, by negotiation. Both parties deprecated war; but one of them would *make* war rather than let the nation survive; and the other would *accept* war rather than let it perish. And the war came.

One eighth of the whole population were colored slaves, not distributed generally over the Union, but localized in the Southern part of it. These slaves constituted a peculiar and powerful interest. All knew that this interest was, somehow, the cause of the war. To strengthen, perpetuate, and extend this interest was the object for which the insurgents would rend the Union, even by war; while the government claimed no right to do more than to restrict the territorial enlargement of it. Neither party expected for the war, the magnitude, or the duration, which it has already attained. Neither anticipated that the *cause* of the conflict might cease with, or even before, the conflict itself should cease. Each looked for an easier triumph, and a result less fundamental and astounding. Both read the same Bible, and pray to the same God; and each invokes His aid against the other. It may seem strange that any men should dare to ask a just God's assistance in wringing their bread from the sweat of other men's faces; but let us judge not that we be not judged. The prayers of both could not be answered; that of neither has been answered fully. The Almighty has his own purposes. "Woe unto the world because of offences! for it must

◆ Build Vocabulary

deprecated (dep´ rə kāt´ id) *v.*: Expressed disapproval of; pleaded against

insurgents (in sʉr´ jənts) *n.*: Rebels; those who revolt against established authority

needs be that offences come; but woe to that man by whom the offence cometh!"[1] If we shall suppose that American Slavery is one of those offences which, in the providence of God,[2] must needs come, but which, having continued through His appointed time, He now wills to remove, and that He gives to both North and South, this terrible war, as the woe due to those by whom the offence came, shall we discern therein any departure from those divine attributes which the believers in a Living God always ascribe to Him? Fondly do we hope—fervently do we pray—that this mighty scourge of war may speedily pass away. Yet, if God wills that it continue, until all the wealth piled by the bond-man's two hundred and fifty years of unrequited toil shall be sunk, and until every drop of blood drawn with the lash, shall be paid by

another drawn with the sword, as was said three thousand years ago, so still it must be said "the judgments of the Lord, are true and righteous altogether."[3]

With malice toward none; with charity for all; with firmness in the right, as God gives us to see the right, let us strive on to finish the work we are in; to bind up the nation's wounds; to care for him who shall have borne the battle, and for his widow, and his orphan—to do all which may achieve and cherish a just and lasting peace, among ourselves, and with all nations.

---

3. **"The judgments . . . altogether":** From Psalm 19:9.

◆ Build Vocabulary

discern (di surn´) v.: Receive or recognize; make out clearly

scourge (skurj) n.: Cause of serious trouble or affliction

malice (mal´ is) n.: Ill will; spite

---

1. **"Woe unto the world . . . offence cometh":** From Matthew 18:7 of the King James Version of the Bible.
2. **providence of God:** Benevolent care or wise guidance of God.

Letter to His Son
Robert E. Lee   *January 23, 1861*

I received Everett's[1] *Life of Washington* which you sent me, and enjoyed its perusal. How his spirit would be grieved could he see the wreck of his mighty labors! I will not, however, permit myself to believe, until all ground of hope is gone, that the fruit of his noble deeds will be destroyed, and that his precious advice and virtuous example will so soon be forgotten by his countrymen. As far as I can judge by the papers, we are between a state of anarchy and civil war. May God avert both of these evils from us! I fear that

mankind will not for years be sufficiently Christianized to bear the absence of restraint and force. I see that four states[2] have declared themselves out of the Union; four more will apparently follow their example. Then, if the border states are brought into the gulf of revolution, one half of the country will be arrayed against the other. I must try and be patient and await the end, for I can do nothing to hasten or retard it.

The South, in my opinion, has been aggrieved by the acts of the North, as you say. I feel the aggression and am willing to take every proper step for redress. It is the principle I contend for, not individual or private benefit. As an American citizen, I take great pride in my country, her prosperity and institutions, and would defend any state if her

---

1. **Everett's:** Referring to Edward Everett (1789–1865), an American scholar and orator who made a long speech at Gettysburg before Lincoln delivered his famous address.

---

2. **four states:** South Carolina, Mississippi, Florida, and Alabama.

rights were invaded. But I can anticipate no greater calamity for the country than a dissolution of the Union. It would be an accumulation of all the evils we complain of, and I am willing to sacrifice everything but honor for its preservation. I hope, therefore, that all constitutional means will be exhausted before there is a resort to force. Secession is nothing but revolution. The framers of our Constitution never exhausted so much labor, wisdom, and forbearance in its formation, and surrounded it with so many guards and securities, if it was intended to be broken by every member of the Confederacy at will. It was intended for "perpetual union," so expressed in the preamble, and for the establishment of a government, not a compact, which can only be dissolved by revolution or the consent of all the people in convention assembled. It is idle to talk of secession. Anarchy would have been established, and not a government, by Washington, Hamilton, Jefferson, Madison, and the other patriots of the Revolution. . . . Still, a Union that can only be maintained by swords and bayonets, and in which strife and civil war are to take the place of brotherly love and kindness, has no charm for me. I shall mourn for my country and for the welfare and progress of mankind. If the Union is dissolved, and the government disrupted, I shall return to my native state and share the miseries of my people; and, save in defense, will draw my sword on none.

◆ **Build Vocabulary**

anarchy (an´ ər kē) *n.*: Absence of government
redress (ri´ dres) *n.*: Atonement; rectification

Guide for Responding

◆ *Literature and Your Life*

Reader's Response What do you think are the most memorable phrases in Lincoln's speeches?
Thematic Focus (a) How does Lincoln use language to soothe and heal his listeners' hearts? (b) Does Lee's aversion to a Union "maintained by swords" justify his decision to place the preservation of Virginia over the preservation of the union?
Journal Entry After the Civil War, Robert E. Lee applied for a complete pardon of his role in leading the Confederate forces against the Union army. If you were a member of Congress, would you have voted to grant it? Why or why not? Explore your answers in a brief journal entry.

☑ **Check Your Comprehension**

1. Briefly describe the occasion on which each of these two Lincoln speeches was delivered.
2. What views about slavery does Lincoln express in these speeches?
3. What choice was Lee considering in his letter?
4. How does Lee define secession?

◆ **Critical Thinking**

INTERPRET
1. (a) Beyond dedicating the battlefield cemetery, what was Lincoln's main purpose in "The Gettysburg Address"? (b) What was his main purpose in the "Second Inaugural Address"? **[Infer]**
2. Lincoln closed both speeches by describing his visions of the nation's eventual rebirth. Considering his purpose, why is this an effective way to structure both speeches? **[Connect]**
3. How does Lincoln attempt to reconcile or reach out to both the North and the South in his speeches? **[Analyze]**
4. In your own words, explain Robert E. Lee's argument against secession. **[Relate]**
5. How does Lee link his acknowledgment of his son's gift to his argument? **[Connect]**
6. What qualities did Lee and Lincoln share? **[Connect]**

APPLY
7. How are Lincoln's speeches different from modern presidential addresses? **[Relate]**

Guide for Responding (continued)

◆ Reading Strategy

USE PRIOR KNOWLEDGE

Although the pieces by Lincoln and Lee reveal important information about events connected to the Civil War, it's not possible to completely understand and appreciate the selections without having some **prior knowledge** of the Civil War era. One way to build on your prior knowledge before reading any literary work is to look at background information related to the subject. Add to your background about the Civil War by reviewing the biographies and Background for Understanding on p. 478. Then answer each question that follows.

1. Why did President Lincoln write such a short speech for his address at Gettysburg?
2. Why did Lincoln connect the honoring of the Gettysburg dead with the goal of continuing the war toward a Union victory?
3. In the "Second Inaugural Address," why did Lincoln suggest that both the war and an end to slavery were God's wish?
4. Why was Lee so opposed to secession?

◆ Build Vocabulary

USING THE WORD ROOT -archy-

Each of the following words contains the root -archy-, meaning "rule" or "government." Use your knowledge of the root and the supplied definitions to write a definition for each word on your paper.

1. monarchy (*mono* = single; one)
2. patriarchy (*patri* = father)
3. oligarchy (*olig* = few)

USING THE WORD BANK

In your notebook, write the letter of the word or phrase that is the best synonym for the first word.

1. consecrate: (a) destroy, (b) bless, (c) join together
2. hallow: (a) honor, (b) greet, (c) enlarge
3. deprecated: (a) condemned, (b) proved, (c) sensed
4. insurgents: (a) patriots, (b) loyal citizens, (c) rebels
5. discern: (a) overlook, (b) understand, (c) disregard
6. scourge: (a) punishment, (b) reward, (c) desire
7. malice: (a) forgiveness, (b) kindness, (c) ill will
8. anarchy: (a) leadership, (b) order, (c) chaos
9. redress: (a) atonement, (b) fear, (c) disturbance

◆ Literary Focus

DICTION

Diction refers to a writer's choice of words. President Lincoln used formal words and phrases to lend elegance and importance to his speeches. General Lee's less formal language creates a more intimate and personal feeling in his letter. Each writer used language that was appropriate to his subject, audience, occasion, and literary form.

1. Find two examples of formal diction in the "Second Inaugural Address."
2. Find two examples of informal, personal diction in Lee's "Letter to His Son."
3. Why is each writer's diction appropriate?

◆ Grammar and Style

PARALLEL STRUCTURE

When President Lincoln told the crowd at Gettysburg, "we cannot dedicate—we cannot consecrate—we cannot hallow—this ground," he was using **parallel structure** to dramatize his point.

> **Parallel structure** is the repeated use of similar ideas expressed in a similar grammatical form.

Practice In your notebook, identify the parallel structures in each of the following examples from Lincoln's speeches. The first one is done for you.

1. ...we cannot dedicate—we cannot consecrate—we cannot hallow—this ground
   Parallel structure: *we cannot* + verb
2. Fondly do we hope—fervently do we pray—that this mighty scourge ...
3. ...until all the wealth piled by the bond-man's ... and until every drop of blood drawn with the lash ...
4. All dreaded it—all sought to avert it.

Writing Application Rewrite a sentence from "Letter to His Son" using parallel structure to emphasize Lee's ideas.

Build Your Portfolio

Idea Bank

Writing

1. **Letter of Response** Assume the role of Lee's son and write an informal letter in which you respond to the ideas in your father's letter. **[Social Studies Link]**

2. **Diary Entry** It is the eve of the address at Gettysburg. Writing as Lincoln, describe the message you are striving to convey in the still-unfinished speech. How do you want it to be remembered?

3. **Newspaper Column** Writing as a journalist covering "The Gettysburg Address," react to the speech in a column. Do you agree with Lincoln, who thought the speech a failure, or with fellow speaker Edward Everett, who greatly admired it? Support your ideas with examples. **[Career Link]**

Speaking and Listening

4. **Reenactment** With a partner, brainstorm about what might have occurred when President Lincoln asked Lee to lead the Union army. Reenact the situation for the class. **[Career Link]**

5. **Mock Court** Stage a mock Supreme Court hearing in which students argue for or against a state's right to secede from the Union. After hearing "lawyers'" arguments, each "judge" should render an opinion. **[Social Studies Link]**

Projects

6. **Memorial Collage** Copy photographs or drawings of the Battle of Gettysburg from library or Internet sources. Combine them with text to create a collage. **[Art Link]**

7. **Web Site** Develop a plan for an Internet Web site providing information and images related to the Civil War. Create a flowchart that illustrates the links you'll include in your site. **[Media Link; Technology Link]**

Writing Mini-Lesson

Research Query

Choose an aspect of Civil War history that interests you, and write a research query, or letter of request, to gather information about it. Address your request to one of the many organizations, libraries, or historical societies that focus on this period of American history. Make your letter effective by using language and format appropriate to a business letter.

> **Writing Skills Focus:
> Appropriate Language for Purpose**
>
> **Appropriate language** ensures that readers understand your request and feel that their efforts are appreciated. Use courteous and formal language. Spell out organization names, choose concise words and phrases, and structure your sentences formally.

Prewriting Identify an organization or individual who can provide the data you want. To help you do so, study on-line or library sources such as the *United States Government Manual* and the *Washington Information Directory*. Answer the questions: What information do I want? Who is the best person to query? How can I narrow my query to elicit the most useful response?

Drafting Begin the letter with your own address, the date, an address containing the name and address of your recipient, and a salutation. In the body of the letter, state your request clearly and briefly. Then thank the recipient, sign the letter, and type or print your name below your signature.

Revising Read your letter aloud, making sure that you have used respectful language appropriate to your audience and purpose and that you've clearly indicated the information you're seeking. In addition, verify that names of people, places, and organizations are spelled correctly.

For What It's Worth
Stephen A. Stills

Thematic Connection

A NATION DIVIDED

The 1860's was a decade of great turmoil for our young nation, which found itself torn by a Civil War that arose from fundamental disagreements between North and South over many issues, including slavery. A century later, the United States was again torn by civil strife, with the Vietnam War and civil rights at the heart of the unrest. Protests were seemingly an everyday occurrence in the 1960's, and the nation once again found itself divided.

Just as the Civil War inspired memorable and enduring songs, the upheavals of the 1960's unleashed an outpouring of protest songs that quickly became an important means of expressing the ideas and feelings of a new generation. For young people openly challenging conventional attitudes and politics, music was more than just a form of entertainment; it was a means of social and political criticism. "For What It's Worth," written by folk-rock singer Stephen Stills, is characteristic of the era that produced such classics as "Where Have All the Flowers Gone?" and "Blowing in the Wind."

STEPHEN A. STILLS
(1945–)

Though a Dallas, Texas, native, double Rock & Roll Hall of Fame inductee Stephen Stills first made his mark on New York's music scene in the mid-1960's. The multi-talented songwriter, vocalist, and musician then moved to Los Angeles in 1966, where he invited fellow musicians Richie Furay and Neil Young to form Buffalo Springfield. Though the band stayed together only two years, Stills wrote one of his most famous songs, "For What It's Worth," for Buffalo Springfield. The song captured the mood of unrest and disenchantment characteristic of the late sixties.

FOR WHAT IT'S WORTH

Words and Music by Stephen A. Stills

There's something happening here
What it is ain't exactly clear
There's a man with a gun over there
Telling me I got to beware
5   I think it's time we stop, children,
     what's that sound
Everybody look what's going down

There's battle lines being drawn
Nobody's right if everybody's wrong
Young people speaking their minds
10 Getting so much resistance from behind

I think it's time we stop, hey,
     what's that sound
Everybody look what's going down

What a field-day for the heat[1]
A thousand people in the street
15 Singing songs and carrying signs
Mostly say, hooray for our side

It's time we stop, hey, what's that sound
Everybody look what's going down

Paranoia strikes deep
20 Into your life it will creep
It starts when you're always afraid
You step out of line,
     the man come and take you away

We better stop, hey, what's that sound
Everybody look what's going down
25 Stop, hey, what's that sound
Everybody look what's going down
Stop, now, what's that sound
Everybody look what's going down
Stop, children, what's that sound
30 Everybody look what's going down

---

1. **the heat:** Slang term for police or law enforcement.

◆ Build Vocabulary

Paranoia (par′ ə noı̆′ ə) *n.*: Mental disorder characterized by delusions, especially of persecution

Guide for Responding

◆ Literature and Your Life

Reader's Response Is this song, which was written three decades ago, relevant to your world? Why or why not?

Thematic Focus How does this song reflect the social unrest that characterized the late 1960's?

Journal Writing What images and scenes come to mind as you read this song? Briefly describe a few of the mental pictures suggested by the lyrics.

☑ Check Your Comprehension

1. What is being described in lines 13–16?
2. According to lines 19–22, what happens to those who openly disagree with the establishment?

◆ Critical Thinking

INTERPRET

1. In lines 3–4, the "man with a gun" who warns the speaker to beware is not a criminal but a military or law enforcement officer. How does this shed new light on your understanding of the chorus? **[Interpret]**
2. According to lines 19–22, what effect do social problems eventually have on individuals? **[Analyze]**
3. What does line 16 imply about the protesters in the streets? **[Infer]**

EVALUATE

4. Is the reference to "battle lines" in line 7 literal or figurative? Explain your reasoning. **[Make a Judgment]**

APPLY

5. Based on these lyrics, how would you characterize the relationship between young people—many of whom shared the point of view presented in this song—and authority figures during the 1960's? Explain. **[Synthesize]**

Thematic Connection

A NATION DIVIDED

The theme of protest is found throughout American history—from the days of the early colonists to the present. Because the right to free speech is protected by our Constitution, Americans have always been able to voice their beliefs and opinions openly. In the 1960's, in particular, musical artists used their place in the media spotlight to take a high-profile stand on issues of concern to their young listeners. Like other protest songs of its day, "For What It's Worth" reached a wide audience of radio listeners, record buyers, and concertgoers, who quickly adopted it as an anthem for the political and antiwar demonstrations of the late sixties.

1. Though "For What It's Worth" never takes a direct stand on a particular issue, it is clearly a protest song. What is Stills protesting, and what action is he trying to bring about on the part of his listeners?
2. How would you make the case for classifying spirituals, such as "Go Down, Moses," as protest songs of the Civil War era?
3. It can be argued that the following works from Part 1 were written as forms of protest. For each of the following selections, explain what is being protested and how the writer conveys his or her opposition. (a) "An Episode of War" (b) "An Occurrence at Owl Creek Bridge."

Idea Bank

Writing

1. **Updated Lyrics** Think about the social, environmental, and political issues of concern to you, your friends, and your classmates. Select one or two and use them as the focus of a modern version of "For What It's Worth." Rewrite the stanzas so that they reflect contemporary events and viewpoints. **[Performing Arts Link]**

2. **Interpretation** Review some of the specific events of the 1960's in an encyclopedia or history text. Write an interpretation of "For What It's Worth" that relates Stills's lyrics to specific events. Explain how you made the connection between the song lyrics and the events. **[Social Studies Link]**

3. **Evaluation** Musical artists continue to use their fame and their songs as a platform for social commentary and protest. How effective is popular music as a means of generating awareness and social change? Explore your response in a essay in which you support your points with examples from real life. **[Music Link]**

Speaking and Listening

4. **Interview/Group Discussion** Interview a parent, relative, family friend, or teacher who remembers the protest era of the 1960's. Prepare a series of questions about the changes taking place in society at that time, the issues and events that concerned young people, the prevalent philosophies and attitudes, and the ways in which people expressed their opposition. Tape-record or videotape your interview, and share it with the class. Afterward, lead a discussion of your classmates' responses to the interview. **[Social Studies Link]**

Projects

5. **Audio/Visual Interpretation** In the medium or form of your choice (painting, collage, sculpture, poster, audio or video montage), illustrate the theme "A Nation Divided" as it relates to the Civil War era, the 1960's, or a combination of the two. The finished work should illustrate both the issues at the heart of the division and their effect on the country. **[Art Link]**

Writing Process Workshop

It is one thing to identify a problem, but quite another to find a workable solution. The works in this section by Lincoln, Lee, and Chief Joseph all present solutions to significant problems: Lincoln, on how best to honor the sacrifices of the Union dead; Lee, on implementing constitutional measures as an alternative to civil war; and Chief Joseph, on resignation as the only possible response to further incursions by white settlers. In each case, the writer, after clearly identifying a problem, explains his strategy and gives the steps necessary for a solution. Follow their example by writing an essay in which you outline solutions to a problem in today's world that concerns you.

The following skills will help you write your essay:

Writing Skills Focus

▶ **Use precise details** to ensure that readers have a clear understanding of both the problem and solutions. (See p. 449.)

▶ **Maintain an objective tone** so that your readers trust the soundness of your solutions. (See p. 477.)

▶ **Organize your thoughts clearly and logically** so that your readers aren't lost in a maze of vaguely stated problems and half-thought-out answers. (See p. 465.)

Robert E. Lee's "Letter to His Son" demonstrates many of these skills:

MODEL FROM LITERATURE

[The dissolution of the Union] would be an accumulation of all the evils we complain of, and I am willing to sacrifice everything but honor for its preservation. ① I hope, therefore, that all constitutional means will be exhausted before there is a resort to force. ② Secession is nothing but revolution. The framers of our Constitution never exhausted so much labor, wisdom, and forbearance in its formation, and surrounded it with so many guards and securities, ③ if it was intended to be broken by every member of the Confederacy at will. ④

① ② The brief statement of the problem and the simple solution suggested make the writer's organization clear.

③ Information on constitutional safeguards adds force to his suggested solution.

④ Despite his southern roots, Lee maintains objectivity by recognizing the importance of constitutional measures.

APPLYING LANGUAGE SKILLS: Active and Passive Voice

A verb is in the **active voice** when the subject of a sentence performs the action (*I hired the clerk*). A verb is in the **passive voice** when the subject of a sentence receives an action—that is, when something is done to the subject (*The clerk was hired by me*).

Usually, the passive voice makes writing seem dull and plodding. Try to maintain the active voice.

Practice On your paper, rewrite each of these sentences in the active voice.

1. Success was attained by Bob by sheer hard work.
2. Training was offered to freshmen by the coach.
3. The secret map was contained in a jewel box under the bed.

Writing Application As you draft your essay, avoid using passive constructions. Rewrite sentences in the passive voice so that the subject performs, rather than receives, the action of the verb.

Writer's Solution Connection Language Lab

For more practice with active and passive voice, complete the Language Lab lesson on Strengthening Sentences.

Prewriting

Choose a Topic With a group of your classmates, brainstorm for a list of problems that affect you or the people around you. After you've created a broad list, discuss ideas for solving each of these problems. Review your notes for possible writing topics, or consider choosing one of the following ideas.

Topic Ideas

- The rising cost of movie tickets
- Pollution
- Slowing the aging process
- A dangerous local intersection

Gather Details Before you can make problems and solutions clear to the reader, you'll need to clarify them for yourself. Consider the following questions:

- What does your audience know about your topic?
- What insights do you bring that will help others understand your topic better?
- How does the situation present a problem? Whom does the problem affect, and how does it affect him or her?
- Is there just one problem or are there several related problems that need to be solved?
- How is your topic important, unique, or special?

Drafting

Identify the Problem Start your essay with a clear explanation of the problem you're addressing. Offer background information that shows why the problem exists and how it affects people.

Outline the Steps of Your Solution Don't assume that your readers can take a vague suggestion and solve a complex problem. Make the path to solution clear. For example, if you are writing about ways to slow the aging process, it is not enough to mention eating a healthy diet and exercising; rather, you should give information about which foods to eat and the amount and types of exercise recommended for a particular age group.

Remain Objective Your credibility hinges on your ability to maintain an even, objective approach. If you write without anger or emotion, you'll inspire the confidence that your solutions are the result of careful, logical reflection.

REVISION MODEL

① *The toll for the past year is sobering: six accidents, five injuries, three fatalities.*

The intersection is a major hazard. ∧ A traffic light would be well worth the safety gained for our community.

② *—in equipment, employees, and traffic delays—*

To implement this, the cost ∧ would be small compared to the benefits of a safer town.

① The writer elaborates with specific, objective information.
② The writer organizes the costs and will use this sentence as the outline for the essay.

Revising

Use a Peer Reviewer Have a classmate read your essay and comment on its logic, clarity, and objectivity. Ask your reviewer to suggest places where you might give more information. After making revisions based on your reviewer's comments, proofread your essay to be sure the grammar, spelling, and punctuation are correct.

Publishing

▶ **Give an Informative Speech to Your Class** A good way to share your essay is to give a class presentation. To prepare, practice reading your essay several times, either in front of a mirror or to a friend. Also, assemble any appropriate charts, diagrams, or maps. When you deliver your speech, remember to speak clearly and make eye contact with your audience.

▶ **Submit Your Essay for Publication** If your essay concerns an issue of importance to your classmates or community, consider submitting it to your school or local newspaper. Enclose a cover letter stating your reasons for wanting your essay to be published. Also, include your name, address, and phone number, in case the editor needs to contact you.

APPLYING LANGUAGE SKILLS: Avoiding Logical Fallacies

Fallacies are illogical conclusions based on unproven assumptions. Avoid these types of faulty logic:

Circular reasoning—restating the same argument in other words

Example: Neil is the richest because he has the most money.

Improved: Neil is the richest because he invested wisely.

Overgeneralization—a statement that is too broad for the evidence that backs it up

Example: Vegetarians are healthier and live longer.

Improved: Scientists found that vegetarians in a controlled study had fewer illnesses and longer lives.

Practice On your paper, identify the logical fallacies in the following statements.

1. People with hobbies are happier than those without.
2. Ann is the best student because she gets the best grades.

Writing Application Review your essay, and weed out any overgeneralizations or circular reasoning.

Writer's Solution Connection Writing Lab

For more information about logical fallacies, see the Drafting section of the Writing Lab Persuasion tutorial.

Real-World Reading Skills Workshop

Strategies for Success

Whether you plan to attend college, join the armed services, or look for a job after high school, you'll need to make important choices. Reading to find specific information can help you gather facts and compare different options.

Define the Search What information do you need? To help focus your search, you need to be able to answer this question. For example, you may want to research college locations, options for financial aid, or academic programs. If you want to learn about several unrelated options, search for them one at a time in order of your interest.

Compare Apples With Apples Develop consistent criteria for reviewing information. For example, look only at colleges in the Southwest with fewer than 5,000 students, or study education packages offered by different branches of the armed services. Don't compare education packages with training requirements.

Read to Find Information Determine how the information is organized. Directories of colleges, for example, may be divided geographically or by size. Use tables of contents and indexes to locate the topics you seek. You may want to create a notebook for your research. For each entry, record the features most important to you, along with the book and page number for future reference.

Apply the Strategy

You're committed to finding a college with between 2,000 and 3,000 students. You'd also like, if possible, to join a sorority or fraternity, to swim competitively, and to major in literature. You also know you won't have a car on campus. Review this information about two fictional colleges. Then answer the questions.

1. Do each of these entries meet your criterion of size? Explain.

Genova College
Location: Mauna, Hawaii
Student Population: 2,548, men and women
Housing: Dormitory
Degrees: Bachelor of Arts; Bachelor of Science
Departments: Literature and Languages; Sciences; Performing and Applied Arts; History
Unique Academic Stresses: Marine biology; Polynesian languages; Hawaiian history
Sports: Varied and well-funded
Sororities/Fraternities: Yes, but no resident facilities
Parking: Ample and free
Setting: Rural
Climate: Warm and seasonally rainy

Southern College
Location: Adour, Louisiana
Student Population: 2,134, men and women
Housing: None
Degrees: Bachelor of Arts; Bachelor of Science
Departments: Literature and Languages; Advanced Technologies; History; Creative Arts
Unique Academic Stresses: Early American literature; Space communications; Special education
Sports: Some facilities; no formal programs
Sororities/Fraternities: None
Parking: Limited spaces assigned by lottery
Setting: Urban
Climate: Hot summers with risk of hurricanes toward fall

2. Is your lack of a car likely to be a problem at either of these schools? Why or why not?

3. What are the sports programs like at each school? Which college might have a swim team?

4. Based on your criteria, which school do you think better suits your needs? Cite specific information to explain.

✔ *Here are other situations in which you'll need to read for specific information:*

▶ *Searching classified ads*
▶ *Making a major purchase, such as a house or a car*
▶ *Comparing job-training programs*

PART 2 *Focus on Literary Forms:*
Diaries, Journals, and Letters

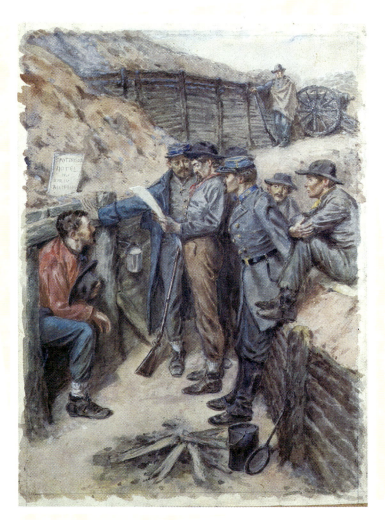

Newspapers in the Trenches '64, William Sheppard,
Museum of the Confederacy, Richmond, Virginia

The Civil War was one of the most painful chapters of American history. The diaries, letters, and journals in this section tell the story of the tragic conflict between the states, allowing readers to experience the events through the eyes of people who experienced them firsthand.

Guide for Interpreting

Civil War Voices

The Civil War was one of the most painful chapters of American history, touching the lives of millions of soldiers and civilians. The following diaries, journals, and letters tell the story of the war through the eyes of just a few of those whose lives were affected by it.

No one was hurt when the opening shots of the war were fired on Fort Sumter on April 12, 1860, but **Mary Boykin Chesnut** (1823–1886) seems to have sensed the carnage to come. The daughter of a cotton plantation owner and United States senator, Mary Boykin was raised in an aristocratic family in Charleston, South Carolina. At the age of seventeen, she married James Chesnut, Jr., a wealthy lawyer and future senator. Her journal entries convey the mingled optimism and dread that marked the opening days of the Civil War.

Men hurried to enlist in what most believed would be a swift and glorious war. Some young men, as we learn from the account of Union soldier **Warren Lee Goss,** saw the military as an opportunity for respect and advancement. The harsh realities of the training camp and battlefield soon taught soldiers on both sides that lives and limbs were the price of glory. The cost was especially high at the Battle of Gettysburg—a stunning defeat for Confederate general Robert E. Lee. In his diary, Confederate soldier **Randolph McKim** recounts the bravery of companions, many of whom were among the 51,000 killed or wounded at Gettysburg.

Confederate general and military strategist **Thomas Jonathan "Stonewall" Jackson** (1824–1863) earned his nickname early in the war for his steadiness and determination during the Battle of Bull Run in 1861. Jackson, who recounted the battle in a letter to his wife, died two years after his great victory; he was accidentally shot by his own troops and died of complications.

The Emancipation Proclamation, issued by President Lincoln on September 22, 1862, changed the purpose of the war. By declaring that all slaves would be freed on January 1, 1863, the Proclamation made the conflict into a war to end slavery, as well as a war to restore the Union. **Reverend Henry M. Turner**, a free-born African American who lived in Washington, D.C., recounts his community's reaction to the news.

When the war ended in 1865, abolitionist **Sojourner Truth** (1797–1883) had only begun to battle discrimination. A preacher and former slave, Truth is also recognized as an advocate of women's rights, temperance, and workplace and prison reform.

◆ Background for Understanding

MEDIA: THE PAST COMES TO LIFE IN *THE CIVIL WAR*

For five nights in early October 1990, Americans sat riveted by a public-television documentary called *The Civil War*. This unexpected hit, which garnered the highest rating of any series in PBS history, presented the story of the war as it had never been told: in the words of those who had lived it. In the course of creating *The Civil War,* filmmaker Ken Burns worked with 2,500 first-person quotations and 16,000 original photographs.

America's fascination with the series is a testament to the power of firsthand accounts to engage and move us. In the companion book, Burns explains how ordinary people captured the many facets of the war as no historian ever could.

"The America that went to war in 1861 was perhaps the most literate nation on earth. Soldiers at the front and civilians at home left an astonishingly rich and moving record of what they saw and felt ... descriptions, reflections, opinions, cries of outrage, cynicism, sorrow, laughter and triumph ... hundreds of voices from across the spectrum of American experience, men and women whose lives were touched or destroyed or permanently changed by the war."

Civil War Diaries, Journals, and Letters

◆ *Literature and Your Life*

CONNECT YOUR EXPERIENCE

In today's world, you can learn about key events almost instantly. You can see news footage that captures the sights and sounds of an event, and hear interviews in which the people involved describe what happened and share their feelings. The Civil War took place long before television cameras were invented, however, so the best way to learn about the war and share the experiences of those involved is through letters, journals, diaries, and photographs.

THEMATIC FOCUS: DIVISION, WAR, AND RECONCILIATION

What insights about the Civil War do these letters, diaries, and journals provide that aren't captured in most history books?

Journal Writing Describe what you already know about the impact of the Civil War on people's lives. When you've finished reading, note any additional insights you've gathered.

◆ Build Vocabulary

PREFIXES: *ob-*

Mary Chesnut uses the word *obstinate* to describe the Union commander's response to a Confederate attack. The word *obstinate* comes from a combination of the prefix *ob-*, meaning "against," and a form of the Latin root *-stare-*, meaning "stand." The adjective describes the commander's stubborn refusal to surrender.

WORD BANK

Preview this list of words from the selections.

| capitulate |
| audaciously |
| foreboding |
| obstinate |
| imprecations |
| serenity |

◆ Grammar and Style

CAPITALIZATION OF PROPER NOUNS

Proper nouns—nouns that name particular persons, places, things, or ideas—should begin with a capital letter. If a proper noun consists of two or more words, capitalize each with the exception of articles, coordinating conjunctions, and prepositions of fewer than four letters. Randolph McKim, for instance, uses capitalized proper nouns throughout his account: They include titles used before or in place of a name (*General Ewell*), particular places (*Culp's Hill*), and the names of specific regiments (*Second Maryland*).

◆ Literary Focus

DIARIES, JOURNALS, AND LETTERS

Diaries and **journals** are personal records of events, thoughts, feelings, and observations. Written on a day-to-day basis, they allow people to record immediate responses to experiences. Because diaries and journals are generally kept for personal use, they are usually written in an informal style that captures the writer's ideas and emotions. Similarly, a personal **letter** is written without the intention of publication. Yet because it is written to another person, it is not entirely private writing.

◆ Reading Strategy

DISTINGUISH FACT FROM OPINION

A fact is a statement that can be proven true; an opinion is a personal judgment that cannot be proved. As you read, **distinguish facts from opinions** by asking yourself whether a statement can be proved or only reflects the writer's bias. Consider this statement by Chesnut:

> Lincoln or Seward have made such silly advances and then far sillier drawings back.

While it is a fact that Union forces made advances and then drew back, the characterization of these actions as "silly" makes this a statement of opinion.

from

Mary Chesnut's Civil War

Mary Chesnut

In the early days of April 1861, the nation held its collective breath as the tension between North and South mounted steadily. On April 12, the opening shots of the Civil War were fired on Fort Sumter, a Union military post in Charleston, South Carolina, as the city's citizens watched from their rooftops. Mary Chesnut captured the emotional upheaval of the time in her journal.

April 7, 1861. Today things seem to have settled down a little.

One can but hope still. Lincoln or Seward[1] have made such silly advances and then far sillier drawings back. There may be a chance for peace, after all.

Things are happening so fast.

My husband has been made an aide-de-camp[2] of General Beauregard.

Three hours ago we were quietly packing to go home. The convention has adjourned.

Now he tells me the attack upon Fort Sumter[3] may begin tonight. Depends upon Anderson and the fleet outside. The *Herald* says that this show of war outside of the bar is intended for Texas.

John Manning came in with his sword and red sash. Pleased as a boy to be on Beauregard's staff while the row goes on. He has gone with Wigfall to Captain Hartstene with instructions.

Mr. Chesnut is finishing a report he had to make to the convention.

Mrs. Hayne called. She had, she said, "but one feeling, pity for those who are not here."

Jack Preston, Willie Alston—"the take-life-easys," as they are called—with John Green, "the big brave," have gone down to the island—volunteered as privates.

Seven hundred men were sent over. Ammunition wagons rumbling along the streets all night. Anderson burning blue lights—signs and signals for the fleet outside, I suppose.

Today at dinner there was no allusion to things as they stand in Charleston Harbor. There was an undercurrent of intense excitement. There could not have been a more brilliant circle. In addition to our usual quartet (Judge Withers, Langdon Cheves, and Trescot) our two governors dined with us, Means and Manning.

These men all talked so delightfully. For once in my life I listened.

That over, business began. In earnest, Governor Means rummaged a sword and red sash from somewhere and brought it for Colonel Chesnut, who has gone to demand the surrender of Fort Sumter.

And now, patience—we must wait.

Why did that green goose Anderson go into Fort Sumter? Then everything began to go wrong.

Now they have intercepted a letter from him, urging them to let him surrender. He paints the horrors likely to ensue if they will not.

He ought to have thought of all that before he put his head in the hole.

April 12, 1861. Anderson will not capitulate.

Yesterday was the merriest, maddest dinner we have had yet. Men were more audaciously wise and witty. We had an unspoken foreboding it was to be our last pleasant

---

1. **Seward:** William Henry Seward (1801–1872), U.S. Secretary of State from 1861 through 1869.
2. **aide-de-camp** (ād´ də kamp´) *n.*: Officer serving as assistant and confidential secretary to a superior.
3. **Fort Sumter:** Fort in Charleston Harbor, South Carolina. At the time, the fort was occupied by Union troops commanded by Major Robert Anderson.

meeting. Mr. Miles dined with us today. Mrs. Henry King rushed in: "The news, I come for the latest news—all of the men of the King family are on the island"—of which fact she seemed proud.

While she was here, our peace negotiator—or envoy—came in. That is, Mr. Chesnut returned—his interview with Colonel Anderson had been deeply interesting—but was not inclined to be communicative, wanted his dinner. Felt for Anderson. Had telegraphed to President Davis[4] for instructions.

What answer to give Anderson, etc., etc. He has gone back to Fort Sumter with additional instructions.

When they were about to leave the wharf, A. H. Boykin sprang into the boat, in great excitement; thought himself ill-used. A likelihood of fighting—and he to be left behind!

I do not pretend to go to sleep. How can I? If Anderson does not accept terms—at four—the orders are—he shall be fired upon.

I count four—St. Michael chimes. I begin to hope. At half-past four, the heavy booming of a cannon.

I sprang out of bed. And on my knees—prostrate—I prayed as I never prayed before.

There was a sound of stir all over the house—pattering of feet in the corridor—all seemed hurrying one way. I put on my double gown and a shawl and went, too. It was to the housetop.

The shells were bursting. In the dark I heard a man say "waste of ammunition."

I knew my husband was rowing about in a boat somewhere in that dark bay. And that the shells were roofing it over—bursting toward the fort. If Anderson was <u>obstinate</u>—he was to order the forts on our side to open fire. Certainly fire had begun. The regular roar of the cannon—there it was. And who could tell what each volley accomplished of death and destruction.

The women were wild, there on the housetop. Prayers from the women and <u>imprecations</u> from the men, and then a shell would light up the scene. Tonight, they say, the forces are to attempt to land.

---

4. **President Davis:** Jefferson Davis (1808–1889), president of the Confederacy (1861–1865).

The *Harriet Lane*[5] had her wheelhouse[6] smashed and put back to sea.

We watched up there—everybody wondered. Fort Sumter did not fire a shot.

Today Miles and Manning, colonels now—aides to Beauregard—dined with us. The latter hoped I would keep the peace. I give him only good words, for he was to be under fire all day and night, in the bay carrying orders, etc.

Last night—or this morning truly—up on the housetop I was so weak and weary I sat down on something that looked like a black stool.
"Get up, you foolish woman—your dress is on fire," cried a man. And he put me out.

It was a chimney, and the sparks caught my clothes. Susan Preston and Mr. Venable then came up. But my fire had been extinguished before it broke out into a regular blaze.

Do you know, after all that noise and our tears and prayers, nobody has been hurt. Sound and fury, signifying nothing.[7] A delusion and a snare. . . .

Somebody came in just now and reported Colonel Chesnut asleep on the sofa in General Beauregard's room. After two such nights he must be so tired as to be able to sleep anywhere. . . .

April 13, 1861. Nobody hurt, after all. How gay we were last night.

Reaction after the dread of all the slaughter we thought those dreadful cannons were making such a noise in doing.

Not even a battery[8] the worse for wear.

---

5. **The *Harriet Lane*:** Federal steamer that had brought provisions to Fort Sumter.
6. **wheelhouse** *n.*: Enclosed place on the upper deck of a ship, in which the helmsman stands while steering.
7. **Sound . . . nothing:** From Shakespeare's *Macbeth,* Act V, Scene v, lines 27–28. Macbeth is contemplating the significance of life and death after learning of his wife's death.
8. **battery** *n.*: Artillery unit.

◆ **Build Vocabulary**

capitulate (kə pich′ ə lāt′) *v.*: Surrender conditionally
audaciously (ô dā′ shəs lē) *adv.*: Boldly or daringly
foreboding (fôr bōd′ iŋ) *n.*: Presentiment
obstinate (äb′ stə nit) *adj.*: Stubborn
imprecations (im′ prə kā′ shənz) *n.*: Curses

Bombardment of Sumter, Harper's Weekly, 1861

▲ **Critical Viewing** How do the figures in this painting seem to be reacting to the bombing of Fort Sumter? [**Analyze**]

April 15, 1861. I did not know that one could live such days of excitement.

They called, "Come out—there is a crowd coming."

A mob indeed, but it was headed by Colonels Chesnut and Manning.

The crowd was shouting and showing these two as messengers of good news. They were escorted to Beauregard's headquarters. Fort Sumter had surrendered.

Those up on the housetop shouted to us, "The fort is on fire." That had been the story once or twice before.

When we had calmed down, Colonel Chesnut, who had taken it all quietly enough—if anything, more unruffled than usual in his <u>serenity</u>—told us how the <u>surrender</u> came about.

Wigfall was with them on Morris Island when he saw the fire in the fort, jumped in a little boat and, with his handkerchief as a white flag, rowed over to Fort Sumter. Wigfall went in through a porthole.

When Colonel Chesnut arrived shortly after and was received by the regular entrance, Colonel Anderson told him he had need to pick his way warily, for it was all mined.

As far as I can make out, the fort surrendered to Wigfall.

But it is all confusion. Our flag is flying there. Fire engines have been sent to put out the fire.

Everybody tells you half of something and then rushes off to tell something else or to hear the last news. . . .

Fort Sumter has been on fire. He has not yet silenced any of our guns. So the aides—still with swords and red sashes by way of uniform—tell us.

But the sound of those guns makes regular meals impossible. None of us go to table. But tea trays pervade the corridors, going everywhere.

Some of the anxious hearts lie on their beds and moan in solitary misery. Mrs. Wigfall and I solace ourselves with tea in my room.

These women have all a satisfying faith.

◆ **Build Vocabulary**
serenity (sə ren´ ə tē) *n.*: Calmness

Recollections of a Private

Warren Lee Goss

In the weeks that followed the attack on Fort Sumter, thousands of men on both sides volunteered to fight. Among the early enlistees was Warren Lee Goss of Massachusetts.

"Cold chills" ran up and down my back as I got out of bed after the sleepless night, and shaved preparatory to other desperate deeds of valor. I was twenty years of age, and when anything unusual was to be done, like fighting or courting, I shaved.

With a nervous tremor convulsing my system, and my heart thumping like muffled drumbeats, I stood before the door of the recruiting office, and before turning the knob to enter read and reread the advertisement for recruits posted thereon, until I knew all its peculiarities. The promised chances for "travel and promotion" seemed good, and I thought I might have made a mistake in considering war so serious after all. "Chances for travel!" I must confess now, after four years of soldiering, that the "chances for travel" were no myth; but "promotion" was a little uncertain and slow.

I was in no hurry to open the door. Though determined to enlist, I was half inclined to put it off awhile; I had a fluctuation of desires; I was fainthearted and brave; I wanted to enlist, and yet—Here I turned the knob, and was relieved. . . .

My first uniform was a bad fit: My trousers were too long by three or four inches; the flannel shirt was coarse and unpleasant, too large at the neck and too short elsewhere. The forage cap[1] was an ungainly bag with pasteboard top and leather visor; the blouse was the only part which seemed decent; while the overcoat made me feel like a little nubbin of corn in a large preponderance of husk. Nothing except "Virginia mud" ever took down my ideas of military pomp quite so low.

After enlisting I did not seem of so much consequence as I had expected. There was not so much excitement on account of my military appearance as I deemed justly my due. I was taught my facings, and at the time I thought the drillmaster needlessly fussy about shouldering, ordering, and presenting arms. At this time men were often drilled in company and regimental evolutions long before they learned the manual of arms, because of the difficulty of obtaining muskets. These we obtained at an early day, but we would willingly have resigned them after carrying them a few hours. The musket, after an hour's drill, seemed heavier and less ornamental than it had looked to be.

The first day I went out to drill, getting tired of doing the same things over and over, I said to the drill sergeant: "Let's stop this fooling and go over to the grocery." His only reply was addressed to a corporal: "Corporal, take this man out and drill him"; and the corporal did! I found that suggestions were not so well appreciated in the army as in private life, and that no wisdom was equal to a drillmaster's "Right face," "Left wheel," and "Right, oblique, march." It takes a raw recruit some time to learn that he is not to think or suggest, but obey. Some never do learn. I acquired it at last, in humility and mud, but it was tough. Yet I doubt if my patriotism, during my first three weeks' drill, was quite knee high. Drilling looks easy to a spectator, but it isn't. After a time I had cut down my uniform so that I could see out of it, and had conquered the drill sufficiently to see through it. Then the word came: on to Washington! . . .

---

1. **forage cap:** Cap worn by infantry soldiers.

A Confederate Account of the Battle of Gettysburg

Randolph McKim

From July 1 to July 3, 1863, Union and Confederate troops fought near the small town of Gettysburg, Pennsylvania. After Union troops gained control of the hills surrounding the town, the Confederate troops commanded by Robert E. Lee launched a risky attack on the strongest Union position. When the attack failed, the Confederate troops were forced to retreat at a great cost of lives. The battle, the first in which troops commanded by Lee were defeated, marked a turning point in the war. In a diary entry, Confederate soldier Randolph McKim described the final day of the battle.

Then came General Ewell's order to assume the offensive and assail the crest of Culp's Hill, on our right. . . . The works to be stormed ran almost at right angles to those we occupied. Moreover, there was a double line of entrenchments, one above the other, and each filled with troops. In moving to the attack we were exposed to enfilading fire[1] from the woods on our left flank, besides the double line of fire which we had to face in front, and a battery of artillery posted on a hill to our left rear opened upon us at short range. . . .

On swept the gallant little brigade, the Third North Carolina on the right of the line, next the Second Maryland, then the three Virginia regiments (10th, 23d, and 37th), with the First North Carolina on the extreme left. Its ranks had been sadly thinned, and its energies greatly depleted by those six fearful hours of battle that morning; but its nerve and spirit were undiminished. Soon, however, the left and center were checked and then repulsed, probably by the severe flank fire from the woods; and the small remnant of the Third North Carolina, with the stronger Second Maryland (I do not recall the banners of any other regiment), were far in advance of the rest of the line. On they pressed to within about twenty or thirty paces of the works—a small but gallant band of heroes daring to attempt what could not be done by flesh and blood.

The end soon came. We were beaten back to the line from which we had advanced with terrible loss, and in much confusion, but the enemy did not make a countercharge. By the strenuous efforts of the officers of the line and of the staff, order was restored, and we reformed in the breastworks[2] from which we had emerged, there to be again exposed to an artillery fire exceeding in violence that of the early morning. It remains only to say that, like Pickett's men[3] later in the day, this single brigade was hurled unsupported against the enemy's works. Daniel's brigade remained in the breastworks during and after the charge, and neither from that command nor from any other had we any support. Of course it is to be presumed that General Daniel acted in obedience to orders. We remained in this breastwork after the charge about an hour before we finally abandoned the Federal entrenchments and retired to the foot of the hill.

---

1. **enfilading** (en´ fə lād iŋ) **fire:** Gunfire directed along the length of a column or line of troops.

2. **breastworks:** Low walls put up quickly as a defense in battle.

3. **Pickett's men:** General George Pickett was a Confederate officer who led the unsuccessful attack on the Union position.

An Account of the Battle of Bull Run

Stonewall Jackson

In this letter to his wife, Confederate General Thomas "Stonewall" Jackson recounts the first southern victory of the war: a battle fought in July 1861, outside Washington, D.C., near a small stream named Bull Run.

Stonewall Jackson at Bull Run

▲ **Critical Viewing** How does the artist's depiction of Jackson enable the viewer to immediately distinguish the general from the officers and soldiers who surround him? **[Analyze]**

My precious pet,

Yesterday we fought a great battle and gained a great victory, for which all the glory is due to God alone. Although under a heavy fire for several continuous hours, I received only one wound, the breaking of the longest finger of my left hand; but the doctor says the finger can be saved. It was broken about midway between the hand and knuckle, the ball passing on the side next [to] the forefinger. Had it struck the center, I should have lost the finger. My horse was wounded, but not killed. Your coat got an ugly wound near the hip, but my servant, who is very handy, has so far repaired it that it doesn't show very much. My preservation was entirely due, as was the glorious victory, to our God, to whom be all the honor, praise and glory. The battle was the hardest that I have ever been in, but not near so hot in its fire. I commanded the center more particularly, though one of my regiments extended to the right for some distance. There were other commanders on my right and left. Whilst great credit is due to other parts of our gallant army, God made my brigade more instrumental than any other in repulsing the main attack. This is for your information only—say nothing about it. Let others speak praise, not myself.

Reaction to the Emancipation Proclamation

Reverend Henry M. Turner

On September 22, 1862, President Lincoln issued the Emancipation Proclamation, declaring that all slaves in states still in rebellion would be free as of January 1, 1863. Because those states were not under Union control at the time, no slaves were actually set free that day. The Proclamation, however, was a powerful symbol of hope for those still in slavery and inspired a wave of Union support from free African Americans. In this account, Reverend Henry M. Turner, a free-born African American living in Washington, D.C., describes his people's reaction to the news of the Proclamation.

Reading the Emancipation Proclamation, Artist unknown

▲ **Critical Viewing** How does this illustration relate to Reverend Turner's account? **[Connect]**

Seeing such a multitude of people in and around my church, I hurriedly sent up to the office of the first paper in which the proclamation of freedom could be printed, known as the *Evening Star*, and squeezed myself through the dense crowd that was waiting for the paper. The first sheet run off with the proclamation in it was grabbed for by three of us, but some active young man got possession of it and fled. The next sheet was grabbed for by several, and was torn into tatters. The third sheet from the press was grabbed for by several, but I succeeded in procuring so much of it as contained the proclamation, and off I went for life and death. Down Pennsylvania Avenue I ran as for my life, and when the people saw me coming with the paper in my hand they raised a shouting cheer that was almost deafening. As many as could get around me lifted me to a great platform, and I started to read the proclamation. I had run the best end of a mile, I was out of breath, and could not read. Mr. Hinton, to whom I handed the paper, read it with great force and clearness. While he was reading every kind of demonstration and gesticulation was going on. Men squealed, women fainted, dogs barked, white and colored people shook hands, songs were sung, and by this time cannons began to fire at the navy yard, and follow in the wake of the roar that had for some time been going on behind the White House. . . . Great processions of colored and white men marched to and fro and passed in front of the White House and congratulated President Lincoln on his proclamation. The President came to the window and made responsive bows, and thousands told him, if he would come out of that palace, they would hug him to death. . . . It was indeed a time of times, and nothing like it will ever be seen again in this life.

An Account of an Experience With Discrimination

Sojourner Truth

Although the Civil War brought an end to slavery, the struggle against racial discrimination was just beginning. In the following letter, written on October 1, 1865, Sojourner Truth describes an encounter with racism.

A few weeks ago I was in company with my friend Josephine S. Griffing, when the conductor of a streetcar refused to stop his car for me, although [I was] closely following Josephine and holding on to the iron rail. They dragged me a number of yards before she succeeded in stopping them. She reported the conductor to the president of the City Railway, who dismissed him at once, and told me to take the number of the car whenever I was mistreated by a conductor or driver. On the 13th I had occasion to go for necessities for the patients in the Freedmen's Hospital where I have been doing and advising for a number of months. I thought now I would get a ride without trouble as I was in company with another friend, Laura S. Haviland of Michigan. As I ascended the platform of the car, the conductor pushed me, saying "Go back—get off here." I told him I was not going off, then "I'll put you off" said he furiously, clenching my right arm with both hands, using such violence that he seemed about to succeed, when Mrs. Haviland told him he was not going to put me off. "Does she belong to you?" said he in a hurried angry tone. she replied, "She does not belong to me, but she belongs to humanity." The number of the car was noted, and conductor dismissed at once upon the report to the president, who advised his arrest for assault and battery as my shoulder was sprained by his effort to put me off. Accordingly I had him arrested and the case tried before Justice Thompson. My shoulder was very lame and swollen, but is better. It is hard for the old slaveholding spirit to die. But die it must. . . .

Guide for Responding

◆ *Literature and Your Life*

Reader's Response In the early days of the Civil War, would you have volunteered to fight? Why or why not?

Thematic Focus In what ways have these selections added to your understanding of the Civil War?

☑ Check Your Comprehension

1. What events does Mary Chesnut describe in her diary entries?
2. Summarize the events described in the accounts of the three soldiers.
3. What is the reaction to the Emancipation Proclamation among the members of Reverend Turner's audience?

◆ Critical Thinking

INTERPRET
1. What does Mary Chesnut's diary reveal about her attitude toward the war? **[Interpret]**
2. How do Private Goss's attitudes and expectations change after he has enlisted? **[Analyze]**
3. How would you describe the tone of (a) Randolph McKim's and (b) Stonewall Jackson's accounts? **[Analyze]**
4. Why did the Emancipation Proclamation have such an emotional effect on African Americans who were already free? **[Speculate]**
5. Given that Truth assumed she could ride a streetcar "without trouble as I was in company with" Laura S. Haviland, what can you reasonably infer about Haviland? **[Infer]**

APPLY
6. How might Chesnut's diary have been different if she had been from the North? **[Modify]**

EXTEND
7. What later leaders and events are foreshadowed by Truth's determination to overcome discrimination? **[Social Studies Link]**

Guide for Responding (continued)

◆ Literary Focus

DIARIES, JOURNALS, AND LETTERS

These **diaries, journals,** and **letters** describe Civil War events and people, as well as the writers' personal responses to them.

1. Many of Mary Chesnut's descriptions are colored by her dislike for the war. Give at least two examples that indicate this dislike.
2. Stonewall Jackson's letter is intended for his wife alone. Find three examples of details or ideas that Jackson probably would have omitted from an account intended for publication.
3. What does Sojourner Truth's letter reveal about her own personality?

◆ Build Vocabulary

USING THE PREFIX *ob-*

Use your understanding of the prefix *ob-*, meaning "against," to match each of the following situations to the word that most closely relates to it.

a. obstruction *(n.)* **b.** obscure *(v.)* **c.** object *(v.)*

1. voice opposition in the courtroom
2. a fallen tree blocking the road
3. cloud an issue with confusing arguments

USING THE WORD BANK

Write each of the following sentences on your paper, filling in the blanks with an appropriate word from the Word Bank.

1. When the rifle jammed, the soldier muttered _____?_____ at his bad luck.
2. There was no _____?_____ to be found in the troubled hearts and minds of soldiers and civilians.
3. As enemy shells exploded in the distance, a sense of _____?_____ hung over the camp like fog.
4. Despite the overwhelming odds facing his brigade, the general refused to _____?_____.
5. What one person would call _____?_____, another person might call courageous.
6. After midnight, the spies crept _____?_____ close to the enemy's encampment.

◆ Reading Strategy

DISTINGUISH FACT FROM OPINION

By reading carefully and asking yourself whether certain assertions can be verified, you can **distinguish fact from opinion.** Each of the following sentences contains elements of fact and opinion. Identify the facts and opinions in each.

1. [Goss:] The forage cap was an ungainly bag with pasteboard top and leather visor; the blouse was the only part which seemed decent; while the overcoat made me feel like a little nubbin of corn in a large preponderance of husk.
2. [Jackson:] Your coat got an ugly wound near the hip, but my servant, who is very handy, has so far repaired it that it doesn't show very much.
3. [Turner:] Mr. Hinton, to whom I handed the paper, read it with great force and clearness.

◆ Grammar and Style

CAPITALIZATION OF PROPER NOUNS

The name of a street, road, town, city, county, or state is considered a **proper noun** and should begin with a **capital letter.** Directional words (east, west, and so on) that are part of the name of a place should also begin with a capital; for example, **N**orth **D**akota.

Practice Rewrite these sentences from the selections, correcting any errors in capitalization.

1. The *herald* says that this show of war outside of the bar is intended for texas.
2. On swept the gallant little brigade, the third north Carolina on the right of the line, next the second maryland, then the three virginia regiments (10th, 23d, and 37th), with the first north carolina on the extreme left.
3. Down Pennsylvania avenue I ran as for my life, and when the People saw me coming with the paper in my hand they raised a shouting cheer that was almost deafening.
4. Accordingly I had him arrested and the Case tried before justice Thompson.

Build Your Portfolio

Idea Bank

Writing

1. **Summary** Write a factual summary of the events described in the excerpt from *Mary Chesnut's Civil War*. Use transitions to link ideas and indicate the time order of events.

2. **Book Jacket** Persuade readers to buy a book of Civil War diary and journal entries and letters by writing a book jacket explaining the unique perspective of the war offered in these accounts.

3. **Reflective Essay** Today, few take the time to correspond or keep a journal. How is this a loss? In an essay, explore the personal benefits and historical value of engaging in this type of writing. Use these selections to illustrate your points.

Speaking and Listening

4. **Persuasive Speech** Speaking as either a Confederate or a Union recruiter, write and deliver a speech to persuade citizens to enlist to fight in the Civil War. **[Performing Arts Link]**

5. **Dramatic Reading** Rev. Turner recounts the emotional impact created by the Emancipation Proclamation. Deliver a dramatic reading of the document, accompanied by music that conveys the tone of your interpretation. **[Music Link]**

Projects

6. **Timeline** By the time Lincoln was inaugurated, seven states had seceded. Research the 1860 presidential election to learn what Lincoln's victory meant to the South. Create a timeline of events leading to the Civil War. **[Social Studies Link]**

7. **Model/Map** Work in a small group to research the Battle of Gettysburg. Create a model or map of the battlefield. Identify the locations of key events with explanatory captions. **[Social Studies Link]**

Writing Mini-Lesson

Firsthand Biography

Do you know someone personally whose accomplishments or experiences are noteworthy? Recount the events of his or her life in a firsthand biography that reflects your perspective on the individual. This brief but revealing profile should include some description of the person, as well as biographical information and your impressions of his or her achievements and personality. Bring your subject to life with action-packed verbs that engage readers.

Writing Skills Focus: Vivid Verbs

Strong, precise verbs, called **vivid verbs**, add liveliness to writing. They name specific actions that help readers envision the events being recounted. This passage from Goss's "Recollections of a Private," for example, would not be nearly as effective if it simply stated that Goss "was nervous." Vivid verbs, however, bring to life his experience as he prepared to enlist in the army.

Model From Private Goss's Account

With a nervous tremor *convulsing* my system, and my heart *thumping* like muffled drumbeats . . .

Prewriting Make a list of your subject's accomplishments or experiences and his or her personal qualities—character, appearance, behavior, and so on. If possible, interview your subject to gather specific biographical information. Then decide which details best reveal your perspective on your subject.

Drafting Focus on the most telling facts, details, and anecdotes. Consider using quotations or dialogue to convey your subject's personality. Keep your writing lively by using vivid verbs.

Revising Compare your draft with your prewriting list. Did you capture the subject as you perceive him or her? Which details should you add? Which seem unnecessary? Where can you replace dull verb choices with vivid verbs?

CONNECTIONS TO TODAY'S WORLD

Gulf War Journal *from* A Woman at War
Molly Moore

Literary Connection

WAR DIARIES, JOURNALS, AND LETTERS

The letters and diary and journal entries in Part 2 tell the story of the Civil War as seen through the eyes of people who experienced it firsthand. Through these intimate literary forms, each of these eyewitnesses—none of whom was a professional writer—presents a personal view of the events of the time.

In her book *A Woman at War*, journalist Molly Moore records her impressions of a modern conflict, the Persian Gulf War between Iraq and a coalition of forces led by the United States. Although Moore, as a newspaper reporter, usually writes objective news stories, this personal account of her experiences as a witness to history makes exciting reading. In this excerpt, she relates her story behind the news story—what it was like to cover the Persian Gulf War from the military zone. Like the personal accounts you have already read, Moore's narrative reveals a human side to war.

Thematic Connection

REVEALING THE HIDDEN FACES OF WAR

The Civil War was a long, bloody conflict that tore the nation apart. Those living outside the war zone, however, never fully comprehended the horror and devastation wrought by the war. Communication was limited and slow. Newspapers, where available, were a key source of information, but the news they contained was often days old. The only way to really understand the impact of the war was to live through it.

In the late 1960's, Americans experienced their first "living-room war" as violent, disturbing footage of the Vietnam War flashed across television screens every evening. The 1991 Persian Gulf War was a full-scale media event that unfolded in real time before the eyes of millions worldwide who watched round-the-clock coverage on satellite and cable news stations. Though viewers were able to "experience" war as never before, there is still something unique and compelling about a personal account by an eyewitness near the action, as journalist Molly Moore was in Saudi Arabia during the Gulf War.

MOLLY MOORE
(1956–   )

Molly Moore has worked for *The Washington Post* since 1981, covering local and state government; the Pentagon (for five years, including the Gulf War); and as a foreign correspondent in South Asia, covering India, Pakistan, Afghanistan, Bangladesh, Nepal, Bhutan and Sri Lanka. She is currently a foreign correspondent based in Mexico City.

Moore says she wrote *A Woman at War* because she came away from the Gulf War believing that most of the world had seen only the television version that was portrayed as a quick and effortless victory by the American armed forces. "That was not the war I witnessed as I accompanied the commanding Marine general on the front lines as he led his troops into Kuwait. There was nothing easy about the ground war. It was a war fraught with mistakes, miscalculations, and human frailty, a war in which each tent and every foxhole was a private battlefield of anguish and emotion."

Gulf War Journal

from

A Woman at War
Molly Moore

▲ **Critical Viewing** Speculate about the events leading up to this photograph taken outside the Dhahran International Hotel. What might the camera operator have been doing that caused the Saudi Arabian security guard to intervene? **[Speculate]**

In August 1990, Iraqi troops under the command of dictator Saddam Hussein invaded neighboring Kuwait, a tiny oil-rich nation on the Persian Gulf. Despite economic sanctions and repeated demands by the United Nations Security Council, Iraq refused to withdraw from Kuwait. In late November 1990, the Council presented the invaders with an ultimatum: leave Kuwait by January 15, 1991, or a coalition of nations, including the United States, would use
"all necessary means" to remove Iraqi troops from Kuwait. Iraq ignored the threat. Early on the morning of January 17, 1991, coalition forces began bombing Iraqi targets, marking the official launch of the Persian Gulf War, also known as Operation Desert Storm. Hundreds of reporters, Molly Moore among them, were gathered at the Dhahran International Hotel in Dhahran, Saudi Arabia, when the airstrike began.

A thunderous roar jarred me out of a light sleep. The hotel windows rattled and the entire building shook. I recognized the sound almost instantly: The U.S. Air Force's 1st Tactical Fighter Wing was taking off outside my window. The fighter jets normally took off in pairs, seldom more than six at a
time. But this was a massive, continuous wave of noise as a dozen or more of the F-15 Eagle fighters fired their afterburners and sped into the night sky. It could mean only one thing: The war had started. I glanced at my watch. It was 1:45 a.m.

Almost simultaneously I heard dozens of

▲ **Critical Viewing** These journalists are presenting their report from atop a tank. Why might the journalists have chosen this location for filming? **[Hypothesize]**

footsteps pounding down the hallways outside my door. The telephone rang. It was my *Washington Post* colleague in the room across the hall.

"It's started," said Guy Gugliotta, a seasoned foreign correspondant who'd been sent to Saudi Arabia to relieve me when I'd returned to Washington in December.

"I just heard the planes take off," I replied, collecting notebooks and a pen from the small desk in my room.

"We just got the first pool report[1] from another air base up north," Gugliotta said. "I'm calling the foreign desk now."

"I'll be upstairs," I told him. "See you there."

I joined the mob surging up the steps to the military's Joint Information Bureau on the third floor of the hotel. Despite the months of waiting and speculation and the more than one hundred stories I'd written dissecting

Operation Desert Shield, the enormity of the moment and the uncertainty of its consequences were almost overwhelming.

So much for "military disinformation." More than three hundred reporters now jammed the Dhahran International's opulent third-floor ballroom, which had been converted into large pressrooms. Reporters squeezed the public affairs officers for details and snatched copies of the media pool reports as soon as they were dictated by the pool of reporters assigned to an air base northwest of Dhahran.

Gugliotta joined me after giving the *Post* the meager information he had from the first pool report. "There's nothing coming out of Washington," he said. "Nobody has announced anything. Cheney[2] is supposed to make a statement later tonight."

An ABC *Nightline* reporter thrust a microphone into my face. "How do you feel about the information the military is providing about the war?"

---

1. **pool report:** During the Persian Gulf War, firsthand information was compiled, or pooled, in reports that then were released to all of the media organizations covering the war.

2. **Cheney** (chā´ nē): U.S. Secretary of Defense Richard Cheney.

I was tempted to say, "What information?" It's always a sure sign that there isn't any real information when reporters start interviewing each other.

"The only information we've gotten so far has been from the reporters on one of the pools," I replied. "At least that worked pretty well. Reporters were at the base where some of the first planes took off and they managed to get to a telephone to dictate a story before Washington even admitted the war had started."

Suddenly an ear-piercing siren wailed through the building.

"What is that?" I shouted to Gugliotta.

"Bomb shelter, get down to the bomb shelter," he yelled.

I followed the herd. As I sprinted down the stairs I noticed the signs that had been added since I'd left six weeks earlier: "To the shelters," with arrows pointing the way.

Almost six hundred hotel guests and staff spilled down the stairwells in near panic. Had the Iraqis launched a counterattack? Were they roaring down the coastal highway toward Dhahran? Had Saddam Hussein fired Scud missiles at us? We'd known since August that the hotel was in a prime target zone. It sat beside the most active military airfield in Saudi Arabia.

In the basement, frantic hotel employees tried to guide the frenzied crowd into half a dozen rooms, including the kitchen. Above the din, Philip Congdon, a former officer of the British special forces, who had been hired as the hotel's defense consultant, threatened, "Sit down or you will be tried!"

I was in a group that was shoved into the kitchen and ordered to lie on the floor. We were surrounded by large plate-glass windows. An explosion would send shards ripping through the air. I crawled beneath a large steel table, thinking it might protect me from flying glass.

"Everyone please sit down and put on your gas masks," directed Congdon, a wiry man who looked to be in his early fifties. Even when giving frightening directives, Congdon had one of those self-assured voices that could calm a hysterical mob.

The people around me were pulling gas masks over their faces. I panicked. I had no

mask. *The Washington Post*'s chemical protection suits had not yet arrived from British Aerospace in London even though we'd ordered them almost two months earlier.

"I don't have a mask," I called in a strained voice to Congdon. He looked at me with exasperation. "Just sit down, I'll get you something," he said impatiently.

Moments later he returned with a crude, spongy contraption that looked somewhat like a surgical mask and covered only my nose and mouth. I slipped it on, knowing it would merely postpone death a microsecond. I sat on the gritty kitchen floor, surrounded by slimy, rotting tomato halves and colleagues in full-face masks. If I could smell the stench of the tomatoes on the floor and the spoiled chicken parts on the counter above me, I figured chemical particles would have no trouble penetrating my pathetic mask.

The information vacuum was almost unbearable. We knew nothing about what was going on at the air base outside our windows or the world outside Saudi Arabia. The siren continued its annoying wail.

Someone pulled out a shortwave radio.

". . . In the event of an attack, there is likely to be a reprisal," the crackly voice said. "There is no reaction from the Iraqi side yet."

I breathed a little easier.

At 3:50 a.m., about thirty minutes after the siren sounded, the hotel security chief called an all clear, the signal that we could remove our gas masks and leave the basement shelter. The civil defense alert had been called because of uncertainty about how the Iraqi military would react to the first bombs dropped on Baghdad. As we pushed our way into the crowded corridors, Congdon warned, "You should be aware that the early stage of an offensive is the most likely time for an attack on Dhahran."

As soon as we were released from our temporary captivity, the JIB began activating emergency media pools in an effort to get reporters across the street to the air base, where pilots would soon be returning with tales of the first bombing runs. The reporters who would serve on these quick-reaction pools had been selected days earlier after acrimonious debates among feuding news organizations. Now, the public affairs officers couldn't find the *New York Times* reporter assigned to the pool. Guy Gugliotta volunteered to take his place. As he collected his sleeping bag and rucksack, Gugliotta rattled off the instructions for operating the satellite telephone the *Post* had leased for our war coverage. For a $53,000 leasing fee, we could have instant communications to Washington from anywhere on the battlefield, including the roof of the Dhahran International Hotel, where the high-tech contraption now sat.

Within the last hour, a convoy of humvees[3]

with machine guns mounted on their roofs had formed a tight ring around the front of the hotel.

I began piecing together the details. At 1:30 a.m., the guided-missile cruiser USS *San Jacinto*, stationed in the Red Sea, had fired the opening shot of the war: a 1.6 ton, twenty-foot-long Tomahawk cruise missile aimed at downtown Baghdad. Minutes later fighter planes based across the street from our hotel, as well as warplanes from bases across the Arabian Peninsula, roared into the sky toward Iraq.

Pool reports from reporters interviewing pilots began trickling into the JIB.

---

3. **humvees:** Large, rugged military vehicles known as High Mobility Multi-Purpose Wheeled Vehicles. The term *humvee* is derived from the acronym HMMWV.

▼ **Critical Viewing** How did computer-guided missiles such as the one in this photograph change the nature of combat? **[Speculate]**

"Baghdad lit up like a Christmas tree," Air Force colonel George Walton told reporters as he climbed out of his F-4G Wild Weasel electronic warfare jet.

"It was the scariest thing I've ever done," Lieutenant Ian Long, a British Tornado pilot, recounted. "Some tracers came off the target[4] down our left-hand side. We tried to avoid that by going right. On our right-hand side was a mass of white explosions, and yellow explosions that looked like flak.[5] You're frightened of failure, you're frightened of dying. You're flying as low as you dare, but high enough to get the weapons off. As the bombs come off, you just run . . . "

I tried to telephone the new details to the *Post*. I dialed and redialed and redialed. The hotel's switchboard was jammed. I raced to the roof of the hotel. Since I had last been there six

weeks earlier, it had become a jungle of satellite dishes, talk-show sets, and camera tripods. The hotel employees called it "Little Hollywood." Wires and electrical cords were coiled and stretched in every direction like a giant plate of spaghetti. It was dark and starting to mist.

I found the *Post* satellite telephone, a midget beside the monster network dishes. Its collapsible dish was about the size of a large umbrella. I pulled out my scribbled instructions and read them in the beam of my flashlight.

"Turn the generator on. The choke is on the back. Give pull one jerk. Adjust the choke." It operated like a lawn mower. Unlike a lawn mower, it started on the first try.

I switched on the telephone, encased in a metal box that looked like a large suitcase, and punched numbers on a keypad until "Indian"—as in Indian Ocean—appeared on a digital readout. I pressed the keypad again to find the designated satellite shore station at Perth, Australia. I dialed a code and *The Washington Post* foreign desk number. I heard three rings. "Foreign desk," said the perfectly clear voice on the other end of the telephone.

---

4. **"Some tracers . . . target:** The Iraqi military bases targeted for bombing responded by firing tracers, ammunition that traces its own course with a visible trail of smoke or fire.
5. **flak** (flak): Antiaircraft gunfire.

Guide for Responding

◆ Literature and Your Life

Reader's Response If you had been in Moore's place, would you have been exhilarated or terrified by the experiences described in this excerpt? Explain.

Thematic Focus How does this passage provide a subjective look at the process of objectively reporting a war?

☑ Check Your Comprehension

1. Why do the author and her colleagues rush to the Joint Information Bureau?
2. Why are the journalists at the Dhahran International Hotel at risk of injury?
3. Why is the civil defense alert called?

◆ Critical Thinking
INTERPRET
1. Given that the Dhahran International Hotel is located in a "prime target zone," why do you think journalists are willing to stay there? **[Infer]**
2. Why is an attack on "the most active military airfield in Saudi Arabia" a real possibility? **[Analyze]**
APPLY
3. Why do you think the author straps on the "pathetic mask," if she knows it will "merely postpone death a microsecond"? **[Speculate]**
EXTEND
4. Based on this journal passage, what personal qualities do you think are necessary for a career as a war correspondent for a newspaper, magazine, or broadcast company? **[Career Link]**

Literary Connection

TWENTIETH-CENTURY DIARIES, JOURNALS, AND LETTERS

Through Civil War letters and journals, you get a "behind the scenes" look at the individuals who were caught up in the war's dramatic events. Similarly, Molly Moore, in her journal of Gulf War experiences, gives readers a glimpse of what daily life was like for the journalists who sent news reports home from the battlefield.

1. How does Molly Moore's role in the war contrast with that of women during the Civil War?
2. What other details of Molly Moore's account confirm that it was written in the 1990's and not the 1860's?

Thematic Connection

REVEALING THE HIDDEN FACES OF WAR

"Official" information about the Civil War was hard to obtain. However, in our own time, information about war is instantly accessible to people far from the battlefields. Sophisticated media technology allows civilians to "witness" the sights, sounds, and harsh realities of conflicts taking place around the globe.

1. Compare and contrast the way Mary Chesnut and Molly Moore get information about the wars.
2. Does Molly Moore's situation in the Dhahran International Hotel more closely resemble the situation of Mary Chesnut or of Randolph McKim? Explain your answer.

Idea Bank

Writing

1. **Telegram** None of the six accounts of the Civil War in Part 2 is written by a journalist. Imagine that you are Molly Moore observing the Battle of Gettysburg firsthand. Compose a telegram to your editor at a Washington newspaper, in which you give information about what you have witnessed. **[Social Studies Link]**

2. **News Story** As a professional journalist, Molly Moore writes objective, factual stories for publication in *The Washington Post*. Write a news story such as Moore might have written about the war-related events described in this journal excerpt. **[Career Link]**

3. **Critical Essay** The accounts in Part 2 offer a personal glimpse of the excitement and confusion that often surround dramatic historic events. Good journalism, however, dictates that news accounts be factually accurate and unbiased. Write an essay in which you discuss the historical value of each type of account—personal/subjective journals and letters versus objective news reports—using the selections in Part 2 as well as your own knowledge of news media to support your points. **[Social Studies Link]**

Speaking and Listening

4. **Debate** In times of war, soldiers' lives often depend on how well military secrets are kept. In a democracy, though, the public has the right to know what policies the government is pursuing—in war as well as in peace. When does the press cross the line between keeping citizens informed and endangering national security? With a group of classmates, organize and stage a debate about the rights and responsibilities of the press during wartime. **[Social Studies Link]**

Projects

5. **Poster** The Civil War and the Persian Gulf War were dramatically different wars in almost every way: why, where, and how they were fought. Research both the American Civil War and the Persian Gulf War. Use your research and your knowledge of the selections to create a poster that compares and contrasts the two wars. Use both words and pictures to show the contrast in at least four areas, such as location, American casualties, weaponry, technology, news coverage, and so on. **[Social Studies Link; Art Link]**

Writing Process Workshop

In this section, you saw how a historical event such as the Civil War can be brought to life through the stories of people who lived through it. Stories that capture or re-create significant events from the past are called historical narratives. Historical narratives can be true stories told from the point of view of people who lived through the events, or they can be written by historians or even fiction writers who piece together events through research. The following skills will help you write your own historical narrative:

Writing Skills Focus

▶ **Use vivid verbs** to capture the action as clearly and precisely as possible. (See p. 505.)

▶ **Establish a mood** that is appropriate to the event you are describing.

▶ **Show, don't tell.** Instead of simply telling what happened, focus on bringing the event to life through dialogue and vivid descriptions of the action.

Warren Lee Goss uses all of these skills to bring his wartime experiences to life.

MODEL FROM LITERATURE

from "Recollections of a Private"
by Warren Lee Goss

"Cold chills" ran up and down my back as I got out of bed after the sleepless night, ① and shaved preparatory to other desperate deeds of valor. I was twenty years of age, and when anything unusual was to be done, like fighting or courting, I shaved.

With a nervous tremor convulsing my system, and my heart thumping ② like muffled drumbeats, ③ I stood before the door of the recruiting office. . . ."

① Goss creates a chilling, suspenseful mood.

② Words like "convulsing" and "thumping" create a vivid picture of the action.

③ Instead of just *telling* the reader "I was so nervous," Goss re-creates his feelings for readers through a detailed description.

APPLYING LANGUAGE SKILLS: Avoiding Shifts in Tense

When writing a narrative, it's important to be careful to avoid shifts in verb tense. For example, if you are writing in the past tense, be careful not to shift into the present.

Incorrect: The private waited as the enemy approached. He is nervous.

Correct: The private waited as the enemy approached. He was nervous.

Practice Identify and correct shifts in verb tense in the following items. Indicate if any are correct as written.

1. My mom walked in. She's amazed to see how clean my room was.

2. All of our energy had drained out of us by the time the game began. There was little chance we'd win.

3. Everyone is laughing as the circus clown ran through the audience.

Writing Application As you draft your narrative, be careful to avoid shifts in tense.

Writer's Solution Connection
Writing Lab

Use the Character Trait Word Bin and the Setting Profile in the Narration tutorial to develop these elements.

Prewriting

Choose a Topic Think of family members, neighbors, and family friends who have had interesting experiences. Interview one or more of them and ask them about their experiences or their memories of historical events. Review the information you've gathered, and choose an event that you think will make an interesting topic. As an alternative, you might consider one of the topic ideas listed here.

> ### Topic Ideas
> - The Califonia gold rush
> - A record-breaking sports event
> - The discovery of a cure for a disease
> - A political scandal

Gather Information If you've chosen a topic from the distant past, you will have to conduct library research to learn more about it. Finding good nonfiction books on your topic or original news stories from the period will provide you with the kind of details you need to write a lively and interesting historical narrative. If your topic is from the recent past, consider conducting personal interviews with people who remember the events about which you are writing.

Drafting

Start Your Narrative A historical narrative, like any other story, should have one or more characters, a setting, and a clear sequence of events. Use one of those elements to grab your readers' attention.

▶ Begin with a vivid description of the setting (Example: a quiet laboratory or a noisy, crowded stadium).

▶ Introduce one of the characters with a catchy bit of dialogue (Example: a politician's comments to a reporter).

▶ Jump right into a high point of the action (Example: the moment a character first strikes gold).

Develop Characters and Setting Drawing from the information you gathered through research, create well-developed characters and a vivid setting. Include details of setting that will give readers a clear picture of time and place of the action. Remember that your setting is most likely very different from the settings with which readers are familiar.

Revising

Use a Checklist Go back to the Writing Skills Focus on the first page of the lesson and use the items as a checklist to evaluate and revise your historical narrative.

▶ Have you created a mood that is appropriate to your subject? Is it suspenseful, comic, serious, tragic, or exciting? *Look for places where you can add or change details to enhance the mood of your narrative.*

▶ Have you used vivid verbs that bring each action to life? *Replace any dull or vague verbs with precise, vivid ones. For example, you might replace the verb "ran" with the more precise verb "sprinted."*

▶ Have you shown the action rather than merely telling about it? *Look for places where you can create a more detailed picture of the action by adding dialogue or vivid descriptive details.*

REVISION MODEL

Before she finished milking the cows, Sarah ~~checked her~~ ① *noticed the sun setting*

~~watch~~ and wondered when Jonah would return from

market. He had been gone for four days, and the journey

~~was~~ usually ~~shorter.~~ ② *took only three.*

① The writer edits out details that do not match the setting.

② This information clarifies the narrative's conflict.

Publishing

Illustrate Your Narrative Illustrations can give your narrative a polished, professional appearance. Aside from embellishing your writing, illustrations can set a mood or help your readers visualize characters, settings, and events. If you like to draw, you might enjoy creating portraits of the characters or bringing major scenes to life through your artwork.

Publish a Class Anthology Collect the finished narratives, and assemble them into an anthology. Bind them together with a table of contents and illustrations. If you have access to a desktop publishing program, reformat the narratives to give your anthology a unified look. Make several copies of your anthology to distribute to other classrooms or the school library.

APPLYING LANGUAGE SKILLS: Punctuating Dialogue

Observe these punctuation rules when writing dialogue:

• Use a comma inside the closing quotation marks when a remark comes before the speaker tag:

"I'm going out," my brother shouted.

• Use a comma before the opening quotation marks when a quoted statement comes after the speaker tag:

He then added, "Come along!"

• When a speaker tag interrupts a direct quotation, use commas to set off the two parts of the quotation.

"I would love to," I responded, "but I have to study for a test."

Practice Correct punctuation errors in the following items.

1. The porter shouted "All aboard!"
2. "Why" he asked "is there a chase in every movie?"
3. "That trail is the most scenic" the guide said.

Writing Application As you review your narrative, check to be sure all dialogue is punctuated correctly.

Writer's Solution Connection Writing Lab

For more on punctuating dialogue, see the Proofreading section of the Writing Lab Narration tutorial.

Real-World Reading Skills Workshop

Strategies for Success

Sports scores, articles, discussion groups, games, images, and more are traveling the Internet every second. Each day, thousands of new words and images are added to this information superhighway. As you view or receive this electronically transmitted data, you must determine what information is useful or reliable and what is not.

Question the Source All Internet sources are not created equal. Remember that anyone with a computer and an Internet linkup can transmit data or create a Home Page. Complete your own review process to determine the reliability of information you find on the Internet.

Sort the Information To evaluate Internet data, examine its content and format. Questions like these can help:

▶ How did you find or receive the information—by browsing or through a secondary source, such as a friend?

▶ What is the source of the information—a respected publisher or organization, a discussion news group, or an individual's Home Page? Are original research sources provided?

▶ What credentials—such as experience in the subject area or affiliation with a recognized organization—does the source have?

▶ Is the source objective or is the organization or individual seeking to persuade you to think or act in a certain way?

▶ Is the information up to date?

Take Action If the source seems reliable, study the actual information. Is it well written? Are statements supported by evidence? Verify information in at least one—and preferably two—additional sources, either on the Internet or elsewhere.

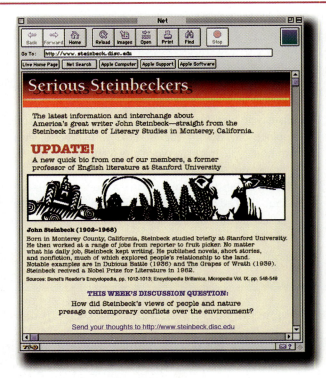

Apply the Strategy

As a fan of author John Steinbeck, you want to learn more about him. A friend referred you to this Steinbeck Home Page. Evaluate the reliability of its information.

1. What credentials support this source? Explain.

2. Would you consider the information printed on this Home Page reliable? Objective? Why or why not?

✔ *Here are other situations in which sorting Internet information is important:*
▶*Conducting research for a school project*
▶*Finding information on hobbies and interests*
▶*Comparing products and services*

PART 3 *Forging New Frontiers*

The Old Stage Coach of the Plains, Frederic Remington, Amon Carter Museum, Fort Worth, Texas

Guide for Interpreting

Mark Twain (1835–1910)

Although Mark Twain is widely regarded as one of the greatest American writers, the world-renowned author once indicated that he would have preferred to spend his life as a famous Mississippi riverboat pilot. Though the comment was probably not entirely serious, Twain so loved life on the river that as a young man, he did in fact work as a riverboat pilot for several years. His childhood on the banks of the Mississippi fostered more than a love of riverboats—it also became the basis for many of his most famous works, including *The Adventures of Tom Sawyer* (1876) and *The Adventures of Huckleberry Finn* (1884).

Life on the River Twain, whose real name is Samuel Langhorne Clemens, felt so closely tied to the Mississippi River that he even took his pen name, Mark Twain, from a river man's call meaning "two fathoms deep," indicating that the river is deep enough for a boat to pass safely. He grew up in the Mississippi River town of Hannibal, Missouri. When he was eleven, his father died, and he left school to become a printer's apprentice. He worked as a printer in a number of different cities before deciding at age twenty-one to pursue a career as a riverboat pilot.

A Traveling Man When the Civil War closed traffic on the Mississippi, Twain went west to Nevada. There he worked as a journalist and lecturer, developing the entertaining writing style that made him famous. In 1865, when he published "The Notorious Jumping Frog of Calaveras County," his version of a tall tale he heard in a mining camp, Twain became an international celebrity.

Following the publication of *The Innocents Abroad* (1869), a successful book of humorous travel letters, Twain moved to Hartford, Connecticut, where he was to make his home for the rest of his life. There he began using his past experiences as raw material for his books. He drew on his travels in the western mining region for *Roughing It* (1872) and turned his childhood experiences on the Mississippi into *The Adventures of Tom Sawyer, Life on the Mississippi,* and *The Adventures of Huckleberry Finn.* The latter title in particular so greatly influenced other writers that Ernest Hemingway praised it with these words:

> *"All modern American literature comes from one book by Mark Twain called Huckleberry Finn."*

Twain traveled widely throughout his career, and his adventures abroad were fuel for a number of books. After living in Europe for several years, he returned home with his family. Following the death of his wife and three of their four children, Twain's writing depicted an increasingly pessimistic view of society and human nature. His work, however, continued to display the same masterful command of language that had already established him as one of America's finest fiction writers.

◆ Background for Understanding

HISTORY: TWAIN WITNESSES AMERICA'S WESTWARD EXPANSION

Twain was an eyewitness to the nineteenth-century expansion of the western frontier. He was a young man when wagon trains left his home state to cross the prairies on the Oregon Trail, and he later saw the transcontinental railroad built. He traveled throughout the rapidly expanding nation, working first on the Mississippi, then in the West, before settling in Connecticut. The rich variety of people and places he observed are reflected in the setting, characters, and dialogue of his uniquely American literature. Twain was working as a gold prospector in California when he heard the story that became "The Notorious Jumping Frog of Calaveras County."

◆ *Literature and Your Life*

CONNECT YOUR EXPERIENCE

Today, the world is changing rapidly through almost daily advancements in technology. During Mark Twain's day, America was also changing at a fast pace—although perhaps not as rapidly as today—as advances in transportation helped settlers venture across the ever-expanding frontier. As these stories illustrate, no writer better captured the flavor of life on the new frontier than Twain.

Journal Writing Jot down your impressions of American frontier life, and explain whether or not you think you would have thrived on the frontier.

THEMATIC FOCUS: FORGING NEW FRONTIERS

As you read, notice what the stories reveal about life on the developing frontier, and compare frontier life to life in today's world.

◆ Build Vocabulary

PREFIXES: *mono-*

Simon Wheeler from "The Notorious Jumping Frog of Calaversas County" is described as a *monotonous* storyteller. Knowing that the prefix *mono-* means "alone," "single," or "one," you might guess that a monotonous storyteller is someone who drones on without varying his or her tone and pace. You'd be close to the actual meaning of the word: "tiresome because unvarying."

WORD BANK

Preview this list of words from the selections.

transient
prodigious
eminence
garrulous
conjectured
monotonous
interminable
ornery

◆ Grammar and Style

DOUBLE NEGATIVES

To capture how people from certain regions speak, writers like Mark Twain sometimes have their characters use **double negatives**—two words with negative meanings when only one is needed. Double negatives are not acceptable in standard English.

Nonstandard: . . . he didn't have no idea what the matter was
Standard: . . . he had no idea what the matter was
    . . . he didn't have any idea what the matter was

Some negative words to watch for are *no, none, never, nobody, not* (and *-n't*), *no one, nothing, nowhere, neither, barely, scarcely,* and *hardly.*

◆ Literary Focus

HUMOR

"The Notorious Jumping Frog of Calaveras County" has become a classic humorous tale. **Humor** is writing intended to evoke laughter. Humorists use a variety of techniques to make their work amusing. Many western humorists of the 1800's, including Mark Twain, exaggerate and embellish certain incidents and details to such an extent that they become comical. Often these incidents are related by a narrator or storyteller in a very serious tone. This tone makes the story even funnier by creating the impression that the storyteller is unaware of the ridiculousness of what he or she is describing.

◆ Reading Strategy

UNDERSTAND REGIONAL DIALECT

Much of the humor in Twain's writing comes not just from exaggeration and embellishment, but also from the language he uses. Twain was a master at using **regional dialect**—language specific to a particular region. You may not at first recognize the words that some of the characters use. By sounding out these words, however, you'll discover that they represent regional pronunciations of words with which you're familiar.

Paddle Steamboat Mississippi, Shelburne Museum, Shelburne, Vermont

from Life on the Mississippi

Mark Twain

The Boys' Ambition

When I was a boy, there was but one permanent ambition among my comrades in our village[1] on the west bank of the Mississippi River. That was, to be a steamboatman. We had <u>transient</u> ambitions of other sorts, but they were only transient.

When a circus came and went, it left us all burning to become clowns; the first Negro minstrel show that came to our section left us all suffering to try that kind of life; now and then we had a hope that if we lived and were good, God would permit us to be pirates. These ambitions faded out, each in its turn; but the ambition to be a steamboatman always remained.

Once a day a cheap, gaudy packet[2] arrived upward from St. Louis, and another downward from Keokuk.[3] Before these events, the day was glorious with expectancy; after them, the day was a dead and empty thing. Not only the boys, but the whole village, felt this. After all these years I can picture that old time to myself now, just as it was then: the white town drowsing in the sunshine of a summer's morning; the streets empty, or pretty nearly so; one or two clerks sitting in front of the Water Street stores, with their splint-bottomed chairs tilted back against the wall,

---

1. **our village:** Hannibal, Missouri.
2. **packet** *n*.: Boat that travels a regular route, carrying passengers, freight, and mail.
3. **Keokuk** (kē′ ə kuk′): Town in southeastern Iowa.

◆ **Build Vocabulary**

transient (tran′ zē ənt) *adj*.: Not permanent

chins on breasts, hats slouched over their faces, asleep—with shingle shavings enough around to show

◆ **Literary Focus**
Notice how the detail about the pigs adds humor to the piece. How do the other details contribute to describing the setting?

what broke them down; a sow and a litter of pigs loafing along the sidewalk, doing a good business in watermelon rinds and seeds; two or three lonely little freight piles scattered about the levee;[4] a pile of skids[5] on the slope of the stone-paved wharf, and the fragrant town drunkard asleep in the shadow of them; two or three wood flats[6] at the head of the wharf, but nobody to listen to the peaceful lapping of the wavelets against them; the great Mississippi, the majestic, the magnificent Mississippi, rolling its mile-wide tide along, shining in the sun; the dense forest away on the other side; the point above the town, and the point below, bounding the river-glimpse and turning it into a sort of sea, and withal a very still and brilliant and lonely one. Presently a film of dark smoke appears above one of those remote points; instantly a Negro drayman,[7] famous for his quick eye and <u>prodigious</u> voice, lifts up the cry, "S-t-e-a-m-boat a-comin'!" and the scene changes! The town drunkard stirs, the clerks wake up, a furious clatter of drays follows, every house and store pours out a human contribution, and all in a twinkling the dead town is alive and moving. Drays, carts, men, boys, all go hurrying from many quarters to a common center, the wharf. Assembled there, the people fasten their eyes upon the coming boat as upon a wonder they are seeing for the first time. And the boat *is* rather a handsome sight, too. She is long and sharp and trim and pretty; she has two tall, fancy-topped chimneys, with a gilded device of some kind swung between them; a fanciful pilothouse, all glass

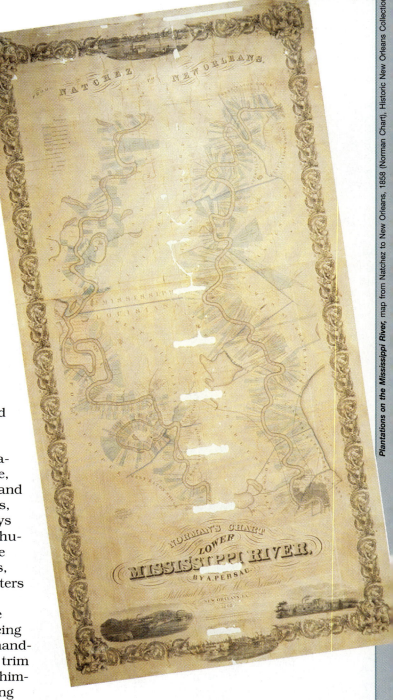

Plantations on the Mississippi River, map from Natchez to New Orleans, 1858 (Norman Chart), Historic New Orleans Collection

---

4. **levee** (lev´ē) *n.*: Landing place along the bank of a river.
5. **skids** *n.*: Low, movable wooden platforms.
6. **flats** *n.*: Small, flat-bottomed boats.
7. **drayman** (drā´ mən) *n.*: Driver of a dray, a low cart with detachable sides.

▲ **Critical Viewing** This map shows the location of plantation lands on the banks of the Mississippi. Why might the river have been a desirable location for plantations, as well as for towns? **[Infer]**

and gingerbread, perched on top of the texas deck[8] behind them; the paddleboxes are gorgeous with a picture or with gilded rays above the boat's name; the boiler deck, the hurricane deck, and the texas deck are fenced and ornamented with clean white railings; there is a flag gallantly flying from the jackstaff;[9] the furnace doors are open and the fires glaring bravely; the upper decks are black with passengers; the captain stands by the big bell, calm, imposing, the envy of all; great volumes of the blackest smoke are rolling and tumbling out of the chimneys—a husbanded grandeur created with a bit of pitch pine just before arriving at a town; the crew are grouped on the forecastle;[10] the broad stage is run far out over the port bow, and an envied deckhand stands picturesquely on the end of it with a coil of rope in his hand; the pent steam is screaming through the gauge cocks; the captain lifts his hand, a bell rings, the wheels stop; then they turn back, churning the water to foam, and the steamer is at rest. Then such a scramble as there is to get aboard, and to get ashore, and to take in freight and to discharge freight, all at one and the same time; and such a yelling and cursing as the mates facilitate it all with! Ten minutes later the steamer is under way again, with no flag on the jackstaff and no black smoke issuing from the chimneys. After ten more minutes the town is dead again, and the town drunkard asleep by the skids once more.

My father was a justice of the peace, and I supposed he possessed the power of life and death over all men and could hang anybody that offended him. This was distinction enough for me as a general thing; but the desire to be a steamboatman kept intruding, nevertheless. I first wanted to be a cabin boy, so that I could come out with a white apron on and shake a tablecloth over the side, where all my old comrades could see me; later I thought I would rather be the deckhand who stood on the end of the stage plank with the coil of rope in his hand, because he was particularly conspicuous. But these were only daydreams—they were too

heavenly to be contemplated as real possibilities. By and by one of our boys went away. He was not heard of for a long time. At last he turned up as apprentice engineer or striker on a steamboat. This thing shook the bottom out of all my Sunday-school teachings. That boy had been notoriously worldly, and I just the reverse; yet he was exalted to this <u>eminence,</u> and I left in obscurity and misery. There was nothing generous about this fellow in his greatness. He would always manage to have a rusty bolt to scrub while his boat tarried at our town, and he would sit on the inside guard and scrub it, where we could all see him and envy him and loathe him. And whenever his boat was laid up he would come home and swell around the town in his blackest and greasiest clothes, so that nobody could help remembering that he was a steamboatman; and he used all sorts of steamboat technicalities in his talk, as if he were so used to them that he forgot common people could not understand them. He would speak of the labboard[11] side of a horse in an easy, natural way that would make one wish he was dead. And he was always talking about "St. Looey" like an old citizen; he would refer casually to occasions when he "was coming down Fourth Street," or when he was "passing by the Planter's House," or when there was a fire and he took a turn on the brakes of "the old Big Missouri"; and then he would go on and lie about how many towns the size of ours were burned down there that day. Two or three of the boys had long been persons of consideration among us because they had been to St. Louis once and had a vague general knowledge of its wonders, but the day of their glory was over now. They lapsed into a humble silence, and

◆ **Reading Strategy**
What does the apprentice engineer's use of riverboat jargon reveal about him?

---

11. **labboard** (labʹ ərd): Larboard, the left-hand side of a ship.

8. **texas deck:** Deck adjoining the officers' cabins, the largest cabins on the ship.
9. **jackstaff** (jakʹ staf) *n.*: Small staff at the bow of a ship for flying flags.
10. **forecastle:** (fōkʹ səl) *n.*: Front part of the upper deck.

◆ **Build Vocabulary**
prodigious (prə dijʹ əs) *adj.*: Of great power or size
eminence (emʹ ə nəns) *n.*: Greatness; celebrity

learned to disappear when the ruthless cub engineer approached. This fellow had money, too, and hair oil. Also an ignorant silver watch and a showy brass watch chain. He wore a leather belt and used no suspenders. If ever a youth was cordially admired and hated by his comrades, this one was. No girl could withstand his charms. He cut out every boy in the village. When his boat blew up at last, it diffused a tranquil contentment among us such as we had not known for months. But when he came home the next week, alive, renowned, and appeared in church all battered up and bandaged, a shining hero, stared at and wondered over by everybody, it seemed to us that the partiality of Providence for an undeserving reptile had reached a point where it was open to criticism.

This creature's career could produce but one result, and it speedily followed. Boy after boy managed to get on the river. The minister's son became an engineer. The doctor's and the postmaster's sons became mud clerks; the wholesale liquor dealer's son became a barkeeper on a boat; four sons of the chief merchant, and two sons of the county judge, became pilots. Pilot was the grandest position of all. The pilot, even in those days of trivial wages, had a princely salary—from a hundred and fifty to two hundred and fifty dollars a month, and no board to pay. Two months of his wages would pay a preacher's salary for a year. Now some of us were left disconsolate. We could not get on the river—at least our parents would not let us.

So by and by I ran away. I said I never would come home again till I was a pilot and could come in glory. But somehow I could not manage it. I went meekly aboard a few of the boats that lay packed together like sardines at the long St. Louis wharf, and very humbly inquired for the pilots, but got only a cold shoulder and short words from mates and clerks. I had to make the best of this sort of treatment for the time being, but I had comforting daydreams of a future when I should be a great and honored pilot, with plenty of money, and could kill some of these mates and clerks and pay for them.

Guide for Responding

◆ Literature and Your Life

Reader's Response Would working on a riverboat appeal to you? Explain why or why not.

Thematic Focus How does Twain's childhood ambition reflect the American desire for expansion and adventure that gave rise to the settlement of new frontiers?

Journal Writing Suppose you lived in Mark Twain's time. Record your ideas about what types of work opportunities might have intrigued you.

☑ Check Your Comprehension

1. What is the one permanent ambition of Twain and his boyhood friends?
2. How do the people of Hannibal respond to the arrival of the steamboat?
3. (a) What happens to the young apprentice engineer's boat? (b) How do the other boys respond?

◆ Critical Thinking

INTERPRET

1. What impression is conveyed by Twain's description of the town and its response to the arrival of the steamboat? **[Interpret]**
2. How does Twain's description of the steamboat reflect his boyhood desire to work on a steamboat? **[Analyze]**
3. How would you describe the attitude of the other boys toward the apprentice engineer? **[Infer]**

APPLY

4. How do you think Twain's love for the Mississippi River contributed to his success as a writer? **[Synthesize]**

EXTEND

5. What career today might be comparable in romance and adventure to being a riverboat pilot in the 1800's? Explain your answer. **[Career Link]**

The Notorious Jumping Frog of Calaveras County

Mark Twain

Mark Twain (Samuel L. Clemens) Riding the Celebrated Jumping Frog

▲ **Critical Viewing** Do you think Mark Twain would have been amused or offended by this caricature of himself? Explain. **[Make a Judgment]**

*I*n compliance with the request of a friend of mine, who wrote me from the East, I called on good-natured, garrulous old Simon Wheeler, and inquired after my friend's friend, Leonidas W. Smiley, as requested to do, and I hereunto append the result. I have a lurking suspicion that *Leonidas W.* Smiley is a myth; that my friend never knew such a personage: and that he only conjectured that if I asked old Wheeler about him, it would remind him of his infamous *Jim* Smiley, and he would go to work and bore me to death with some exasperating reminiscence of him as long and as tedious as it should be useless to me. If that was the design, it succeeded.

I found Simon Wheeler dozing comfortably by the barroom stove of the dilapidated tavern in the decayed mining camp of Angel's, and I noticed that he was fat and baldheaded, and had an expression of winning gentleness and simplicity upon his tranquil countenance. He roused up, and gave me good day. I told him a friend of mine had commissioned me to make some inquiries about a cherished companion of his boyhood named *Leonidas W.* Smiley—*Rev. Leonidas W.* Smiley, a young minister of the Gospel, who he had heard was at one time a resident of Angel's Camp. I added that if Mr. Wheeler could tell me anything about this Rev. Leonidas W. Smiley, I would feel under many obligations to him.

Simon Wheeler backed me into a corner and blockaded me there with his chair, and then sat down and reeled off the monotonous narrative which follows this paragraph. He never smiled, he never frowned, he never changed his voice from the gentle-flowing key to which he tuned his initial sentence, he never betrayed the slightest suspicion of enthusiasm; but all through the interminable narrative there ran a vein of impressive earnestness and sincerity, which showed me plainly that, so far from his

imagining that there was anything ridiculous or funny about his story, he regarded it as a really important matter, and admired its two heroes as men of transcendent genius in *finesse*. I let him go on in his own way, and never interrupted him once.

"Rev. Leonidas W. H'm, Reverend Le— well, there was a feller here once by the name of *Jim Smiley*, in the winter of '49—or maybe it was the spring of '50—I don't recollect exactly, somehow, though what makes me think it was one or the other is because I remember the big flume[1] warn't finished when he first come to the camp; but anyway, he was the curiousest man about always betting on anything that turned up you ever see, if he could get anybody to bet on the other side; and if he couldn't he'd change sides. Any way that suited the other man would suit *him*—any way just so's he got a bet, *he* was satisfied. But still he was lucky, uncommon lucky; he most always come out winner. He was always ready and laying for a chance; there couldn't be no solit'ry thing mentioned but that feller'd offer to bet on it, and take ary side you please, as I was just telling you. If there was a horse race, you'd find him flush or you'd find him busted at the end of it; if there was a dogfight, he'd bet on it; if there was a cat fight, he'd bet on it; if there was a chicken fight, he'd bet on it; why, if there was two birds setting on a fence, he would bet you which one would fly first; or if there was a camp meeting,[2] he would be there reg'lar to bet on Parson Walker, which he judged to be the best exhorter about here and so he was too, and a good man. If he even see a straddle bug[3] start to go anywheres, he would bet you how long it would take him to get to—to wherever he was going to, and if you took him up, he would foller that straddle bug to Mexico but what he would find out where he was bound for and how long he was on the road. Lots of the boys here has seen that Smiley, and can tell you about him. Why, it never made no difference to *him*—he'd bet on *any* thing—the dangdest feller. Parson Walker's wife laid very sick once,

for a good while, and it seemed as if they warn't going to save her; but one morning he come in, and Smiley up and asked him how she was, and he said she was considable better—thank the Lord for his inf'nite mercy—and coming on so smart that with the blessing of Prov'dence she'd get well yet; and Smiley, before he thought, says, 'Well, I'll resk two-and-a-half she don't anyway.'

Thish-yer Smiley had a mare—the boys called her the fifteen-minute nag, but that was only in fun, you know, because of course she was faster than that—and he used to win money on that horse, for all she was so slow and always had the asthma, or the distemper, or the consumption, or something of that kind. They used to give her two or three hundred yards start, and then pass her under way; but always at the fag end[4] of the race she'd get excited and desperate like, and come cavorting and straddling up, and scattering her legs around limber, sometimes in the air, and sometimes out to one side among the fences, and kicking up m-o-r-e dust and raising m-o-r-e racket with her coughing and sneezing and blowing her nose—and *always* fetch up at the stand just about a neck ahead, as near as you could cipher it down.

And he had a little small bull-pup, that to look at him you'd think he warn't worth a cent but to set around and look <u>ornery</u> and lay for a chance to steal something. But as soon as money was up on him he was a different dog; his under-jaw'd begin to stick out like the fo'-castle[5] of a steamboat, and his teeth would uncover and shine like the furnaces. And a dog might tackle him and bullyrag him, and bite him, and throw him over his shoulder two or three times, and Andrew Jackson—which was the name of the pup—Andrew Jackson would never let on but what *he* was satisfied, and hadn't expected nothing else—and the bets being doubled and doubled on the other side all the time, till the money was all up; and then all of a sudden he would grab that other dog jest

---

1. **flume** (floom) *n.*: Artificial channel for carrying water to provide power and transport objects.
2. **camp meeting:** Religious gathering at the mining camp.
3. **straddle bug:** Insect with long legs.

---

4. **fag end:** Last part.
5. **fo'castle** (fōk′ səl) *n.*: Forecastle; the forward part of the upper deck.

 **Build Vocabulary**

ornery (ôr′ nər ē) *adj.*: Having a mean disposition

by the j'int of his hind leg and freeze to it—not chaw, you understand, but only just grip and hang on till they throwed up the sponge, if it was a year. Smiley always come out winner on that pup, till he harnessed a dog once that didn't have no hind legs, because they'd been sawed off in a circular saw, and when the thing had gone along far enough, and the money was all up, and he come to make a snatch for his pet holt,[6] he see in a minute how he'd been imposed on, and how the other dog had him in the door, so to speak, and he 'peared surprised, and then he looked sorter discouraged-like, and didn't try no more to win the fight, and so he got shucked out bad. He give Smiley a look, as

much as to say his heart was broke, and it was *his* fault, for putting up a dog that hadn't no hind legs for him to take holt of, which was his main dependence in a fight, and then he limped off a piece and laid down and died. It was a good pup, was that Andrew Jackson, and would have made a name for hisself if he'd lived, for the stuff was in him and he had genius—I know it, because he hadn't no opportunities to speak of, and it don't stand to reason that a dog could make such a fight as he could under them circumstances if he hadn't no talent. It always makes me feel sorry when I think of that last fight of his'n, and the way it turned out.

Well, thish-yer Smiley had rat terriers,[7] and chicken cocks,[8] and tomcats and all them kind of things, till you couldn't rest, and you couldn't fetch nothing for him to bet on but he'd match you. He ketched a frog one day, and took him home, and said he cal'lated to educate him; and

---

6. **holt:** Hold.

7. **rat terriers:** Dogs skilled in catching rats.
8. **chicken cocks:** Roosters trained to fight.

so he never done nothing for three months but set in his back yard and learn that frog to jump. And you bet you he *did* learn him, too. He'd give him a little punch behind, and the next minute you'd see that frog whirling in the air like a doughnut—see him turn one summerset, or maybe a couple, if he got a good start, and come down flatfooted and all right, like a cat. He got him up so in the matter of ketching flies, and kep' him in practice so constant, that he'd nail a fly every time as fur as he could see him. Smiley said all a frog wanted was education, and he could do 'most anything—and I believe him. Why, I've seen him set Dan'l Webster down here on this floor—Dan'l Webster was the name of the frog—and sing out, "Flies, Dan'l, flies!" and quicker'n you could wink he'd spring straight up and snake a fly off'n the counter there, and flop down on the floor ag'in as solid as a gob of mud, and fall to scratching the side of his head with his hind foot as indifferent as if he hadn't no idea he'd been doin' any more'n any frog might do. You never see a frog so modest and straightfor'ard as he was, for all he was so gifted. And when it come to fair and square jumping on a dead level, he could get over more ground at one straddle than any animal of his breed you ever see. Jumping on a dead level was his strong suit, you understand; and when it come to that, Smiley would ante up money on him as long as he had a red.[9] Smiley was monstrous proud of his frog, and well he might be, for fellers that had traveled and been everywheres all said he laid over any frog that ever *they* see.

Well, Smiley kep' the beast in a little lattice box, and he used to fetch him downtown sometimes and lay for a bet. One day a feller—a stranger in the camp, he was—come across him with his box, and says:

'What might it be that you've got in the box?'

And Smiley says, sorter indifferent-like, 'It might be a parrot, or it might be a canary, maybe, but it ain't—it's only just a frog.'

And the feller took it, and looked at it

◆ **Literary Focus**
How do these embellishments heighten the comical effect of this passage?

careful, and turned it round this way and that, and says, 'H'm—so 'tis. Well, what's *he* good for?'

'Well,' Smiley says, easy and careless, 'he's good enough for *one* thing, I should judge—he can outjump any frog in Calaveras county.'

The feller took the box again, and took another long, particular look, and give it back to Smiley, and says, very deliberate, 'Well,' he says, 'I don't see no p'ints about that frog that's any better'n any other frog.'

'Maybe you don't,' Smiley says. 'Maybe you understand frogs and maybe you don't understand 'em; maybe you've had experience, and maybe you ain't only a amature, as it were. Anyways, I've got *my* opinion, and I'll resk forty dollars that he can outjump any frog in Calaveras county.'

And the feller studied a minute, and then says, kinder sad like, 'Well, I'm only a stranger here, and I ain't got no frog; but if I had a frog, I'd bet you.'

And then Smiley says, 'That's all right—that's all right—if you'll hold my box a minute, I'll go and get you a frog.' And so the feller took the box, and put up his forty dollars along with Smiley's, and set down to wait.

So he set there a good while thinking and thinking to hisself, and then he got the frog out and prized his mouth open and took a teaspoon and filled him full of quailshot[10] —filled him pretty near up to his chin—and set him on the floor. Smiley he went to the swamp and slopped around in the mud for a long time, and finally he ketched a frog, and fetched him in, and give him to this feller, and says:

'Now, if you're ready, set him alongside of Dan'l, with his forepaws just even with Dan'l's, and I'll give the word.' Then he says, 'One—two—three—*git*!' and him and the feller touched up the frogs from behind, and the new frog hopped off lively, but Dan'l give a heave, and hysted up his shoulders—so—like a Frenchman, but it warn't no use—he couldn't budge; he was planted as solid as a church, and he couldn't no more stir than if he was anchored out. Smiley was a good deal surprised, and he was disgusted too, but he didn't have no idea what the matter was, of course.

---

9. a red: Red cent; colloquial expression for "any money at all."

10. quailshot: Small lead pellets used for shooting quail.

The feller took the money and started away; and when he was going out at the door, he sorter jerked his thumb over his shoulder—so—at Dan'l, and says again, very deliberate, 'Well,' he says, 'I don't see no p'ints about that frog that's any better'n any other frog.'

Smiley he stood scratching his head and looking down at Dan'l a long time, and at last he says, 'I do wonder what in the nation that frog throw'd off for—I wonder if there ain't something the matter with him—he 'pears to look mighty baggy, somehow.' And he ketched Dan'l by the nap of the neck, and hefted him, and says, 'Why blame my cats if he don't weigh five pound!' and turned him upside down and he belched out a double handful of shot. And then he see how it was, and he was the maddest man—he set the frog down and took out after that feller, but he never ketched him. And—"

Here Simon Wheeler heard his name called from the front yard, and got up to see what was wanted. And turning to me as he moved away, he said: "Just set where you are, stranger, and rest easy—I ain't going to be gone a second."

But, by your leave, I did not think that a continuation of the history of the enterprising vagabond *Jim* Smiley would be likely to afford me much information concerning the Rev. *Leonidas W.* Smiley, and so I started away.

At the door I met the sociable Wheeler returning, and he button-holed me and recommenced:

"Well, thish-yer Smiley had a yaller one-eyed cow that didn't have no tail, only just a short stump like a bannanner, and—"

However, lacking both time and inclination, I did not wait to hear about the afflicted cow, but took my leave.

> ◆ *Literature and Your Life*
>
> If you were the narrator, what would you have done at this point? Explain.

Guide for Understanding

◆ *Literature and Your Life*

Reader's Response If Mark Twain were a stand-up comic today, would you want to see him perform? Why or why not?

Thematic Focus Telling tall tales was a common form of entertainment on the western frontier. What does this tale suggest about the setting and characters of the developing West?

Group Activity Imagine that you and your classmates are set designers for the film industry. Describe a movie set that might be used as a backdrop for this story.

☑ Check Your Comprehension

1. What prompts Simon Wheeler to tell the story of Jim Smiley?
2. What was Jim Smiley's response to any event?
3. Why was Smiley so proud of his frog?
4. How did the stranger outwit Smiley?

◆ Critical Thinking

INTERPRET
1. Why had the narrator's friend suggested he ask Wheeler about Leonidas Smiley? Explain. **[Infer]**
2. Based on the way they use language, compare the personality of the anonymous narrator with that of Simon Wheeler. **[Compare and Contrast]**
3. Why did Twain have Wheeler, rather than the narrator, relay the story of Jim Smiley? **[Draw Conclusions]**

EVALUATE
4. Does "The Notorious Jumping Frog . . ." succeed in conveying the character of Simon Wheeler as effectively as it conveys the character of Jim Smiley, the subject of the tale? Explain. **[Evaluate]**

EXTEND
5. With what other tall tales are you familiar? Why do people generally enjoy telling and hearing tall tales? **[Literature Link]**

Guide for Responding (continued)

◆ Reading Strategy

UNDERSTAND REGIONAL DIALECT

The **regional dialect** you encountered in these stories can both amuse and confuse readers. Some regional expressions may be unfamiliar, and certain words may not be spelled as they are in standard English. However, by reading aloud to yourself, you can usually decipher the meaning of the passages and better appreciate their comic effect. In your own words, explain the meaning of each of the following excerpts.

1. "...he 'peared surprised, and then he looked sorter discouraged-like, and didn't try no more to win the fight, and so he got shucked out bad."

2. "He got him up so in the matter of ketching flies, and kep' him in practice so constant, that he'd nail a fly every time as fur as he could see him."

3. "Well, thish-yer Smiley had a yaller one-eyed cow that didn't have no tail, only just a short stump like a bannanner ..."

◆ Build Vocabulary

USING THE PREFIX mono-

The prefix *mono-* means "alone" or "single." Add the prefix *mono-* to each of these word roots. Use your understanding of the prefix along with the definition of the root to tell the meaning of the new word.

1. *theism* = belief in god
2. *logue* = speaking
3. *lith* = stone
4. *chrome* = color

USING THE WORD BANK

Write the letter of the word in the right column that is the best antonym of the Word Bank word in the left column.

1. transient   a. varied
2. prodigious   b. meager
3. eminence   c. quiet
4. garrulous   d. permanent
5. conjectured   e. kind
6. monotonous   f. verified
7. interminable   g. obscurity
8. ornery   h. brief

◆ Literary Focus

HUMOR

Twain uses a broad range of techniques, including exaggeration, embellishment, and regional dialect, to amuse and entertain readers. "The Notorious Jumping Frog" is a particularly good example of Twain's special brand of **humor**, though there are plenty of amusing details and tongue-in-cheek observations to be found in "The Boys' Ambition," as well.

1. In "The Boys' Ambition," Twain daydreams about the "heavenly" steamboat duties of shaking out a tablecloth or holding a rope. How does his description of these everyday activities add to the humor of his narrative?

2. Find at least two examples of exaggeration in "The Notorious Jumping Frog," and explain why each is amusing.

3. Why would "The Notorious Jumping Frog" be less effective if Wheeler spoke in standard English?

◆ Grammar and Style

DOUBLE NEGATIVES

The use of **double negatives**—two negative words in a sentence where only one is needed—can change the intended meaning of a sentence; in effect, the words cancel each other out. Pay special attention to the words *neither, barely, scarcely*, and *hardly*. It is easy to forget that they are negative words and should not be combined with another negative word.

Looking at Style Explain how Simon Wheeler's frequent use of double negatives fits his character and contributes to the story's humor.

Writing Application In your notebook, rewrite the following sentences from the story, revising them as necessary to eliminate double negatives.

1. Why, it never made no difference to him. . . .

2. . . . you couldn't fetch nothing for him to bet on but he'd match you.

3. . . . maybe you've had experience and maybe you ain't only a amature.

4. . . . it warn't no use—he couldn't budge.

Build Your Portfolio

 ## Idea Bank

Writing

1. **Cartoon** Develop one of the shorter anecdotes in Simon Wheeler's tale into a cartoon strip. Create a caption and an illustration for each frame.

2. **Obituary** Write a newspaper obituary for the famous jumping frog, Dan'l Webster, in which you relate his accomplishments. Use exaggeration to make it funny.

3. **Analytic Essay** Mark Twain wrote, "The humorous story may be spun out to great length, and may wander around as much as it pleases, and arrive nowhere in particular. . . . [It] is told gravely; the teller does his best to conceal the fact that he even dimly suspects there is anything funny about it." In an essay, discuss how these techniques were applied to "Jumping Frog."

Speaking and Listening

4. **Interview** Prepare a list of questions about a career that interests you. Then interview someone in the field to obtain answers. Present your findings to the class. **[Career Link]**

5. **Oral Interpretation** Much of the humor in "Jumping Frog" is in the speaker's deadpan delivery. With a partner, practice a part of the story and role-play the characters, Simon Wheeler and the narrator. **[Performing Arts Link]**

Projects

6. **Multimedia Presentation** Create a multimedia report on Mississippi riverboats. Use text, visual images, and video or audio clips to convey the sights and sounds of nineteenth-century riverboat life. **[Social Studies Link]**

7. **Illustration** Select a scene from either work and illustrate it. Include an extended caption describing the events depicted. **[Art Link]**

 ## Writing Mini-Lesson

Humorous Anecdote

Choose a funny event that you have heard about or that happened to you. Then develop it into an amusing anecdote. Create humor by making the characters amusing and by using exaggeration where appropriate. Also keep the following in mind:

Writing Skills Focus: Elaboration for Vividness

As you develop your anecdote, **elaborate for vividness** by adding details that make the events come alive. Elaboration can take the form of sensory details, unexpected comparisons, or restatements. Twain brings Simon Wheeler to life by filling his dialogue with a stream of unexpected details, asides, and comparisons.

Model From the Story

Thish-yer Smiley had a mare—the boys called her the fifteen-minute nag, but that was only in fun, you know, because of course she was faster than that—and he used to win money on that horse, for all she was so slow and always had the asthma, or the distemper, or the consumption, or something of that kind.

Prewriting Select an event on which to base your humorous anecdote. Then, in a web like this one, note details that will make the story funny.

Drafting Use your completed word web to help you write a draft of your anecdote. Include unusual comparisons and sensory details that will make the characters and events especially vivid.

Revising Use these questions to guide your revision: Is the sequence of events clear? How can I make the characters more humorous? How effectively have I used exaggeration?

Guide for Interpreting

Bret Harte (1836–1902)

A literary pioneer, Bret Harte played a key role in creating a vivid, lasting portrait of the Old West. His stories, filled with picturesque characters and colorful dialogue, provided much of post-Civil War America with its first glimpse of western life and established the Old West as a popular fictional setting.

In many ways, the roots of the Hollywood western can be traced back to Harte's tales.

Heading West Harte was born and raised in Albany, New York. In 1854, when he was eighteen, he traveled to California, a land undergoing a turbulent period of rapid growth due to the discovery of gold in 1848. During his first few years in California, Harte worked as a schoolteacher, messenger, clerk, and prospector. While Harte's life seemed to have little direction at the time, his observations of the rugged, often violent life in the mining camps and the towns and cities of the new frontier provided him with the inspiration for his most successful short stories.

A Career of Ups and Downs After working as a typesetter and writer for two California periodicals and publishing two books of verse, *Outcroppings* (1865) and *The Last Galleon* (1867), Harte became the editor in 1868 of the *Overland Monthly*. When he published his story "The Luck of Roaring Camp" in the magazine's second issue, he immediately became famous. The American public, eager to learn about life in the new frontier, responded to the story with enthusiasm. Over the next two years, Harte published "The Outcasts of Poker Flat" and other stories about life in the frontier, and his popularity grew at a rapid pace.

Following the publication of *The Luck of Roaring Camp and Other Sketches* in 1870, Harte's popularity reached its peak. In 1871, *The Atlantic Monthly,* a distinguished literary magazine, contracted to pay Harte the large sum of $10,000 for any twelve sketches or stories he contributed over the next year. Harte returned to the East to fulfill his contract, but the stories he wrote were flat and disappointing compared with his earlier work. His celebrity waned almost as quickly as it had grown.

A Political Appointment Harte continued to publish stories, short novels, and plays during the next twenty years, but most of his later work was unsuccessful. Some friends helped him land a diplomatic post, however, and from 1878 to 1885, Harte served as a United States consul in Germany and Scotland. He retired to London for the remainder of his life.

◆ Background for Understanding

LITERATURE: THE REAL MR. OAKHURST

Mr. Oakhurst, a gambler and the main character of "The Outcasts of Poker Flat," is a generous, genial man who is seemingly nonchalant in the face of danger. As you read the story, you may wonder how true-to-life Mr. Oakhurst is.

Harte's biographer, Henry Childs Merwin, described a gambler named Lucky Bill who demonstrated traits similar to Mr. Oakhurst's. According to Merwin, "Lucky Bill was noted for his generosity, and, though finally hanged by a vigilance committee, he made a 'good end,' for, on the scaffold, he exhorted his son who was among the spectators, to avoid bad company, to keep away from saloons, and to lead an industrious and honest life."

The Outcasts of Poker Flat

◆ Literature and Your Life

CONNECT YOUR EXPERIENCE

The "outcasts" in Bret Harte's story are tested by circumstances. Think of a time you—or someone you know—used the words, "It was a real test of character." What was the situation? What qualities did it bring out in the people involved?

THEMATIC FOCUS: FORGING NEW FRONTIERS

Stories of the Old West have endured in popularity. As you read, think about the qualities of frontier life depicted in this story that make the Old West so interesting to modern readers.

Journal Writing List some the characteristics that you associate with a western hero.

◆ Literary Focus

REGIONALISM

Bret Harte's early stories about frontier life helped to fuel a new literary movement known as **Regionalism**—a movement in which writers attempted to capture the "local color" of a region by accurately depicting the distinctive qualities of its people and its physical environment. The interest in regional literature was driven by the fact that during the mid- to late-1800's, the country was expanding at a rapid pace—both in population and in geographical area. Yet, there were then few ways for people to learn about life in regions other than their own—photography had just been developed and television was still decades away from becoming a reality. However, stories like "The Outcasts of Poker Flat" painted a vivid and engaging portrait of what life was like in the far reaches of the land.

◆ Grammar and Style

COORDINATING CONJUNCTIONS IN COMPOUND SENTENCES

Coordinating conjunctions—*and, or, but, nor, for, so,* and *yet*—connect words or phrases of equal weight. In compound sentences, they connect two or more independent clauses to form a single sentence. They also indicate the relationship between the ideas expressed. In this example, *but* indicates a contrast:

Tommy, you're a good little man, *but* you can't gamble worth a cent.

◆ Reading Strategy

QUESTION THE TEXT

When you read any piece of literature—from an essay to a short story—**question the text.** Ask yourself, What's happening? What's the author's purpose here? What is the motive for this character's action? Will this idea be further developed? Consider this description of the place known as Poker Flat:

There was a Sabbath lull in the air which, in a settlement unused to Sabbath influences, looked ominous.

Here you might ask yourself, Where will this ominous mood lead? What makes Poker Flat a place of doubtful virtue? Look for answers to these and other questions as you read.

◆ Build Vocabulary

WORD ROOTS: -bel-

In this story, a character is described as being "in a *bellicose* state." You might already be familiar with the word *belligerent,* which also contains the root *-bel-* and which is close in meaning. The root *-bel-* means "war." Both *belligerent* and *bellicose* mean "warlike" or "ready to fight or quarrel."

WORD BANK

Preview this list of words from the story.

expatriated
anathema
bellicose
recumbent
equanimity
vociferation
vituperative
querulous

As Mr. John Oakhurst, gambler, stepped into the main street of Poker Flat on the morning of the twenty-third of November, 1850, he was conscious of a change in its moral atmosphere since the preceding night. Two or three men, conversing earnestly together, ceased as he approached, and exchanged significant glances. There was a Sabbath lull in the air which, in a settlement unused to Sabbath influences, looked ominous.

Mr. Oakhurst's calm, handsome face betrayed small concern in these indications. Whether he was conscious of any predisposing cause was another question. "I reckon they're after somebody," he reflected; "likely it's me." He returned to his pocket the handkerchief with which he had been whipping away the red dust of Poker Flat from his neat boots, and quietly discharged his mind of any further conjecture.

In point of fact, Poker Flat was "after somebody." It had lately suffered the loss of several

The Outcasts of Poker Flat

❧ Bret Harte ❧

done permanently in regard of two men who were then hanging from the boughs of a sycamore in the gulch, and temporarily in the banishment of certain other objectionable characters. I regret to say that some of these were ladies. It is but due to the sex, however, to state that their impropriety was professional, and it was only in such easily established standards of evil that Poker Flat ventured to sit in judgment.

Mr. Oakhurst was right in supposing that he was included in this category. A few of the committee had urged hanging him as a possible example, and a sure method of reimbursing themselves from his pockets of the sums he had won from them. "It's agin justice," said Jim Wheeler, "to let this yer young man from Roaring Camp—an entire stranger—carry away our money." But a crude sentiment of equity residing in the breasts of those who had been fortunate enough to win from Mr. Oakhurst overruled this narrower local prejudice.

◆ Literary Focus
What does this passage reveal about some of the inhabitants of Poker Flat?

Mr. Oakhurst received his sentence with philosophic calmness, none the less coolly that

▲ **Critical Viewing** How does the mood of this painting echo the mood of the story's opening paragraphs? [Compare]

thousand dollárs, two valuable horses, and a prominent citizen. It was experiencing a spasm of virtuous reaction, quite as lawless and ungovernable as any of the acts that had provoked it. A secret committee had determined to rid the town of all improper persons. This was

he was aware of the hesitation of his judges. He was too much of a gambler not to accept Fate. With him life was at best an uncertain game, and he recognized the usual percentage in favor of the dealer.

A body of armed men accompanied the deported wickedness of Poker Flat to the outskirts of the settlement. Besides Mr. Oakhurst, who was known to be a coolly desperate man, and for whose intimidation the armed escort was intended, the expatriated party consisted of a young woman familiarly known as the "Duchess"; another, who had won the title of "Mother Shipton";[1] and "Uncle Billy," a suspected sluice robber[2] and confirmed drunkard. The cavalcade provoked no comments from the spectators, nor was any word uttered by the escort. Only, when the gulch which marked the uttermost limit of Poker Flat was reached, the leader spoke briefly and to the point. The exiles were forbidden to return at the peril of their lives.

As the escort disappeared, their pent-up feelings found vent in a few hysterical tears from the Duchess, some bad language from Mother Shipton, and a Parthian volley of expletives[3] from Uncle Billy. The philosophic Oakhurst alone remained silent. He listened calmly to Mother Shipton's desire to cut somebody's heart out, to the repeated statements of the Duchess that she would die in the road, and to the alarming oaths that seemed to be bumped out of Uncle Billy as he rode forward. With the easy good humor characteristic of his class, he insisted upon exchanging his own riding horse, "Five Spot," for the sorry mule which the Duchess rode. But even this act did not draw the party into any closer sympathy. The young woman readjusted her somewhat draggled plumes with a feeble, faded coquetry; Mother Shipton eyed the possessor of "Five Spot" with malevolence, and Uncle Billy included the whole party in one sweeping anathema.

The road to Sandy Bar—a camp that, not having as yet experienced the regenerating influences of Poker Flat, consequently seemed to offer some invitation to the emigrants—lay over a steep mountain range. It was distant a day's severe travel. In that advanced season, the party soon passed out of the moist, temperate regions of the foothills into the dry, cold, bracing air of the Sierras.[4] The trail was narrow and difficult. At noon the Duchess, rolling out of her saddle upon the ground, declared her intention of going no farther, and the party halted.

The spot was singularly wild and impressive. A wooded amphitheater, surrounded on three sides by precipitous cliffs of naked granite, sloped gently toward the crest of another precipice that overlooked the valley. It was, undoubtedly, the most suitable spot for a camp, had camping been advisable. But Mr. Oakhurst knew that scarcely half the journey to Sandy Bar was accomplished, and the party were not equipped or provisioned for delay. This fact he pointed out to his companions curtly, with a philosophic commentary on the folly of "throwing up their hand before the game was played out." But they were furnished with liquor, which in this emergency stood them in place of food, fuel, rest, and prescience. In spite of his remonstrances, it was not long before they were more or less under its influence. Uncle Billy passed rapidly from a bellicose state into one of stupor, the Duchess became maudlin, and Mother Shipton snored. Mr. Oakhurst alone remained erect, leaning against a rock calmly surveying them.

◆ **Literary Focus**
What does this passage reveal about difficulties related to travel in the Old West?

---

1. **"Mother Shipton":** English woman who lived in the sixteenth century and was suspected of being a witch.
2. **sluice robber:** Person who steals gold from sluices— long troughs used for sifting gold.
3. **Parthian . . . expletives:** Hostile remarks made while leaving. The Parthians were an ancient society whose cavalrymen usually shot at the enemy while retreating or pretending to retreat.

4. **Sierras** (sē er´ əz): Mountains in eastern California, also called the Sierra Nevadas.

◆ **Build Vocabulary**

expatriated (eks pā´ trē āt´ id) adj.: Deported; driven from one's native land

anathema (ə nath´ ə mə) n.: Curse

bellicose (bel´ ə kōs) adj.: Quarrelsome

recumbent (ri kum´ bənt) adj.: Resting

equanimity (ek´ wə nim ə tē) n.: Composure

Mr. Oakhurst did not drink. It interfered with a profession which required coolness, impassiveness, and presence of mind, and, in his own language, he "couldn't afford it." As he gazed at his <u>recumbent</u> fellow exiles, the loneliness begotten of his pariah trade, his habits of life, his very vices, for the first time seriously oppressed him. He bestirred himself in dusting his black clothes, washing his hands and face, and other acts characteristic of his studiously neat habits, and for a moment forgot his annoyance. The thought of deserting his weaker and more pitiable companions never perhaps occurred to him. Yet he could not help feeling the want of that excitement which singularly enough, was most conducive to that calm <u>equanimity</u> for which he was notorious. He looked at the gloomy walls that rose a thousand feet sheer above the circling pines around him; at the sky, ominously clouded; at the valley below, already deepening into shadow. And, doing so, suddenly he heard his own name called.

A horseman slowly ascended the trail. In the fresh, open face of the newcomer Mr. Oakhurst recognized Tom Simson, otherwise known as the "Innocent" of Sandy Bar. He had met him some months before over a "little game," and had, with perfect equanimity, won the entire fortune—amounting to some forty dollars—of that guileless youth. After the game was finished, Mr. Oakhurst drew the youthful speculator behind the door and thus addressed him: "Tommy, you're a good little man, but you can't gamble worth a cent. Don't try it over again." He then handed him his money back, pushed him gently from the room, and so made a devoted slave of Tom Simson.

There was a remembrance of this in his boyish and enthusiastic greeting of Mr. Oakhurst. He had started, he said, to go to Poker Flat to seek his fortune. "Alone?" No, not exactly alone; in fact (a giggle), he had run away with Piney Woods. Didn't Mr. Oakhurst remember Piney? She that used to wait on the table at the Temperance House? They had been engaged a long time, but old Jake Woods had objected, and so they had run away, and were going to Poker Flat to be married, and here they were. And they were tired out, and how lucky it was they had found a place to camp and company. All this the Innocent delivered rapidly, while

Piney, a stout, comely damsel of fifteen, emerged from behind the pine tree, where she had been blushing unseen, and rode to the side of her lover.

Mr. Oakhurst seldom troubled himself with sentiment, still less with propriety; but he had a vague idea that the situation was not fortunate. He retained, however, his presence of mind sufficiently to kick Uncle Billy, who was about to say something, and Uncle Billy was sober enough to recognize in Mr. Oakhurst's kick a superior power that would not bear trifling. He then endeavored to dissuade Tom Simson from delaying further, but in vain. He even pointed out the fact that there was no provision, nor means of making a camp. But, unluckily, the Innocent met this objection by assuring the party that he was provided with an extra mule loaded with provisions and by the discovery of a rude attempt at a log house near the trail. "Piney can stay with Mrs. Oakhurst," said the Innocent, pointing to the Duchess, "and I can shift for myself."

Nothing but Mr. Oakhurst's admonishing foot saved Uncle Billy from bursting into a roar of laughter. As it was, he felt compelled to retire up the canyon until he could recover his gravity. There he confided the joke to the tall pine trees, with many slaps of his leg, contortions of his face, and the usual profanity. But when he returned to the party, he found them seated by a fire—for the air had grown strangely chill and the sky overcast—in apparently amicable conversation. Piney was actually talking in an impulsive, girlish fashion to the Duchess, who was listening with an interest and animation she had not shown for many days. The Innocent was holding forth, apparently with equal effect, to Mr. Oakhurst and Mother Shipton, who was actually relaxing into amiability. "Is this yer a d——d picnic?" said Uncle Billy with inward scorn as he surveyed the sylvan[5] group, the glancing firelight, and the tethered animals in the foreground. Suddenly an idea mingled with the alcoholic fumes that disturbed his brain. It was apparently of a jocular nature, for he felt impelled to slap his leg again and cram his fist into his mouth.

As the shadows crept slowly up the mountain, a slight breeze rocked the tops of the pine

---

5. **sylvan:** (sil´ vən) adj.: Characteristic of the forest.

trees, and moaned through their long and gloomy aisles. The ruined cabin, patched and covered with pine boughs, was set apart for the ladies. As the lovers parted, they unaffectedly exchanged a kiss, so honest and sincere that it might have been heard above the swaying pines. The frail Duchess and the malevolent Mother Shipton were probably too stunned to remark upon this last evidence of simplicity, and so turned without a word to the hut. The fire was replenished, the men lay down before the door, and in a few minutes were asleep.

Mr. Oakhurst was a light sleeper. Toward morning he awoke benumbed and cold. As he stirred the dying fire, the wind, which was now blowing strongly, brought to his cheek that which caused the blood to leave it—snow!

He started to his feet with the intention of awakening the sleepers, for there was no time to lose. But turning to where Uncle Billy had been lying, he found him gone. A suspicion leaped to his brain and a curse to his lips. He ran to the spot where the mules had been tethered; they were no longer there. The tracks were already rapidly disappearing in the snow.

◆ Reading Strategy
What is the meaning behind Uncle Billy's disappearance? Identify one or more clues that point to the answer.

The momentary excitement brought Mr. Oakhurst back to the fire with his usual calm. He did not waken the sleepers. The Innocent slumbered peacefully, with a smile on his good-humored, freckled face; the virgin Piney slept beside her frailer sisters as sweetly as though attended by celestial guardians; and Mr. Oakhurst, drawing his blanket over his shoulders, stroked his mustaches and waited for the dawn. It came slowly in a whirling mist of snowflakes that dazzled and confused the eye. What could be seen of the landscape appeared magically changed. He looked over the valley, and summed up the present and future in two words—"snowed in!"

A careful inventory of the provisions, which, fortunately for the party, had been stored within the hut and so escaped the felonious fingers of Uncle Billy, disclosed the fact that with care and prudence they might last ten days longer. "That is," said Mr. Oakhurst, sotto voce[6] to the Innocent, "if you're willing to board

us. If you ain't—and perhaps you'd better not—you can wait till Uncle Billy gets back with provisions." For some occult reason, Mr. Oakhurst could not bring himself to disclose Uncle Billy's rascality, and so offered the hypothesis that he had wandered from the camp and had accidentally stampeded the animals. He dropped a warning to the Duchess and Mother Shipton, who of course knew the facts of their associate's defection. "They'll find out the truth about us *all* when they find out anything," he added, significantly, "and there's no good frightening them now."

Tom Simson not only put all his worldly store at the disposal of Mr. Oakhurst, but seemed to enjoy the prospect of their enforced seclusion. "We'll have a good camp for a week, and then the snow'll melt, and we'll all go back together." The cheerful gaiety of the young man, and Mr. Oakhurst's calm, infected the others. The Innocent with the aid of pine boughs extemporized a thatch for the roofless cabin, and the Duchess directed Piney in the rearrangement of the interior with a taste and tact that opened the blue eyes of that provincial maiden to their fullest extent. "I reckon now you're used to fine things at Poker Flat," said Piney. The Duchess turned away sharply to conceal something that reddened her cheek through its professional tint, and Mother Shipton requested Piney not to "chatter." But when Mr. Oakhurst returned from a weary search for the trail, he heard the sound of happy laughter echoed from the rocks. He stopped in some alarm, and his thoughts first naturally reverted to the whisky, which he had prudently cached.[7] "And yet it don't somehow sound like whisky," said the gambler. It was not until he caught sight of the blazing fire through the still-blinding storm and the group around it that he settled to the conviction that it was "square fun."

Whether Mr. Oakhurst had cached his cards with the whisky as something debarred the free access of the community, I cannot say. It was certain that, in Mother Shipton's words, he "didn't say cards once" during that evening. Haply the time was beguiled by an accordion, produced somewhat ostentatiously by Tom Simson from his pack. Notwithstanding some

---

6. **sotto voce** (sät′ ō vō′ chē): In an undertone.

7. **cached** (kasht) v.: Hidden.

difficulties attending the manipulation of this instrument, Piney Woods managed to pluck several reluctant melodies from its keys, to an accompaniment by the Innocent on a pair of bone castanets. But the crowning festivity of the evening was reached in a rude camp-meeting hymn, which the lovers, joining hands, sang with great earnestness and <u>vociferation</u>. I fear that a certain defiant tone and Covenanter's[8] swing to its chorus, rather than any devotional quality, caused it speedily to infect the others, who at last joined in the refrain:

◆ **Literary Focus**
What aspects of "local color" does this passage convey?

"I'm proud to live in the
   service of the Lord,
And I'm bound to die in
   His army."[9]

The pines rocked, the storm eddied and whirled above the miserable group, and the flames of their altar leaped heavenward as if in token of the vow.

At midnight the storm abated, the rolling clouds parted, and the stars glittered keenly above the sleeping camp. Mr. Oakhurst, whose professional habits had enabled him to live on the smallest possible amount of sleep, in dividing the watch with Tom Simson somehow managed to take upon himself the greater part of that duty. He excused himself to the Innocent by saying that he had "often been a week without sleep." "Doing what?" asked Tom. "Poker!" replied Oakhurst, sententiously; "when a man gets a streak of luck, he don't get tired. The luck gives in first. Luck," continued the gambler, reflectively, "is a mighty queer thing. All you know about it for certain is that it's bound to change. And it's finding out when it's going to change that makes you. We've had a streak of bad luck since we left Poker Flat—you come along, and slap you get into it, too. If you can hold your cards right along you're all right. For," added the gambler, with cheerful irrelevance,

" 'I'm proud to live in the service
   of the Lord,

---

8. **Covenanter's** (kuv´ ə nan´ tərz): Seventeenth-century Scottish Presbyterians who resisted the rule of the Church of England.
9. **"I'm . . . army:** Lines from the early American spiritual "Service of the Lord."

And I'm bound to die in
   His army.' "

The third day came, and the sun, looking through the white-curtained valley, saw the outcasts divide their slowly decreasing store of provisions for the morning meal. It was one of the peculiarities of that mountain climate that its rays diffused a kindly warmth over the wintry landscape, as if in regretful commiseration of the past. But it revealed drift on drift of snow piled high around the hut—a hopeless, uncharted, trackless sea of white lying below the rocky shores to which the castaways still clung. Through the marvelously clear air the smoke of the pastoral village of Poker Flat rose miles away. Mother Shipton saw it, and from a remote pinnacle of her rocky fastness hurled in that direction a final malediction. It was her last <u>vituperative</u> attempt, and perhaps for that reason was invested with a certain degree of sublimity. It did her good, she privately informed the Duchess. "Just you go out there and cuss, and see." She then set herself to the task of amusing "the child," as she and the Duchess were pleased to call Piney. Piney was no chicken, but it was a soothing and original theory of the pair thus to account for the fact that she didn't swear and wasn't improper.

When night crept up again through the gorges, the reedy notes of the accordion rose and fell in fitful spasms and long-drawn gasps by the flickering campfire. But music failed to fill entirely the aching void left by insufficient food, and a new diversion was proposed by Piney—storytelling. Neither Mr. Oakhurst nor his female companions caring to relate their personal experiences, this plan would have failed too but for the Innocent. Some months before he had chanced upon a stray copy of Mr. Pope's[10] ingenious translation of the *Iliad*.[11] He now proposed to narrate the principal incidents

---

10. **Mr. Pope:** English poet Alexander Pope (1688–1744).
11. **Iliad** (il´ ē əd): Greek epic poem written by Homer that tells the story of the Trojan War.

◆ **Build Vocabulary**
vociferation (vō sif´ ər ā´ shən) *n*.: Loud or vehement shouting
vituperative (vī too´ pər ə tiv) *adj*.: Spoken abusively

◀ **Critical Viewing** Compare and contrast this photograph with the group's wintry surroundings. [**Compare and Contrast**]

to replenish their fires, even from the fallen trees beside them, now half-hidden in the drifts. And yet no one complained. The lovers turned from the dreary prospect and looked into each other's eyes, and were happy. Mr. Oakhurst settled himself coolly to the losing game before him. The Duchess, more cheerful than she had been, assumed the care of Piney. Only Mother Shipton—once the strongest of the party—seemed to sicken and fade. At midnight on the tenth day she called Oakhurst to her side. "I'm going," she said, in a voice of <u>querulous</u> weakness, "but don't say anything about it. Don't waken the kids. Take the bundle from under my head and open it." Mr. Oakhurst did so. It contained Mother Shipton's rations for the last week, untouched. "Give 'em to the child," she said, pointing to the sleeping Piney. "You've starved yourself," said the gambler. "That's what they call it," said the woman, querulously, as she lay down again and, turning her face to the wall, passed quietly away.

The accordion and the bones were put aside that day, and Homer was forgotten. When the body of Mother Shipton had been committed to the snow, Mr. Oakhurst took the Innocent aside, and showed him a pair of snowshoes, which he had fashioned from the old pack saddle. "There's one chance in a hundred to save her yet," he said, pointing to Piney; "but it's there," he added, pointing toward Poker Flat. "If you can reach there in two days she's safe." "And you?" asked Tom Simson. "I'll stay here," was the curt reply.

The lovers parted with a long embrace. "You are not going, too?" said the Duchess as she saw Mr. Oakhurst apparently waiting to accompany him. "As far as the canyon," he replied. He turned suddenly, and kissed the Duchess, leaving her pallid face aflame and her trembling limbs rigid with amazement.

of that poem—having thoroughly mastered the argument and fairly forgotten the words—in the current vernacular of Sandy Bar. And so for the rest of that night the Homeric demigods again walked the earth. Trojan bully and wily Greek wrestled in the winds, and the great pines in the canyon seemed to bow to the wrath of the son of Peleus.[12] Mr. Oakhurst listened with quiet satisfaction. Most especially was he interested in the fate of "Ash-heels," as the Innocent persisted in denominating the "swift-footed Achilles."

So with small food and much of Homer and the accordion, a week passed over the heads of the outcasts. The sun again forsook them, and again from leaden skies the snowflakes were sifted over the land. Day by day closer around them drew the snowy circle, until at last they looked from their prison over drifted walls of dazzling white that towered twenty feet above their heads. It became more and more difficult

---

12. **son of Peleus** (pē′ lē əs): Achilles (ə kil′ ēz), the Greek warrior hero in the *Iliad*.

◆ **Build Vocabulary**

 **querulous** (kwer′ ə ləs) *adj*.: Inclined to find fault

Night came, but not Mr. Oakhurst. It brought the storm again and the whirling snow. Then the Duchess, feeding the fire, found that someone had quietly piled beside the hut enough fuel to last a few days longer. The tears rose to her eyes, but she hid them from Piney.

The women slept but little. In the morning, looking into each other's faces, they read their fate. Neither spoke; but Piney, accepting the position of the stronger, drew near and placed her arm around the Duchess's waist. They kept this attitude for the rest of the day. That night the storm reached its greatest fury, and, rending asunder the protecting pines, invaded the very hut.

Toward morning they found themselves unable to feed the fire, which gradually died away. As the embers slowly blackened, the Duchess crept closer to Piney, and broke the silence of many hours: "Piney, can you pray?" "No, dear," said Piney, simply. The Duchess, without knowing exactly why, felt relieved, and, putting her head upon Piney's shoulder, spoke no more. And so reclining, the younger and purer pillowing the head of her soiled sister upon her virgin breast, they fell asleep.

The wind lulled as if it feared to waken them. Feathery drifts of snow, shaken from the long pine boughs, flew like white-winged birds, and settled about them as they slept. The moon through the rifted clouds looked down upon what had been the camp. But all human stain, all trace of earthly travail, was hidden beneath the spotless mantle mercifully flung from above.

They slept all that day and the next, nor did they waken when voices and footsteps broke the silence of the camp. And when pitying fingers brushed the snow from their wan faces, you could scarcely have told from the equal peace that dwelt upon them which was she that had sinned. Even the law of Poker Flat recognized this, and turned away, leaving them still locked in each other's arms.

But at the head of the gulch, on one of the largest pine trees, they found the deuce of clubs pinned to the bark with a bowie knife. It bore the following, written in pencil, in a firm hand:

> BENEATH THIS TREE
> LIES THE BODY
> OF
> JOHN OAKHURST,
> WHO STRUCK A STREAK OF BAD LUCK
> ON THE 23D OF NOVEMBER, 1850
> AND
> HANDED IN HIS CHECKS
> ON THE 7TH DECEMBER, 1850.

And pulseless and cold, with a Derringer [13] by his side and a bullet in his heart, though still calm as in life, beneath the snow lay he who was at once the strongest and yet the weakest of the outcasts of Poker Flat.

---

13. **Derringer:** Small pistol.

Guide for Responding

◆ Literature and Your Life

Reader's Response Which character did you admire the most? Why?

Thematic Focus Would you like to be transported back in time to the western frontier that Harte depicts? Why or why not?

Group Discussion As a group, brainstorm for two lists: one showing the traits you associate with heroes from movie and television westerns, and one showing traits you found in Mr. Oakhurst. Compare and discuss the two lists. Do the similarities outweigh the differences?

☑ Check Your Comprehension

1. At the opening of the story, what has the secret committee of Poker Flat decided?
2. Who joins the outcasts at their camp?
3. What does Mr. Oakhurst discover when he awakens after his first night at the camp?
4. What does Mother Shipton do with her rations?
5. What does the rescue party discover?

Guide for Understanding (continued)

◆ Critical Thinking

INTERPRET

1. What motivates the committee to take action against Mr. Oakhurst? **[Infer]**
2. What effect do Tom and Piney have on all the outcasts except Uncle Billy? Why? **[Analyze]**
3. What does Harte mean in writing that Oakhurst "was at once the strongest and yet the weakest of the outcasts of Poker Flat"? **[Interpret]**
4. What is contradictory about the identity of the "good guys" and the "bad guys" in this tale? **[Interpret]**

APPLY

5. Though the characters in this story have little in common, they band together. Why might people tend to draw together in life? **[Generalize]**

EXTEND

6. Based on the story, what conclusions can you draw about law in settlements that sprang up during the Gold Rush? **[Social Studies Link]**

◆ Literary Focus

REGIONALISM

Harte's portrait of Poker Flat and its outcasts is an example of **Regionalism,** which attempts to capture the "local color" of an area.

1. Find a passage in which Harte describes the physical environment. What specific details help you picture the California landscape?
2. Find three examples of distinctly western speech.

◆ Reading Strategy

QUESTION THE TEXT

If you **question** important ideas, plot developments, and the author's purpose in a text, you can get more out of your reading. Review this passage:

> There was a Sabbath lull in the air which, in a settlement unused to Sabbath influences, looked ominous.

1. What turned out to be the cause of the ominous lull in the air?
2. Cite a passage that helped you determine the cause.

◆ Grammar and Style

COORDINATING CONJUNCTIONS IN COMPOUND SENTENCES

Place a comma before a **coordinating conjunction** that joins the independent clauses in a compound sentence.

> In compound sentences, **coordinating conjunctions** —and, or, but, nor, for, so, and yet— connect two or more independent clauses to form a single sentence.

Writing Application In your notebook, combine each pair of sentences to form a compound sentence. Use the coordinating conjunction given in parentheses.

1. She felt he wasn't joking. She continued to laugh. (*yet*)
2. He raced to the gate. The plane was about to depart. (*for*)
3. Vitamins can be good supplements. They are no substitute for a healthy diet. (*but*)

◆ Build Vocabulary

USING THE WORD ROOT -*bel*-

On your paper, write the letter of the item that best defines the italicized word in each sentence.

a. quick to pick a fight   **b.** an instance of resistance

1. The *rebellion* known as the Boston Tea Party was the result of opposition to British taxation.
2. He must control his rage and not be so *bellicose*.

USING THE WORD BANK

On your paper, write the letter of the word whose meaning is closest to that of the first word.

1. expatriated: (a) honored, (b) ignored, (c) expelled
2. anathema: (a) curse, (b) riddle, (c) chant
3. bellicose: (a) strong, (b) quarrelsome, (c) beautiful
4. recumbent: (a) full, (b) reclining, (c) unnecessary
5. equanimity: (a) fairness, (b) precision, (c) serenity
6. vociferation: (a) uncertainty, (b) loudness, (c) cleverness
7. vituperative: (a) scolding, (b) healthful, (c) complex
8. querulous: (a) trustworthy, (b) mysterious, (c) disagreeable

Build Your Portfolio

Idea Bank

Writing

1. **Visitor's Guide** Create a visitor's guide to the three main sites in the story: Poker Flat, Sandy Bar, and the slope where the outcasts become stranded. Briefly describe each site, and explain its significance in the story.

2. **Review** Write a critical review of the story to appear in a magazine targeted at fans of westerns. Present and support your opinion of the story.

3. **Newspaper Editorial** Put yourself in the place of the editor of a newspaper serving Poker Flat and several other frontier camps. Write an editorial about the outcasts and their fate.

Speaking and Listening

4. **Literary Discussion** With a classmate, prepare and act out a dialogue in which two friends living in the East in 1870 discuss their reactions to frontier life as depicted in "The Outcasts of Poker Flat." **[Social Studies Link]**

5. **Eulogy** As Tom Simson, the only survivor of the stranded group, prepare and deliver a eulogy—a speech in honor of someone who has died—for Mr. Oakhurst. **[Performing Arts Link]**

Projects

6. **Boom Towns** Research Helena, Montana; San Francisco, California; or Denver, Colorado. Then write a brief history of one of the cities, including a discussion of the role that the discovery of gold played in its founding. **[Social Studies Link]**

7. **In Search of Gold** Use library or Internet sources to learn about prospecting and mining. Then give a brief oral report in which you identify the main steps in each of these processes. **[Science Link]**

Writing Mini-Lesson

Description of a Place

Bret Harte's stories transported readers to the rugged landscapes and rough, dusty settlements of the western frontier. Think of a place you would like to share with others; then write a description that will make your readers feel as though they've been there themselves.

Writing Skills Focus: Precise Details
Use **precise details**—details that deliver concrete information—to make your description of a place as true-to-life as possible. Notice, for example, that Bret Harte does not simply mention the *dust* or *trees* around Poker Flat, he also supplies precise images: the *red* dust, the *sycamore*, the *pines*. Notice Harte's use of the precise details:

Model From the Story

A wooded amphitheater, surrounded on three sides by precipitous cliffs of naked granite, sloped gently toward the crest of another precipice. . . .

Try to capture the look and feel of a place you know well by zooming in on precise details.

Prewriting Revisit in your mind the place you have chosen. Jot down some words that describe its distinctive atmosphere or qualities. Then note the specific physical features that help to produce this atmosphere.

Drafting Identify your place early in your description so that readers can get their bearings. Use the precise details you gathered in the prewriting stage to build up a sense of its physical reality as well as to reveal its "personality."

Revising Reread your description from the point of view of someone who has never been to the place it presents. Have you overlooked any essential details? Is there anything you can do to make the details you included more vivid and more precise?

Guide for Interpreting

Chief Joseph (1840–1904)

In 1871, Chief Joseph succeeded his father as the leader of the Nez Percé (nez' pʉrs' or pər sā') nation. At that time, the United States government was trying to force the Nez Percé to relocate to Idaho. The Nez Percé had signed a treaty in 1863 giving the government control of the tribe's land, but Chief Joseph felt that the treaty was illegal and refused to recognize it.

A Reluctant Warrior

In 1877, the dispute between the Nez Percé and the United States government erupted into war. Chief Joseph, hoping to join forces with the Sioux, led his people on a long march through Idaho and Montana, during which the outnumbered Nez Percé frequently clashed with federal troops.

The Bitter End

By October 1877, the Nez Percé were cold, starving, and scattered. Chief Joseph accepted reasonable terms of surrender, which the United States government failed to honor. Instead, the Nez Percé were sent to a barren Oklahoma territory where many of them became ill and died.

The speech in which Chief Joseph finally accepted defeat contains some of the most achingly sad and beautiful words ever spoken. Because of the widespread attention his words received, Chief Joseph became for many a symbol of the Nez Percé and their tragic plight.

Miriam Davis Colt (1815–c.1900)

Miriam Davis Colt was one of a quarter of a million Americans who traveled across the United States in the mid-1800's to forge a new frontier. These pioneers knew they were making history, and hundreds of them kept diaries to send to relatives back east or to pass down to their children.

The Women's Perspective

Usually, the pioneer men, filled with a sense of destiny and excitement, made the decision to sell their homes and move their families west. The women's diaries, however, reveal a different point of view. Many women describe their anguish at leaving home, their struggle to maintain some sort of domestic comfort in the harsh conditions, and their fear of the dangers that lay ahead.

A Vision of the Future

The women, nevertheless, did share their husbands' belief that they were building a better future for their children. The path to that future might be hard, but it was also filled with moments of sudden beauty, like the "crab-apple trees . . . blooming in sheets of whiteness" that Colt saw by the side of a Kansas road as she and her family traveled toward a new life in a "city" established by a group of vegetarians. Her family was one of many that invested money in the creation of this new settlement, where they hoped to live with people "whose tastes and habits" would coincide with their own.

◆ Background for Understanding

CULTURE: THIS LAND IS WHOSE LAND?

"The earth is the mother of all people, and all people should have equal rights upon it." Chief Joseph's words express the point of view of Native Americans, who saw themselves as using land but never owning it. Because they were a culture of hunters, the Nez Percé ranged over a vast territory. Settlers like Miriam Davis Colt, however, were farmers, and they had a very different view of the land. They wanted individual plots to cultivate, and they considered the land they settled as their own. These opposing viewpoints were a source of ongoing strife in frontier America.

◆ Literature and Your Life

CONNECT YOUR EXPERIENCE

For very different reasons, both Chief Joseph and Miriam Davis Colt had to say goodbye to the places they called home. Think about how you would feel if you suddenly had to leave everything that you loved, with no possibility of ever returning.

THEMATIC FOCUS: FORGING NEW FRONTIERS

Saying goodbye to one home and one way of life means standing on the frontier of a new world. As you read these selections, consider how Chief Joseph and Miriam Davis Colt felt on the frontier of a new existence. How and why did their emotions differ?

Journal Writing If you could take only a few possessions to a new home, what would they be? List them in your journal.

◆ Build Vocabulary

WORDS FROM LATIN: *TERRA FIRMA*

In "Heading West," you'll find *terra firma*, a Latin term meaning "solid ground." If you encounter an unfamiliar Latin word or phrase when reading, you can often find its meaning in a dictionary.

WORD BANK

Preview this list of words before you read.

genial
pervading
terra firma
emigrants
profusion
depredations
nonplused

◆ Grammar and Style

SENTENCE FRAGMENTS

The early entries in Miriam Colt's diary are written in complete sentences, whereas many of the later entries contain **sentence fragments**—incomplete sentences that may lack either a subject or a verb. As Colt heads west, she begins dropping the subjects of her sentences as a form of shorthand—an effort to hurriedly record her impressions during her few quiet moments. In polished writing, however, fragments are not acceptable. Use only complete sentences, which contain a subject and a verb.

Sentence Fragment: Have been on the cars again since yesterday morning. (no subject)

Complete Sentence: We have been on the cars again since yesterday morning. (subject, *We,* has been added)

◆ Literary Focus

TONE

A writer's attitude toward his or her subject, characters, or audience comes through in the **tone** of a work. As you read, pay careful attention to tone, just as you would when listening to a speaker. The tone of a nonfiction work is established by the writer's use of descriptive words and choice of details. The tone of "I Will Fight No More Forever" clearly reflects the desolate situation in which the speech was made. Different entries in "Heading West" have different tones, depending on Miriam Davis Colt's feelings when she wrote them.

◆ Reading Strategy

RESPOND

As you read "I Will Fight No More Forever" and "Heading West," pay close attention to your personal responses. What emotions do you feel? What images do you see? What words and phrases have the most striking effects on you? You will get much more from your reading when you take the time to note how you **respond** to a piece of literature. Both of the selections you are about to read describe life-changing situations, the kind that are sure to evoke responses that will affect your understanding and appreciation of the works.

HEADING WEST

Miriam Davis Colt

▲ **Critical Viewing** Which details of this photograph of pioneers stopping for lunch seem surprising or out of place? **[Analyze]**

January 5th, 1856. We are going to Kansas. The Vegetarian Company that has been forming for many months, has finally organized, formed its constitution, elected its directors, and is making all necessary preparations for the spring settlement. . . . We can have, I think, good faith to believe, that our directors will fulfill on their part; and we, as settlers of a new country, by going in a company will escape the hardships attendant on families going in singly, and at once find ourselves surrounded by improving society in a young and flourishing city. It will be better for ourselves pecuniarily,[1] and better in the future for our children.

My husband has long been a practical

vegetarian, and we expect much from living in such a <u>genial</u> clime, where fruit is so quickly grown, and with people whose tastes and habits will coincide with our own.

January 15th. We are making every necessary preparation for our journey, and our home in Kansas. My husband has sold his farm, purchased shares in the company, sent his money as directed by H.S. Clubb. . . . I am very busy in repairing all of our clothing, looking over bags of pieces, tearing off and reducing down, bringing everything into as small a compass as possible, so that we shall have no unnecessary baggage.

April 15th. Have been here in West Stockholm, at my brother's, since Friday last. Have visited Mother very hard, for, in all probability,

---

1. **pecuniarily** (pi kyoo′ nē er′ i lē) *adv.*: Financially.

◆ **Build Vocabulary**
genial (jēn′ yəl) *adj.*: Promoting life and growth

it is the last visit we shall have until we meet where parting never comes—believe we have said everything we can think of to say.

April 16th. Antwerp, N.Y. Bade our friends good bye, in Potsdam, this morning, at the early hour of two o'clock.

April 22nd. Have been on the cars[2] again since yesterday morning. Last night was a lovely moonlit night, a night of thought, as we sped almost with lightning speed, along in the moonlight, past the rail fences.

Found ourselves in this miserable hotel before we knew it. Miserable fare—herring boiled with cabbage—miserable, dirty beds, and an odor <u>pervading</u> the house that is not at all agreeable. Mistress gone.

April 23rd. On board streamer "Cataract," bound for Kansas City.

April 24th. A hot summer day. The men in our company are out in the city, purchasing wagons and farming implements, to take along on the steamer up to Kansas City.

April 28th. The steamer struck a "snag" last night; gave us a terrible jar; tore off a part of the kitchen; ladies much frightened. Willie is not very well; the water is bad; it affects all strangers.

April 30th. Here we are, at Kansas City, all safely again on <u>terra firma</u>. Hasten to the hotel—find it very much crowded. Go up, up, up, and upstairs to our lodging rooms.

May 1st. Take a walk out onto the levee—view the city, and see that it takes but a few buildings in this western world to make a city. The houses and shops stand along on the levee, extending back into the hillsides. The narrow street is literally filled with huge merchandise wagons bound for Santa Fe. The power attached to these wagons is seven or eight and sometimes nine pair of long-eared mules, or as many pair of oxen, with a Mexican driver who wields a whip long enough to reach the foremost pair, and who

does not hesitate to use it with severity, and a noise, too.

Large droves of cattle are driven into town to be sold to <u>emigrants</u>, who like us, are going into the Territory. Our husbands are all out today buying oxen, provisions and cooking utensils for our ox-wagon journey into the Territory.

This is the anniversary of my wedding-day, and as I review the past pleasant years as they have passed, one after an other, until they now number eleven, a shadow comes over me, as I try to look away into the future and ask, "What is my destiny?"

Ah! away with all these shadowings. We shall be very busy this year in making our home comfortable, so that no time can be spared for that dreaded disease, "home-sick ness," to take hold of us, and we mean to obey physical laws,[3] thereby securing to ourselves strength of body and vigor of mind.

◆ *Literature and Your Life*

Do you ever feel fearful when you try to imagine your future? How do you try to reassure yourself when you get nervous about your "destiny"?

May 2nd. A lovely day. Our husbands are loading the ox-wagons. . . . Women and children walk along up the hill out of this "Great City," wait under a tree—what a beautiful country is spread out before us! Will our Kansas scenery equal this . . .?

One mile from the city, and Dr. Thorn has broke his wagon tongue;[4] it must be sent back to Kansas City to be mended. Fires kindled—women cooking—supper eaten sitting round on logs, stones and wagon tongues. This I am sure is a "pic-nic." We expect "pic-nic" now all the time. We are shaded by the horse-chestnut,

---

3. **physical laws:** Community's by-laws that dictated members abstain from alcohol and meat.
4. **wagon tongue:** Harnessing pole attached to the front axle of a horse-drawn vehicle.

◆ Build Vocabulary

pervading (pər vād´ iŋ) *adj.*: Spreading throughout

terra firma (ter´ ə fur´ mə) *n.*: Firm earth; solid ground (Latin)

emigrants (em´ i grəntz) *n.*: People who leave one area to move to another

---

2. **cars:** Train cars.

sweet walnut, and spreading oak; flowers blooming at our feet, and grasshoppers in profusion hopping in every direction. This is summer time.

May 3rd. The women and children, who slept in their wagons last night, got a good drenching from the heavy shower. It was fortunate for mother, sister, myself and children, that lodgings were found for us in a house. My husband said not a rain drop found him; he had the whole wagon to himself, besides all of our Indian blankets. Father, it seems, fell back a little and found a place to camp in a tavern (not a hotel), where he fell in with the scores of Georgians who loaded a steamer and came up the river the same time that we did. He said he had to be very shrewd indeed not to have them find out that he was a "Free States"[5] man. These Bandits have been sent in here, and will commit all sorts of depredations on the Free State settlers, and no doubt commit many a bloody murder.

◆ **Literary Focus**
What is Colt's tone as she discusses the Georgians who have come up river at the same time as her party?

Have passed Westport, the foothold for Border-Ruffianism. The town looks new, but the hue is dingy. Our drivers used their goads to hurry up the oxen's heavy tread, for we felt somewhat afraid, for we learned the Georgians had centered here. Here, too, came in the Santa Fe and Indian trade—so here may be seen the huge Mexican wagon, stubborn mule, swarthy driver with his goad-like whip, and the red man of the prairie on his fleet Indian pony, laden with dried meat, furs, and buffalo robes.

"What! fast in the mud, and with our wagon tongue broke?" "Why yes, to be sure." So a long time is spent before my husband and Dr. House can put our vehicle in moving order again. Meanwhile, we women folks and children must sit quietly in the wagon to keep out of the rain—lunch on soda biscuit, look at the deep, black mud in which our wagon is set, and inhale the sweet odor that comes from the blossoms of the crab-apple trees that are blooming in sheets of whiteness along the roadside. . . .

May 6th. Dined on the prairie, and gathered flowers, while our tired beasts filled themselves with the fresh, green grass. . . . Have driven 18 miles to-day . . . so here we are, all huddled into this little house 12 by 16—cook supper over the fire . . . fill the one bed lengthwise and crosswise; the family of the house take to the trundle-bed,[6] while the floor is covered . . . with men, women and children, rolled in Indian blankets like silk worms in cocoons.

May 11th. "Made" but a few miles yesterday. Forded the Little Osage; the last river, they say, we have to ford . . . our "noble lords" complained of the great weight of the wagons. . . . That our wagon is heavily loaded, have only to make a minute of what we have stowed away in it—eight trunks, one valise, three carpet bags, a box of soda crackers, 200 lbs. flour, 100 lbs. corn meal, a few lbs. of sugar, rice, dried apple, one washtub of little trees, utensils for cooking, and two provision boxes—say nothing of mother, a good fat sister, self, and two children, who ride through the rivers. . . .

At nightfall came to a log-cabin at the edge of the wood, and inquired of the "Lord of the Castle" if some of the women and children could take shelter under his roof for the night; the masculine number and whichever of the women that chose, couching in the wagons and under them. He said we could. His lady, who was away, presently came, with bare feet, and a white sack twisted up and thrown over her shoulder, with a few quarts of corn meal in the end that hung down her back. I said to myself—"Is that what I have got to come to?" She seemed pleased to have company—allowed us the first chance of the broad, Dutch-backed fireplace with its earthy hearth, and without pot hooks or trammels,[7] to make ready our simple evening repast. . . .

---

6. **trundle-bed:** Low, portable bed that can be stored beneath a larger bed.
7. **trammels** (tram´ əlz) *n.*: Devices for hanging several pothooks in a fireplace.

◆ **Build Vocabulary**
profusion (prō fyo͞o´ zhən) *n.*: Abundance; rich supply
depredations (dep´ rə dā´ shənz) *n.*: Acts of robbing or plundering

---

5. **"Free States":** Free Soil movement; a group whose goal was to keep slavery out of the western territories.

Covered wagons on Main Street in Ottawa, Kansas, 1866, Kansas State Historical Society

▲ **Critical Viewing** This 1866 photograph shows covered wagons on Main Street in Ottawa, Kansas. How does the diary suggest that towns like this one were important to the wagon trains of settlers traveling westward? [**Draw Conclusions**]

Are now [May 11th] crossing the 20 mile prairie, no roads—Think Mrs. Voorhees will get walking enough crossing this prairie. She is quite a pedestrian, surely, for she has walked every bit of the way in, so far, from Kansas City, almost 100 miles.

Arrive at Elm Creek—no house to lodge in tonight—campfire kindled—supper cooked, and partaken of with a keen relish, sitting in family groups around the "great big" fire. Some will sleep in wagons, others under the canopy of the blue vault of Heaven. The young men have built some shady little bowers of the green boughs; they are looking very cosily under them, wrapped in their white Indian blankets.

We ladies, or rather, "emigrant women," are having a chat around the camp-fire—the bright stars are looking down upon us—we wonder if

we shall be neighbors to each other in the great "Octagon City. . . ."

May 12th. Full of hope, as we leave the smoking embers of our camp-fire this morning. Expect tonight to arrive at our new home.

It begins to rain, rain, rain, like a shower; we move slowly on, from high prairie, around the deep ravine—are in sight of the timber that skirts the Neosho river. Have sent three men in advance to announce our coming; are looking for our Secretary, (Henry S. Clubb) with an escort to welcome us into the embryo city. If the booming of cannon is not heard at our approach, shall expect a salute from the firing of Sharp's rifles, certainly.

No escort is seen! no salute is heard! We move slowly and drippingly into town just at nightfall—feeling not a little <u>nonplused</u> on learning that our worthy, or <u>unworthy</u>

◆ **Build Vocabulary**
nonplused (nän′ plüsd′) *adj.*: Bewildered; perplexed

Heading West ◆ 549

Secretary was out walking in the rain with his *dear* wife. We leave our wagons and make our way to the large camp-fire. It is surrounded by men and women cooking their suppers—while others are busy close by, grinding their hominy[8] in hand mills.

Look around, and see the grounds all around the camp-fire are covered with tents, in which the families are staying. Not a house is to be seen. In the large tent here is a cook stove—they have supper prepared for us; it consists of hominy, soft Johnny cake (or corn bread, as it is called here), stewed apple, and tea. We eat what is set before us, "asking no questions for conscience' sake."

The ladies tell us they are sorry to see us come to this place; which shows us that all is not right. Are too weary to question, but with hope depressed go to our lodgings, which we find around in the tents, and in our wagons.

May 13th. Can anyone imagine our disappointment this morning, on learning from this and that member, that no mills have been built; that the directors, after receiving our money to build mills, have not fulfilled the trust reposed in them, and that in consequence, some families have already left the settlement . . . ?

As it is, we find the families, some living in tents of cloth, some of cloth and green bark just peeled from the trees, and some wholly of green barn, stuck up on the damp ground, without floors or fires. Only two stoves in the company. . . .

We see that the city grounds, which have been surveyed . . . contain only one log cabin, 16 by 16, muddled between the logs on the inside, instead of on the outside; neither door nor window; the roof covered with "shakes" (western shingles), split out of oak I should think, 3 ½ feet in length, and about as wide as a sheet of fools cap paper.[9]

---

8. **hominy** (häm´ ə nē) *n.:* Dry corn, usually ground and boiled for food.

9. **fools cap paper:** Writing paper usually measuring 13 by 16 inches.

Guide for Responding

◆ *Literature and Your Life*

Reader's Response Would you have had the courage and determination to leave your home and family to become a pioneer?

Thematic Focus How was the promise of a new life in the West both attractive and frightening for Colt and thousands like her?

Journal Writing If you could move to a new home anywhere in the world, where would it be? How do you imagine your life would be different?

☑ Check Your Comprehension

1. List two ways in which Miriam Davis Colt expects her new way of life to be an improvement from her life in New York.

2. What are the three modes of transportation required to reach the Octagon City settlement?

3. Why have some families already left the settlement by the time Colt and her family arrive?

◆ Critical Thinking

INTERPRET

1. (a) What does Colt think of the appearance of the settler woman who appears with bare feet and a sack flung over her back? (b) What does this settler woman suggest to Colt about her own future? **[Infer; Interpret]**

2. How does Colt's expectation about life at Octagon City compare with the realities? **[Compare and Contrast]**

EVALUATE

3. Were Colt and her husband too naive and trusting in making their plans? Explain. **[Assess]**

APPLY

4. Based on Colt's experiences, explain which character traits you feel were necessary to being a successful pioneer. **[Synthesize]**

I Will Fight No More Forever

Chief Joseph

Tell General Howard I know his heart. What he told me before, I have in my heart. I am tired of fighting. Our chiefs are killed. Looking Glass is dead. Toohoolhoolzote is dead. The old men are all dead. It is the young men who say yes and no. He who led on the young men is dead. It is cold and we have no blankets. The little children are freezing to death. My people, some of them, have run away to the hills and have no blankets, no food; no one knows where they are—perhaps freezing to death. I want to have time to look for my children and see how many I can find. Maybe I shall find them among the dead. Hear me, my chiefs. I am tired; my heart is sick and sad. From where the sun now stands I will fight no more forever.

Guide for Responding

◆ Literature and Your Life

Reader's Response In the opening to his speech, Chief Joseph speaks of knowing his enemy's heart and having the general's words in his heart. Have you ever felt as if you knew something with your heart rather than with your head? What is the difference?

Thematic Focus Chief Joseph stands on the brink of a new and unpromising life. What are his limited hopes for the future?

Group Discussion As a group, discuss the different ways of thinking and knowing (intellectually, emotionally, physically). How do they differ? Why is each way important?

☑ Check Your Comprehension

1. At the time of Chief Joseph's surrender, what has happened to the other chiefs of the Nez Percé?
2. Why is it urgent that Chief Joseph get immediate help for his people?

◆ Critical Thinking

INTERPRET
1. Based on this speech, how would you describe Chief Joseph's relationship to his people? Explain. **[Infer]**
2. Although Chief Joseph delivered his speech to notify federal troops of his tribe's surrender, the speech had another, equally important purpose. What was that purpose? **[Interpret]**

EVALUATE
3. Would Chief Joseph's speech have been more or less effective if it had contained longer, more detailed explanations of the reasons for his decision to surrender? Explain your answer. **[Evaluate]**

EXTEND
4. What effects do the physical conditions of fatigue, hunger, and cold have on people's emotional states? **[Health Link]**

Guide for Responding (continued)

◆ Reading Strategy

RESPOND

As you read, you paid close attention to how you felt about the people and the events in the selections. Did the way in which you **responded** to a work affect your appreciation of it?

For each selection, cite one passage that affected you strongly, and describe your response to it.

◆ Literary Focus

TONE

To fully understand the meaning of a literary work, you must appreciate the **tone,** or attitude, the writer wishes to convey. Chief Joseph's simple language and delivery establishes a tone that communicates more than the message contained in the words alone. The journal entries of Miriam Davis Colt are not an objective telling of her experiences; the tone of her writing reveals her attitudes about the people and situations she encounters.

1. A military leader might adopt many tones when admitting defeat. (a) What is the overall tone of Chief Joseph's surrender? (b) What contributes to this tone?
2. Find two examples of an upbeat, positive tone in Miriam Davis Colt's diary entries.
3. Find two examples of a negative tone in "Heading West."

Beyond Literature

History Connection

Moving West The pioneers who flocked to the Oregon Country and California in the 1840's and 1850's faced great difficulties. The trip through the Rocky Mountains could last up to six months, and life on the trail was difficult and dangerous. Sickness—cholera and other diseases—not only wiped out entire wagon trains, but devastated the Native American communities along the routes. Why did so many people emigrate to the West despite the dangers?

◆ Build Vocabulary

USING THE LATIN TERM *TERRA FIRMA*

Follow the directions for each item by writing a sentence that contains the Latin term *terra firma,* meaning "firm earth" or "solid ground."

1. Describe the Pilgrims landing on Plymouth Rock after months at sea in a tiny boat.
2. Describe a hot-air balloon safely touching down after a rough flight.

USING THE WORD BANK

Select the word from the Word Bank that best describes or relates to each "situation."

1. People who left America to live in another country
2. Acts committed by hostile invading troops
3. The personality of a pleasant host
4. The scents in a perfume shop
5. A buffet of more than fifty desserts
6. An auto mechanic perplexed by a car he is unable to fix

◆ Grammar and Style

SENTENCE FRAGMENTS

Though they are an effective way to lend a sense or urgency or immediacy to a piece of writing, **sentence fragments** are not acceptable in formal English.

> A **sentence fragment** is a part of a sentence used in place of a complete sentence. It may lack a subject, a predicate, or both.

Practice Read these passages from "Heading West." If a sentence is complete, write "correct" on your paper; if it is incomplete, write "fragment." Rewrite each fragment as a complete sentence.

1. A hot summer day.
2. Have been here in West Stockholm, at my brother's, since Friday last.
3. Hasten to the hotel—find it very much crowded.

Looking at Style Miriam Davis Colt uses many sentence fragments in her writing. As a reader, evaluate the effect of that style on your understanding of her experiences.

Build Your Portfolio

 Idea Bank

Writing

1. **Poem** Write a poem using the refrain "I will fight no more forever." The subject may be a historic, contemporary, or personal conflict.

2. **Character Sketch** Describe the characteristics of Miriam Davis Colt's personality, and explain how you inferred them from the actions and comments recorded in her diary.

3. **Speech** Write a speech in which you express your thoughts on an issue or current event that interests you. Strive for the simplicity of language that makes Chief Joseph's speech so effective. **[Social Studies Link]**

Speaking and Listening

4. **Oral Interpretation** Chief Joseph's speech so moved the officers present that they were unable to speak. Recite the speech for the class as you imagine Chief Joseph did. **[Performing Arts Link]**

5. **Critique** Have a librarian help you locate original recordings of famous speeches. Select two or three excerpts from different speeches, and play them for the class. Lead a class discussion comparing the speakers' tones and styles. How do you imagine they differ from Chief Joseph's?

Projects

6. **Brochure** Write and produce a marketing brochure to attract members to the vegetarian community the Colts joined. Describe its goals, location, attitudes, and practices. **[Career Link]**

7. **Quilt** Use colored pencils or markers to draw a design for a story quilt that Miriam Davis Colt might have made to commemorate her trip. Each square should represent a different step on the journey. **[Art Link]**

 Writing Mini-Lesson

Position Paper on Development

The great open stretches of frontier land where both Chief Joseph and Miriam Davis Colt made their homes are increasingly rare today. Imagine that you live in a community whose only undeveloped section of land is about to be turned into a shopping mall. The mall would be a boost to the local economy, but it would also mean the loss of a beautiful stretch of land. Support or oppose the planned development in a position paper—a formal piece of writing that argues one side of a controversial issue. Your readers will grasp your point quickly if you present a coherent argument.

Writing Skills Focus: Coherence

A position paper must have **coherence** in order to be persuasive. In a coherent piece of writing, ideas are logically organized and clearly explained. Here are tips for writing coherently:
- Pick an organizational method (for example, chronological order, comparison and contrast, or cause and effect) and use it consistently.
- Use transition words to show relationships.
- Use specific rather than vague terminology.
- Repeat words and grammatical structures to emphasize important points.

Prewriting List the reasons you support or oppose the project, along with facts to back up your reasons.

Drafting Begin your paper with a clear statement of your position. Then give the reasons for your stand. Follow up with specific details to support your case, and end with a persuasive conclusion.

Revising Check your paper for coherence. Does your argument proceed logically and flow smoothly from one paragraph to the next? Do you provide convincing reasons and back up opinions with facts?

Guide for Interpreting

Jack London (1876–1917)

Jack London had endured more hardships by the age of twenty-one than most people experience in a lifetime. His struggles developed in him a sympathy for the working class and a lasting dislike of drudgery and provided inspiration for his career as a writer.

Difficult Beginnings London grew up in San Francisco in extreme poverty. At an early age, he left school and supported himself through a succession of unskilled jobs—working as a paper boy, in bowling alleys, on ice wagons, and in canneries and mills. Despite working long hours at these jobs, London was able to read constantly, borrowing travel and adventure books from the library.

The books London read inspired him to travel, and his job experiences led him to become active in fighting for the rights of workers. He sailed to Japan on a sealing expedition and joined a cross-country protest march with a group of unemployed workers. After being arrested for vagrancy near Buffalo, New York, London decided to educate himself and reshape his life. He quickly completed high school and entered the University of California.

After only one semester, however, the lure of fortune and adventure proved irresistible. London abandoned his studies and traveled to the Alaskan Yukon in 1897 in search of gold. Although he was unsuccessful as a miner, London's experiences in Alaska taught him about the human desire for wealth and power and about humankind's inability to control the forces of nature. While in Alaska, London also absorbed memories and stories that would make his name known one hundred years later.

A Writing Life Once back in California, London became determined to earn a living as a writer. He rented a typewriter and worked up to fifteen hours a day, spinning his Alaskan adventures into short stories and novels.

According to legend, London's stack of rejection slips from publishers grew to five feet in height!

Even so, London persevered. In 1903, he earned national fame when he published the popular novel *The Call of the Wild*. He soon became the highest paid and most industrious writer in the country. During his career, he produced more than fifty books and earned more than a million dollars. Several of his novels, including *The Call of the Wild* (1903), *The Sea-Wolf* (1904), and *White Fang* (1906), have become American classics. His best works depict a person's struggle for survival against the powerful forces of nature. "To Build a Fire," for example, tells the story of a man's fight to survive the harsh cold of the Alaskan winter.

◆ Background for Understanding

HISTORY: LONDON AND THE GOLD RUSH

The United States Secretary of State William Seward purchased Alaska from Russia in 1867 for two cents an acre. Many Americans, believing it to be nothing but a frozen barren wasteland, called the purchase "Seward's Folly."

In 1896 the discovery of a rich lode of gold in the Yukon, part of the Arctic wilderness, led to the Klondike stampede of 1897–1898. Thousands of prospectors headed for the frozen north, lured by the promise of quick riches from gold and other natural resources.

Jack London was among the first of these prospectors. He may have searched for more than gold, however. London once commented, "True, the new territory was mostly barren; but its several hundred thousand square miles of frigidity at least gave breathing space to those who else would have suffocated at home."

To Build a Fire

◆ Literature and Your Life

CONNECT YOUR EXPERIENCE

Some people enjoy pushing themselves to their physical limits through sports such as rock climbing and sky diving. In some cases, as in this story, people push themselves to such extremes that they actually place their lives in jeopardy.

Journal Writing Describe a time when you endured extreme weather or engaged in a physically demanding activity.

THEMATIC FOCUS: FORGING NEW FRONTIERS

Jack London, along with thousands of other prospectors, helped establish the Alaskan frontier. Like the main character of "To Build a Fire," they were drawn to a brutal setting by the lure of gold. What qualities are key to survival in this frozen frontier?

◆ Reading Strategy

PREDICT

The main character in this story fails to notice signs of danger and take proper precautions. A more alert person might have anticipated the dangers. As a reader, you too can anticipate, or **predict,** what will happen by taking note of clues that hint at later events. The clues in this story include the repeated references to the frigid temperatures and the man's determination to reach his goal. As you read, use a chart like this to note clues and record your predictions. Revise your predictions as you encounter new information.

As you read, take note of clues and chart your own predictions.

Clues	Prediction	Outcome

◆ Grammar and Style

ADVERB CLAUSES

"Day had broken cold and gray, exceedingly cold and gray, *when the man turned aside from the main Yukon trail* . . . There was no sun nor hint of sun, *though there was not a cloud in the sky.*" The italicized portions of this passage from the story are adverb clauses. An **adverb clause** is a subordinate clause—a group of words with a subject and a verb that cannot stand by itself as a sentence—that describes *how, when, where, why, under what circumstances,* and *to what extent* an action occurs. The first adverb clause tells when the action occurred; the second tells under what circumstances.

◆ Literary Focus

CONFLICT

With only a dog for company, an unnamed man struggles to survive in the frigid Alaskan wilderness. This man is in the throes of a **conflict,** a struggle between two opposing forces. Conflicts may be **external**—between a character and an outside force such as nature or another person—or **internal**—a struggle within an individual. A character's struggle to resolve these conflicts forms the basis for the plot of a literary work. As you read, identify the conflicting forces at work in "To Build a Fire."

◆ Build Vocabulary

WORD ROOTS: -ject-

The main character in this story *rejects* an old-timer's advice not to travel alone and fails to *conjecture* about the consequences. The root *-ject-* means "to throw." When you *conjecture,* you throw out a guess. If you *reject* an idea, you throw it back. What other words do you know that contain the root *-ject-?*

WORD BANK

Preview this list of words before you read the story.

conjectural
unwonted
conflagration
peremptorily

To Build a Fire

Jack London

Day had broken cold and gray, exceedingly cold and gray, when the man turned aside from the main Yukon[1] trail and climbed the high earth-bank, where a dim and little-traveled trail led eastward through the fat spruce timberland. It was a steep bank, and he paused for breath at the top, excusing the act to himself by looking at his watch. It was nine o'clock. There was no sun nor hint of sun, though there was not a cloud in the sky. It was a clear day, and yet there seemed an intangible pall over the face of things, a subtle gloom that made the day dark, and that was due to the absence of sun. This fact did not worry the man. He was used to the lack of sun. It had been days since he had seen the sun, and he knew that a few more days must pass before that cheerful orb, due south, would just peep above the skyline and dip immediately from view.

The man flung a look back along the way he had come. The Yukon lay a mile wide and hidden under three feet of ice. On top of this ice were as many feet of snow. It was all pure white, rolling in gentle undulations where the ice jams of the freeze-up had formed. North and south, as far as his eye could see, it was unbroken white, save for a dark hairline that curved and twisted from around the spruce-covered island to the south, and that curved and twisted away into the north, where it dis-appeared behind another spruce-covered is-land. This dark hairline was the trail—the main trail—that led south five hundred miles to the Chilcoot Pass, Dyea,[2] and salt water; and that led north seventy miles to Dawson, and still on to the north a thousand miles to Nulato,[3] and finally to St. Michael on Bering Sea, a thousand miles and half a thousand more.

But all this—the mysterious, far-reaching hairline trail, the absence of sun from the sky, the tremendous cold, and the strangeness and weirdness of it all—no impression on the man. It was not because he was long used to it. He was a newcomer in the land, a *chechaquo*,[4] and this was his first winter. The trouble with him was that he was without imagination. He was quick and alert in the things of life, but only in the things, and not in the significances. Fifty degrees below zero meant eighty-odd degrees of frost. Such fact impressed him as being cold and uncomfortable, and that was all. It did not lead him to meditate upon his frailty as a creature of temperature, and upon man's frailty in general, able only to live within certain narrow limits of heat and cold; and from there on it did not lead him to the conjectural field of immortality and man's place in the universe. Fifty

---

1. **Yukon** (yŏŏ´ kän): Territory in northwestern Canada, east of Alaska; also, a river.

2. **Dyea** (dī´ ā): Former town in Alaska at the start of the Yukon trail.
3. **Dawson . . . Nulato:** Former gold-mining villages in the Yukon.
4. *chechaquo* (chē chä´ kwō): Slang for newcomer.

degrees below zero stood for a bite of frost that hurt and that must be guarded against by the use of mittens, earflaps, warm moccasins, and thick socks. Fifty degrees below zero was to him just precisely fifty degrees below zero. That there should be anything more to it than that was a thought that never entered his head.

As he turned to go on, he spat speculatively. There was a sharp, explosive crackle that startled him. He spat again. And again, in the air, before it could fall to the snow, the spittle crackled. He knew that at fifty below spittle crackled on the snow, but this spittle had crackled in the air. Undoubtedly it was colder than fifty below—how much colder he did not know. But the temperature did not matter. He was bound for the old claim on the left fork of Henderson Creek, where the boys were already. They had come over across the divide from the Indian Creek country, while he had come the roundabout way to take a look at the possibilities of getting out logs in the spring from the islands in the Yukon. He would be in to camp by six o'clock; a bit after dark, it was true, but the boys would be there, a fire would be going, and a hot supper would be ready. As for lunch, he pressed his hand against the protruding bundle under his jacket. It was also under his shirt, wrapped up in a handkerchief and lying against the naked skin. It was the only way to keep the biscuits from freezing. He smiled agreeably to himself as he thought of those biscuits, each cut open and sopped in bacon grease, and each enclosing a generous slice of fried bacon.

He plunged in among the big spruce trees. The trail was faint. A foot of snow had fallen since the last sled had passed over, and he was glad he was without a sled, traveling light. In fact, he carried nothing but the lunch wrapped in the handkerchief. He was surprised, however, at the cold. It certainly was cold, he concluded, as he rubbed his numb nose and cheekbones with his mittened hand. He was a warm-whiskered man, but the hair on his face did not protect the high cheekbones and the eager nose that thrust itself aggressively into the frosty air.

At the man's heels trotted a dog, a big native husky, the proper wolf dog, gray-coated and without any visible or temperamental difference from its brother, the wild wolf. The animal was depressed by the tremendous cold. It knew that it was no time for traveling. Its instinct told it a truer tale than was told to the man by the man's judgment. In reality, it was not merely colder than fifty below zero; it was colder than sixty below, than seventy below. It was seventy-five below zero. Since the freezing point is thirty-two above zero, it meant that one hundred and seven degrees of frost obtained. The dog did not know anything about thermometers. Possibly in its brain there was no sharp consciousness of a condition of very cold such as was in the man's brain. But the brute had its instinct. It experienced a vague but menacing apprehension that subdued it and made it slink along at the man's heels, and that made it question eagerly every unwonted movement of the man as if expecting him to go into camp or to seek shelter somewhere and build a fire. The dog had learned fire, and it wanted fire, or else to burrow under the snow and cuddle its warmth away from the air.

The frozen moisture of its breathing had settled on its fur in a fine powder of frost, and especially were its jowls, muzzle, and eyelashes whitened by its crystalled breath. The man's red beard and mustache were likewise frosted, but more solidly, the deposit taking the form of ice and increasing with every warm, moist breath he exhaled. Also, the man was chewing tobacco, and the muzzle of ice held his lips so rigidly that he was unable to clear his chin when he expelled the juice. The result was that a crystal beard of the color and solidity of amber was increasing its length on his chin. If he fell down it would shatter itself, like glass, into brittle fragments. But he did not mind the appendage. It was the penalty all tobacco-chewers paid in that country, and he had been out before in two cold snaps. They had not been so cold as this, he knew, but by

♦ **Build Vocabulary**
conjectural (kən jek′ chər əl) *adj.*: Based on guesswork
unwonted (un wän′ tid) *adj.*: Unusual; unfamiliar

♦ **Literary Focus**
The great elaboration on the cold points out the central conflict in this story. With what or whom is the man in conflict?

the spirit thermometer[5] at Sixty Mile he knew they had been registered at fifty below and at fifty-five.

He held on through the level stretch of woods for several miles, crossed a wide flat, and dropped down a bank to the frozen bed of a small stream. This was Henderson Creek, and he knew he was ten miles from the forks. He looked at his watch. It was ten o'clock. He was making four miles an hour, and he calculated that he would arrive at the forks at half past twelve. He decided to celebrate that event by eating his lunch there.

The dog dropped in again at his heels, with a tail drooping discouragement, as the man swung along the creek bed. The furrow of the old sled trail was plainly visible, but a dozen inches of snow covered the marks of the last runners. In a month no man had come up or down that silent creek. The man held steadily on. He was not much given to thinking, and just then particularly he had nothing to think about save that he would eat lunch at the forks and that at six o'clock he would be in camp with the boys. There was nobody to talk to; and, had there been, speech would have been impossible because of the ice-muzzle on his mouth. So he continued monotonously to chew tobacco and to increase the length of his amber beard.

Once in a while the thought reiterated itself that it was very cold and that he had never experienced such cold. As he walked along he rubbed his cheekbones and nose with the back of his mittened hand. He did this automatically, now and again changing hands. But rub as he would, the instant he stopped his cheekbones went numb, and the following instant the end of his nose went numb. He was sure to frost his cheeks; he knew that, and experienced a pang of regret that he had not devised a nose strap of the sort Bud wore in cold snaps. Such a strap passed across the cheeks, as well, and saved them. But it didn't matter much, after

▲ **Critical Viewing** Which words or passages from the story could be used to describe this scene? [Analyze]

all. What were frosted cheeks? A bit painful, that was all: they were never serious.

Empty as the man's mind was of thoughts, he was keenly observant, and he noticed the changes in the creek, the curves and bends and timber jams, and always he sharply noted where he placed his feet. Once, coming around a bend, he shied abruptly, like a startled horse, curved away from the place where he had been walking, and retreated several paces back along the trail. The creek he knew was frozen clear to the bottom—no creek could contain water in that arctic winter—but he knew also that there were springs that bubbled out from the hillsides and ran along under the snow and on top the ice of the creek. He knew that the coldest snaps never froze these springs, and he knew likewise their danger. They were traps. They hid pools of water under the snow that might be three inches deep, or three feet. Sometimes a skin of ice half an inch thick covered them, and in turn was covered by the snow. Sometimes there were alternate layers of water and ice skin, so that when one broke through he kept on breaking through for a while, sometimes wetting himself to the waist.

That was why he had shied in such panic. He had felt the give under his feet and heard the

◆ **Reading Strategy**
Based on this passage, what can you predict might happen?

5. **spirit thermometer:** Thermometer containing alcohol; used in extreme cold.

crackle of a snow-hidden ice skin. And to get his feet wet in such a temperature meant trouble and danger. At the very least it meant delay, for he would be forced to stop and build a fire, and under its protection to bare his feet while he dried his socks and moccasins. He stood and studied the creek bed and its banks, and decided that the flow of water came from the right. He reflected awhile, rubbing his nose and cheeks, then skirted to the left, stepping gingerly and testing the footing for each step. Once clear of the danger, he took a fresh chew of tobacco and swung along at his four-mile gait.

◆ **Literary Focus**

Until now, the man has struggled with the frigid air temperature. What other element of conflict is introduced here?

In the course of the next two hours he came upon several similar traps. Usually the snow above the hidden pools had a sunken, candied appearance that advertised the danger. Once again, however, he had a close call; and once, suspecting danger, he compelled the dog to go on in front. The dog did not want to go. It hung back until the man shoved it forward, and then it went quickly across the white, unbroken surface. Suddenly it broke through, floundered to one side, and got away to firmer footing. It had wet its forefeet and legs, and almost immediately the water that clung to it turned to ice. It made quick efforts to lick the ice off its legs, then dropped down in the snow and began to bite out the ice that had formed between the toes. This was a matter of instinct. To permit the ice to remain would mean sore feet. It did not know this. It merely obeyed the mysterious prompting that arose from the deep crypts of its being. But the man knew, having achieved a judgment on the subject, and he removed the mitten from his right hand and helped tear out the ice particles. He did not expose his fingers more than a minute, and was astonished at the swift numbness that smote them. It certainly was cold. He pulled on the mitten hastily, and beat the hand savagely across his chest.

At twelve o'clock the day was at its brightest. Yet the sun was too far south on its winter journey to clear the horizon. The bulge of the earth intervened between it and Henderson Creek, where the man walked under a clear sky at noon and cast no shadow. At half-past twelve, to the minute, he arrived at the forks of the creek. He was pleased at the speed he had made. If he kept it up, he would certainly be with the boys by six. He unbuttoned his jacket and shirt and drew forth his lunch. The action consumed no more than a quarter of a minute, yet in that brief moment the numbness laid hold of the exposed fingers. He did not put the mitten on, but, instead, struck the fingers a dozen sharp smashes against his leg. Then he sat down on a snow-covered log to eat. The sting that followed upon the striking of his fingers against his leg ceased so quickly that he was startled. He had had no chance to take a bite of biscuit. He struck the fingers repeatedly and returned them to the mitten, baring the other hand for the purpose of eating. He tried to take a mouthful, but the ice muzzle prevented. He had forgotten to build a fire and thaw out. He chuckled at his foolishness, and as he chuckled he noted the numbness creeping into the exposed fingers. Also, he noted that the stinging which had first come to his toes when he sat down was already passing away. He wondered whether the toes were warm or numb. He moved them inside the moccasins and decided that they were numb.

He pulled the mitten on hurriedly and stood up. He was a bit frightened. He stamped up and down until the stinging returned into the feet. It certainly was cold, was his thought. That man from Sulphur Creek had spoken the truth when telling how cold it sometimes got in the country. And he had laughed at him at the time! That showed one must not be too sure of things. There was no mistake about it, it *was* cold. He strode up and down, stamping his feet and threshing his arms, until reassured by the returning warmth. Then he got out matches and proceeded to make a fire. From the undergrowth, where high water of the previous spring had lodged a supply of seasoned twigs, he got his firewood. Working carefully from a small beginning, he soon had a roaring fire, over which he thawed the ice from his face and in the protection of which he ate his biscuits. For the moment the cold of space was outwitted.

The dog took satisfaction in the fire, stretching out close enough for warmth and far enough away to escape being singed.

When the man had finished, he filled his pipe and took his comfortable time over a smoke. Then he pulled on his mittens, settled the earflaps of his cap firmly about his ears, and took the creek trail up the left fork. The dog was disappointed and yearned back toward the fire. This man did not know cold. Possibly all the generations of his ancestry had been ignorant of cold, of real cold, of cold one hundred and seven degrees below freezing point. But the dog knew; all its ancestry knew, and it had inherited the knowledge. And it knew that it was not good to walk abroad in such fearful cold. It was the time to lie snug in a hole in the snow and wait for a curtain of cloud to be drawn across the face of outer space whence this cold came. On the other hand, there was no keen intimacy between the dog and the man. The one was the toil slave of the other, and the only caresses it had ever received were the caresses of the whiplash and of harsh and menacing throat sounds that threatened the whiplash. So the dog made no effort to communicate its apprehension to the man. It was not concerned in the welfare of the man; it was for its own sake that it yearned back toward the fire. But the man whistled, and spoke to it with the sound of whiplashes, and the dog swung in at the man's heels and followed after.

The man took a chew of tobacco and proceeded to start a new amber beard. Also, his moist breath quickly powdered with white his mustache, eyebrows, and lashes. There did not seem to be so many springs on the left fork of the Henderson, and for half an hour the man saw no signs of any. And then it happened. At a place where there were no signs, where the soft, unbroken snow seemed to advertise solidity beneath, the man broke through. It was not deep. He wet himself halfway to the knees before he floundered out to the firm crust.

He was angry, and cursed his luck aloud. He had hoped to get into camp with the boys at six o'clock, and this would delay him an hour, for he would have to build a fire and dry out his footgear. This was imperative at that low temperature—he knew that much; and he turned aside to the bank, which he climbed. On top, tangled in the underbrush about the trunks of several small spruce trees, was a high-water deposit of dry firewood—sticks and twigs, principally, but also larger portions of seasoned branches and fine, dry, last year's grasses. He threw down several large pieces on top of the snow. This served for a foundation and prevented the young flame from drowning itself in the snow it otherwise would melt. The flame he got by touching a match to a small shred of birch bark that he took from his pocket. This burned even more readily than paper. Placing it on the foundation, he fed the young flame with wisps of dry grass and with the tiniest dry twigs.

He worked slowly and carefully, keenly aware of his danger. Gradually, as the flame grew stronger, he increased the size of the twigs with which he fed it. He squatted in the snow, pulling the twigs out from their entanglement in the brush and feeding directly to the flame. He knew there must be no failure. When it is seventy-five below zero, a man must not fail in his first attempt to build a fire—that is, if his feet are wet. If his feet are dry, and he fails, he can run along the trail for half a mile and restore his circulation. But the circulation of wet and freezing feet cannot be restored by running when it is seventy-five below. No matter how fast he runs, the wet feet will freeze the harder.

All this the man knew. The old-timer on Sulphur Creek had told him about it the previous fall, and now he was appreciating the advice. Already all sensation had gone out of his feet. To build the fire he had been forced to remove his mittens, and the fingers had quickly gone numb. His pace of four miles an hour had kept his heart pumping blood to the surface of his body and to all the extremities. But the instant he stopped, the action of the pump eased down. The cold of space smote the unprotected tip of the planet, and he, being on that unprotected tip, received the full force of the blow. The blood of his body recoiled before it. The blood was alive, like the dog, and like the dog it wanted to hide away and cover itself up from the fearful cold. So long as he walked four miles an hour, he pumped that blood, willy-nilly, to the surface; but now it ebbed away and sank down into the recesses of his body. The extremities were the first to feel its absence. His wet feet froze the faster, and his exposed fingers numbed the faster, though they had not yet begun to freeze. Nose and cheeks were already freezing, while the skin of all his body chilled as it lost its blood.

But he was safe. Toes and nose and cheeks would be only touched by the frost, for the fire was beginning to burn with strength. He was feeding it with twigs the size of his finger. In another minute he would be able to feed it with branches the size of his wrist, and then he could remove his wet foot-gear, and, while it dried, he could keep his naked feet warm by the fire, rubbing them at first, of course, with snow. The fire was a success. He was safe. He remembered the advice of the old-timer on Sulphur Creek, and smiled. The old-timer had been very serious in laying down the law that no man must travel alone in the Klondike after fifty below. Well, here he was; he had had the accident; he was alone; and he had saved himself. Those old-timers were rather womanish, some of them, he thought. All a man had to do was to keep his head, and he was all right. Any man who was a man could travel alone. But it was surprising, the rapidity with which his

◆ Reading Strategy
Has the man saved himself? What do you predict will happen?

cheeks and nose were freezing. And he had not thought his fingers could go lifeless in so short a time. Lifeless they were, for he could scarcely make them move together to grip a twig, and they seemed remote from his body and from him. When he touched a twig, he had to look and see whether or not he had hold of it. The wires were pretty well down between him and his finger ends.

All of which counted for little. There was the fire, snapping and crackling and promising life with every dancing flame. He started to untie his moccasins. They were coated with ice; the thick German socks were like sheaths of iron halfway to the knees; and the moccasin strings were like rods of steel all twisted and knotted as by some conflagration. For a moment he tugged with his numb fingers, then, realizing the folly of it, he drew his sheath-knife.

But before he could cut the strings, it happened. It was his own fault or, rather, his mistake. He should not have built the fire under the spruce tree. He should have built it in the open. But it had been easier to pull the twigs from the brush and drop them directly on the fire. Now the tree under which he had done this carried a weight of snow on its boughs. No wind had blown for weeks, and each bough was fully freighted. Each time he had pulled a twig he had communicated a slight agitation to the tree—an imperceptible agitation, so far as he was concerned, but an agitation sufficient to bring about the disaster. High up in the tree one bough capsized its load of snow. This fell on the boughs beneath, capsizing them. This process continued, spreading out and involving the whole tree. It grew like an avalanche, and it descended without warning upon the man and the fire, and the fire was blotted out! Where it had burned was a mantle of fresh and disordered snow.

The man was shocked. It was as though he had just heard his own sentence of death. For a moment he sat and stared at the spot where the fire had been. Then he grew very calm. Perhaps the old-timer on Sulphur Creek was right. If he had only had a trail mate he would have been in no danger now. The trail mate could have built the fire. Well, it was up to him to build the fire over again, and this second time there must be no failure. Even if he succeeded, he would most likely lose some toes. His feet must be badly frozen by now, and there would be some time before the second fire was ready.

Such were his thoughts, but he did not sit and think them. He was busy all the time they were passing through his mind. He made a new foundation for a fire, this time in the open, where no treacherous tree could blot it out. Next, he gathered dry grasses and tiny twigs from the high-water flotsam. He could not bring his fingers together to pull them out, but he was able to gather them by the handful. In

◆ **Build Vocabulary**
conflagration (kän′ flə grā′ shən) *n*.: Big, destructive fire

this way he got many rotten twigs and bits of green moss that were undesirable, but it was the best he could do. He worked methodically, even collecting an armful of the larger branches to be used later when the fire gathered strength. And all the while the dog sat and watched him, a certain yearning wistfulness in its eyes, for it looked upon him as the fire provider, and the fire was slow in coming.

When all was ready, the man reached in his pocket for a second piece of birch bark. He knew the bark was there, and, though he could not feel it with his fingers, he could hear its crisp rustling as he fumbled for it. Try as he would, he could not clutch hold of it. And all the time, in his consciousness, was the knowledge that each instant his feet were freezing. This thought tended to put him in a panic, but he fought against it and kept calm. He pulled on his mittens with his teeth, and threshed his arms back and forth, beating his hands with all his might against his sides. He did this sitting down, and he stood up to do it; and all the while the dog sat in the snow, its wolf brush of a tail curled around warmly over its forefeet, its sharp wolf ears pricked forward intently as it watched the man. And the man, as he beat and threshed with his arms and hands, felt a great surge of envy as he regarded the creature that was warm and secure in its natural covering.

▲ **Critical Viewing** Study the eyes of this husky. What human characteristics would you attribute to its eyes? Which, if any, of those characteristics apply to the dog in the story? **[Infer; Relate]**

After a time he was aware of the first faraway signals of sensation in his beaten fingers. The faint tingling grew stronger till it evolved into a stinging ache that was excruciating, but which the man hailed with satisfaction. He stripped the mitten from his right hand and fetched forth the birch bark. The exposed fingers were quickly going numb again. Next he brought out his bunch of sulphur matches. But the tremendous cold had already driven the life out of his fingers. In his effort to separate one match from the others, the whole bunch fell in the snow. He tried to pick it out of the snow, but failed. The dead fingers could neither touch nor clutch. He was very careful. He drove the thought of his freezing feet, and nose, and cheeks, out of his mind, devoting his whole soul to the matches. He watched, using the sense of vision in place of that of touch, and when he saw his fingers on each side the bunch, he closed them—that is, he willed to close them, for the wires were down, and the fingers did not obey. He pulled the mitten on the right hand, and beat it fiercely against his knee. Then, with both mittened hands, he scooped the bunch of matches, along with much snow, into his lap. Yet he was no better off.

After some manipulation he managed to get the bunch between the heels of his mittened hands. In this fashion he carried it to his mouth. The ice crackled and snapped when by a violent effort he opened his mouth. He drew the lower jaw in, curled the upper lip out of the way, and scraped the bunch with his upper teeth in order to separate a match. He succeeded in getting one, which he dropped on his lap. He was no better off. He could not pick it up. Then he devised a way. He picked it up in his teeth and scratched it on his leg. Twenty times he scratched before he succeeded in lighting it. As it flamed he held it with his teeth to the birch bark. But the burning brimstone went up his nostrils and into his lungs, causing him to cough spasmodically. The match fell into the snow and went out.

The old-timer on Sulphur Creek was right, he thought in the moment of controlled despair that ensued: after fifty below, a man should travel with a partner. He beat his hands, but failed in exciting any sensation. Suddenly he bared both hands, removing the mittens with his teeth. He caught the whole bunch between the heels of his hands. His arm muscles not being frozen enabled him to press the hand heels tightly against the matches. Then he scratched the bunch along his leg. It flared into flame, seventy sulphur matches at once! There was no wind to blow them out. He kept his head to one side to escape the strangling fumes, and held the blazing bunch to the birch bark. As he so held it, he became aware of sensation in his hand. His flesh was burning. He could smell it. Deep down below the surface he could feel it. The sensation developed into pain that grew acute. And still he endured it, holding the flame of the matches clumsily to the bark that would not light readily because his own burning hands were in the way, absorbing most of the flame.

At last, when he could endure no more, he jerked his hands apart. The blazing matches fell sizzling into the snow, but the birch bark was alight. He began laying dry grasses and the tiniest twigs on the flame. He could not pick and choose, for he had to lift the fuel between the heels of his hands. Small pieces of rotten wood and green moss clung to the twigs, and he bit them off as well as he could with his teeth. He cherished the flame carefully and awkwardly. It meant life, and it must not perish. The withdrawal of blood from the surface of his body now made him begin to shiver, and he grew more awkward. A large piece of green moss fell squarely on the little fire. He tried to poke it out with his fingers, but his shivering frame made him poke too far, and he disrupted the nucleus of the little fire, the burning grasses and tiny twigs separating and scattering. He tried to poke them together again, but in spite of the tenseness of the effort, his shivering got away with him, and the twigs were hopelessly scattered. Each twig gushed a puff of smoke and went out. The fire provider had failed. As he looked apathetically about him, his eyes chanced on the dog, sitting across the ruins of the fire from him, in the snow, making restless, hunching movements, slightly lifting one forefoot and then the other, shifting its weight back and forth on them with wistful eagerness.

The sight of the dog put a wild idea into his head. He remembered the tale of the man, caught in a blizzard, who killed a steer and crawled inside the carcass, and so was saved. He would kill the dog and bury his hands in the warm body until the numbness went out of them. Then he could build another fire. He spoke to the dog, calling it to him; but in his voice was a strange note of fear that frightened the animal, who had never known the man to speak in such way before. Something was the matter, and its suspicious nature sensed danger—it knew not what danger, but somewhere, somehow, in its brain arose an apprehension of the man. It flattened its ears down at the sound of the man's voice, and its restless, hunching movements and the liftings and shiftings of its forefeet became more pronounced; but it would not come to the man. He got on his hands and knees and crawled toward the dog. This unusual posture again excited suspicion, and the animal sidled mincingly away.

The man sat up in the snow for a moment and struggled for calmness. Then he pulled on his mittens, by means of his teeth, and got upon his feet. He glanced down at first in order to assure himself that he was really standing up, for the absence of sensation in his feet left him unrelated to the earth. His erect position in itself started to drive the webs of suspicion from the dog's mind; and when he spoke peremptorily, with the sound of whiplashes in his voice, the dog rendered its customary allegiance and came to him. As it came within reaching distance, the man lost his control. His arms flashed out to the dog, and he experienced genuine surprise when he discovered that his hands could not clutch, that there was neither bend nor feeling in the fingers. He had forgotten for the moment that they were frozen and that they were freezing more and more. All this happened quickly, and before the animal could get away, he encircled its body with his arms. He sat down in the snow, and in this fashion held the dog, while it snarled and whined and struggled.

◆ **Build Vocabulary**

peremptorily (pər emp′ tər ə lē) *adj.*: Decisively; commandingly

But it was all he could do, hold its body encircled in his arms and sit there. He realized that he could not kill the dog. There was no way to do it. With his helpless hands he could neither draw nor hold his sheath-knife nor throttle the animal. He released it, and it plunged wildly away, with tail between its legs, and still snarling. It halted forty feet away and surveyed him curiously, with ears sharply pricked forward. The man looked down at his hands in order to locate them, and found them hanging on the ends of his arms. It struck him as curious that one should have to use his eyes in order to find out where his hands were. He began threshing his arms back and forth, beating the mittened hands against his sides. He did this for five minutes, violently, and his heart pumped enough blood up to the surface to put a stop to his shivering. But no sensation was aroused in the hands. He had an impression that they hung like weights on the ends of his arms, but when he tried to run the impression down, he could not find it.

A certain fear of death, dull and oppressive, came to him. This fear quickly became poignant as he realized that it was no longer a mere matter of freezing his fingers and toes, or of losing his hands and feet, but that it was a matter of life and death with the chances against him. This threw him into a panic, and he turned and ran up the creek-bed along the old, dim trail. The dog joined in behind and kept up with him. He ran blindly, without intention, in fear such as he had never known in his life. Slowly, as he plowed and floundered through the snow, he began to see things again—the banks of the creek, the old timber jams, the leafless aspens, and the sky. The running made him feel better. He did not shiver. Maybe, if he ran on, his feet would thaw out; and, anyway, if he ran far enough, he would reach camp and the boys. Without doubt he would lose some fingers and toes and some of his face; but the boys would take care of him, and save the rest of him when he got there. And at the same time there was another thought in his mind that said he would never

◆ **Reading Strategy**
Does the man still have a chance for survival? Explain why or why not.

get to the camp and the boys; that it was too many miles away, that the freezing had too great a start on him, and that he would soon be stiff and dead. This thought he kept in the background and refused to consider. Sometimes it pushed itself forward and demanded to be heard, but he thrust it back and strove to think of other things.

It struck him as curious that he could run at all on feet so frozen that he could not feel them when they struck the earth and took the weight of his body. He seemed to himself to skim along above the surface, and to have no connection with the earth. Somewhere he had once seen a winged Mercury,[6] and he wondered if Mercury felt as he felt when skimming over the earth.

His theory of running until he reached camp and the boys had one flaw in it: he lacked the endurance. Several times he stumbled, and finally he tottered, crumpled up, and fell. When he tried to rise, he failed. He must sit and rest, he decided, and next time he would merely walk and keep on going. As he sat and regained his breath, he noted that he was feeling quite warm and comfortable. He was not shivering, and it even seemed that a warm glow had come to his chest and trunk. And yet, when he touched his nose or cheeks, there was no sensation. Running would not thaw them out. Nor would it thaw out his hands and feet. Then the thought came to him that the frozen portions of his body must be extending. He tried to keep this thought down, to forget it, to think of something else; he was aware of the panicky feeling that it caused, and he was afraid of the panic. But the thought asserted itself, and persisted, until it produced a vision of his body totally frozen. This was too much, and he made another wild run along the trail. Once he slowed down to a walk, but the thought of the freezing extending itself made him run again.

And all the time the dog ran with him, at his heels. When he fell down a second time, it curled its tail over its forefeet and sat in front of him, facing him, curiously eager and intent. The warmth and security of the animal angered him, and he cursed it till it flattened down its

---

6. **Mercury:** From Roman mythology, the wing-footed messenger of the gods.

ears appeasingly. This time the shivering came more quickly upon the man. He was losing in his battle with the frost. It was creeping into his body from all sides. The thought of it drove him on, but he ran no more than a hundred feet, when he staggered and pitched headlong. It was his last panic. When he had recovered his breath and control, he sat up and entertained in his mind the conception of meeting death with dignity. However, the conception did not come to him in such terms. His idea of it was that he had been making a fool of himself, running around like a chicken with its head cut off—such was the simile that occurred to him. Well, he was bound to freeze anyway, and he might as well take it decently. With this new-found peace of mind came the first glimmerings of drowsiness. A good idea, he thought, to sleep off to death. It was like taking an anaesthetic. Freezing was not so bad as people thought. There were lots worse ways to die.

He pictured the boys finding his body next day. Suddenly he found himself with them, coming along the trail and looking for himself. And, still with them, he came around a turn in the trail and found himself lying in the snow. He did not belong with himself any more, for even then he was out of himself; standing with the boys and looking at himself in the snow. It certainly was cold, was his thought. When he got back to the States he could tell the folks what real cold was. He drifted on from this to a vision of the old-timer on Sulphur Creek. He could see him quite clearly, warm and comfortable, and smoking a pipe.

"You were right, old hoss; you were right," the man mumbled to the old-timer of Sulphur Creek.

Then the man drowsed off into what seemed to him the most comfortable and satisfying sleep he had ever known. The dog sat facing him and waiting. The brief day drew to a close in a long, slow twilight. There were no signs of a fire to be made, and, besides, never in the dog's experience had it known a man to sit like that in the snow and make no fire. As the twilight drew on, its eager yearning for the fire mastered it, and with a great lifting and shifting of forefeet, it whined softly, then flattened its ears down in anticipation of being chidden[7] by the man. But the man remained silent. Later, the dog whined loudly. And still later it crept close to the man and caught the scent of death. This made the animal bristle and back away. A little longer it delayed, howling under the stars that leaped and danced and shone brightly in the cold sky. Then it turned and trotted up the trail in the direction of the camp it knew, where were the other food providers and fire providers.

---

7. **chidden:** Scolded.

Guide for Responding

◆ Literature and Your Life

Reader's Response Could you imagine yourself falling into the same circumstances as the man? How could you avoid them?

Thematic Focus Adventurers seek different things when they challenge themselves. Are the risks worth the possible consequences?

Group Discussion With a group, discuss your attitudes toward the positives and negatives of high-risk sports and adventures.

☑ Check Your Comprehension

1. What advice from an old-timer does the man choose to ignore?
2. (a) What traps does the man try to avoid? (b) What happens despite his precautions?
3. What careless mistake does the man make when he tries to build a fire to thaw out his feet?
4. Why is the man unable to build another fire?
5. What happens to the man and the dog at the end of the story?

Guide for Responding (continued)

◆ Critical Thinking

INTERPRET

1. Why does the extreme cold "make no impression" on the man? **[Deduce]**
2. Compare the dog's relationship with nature to the man's relationship with nature. Which is better equipped to survive? **[Compare]**
3. Why might London have chosen not to give the man in the story a name? **[Speculate]**
4. What does the story suggest about humanity's place in the natural world? **[Draw Conclusions]**

EVALUATE

5. At one point, the man gets angry and curses his fate. Is the outcome of the story due to fate or something within the man? Explain. **[Evaluate]**

EXTEND

6. How might the outcome of the story be different if it were set in today's world? Why? **[Connect]**

◆ Reading Strategy

PREDICT

Jack London includes a variety of clues that can help you **predict**, or make educated guesses about, the outcome of the story.

1. How do the man's recollections of his conversation with the old man from Sulphur Creek help you predict the end of the story?
2. (a) At what point did you first predict that the man would not survive his journey? (b) On what clues did you base your prediction?

◆ Literary Focus

CONFLICT

Conflict—a struggle between two opposing forces—may be **internal,** occurring in the mind of a character, or **external,** occurring between a character and society, a character and nature, or between a character and fate.

1. What external conflict is central to the plot of "To Build a Fire"?
2. How does the conflict intensify as the plot unfolds and how is it resolved?
3. Describe the internal conflict that develops as the story progresses.

◆ Build Vocabulary

USING THE WORD ROOT -ject-

Each word below contains the root -ject-, meaning "to throw." Use the clues to match each word with the situation to which it applies.

1. reject (*re* = again; back)
2. object (*ob* = toward; over; against)
3. conjecture (*con* = with; *ure* = noun of action)
4. abject (*ab* = away from)

a. you throw your thoughts in with others
b. you throw back fish that are too small
c. you speak out against something
d. you feel this way when your friends shun you

USING THE WORD BANK

Copy this passage. Then fill in the blanks with the appropriate vocabulary words from the Word Bank.

A lightning storm in the parched woodland sparked a ____?____. The mild-mannered fire chief acted with ____?____ speed and authority, ____?____ ordering all firefighters to work round the clock, though his estimates of how long it would take to overcome the fire were ____?____, at best.

◆ Grammar and Style

ADVERB CLAUSES

Adverb clauses modify verbs, adjectives, or other adverbs, explaining *how, where, when, why, to what extent,* or *under what circumstances.*

Practice Identify the adverb clause in each item and indicate whether it tells *where, when, why, how, to what extent,* or *under what circumstances.*

1. North and south, as far as the eye could see, it was unbroken white . . .
2. A foot of snow had fallen since the last sled had passed over.
3. He made a new foundation for a fire, this time in the open, where no treacherous tree could blot it out.
4. If he kept it up, he would certainly be with the boys by six.

Writing Application Write a brief description of extreme weather. Use at least four adverb clauses.

Build Your Portfolio

 ## Idea Bank

Writing

1. **Diary Entry** Imagine that you are the man in the story, keeping a diary of your journey. Write the last entry that you'd be capable of creating.

2. **Sequel** Add another episode to the story in which you describe the dog's journey to the camp and the reactions of the campers on seeing him.

3. **Character Analysis** London tells us little about the main character of his story, but the man's decisions and actions are revealing. Write an analysis of the man's character, citing examples from the story to support your conclusions.

Speaking and Listening

4. **Soliloquy** If the dog could voice its thoughts about the man's behavior, what would it say? Write and present your version of what the dog might be thinking as a particular scene from the story unfolds. **[Performing Arts Link]**

5. **Oral Storytelling** Given his warnings, how might the old-timer from Sulphur Creek have reacted to the news of the man's death? Tell the tale of the man's fate as the old-timer would have told it by the campfire. **[Performing Arts Link]**

Projects

6. **Board Game** Create a game board, playing pieces, and rules for a game based on the events of this story. Each player's goal: to reach camp safely by avoiding hazards and seizing opportunities. Have players answer questions about the story in order to advance their game pieces.

7. **Pamphlet** The man in the story died from hypothermia, or subnormal body temperature. Research this condition, then create a booklet of tips and guidelines for avoiding hypothermia and detecting its warning signs. **[Health Link]**

 ## Writing Mini-Lesson

Literary Analysis

Although "To Build a Fire" remains a classic story, many of London's works are no longer as highly regarded. Public opinion of fiction is often swayed by critiques and literary analyses. A **literary analysis** explores how the different elements of a piece of literature—such as plot, setting, characters, point of view, and theme—work together to convey a message or create an overall effect. Write a literary analysis in which you explain the message that London conveys in "To Build a Fire" and discuss how the various story elements contribute to this message.

Writing Skills Focus: Elaborate to Support an Argument

Unlike a book report that simply restates what happened in a literary work, a literary analysis digs beneath the surface to present an individual interpretation of the work or an aspect of the work. This interpretation forms the thesis, or main point, of the analysis. To write an effective literary analysis effective, you have to present an argument to back up the thesis. **Elaborate on each point in your argument** by providing details and passages from the literature that back up what you are saying.

Prewriting First review the story to identify its message. What is London saying about the relationship between humanity and nature? Gather details and passages that support your interpretation.

Drafting Start with an introduction in which you state your thesis in a single sentence and outline each of your main points. Focus each body paragraph on one main point. Cite supporting passages and details from the story.

Revising Read your draft as though seeing it for the first time. Is your thesis clear? Is your support convincing? Look for opportunities to elaborate on your key points.

Guide for Interpreting

Oral Tradition: Tales of the Old West

Tall tales with larger-than-life-heroes, folk tales, and ballads are all part of the oral tradition—tales that have been passed down from generation to generation. In America, this oral tradition has preserved myths of Native Americans, folk tales, spirituals, legends, and ballads. All were originally spoken and memorized rather than written down. Most oral works have changed over time as their tellers elaborate, exaggerate, and add and subtract details. The folk literature that follows includes a folk tale, a legend, and a ballad that will give you a glimpse into life in the Old West.

Folk Tales

Folk tales are traditional stories, often based on fanciful heroes with mythical qualities. Pecos Bill, whom you'll read about here, Paul Bunyan, and Febold Feboldson are a few well-known subjects of folk tales. Folk tale heroes are frequently common people who display extraordinary strength and perform great acts of courage.

Courtesy of the Museum of Texas Tech University

Legends

Legends are traditional stories that often deal with a particular person, such as King Arthur or Gregorio Cortez (gre gōr´ ē ō kôr tez´), the Mexican hero you'll soon read about. Legends typically reflect the cultural values of the people who originally told them. For example, "The Legend of Gregorio Cortez," told in the form of a ballad, gives you a taste of what life was like for Mexicans living in Texas at the beginning of the 1900's. By emphasizing the heroic qualities of their subjects, legends have immortalized many figures who were famous in their own time, such as Daniel Boone, Davy Crockett, Calamity Jane, and Gregorio Cortez.

Ballads

Ballads are song-like poems that tell a story, often dealing with adventure and romance. Folk ballads, such as "The Streets of Laredo," which features an unnamed gunman, originated in the oral tradition and were passed down over time. Ballads usually feature simple language, four- or six-line stanzas, rhyme, and regular meter—all characteristics of "The Streets of Laredo."

◆ Background for Understanding

HISTORY: GREGORIO CORTEZ

"The Legend of Gregorio Cortez" centers on a Mexican man who became a famous fugitive in Texas at the turn of the century, a time when tensions around the United States–Texas border ran high, fueled by the lynching of Mexicans. On June 12, 1901, Cortez shot and killed Sheriff Brack Morris in retribution for Morris's having killed Cotez's brother while trying to arrest him for a crime he didn't commit. In his flight to the Mexican border, Cortez walked more than 100 miles and rode another 400 miles—killing another sheriff along the way. Three hundred men searched for Cortez with no luck. Finally, he was captured, exhausted and out of ammunition. He was acquitted for killing the first sheriff, but sentenced to life for killing the second. After serving twelve years for his crime, Cortez was pardoned by the governor of Texas in 1913.

◆ *Literature and Your Life*

CONNECT YOUR EXPERIENCE

Think about your favorite cultural heroes. Do they stand for your idea of America today? Frequently faced with danger, the folk heroes of the American West exhibited courage and strength. As you read, compare their behavior with that of the people you think of as heroes. Ask yourself whether the people you admire are likely to become tomorrow's legendary heroes.

Journal Writing List characteristics that you think would make someone a hero of legendary proportions today.

THEMATIC FOCUS: FORGING NEW FRONTIERS

The many dangers awaiting frontier settlers often required the bold and heroic actions that inspired much of our culture's folk literature.

◆ Build Vocabulary

SUFFIXES: *-ance* AND *-ence*

The suffixes *-ance* and *-ence,* which indicate a quality or state of being, change adjectives into nouns. For words ending in *-ent* or *-ant,* drop the *t* and add only *ce.* For example, the adjective *defiant,* meaning "refusing to submit," becomes the noun *defiance*—a quality Bull Rattlesnake displays in this tale about Pecos Bill.

WORD BANK

Preview these words from the selections.

> defiance
> pall

◆ Grammar and Style

COMPOUND PREDICATES

Picture a storyteller spinning a long, drawn-out tale. The sentences might well include some **compound predicates**—two or more verbs that share the same subject. Using compound predicates avoids the necessity of having to repeat the subject. The following examples of compound predicates come from "Pecos Bill Becomes a Coyote."

- He *became* a member of a pack of wild coyotes, and . . . *believed* that his name was Cropear . . .
- Later he *discovered* that he was a human being and very shortly thereafter *became* the greatest cowboy . . .

◆ Literary Focus

FOLK LITERATURE

Folk literature—stories and ballads handed down orally—originated in a time before electronic media or the printing press. This literature was often passed along by people who did not read or write. Most folk literature is not attributed to any one person because the first teller of the tale has long been forgotten. However, people have written down particular versions of many tales, making them permanent. They do not tell the tale for the first time, but *retell* it. James Bowman, for example, retells "Pecos Bill," stamping his own special mark on this famous folk tale.

◆ Reading Strategy

RECOGNIZE CULTURAL DETAILS

Just by looking up from this page, you'll notice **cultural details** that root you to your time and place. Perhaps you see a computer. The mention of a computer in writing is a cultural detail because it reveals something about modern society—just as mention of a fife in "The Streets of Laredo" reveals something about the culture of Laredo at the time the ballad was written. Notice other cultural details that show what life was like during the late nineteenth century.

Pecos Bill Becomes a Coyote

RETOLD BY JAMES CLOYD BOWMAN

Pecos Bill had the strangest and most exciting experience any boy ever had. He became a member of a pack of wild Coyotes, and until he was a grown man, believed that his name was Cropear, and that he was a full-blooded Coyote. Later he discovered that he was a human being and very shortly thereafter became the greatest cowboy of all time. This is how it all came about.

Pecos Bill's family was migrating westward through Texas in the early days, in an old covered wagon with wheels made from cross sections of a sycamore log. His father and mother were riding in the front seat, and his father was driving a wall-eyed, spavined[1] roan horse and a red and white spotted milch cow hitched side by side. The eighteen children in the back of the wagon were making such a medley of noises that their mother said it wasn't possible even to hear thunder.

Just as the wagon was rattling down to the ford across the Pecos River, the rear left wheel bounced over a great piece of rock, and Bill, his red hair bristling like porcupine quills, rolled out of the rear of the wagon, and landed, up to his neck, in a pile of loose sand. He was only four years old at the time, and he lay dazed until the wagon had crossed the river and disappeared into the sage brush. It wasn't until his mother rounded up the family for the noonday meal that Bill was missed. The last anyone remembered seeing him was just before they had forded the river.

The mother and eight or ten of the older children hurried back to the river and hunted everywhere, but they could find no trace of the lost boy. When evening came, they were forced to go back to the covered wagon, and later, to continue their journey without him. Ever after, when they thought of Bill, they remembered the river, and so they naturally came to speak of him as Pecos Bill.

What had happened to Bill was this. He had strayed off into the mesquite,[2] and a few hours later was found by a wise old Coyote, who was the undisputed leader of the Loyal and Approved Packs of the Pecos and Rio Grande Valleys. He was, in fact, the Granddaddy of the entire race of Coyotes, and so his followers, out of affection to him, called him Grandy.

When he accidentally met Bill, Grandy was curious, but shy. He sniffed and he yelped, and he ran this way and that, the better to get the scent, and to make sure there was no danger. After a while he came quite near, sat up on his haunches, and waited to see what the boy would do. Bill trotted up to Grandy and began running his hands through the long shaggy hair.

---

1. **spavined** (spav´ ind) *adj.*: Afflicted with spavin, a horse disease that can cause lameness.

2. **mesquite** (mes kēt´) *n.*: Thorny trees or shrubs commonly found in the southwestern United States and Mexico.

▶ **Critical Viewing** How does this story's description of Pecos Bill as a child hint at the extraordinary adult he was to become? [Connect]

"What a nice doggy you are," he repeated again and again.

"Yes, and what a nice Cropear you are," yelped Grandy joyously.

And so, ever after, the Coyotes called the child Cropear.

Grandy was much pleased with his find and so, by running ahead and stopping and barking softly, he led the boy to the jagged side of Cabezon, or the Big Head, as it was called. This was a towering mass of mountain that rose abruptly, as if by magic, from the prairie. Around the base of this mountain the various families of the Loyal and Approved Packs had burrowed out their dens.

Here, far away from the nearest human dwelling, Grandy made a home for Cropear, and taught him all the knowledge of the wild out-of-doors. He led Cropear to the berries that were good to eat, and dug up roots that were sweet and spicy. He showed the boy how to break open the small nuts from the piñon;[3] and

---

3. **piñon** (pēn´ yän´) *n.*: Small pine trees with large, edible seeds or nuts.

when Cropear wanted a drink, he led him to a vigorous young mother coyote who gave him of her milk. Cropear thus drank the very life blood of a thousand generations of wild life and became a native beast of the prairie, without at all knowing that he was a man-child.

Grandy became his teacher and schooled him in the knowledge that had been handed down through thousands of generations of the Pack's life. He taught Cropear the many signal calls, and the code of right and wrong, and the gentle art of loyalty to the leader. He also trained him to leap long distances and to dance; and to flip-flop and to twirl his body so fast that the eye could not follow his movements. And most important of all, he instructed him in the silent, rigid pose of invisibility, so that he could see all that was going on around him without being seen.

And Cropear grew tall and strong, he became the pet of the Pack. The Coyotes were always bringing him what they thought he would like to eat, and were ever showing him the many secrets of the fine art of hunting. They taught him where the Field-mouse nested, where the Song Thrush hid her eggs, where the Squirrel stored his nuts; and where the Mountain Sheep concealed their young among the towering rocks.

When the Jack-rabbit was to be hunted, they gave Cropear his station and taught him to do his turn in the relay race. And when the prong-horn Antelope was to be captured, Cropear took his place among the encircling pack and helped bring the fleeting animal to bay and pull him down, in spite of his darting, charging antlers.

Grandy took pains to introduce Cropear to each of the animals and made every one of them promise he would not harm the growing man-child. "Au-g-gh!" growled the Mountain Lion, "I will be as careful as I can. But be sure to tell your child to be careful, too!"

"Gr-r-rr!" growled the fierce Grizzly Bear, "I have crunched many a marrow bone, but I will not harm your boy. Gr-r-rr!"

"Yes, we'll keep our perfumery and our quills in our inside vest pockets," mumbled the silly Skunk and Porcupine, as if suffering from adenoids.[4]

But when Grandy talked things over with the Bull Rattlesnake, he was met with the <u>defiance</u> of hissing rattles. "Nobody will ever make me promise to protect anybody or anything! S-s-s-s-ss! I'll do just as I please!"

"Be careful of your wicked tongue," warned Grandy, "or you'll be very sorry."

But when Grandy met the Wouser, things were even worse. The Wouser was a cross between the Mountain Lion and the Grizzly Bear, and was ten times larger than either. Besides that, he was the nastiest creature in the world. "I can only give you fair warning," yowled the Wouser, "and if you prize your man-child, as you say you do, you will have to keep him out of harm's way!" And as the Wouser continued, he stalked back and forth, lashing his tail and gnashing his jaws, and acting as if he were ready to snap somebody's head off. "What's more, you know that nobody treats me as a friend. Everybody runs around behind my back spreading lies about me. Everybody says I

carry hydrophobia[5]—the deadly poison—about on my person, and because of all these lies, I am shunned like a leper. Now you come sneaking around asking me to help you. Get out of my sight before I do something I shall be sorry for!"

"I'm not sneaking," barked Grandy in defiance, "and besides, you're the one who will be sorry in the end."

So it happened that all the animals, save only the Bull Rattlesnake and the Wouser, promised to help Cropear bear a charmed life so that no harm should come near him. And by good fortune, the boy was never sick. The vigorous exercise and the fresh air and the constant sunlight helped him to become the healthiest, strongest, most active boy in the world.

When Pecos Bill, the Coyotes' *Cropear,* met Chuck, a cowpuncher, and discovered that he was human, he learned to speak and joined Chuck's company of cowpunchers at the I. X. L. Ranch.

---

4. **adenoids** (ad´ ən oidz´) *n.*: Growth of lymph tissue in the upper part of the throat that, when swollen, can obstruct breathing and result in nasal-sounding speech.

5. **hydrophobia** (hī´ drō fō´ bē ə) *n.*: Rabies.

◆ **Build Vocabulary**

defiance (dē fī´ əns) *n.*: Act of defying authority or opposition; open, bold resistance

---

◆ *Guide for Responding*

◆ *Literature and Your Life*

Reader's Response What are your impressions of Grandy as a caretaker? Explain why you would or would not want him to care for you as a young child.

Thematic Focus Do you think the animals in this tale were the kinds that populated the western frontier? Explain.

Group Discussion What unique lessons does the animal world teach? With a group, discuss how each of these lessons would be useful to Pecos Bill.

☑ Check Your Comprehension

1. How did Pecos Bill get his name?
2. Who raised the boy?
3. How did Pecos Bill discover that he was a human?

◆ Critical Thinking

INTERPRET

1. What evidence in this tale suggests Pecos Bill may have problems in the future? **[Support]**
2. Why do most of the animals agree not to harm Cropear? **[Infer]**
3. What are one or two underlying reasons for Wouser's behavior? **[Analyze]**

EVALUATE

4. Do you think Pecos Bill is a good example of a folk hero? Support your answer. **[Evaluate]**

EXTEND

5. Where in the United States would you be likely to find wildlife like that which appears in this tale? Explain. **[Science Link]**

The Legend Of Gregorio Cortez

Translated by Amérigo Paredes

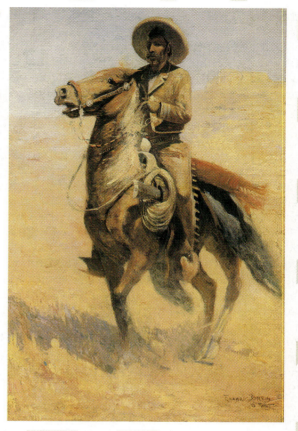

Headin' Up the Range, Edward Borein, Gerald Peters Gallery, Sante Fe, New Mexico

In the country of El Carmen
A great misfortune befell;
The Major Sheriff is dead;
Who killed him no one can tell.

5   At two in the afternoon
In half an hour or less,
They knew that the man who killed
Had been Gregorio Cortez.

They let loose the bloodhound dogs;
10   They followed him from afar.
But trying to catch Cortez
Was like following a star.

All the rangers of the county
Were flying, they rode so hard;
15   What they wanted was to get
The thousand-dollar reward.

And in the county of Kiansis
They cornered him after all;
Though they were more than three hundred
20   He leaped out of their corral.

Then the Major Sheriff said,
As if he was going to cry,
"Cortez, hand over your weapons;
We want to take you alive."

25   Then said Gregorio Cortez,
And his voice was like a bell,
"You will never get my weapons
Till you put me in a cell."

Then said Gregorio Cortez,
30   With his pistol in his hand,
"Ah, so many mounted Rangers
Just to take one Mexican!"

▲ **Critical Viewing:**
How does this painting convey the fiery spirit of Cortez? [**Analyze**]

The Streets of Laredo

Anonymous

As I walked out in the streets of Laredo,
As I walked out in Laredo one day,
I spied a poor cowboy all wrapped in white linen,
All wrapped in white linen as cold as the clay.

5 "I see by your outfit that you are a cowboy,"
These words he did say as I calmly went by.
"Come sit down beside me and hear my sad
    story,
I'm shot in the breast and I know I must die."

"It was once in the saddle I used to go dashing,
10 With no one as quick on the trigger as I.
I sat in a card-game in back of the bar-room,
Got shot in the back and today I must die."

"Get six of my buddies to carry my coffin,
And six pretty maidens to sing a sad song,
15 Take me to the valley and lay the sod o'er me,
For I'm a young cowboy who played the game
    wrong."

"Oh, beat the drum slowly and play the fife lowly,
And play the dead march as they carry my <u>pall</u>.
Put bunches of roses all over my coffin,
20 The roses will deaden the clods as they fall."

"Go gather around you a crowd of young
    cowboys,
And tell them the story of this my sad fate.
Tell one and the other before they go further,
To stop their wild roving before it's too late."

25 "Go fetch me a cup, just a cup of cold water,
To cool my parched lips," the cowboy then said.
Before I returned, his brave spirit had left him,
And gone to his Master, the cowboy was dead.

◆ Build Vocabulary

pall (pôl) *n*.: Cloth used to cover a coffin;
used here to represent a draped coffin

Guide for Responding

◆ Literature and Your Life

Reader's Response Not everyone
would agree that Gregorio Cortez is a
hero. What's your opinion on Cortez's status as a hero? Explain your answer.

Thematic Focus Judging by this legend
and ballad, violence seems to have been
rampant on the western frontier. Why do
you think this was so?

☑ Check Your Comprehension

1. Why did the rangers chase after Gregorio Cortez?
2. What did Cortez do to escape three
   hundred men?
3. Under what circumstances did the
   Laredo cowboy get shot?

◆ Critical Thinking

INTERPRET

1. What evidence suggests that Cortez
   was unwilling to give himself up?
   [Support]
2. What does the last line of "The Legend
   of Gregorio Cortez" suggest about
   Cortez's attitude toward his national-
   ity? **[Infer]**
3. What is the central message of "The
   Streets of Laredo?" **[Interpret]**

EVALUATE

4. Did Cortez or the Laredo cowboy deserve their fates? Explain. **[Make a
   Judgment]**

EXTEND

5. Name one or two other pieces of literature you know in which the "heroes"
   are not necessarily positive role models.
   Explain. **[Literature Link]**

Guide for Responding (continued)

◆ Reading Strategy

RECOGNIZE CULTURAL DETAILS

Literature set in a different time or place from your own can reveal much through cultural details. Think of **cultural details**—such as mention of a clothing or furniture style, kind of music or food, or slang expression—as clues that show the way people lived and what they regarded as important in their lives.

1. What does mention of the relay race in "Pecos Bill Becomes a Coyote" tell you about the culture of the time and place?
2. Find two cultural details in "The Streets of Laredo" that indicate cowboys led reckless lives.

◆ Literary Focus

FOLK LITERATURE

Each of these selections represents a different form of folk literature. "Pecos Bill Becomes a Coyote" is a **folk tale** because it focuses upon a fanciful hero who possesses mythical qualities. It can be further characterized as a **tall tale** because it exaggerates the attributes of the hero. "The Legend of Gregorio Cortez" has typical features of a **legend:** It's about a person who really existed, and it emphasizes that person's heroic qualities. "The Streets of Laredo" is a **ballad**—a rhymed, songlike poem that tells a story.

Having been passed down from generation to generation, these pieces preserve aspects of an important period in American history—the settling of the West.

1. What characteristics of Pecos Bill and Gregorio Cortez are exaggerated or fanciful?
2. How does the ballad format of "The Streets of Laredo" enhance your appreciation of the story?
3. What are some pros and cons of reading folk literature to gain information about a period in history?
4. Based on the examples you read in this group, which form of folk literature do you prefer? Explain your choice.

◆ Build Vocabulary

USING THE SUFFIXES -ance AND -ence

Using the suffix -ance or -ence, rewrite the following adjectives so that they become nouns indicating a state of being. Use each new noun in a sentence in your notebook.

1. significant (full of meaning)
2. diligent (hard-working)
3. defiant (refusing to submit)
4. munificent (very generous)
5. independent (free from the rule of another)

USING THE WORD BANK

Copy the following passage in your notebook, filling the blanks with appropriate words from the Word Bank.

In _____?_____ of the sheriff's orders, the townsfolk filled the streets as the outlaw's _____?_____-draped coffin was carried to the graveyard.

◆ Grammar and Style

COMPOUND PREDICATES

Using **compound predicates** helps you to avoid repeating subjects in your sentences.

> **Compound predicates** combine two or more verbs with the same subject into one sentence.

Practice In your notebook, rewrite each group of sentences as one sentence with a compound predicate.

1. The Coyotes were always bringing him what they thought he would like to eat. The Coyotes were ever showing him the many secrets of the fine art of hunting.
2. After a while he came quite near. He sat up on his haunches. He waited to see what the boy would do.
3. Grandy made a home for Cropear. Grandy taught him all about the out-of-doors.

Build Your Portfolio

Idea Bank

Writing

1. **Fantasy Creature** A cross between two animals, Wouser is the only fantasy creature in the folk tale about Pecos Bill. Write a paragraph describing another fantasy creature. Decide which animals this creature combines and describe the new animal's personality and characteristics.

2. **Dialogue** Several heroes in these pieces brag or exaggerate. Choose two characters from among the tales, and write a dialogue in which they boast to each other about their feats.

3. **Analytic Essay** Based on these selections, what was society like in the early American West? Considering issues such as violence, roles of women, and attitudes about work, write a brief social analysis of the times.

Speaking and Listening

4. **Oral Report** Research another legendary figure of the western frontier, such as Davy Crockett, Kit Carson, or Paul Bunyan and report to the class on your findings. **[Social Studies Link]**

5. **Prosecution Argument** As a prosecuting attorney, deliver a closing argument to convince a jury to convict Gregorio Cortez for murder. **[Social Studies Link]**

Projects

6. **Western Ballads** Find a collection of folk songs that includes western ballads. Sing or play one or more of the songs for your classmates; then lead a discussion on the cultural details revealed in the ballads. **[Music Link]**

7. **Timeline** Research events that occurred in Texas around the time Cortez murdered the sheriffs. Create a timeline of important events, including Cortez's crime. **[History Link]**

Writing Mini-Lesson

Legend About a Heroic Figure

Now is your chance to create a legend about your favorite heroic figure. Choose someone known for a particular act of courage or greatness. Then write a legend about that person, filling in for your audience all the details about why your hero is heroic.

Writing Skills Focus: Elaboration to Entertain

One technique for making writing entertaining is **elaborating**—adding vivid details or exaggerating. Notice how James Cloyd Bowman elaborates in his retelling of the Pecos Bill tale:

Model From the Selection

Just as the wagon was rattling down to the ford across the Pecos River, the rear left wheel bounced over a great piece of rock, and Bill, his red hair bristling like porcupine quills, rolled out of the rear of the wagon, and landed, up to his neck, in a pile of loose sand.

Prewriting Before you begin to write, brainstorm for a list of physical traits, qualities, and actions that make your hero legendary in your eyes. Then list several specific details that reinforce each trait, quality, or action.

Drafting Develop your ideas into a written legend. Begin with an exciting event or an engaging bit of dialogue to hook your readers. Then refer to your prewriting notes to help you find interesting ways to elaborate on the main accomplishments of your hero.

Revising Read your legend aloud as if you were telling it to someone, and listen to the way the words work together. Be sure your characterization reveals the heroic qualities of your hero. Look for ways to clarify the action, heighten the suspense, and make the dialogue sound more natural or realistic.

CONNECTIONS TO TODAY'S WORLD

from Lonesome Dove
Larry McMurtry

Thematic Connection

FORGING NEW FRONTIERS

Americans have been heading west ever since the first immigrants crossed the Atlantic to reach this country. In the 1700's, adventurers left the settled East for the wilds of Kentucky and Ohio. Gradually, Americans pushed on toward the Mississippi, and by the mid-1800's, they were thronging the 2,000-mile trail that led from the Missouri River to Oregon.

COWBOYS AND THE LONG TRAIL

Among the greatest legends of the American West were the cowboys, who drove longhorn cattle from the open ranges of Texas up to the railroad yards in Kansas. As they made the two- or three-month journey, cowboys faced loneliness, and danger— yet they seemed glamourous to those who lived more settled lives. As more of the wilderness was tamed, the cowboy came to symbolize a side of the American dream that was being lost.

Toward the end of the nineteenth century, the spread of the railroads and the fencing of the range spelled the end for most working cowboys. However, the national obsession with the cowboy myth refused to die.

THE WESTERN

For most of the twentieth century, fictional cowboys pursued their lonely quests in thousands of books and movies. Beginning in 1912, an Ohio dentist named Zane Grey published over eighty westerns, many of which are still popular today. The first western movie, *The Great Train Robbery,* was made in 1903, and hundreds of low-budget, hugely popular westerns were filmed in the decades that followed. In all of them, the cowboy was a mythical American figure: a solitary hero forced to prove himself in the wilderness.

Contemporary writers like Larry McMurtry and Cormac McCarthy have tapped into a uniquely American interest. Their novels set in the West have captured the public's imagination and enjoyed both popular and critical success.

LARRY McMURTRY
(1936–   )

Larry McMurtry, a descendant of Texas cattle ranchers, published his first western when he was only twenty-six. In his many novels, McMurtry has trained a humorous, critical eye on the culture of the American West, which, he believes, tries to create a tradition out of rootlessness.

Labeled by some critics as the creator of the "urban western," McMurtry first attracted attention as a new kind of writer of western novels, who mixed the traditional elements of the genre with sharp social observation and a strong dose of dark humor.

When it was published in 1985, *Lonesome Dove* and its portrayal of the frontier heritage of the West were seen as a dramatic departure from McMurtry's earlier works—such as *The Last Picture Show* (1966), *Moving On* (1970), and *Terms of Endearment* (1975)—which focus on the ever-changing character of contemporary life.

from

LONESOME DOVE

Larry McMurtry

Captain Woodrow Call and Augustus McCrae are two former Texas Rangers who helped bring peace to the Texas frontier. Call now feels a yearning for adventure. With his friend Augustus, he gathers together a ragtag bunch of cowboys and embarks on a cattle drive from Lonesome Dove, Texas, on the Rio Grande, to the wilderness of Montana.

n the late afternoon they strung a rope corral around the remuda,[1] so each hand could pick himself a set of mounts, each being allowed four picks. It was slow work, for Jasper Fant and Needle Nelson could not make up their minds. The Irishmen and the boys had to take what was left after the more experienced hands had chosen.

Augustus did not deign to make a choice at all. "I intend to ride old Malaria all the way," he said, "or if not I'll ride Greasy."

Once the horses were assigned, the positions had to be assigned as well.

"Dish, you take the right point," Call said. "Soupy can take the left and Bert and Needle will back you up."

Dish had assumed that, as a top hand, he would have a point, and no one disputed his right, but both Bert and Needle were unhappy that Soupy had the other point. They had been with the outfit longer, and felt aggrieved.

The Spettle boys were told to help Lippy with the horse herd, and Newt, the Raineys and the Irishmen were left with the drags. Call saw that each of them had bandanas, for the dust at the rear of the herd would be bad.

They spent an hour patching on the wagon, a vehicle Augustus regarded with scorn. "That dern wagon won't get us to the Brazos,"[2] he said.

"Well, it's the only wagon we got," Call said.

"You didn't assign me no duties, nor yourself either," Augustus pointed out.

---

2. **the Brazos** (brä′ zəs): River in central and southeastern Texas.

◆ **Build Vocabulary**

aggrieved (ə grēvd′) *adj*.: Offended; wronged

---

1. **remuda** (rə mōō′ də) *n.:* Group of extra saddle horses kept as a supply of remounts.

Open Range, 1942, Maynard Dixon, Museum of Western Art, Denver, Colorado

◀ **Critical Viewing** Based on the descriptions in the selection, would you characterize this depiction of a cattle drive as realistic or romanticized? Explain. **[Distinguish]**

"That simple," Call said. "I'll scare off bandits and you can talk to Indian chiefs."

"You boys let these cattle string out," he said to the men. "We ain't in no big hurry."

Augustus had ridden through the cattle and had come back with a count of slightly over twenty-six hundred.

"Make it twenty-six hundred cattle and two pigs," he said. "I guess we've seen the last of the dern Rio Grande. One of us ought to make a speech, Call. Think of how long we've rode this river."

Call was not willing to indulge him in any dramatics. He mounted the mare and went over to help the boys get the cattle started. It was not a hard task. Most of the cattle were still wild as antelope and instinctively moved away from the horsemen. In a few minutes they were on the trail, strung out for more than a mile. The point riders soon disappeared in the low brush.

Lippy and the Spettle boys were with the wagon. With the dust so bad, they intended to keep the horses a fair distance behind.

Bolivar sat on the wagon seat, his ten-gauge across his lap. In his experience trouble usually came quick, when it came, and he meant to keep the ten-gauge handy to discourage it.

Newt had heard much talk of dust, but had paid little attention to it until they actually started the cattle. Then he couldn't help noticing it, for there was nothing else to notice. The grass was sparse, and every hoof sent up its little spurt of dust. Before they had gone a mile he himself was white with it, and for moments actually felt lost, it was so thick. He had to tie the bandana around his nose to get a good breath. He understood why Dish and the other boys were so anxious to draw assignments near the front of the herd. If the dust was going to be that bad all the way, he might as well be riding to Montana with his eyes shut. He would see nothing but his own horse and the few cattle that happened to be within ten yards of him. A grizzly bear could walk in and eat him and his horse both, and they wouldn't be missed until breakfast the next day.

But he had no intention of complaining. They were on their way, and he was part of the outfit. After waiting for the moment so long, what was a little dust?

Once in a while, though, he dropped back a little. His bandana got sweaty, and the dust caked on it so that he felt he was inhaling mud. He had to take it off and beat it against his leg once in a while. He was riding Mouse, who looked like he could use a bandana of his own. The dust seemed to make the heat worse, or else the heat made the dust worse.

The second time he stopped to beat his bandana, he happened to notice Sean leaning off his horse as if he were trying to vomit. The horse and Sean were both white, as if they had been rolled in powder, though the horse Sean rode was a dark bay.

"Are you hurt?" he asked anxiously.

"No, I was trying to spit," Sean said. "I've got some mud in my mouth. I didn't know it would be like this."

"I didn't either," Newt said.

"Well, we better keep up," he added nervously—he didn't want to neglect his responsibilities. Then to his dismay, he looked back and saw twenty or thirty cattle standing behind them. He had ridden right past them in the dust. He immediately loped back to get them, hoping the Captain hadn't noticed. When he turned back, two of the wild heifers spooked. Mouse, a good cow horse, twisted and jumped a medium-sized chaparral[3] bush in an effort to gain a step on the cows. Newt had not expected the jump and lost both stirrups, but fortunately diverted the heifers so that they turned back into the main herd. He found his heart was beating fast, partly because he had almost been thrown and partly because he had nearly left thirty cattle behind. With such a start, it seemed to him he would be lucky to get to Montana without disgracing himself.

Call and Augustus rode along together, some distance from the herd. They were moving through fairly open country, flats of chaparral with only here and there a strand of mesquite.[4] That would soon change: the first challenge would be the brush country, an almost impenetrable band of thick mesquite between them and San Antonio. Only a few of the hands were experienced in the brush, and a bad run of some kind might cost them hundreds of cattle.

"What do you think, Gus?" Call asked. "Think we can get through the brush, or had we better go around?"

Augustus looked amused. "Why, these cattle are like deer, only faster." he said. "They'll get through the brush fine. The problem will be with the hands. Half of them will probably get their eyes poked out."

"I still don't know what you think," Call said.

"The problem is, I ain't used to being consulted," Augustus said. "I'm usually sitting on the porch drinking whiskey at this hour. As for the brush, my choice would be to go through. It's that or go down to the coast and get et by the mosquitoes."

"Where do you reckon Jake will end up?" Call asked.

"In a hole in the ground, like you and me," Augustus said.

"I don't know why I ever ask you a question," Call said.

"Well, last time I seen Jake he had a thorn in his hand," Augustus said. "He was wishing he'd stayed in Arkansas and taken to his hanging."

They rode up on a little knobby hill and stopped for a moment to watch the cattle. The late sun shone through the dust cloud, making the white dust rosy. The riders to each side of the herd were spread wide, giving the cattle lots of room. Most of them were horned stock, thin and light, their hides a mixture of colors. The riders at the rear were all but hidden in the rosy dust.

"Them boys on the drags won't even be able to get down from their horses unless we take a spade and spade 'em off a little," Augustus said.

"It won't hurt 'em," Call said. "They're young."

In the clear late afternoon light they could see all the way back to Lonesome Dove and the river and Mexico. Augustus regretted not tying a jug to his saddle—he would have liked to sit on the little hill and drink for an hour. Although Lonesome Dove had not been much of a town, he felt sure that a little whiskey would have made him feel sentimental about it. Call merely sat on the hill, studying the cattle. It was clear to Augustus that he was not troubled in any way by leaving the border or the town.

"It's odd I partnered with a man like you, Call," Augustus said. "If we was to meet now

---

3. **chaparral** (chap′ ə ral′) *n.*: Thicket of shrubs or thorny bushes.
4. **mesquite** (mes kēt′) *n.*: Type of small, thorny tree.

instead of when we did, I doubt we'd have two words to say to one another."

"I wish it could happen, then, if it would hold you to two words," Call said. Though everything seemed peaceful, he had an odd, confused feeling at the thought of what they had undertaken. He had quickly convinced himself it was necessary, this drive. Fighting the Indians had been necessary, if Texas was to be settled. Protecting the border was necessary, else the Mexicans would have taken south Texas back.

A cattle drive, for all its difficulty, wasn't so imperative. He didn't feel the old sense of adventure, though perhaps it would come once they got beyond the settled country.

Augustus, who could almost read his mind, almost read it as they were stopped on the little knob of a hill.

"I hope this is hard enough for you, Call," he said. "I hope it makes you happy. If it don't, I give up. Driving all these skinny cattle all that way is a funny way to maintain an interest in life, if you ask me."

"Well, I didn't," Call said.

"No, but then you seldom ask," Augustus said. "You should have died in the line of duty, Woodrow. You'd know how to do that fine. The problem is you don't know how to live."

"Whereas you do?" Call asked.

"Most certainly," Augustus said. "I've lived about a hundred to your one. I'll be a little riled if I end up being the one to die in the line of duty, because this ain't my duty and it ain't yours, either. This is just fortune hunting."

"Well, we wasn't finding one in Lonesome Dove," Call said. He saw Deets returning from the northwest, ready to lead them to the bedground. Call was glad to see him—he was tired of Gus and his talk. He spurred the mare on off the hill. It was only when he met Deets that he realized Augustus hadn't followed. He was still sitting on old Malaria, back on the little hill, watching the sunset and the cattle herd.

Guide for Responding

◆ Literature and Your Life

Reader's Response If you had been invited to go along on a cattle drive, would you have accepted? Why or why not?

Thematic Focus Augustus implies that the cattle drive has a purpose beyond making money. What is its symbolic meaning for Call and himself, and how does it relate to the romance of the West?

Journal Entry With which character do you identify more—Augustus or Call? List the qualities you share with this character.

☑ Check Your Comprehension

1. Why is riding point a more desirable position than riding at the back of the herd?
2. Why is Call concerned about the stretch of the trail that the cowboys are about to reach?
3. At the end, at what is Augustus staring?

◆ Critical Thinking

INTERPRET

1. Who seems to be more in charge of the cattle drive—Call or Augustus? How can you tell? **[Analyze]**
2. How do you know that the cowboys face danger as well as discomfort? Cite two clues from the story. **[Draw Conclusions]**
3. Give two examples of humor from this selection. **[Analyze]**

EVALUATE

4. How effective is McMurtry in painting a picture of the cattle drive? **[Make a Judgment]**

APPLY

5. List examples of famous people or people whom you know who seem to need a major challenge in order to enjoy life. **[Synthesize]**

Thematic Connection

FORGING NEW FRONTIERS

Lonesome Dove, Larry McMurtry's Pulitzer Prize-winning novel, was written in the 1980's. However, it was set over a century earlier and describes an 1870 cattle drive from the Rio Grande River to Northern Montana.

The reality of the West often differed dramatically from the romanticized vision of the West held by so many people.

1. How does the cattle drive on which Woodrow Call has embarked fail to live up to his romantic expectations?
2. How does this fictional story compare with Miriam Davis Colt's account "Heading West"? Explain.
3. Not all historical periods capture the modern imagination. Why do you think stories about the American West are still popular today?

 Idea Bank

Writing

1. **Western Scenario** Write a scenario that could serve as the basis for a classic western movie. Identify basic elements, such as a lonely and heroic protagonist, a wild and desolate setting, and some kind of conflict that the protagonist must win alone using his bravery and skill. Explain your premise. Then briefly outline the hero's situation and how the story would unfold.

2. **Literary Critique** *Lonesome Dove* won the Pulitzer Prize—a major literary award. Such awards are given on the basis of many criteria, including literary style. Evaluate McMurtry's style, and explain whether or not you think it deserves to win an award.

Speaking and Listening

3. **Audition** *Lonesome Dove* is full of dialogue that is both entertaining and revealing of character. "Audition" for the role of either Call or Augustus. Read a few lines of dialogue for your classmates. When everyone is finished, discuss which readings best seem to convey each character. **[Performing Arts Link]**

Projects

4. **Report** Though there are far fewer today than a century ago, professional cowboys still exist. What functions do they perform? What skills must they have? Where and how do they live? Research the answers to these questions, and present your findings in a written report. You may find it helpful to visit cowboy-related Internet Web sites, such as the Home Page of the professional Rodeo Cowboys Association at http://www. ProRodeo. com. **[Career Link]**

5. **Annotated Movie List** To study a unique genre of film, watch several westerns. Develop a set of criteria to use as you evaluate each film. Then rate each film and create an annotated list for classmates. In each entry, identify the name of the film, the year it was made, and any comments. You might devise a rating system—four lassos—to help organize your list. **[Media Link]**

Writing Process Workshop

In *Life on the Mississippi*, Mark Twain captures the glamour and excitement of life aboard a steamboat by contrasting it with the humdrum life in Hannibal, Missouri. As Twain's writing illustrates, comparisons are one of the most effective ways to give readers a clear sense of one or more subjects. Develop your ability to create comparisons by writing a comparison-and-contrast essay—an essay that examines the similarities and differences between two or more persons, places, things, or ideas. The following skills, introduced in this section's Writing Mini-Lessons, will help you.

Writing Skills Focus

▶ **Use precise details** to make your comparisons clear to readers. (See p. 543.)
▶ **Elaborate for vividness**. Provide enough details so readers will get a complete picture. (See p. 531.)
▶ **Write coherently.** Use a logical organization and provide transitions to connect your details. (See p. 553.)

Look at Twain's use of comparisons in his description of a boy who had left home to work on a steamboat.

MODEL FROM LITERATURE

from *Life on the Mississippi*
by Mark Twain

By and by one of our boys went away. He was not heard of for a long time. At last he turned up as apprentice engineer or striker on a steamboat. This thing shook the bottom out of all my Sunday-school teachings. ① That boy had been notoriously worldly, and I just the reverse: yet he was exalted to this eminence, and I left in obscurity and misery. ② He would always manage to have a rusty bolt to scrub while his boat tarried at our town, and he would sit on the inside guard and scrub it, where we could all see him and envy him and loathe him. . . . ③

① Twain captures the intensity of his reaction to the reappearance of the boy.
② Here, Twain creates a clear contrast by alternating descriptions of "that boy" and himself.
③ The precise details "rusty bolt to scrub" and "sit on the inside guard" sharpen the picture of the striker.

APPLYING LANGUAGE SKILLS: Avoiding Faulty Logic

Be careful to avoid making incomplete comparisons, such as these:

Incomplete Comparisons:

Dent-o toothpaste is better for tartar control. (Better than what?)

Dent-o toothpaste is the best. (The best compared to what, and in what way?)

Revised Comparisons:

Dent-o toothpaste is better than Smilex for tartar control.

Dent-o toothpaste is the best of all the leading brands for tartar control.

Practice Correct any flaws you see in the following comparisons.

1. Vote for Tino for class president. He's better than Melissa.
2. Senator Woolf's budget proposal is far superior.
3. Health care is not as big an issue in the campaign.

Writing Application As you draft and revise your essay, be sure that your comparisons are complete.

Writer's Solution Connection Writing Lab

For help gathering your details, use the Venn diagram in the Exposition tutorial.

Prewriting

Choose a Topic To select a topic for a comparison-and-contrast essay, note interesting places, things, and people that are in some ways similar. Review your notes, and focus on the topic that you think will most appeal to others. You may also choose one of the topic ideas listed here.

Topic Ideas

- Earth and Mars
- Movies and stage plays
- Two rock stars
- Two sports

Gather Details Use a Venn diagram to help you identify the similarities and differences between your subjects. Draw two circles that overlap each other. Label each with one of your two subjects. In each nonoverlapping portion, list the characteristics unique to each subject. In the overlapping portion, list the shared characteristics. Refer to your Venn diagram as you develop and draft your paper.

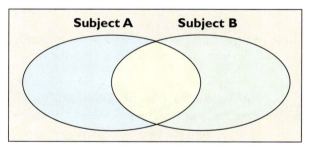

Drafting

Introduce Your Main Points Begin your essay with an introduction in which you present your overall conclusions about the similarities and differences between your subjects.

Organize Your Details Clearly As you develop your body paragraphs, use a clear organization to avoid getting details jumbled and confused. You might discuss all the aspects of one subject fully before going on to the next subject, or you might move back and forth between your two subjects, explaining each point of similarity or difference.

Mark Places to Add Precise Details If you can't come up with the right word to describe an aspect of one of your subjects, simply mark the spot and move on.

Revising

Use a Checklist Use these questions to help you revise your essay:

▶ Where can you add details or replace vague words with more precise language to make your comparisons more clear? Remember to fill in details or replace words in passages that you marked while drafting.

▶ How can you improve the organization of your essay to make it easier for readers to follow?

▶ Where can you add transitions, such as *in contrast, as opposed to,* and *similarly,* to make your comparisons more obvious to readers?

REVISION MODEL

① You can put out the litter box and a big bowl of food and take off for the weekend.

Cats are easy to care for. Dogs require more attention.

② —regular walking and scheduled feeding are a must—

but they repay your efforts many times over because they

③ : while your cat checks in for an occasional nuzzle on his schedule, your dog is always there for you, with a sloppy, consoling lick at the ready.

are more affectionate.

①② The addition of these precise details makes the comparison clear for the reader.

③ The vivid images in this sentence develop the comparison in an amusing and entertaining way.

Use a Peer Reviewer Once you've finished revising your essay on your own, have a classmate read your paper. Ask your peer to suggest where you might add details to make your comparisons more complete and to suggest how you can improve your organization. Encourage your classmate to be as specific as possible in making suggestions.

Publishing

Read Your Essay Aloud to the Class A great way to share your ideas with others is to read your essay aloud. Before delivering your reading, practice on your own or with a friend or family member. Work on varying the volume and tone of your voice and on using hand gestures to emphasize key points. In addition, practice looking up from your paper to meet the eyes of the members of your audience. After you present your essay, hold a question-and-answer session.

APPLYING LANGUAGE SKILLS: Inverted Sentences

In most sentences, the subject comes before the verb. In inverted sentences, the subject comes after the verb, but the subject and verb must still agree in number. Many inverted sentences start with *here, there,* or *where.*

Incorrect:
Here comes the happy winners.

Correct:
Here come the happy winners.

Practice On your paper, correct any errors in subject-verb agreement in the following inverted sentences.

1. Here in this magazine is two great articles.
2. Down the hillside rumbles the huge boulders.
3. There has to be three cookies left.

Writing Application Review your essay to be sure that all sentences with inverted word order have correct subject-verb agreement.

Writer's Solution Connection
Language Lab

For more practice, complete the Language Lab lesson on Correct and Effective Use of Verbs.

Real-World Reading Skills Workshop

Strategies for Success

Road signs use both words and symbols to indicate road conditions, street directions, speed limits, and other key information. Whether you're the navigator on a family trip or riding your bike to work, reading road signs is important to a safe and successful journey.

Know the Different Signs As you travel around the community, observe the various types of road signs. Ask an adult driver about any that are unclear. Become familiar with symbols and what they mean. Note the colors and shapes of road signs—they can often help you determine the purpose of the sign:

- Green rectangle with white lettering = City/town destination
- Yellow diamond = Warning
- Orange diamond = Construction
- Red octagonal = Stop
- Inverted triangle = Yield
- Red circle inside white square = Do not enter

Learn to Recognize Symbols Many signs use symbols, rather than words, to alert drivers to changes in the road or possible dangers. A black arrow symbolizes the course of the roadway; for example, as it flows around a divider, curves dangerously, or merges with another road. A symbol of a horse indicates a horse crossing ahead. Numbered symbols represent roadways and routes. When these symbols appear on exit signs, they alert drivers that the exit connects with those roadways. The numbers on a destination sign usually indicate distance in miles.

Read Road Signs Determine the overall focus of the sign. Is it about road conditions? Should you drive differently—more slowly, for instance—after reading it? Does it direct you to destinations or to other roads?

Apply the Strategy

You're the leader of a youth bicycle trip. Everyone is following you. Your group encounters the above signs along the course.

1. Explain the meaning of each sign.
2. Which signs might indicate the need to slow down?
3. What roadways can you reach by taking Exit 14 Oak Street?
4. What should you do in order to get to Route 5 South at the junction indicated in sign #7?

✔ *Here are other situations in which reading road signs can be important:*
  ▶ *Creating directions to your home*
  ▶ *Locating emergency or other services*
  ▶ *Calculating travel time to destinations*

Living in a
Changing World

Channel to the Mills, 1913,
Edwin M. Dawes, Minneapolis Institute of Arts

Guide for Interpreting

Kate Chopin (1851–1904)

Despite her conservative, aristocratic upbringing, Kate Chopin (shō´ pan) became one of the most powerful and controversial writers of her time. In her stories, sketches, and novels, she not only captured the local color of Louisiana, but also boldly explored the role of women in society.

Family Life Kate O'Flaherty, who was born in St. Louis, Missouri, married Oscar Chopin, a Louisiana cotton trader, when she was only nineteen. She moved with her husband to New Orleans, where they lived for ten years before settling on a plantation in rural Louisiana. In 1883, Chopin's husband died, leaving her to raise their six children alone. She managed the plantation on her own for a year, developing her financial and business skills. Eventually, however, she gave in to her mother's urging to sell her home and return with her children to St. Louis.

Her mother's sudden death in 1885 left Chopin in deep sorrow. It was at the suggestion of a family doctor, who was concerned about her emotional health, that she began to write fiction. Chopin kept St. Louis as her home and devoted much of her energy to writing.

Chopin the Writer and Rebel Chopin's writing is noted for its ability to present the essence of Louisiana life. Like most of her works, Chopin's first novel, *At Fault* (1890), was set in a Louisiana town inhabited by Creoles, descendants of the original French and Spanish settlers, and Cajuns, descendants of French Canadian settlers who arrived later. Through vivid descriptions and dialect, Chopin captured the local color of the region. Her stories, published in *Bayou Folk* (1894) and *Acadie* (1897), exhibited a deep understanding of the different attitudes of the Louisiana natives.

Kate Chopin's charming portraits of Louisiana life often obscured their underlying radical themes.

She examined the nature of marriage, racial prejudice, and women's desire for social, economic and political equality. "The Story of an Hour" explores several of these issues.

Chopin's finest novel, *The Awakening* (1899), is an account of a woman's search for independence and fulfillment. The novel aroused a storm of protest and was eventually banned. Her reputation was so badly damaged that her work was ignored for decades after her death. Today, however, she is widely respected for her portrayal of the psychology of women and her ability to capture local color.

◆ Background for Understanding

CULTURE: CHOPIN'S WORKS STIR THE SOCIAL CONSCIENCE OF A NATION

"The Story of an Hour" was considered daring in the nineteenth century. At least two magazines refused the story because they thought it was unethical. They wanted Chopin to soften her female characters, to make them less independent and assertive. Undaunted, she continued to deal with issues of women's growth and emancipation in her writing, advancing ideas that are widely accepted today.

In Chopin's time, however, activists were just beginning to stir the national conscience. Women and minorities were seeking to expand their civil rights. In addition, psychologists such as William James were debating free will, the ability of individuals to control their own destiny. These developments began a social revolution whose effects are still being felt today.

The Story of an Hour

◆ *Literature and Your Life*

CONNECT YOUR EXPERIENCE

Often, life-changing events sneak up on us unexpectedly—a chance encounter with someone who becomes important in our lives, the loss of a loved one, a change in a parent's employment situation, a sudden move to a new place. The story you're about to read focuses on a woman's surprising reaction to a shocking piece of news.

THEMATIC FOCUS: LIVING IN A CHANGING WORLD

As you read this story, remember that it was very controversial in its time. However, the inner transformation of the main character foreshadows great social changes that would soon transform the nation.

Journal Writing In a journal entry, explore one facet of life in our culture that has changed significantly since the late nineteenth century.

◆ Literary Focus

IRONY

Irony is a contrast between what is stated and what is intended or between what is expected and what actually happens. There are a number of different types of irony to be found in literature. **Verbal irony** is the use of words to suggest the opposite of their usual meaning. **Dramatic irony** occurs when readers are aware of something that a character in a literary work does not know. **Situational irony** occurs when the outcome of an action or situation is quite different from what one expects. As you read, decide which type of irony best describes the events in this story.

◆ Reading Strategy

RECOGNIZE IRONIC DETAILS

A story's details often lead readers to have certain expectations. When events don't turn out as details lead us to expect, it creates irony. As you read "The Story of an Hour," use a chart like this one to note how specific details imply certain feelings, circumstances, or events that may not, in fact, be what they appear. After reading the story, note whether your expectations were or were not met.

Detail	Expected Outcome	Actual Outcome
Care is taken to reveal bad news to Mrs. Mallard.	She would be upset.	

◆ Build Vocabulary

USING THE PREFIX *fore-*

If you have *foreknowledge* of an event, you can take steps to prepare for it or even to *forestall* it. The prefix *fore-* means "before," either in time, place, or condition. Words with this prefix include *foreshadow, forethought* (time); *forearm, forehead, forecourt* (place); *foremost, forefront* (condition). In which category does *forestall* fit?

WORD BANK

Preview this list of words from "The Story of an Hour."

| forestall |
| repression |
| elusive |
| tumultuously |
| importunities |

◆ Grammar and Style

APPOSITIVES AND APPOSITIVE PHRASES

An **appositive** is a noun or pronoun placed near another noun or pronoun to provide more information about it. When an appositive is accompanied by its own modifiers, it forms an **appositive phrase.** Look at this example from "The Story of an Hour."

> What could love, the unsolved mystery, count for in the face of this possession . . . (appositive phrase renaming *love*)

The Story of an Hour

Kate Chopin

Knowing that Mrs. Mallard was afflicted with a heart trouble, great care was taken to break to her as gently as possible the news of her husband's death.

It was her sister Josephine who told her, in broken sentences; veiled hints that revealed in half concealing.

▶ **Critical Viewing** How does the light shining through the uncovered portion of the window reflect the "subtle and elusive" revelation that will come to Mrs. Mallard? [**Connect**]

Afternoon in Piedmont, Xavier Martinez, Courtesy of the Oakland Museum

Her husband's friend Richards was there, too, near her. It was he who had been in the newspaper office when intelligence of the railroad disaster was received, with Brently Mallard's name leading the list of "killed." He had only taken the time to assure himself of its truth by a second telegram, and had hastened to forestall any less careful, less tender friend in bearing the sad message.

She did not hear the story as many women have heard the same, with a paralyzed inability to accept its significance. She wept at once, with sudden, wild abandonment, in her sister's arms. When the storm of grief had spent itself she went away to her room alone. She would have no one follow her.

There stood, facing the open window, a comfortable, roomy armchair. Into this she sank, pressed down by a physical exhaustion that haunted her body and seemed to reach into her soul.

She could see in the open square before her house the tops of trees that were all aquiver with the new spring life. The delicious breath of rain was in the air. In the street below a peddler was crying his wares. The notes of a distant song which someone was singing reached her faintly, and countless sparrows were twittering in the eaves.

There were patches of blue sky showing here and there through the clouds that had met and piled one above the other in the west facing her window.

She sat with her head thrown back upon the cushion of the chair, quite motionless, except when a sob came up into her throat and shook her, as a child who has cried itself to sleep continues to sob in its dreams.

She was young, with a fair, calm face, whose lines bespoke repression and even a certain strength. But now there was a dull stare in her eyes, whose gaze was fixed away off yonder on one of those patches of blue sky. It was not a glance of reflection, but rather indicated a suspension of intelligent thought.

There was something coming to her and she was waiting for it, fearfully. What was it? She did not know; it was too subtle and elusive to name. But she felt it, creeping out of the sky, reaching toward her through the sounds, the scents, the color that filled the air.

Now her bosom rose and fell tumultuously. She was beginning to recognize this thing that was approaching to possess her, and she was striving to beat it back with her will—as powerless as her two white slender hands would have been.

When she abandoned herself, a little whispered word escaped her slightly parted lips. She said it over and over under her breath: "free, free, free!" The vacant stare and the look of terror that had followed it went from her eyes. They stayed keen and bright. Her pulses beat fast, and the coursing blood warmed and relaxed every inch of her body.

She did not stop to ask if it were or were not a monstrous joy that held her. A clear and exalted perception enabled her to dismiss the suggestion as trivial.

She knew that she would weep again when she saw the kind, tender hands folded in death; the face that had never looked save with love upon her, fixed and gray and dead. But she saw beyond that bitter moment a long procession of years to come that would belong to her absolutely. And she opened and spread her arms out to them in welcome.

There would be no one to live for her during those coming years; she would live for herself. There would be no powerful will bending hers in that blind persistence with which men and women believe they have a right to impose a private will upon a fellow creature. A kind intention or a cruel intention made the act seem no less a crime as she looked upon it in that brief moment of illumination.

◆ Build Vocabulary

forestall (fôr stôl´) v.: Prevent by acting ahead of time

repression (ri presh´ ən) n.: Restraint

elusive (ē lo͞o´ siv) adj.: Hard to grasp

tumultuously (to͞o mul´ cho͞o wəs lē) adv.: In an agitated way

importunities (im´ pôr to͞on´ ə tēz) n.: Persistent requests or demands

And yet she had loved him—sometimes. Often she had not. What did it matter! What could love, the unsolved mystery, count for in face of this possession of self-assertion which she suddenly recognized as the strongest impulse of her being!

◆ **Literary Focus**
Why is Josephine's reaction an example of dramatic irony?

"Free! Body and soul free!" she kept whispering.

Josephine was kneeling before the closed door with her lips to the keyhole, imploring for admission. "Louise, open the door! I beg; open the door—you will make yourself ill. What are you doing, Louise? For heaven's sake open the door."

"Go away. I am not making myself ill." No; she was drinking in a very elixir of life[1] through that open window.

Her fancy was running riot along those days ahead of her. Spring days, and summer days, and all sorts of days that would be her own.

She breathed a quick prayer that life might be long. It was only yesterday she had thought with a shudder that life might be long.

She arose at length and opened the door to her sister's <u>importunities</u>. There was a feverish triumph in her eyes, and she carried herself unwittingly like a goddess of Victory. She clasped her sister's waist, and together they descended the stairs. Richards stood waiting for them at the bottom.

Someone was opening the front door with a latchkey. It was Brently Mallard who entered, a little travel-stained, composedly carrying his gripsack[2] and umbrella. He had been far from the scene of accident, and did not know there had been one. He stood amazed at Josephine's piercing cry; at Richards's quick motion to screen him from the view of his wife.

But Richards was too late.

When the doctors came they said she had died of heart disease—of joy that kills.

---

1. **elixir of life** (i lik′ sər): Imaginary substance believed in medieval times to prolong life indefinitely.

2. **gripsack** (grip′ sak) *n*.: Small bag for holding clothes.

Guide for Responding

◆ Literature and Your Life

Reader's Response Were you surprised by the end of the story? Explain why or why not.

Thematic Focus Kate Chopin lived and wrote in a time in which great social changes were brewing. How might Mrs. Mallard's life been different if the story were set in the late twentieth century?

Journal Writing What did you feel as you read about Mrs. Mallard's joy at her husband's death? Why? Describe your response in a journal entry.

☑ Check Your Comprehension

1. How does Mrs. Mallard react at first?
2. How does Mrs. Mallard's reaction change?
3. (a) What happens to Mrs. Mallard at the end of the story? (b) What prompts this occurrence?

◆ Critical Thinking

INTERPRET

1. At the beginning of the story, the author writes that Mrs. Mallard was afflicted with "a heart trouble." What, in addition to a medical condition, might she mean by this statement? **[Interpret]**
2. How does the scene outside Mrs. Mallard's window foreshadow the feelings that sweep over her as she sits in her chair? **[Connect]**
3. What has Mrs. Mallard apparently resented about her marriage? **[Infer]**
4. What do you believe is the actual reason for Mrs. Mallard's death? **[Draw a Conclusion]**

EVALUATE

5. Would "The Story of an Hour" seem believable as a modern tale? Explain. **[Evaluate]**

Guide for Responding (continued)

◆ Literary Focus

IRONY

Irony is the contrast between what is stated and what is meant or between what is expected and what actually happens. "The Story of an Hour" contains both **dramatic irony,** which occurs when the reader knows something a character does not, and **situational irony,** which occurs when a reader is surprised by an unexpected turn of events.

1. How is Mrs. Mallard's reaction to her husband's death an example of situational irony?
2. Why is Mrs. Mallard's sudden death also an example of situational irony?
3. Where is the dramatic irony in the diagnosis of Mrs. Mallard's cause of death?

◆ Build Vocabulary

USING THE PREFIX *fore-*

Knowing that the prefix *fore-* means "before," select the word from the box below that you could expect to find in each of these book titles.

foretell	foreman	forestall	forefathers

1. *Why Pay Taxes Now When You Can Pay Them Later?*
2. *Amazing Predictions for the Twenty-first Century*
3. *Twenty Years on an Assembly Line*
4. *How to Trace Your Family History*

USING THE WORD BANK

Write the following sentences in your notebook, replacing the italicized word or phrase in each with the appropriate word from the Word Bank.

1. After her husband's death, Kate Chopin gave in to her mother's *insistent pleas* and returned to live in St. Louis.
2. Following her mother's death, a doctor suggested Chopin take up writing in the hope that it would *head off* a slide into depression.
3. Kate Chopin strove in her writing to expose the social conventions that kept women in a state of near constant *restraint.*
4. Her characters often lived *in a state of agitation*, their lives fraught with upheaval and change.
5. Though she initially enjoyed success as a writer, outrage over her finest novel taught Chopin that lasting acclaim is *difficult to hold on to.*

◆ Reading Strategy

RECOGNIZE IRONIC DETAILS

"The Story of an Hour" is filled with **details** that lead the reader to have certain expectations. When readers draw conclusions or make predictions based on the details, the actual turn of events is often surprising.

1. What detail leads you to believe that Mrs. Mallard will be truly grieved by her husband's death?
2. Which detail in the second paragraph makes Mr. Mallard's arrival at the end all the more ironic?
3. Identify two details that help create the surprise of Mrs. Mallard's death.

◆ Grammar and Style

APPOSITIVES AND APPOSITIVE PHRASES

If an **appositive** can be omitted from a sentence without altering the sentence's basic meaning, it must be set off by commas. If, however, the appositive is essential to the meaning of the sentence, commas are not used. **Appositive phrases** are always set off by commas or dashes.

> An **appositive** is a noun or pronoun placed near another noun or pronoun to provide more information about it. When an appositive is accompanied by its own modifiers, it forms an **appositive phrase.**

Writing Application Combine the information in each pair of sentences into a single sentence containing an appositive. The first one has been done for you.

1. Mrs. Mallard was not grieved by her husband's death. She was an unconventional woman.
   Mrs. Mallard, *an unconventional woman,* was not grieved by her husband's death.
2. She sank gratefully into the chair. The chair was a comfortable, roomy armchair.
3. She felt like a new woman as she left her room. She felt like the goddess of Victory.
4. Her husband's friend tried to shield the visitor from Mrs. Mallard's sight. The friend's name was Richards.

*B*uild *Y*our *P*ortfolio

 ## Idea Bank

Writing

1. **Diary Entry** Imagine that Louise Mallard survives the shock of her husband's return. Writing as Mrs. Mallard, create a diary entry describing the day's emotional ordeal.

2. **New Version** Write a new version of the story, setting it in modern times. Consider how the details and Mrs. Mallard's options might be different.

3. **Commentary** Shortly after completing this story, Chopin wrote that if she could get her husband back, she would be willing to give up "...the past ten years of [her] growth—[her] real growth." In a brief essay, explain how her comment affects your interpretation of "The Story of an Hour."

Speaking and Listening

4. **Soliloquy** What might Mrs. Mallard have made of her life if her husband had not returned? Present a soliloquy in which she reflects on her life and thoughts ten years later. Have the years fulfilled their promise? **[Performing Arts Link]**

5. **Oral Presentation** Give an oral presentation comparing the roles of women in the United States today with those of women in a culture or country that interests you. Encourage the class to discuss its reactions. **[Social Studies Link]**

Projects

6. **Visual Interpretation** Create a work of art that expresses the joy of freedom experienced by Mrs. Mallard. Be prepared to explain your piece, in particular any symbolism that reflects details or events from the story. **[Art Link]**

7. **Mime** With a small group, act out "The Story of an Hour" using facial expressions and gestures but no dialogue. **[Performing Arts Link]**

 ## Writing Mini-Lesson

Reflective Essay

In a reflective essay, a writer describes personal experiences or pivotal events and conveys his or her feelings about them. In addition, the writer often reflects on the significance of his or her subject. Draw upon your memory and your observations to come up with a topic for a reflective essay. Recall interesting people, places, and events; think about issues of importance to you. In writing your essay, use a personal tone.

Writing Skills Focus: Personal Tone

Just as your tone of voice can convey your attitude about an event or a situation, the tone of your writing can convey how you feel about your topic. You can achieve a **personal tone** in your reflective essay by incorporating these strategies:
- Write in the first person.
- Use an informal conversational style.
- Include your personal opinions and feelings about your topic.

Prewriting To gather details for your reflective essay, use a sunburst diagram like this one. Write your topic in the center circle; then write your observations and feelings about the topic on spokes radiating from the circle.

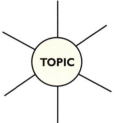

Drafting Organize your details in a way that fits your topic; consider chronological order or order of importance. As you write, use a personal tone that reflects your attitude toward your subject. To keep the tone of your essay informal, avoid high-level vocabulary.

Revising Read over your essay, focusing on parts that could be made clearer. Add or eliminate details as necessary to strengthen the impression you wish to convey to your readers.

Guide for Interpreting

Paul Laurence Dunbar

(1872–1906)

The first African American to support himself entirely by writing, Paul Laurence Dunbar displayed great versatility as a writer throughout his short career.

Dunbar was born in Dayton, Ohio, the son of former slaves. Encouraged by his mother, he began writing poetry at an early age. During high school, Dunbar, who was the only African America student in his class, frequently recited his poetry before school assemblies. He also served as the president of the literary society, as class poet, and as editor of the school newspaper. Following his graduation, he supported himself by working as an elevator operator while continuing to write. He first earned recognition when he gave a poetry reading during a meeting of the Western Association of Writers.

Characters, Themes, and Forms In his lifetime, he published seven volumes of poetry, four novels, and four volumes of short stories. Dunbar's writing cast a nostalgic light on the lost world of the southern plantation. Dunbar also focused on social problems facing African Americans at the turn of the century. His characters included farmers, politicians, preachers, traders, entertainers, and professional people.

By his late twenties, Dunbar was a nationally prominent poet. His reputation resulted largely from the readings he gave throughout the United States and Europe.

Popularity at a Price Dunbar composed poems in two styles—one formal, elegant, and serious; the other, a rural dialect. This split was echoed in people's reactions to his work. Called the "Poet Laureate of the Negro Race" by Booker T. Washington, Dunbar was criticized by some blacks who believed that his dialect poems pandered to white readers' desire for sentimental stereotypes of prewar African Americans.

Despite his success as a poet, Dunbar was disillusioned by the critics' tendency to focus on the poetry he wrote in black dialect, while virtually ignoring the poetry he wrote in more formal verse.

By the end of his life, his poetry was so popular that he was able to write from Florida, "Down here one finds my poems recited everywhere."

In poems such as "Douglass" and "We Wear the Mask," Dunbar demonstrates a command of the English language that was often overlooked, capturing the despair of African Americans in a dignified, graceful manner.

◆ Background for Understanding

CULTURE: DUNBAR AND INDEPENDENCE DAY

Dunbar wrote during a period of racial injustice. In a July 1903 letter, he uses bitter irony to express his feelings about observing Independence Day as a black American. Parts of the letter follow.

[W]e have celebrated the Nation's birthday. Yes, and we black folks have celebrated. . . . Like a dark cloud, pregnant with terror and destruction, disenfranchisement has spread its wings over our brethren of the South. Like the same dark cloud, industrial

prejudice glooms about us in the North . . . And yet we celebrate. . . .

With bleeding hands uplifted, still sore and smarting from long beating at the door of opportunity, we raise our voices and sing, "My Country, Tis of Thee"; . . . while from the four points of the compass comes our brothers' unavailing cry, and so we celebrate.

◆ Literature and Your Life

CONNECT YOUR EXPERIENCE

At the end of most sporting events, the competitors shake hands. Despite anger or frustration, the loser usually smiles and congratulates the winner. The rules of courtesy often dictate that people smile even when they really feel sad or disappointed. Paul Laurence Dunbar describes such a reaction in his poems as he explores conflicts arising from the struggle for identity and truth.

Journal Writing Write about a time when your appearance or behavior was contrary to the way you felt inside.

THEMATIC FOCUS: LIVING IN A CHANGING WORLD

Dunbar was among the first generation of African Americans born into a nation that no longer tolerated slavery. However, change came slowly for African Americans and brought with it struggle and self-doubt. In these poems, Dunbar confronts directly some of the difficulties and anxieties of living in a changing world.

◆ Build Vocabulary

RELATED WORDS: FORMS OF GUILE

The word *guile* is a noun meaning "craftiness." By adding one or more prefixes or suffixes to *guile,* you can form related words, such as the adjective *guileless,* meaning "innocent or naive," and the verb *beguile,* meaning "to mislead or trick."

salient
tempest
stark
guile
myriad

WORD BANK

Preview this list of words from the poems.

◆ Grammar and Style

PUNCTUATION OF INTERJECTIONS

Dunbar writes, "Ah, Douglass, we have fall'n on evil days . . ." In this line, *Ah* is an **interjection**—a word or phrase used to express emotion. An interjection has no grammatical relation to other words in a sentence. Depending on the degree of emotion being expressed, you can use either an exclamation point or a comma after an interjection. For example:

No! Don't touch that doorknob!

Yes, she agrees with me.

◆ Literary Focus

RHYME

Rhyme—which gives poetry a musical quality—is the repetition of sounds in the accented syllables of two or more words appearing close to each other. In a **true rhyme,** the vowel sounds and any consonants that appear after them must be the same, as in *flag* and *stag.* A **slant rhyme** links two similar (but not exact) vowel sounds, as in *prove* and *love.*

Poets use rhyme in different ways. **End rhymes** occur at the ends of two or more poetic lines; an **internal rhyme** appears within a single line.

◆ Reading Strategy

INTERPRET

Poets often mean much more than their lines say literally. To **interpret** the poet's words, you have to read between and beyond the lines to discover what the poet really means.

For example, in order to interpret "We Wear the Mask," you must consider who "we" refers to. It also helps to know the time and historical context in which the poem was written. Then you need to consider what a mask suggests and what it might cover.

Thinking about these issues as you read the poem will help you to interpret it.

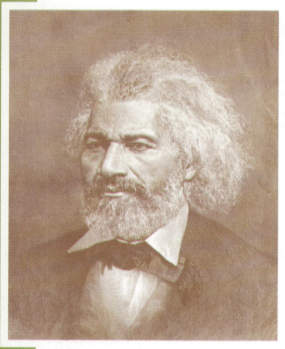

DOUGLASS

Paul Laurence Dunbar

Ah, Douglass,[1] we have fall'n on evil days,
  Such days as thou, not even thou didst know,
  When thee, the eyes of that harsh long ago
Saw, <u>salient</u>, at the cross of devious ways,
5 And all the country heard thee with amaze.
  Not ended then, the passionate ebb and flow.
  The awful tide that battled to and fro;
We ride amid a <u>tempest</u> of dispraise.

Now, when the waves of swift dissension swarm,
10   And Honor, the strong pilot, lieth[2] <u>stark</u>,
Oh, for thy voice high-sounding o'er the storm,
  For thy strong arm to guide the shivering bark,[3]
The blast-defying power of thy form,
  To give us comfort through the lonely dark.

---

1. **Douglass:** Frederick Douglass, an American abolitionist (1817?–1895).
2. **lieth** (lī´ eth) *v.*: Lies.
3. **bark:** Boat.

◆ **Build Vocabulary**

salient (sāl´ yənt) *adj.*: Standing out from the rest

tempest (tem´ pist) *n.*: Violent storm

stark (stärk) *adj.*: Stiff or rigid, as a corpse

We Wear the Mask

Paul Laurence Dunbar

We wear the mask that grins and lies,
It hides our cheeks and shades our eyes—
This debt we pay to human guile;
With torn and bleeding hearts we smile,
5   And mouth with myriad subtleties.

Why should the world be overwise,
In counting all our tears and sighs?
Nay, let them only see us, while
   We wear the mask.

10   We smile, but, O great Christ, our cries
To thee from tortured souls arise.
We sing, but oh the clay is vile
Beneath our feet, and long the mile;
But let the world dream otherwise,
15   We wear the mask!

◆ **Build Vocabulary**
guile (gīl) *n.*: Craftiness
myriad (mir´ ē əd) *adj.*: Countless

Guide for Responding

◆ Literature and Your Life

Reader's Response How do you feel when you must appear or behave as others want you to?

Thematic Focus How might Paul Laurence Dunbar like to see the world change?

Group Activity Dunbar may consider Douglass a hero or role model. With a small group, generate a list of people your generation admires in the same way.

☑ Check Your Comprehension

1. According to the speaker of "Douglass," when was Frederick Douglass's voice heard by the whole nation?
2. Why does the speaker wish that Douglass were alive to "guide the shivering bark"?
3. According to the speaker of "We Wear the Mask," what emotions does the mask hide?

Guide for Responding (continued)

◆ Critical Thinking

INTERPRET

1. (a) Who is the speaker of "We Wear the Mask"? (b) How would you describe the speaker's emotional condition? **[Analyze]**
2. (a) What does the mask symbolize? (b) Whom does it deceive? **[Interpret]**
3. To what does the speaker of "Douglass" compare the plight of African Americans?
4. Summarize the main idea of "Douglass." **[Draw Conclusions]**

EXTEND

5. How do you think Dunbar might have characterized the situation of African Americans in the 1990's? **[Social Studies Link]**

◆ Literary Focus

RHYME

Rhyme occurs in two or more words that have similar or identical vowel and final consonant sounds in their accented syllables. For example, in the first two lines of "We Wear the Mask," Paul Laurence Dunbar rhymes the words *lies* and *eyes*.

1. List all the words in "We Wear the Mask" that are true rhymes with the word *lies*.
2. What slant rhyme does Dunbar use in this poem?
3. The **rhyme scheme** or pattern of rhyme in the first stanza of "Douglass" can be expressed as ABBAABBA (A stands for words rhyming with *days* and B stands for words rhyming with *know*.) What is the rhyme scheme for the second stanza?

◆ Reading Strategy

INTERPRET

As you **interpret** a work of literature, you explain its meaning and significance. Interpreting a work of literature can reveal several layers of meaning.

1. How might you interpret "We Wear the Mask" on the level of Dunbar's personal experience?
2. What situation might he be describing for African Americans in general?
3. In "Douglass," how would you interpret the situation described in lines 6–10?

◆ Build Vocabulary

USING FORMS OF *GUILE*

Several English words are related to the noun *guile*. Combine *guile*, meaning "craftiness," with the suffixes *-ful*, *-fully*, *-fullness*, *-less*, *-lessly*, and *-lessness* to create six words. Label each word's part of speech.

USING THE WORD BANK

On your paper, match each word in the left column with its antonym in the right column.

1. guile   a. tranquility; stillness
2. tempest   b. not many
3. salient   c. elastic; flexible
4. stark   d. unimportant
5. myriad   e. honesty

◆ Grammar and Style

PUNCTUATION OF INTERJECTIONS

Interjections are grammatically unrelated to the other words in a sentence. Use a comma to punctuate an interjection that expresses mild emotion. Use an exclamation point to punctuate an interjection that expresses strong emotion. Note that any words following the exclamation point constitute a new sentence, which must begin with a capital letter.

> An **interjection** is a word or phrase that expresses emotion in a sentence.

Practice Add a comma or an exclamation point to correct the punctuation of the interjections in each of the following sentences. Capitalize the sentences as necessary.

1. Hey don't leave without me!
2. Ah this warm bath feels soothing.
3. No I'm afraid I won't be able to attend your party.
4. (a) Oh is that what you think? (b) Well you should know you're wrong.
5. Yes you've got to hurry!

Build Your Portfolio

Idea Bank

Writing

1. Diary Entry Imagine that you are the speaker of "We Wear the Mask." Write a diary entry describing a day in your life. Focus on encounters in which you are required to "wear the mask."

2. Report Research one aspect of racial discrimination in the United States during Dunbar's lifetime. Present your findings in a written report. **[Social Studies Link]**

3. Literary Analysis Choose one Dunbar poem, and write a literary analysis in which you examine the imagery, word choice, rhyme, and rhythm and show how, together, these elements convey Dunbar's thoughts and feelings.

Speaking and Listening

4. Panel Discussion With several of your classmates, stage a panel discussion on how important figures in history can affect the generations that follow them. **[Social Studies Link]**

5. Oral Interpretation Prepare an oral interpretation of one of the two Dunbar poems. Begin by analyzing the meaning and form of each line. Then read the poem aloud many times, trying different tones of voice and cadences. Present your interpretation to the class. **[Drama Link]**

Projects

6. Model/Drawing Since the Stone Age, human beings have constructed and worn masks. Explore types of masks used around the world; then create a replica or drawing of a mask that you find particularly interesting. **[Art Link]**

7. Timeline Research the life of activist Frederick Douglass; then create a timeline showing the important events and achievements of his career. **[Social Studies Link]**

Writing Mini-Lesson

Poem to Honor a Hero

In "Douglass," Paul Laurence Dunbar expresses the wish that his hero were still alive to help comfort and guide African Americans through continuing difficult times. Think of another historical figure who, if alive today, might help solve some of society's problems. Compose a poem in which you address this hero as Dunbar addresses Douglass.

Writing Skills Focus: Main Impression

The ideas and details in your poem should combine to create a single, dominant impression of your subject. Use language and images that contribute to the impression you're striving for, and avoid details that do not. Notice how the images in "Douglass" work together to convey the sense of the subject as a powerful figure.

Model from the Poem

Oh, for thy voice high-sounding o'er the storm, / For thy strong arm to guide the shivering bark . . .

Prewriting First, list the accomplishments and character traits that contributed to your subject's heroism. Then brainstorm for sensory words and images that relate this person to aspects of today's world that your hero might affect.

Drafting Choose a form for your poem—a regular rhythm and rhyme scheme or free verse, for example. Use images and sound devices that convey a vivid main impression of your subject.

Revising Reread your poem. What details should you add or eliminate to sharpen the impression of your subject? How can you improve your sound devices, such as rhyme or alliteration? How can you use images and figurative language—similes and metaphors—to convey your ideas more effectively?

Guide for Interpreting

Edwin Arlington Robinson (1869–1935)

As a New York City subway inspector in his mid-thirties, Edwin Arlington Robinson earned twenty cents an hour. Yet friends helped him arrange the private printing of three books of poetry during these lean times, helping Robinson establish himself as the most successful American poet of the 1920's. Robinson grew up in Gardiner, Maine, a small town that was the model for Tilbury Town, the fictional setting of many of his poems. He attended college for two years, but he was forced to return to Gardiner after his father's death. Upon his return, Robinson began writing poetry; by the time he moved to New York four years later, he had established his poetic voice. Most of Robinson's best poems focus on people's inner struggles. They paint portraits of desperate characters who view their lives as trivial and meaningless or who long to live in another place or time.

Robinson lived and worked in New York for many years before achieving success with *The Town Down the River* in 1910. He went on to publish many acclaimed books, including *The Man Against the Sky* (1915) and *Avon's Harvest* (1922), and received three Pulitzer Prizes.

Edgar Lee Masters (1868–1950)

For years, Edgar Lee Masters practiced criminal law by day in a successful Chicago firm and wrote poems, plays, and essays by night. In 1915, he published *Spoon River Anthology,* a series of poems about the lives of people in rural southern Illinois. The volume was so successful that Masters decided to quit his law career and move to New York City to earn a living as a writer.

Masters went on to produce many other volumes of poetry, in addition to novels, biographies, and his autobiography, *Across Spoon River.* However, he is still remembered almost exclusively for *Spoon River Anthology*, and the collection is widely regarded as his masterpiece.

The *Anthology* consists of 244 epitaphs for characters buried in the mythical Spoon River cemetery. The dead themselves serve as the speakers of the poems, often revealing secrets they kept hidden during their lifetimes. Many types of people are represented, including storekeepers, housewives, and murderers. Some of the characters lived happy lives, but many more lived lives filled with frustration and despair. Presented together, the epitaphs paint a vivid portrait of what life was like in small midwestern towns around the turn of the century.

◆ Background for Understanding

LITERATURE: THE ROOTS OF MASTERS'S SPOON RIVER

In his essay "The Genesis of Spoon River," Edgar Lee Masters describes experiences from his youth that contributed to his writing of the *Spoon River Anthology*. He points out that the characters are based on a variety of interesting and unusual people he observed as a boy. He also explains that no one single town inspired his famous fictional village. Instead, he refers to the general area lining the Spoon River, which flows through west-central Illinois:

People ask me over and over where the town of Spoon River is located. As there is no such town, I have to answer that there is only a river. And what a river! . . . It goes by little towns as ugly and lonely as the tin-roofed hamlets of Kansas. Yet this is the town, or one of the towns, and this is the river and the country from which I extracted whatever beauty there is in that part of *Spoon River Anthology* which relates to a village depiction. . . .

Luke Havergal ◆ Richard Cory
Lucinda Matlock ◆ Richard Bone

◆ *Literature and Your Life*

CONNECT YOUR EXPERIENCE

Have you ever wondered how you'll be remembered a century from now? Perhaps you'd like to be remembered for professional achievements or for your personal characteristics. The following poems create a memorable impression of four characters from small-town America one hundred years ago. How do your impressions of them compare with the impression you'd like to leave behind?

Journal Writing Jot down your thoughts about how you'd like to be remembered one hundred years from now.

THEMATIC FOCUS: LIVING IN A CHANGING WORLD

The characters in these poems lived in a time when our nation was changing from an agricultural to an industrial society. How do the poems capture both a sense of change and a sense of tradition?

◆ Build Vocabulary

WORD ROOTS: -pose-

Edgar Lee Masters uses the word *repose* to describe Lucinda Matlock's death. This word combines the Latin root -pose- ("place" or "rest") with the prefix *re-* ("back"); the word *repose* can be defined as "the state of being at rest."

WORD BANK

Preview this list of words before you read.

> imperially
> repose
> degenerate
> epitaph

◆ Grammar and Style

NOUN CLAUSES

These poems contain **noun clauses**—subordinate clauses (word groups with subjects and verbs that cannot stand alone as sentences) used as nouns in sentences. Noun clauses can act as a subject, direct or indirect object, predicate nominative, or object of a preposition.

Direct Object: In fine, we thought *that he was everything*

Object of a Preposition: . . . wait for *what will come.*

Noun clauses are commonly introduced by: *that, which, whomever, how, where, what, who, whose, whether, whatever, whoever, when,* and *why.*

◆ Literary Focus

SPEAKER

The **speaker** is the voice of a poem. Although the speaker is often the poet, it can also be a fictional character or some non-human entity. For example, the speakers of the poems in Masters's *Spoon River Anthology* are characters buried in a cemetery in fictional Spoon River. Instead of using a neutral speaker, Masters lets characters speak candidly for themselves. In this way, the poet can delve deeply into the minds and hearts of Spoon River's former citizens.

◆ Reading Strategy

RECOGNIZE ATTITUDES

The attitudes and beliefs of a poem's speaker—whether the speaker is the poet or a fictional character—are likely to color the depiction of the characters, settings, and events in the poem. As you read a poem, determine who the speaker is and look for clues to the speaker's outlook on life and **attitudes** toward the poem's subject. For example, "Lucinda Matlock" includes the lines, "Degenerate sons and daughters,/Life is too strong for you—" These lines suggest that the speaker, Lucinda Matlock, believes that the younger generation isn't as tough and hard-working as she was.

Luke Havergal

Edwin Arlington Robinson

Go to the western gate, Luke Havergal,
There where the vines cling crimson on the wall,
And in the twilight wait for what will come.
The leaves will whisper there of her, and some,
5   Like flying words, will strike you as they fall;
But go, and if you listen she will call.
Go to the western gate, Luke Havergal—
Luke Havergal.

No, there is not a dawn in eastern skies
10   To rift the fiery night that's in your eyes;
But there, where western glooms are gathering,
The dark will end the dark, if anything:
God slays Himself with every leaf that flies,
And hell is more than half of paradise.
15   No, there is not a dawn in eastern skies—
In eastern skies.

Out of a grave I come to tell you this,
Out of a grave I come to quench the kiss
That flames upon your forehead with a glow
20   That blinds you to the way that you must go.
Yes, there is yet one way to where she is,
Bitter, but one that faith may never miss.
Out of a grave I come to tell you this—
To tell you this.

25   There is the western gate, Luke Havergal,
There are the crimson leaves upon the wall.
Go, for the winds are tearing them away,—
Nor think to riddle the dead words they say,
Nor any more to feel them as they fall;
30   But go, and if you trust her she will call.
There is the western gate, Luke Havergal—
Luke Havergal.

▲ **Critical Viewing**
Picture this gate as Luke Havergal will see it: at twilight with the winds whipping the dead leaves from the trees. Describe the mood evoked by that image. **[Analyze]**

Richard Cory

Edwin Arlington Robinson

The Thinker (Portrait of Louis N. Kenton, 1900), Thomas Eakins, The Metropolitan Museum of Art

Whenever Richard Cory went down town,
We people on the pavement looked at him:
He was a gentleman from sole to crown,
Clean favored, and <u>imperially</u> slim.

5 And he was always quietly arrayed,
   And he was always human when he talked;
   But still he fluttered pulses when he said,
   "Good-morning," and he glittered when he walked.

   And he was rich—yes, richer than a king—
10 And admirably schooled in every grace:
   In fine, we thought that he was everything
   To make us wish that we were in his place.

   So on we worked, and waited for the light,
   And went without the meat, and cursed the bread;
15 And Richard Cory, one calm summer night,
   Went home and put a bullet through his head.

▲ **Critical Viewing** Is this painting an appropriate illustration for "Richard Cory"? Explain. **[Evaluate]**

◆ **Build Vocabulary**

imperially (im pir′ ē əl ē) *adv.*: Majestically

Guide for Responding

◆ *Literature and Your Life*

Reader's Response Would you like to read more poems about the residents of Tilbury Town? Why or why not?

Thematic Focus What characteristics does a person need in order to thrive in a changing world?

☑ **Check Your Comprehension**

1. According to the speaker, why should Luke Havergal go to the western gate?

2. In "Luke Havergal," from where has the speaker come to deliver a message?

3. Why was Richard Cory envied?

4. What does he do "one calm summer night"?

◆ **Critical Thinking**

INTERPRET

1. What do you think was Luke Havergal's relationship to the woman? Why? **[Speculate]**

2. (a) What might the western gate symbolize? (b) What might the "dawn in eastern skies" symbolize? **[Interpret]**

3. Would the townspeople have expected Richard Cory to take his life? Why or why not? **[Support]**

APPLY

4. (a) Why do you think a person like Richard Cory might be miserable? (b) What do you think are the keys to a person's happiness? **[Relate]**

Barn Dance, Grandma Moses, © 1989, Grandma Moses Properties Co., New York

◄ **Critical Viewing**
In what ways does this painting reflect the life of Lucinda Matlock? [Connect]

Lucinda Matlock

Edgar Lee Masters

I went to the dances at Chandlerville,
And played snap-out[1] at Winchester.
One time we changed partners,
Driving home in the moonlight of middle June,
5   And then I found Davis.
We were married and lived together for seventy years,
Enjoying, working, raising the twelve children,
Eight of whom we lost
Ere I had reached the age of sixty.
10 I spun, I wove, I kept the house, I nursed the sick,
I made the garden, and for holiday
Rambled over the fields where sang the larks,
And by Spoon River gathering many a shell,
And many a flower and medicinal weed—
15 Shouting to the wooded hills, singing to the green valleys.
At ninety-six I had lived enough, that is all,
And passed to a sweet repose.
What is this I hear of sorrow and weariness,
Anger, discontent and drooping hopes?
20 Degenerate sons and daughters,
Life is too strong for you—
It takes life to love Life.

---

1. **Snap-out:** Game often referred to as Crack-the-Whip, in which a long line of players who are holding hands spin around in a circle, causing the players on the ends to be flung off by centrifugal force.

◆ **Build Vocabulary**

repose (ri pōz´) *n*.: State of being at rest

degenerate (dē jen´ ər it) *adj*.: Morally corrupt

Richard Bone

Edgar Lee Masters

When I first came to Spoon River
I did not know whether what they told me
Was true or false.
They would bring me the epitaph
5   And stand around the shop while I worked
and say "He was so kind," "He was wonderful,"
"She was the sweetest woman," "He was a consistent Christian."
And I chiseled for them whatever they wished,
All in ignorance of its truth.
10   But later, as I lived among the people here,
I knew how near to the life
Were the epitaphs that were ordered for them as they died.

But still I chiseled whatever they paid me to chisel
and made myself party to the false chronicles
15   Of the stones,
Even as the historian does who writes
Without knowing the truth,
Or because he is influenced to hide it.

◆ **Build Vocabulary**

epitaph (ep´ ə taf´) *n.*: Inscription on a tombstone or grave marker

---

Guide for Responding

◆ *Literature and Your Life*

Reader's Response (a) What is your opinion of Lucinda Matlock? (b) Is she someone you would strive to emulate? Why or why not?

Thematic Focus How do Lucinda Matlock and Richard Bone deal with change in a similar manner?

☑ Check Your Comprehension

1. (a) Who is the speaker of "Lucinda Matlock"?
   (b) How old was Matlock when she died?
   (c) Use the poem to write a summary of Matlock's life.
2. (a) What is Richard Bone's occupation? (b) What change occurs in Bone after years of living in Spoon River?

◆ Critical Thinking

INTERPRET

1. (a) Characterize Lucinda Matlock's life. (b) What is her attitude about her life? **[Analyze]**
2. (a) Who are the "sons and daughters" Matlock addresses? (b) What is the meaning of her message to them? **[Interpret]**
3. Why do you think the townspeople in "Richard Bone" composed false epitaphs for their loved ones? **[Analyze]**

APPLY

4. How might Lucinda Matlock respond to the complaint that life today is too complex? **[Relate]**
5. Why do you think two generations' attitudes toward life are often so different? **[Speculate]**

Guide for Responding (continued)

◆ Literary Focus

SPEAKER

The **speaker** is the the voice of a poem. A poem's speaker may be the poet or a fictional character, an animal, or even an inanimate object. The speaker in "Lucinda Matlock" is Lucinda Matlock herself.

1. How can you tell that the speaker of "Richard Cory" is speaking for the entire town?
2. How does the fact that the speaker admires Richard Cory add to the impact of the poem?
3. How would "Lucinda Matlock" be different if Masters had used a different speaker?
4. Lucinda Matlock, Richard Bone, and the other speakers in *Spoon River Anthology* are dead. Why might this allow them to discuss their lives more openly than if they were alive?

◆ Grammar and Style

NOUN CLAUSES

A **noun clause** is a subordinate clause used as a noun. A noun clause can be used as a subject, predicate noun, direct object, indirect object, or object of a preposition.

Practice On your paper, write the following sentences and underline the noun clause in each. Explain the function of each noun clause.

1. There is yet one way to where she is.
2. I chiseled for them whatever they wished.
3. I did not know whether what they told me was true or false.
4. I knew how near to the life were the epitaphs that were ordered.
5. I chiseled whatever they paid me to chisel.

Writing Application Combine the following pairs of sentences by turning one of the sentences into a noun clause.

1. The speaker knew what was right. Luke Havergal must go to the western gate.
2. Lucinda Matlock gave advice. She would give it to anyone who would listen.

◆ Reading Strategy

RECOGNIZE ATTITUDES

To fully understand a person, you have to be aware of his or her outlook on life. The same is true of a poem's speaker. When you read a poem, look closely at the choice of words and the presentation of details, and think about what they reveal about the speaker's attitudes and beliefs. **Recognizing the speaker's attitudes** will help you unlock the meaning of the poem.

1. In "Richard Cory," how does the speaker's attitude toward Richard Cory differ from Cory's attitude toward himself? Support your answer.
2. What do you think might have been Richard Cory's attitude toward the townspeople?
3. How would you describe the attitude of the speaker in "Richard Bone"? Support your answer.
4. How would you describe Lucinda Matlock's outlook on life?
5. What seems to be Lucinda Matlock's attitude toward the people who have survived her? Support your answer.

◆ Build Vocabulary

USING THE WORD ROOT -pose-

Use each of these words containing the root -pose-, meaning "place" or "rest," to complete one of the sentences.

a. depose   **b.** impose   **c.** interpose

1. He hated to ____?____ on his friends, but he was unable to find a hotel room.
2. Each time audience members ____?____ comments, the speaker loses his train of thought.
3. When we ____?____ the prime minister, we will set this nation on a course toward true freedom.

USING THE WORD BANK

Write the letter of the best synonym for the first word.

1. imperially: (a) grandly, (b) scornfully, (c) strongly
2. repose: (a) model, (b) silence, (c) ease
3. degenerate: (a) evil, (b) degraded, (c) slow
4. epitaph: (a) inscription, (b) homily, (c) graph

Build Your Portfolio

Idea Bank

Writing

1. **Biographical Sketch** Using details from the poems, along with additional details that you concoct in your imagination, write a biographical sketch of one of the characters in these poems.

2. **Comparison/Contrast** Write an essay comparing and contrasting the poems of Robinson and Masters. Explore similarities and differences in the settings, characters, moods, and themes.

3. **Persuasive Letter** How would you convince Lucinda Matlock that her assessment of the younger generation is wrong? Look closely at the last few lines of the poem. Then write a persuasive letter to Matlock convincing her that life is not "too strong" for today's younger generation.

Speaking and Listening

4. **Music Appreciation** Find a copy of folk duo Simon and Garfunkel's adaptation of "Richard Cory," and play it for the class. Lead a discussion of the song's effectiveness. **[Music Link]**

5. **Dramatic Reading** Read one of the poems aloud to the class in a way that you think fits the poem's speaker and subject matter. For example, if you read "Lucinda Matlock," try to capture how you imagine the poem's speaker would sound. **[Performing Arts Link]**

Projects

6. **Illustration** Create or find an illustration that could accompany one of the four poems in a poetry collection. **[Art Link]**

7. **Map** Like Robinson and Masters, many American writers have focused their works on one specific location. Conduct research to learn about places associated with various writers. Then create a literary map identifying these locations.

Writing Mini-lesson

Firsthand Biography

Poems like Robinson's and Masters's are one way to create vivid portraits of people. Another way to present a portrait of a person is through a firsthand biography—a story about events in the life of a person with whom the writer has a personal relationship. Think of an interesting, special, or unusual person who stands out in your memory. Then write a firsthand biography in which you share your impressions of the person and describe one or more events that capture his or her personality.

Writing Skills Focus: Transitions to Show Order of Importance

In your firsthand biography, you'll want to give readers a strong impression of the personality traits and details of the person's life that stand out most in your own mind. One way to make it clear to readers which details are most important is to use **transitional words that show order of importance.** These words include: *first, second, more importantly, least importantly, mainly, last, finally, good, better, best, primarily, secondarily, above all, worst of all, few, most effective,* and *unnecessary.*

Prewriting After you've decided on your subject, list key personality traits and events in the person's life that illustrate the personality traits. Then arrange these details in their order of importance.

Drafting Focus your firsthand biography on a single event or a series of events that illustrate the person's most important personality traits. As you describe the event or events, include your own impressions of the person. Use transitional words to indicate which impressions are most important.

Revising Have you included details that reveal your subject's personality? Review your biography to make sure that it conveys the impression of your subject that you intended.

Guide for Interpreting

Willa Cather (1873–1947)

Although Willa Cather lived more than half her life in New York City, she turned again and again to the Nebraska prairie of her youth—at the time, a recently settled area of the American frontier—for inspiration and material for her writing.

Cather captured with unflinching honesty the difficulties of life on the expanding frontier.

A Prairie Childhood Born in a small town in western Virginia, Cather moved to the Nebraska frontier when she was ten. Many of her new neighbors were immigrants struggling to build new lives while preserving their native cultures. Commenting on the diversity that surrounded her during her childhood, Cather once wrote: "On Sundays we could drive to a Norwegian church and listen to a sermon in that language, or to a Danish or Swedish church. We could go to a French Catholic settlement or into a Bohemian township and hear one in Czech, or we could go to the church with the German Lutherans." In addition to all that she learned from observing the diverse group of people who surrounded her, Cather received a rich formal education, studying foreign languages, history, classical music, and opera.

The Making of a Literary Giant After graduating from the University of Nebraska in 1895, Cather worked as an editor at a Pittsburgh newspaper, while writing poems and short stories in her spare time. In 1904, she moved to New York, where she joined the editorial staff of *McClure's Magazine.* Her first collection of stories, *The Troll Garden,* was published in 1905. After her first novel, *Alexander's Bridge,* was published in 1911, Cather left *McClure's* to devote herself to writing.

Over the next 35 years, Cather produced some ten novels, two short-story collections, and two collections of essays. Among her outstanding works are *O Pioneers!* (1913), *My Antonia* (1918), and *One of Ours* (1922), which capture the flavor of life on the midwestern prairie. *One of Ours* won Cather the Pulitzer Prize in 1923.

Portraits of Prairie Life Although Cather's fiction was by no means limited to "prairie stories"—her fictional settings ranged from contemporary New York City to the American Southwest to seventeenth-century Quebec—it was her stories about Nebraska immigrants that most appealed to readers and critics. In these stories, she displayed her admiration for the courage and spirit of the immigrants and other settlers of the frontier. At the same time, she conveyed an intense awareness of the loss felt by the pioneers and the loneliness and isolation from which they suffered. In "A Wagner Matinée," Cather captures this sense of loneliness and isolation by contrasting the stark realities of frontier life with the possibilities of life in a more cultured world.

◆ Background for Understanding

MUSIC: THE OPERAS OF RICHARD WAGNER

When "A Wagner Matinée" first appeared in 1904, Cather's readers would have been as familiar with Richard Wagner (Väg nər) as people are today with the Beatles. Wagner, who was German, was one of the nineteenth century's greatest composers. His operas are characterized by their adventurous harmonic language and their innovative intermarriage of music and drama. Although many critics judged Wagner's music unfavorably during his lifetime, his operas became enormously popular after his death in 1883.

A Wagner Matinée

◆ Literature and Your Life

CONNECT YOUR EXPERIENCE

Have you ever heard a song that grabbed at your emotions, pulling you out of the moment and into another time or place? Music can exert a powerful pull on our feelings, memories, and fantasies. In this story, a woman experiences a flood of long-buried emotions when she attends a special concert.

Journal Writing Briefly describe a time when a song or piece of music stirred up your emotions.

THEMATIC FOCUS: LIVING IN A CHANGING WORLD

The music that this story's central character hears stirs up memories of the world she left behind when she and her husband headed to the frontier. Why do you think people often feel isolated or disillusioned when they undergo major changes in their lives?

◆ Build Vocabulary

WORDS FROM MUSIC: *PRELUDE*

Vocabulary from the field of music can often have two meanings—one specific musical meaning and one for use in a nonmusical context. A *prelude*, for example, is a musical introduction. However, *prelude* also refers to any preparation for an important matter.

WORD BANK

Before you read, preview this list of words from the selection.

> reverential
> tremulously
> semi-somnambulant
> inert
> prelude
> jocularity

◆ Grammar and Style

REFLEXIVE AND INTENSIVE PRONOUNS

Reflexive pronouns end in *-self* or *-selves*, refer to the subject, and are necessary to complete the meaning of a sentence. **Intensive pronouns**, which also end in *-self* or *-selves*, simply add emphasis to a noun or pronoun in the same sentence and can be omitted without changing the meaning of the sentence.

> **Reflexive Pronoun:** . . . she had surrendered *herself* unquestioningly into the hands of a country dressmaker.
> **Intensive Pronoun:** *Myself*, I saw my aunt's misshapen figure with that feeling of awe and respect . . .

◆ Literary Focus

CHARACTERIZATION

Characterization is the means by which a writer reveals a character's personality. Writers generally develop characters through one of the following methods: direct statements about the character, physical descriptions of the character, actions of the character, thoughts and comments of the character, or comments about the character made by other characters. As you read, look for the ways in which this story's main character is developed.

◆ Reading Strategy

CLARIFYING

Cather's story is packed with details about its main character. To fully understand the character's actions, it is important to **clarify**—check your understanding of—the details that are provided. This may simply involve reading a footnote or looking up a word in the dictionary. In other instances, you may need to reread a passage to refresh your memory about previous details. In still other cases, when you come across a passage you don't fully understand, you may want to read ahead to find details that clarify its meaning.

A Wagner Matinée

Willa Cather

I received one morning a letter written in pale ink, on glassy, blue-lined notepaper, and bearing the postmark of a little Nebraska village. This communication, worn and rubbed, looking as though it had been carried for some days in a coat pocket that was none too clean, was from my Uncle Howard. It informed me that his wife had been left a small legacy by a bachelor relative who had recently died, and that it had become necessary for her to come to Boston to attend to the settling of the estate. He requested me to meet her at the station, and render her whatever services might prove necessary. On examining the date indicated as that of her arrival, I found it no later than to-morrow. He had characteristically delayed writing until, had I been away from home for a day, I must have missed the good woman altogether.

The name of my Aunt Georgiana called up not alone her own figure, at once pathetic and grotesque, but opened before my feet a gulf of recollections so wide and deep that, as the letter dropped from my hand, I felt suddenly a stranger to all the present conditions of my existence, wholly ill at ease and out of place amid the surroundings of my study. I became, in short, the gangling farmer boy my aunt had known, scourged with chilblains and bashfulness, my hands cracked and raw from the corn husking. I felt the knuckles of my thumb tentatively, as though they were raw again. I sat again before her parlor organ, thumbing the scales with my stiff, red hands, while she beside me made canvas mittens for the huskers.

The next morning, after preparing my landlady somewhat, I set out for the station. When

From Arkansas, George Schreiber, Sheldon Swope Art Museum, Terre Haute, Indiana

▲ **Critical Viewing** In what ways does the woman in the painting seem like Aunt Georgiana? **[Connect; Interpret]**

the train arrived I had some difficulty in finding my aunt. She was the last of the passengers to alight, and when I got her into the carriage she looked not unlike one of those charred, smoked bodies that firemen lift from the *débris* of a burned building. She had come all the way in a day coach; her linen duster[1] had become black with soot and her black bonnet gray with dust during the journey. When we arrived at my

---

1. **duster** *n.*: Short, loose smock worn to protect clothing from dust.

boardinghouse the landlady put her to bed at once, and I did not see her again until the next morning.

Whatever shock Mrs. Springer experienced at my aunt's appearance she considerately concealed. Myself, I saw my aunt's misshapen figure with that feeling of awe and respect with which we behold explorers who have left their ears and fingers north of Franz Josef Land,[2] or their health somewhere along the upper Congo.[3] My Aunt Georgiana had been a music teacher at the Boston Conservatory, somewhere back in the latter sixties. One summer, which she had spent in the little village in the Green Mountains[4] where her ancestors had dwelt for generations, she had kindled the callow[5] fancy of the most idle and shiftless of all the village lads, and had conceived for this Howard Carpenter one of those absurd and extravagant passions which a handsome country boy of twenty-one sometimes inspires in a plain, angular, spectacled woman of thirty. When she returned to her duties in Boston, Howard followed her; and the upshot of this inexplicable infatuation was that she eloped with him, eluding the reproaches of her family and the criticism of her friends by going with him to the Nebraska frontier. Carpenter, who of course had no money, took a homestead in Red Willow County,[6] fifty miles from the railroad. There they measured off their eighty acres by driving across the prairie in a wagon, to the wheel of which they had tied a red cotton handkerchief, and counting its revolutions. They built a dugout in the red hillside, one of those cave dwellings whose inmates usually reverted to the conditions of primitive savagery. Their water they got from the lagoons where the buffalo drank, and their slender stock of provisions was always at the mercy of

◆ **Literary Focus**
What do the contrasting details of Aunt Georgiana's life in Boston and Nebraska reveal about her character?

bands of roving Indians. For thirty years my aunt had not been farther than fifty miles from the homestead.

But Mrs. Springer knew nothing of all this, and must have been considerably shocked at what was left of my kinswoman. Beneath the soiled linen duster, which on her arrival was the most conspicuous feature of her costume, she wore a black stuff dress whose ornamentation showed that she had surrendered herself unquestioningly into the hands of a country dressmaker. My poor aunt's figure, however, would have presented astonishing difficulties to any dressmaker. Her skin was yellow from constant exposure to a pitiless wind, and to the alkaline water which transforms the most transparent cuticle into a sort of flexible leather. She wore ill-fitting false teeth. The most striking thing about her physiognomy, however, was an incessant twitching of the mouth and eyebrows, a form of nervous disorder resulting from isolation and monotony, and from frequent physical suffering.

In my boyhood this affliction had possessed a sort of horrible fascination for me, of which I was secretly very much ashamed, for in those days I owed to this woman most of the good that ever came my way, and had a <u>reverential</u> affection for her. During the three winters when I was riding herd for my uncle, my aunt, after cooking three meals for half a dozen farmhands, and putting the six children to bed, would often stand until midnight at her ironing board, hearing me at the kitchen table beside her recite Latin declensions and conjugations, and gently shaking me when my drowsy head sank down over a page of irregular verbs. It was to her, at her ironing or mending, that I read my first Shakespeare; and her old textbook of mythology was the first that ever came into my empty hands. She taught me my scales and exercises, too, on the little parlor organ which her husband had bought her after fifteen years, during which she had not so much as seen any instrument except an accordion, that belonged to one of the

---

2. **Franz Josef Land:** Group of islands in the Arctic Ocean.
3. **Congo:** River in central Africa.
4. **Green Mountains:** Mountains in Vermont.
5. **callow** (kal' ō) *adj.*: Immature; inexperienced
6. **Red Willow County:** County in southwestern Nebraska that borders on Kansas.

◆ **Build Vocabulary**
reverential (rev´ ə ren´ shəl) *adj.*: Showing or caused by a feeling of deep respect, love, and awe

Norwegian farmhands. She would sit beside me by the hour, darning and counting, while I struggled with the "Harmonious Blacksmith"; but she seldom talked to me about music, and I understood why. She was a pious woman; she had the consolation of religion; and to her at least her martyrdom was not wholly sordid. Once when I had been doggedly beating out some passages from an old score of "Euryanthe" I had found among her music books, she came up to me and, putting her hands over my eyes, gently drew my head back upon her shoulder, saying <u>tremulously</u>, "Don't love it so well, Clark, or it may be taken from you. Oh! dear boy, pray that whatever your sacrifice be it is not that."

When my aunt appeared on the morning after her arrival, she was still in a <u>semi-somnambulant</u> state. She seemed not to realize that she was in the city where she had spent her youth, the place longed for hungrily for half a lifetime. She had been so wretchedly trainsick throughout the journey that she had no recollection of anything but her discomfort, and, to all intents and purposes, there were but a few hours of nightmare between the farm in Red Willow County and my study on Newbury Street. I had planned a little pleasure for her that afternoon, to repay her for some of the glorious moments she had given me when we used to milk together in the straw-thatched cowshed, and she, because I was more than usually tired, or because her husband had spoken sharply to me, would tell me

of the splendid performance of Meyerbeer's *Les Huguenots*[7] she had seen in Paris in her youth. At two o'clock the Boston Symphony Orchestra was to give a Wagner[8] program, and I intended to take my aunt, though as I conversed with her I grew doubtful about her enjoyment of it. Indeed, for her own sake, I could only wish her taste for such things quite dead, and the long struggle mercifully ended at last. I suggested our visiting the Conservatory and the Common[9] before lunch, but she seemed altogether too timid to wish to venture out. She questioned me absently about various changes in the city, but she was chiefly concerned that she had forgotten to leave instructions about feeding half-skimmed milk to a certain weakling calf, "Old Maggie's calf, you know, Clark," she explained, evidently having forgotten how long I had been away. She was further troubled because she had neglected to tell her daughter about the freshly opened kit of mackerel in the cellar, that would spoil if it were not used directly.

---

7. *Les Huguenots* (lāz hyo͞o′ gə nät′): Opera written in 1836 by Giacomo Meyerbeer (1791–1864).
8. **Wagner** (väg′ nər): Richard Wagner (1813–1883), a great German composer who is responsible for the development of the musical drama.
9. **Common:** Boston Common, a small park in Boston.

◆ **Build Vocabulary**
tremulously (trem′ yo͞o ləs lē) *adv.*: Fearfully; timidly
semi-somnambulant (sem′ i säm nam′ byo͞o lənt) *adj.*: Half-sleepwalking

I asked her whether she had ever heard any of the Wagnerian operas, and found that she had not, though she was perfectly familiar with their respective situations and had once possessed the piano score of *The Flying Dutchman*. I began to think it would have been best to get her back to Red Willow County without waking her, and regretted having suggested the concert.

From the time we entered the concert hall, however, she was a trifle less passive and <u>inert</u>, and seemed to begin to perceive her surroundings. I had felt some trepidation[10] lest one might become aware of the absurdities of her attire, or might experience some painful embarrassment at stepping suddenly into the world to which she had been dead for a quarter of a century. But again I found how superficially I had judged her. She sat looking about her with eyes as impersonal, almost as stony, as those with which the granite Ramses[11] in a museum watches the froth and fret that ebbs and flows about his pedestal, separated from it by the lonely stretch of centuries. I have seen this same aloofness in old miners who drift into the Brown Hotel at Denver, their pockets full of bullion, their linen soiled, their haggard faces unshorn, and who stand in the thronged corridors as solitary as though they were still in a frozen camp on the Yukon, or in the yellow blaze of the Arizona desert, conscious that certain experiences have isolated them from their fellows by a gulf no haberdasher could conceal.

The audience was made up chiefly of women. One lost the contour of faces and figures, indeed any effect of line whatever, and there was only the color contrast of bodices past counting, the shimmer and shading of fabrics soft and firm, silky and sheer, resisting and yielding: red, mauve, pink, blue, lilac, purple, ecru, rose, yellow, cream, and white, all the colors that an impressionist finds in a sunlit landscape, with here and there the dead black shadow of a frock coat. My Aunt Georgiana regarded them as

though they had been so many daubs of tube paint on a palette.

When the musicians came out and took their places, she gave a little stir of anticipation, and looked with quickening interest down over the rail at that invariable grouping; perhaps the first wholly familiar thing that had greeted her eye since she had left old Maggie and her weakling calf. I could feel how all those details sank into her soul, for I had not forgotten how they had sunk into mine when I came fresh from plowing forever and forever between green aisles of corn, where, as in a treadmill, one might walk from daybreak to dusk without perceiving a shadow of change in one's environment. I reminded myself of the impression made on me by the clean profiles of the musicians, the gloss of their linen; the dull black of their coats, the beloved shapes of the instruments, the patches of yellow light thrown by the green-shaded stand-lamps on the smooth, varnished bellies of the cellos and the bass viols in the rear, the restless, wind-tossed forest of fiddle necks and bows; I recalled how, in the first orchestra I had ever heard, those long bow strokes seemed to draw the soul out of me, as a conjuror's stick reels out paper ribbon from a hat.

The first number was the Tannhäuser overture. When the violins drew out the first strain of the Pilgrims' chorus, my Aunt Georgiana clutched my coat sleeve. Then it was that I first realized that for her this singing of basses and stinging frenzy of lighter strings broke a silence of thirty years, the inconceivable silence of the plains. With the battle between the two motifs, with the bitter frenzy of the Venusberg[12] theme and its ripping of strings, came to me an overwhelming sense of the waste and wear we are so powerless to combat. I saw again the tall, naked house on the prairie, black and grim as a wooden fortress; the black pond where I had learned to swim, the rain-gullied clay about the naked house; the four dwarf ash seedlings on

♦ **Literary Focus**

What does Aunt Georgiana's excitement about the upcoming performance reveal about her?

10. **trepidation** (trep´ ə dā´ shən) *n.*: Fearful anxiety; apprehension.

11. **Ramses** (ram´ sēz): One of the eleven Egyptian kings by that name who ruled from c. 1315 to c. 1090 B.C.

♦ **Build Vocabulary**

inert (in urt´) *adj.*: Motionless

12. **Venusberg** (vē´ nəs burg´): Legendary mountain in Germany where Venus, the Roman goddess of love, held court.

which the dishcloths were always hung to dry before the kitchen door. The world there is the flat world of the ancients; to the east, a cornfield that stretched to daybreak; to the west, a corral that stretched to sunset; between, the sordid conquests of peace, more merciless than those of war.

The overture closed. My aunt released my coat sleeve, but she said nothing. She sat staring at the orchestra through a dullness of thirty years, through the films made, little by little, by each of the three hundred and sixty-five days in every one of them. What, I wondered, did she get from it? She had been a good pianist in her day, I knew, and her musical education had been broader than that of most music teachers of a quarter of a century ago. She had often told me of Mozart's operas and Meyerbeer's, and I could remember hearing her sing, years ago, certain melodies of Verdi. When I had fallen ill with a fever she used to sit by my cot in the evening, while the cool night wind blew in through the faded mosquito netting tacked over the window, and I lay watching a bright star that burned red above the cornfield, and sing "Home to our mountains, oh, let us return!" in a way fit to break the heart of a Vermont boy near dead of homesickness already.

I watched her closely through the <u>prelude</u> to *Tristan and Isolde*, trying vainly to conjecture what that warfare of motifs, that seething turmoil of strings and winds, might mean to her. Had this music any message for her? Did or did not a new planet swim into her ken? Wagner had been a sealed book to Americans before the sixties. Had she anything left with which to comprehend this glory that had flashed around the world since she had gone from it? I was in a fever of curiosity, but Aunt Georgiana sat silent upon her peak in Darien.[13] She preserved this utter immobility throughout the numbers from the *Flying Dutchman*, though her fingers worked mechanically upon her black dress, as though of themselves they were recalling the piano score they had once played. Poor old hands! They were stretched and pulled and twisted into mere tentacles to hold, and lift, and knead with; the palms unduly swollen, the fingers bent and knotted, on one of them a thin worn band that had once been a wedding ring. As I pressed and gently quieted one of those groping hands, I remembered, with quivering eyelids, their services for me in other days.

Soon after the tenor began the "Prize Song," I heard a quick-drawn breath, and turned to my aunt. Her eyes were closed, but the tears were glistening on her cheeks, and I think in a moment more they were in my eyes as well. It never really dies, then, the soul? It withers to the outward eye only, like that strange moss which can lie on a dusty shelf half a century and yet, if placed in water, grows green again. My aunt wept gently throughout the development and elaboration of the melody.

During the intermission before the second half of the concert, I questioned my aunt and found that the "Prize Song" was not new to her. Some years before there had drifted to the farm in Red Willow County a young German, a tramp cow puncher who had sung in the chorus at Bayreuth,[14] when he was a boy, along with the other peasant boys and girls. Of a Sunday morning he used to sit on his blue gingham-sheeted bed in the hands' bedroom, which opened off the kitchen, cleaning the leather of his boots and saddle, and singing the "Prize Song," while my aunt went about her work in the kitchen. She had hovered about him until she had prevailed upon him to join the country church, though his sole fitness for this step, so far as I could gather, lay in his boyish face and his possession of this divine melody. Shortly afterward he had gone to town on the Fourth of July, lost his money at a faro[15] table, ridden a saddled Texas steer on a

---

13. **peak in Darien** (der´ ē ən): Mountain on the Isthmus of Panama; from "On First Looking at Chapman's Homer" by English poet John Keats (1795–1821).

14. **Bayreuth** (bī roit´): City in Germany known for its annual Wagnerian music festivals.

15. **faro** (fer´ ō): Gambling game in which players bet on the cards to be turned up from the top of the dealer's deck.

◆ **Build Vocabulary**

prelude (prel´ yŏod) *n*.: Introductory section or movement of a suite, fugue, or work of music

bet, and disappeared with a fractured collar-bone.

"Well, we have come to better things than the old *Trovatore* at any rate, Aunt Georgie?" I queried, with well-meant jocularity.

Her lip quivered and she hastily put her handkerchief up to her mouth. From behind it she murmured, "And you've been hearing this ever since you left me, Clark?" Her question was the gentlest and saddest of reproaches.

"But do you get it, Aunt Georgiana, the astonishing structure of it all?" I persisted.

"Who could?" she said, absently; "why should one?"

The second half of the program consisted of four numbers from the *Ring*. This was followed by the forest music from *Siegfried*[16] and the program closed with Siegfried's funeral march. My aunt wept quietly, but almost continuously. I was perplexed as to what measure of musical comprehension was left to her, to her who had heard nothing for so many years but the singing of gospel hymns in Methodist services at the square frame schoolhouse on Section Thirteen. I was unable to gauge how much of it had been dissolved in soapsuds, or worked into bread, or milked into the bottom of a pail.

---

16. ***Siegfried*** (sēg´ frēd): Opera based on the adventures of Siegfried, a legendary hero in medieval German literature.

The deluge of sound poured on and on; I never knew what she found in the shining current of it; I never knew how far it bore her, or past what happy islands, or under what skies. From the trembling of her face I could well believe that the *Siegfried* march, at least, carried her out where the myriad graves are, out into the gray, burying grounds of the sea; or into some world of death vaster yet, where, from the beginning of the world, hope has lain down with hope, and dream with dream and, renouncing, slept.

The concert was over; the people filed out of the hall chattering and laughing, glad to relax and find the living level again, but my kinswoman made no effort to rise. I spoke gently to her. She burst into tears and sobbed pleadingly, "I don't want to go, Clark, I don't want to go!"

I understood. For her, just outside the door of the concert hall, lay the black pond with the cattle-tracked bluffs, the tall, unpainted house, naked as a tower, with weather-curled boards; the crook-backed ash seedlings where the dishcloths hung to dry, the gaunt, moulting turkeys picking up refuse about the kitchen door.

◆ **Build Vocabulary**

jocularity (jäk´ yə lar´ ə tē) *n.*: Joking good humor

Guide for Responding

◆ *Literature and Your Life*

Reader's Response Did you feel sorry for Aunt Georgiana? Why or why not?

Thematic Focus At one point, the narrator suggests that it would have been better to have sent Aunt Georgiana back to Red Willow "without waking her." Do you agree? Why or why not?

Group Discussion Aunt Georgiana gave up her greatest joy—music—for the chance to marry the man she loved. Did she make the right choice? Discuss the question in a small group.

☑ Check Your Comprehension

1. Summarize the sequence of events leading up to the matinée.
2. Describe Aunt Georgiana in your own words.
3. When and under what circumstances did the narrator live with Aunt Georgiana?
4. What happens to make the narrator realize that "it never really dies, then, the soul"?
5. How does Aunt Georgiana react when the concert ends?

Guide for Responding (continued)

◆ Critical Thinking

INTERPRET

1. Contrast the impression the story conveys of life in Red Willow County with life in Boston. **[Compare and Contrast]**
2. What does Aunt Georgiana mean when she says "Don't love it so well, Clark, or it may be taken from you"? **[Interpret]**
3. (a) Why does the opera have such a powerful effect on Aunt Georgiana? **[Analyze]** (b) How does her reaction, in turn, awaken Clark? **[Connect]**

EVALUATE

4. Would it have been better for Aunt Georgiana if she had not come to Boston? Explain. **[Speculate]**

APPLY

5. How are people's personalities shaped by the environment in which they live? **[Apply]**

◆ Reading Strategy

CLARIFYING

To understand Aunt Georgiana's actions in this story, it is important to **clarify**—check your understanding of—the details that Cather provides about her background.

Review the details that Cather provides about Aunt Georgiana's life on the frontier. How do these details help explain how she behaves in Boston?

◆ Literary Focus

CHARACTERIZATION

Characterization is the means by which an author reveals a character's personality. Because of Cather's use of a first-person narrator, much of what we learn about Aunt Georgiana comes from Clark's thoughts and feelings about her.

1. What is revealed about Aunt Georgiana through descriptions of her appearance?
2. What does Aunt Georgiana's reaction to the opera reveal about her personality?
3. What is revealed about Clark's personality through his thoughts and feelings about his aunt?
4. How does the fact that much of what we learn about Aunt Georgiana is revealed through Clark's thoughts help us shape our impressions of her?

◆ Build Vocabulary

USING WORDS FROM MUSIC

Look at the following definitions. Then choose the response to each item that better fits the situation.

overture: (a) an introductory movement to an extended musical work, (b) any first move

concert: (a) a public performance of several short compositions, (b) the act of working together

1. **concerted** effort: (a) competitive, (b) united
2. **overture** at a car sale: (a) "Would you like to take a test drive?" (b) "Step away from the car."

USING THE WORD BANK

Answer the following questions in your notebook.

1. If students are *reverential* toward a teacher, do they ignore her, worship her, or avoid her?
2. Who is most likely to speak *tremulously*—a musician, a truck driver, or a child?
3. Does *semi-somnambulant* describe someone who is angry, dazed, or busy?
4. Is an *inert* substance motionless or weightless?
5. Is *jocularity* the trademark of a funeral director, a talk-show host, or a surgeon?
6. As a *prelude* to bad news, would you expect humor or seriousness?

◆ Grammar and Style

REFLEXIVE AND INTENSIVE PRONOUNS

Reflexive and **intensive pronouns** end in -*self* or -*selves* but function differently. Reflexive pronouns refer to the subject and are necessary to the meaning of the sentence. Intensive pronouns emphasize a word mentioned earlier. They can be omitted without changing the meaning of the sentence.

Practice Identify the reflexive or intensive pronouns in these sentences.

1. Cather quit her job to devote herself to writing.
2. If you're a writer, you have to ask yourself whether you would have the courage to do the same.
3. For Cather, writing was itself a full-time job.
4. Writing is hard—books don't write themselves.

Writing Application Write four sentences describing some of your interests. Use two reflexive and two intensive pronouns.

Build Your Portfolio

Idea Bank

Writing

1. **Diary Entry** For the most part, Clark cannot gauge the effect of the music on his aunt. Let Aunt Georgiana speak for herself. Write a diary entry recording her reactions to the matinée.

2. **School Brochure** Aunt Georgiana has decided to open a music school in Red Willow County. Create an informational brochure aimed at convincing Nebraskans to send their children to the school. **[Media Link]**

3. **Editorial** "A Wagner Matinée" provoked an outcry among Nebraskans who felt Cather had portrayed the state unfairly. Cather said the story was a tribute to pioneer strength and endurance. As the editor of a Nebraska newspaper, write an editorial stating and defending your view.

Speaking and Listening

4. **Debate** Create two teams to debate the question: Which is a healthier environment, the Nebraska frontier or Boston?

5. **Oral Storytelling** Tell the story of Aunt Georgiana's visit as you imagine Clark would have described it to friends after his aunt left.

Projects

6. **A Wagner Matinée** Organize your own Wagner matinée. Locate recordings of two or more operas by Wagner. Research the pieces so that you can introduce them. Play the music for the class. **[Music Link]**

7. **Research Project** Find out how the Homestead Act of 1862 opened the frontier for settlement. Does Cather present an accurate portrait of life on a homestead? Use your findings to create an oral report. **[Social Studies Link]**

Writing Mini-Lesson

Travel Brochure

Cather's rendering of Aunt Georgiana's Nebraska homestead is strikingly vivid, but it doesn't exactly make you want to visit. Think of a place that captures your imagination—a place you've visited, seen on television, or read about—and create a travel brochure that does make people want to visit.

Writing Skills Focus: Sensory Details

Travel brochures use description to make vacation destinations seem appealing. Make your descriptions rich and vivid by including **sensory details**—details that appeal to one or more of the five senses—as Cather does in this description of the matinée audience.

Model From the Selection

. . . there was only the color contrast of bodices past counting, the shimmer and shadowing of fabrics soft and firm, silky and sheer, resisting and yielding: red mauve, pink, blue, lilac, purple, ecru, rose, yellow, cream, and white.

Prewriting Once you've chosen a place, think about the features you might describe, such as culture, architecture, music, foods, museums, or scenic locales. Gather and list sensory details you could use to describe them. Then find photographs and other visuals you can include in your brochure.

Drafting Arrange the visuals you've gathered into an order that makes sense. Then write a paragraph to accompany each visual. In each paragraph, focus on presenting vivid descriptions that will make your readers want to visit the destination.

Revising Review your draft, looking for places where you can add or change sensory details to make the descriptions more vivid and appealing.

CONNECTIONS TO TODAY'S WORLD

Cats
Anna Quindlen

Thematic Connection

LIVING IN A CHANGING WORLD

Writer Joyce Carol Oates once described Willa Cather as "a passionate chronicler of her time and place." The same can be said of novelist and former *New York Times* columnist Anna Quindlen. Although separated by nearly a century, both writers explore similar emotional terrain, charting the inner struggles and conflicts of the individual in a changing society.

A NEW LITERARY SENSIBILITY

The America of Willa Cather's youth was a nation in the midst of rapid and massive change. Industry and technology were booming. Immigrants swelled urban populations and fanned out westward across the plains. Cities burgeoned, and the pace of life quickened.

Confronted by these changes in society and its values, many writers struggled to find meaning in lives that were isolated from others. Out of this struggle, a new literary movement, known as Realism, emerged. Realism emphasized the honest rendering of life, and the works of the Realists were often colored by loneliness and alienation.

A LOSS OF COMMUNITY

With the Information Age dawning, America is again undergoing a transformation, and many find the changes exciting. However, for some, the loneliness and alienation of a century ago are still a reality.

The symptoms aren't hard to spot. People log anonymously onto chat rooms or spend hours watching television instead of chatting with flesh-and-blood neighbors. They pursue high-powered careers that leave little time for an emotional life. They move every few years in pursuit of better jobs, but at the expense of family and community ties.

The emotional isolation that results is the subtext of many of Anna Quindlen's columns. In her column "Life in the '30s," Quindlen took the school, the neighborhood, and the office as her territory. These are the places where human bonds should be strongest. Yet, as Quindlen reveals, there is a profound underside of loneliness and isolation.

ANNA QUINDLEN
(1953–   )

Anna Quindlen was a *New York Times* reporter and editor and an aspiring novelist when the *Times* asked her to write a weekly column. She accepted the offer, never dreaming of where it might lead. "I thought of the column as a way to make a little bit of money while writing my novel," she said. "I was just trying hard not to disgrace myself."

Far from it. Quindlen's column, "Life in the '30s," was a well-loved *Times* feature for five years, beginning in 1990. Quindlen's approach to the column—honest, personal, empathetic, astute—helps explain its immense popularity. She also had a knack for pinpointing the concerns of her readers. "I think of a column as having a conversation with a person that it just so happens I can't see," Quindlen said after winning a Pulitzer Prize for commentary in 1992. "It's nice to know that my end of the conversation was heard."

Cats

Anna Quindlen

The cats came with the house. They lived in the backyards, tiger gray, orange marmalade, calico, black. They slithered through the evergreens at the back perimeter, and during mating season their screams were terrible. Sometimes I shook black pepper along the property line, and for a night or two all was still. Then the rain came and they were back.

The cats came because of the woman next door. She and her husband, said to be bedridden, had lived on the third floor for many years. Every evening after dinner she went into the alley with a foil pie plate heaped with cat food and scraps: cabbage, rice, the noodles from chicken noodle soup, whatever they had had for dinner. Before she would even get to the bottom of the stairs the cats would begin to assemble, narrowing their eyes. She would talk to them roughly in a voice like sandpaper, coarse from years of cigarette smoke. ". . . Cats," she grumbled as she bent to put the food down.

She had only two interests besides the cats: my son and her own. She and her husband had one grown child. I never heard her say a bad word about him. He had reportedly walked and talked early, been as beautiful as a child star, never given a bit of trouble. He always sent a large card on Mother's Day, and each Christmas a poinsettia came, wrapped in green foil with a red bow. He was in the military, stationed here and there. During the time we lived next door to her, he came home once. She said it broke his heart not to see his father more. She said they had always been close when he lived at home, that he played baseball for the high school team and that his father never missed a game. He was a crack shortstop, she said, and a superior hitter.

She called my son "Bop Bop" because of the way he bounced in my arms. It was one of the first things he learned to say, and when he was in the backyard on summer evenings he would call "Bop Bop" plaintively until she came to her apartment window. As she raised the screen the cats would begin to mass in a great Pavlovian[1] gesture at the head of the alley. "Are you being a good boy?" she would call down. Bop Bop would smile up, his eyes shining. "Cat," he said, pointing, and the cats looked, too. Some summer nights she and my little boy would sit together companionably on the front stoop, watching the cars go by. She did not talk to him very much, and she wasn't tender, but when he was very good and not terribly dirty she sometimes said he looked just like her own little boy, only his hair wasn't quite as thick.

Last year she fell on the street and broke her hip, but while she was in the hospital, they found that she had fallen because she had had a stroke, and she had had a stroke because

---

1. **Pavlovian** (pav lō´ vē ən) *adj.*: Referring to Russian physiologist Ivan Pavlov (1849–1936), who showed that acquired habits depend on chains of conditioned reflexes.

of brain cancer. I went to see her in the hospital, and brought a picture of my son. She propped it against the water pitcher. She asked me to take care of her parakeet until she came home, to look in on her husband and to feed the cats. At night, when I came back from work, they would be prowling the yards, crying pitifully. My dogs lunged at the back windows.

When the ambulance brought her home, she looked like a scarecrow, her arms broomsticks in the armholes of her housecoat, her white hair wild. A home health-care aide came and cared for her and her husband. The woman across the street told me she was not well enough to take the bird back. The cats climbed the fire escape and banged against the screens with their bullet heads, but the aide shooed them away. My son would stand in the backyard and call "Bop Bop" at the window. One evening she threw it open and leaned out, a death's head, and shouted at him, and he cried. "Bop Bop is very sick," I said, and gave him a Popsicle.

She died this winter, a month after her husband. Her son came home for the funerals with

his wife, and together they cleaned out the apartment. We sent roses to the funeral home, and the son's wife sent a nice thank-you note. The bird died the next month. Slowly the cats began to disperse. The two biggest, a tom and a female, seem to have stayed. I don't really feed them, but sometimes my son will eat lunch out back; if he doesn't finish his food, I will leave it on the table. When I look out again it is gone, and the dogs are a little wild.

My son likes to look through photo albums. In one there is a picture of her leaning out the window, and a picture of him looking up with a self-conscious smile. He calls them both "Bop Bop." I wonder for how long he will remember, and what it will mean to him, years from now, when he looks at the picture and sees her at her window, what reverberations will begin, what lasting lessons will she have subliminally taught him, what lasting lessons will she not so subliminally have taught me.

Guide for Responding

◆ Literature and Your Life

Reader's Response Did you feel sorry for the woman next door? Why or why not?

Thematic Focus Is "Cats" really about cats? What changes result from the neighbor's illness and eventual death?

Journal Entry Think about someone to whom you are emotionally close. Briefly describe your relationship, and tell what makes you so close to the other person.

☑ Check Your Comprehension

1. What are the main interests of the neighbor?
2. How does the woman express her affection for Quindlen's son?
3. What happens to the woman to end her relationship with Quindlen and her son?

◆ Critical Thinking

INTERPRET

1. What role do the cats play in the life of the woman next door? **[Interpret]**
2. Why is the woman so interested in Quindlen's son? **[Infer]**
3. Does the woman's perception of her own son equate with his actions? Support your answer with examples from the text. **[Analyze; Support]**

EVALUATE

4. Is the neighbor's son really a "good son"? Explain. **[Criticize]**

APPLY

5. What "lasting lessons" do you think Quindlen might have learned from her neighbor? **[Generalize]**

Thematic Connection

LIVING IN A CHANGING WORLD

An old woman sickens and dies, estranged from her only son. Another woman, after years of physical and mental isolation, weeps inconsolably when that isolation is broken. A rich and successful man stuns his community by taking his own life.

What do these scenarios—taken from the selections in this section—have in common? They all show people in emotional pain, people who are disconnected from other people. Although all but one are drawn from the fiction and poetry of the past, it's not hard to imagine them taking place today, just about anywhere in the United States.

People in every age have suffered from loneliness; our need for other people is part of what makes us human. However, alienation—withdrawal or disconnection from society—is a modern condition, peculiar to highly developed, fast-paced, industrial and post-industrial societies. The authors in this section, all writing at the dawn of this century, searched for meaning in the emotional detachment and suffering of ordinary people. As the century comes to a close, the search goes on.

1. How does Quindlen's neighbor try to give meaning to her lonely life?
2. With which character from the selections in this section does Quindlen's neighbor have the most in common? Explain.
3. Could "Cats" have been written a hundred years ago? Why or why not?

 Idea Bank

Writing

1. **Epitaph** In *Spoon River Anthology*, Edgar Lee Masters lets the dead speak for themselves in their own revealing epitaphs. Using them as a model, write an epitaph for Quindlen's neighbor.

2. **Letter to the Editor** "Cats" originally appeared as a "Life in the 30's" column in the *New York Times*. Write a letter to the editor of the *New York Times* expressing your reaction to "Cats." **[Media Link]**

3. **Song** Drawing on any of the situations and characters in this section, write a song about loneliness. **[Music Link]**

4. **Character Sketch** Write a character sketch of a lonely or isolated person—either real or imaginary. In the sketch, suggest the reasons for the person's situation.

Speaking and Listening

5. **Dramatic Monologue** Write and deliver a monologue in which you, as Quindlen's neighbor, reveal your inner feelings about your son and his behavior toward you. Alternatively, take the role of the son, and write and perform a dramatic monologue in which you reveal your feelings and the history of your relationship with your mother.

Projects

6. **Report** The writers in this section have drawn on experience and creative imagination for their portrayals of the effects of social and emotional isolation, but have the effects of isolation been scientifically documented? Do research to find out what kinds of effects isolation can have on people. Present your findings in the form of an oral or written report. **[Science Link]**

Writing Process Workshop

A character sketch describes the physical appearance and personality of a real person or a fictional character and often provides insights into the subject's behavior and motivations. The sketch might also include other people's or characters' responses to the subject. Although character studies are usually prose pieces, a poem can be an equally effective vehicle for this purpose: Witness Edward Arlington Robinson's arresting poetic portraits of Miniver Cheevy and Richard Cory, and Edgar Lee Master's study of Lucinda Matlock.

The following skills, introduced in this section's Writing Mini-Lessons, will help you write a character sketch:

Writing Skills Focus

▶ **Create a main impression** of your subject. Focus on presenting details that support this impression. (See p. 603.)

▶ **Use sensory details** to make your subject's appearance and personality come alive for your readers. (See p. 621.)

▶ **Use a personal tone** that conveys your attitude toward your subject. (See p. 597.)

▶ **Use transitions** to make clear connections among the details you include. (See p. 597.)

Edward Arlington Robinson uses all these skills in his poetic character sketch of the fictional Richard Cory.

① Robinson establishes a main impression of Cory in the opening line.

② Transitions such as "and" and "but" make clear connections among the details.

③ Sensory details such as "imperially slim," and "glittered" help to create a portrait of Cory's physical appearance.

MODEL FROM LITERATURE

He was a gentleman from sole to crown, ①
Clean favored, and imperially slim,
And he was always quietly arrayed,
And he was always human when he talked;
But ② still he fluttered pulses when he said,
"Good-morning," and he glittered ③ when he
    walked.

Prewriting

Choose a Topic Search your memory to identify the most interesting or unusual people you've encountered at some time in your life. Choose one of these individuals as the subject for your character profile, or consider one of the following topic ideas:

> **Topic Ideas**
> - An inspiring coach or teacher
> - A character in a mystery
> - A family member or close friend

Gather Sensory Details Use a cluster diagram like the one below to gather details that vividly capture your subject's physical appearance and personality:

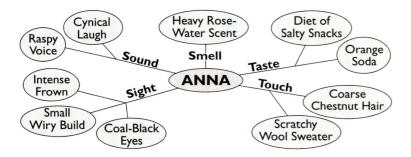

Drafting

Create a Main Impression All of the details in your profile should work together to create a single impression of the subject. Focus on capturing physical characteristics and personality traits that contribute to the impression you're striving to convey to readers.

Organize by Order of Importance When you organize by order of importance, you place details from the least to most important, or vice versa. Decide which order will help you portray your subject most effectively. Then use appropriate transition words to clarify the order you've chosen and guide your readers from point to point. These transition words show order of importance:

and, but, first, second, more importantly, most importantly, less importantly, least importantly, mainly, last, finally, even better, not as good, primarily, secondarily, above all, worst of all.

APPLYING LANGUAGE SKILLS: Using Quotations

Including appropriate quotations from or about your subject is a great way to capture his or her personality.

Description: Mrs. Drake was a kindly woman who cared for stray cats. She seemed to love the animals and worry about their welfare.

Enhanced With a Quotation: Mrs. Drake was a kindly woman who cared for stray cats. She once lamented, "I worry so about all the poor, homeless kitties. If I can give a few of them some food and a place to stay, I feel I've done some good."

Practice Enhance each of the following descriptions by adding a quotation or two or three lines of dialogue.

1. When Zoltron got angry, he roared at his crew, and they tried to calm him.
2. Coach Jones revved us up with his weekly pep talks.

Writing Application As you draft your character sketch, look for places where you can include dialogue or quotations.

Writer's Solution Connection Writing Lab

To help you gather details, use the Character Trait Word Bin in the Description tutorial.

APPLYING LANGUAGE SKILLS:
Combining Sentences

To avoid choppy writing, look for places to combine two or more short sentences into one longer one by using a coordinating conjunction (*and, but, or*) or a subordinating conjunction (*if, after, because,* and so on).

Short Sentences:

Tom lifts weights every day. He also runs three miles.

Revised Sentences:

Tom is dedicated to keeping fit. He eats nutritious meals.

Tom lifts weights <u>and</u> runs three miles every day.

<u>Because</u> Tom is dedicated to keeping fit, he eats nutritious meals.

Practice Combine each of the following pairs of short sentences into a longer sentence.

1. Zoe's blue eyes twinkle. Her brown hair glistens.

2. Grandpa reads the morning paper. Then he goes for a stroll.

Writing Application As you revise your character sketch, smooth your writing by combining short, choppy sentences into longer ones.

Writer's Solution Connection
Writing Lab

For help revising your profile, use the Vague Adjective Checker in the Description tutorial.

Revising

Use a Checklist Use the following checklist to help you revise your character sketch:

▶ How can you strengthen the main impression of your subject?

▶ Where can you add sensory details to sharpen the picture of your subject's appearance and personality?

▶ What details might you delete?

▶ What transitions can you add to connect your paragraphs more smoothly and clarify the relationships among your ideas?

REVISION MODEL

① *one of the kindest, most considerate people I know*
Kathy is ~~a nice person~~. She's always trying to do things to

② *For example,*   ③ *to Hawaii she'd been planning for years*
help other people. She canceled a ~~planned~~ vacation to take

recently
care of a close friend who was sick.

① Notice how the writer clarifies her main impression of her subject.

② The writer adds this transition to introduce an example.

③ This precise detail helps the reader to understand the sacrifice that was made.

Consult a Peer Reviewer Have a classmate read your profile and jot down his or her key impressions of your subject based on your paper. Check to see that the main impressions your peer reviewer has noted match the impressions you were trying to convey. If not, consult with your classmate to find ways that you can strengthen your writing to better achieve your purpose.

Publishing

Prepare a Documentary If your subject is nearby, consider creating a documentary-style character portrait on video, adapting your written text for use as a voice-over narration. You might even include an on-camera interview. Show the video in class.

Create a Bulletin Board Display Assemble the character sketches from your classmates and display them on a wall or bulletin board, together with photographs and drawings of the subjects.

Real-World Reading Skills Workshop

Strategies for Success

Summer job applications, standardized test forms, warranty registrations, club memberships—all these require you to fill out application forms. While some forms are more complex than others, correctly reading any application helps you complete it accurately and completely.

Know What You're Being Asked

Determine the purpose of the application. Is it intended to gather information about your personal life, your medical history, or your employment experience? Will you gain access to services or privileges by completing the form, or does it merely identify you and your work for reviewers? Recognizing what information an application is seeking will help you focus your answers.

Verify the Form Confirm that you are completing the correct form. Check its title, and briefly scan labeled boxes or lines. Quickly skim any directions before writing.

Read the Application Once you're sure you have the correct form, read the directions thoroughly. Check the information requested against the purpose of the form. If you're applying for a job in another city, for example, you'll want to include an address in that city along with your home address. Work slowly and carefully.

Apply the Strategy

Hoping to work at the next national political convention, you must complete this application for an internship position.

1. What is this form entitled?
2. Complete the application, using a separate piece of paper.
3. After you complete the application, what else must you do if you were actually submitting it?

Internship Application Form

Name _____

Address _____

_____

SS# ____-___-____ date of birth __/__/__

Phone _____

Health restrictions _____

Will you need housing in Convention City?

Yes ____ No ____ (If *no*, please list your Convention City address.) _____

How many hours per day are you available to work? _____

Check all the communications operations with which you are familiar. ___ word processing ___ e-mail ___ live broadcast ___ still photography ___ video recording ___ cell telephones

Write a brief paragraph explaining why you want to work as an intern and listing some experiences you think qualify you for the job.

✔ *Here are other situations in which reading an application form can be important.*
- ▶ *Armed services entry*
- ▶ *Sports or activity tryouts*
- ▶ *Automobile or home loan qualification*

Speaking and Listening Workshop

Problems arise—it's a fact of life. You *will* sometimes find yourself in conflict with others over ideas, actions, or issues. How you behave in these situations is very important.

Listen and Reflect One way to avoid conflict is to be a polite and interested listener. When you listen carefully to what other people say, you will understand their ideas accurately and avoid a snap judgment or response.

Think Before You Speak The more heated the conversation gets, the more important it is to pause before speaking. When you do speak, stick to the facts and avoid inflammatory remarks. It's never productive to hurt people's feelings or insult their ideas.

Suppose you are out with a group of friends. Some want to go to the movies, while others want to head for the town swimming pool. You'd like to go to the mall. How will you resolve the conflict?

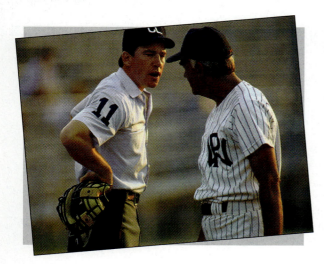

Keep an Open Mind Perhaps you will see some merit in alternative views. As you consider others' ideas, identify areas where you feel comfortable compromising. Look for ways to offer everyone in the conflict some of what they seek.

✔ Tips for Conflict Resolution

▶ Take turns talking—one at a time.
▶ At school, take advantage of any formal conflict-resolution programs or approaches.
▶ Consider any reasonably stated option.
▶ Be courteous and respectful.
▶ Ask someone outside the conflict to mediate the discussion.

Apply the Strategies

Practice these conflict-resolution techniques as you complete one or more of the following activities.

1. With a group of classmates, brainstorm for several possible causes of conflicts. Then role-play constructive resolutions.

2. Participate in a session of your school's conflict-resolution program. Use the techniques outlined on this page to make a productive contribution.

3. Recount a recent conflict with your parents or other adults. Identify ways you used or could have used conflict-resolution strategies.

Find out about conflict-resolution programs in your school, through your parents' workplace, or in the community government. Add your own ideas to these programs or develop your own complete program.

Extended Reading Opportunities

The literature of 1850–1914 reflects the growing pains the nation experienced as it rose to the challenges of a divisive war and an untamed frontier. These are just a few possibilities for extending your understanding of this electrifying period of history.

Suggested Titles

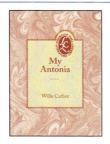

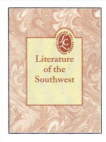

The Adventures of Huckleberry Finn
Mark Twain

Widely regarded as Twain's masterpiece, this action-packed novel captures the adventures of a young white orphan and a runaway slave. *Huckleberry Finn* is more than just a great story, however—its uniquely American characters and speech convey the vitality of life in the United States as no other novel ever has. Read this book, and you'll understand why it's credited with changing the course of American literature.

My Antonia
Willa Cather

The road to adulthood is never easy, especially when you live in the desolate wilderness described in Willa Cather's novel *My Antonia*. For young Bohemian immigrant Antonia Shimerdas, the unforgiving, primitive Nebraska heartland is now home. Tough, self-sufficient, and spirited, she meets the daily challenges of frontier life with courage and determination. *My Antonia* is a celebration of the pioneer spirit that realistically portrays both the beauty and hardship of life on the American frontier.

Literature of the Southwest

What comes to mind when you think of the American Southwest? For most, it's blue skies, sandy deserts and plains, cactuses, coyotes, and, of course, cowboys. Experience this exciting region through its literature—stories, tall tales, and songs that capture a time and place where people and events were larger than life.

Other Possibilities

Gone With the Wind	Margaret Mitchell
The Civil War	Geoffrey C. Ward
The Life and Times of Frederick Douglass	Frederick Douglass
A Treasury of Civil War Tales	Webb Garrison, Editor
The Jungle	Upton Sinclair
Sister Carrie	Theodore Dreiser
Washington Square	Henry James

Nighthawks, 1942, Edward Hopper, The Art Institute of Chicago

Disillusion, Defiance, and Discontent (1914–1946)

> "We asked the cyclone
> to go around our barn but
> it didn't hear us."
>
> —Carl Sandburg
> *from* The People, Yes

Timeline
1915–1945

American Events

- **1915** Olympic track and field champion Jim Thorpe begins his professional football career. ◀
- **1916** *Chicago Poems* by Carl Sandburg appears.
- **1917** United States enters World War I.
- **1918** President Wilson announces his 14 Points in peace plan. ▼
- **1919** Prohibition becomes law; repealed in 1933.
- **1919** Sherwood Anderson publishes *Winesburg, Ohio.*

- **1920** Nineteenth Amendment to Constitution gives U.S. women the right to vote. ▼

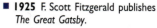

- **1922** T. S. Eliot publishes *The Waste Land.*
- **1923** Wallace Stevens publishes *Harmonium.*

- **1925** F. Scott Fitzgerald publishes *The Great Gatsby.*
- **1926** Langston Hughes publishes *The Weary Blues.*
- **1926** Ernest Hemingway publishes *The Sun Also Rises.*
- **1927** Charles Lindbergh flies solo and nonstop from New York to Paris.
- **1929** Stock market crashes in October, followed by Great Depression of the 1930's. ▶

World Events

- **1914** Panama: Built by the United States, the Panama Canal is opened. ▲
- **1915** England: Because of the war in Europe, travelers are cautioned against transatlantic voyages. *The Lusitania* would be sunk despite these warnings. ◀
- **1917** Russia: Bolsheviks seize control of Russia in October Revolution.
- **1918** Worldwide influenza epidemic kills as many as 20 million people.
- **1919** France: Treaty of Versailles ends World War I. ▶

- **1921** England: D. H. Lawrence publishes *Women in Love.*
- **1922** Ireland: James Joyce publishes *Ulysses.* ▲
- **1924** Germany: Thomas Mann publishes *The Magic Mountain.*

- **1925** England: Virginia Woolf publishes *Mrs. Dalloway.*
- **1928** China: Chiang Kai-shek becomes head of Nationalist government. ▼
- **1928** Germany: Kurt Weill and Bertolt Brecht write and produce *The Threepenny Opera.*

1930　　　　　　　　**1940**　　　　　　　　　　**1945**

■ **1930** Katherine Anne Porter publishes *Flowering Judas.*

■ **1933** President Roosevelt closes banks; Congress passes New Deal laws. ▲

■ **1938** Thornton Wilder's play *Our Town* opens.

■ **1939** John Steinbeck publishes *The Grapes of Wrath.*

■ **1939** *The Wizard of Oz* and *Gone With the Wind* appear in movie theaters. ▼

■ **1939** United States declares neutrality as World War II breaks out in Europe.

■ **1940** Richard Wright publishes *Native Son.*

■ **1940** Civil Aeronautics Board is created to regulate U.S. commercial air traffic.

■ **1941** Federal Communications Commission grants first commercial television station licenses to NBC and CBS in New York.

■ **1941** *A Curtain of Green* by Eudora Welty appears.

■ **1941** Japanese bomb American naval base at Pearl Harbor, bringing U.S. into World War II. ▼

■ **1944** Roosevelt is reelected president for an unprecedented fourth term.

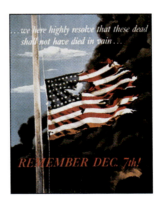

...we here highly resolve that these dead shall not have died in vain...

REMEMBER DEC. 7th!

American Events

■ **1945** First atomic bomb is successfully exploded by U.S. in secret test, July 16.

■ **1945** Truman declares September 2 V-J Day, or Victory Over Japan Day. World War II ends. ▼

■ **1945** Karl Shapiro's collection *V-Letter and Other Poems* wins Pulitzer Prize for poetry.

World Events

■ **1930** India: Mahatma Gandhi leads famous march to the sea to protest British tax on salt. ◄

■ **1931** Spain: Salvador Dali paints *Persistence of Memory.* ▶

■ **1933** Germany: Adolf Hitler becomes German chancellor.

■ **1936** USSR: Stalin starts Great Purge to rid government and armed forces of opposition.

■ **1936** Spain: Spanish Civil War begins.

■ **1939** Poland: German blitzkrieg invasion of Poland sets off World War II.

■ **1940** France: French government signs armistice with Germany.

■ **1942** France: Albert Camus completes *The Stranger.*

■ **1944** Poland: Warsaw uprising. Polish underground unsuccessfully attempts to capture Warsaw from Germans before Soviets can take city.

■ **1945** Germany: Dresden is hit by Allied firebombing raid. Firestorm virtually destroys city.

■ **1945** Germany: First attempt at manned rocket flight. Pilot is killed.

■ **1945** United Nations Charter signed at end of World War II. ▼

The Story of the Times
1914–1946

The America that entered the twentieth century was a nation achieving world dominance, but at the same time losing some of its youthful innocence and brash confidence. Two world wars, a dizzying decade of prosperity, and a devastating worldwide depression marked this era. With these events came a new age in American literature. The upheavals of the early twentieth century ushered in a period of artistic experimentation and lasting literary achievement.

Historical Background

The years immediately preceding World War I were characterized by an overwhelming sense of optimism. Numerous technological advances occurred, dramatically affecting people's lives and creating a sense of promise for the future. While a number of serious social problems still existed, reforms aimed at solving these problems began to be instituted. When World War I broke out in 1914, however, President Woodrow Wilson was forced to turn his attention away from the troubles at home and focus on the events in Europe.

War in Europe World War I was one of the bloodiest and most tragic conflicts ever to occur. The introduction of the machine gun changed the methods of battle, and the war dragged on for several years, claiming almost an entire generation of European men.

President Wilson wanted the United States to remain neutral in the war, but that proved impossible. In 1915, a German submarine sank the *Lusitania*, pride of the British merchant fleet. More than 1,200 people on board lost their lives, including 128 Americans. After the sinking, American public opinion favored the Allies—England, France, Italy, and Russia. When Germany resumed unrestricted submarine warfare two years later, the United States joined the Allied cause.

▲ **Evaluate an Advertisement**
Recruiting posters like this one urged Americans to help the war effort during World War I by joining the armed forces. Why do you think this poster would or would not have been effective in persuading people to enlist?

▲ **Hypothesize** As World War I took men away from home industries, women took over their jobs. These shipyard workers are holding the tools they used to work with red-hot steel rivets. How do you think their wartime work helped women win the right to vote after the war?

Americans were confident and carefree as the troops set off overseas. That cheerful mood soon passed. A number of famous American writers saw the war firsthand and learned of its horror. E. E. Cummings, Ernest Hemingway, and John Dos Passos served as ambulance drivers. Hemingway later served in the Italian infantry and was seriously wounded.

Prosperity and Depression The end of the Great War in November 1918 brought little peace to the big cities of America. In 1919, Prohibition made the sale of liquor illegal, leading to bootlegging, speak-easies, widespread law breaking, and sporadic warfare among competing gangs.

Throughout the 1920's, the nation seemed on a binge. After a brief recession in 1920 and 1921, the economy boomed. New buildings rose everywhere, creating new downtown sections in many cities—Omaha, Des Moines, and Minneapolis among them. Radio arrived, and so did jazz. Movies became big business, and spectacular movie palaces sprang up across the country. Fads abounded: raccoon coats, flagpole sitting, a dance called the Charleston. The great literary interpreter of the Roaring Twenties was F. Scott Fitzgerald. In *This Side of Paradise* and *The Great Gatsby,* Fitzgerald vividly captured the essence of life during this frenzied decade.

In late October 1929, the stock market crashed, marking the beginning of the Great Depression. By mid-1932, about 12 million people—one quarter of the work force—were out of work. Even as bread lines formed and the numbers of unemployed grew, most business leaders remained optimistic. However, the situation continued to worsen. In the presidential election of 1932, New York's governor Franklin D. Roosevelt defeated incumbent president Herbert Hoover. Roosevelt initiated a package of major economic reforms, the New Deal, to turn the economic tide. Roosevelt's policies helped bring an end to the Depression and earned him reelection in 1936 and again in 1940.

World War II Only twenty years after the Treaty of Versailles had ended World War I, the German invasion of Poland touched off World War II. As in the earlier war, most Americans wanted to remain neutral. When the Japanese

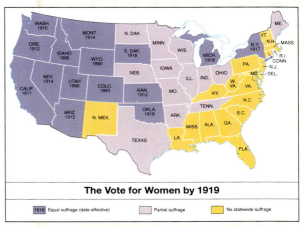

The Vote for Women by 1919

1918 Equal suffrage (date effective)　Partial suffrage　No statewide suffrage

▲ **Read a Map** By 1919, women in most states had won the right to vote in state and local elections. (a) Which state was the first to grant women full suffrage? (b) Using the information on this map, make a generalization about the relationship between women's suffrage and regions of the country.

You will always be glad you bought a Glenwood

Gold Medal **Glenwood** *Pearl Gray*

▲ **Make an Inference** In the 1920's, Americans were eager to buy new devices that made life easier. What does the clothing the model is wearing suggest about lifestyles at that time?

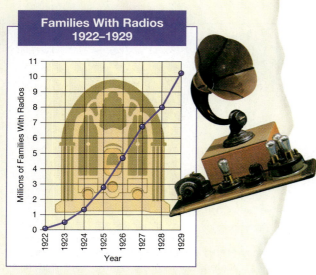

Families With Radios 1922–1929

(Millions of Families With Radios vs. Year)

▲ **Read a Graph** The 1920's could be called the age of radio. Millions of American families bought radios and listened to popular programming. About how many families had radios in 1924? In 1928? What later trends in home entertainment did the growth in popularity of the radio foreshadow?

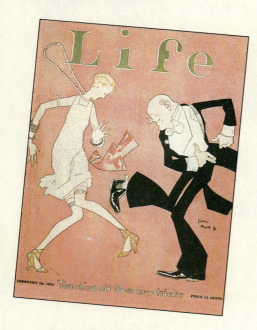

Life

February 28, 1926   Teaching old Dogs new tricks   PRICE 15 CENTS

▲ **Make an Inference** The Charleston was a popular dance during the Roaring Twenties. Why do nightclubs featuring music and dance flourish during periods of prosperity?

attacked Pearl Harbor in Hawaii on December 7, 1941, however, America could stay neutral no longer. The United States declared war on the Axis powers—Japan, Germany, and Italy.

After years of bitter fighting on two fronts, the Allies—including the United States, Great Britain, the Soviet Union, and France—defeated Nazi Germany. Japan surrendered three months later, after the United States had dropped atomic bombs on two Japanese cities. Peace, and the atomic age, had arrived.

Literature of the Period

The Birth of Modernism The devastation of World War I left many people with a feeling of uncertainty and disillusionment. No longer trusting the ideas and values of the world out of which the war had developed, people sought to find new ideas that better suited twentieth-century life. A major literary movement known as Modernism was born. Modernists experimented with a wide variety of new approaches and techniques, producing a remarkably diverse body of literature. Yet, the Modernists shared a common purpose. They sought to capture the essence of modern life in both the form and content of their work. To reflect the fragmentation of the modern world, the Modernists constructed their works out of fragments, omitting the expositions, transitions, resolutions, and explanations used in traditional literature. The themes of their works were usually implied, rather than directly stated, creating a sense of uncertainty and forcing readers to draw their own conclusions.

Imagism The Modernist movement was ushered in by a poetic movement known as Imagism. This movement, which lasted from 1909 to 1917, attracted followers in both the United States and England. The Imagists rebelled against the sentimentality of nineteenth-century poetry. They demanded instead hard, clear expression, concrete images, and the language of everyday speech. Their models came from Greek and Roman classics, Chinese and Japanese poetry, and the free verse of the French poets of their day. The early leader of the Imagist movement was Ezra Pound. When Pound abandoned Imagism, other Imagists assumed leadership, among them the poet H. D. (Hilda Doolittle).

The Expatriates Postwar disenchantment led a number of American writers to become expatriates, or exiles. Many of these writers settled in Paris, where they were influenced by Gertrude Stein, the writer who coined the phrase "lost generation" to describe those who were disillusioned by World War I. Stein lived in Paris from 1902 until her death in 1946, and her home attracted many major authors, including Sherwood Anderson, F. Scott Fitzgerald, and Ernest Hemingway.

Fitzgerald and Hemingway are the best known of the expatriates, but they are by no means the only ones. Ezra Pound spent most of his adult life in England, France, and Italy. T. S. Eliot, born in St. Louis, went to Europe in 1914 and died in London in 1965. Some critics have called Eliot's long, despairing poem *The Waste Land* the most important poem of the century.

New Approaches During the years between the two world wars, writers in both the United States and Europe explored new literary territories. Influenced by developments in modern psychology, writers began using the stream-of-consciousness technique, attempting to recreate the natural flow of a character's thoughts. Named by psychologist William James, the stream-of-consciousness technique involves the presentation of a series of thoughts, memories, and insights, connected only by a character's natural associations. The landmark stream-of-consciousness novel is *Ulysses*, published in 1922 by the Irish writer James Joyce. A number of American novelists soon adopted the technique, most notably William Faulkner in *The Sound and the Fury*. Katherine Anne Porter's short stories also employ stream of consciousness.

Poets also sought to stretch the old boundaries. E. E. Cummings's poems attracted special attention because of their wordplay, unique typography, and special punctuation. These devices are more than mere oddities in Cummings's poetry. They are vital to its intent and its meaning. William Carlos Williams, a

▲ **Analyze Art** Aaron Douglas, an African American artist who lived and painted during the Harlem Renaissance, became one of the nation's leading muralists. How does "From Slavery Through Reconstruction," the painting shown here, communicate the experience of African Americans?

▲ **Make an Inference** The government
▼ struggled to stop the illegal flow of liquor during Prohibition. In the photograph below, federal agents destroy cases of beer found during a raid in Philadelphia. The two men in disguise in the picture above were among the most effective Prohibition agents. Working undercover, the partners made more than 4,000 arrests. Given the many advances during this period of history, why do you think many Americans supported Prohibition?

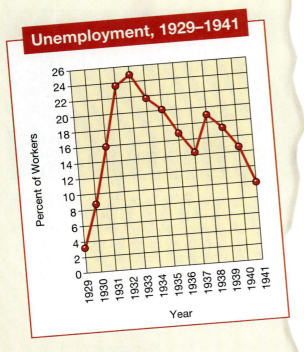

Unemployment, 1929–1941

(Graph: Percent of Workers vs. Year, 1929–1941)

▲ **Interpret a Pattern** During the Depression, millions of Americans were out of work. According to the graph, in which year was unemployment the highest? What happened to unemployment between 1936 and 1941?

▲ **Draw a Conclusion** During the Depression, photographers captured the suffering of the rural poor in powerful pictures. Dorothea Lange took this photograph, which has become a symbol of the Great Depression. Why do you think photographs are such valuable records of the times?

and its meaning. William Carlos Williams, a New Jersey physician and poet, wrote poetry so spare and cryptic that one cannot say for sure what the poems "mean." This obscurity of meaning did not bother Williams. Likewise, it did not concern other poets who shared Archibald MacLeish's belief that "a poem should not mean but be."

Writers of International Renown The Modernists dramatically altered the complexion of American literature. At the same time, many of these writers earned international acclaim that equaled that of their European literary contemporaries.

The Nobel Prize for Literature is an international award. It was established in 1901 with funds bequeathed by Alfred Nobel, the Swedish inventor of dynamite. The first American to win the Nobel Prize for Literature was Sinclair Lewis. A native of Minnesota, Lewis fictionalized his hometown in his first important novel, *Main Street*.

Lewis's Nobel Prize in 1930 was the first of many for American writers. In 1936, the prize went to Eugene O'Neill, ranked by most critics as America's greatest playwright. Among his best-known plays are *Desire Under the Elms*, *The Iceman Cometh*, and *Long Day's Journey Into Night*. O'Neill's plays are sometimes autobiographical, generally tragic, and often experimental.

In 1938, the Nobel Prize for Literature went to Pearl S. Buck, an American who spent her early years in China. Buck wrote about that country with understanding and compassion. *The Good Earth* is considered her finest work.

T. S. Eliot, who had become a British subject in 1927, won the award in 1948. William Faulkner won it the following year. In addition to *The Sound and the Fury*, Faulkner wrote such enduring works as *Light in August* and *The Hamlet*.

In later years, Ernest Hemingway and John Steinbeck also won Nobel Prizes for Literature. Hemingway's simple, direct, journalistic style of writing, evident in such novels as *The Sun Also Rises* and *A Farewell to Arms*, influenced a generation of young writers. Much of his best writing captures aspects of World War I and its aftermath. Many of Steinbeck's works depict the Depression, especially as it affected migrant workers and dust-bowl farmers. Two of Steinbeck's most memorable novels are *Of Mice and Men* and *The Grapes of Wrath.*

The Harlem Renaissance A new literary age was dawning—not only in Greenwich Village and among expatriates in Paris, but also in northern Manhattan, in Harlem. African American writers, mostly newcomers from the South, were creating their own renaissance there. It began in 1921 with the publication of Countee Cullen's "I Have a Rendezvous With Life (with apologies to Alan Seeger)." Another poem by a promising young African American writer—"The Negro Speaks of Rivers," by Langston Hughes—followed six months later.

What occurred thereafter would come to be known as the Harlem Renaissance. It was a burst of creative activity by black writers and artists, few of whom, other than Cullen, had been born in New York City. Most of those involved in the movement moved to Harlem during the renaissance. Claude McKay, for example, was from Jamaica. His most famous book was *Harlem Shadows*, a collection of poems published in 1922. A year later came Jean Toomer's *Cane*, a collection of stories, verses, and a play.

The Harlem phenomenon continued throughout the 1920's and into the 1930's, producing a body of exceptional works. In addition, Harlem Renaissance artists opened the door for later generations of African American writers who would follow them.

A Continuing Tradition World War II did not end the literary revival that had begun after World War I. Many of the older writers continued to produce novels, short stories, plays, and poems. Meanwhile, a new generation of writers arose after World War II to keep American literature at the leading edge of the world's artistic achievement.

▲ Draw a Conclusion This photograph was taken soon after the surprise bombing of Pearl Harbor, December 7, 1941. Within hours, newspaper "extras" were on the street with the story of the Japanese sneak attack. Why would such an attack make the United States entry into WWII inevitable?

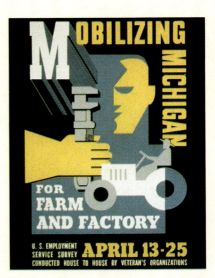

▲ Draw a Conclusion The Works Progress Administration (WPA) employed men and women to build hospitals, schools, parks, and airports. The WPA also employed artists, writers, and musicians. How would this program benefit both the government and the unemployed?

The Development of American English

SLANG AS IT IS SLUNG

by Richard Lederer

Slang is hot and slang is cool. Slang is nifty and slang is wicked. Slang is the bee's knees and the cat's whiskers. Slang is far out, groovy, and outa sight. Slang is fresh, fly, and phat. Slang is bodacious and fantabulous. Slang is ace, awesome, copacetic, the max, and totally tubular.

Those are many ways of saying that, if variety is the spice of life, slang is the spice of language. Slang adds gusto to the feast of words, as long as speakers and writers remember that too much spice can kill the feast of any dish.

Slang has added spice to the feast of American literature as American writers have increasingly written in an American voice, with the words and rhythms of everyday American discourse. Listen to the Harlem Renaissance poet Langston Hughes:

Good morning, daddy!
Ain't you heard
The boogie-woogie rumble
Of a dream deferred?

Defining the "Lingo" What is slang? In the preface to their *Dictionary of American Slang*, Harold Wentworth and Stuart Berg Flexner define slang as "the body of words and expressions frequently used by or intelligible to a rather large portion of the general American public, but not accepted as good, formal usage by the majority." Slang, then, is seen as a kind of vagabond language that prowls the outskirts of respectable speech, yet few of us can get along without it. Even our statespersons have a hard time getting by without such colloquial or slang expressions as "hit the nail on the head," "team effort," or "pass the buck."

What's in This Name? Nobody is quite sure where the word *slang* comes from. According to H. L. Mencken, the word *slang* developed in the eighteenth century (it was first recorded in 1756) either from an erroneous past tense of *sling* (*sling-slang-slung*) or from *language* itself, as in *(thieve)s'lang(uage)* and *(beggar)s'lang(uage)*. The second theory makes the point that jargon and slang originate and are used by a particular trade or class group, but slang words come to be slung around to some extent by a whole population.

Slang is a prominent part of our American wordscape. In fact, *The Dictionary of American Slang* estimates that slang makes up perhaps a fifth of the words we use. Many of our most valuable and pungent words have begun their lives keeping company with thieves, vagrants, and hipsters. As Mr. Dooley, a fictional Irish saloon keeper, once observed, "When we Americans get through with the English language, it will look as if it has been run over by a musical comedy."

Activity

Student slang is a rich vein of metaphor and word formation. With your classmates, compile a glossary of the slang used in your school.

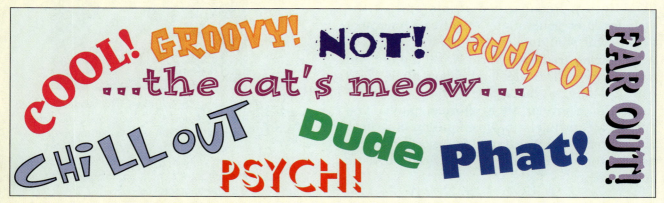

PART **1** *Facing Troubled Times*

No Place to Go, 1935, Maynard Dixon, The Herald Clark
Memorial Collection, Courtesy of Brigham Young University
Museum of Fine Arts

The devastation of World War I and the calamity of
the Great Depression left many Americans disillusioned
with the world. However, as in other chapters of our
nation's history, Americans showed the ability to endure
these troubled times and to build something positive out
of them. One of the positive effects was a new brand of
experimental literature that carried the American literary
tradition to new heights.

Guide for Interpreting

T. S. Eliot (1888–1965)

Always somberly attired and well-spoken, Thomas Stearns Eliot was outwardly the model of convention. His work, in contrast, was revolutionary in both form and content.

Beginnings Born into a wealthy family in St. Louis, Missouri, Eliot grew up in an environment that promoted his intellectual development. He attended Harvard University, and in 1910, the year he received his master's degree in philosophy, he completed "The Love Song of J. Alfred Prufrock."

A Literary Sensation When World War I broke out, Eliot moved to England. There he became acquainted with Ezra Pound, another young American poet. Pound helped influence a magazine editor to publish "Prufrock," making Eliot's work available to the public for the first time. A short time later, Eliot published a collection, *Prufrock and Other Observations* (1917), that contained "Prufrock" and a variety of other poems. The book caused a sensation, earning Eliot a lasting place among the finest writers of this century.

> *Eliot's exploration of the uncertainty of modern life struck a chord among readers, who were stunned by his revolutionary poetic imagery.*

In 1922, Eliot published *The Waste Land*, his most celebrated work. Although Eliot himself once dismissed *The Waste Land* as "a piece of rhythmical grumbling," most readers saw it as a profound critique of the spiritual barrenness of the modern world. The poem, which had an enormous impact on writers and critics, was a crowning achievement of the Modernist literary movement and is still considered one of the finest works ever written.

A Return to Tradition In his search for something beyond the "waste land" of modern society, Eliot became a member of the Church of England in 1927. He began to explore religious themes in poems such as "Ash Wednesday" (1930) and *Four Quartets* (1943)—works which suggest that he believed religion could heal the wounds inflicted by society. In later years, he wrote several plays, including *Murder in the Cathedral* (1935) and *The Cocktail Party* (1950).

◆ Background for Understanding

LITERATURE: ELIOT AND THE MODERNIST MOVEMENT

Telephones, radios, automobiles—all were transforming life at an unprecedented pace in the early decades of the twentieth century. Long-held traditions seemingly had no place in this new and modern way of life. Uncertain and disillusioned with the values and ideologies that produced the devastation of World War I, many people were searching for new ideas, values, and ways of looking at life.

Within the literary world, the quest for all things new gave rise to Modernism, a movement that represented a break with literary traditions. In an effort to reflect a world that no longer held simple answers or permanent truths, Modernist leaders T. S. Eliot and Ezra Pound began creating literature that was often fragmented in structure and avoided providing directly stated themes. Rather than providing answers, the Modernists most often left it up to readers to draw their own conclusions about the meaning of a work. In some works, including "Prufrock," Eliot and other Modernists used a technique known as stream of consciousness, in which they tried to reproduce the natural tendency of the human mind to jump from association to association.

The Love Song of J. Alfred Prufrock

◆ *Literature and Your Life*

CONNECT YOUR EXPERIENCE

Think of the times you have wished you had a different personality. Maybe you would have preferred to be more outgoing or more assertive, the type of person who "makes things happen." The character J. Alfred Prufrock speaks to this feeling in all of us.

Journal Writing Recall an occasion in which you wish you had behaved more boldly. What actually happened? Describe the scenario you wish you had acted out.

THEMATIC FOCUS: FACING TROUBLED TIMES

J. Alfred Prufrock's public face is that of a proper gentleman, a member of society. Inwardly, however, he is lonely and suffering, paralyzed by his inability to act in ways that might bring meaning to his empty life. He is discontented by his timidity, his physical imperfections, and his insignificance; he is also disillusioned with other people. Prufrock symbolizes all of the characteristics that the Modernists associated with life in the early 1900's.

◆ Build Vocabulary

PREFIXES: *di-*

The prefix *di-* (or *dis-*) means "apart" or "away." You'll notice that this prefix appears in the word *digress*, meaning "to turn aside from," in Eliot's poem. How does the prefix contribute to the overall meaning of the word? What other words include this prefix?

WORD BANK

Before you read, preview this list of words from "The Love Song of J. Alfred Prufrock."

insidious
digress
malingers
meticulous
obtuse

◆ Grammar and Style

ADJECTIVAL MODIFIERS

There are many different grammatical structures that can function as adjectives to modify nouns or pronouns. For example, Eliot uses a variety of phrases and clauses to modify nouns:

Prepositional Phrases: sawdust restaurants *with oyster-shells*
Participial Phrases: a patient *etherized upon a table*
Adjective Clauses: Streets *that follow like a tedious argument*
Infinitive Phrases: prepare a face *to meet the faces that you meet*

◆ Literary Focus

DRAMATIC MONOLOGUE

A troubled J. Alfred Prufrock invites an unidentified companion—perhaps a part of his own personality—to walk with him as he reflects aloud about his inhibitions and the bitter realization that life and love are passing him by. Prufrock's so-called love song is actually a **dramatic monologue**— a poem or speech in which a character addresses a silent listener at a critical point in the speaker's life.

As you read Eliot's dramatic monologue, use a chart like the one below to record Prufrock's observations about life, along with details about his personality and the situation that he faces.

Prufrock's Situation	Personality Traits	Observations About Life

Reading for Success

Strategies for Reading Poetry

Poetry is one of the richest and most mysterious forms of literature. Because a poem generally comes at the truth sideways rather than head on, you must use a number of strategies to help you unravel the meaning the poet has hidden within the lines. Here are several:

Identify the poem's speaker.

Identifying its speaker is an important first step in gaining insight into a poem. The speaker may be the poet or a fictional character created by the poet. What is the speaker's outlook on life? How is it reflected in the poem?

Engage your senses.

Poems, especially the Imagist poems you will study in this unit, use images—words or phrases that appeal to the five senses—to convey meaning. As you read, picture the visual images in all their detail. Hear the sounds described, and imagine the textures and scents. When you engage your senses, you will find greater enjoyment and meaning in the poem.

Relate structure to meaning.

A poem's structure—the length of its lines, the way it is broken into lines and stanzas—is often closely tied to its meaning. Avoid the temptation to read a poem rigidly, pausing or stopping at the end of each line. Notice where sentences begin and end and how ideas are grouped into stanzas; the start of a new stanza can signal the introduction of a new thought or idea.

Paraphrase.

Pause every so often and try restating passages in your own words. How might you describe the speaker's experiences and feelings?

Respond.

Think about what the poem is saying. How does it make you feel? What thoughts does it set off in your mind?

Apply historical context.

Understanding the social, political, economic, and literary environment in which a poem was written will help you grasp its meaning. To help you better understand each poem, review the background in the unit introduction.

Listen.

To fully appreciate a poem, you must listen to it. Try reading the poem aloud. Pay attention to its rhythms and to the repetition of certain sounds. Consider how they contribute to the mood and meaning of the work.

As you read "The Love Song of J. Alfred Prufrock," look at the notes along the side of each page. They demonstrate how to apply these strategies.

The Love Song of J. Alfred Prufrock

T. S. Eliot

S'io credessi che mia risposta fosse
a persona che mai tornasse al mondo,
questa fiamma staria senza più scosse.
Ma per ciò che giammai di questo fondo
non tornò vivo alcun, s'i'odo il vero,
senza tema d'infamia ti rispondo.[1]

Let us go then, you and I,
When the evening is spread out against the sky
Like a patient etherized[2] upon a table;
Let us go, through certain half-deserted streets,
5   The muttering retreats
Of restless nights in one-night cheap hotels
And sawdust restaurants with oyster-shells:
Streets that follow like a tedious argument
Of <u>insidious</u> intent
10 To lead you to an overwhelming question . . .
Oh, do not ask, "What is it?"
Let us go and make our visit.

In the room the women come and go
Talking of Michelangelo.[3]

> Who is the "I" referred to in this line? Is it the poet, T. S. Eliot, or a character in the poem? The poem's title provides a clue to **identifying the poem's speaker,** J. Alfred Prufrock.

---

1. *S'io credessi . . . ti rispondo:* The epigraph is a passage from Dante's *Inferno,* in which one of the damned, upon being requested to tell his story, says: "If I believed my answer were being given to someone who could ever return to the world, this flame (his voice) would shake no more. But since no one has ever returned alive from this depth, if what I hear is true, I will answer you without fear of disgrace."
2. etherized (ē´ thə rīzd) *v.*: Anesthetized with ether.
3. Michelangelo (mī´ kəl an´ jə lō): A famous Italian artist and sculptor (1475–1564).

◆ Build Vocabulary

insidious (in sid´ ē əs) *adj.*: Secretly treacherous

Moonlight, Dovehouse Street, Chelsea, Algernon Newton, Fine Art Society, London

▶ **Critical Viewing** In what ways does this painting reflect aspects of the poem? [**Analyze**]

15   The yellow fog that rubs its back upon the window-panes,
      The yellow smoke that rubs its muzzle on the window-panes,
      Licked its tongue into the corners of the evening,
      Lingered upon the pools that stand in drains,
      Let fall upon its back the soot that falls from chimneys,
20   Slipped by the terrace, made a sudden leap,
      And seeing that it was a soft October night,
      Curled once about the house, and fell asleep.

      And indeed there will be time⁴
      For the yellow smoke that slides along the street
25   Rubbing its back upon the window-panes;
      There will be time, there will be time
      To prepare a face to meet the faces that you meet;
      There will be time to murder and create,
      And time for all the works and days⁵ of hands
30   That lift and drop a question on your plate;
      Time for you and time for me,
      And time yet for a hundred indecisions,
      And for a hundred visions and revisions.
      Before the taking of a toast and tea.

35   In the room the women come and go
      Talking of Michelangelo.

> **Relate the structure of the poem to its meaning** by recognizing that these eight lines are part of a single sentence describing the actions of the fog.

---

4. there will be time: Echoes the narrator's plea in English poet Andrew Marvell's "To His Coy Mistress": "Had we but world enough and time . . ."
5. works and days: Ancient Greek poet Hesiod wrote a poem about farming called "Works and Days."

And indeed there will be time
To wonder, "Do I dare?" and, "Do I dare?"
Time to turn back and descend the stair,
40 With a bald spot in the middle of my hair—
(They will say: "How his hair is growing thin!")
My morning coat, my collar mounting firmly to the chin,
My necktie rich and modest, but asserted by a simple pin—
(They will say: "But how his arms and legs are thin!")
45 Do I dare
Disturb the universe?
In a minute there is time
For decisions and revisions which a minute will reverse.

For I have known them all already, known them all—
50 Have known the evenings, mornings, afternoons,
I have measured out my life with coffee spoons;
I know the voices dying with a dying fall
Beneath the music from a farther room.
    So how should I presume?

55 And I have known the eyes already, known them all—
The eyes that fix you in a formulated phrase,
And when I am formulated, sprawling on a pin,
When I am pinned and wriggling on the wall,
Then how should I begin
60 To spit out all the butt-ends of my days and ways?
    And how should I presume?

And I have known the arms already, known them all—
Arms that are braceleted and white and bare
(But in the lamplight, downed with light brown hair!)
65 Is it perfume from a dress
That makes me so digress?
Arms that lie along a table, or wrap about a shawl.
    And should I then presume?
    And how should I begin?

    . . . . . .

70 Shall I say, I have gone at dusk through narrow streets
And watched the smoke that rises from the pipes
Of lonely men in shirt-sleeves, leaning out of windows? . . .

I should have been a pair of ragged claws
Scuttling across the floors of silent seas.[6]

    . . . . . .

---

6. I should . . . seas: In Shakespeare's *Hamlet*, the hero, Hamlet, mocks the aging Lord Chamberlain, Polonius, saying, "You yourself, sir, should be old as I am, if like a crab you could go backward" (II.ii. 205–206).

◆ Build Vocabulary

digress (dī gres´) *v.*: Depart temporarily from the main subject

Respond emotionally to the speaker's indecisiveness and self-consciousness. Do you empathize with him or not?

Engage your senses by imagining the sounds of "voices dying" and music coming "from a farther room." They suggest that Prufrock feels removed from other people.

To help you understand the speaker's feelings, you might **paraphrase** lines 55–61 in these words: "I know what it feels like to have people inspect and discuss me like an insect on display in a collection. I feel exposed, helpless, and unable to explain myself."

75 And the afternoon, the evening, sleeps so peacefully!
    Smoothed by long fingers,
    Asleep . . . tired . . . or it <u>malingers</u>,
    Stretched on the floor, here beside you and me.
    Should I, after tea and cakes and ices,
80 Have the strength to force the moment to its crisis?
    But though I have wept and fasted, wept and prayed,
    Though I have seen my head (grown slightly bald) brought in
        upon a platter,[7]
    I am no prophet—and here's no great matter;
    I have seen the moment of my greatness flicker,
85 And I have seen the eternal Footman[8] hold my coat, and
        snicker.
    And in short, I was afraid.

    And would it have been worth it, after all,
    After the cups, the marmalade, the tea,
    Among the porcelain, among some talk of you and me,
90 Would it have been worth while,
    To have bitten off the matter with a smile,
    To have squeezed the universe into a ball
    To roll it towards some overwhelming question.
    To say: "I am Lazarus,[9] come from the dead,
95 Come back to tell you all. I shall tell you all"—
    If one, settling a pillow by her head,
        Should say: "That is not what I meant at all.
        That is not it, at all."

    And would it have been worth it, after all,
100 Would it have been worth while,
    After the sunsets and the dooryards and the sprinkled streets,
    After the novels, after the teacups, after the skirts that trail
        along the floor—
    And this, and so much more?—
    It is impossible to say just what I mean!
105 But as if a magic lantern[10] threw the nerves in patterns on a
        screen:
    Would it have been worth while
    If one, settling a pillow or throwing off a shawl,
    And turning toward the window, should say:

---

7. **head . . . platter:** A reference to the prophet John the Baptist, whose head was delivered on a platter to Salome as a reward for her dancing (Matthew 14:1–11).

8. **eternal Footman:** Death.

9. **Lazarus** (laz´ ə rəs): Lazarus is resurrected from the dead by Jesus in John 11:1–44.

10. **magic lantern:** An early device used to project images on a screen.

◆ **Build Vocabulary**

malingers (mə liŋ´ gərz) v.: Pretends to be ill

meticulous (mə tik´ yŏŏ ləs) adj.: Extremely careful about details

obtuse (äb tŏŏs´) adj.: Slow to understand or perceive

"That is not it at all,
110   That is not what I meant, at all."

      .   .   .   .   .   .

      No! I am not Prince Hamlet, nor was meant to be;
      Am an attendant lord, one that will do
      To swell a progress,[11] start a scene or two,
      Advise the prince; no doubt, an easy tool,
115   Deferential, glad to be of use,
      Politic, cautious, and <u>meticulous</u>;
      Full of high sentence,[12] but a bit <u>obtuse</u>;
      At times, indeed, almost ridiculous—
      Almost, at times, the Fool.

120   I grow old . . . I grow old . . .
      I shall wear the bottoms of my trousers rolled.

      Shall I part my hair behind? Do I dare to eat a peach?
      I shall wear white flannel trousers, and walk upon the beach.
      I have heard the mermaids singing, each to each.

125   I do not think that they will sing to me.

      I have seen them riding seaward on the waves
      Combing the white hair of the waves blown back
      When the wind blows the water white and black.

      We have lingered in the chambers of the sea
130   By sea-girls wreathed with seaweed red and brown
      Till human voices wake us, and we drown.

---

11. To swell a progress: To add to the number of people in a parade or scene from a play.
12. Full of high sentence: Speaking in a very ornate manner, often offering advice.

> **Listen** to the musical quality of line 130. Notice how the soft "s" sounds mimic the rhythmic sound of ocean waves.

Guide for Responding

◆ *Literature and Your Life*

Reader's Response What do you mostly feel for Prufrock: pity or irritation? Why? What advice would you give him if he were your friend?

Thematic Focus In what way does Prufrock represent many modern people?

Journal Writing How do the particular disillusionments and discontents of our present age affect you as an individual? Explore your answer in a journal entry.

☑ Check Your Comprehension

1. What time of day is it when the poem begins?
2. What is the weather like?
3. In roughly what stage of life is Prufrock?
4. To which character from Shakespeare does Prufrock unfavorably compare himself?
5. At the end of the poem, whom does Prufrock hear singing?

Guide for Responding (continued)

◆ Critical Thinking

INTERPRET

1. What does the opening quotation from Dante's *Inferno* suggest about the content of the poem that follows? **[Interpret]**
2. Prufrock, who is on his way to a tea party, is trying to raise the courage to tell a woman of his love for her. How does he convey his apprehension and uncertainty in lines 23–48? **[Analyze]**
3. (a) What feelings about the other guests he expects to find at the party does Prufrock express in lines 49–69? (b) How does he expect to be treated by the other guests? **[Interpret]**
4. (a) In lines 87–109, how does Prufrock convey the fact that he has decided not to express his love? (b) How does he justify his decision? **[Analyze]**
5. (a) Contrast the vision at the end of the poem with the images at the beginning. (b) How does the final line suggest that reality has intruded on Prufrock's thoughts? **[Compare and Contrast; Interpret]**

EVALUATE

6. Toward the end of the poem, Prufrock labels himself "almost ridiculous." Explain whether you believe his self-assessment is accurate. **[Assess]**

APPLY

7. When Eliot writes that the mermaids, who represent beauty and happiness, will not sing for Prufrock, what might he be suggesting about his entire generation? **[Generalize]**

◆ Literary Focus

DRAMATIC MONOLOGUE

Although Prufrock's thoughts are presented in a sometimes disjointed and confusing stream and he says little about the actual circumstances and events of his life, Eliot's **dramatic monologue** does build a detailed portrait of the speaker's personality.

1. What can you infer about Prufrock's outlook on life from the images he uses in lines 1–12?
2. How does the monologue reveal that Prufrock sees himself as a man divided in two parts?
3. (a) Do you think Prufrock has ever been in a successful relationship? (b) How do you know?

◆ Reading Strategy

STRATEGIES FOR READING POETRY

Review the strategies outlined for reading poetry.

1. What is suggested by the image of the "yellow fog" described in lines 15–22?
2. How does the structure of the poem signal that Prufrock is jumping to a new thought in the lines "In the room the women come and go / Talking of Michelangelo."
3. Paraphrase the line, "And I have seen the eternal Footman hold my coat, and snicker."

◆ Build Vocabulary

USING THE PREFIX *di-*

Each of the following sentences includes a word that contains the prefix *di-*, meaning "away" or "apart." Decide whether each is true or false.

1. A path *diverges* if it branches off.
2. When you *divide* something, you join its parts.
3. When you are *diverted,* your attention is focused.
4. A *diverse* menu features many similar foods.

USING THE WORD BANK

On your paper, write the letter of the word that is the best synonym of the first word.

1. insidious: (a) innocent, (b) wealthy, (c) dangerous
2. digress: (a) wander, (b) contain, (c) hesitate
3. malingers: (a) fakes, (b) studies, (c) boasts
4. meticulous: (a) messy, (b) absurd, (c) careful
5. obtuse: (a) wide, (b) stupid, (c) friendly

◆ Grammar and Style

ADJECTIVAL MODIFIERS

Eliot creates vivid images in his poems by using a variety of phrases and clauses to modify nouns.

Practice Copy each sentence below. Underline the adjectival modifier, and circle the noun it modifies.

1. The cups full of tea sat on the tray.
2. The guests talking in the next room were gossiping about J. Alfred Prufrock.
3. People who secretly disliked each other chatted politely.
4. The hostess announced it was time to serve tea.

Build Your Portfolio

Idea Bank

Writing

1. **Letter** Imagine that an aged J. Alfred Prufrock finally summons the courage to tell the woman he loves of his feelings. Write a letter to her in which he explains why he hid his feelings for so long.

2. **Character Analysis** Write an analysis of Prufrock's character in which you describe his personal and physical qualities. How does he appear to others? How does he perceive himself?

3. **Allusions Essay** The poem contains several allusions—references to other literary, historic, religious, or mythological people or events. Identify two allusions and research their origins. Use your findings to write an essay in which you interpret what each means within the context of the poem.

Speaking and Listening

4. **Oral Interpretation** Read the poem aloud for the class as Prufrock might have spoken it. Lead a class discussion about your interpretation. Did anyone notice anything new about the poem as a result of hearing it? **[Performing Arts Link]**

5. **Role Play** With a fellow student, role-play a talk-show host's interview with Prufrock. Explore the reasons for Prufrock's poor self-esteem, and try to build his self-image. **[Media Link]**

Projects

6. **Report** Modernism has had a lasting effect on art, literature, and popular culture. Research the movement and its impact, and present your findings in a report. **[Social Studies Link]**

7. **Art Exhibit** Locate reproductions of artworks produced around the same time as "Prufrock." Create a classroom exhibit of works that share the poem's themes, images, or moods. **[Art Link]**

Writing Mini-Lesson

A Day-in-the-Life Monologue

Through J. Alfred Prufrock's dramatic monologue, we learn much about the character's daily life—how he passed his days taking tea with people he disliked and who cared little for him. Create your own dramatic monologue describing a typical day in the life of a character—either one from another literary work or one of your own creation. Focus on conveying the character's personality and capturing his or her observations about life. Remember that it is your character, not you, who is speaking.

Writing Skills Focus: Consistent Point of View

To make your dialogue believable, you must maintain a **consistent point of view** by conveying all of your information from the point of view of the individual who is supposed to be talking. Be careful not to slip into your own voice; relate all of the events as the character would perceive them. Any information you include should fit within the context of
- what the character would see and know
- how he or she would feel about the events
- how she or he would use language

Prewriting Jot down notes on your character's age, personality, occupation, place of origin, and so on. Then imagine what that character would do on a typical day. Think about how you might reveal his or her personality through the description of those events.

Drafting Describe the character's day in her or his own words. Portray events as the character would perceive them, and avoid using language or statements inconsistent with his or her point of view.

Revising Does the monologue consistently reflect only your character's point of view? Does it reveal anything about your character's personality? Refer to your prewriting notes to guide your revisions.

Guide for Interpreting

Ezra Pound *(1885–1972)*

More than any other poet of his day, Ezra Pound inspired the dramatic changes in American poetry that characterized the Modern Age. Pound's insistence that writers "make it new" led many poets to discard the forms, techniques, and ideas of the past and to experiment with new approaches to poetry.

Pound influenced the work of the noted Irish poet William Butler Yeats and that of many American writers, including T. S. Eliot, William Carlos Williams, H. D., Marianne Moore, and Ernest Hemingway— a "who's who" of the literary voices of the age. Pound spent most of his life in Europe, where he became a vital part of the Modernist movement. He is perhaps best remembered, however, for his role in the development of Imagism, a literary movement that included H. D., Williams, and Moore.

Despite his preoccupation with originality and inventiveness, Pound's work often drew upon the poetry of ancient cultures. Many of his poems are filled with literary and historical allusions, which can make the poems difficult to interpret without having the appropriate background information.

After 1920, Pound focused his efforts on writing *The Cantos,* a long poetic sequence in which he expresses his beliefs, reflects upon history and politics, and alludes to a variety of foreign languages and literatures. In all, he produced 116 cantos of varying quality.

Fall From Grace

In 1925, Pound settled in Italy. Motivated by the mistaken belief that a country governed by a powerful dictator was the most conducive environment for the creation of art, Pound became an outspoken supporter of Italian dictator Benito Mussolini during World War II. In 1943, the American government indicted Pound for treason; in 1945, he was arrested by American troops and imprisoned. After being flown back to the United States in 1945, he was judged psychologically unfit to stand trial and was confined to a hospital for the criminally insane. There he remained until 1958, when he was released due largely to the efforts of the literary community. He returned to Italy, where he lived until his death.

William Carlos Williams *(1883–1963)*

Unlike his fellow Imagists, William Carlos Williams spent most of his life in the United States, where he pursued a double career as a poet and a pediatrician in New Jersey. He felt that his experiences as a doctor helped provide him with inspiration as a poet, crediting medicine for his ability to "gain entrance to . . . the secret gardens of the self."

Although his father was English and his mother Puerto Rican, Williams was enamored of American language and life. He rejected the views of his college friend, Ezra Pound, who believed in using allusions to history, religion, and ancient literature. Williams focused instead on capturing the essence of modern American life by depicting a variety of ordinary people, objects, and experiences using current, everyday language.

The Poetry of Daily Life

In volumes such as *Spring and All* (1923) and *In the American Grain* (1925), Williams captured the essence of American life by using commonplace objects and experiences in writing his poetry. He avoided presenting explanations, remarking that a poet should deal in "No ideas but in things"—concrete images that speak for themselves, evoking emotions and ideas.

Williams continued to write even after his failing health forced him to give up his medical practice. In 1963, he received a Pulitzer Prize for *Pictures from Breughel and Other Poems,* his final volume of poetry.

The Imagist Poets

H. D. (Hilda Doolittle) *(1886–1961)*

In 1913, when Ezra Pound re-shaped three of Hilda Doolittle's poems and submitted them to *Poetry* magazine under the name "H. D., Imagiste," the Imagist movement was born. The publication of the poems also served to launch the successful career of the young poet, who continued to publish under the name H. D. throughout her life.

Born in Pennsylvania, Doolittle was only fifteen when she first met Ezra Pound, who was studying at the University of Pennsylvania. In 1911, Doolittle moved to London and renewed her acquaintance with Pound. She married a close friend of his, English poet Richard Aldington, but the marriage failed during World War I when Aldington left to fight in France. Doolittle remained a short while in London, where she became a leader of the Imagist group. She returned to the United States and settled in California , where she remained for a year before going back to England. In 1921, she moved to Switzerland, where she lived until her death.

Classically Inspired Like the Greek lyrics that she so greatly admired, H. D.'s early poems were brief, precise, and direct. Often emphasizing light, color, and physical textures, she created vivid, emotive images. She also abandoned traditional rhythmical patterns, instead creating innovative musical rhythms in her poetry.

In 1925, almost all of H. D.'s early poems were gathered in *Collected Poems,* a volume that also contained her translations from the *Odyssey* and from the Greek poet Sappho. She also wrote a play, *Hippolytus Temporizes,* which appeared in 1927, and two prose works: *Palimpsest* (1926) and *Hedylus* (1928). During the later stages of her career, she focused on writing longer works, including an epic poem. H. D. is best remembered, however, for her early Imagist poetry.

◆ Background for Understanding

LITERATURE: THE IMAGIST MOVEMENT

Imagism was a literary movement established in the early 1900's by Ezra Pound and other poets. As the name suggests, the Imagists concentrated on the direct presentation of images, or word pictures. An Imagist poem expressed the essence of an object, person, or incident, without providing explanations. Through the spare, clean presentation of an image, the Imagists hoped to evoke an emotional response—they hoped to freeze a single moment in time and to capture the emotions of that moment. To accomplish this purpose, the Imagists used the language of everyday speech, carefully choosing each word and avoiding unnecessary words. In addition, they also shied away from traditional poetic patterns, focusing instead on creating new, musical rhythms in their poetry.

The Imagists were strongly influenced by traditional Chinese and Japanese poetry. Many Imagist poems bear a close resemblance to the Japanese verse forms of haiku and tanka. The haiku consists of three lines of five, seven, and five syllables. The tanka consists of five lines of five, seven, five, seven, and five syllables. Like Imagist poems, haiku and tanka generally evoke an emotional response through the presentation of a single image or a pair of contrasting images.

The Imagist movement was short-lived, lasting only until about 1918. However, for many years that followed, the poems of Pound, Williams, H. D., and other Imagists continued to influence the works of other poets, including Wallace Stevens, T. S. Eliot, and Hart Crane.

Guide for Interpreting (continued)

◆ Literature and Your Life

CONNECT YOUR EXPERIENCE

You may know what it's like to have a song stick in your mind for hours, but have you ever had an *image* lodge there? The poems you're about to read capture in words some of the striking images that lodged in the minds and emotions of the Imagists.

Journal Writing Think of an image that you find striking—a skyscraper, a shiny new car, sunset, a pizza hot from the oven. List sensory details that vividly convey this image. What emotions do you associate with the image?

THEMATIC FOCUS: FACING TROUBLED TIMES

The first decades of the twentieth century were times of great change in the social and literary worlds. How do these works reflect a new and unique way of seeing both poetry and everyday life?

◆ Literary Focus

IMAGIST POETRY

Imagist poems focus on evoking emotion and sparking the reader's imagination through the vivid presentation of a limited number of images. "In a Station of the Metro," for example, presents just two images, and consists of only two lines and fourteen words. The words were chosen with extreme precision, however. They paint a vivid picture of each image and prompt the reader to consider the meaning of each word and to think about the connection between the two images. Few poems have ever been written that convey so much meaning in so few words.

◆ Grammar and Style

CONCRETE AND ABSTRACT NOUNS

A **concrete noun** names something that can be perceived with one or more of the five senses. An **abstract noun** names something that cannot be seen, heard, smelled, tasted, or touched. By their very nature, Imagist poems tend to include more concrete than abstract nouns. For instance, there are thirteen nouns in the first stanza of "The River-Merchant's Wife." Two of these—*dislike* and *suspicion*—are abstract, whereas the remainder—words such as *hair*, *forehead*, and *gate*—are concrete nouns.

◆ Reading Strategy

ENGAGE YOUR SENSES

These poems are filled with vivid imagery—words or phrases that appeal to one or more of the five senses. As you encounter each image, **engage your senses**—experience in your mind the sights, sounds, smells, tastes, and physical sensations associated with the image. Recreating these sensations will enrich your enjoyment and understanding of the work.

While you might think of images as being primarily visual, many appeal to more than one sense. For example, you can almost see and feel the thickness of the air as H. D. calls on the wind in "Heat": "Cut the heat— / plow through it, / turning it on either side / of your path."

◆ Build Vocabulary

FORMS OF *APPEAR*

Ezra Pound uses the word *apparition* in his description of people standing in a train station. This noun is based on the verb *appear*, meaning "to come into sight or into being" or "to become understood." What do you think *apparition* means?

WORD BANK

Before you read, preview this list of words from the poems.

> voluminous
> dogma
> apparition

A Few Don'ts by an

IMAGISTE[1]

Ezra Pound

An "Image" is that which presents an intellectual and emotional complex in an instant of time. I use the term "complex" rather in the technical sense employed by the newer psychologists, such as Hart, though we might not agree absolutely in our application.

It is the presentation of such a "complex" instantaneously which gives that sense of sudden liberation; that sense of freedom from time limits and space limits; that sense of sudden growth, which we experience in the presence of the greatest works of art.

It is better to present one Image in a life-time than to produce voluminous works.

All this, however, some may consider open to debate. The immediate necessity is to tabulate A LIST OF DON'TS for those beginning to write verses. But I can not put all of them into Mosaic negative.[2]

To begin with, consider the three rules recorded by Mr. Flint,[3] . . . not as dogma—never consider anything as dogma—but as

---

1. Imagiste: French for *Imagist*.
2. Mosaic negative: Refers to the ten commandments presented by Moses to the Israelites in the Old Testament of the Bible. Many of the commandments are in the negative and begin with the words "Thou shalt not . . ."
3. the three rules recorded by Mr. Flint: English Imagist poet Frank Stuart Flint noted that Imagist poets adhered to the following three rules or guidelines.
1. Direct treatment of the "thing," whether subjective or objective.
2. To use absolutely no word that did not contribute to the presentation.
3. As regarding rhythm: to compose in sequence of the musical phrase, not in sequence of a metronome.

▲ **Critical Viewing** How might an Imagist describe the scene depicted in this portrait of Ezra Pound? [**Synthesize**]

the result of long contemplation, which, even if it is some one else's contemplation, may be worth consideration. . . .

LANGUAGE

Use no superfluous word, no adjective, which does not reveal something.

Don't use such an expression as "dim lands *of peace.*" It dulls the image. It mixes an abstraction with the concrete. It comes from the writer's not realizing that the natural object is always the *adequate* symbol.

Go in fear of abstractions. Don't retell in mediocre verse what has already been done in good prose. Don't think any intelligent person is going to be deceived when you try to shirk all the difficulties of the unspeakably difficult art of good prose by chopping your composition into line lengths. . . .

Don't imagine that the art of poetry is any simpler than the art of music, or that you can please the expert before you have spent at least as much effort on the art of verse as the average piano teacher spends on the art of music. . . .

RHYTHM AND RHYME

. . . Don't imagine that a thing will "go" in verse just because it's too dull to go in prose.

Don't be "viewy"—leave that to the writers of pretty little philosophic essays. Don't be descriptive; remember that the painter can describe a landscape much better than you can, and that he has to know a deal more about it.

When Shakespeare talks of the "Dawn in russet mantle clad" he presents something which the painter does not present. There is in this line of his nothing that one can call description; he presents. . . .

Don't chop your stuff into separate *iambs.*[4] Don't make each line stop dead at the end, and then begin every next line with a heave. Let the beginning of the next line catch the rise of the rhythm wave, unless you want a definite longish pause.

In short, behave as a musician, a good musician, when dealing with that phase of your art which has exact parallels in music. The same laws govern, and you are bound by no others. . . .

A rhyme must have in it some slight element of surprise if it is to give pleasure; it need not be bizarre or curious, but it must be well used if used at all. . . .

Don't mess up the perception of one sense by trying to define it in terms of another. This is usually only the result of being too lazy to find the exact word. To this clause there are possibly exceptions.

The first three simple proscriptions[5] will throw out nine-tenths of all the bad poetry now accepted as standard and classic; and will prevent you from many a crime of production. . . .

---

4. **iambs** (ī′amz′) *n.*: Metrical feet consisting of two syllables, the first unaccented, the other accented.

5. **The first three simple proscriptions:** Reference to Flint's three rules outlined in footnote #3.

Guide for Responding

◆ Literature and Your Life

Reader's Response What is your reaction to Ezra Pound's ideas about great poetry?

Thematic Focus Why might you expect that new literary movements develop during periods of societal change?

☑ Check Your Comprehension

1. How did the Imagists measure the success of a poetic career?
2. What do the Imagists consider preferable to abstractions?
3. Summarize Pound's attitude toward adjectives.
4. With which other art does Pound compare the art of poetry?

◆ Critical Thinking

INTERPRET

1. Why do you think Pound preferred a list of "don'ts" to a list of "do's"? **[Speculate]**
2. Name at least two stated or implied differences between prose and poetry, according to Pound. **[Interpret]**
3. (a) Does Pound consider Shakespeare's image of "Dawn in russet mantle clad" as an example of description or presentation? (b) According to Pound, how are the two different? **[Distinguish]**

EVALUATE

4. Do you think following Pound's rules would make it easier or more difficult to write poetry? Explain. **[Evaluate]**

The River-Merchant's Wife: A Letter

Ezra Pound

While my hair was still cut straight across my forehead
I played about the front gate, pulling flowers.
You came by on bamboo stilts, playing horse,
You walked about my seat, playing with blue plums.
5   And we went on living in the village of Chokan:[1]
Two small people, without dislike or suspicion.

At fourteen I married My Lord you.
I never laughed, being bashful.
Lowering my head, I looked at the wall.
10 Called to, a thousand times, I never looked back.

At fifteen I stopped scowling,
I desired my dust to be mingled with yours
Forever and forever and forever.
Why should I climb the lookout?

15 At sixteen you departed,
You went into far Ku-to-yen,[2] by the river of swirling eddies,
And you have been gone five months.
The monkeys make sorrowful noise overhead.

You dragged your feet when you went out.
20 By the gate now, the moss is grown, the different mosses,
Too deep to clear them away!
The leaves fall early this autumn, in wind.
The paired butterflies are already yellow with August
Over the grass in the West garden;
25 They hurt me. I grow older.
If you are coming down through the narrows of the river Kiang,

Please let me know beforehand,
And I will come out to meet you
   As far as Cho-fu-Sa.[3]

By Rihaku

---

1. **Chokan** (chō´ kän´): A suburb of Nanking, a city in the People's Republic of China.
2. **Ku-to-yen** (kōō´ tō´ yen´): An island in the Yangtze (yäng´ tsē) River.
3. **Cho-fu-Sa** (chō´ fōō´ sä´): A beach along the Yangtze River, several hundred miles from Nanking.

▼ **Critical Viewing** How does the mood of this drawing mirror the mood of "The River-Merchant's Wife: A Letter"? **[Analyze]**

Landscape Album in Various Styles, Ch'a Shih-piao, The Cleveland Museum of Art

In a Station of the Metro[1]

Ezra Pound

The apparition of these faces in the crowd;
Petals on a wet, black bough.

_____

1. **Metro:** The Paris subway.

◆ **Build Vocabulary**

apparition (ap´ ə rish´ ən) *n*.: The act of appearing or becoming visible

Guide for Responding

◆ *Literature and Your Life*

Reader's Response Of all the images contained in these two poems, which did you find the most striking? Why?

Thematic Focus What troubled times does the river-merchant's wife face?

☑ **Check Your Comprehension**

1. Summarize the events in the life of the river-merchant's wife.

2. Describe in your own words the setting of "In a Station of the Metro."

◆ **Critical Thinking**

1. (a) How did the river-merchant's wife feel at the time of her marriage? (b) How have her feelings for her husband changed since then? **[Analyze]**

2. (a) How does she feel about her husband's absence? (b) How do the descriptions of the animals and insects reflect her feelings? **[Analyze]**

3. What does the comparison Pound makes in "In a Station of the Metro" suggest about how society affects individuality? **[Interpret]**

EXTEND

4. Many cultures have practiced the custom of arranged marriages. What are its potential benefits and drawbacks? **[Social Studies Link]**

The Red Wheelbarrow

William Carlos Williams

so much depends
upon

a red wheel
barrow

5   glazed with rain
water

beside the white
chickens.

The Great Figure

William Carlos Williams

Among the rain
and lights
I saw the figure 5
in gold
5   on a red
fire truck
moving
tense
unheeded
10   to gong clangs
siren howls
and wheels rumbling
through the dark city.

The Figure 5 in Gold, Charles Demuth, Metropolitan Museum of Art

▲ **Critical Viewing** Artist Charles Demuth created this work of art to accompany his friend Williams's poem. How does his illustration convey the energy and clamor of "gong clangs / siren howls / and wheels rumbling / through the dark city"? **[Connect]**

This Is Just to Say

I have eaten
the plums
that were in
the icebox
5   and which
you were probably
saving
for breakfast

Forgive me
10 they were delicious
so sweet
and so cold

William Carlos Williams

Guide for Responding

◆ Literature and Your Life

Reader's Response Which of these three poems evokes the strongest emotional response in you? Why?

Thematic Focus How is everyday life transformed in Williams's poetry?

Journal Writing Choose another food to take the place of "the plums" in line two of "This Is Just to Say" and revise the poem accordingly. Is your new poem more or less effective than the original?

☑ Check Your Comprehension

1. To what sense do the images in "The Red Wheelbarrow" directly appeal?
2. What detail is the focus of the speaker's experience of the fire truck?
3. What is the intention of the speaker in "This Is Just to Say"?

◆ Critical Thinking

INTERPRET

1. In your view, *what* depends on the red wheelbarrow? **[Speculate]**
2. In "The Great Figure," what might Williams be saying about (a) beauty? (b) modern life? **[Interpret]**
3. (a) Why is the incident in "This Is Just to Say" important to the speaker? (b) How do lines 10–12 reveal its importance? **[Infer, Analyze]**

APPLY

4. How would you describe the philosophy of life suggested by "This Is Just to Say"? **[Synthesize]**

EXTEND

5. Imagine that Williams had been a painter, not a poet. Describe the kinds of subjects he might have chosen to paint. **[Art Link]**

Pear Tree H. D.

Silver dust
lifted from the earth,
higher than my arms reach,
you have mounted,
5   O silver,
higher than my arms reach
you front us with great mass;

no flower ever opened
so staunch a white leaf,
10   no flower ever parted silver
from such rare silver;

O white pear,
your flower-tufts
thick on the branch
15   bring summer and ripe fruits
in their purple hearts.

Heat
H. D.

Overhanging Cloud in July, (1947/1959), Charles Burchfield, Watercolor on paper, 39 1/2" x 35 1/2", Collection of Whitney Museum of American Art, Purchase, with funds from the Friends of the Whitney Museum of American Art

O wind, rend open the heat,
cut apart the heat,
rend it to tatters.

5   Fruit cannot drop
through this thick air—
fruit cannot fall into heat
that presses up and blunts
the points of pears
and rounds the grapes.

10   Cut the heat—
plow through it,
turning it on either side
of your path.

◀ **Critical Viewing** Does this painting capture the oppressive heat of a humid summer day as effectively as the poem does? Explain. **[Evaluate]**

Guide for Responding

◆ Literature and Your Life

Reader's Response How do these two poems by H. D. make you feel?

Thematic Focus In the world presented in "Heat," are troubles natural or man-made?

Journal Writing What images do you associate with summer? Jot down your ideas in a journal entry.

☑ Check Your Comprehension

1. What is the "silver dust" referred to in the first stanza of "Pear Tree"?
2. According to the speaker of "Heat," how is wind potentially stronger than heat?

◆ Critical Thinking

INTERPRET
1. In "Pear Tree," in what sense is the silver dust "lifted from the earth"? **[Interpret]**
2. (a) What time of year is the speaker describing in "Pear Tree"? (b) How is this information conveyed? **[Infer, Analyze]**
3. What specific type of heat is the speaker in "Heat" describing? **[Interpret]**
4. How does H. D. create the impression that heat is almost a solid substance? **[Analyze]**

APPLY
5. H. D. uses the color silver several times. What associations do you have with this color? **[Relate]**

Guide for Responding (continued)

◆ Reading Strategy

ENGAGE YOUR SENSES

By **engaging your senses** to fully experience the images created by a writer, you can deepen your involvement in a literary work. For instance, experiencing the range of sensations brought to life in "The Red Wheelbarrow" may trigger a range of associations from experiences with rainstorms to memories of a childhood.

1. What other senses, besides sight, can you engage to recreate the image of "Petals on a wet, black bough"? Explain.
2. Give examples of two passages in "The River-Merchant's Wife" where you were able to engage the sense of smell.
3. List each of the images in "The Great Figure" and identify the sense or senses to which each appeals.

◆ Literary Focus

IMAGIST POETRY

Imagism was a literary movement that focused on presenting unadorned images in poetry. The Imagists used common language, which emphasized the creation of new poetic rhythms. They chose words with great precision in the belief that a single, well-crafted image could spark readers' associations and evoke powerful emotions.

1. Based on what you've learned of Imagism, does "The River-Merchant's Wife: A Letter" qualify as a purely Imagist poem? Why or why not?
2. How does Pound's choice of the word *apparition*—which is commonly used to describe a ghostly figure—to mean *appearance* contribute to the emotional impact of the image of "In a Station of the Metro"?
3. What types of feelings do H.D.'s images evoke in "Heat"?
4. Use your understanding of "A Few Don'ts by an Imagiste" to explain whether you agree or disagree with this comment about H. D. made by poet and critic Louis Untermeyer: "She was the only one who steadfastly held to the letter as well as the spirit of [the Imagist] *credo*."

◆ Build Vocabulary

USING FORMS OF *APPEAR*

Several common English words are forms of the word *appear*. Complete each of the following sentences with the correct word from the box below.

apparent   appearance   apparition

1. He made a brief ___?___ at the awards dinner—just long enough to pick up his trophy and say a few words.
2. When midnight found the toddlers still running around the house, it became ___?___ that the babysitter was no longer in control.
3. The ___?___ of a face at the window nearly stopped her heart with fear.

USING THE WORD BANK

On your paper, write the letter of the best synonym for the first word.

1. dogma: (a) doctrine, (b) legality, (c) statement
2. voluminous: (a) loud, (b) arrogant, (c) comprehensive
3. apparition: (a) suspicion, (b) vision, (c) face

◆ Grammar and Style

CONCRETE AND ABSTRACT NOUNS

A **concrete noun** names a physical thing that can be perceived with one of the five senses. An **abstract noun** names something that cannot be seen, heard, felt, tasted, or touched.

Practice On your paper, label the italicized noun(s) in each passage as *concrete* or *abstract*.

1. Don't use such an expression as "dim lands of *peace*."
2. The *leaves* fall early this autumn, in *wind*.
3. Among the *rain* and lights I saw the figure 5 in gold on a red firetruck moving tense unheeded to gong *clangs* siren howls and wheels rumbling through the dark *city*.
4. Cut the *heat*—plow through it, turning it on either side of your *path*.

Looking at Style Explain why you'd expect to find mainly concrete nouns in an Imagist poem.

Build Your Portfolio

Idea Bank

Writing

1. **Description** Critic Louis Untermeyer claims that in "Heat," H. D. goes beyond describing heat; rather, she presents "the effect of it." Write a description that captures the effect of heat, cold, or some other weather condition. **[Science Link]**

2. **Poem** Capture the essence of an object, person, or incident in a brief Imagist poem of your own. Use language that is precise and suggestive.

3. **Critical Essay** Select one of the poems you have just read, and write a critical essay explaining how it meets—or fails to meet—each of the key guidelines for Imagist poetry set forth in Pound's "A Few Don'ts."

Speaking and Listening

4. **Informal Debate** Discussing "The Red Wheelbarrow," critic Roy Harvey Pearce comments: "At its worst this is togetherness in a chickenyard. At its best it is an exercise in the creation of the poetic out of the anti-poetic." To which view do you subscribe? Defend your assessment of Williams's poem in an informal debate with classmates.

5. **Oral Interpretation** What type of music elicits the feel of a hot summer day? Select a piece of music that suggests the effect of heat and play it as you read "Heat" aloud. **[Music Link]**

Projects

6. **Art** Draw or paint the way *you* envision the image of "In a Station of the Metro." **[Art Link]**

7. **Poetry Collection** Explore the poetry of Pound, Williams, H. D., and other Imagists. Create a collection of your favorite Imagist poems. Accompany each poem with a brief explanation of why you chose it. Share copies with the class.

Writing Mini-Lesson

An Editor's Review of Manuscript

Magazine editors (such as Ezra Pound was) receive manuscripts from writers. An editor reviews each manuscript, makes a decision about publishing it, and sends a letter of acceptance or rejection to the writer. Often these letters contain constructive criticism about the work's merits and weaknesses. Imagine that you are a literary magazine editor who has just received a manuscript from an Imagist poet. Critique the poems of Pound, Williams, or H. D., in a letter explaining why you will or will not publish this work. Make your points clearly and concisely in a professional manner.

Writing Skills Focus: Brevity and Clarity

A business letter—like most examples of good prose—should present ideas with **brevity and clarity**. Here are a few tips to keep your letter precise and to the point:

- Avoid general, vague nouns. Instead, use specific, concrete words that express ideas exactly.
- Eliminate unnecessary words or sentences.
- Present your ideas in a logical sequence—don't jump from point to point.

Prewriting Decide to which of the three poets you will address your review, then reread his or her poems. As you read, take notes on the strengths and weaknesses of each poem, noting relevant passages.

Drafting Draft a letter that briefly and clearly explains why you will or will not publish the poems. Discuss what you particularly liked or disliked about each poem, citing examples from the work. Be simple, honest, and kind in your analysis.

Revising Trim any excess words, sharpen your word choices, and then read your letter aloud as if you were the recipient. Do you understand exactly what the editor thought of your writing?

Guide for Interpreting

F. Scott Fitzgerald (1896–1940)

When you open the pages of F. Scott Fitgerald's books, you're transported back in time to the Roaring 20's, a frantic decade unlike any other in American history. Fitzgerald was able to successfully capture the glittering, materialistic, and often self-destructive lifestyle of the time because he actually lived it. Like many of his characters, he led a fast-paced life and longed to attain the wealth and social status of the upper class.

A Quick Rise to Fame Francis Scott Key Fitzgerald was born in St. Paul, Minnesota, into a family with high social aspirations but little money. He entered Princeton University in 1913, where he began leading the type of high profile social life for which he'd become famous in the 1920's.

His first novel, *This Side of Paradise* (1920), published shortly after his discharge from army service, was an instant success. With the fame and wealth the novel brought him, Fitzgerald was able to persuade Zelda Sayre, a lovely southern belle with whom he had fallen in love while in the army, to be his wife. Together, they blazed an extravagant trail across the societies of both New York and Europe, mingling with rich and famous artists and aristocrats and spending money recklessly. Despite the couple's pleasure-seeking lifestyle, Fitzgerald remained a productive writer, publishing dozens of short stories. In 1925 he published his most successful novel, *The Great Gatsby*, the story of a self-made man whose dreams of love and social acceptance lead to scandal and corruption and ultimately end in tragedy. The novel displayed Fitzgerald's fascination with and growing distrust of the wealthy society he had embraced.

Fortunes Turn After the 1929 stock-market crash, Fitzgerald's world began to crumble. His wife suffered a series of nervous breakdowns, his reputation as a writer declined, and financial setbacks forced him to seek work as a Hollywood screenwriter. Despite these setbacks, however, he managed to produce many more short stories and a fine second novel, *Tender Is the Night (1934)*. Focusing on the decline of a young American psychiatrist following his marriage to a wealthy patient, the novel reflects Fitzgerald's growing awareness of the tragedy that can result from an obsession with wealth and social status.

Fitzgerald was in the midst of writing a novel about a Hollywood film mogul, *The Last Tycoon*, when he died of a heart attack in 1940.

◆ Background for Understanding

CULTURE: FITZGERALD AS THE VOICE OF THE JAZZ AGE

After World War I—a war that politicians had once promised would end war forever but turned out to be the bloodiest war in history—it seemed to many that modern advances had created more problems rather than solving those that already existed. Frustrated and disappointed, Americans were desperate for a good time. They roared into the 1920's at breakneck pace, overthrowing rules about clothing and personal style. Shorter dresses, sporty automobiles, and dancing until dawn were just a few of the hallmarks of the age.

Another feature of the time was the quest for personal fulfillment through material wealth. The restricted world of America's established wealthy families had begun to open its doors. Making money—rather than inheriting it—became honorable and admired. Yet there was something frantic and despairing about the urgent quest for pleasure and money. F. Scott Fitzgerald's work and life reflected both the gaiety and the emptiness of this time—named "The Jazz Age" after the free-flowing music that dominated the time.

Winter Dreams

◆ Literature and Your Life

CONNECT YOUR EXPERIENCE

What you long for isn't always what's good for you. The little voice inside your head tells you that someone or something—as much as you want it—isn't right for you, but you still go on wanting.

Journal Writing Think of an episode in your own life when your desire for something left you caught in a struggle between reason and emotion. Write a dialogue that tells what the two voices in your head were saying to you.

THEMATIC FOCUS: FACING TROUBLED TIMES

The battle between the voice of reason and the voice of desire sometimes leaves scars. In this story of destructive love, a young man, Dexter Green, defies convention and sensibility to pursue his romantic ideal—a woman who embodies the wealth and social standing for which he yearns. Consider how Green's devotion to that ideal comes at the cost of his own happiness.

◆ Literary Focus

CHARACTERIZATION

As Dexter and Judy's story unfolds, you'll feel you have known them a long time. Fitzgerald creates this feeling of intimacy through **characterization**—the revelation of characters' personalities. In **direct characterization,** the writer directly states the traits of the characters. In **indirect characterization,** characters' traits are revealed through their own words, thoughts, and actions and by what other characters say to or about them. Notice how Fitzgerald brings the personalities of Dexter and Judy into sharp focus through a variety of methods of characterization.

◆ Grammar and Style

DASHES

Dashes (—), which create a longer, more emphatic pause than commas, signal information that interrupts the flow of text. As you'll discover in this story, dashes tend to draw readers' attention to the information they set off. Look at this example:

When he was twenty-three, Mr. Hart—*one of the gray-haired men who liked to say "Now there's a boy"*—gave him a guest card to the Sherry Island Golf Club for a weekend.

◆ Reading Strategy

DRAW CONCLUSIONS ABOUT CHARACTERS

F. Scott Fitzgerald paints a vivid picture of Dexter's and Judy's personalities but sometimes leaves it up to you to draw conclusions about their motivations and emotions. To **draw conclusions,** combine information from the story with your own knowledge of human behavior. Look at the example:

Dexter stood perfectly still . . . if he moved forward a step his stare would be in her line of vision—if he moved backward he would lose his full view of her face.

If you've ever wanted to hide your own interest in someone but couldn't stop looking, you can conclude from his behavior that Dexter is enthralled by Judy's beauty.

◆ Build Vocabulary

WORD ROOTS: -somn-

The word *somnolent* in this story is built on the word root -somn-, which means "sleep." Knowing its meaning is related to sleep can help you define *somnolent*—it means "sleepy or likely to induce sleep"—and other words that contain -somn-.

WORD BANK

Before you read, preview this list of words.

fallowness
preposterous
fortuitous
sinuous
mundane
poignant
pugilistic
somnolent

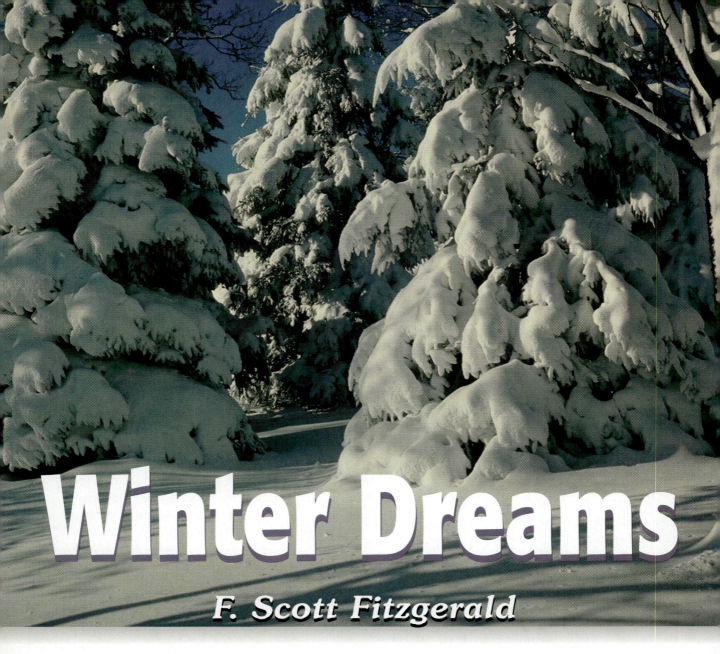

Winter Dreams

F. Scott Fitzgerald

I

Some of the caddies were poor as sin and lived in one-room houses with a neurasthenic[1] cow in the front yard, but Dexter Green's father owned the second best grocery store in Black Bear—the best one was "The Hub," patronized by the wealthy people from Sherry Island—and Dexter caddied only for pocket money.

In the fall when the days became crisp and gray, and the long Minnesota winter shut down like the white lid of a box, Dexter's skis moved over the snow that hid the fairways of the golf course. At these times the country gave him a feeling of profound melancholy—it offended him that the links should lie in enforced <u>fallowness</u>,

---

1. **neurasthenic** (noor´ əs then´ ik) *adj.*: Here, weak, tired.

haunted by ragged sparrows for the long season. It was dreary, too, that on the tees where the gay colors fluttered in summer there were now only the desolate sandboxes knee deep in crusted ice. When he crossed the hills the wind blew cold as misery, and if the sun was out he tramped with his eyes squinted up against the hard dimensionless glare.

In April the winter ceased abruptly. The snow ran down into Black Bear Lake scarcely tarrying for the early golfers to brave the season with red and black balls. Without elation, without an interval of moist glory, the cold was gone. Dexter knew that there was something dismal about this Northern spring, just as he knew there was something gorgeous about the fall. Fall made him clinch his hands and tremble and repeat idiotic sentences to himself, and make brisk abrupt gestures of command to imaginary audiences and armies. October filled him with hope which November raised to a sort of ecstatic triumph, and in this mood the fleeting brilliant impressions of the summer at Sherry Island were ready grist to his mill. He became a golf champion and defeated Mr. T. A. Hedrick in a marvelous match played a hundred times over the fairways of his imagination, a match each detail of which he changed about untiringly—sometimes he won with almost laughable ease, sometimes he came up magnificently from behind. Again, stepping from a Pierce-Arrow automobile, like Mr. Mortimer Jones, he strolled frigidly into the lounge of the Sherry Island Golf Club—or perhaps, surrounded by an admiring crowd, he gave an exhibition of fancy diving from the springboard of the club raft. . . . Among those who watched him in openmouthed wonder was Mr. Mortimer Jones.

And one day it came to pass that Mr. Jones—himself and not his ghost—came up to Dexter with tears in his eyes and said that Dexter was the——best caddy in the club, and wouldn't he decide not to quit if Mr. Jones made it worth his while, because every other——caddy in the club lost one ball a hole for him—regularly——

"No, sir," said Dexter decisively, "I don't want to caddy any more." Then, after a pause: "I'm too old."

"You're not more than fourteen. Why the devil did you decide just this morning that you wanted to quit? You promised that next week you'd go over to the state tournament with me."

"I decided I was too old."

Dexter handed in his "A Class" badge, collected what money was due him from the caddy master, and walked home to Black Bear Village.

"The best——caddy I ever saw," shouted Mr. Mortimer Jones over a drink that afternoon. "Never lost a ball! Willing! Intelligent! Quiet! Honest! Grateful!"

The little girl who had done this was eleven—beautifully ugly as little girls are apt to be who are destined after a few years to be inexpressibly lovely and bring no end of misery to a great number of men. The spark, however, was perceptible. There was a general ungodliness in the way her lips twisted down at the corners when she smiled, and in the—Heaven help us!—in the almost passionate quality of her eyes. Vitality is born early in such women. It was utterly in evidence now, shining through her thin frame in a sort of glow.

She had come eagerly out on to the course at nine o'clock with a white linen nurse and five small new golf clubs in a white canvas bag which the nurse was carrying. When Dexter first saw her she was standing by the caddy house, rather ill at ease and trying to conceal the fact by engaging her nurse in an obviously unnatural conversation graced by startling and irrelevant grimaces from herself.

"Well, it's certainly a nice day, Hilda," Dexter heard her say. She drew down the corners of her mouth, smiled, and glanced furtively around, her eyes in transit falling for an instant on Dexter.

Then to the nurse:

"Well, I guess there aren't very many people out here this morning, are there?"

The smile again—radiant, blatantly artificial—convincing.

"I don't know what we're supposed to do now," said the nurse looking nowhere in particular.

"Oh, that's all right. I'll fix it up."

Dexter stood perfectly still, his mouth slightly ajar. He knew that if he moved forward a step his stare would be in her line of vision— if he moved backward he would lose his full view of her face. For a moment he had not realized how young she was. Now he remembered having seen her several times the year before— in bloomers.

Suddenly, involuntarily, he laughed, a short abrupt laugh—then, startled by himself, he turned and began to walk quickly away.

"Boy!"

Dexter stopped.

"Boy——"

Beyond question he was addressed. Not only that, but he was treated to that absurd smile, that preposterous smile—the memory of which at least a dozen men were to carry into middle age.

"Boy, do you know where the golf teacher is?"

"He's giving a lesson."

"Well, do you know where the caddy master is?"

"He isn't here yet this morning."

"Oh." For a moment this baffled her. She stood alternately on her right and left foot.

"We'd like to get a caddy," said the nurse. "Mrs. Mortimer Jones sent us out to play golf, and we don't know how without we get a caddy."

Here she was stopped by an ominous glance from Miss Jones, followed immediately by the smile.

"There aren't any caddies here except me," said Dexter to the nurse, "and I got to stay here in charge until the caddy master gets here."

"Oh."

Miss Jones and her retinue now withdrew, and at a proper distance from Dexter became involved in a heated conversation, which was concluded by Miss Jones taking one of the clubs and hitting it on the ground with violence. For further emphasis she raised it again and was about to bring it down smartly upon the nurse's bosom, when the nurse seized the club and twisted it from her hands.

"You little mean old *thing*!" cried Miss Jones wildly.

Another argument ensued. Realizing that the elements of the comedy were implied in the scene, Dexter several times began to laugh, but each time restrained the laugh before it reached audibility. He could not resist the monstrous conviction that the little girl was justified in beating the nurse.

The situation was resolved by the <u>fortuitous</u> appearance of the caddy master, who was appealed to immediately by the nurse.

"Miss Jones is to have a little caddy, and this one says he can't go."

"Mr. McKenna said I was to wait here till you came," said Dexter quickly.

"Well, he's here now." Miss Jones smiled cheerfully at the caddy master. Then she dropped her bag and set off at a haughty mince toward the first tee.

"Well?" The caddy master turned to Dexter. "What you standing there like a dummy for? Go pick up the young lady's clubs."

"I don't think I'll go out today," said Dexter.

"You don't——"

"I think I'll quit."

The enormity of his decision frightened him. He was a favorite caddy, and the thirty dollars a month he earned through the summer were not to be made elsewhere around the lake. But he had received a strong emotional shock,

◆ **Literary Focus**

What methods of characterization does Fitzgerald use to introduce the character of Judy Jones?

◆ **Build Vocabulary**

preposterous (pri päs´ tər əs) *adj.*: Ridiculous
fortuitous (fôr tōō´ ə təs) *adj.*: Fortunate

and his perturbation required a violent and immediate outlet.

It is not so simple as that, either. As so frequently would be the case in the future, Dexter was unconsciously dictated to by his winter dreams.

II

Now, of course, the quality and the seasonability of these winter dreams varied, but the stuff of them remained. They persuaded Dexter several years later to pass up a business course at the State university—his father, prospering now, would have paid his way—for the precarious advantage of attending an older and more famous university in the East, where he was bothered by his scanty funds. But do not get the impression, because his winter dreams happened to be concerned at first with musings on the rich, that there was anything merely snobbish in the boy. He wanted not association with glittering things and glittering people—he wanted the glittering things themselves. Often he reached out for the best without knowing why he wanted it—and sometimes he ran up against the mysterious denials and prohibitions in which life indulges. It is with one of those denials and not with his career as a whole that this story deals.

He made money. It was rather amazing. After college he went to the city from which Black Bear Lake draws its wealthy patrons. When he was only twenty-three and had been there not quite two years, there were already people who liked to say: "Now *there's* a boy—" All about him rich men's sons were peddling bonds precariously, or investing patrimonies precariously, or plodding through the two dozen volumes of the "George Washington Commercial Course," but Dexter borrowed a thousand dollars on his college degree and his confident mouth, and bought a partnership in a laundry.

It was a small laundry when he went into it, but Dexter made a specialty of learning how the English washed fine woolen golf stockings without shrinking them, and within a year he was catering to the trade that wore knickerbockers. Men were insisting that their

◆ **Reading Strategy**
What conclusion can you draw about Dexter from his high standards for his laundry business?

Shetland hose and sweaters go to his laundry, just as they had insisted on a caddy who could find golf balls. A little later he was doing their wives' lingerie as well—and running five branches in different parts of the city. Before he was twenty-seven he owned the largest string of laundries in his section of the country. It was then that he sold out and went to New York. But the part of his story that concerns us goes back to the days when he was making his first big success.

When he was twenty-three Mr. Hart—one of the gray-haired men who like to say "Now there's a boy"—gave him a guest card to the Sherry Island Golf Club for a weekend. So he signed his name one day on the register, and that afternoon played golf in a foursome with Mr. Hart and Mr. Sandwood and Mr. T. A. Hedrick. He did not consider it necessary to remark that he had once carried Mr. Hart's bag over this same links, and that he knew every trap and gully with his eyes shut—but he found himself glancing at the four caddies who trailed them, trying to catch a gleam or gesture that would remind him of himself, that would lessen the gap which lay between his present and his past.

It was a curious day, slashed abruptly with fleeting, familiar impressions. One minute he had the sense of being a trespasser—in the next he was impressed by the tremendous superiority he felt toward Mr. T. A. Hedrick, who was a bore and not even a good golfer any more.

Then, because of a ball Mr. Hart lost near the fifteenth green, an enormous thing happened. While they were searching the stiff grasses of the rough there was a clear call of "Fore!" from behind a hill in their rear. And as they all turned abruptly from their search a bright new ball sliced abruptly over the hill and caught Mr. T. A. Hedrick in the abdomen.

"By Gad!" cried Mr. T. A. Hedrick, "they ought to put some of these crazy women off the course. It's getting to be outrageous."

A head and a voice came up together over the hill:

"Do you mind if we go through?"

"You hit me in the stomach!" declared Mr. Hedrick wildly.

"Did I?" The girl approached the group of men. "I'm sorry. I yelled 'Fore!' "

Her glance fell casually on each of the men—then scanned the fairway for her ball.

Golf Course–California, 1917, George Wesley Bellows, Cincinnati Art Museum

▲ **Critical Viewing** Golf was once a game reserved for the wealthy. It is on a golf course like the one in this painting that Dexter meets Judy for the first time, then again nine years later. How might this setting have affected Dexter's perception of Judy? [**Analyze**]

"Did I bounce into the rough?"

It was impossible to determine whether this question was ingenuous or malicious. In a moment, however, she left no doubt, for as her partner came up over the hill she called cheerfully:

"Here I am! I'd have gone on the green except that I hit something."

As she took her stance for a short mashie shot, Dexter looked at her closely. She wore a blue gingham dress, rimmed at throat and shoulders with a white edging that accentuated her tan. The quality of exaggeration, of thinness, which had made her passionate eyes and down-turning mouth absurd at eleven, was gone now. She was arrestingly beautiful. The color in her cheeks was centered like the color in a picture—it was not a "high" color, but a sort of fluctuating and feverish warmth, so shaded that it seemed at any moment it would recede and disappear. This color and the mobility of her mouth gave a continual impression of flux, of intense life, of passionate vitality—balanced only partially by the sad luxury of her eyes.

She swung her mashie impatiently and without interest, pitching the ball into a sand pit on the other side of the green. With a quick, insincere smile and a careless "Thank you!" she went on after it.

"That Judy Jones!" remarked Mr. Hedrick on the next tee, as they waited—some moments—for her to play on ahead. "All she needs is to be turned up and spanked for six months and then to be married off to an old-fashioned cavalry captain."

"My God, she's good looking!" said Mr. Sandwood, who was just over thirty.

"Good looking!" cried Mr. Hedrick contemptuously, "she always looks as if she wanted to be kissed! Turning those big coweyes on every calf in town!"

It was doubtful if Mr. Hedrick intended a reference to the maternal instinct.

"She'd play pretty good golf if she'd try," said Mr. Sandwood.

"She has no form," said Mr. Hedrick solemnly.

"She has a nice figure," said Mr. Sandwood.

"Better thank the Lord she doesn't drive a swifter ball," said Mr. Hart, winking at Dexter.

Later in the afternoon the sun went down with a riotous swirl of gold and varying blues and scarlets, and left the dry, rustling night of Western summer. Dexter watched from the veranda of the golf club, watched the even overlap of the waters in the little wind, silver molasses under the harvest moon. Then the moon held a finger to her lips and the lake became a clear pool, pale and quiet. Dexter put on his bathing suit and swam out to the farthest raft, where he stretched dripping on the wet canvas of the springboard.

There was a fish jumping and a star shining and the lights around the lake were gleaming. Over on a dark peninsula a piano was playing the songs of last summer and of summers before that—songs from *Chin-Chin* and *The Count of Luxemburg* and *The Chocolate Soldier*[2]—and because the sound of a piano over a stretch of water had always seemed beautiful to Dexter he lay perfectly quiet and listened.

The tune the piano was playing at that moment had been gay and new five years before when Dexter was a sophomore at college. They had played it at a prom once when he could not afford the luxury of proms, and he had stood outside the gymnasium and listened. The sound of the tune precipitated in him a sort of ecstasy and it was with that ecstasy he viewed what happened to him now. It was a mood of intense appreciation, a sense that, for once, he was magnificently attuned to life and that everything about him was radiating a brightness and a glamor he might never know again.

A low, pale oblong detached itself suddenly from the darkness of the Island, spitting forth the reverberate sound of a racing motorboat. Two white streamers of cleft water rolled themselves out behind it and almost immediately the boat was beside him, drowning out the hot tinkle of the piano in the drone of its spray. Dexter raising himself on his arms was aware of a figure standing at the wheel, of two dark eyes regarding him over the lengthening space of water—then the boat had gone by and was sweeping in an immense and purposeless circle of spray round and round in the middle of the lake. With equal eccentricity one of the circles flattened out and headed back toward the raft.

"Who's that?" she called, shutting off her motor. She was so near now that Dexter could see her bathing suit, which consisted apparently of pink rompers.

The nose of the boat bumped the raft, and as the latter tilted rakishly he was precipitated toward her. With different degrees of interest they recognized each other.

"Aren't you one of those men we played through this afternoon?" she demanded.

He was.

"Well, do you know how to drive a motorboat? Because if you do I wish you'd drive this one so I can ride on the surfboard behind. My name is Judy Jones"—she favored him with an absurd smirk—rather, what tried to be a smirk, for, twist her mouth as she might, it was not grotesque, it was merely beautiful—"and I live in a house over there on the Island, and in that house there is a man waiting for me. When he drove up at the door I drove out of the dock because he says I'm his ideal."

There was a fish jumping and a star shining and the lights around the lake were gleaming. Dexter sat beside Judy Jones and she explained how her boat was driven. Then she was in the water, swimming to the floating surfboard with a <u>sinuous</u> crawl. Watching her was without effort to the eye, watching a branch waving or a sea gull flying. Her arms, burned to butternut, moved sinuously among the dull platinum ripples, elbow appearing first, casting the forearm back with a cadence of falling water, then reaching out and down, stabbing a path ahead.

They moved out into the lake; turning, Dexter saw that she was kneeling on the low rear of the now uptilted surfboard.

"Go faster," she called, "fast as it'll go."

Obediently he jammed the lever forward and the white spray mounted at the bow. When he looked around again the girl was standing up on the rushing board, her arms spread wide, her eyes lifted toward the moon.

"It's awful cold," she shouted. "What's your name?"

He told her.

"Well, why don't you come to dinner tomorrow night?"

His heart turned over like the flywheel of the boat, and, for the second time, her casual whim gave a new direction to his life.

III

Next evening while he waited for her to come downstairs, Dexter peopled the soft deep summer room and the sun porch that opened from it with the men who had already loved Judy Jones. He knew the sort of men they were—the men who when he first went to college had entered from the great

---

2. ***Chin-Chin . . . The Chocolate Soldier***: Popular operettas of the time.

◆ **Build Vocabulary**

sinuous (sin´ yōo wəs) *adj.*: Moving in and out; wavy

prep schools with graceful clothes and the deep tan of healthy summers. He had seen that, in one sense, he was better than these men. He was newer and stronger. Yet in acknowledging to himself that he wished his children to be like them he was admitting that he was but the rough, strong stuff from which they eternally sprang.

When the time had come for him to wear good clothes, he had known who were the best tailors in America, and the best tailors in America had made him the suit he wore this evening. He had acquired that particular reserve peculiar to his university, that set it off from other universities. He recognized the value to him of such a mannerism and he had adopted it; he knew that to be careless in dress and manner required more confidence than to be careful. But carelessness was for his children. His mother's name had been Krimelich. She was a Bohemian of the peasant class and she had talked broken English to the end of her days. Her son must keep to the set patterns.

At a little after seven Judy Jones came downstairs. She wore a blue silk afternoon dress, and he was disappointed at first that she had not put on something more elaborate. This feeling was accentuated when, after a brief greeting, she went to the door of a butler's pantry and pushing it open called: "You can serve dinner, Martha." He had rather expected that a butler would announce dinner, that there would be a cocktail. Then he put these thoughts behind him as they sat down side by side on a lounge and looked at each other.

"Father and mother won't be here," she said thoughtfully.

He remembered the last time he had seen her father, and he was glad the parents were not to be here tonight—they might wonder who he was. He had been born in Keeble, a Minnesota village fifty miles farther north, and he always gave Keeble as his home instead of Black Bear Village. Country towns were well enough to come from if they weren't inconveniently in sight and used as footstools by fashionable lakes.

They talked of his university, which she had visited frequently during the past two years, and of the nearby city which supplied Sherry Island with its patrons,

and whither Dexter would return next day to his prospering laundries.

During dinner she slipped into a moody depression which gave Dexter a feeling of uneasiness. Whatever petulance she uttered in her throaty voice worried him. Whatever she smiled at—at him, at a chicken liver, at nothing—it disturbed him that her smile could have no root in mirth, or even in amusement. When the scarlet corners of her lips curved down, it was less a smile than an invitation to a kiss.

Then, after dinner, she led him out on the dark sun porch and deliberately changed the atmosphere.

"Do you mind if I weep a little?" she said.

"I'm afraid I'm boring you," he responded quickly.

"You're not. I like you. But I've just had a terrible afternoon. There was a man I cared about, and this afternoon he told me out of a clear sky that he was poor as a church mouse. He'd never even hinted it before. Does this sound horribly mundane?"

"Perhaps he was afraid to tell you."

"Suppose he was," she answered. "He didn't start right. You see, if I'd thought of him as poor—well, I've been mad about loads of poor men, and fully intended to marry them all. But in this case, I hadn't thought of him that way, and my interest in him wasn't strong enough to survive the shock. As if a girl calmly informed her fiancé that she was a widow. He might not object to widows, but——"

"Let's start right," she interrupted herself suddenly. "Who are you, anyhow?"

For a moment Dexter hesitated. Then:

"I'm nobody," he announced. "My career is largely a matter of futures."

"Are you poor?"

"No," he said frankly, "I'm probably making more money than any man my age in the Northwest. I know that's an obnoxious remark, but you advised me to start right."

There was a pause. Then she smiled and the corners of her mouth drooped and an al-

◆ **Literary Focus**
What does this conversation reveal to you about the personalities of Dexter and Judy?

◆ **Build Vocabulary**

mundane (mun dān´) *adj.*: Commonplace; ordinary

The Morning Sun, © 1920, Pauline Palmer, Rockford Art Museum

most imperceptible sway brought her closer to him, looking up into his eyes. A lump rose in Dexter's throat, and he waited breathless for the experiment, facing the unpredictable compound that would form mysteriously from the elements of their lips. Then he saw—she communicated her excitement to him, lavishly, deeply, with kisses that were not a promise but a fulfillment. They aroused in him not hunger demanding renewal but surfeit that would demand more surfeit . . . kisses that were like charity, creating want by holding back nothing at all.

It did not take him many hours to decide that he had wanted Judy Jones ever since he was a proud, desirous little boy.

IV

It began like that—and continued, with varying shades of intensity, on such a note right up to the denouement. Dexter surrendered a part of himself to the most direct and unprincipled personality with which he had ever come in contact. Whatever Judy wanted, she went after with the full pressure of her charm. There was no divergence of method, no jockeying for position or premeditation of effects—there was a very little mental side to any of her affairs. She simply made men conscious to the highest degree of her physical loveliness. Dexter had no desire to change her. Her deficiencies were knit up with a passionate energy that transcended and justified them.

When, as Judy's head lay against his shoulder that first night, she whispered, "I don't know what's the matter with me. Last night I thought I was in love with a man and tonight I think I'm in love with you——" it seemed to him a beautiful and romantic thing to say.

It was the exquisite excitability that for the moment he controlled and owned. But a week later he was compelled to view this same quality in a different light. She took him in her roadster to a picnic supper, and after supper she disappeared, likewise in her roadster, with another man. Dexter became enormously upset and was scarcely able to be decently civil to the other people present. When she assured him that she had not kissed the other man, he knew she was lying—yet he was glad that she had taken the trouble to lie to him.

He was, as he found before the summer ended, one of a varying dozen who circulated about her. Each of them had at one time been favored above all others—about half of them still basked in the solace of occasional sentimental revivals. Whenever one showed signs of dropping out through long neglect, she granted him a brief honeyed hour, which encouraged him to tag along for a year or so longer. Judy made these forays upon the helpless and defeated without malice, indeed half unconscious that there was anything mischievous in what she did.

When a new man came to town everyone dropped out—dates were automatically canceled.

The helpless part of trying to do anything about it was that she did it all herself. She was not a girl who could be "won" in the kinetic sense—she was proof against cleverness, she was proof against charm; if any of these assailed her too strongly she would immediately resolve the affair to a physical basis, and under the magic of her physical splendor the strong as well as the brilliant played her game and not their own. She was entertained only by the gratification of her desires and by the direct exercise of her own charm. Perhaps from so much youthful love, so many youthful lovers, she had come, in self-defense, to nourish herself wholly from within.

Succeeding Dexter's first exhilaration came restlessness and dissatisfaction. The helpless ecstasy of losing himself in her was opiate rather than tonic. It was fortunate for his work during the winter that those moments of ecstasy came infrequently. Early in their acquaintance it had seemed for a while that there was a deep and spontaneous mutual attraction—that first August, for example—three days of long evenings on her dusky veranda, of strange wan kisses through the late afternoon, in shadowy alcoves or behind the protecting trellises of the garden arbors, of mornings when she was fresh as a dream and almost shy at meeting him in the clarity of the rising day. There was all the ecstasy of an engagement about it, sharpened by his realization that there was no engagement. It was during those three days that, for the first time, he had asked her to marry him. She said "maybe some day," she said "kiss me," she said, "I'd like to marry you," she said "I love you"—she said—nothing.

The three days were interrupted by the arrival of a New York man who visited at her house for half September. To Dexter's agony, rumor engaged them. The man was the son of the president of a great trust company. But at the end of a month it was reported that Judy was yawning. At a dance one night she sat all evening in a motorboat with a local beau, while the New Yorker searched the club for her frantically. She told the local beau that she was bored with her visitor, and two days later he left. She was seen with him at the station, and it was reported that he looked very mournful indeed.

On this note the summer ended. Dexter was twenty-four, and he found himself increasingly in a position to do as he wished. He joined two clubs in the city and lived at one of them. Though he was by no means an integral part of the stag lines at these clubs, he managed to be on hand at dances where Judy Jones was likely to appear. He could have gone out socially as much as he liked—he was an eligible young man, now, and popular with downtown fathers. His confessed devotion to Judy Jones had rather solidified his position. But he had no social aspirations and rather despised the dancing men who were always on tap for the Thursday or Saturday parties and who filled in at dinners with the younger married set. Already he was playing with the idea of going East to New York. He wanted to take Judy Jones with him. No disillusion as to the world in which she had grown up could cure his illusion as to her desirability.

Remember that—for only in the light of it can what he did for her be understood.

◆ Reading Strategy
What does this observation reveal about the way in which Dexter regards Judy?

Eighteen months after he first met Judy Jones he became engaged to another girl. Her name was Irene Scheerer, and her father was one of the men who had always believed in Dexter. Irene was light-haired and sweet and honorable, and a little stout, and she had two suitors whom she pleasantly relinquished when Dexter formally asked her to marry him.

Summer, fall, winter, spring, another summer, another fall—so much he had given of his active life to the incorrigible lips of Judy Jones. She had treated him with interest, with encouragement, with malice, with indifference, with contempt. She had inflicted on him the innumerable little slights and indignities possible in such a case—as if in revenge for having ever cared for him at all. She had beckoned him and yawned at him and beckoned him again and he had responded often with bitterness and narrowed eyes. She had brought him ecstatic happiness and intolerable agony of spirit. She had caused him untold inconvenience and not a little trouble. She had insulted him, and she had ridden over him, and she had played his interest in her against his interest in his work—for fun. She had done everything to him except to criticize him—this she had not done—it seemed to him only because it might have sullied the utter indifference she manifested and sincerely felt toward him.

When autumn had come and gone again it occurred to him that he could not have Judy Jones. He had to beat this into his mind but he convinced himself at last. He lay awake at night for a while and argued it over. He told himself the trouble and the pain she had caused him, he enumerated her glaring deficiencies as a wife. Then he said to himself that he loved her, and after a while he fell asleep. For a week, lest he imagined her husky voice over the telephone or her eyes opposite him at lunch, he worked hard and late, and at night he went to his office and plotted out his years.

At the end of a week he went to a dance and cut in on her once. For almost the first time since they had met he did not ask her to sit out with him or tell her that she was lovely. It hurt him that she did not miss these things—that was all. He was not jealous when he saw that there was a new man tonight. He had been hardened against jealousy long before.

He stayed late at the dance. He sat for an hour with Irene Scheerer and talked about books and about music. He knew very little about either. But he was beginning to be master of his own time now, and he had a rather priggish[3] notion that he—the young and already fabulously successful Dexter Green—should know more about such things.

That was in October, when he was twenty-five. In January, Dexter and Irene became engaged. It was to be announced in June, and they were to be married three months later.

The Minnesota winter prolonged itself interminably, and it was almost May when the winds came soft and the snow ran down into Black Bear Lake at last. For the first time in over a year Dexter was enjoying a certain tran-

quility of spirit. Judy Jones had been in Florida, and afterward in Hot Springs, and somewhere she had been engaged, and somewhere she had broken it off. At first, when Dexter had definitely given her up, it had made him sad that people still linked them together and asked for news of her, but when he began to be placed at dinner next to Irene Scheerer people didn't ask him about her any more—they told him about her. He ceased to be an authority on her.

May at last. Dexter walked the streets at night when the darkness was damp as rain, wondering that so soon, with so little done, so much of ecstasy had gone from him. May one year back had been marked by Judy's poignant, unforgivable, yet forgiven turbulence—it had been one of those rare times when he fancied she had grown to care for him. That old penny's worth of happiness he had spent for this bushel of content. He knew that Irene would be no more than a curtain spread behind him, a hand moving among gleaming teacups, a voice calling to children . . . fire and loveliness were gone, the magic of nights and the wonder of the varying hours and seasons . . . slender lips, down-turning, dropping to his lips and bearing him up into a heaven of eyes . . . The thing was deep in him. He was too strong and alive for it to die lightly.

In the middle of May when the weather balanced for a few days on the thin bridge that led to deep summer he turned in one night at Irene's house. Their engagement was to be announced in a week now—no one would be surprised at it. And tonight they would sit together on the lounge at the University Club and look on for an hour at the dancers. It gave him a sense of solidity to go with her—she was so sturdily popular, so intensely "great."

He mounted the steps of the brownstone house and stepped inside.

"Irene," he called.

Mrs. Scheerer came out of the living room to meet him.

---

3. **priggish** (prig´ ish) *adj.*: Excessively proper and smug.

◆ **Build Vocabulary**

poignant (poin´ yənt) *adj.*: Sharply painful to the feelings

"Dexter," she said, "Irene's gone upstairs with a splitting headache. She wanted to go with you but I made her go to bed."

"Nothing serious, I——"

"Oh, no. She's going to play golf with you in the morning. You can spare her for just one night, can't you, Dexter?"

Her smile was kind. She and Dexter liked each other. In the living room he talked for a moment before he said good night.

Returning to the University Club, where he had rooms, he stood in the doorway for a moment and watched the dancers. He leaned against the doorpost, nodded at a man or two—yawned.

"Hello, darling."

The familiar voice at his elbow startled him. Judy Jones had left a man and crossed the room to him—Judy Jones, a slender enameled doll in cloth of gold: gold in a band at her head, gold in two slipper points at her dress's hem.

The fragile glow of her face seemed to blossom as she smiled at him. A breeze of warmth and light blew through the room. His hands in the pockets of his dinner jacket tightened spasmodically. He was filled with a sudden excitement.

"When did you get back?" he asked casually.

"Come here and I'll tell you about it."

She turned and he followed her. She had been away—he could have wept at the wonder of her return. She had passed through enchanted streets, doing things that were like provocative music. All mysterious happenings, all fresh and quickening hopes, had gone away with her, come back with her now.

She turned in the doorway.

"Have you a car here? If you haven't, I have."

"I have a coupé."

In then, with a rustle of golden cloth. He slammed the door. Into so many cars she had stepped—like this—like that—her back against the leather, so—her elbow resting on the door—waiting. She would have been soiled long since had there been anything to soil her—except herself—but this was her own self outpouring.

With an effort he forced himself to start the car and back into the street. This was nothing, he must remember. She had done this before, and he had put her behind him, as he would have crossed a bad account from his books.

He drove slowly downtown and, affecting abstraction, traversed the deserted streets of the business section, peopled here and there where a movie was giving out its crowd or where consumptive or pugilistic youth lounged in front of pool halls. The clink of glasses and the slap of hands on the bars issued from saloons, cloisters of glazed glass and dirty yellow light.

She was watching him closely and the silence was embarrassing, yet in this crisis he could find no casual word with which to profane the hour. At a convenient turning he began to zigzag back toward the University Club.

"Have you missed me?" she asked suddenly.

"Everybody missed you."

He wondered if she knew of Irene Scheerer. She had been back only a day—her absence had been almost contemporaneous with his engagement.

"What a remark!" Judy laughed sadly—without sadness. She looked at him searchingly. He became absorbed in the dashboard.

"You're handsomer than you used to be," she said thoughtfully. "Dexter, you have the most rememberable eyes."

He could have laughed at this, but he did not laugh. It was the sort of thing that was said to sophomores. Yet it stabbed at him.

"I'm awfully tired of everything, darling." She called everyone darling, endowing the endearment with careless, individual camaraderie.[4] "I wish you'd marry me."

The directness of this confused him. He should have told her now that he was going to marry another girl, but he could not tell her. He could as easily have sworn that he had never loved her.

"I think we'd get along," she continued, on the same note, "unless probably you've forgotten me and fallen in love with another girl."

Her confidence was obviously enormous. She had said, in effect, that she found such a thing

---

4. **camaraderie** (käm´ ə räd´ ər ē) *n*.: Warm, friendly feelings.

◆ *Literature and Your Life*

Like Dexter, have you ever kept quiet when you knew that telling the truth was the right thing to do?

impossible to believe, that if it were true he had merely committed a childish indiscretion—and probably to show off. She would forgive him, because it was not a matter of any moment but rather something to be brushed aside lightly.

"Of course you could never love anybody but me," she continued, "I like the way you love me. Oh, Dexter, have you forgotten last year?"

"No, I haven't forgotten."

"Neither have I!"

Was she sincerely moved—or was she carried along by the wave of her own acting?

"I wish we could be like that again," she said, and he forced himself to answer:

"I don't think we can."

"I suppose not. . . . I hear you're giving Irene Scheerer a violent rush."

There was not the faintest emphasis on the name, yet Dexter was suddenly ashamed.

"Oh, take me home," cried Judy suddenly; "I don't want to go back to that idiotic dance—with those children."

Then, as he turned up the street that led to the residence district, Judy began to cry quietly to herself. He had never seen her cry before.

The dark street lightened, the dwellings of the rich loomed up around them, he stopped his coupé in front of the great white bulk of the Mortimer Joneses' house, <u>somnolent</u>, gorgeous, drenched with the splendor of the damp moonlight. Its solidity startled him. The strong walls, the steel of the girders, the breadth and beam and pomp of it were there only to bring out the contrast with the young beauty beside him. It was sturdy to accentuate her slightness—as if to show what a breeze could be generated by a butterfly's wing.

He sat perfectly quiet, his nerves in wild clamor, afraid that if he moved he would find her irresistibly in his arms. Two tears had rolled down her wet face and trembled on her upper lip.

"I'm more beautiful than anybody else," she said brokenly, "why can't I be happy?" Her moist eyes tore at his stability— her mouth turned slowly downward with an exquisite sadness: "I'd like to marry you if you'll have me, Dexter. I suppose you think I'm not worth having, but I'll be so beautiful for you, Dexter."

A million phrases of anger, pride, passion, hatred, tenderness fought on his lips. Then a perfect wave of emotion washed over him, carrying off with it a sediment of wisdom, of convention, of doubt, of honor. This was his girl who was speaking, his own, his beautiful, his pride.

"Won't you come in?" He heard her draw in her breath sharply.

Waiting.

"All right," his voice was trembling, "I'll come in."

V

It was strange that neither when it was over nor a long time afterward did he regret that night. Looking at it from the perspective of ten years, the fact that Judy's flare for him endured just one month seemed of little importance. Nor did it matter that by his yielding he subjected himself to a deeper agony in the end and gave serious hurt to Irene Scheerer and to Irene's parents, who had befriended him. There was nothing sufficiently pictorial about Irene's grief to stamp itself on his mind.

Dexter was at bottom hard-minded. The attitude of the city on his action was of no importance to him, not because he was going to leave the city, but because any outside attitude on the situation seemed superficial. He was completely indifferent to popular opinion. Nor, when he had seen that it was no use, that he did not possess in himself the power to move fundamentally or to hold Judy Jones, did he bear any malice toward her. He loved her, and he would love her until the day he was too old for loving—but he could not have her. So he tasted the deep pain that is reserved only for the strong, just as he had tasted for a little while the deep happiness.

Even the ultimate falsity of the grounds upon which Judy terminated the engagement that she did not want to "take him away" from Irene—Judy who had wanted nothing else—did

---

◆ **Literary Focus**

How does this wistful remark add to Fitzgerald's portrait of Judy's character? Do you think Judy has changed?

◆ **Build Vocabulary**

pugilistic (pyo͞o′ jə lis′ tik) *adj.*: Looking for a fight

somnolent (säm′ nə lənt) *adj.*: Sleepy; drowsy

---

not revolt him. He was beyond any revulsion or any amusement.

He went East in February with the intention of selling out his laundries and settling in New York—but the war came to America in March and changed his plans. He returned to the West, handed over the management of the business to his partner, and went into the first officers' training camp in late April. He was one of those young thousands who greeted the war with a certain amount of relief, welcoming the liberation from webs of tangled emotion.

VI

This story is not his biography, remember, although things creep into it which have nothing to do with those dreams he had when he was young. We are almost done with them and with him now. There is only one more incident to be related here, and it happens seven years farther on.

It took place in New York, where he had done well—so well that there were no barriers too high for him. He was thirty-two years old, and, except for one flying trip immediately after the war, he had not been West in seven years. A man named Devlin from Detroit came into his office to see him in a business way, and then and there this incident occurred, and closed out, so to speak, this particular side of his life.

"So you're from the Middle West," said the man Devlin with careless curiosity. "That's funny—I thought men like you were probably born and raised on Wall Street. You know—wife of one of my best friends in Detroit came from your city. I was an usher at the wedding."

Dexter waited with no apprehension of what was coming.

"Judy Simms," said Devlin with no particular interest; "Judy Jones she was once."

"Yes, I knew her." A dull impatience spread over him. He had heard, of course, that she was married—perhaps deliberately he had heard no more.

"Awfully nice girl," brooded Devlin meaninglessly, "I'm sort of sorry for her."

"Why?" Something in Dexter was alert, receptive, at once.

"Oh, Lud Simms has gone to pieces in a way. I don't mean he ill-uses her, but he drinks and runs around——"

"Doesn't she run around?"

"No. Stays at home with her kids."

"Oh."

"She's a little too old for him," said Devlin.

"Too old!" cried Dexter. "Why, man, she's only twenty-seven."

He was possessed with a wild notion of rushing out into the streets and taking a train to Detroit. He rose to his feet spasmodically.

"I guess you're busy," Devlin apologized quickly. "I didn't realize——"

"No, I'm not busy," said Dexter, steadying his voice. "I'm not busy at all. Not busy at all. Did you say she was—twenty-seven? No, I said she was twenty-seven."

"Yes, you did," agreed Devlin dryly.

"Go on, then. Go on."

"What do you mean?"

"About Judy Jones."

Devlin looked at him helplessly.

"Well, that's—I told you all there is to it. He treats her like the devil. Oh, they're not going to get divorced or anything. When he's particularly outrageous she forgives him. In fact, I'm inclined to think she loves him. She was a pretty girl when she first came to Detroit. "

A pretty girl! The phrase struck Dexter as ludicrous.

"Isn't she—a pretty girl, anymore?"

"Oh, she's all right."

"Look here," said Dexter, sitting down suddenly. "I don't understand. You say she was a 'pretty girl' and now you say she's 'all right.' I don't understand what you mean—Judy Jones wasn't a pretty girl, at all. She was a great beauty. Why, I knew her. I knew her. She was ——"

Devlin laughed pleasantly.

"I'm not trying to start a row," he said. "I think Judy's a nice girl and I like her. I can't understand how a man like Lud Simms could fall madly in love with her, but he did." Then he added: "Most of the women like her."

Dexter looked closely at Devlin, thinking wildly that there must be a reason for this, some insensitivity in the man or some private malice.

"Lots of women fade just like *that*," Devlin snapped his fingers. "You must have seen it happen. Perhaps I've forgotten how pretty she was at her wedding. I've seen her so much since then, you see. She has nice eyes."

A sort of dullness settled down upon Dexter.

For the first time in his life he felt like getting very drunk. He knew that he was laughing loudly at something Devlin had said, but he did not know what it was or why it was funny. When, in a few minutes, Devlin went he lay down on his lounge and looked out the window at the New York skyline into which the sun was sinking in dull lovely shades of pink and gold.

He had thought that having nothing else to lose he was invulnerable at last—but he knew that he had just lost something more, as surely as if he had married Judy Jones and seen her fade away before his eyes.

The dream was gone. Something had been taken from him. In a sort of panic he pushed the palms of his hands into his eyes and tried to bring up a picture of the waters lapping on Sherry Island and the moonlit veranda, and gingham on the golf links and the dry sun and the gold color of her neck's soft down. And her mouth damp to his kisses and her eyes plaintive with melancholy and her freshness like new fine linen in the morning. Why, these things were no longer in the world! They had existed and they existed no longer.

For the first time in years the tears were streaming down his face. But they were for himself now. He did not care about mouth and eyes and moving hands. He wanted to care, and he could not care. For he had gone away and he could never go back any more. The gates were closed, the sun was gone down, and there was no beauty but the gray beauty of steel that withstands all time. Even the grief he could have borne was left behind in the country of illusion, of youth, of the richness of life, where his winter dreams had flourished.

"Long ago," he said, "long ago, there was something in me, but now that thing is gone. Now that thing is gone, that thing is gone. I cannot cry. I cannot care. That thing will come back no more."

Guide for Responding

◆ *Literature and Your Life*

Reader's Response Do you feel sorry for Judy? For Dexter? Why or why not?

Thematic Response How do Dexter's feelings for Judy dictate the course of his life?

Informal Debate Fitzgerald suggests that Dexter is destroyed by his "winter dreams." Stage an informal debate in which you make a case for or against the need for winter dreams.

☑ Check Your Comprehension

1. (a) What action does Dexter take as a result of his first meeting with Judy Jones? (b) What happens the second time they meet?
2. How does Judy behave during her romance with Dexter?
3. Why does Dexter become engaged to another woman but later break the engagement?
4. What happens to Dexter and Judy's relationship after he breaks his engagement with Irene?
5. How does Devlin shatter Dexter's image of Judy?

◆ Critical Thinking

INTERPRETING
1. What are Dexter's "winter dreams," and how does Judy fit into those dreams? **[Interpret]**
2. Find two examples in the story that demonstrate how Judy's casual decisions or behavior changes Dexter's life in important ways. **[Connect]**
3. What does the decision to become engaged to Irene symbolize for Dexter? **[Infer]**
4. (a) What does Judy represent to Dexter? (b) Why does Dexter keep loving Judy even after he has lost her? **[Analyze]**

EVALUATE
5. Are Dexter's values and ideals influenced by the times in which he lived, or would his feelings for Judy Jones have been the same in any era? Explain. **[Assess]**

APPLY
6. How might the story have been different if Dexter had married Judy? **[Modify]**

Guide for Responding (continued)

◆ Literary Focus

CHARACTERIZATION

Fitzgerald uses **characterization**—a variety of techniques that reveal characters' personalities—to paint multi-dimensional portraits of Judy and Dexter. We learn about Judy and Dexter through **direct characterization**—the narrator's comments about their personalities—as well as through **indirect characterization**—their own actions and words and other characters' reactions to them.

1. Cite at least two examples from the story of Fitzgerald's use of direct characterization to characterize Judy and Dexter.
2. Cite two examples of indirect characterization of Judy and Dexter, and explain what you learn from each example.
3. (a) In what ways are Dexter and Judy alike? (b) In what ways are they different? (c) Explain which details of characterization lead you to draw your conclusions.

◆ Build Vocabulary

USING THE WORD ROOT -somn-

The word root -somn- means "sleep." Using each of the words defined below, write a brief paragraph about a student who keeps nodding off in class because he or she can't sleep at night.

insomnia *n.*: Prolonged inability to sleep
somnolent *adj.*: Sleepy; drowsy
somniloquist *n.*: One who talks in his or her sleep
somnambulation *n.*: The action of walking while sleeping

USING THE WORD BANK

On a separate sheet of paper, write the letter of the word that is the best antonym of the given word.

1. **fallowness**   (a) activity   (b) emptiness
2. **preposterous**   (a) serious   (b) sarcastic
3. **fortuitous**   (a) wealthy   (b) cursed
4. **sinuous**   (a) straight   (b) slippery
5. **mundane**   (a) legal   (b) amazing
6. **poignant**   (a) dull   (b) moving
7. **pugilistic**   (a) tough   (b) peace-loving
8. **somnolent**   (a) alert   (b) hard

◆ Reading Strategy

DRAW CONCLUSIONS ABOUT CHARACTER

As you read, you **drew conclusions** about Judy and Dexter. You gathered details about their actions and words and, using your own knowledge of human behavior, read between the lines to infer emotions and motivations not directly stated. Now demonstrate what you have learned by writing an account of Dexter and Judy's last meeting. What did they say and how did they act as she broke off their engagement? Use the conclusions you have drawn to help you develop your descriptions of their behavior. Include dialogue in your account.

◆ Grammar and Style

DASHES

Fitzgerald makes abundant use of dashes to introduce asides that seem to compete for the reader's attention. These dashes reflect the frenetic competition for the spotlight that characterized the writer's life and times. In your writing, use dashes only occasionally for dramatic effect, to surprise, or to emphasize.

> **Dashes** are punctuation marks that set off information that interrupts the flow of a sentence. Dashes are stronger and more emphatic than commas.

Practice In your notebook, write the following sentences. Insert dashes where necessary to set off dramatic ideas or abrupt changes in thought.

1. Mr. Hart one of those golfers who like to yell *Fore!* at the top of their lungs gave him a guest card to a prestigious local golf club.
2. He was glad her parents were not there they might wonder who he was.
3. Whatever she smiled at at him, at a chicken liver, at nothing it disturbed him that her smile could have no root in mirth.
4. He had the notion that she and this was the really strange part actually had feelings for him.

Writing Application Write a brief description of someone you admire. Use dashes to set off a few pieces of information you want readers to notice.

Build Your Portfolio

Idea Bank

Writing

1. **Diary Entry** Fitzgerald never tells us what Judy thinks of or feels for Dexter. Write the diary entry she might have written to describe their meeting on the lake. What are her impressions?

2. **Résumé** Consider the skills and character traits Dexter demonstrates in the story. Then write a résumé that he might use to be considered for a management job. **[Career Link]**

3. **Essay** According to one critic, Fitzgerald's best work "caught not only the irresponsibility of the years following [World War I] but pointed also to the sources of personal and moral corruption implicit in a society based upon the social and moral prerogatives of wealth." Write an essay in which you demonstrate how this observation applies to "Winter Dreams."

Speaking and Listening

4. **Dialogue** Imagine that Dexter and Judy meet a month after the story's close. With a partner, write and perform the conversation they might have. **[Performing Arts Link]**

5. **Musical Interpretation** Select a song that might remind Dexter of his relationship with Judy. Play the song for the class, and discuss why it is appropriate. **[Music Link]**

Projects

6. **Montage** Create a montage of words and images that reflect the values, fads, and fashions of the "Roaring Twenties." **[Social Studies Link]**

7. **Report** Research the lives of F. Scott and Zelda Fitzgerald. Then write a report on the couple's relationship and lifestyle and how they may have influenced Fitzgerald's works.

Writing Mini-Lesson

Character Analysis

Dexter Green comes vividly to life because F. Scott Fitzgerald portrays him as a fully-rounded character with believable thoughts and feelings, strengths and weaknesses. Explore Dexter's behavior, motivations, and weak and strong traits in a character analysis. Support your ideas with specific examples from the story.

> ### Writing Skills Focus: Elaboration to Give Information
> **Elaborate** by providing information that supports your analysis of Dexter's personality:
> - After making general statements about the character's personality, elaborate with precise details from the story.
> - Describe Dexter's behavior with specific examples.
> - Paraphrase or quote exactly from the text to support your judgments of the character.
> - Identify Dexter's strengths and weaknesses, using the reactions of other characters to him.

Prewriting Scan the story for examples of Dexter's appearance, words, actions, and motivations. Note how he changes during the story and whether his actions seem heroic or simply foolish.

Drafting In your opening statement, name the author and title of the work, identify the character to be discussed, then grab readers' attention by stating your most important idea about the character. You might organize the rest of your analysis around strengths and weaknesses, addressing first one and then the other.

Revising Read your essay. Have you conveyed your opinion? Have you supported your view with elaboration? Where needed, add specific quotations or other details to support your points.

Guide for Interpreting

John Steinbeck *(1902–1968)*

No writer more vividly captures what it was like to live through the Great Depression of the 1930's than John Steinbeck.

His stories and novels, many of which are set in the agricultural region of Northern California where he grew up, capture the poverty, desperation, and social injustice experienced by many working class Americans during this bleak period in our nation's history. As in the works of Naturalist writers like Stephen Crane and Jack London, Steinbeck's characters struggle desperately against forces beyond their understanding or control. Many of his characters suffer tragic fates, yet they almost always manage to exhibit bravery and retain a sense of dignity throughout their struggles.

Modest Beginnings Steinbeck was born in Salinas, California, the son of a county official and a schoolteacher. By his late teens, he was already supporting himself by working as a laborer. After graduating from high school, he enrolled at Stanford University. He left before graduating, however, and spent the next five years drifting across the country, working as a fish hatcher, fruit picker, and apprentice painter. Through these experiences, Steinbeck discovered firsthand what it means to survive by manual labor.

Steinbeck also gathered material that he would later be able to use in his literary works to create authentic portraits of working-class life.

Even before he was paid for his words, Steinbeck always found time to write. However, he had little success as a writer until 1935 when he published *Tortilla Flat*, his third novel. Two years later, he earned widespread recognition and critical acclaim with *Of Mice and Men* (1937). This novel, which portrays two migrant workers whose dream of owning a farm ends in tragedy, became a best seller and was made into a Broadway play and a movie.

The Great American Novel

Steinbeck went on to write what is generally regarded as his finest novel. *The Grapes of Wrath* (1939) is the accurate and emotional story of the Joad family, Oklahoma farmers dispossessed of their land and forced to become migrant farmers in California. "The Turtle" is an excerpt from the opening pages of this novel which won the National Book Award and the Pulitzer Prize. The book established Steinbeck as one of the most highly regarded writers of his day.

Steinbeck produced several more successful works during his later years, including *Cannery Row* (1945), *The Pearl* (1947), *East of Eden* (1951), and *The Winter of Our Discontent* (1961). Steinbeck received the Nobel Prize for Literature in 1962.

◆ Background for Understanding

HISTORY: THE GREAT DEPRESSION

The Great Depression of the 1930's was a time of unparalleled financial hardship. In 1932 a quarter of Americans—at least 12 million—were out of work. One of many factors contributing to the Depression was a massive drought in Oklahoma. The drought was so bad that farmlands literally blew away in massive dust storms that sometimes lasted several days. Many farmers fled the land for the city, hoping to find relief away from nature's failure. This is the situation faced by the Joad family who, like the turtle in this piece, are repelled by a commercial world that cares nothing for them.

The Turtle

◆ Literature and Your Life

CONNECT YOUR EXPERIENCE

Sometimes a single event can seem to mirror all of life. For example, one long and complicated journey with many detours and wrong turns might be seen as representing the experience of growing up. As you read, think about how the small events in this story could reflect something much bigger about the times in which the story takes place.

Journal Writing Describe a past experience that seemed to reflect the way your life was going at the time. What qualities made the experience seem so loaded with meaning?

THEMATIC FOCUS: FACING TROUBLED TIMES

In this tale, a turtle perseveres in the face of many obstacles. As you move through the story, remember what you've read about the Joads and other Oklahoma farmers. How might the turtle's plight relate to their struggle in the Great Depression?

◆ Build Vocabulary

PREFIXES: pro-

In this story, Steinbeck uses the word *protruded*, which begins with the prefix *pro-*, meaning "forward." Knowing this meaning helps you to define the whole word *protruded*—"thrust forward"—and other words beginning with the prefix *pro-*.

WORD BANK

Preview this list of words from the story.

embankment
protruded

◆ Grammar and Style

PARALLEL STRUCTURE

Parallel structure—the expression of similar ideas in similar grammatical form—helps to emphasize key ideas and link similar concepts. In this story, Steinbeck uses parallel structure to draw attention to the details in his descriptions and to give equal weighting to these details. In this example he uses parallel infinitive phrases:

. . . the grass heads were heavy with oat beards *to catch on a dog's coat*, and foxtails *to tangle in a horse's fetlocks*, and clover burrs *to fasten in sheep's wool* . . .

◆ Literary Focus

THEME

John Steinbeck's story about a brief episode in a turtle's life conveys an important **theme,** or insight into life. An author's theme is rarely directly stated. Instead, it is revealed indirectly through the characters' comments and actions, the events in the plot, and the author's use of literary devices, such as symbols. Sometimes, even small details can serve an important role in conveying a theme.

◆ Reading Strategy

FIND CLUES TO THEME

The process of interpreting the theme of a story is almost like being a detective—you have to look carefully for **clues to the theme** in the writer's choice of details, in the comments that characters make, in the ways they react to one another, and so on. In a brief story like this one, each detail is especially important. For example, Steinbeck includes only slight descriptions of how two motorists react when they encounter the turtle. However, these brief descriptions are important clues to the theme. When you encounter such clues, ask yourself: What broader or underlying meaning do the clues suggest?

The Turtle

John Steinbeck

The concrete highway was edged with a mat of tangled, broken, dry grass, and the grass heads were heavy with oat beards to catch on a dog's coat, and foxtails to tangle in a horse's fetlocks, and clover burrs to fasten in sheep's wool; sleeping life waiting to be spread and dispersed, every seed armed with an appliance of dispersal, twisting darts and parachutes for the wind, little spears and balls of tiny thorns, and all waiting for animals or the hem of a woman's skirt, all passive but armed with appliances of activity, still, but each possessed of the anlage[1] of movement.

The sun lay on the grass and warmed it, and in the shade under the grass the insects moved, ants and ant lions to set traps for them, grasshoppers to jump into the air and flick their yellow wings for a second, sow bugs like little armadillos, plodding restlessly on many tender

---

1. anlage (än´ lä´gə) *n*.: Foundation; basis; the initial cell structure from which an embryonic part develops.

▲ **Critical Viewing** What elements of this turtle's anatomy make it especially suited for the landscape Steinbeck describes? **[Connect]**

feet. And over the grass at the roadside a land turtle crawled, turning aside for nothing, dragging his high-domed shell over the grass: His hard legs and yellow-nailed feet threshed slowly through the grass, not really walking, but boosting and dragging his shell along. The barley beards slid off his shell, and the clover burrs fell on him and rolled to the ground. His horny beak was partly opened, and his fierce, humorous eyes, under brows like fingernails, stared straight ahead. He came over the grass leaving a beaten trail behind him, and the hill, which was the highway embankment, reared up ahead of him. For a moment he stopped, his head held high. He blinked and looked up and down. At last he started to climb the embankment. Front clawed feet reached forward but did not touch. The hind feet kicked his shell along, and it scraped on the grass, and on the gravel. As the embankment grew steeper and steeper, the more frantic were the efforts of the land turtle. Pushing hind legs strained and slipped, boosting the shell along, and the horny head protruded as far as the neck could stretch. Little by little the shell slid up the embankment until at last a parapet[2] cut straight across its line of march, the shoulder of the road, a concrete wall four inches high. As though they worked independently the hind legs pushed the shell against the wall. The head upraised and peered over the wall to the broad smooth plain of cement. Now the hands, braced on top of the wall, strained and lifted, and the shell came slowly up and rested its front end on the wall. For a moment the turtle rested. A red ant ran into the shell, into the soft skin inside the shell, and suddenly head and legs snapped in, and the armored tail clamped in sideways. The red ant was crushed between body and legs. And one head of wild oats was clamped into the shell by a front leg. For a long moment the turtle lay still, and then the neck crept out and the old humorous frowning eyes looked about and the legs and tail came out. The back legs went to work, straining like elephant legs, and the shell tipped to an angle so that the front legs could not reach the level cement plain. But higher and higher the hind legs boosted it, until at last the center of balance was reached, the front tipped down, the front legs scratched at the pavement, and it was up. But the head of wild oats was held by its stem around the front legs.

Now the going was easy, and all the legs worked, and the shell boosted along, waggling from side to side. A sedan driven by a forty-year-old woman approached. She saw the turtle and swung to the right, off the highway, the wheels screamed and a cloud of dust boiled up. Two wheels lifted for a moment and then settled. The car skidded back onto the road, and went on, but more slowly. The turtle had jerked into its shell, but now it hurried on, for the highway was burning hot.

And now a light truck approached, and as it came near, the driver saw the turtle and swerved to hit it. His front wheel struck the edge of the shell, flipped the turtle like a tiddly-wink, spun it like a coin, and rolled it off the highway. The truck went back to its course along the right side. Lying on its back, the turtle was tight in its shell for a long time. But at last its legs waved in the air, reaching for something to pull it over. Its front foot caught a piece of quartz and little by little the shell pulled over and flopped upright. The wild oat head fell out and three of the spearhead seeds stuck in the ground. And as the turtle crawled on down the embankment, its shell dragged dirt over the seeds. The turtle entered a dust road and jerked itself along, drawing a wavy shallow trench in the dust with its shell. The old humorous eyes looked ahead, and the horny beak opened a little. His yellow toe nails slipped a fraction in the dust.

---

2. **parapet** (par´ ə pet´) n.: A low, protective wall or edge of a roof, balcony, or similar structure.

◆ Build Vocabulary

embankment (em bangk´ mənt) n.: A mound of earth or stone built to hold back water or support a roadway

protruded (prō trōōd´ id) v.: Pushed or thrusted outward

Guide for Responding

◆ *Literature and Your Life*

Reader's Response Describe how you felt as you watched the turtle slowly proceed.

Thematic Response Identify two challenges the turtle faces that might symbolize the plight of ordinary Americans facing the uncaring modern world.

☑ Check Your Comprehension

1. What is the turtle's goal?
2. What obstacles does the turtle encounter?
3. How does the turtle react to the final obstacles?
4. What happens to the wild oat head at the end of the story?

Guide for Responding *(continued)*

◆ Critical Thinking

INTERPRET

1. Why is the turtle so persistent in working toward his goal? **[Analyze]**
2. Compare and contrast the actions of the two vehicle drivers in this story. **[Compare and Contrast]**

EVALUATE

3. Do you think the turtle made the right decision in retreating from the embankment? Why or why not? **[Make a Judgment]**
4. Do you think the turtle would make an effective symbol of the experiences of ordinary people during the Great Depression of the 1930's? Explain. **[Evaluate]**

EXTEND

5. How would the personal qualities of the turtle be advantageous or disadvantageous in today's business world? **[Career Link]**

◆ Reading Strategy

FIND CLUES TO THEME

To arrive at an understanding of a story's theme, or central insight into life, it is important to analyze the writing carefully. Look for **clues to the theme** by considering each detail the writer provides and thinking about whether it might have a broader or underlying meaning.

1. (a) List three obstacles the turtle faces. (b) How does the turtle respond to each obstacle? (c) What underlying meaning can you find in these obstacles and the turtle's responses to them?
2. Steinbeck uses the words *dragging, turning aside for nothing,* and *thrashed slowly* to describe the turtle. (a) What effect do these words have on how the reader perceives the turtle? (b) How do you think Steinbeck wants readers to respond to the turtle?
3. (a) Which story characters can be seen as representing nature—or the simple life—and which represent the modern commercial world? Give reasons for your choices. (b) What do you think Steinbeck feels is more important? Explain.

◆ Literary Focus

THEME

Although it is an extremely brief piece, "The Turtle" conveys an important **theme**, or central message about life. This message is closely tied to the overall theme of Steinbeck's novel *The Grapes of Wrath,* for which "The Turtle" serves as an introduction.

1. How can the experiences of the turtle be connected to human experiences?
2. Explain the significance of the wild oat seed. How might it relate to the story's theme?
3. Using your answers to the previous questions, state the theme of the story.

◆ Build Vocabulary

USING THE PREFIX *pro-*

Add the prefix *pro-* meaning "forward" to these word roots. Then use each word in a sentence.

1. -ject   **2.** -ceed   **3.** -gress   **4.** -hibit

USING THE WORD BANK

Using your knowledge of the word bank words, decide if these statements are true or false.

1. An **embankment** is at the bottom of a lake.
2. When the cat's paw **protruded** from the cat carrier, it stuck out.

◆ Grammar and Style

USING PARALLEL STRUCTURE

Writers use **parallel structure**—the expression of similar ideas in similar grammatical form—to emphasize key ideas and link similar concepts.

Practice On your paper, write these passages. Underline the parallel grammatical elements.

1. . . . all waiting for animals and for the wind, for a man's trouser cuff. . .
2. . . . a land turtle crawled, turning aside for nothing, dragging his high-domed shell over the grass.
3. His front wheel struck the edge of the shell, flipped the turtle like a tiddly-wink, spun it like a coin, and rolled it off the highway.

Writing Application Write a short description of an event in nature. Use parallel structure to call attention to the key details in your description.

Build Your Portfolio

 ## Idea Bank

Writing

1. **Description** Write a description of the events in the story from the point of view of one of the two motorists.

2. **Literary Analysis** Write a brief essay in which you analyze the theme of "The Turtle." Cite passages and details from the story to support your interpretation.

3. **Essay About Historical Context** Research the Great Depression. Then write an essay in which you connect the events described in "The Turtle" to the experiences of ordinary people during the 1930's. **[Social Studies Link]**

Speaking and Listening

4. **Interview** After preparing a list of questions, interview someone who lived through the Great Depression. Ask open-ended questions and encourage detailed answers. Share your findings with the class. **[Social Studies Link]**

5. **Monologue** Imagine you're the turtle in the story, and you're talking to yourself as you proceed on your journey. Present a monologue of your interior speech. **[Performing Arts Link]**

Projects

6. **Environmental Report** Research the impact of human settlement on a particular turtle population. Gather data about species type, anatomy, movement, and feeding habits. Present your findings in an oral report with visuals. **[Science Link]**

7. **Cartoon** With a partner, pare "The Turtle" down to its essential thematic message. Write and illustrate a cartoon conveying that message. **[Art Link]**

 ## Writing Mini-Lesson

Scientific Observation

John Steinbeck describes the turtle's progress up the embankment with specific language that accounts for everything the reptile does. Observe an animal of your choice as it completes a specific task. Then create a piece of writing in which you present your observations.

Writing Skills Focus: Clear Sequence of Events

Arrange your details in chronological order to make it easy for readers to follow the sequence of events in your observation. Use signal words such as *first, next, now,* and *at last* to clearly place each step in sequence. Notice how Steinbeck uses time order words to trace the turtle's progress across the grass:

Model From the Story

For a moment he stopped, his head held high . . . *At last* he started to climb the embankment. . . . *Now* the hands . . . lifted

Prewriting Choose an animal to describe. For example, you might describe a dog exploring its surroundings during a walk or a fish reacting to feeding time. Then carefully observe the animal you've chosen, recording as many details as you can.

Drafting Begin your observation with a detailed description of the animal's physical appearance. Then follow with a detailed, step-by-step description of its actions. Use precise nouns and verbs; avoid using an excessive number of adjectives and adverbs.

Revising As you revise, look for any details you might have left out. Also make sure that the sequence of events is clear. Where possible, add transitions to clarify the connection among details.

Guide for Interpreting

E. E. Cummings (1894–1962)

After working in the French ambulance corps and spending three months behind bars as a political prisoner during World War I, Edward Estlin Cummings studied painting in Paris and then began writing poetry in New York City. Though some critics attacked the unconventional style of his first published poems, Cummings's work was popular with general readers. People admired his playful use of language, his distinctive approach to using grammar and punctuation, and his interest in a poem's appearance—an interest that might have stemmed from his gifts as a painter.

Although Cummings's poems tend to be unconventional in form and style, they generally embody traditional thought. In his finest poems, Cummings explores love and nature while innovatively using grammar and punctuation to reinforce meaning. Many of his poems also contain a touch of humor, as Cummings addresses the confusing aspects of modern life.

Cummings received a number of awards for his work, including the Boston Fine Arts Poetry Festival Award and the Bollingen Prize in Poetry. In 1968, six years after his death, a complete volume of his poetry, *The Complete Poems, 1913–1968,* was published.

W. H. Auden (1907–1973)

Although he was influenced by the Modernist poets, Wystan Hugh Auden adopted only those aspects of Modernism with which he felt comfortable. At the same time, he maintained many elements of traditional poetry. Throughout his career, he wrote with insight about people struggling to preserve their individuality in an increasingly conformist society.

Auden was born in England, and attended Oxford University. At age twenty-three, W. H. Auden published his first volume of poems and developed a passionate interest in politics. He spoke out against poverty in England and the rise of Nazism in German.

Just before World War II, in 1939, Auden moved from England to the United States, and around that same time he rediscovered his Christian beliefs. He expressed his beliefs in *Double Man* (1941) and *For the Times Being* (1944), depicting religion as a way of coping with the disjointedness of modern society.

Auden earned the Pulitzer Prize in 1948 for his long narrative poem *The Age of Anxiety* (1947) which explores the confusion associated with post-World War II life. He went on to produce several more volumes of poetry and a large body of literary criticism.

◆ Background for Understanding

LITERATURE: E. E. CUMMINGS'S STYLE

Cummings's style is among the most distinctive of any American poet. He molded his poems into unconventional shapes by varying line lengths and inserting unusual spaces between letters and lines. He also wrote **concrete poetry**—poetry in which the shape of the poem reinforces its meaning. For example, his poem about a grasshopper, "r-p-o-p-h-e-s-s-a-g-r" forms the shape of a grasshopper hopping and reforming itself.

Many of E. E. Cummings's poems contain little punctuation; the few marks that do appear often highlight important ideas. In addition, Cummings rarely used capital letters, except for emphasis. Another distinguishing mark of his style was his use of a lower-case *i* when his speakers refer to themselves. This small *i* was meant to convey the idea of the self as a small part of mass society and Cummings's belief in the need for modesty.

◆ *Literature and Your Life*

CONNECT YOUR EXPERIENCE

In this country, you are both an individual and a member of a vast society. Have you ever felt a conflict between asserting your individuality and maintaining your responsibility toward society? Do you wonder how you can distinguish yourself from the rest of humanity—or even from a group of your friends? The following poems address these issues.

> **Journal Writing** Jot down examples of television, radio, and print advertising that encourage people to conform to certain ways of thought, appearance, and behavior.

THEMATIC FOCUS: FACING TROUBLED TIMES

As you read, think about what these poems suggest about some of the negative aspects of today's world. Does modern society sometimes lose track of the needs of certain individuals?

◆ Literary Focus

SATIRE

Satire is writing in which an author uses humor to ridicule or criticize certain individuals, institutions, types of behavior, or even humanity. Satire ranges in tone; it might be tolerant, humorous, or bitter. The purpose of satire is to promote changes in society or humanity. Satirists write about what they perceive to be problems in the world. By poking fun at these problems, they use the force of laughter to persuade readers to accept their point of view.

◆ Reading Strategy

RELATE STRUCTURE TO MEANING

You can often relate a poem's **structure**—the way it is put together in words, lines, and stanzas—to its **meaning**—the central ideas the poet wants you to take away. For example, you'll see that Cummings's poems play typographical games and break rules of grammar and syntax. "Look at me," the structure of the poems seems to say, "I'm an individual." It is no coincidence that the meaning of many of Cummings's poems *also* centers on the individual challenging conventional boundaries.

◆ Build Vocabulary

WORD ROOTS: *-psych-*

The name Psyche—a heroine in a Greek myth—comes from a Greek word meaning "breath" or "soul." The Greek root *-psych-* means "soul" or "mind," and it forms the basis for a number of English words, including *psychology,* which appears in Auden's poem.

WORD BANK

Preview this list before you read.

statistics
psychology

◆ Grammar and Style

PARENTHESES

Generally, **parentheses**, ( ), are used to enclose extra information. They set off material that does not merit special attention but is relevant enough to be included in a sentence.

Although E. E. Cummings uses parentheses conventionally, he also uses them for his own stylistic purposes. In "old age sticks," for example, he uses parentheses to highlight the contrast in attitudes between the old and young.

E. E. Cummings

anyone lived in a pretty how town
(with up so floating many bells down)
spring summer autumn winter
he sang his didn't he danced his did.

5   Women and men(both little and small)
cared for anyone not at all
they sowed their isn't they reaped their same
sun moon stars rain

children guessed(but only a few
10   and down they forgot as up they grew
autumn winter spring summer)
that noone loved him more by more

when by now and tree by leaf
she laughed his joy she cried his grief
15   bird by snow and stir by still
anyone's any was all to he

someones married their everyones
laughed their cryings and did their dance
(sleep wake hope and then)they
20   said their nevers they slept their dream

stars rain sun moon
(and only the snow can begin to explain
how children are apt to forget to remember
with up so floating many bells down)

25   one day anyone died i guess
(and noone stooped to kiss his face)
busy folk buried them side by side
little by little and was by was

all by all and deep by deep
30   and more by more they dream their sleep
noone and anyone earth by april
wish by spirit and if by yes.

Women and men(both dong and ding)
summer autumn winter spring
35   reaped their sowing and went their came
sun moon stars rain

old age sticks
E. E. Cummings

old age sticks
up Keep
Off
signs)&

5   youth yanks them
down(old
age
cries No

Tres)&(pas)
10 youth laughs
(sing
old age

scolds Forbid
den Stop
15 Must
n't Don't

&)youth goes
right on
gr
20 owing old

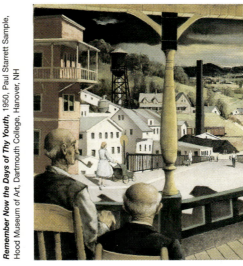

Remember Now the Days of Thy Youth, 1950, Paul Starrett Sample, Hood Museum of Art, Dartmouth College, Hanover, NH

▲ **Critical Viewing** Do you think that the elderly men in this painting belong to the group that Cummings describes or are they a different sort? On what details did you base your conclusion? **[Speculate]**

Guide for Responding

◆ *Literature and Your Life*

Reader's Response Did you enjoy the language play in these poems? Why, or why not?

Thematic Focus In what sense does Cummings address the issue of personal or national identity?

☑ Check Your Comprehension

1. In "anyone lived in a pretty how town," what does "anyone" sing and dance?
2. (a) In "old age sticks," what actions does old age take? (b) What are youth's three responses to old age's actions?

◆ Critical Thinking

INTERPRET
1. (a) In "anyone lived in a pretty how town," why might Cummings have chosen the names "anyone" for the man and "noone" for his wife? **[Speculate]**
2. What is the meaning of "laughed their cryings" and "slept their dream"? **[Interpret]**
3. In "old age sticks," explain the difference Cummings is pointing out between youth and old age. **[Compare and Contrast]**
4. Explain the irony in the final stanza of "old age sticks." **[Interpret]**

The Unknown Citizen

W. H. Auden

(To JS/07/M/378 This Marble Monument Is Erected by the State)

He was found by the Bureau of <u>Statistics</u> to be
One against whom there was no official complaint,
And all the reports on his conduct agree
That, in the modern sense of an old-fashioned word, he was a saint,
5   For in everything he did he served the Greater Community.
Except for the War till the day he retired
He worked in a factory and never got fired,
But satisfied his employers, Fudge Motors Inc.
Yet he wasn't a scab[1] or odd in his views,
10   For his Union reports that he paid his dues,
(Our report on his Union shows it was sound)
And our Social <u>Psychology</u> workers found
That he was popular with his mates and liked a drink.
The Press are convinced that he bought a paper every day
15   And that his reactions to advertisements were normal in every way.
Policies taken out in his name prove that he was fully insured,
And his Health-card shows he was once in hospital but left it cured.
Both Producers Research and High-Grade Living declare
He was fully sensible to the advantages of the Installment Plan
20   And had everything necessary to the Modern Man,
A phonograph, a radio, a car and a frigidaire.
Our researchers into Public Opinion are content
That he held the proper opinions for the time of year;
When there was peace, he was for peace; when there was war, he went.

---

1.   **scab** *n.*: A worker who refuses to strike or takes the place of a striking worker.

► Critical Viewing
In what ways does the man in this painting appear to fit Auden's description of "the unknown citizen"?
[Analyze]

Turret Lathe Operator, Grant Wood, Cedar Rapids Museum of Art, Cedar Rapids, Iowa. Courtesy Associated American Artists, © Estate of Grant Wood/Licensed by VAGA, New York, NY

25   He was married and added five children to the population,
Which our Eugenist[2] says was the right number for a parent of his generation,
And our teachers report that he never interfered with their education.
Was he free? Was he happy? The question is absurd:
Had anything been wrong, we should certainly have heard.

---

2. **Eugenist** (yo͞o jen´ ist) *n.*: A specialist in eugenics, the movement devoted to improving the human species through genetic control.

◆ **Build Vocabulary**

statistics (sta tis´ tiks) *n.*: The science of collecting and arranging facts about a particular subject in the form of numbers

psychology (sī käl´ ə jē) *n.*: The science dealing with the mind and with mental and emotional processes

Beyond Literature

Math Connection

The Census In "The Unknown Citizen," W.H. Auden pokes fun at the amount of data collected on people in the United States. One of the most basic means of collecting such data is through the census. In the United States, a population census—a count of the number of people—is taken every ten years. The census was provided for by the United States Constitution. The first United States Census was a population count that began in 1790. At that time, the data collection lasted about eighteen months and revealed that fewer than four million people lived in the country. Since then, the country's population—and the way it is counted—has grown.

The census is now conducted by the Bureau of the Census, which is an agency of the Department of Commerce. In 1990, the U.S. population was more than 280 million. Data collected in that census included information such as population, age, sex, ethnicity, marital status, and more.

Why is the information collected by the census useful to the government and the American people?

Guide for Responding

◆ Literature and Your Life

Reader's Response Have you ever felt reduced to a number? Explain your answer.

Thematic Focus How have large bureaucracies, such as government offices and some corporations, affected our sense of American identity?

☑ Check Your Comprehension

Name four groups that report on the unknown citizen's activities.

◆ Critical Thinking

INTERPRET

1. (a) What is suggested by the numbers and letters referring to the citizen? (b) How is the citizen "unknown" to the state? **[Interpret]**
2. (a) Describe the nature of the the state's interest in the citizen in this poem. (b) What do the concerns of the state and the group reveal about society as a whole? **[Infer; Interpret]**
3. Why might the state have heard nothing about the citizen's freedom and happiness? **[Deduce]**

APPLY

4. What aspects of the society portrayed in the poem are like contemporary American society? What aspects are different? **[Relate]**

Guide for Responding (continued)

◆ Literary Focus

SATIRE

In **satire,** a writer ridicules specific individuals or institutions or human behavior or society in general in a humorous manner. In "The Unknown Citizen," for example, W. H. Auden criticizes the impersonal and bureaucratic nature of modern society by presenting an exaggerated vision of a state in which people are stripped of their individuality.

1. Describe the tone in Cummings's satiric poem "anyone lived in a pretty how town." Give reasons or examples to support your answer.
2. What is Auden's attitude toward the type of society portrayed in his poem?
3. How do the final two lines clarify his attitude?
4. Considering Auden's attitude toward the society he portrays, what type of society do you think he supports? Provide details from the poem to support your answer.

◆ Build Vocabulary

USING WORD ROOTS: *psyche*

The root -*psych*- derives from the mythological Greek heroine Psyche and means "mind" or "soul." Using a dictionary, write definitions in your notebook for the following -*psych*- words. Then write a sentence using each word.

1. psychiatry   3. psychotic   5. psychodrama
2. psychosomatic 4. psychiatrist

USING THE WORD BANK

The word *psychology* refers to the science dealing with mental and emotional processes. The word *statistics* refers to the science of tabulation or counting. In a small group, discuss whether each of the following descriptions relates more closely to psychology or statistics.

1. Teacher assigns class lesson on grieving process.
2. Teacher keeps records of completed assignments.
3. You explain your dream to a friend.
4. Scientist publishes paper on blood diseases in New York State.
5. A star athlete's endorsement boosts product sales.

◆ Reading Strategy

RELATE STRUCTURE TO MEANING

You can often relate a poem's **structure**—the way it is put together in words, lines, and stanzas—to its **meaning**—the central ideas the poet wants you to take away. For example, E. E. Cummings uses regular stanzas, rhythms, and rhymes in "anyone lived in a pretty how town," yet he also uses little punctuation and only two capital letters. This blend of formal and informal structural elements echoes Cummings's central ideas about the lives being led in "a pretty how town."

1. How does the structure of "old age sticks" relate to the idea of rules and rule-breaking as it is presented in the poem? Use examples to support your answer.
2. Discuss how Auden's style of capitalization affects the meaning and tone of his poems.

◆ Grammar and Style

PARENTHESES

Parentheses are used for slightly different purposes than commas and dashes. Use commas to set off material that is especially closely connected to the rest of a sentence. Dashes are appropriate if you want to call attention to the extra information.

> **Parentheses** enclose extra material that does not deserve special attention but is relevant enough to be included in a sentence.

You should use parentheses when the material is interruptive (but not deserving of special attention) or loosely related to the rest of the sentence.

Practice Rewrite each of the following sentences, adding parentheses to improve the clarity.

1. No person at least no sensible person could accuse Cummings of being a conformist.
2. Cummings's poetry except for the love poems can be silly and serious at the same time.
3. Auden's poetry especially when read by an actor always affects listeners.
4. Auden's political viewpoints I'd guess were formed over time.

Build Your Portfolio

Idea Bank

Writing

1. **Summary** Write a paragraph summarizing the events described in "anyone lived in a pretty how town." Follow with a paragraph explaining how the impact of reading your summary compares to the impact of reading the poem.

2. **Double Diary Entry** Write a diary entry describing a recent experience. Then write a second account of the same experience as if you knew someone were monitoring your diary.

3. **Critical Essay** Write an essay in which you explain how Cummings's style reinforces the meaning in his poems. Use at least one passage from each poem to support your argument.

Speaking and Listening

4. **Poetry Reading** You are at a poetry reading in a New York coffee house in the 1920's. Choose your favorite poems from the early twentieth century. Then, read them aloud to your audience of fellow artists and intellectuals.

5. **Group Discussion** How might "anyone lived in a pretty how town" be different if it were set in a city? Discuss this question with a group of classmates. To start, suggest points of revision.

Projects

6. **Internet Research** Auden speaks out against totalitarianism, or a system in which the government takes complete control. Use the Internet to investigate totalitarian governments in Europe after World War I. Share your findings in an informal oral report. **[Social Studies Link]**

7. **Art** Choose one of the three poems, and capture and create a piece of art that could accompany it in a poetry collection. **[Art Link]**

Writing Mini-Lesson

Introduction to a Poetry Reading

Poetry readings—oral readings of poetry often held in bookstores, libraries, coffee houses, and community centers—often feature the work of more than one writer. Image that you've been asked to organize a reading of several poems by E. E. Cummings and W. H. Auden. Write an introduction that welcomes your audience and provides brief background information on the poets and a comparison of their work.

Writing Skills Focus: Types of Support—Details

To support or illustrate general statements about literary works, provide quotations and other specific details from the works. Consider using examples that show the poets' themes, as well as their use of rhythm, sound devices, imagery, structure, and figurative language. For instance, you'll probably want to share several examples of E. E. Cummings's unique writing style.

Prewriting Reread the poems. Develop a central idea about how the works of Cummings and Auden are related. Then jot down details or examples from the poems that support this main idea.

Drafting Keep your audience in mind as you draft your introduction. Make your remarks about the poems brief but informative. Remember that you'll be reading your introduction aloud, so use a conversational writing style and keep in mind the sound of the language you choose.

Revising Ask a classmate to read your introduction aloud. As you're listening, ask yourself if your ideas can be clearly understood. Do you prepare your audience adequately for the poetry they're about to hear? Are the details that support your main points relevant and important?

Guide for Interpreting

Thomas Wolfe (1900–1938)

A man of tremendous energy, appetites, and size, Thomas Wolfe poured out thousands of pages of fiction during his brief career.

Wolfe was driven by the desire to experience all life had to offer.

He sought a range of experiences throughout his life: living in the city and in the country, in America and in Europe, in the North and in the South. He reflected them in his work: in its sheer volume, in the expanses of time and territory it covers, in his characters who were symbols of greater humanity.

An Instant Success Born in Asheville, North Carolina, Wolfe grew up in a large, eccentric family whose members later served as models for his fiction. He attended the University of North Carolina. There he became interested in playwriting, a focus he pursued during and after his postgraduate studies at Harvard. Wolfe eventually moved to New York City where he taught composition at New York University and wrote plays in his spare time. Unable to find suc-

cess as a playwright, Wolfe turned to writing fiction. With the assistance of Maxwell Perkins, the leading editor of the time, Wolfe published his first novel, the loosely autobiographical *Look Homeward, Angel,* in 1929. The novel was a critical and financial success and earned Wolfe widespread recognition.

A New Direction Inspired by the success of his first novel, Wolfe began working on a sequel. Once again Perkins helped him to shorten and shape the novel, which was published as *Of Time and the River* in 1935. The novel sold well, yet Wolfe was criticized for basing his work too closely on his own life and for his reliance on Perkins. Stung by the criticism, Wolfe switched publishers and struck out on a new course, obsessed with the idea that his duty as a writer was to act as a social historian, to interpret his time and place. Unfortunately, he died of a brain infection before he could finish another novel. He did, however leave several thousand pages of manuscript in the hands of another editor, Edward Aswell, who shaped them into two more books, *The Web and the Rock* (1939) and *You Can't Go Home Again* (1940).

◆ Background for Understanding

HISTORY: AMERICA'S ROMANCE WITH THE RAILROAD

With the driving of the "golden spike" on May 10, 1869, at Promontory, Utah, the first transcontinental rail link was completed. Finishing the western half had taken more than six years, the work of thousands, and the lives of many. With its completion, America's love affair with the railways had officially begun. Now people could travel the young nation in relative comfort; they could strike out for the inexpensive land available to homesteaders; they could return East to visit relatives. The railroad also gave western farmers and ranchers access to the markets of the East.

Songs and literature about the emerging railroad abounded, including folksongs like "I've Been Working on the Railroad." The railroad influenced more than popular culture, however; it also affected the development of the United States. The nation grew smaller and in some ways more united. Cities grew at railroad hubs such as Chicago and St. Louis. As the railroad crisscrossed the nation, untamed land and lifestyles, like those of cowboys, disappeared. America was becoming a nation of towns like the one the engineer in "The Far and the Near" observes from his perch in the train engine.

The Far and the Near

◆ *Literature and Your Life*

CONNECT YOUR EXPERIENCE

At some time in your life, you've probably looked forward to an experience for days, weeks, even months, only to find that it wasn't all you had hoped it would be. In this story a character actually spends years eagerly anticipating an event and building it up in his mind. Do you think it will live up to his expectations?

Journal Writing Describe a time in your life when an anticipated experience proved disappointing.

THEMATIC FOCUS: FACING TROUBLED TIMES

In this story of one man's very personal experience, you can find a nation's disillusionment with a future it thought endlessly bright.

◆ Literary Focus

CLIMAX AND ANTICLIMAX

The **climax** is the high point of interest or suspense in a story, the moment at which the conflict is resolved. When that resolution is unexpectedly disappointing, ridiculous, or trivial, it is called an **anticlimax.** Like a climax, an anticlimax is the biggest moment of the story, but it is more a low point than a high point in the action. The reader, who has been led to expect that something important or serious is about to occur, is suddenly confronted with the letdown of a seemingly inappropriate resolution. When used intentionally and effectively, anticlimax can create a variety of effects, from pathos—sorrow or sympathy—to humor.

◆ Grammar and Style

RESTRICTIVE AND NONRESTRICTIVE PARTICIPIAL PHRASES

A **participle** is a form of a verb that acts as an adjective. A **participial phrase** consists of a participle and its modifiers or complements. The entire phrase acts as an adjective. If the phrase is essential to the meaning of the sentence, it is **restrictive** and not set off by commas. If the phrase is not essential to the sentence, it is **nonrestrictive** and should be set off by commas.

Restrictive: a light spring wagon *filled with children.*

Nonrestrictive: And finally, *stammering a crude farewell,* he departed.

◆ Reading Strategy

PREDICT

This story about a train engineer's life is a bit like a real train ride—signposts guide the way to the final destination. These clues enable you to **predict,** or make educated guesses about, upcoming events and outcomes. Watch for signals in statements about characters, in the author's use of language, and in events you can associate with your own experiences. You'll find that they can help you predict where the story is headed. For example:

Detail Every day, a few minutes after two o'clock in the afternoon, the limited express . . . passed this spot.

Prediction The story will involve "this spot" in a way different from "every day."

◆ Build Vocabulary

WORD ROOTS: *-temp-*

Wolfe uses the word *tempo* to describe the timing of the train's noises. Built on the Latin root *-temp-*, meaning "time," *tempo* means "pace" or "the rate of activity of a sound or motion." What other *-temp-* words can you think of?

WORD BANK

Preview these words before you

tempo
sallow
sullen
timorous
visage

The Far and the Near

Thomas Wolfe

On the outskirts of a little town upon a rise of land that swept back from the railway there was a tidy little cottage of white boards, trimmed vividly with green blinds. To one side of the house there was a garden neatly patterned with plots of growing vegetables, and an arbor for the grapes which ripened late in August. Before the house there were three mighty oaks which sheltered it in their clean and massive shade in summer, and to the other side there was a border of gay flowers. The whole place had an air of tidiness, thrift, and modest comfort.

Stone City, Iowa, Grant Wood, Joslyn Art Museum, Omaha, Nebraska, © Estate of Grant Wood/Licensed by VAGA, New York, NY

▲ **Critical Viewing** How does this painting reflect the engineer's perspective on the farms and villages he sees along his train route? **[Analyze]**

Every day, a few minutes after two o'clock in the afternoon, the limited express between two cities passed this spot. At that moment the great train, having halted for a breathing space at the town nearby, was beginning to lengthen evenly into its stroke, but it had not yet reached the full drive of its terrific speed. It swung into view deliberately, swept past with a powerful swaying motion of the engine, a low smooth rumble of its heavy cars upon pressed steel, and then it vanished in the cut. For a moment the progress of the engine could be marked by heavy bellowing puffs of smoke that burst at spaced intervals above the edges of the meadow grass, and finally nothing could be heard but the solid clacking tempo of the wheels receding into the drowsy stillness of the afternoon.

Every day for more than twenty years, as the train had approached this house, the engineer had blown on the whistle, and every day, as soon as she heard this signal, a woman had appeared on the back porch of the little house and waved to him. At first she had a small child clinging to her skirts, and now this child had grown to full womanhood, and every day she, too, came with her mother to the porch and waved.

The engineer had grown old and gray in service. He had driven his great train, loaded with its weight of lives, across the land ten thousand times. His own children had grown up and married, and four times he had seen before him on the tracks the ghastly dot of

◆ **Build Vocabulary**

tempo (tem´ pō) *n.*: Rate of activity of a sound or motion; pace

tragedy converging like a cannon ball to its eclipse of horror at the boiler head[1]—a light spring wagon filled with children, with its clustered row of small stunned faces; a cheap automobile stalled upon the tracks, set with the wooden figures of people paralyzed with fear; a battered hobo walking by the rail, too deaf and old to hear the whistle's warning; and a form flung past his window with a scream—all this the man had seen and known. He had known all the grief, the joy, the peril and the labor such a man could know; he had grown seamed and weathered in his loyal service, and now, schooled by the qualities of faith and courage and humbleness that attended his labor, he had grown old, and had the grandeur and the wisdom these men have.

But no matter what peril or tragedy he had known, the vision of the little house and the women waving to him with a brave free motion of the arm had become fixed in the mind of the engineer as something beautiful and enduring, something beyond all change and ruin, and something that would always be the same, no matter what mishap, grief or error might break the iron schedule of his days.

The sight of the little house and of these two women gave him the most extraordinary happiness he had ever known. He had seen them in a thousand lights, a hundred weathers. He had seen them through the harsh bare light of wintry gray across the brown and frosted stubble of the earth, and he had seen them again in the green luring sorcery of April.

He felt for them and for the little house in which they lived such tenderness as a man might feel for his own children, and at length the picture of their lives was carved

so sharply in his heart that he felt that he knew their lives completely, to every hour and moment of the day, and he resolved that one day, when his years of service should

◆ **Reading Strategy**

Can you predict what will happen when the engineer carries out his resolution?

be ended, he would go and find these people and speak at last with them whose lives had been so wrought into his own.

That day came. At last the engineer stepped from a train onto the station platform of the town where these two women lived. His years upon the rail had ended. He was a pensioned servant of his company, with no more work to do. The engineer walked slowly through the station and out into the streets of the town. Everything was as strange to him as if he had never seen this town before. As he walked on, his sense of bewilderment and confusion grew. Could this be the town he had passed ten thousand times? Were these the same houses he had seen so often from the high windows of his cab? It was all as unfamiliar, as disquieting as a city in a dream, and the perplexity of his spirit increased as he went on.

Presently the houses thinned into the straggling outposts of the town, and the street faded into a country road—the one on which the women lived. And the man plodded on slowly in the heat and dust. At length he stood before the house he sought. He knew at once that he had found the proper place. He saw the lordly oaks before the house, the flower beds, the garden and the arbor, and farther off, the glint of rails.

Yes, this was the house he sought, the place he had passed so many times, the destination he had longed for with such happiness. But now that he had found it, now that he was here, why did his hand falter on the gate; why had the town, the road, the earth, the very entrance to this place he loved turned unfamiliar as the landscape of some ugly dream? Why did he now feel this sense of confusion, doubt and hopelessness?

At length he entered by the gate, walked slowly up the path and in a moment more had mounted three short steps that led up to the porch, and was knocking at the door. Presently he heard steps in the hall, the door was opened, and a woman stood facing him.

And instantly, with a sense of bitter loss and grief, he was sorry he had come. He knew at once that the woman who stood there looking at him with a mistrustful eye was the same woman who had waved to

---

1. **boiler head:** The front section of a steam locomotive.

him so many thousand times. But her face was harsh and pinched and meager; the flesh sagged wearily in <u>sallow</u> folds, and the small eyes peered at him with timid suspicion and uneasy doubt. All the brave freedom, the warmth and the affection that he had read into her gesture, vanished in the moment that he saw her and heard her unfriendly tongue.

◆ **Literary Focus**
How is the woman's appearance anticlimactic?

And now his own voice sounded unreal and ghastly to him as he tried to explain his presence, to tell her who he was and the reason he had come. But he faltered on, fighting stubbornly against the horror of regret, confusion, disbelief that surged up in his spirit, drowning all his former joy and making his act of hope and tenderness seem shameful to him.

At length the woman invited him almost unwillingly into the house, and called her daughter in a harsh shrill voice. Then, for a brief agony of time, the man sat in an ugly little parlor, and he tried to talk while the two women stared at him with a dull, bewildered hostility, a <u>sullen</u>, <u>timorous</u> restraint.

And finally, stammering a crude farewell, he departed. He walked away down the path and then along the road toward town, and suddenly he knew that he was an old man. His heart, which had been brave and confident when it looked along the familiar vista of the rails, was now sick with doubt and horror as it saw the strange and unsuspected <u>visage</u> of an earth which had always been within a stone's throw of him, and which he had never seen or known. And he knew that all the magic of that bright lost way, the vista of that shining line, the imagined corner of that small good universe of hope's desire, was gone forever, could never be got back again.

◆ **Build Vocabulary**
sallow (sal′ ō) *adj*.: Sickly; pale yellow
sullen (sul′ ən) *adj*.: Sulky; glum
timorous (tim′ ər əs) *adj*.: Full of fear
visage (viz′ ij) *n*.: Appearance

Guide for Responding

◆ *Literature and Your Life*

Reader's Response As you read about the engineer's approaching visit to the little town, what did you hope he would find?

Thematic Focus The engineer is crushed when he discovers that his optimism was falsely based. Is it possible to confront reality and remain hopeful about life? Explain.

☑ **Check Your Comprehension**

1. Describe the engineer's daily experience for the last twenty years.
2. How does the engineer feel about the little house and the two women?
3. How does the engineer's life change during the story?
4. What realization does the engineer come to at the end of the story?

◆ **Critical Thinking**

INTERPRET
1. The narrator uses the phrase "every day" several times in the opening paragraphs. What does this tell you about the engineer's life? **[Interpret]**
2. What does the house represent to the engineer? **[Infer]**
3. When does the engineer first sense that his experience is unlikely to match his expectations? **[Connect]**
4. How do the engineer's observations in the final scene contrast with his expectations? **[Contrast]**
5. How does the title of the story relate to its content? **[Interpret]**

APPLY
6. What is Wolfe saying about life through this story? **[Generalize]**

Guide for Responding (continued)

◆ Reading Strategy

PREDICT

"The Far and the Near" offered several clues to help you **predict** upcoming events or emotions. Use those clues to answer these questions.

1. When you read about the engineer's resolution to visit the two women after retiring, what did you think would happen? Identify the details from the story that support the prediction you made.
2. Based on your own experience, how did you predict the engineer's view of the world would change when he stepped down from the "high windows of his cab"?
3. (a) What prediction did you make about the woman's likely reception of the engineer? (b) How, if at all, did you revise your prediction as you read the story's ending?

◆ Build Vocabulary

USING THE WORD ROOT -*temp*-

The word root -*temp*- means "time." Use your knowledge of this root to replace the italicized word or phrase in each of the following sentences with the appropriate word from the box below.

temporary	extemporaneous
tempo	contemporary

1. The band slowed the *pace* of the music.
2. His *spur of the moment* wedding proposal caught his girlfriend off guard.
3. Judging from the age of the paper, these two documents appear to be *of the same time period*.
4. I have to walk to school until the car is fixed, but I'm hoping that it will be just *for a short time*.

USING THE WORD BANK

For each item, follow the directions by writing a sentence using a word from the word bank.

1. Describe a man who has been ill for many weeks.
2. Describe how a child might feel before visiting the dentist.
3. Describe a student giving an outrageous reason for not having completed her research paper.
4. Write the first sentence of a story about a girl who is unhappy and angry about her life.
5. Describe activity in a busy office.

◆ Literary Focus

CLIMAX AND ANTICLIMAX

Although you might have predicted that all would not turn out exactly as the engineer hoped, the reception he receives at the "tidy little cottage" is a devastating **anticlimax**.

1. Explain how the rising action of the story makes the story's resolution an anticlimax rather than a climax.
2. What effect does the anticlimax have on the engineer and on the reader?

◆ Grammar and Style

RESTRICTIVE AND NONRESTRICTIVE PARTICIPIAL PHRASES

Participial phrases can help writers insert action into a description. A **participle** is a form of a verb that acts as an adjective. A **participial phrase** consists of a participle and its modifiers or complements. The entire phrase acts as an adjective.

If a participial phrase is essential to the meaning of the sentence, it is **restrictive** and not set off by commas. If the phrase is not essential to the sentence, it is **nonrestrictive** and should be set off by commas.

Practice Write the following passages on your paper. Underline the participial phrases and add commas as necessary.

1. . . . and now schooled by the qualities of faith and courage and humbleness that attended his labor he had grown old . . .
2. . . . four times he had seen before him on the tracks the ghastly dot of tragedy converging like a cannon ball to its eclipse of horror at the boiler head . . .
3. . . . He had driven his great train loaded with its weight of lives across the land ten thousand times.
4. . . . nothing could be heard but the solid clacking tempo of the wheels receding into the drowsy stillness of the afternoon.

Looking at Style Explain how each of the participial phrases in the Practice enables Wolfe to insert action into a description.

Build Your Portfolio

Idea Bank

Writing

1. **Description** Using details from the story and your imagination, write a description of the countryside and sights the engineer sees as he travels his daily train route.

2. **First-Person Account** What did the woman who lives in the green and white cottage think of the engineer's visit? Write an account of the visit as she might have described it to a neighbor.

3. **Comparison-and-Contrast Essay** Write an essay in which you compare the two viewpoints suggested by the title "The Far and the Near." How does the engineer's view of his world depend on his proximity to it? What does the story suggest about the dreams we dream from afar?

Speaking and Listening

4. **Interview** Is there really something special about train travel? Interview someone who has traveled great distances by train about their experiences. Share your findings with the class.

5. **Music Critique** Locate recordings of several songs about trains. Play them for the class, then lead a discussion on how rail travel is portrayed. Are the songs realistic? Romantic? **[Music Link]**

Projects

6. **Railroad Report** Research the evolution of the railroad and the nation's love affair with it. In a written report, explain one aspect of the history of the railroad and the changes that have taken place in recent decades. **[Social Studies Link]**

7. **Map** Create a map or three-dimensional diagram of a train route, and embellish it with real or imagined details. The route may be short—between two towns—or long. **[Geography Link]**

Writing Mini-Lesson

Brochure on Train Travel

"The Far and the Near" is built on the simple premise that the world can appear better than it really is when viewed from a train. Think like a salesperson and use this insight to promote rail travel. Write a brochure to encourage people to travel by train rather than by car, bus, or plane. Describe the benefits of seeing America by rail. Be careful, however, to keep your brochure believable by insuring that all your information is accurate.

Writing Skills Focus: Accuracy

Accuracy in your brochure is essential. Tell the truth so that the readers you convince to travel by train won't be disappointed. Keep these tips in mind:

- Don't exaggerate benefits or make unrealistic promises about services that train travel could never realistically deliver.
- Gather facts from reliable sources, and verify information obtained from unofficial sources.
- Include quotations from real people, recorded accurately word for word.

Prewriting Research information about train travel, focusing if you like on a particular area of the country. Note facts about routes, schedules, prices, seating and sleeping accommodations, and meals. Then jot down sensory details you might use to flesh out your descriptions.

Drafting Open with an anecdote, a quotation about train travel, or a vivid description of a place viewed from a train. Use your notes to highlight each of the features you identified, adding descriptive and sensory words to entice passengers.

Revising Read your brochure aloud, checking for promises that sound "too good to be true." Can you verify the accuracy of your statements?

Guide for Interpreting

Wallace Stevens (1879–1955)

Wallace Stevens believed that the goal of poetry was to capture the interaction of fantasy and reality. He spent his career writing poems that delve into the ways in which the imagination can shape the way in which we perceive the physical world.

Stevens was born and raised in Reading, Pennsylvania. After completing his education, he took a job at an insurance company in Hartford, Connecticut, and eventually became the company's vice president. He didn't publish his first collection of poetry, *Harmonium* (1923), until he was over forty. In this book, Stevens uses dazzling imagery to capture the beauty of the physical world, while expressing the dependence of that beauty on the perceptions of the observer. Although the book received little public attention, it was praised by critics and launched Stevens into a successful literary career.

Stevens went on to publish many volumes of poetry, including *Ideas of Order* (1935), *Parts of a World* (1942), *Transport to Summer* (1947), and *The Auroras of Autumn* (1950). His *Collected Poems* earned him the Pulitzer Prize in 1955. Despite his success as a poet, however, Stevens continued his career in insurance. He rarely appeared in public and only began giving readings toward the end of his life.

Archibald MacLeish (1892–1982)

Archibald MacLeish was trained as a lawyer, but unlike Stevens, he turned his back on his first career to devote himself completely to poetry. MacLeish's early poems, such as "Ars Poetica," are experimental in form, reflecting the influence of the Modernists. However, in an effort to help his readers more easily understand his work, he later tried to make his poems more traditional. As unrest spread through the world in the 1930's, MacLeish used poetry to explore political and social issues.

Marianne Moore (1887–1972)

Born in Kirkwood, Missouri, Marianne Moore first became an influential literary figure when she became the editor of *The Dial*, a highly regarded literary journal. In that role, she encouraged many new writers by publishing their work. However, she was hesitant to publish her own work, despite the fact that it had been read and admired by many noted poets. In fact, her first book, *Poems* (1921), was published without her knowledge.

◆ Background for Understanding

LITERATURE: STEVENS'S VIEWS OF POETRY

Stevens believed that the Modern Age was a time of uncertainty and that it was the duty of the poet to provide new ways of understanding the world. His views of poetry reflect the influence of Symbolism, a literary movement that originated in France in the last half of the nineteenth century. Because people perceive the physical world in different ways, the Symbolist poets believed that the ideas and emotions that people experience are personal and difficult to communicate. As a result, these poets avoided directly stating their ideas in their poetry. Instead, they tried to convey meaning through clusters of symbols—people, places, and objects that have meanings in themselves and also represent something larger than themselves. Because of this reliance on symbols, Symbolist poems—and the works of Stevens—can often be interpreted in a number of different ways.

Of Modern Poetry ◆ Anecdote of the Jar
Ars Poetica ◆ Poetry

◆ *Literature and Your Life*

CONNECT YOUR EXPERIENCE

You probably have your own special ways of looking at the activities you care about most deeply. Maybe you have strong views of what makes good music or a unique way of looking at your favorite sport. In the selections you're about to read, the writers present their views on a subject that they are passionate about: poetry.

Journal Writing Although people have debated the rules of the genre for ages, poetry defies definition. What is your definition of poetry?

THEMATIC FOCUS: FACING TROUBLED TIMES

During the time in which these poets lived, technological advances and wars with an unparalleled scale of destruction changed how people viewed the world. At the same time, the arts, including literature, underwent major changes. With these changes, writers had to develop new ways of defining literary forms and techniques. These selections present new ways of looking at poetry.

◆ Literary Focus

SIMILE

A **simile** is a comparison between two seemingly dissimilar things. A signal word such as "like" or "as" indicates the comparison. For example, the word *like* signals the comparison in the following simile:

The sound of the explosion echoed through the air *like thunder.*

Like poetry itself, similes enable us to see the world in startling new ways.

◆ Grammar and Style

SUBJECT COMPLEMENTS

A **subject complement** follows a linking verb and identifies or describes the subject. It may be a noun, a pronoun, or an adjective. Sentences containing subject complements are especially effective when a writer's purpose is to define something. For example, in several of the selections that follow, the poets use subject complements in defining poetry. Look at this example:

A poem should be <u>wordless</u> . . .

◆ Reading Strategy

PARAPHRASE

Because poetry is written in verse and is likely to contain unexpected words and images, it can be difficult to understand. One way to make sure that you grasp what you are reading is to **paraphrase**—to identify key ideas and restate them. For example, you might restate the opening lines of Moore's "Poetry" *(I, too, dislike it: there are things that are important beyond/all this fiddle.")* as "I also dislike poetry. It's nonsense, and a lot of other things are more important." Paraphrasing can remove barriers that make some poems seem too difficult to understand.

◆ Build Vocabulary

WORD ROOTS: *-satis-*

In "Of Modern Poetry," Wallace Stevens uses the word *insatiable*. This word contains the root *-satis-*, which means "enough." How does the root contribute to the meaning of insatiable— "constantly wanting more"? What other words can you think of that contain this root?

WORD BANK

Preview this list of words.

suffice
insatiable
slovenly
dominion
palpable
derivative
literalists

Of Modern Poetry

Wallace Stevens

The poem of the mind in the act of finding
What will suffice. It has not always had
To find: the scene was set; it repeated what
Was in the script.
                  Then the theatre was changed
5   To something else. Its past was a souvenir.

It has to be living, to learn the speech of the place.
It has to face the men of the time and to meet
The women of the time. It has to think about war
And it has to find what will suffice. It has
10   To construct a new stage. It has to be on that stage
And, like an insatiable actor, slowly and
With meditation, speak words that in the ear,
In the delicatest ear of the mind, repeat,
Exactly, that which it wants to hear, at the sound
15   Of which, an invisible audience listens,
Not to the play, but to itself, expressed
In an emotion as of two people, as of two
Emotions becoming one. The actor is
A metaphysician[1] in the dark, twanging
20   An instrument, twanging a wiry string that gives
Sounds passing through sudden rightnesses, wholly
Containing the mind, below which it cannot descend,
Beyond which it has no will to rise.
                         It must
Be the finding of a satisfaction, and may
25   Be of a man skating, a woman dancing, a woman
Combing. The poem of the act of the mind.

---

1. metaphysician (met′ ə fə zish′ ən) *n*.: A person versed in philosophy, especially those branches that seek to explain the nature of being or of the universe.

◆ Build Vocabulary

suffice (sə fīs′) *v*.: Be adequate; meet the needs of

insatiable (in sā′ shə bəl) *adj*.: Constantly wanting more; unable to be satisfied

Anecdote of the Jar

Wallace Stevens

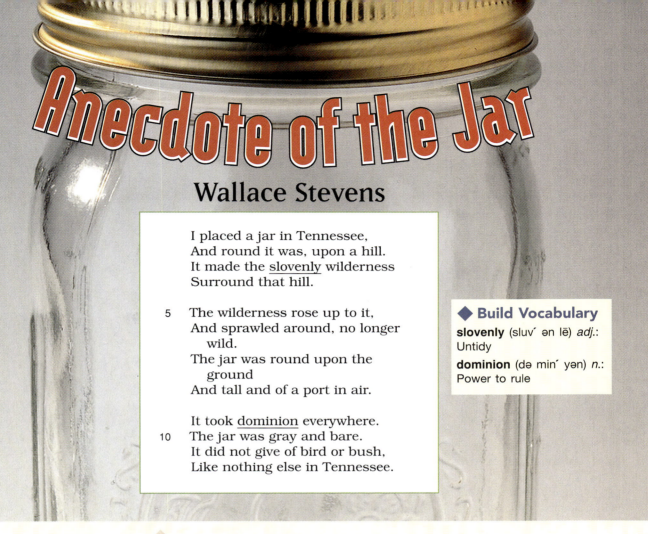

I placed a jar in Tennessee,
And round it was, upon a hill.
It made the <u>slovenly</u> wilderness
Surround that hill.

5   The wilderness rose up to it,
And sprawled around, no longer
     wild.
The jar was round upon the
     ground
And tall and of a port in air.

It took <u>dominion</u> everywhere.
10   The jar was gray and bare.
It did not give of bird or bush,
Like nothing else in Tennessee.

◆ **Build Vocabulary**

slovenly (sluv´ ən lē) *adj*.:
Untidy

dominion (də min´ yən) *n*.:
Power to rule

Guide for Responding

◆ Literature and Your Life

Reader's Response What is your reaction to the ideas Stevens presents in "Of Modern Poetry"? Why?

Thematic Focus In "Of Modern Poetry," what does Stevens mean by the line, "Then the theater was changed"?

☑ Check Your Comprehension

1. What does "Of Modern Poetry" suggest about the relationship modern poetry needs to have with the people of its time?
2. Where does the speaker in "Anecdote of the Jar" place the jar?

◆ Critical Thinking

INTERPRET

1. Describe the jar's effect on the wilderness in "Anecdote of the Jar." **[Analyze]**
2. How is the impression of the jar that the speaker conveys in the third stanza different from that conveyed in the first two stanzas? **[Compare and Contrast]**
3. Find evidence in "Anecdote of the Jar" to support this interpretation: The jar symbolizes the human imagination, and the poem says nature is shaped by our perceptions. **[Support]**
4. Find two lines from "Of Modern Poetry" that suggest that writing poetry requires effort and precision. **[Support]**

Ars Poetica[1]

Archibald MacLeish

A poem should be <u>palpable</u> and mute
As a globed fruit.

Dumb
As old medallions to the thumb,

5   Silent as the sleeve-worn stone
Of casement ledges where the moss has grown—

A poem should be wordless
As the flight of birds.

A poem should be motionless in time
10 As the moon climbs,

Leaving, as the moon releases
Twig by twig the night-entangled trees,

---

1. Ars Poetica: The title is an allusion to Horace's "Ars Poetica," or "The Art of Poetry," which was composed about 20 B.C.

▶ **Critical Viewing**
Which of the poem's images can be found in this photograph? **[Interpret]**

Leaving, as the moon behind the winter leaves.
Memory by memory the mind—

15   A poem should be motionless in time
As the moon climbs.

A poem should be equal to:
Not true.

For all the history of grief
20   An empty doorway and a maple leaf.

For love
The leaning grasses and two lights above the sea—

A poem should not mean
But be.

◆ **Build Vocabulary**

palpable (pal´ pə bəl) *adj*.: Able to be touched, felt, or handled

Poetry

Marianne Moore

Untitled, 1984, Alexander Calder, Solomon R. Guggenheim Museum, New York

▶ **Critical Viewing**
How does this modern image compare or contrast with the ideas in Moore's poem? **[Draw Conclusions]**

I, too, dislike it: there are things that are important beyond
　　all this fiddle.
　　　　Reading it, however, with a perfect contempt for it, one
　　　　　　discovers in
　　it after all, a place for the genuine.
　　　　　　Hands that can grasp, eyes
5　　　　　　that can dilate, hair that can rise
　　　　　　if it must, these things are important not because a

　　high-sounding interpretation can be put upon them but
　　　　because they are
　　　　useful. When they become so <u>derivative</u> as to become
　　　　　　unintelligible,
　　the same thing may be said for all of us, that we do not
　　　　admire what
10　　　　　　we cannot understand: the bat
　　　　　　　holding on upside down or in quest of something to

　　eat, elephants pushing, a wild horse taking a roll, a
　　　　tireless wolf under
　　　　a tree, the immovable critic twitching his skin like a
　　　　　　horse that feels a flea, the base-
　　　　ball fan, the statistician—
15　　　　　　nor is it valid
　　　　　　　to discriminate against "business documents and

　　schoolbooks"; all these phenomena are important. One
　　　　must make a distinction
　　　　however: when dragged into prominence by half poets,
　　　　　　the result is not poetry,
　　nor till the poets among us can be

20   "<u>literalists</u> of
        the imagination"—above
           insolence and triviality and can present

      for inspection, "imaginary gardens with real toads in
        them," shall we have
        it. In the meantime, if you demand on the one hand,
25   the raw material of poetry in
        all its rawness and
        that which is on the other hand
           genuine, you are interested in poetry.

◆ Build Vocabulary

derivative (də riv´ ə tiv) *adj*.: Not original; based on something else

literalists (lit´ ər əl ists) *n*.: People who insist on taking words at their exact meaning

Guide for Responding

◆ *Literature and Your Life*

Reader's Response (a) Are you interested in poetry? Explain. (b) In your opinion, which word or phrase best describes Moore's poem—"fiddle," "derivative," or "genuine"? Explain.

Thematic Focus According to Marianne Moore, what characteristics make poetry useful to its readers?

Group Discussion Some have suggested that the lyrics of popular music are the poetry of today's generation. With classmates, discuss this assertion.

☑ Check Your Comprehension

1. (a) To what does the speaker of "Ars Poetica" compare a poem? (b) How should a poem show the history of grief? (c) How should it show love?
2. (a) What does the speaker of "Poetry" say a person discovers when reading poetry "with a perfect contempt for it"? (b) What happens when poetry is "dragged into prominence by half poets"?

◆ Critical Thinking

INTERPRET

1. What do you think the speaker of "Ars Poetica" means by saying that a poem should be (a) "palpable and mute" (line 1); (b) "wordless" (line 7); and (c) "motionless in time" (line 9)? **[Analyze]**
2. Why do you think MacLeish chose to focus on the emotions of love and grief? **[Infer]**
3. How does the final line of "Ars Poetica" sum up the ideas expressed in the poem? **[Analyze]**
4. What type of poetry does the speaker of "Poetry" dislike? **[Interpret]**
5. (a) What does the speaker mean by saying that poets should be "literalists of the imagination"? (b) What is meant by "imaginary gardens with real toads in them"? **[Interpret]**
6. What qualities does the speaker believe good poetry should possess? **[Interpret]**

APPLY

7. Explain the similarities and the differences between Moore's views of poetry and MacLeish's label. **[Compare and Contrast]**

Guide for Responding (continued)

◆ Literary Focus

SIMILE

A **simile** is an explicit comparison between two seemingly dissimilar things, clearly indicated by a connecting word such as *like* or *as*. For example, MacLeish presents a simile in lines 1 and 2 in which he compares a poem to a globed fruit.

1. What does "globed" suggest about a poem?
2. In what ways can a poem be like a fruit?
3. Find three other similes in "Ars Poetica" and interpret their meaning.
4. How do all of the similes work together to create a vision of poetry as something that "should not mean/But be"?

◆ Reading Strategy

PARAPHRASING

When you **paraphrase**, you identify key ideas in a passage and restate them in your own words. Paraphrase the following passages from the poems. Try to make your paraphrased version as straightforward, direct, and comprehensible as possible.

1. The wilderness rose up to it,
   And sprawled around, no longer wild.
   The jar was round upon the ground
   And tall and of a port in air.

2. A poem should be motionless in time
   As the moon climbs.

   As poem should be equal to:
   Not true.

3. A poem should not mean
   But be.

4. . . . these things are important not because a
   high sounding interpretation can be put upon
          them but
       because they are
       useful. . .

5. . . . In the meantime, if you demand on the one
          hand,
       the raw material of poetry in
       all its rawness and
       that which is on the other hand
          genuine, you are interested in poetry.

◆ Build Vocabulary

USING THE WORD ROOT *-satis-*

Each of the following words contains the root -*satis*-, meaning "enough." Use your knowledge of the root to guess their meanings—and use a dictionary to confirm the precise definition. Then use each of the words correctly in a sentence.

1. satisfy	3. satiate
2. satisfactory	4. satiety

USING THE WORD BANK

Follow the instructions below by writing a sentence for each item that uses one word from the Word Bank. Use each word once.

1. Describe someone who has no imagination.
2. Define the territory governed by a king.
3. Describe the quality of a peach in a beautiful painting.
4. Explain why a friend's room is such a mess.
5. Criticize a musician who lacks originality.
6. Explain why a certain amount of food is not enough to maintain one's health.
7. Criticize a sibling who always wants more possessions.

◆ Grammar and Style

SUBJECT COMPLEMENTS

Subject complements are nouns, pronouns, or adjectives that follow linking verbs (often forms of the verb "to be") and identify or describe the subject of a sentence. Sentences containing subject complements are especially effective when a writer's purpose is to define something.

Practice Copy each of the following sentences. Underline the subject complement and label it as a noun, pronoun, or adjective.

1. The winner of this year's poetry prize is you!
2. The subject of the poem was a waterfall.
3. Good poetry should be thrilling.
4. Poets are deep thinkers.
5. The oldest book in the library is a volume of poems.

Writing Application Write a brief descriptive poem about a familiar person or object. Begin each line with the name of the person or object. Follow it with a linking verb and a noun, pronoun, or adjective that renames or describes the person or object.

Build Your Portfolio

 ## Idea Bank

Writing

I. Ars Poetica MacLeish's poem is a listing of the different characteristics a poem should have. Using his similes as a model, write five new couplets (two-line verses) that express your ideas about the characteristics of a good poem.

2. Comparison and Contrast Write an essay in which you compare and contrast two of the definitions of poetry presented in this group. Cite passages from the poems to support your points.

3. Response to Criticism Wallace Stevens felt that the goal of a poet is "to help people live their lives." Choose one of Stevens's poems. Then write an essay in which you discuss how effectively that poem achieves this goal. Support your argument with passages from the poem.

Speaking and Listening

4. Round Table Discussion With a small group, analyze the views of poetry held by the different poets. Then stage a round table discussion on the issue "What Is Poetry?" Each group member should take the position of one of the poets.

5. Introduction When poets read their work, they often introduce each poem with a brief explanation of it. Plan and present remarks to introduce one of these poems.

Projects

6. Illustration Create an illustration that captures the scene in "Anecdote of the Jar." **[Art Link]**

7. Poetry Collection These poems focus on a specific topic: What is poetry? Create a collection of poems on another topic—such as sports or nature. Include an introduction that explains how the poems relate to one another.

 ## Writing Mini-Lesson

Definition

In these selections, Stevens, MacLeish, and Moore define something about which they care very deeply: poetry. Choose something that you care deeply about—for example, your favorite type of music, your favorite ice cream, or your favorite season—and write a definition of it in which you use one or more striking comparisons to capture how you feel about the subject. Keep this tip in mind as you develop your definition.

Writing Skills Focus: Necessary Background

When you write a definition, it's essential that you provide readers with any necessary background information about your subject. Think about what someone who is not an expert on your topic would and wouldn't know about it. You'll need to provide any details that your audience wouldn't already know. In addition, you'll need to define any specialized terms with which your audience is likely to be unfamiliar.

Prewriting Freewrite about what your topic means to you. What aspects of it interest you most? Review what you've written and underline details that you can use in your definition. Then create comparisons that you can use to capture what your topic means to you.

Drafting You can either develop your definition around a single comparison, or present a series of comparisons. Whichever approach you choose, make sure to include enough details to give your readers a clear understanding of your topic.

Revising Give your definition to a classmate who is not familiar with your topic. Ask your reader to suggest places where you can add details to make it more clear.

Allentown
Billy Joel

Thematic Connection

TROUBLED TIMES

Through their novels and stories, Fitzgerald, Steinbeck, and other writers spoke for many Americans who felt confused and alienated in the period between the two world wars. The brutality and carnage of World War I had shocked our still young nation. The war highlighted the most destructive capabilities of modern technology and made many people begin to question whether traditional values could still be applied to the modern world.

More recent American writers have also addressed social problems and their effects. The Vietnam War and the unrest it caused, the issues relating to civil rights and inequality, concern for the environment—these are all themes that contemporary American writers have dealt with in recent years. Every age has its troubles, and writers often give voice to these concerns, moving readers to deeper reflection and sometimes to action.

Singers also frequently address social concerns. One such artist is Billy Joel, who addressed some of the dominant issues of the 1980's. For many Americans, this period was one of economic prosperity, with average incomes rising and the financial markets booming. Yet for others, the 1980's was the decade when the American dream died. Factories, which had long been a reliable source of employment, began to streamline their work forces, move overseas to take advantage of cheap labor, or close down altogether. Many skilled laborers were forced to take lower-paying service jobs. A sense of betrayal and confusion permeated towns that had long been dominated by huge steel mills, automobile manufacturing plants, and other large industries.

The lyrics of many of Billy Joel's songs written during this period show the plight of legions of abandoned workers. Through words and music, Joel drew attention to situations that some would prefer to overlook. Like many writers before him, Joel had the courage and compassion to write movingly of those who were left behind.

BILLY JOEL (1949–   )

The son of Jewish immigrants, Billy Joel grew up in Hicksville, New York. When Joel was a child, his engineer father left the family, forcing his mother to raise her two children on a secretary's salary. Although the family was poor, Joel had a rich cultural life learning to play the piano and going to classical concerts with his grandfather. He also boxed and spent time with friends.

At age sixteen, Joel became the pianist for a local band called the Hassles. He worked a lot of late nights, earning money that helped his mother pay the mortgage.

His first album was a failure, but his second album, released in 1973, was the hugely successful *Piano Man*. Hit song after hit song has followed. Yet Joel warns people against assessing him as a "pop meister who just churns out these hit singles." Unlike many pop artists, Joel has tackled a range of social issues from unemployment to the legacy of the Vietnam War.

In the late 1980's, Joel toured Russia, playing songs that emphasized similarities between people despite political divisions. More recently, he has lectured at colleges to help young musicians learn from his experiences.

Allentown

Words and Music
by Billy Joel

Well we're living here in Allentown[1]
And they're closing all the factories down
Out in Bethlehem[2] they're killing time
Filling out forms
5   Standing in line

Well our fathers fought the Second World War
Spent their weekends on the Jersey shore

---

1. Allentown: A city on the Lehigh River in eastern Pennsylvania, once home to a thriving steel industry that began to collapse during the 1970's, leaving thousands of workers unemployed.
2. Bethlehem: A neighboring city located within the Allentown, Pennsylvania, metropolitan area.

Met our mothers in the USO[3]
Asked them to dance
10 Danced with them slow

And we're living here in Allentown
But the restlessness was handed down
and it's getting very hard to stay

Well we're waiting here in Allentown
15 For the Pennsylvania we never found
For the promises our teachers gave
If we worked hard
If we behaved
So the graduations hang on the wall
20 But they never really helped us at all
No they never told us what was real
Iron and coke[4]
And chromium steel

And we're waiting here in Allentown
25 But they've taken all the coal from the ground
And the union people crawled away

▲ **Critical Viewing** Lines of unemployed workers were a common sight in "steel towns" like Allentown during the 1970's and early 1980's. Which lines of the song describe a scene like this one? **[Connect]**

---

3. USO: Refers to a social club sponsored by the United Service Organizations, a group that provides entertainment and many other services to U.S. military personnel and their families worldwide.
4. coke: A form of coal used as industrial fuel.

Every child had a pretty good shot
To get at least as far as their old man got
But something happened on the way to that place
30   They threw an American flag in our face

Well I'm waiting here in Allentown
And it's hard to keep a good man down
But I won't be getting up today
And it's getting very hard to stay
35   And we're living here in Allentown

Guide for Responding

◆ Literature and Your Life

Reader's Response If you were the speaker in this song, would you stay in Allentown? Explain.

Thematic Focus Which has a greater influence on a person's fate—his or her character or the surrounding environment? Support your opinion.

☑ Check Your Comprehension

1. For what is Allentown famous?
2. According to the speaker, what is "real" inAllentown?
3. What happened to the union in Allentown?
4. What did the speaker expect to do for a living?

◆ Critical Thinking

INTERPRET

1. According to the speaker, how did his education fail him? **[Interpret]**
2. Why does the speaker mention his father's war experience? **[Connect]**
3. What is the speaker's attitude toward America? **[Draw Conclusions]**

EVALUATE

4. Is the speaker's attitude justified? Explain. **[Assess]**

EXTEND

5. What might Stevens, MacLeish, or Moore think of "Allentown"? Explain. **[Literature Link]**

Thematic Connection

TROUBLED TIMES

Economic and social changes can happen quickly. Sometimes individuals have to struggle to keep up. Sometimes whole cities find themselves without the resources to keep up. This was the case for Allentown, Pennsylvania, which lost its most important industry—the steel industry that had once been vital to our nation's prosperity.

Joel's song expresses the inner turmoil of a man living in troubled times. In addition to suffering from financial problems, the speaker suffers spiritually— his most deeply rooted beliefs are being held up to question. He has lost the security of a world where "Every child had a pretty good shot / To get at least as far as their old man got." Many people feel the same even today.

Billy Joel's song might leave you with the question: Will the speaker remake himself, or will he surrender?

1. What is the mood of "Allentown"? Give examples to support your answer.
2. Do you think the speaker could have changed his destiny? Why or why not?
3. What does the future seem to hold for the speaker and the town? Support your answer with evidence from the song.

 Idea Bank

Writing

1. **Application Essay** You are the speaker in the song "Allentown," and you've decided to seek training for another career. Write an application essay for a technical school or training program. Stress the experience and personal qualities that would make you a good student. **[Career Link]**

2. **Letter to Congress** As the speaker in "Allentown," write a letter to your Congressional representative. Summarize the state of the local economy and its effect upon the population. Make suggestions about what the government might do to help. **[Social Studies Link]**

3. **Newspaper Interview** You are a journalist assigned the task of profiling an individual personally affected by economic changes. With this goal in mind, write up an interview with the speaker of "Allentown." **[Media Link]**

Speaking and Listening

4. **Role Play** With a partner, role-play two retired steel workers reminiscing about their working days. They might recall working conditions, union strikes, or financial matters. **[Social Studies Link]**

5. **Interview** Interview an adult who lived through—or knew someone who lived through—financial hard times resulting from an economic change or a job lay-off. Relate what you learn. **[Social Studies Link]**

Projects

6. **Diagram** Research the process of manufacturing steel. Create a diagram illustrating the basic steps in the process. **[Science Link]**

7. **City Profile** Research Allentown before and after the collapse of the steel industry. If possible, find pictures. Share your findings with the class. **[Social Studies Link]**

Writing Process Workshop

During the Modern Age, many fiction writers and poets abandoned traditional structures and began experimenting with new forms and techniques. You can also experiment with forms and techniques when you write creatively. When you write an essay for a test, however, it is essential that your writing fit into the format that the test dictates. In addition, you must work quickly and efficiently, outlining your ideas, crafting your essay, and making revisions within a matter of minutes.

The following skills, introduced in this section's Writing Mini-Lessons, will help you write a concise, complete test essay.

Writing Skills Focus

▶ **Elaborate** on your key points. Provide enough facts and details to thoroughly answer the question. (See p. 685.)

▶ **Maintain brevity and clarity.** Make sure your essay is clear and direct. Avoid including unnecessary details, and check to see that each word conveys your intended meaning. (See p. 667.)

▶ **Pay attention to accuracy.** Make sure that any facts, names, and dates you cite are correct. (See p. 707.)

▶ **Provide necessary background information.** Present definitions and historical details that give a framework for your answer. (See p. 717.)

Consider how the following essay demonstrates these skills:

WRITING MODEL

Excerpt from a test essay on the importance of voting

I believe that all eligible citizens should vote in every election. ① The right to vote is a freedom that we should not take for granted. . . . Even in this country, people could not always vote. For example, African American men could not vote until after the Civil War. Women could not vote until early in this century. ② History tells of several presidential elections that were determined by no more than a hundred thousand votes . . . a very small margin. ③

① The writer begins with a clear statement of his thesis, or main point.

② The writer accurately cites historical details that support his thesis.

③ This fact further elaborates on the essay's main point.

APPLYING LANGUAGE SKILLS: Sentence Fragments

A **sentence fragment** is a group of words incorrectly punctuated as a sentence. Most often, fragments are missing a subject, a verb, or both.

Missing Subject and Verb:
Responsible for changes in American poetry.

Missing Subject:
Writes about a pear tree in spring.

Missing Verb:
W. H. Auden, known for his use of satire to comment on modern society.

To correct a fragment, supply the missing element or combine the fragment with a nearby sentence.

Practice Rewrite the examples as complete sentences.

Writing Application In a timed situation, use complete sentences when you are outlining your essay to give you a head start on your draft.

Writer's Solution Connection
Language Lab

For additional practice correcting sentence fragments, complete the Fragments and Run-on Sentences lesson in the Sentence Errors unit.

Prewriting

Choose a Topic Some tests provide a highly structured topic; others offer a general question that requires you to narrow the topic. It is a good idea to be prepared for all types of questions by practicing ahead of time. Practice writing a test essay either by responding to a question you think you're likely to be asked on an upcoming test or by using one of the suggestions given below.

Topic Ideas

- Explain how Modernist writers were influenced by events of the time.
- Compare and contrast the works of two Modernist poets.

Develop Your Thesis With an Outline Allow yourself five minutes to outline your essay. Begin by quickly brainstorming for all the details that you can remember about your topic. Jot them down, then organize them in logical categories. Develop and state your thesis—the statement that summarizes your main idea. Use the following outline format to organize details and ideas for your essay, or adapt it to fit your topic:

  I. Introduction/Thesis Statement
 II. Background
     A. Detail
     B. Detail
III. Supporting Information
     A. Detail
     B. Detail
 IV. Conclusion/Restatement of Thesis

Drafting

Focus Your Response Because time is limited, a test essay must be concise. Begin with a brief introduction that states your thesis. In the body of the essay, present those details that most effectively support your thesis statement. Summarize your main points in a conclusion.

Mark Places for Factual Details In a timed situation, it is easy to stall over a name, title, or other detail. If this happens to you, mark the place with a check in the margin and continue writing. When you have completed your draft, go back and add missing information. If you are still unable to remember, adjust your essay to include a different, but equally relevant, detail.

Revising

Do a Quick Check While you won't have time to do a full-scale revision, take a few minutes at the end of the test to do a quick scan of your essay. Whenever you revise a test essay, use questions like these to guide your editing:

▶ Have you left out any important facts or details? *Add any information that will improve your argument.*

▶ Are all of your facts accurate? *Eliminate or replace any facts about which you are unsure.*

▶ Is the writing legible? *If there are any words that can't be read, take the time to make them more clear.*

▶ Are all your ideas expressed in full sentences? *Revise any sentence fragments or run-ons.*

▶ Is the order of extra pages clear? *Take a minute to number the pages so your reader reads the information in the way that you intend.*

REVISION MODEL

① *during the time between the two world wars,*

Influenced by developments in modern psychology ∧ writers

began using the stream-of-consciousness technique.

~~The term originated with American psychologist William~~

~~James.~~ ② The technique, unlike traditional literary forms,

attempts to present thoughts, memories, and insights

connected by a character's natural associations.

~~James Joyce~~ ③ and William Faulkner, *an* American novelists,

④ *Other prose authors who employed this technique include Katherine Anne Porter and John Dos Passos.*

used stream of consciousness successfully. ∧

① The author adds a historical detail to clarify the time frame of the events.

② By deleting a detail that is not necessary or true, the author maintains a clear, brief presentation.

③ The author deletes a factually incorrect detail: James Joyce was Irish.

④ Additional details help support the thesis.

Publishing

▶ **Share Your Essay** Ask family members to read your essay and give their reactions. Did they learn something new?

APPLYING LANGUAGE SKILLS: Language Variety

Avoid repeating the same words and phrases. Think of synonyms or alternative ways to structure your sentences. Notice how the example is improved:

Example:

Many of the expatriates settled in Paris. The expatriates were named the "lost generation" by Gertrude Stein, who influenced the writing of many of the expatriates.

Revision:

The expatriate writers were named "the lost generation" by Gertrude Stein. Much of their writing was influenced by Stein, who entertained them at her Paris home.

Practice Revise the following to improve language variety.

Thomas Wolfe is a native of Asheville, N.C. He is best known for his first novel, *Look Homeward Angel*. Thomas Wolfe's novel is about his experiences in Asheville, N.C.

Writer's Solution Connection
Writing Lab

For more help on test essays, use the instruction and activities in the tutorial on Practical and Technical Writing in the Writing Lab CD-ROM.

Strategies for Success

Don't believe everything you read! Many types of writing openly seek to influence your ideas. Others reflect the subjective viewpoint or agenda of the writer. Challenging the text helps you evaluate the reliability and objectivity of what you read.

Define the Purpose First of all, determine the writer's purpose in the text. Does the material seek to persuade, entertain, inform, or describe? Choose your focus accordingly: for example, challenging factual accuracy in an informative article.

Consider the Issues Bring some skepticism along as you challenge texts. These tips can help you examine statements, data, and description:

▶ Look for language with either negative or positive connotations.

▶ Note evidence of bias in the text.

▶ Identify unsupported opinions.

▶ Question the writer's focus—are you hearing the whole story or just a fragment?

Challenge the Text Consider alternate points of view and pieces of evidence not included in the text. Are other options plausible? Is there just as much reason to believe your alternative points of view as there is to believe the one in the text? Once you've exposed whatever weak points exist in the original text, you can decide whether you still accept the statements it presents. If you wish, broadcast your reactions in writing as an editorial or a letter to the editor, for example, or present them orally by speaking out in a town meeting.

Apply the Strategy

As a member of the debate team, you'll be arguing against TV sitcoms as valuable cultural vehicles. An opponent makes this statement in support of this art form. Challenge the text.

from **The Case of the Missing Laugh Track**
by Terry Teachout

A Russian [immigrant] once seized my lapel over lunch and informed me, in the ripest possible accent, that the half-hour situation comedy was television's only truly original contribution to the art of storytelling. . . . Although he had his history askew—sitcoms began in the days of radio—his heart was in the right place. From *I Love Lucy* to *King of the Hill*, much of what network television has to offer during its first half-century has come in the form of 30-minute playlets, with continuing casts, whose sole purpose is to make you laugh. Situation comedies are to television as westerns are to movies. Some are wonderful, some appalling, most indifferent, but taken together, they do more than anything else to sum up what the medium is about.

1. What is the purpose of this text? Explain.

2. Cite and explain words with negative or positive connotations.

3. Which, if any, of the writer's opinions are unsupported?

4. Develop a statement refuting the positions in this text.

✔ **Here are other situations in which challenging the text is important:**
▶ Sales promotional literature
▶ Travel brochures
▶ Political speeches

PART 2

Focus on Literary Forms:
The Short Story

Do It Yourself Landscape,
Andy Warhol, Museum Ludwig, Cologne,
photo courtesy of Rheinisches Bildarchiv Köln

The short story has been a part of American literature since Edgar Allan Poe defined the genre in the 1800's. Every generation of writers brings a new energy to the form, revitalizing it by reflecting the changing values, attitudes and issues of the times. The Modern Age was a critical period in the growth of the American short story, as writers such as Hemingway and Fitzgerald carried the form to new heights.

Guide for Interpreting

Ernest Hemingway *(1899–1961)*

In his short stories, Ernest Hemingway vividly and forcefully expressed the sentiments of many members of the post-World War I generation. Using a concise, direct style, he wrote about people's struggles to maintain a sense of dignity while living in a seemingly hostile and confusing world.

After graduating from high school, Hemingway got a job as a reporter for the *Kansas City Star.* Eager to serve in World War I, however, he joined the Red Cross ambulance corps in 1918 and was sent to the Italian front. Shortly after his arrival, he was severely wounded and he spent several months recovering in a Milan hospital. His experiences during the war shaped his views and provided material for his writing.

After the war, Hemingway had an especially hard time readjusting to life in the United States. Hoping to find personal contentment and establish himself as a writer, he went to Paris where he became friends with Ezra Pound, Gertrude Stein, and other expatriate writers and artists. His new friends provided him with valuable advice and helped him to develop his writing style.

In 1925, Hemingway published his first major work, *In Our Time*, a series of loosely connected short stories. A year later he published *The Sun Also Rises*, a novel about a group of British and American expatriates trying to overcome the pain and disillusionment of life in the modern world. The novel earned him international acclaim and he remained famous for the rest of his life.

Hemingway was as well known for his lifestyle as he was for his writing.

Constantly pursuing adventure, he hunted in Africa, fished in the Caribbean, and skied in Europe.

The full body of Hemingway's work—including *A Farewell to Arms* (1929), *For Whom the Bell Tolls* (1940) and *The Old Man and the Sea* (1952)—earned him the Nobel Prize for Literature in 1954.

Sherwood Anderson *(1876–1941)*

Sherwood Anderson was one of the most influential writers of the modern age. Born and raised in a small town in Ohio, Anderson used his boyhood observations and experiences as material for his best-known work: *Winesburg, Ohio* (1919), a unified collection of short stories. In this work, Anderson presents a portrait of small-town life that is strikingly different from the portraits presented in most earlier works of literature. He captures the sense of isolation hidden beneath the surface of the characters' seemingly uneventful lives. He also uses everyday language to capture the true flavor of his characters—a technique that influenced such other twentieth-century writers as Ernest Hemingway.

Success in the City

In his own life, Anderson eventually left small-town life behind, moving to Chicago, to pursue a writing career. There, he met Carl Sandburg, Theodore Dreiser, Edgar Lee Masters, and other writers. When he saw the success of Masters's *Spoon River Anthology*, he began to write about life in rural America.

Psychology and Literature

While he was concerned with the troubles of modern life, Anderson was one of the first American writers to incorporate the ideas of contemporary psychology in his works. Inspired by the insights of Austrian psychologist Sigmund Freud, Anderson developed a type of character known as *grotesque* that had a singular focus on one truth, value, or assumption.

Although Anderson's reputation rests mainly on the success of *Winesburg, Ohio*, he published several other books, including *Windy McPherson's Son* (1916), *The Triumph of the Egg* (1921), *Horses and Men* (1923), and *Death in the Woods and Other Stories* (1933).

Eudora Welty *(1909–)*

In her short stories and novels. Eudora Welty vividly captures life in the deep South, creating powerful images of the landscape and conveying the shared attitudes and values of the people. She often confronts the hardships and sorrows of life in poor rural areas.

Despite her awareness of people's suffering, her outlook remains positive and optimistic.

Welty was born in Jackson, Mississippi, where she has spent most of her life. She attended Mississippi State College for Women before transferring to the University of Wisconsin, from which she graduated in 1929. Hoping to pursue a career in advertising, she moved to New York and enrolled at Columbia University School of Business. However, because of the worsening Depression, she was unable to find a steady job and returned to Jackson in 1931.

After accepting a job as a publicist for a government agency, she spent several years traveling throughout Mississippi, taking photographs and interviewing people. Her experiences and observations inspired her to write fiction, and in 1936, her first short story, "Death of a Travelling Salesman," was published in a small magazine.

Throughout her work, Welty displays an acute sense of detail and a deep sense of compassion toward her characters. In "A Worn Path," for example, she paints a sympathetic portrait of an old woman whose feelings of love and sense of duty motivate her to make a long, painful journey through the woods.

Welty is one of the leading American writers of the twentieth century. Over the years, she has published numerous collections of short stories and novels. In 1973, her novel *The Optimist's Daughter* won the Pulitzer Prize.

◆ Background for Understanding

HISTORY: WORLD WAR I

World War I was the first truly global war, involving nations on every continent but Antarctica. The Great War, as it was also called, began in Europe in 1914, sparked by nationalistic pride and systems of alliances among nations. The Central Powers (Germany, Austria, Turkey) fought the Allies (England, France, Russia) with other nations joining one side or the other. Italy, where Hemingway's "In Another Country" takes place, was not strategically important but helped the Allies by drawing Central Power troops away from other battle areas.

The war lasted four brutal years and took the lives of nine million soldiers. Throughout most of the conflict, a stalemate existed. Both sides were dug into trenches and took turns rushing one another. Each rush was greeted by a barrage of machine fire, with thousands falling dead. Other soldiers fell to new weapons of killing—inventions such as airplanes, long-range artillery, and poison gas, which many people had hoped would deter aggressors and prevent war. Many of the wounded

were saved, however, by advances in medical treatment, such as surgically disinfected wounds, plastic surgery, and rehabilitation to strengthen injured limbs. Ironically, despite the war's devastation, modern medicine leapt forward during World War I.

Guide for Interpreting (continued)

◆ Literature and Your Life

CONNECT YOUR EXPERIENCE

During the course of your life, you'll journey to countless places. Through these journeys you'll learn about yourself and the world around you. In each of these stories, you'll encounter characters who make journeys that dramatically impact their lives. How do their journeys compare to ones you've made?

Journal Writing Jot down some thoughts you might have during a journey. Your journey may be real or imagined.

THEMATIC FOCUS: FACING TROUBLED TIMES

War, poverty, illness—such hardships affect people's personal journeys. How are these story characters affected by hardships?

◆ Literary Focus

POINT OF VIEW

Each of these stories is told from a different **point of view,** or perspective. "In Another Country" features a narrator who is the central character in the story. He uses the **first-person point of view** referring to himself as "I" and telling the story in his own words. "The Corn Planting" also uses the first-person point of view but the narrator is a minor character. In both these stories, readers learn only what is in the narrator's range of experience. "A Worn Path" is told from the **limited third-person point of view,** in which a narrator who doesn't participate in the action tells the story and conveys the thoughts of one of the characters.

◆ Grammar and Style

PUNCTUATING DIALOGUE

Like most short stories, these pieces include dialogue. Notice that the dialogue follows these rules.

Quotation marks appear immediately before and after a character's words. When a quotation is inserted into a longer sentence, place a comma before each set of marks. ("*Dance old scarecrow,*" *she said,* "*while I dance with you.*") **Periods** are placed inside the quotation marks. **Question** and **exclamation marks** appear inside the quotation marks if they are part of the quoted material. ("*How could we?*" *he said.*) Place them outside the marks if they belong to the overall sentence. (*Did he really mean,* "*I loved that story*"?)

◆ Reading Strategy

IDENTIFY WITH CHARACTERS

Even if your journeys have differed greatly from the ones taken by these characters, you might feel as if you know them. When you **identify with characters,** you try to relate to their thoughts and feelings, and make connections to your own experience. For example, when the doctor consoles the injured soldier in this story, you might find yourself remembering an injury *you* recovered from, or you may just feel you know what the soldier feels like. In either case, you're identifying with the character—taking him into your personal world.

◆ Build Vocabulary

WORD ROOTS: -val-

The word *invalided* means "removed from active duty by illness or injury." You can construct this meaning—and the meaning of other *-val-* words—with the help of the word root *-val-*, which means "strength or value."

WORD BANK

Preview this list of words from the stories.

invalided
grave
limber
obstinate

In Another Country

Ernest Hemingway

In the fall the war[1] was always there, but we did not go to it any more. It was cold in the fall in Milan[2] and the dark came very early. Then the electric lights came on, and it was pleasant along the streets looking in the windows. There was much game hanging outside the shops, and the snow powdered in the fur of the foxes and the wind blew their tails. The deer hung stiff and heavy and empty, and small birds blew in the wind and the wind turned their feathers. It was a cold fall and the wind came down from the mountains.

We were all at the hospital every afternoon, and there were different ways of walking across the town through the dusk to the hospital. Two of the ways were alongside canals, but they were long. Always, though, you crossed a bridge across a canal to enter the hospital. There was a choice of three bridges. On one of them a woman sold roasted chestnuts. It was warm, standing in front of her charcoal fire, and the chestnuts were warm afterward in your pocket. The hospital was very old and very beautiful, and you entered through a gate and walked across a courtyard and out a gate on the other side. There were usually funerals starting from the courtyard. Beyond the old hospital were the new brick pavilions, and there we met every afternoon and were all very polite and interested in what was the matter, and sat in the machines that were to make so much difference.

The doctor came up to the machine where I was sitting and said: "What did you like best to do before the war? Did you practice a sport?"

I said: "Yes, football."

"Good," he said. "You will be able to play football again better than ever."

My knee did not bend and the leg dropped straight from the knee to the ankle without a calf, and the machine was to bend the knee and make it move as in riding a tricycle. But it did not bend yet, and instead the machine lurched when it came to the bending part. The doctor said: "That will all pass. You are a fortunate young man. You will play football again like a champion."

In the next machine was a major who had a little hand like a baby's. He winked at me when the doctor examined his hand, which was between two leather straps that bounced up and down and flapped the stiff fingers, and said: "And will I too play football, captain-doctor?" He had been a very great fencer, and before the war the greatest fencer in Italy.

The doctor went to his office in a back room and brought a photograph which showed a hand that had been withered almost as small as the major's, before it had taken a machine course, and after was a little larger. The major held the photograph with his good hand and

---

1. **the war:** World War I (1914–1918).
2. **Milan** (mi lan´): A city in northern Italy.

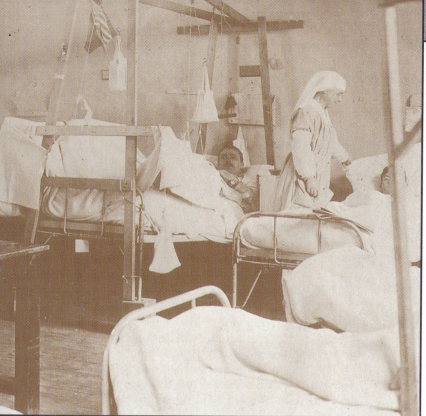

◀ **Critical Viewing** How does the World War I military hospital in this photo compare with the hospital Hemingway describes? [**Compare and Contrast**]

we passed. Another boy who walked with us sometimes and made us five wore a black silk handkerchief across his face because he had no nose then and his face was to be rebuilt. He had gone out to the front from the military academy and been wounded within an hour after he had gone into the front line for the first time. They rebuilt his face, but he came from a very old family and they could never get the nose exactly right. He went to South America and worked in a bank. But this was a long time ago, and then we did not any of us know how it was going to be afterward. We only knew then that there was always the war, but that we were not going to it any more.

We all had the same medals, except the boy with the black silk bandage across his face, and he had not been at the front long enough to get any medals. The tall boy with a very pale face who was to be a lawyer had been a lieutenant of Arditi[5] and had three medals of the sort we each had only one of. He had lived a very long time with death and was a little detached. We were all a little detached, and there was nothing that held us together except that we met every afternoon at the hospital. Although, as we walked to the Cova through the tough part of town, walking in the dark, with light and singing coming out of the wineshops, and sometimes having to walk into the street when the men and women would crowd together on the sidewalk so that we would have had to jostle them to get by, we felt held together by there being something that had happened that they, the people who disliked us, did not understand.

looked at it very carefully. "A wound?" he asked.

"An industrial accident," the doctor said.

"Very interesting, very interesting," the major said, and handed it back to the doctor.

"You have confidence?"

"No," said the major.

There were three boys who came each day who were about the same age I was. They were all three from Milan, and one of them was to be a lawyer, and one was to be a painter, and one had intended to be a soldier, and after we were finished

◆ **Literary Focus**
Who is telling this story? How is the narrator identified?

with the machines, sometimes we walked back together to the Café Cova, which was next door to the Scala.[3] We walked the short way through the communist quarter because we were four together. The people hated us because we were officers, and from a wine-shop someone called out, "A basso gli ufficiali!"[4] as

---

3. **the Scala** (skä´ la): An opera house in Milan.
4. **"A basso gli ufficiali!"** (a ba´ so lye oo fe cha´ le): "Down with officers!" (Italian).

5. **Arditi** (är dē´ tē): A select group of soldiers chosen specifically for dangerous campaigns.

We ourselves all understood the Cova, where it was rich and warm and not too brightly lighted, and noisy and smoky at certain hours, and there were always girls at the tables and the illustrated papers on a rack on the wall. The girls at the Cova were very patriotic, and I found that the most patriotic people in Italy were the café girls—and I believe they are still patriotic.

The boys at first were very polite about my medals and asked me what I had done to get them. I showed them the papers, which were written in very beautiful language and full of *fratellanza* and *abnegazione*,[6] but which really said, with the adjectives removed, that I had been given the medals because I was an American. After that their manner changed a little toward me, although I was their friend against outsiders. I was a friend, but I was never really one of them after they had read the citations, because it had been different with them and they had done very different things to get their medals. I had been wounded, it was true; but we all knew that being wounded, after all, was really an accident. I was never ashamed of the ribbons, though, and sometimes, after the cocktail hour, I would imagine myself having done all the things they had done to get their medals; but walking home at night through the empty streets with the cold wind and all the shops closed, trying to keep near the street lights, I knew that I would never have done such things, and I was very much afraid to die, and often lay in bed at night by myself, afraid to die and wondering how I would be when I went back to the front again.

The three with the medals were like hunting-hawks; and I was not a hawk, although I might seem a hawk to those who had never hunted; they, the three, knew better and so we drifted apart. But I stayed good friends with the boy who had been wounded his first day at the front, because he would never know now how he would have turned out; so he could never be accepted either, and I liked him because I thought perhaps he would not have turned out to be a hawk either.

The major, who had been the great fencer, did not believe in bravery, and spent much time while we sat in the machines correcting my grammar. He had complimented me on how I spoke Italian, and we talked together very easily. One day I had said that Italian seemed such an easy language to me that I could not take a great interest in it; everything was so easy to say. "Ah yes," the major said. "Why, then, do you not take up the use of grammar?" So we took up the use of grammar, and soon Italian was such a difficult language that I was afraid to talk to him until I had the grammar straight in my mind.

The major came very regularly to the hospital. I do not think he ever missed a day, although I am sure he did not believe in the machines. There was a time when none of us believed in the machines, and one day the major said it was all nonsense. The machines were new then and it was we who were to prove them. It was an idiotic idea, he said, "a theory, like another." I had not learned my grammar, and he said I was a stupid impossible disgrace, and he was a fool to have bothered with me. He was a small man and he sat straight up in his chair with his right hand thrust into the machine and looked straight ahead at the wall while the straps thumped up and down with his fingers in them.

"What will you do when the war is over if it is over?" he asked me. "Speak grammatically!"

"I will go to the States."

"Are you married?"

"No, but I hope to be."

"The more of a fool you are," he said. He seemed very angry. "A man must not marry."

"Why, Signor Maggiore?"[7]

"Don't call me 'Signor Maggiore.'"

"Why must not a man marry?"

"He cannot marry. He cannot marry," he said angrily. "If he is to lose everything, he should not place himself in a position to lose that. He should not place himself in a position to lose. He should find things he cannot lose."

He spoke very angrily and bitterly, and looked straight ahead while he talked.

---

6. *fratellanza* (frä tāl än′ tsä) and *abnegazione* (äb′ nā gä tzyō′ nā): "Brotherhood" and "self-denial" (Italian).

7. **Signor Maggiore** (sēn yōr′ mäj jō′ rā): "Mr. Major" (Italian); a respectful way of addressing an officer.

"But why should he necessarily lose it?"

"He'll lose it," the major said. He was looking at the wall. Then he looked down at the machine and jerked his little hand out from between the straps and slapped it hard against his thigh. "He'll lose it," he almost shouted. "Don't argue with me!" Then he called to the attendant who ran the machines. "Come and turn this damned thing off."

He went back into the other room for the light treatment and the massage. Then I heard him ask the doctor if he might use his telephone and he shut the door. When he came back into the room, I was sitting in another machine. He was wearing his cape and had his cap on, and he came directly toward my machine and put his arm on my shoulder.

"I am so sorry," he said, and patted me on the shoulder with his good hand. "I would not be rude. My wife has just died. You must forgive me."

"Oh—" I said, feeling sick for him. "I am so sorry."

He stood there biting his lower lip. "It is very difficult," he said. "I cannot resign myself."

He looked straight past me and out through the window. Then he began to cry. "I am utterly unable to resign myself," he said and choked. And then crying, his head up looking at nothing, carrying himself straight and soldierly, with tears on both his cheeks and biting his lips, he walked past the machines and out the door.

The doctor told me that the major's wife, who was very young and whom he had not married until he was definitely underlined invalided /underlined out of the war, had died of pneumonia. She had been sick only a few days. No one expected her to die. The major did not come to the hospital for three days. Then he came at the usual hour, wearing a black band on the sleeve of his uniform. When he came back, there were large framed photographs around the wall of all sorts of wounds before and after they had been cured by the machines. In front of the machine the major used were three photographs of hands like his that were completely restored. I do not know where the doctor got them. I always understood we were the first to use the machines. The photographs did not make much difference to the major because he only looked out of the window.

◆ **Build Vocabulary**

invalided (in´ və lid´ id) *v.*: Released because of illness or disability

Guide for Responding

◆*Literature and Your Life*

Reader's Response What emotion did this story arouse most strongly in you? Explain.

Thematic Focus What qualities allow the characters in this story to deal with hardship? Explain.

Journal Writing Describe what you learned about World War I from the story.

☑ Check Your Comprehension

1. Why does the narrator go to the hospital every afternoon?
2. How do the people in the communist quarter react to the officers as they walked by?
3. (a) What happens to the major's wife? (b) How does he react?

◆ Critical Thinking

INTERPRET

1. How would you describe the story's mood? **[Deduce]**
2. How do the three boys' attitude about the war relate to their nationalities? **[Connect]**
3. What might be the significance of the major's interest in grammar? **[Interpret]**
4. Find examples to support this statement: In this story, the machines symbolize the false hopes and promises of the Modern Age. **[Support]**
5. What is ironic, or surprising, about the major's wife's death? **[Analyze]**

APPLY

6. How does the story reflect the sense of disillusionment that arose during World War I? **[Apply]**

The Corn Planting

Sherwood Anderson

The farmers who come to our town to trade are a part of the town life. Saturday is the big day. Often the children come to the high school in town.

It is so with Hatch Hutchenson. Although his farm, some three miles from town, is small, it is known to be one of the best-kept and best-worked places in all our section. Hatch is a little gnarled old figure of a man. His place is on the Scratch Gravel Road and there are plenty of poorly kept places out that way.

Hatch's place stands out. The little frame house is always kept painted, the trees in his orchard are whitened with lime halfway up the trunks, and the barn and sheds are in repair, and his fields are always clean-looking.

Hatch is nearly seventy. He got a rather late start in life. His father, who owned the same farm, was a Civil War man and came home badly wounded, so that, although he lived a long time after the war, he couldn't work much. Hatch was the only son and stayed at home, working the place until his father died. Then, when he was nearing fifty, he married a schoolteacher of forty, and they had a son. The schoolteacher was a small one like Hatch. After they married, they both stuck close to the land. They seemed to fit into their farm life as certain people fit into the clothes they wear. I have noticed something about people who make a go of marriage. They grow more and more alike. Then even grow to look alike.

Their one son, Will Hutchenson, was a small but remarkably strong boy. He came to our high school in town and pitched on our town baseball team. He was a fellow always cheerful, bright and alert, and a great favorite with all of us.

For one thing, he began as a young boy to make amusing little drawings. It was a talent. He made drawings of fish and pigs and cows, and they looked like people you knew. I never did know, before, that people could look so much like cows and horses and pigs and fish.

When he had finished in the town high school, Will went to Chicago, where his mother had a cousin living, and he became a student in the Art Institute out there. Another young fellow from our town was also in Chicago. He really went two years before Will did. His name was Hal Weyman, and he was a student at the University of Chicago. After he graduated, he came home and got a job as principal of our high school.

Hal and Will Hutchenson hadn't been close friends before, Hal being several years older than Will, but in Chicago they got together, went together to see plays, and, as Hal later told me, they had a good many long talks.

I got it from Hal that, in Chicago, as at home here when he was a young boy, Will was immediately popular. He was good-looking, so the girls in the art school liked him, and he had a straightforwardness that made him popular with all the young fellows.

Hal told me that Will was out to some party nearly every night, and right away he began to sell some of his amusing little drawings and to make money. The drawings were used in advertisements, and he was well paid.

He even began to send some money home. You see, after Hal came back here, he used to go quite often out to the Hutchenson place to see Will's father and mother. He would walk or drive out there in the afternoon or on summer evenings and sit with them. The talk was always of Will.

Hal said it was touching how much the father and mother depended on their one son, how much they talked about him and dreamed of his future. They had never been people who went about much with the town folks or even with their neighbors. They were of the sort who work all the time, from early morning till late in the evenings, and on moonlight nights, Hal said, and after the little old wife had got the supper, they often went out into the fields and worked again.

You see, by this time old Hatch was nearing seventy and his wife would have been ten years younger. Hal said that whenever he went out to the farm they quit work and came to sit with him. They might be in one of the fields, working together, but when they saw him in the road, they came running. They had got a letter from Will. He wrote every week.

The little old mother would come running following the father. "We got another letter, Mr. Weyman," Hatch would cry, and then his wife, quite breathless, would say the same thing, "Mr. Weyman, we got a letter."

The letter would be brought out at once and read aloud. Hal said the letters were always delicious. Will larded them with little sketches. There were humorous drawings of people he had seen or been with, rivers of automobiles on Michigan Avenue in Chicago, a policeman at a street crossing, young stenographers hurrying into office buildings. Neither of the old people had ever been to the city and they were curious and eager. They wanted the drawings explained, and Hal said they were like two children wanting to know every little detail Hal could remember about their son's life in the big city. He was always at them to come there on a visit and they would spend hours talking of that.

◆ **Literary Focus**
How does the narrator interact with other characters?

"Of course," Hatch said, "we couldn't go."

"How could we?" he said. He had been on that one little farm since he was a boy. When he was a young fellow, his father was an invalid and so Hatch had to run things. A farm, if you run it right, is very exacting. You have to fight weeds all the time. There are the farm animals to take care of. "Who would milk our cows?" Hatch said. The idea of anyone but him or his wife touching one of the Hutchenson cows seemed to hurt him. While he was alive, he didn't want anyone else plowing one of his fields, tending his corn, looking after things about the barn. He felt that way about his farm. It was a thing you couldn't explain, Hal said. He seemed to understand the two old people.

It was a spring night, past midnight, when Hal came to my house and told me the news. In our town we have a night telegraph operator at the railroad station and Hal got a wire. It was really addressed to Hatch Hutchenson, but the operator brought it to Hal. Will Hutchenson was dead, had been killed. It turned out later that he was at a party with some other young fellows and there might have been some drinking. Anyway, the car was wrecked, and Will Hutchenson was killed. The operator wanted Hal to go out and take the message to Hatch and his wife, and Hal wanted me to go along.

I offered to take my car, but Hal said no, "Let's

◀ **Critical Viewing** What does a harvest usually symbolize? How does corn play an important part of this story? **[Connect]**

Farm Landscape, Grant Wood, Coe College, Cedar Rapids, Iowa,
© Estate of Grant Wood/Licensed by VAGA, New York, NY

walk out," he said. He wanted to put off the moment, I could see that. So we did walk. It was early spring, and I remember every moment of the silent walk we took, the little leaves just coming on the trees, the little streams we crossed, how the moonlight made the water seem alive. We loitered and loitered, not talking, hating to go on.

Then we got out there, and Hal went to the front door of the farmhouse while I stayed in the road. I heard a dog bark, away off somewhere. I heard a child crying in some distant house. I think that Hal, after he got to the front door of the house, must have stood there for ten minutes, hating to knock.

Then he did knock, and the sound his fist made on the door seemed terrible. It seemed like guns going off. Old Hatch came to the door, and I heard Hal tell him. I know what happened. Hal had been trying, all the way out from town, to think up words to tell the old couple in some gentle way, but when it came to the scratch, he couldn't. He blurted everything right out, right into old Hatch's face.

That was all. Old Hatch didn't say a word. The door was opened, he stood there in the moonlight, wearing a funny long white nightgown, Hal told him, and the door went shut again with a bang, and Hal was left standing there.

He stood for a time, and then came back out

▲ **Critical Viewing** How does the mood of this idealized image of a farm compare with the mood conveyed in the story? Explain.**[Compare and Contrast]**

into the road to me. "Well," he said, and "Well," I said. We stood in the road looking and listening. There wasn't a sound from the house.

And then—it might have been ten minutes or it might have been a half-hour—we stood silently, listening and watching, not knowing what to do—we couldn't go away——"I guess they are trying to get so they can believe it," Hal whispered to me. I got his notion all right. The two old people must have thought of their son Will always only in terms of life, never of death.

We stood watching and listening, and then, suddenly, after a long time, Hal touched me on the arm. "Look," he whispered. There were two white-clad figures going from the house to the barn. It turned out, you see, that old Hatch had been plowing that day. He had finished plowing and harrowing a field near the barn.

The two figures went into the barn and presently came out. They went into the field, and Hal and I crept across the farmyard to the barn and got to where we could see what was going on without being seen.

It was an incredible thing. The old man had got a hand corn-planter out of the barn and his wife had got a bag of seed corn, and there, in the moonlight, that night, after they got that news, they were planting corn.

It was a thing to curl your hair—it was so ghostly. They were both in their nightgowns. They would do a row across the field, coming quite close to us as we stood in the shadow of the barn, and then, at the end of each row, they would kneel side by side by the fence and stay silent for a time. The whole thing went on in silence. It was the first time in my life I ever understood something, and I am far from sure now that I can put down what I understood and felt that night—I mean something about the connection between certain people and the earth—a kind of silent cry, down into the earth, of these two old people, putting corn down into the earth. It was as though they were putting death down into the ground that life might grow again—something like that.

They must have been asking something of the earth, too. But what's the use? What they were up to in connection with the life in their field and the lost life in their son is something you can't very well make clear in words. All I know is that Hal and I stood the sight as long as we could, and then we crept away and went back to town, but Hatch Hutchenson and his wife must have got what they were after that night, because Hal told me that when he went out in the morning to see them and to make the arrangements for bringing their dead son home, they were both curiously quiet and Hal thought in command of themselves. Hal said he thought they had got something. "They have their farm and they have still got Will's letters to read," Hal said.

◆ *Literature and Your Life*

Use empathy and your own experience to explain why Hal and the narrator find it difficult to watch the Hutchensons plant corn.

Guide for Responding

◆ *Literature and Your Life*

Reader's Response Which character did you identify the most with in this story? Why?

Thematic Focus If you were Mr. or Mrs. Hutchenson, how would you have faced the terrible news of Will's death?

Journal Writing Each person has his or her own way of dealing with grief. In a journal entry, discuss coping methods you have used or observed.

☑ Check Your Comprehension

1. Why didn't Hatch Hutchenson go off to make his own way in the world?
2. What did the Hutchensons always do when Hal came to visit?
3. Why is Hal given the task of bringing the bad news to the Hutchensons?

◆ Critical Thinking

INTERPRET

1. Why do the Hutchensons spend so much time working in their fields? **[Infer]**
2. Why do the Hutchensons react as they do to the news Hal Weyman brings? **[Interpret]**
3. Compare the Hutchensons at the story's beginning and at its end. **[Compare and Contrast]**
4. What message about life does this story convey? Support your answer. **[Draw Conclusions]**

EVALUATE

5. Do you think Hal did a good job of telling the Hutchensons about Will's death? Why or why not? **[Make a Judgment]**

EXTEND

6. Compare and contrast this story with others you've read that deal with grief. **[Literature Link]**

A Worn Path

Eudora Welty

It was December—a bright frozen day in the early morning. Far out in the country there was an old Negro woman with her head tied in a red rag, coming along a path through the pinewoods. Her name was Phoenix Jackson. She was very old and small and she walked slowly in the dark pine shadows, moving a little from side to side in her steps, with the balanced heaviness and lightness of a pendulum in a grandfather clock. She carried a thin, small cane made from an umbrella, and with this she kept tapping the frozen earth in front of her. This made a grave and persistent noise in the still air, that seemed meditative like the chirping of a solitary little bird.

She wore a dark striped dress reaching down to her shoe tops, and an equally long apron of bleached sugar sacks, with a full pocket all neat and tidy, but every time she took a step she

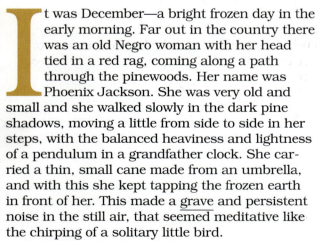

▲ **Critical Viewing** Use the third and fourth paragraphs of the story to decide whether this image accurately represents the path Phoenix travels. [Evaluate]

might have fallen over her shoelaces, which dragged from her unlaced shoes. She looked straight ahead. Her eyes were blue with age. Her skin had a pattern all its own of numberless branching wrinkles and as though a whole little tree stood in the middle of her forehead, but a golden color ran underneath, and the two knobs of her cheeks were illumined by a yellow burning under the dark. Under the red rag her hair came down on her neck in the frailest of ringlets, still black, and with an odor like copper.

Now and then there was a quivering in the thicket. Old Phoenix said, "Out of my way, all you foxes, owls, beetles, jack rabbits, coons

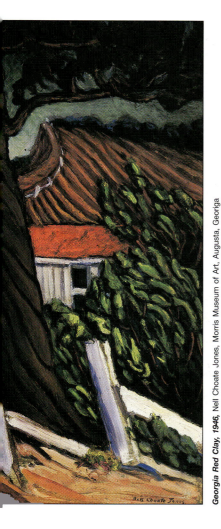

Georgia Red Clay, 1946, Nell Choate Jones, Morris Museum of Art, Augusta, Georiga

and wild animals! . . . Keep out from under these feet, little bobwhites[1]. . . . Keep the big wild hogs out of my path. Don't let none of those come running my direction. I got a long way." Under her small black-freckled hand her cane, <u>limber</u> as a buggy whip, would switch at the brush as if to rouse up any hiding things. On she went. The woods were deep and still. The sun made the pine needles almost too bright to look at, up where the wind rocked. The cones dropped as light as feathers.

Down in the hollow was the mourning dove—it was not too late for him.

The path ran up a hill. "Seem like there is chains about my feet, time I get this far," she said, in the voice of argument old people keep to use with themselves. "Something always take a hold of me on this hill—pleads I should stay."

After she got to the top she turned and gave a full, severe look behind her where she had come. "Up through pines," she said at length. "Now down through oaks."

Her eyes opened their widest, and she started down gently. But before she got to the bottom of the hill a bush caught her dress.

Her fingers were busy and intent, but her skirts were full and long, so that before she could pull them free in one place they were caught in another. It was not possible to allow the dress to tear. "I in the thorny bush," she said. "Thorns, you doing your appointed work. Never want to let folks pass, no sir. Old eyes thought you was a pretty little *green* bush."

Finally, trembling all over, she stood free, and after a moment dared to stoop for her cane.

"Sun so high!" she cried, leaning back and looking, while the thick tears went over her eyes. "The time getting all gone here."

At the foot of this hill was a place where a log was laid across the creek.

"Now comes the trial," said Phoenix.

Putting her right foot out, she mounted the log and shut her eyes. Lifting her skirt, leveling her cane fiercely before her, like a festival figure in some parade, she began to march across. Then she opened her eyes and she was safe on the other side.

"I wasn't as old as I thought," she said.

But she sat down to rest. She spread her skirts on the bank around her and folded her hands over her knees. Up above her was a tree in a pearly cloud of mistletoe. She did not dare to close her eyes, and when a little boy brought her a plate with a slice of marble cake on it she spoke to him. "That would be acceptable," she said. But when she went to take it there was just her own hand in the air.

So she left that tree, and had to go through a barbed-wire fence. There she had to creep and crawl, spreading her knees and stretching her fingers like a baby trying to climb the steps. But she talked loudly to herself: she could not let her dress be torn now, so late in the day, and she could not pay for having her arm or her leg sawed off if she got caught fast where she was.

At last she was safe through the fence and risen up out in the clearing. Big dead trees, like black men with one arm, were standing in the purple stalks of the withered cotton field. There sat a buzzard.

"Who you watching?"

In the furrow she made her way along.

"Glad this not the season for bulls," she said, looking sideways, "and the good Lord made his

---

1. **bobwhites** *n.*: Partridges.

◆ **Build Vocabulary**

grave (grāv) *adj.*: Serious; solemn
limber (lim´ bər) *adj.*: Flexible

snakes to curl up and sleep in the winter. A pleasure I don't see no two-headed snake coming around that tree, where it come once. It took a while to get by him, back in the summer."

She passed through the old cotton and went into a field of dead corn. It whispered and shook and was taller than her head. "Through the maze now," she said, for there was no path.

Then there was something tall, black, and skinny there, moving before her.

At first she took it for a man. It could have been a man dancing in the field. But she stood still and listened, and it did not make a sound. It was as silent as a ghost.

"Ghost," she said sharply, "who be you the ghost of? For I have heard of nary death close by."

But there was no answer—only the ragged dancing in the wind.

She shut her eyes, reached out her hand, and touched a sleeve. She found a coat and inside that an emptiness, cold as ice.

"You scarecrow," she said. Her face lighted. "I ought to be shut up for good," she said with laughter. "My senses is gone. I too old. I the oldest people I ever know. Dance, old scarecrow," she said, "while I dancing with you."

◆ **Literary Focus**

From what point of view is the story being told? How do you know?

She kicked her foot over the furrow, and with mouth drawn down, shook her head once or twice in a little strutting way. Some husks blew down and whirled in streamers about her skirts.

Then she went on, parting her way from side to side with the cane, through the whispering field. At last she came to the end, to a wagon track where the silver grass blew between the red ruts. The quail were walking around like pullets, seeming all dainty and unseen.

"Walk pretty," she said. "This the easy place. This the easy going."

She followed the track, swaying through the quiet bare fields, through the little strings of trees silver in their dead leaves, past cabins silver from weather, with the doors and windows boarded shut, all like old women under a spell sitting there. "I walking in their sleep," she said, nodding her head vigorously.

In a ravine she went where a spring was silently flowing through a hollow log. Old Phoenix bent and drank. "Sweet gum[2] makes the water sweet," she said, and drank more. "Nobody know who made this well, for it was here when I was born."

The track crossed a swampy part where the moss hung as white as lace from every limb. "Sleep on, alligators, and blow your bubbles." Then the track went into the road.

Deep, deep the road went down between the high green-colored banks. Overhead the live-oaks met, and it was as dark as a cave.

A black dog with a lolling tongue came up out of the weeds by the ditch. She was meditating, and not ready, and when he came at her she only hit him a little with her cane. Over she went in the ditch, like a little puff of milkweed.[3]

Down there, her senses drifted away. A dream visited her, and she reached her hand up, but nothing reached down and gave her a pull. So she lay there and presently went to talking. "Old woman," she said to herself, "that black dog come up out of the weeds to stall you off, and now there he sitting on his fine tail, smiling at you."

A white man finally came along and found her—a hunter, a young man, with his dog on a chain.

"Well, Granny!" he laughed. "What are you doing there?"

"Lying on my back like a June bug waiting to be turned over, mister," she said, reaching up her hand.

He lifted her up, gave her a swing in the air, and set her down. "Anything broken, Granny?"

"No sir, them old dead weeds is springy enough," said Phoenix, when she had got her breath. "I thank you for your trouble."

"Where do you live, Granny?" he asked, while the two dogs were growling at each other.

"Away back yonder, sir, behind the ridge. You can't even see it from here."

"On your way home?"

"No sir, I going to town."

"Why, that's too far! That's as far as I walk when I come out myself, and I get something for my trouble." He patted the stuffed bag he carried, and there hung down a little closed claw. It was one of the bobwhites, with its beak

---

2. **sweet gum** *n*.: A tree that produces a fragrant juice.
3. **milkweed** *n*.: A plant with pods that, when ripe, release feathery seeds.

hooked bitterly to show it was dead. "Now you go on home, Granny!"

"I bound to go to town, mister," said Phoenix. "The time come around."

He gave another laugh, filling the whole landscape. "I know you old colored people! Wouldn't miss going to town to see Santa Claus!"

But something held old Phoenix very still. The deep lines in her face went into a fierce and different radiation. Without warning, she had seen with her own eyes a flashing nickel fall out of the man's pocket onto the ground.

"How old are you, Granny?" he was saying.

◆ **Literary Focus**
What might you learn about the young man's thoughts if the story were told from his point of view?

"There is no telling, mister," she said, "no telling."

Then she gave a little cry and clapped her hands and said, "Git on away from here, dog! Look! Look at that dog!" She laughed as if in admiration. "He ain't scared of nobody. He a big black dog." She whispered, "Sic him!"

"Watch me get rid of that cur," said the man. "Sic him, Pete! Sic him!"

Phoenix heard the dogs fighting, and heard the man running and throwing sticks. She even heard a gunshot. But she was slowly bending forward by that time, further and further forward, the lids stretched down over her eyes, as if she were doing this in her sleep. Her chin was lowered almost to her knees. The yellow palm of her hand came out from the fold of her apron. Her fingers slid down and along the ground under the piece of money with the grace and care they would have in lifting an egg from under a setting hen. Then she slowly straightened up, she stood erect, and the nickel was in her apron pocket. A bird flew by. Her lips moved. "God watching me the whole time. I come to stealing."

The man came back, and his own dog panted about them. "Well, I scared him off that time," he said, and then he laughed and lifted his gun and pointed it at Phoenix.

She stood straight and faced him.

"Doesn't the gun scare you?" he said, still pointing it.

"No, sir, I seen plenty go off closer by, in my day, and for less than what I done," she said, holding utterly still.

Miz Emily, Joseph Holston, Holston Reproductions

▲ Critical Viewing What details in this image suggest the woman's strong character? What details in the story suggest Phoenix's strong character? [**Connect**]

He smiled, and shouldered the gun. "Well, Granny," he said, "you must be a hundred years old, and scared of nothing. I'd give you a dime if I had any money with me. But you take my advice and stay home, and nothing will happen to you."

"I bound to go on my way, mister," said Phoenix. She inclined her head in the red rag. Then they went in different directions, but she could hear the gun shooting again and again over the hill.

She walked on. The shadows hung from the oak trees to the road like curtains. Then she smelled woodsmoke, and smelled the river, and she saw a steeple and the cabins on their steep steps. Dozens of little black children whirled around her. There ahead was Natchez[4] shining. Bells were ringing. She walked on.

In the paved city it was Christmas time. There were red and green electric lights strung and criss-crossed everywhere, and all turned on in the daytime. Old Phoenix would have been lost if she had not distrusted her eyesight and depended on her feet to know where to take her.

She paused quietly on the sidewalk where people were passing by. A lady came along in the crowd, carrying an armful of red-, green- and silver-wrapped presents; she gave off perfume like the red roses in hot summer, and Phoenix stopped her.

"Please, missy, will you lace up my shoe?" She held up her foot.

"What do you want, Grandma?"

"See my shoe," said Phoenix. "Do all right for out in the country, but wouldn't look right to go in a big building."

"Stand still then, Grandma," said the lady. She put her packages down on the sidewalk beside her and laced and tied both shoes tightly.

"Can't lace em with a cane," said Phoenix. "Thank you, missy. I doesn't mind asking a nice lady to tie up my shoe, when I gets out on the street."

Moving slowly and from side to side, she went into the big building, and into a tower of steps, where she walked up and around and around until her feet knew to stop.

She entered a door, and there she saw nailed up on the wall the document that had been stamped with the gold seal and framed in the gold frame, which matched the dream that was hung up in her head.

"Here I be," she said. There was a fixed and ceremonial stiffness over her body.

"A charity case, I suppose," said an attendant who sat at the desk before her.

But Phoenix only looked above her head. There was sweat on her face, the wrinkles in her skin shone like a bright net.

"Speak up, Grandma," the woman said. "What's your name? We must have your history, you know. Have you been here before? What seems to be the trouble with you?"

Old Phoenix only gave a twitch to her face as if a fly were bothering her.

"Are you deaf?" cried the attendant.

But then the nurse came in.

"Oh, that's just old Aunt Phoenix," she said. "She doesn't come for herself—she has a little grandson. She makes these trips just as regular as clockwork. She lives away back off the Old Natchez Trace." She bent down. "Well, Aunt Phoenix, why don't you just take a seat? We won't keep you standing after your long trip." She pointed.

The old woman sat down, bolt upright in the chair.

"Now, how is the boy?" asked the nurse.

Old Phoenix did not speak.

"I said, how is the boy?"

But Phoenix only waited and stared straight ahead, her face very solemn and withdrawn into rigidity.

"Is his throat any better?" asked the nurse. "Aunt Phoenix, don't you hear me? Is your grandson's throat any better since the last time you came for the medicine?"

With her hands on her knees, the old woman waited, silent, erect and motionless, just as if she were in armor.

"You mustn't take up our time this way, Aunt Phoenix," the nurse said. "Tell us quickly about your grandson, and get it over. He isn't dead, is he?"

At last there came a flicker and then a flame of comprehension across her face, and she spoke.

"My grandson. It was my memory had left me. There I sat and forgot why I made my long trip."

"Forgot?" The nurse frowned. "After you came so far?"

Then Phoenix was like an old woman begging a dignified forgiveness for waking up frightened in the night. "I never did go to school. I was too old at the Surrender,"[5] she said in a soft voice. "I'm an old woman without an education. It was my memory fail me. My little grandson, he is just the same, and I forgot it in the coming."

"Throat never heals, does it?" said the nurse, speaking in a loud, sure voice to old Phoenix. By now she had a card with something written on it, a little list. "Yes. Swallowed lye. When was it?—January—two-three years ago—"

Phoenix spoke unasked now. "No, missy, he not dead, he just the same. Every little while his

---

4. **Natchez** (nach′ iz): A town in southern Mississippi.

5. **the Surrender:** The surrender of the Confederate army, which ended the Civil War.

throat begin to close up again, and he not able to swallow. He not get his breath. He not able to help himself. So the time come around, and I go on another trip for the soothing medicine."

"All right. The doctor said as long as you came to get it, you could have it," said the nurse. "But it's an <u>obstinate</u> case."

"My little grandson, he sit up there in the house all wrapped up, waiting by himself," Phoenix went on. "We is the only two left in the world. He suffer and it don't seem to put him back at all. He got a sweet look. He going to last. He wear a little patch quilt and peep out holding his mouth open like a little bird. I remembers so plain now. I not going to forget him again, no, the whole enduring time. I could tell him from all the others in creation."

◆ **Reading Strategy**
Can you identify with Phoenix Jackson's feelings in this situation?

"All right." The nurse was trying to hush her now. She brought her a bottle of medicine. "Charity," she said, making a check mark in a book.

Old Phoenix held the bottle close to her eyes, and then carefully put it into her pocket.

"I thank you," she said.

"It's Christmas time, Grandma," said the attendant. "Could I give you a few pennies out of my purse?"

"Five pennies is a nickel," said Phoenix stiffly.

"Here's a nickel," said the attendant.

Phoenix rose carefully and held out her hand. She received the nickel and then fished the other nickel out of her pocket and laid it beside the new one. She stared at her palm closely, with her head on one side.

Then she gave a tap with her cane on the floor.

"This is what come to me to do," she said. "I going to the store and buy my child a little windmill they sells, made out of paper. He going to find it hard to believe there such a thing in the world. I'll march myself back where he is waiting, holding it straight up in this hand."

She lifted her free hand, gave a little nod, turned around, and walked out of the doctor's office. Then her slow step began on the stairs, going down.

◆ **Build Vocabulary**

obstinate (äb′ stə nit) *adj.*: Stubborn

Guide for Responding

◆ *Literature and Your Life*

Reader's Response Do you think Welty's use of language suits her story, or would you have used language differently? Explain.

Thematic Focus In what specific ways has a life of troubled times shaped Phoenix Jackson's character?

Group Activity With a small group, discuss the emotions this story evokes in you.

☑ Check Your Comprehension

1. Why does Phoenix make her journey?

2. What obstacles does Phoenix Jackson encounter on her journey?

3. (a) What does the nurse ask Phoenix? (b) How does Phoenix explain her inability to answer?

◆ **Critical Thinking**

INTERPRET

1. Compare and contrast the attitudes of the hunter, the attendant, and the nurse toward Phoenix. **[Compare and Contrast]**

2. Why do you think Phoenix does not immediately respond to the questions of the nurse and the attendant? **[Infer]**

3. What is the significance of the story's taking place at Christmas time? **[Interpret]**

4. What does Phoenix's journey symbolize, or represent? **[Draw Conclusions]**

EVALUATE

5. Do you think Phoenix sees herself as others see her? Explain. **[Assess]**

EXTEND

6. How might this story change if the setting were changed? **[Social Studies Link]**

Guide for Responding (continued)

◆ Literary Focus

POINT OF VIEW

Point of view refers to the perspective from which a narrative is told. Each of these stories is told from a different point of view. "In Another Country" is told by a main character from a **first-person point of view**. "The Corn Planting" is told from a first-person point of view by a minor character who primarily observes. "A Worn Path" is told from a **limited third-person point of view** by an outside narrator who reveals the thoughts of one character. In each case, the story's point of view determines the level of information you receive about the characters and events.

1. (a) List three details that you learn about the thoughts, feelings, or emotions of the narrator of "In Another Country." (b) How would the story be different if Hemingway had used a third-person point of view?
2. In what ways is the narrator of "The Corn Planting" the best character to tell the story?
3. How would "A Worn Path" be different if Welty had told the story from Phoenix Jackson's point of view?
4. Choose one of the stories in this grouping. Using a different point of view from the original, rewrite one of the paragraphs. Then compare the two versions. (a) What is gained in your version? (b) What is lost?

◆ Reading Strategy

IDENTIFY WITH CHARACTERS

When you **identify with characters** such as Phoenix Jackson, the Hutchensons, or the disillusioned soldiers, you place yourself in their shoes and try to see life as they do. You can imagine yourself behaving or feeling as they do, and consider how you'd react in their situation.

1. Among the three stories, choose the characters with whom you identify the most *and* the least. Give reasons in both cases.
2. For a reader to identify with a character, that character needs to be sympathetic—able to arouse feelings in others. Discuss why Phoenix Jackson is—or isn't—a sympathetic character.

◆ Build Vocabulary

USING THE WORD ROOT -val-

The root -val- means "strength" or "value." Use a dictionary to define each of the words below. Then write a sentence explaining how each word's definition might relate to the meaning of -val-.

1. valid
2. equivalent
3. valor
4. prevail

USING THE WORD BANK

On your paper, answer yes or no to each question. Explain each of your answers.

1. If a soldier is **invalided**, has he or she been transferred to combat duty?
2. Would someone bringing **grave** news be smiling?
3. Would a gymnast need to be **limber** before performing?
4. Would you want to pair up for a project with someone described as **obstinate**?

◆ Grammar and Style

PUNCTUATING DIALOGUE

In these stories, dialogue brings the characters to life by letting readers "hear" the characters' own words. Because each writer carefully punctuated the **dialogue**, you could easily tell who was speaking each line.

Practice The punctuation marks in the following pieces of dialogue have been misplaced. Rewrite each item, correctly placing punctuation marks.

1. "No", said the major.
2. "Well," he said, and "Well", I said.
3. "Don't argue with me"!
4. I offered to take my car, but Hal said no ",Let's walk out," he said.
5. "How old are you, Granny"? he was saying.
6. "Very interesting, very interesting", the major said, and handed it back to the doctor.

Looking at Style When you compare the amount of dialogue in these three stories, you'll notice that "The Corn Planting" has the least dialogue. How does this difference affect the way you relate to the characters? Explain.

Build Your Portfolio

Idea Bank

Writing

1. **Memorial Speech** As Hal Weyman in "The Corn Planting," write a speech you might give at Will's memorial service. In your remarks, acknowledge both Will's family and his dreams.

2. **Magazine Article** Write a feature article about the hospital machines in the story "In Another Country." Explain why World War I doctors were hopeful about this new medical technology.

3. **Grant Proposal** Assume the role of a fundraiser for a social service agency, and use Phoenix Jackson's story to generate support. Write a proposal for a program to help grandparents who raise grandchildren alone.

Speaking and Listening

4. **Oral Story** What happens to Phoenix Jackson when she gets home? Use your imagination to come up with a plot for the events that might occur. Present your story orally to classmates.

5. **Role Play** With a partner, role-play the conversations that may have occurred between Hatch Hutchenson and his wife—in the house or the cornfield—after they learn of Will's death.

Projects

6. **Report on Rehabilitation** Gather information about current practices in rehabilitation medicine. Present your findings in a brief written report with visuals. **[Science/Health Link]**

7. **Military Report** Hemingway's story drew upon his service in the Italian Arditi (volunteer infantry). Report on the role of the Italian Arditi in World War I, as well as Hemingway's participation in it. Use maps and charts in presenting your findings. **[Social Studies Link]**

Writing Mini-Lesson

Personal Narrative

Each of the three stories you've just read recounts a memorable event or time in one character's personal experience. Write a personal narrative highlighting a memorable event in your life. Help readers appreciate what the experience meant to you by using elaboration to add emotional depth.

Writing Skills Focus: Elaboration to Add Emotional Depth

Use these tips to **elaborate** upon the event:
1. Create sensory descriptions to help put your reader at the scene of your experience.
2. Carefully describe your true feelings. Your readers might have had similar feelings, and they'll identify with you.
3. Let other people speak in their own words. Honest dialogue often moves readers.

Prewriting Off the top of your head, write the names of four or five events that have made major impressions on you. Under each, write two or three reasons why the events might interest others. Then decide which event you'll describe.

Drafting Writing in the first-person, you may want to begin your narrative with a remembered detail or an observation. To create a mood suited to the event you describe, use carefully chosen language and details.

Revising Ask a partner to read your narrative, and summarize what its topic means to you. Check your partner's response against your own perception. Does he or she understand the importance of the experience? If not, ask what changes you can make to help your reader identify with your experience.

CONNECTIONS TO TODAY'S WORLD

Anxiety
Grace Paley

Thematic Connection

FACING TROUBLED TIMES

The Modernists writing after World War I had a deep sense of uncertainty about their time. The war that had cost the world dearly seemed to have accomplished little. Technology such as airplanes and long-range artillery expected to help prevent war instead caused terrible suffering within war. Searching for values suited to a new era, Modernists focused on themes of confusion and the apparent meaninglessness of life. Their themes were often implied, not directly stated, and readers were expected to draw their own conclusions. Modernist stories had fragmented structures, seeming to begin arbitrarily and to end without resolution.

For contemporary Americans, the world is even more fragmented, with rapid technological advances, shifting national boundaries, and terrorist threats. Grace Paley's story "Anxiety," with its implied theme of world doom, reflects the uncertainty brought about by these changes.

Literary Connection

CONTEMPORARY SHORT STORIES

Ernest Hemingway, Sherwood Anderson, Eudora Welty, and Grace Paley all wrote **short stories**—brief fictional narratives with a limited number of characters and settings. The short story genre remains popular in current times—suited to the fast-paced lives of readers who sometimes have limited time to satisfy their literary appetites.

As twentieth-century stories, the four examples in this section share common themes of uncertainty, ambiguity, and some disillusionment. However, you'll notice some differences, too. Welty and Anderson's stories unfold in small-town America, and their characters reflect its values. In contrast, Paley's contemporary short story is set in a city, and its straight-to-the-point style reflects the pace of our increasingly urban culture. Additionally, Paley's story raises new issues of concern—nuclear warfare, for example—and, consisting almost entirely of unpunctuated dialogue, blurs structural form further than the other stories.

GRACE PALEY (1922–)

Grace Paley is a New Yorker through and through. Born, raised, and often living in the boisterous city, Paley has a strong concern for urban community life. This concern, along with her interest in social issues, is reflected in her highly praised short story collections, such as *Enormous Changes at the Last Minute* (1974) and *Later the Same Day* (1985).

Sometimes referred to as a writer's writer, Paley is often studied in writing workshops. Her style is crisp and deceptively simple. Nonetheless, "Anxiety" embodies an implicit theme of moral concern worth consideration in our age.

ANXIETY

Grace Paley

Woman in a Window, Richard Diebenkorn, Albright-Knox Art Gallery, Buffalo, New York

▶ **Critical Viewing** How do the colors in this image create a sense of anxiety? [Support]

The young fathers are waiting outside the school. What curly heads! Such graceful brown mustaches. They're sitting on their haunches eating pizza and exchanging information. They're waiting for the 3 P.M. bell. It's springtime, the season of first looking out the window. I have a window box of greenhouse marigolds. The young fathers can be seen through the ferny leaves.

The bell rings. The children fall out of school, tumbling through the open door. One of the fathers sees his child. A small child. Is she Chinese? A little. Up u-u-p, he says and hoists her to his shoulders. U-u-p, says the second father, and hoists his little boy. The little boy sits on top of his father's head for a couple of seconds before sliding to his shoulders. Very funny, says the father.

They start off down the street, right under and past my window. The two children are still laughing. They try to whisper a secret. The fathers haven't finished their conversation. The frailer father is uncomfortable; his little girl wiggles too much.

Stop it this minute, he says.

Oink oink, says the little girl.

What'd you say?

Oink oink, she says.

The young father says What! three times. Then he seizes the child, raises her high above his head, and sets her hard on her feet.

What'd I do so bad, she says, rubbing her ankle. Just hold my hand, screams the frail and angry father.

I lean far out the window. Stop! Stop! I cry.

The young father turns, shading his eyes, but sees. What? he says. His friend says, Hey? Who's that? He probably thinks I'm a family friend, a teacher maybe.

Who're you? he says.

I move the pots of marigold aside. Then I'm able to lean my elbow way out into unshadowed visibility. Once, not too long ago, the tenements were speckled with women like me in every third window up to the fifth story, calling the children from play to receive orders and instruction. This memory enables me to say strictly, Young man, I am an older person who feels free because of that to ask questions and give advice.

Oh? he says, laughs with a little embarrassment, says to his friend, Shoot if you will that old gray head.[1] But he's joking, I know,

because he has established himself, legs apart, hands behind his back, his neck arched to see and hear me out.

How old are you? I call. About thirty or so? Thirty-three.

First I want to say you're about a generation ahead of your father in your attitude and behavior toward your child.

Really? Well? Anything else, ma'am.

Son, I said, leaning another two, three dangerous inches toward him. Son, I must tell you that madmen intend to destroy this beautifully made planet. That the murder of our children by these men has got to become a terror and a sorrow to you, and starting now, it had better interfere with any daily pleasure.

Speech, speech, he called.

I waited a minute, but he continued to look up. So, I said, I can tell by your general appearance and loping walk that you agree with me.

I do, he said, winking at his friend; but turning a serious face to mine, he said again, Yes, yes, I do.

Well then, why do you become so angry at that little girl whose future is like a film which suddenly cuts to white. Why did you nearly slam this little doomed person to the ground in your uncontrollable anger.

Let's not go too far, said the young father. She *was* jumping around on my poor back and hollering oink oink.

When were you angriest—when she wiggled and jumped or when she said oink?

He scratched his wonderful head of dark well-cut hair. I guess when she said oink.

Have you ever said oink oink? Think carefully. Years ago, perhaps?

No. Well maybe. Maybe.

Whom did you refer to in this way?

He laughed. He called to his friend, Hey Ken, this old person's got something. The cops. In a demonstration. Oink oink, he said, remembering, laughing.

The little girl smiled and said, Oink oink.

Shut up, he said.

What do you deduce from this?

That I was angry at Rosie because she was

---

1. **Shoot . . . head:** A reference to John Greenleaf Whittier's 1864 Civil War poem, "Barbara Frietchie," which contains the line, "'Shoot, if you must, this old gray head,/But spare your country's flag,' she said."

dealing with me as though I was a figure of authority, and it's not my thing, never has been, never will be.

I could see his happiness, his nice grin, as he remembered this.

So, I continued, since those children are such lovely examples of what may well be the last generation of humankind, why don't you start all over again, right from the school door, as though none of this had ever happened.

Thank you, said the young father. Thank you. It would be nice to be a horse, he said, grabbing little Rosie's hand. Come on Rosie, let's go. I don't have all day.

U-up, says the first father. U-up, says the second.

Giddap, shout the children, and the fathers yell neigh neigh, as horses do. The children kick their fathers' horsechests,

screaming giddap giddap, and they gallop wildly westward.

I lean way out to cry once more, Be careful! Stop! But they've gone too far. Oh, anyone would love to be a fierce fast horse carrying a beloved beautiful rider, but they are galloping toward one of the most dangerous street corners in the world. And they live beyond that trisection across other dangerous avenues.

So I must shut the window after patting the April-cooled marigolds with their rusty smell of summer. Then I sit in the nice light and wonder how to make sure that they gallop safely home through the airy scary dreams of scientists and the bulky dreams of automakers. I wish I could see just how they sit down at their kitchen tables for a healthy snack (orange juice or milk and cookies) before going out into the new spring afternoon to play.

Guide for Responding

◆ *Literature and Your Life*

Reader's Response What was your first response to the old woman in the story? Explain.

Thematic Focus Which time period do you find more uncertain and troubling—post-World War I or Grace Paley's nuclear age? Why?

☑ Check Your Comprehension

1. What do the young fathers do while they are waiting outside the school?
2. Explain the circumstances in which the young father said "oink oink" when he was a young man.
3. The young father eventually says he was angry at his daughter. What does he discover was the underlying reason for his anger?

◆ Critical Thinking

INTERPRET

1. What does the father's response to the narrator's remarks reveal about his character? **[Interpret]**
2. What makes the narrator anxious? **[Draw Conclusions]**

APPLY

3. What does this story suggest to you about the emotional climate of the late twentieth century? **[Generalize]**

EXTEND

4. What social and political circumstances suggested in Hemingway's story would most concern the narrator of "Anxiety"? Why? **[Literature Link]**

Thematic Connection

**FACING TROUBLED TIMES:
AN UNCERTAIN FUTURE**

The short stories written just after World War I and those written today share a sense of disillusionment and anxiety about the future.

1. Compare and contrast how Paley's narrator, Hemingway's soldiers, and Anderson's Hutchensons respond to the advancing technology of their eras. Give examples.

2. How are the concerns of the post-World War II era—when Paley wrote—different from those of the period following World War I?

3. Explain how the title "Anxiety" might fit the stories by Hemingway, Anderson, and Welty. What issues concern key characters in each of these stories?

Literary Connection

CONTEMPORARY SHORT STORIES

The world created within a short story is defined by limitations of plot complexity and numbers of characters and settings. In contrast to longer works, elements of character, setting, and mood become key parts of the story. As you reflect on Grace Paley's portrait of modern anxiety, think about how each of these key elements contributes to the overall effect of the story. Compare and contrast the characters, setting, and moods with those created by Hemingway, Anderson, and Welty in their stories.

1. Explain how you think the central characters in each story view their world.

2. Cite three descriptive words in each story that help evoke the story's mood.

 Idea Bank

Writing

1. **Dialogue** Write a dialogue between the Hutchensons in Sherwood Anderson's story and the old woman in "Anxiety." The Hutchensons should argue for coping with modern uncertainty by burying oneself in work. The old woman should advocate combating uncertainty by taking action to change society.

2. **Expository Essay** A common generalization calls the period following World War II an age of anxiety. Identify the world, national, social, and personal factors that might lead to this growing sense of anxiety. In an essay, explain how these factors might affect the people living at this time.

3. **Critical Analysis** Grace Paley has said, "There isn't a story written that isn't about blood and money. People and their relationships to each other is the blood, the family. And how they live, the money of it." Write a brief essay in which you connect this idea to specific issues and examples in Paley's story "Anxiety."

Speaking and Listening

4. **Interview** Interview two or three adults—family members or others—about the threat of nuclear war. How do they feel about it? Ask what has been done—and what can yet be done—to minimize the threat.
[Social Studies Link; Science Link]

Projects

5. **Historical Newspaper** With a group, research the times and settings of the stories you've read in this section. Create the front page of a historical newspaper; then devote one page to the time period of each story. Fill each page with news, pictures, and advertisements that would be typical of the times. [Social Studies Link]

6. **Future Projection** Think about the rate at which technology advanced from the time of Hemingway's story to Grace Paley's. Create a presentation explaining and showing (with drawings and graphs) where technology is expected to be in twenty-five years. [Science Link]

Any one of the short stories in this section would make an excellent topic for a literary analysis—a formal piece of writing that examines the underlying meaning or significance of one or more elements of a literary work or of the work as a whole. By writing a literary analysis, you can demonstrate your ability to think critically about what you read and to dig beneath the surface to unlock meaning. The skills below and the instructions on the following pages will help you develop an effective literary analysis of any work you choose.

The skills below will help you write a literary analysis.

Writing Skills Focus

▶ **Use an appropriate level of formality.** Use formal language and a serious, thoughtful tone.

▶ **Present a clear thesis statement** in which you offer your interpretation of the literary work or an element of that work.

▶ **Use precise details** from the literary work to support your thesis—the main idea of your analysis. Wherever possible, use direct quotations from the work.

▶ **Elaborate** by discussing how the elements in a work of literature elicit an emotional response. (See p. 747.)

This excerpt from an introduction to a literary analysis of "Winter Dreams" includes some of the features of a strong analysis:

WRITING MODEL

F. Scott Fitzgerald's "Winter Dreams" suggests that a single-minded pursuit of wealth and social status is unlikely to lead to personal fulfillment. ① The story's main character, Dexter Green, accumulates great wealth, yet is unable to find happiness because of his obsession with Judy Jones, a beautiful woman who symbolizes for Dexter all that is exciting and glamourous about upper-class life. ② ③

① The writer opens with her thesis statement.

② The writer then develops her thesis statement with details from the story.

③ A formal vocabulary and presentation lend an authoritative tone to the essay.

APPLYING LANGUAGE SKILLS: Parallel Structure

Parallel structure is the placement of equal ideas in words, phrases, or clauses of similar types. Notice that all of the elements must be parallel.

First Draft: Fads of the Roaring Twenties included the Charleston, raccoon coats, and they sat on flagpoles.

Revision: Fads of the Roaring Twenties included the Charleston, raccoon coats, and flagpole sitting.

Practice Correct the faulty parallelism in each sentence:

1. The writer Eudora Welty is also a photographer and paints pictures.
2. Many American writers were affected by experiencing the horrors of WWI firsthand or they heard about them from friends who served in the military.
3. After the end of WWII, President Truman ordered full restoration of civilian consumer production and to return to free markets.

Writer's Solution Connection
Language Lab

For help on parallel structure, see the Strengthening Sentences lesson in the Writing Style unit.

Prewriting

Choose a Topic If you found one of the stories in this section especially thought-provoking, you may want to use that story as the focus of your literary analysis. As an alternative, choose another literary work that you've recently read that had a strong impact on you.

Review the Literature Carefully review the literary work you've selected. Jot down answers to the following questions:

▶ Which of the characters stand out? Why? What motivates the characters actions?
▶ How does the setting shape the characters and the plot?
▶ Which images are most striking? Why? What associations do these images call to mind? Which images seem to have an underlying meaning?
▶ What if any symbolic meaning can be found in the characters, setting, or events?
▶ What lessons can be learned from the characters and events that can be applied to real life?

Review your answers to these questions. Then decide whether to focus your analysis on one or more elements of the work or to concentrate on analyzing the work as a whole.

Gather Precise Details Once you've decided on the focus of your analysis, write a sentence or two stating the main point that you'll make in your paper. Then gather details and passages from the work that you can use to support this thesis.

Drafting

Begin With a Strong Introduction Your introduction should have an attention-grabbing beginning, a statement of the title and author of the work to be discussed, and a clearly stated thesis. Notice how the following example meets all three criteria:

> Will Phoenix rise again? In her story "A Worn Path," Eudora Welty's use of the name Phoenix for her main character is an allusion to the phoenix that rises from the ashes in ancient Egyptian mythology. Like the mythological phoenix, the character Phoenix Jackson is able to endure and rise above the hardships that her life presents to her.

Maintain a Serious Tone A literary analysis calls for formal sentence structure and a serious tone. Avoid slang and familiar, informal language and use a more scholarly tone.

Revising

Check Your Language Variety Reread your essay to determine whether you overuse any words. For example, if you use the word "writer" too frequently, revise by inserting synonyms or the author's name. You may want to rewrite some sentences to improve language variety.

Consult a Peer Reviewer Ask a classmate who is familiar with your topic to read your literary analysis. Provide your peer reviewer with a checklist based on the following points:

- ▶ How can you more clearly express the thesis in the introduction of the analysis?
- ▶ What quotations or other details could you add in the body of the analysis to strengthen support for your ideas?
- ▶ Have you restated the thesis in your conclusion?
- ▶ What personal reactions should you include?
- ▶ Have you been consistently and appropriately formal?

REVISION MODEL

Welty leaves unanswered the question of whether Phoenix Jackson's grandson is still alive. ~~On one hand~~, ① a nurse at the clinic to which Phoenix walks says, "She doesn't come in for herself—she has a little grandson." ② *However,* Later in the story, the ③ *, "Tell us about your grandson. . . . He's dead, isn't he?"* same nurse asks if ~~Phoenix's granson is dead~~ In an essay on this topic, Welty herself answers the question by stating, "*Phoenix* is alive."

① The writer deletes this awkward transition.
② Here, a transition is added to make a smoother connection between sentences.
③ A quotation from the work replaces a vague reference.

Publishing

▶**Literary Magazine** Create a class literary magazine featuring the literary analyses of several members of the class. Organize the analyses by time period, author, or genre; include a table of contents; and consider adding illustrations.

APPLYING LANGUAGE SKILLS: Infinitives and Infinitive Phrases

An **infinitive** is the base form of a verb—usually preceded by the word *to* as in *to sing.* An **infinitive phrase** consists of an infinitive plus complements and/or modifiers (*to sing a song merrily*). Both an infinitive and an infinitive phrase can function as a noun, an adjective, or an adverb.

Examples:

To write [n] was her dream. She had the will to succeed [adj]. Still, she found it hard to complete [adv] her first novel.

Practice Identify the infinitive phrases in the following sentences, and label their function (noun, adjective, or adverb).

1. I like to read literature about the South.
2. My career goal is to be a published writer.

Writing Application Use infinitive phrases to avoid dull, repetitious writing.

Writer's Solution Connection Writing Lab

For help revising your analysis, view the video tip from writer Ralph Ellison in the Revising and Editing section of the tutorial on Response to Literature.

Real-World Reading Skills Workshop

Strategies for Success

This book is filled with brief literary works, most of which can be read in a single sitting. A novel, a nonfiction biography, a how-to guide, or a full-length play, on the other hand, may be read over an extended period of time.

Define Your Interest Before you tackle a lengthy reading project, read jacket and flap copy, author's notes or foreword, and reviewer's comments to assess your interest in the work.

Get an Overview Survey the structure. Are there parts or sections? Is the text divided into chapters? Look at the table of contents, prologue or foreword, and other explanatory notes that may shed light on the organization of the work.

Read the Work The way you approach and read a longer work will determine how much you get from the experience. Use these questions to keep you on track:

Before you read:
- ▶ What does the title suggest about the book's contents or point of view?
- ▶ How do chapter titles explain early text or prepare you for later chapters?
- ▶ Identify the section organization to monitor events and ideas.

As you read:
- ▶ Notice the changes that take place over the course of a longer work. How much time passes from one chapter to the next? How do characters change?
- ▶ Appreciate the details and descriptive passages you'll find in longer works.

Apply the Strategy

You pick up the latest novel by a favorite author. Evaluate the book's cover and table of contents to help you determine what to expect as you read.

"The Element of Surprise lives up to its name. More than just the story of a boy's childhood, it brings to life the surprises—both humorous and touching—that await us each day."
San Antonio Book News

The Element of Surprise
by Marin Cresstall

1. Based on the cover, what do you think this book is about? Explain.
2. How is the book organized?
3. What does the structure suggest to you about the story?
4. Based on the organization and the chapter titles, how do you think central characters change as the story progresses? Explain.

✔ *Here are situations in which strategies for reading novels and longer works are useful:*
- ▶ *Reading a novel for pleasure*
- ▶ *Selecting and reading a book for a book report*
- ▶ *Reading nonfiction for a research report*

PART 3

From Every Corner of the Land

The Tower, Charles Demuth, Columbus Museum of Art, Ohio

Guide for Interpreting

Edith Wharton (1862–1937)

Colorful Old New York, the high society of London and Paris, The French Riviera—these settings from the late nineteenth century through the 1930's were all part of Edith Wharton's world. They also played an important role in the making of her books—more than fifty published volumes—and her remarkable literary career.

Wharton was a master at re-creating the staid, rule-bound atmosphere of the up-per-class society of her time.

A Daughter of Privilege
Born Edith Newbold Jones, Wharton was the daughter of a socially prominent New York City family. Educated privately in New York and Europe, she married Edward Wharton, a Boston banker, in 1885. The couple spent the next few years immersing themselves in the social life of the high society in Newport, Rhode Island; in Lenox, Massachusetts; and in Europe.

Interestingly, it was on the advice of a doctor that Wharton began to write fiction. Wharton was caring for her husband, known as Teddy, who had become chronically ill, and the doctor advised Wharton to take up writ-ing as a way to relieve stress. Her first stories appeared in *Scribner's* magazine, and several volumes of her fiction were published around the turn of the century. However, it was her best-selling novel *The House of Mirth* (1905)—a devastating portrait of a young woman who tries and fails to survive in New York high society—that established her as an important writer.

An Expatriate Writer
In 1913, Wharton moved to Paris. She began a friendship with the novelist Henry James and other writers who helped her refine her work. As World War I loomed, she produced some of her finest novels: *Ethan Frome* (1911), *The Reef* (1912), and *The Custom of the Country* (1913). During the war, Wharton remained in France, organizing aid for Belgian refugees. In 1920, her novel *The Age of Inno-cence*—which was recently made into a popular movie—won the Pulitzer Prize. Wharton also published *Old New York* (1924), *The Mothers Recompense* (1925), and 85 short stories. In addition, she published an autobiography, *A Backward Glance*, in 1934.

In her fiction, which continues to attract readers and earn critical acclaim, Wharton explores the conflict be-tween money and morality and exposes the cruelty of the social "game," with its rivalries, rules, and punishments.

◆ Background for Understanding

HISTORY: PUBLISHING AT THE TURN OF THE CENTURY

The publishing world of the late nineteenth and early twentieth centuries was far different from today's book world. If Wharton's novels were published today, they would stand on bookstore shelves crowded with many other novels. Wharton's publisher would probably send her on a whirlwind book tour; perhaps she'd appear on Oprah Winfrey's show. You could even hear her books read on audiotape by a famous actor.

Around the turn of century, however, things were different. Novels were customarily serialized in magazines and newspapers. *The House of Mirth*, one of Wharton's most famous novels, appeared in *Scribner's* magazine before it was published as a book in 1905. Readers of the time would eagerly await the next monthly installment of the latest novel by their favorite author. Some great writers, including England's Charles Dickens earlier in the century, established their reputations this way.

◆ *Literature and Your Life*

CONNECT YOUR EXPERIENCE

You submit a poem to a literary magazine or audition for the lead in the play. Suddenly, you seem to be waiting for a world of strangers to pass judgment. It takes courage to risk having your work criticized or rejected. In this story, a young writer braves the world of publishing—and gets not one surprise, but two.

Journal Writing Do you ever dream of being "discovered" and shooting to fame? Describe your dream.

THEMATIC FOCUS: FROM EVERY CORNER OF THE LAND

Most of this story is set in a small Massachusetts town where neighbors know one another. As you read, think how the story would be different if all the action had taken place in the city of Boston.

◆ Literary Focus

ELEMENTS OF PLOT

Like most short story writers, Wharton brings together the **elements of plot** to lead readers through the events of a story. The **exposition** introduces the story's characters, setting, and situation. This is followed by an event that sets out the **conflict**, or struggle, whether internal or external. The conflict increases until it reaches a **climax,** or high point of suspense. The events leading up to the climax comprise the **rising action.** The climax is followed by the end, or **resolution,** of the central conflict. Anything that occurs after the resolution is the **denouement,** or **falling action.** Use a chart like this one to record the elements of plot.

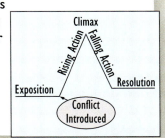

◆ Build Vocabulary

PREFIXES: *man-, manu-*

The word *manuscript* is formed from the prefix *manu-*, derived from the Latin word *manus* meaning "hand" and the Latin root *-script-* meaning "write." Using this information, you might guess that *manuscript* means "a handwritten document."

admonitory
retrospective
antagonism
contrition
manuscript
commiseration

WORD BANK

Preview this list of words from the story.

◆ Reading Strategy

ANTICIPATE EVENTS

As you read "April Showers," you will probably find yourself **anticipating events**—eagerly looking forward to what is going to happen. Anticipating events differs from predicting in that it's less a conscious mental process and more an emotional one. When you anticipate events, you forge a connection to characters who, like you, are watching their lives unfold.

As you read this story, join the central character, Theodora, in anticipating what will happen.

◆ Grammar and Style

GERUND PHRASES

A **gerund** is a verb form that ends in -*ing* and is used as a noun. A **gerund phrase,** which also serves as a noun, includes a gerund and any modifiers or complements. Like nouns, gerund phrases function as subjects, direct objects, subject complements, and objects of prepositions. This gerund phrase functions as an object of the preposition *in.*

I don't believe in *feeding* youngsters on sentimental trash; . . .

As you read, notice the author's frequent use of gerund phrases.

April Showers

Edith Wharton

"But Guy's heart slept under the violets on Muriel's grave."

It was a beautiful ending; Theodora had seen girls cry over last chapters that weren't half as pathetic. She laid her pen aside and read the words over, letting her voice linger on the fall of the sentence; then, drawing a deep breath, she wrote across the foot of the page the name by which she had decided to become known in literature—Gladys Glyn.

Downstairs the library clock struck two. Its muffled thump sounded like an admonitory knock against her bedroom floor. Two o'clock! and she had promised her mother to be up early enough to see that the buttons were sewn on Johnny's reefer, and that Kate had her cod-liver oil before starting for school!

Lingeringly, tenderly she gathered up the pages of her novel—there were five hundred of them—and tied them with the blue satin ribbon that her Aunt Julia had given her. She had meant to wear the ribbon with her new dotted muslin on Sundays, but this was putting it to a nobler use. She bound it round her manuscript, tying the ends in a pretty bow. Theodora was clever at making bows, and could have trimmed hats beautifully, had not all her spare moments been given to literature. Then, with a last look at the precious pages, she sealed and addressed the package. She meant to send it off next morning to the *Home Circle.* She knew it would be hard to obtain access to a paper which numbered so many popular authors among its contributors, but she had been encouraged to make the venture by something her Uncle James had said the last time he had come down from Boston.

He had been telling his brother, Doctor Dace, about his new house out at Brookline. Uncle James was prosperous, and was always moving into new houses with more "modern improvements." Hygiene was his passion, and he migrated in the wake of sanitary plumbing.

"The bathrooms alone are worth the money," he was saying, cheerfully, "although it *is* a big rent. But then, when a man's got no children to save up for—" he glanced compassionately round Doctor Dace's crowded table "—and it is something to be in a neighborhood where the drainage is A-one. That's what I was telling our neighbor. Who do you suppose she is, by the way?" He smiled at Theodora. "I rather think that young lady knows all about her. Ever heard of Kathleen Kyd?"

Kathleen Kyd! The famous "society novelist," the creator of more "favorite heroines" than all her predecessors put together had ever turned out, the author of *Fashion and Passion, An American Duchess, Rhona's Revolt.* Was there any intelligent girl from Maine to California whose heart would not have beat faster at the mention of that name?

"Why, yes," Uncle James was saying, "Kathleen Kyd lives next door. Frances G. Wollop is her real name, and her husband's a dentist. She's a very pleasant, sociable kind of woman; you'd never think she was a writer. Ever hear how she began to write? She told me the whole story. It seems she was a saleswoman in a store, working on starvation wages, with a mother and a consumptive sister to support. Well, she wrote a story one day, just for fun, and sent it to the *Home Circle*. They'd never heard of her, of course, and she never expected to hear from them. She did, though. They took the story and passed their plate for more. She became a regular contributor and eventually was known all over the country. Now she tells me her books bring her in about ten thousand a year. Rather more than you and I can boast of, eh, John? Well, I hope *this* household doesn't contribute to her support." He glanced sharply at Theodora. "I don't believe in feeding youngsters on sentimental trash; it's like sewer gas—doesn't smell bad, and infects the system without your knowing it."

Theodora listened breathlessly. Kathleen Kyd's first story had been accepted by the *Home Circle*, and they had asked for more! Why should Gladys Glyn be less fortunate? Theodora had done a great deal of novel reading—far more than her parents were aware of—and felt herself competent to pronounce upon the quality of her own work. She was almost sure that "April Showers" was a remarkable book. If it lacked Kathleen Kyd's lightness of touch, it had an emotional intensity never achieved by that brilliant writer. Theodora did not care to amuse her readers; she left that to more frivolous talents. Her aim was to stir the depths of human nature, and she felt she had succeeded. It was a great thing for a girl to be able to feel that about her first novel. Theodora was only seventeen; and she remembered, with a touch of retrospective compassion, that George Eliot[1] had not become famous till she was nearly forty.

No, there was no doubt about the merit of "April Showers." But would not an inferior work

Memories, 1885–86, William Merritt Chase, Munson-Williams-Proctor Institute Museum of Art, Utica, New York

▲ **Critical Viewing** What emotions are evoked by this portrait? How do they relate to Theodora's literary hopes and dreams? **[Connect]**

have had a better chance of success? Theodora recalled the early struggles of famous authors, the notorious antagonism of publishers and editors to any new writer of exceptional promise. Would it not be wiser to write the book down to the average reader's level, reserving for some later work the great "effects" into which she had thrown all the fever of her imagination? The thought was sacrilege! Never would she lay hands on the sacred structure she had reared; never would she resort to the inartistic expedient of modifying her work to suit the popular taste. Better obscure failure than a vulgar triumph. The great authors never stooped to such concessions, and Theodora felt herself included in their ranks by the firmness with which she rejected all thought of conciliating an unappreciative public. The manuscript should be sent as it was.

She woke with a start and a heavy sense of apprehension. The *Home Circle* had refused "April Showers!" No, that couldn't be it; there lay the precious manuscript, waiting to be posted. What was it, then? Ah, that ominous thump below stairs—nine o'clock striking! It was Johnny's buttons!

She sprang out of bed in dismay. She had been so determined not to disappoint her mother about Johnny's buttons! Mrs. Dace, helpless from chronic rheumatism, had to entrust the care of the household to her

◆ **Literary Focus**
Where does the exposition end and the rising action begin?

◆ **Build Vocabulary**
admonitory (ad män´ i tôr ē) *adj.*: Warning
retrospective (re trə spek´ tiv) *adj.*: Looking back on or directed to the past
antagonism (an tag´ ə niz´ əm) *n.*: Hostility

---

1. **George Eliot:** Pseudonym of Mary Ann Evans (1819–1880), a celebrated English novelist.

eldest daughter; and Theodora honestly meant to see that Johnny had his full complement of buttons, and that Kate and Bertha went to school tidy. Unfortunately, the writing of a great novel leaves little time or memory for the lesser obligations of life, and Theodore usually found that her good intentions matured too late for practical results.

Her <u>contrition</u> was softened by the thought that literary success would enable her to make up for all the little negligences of which she was guilty. She meant to spend all her money on her family; and already she had visions of a wheeled chair for her mother, a fresh wallpaper for the doctor's shabby office, bicycles for the girls, and Johnny's establishment at a boarding school where sewing on his buttons would be included in the curriculum. If her parents could have guessed her intentions, they would not have found fault with her as they did; and Doctor Dace, on this particular morning, would not have looked up to say, with his fagged, ironical air:

"I suppose you didn't get home from the ball till morning?"

Theodora's sense of being in the right enabled her to take the thrust with a dignity that would have awed the unfeeling parent of fiction.

"I'm sorry to be late, father," she said.

Doctor Dace, who could never be counted on to behave like a father in a book, shrugged his shoulders impatiently.

"Your sentiments do you credit, but they haven't kept your mother's breakfast warm."

"Hasn't mother's tray gone up yet?"

"Who was to take it, I should like to know? The girls came down so late that I had to hustle them off before they'd finished breakfast, and Johnny's hands were so dirty that I sent him back to his room to make himself decent. It's a pretty thing for the doctor's children to be the dirtiest little savages in Norton!"

Theodora had hastily prepared her mother's tray, leaving her own breakfast untouched. As she entered the room upstairs, Mrs. Dace's patient face turned to her with a smile much harder to bear than her father's reproaches.

"Mother, I'm *so* sorry——"

"No matter, dear. I suppose Johnny's buttons

kept you. I can't think what they boy does to his clothes!"

Theodora sat the tray down without speaking. It was impossible to own to having forgotten Johnny's buttons without revealing the cause of her forgetfulness. For a few weeks longer she must bear to be misunderstood; then—ah, then if her novel were accepted, how gladly would she forget and forgive! But what if it were refused? She turned aside to hide the dismay that flushed her face. Well, then she would admit the truth—she would ask her parents' pardon, and settle down without a murmur to an obscure existence of mending and combing.

She had said to herself that after the <u>manuscript</u> had been sent, she would have time to look after the children and catch up with the mending; but she had reckoned without the postman. He came three times a day; for an hour before each ring she was too excited to do anything but wonder if he would bring an answer this time, and for an hour afterward she moved about in a leaden stupor of disappointment. The children had never been so trying. They seemed to be always coming to pieces, like cheap furniture; one would have supposed they had been put together with bad glue. Mrs. Dace worried herself ill over Johnny's tatters, Bertha's bad marks at school, and Kate's open abstention from cod-liver oil; and Doctor Dace, coming back late from a long round of visits to a fireless office with a smoky lamp, called out furiously to know if Theodora would kindly come down and remove the "East, West, home's best" that hung above the empty grate.

In the midst of it all, Miss Sophy Brill called. It was very kind of her to come, for she was the busiest woman in Norton. She made it her duty to look after other people's affairs, and there was not a house in town but had the benefit of her personal supervision. She generally came when things were going wrong, and the sight of her bonnet on the doorstep was a surer sign of calamity than a crepe bow on the bell. After she left, Mrs. Dace looked very sad, and the doctor punished Johnny for warbling down the entry:

"Miss Sophy Brill
Is a bitter pill!"

> *She turned aside to hide the dismay that flushed her face.*

while Theodora, locking herself in her room, resolved with tears that she would never write another novel.

The week was a long nightmare. Theodora could neither eat nor sleep. She was up early enough, but instead of looking after the children and seeing that breakfast was ready, she wandered down the road to meet the postman, and came back wan and empty-handed, oblivious of her morning duties. She had no idea how long the suspense would last; but she didn't see how authors could live if they were kept waiting more than a week.

Then, suddenly, one afternoon—she never quite knew how or when it happened—she found herself with a *Home Circle* envelope in her hands, and her dazzled eyes flashing over a wild dance of words that wouldn't settle down and make sense.

"Dear Madam:" [They called her *Madam!* And then; yes, the words were beginning to fall into line now.] "Your novel, 'April Showers,' has been received, and we are glad to accept it on the usual terms. A serial on which we were counting for immediate publication has been delayed by the author's illness, and the first chapters of 'April Showers' will therefore appear in our midsummer number. Thanking you for favoring us with your manuscript, we remain," and so forth.

Theodora found herself in the wood beyond the schoolhouse. She was kneeling on the ground, brushing aside the dead leaves and pressing her lips to the little bursting green things that pushed up eager tips through last year's decay. It was spring—spring! Everything was crowding toward the light and in her own heart hundreds of germinating hopes had burst into sudden leaf. She wondered if the thrust of those little green fingers hurt the surface of the earth as her springing raptures hurt—yes, actually hurt!—her hot, constricted breast! She looked up through interlacing boughs at a tender, opaque blue sky full of the coming of a milky moon. She seemed enveloped in an atmosphere of loving comprehension. The brown earth throbbed with her joy, the treetops trembled with it, and a sudden star broke through the branches with an audible "I know!"

◆ **Reading Strategy**
Here, Theodora begins to anticipate the publication of her story. What do you feel?

Theodora, on the whole, behaved very well. Her mother cried, her father whistled and said he supposed he must put up with grounds in his coffee now, and be thankful if he ever got a hot meal again; while the children took the most deafening and harassing advantage of what seemed a sudden suspension of the laws of nature.

Within a week everybody in Norton knew that Theodora had written a novel, and that it was coming out in the *Home Circle*. On Sundays, when she walked up the aisle, her friends dropped their prayer books and the soprano sang false in her excitement. Girls with more pin money than Theodora had ever dreamed of copied her hats and imitated her way of speaking. The local paper asked her for a poem; her old school teachers stopped to shake hands and grew shy over their congratulations; and Miss Sophy Brill came to call. She had put on her Sunday bonnet and her manner was almost abject. She ventured, very timidly, to ask her young friend how she wrote, whether it "just came to her," and if she had found that the kind of pen she used made any difference; and wound up by begging Theodora to write a sentiment in her album.

Even Uncle James came down from Boston to talk the wonder over. He called Theodora a "sly baggage," and proposed that she should give him her earnings to invest in a new patent grease-trap company. From what Kathleen Kyd had told him, he thought Theodora would probably get a thousand dollars for her story. He concluded by suggesting that she should base her next romance on the subject of sanitation, making the heroine nearly die of sewer gas poisoning because her parents won't listen to the handsome young doctor next door, when he warns them that their plumbing is out of order. That was a subject that would interest everybody, and do a lot more good than the sentimental trash most women wrote.

◆ **Build Vocabulary**

contrition (kən trish′ ən) *n*.: Remorse for having done wrong

manuscript (man′ yōō skript′) *n*.: Written or typed document, especially one submitted to a publisher or printer

At last the great day came. Theodora had left an order with the bookseller for the midsummer number of the *Home Circle* and before the shop was open she was waiting on the sidewalk. She clutched the precious paper and ran home without opening it. Her excitement was almost more than she could bear. Not heeding her father's call to breakfast, she rushed upstairs and locked herself in her room. Her hands trembled so that she could hardly turn the pages. At last—yes, there it was: "April Showers."

The paper dropped from her hands. What name had she read beneath the title? Had her emotion blinded her?

"April Showers, by *Kathleen Kyd.*"

Kathleen Kyd! Oh, cruel misprint! Oh, dastardly typographer! Through tears of rage and disappointment Theodora looked again; yes, there was no mistaking the hateful name. Her glance ran on. She found herself reading a first paragraph that she had never seen before. She read farther. All was strange. The horrible truth burst upon her: *It was not her story!*

She never knew how she got back to the station. She struggled through the crowd on the platform, and a gold-banded arm pushed her into the train just starting for Norton. It would be dark when she reached home; but that didn't matter—nothing mattered now. She sank into her seat, closing her eyes in the vain attempt to shut out the vision of the last few hours; but minute by minute memory forced her to relive it; she felt like a rebellious school child dragged forth to repeat the same detested "piece."

Although she did not know Boston well, she had made her way easily enough to the *Home Circle* building; at least, she supposed she had, since she remembered nothing till she found herself ascending the editorial stairs as easily as one does incredible things in dreams. She must have walked very fast, for her heart was beating furiously, and she had barely breath to whisper the editor's name to a young man who looked out at her from a glass case, like a zoological specimen. The young man led her past other glass cases containing similar specimens to an inner enclosure which seemed filled by an enormous presence. Theodora felt herself enveloped in the presence, submerged by it, gasping for air as she sank under its rising surges.

Gradually fragments of speech floated to the surface. "'April Showers?' Mrs. Kyd's new serial? *Your* manuscript, you say? You have a letter from me? The name, please? Evidently some unfortunate misunderstanding. One moment." And then a bell ringing, a zoological specimen ordered to unlock a safe, her name asked for again, the manuscript, her own precious manuscript, tied with Aunt Julia's ribbon, laid on the table before her, and her outcries, her protests, her interrogations, drowned in a flood of bland apology: "An unfortunate accident—Mrs. Kyd's manuscript received the same day—extraordinary coincidence in the choice of a title—duplicate answers sent by mistake—Miss Dace's novel hardly suited to their purpose—should of course have been returned—regrettable oversight—accidents would happen—sure she understood."

The voice went on, like the steady pressure of a surgeon's hand on a shrieking nerve. When it stopped she was in the street. A cab nearly ran her down, and a car bell jangled furiously in her ears. She clutched her manuscript, carrying it tenderly through the crowd, like a live thing that had been hurt. She could not bear to look at its soiled edges and the ink stain on Aunt Julia's ribbon.

The train stopped with a jerk and she opened her eyes. It was dark, and by the windy flare of gas on the platform she saw the Norton passengers getting out. She stood up stiffly and followed them. A warm wind blew into her face the fragrance of the summer woods, and she remembered how, two months earlier, she had knelt among the dead leaves, pressing her lips to the first shoots of green. Then for the first time she thought of home. She had fled away in the morning without a word, and her heart sank at the thought of her mother's fears. And her father—how angry he would be! She bent her head under the coming storm of his derision.

The night was cloudy, and as she stepped into the darkness beyond the station a hand was slipped in hers. She stood still, too weary to feel frightened, and a voice said, quietly:

"Don't walk so fast, child. You look tired."

"Father!" Her hand dropped from his, but he recaptured it and drew it through his arm. When she found voice, it was to whisper, "You

◆ **Literary Focus**
What is the resolution of the central conflict?

◆ Reading Strategy

Theodora is anticipating a negative reaction from her father. What are you anticipating?

were at the station?"

"It's such a good night I thought I'd stroll down and meet you."

Her arm trembled against his. She could not see his face in the dimness, but the light of his cigar looked down on her like a friendly eye, and she took courage to falter out: "Then you knew—"

"That you'd gone to Boston? Well, I rather thought you had."

They walked on slowly, and presently he added, "You see, you left the *Home Circle* lying in your room."

How she blessed the darkness and the muffled sky! She could not have borne the scrutiny of the tiniest star.

"Then mother wasn't very much frightened?"

"Why, no, she didn't appear to be. She's been busy all day over some toggery of Bertha's."

Theodora choked. "Father, I'll—" She groped for words, but they eluded her. "I'll do things—differently; I haven't meant—" Suddenly she heard herself bursting out: "It was all a mistake, you know—about my story. They didn't want it; they won't have it!" and she shrank back involuntarily from his impending mirth.

She felt the pressure of his arm, but he didn't speak, and she figured his mute hilarity. They moved on in silence. Presently he said:

"It hurts a bit just at first, doesn't it?"

"O father!"

He stood still, and the gleam of his cigar showed a face of unexpected participation.

"You see I've been through it myself."

"You, father? You?"

"Why, yes. Didn't I ever tell you? I wrote a novel once. I was just out of college, and didn't want to be a doctor. No; I wanted to be a genius, so I wrote a novel."

The doctor paused, and Theodora clung to him in a mute passion of commiseration. It was as if a drowning creature caught a live hand through the murderous fury of the waves.

"Father—O father!"

"It took me a year—a whole year's hard work; and when I'd finished it the public wouldn't have it, either; not at any price and that's why I came down to meet you, because I remembered my walk home."

◆ **Build Vocabulary**

commiseration (kə miz´ ər ā´ shən) *n.*: Sympathy; condolence

Guide for Responding

◆ *Literature and Your Life*

Reader's Response Did this story surprise you? Explain.

Thematic Focus How might "April Showers" have been different if it had been set in a different region of the country?

☑ **Check Your Comprehension**

1. What is Theodora's job in the family?
2. What is Theodora planning to do when the story begins?
3. How does the acceptance of Theodora's story change the way others behave toward her?
4. What does Theodora do when she sees that the story in the magazine is not her story?
5. What is her father's reaction to the mistake?

◆ **Critical Thinking**

INTERPRET

1. (a) What is the author's tone in "April Showers"? (b) How does the author's tone influence your view of Theodora? **[Analyze]**
2. How does Theodora change during the story? **[Compare and Contrast]**
3. Does this story support the saying: "If it seems too good to be true, it probably is"? Explain. **[Support]**

EVALUATE

4. What is the importance of Doctor Dace as a character in the story? **[Assess]**

APPLY

5. What lesson(s) from this story might apply to your own life? **[Generalize]**

Guide for Responding (continued)

◆ Reading Strategy

ANTICIPATE EVENTS

As you read, you—along with Theodora—**anticipated events**, or looked forward to what was going to happen. Anticipating can take a variety of forms: eagerness, excitement, uncertainty, dread, or foreboding are a few examples.

1. (a) What was your emotional response to the letter Theodora got from *Home Circle*? Why? (b) What did you think would happen next?
2. How did the news that *Home Circle* had published the wrong story affect your sense of anticipation?

◆ Literary Focus

ELEMENTS OF PLOT

The anticipation you felt when reading "April Showers" was partly a result of the twists and turns of the plot. The author skillfully handles the **elements of plot**—exposition, conflict, rising action, climax, resolution, denouement—to evoke curiosity, surprise, and empathy in the reader.

1. (a) Describe the central conflict of the story. (b) What incident introduces this conflict?
2. What is the climax of the story? Explain.
3. Does this story have a denouement? Explain.

Beyond Literature

Career Connection

Careers in Publishing Modern publishing is a vast and vital field. It encompasses print media, such as newspapers, books, and magazines, as well as multimedia produced for CD-ROM and the Internet.

Career roles in publishing have expanded since Wharton's time. Today you might edit novels, design a magazine, produce a publication for a high-tech corporation, design and maintain web sites, or even arrange the manufacture of toys from book characters. The opportunities seem endless. If Theodora had decided on a publishing career today, what specific job might she have pursued? Why?

◆ Build Vocabulary

USING THE PREFIXES *man-, manu-*

Replace the italicized word or phrase in each sentence with a word from the box that contains the prefix *man-* (also spelled *manu-*).

manufactures	manual	manipulated	emancipate

1. A hammer is a *hand-operated* tool.
2. He decided to *free* his caged birds *from restraint*.
3. The potter *kneaded* the clay *with his hands* until it was soft.
4. That company *makes* motorcycles *into finished products*.

USING THE WORD BANK

Write the letter of the word closest in meaning to each of the following words from the word bank.

1. admonitory: (a) sorry, (b) warning, (c) financial
2. retrospective: (a) futuristic, (b) under, (c) back
3. antagonism: (a) hostility, (b) fright, (c) arrogance
4. contrition: (a) regret, (b) jocularity, (c) passivity
5. manuscript: (a) draft, (b) map, (c) autograph
6. commiseration: (a) wrath, (b) sympathy, (c) angst

◆ Grammar and Style

GERUND PHRASES

"April Showers" includes **gerund phrases**, which perform as subjects, direct objects, subject complements, and objects of prepositions.

Practice Copy these examples into your notebook. For each one, underline at least one gerund phrase and identify how it is used in the sentence.

> A **gerund phrase** is a group of words serving as a noun and consisting of a gerund (*-ing* verb form that is used as a noun) and any modifiers or complements.

1. Unfortunately, the writing of a great novel leaves little time or memory for the lesser obligations of life . . .
2. . . . instead of looking after the children and seeing that breakfast was ready . . .
3. Theodora's sense of being in the right enabled her . . .
4. . . . there was no mistaking the hateful name.

Build Your Portfolio

Idea Bank

Writing

1. **Flier Copy** Theodora could have been in a writer's group—a group where writers read and appraise one another's work. Create a flier to advertise such a group and explain its benefits.

2. **Movie Scene** Choose one scene from the story to adapt for the big screen. Write a script based on the scene. Include set descriptions, camera directions, and dialogue.

3. **Critical Response** Wharton's publishers wrote that she had a "magnificent gift of story telling, pure and simple." Based on your reading of "April Showers," write an essay in which you critically respond to this appraisal.

Speaking and Listening

4. **Casting Discussion** In a small group, list the roles necessary for a movie version of "April Showers." Then discuss which actors would be right for each role, and why. **[Media Link]**

5. **Dramatic Monologue** Imagine that Theodora's neighbors throw a surprise party to celebrate her story. As Theodora, deliver a brief speech explaining to your neighbors what happened in Boston. **[Performing Arts Link]**

Projects

6. **Interior Design Project** Wharton had a special interest in interior decoration. Research principles of interior decor of the time the story was set, and create an oral and visual presentation showing what Theodora's house might have looked like. **[Art Link; Social Studies Link]**

7. **Contest Announcement** For *Home Circle*'s new story contest, write and design an eye-catching ad detailing submission guidelines and announcing awards for winning stories. **[Media Link]**

Writing Mini-Lesson

Short Story

Theodora might have done better to launch her writing career with a short story—a brief fictional narrative. Using a single setting, a simple plot, and just a few characters, write a short story that will succeed as well as "April Showers" does in holding audience attention.

Writing Skills Focus: Creating a Mood

Your single setting should include details that convey a particular **mood**, or atmosphere, as well as a sense of time and place.

Model From the Story

Downstairs the library clock struck two. Its muffled thump sounded like an admonitory knock against her bedroom floor. Two o'clock! and she had promised her mother to be up early . . .

In this passage, the author creates a hushed atmosphere with the words *muffled* and *admonitory*. The exclamation *Two o'clock!* throws a bit of fright into the mood. Choose vivid details to create a mood for your story.

Prewriting Ask yourself: What central idea do I want to convey? Who is my audience? Then decide on the narrative elements of your story: plot, characters, setting, theme, narrator, and point of view.

Drafting Begin your draft by describing your setting and creating a mood. Use vivid language to make your setting and mood enticing. Then introduce the characters and the conflict. Be sure to bring the conflict to a climax and resolution.

Revising Think about ways to strengthen your story. For example, can the plot and conflict be made clearer? You may go through several rounds of revision before you are satisfied with your story.

Guide for Interpreting

Carl Sandburg (1878–1967)

You may know the work of a contemporary poet or songwriter who seems to speak right to you. The poetry of Carl Sandburg seemed to speak directly to many of the people of his time. It celebrated the lives and the spirit of ordinary Americans of that era.

Modest Beginnings The son of Swedish immigrants, Sandburg was born and raised in Galesburg, Illinois. Forced to go to work at an early age, Sandburg attended school on an irregular basis. As an adolescent, he knew firsthand the life of a laborer.

> *By writing about mills and factories, Sandburg paid tribute to the struggles and hopes of the poor.*

After spending six years working at a variety of jobs, Sandburg enlisted in the army in 1898, at the time of the Spanish-American War. After the war, he attended college, but dropped out before graduating. He then spent several years traveling around the country, again working at a variety of jobs.

The Bard of Chicago In 1912, Sandburg settled in Chicago, one of the nation's great industrial cities. He worked as a newspaper reporter and began to publish poetry. His first book, *Chicago Poems*, published in 1916, met with success. Sandburg soon earned widespread recognition, and helped establish Chicago as a leading literary center. During the next ten years, Sandburg published three more successful collections of poetry: *Cornhuskers* (1918), *Smoke and Steel* (1920), and *Slabs of the Sunburst West* (1922). While continuing to write poetry, Sandburg then began touring the country delivering lectures on Walt Whitman and Abraham Lincoln—two men whom he greatly admired—and started a career as a folk singer. He also spent a great deal of time collecting material for a biography of Lincoln and he prepared an anthology of American folk songs, *The American Songbook* (1927). In 1940, Carl Sandburg received a Pulitzer Prize for his multi-volume biography of Lincoln, and in 1951 he received a second Pulitzer Prize for his *Complete Poems*.

Power of Positive Thinking Sandburg was an optimist who believed in the power of ordinary Americans to fulfill their dreams. Throughout his career, Sandburg reached out to his readers with poems that were concrete and direct. He was not interested in experimenting with complicated syntax or images, as were some other poets of his generation.

Sandburg offered a variety of definitions of poetry, among them these two: "Poetry is a search for syllables to shoot at the barriers of the unknown and the unknowable" and "Poetry is the opening and closing of a door, leaving those who look through to guess about what is seen during a moment."

◆ Background for Understanding

SOCIAL STUDIES: SANDBURG AND 1920'S AMERICA

The 1920's, the decade when Sandburg wrote many of his greatest poems, was a time of activity and excitement in America. The economy was booming, jazz filled the airwaves, the Charleston was the rage at dance halls, and Hollywood started producing talking films. Called the Roaring Twenties, this decade was celebrated in the literature of F. Scott Fitzgerald, among other writers.

Sandburg's poems, too, reflected what many Americans believed in the 1920's: There was no limit to what they could achieve. However, Sandburg also focused attention on the lives of those who weren't getting rich: workers in meatpacking houses, mills, and factories. The result was a simple and straightforward verse that captured the energy of industrial America.

Chicago ◆ Grass

◆ Literature and Your Life

CONNECT YOUR EXPERIENCE

If you've ever celebrated the comeback of someone who seemed to have been defeated—a team scoring four runs in the bottom of the ninth, for example—then you understand the spirit in which Carl Sandburg wrote. In reading these poems, you'll see that Sandburg recognized people's (and cities') failures—but he cheered the invincibility of their souls.

Journal Writing Do you think that most of the residents of your town or city have a strong spirit? Write about one or two events that illustrate their general outlook on life.

THEMATIC FOCUS: FROM EVERY CORNER OF THE LAND

Carl Sandburg paid special attention to the voices of industrial workers in the nation's heartland. Think about the ways in which these voices differ from those in other regions of the country.

◆ Build Vocabulary

RELATED WORDS: *BRUTAL*

Sandburg uses the word *brutal* to refer to Chicago. Knowing the meaning of *brutal*—cruel or harsh—can help you determine the meanings of related words such as *brute*, *brutality*, and *brutish*.

WORD BANK

Preview this list of words from the poems.

| brutal |
| wanton |
| cunning |

◆ Grammar and Style

FOUR TYPES OF SENTENCES

In these poems, Sandburg uses all four types of sentences:

I am the grass. This sentence is **declarative** because it makes a statement and ends with a period.

What place is this? This sentence is **interrogative** because it asks a question and ends with a question mark.

Pile the bodies high at Austerlitz and Waterloo. This sentence is **imperative** because it is a statement that gives a command or makes a request.

…under his wrist is the pulse, and under his ribs the heart of the people, Laughing! This sentence is **exclamatory** because it expresses a strong emotion and ends with an exclamation point.

◆ Literary Focus

APOSTROPHE

Apostrophe is a literary device in which the speaker or narrator directly addresses a person or thing. For example, in "Chicago," Sandburg addresses the city as if it were a person:

> They tell me you are wicked
> and I believe them . . .

> And they tell me you are
> crooked and I answer:
> Yes . . .

As you read "Chicago," think about the effect this technique creates. Why do you think Sandburg chose to speak directly to the city of Chicago?

◆ Reading Strategy

RESPOND

When you **respond** to a poem, you think about the message that the poet has conveyed and reflect on how you personally feel about the topic. Consider how the poet's message relates to your own life and to the world in which you live, and think about how you can use or apply what you learned from the poem.

As you read these poems, connect your own experiences to the images and ideas presented, and react to the message Sandburg conveys.

CHICAGO

CARL SANDBURG

Hog Butcher for the World
Tool Maker, Stacker of Wheat,
Player with Railroads and the Nation's Freight Handler;
Stormy, husky, brawling,
5   City of the Big Shoulders:

They tell me you are wicked and I believe them, for I have seen
    your painted women under the gas lamps luring the farm
    boys.
And they tell me you are crooked and I answer: Yes, it is true
    I have seen the gunman kill and go free to kill again.
And they tell me you are brutal and my reply is: On the faces
    of women and children I have seen the marks of wanton
    hunger.
And having answered so I turn once more to those who sneer
    at this my city, and I give them back the sneer and say to
    them:
10   Come and show me another city with lifted head singing so
    proud to be alive and coarse and strong and cunning.
Flinging magnetic curses amid the toil of piling job on job,
    here is a tall bold slugger set vivid against the little soft
    cities;
Fierce as a dog with tongue lapping for action, cunning as a
    savage pitted against the wilderness,
        Bareheaded,
        Shoveling,
15   Wrecking,
        Planning,
        Building, breaking, rebuilding,

Under the smoke, dust all over his mouth, laughing with
    white teeth,
Under the terrible burden of destiny laughing as a young man
    laughs,
20   Laughing even as an ignorant fighter laughs who has never
    lost a battle,
Bragging and laughing that under his wrist is the pulse, and
    under his ribs the heart of the people,
                Laughing!
Laughing the stormy, husky, brawling laughter of Youth, half-
    naked, sweating, proud to be a Hog Butcher, Tool Maker,
    Stacker of Wheat, Player with Railroads and Freight Handler
    to the Nation.

GRASS
CARL SANDBURG

Pile the bodies high at Austerlitz and Waterloo.[1]
Shovel them under and let me work—
   I am the grass; I cover all.

And pile them high at Gettysburg
5 And pile them high at Ypres and Verdun.[2]
Shovel them under and let me work.
Two years, ten years, and passengers ask the conductor:
   What place is this?
   Where are we now?

10   I am grass.
     Let me work.

---

1. **Austerlitz** (ôs′ tər lits′) **and Waterloo**: Sites of battles of the Napoleonic Wars.
2. **Ypres** (ē′ pr) **and Verdun** (vər dun′): Sites of battles of World War I.

◆ **Build Vocabulary**

brutal (br$\overline{oo}$t′ əl) *adj*.: Cruel and without feeling; savage; violent

wanton (wän′ tən) *adj*.: Senseless; unjustified

cunning (kun′ iŋ) *adj*.: Skillful in deception; crafty; sly

Guide for Responding

◆ Literature and Your Life

Reader's Response Unlike some poets, Sandburg tells you what to feel and what to think. How do you react to this directness? Do you enjoy, admire, or resent it? Why?

Thematic Focus How does Chicago differ from your town? (Or, if you live in Chicago, how does Sandburg's Chicago differ from the city you know?)

☑ Check Your Comprehension

1. What do the different places mentioned in "Grass" have in common?
2. Name two of the industries for which Chicago was famous.

◆ Critical Thinking

INTERPRET

1. According to the speaker, how do other people see Chicago? Support your answer. **[Interpret]**
2. Why does the speaker appreciate Chicago? **[Interpret]**
3. What does "Grass" say about the end result of war? **[Draw Conclusions]**
4. What does "Grass" say about the relationship between people and nature? **[Draw Conclusions]**

EVALUATE

5. In "Grass," Sandburg uses only 11 lines to get his message across. Does he achieve his goal? Explain. **[Make a Judgment]**

Guide for Responding (continued)

◆ Reading Strategy

RESPOND

To **respond** to a poem, think about what the writing says. Consider how the poem makes you feel, and notice what thoughts the poem sets off in your mind.

Combine your knowledge with your emotional reactions to "Grass" and "Chicago" to answer these questions.

1. (a) What is Sandburg's message in "Grass"?
   (b) How do you react to that message? Why?
2. (a) What senses did you draw upon to respond to the description "Under the smoke, dust all over his mouth, laughing with white teeth" from "Chicago"? (b) What was your response to the description? Explain.

◆ Build Vocabulary

USING RELATED WORDS: *BRUTAL*

The word *brutal* means "cruel; crude; harsh." Use this knowledge and what you know about parts of speech to complete each sentence with *brutish, brutalize, brute,* or *brutality*.

1. Sam was so rough with my brother that I told him he was behaving like a ___?___ and asked him to leave.
2. Many who participated in World War I were stunned by the ___?___ on the front lines.
3. Use your knife and fork, and stop that ___?___ behavior at once!
4. Those who ___?___ innocent animals should receive the harshest punishment.

USING THE WORD BANK

Write the letter of the word closest in meaning to each of the following words from the word bank:

1. brutal: (a) unwise, (b) violent, (c) heavy
2. cunning: (a) suspicious, (b) diligent, (c) crafty
3. wanton: (a) rapid, (b) kind, (c) rash

◆ Literary Focus

APOSTROPHE

Carl Sandburg uses **apostrophe**—the literary technique of directly addressing a person or thing—to make the city of Chicago come alive. By addressing Chicago as *you*, Sandburg shows us that his relationship with the city resembles a close relationship with a person.

1. Identify the lines in which Sandburg uses apostrophe.
2. Compare the lines that directly address the city with those that are addressed to the people who criticize Chicago. (a) Which section contains more positive images? (b) Analyze the difference between the two sections.
3. Identify at least one feeling Sandburg has for Chicago that he might feel toward a close friend. Support your answer with examples from the poem.

◆ Grammar and Style

SENTENCE TYPES

By varying sentence types, writers can add interest to their creative works.

> The four types of sentences are **declarative, imperative, interrogative,** and **exclamatory**.

Practice On your paper, write each sentence, add the correct end punctuation, and label the sentence type.

1. Shovel me under and let me work
2. I am the grass
3. Where are we now
4. Come and show me another city
5. What place is this

Writing Application Write an essay in which you praise and/or criticize your city or town. Use all four types of sentences in your essay.

Build Your Portfolio

 ## Idea Bank

Writing

1. Postcard Imagine that you've traveled to Chicago, and write a postcard to a friend back home, describing your impressions of the city.

2. Apostrophe Write a poem to the place that means the most to you, making sure to address the place as *you*. In your poem, reflect upon the positive and negative aspects of the place.

3. Analysis of Repetition Sandburg is famous for repetition. Using either of his poems, write an analysis that explains the effect that the repeated elements (words, phrases, sentence structure, grammatical elements, and so on) have on the overall effect of the poem.

Speaking and Listening

4. Disagreement With a partner, role-play a disagreement between two Chicago residents. One defends the city, and one attacks it. Use the opinions expressed in "Chicago" as a guide.

5. Stand-up Routine Acting as the city of Chicago, deliver a comedy routine. You can either brag about how tough you are or whine about how everyone criticizes you. **[Performing Arts Link]**

Projects

6. Research Project "Grass" mentions two battles from the Napoleonic Wars. Conduct research to learn more about these wars. Present your findings in a report along with illustrations or other graphic aids. **[Social Studies Link]**

7. Population Breakdown Using the Internet or the library, find the total population of Chicago. Collect statistics related to that population (male/female totals, totals by ethnic group, and so on). Calculate percentages of the total represented by each category. **[Math Link]**

 ## Writing Mini-Lesson

Description for a Travel Guide

In "Chicago," Carl Sandburg conveys that city's energy through descriptive details of the activities that go on there. As a writer assigned to produce a travel guide, write a vivid, exciting description of a place you want to sell to an audience of travelers.

Writing Skills Focus: Precise Details

Use specific examples to create a vivid and precise picture of a place. Don't just say a city has great ethnic restaurants; tell your readers they can find Mexican, Thai, and Ethiopian food there. *Describe* that food.

Take "Chicago" as your example. Sandburg doesn't just say the city resembles a powerful young laborer; he uses verbs that show the power:

Model From the Poem

Bareheaded,/Shoveling,/Wrecking,/Planning,/Building, breaking, rebuilding, . . .

Prewriting Think of a place you know well. On a chart like this one, jot down its most positive features—interesting architecture, great museums, crystal-clear freshwater lakes. Then list specific examples of each.

Features	Examples

Drafting You might want to chose your subject's strongest feature first. Describe exactly why visitors must see this feature, and why it reflects the place as a whole.

Revising Review your draft. Did you bring a place alive with description? Check to see where you can replace vague or general language with precise nouns and vivid verbs.

*G*uide for Interpreting

Katherine Anne Porter
(1890–1980)

The exceptionally well-crafted fiction of Katherine Anne Porter focuses primarily on human relationships and on people's varied responses to a rapidly changing world.

In her writing, Porter sought to understand people's motivations and emotions.

Porter's dual interests in people's religious attitudes and the rural South—pursued in much of her work—may have originated in her childhood. Born in Indian Creek, Texas, she was raised in poverty and haphazardly educated in convent schools.

Beginnings as a Writer Porter began writing at an early age; as a young adult, she worked as a journalist. Her work took her to many places, including Mexico City, where she lived for eight years. There she developed an interest in writing fiction and in 1922 she published her first story, "María Concepción," in *Century*, a highly regarded literary magazine. Eight years later, she published her first book, *Flowering Judas* (1930). The book, a collection of six short stories, was praised by critics and earned Porter widespread recognition. *Flowering Judas and Other Stories*, an expanded edition of the book containing ten stories, was published in 1935.

Literary Achievements Katherine Anne Porter went on to produce several other major works, including *Noon Wine* (1937), *Pale Horse, Pale Rider* (1939), *No Safe Harbor* (1941), *The Leaning Tower and Other Stories* (1944), and *Ship of Fools* (1962)— Porter's only novel. Although her body of work was relatively small in comparison to some of the other major writers of her time, her works consistently received high praise from critics and earned her a place among the finest writers of this century. Her *Collected Stories* (1965), was awarded the Pulitzer Prize and the National Book Award. In addition, her novel, *Ship of Fools*, was made into a popular film.

In his review of *The Leaning Tower and Other Stories,* critic Edmund Wilson tried to account for the "elusive" quality that made Porter an "absolutely first-rate artist." He said, "These stories are not illustrations of anything that is reducible to a moral law or a political or social analysis or even a principle of human behavior. What they show us are human relationships in their constantly shifting phases and in the moments of which their existence is made. There is not place for general reflections; you are to live through the experiences as the characters do." You'll discover that Wilson's observations can be applied to "The Jilting of Granny Weatherall," which takes readers on a journey through the various phases of an old woman's life in the moments leading up to her death.

◆ Background for Understanding

CULTURE: POST-WAR DESPAIR

Katherine Anne Porter's life view was shaped by the universal sense of disillusionment resulting from World War I, the despair of the Great Depression, and the World War II horrors of Nazism and nuclear warfare. In her words, she lived life "under the heavy threat of world catastrophe." In response, Porter poured all her energies into "the effort to grasp the meaning of those threats...." Sometimes, as in the novel *Ship of Fools,* this exploration focused on large-scale social and political issues such as Nazism. In contrast, works like "The Jilting of Granny Weatherall" pinpointed the drifting and dissolving families and communities of the modern age.

The Jilting of Granny Weatherall

◆ Literature and Your Life

CONNECT YOUR EXPERIENCE

Think about the memories and images your mind offers up just as you're falling asleep. They are probably strange, disjointed, and a little fuzzy. If you can remember these semi-conscious thoughts of yours, you may be able to understand Granny Weatherall a little better. The old woman in this story is being visited by a host of images from her past. As you read, try to piece together the meaning of those memories.

Journal Writing Choose an event from the recent past. Without trying to write perfectly formed sentences, write down some associations that flow through your mind.

THEMATIC FOCUS: FROM EVERY CORNER OF THE LAND

This story is set in the rural South where families often lived far from town. In what specific ways does the setting capture a sense of isolation?

◆ Reading Strategy

CLARIFY SEQUENCE OF EVENTS

This story evokes many different time periods as Granny Weatherall drifts in and out of the present. To stay oriented, you should **clarify the sequence of events**. Watch for jumps in Granny Weatherall's thinking, often signaled by a shift from present-moment dialogue to Granny's inner thoughts. Notice flashbacks, in which Granny's thoughts return to an earlier time in her life. List key moments in a chart under the headings Past and Present. Number them in order as you unravel the sequence of Granny's life.

Past	Present

◆ Build Vocabulary

PREFIXES: *dys-*

You'll find the word *dyspepsia*, which means "indigestion," in this story. The word contains the prefix *dys-*, meaning "difficult" or "bad." How does the prefix contribute to the overall meaning of the word?

WORD BANK

Preview this list of words from the story.

piety
frippery
dyspepsia

◆ Literary Focus

STREAM OF CONSCIOUSNESS

People's thoughts don't usually flow in a neat, organized manner. Instead, they proceed in an unorganized flow of insights, memories, and reflections. During the early 1900's some writers began using a literary device called **stream of consciousness,** in which they tried to capture the natural flow of people's thoughts. When writers use this technique, they present a sequence of thoughts as if they were coming directly from a character's mind. Transitions found in ordinary prose are omitted, and details are connected only by a character's associations.

◆ Grammar and Style

IMPERATIVE SENTENCES

To portray Granny Weatherall's attempt to regain control of her life—and death—Katherine Anne Porter uses imperative sentences. An **imperative sentence** states a request, or, in Granny Weatherall's case, gives an order. The subject, *you,* is understood, not stated. Look at the example from the story:

The word *you,* or a character's name, is implied here.

"Get along now, take your schoolbooks and go."

The Jilting of Granny Weatherall

Katherine Anne Porter

She flicked her wrist neatly out of Doctor Harry's pudgy careful fingers and pulled the sheet up to her chin. The brat ought to be in knee breeches. Doctoring around the country with spectacles on his nose! "Get along now, take your schoolbooks and go. There's nothing wrong with me."

Doctor Harry spread a warm paw like a cushion on her forehead where the forked green vein danced and made her eyelids twitch. "Now, now, be a good girl, and we'll have you up in no time."

"That's no way to speak to a woman nearly eighty years old just because she's down. I'd have you respect your elders, young man."

"Well, Missy, excuse me," Doctor Harry patted her cheek. "But I've got to warn you, haven't I? You're a marvel, but you must be careful or you're going to be good and sorry."

"Don't tell me what I'm going to be. I'm on my feet now, morally speaking. It's Cornelia. I had to go to bed to get rid of her."

Her bones felt loose, and floated around in her skin, and Doctor Harry floated like a balloon around the foot of the bed. He floated and pulled down his waistcoat and swung his glasses on a cord. "Well, stay where you are, it certainly can't hurt you."

"Get along and doctor your sick," said Granny Weatherall. "Leave a well woman alone. I'll call for you when I want you. . . . Where were you forty years ago when I pulled through milk leg[1] and double pneumonia? You weren't even born. Don't let Cornelia lead you on," she shouted, because Doctor Harry appeared to float up to the ceiling and out. "I pay my own bills, and I don't throw my money away on nonsense!"

She meant to wave good-bye, but it was too much trouble. Her eyes closed of themselves, it was like a dark curtain drawn around the bed. The pillow rose and floated under her, pleasant as a hammock in a light wind. She listened to the leaves rustling outside the window. No, somebody was swishing newspapers: no, Cornelia and Doctor Harry were whispering together. She leaped broad awake, thinking they whispered in her ear.

"She was never like this, never like this!" "Well, what can we expect?" "Yes, eighty years old. . . ."

Well, and what if she was? She still had ears. It was like Cornelia to whisper around doors. She always kept things secret in such a public way. She was always being tactful and kind. Cornelia was dutiful; that was the trouble with her. Dutiful and good: "So good and dutiful," said Granny, "that I'd like to spank her." She saw herself spanking Cornelia and making a fine job of it.

"What'd you say, Mother?"

Granny felt her face tying up in hard knots.

"Can't a body think, I'd like to know?"

"I thought you might want something."

"I do. I want a lot of things. First off, go away and don't whisper."

She lay and drowsed, hoping in her sleep that the children would keep out and let her rest a minute. It had been a long day. Not that she was tired. It was always pleasant to snatch a minute now and then. There was always so much to be done, let me see: tomorrow.

---

1. **milk leg:** Painful swelling of the leg.

Tomorrow was far away and there was nothing to trouble about. Things were finished somehow when the time came; thank God there was always a little margin over for peace: then a person could spread out the plan of life and tuck in the edges orderly. It was good to have everything clean and folded away, with the hair brushes and tonic bottles sitting straight on the white embroidered linen: the day started without fuss and the pantry shelves laid out with rows of jelly glasses and brown jugs and white stone-china jars with blue whirligigs and words painted on them: coffee, tea, sugar, ginger, cinnamon, allspice: and the bronze clock with the lion on top nicely dusted off. The dust that lion could collect in twenty-four hours! The box in the attic with all those letters tied up, well, she'd have to go through that tomorrow. All those letters—George's letters and John's letters and her letters to them both—lying around for the children to find afterwards made her uneasy. Yes, that would be tomorrow's business. No use to let them know how silly she had been once.

While she was rummaging around she found death in her mind and it felt clammy and unfamiliar. She had spent so much time preparing for death there was no need for bringing it up again. Let it take care of itself now. When she was sixty she had felt very old, finished, and went around making farewell trips to see her children and grandchildren, with a secret in her mind: This is the very last of your mother, children! Then she made her will and came down with a long fever. That was all just a notion like a lot of other things, but it was lucky too, for she had once for all got over the idea of dying for a long time. Now she couldn't be worried. She hoped she had better sense now. Her father had lived to be one hundred and two years old and had drunk a noggin of strong hot toddy on his last birthday. He told the reporters it was his daily habit, and he owed his long life to that. He had made quite a scandal and was very pleased about it. She believed she'd just plague Cornelia a little.

"Cornelia! Cornelia!" No footsteps, but a

Garden of Memories, Charles Burchfield, The Museum of Modern Art

▲ **Critical Viewing** How might the figure in this surreal illustration of an old woman in her "garden of memories" represent Granny Weatherall? **[Connect]**

sudden hand on her cheek. "Bless you, where have you been?"

"Here, mother."

"Well, Cornelia, I want a noggin of hot toddy."

"Are you cold, darling?"

"I'm chilly, Cornelia. Lying in bed stops the circulation. I must have told you that a thousand times."

Well, she could just hear Cornelia telling her husband that Mother was getting a little childish and they'd have to humor her. The thing that most annoyed her was that Cornelia thought she was deaf, dumb, and blind. Little hasty glances and tiny gestures tossed around her and over her head saying, "Don't cross her, let her have her way, she's eighty years old," and she sitting there as if she lived in a thin glass cage. Sometimes Granny almost made up her mind to pack up and move back to her own house where nobody could remind her every minute that she was old. Wait, wait, Cornelia, till your own children whisper behind your back!

In her day she had kept a better house and had got more work done. She wasn't too old yet for Lydia to be driving eighty miles for advice when one of the children jumped the track, and Jimmy still dropped in and talked things over: "Now, Mammy, you've a good business head, I want to know what you think of this?. . . " Old. Cornelia couldn't change the furniture around without asking. Little things, little things! They had been so sweet when they were little. Granny wished the old days were back again with the children young and everything to be done over. It had been a hard pull, but not too much for her. When she thought of all the food she had cooked, and all the clothes she had cut and sewed, and all the gardens she had made—well, the children showed it. There they were, made out of her, and they couldn't get away from that. Sometimes she wanted to see John again and point to them and say, Well, I didn't do so badly, did I? But that would have to wait. That was for tomorrow. She used to think of him as a man, but now all the children were older than their father, and he would be a child beside her if she saw him now. It seemed strange and there was something wrong in the idea. Why, he couldn't possibly recognize her. She had fenced in a hundred acres once, digging the post holes herself and clamping the wires with just a negro boy to help. That changed a woman. John would be looking for a young woman with the peaked Spanish comb in her hair and the painted fan. Digging post holes changed a woman. Riding country roads in the winter when women had their babies was another thing: sitting up nights with sick horses and sick children and hardly ever losing one. John, I hardly ever lost one of them! John

◆ **Literary Focus**

Notice the random path of Granny's thoughts. What are some topics she touches on, and how are they linked in her mind?

> **Granny wished the old days were back again with the children young and everything to be done over.**

would see that in a minute, that would be something he could understand, she wouldn't have to explain anything!

It made her feel like rolling up her sleeves and putting the whole place to rights again. No matter if Cornelia was determined to be everywhere at once, there were a great many things left undone on this place. She would start tomorrow and do them. It was good to be strong enough for everything, even if all you made melted and changed and slipped under your hands, so that by the time you finished you almost forgot what you were working for. What was it I set out to do? she asked herself intently, but she could not remember. A fog rose over the valley, she saw it marching across the creek swallowing the trees and moving up the hill like an army of ghosts. Soon it would be at the near edge of the orchard, and then it was time to go in and light the lamps. Come in, children, don't stay out in the night air.

Lighting the lamps had been beautiful. The children huddled up to her and breathed like little calves waiting at the bars in the twilight. Their eyes followed the match and watched the flame rise and settle in a blue curve, then they moved away from her. The lamp was lit, they didn't have to be scared and hang on to mother any more. Never, never, never more. God, for all my life I thank Thee. Without Thee, my God, I could never have done it. Hail Mary, full of grace.

I want you to pick all the fruit this year and see that nothing is wasted. There's always someone who can use it. Don't let good things rot for want of using. You waste life when you waste good food. Don't let things get lost. It's bitter to lose things. Now, don't let me get to thinking, not when I am tired and taking a little nap before supper. . . .

The pillow rose about her shoulders and pressed against her heart and the memory was being squeezed out of it: oh, push down the pillow, somebody: it would smother her if she tried to hold it. Such a fresh breeze blowing and such a green day with no threats in it. But he had not come, just the same. What does a woman do when she has put on the white veil and set out the white cake for a man and he doesn't come? She tried to remember. No, I swear he never harmed me but in that. He never harmed me but in that . . . and what if he did? There was the day, the day, but a whirl of dark smoke rose and covered it, crept up and over into the bright field where everything was planted so carefully in orderly rows. That was hell, she knew hell when she saw it. For sixty years she had prayed against remembering him and against losing her soul in the deep pit of hell, and now the two things were mingled in one and the thought of him was a smoky cloud from hell that moved and crept in her head when she had just got rid of Doctor Harry and was trying to rest a minute. Wounded vanity, Ellen, said a sharp voice in the top of her mind. Don't let your wounded vanity get the upper hand of you. Plenty of girls get jilted. You were jilted, weren't you? Then stand up to it. Her eyelids wavered and let in streamers of blue-gray light like tissue paper over her eyes. She must get up and pull the shades down or she'd never sleep. She was in bed again and the shades were not down. How could that happen? Better turn over, hide from the light, sleeping in the light gave you nightmares. "Mother, how do you feel now?" and a stinging wetness on her forehead. But I don't like having my face washed in cold water!

Hapsy? George? Lydia? Jimmy? No, Cornelia, and her features were swollen and full of little puddles. "They're coming, darling, they'll all be here soon." Go wash your face, child, you look funny.

Instead of obeying, Cornelia knelt down and put her head on the pillow. She seemed to be talking but there was no sound. "Well, are you tongue-tied? Whose birthday is it? Are you going to give a party?"

Cornelia's mouth moved urgently in strange shapes. "Don't do that, you bother me, daughter."

"Oh, no, Mother. Oh, no. . . ."

Nonsense. It was strange about children. They disputed your every word. "No what, Cornelia?"

"Here's Doctor Harry."

"I won't see that boy again. He just left five minutes ago."

"That was this morning, Mother. It's night now. Here's the nurse."

"This is Doctor Harry, Mrs. Weatherall. I never saw you look so young and happy!"

"Ah, I'll never be young again—but I'd be happy if they'd let me lie in peace and get rested."

She thought she spoke up loudly, but no one answered. A warm weight on her forehead, a warm bracelet on her wrist, and a breeze went on whispering, trying to tell her something. A shuffle of leaves in the everlasting hand of God, He blew on them and they danced and rattled. "Mother, don't mind, we're going to give you a little hypodermic." "Look here, daughter, how do ants get in this bed? I saw sugar ants yesterday." Did you send for Hapsy too?

It was Hapsy she really wanted. She had to go a long way back through a great many rooms to find Hapsy standing with a baby on her arm. She seemed to herself to be Hapsy also, and the baby on Hapsy's arm was Hapsy and himself and herself, all at once, and there was no surprise in the meeting. Then Hapsy melted from within and turned flimsy as gray gauze and the baby was a gauzy shadow, and Hapsy came up close and said, "I thought you'd never come," and looked at her very searchingly and said, "You haven't changed a bit!" They leaned forward to kiss, when Cornelia began whispering from a long way off, "Oh, is there anything you want to tell me? Is there anything I can do for you?"

Yes, she had changed her mind after sixty years and she would like to see George. I want you to find George. Find him and be sure to tell him I forgot him. I want him to know I had my husband just the same and my children and my house like any other woman. A good house too and a good husband that I loved and fine children out of him. Better than I hoped for even. Tell him I was given back everything he took away and more. Oh, no, oh, God, no, there was something else besides the house and the man and the children. Oh, surely they were not all? What was it? Something not given back. . . . Her breath crowded down under her ribs and grew into a monstrous frightening shape with cutting

◆ Reading Strategy
Who are George and John, and in what sequence did they appear in Granny's life?

edges; it bored up into her head, and the agony was unbelievable: Yes, John, get the Doctor now, no more talk, my time has come.

When this one was born it should be the last. The last. It should have been born first, for it was the one she had truly wanted. Everything came in good time. Nothing left out, left over. She was strong, in three days she would be as well as ever. Better. A woman needed milk in her to have her full health.

"Mother, do you hear me?"

"I've been telling you—"

"Mother, Father Connolly's here."

"I went to Holy Communion only last week. Tell him I'm not so sinful as all that."

"Father just wants to speak to you."

He could speak as much as he pleased. It was like him to drop in and inquire about her soul as if it were a teething baby, and then stay on for a cup of tea and a round of cards and gossip. He always had a funny story of some sort, usually about an Irishman who made his little mistakes and confessed them, and the point lay in some absurd thing he would blurt out in the confessional showing his struggles between native piety and original sin. Granny felt easy about her soul. Cornelia, where are your manners? Give Father Connolly a chair. She had her secret comfortable understanding with a few favorite saints who cleared a straight road to God for her. All as surely signed and sealed as the papers for the new Forty Acres. Forever . . . heirs and assigns[2] forever. Since the day the wedding cake was not cut, but thrown out and wasted. The whole bottom dropped out of the world, and there she was blind and sweating with nothing under her feet and the walls falling away. His hand had caught her under the breast, she had not fallen, there was the freshly polished floor with the green rug on it, just as before. He had cursed like a sailor's parrot and said, "I'll kill him for you." Don't lay a hand on him, for my sake leave something to God. "Now, Ellen, you must believe what I tell you. . . ."

So there was nothing, nothing to worry about any more, except sometimes in the night one of the children screamed in a nightmare, and they both hustled out shaking and hunting for the matches and calling, "There, wait a minute, here we are!" John, get the doctor now,

Hapsy's time has come. But there was Hapsy standing by the bed in a white cap. "Cornelia, tell Hapsy to take off her cap. I can't see her plain."

Her eyes opened very wide and the room stood out like a picture she had seen somewhere. Dark colors with the shadows rising towards the ceiling in long angles. The tall black dresser gleamed with nothing on it but John's picture, enlarged from a little one, with John's eyes very black when they should have been blue. You never saw him, so how do you know how he looked? But the man insisted the copy was perfect, it was very rich and handsome. For a picture, yes, but it's not my husband. The table by the bed had a linen cover and a candle and a crucifix. The light was blue from Cornelia's silk lampshades. No sort of light at all, just frippery. You had to live forty years with kerosene lamps to appreciate honest electricity. She felt very strong and she saw Doctor Harry with a rosy nimbus around him.

"You look like a saint, Doctor Harry, and I vow that's as near as you'll ever come to it."

"She's saying something."

"I heard you, Cornelia. What's all this carrying on?"

"Father Connolly's saying—"

Cornelia's voice staggered and bumped like a cart in a bad road. It rounded corners and turned back again and arrived nowhere. Granny stepped up in the cart very lightly and reached for the reins, but a man sat beside her and she knew him by his hands, driving the cart. She did not look in his face, for she knew without seeing, but looked instead down the road where the trees leaned over and bowed to each other and a thousand birds were singing a Mass. She felt like singing too, but she put her hand in the bosom of her dress and pulled out a rosary, and Father Connolly murmured Latin in a very solemn voice and tickled her feet.[3] My God, will you stop that nonsense? I'm a married woman. What if he did run away and leave me to face the priest by myself? I found another a whole world better. I wouldn't have exchanged my husband for anybody except St. Michael[4] himself, and you may tell him that

---

2. **assigns:** Persons to whom property is transferred.

3. **murmured . . . feet:** Administered the last rites of the Catholic Church.
4. **St. Michael:** One of the archangels.

for me with a thank you in the bargain.

Light flashed on her closed eyelids, and a deep roaring shook her. Cornelia, is that lightning? I hear thunder. There's going to be a storm. Close all the windows. Call the children in. . . . "Mother, here we are, all of us." "Is that you, Hapsy?" "Oh, no, I'm Lydia. We drove as fast as we could." Their faces drifted above her, drifted away. The rosary fell out of her hands and Lydia put it back. Jimmy tried to help, their hands fumbled together, and Granny closed two fingers around Jimmy's thumb. Beads wouldn't do, it must be something alive. She was so amazed her thoughts ran round and round. So, my dear Lord, this is my death and I wasn't even thinking about it. My children have come to see me die. But I can't, it's not time. Oh, I always hated surprises. I wanted to give Cornelia the amethyst set—Cornelia, you're to have the amethyst set, but Hapsy's to wear it when she wants, and, Doctor Harry, do shut up. Nobody sent for you. Oh, my dear Lord, do wait a minute. I meant to do something about the Forty Acres, Jimmy doesn't need it and Lydia will later on, with that worthless husband of hers. I meant to finish the altar cloth and send six bottles of wine to Sister Borgia for her dyspepsia. I want to send six bottles of wine to Sister Borgia, Father Connolly, now don't let me forget.

Cornelia's voice made short turns and tilted over and crashed. "Oh, Mother, oh, Mother, oh Mother. . . ."

"I'm not going, Cornelia. I'm taken by surprise. I can't go."

You'll see Hapsy again. What about her? "I thought you'd never come." Granny made a long journey outward, looking for Hapsy. What if I don't find her? What then? Her heart sank down and down, there was no bottom to death, she couldn't come to the end of it. The blue light from Cornelia's lampshade drew into a tiny point in the center of her brain, it flickered and winked like an eye, quietly it fluttered and dwindled. Granny lay curled down within herself, amazed and watchful, staring at the point of light that was herself; her body was now only a deeper mass of shadow in an endless darkness and this darkness would curl around the light and swallow it up. God, give a sign!

For the second time there was no sign. Again no bridegroom and the priest in the house. She could not remember any other sorrow because this grief wiped them all away. Oh, no, there's nothing more cruel than this—I'll never forgive it. She stretched herself with a deep breath and blew out the light.

◆ **Build Vocabulary**

piety (pī′ ə tē) *n.*: Devotion to religious duties

frippery (frip′ ər ē) *n.*: Showy display of elegance

dyspepsia (dis pep′ shə) *n.*: Indigestion

Guide for Responding

◆ *Literature and Your Life*

Reader's Response If you were at Granny Weatherall's deathbed, what would you say to help comfort her?

Thematic Focus Identify three clues from the story that indicate it is set in a rural area.

Journal Entry Write a paragraph explaining why the portrayal of Granny Weatherall's final hours seems—or does not seem—plausible to you.

☑ **Check Your Comprehension**

1. (a) Which memory is most painful to Granny as she reviews her life? (b) With what thought does this memory become mingled?
2. How does Granny respond to her children's arrival?
3. What happens at the end of the story just before Granny blows "out the light"?

◆ Critical Thinking

INTERPRET

1. Why is "Weatherall" an appropriate surname for Granny? **[Interpret]**
2. How might Granny summarize the important turning point of her life? **[Synthesize]**
3. What is ironic or surprising about Granny's desire to find George to tell him she has forgotten him? **[Interpret]**
4. What has George taken from Granny that she hopes to regain as the story ends? **[Analyze]**
5. At the end of the story, Granny says "I'll never forgive it." What is *it*, and what does her comment reveal about her? **[Draw Conclusions]**
6. What does the light referred to in the last two paragraphs symbolize? **[Draw Conclusions]**

APPLY

7. How might this story have been different if Granny had confronted George after he jilted her? **[Hypothesize]**

◆ Literary Focus

STREAM OF CONSCIOUSNESS

Porter's **stream-of-consciousness** technique captures the natural flow of Granny Weatherall's thoughts. She deliberately avoids using transition phrases such as *when she was younger* or *looking back at it now*. Rather, Porter lets Granny's associations bridge the gap between thoughts.

Cite two examples in which Granny's thoughts drift from one subject to a seemingly unrelated subject. For each example, explain the natural associations that connect Granny's thoughts.

◆ Reading Strategy

CLARIFY SEQUENCE OF EVENTS

When the stream-of-consciousness technique is used in a story, events are organized according to a character's associations, rather than in chronological order. This means that the narrative jumps around in time. As a result, to understand the **sequence**, you must be able to reorganize the events in the order in which they occurred.

Rearrange the events presented in "The Jilting of Granny Weatherall" in chronological order.

◆ Build Vocabulary

USING THE PREFIX *dys*-

The prefix *dys*- means "difficult" or "bad." Add this meaning to each of the clues in parentheses to define the numbered words. Check your definitions in the dictionary. Revise if necessary.

1. dysentery (*entery* = intestine)
2. dysfunctional (*functional* = working properly)
3. dyslexia (*lexis* = word or speech)

USING THE WORD BANK

On your paper, write the word from the word bank that fits best in each sentence.

1. Kelly showed her ____?____ by attending religious services daily.
2. "Pizza aggravates my ____?____," said Mr. Otis.
3. The skaters strutted by, displaying their ____?____ for all to admire.

◆ Grammar and Style

USING IMPERATIVE SENTENCES

Each time Granny Weatherall gives a command in this story, she is using an **imperative sentence**—a sentence that gives an order or states a request.

Practice On your paper, write the letter of the imperative sentence.

1. **a.** Will you get along and doctor your sick?
   b. Your sick need doctoring.
   c. Get along and doctor your sick.
2. **a.** Could you stay where you are?
   b. I want you to stay where you are.
   c. Stay where you are.
3. **a.** They shouldn't be whispering.
   b. Go away and don't whisper.
   c. I wish they wouldn't whisper.

Looking at Style Explain what Granny's use of imperative sentences reveals about her character.

Writing Application Rewrite these sentences to make them imperative sentences.

1. Won't you please leave a well woman alone?
2. You shouldn't let Cornelia lead you on.
3. Can't a body think?

Build Your Portfolio

 ## Idea Bank

Writing

1. **Doctor's Report** Imagine you're Doctor Harry. Write a report describing the physical and mental changes you've observed in Granny over the course of the day.

2. **Letter to George** As Cornelia, write a letter to George informing him of Granny's death. In whatever tone you choose, discuss the impact he had on Granny's life.

3. **Course Description** For a college catalog, write a page-long description of a course on stream-of-consciousness writing. Use examples from Porter's story to support your points.

Speaking and Listening

4. **Conversation** Suppose that Granny and George happened to meet ten years after the jilting. With a partner, role-play a conversation between them. **[Performing Arts Link]**

5. **Lecture** You are Doctor Harry fifteen years after Granny's death. More experience has taught you better ways of interacting with the elderly and infirm. In a lecture to a group of colleagues, share what you've learned. **[Health Link]**

Projects

6. **Free Painting** In a painting, illustrate the stream-of-consciousness writing technique. Using the medium of your choice, make a painting of free-associated images. Listening to music might help you to paint from your subconscious. **[Art Link; Music Link]**

7. **Report on Hospice Care** Hospice care—benevolent care of terminally ill people—is a growing area of medical specialization. Prepare a report detailing how Granny might have been cared for in a modern hospice. **[Health Link]**

 ## Writing Mini-Lesson

Dramatic Monologue

A **dramatic monologue** is a speech in which an imaginary character speaks to a silent listener. It might be said that Granny Weatherall's silent listener is herself, or her younger self.

Create a character who interests you; it may or may not be an elderly person. Write a dramatic monologue incorporating that character's stream-of-consciousness thoughts and memories. As you write, focus on effective characterizations that reveal what the character is like as a person.

Writing Skills Focus: Characterization

Choose memories, thoughts, language, and details that contribute to your characterization. For example, notice that Porter returns again and again to the incident of the jilting to show its impact on Granny's character and attitudes. Knowing what has hurt Granny helps readers know her better.

If your character is dominated by a particular emotion, show a memory that clearly and consistently explains the reason for that emotion.

Prewriting List descriptive words you associate with your character. Group these under "Actions," "Feelings," "Comments," and "Attitudes."

Drafting Select one or two key memories, events, or details around which to organize your monologue. Introduce one of these early in your draft. Experiment with the stream-of-consciousness technique by writing without transitions.

Revising Read your dramatic monologue aloud to yourself. Does it sound like the voice in someone's head? If you have been successful in making the sequence of events sound as though it were entirely random, you may want to add clues to help your audience follow the thought stream and clarify the purpose of the character's monologue.

Guide for Interpreting

William Faulkner (1897–1962)

For some writers, the place of their roots is a wellspring of story material. Oxford, Mississippi, was such a place for William Faulkner. It became the basis for the imaginary world of Yoknapatawpha County—the setting of many of his novels.

A Writer's Roots Although Faulkner never finished high school, he read a great deal and developed an interest in writing from an early age. In 1918, he enlisted in the British Royal Flying Corps and was sent to Canada for training. However, World War I ended before he had a chance to see combat, and he returned to Mississippi. A few years later, longing for a change of scene, Faulkner moved to New Orleans. There he became friends with Sherwood Anderson, who offered encouragement and helped get Faulkner's first novel, *A Soldier's Pay,* published. In 1926, he returned home to Oxford, Mississippi, to devote himself to his writing.

A Gold Mine of Inspiration In what he called his "own little postage stamp of native soil," Faulkner uncovered a "gold mine" of inspiration. From there, he wrote a series of novels about the decay of traditional values as small communities became swept up in the changes of the modern age. Faulkner saw immense dramas acted out in his small, rural environment, and he used jumbled time sequences, stream-of-consciousness narration, dialect, and other difficult techniques to show what he called "the human heart in conflict with itself."

A Slow Spread of Recognition For many years, Faulkner was dismissed as an eccentric—an unimportant regional writer. Gradually, however, critics began to take him seriously.

Today, Faulkner is generally considered the most innovative writer of his time.

The novel that first earned him critical acclaim was *The Sound and the Fury* (1929), a complex novel exploring the downfall of an old southern family. A year later, he published *As I Lay Dying*, the story of a poor family's six-day journey to bury their mother. Told from fifteen different points of view and exploring people's varying perspectives of death, the novel was a masterpiece in narrative experimentation. Other innovative works followed, including *Absalom, Absalom!* (1936), which is told by four speakers with different interpretations of events.

Despite the critical success of his works, Faulkner did not earn widespread public recognition until 1946, when *The Portable Faulkner*—an anthology in which many of his writings about Yoknapatawpha County were presented in chronological order—was published. Four years later, he was awarded the Nobel Prize following the publication of *Intruder in the Dust* (1948), a novel in which he confronted the issue of racism.

◆ Background for Understanding

LITERATURE: THE NOBEL PRIZE

Alfred Nobel, a Swedish chemist, first earned fame as the inventor of dynamite, and at one time many people associated him with death. Nobel had intended dynamite to be used safely in mining and construction, but disasters often occurred. Nobel was determined to make dynamite safer, and he eventually succeeded in his goal. Later, he sought to use his success to help bring about good in the world by establishing a multimillion-dollar foundation to encourage achievement and diplomacy by awarding annual prizes in the fields of physics, chemistry, medicine, literature, and world peace.

◆ Race at Morning ◆
Nobel Prize Acceptance Speech

◆ *Literature and Your Life*

CONNECT YOUR EXPERIENCE

People's interests are often determined largely by where they live. For example, if you live in the city, your idea of fun might be a pick-up basketball game. In contrast, if you live in the country, you might choose to spend a free afternoon fishing in a local stream. "Race at Morning" captures one of the favorite activities of a group of characters from rural Mississippi—an annual hunting expedition.

Journal Writing Think of an activity you have enjoyed that was somehow linked to a particular place. Describe the place and the activity.

THEMATIC FOCUS: FROM EVERY CORNER OF THE LAND

In this story, Faulkner creates a vivid portrait of life in rural Mississippi. As you read, take note of how the characteristics of the setting and the characters contribute to the flavor of the story.

◆ Build Vocabulary

SUFFIXES: *-ery*

"Race at Morning" includes the word *distillery,* which contains the suffix *-ery* (sometimes spelled *-ry*). The suffix, meaning "state or quality of" or "place of," is used to form nouns from verbs or other nouns. The verb *distill* means "to refine" or "to extract." The noun *distillery* means a place where something is distilled.

WORD BANK

Preview this list of words.

bayou
distillery
buck
moiling
switch
scrabbling
swag
glade

◆ Grammar and Style

CORRECT USE OF IRREGULAR VERB FORMS

The narrator of "Race at Morning" is an uneducated boy who often mistakenly conjugates **irregular verbs**—verbs whose past tenses and past participles are *not* formed by adding *-ed* or *-d* to the present form—as regular verbs. Notice how examples such as this one help capture the narrator's dialect.

Incorrect: I *knowed* it was him.

Correct: I *knew* it was he.

◆ Literary Focus

DIALECT

One way in which Faulkner captures the flavor of life in rural Mississippi is by using **dialect,** a manner of speaking that is common to a particular region or group. Dialect affects pronunciation, word choice, and grammatical structure. Look at this example:

> It was *jest dust-dark*; I had *jest* fed the horses and *clumb* back down the bank. . .

Jest is the way the speaker pronounces *just. Dust-dark* is his word for *dusk,* and *clumb* is the way he forms the past participle of *climb.*

◆ Reading Strategy

BREAK DOWN LONG SENTENCES

Faulkner is famous for his use of long sentences, which can make his works difficult to read. To avoid letting the length of his sentences cause confusion or disrupt your enjoyment of his stories, **break each long sentence down** into smaller units of meaning. Using the punctuation as a guide, divide the sentence into sections. Determine the meaning of each section. Then look for transitions that show how the sections fit together. With an extremely long sentence, you may find it helpful to divide the sentence into a series of shorter ones.

Race at MORNING

William Faulkner

Buck and Doe Alerted, Arthur Fitzwilliam Tait, Superstock

▲ **Critical Viewing** Compare the mood of this painting with the feeling you get from the narrator's description of the bayou on page 788. [Compare]

I was in the boat when I seen him. It was jest dust-dark; I had jest fed the horses and clumb back down the bank to the boat and shoved off to cross back to camp when I seen him, about half a quarter up the river, swimming; just his head above the water, and it no more than a dot in that light. But I could see that rocking chair he toted on it and I knowed it was him, going right back to that canebrake[1] in the fork of the bayou where he

1. **canebrake** *n.*: Area overgrown with the tall, woody reeds of cane plants.

lived all year until the day before the season opened, like the game wardens had give him a calendar, when he would clear out and disappear, nobody knowed where, until the day after the season closed. But here he was, coming back a day ahead of time, like maybe he had got mixed up and was using last year's calendar by mistake. Which was jest too bad for him, because me and Mister Ernest would be setting on the horse right over him when the sun rose tomorrow morning.

So I told Mister Ernest and we et supper and fed the dogs, and then I holp Mister Ernest in the poker game, standing behind his chair until about ten o'clock, when Roth Edmonds said, "Why don't you go to bed, boy?"

"Or if you're going to set up," Willy Legate said, "why don't you take a spelling book to set up over? He knows every cuss word in the dictionary, every poker hand in the deck and every whisky label in the distillery, but he can't even write his name. Can you?" he says to me.

"I don't need to write my name down," I said. "I can remember in my mind who I am."

"You're twelve years old," Walter Ewell said. "Man to man now, how many days in your life did you ever spend in school?"

"He ain't got time to go to school," Willy Legate said. "What's the use in going to school from September to middle of November, when he'll have to quit then to come in here and do Ernest's hearing for him? And what's the use in going back to school in January, when in jest eleven months it will be November fifteenth again and he'll have to start all over telling Ernest which way the dogs went?"

"Well, stop looking into my hand, anyway," Roth Edmonds said.

"What's that? What's that?" Mister Ernest said. He wore his listening button in his ear all the time, but he never brought the battery to camp with him because the cord would bound to get snagged ever time we run through a thicket.

"Willy says for me to go to bed!" I hollered.

"Don't you never call nobody 'mister'?" Willy said.

"I call Mister Ernest 'mister.'" I said.

"All right," Mister Ernest said. "Go to bed then. I don't need you."

"That ain't no lie," Willy said. "Deaf or no deaf, he can hear a fifty-dollar raise if you don't even move your lips."

So I went to bed, and after a while Mister Ernest come in and I wanted to tell him again how big them horns looked even half a quarter away in the river. Only I would 'a' had to holler, and the only time Mister Ernest agreed he couldn't hear was when we would be setting on Dan, waiting for me to point which way the dogs was going. So we jest laid down, and it wasn't no time Simon was beating the bottom of the dishpan with the spoon, hollering, "Raise up and get your four-o'clock coffee!" and I crossed the river in the dark this time, with the lantern, and fed Dan and Roth Edmondziz horse. It was going to be a fine day, cold and bright; even in the dark I could see the white frost on the leaves and bushes—jest exactly the kind of day that big old son of a gun laying up there in that brake would like to run.

Then we et, and set the stand-holder across for Uncle Ike McCaslin to put them on the stands where he thought they ought to be, because he was the oldest one in camp. He had been hunting deer in these woods for about a hundred years, I reckon, and if anybody would know where a buck would pass, it would be him. Maybe with a big old buck like this one, that had been running the woods for what would amount to a hundred years in a deer's life, too, him and Uncle Ike would sholy manage to be at the same place at the same time this morning—provided, of course, he managed to git away from me and Mister Ernest on the jump. Because me and Mister Ernest was going to git him.

Then me and Mister Ernest and Roth Edmonds sent the dogs over, with Simon holding Eagle and the other old dogs on leash because the young ones, the puppies, wasn't going nowhere until Eagle let him, nohow. Then me and Mister Ernest and Roth saddled up, and Mr. Ernest got up and I handed him up his

◆ Build Vocabulary

bayou (bī′ ōō) *n*.: Sluggish, marshy inlet

distillery (dis til′ ə rē) *n*.: Place where alcoholic liquors are distilled

buck (bək) *n*.: Male animal, especially a male deer

pump gun and let Dan's bridle[2] go for him to git rid of the spell of bucking he had to git shut of ever morning until Mister Ernest hit him between the ears with a gun barrel. Then Mister Ernest loaded the gun and give me the stirrup,[3] and I got up behind him and we taken the fire road up toward the bayou, the four big dogs dragging Simon along in front with his single-barrel britch-loader slung on a piece of plow line across his back, and the puppies <u>moiling</u> along in ever'body's way. It was light now and it was going to be jest fine; the east already yellow for the sun and our breaths smoking in the cold still bright air until the sun would come up and warm it, and a little skim of ice in the ruts, and ever leaf and twig and <u>switch</u> and even the frozen clods frosted over, waiting to sparkle like a rainbow when the sun finally come up and hit them. Until all my insides felt light and strong as a balloon, full of that light cold strong air, so that it seemed to me like I couldn't even feel the horse's back I was straddle of—jest the hot strong muscles moving under the hot strong skin, setting up there without no wait atall, so that when old Eagle struck and jumped, me and Dan and Mister Ernest would go jest like a bird, not even touching the ground. It was jest fine. When that big old buck got killed today, I knowed that even if he had put it off another ten years, he couldn't 'a' picked a better one.

And sho enough, as soon as we come to the bayou we seen his foot in the mud where he had come up out of the river last night, spread in the soft mud like a cow's foot, big as a cow's, big as a mule's, with Eagle and the other dogs laying into the leash rope now until Mister Ernest told me to jump down and help Simon hold them. Because me and Mister Ernest knowed exactly where he would be—a little canebrake island in the middle of the bayou, where he could lay up until whatever doe or little deer the dogs had happened to jump could go up or down the bayou in either direction and take the dogs on away, so he could steal out and creep back down the bayou to the river and swim it, and leave the country like he always done the day the season opened.

Which is jest what we never aimed for him to do this time. So we left Roth on his horse to cut him off and turn him over Uncle Ike's standers if he tried to slip back down the bayou, and me and Simon, with the leashed dogs, walked on up the bayou until Mister Ernest on the horse said it was fur enough; then turned up into the woods about half a quarter above the brake because the wind was going to be south this morning when it riz, and turned down toward the brake, and Mister Ernest give the word to cast them,[4] and we slipped the leash and Mr. Ernest give me the stirrup again and I got up.

Old Eagle had done already took off because he knowed where that old son of a gun would be laying as good as we did, not making no racket atall yet, but jest boring on through the buck vines with the other dogs trailing along behind him, and even Dan seemed to know about that buck, too, beginning to souple up and jump a little through the vines, so that I taken my holt in Mister Ernest's belt already before the time had come for Mister Ernest to touch him. Because when we got strung out, going fast behind a deer, I wasn't on Dan's back much of the time nohow, but mostly jest strung out from my holt on Mister Ernest's belt, so that Willy Legate said that when we was going through the woods fast, it looked like Mister Ernest had a boy-size pair of empty overalls blowing out of his hind pocket.

So it wasn't even a strike, it was a jump. Eagle must 'a' walked right up behind him or maybe even stepped on him while he was laying there still thinking it was day after tomorrow. Eagle jest throwed his head back and up and said, "There he goes," and we even heard the buck crashing through the first of the cane. Then all the other dogs was hollering behind him, and Dan give a squat to jump, but it was against the curb[5] this time, not jest the snaffle,[6] and Mister Ernest let him down into

◆ **Literary Focus**
Which word here shows the speaker is using dialect, and what does the word mean in standard English?

---

2. **bridle** *n*.: Headgear with which a horse is guided.
3. **stirrup** *n*.: Rings or other devices attached to the saddle of a horse and used to support the rider's feet.

4. **cast them:** Send them ranging overland in search of a trail.
5. **curb** *n*.: Chain or strap used to restrain a horse.
6. **snaffle** *n*.: The part of a bridle that is inserted into the mouth of a horse.

the bayou and swung him around the brake and up the other bank. Only he never had to say, "Which way?" because I was already pointing past his shoulder, freshening my holt on the belt jest as Mister Ernest touched Dan with that big old rusty spur on his nigh heel, because when Dan felt it he would go off jest like a stick of dynamite, straight through whatever he could bust and over and under what he couldn't, over it like a bird or under it crawling on his knees like a mole or a big coon, with Mister Ernest still on him because he had the saddle to hold on to, and me still there because I had Mister Ernest to hold on to; me and Mister Ernest not riding him, but jest going along with him, provided we held on. Because when the jump come, Dan never cared who else was there neither; I believe to my soul he could 'a' cast and run them dogs by hisself, without me or Mister Ernest or Simon or nobody.

That's what he done. He had to; the dogs was already almost out of hearing. Eagle must 'a' been looking right up that big son of a gun's tail until he finally decided he better git on out of there. And now they must 'a' been getting pretty close to Uncle Ike's standers, and Mister Ernest reined Dan back and held him, squatting and bouncing and trembling like a mule having his tail roached,[7] while we listened for the shots. But never none come, and I hollered to Mister Ernest we better go on while I could still hear the dogs, and he let Dan off, but still there wasn't no shots, and now we knowed the race had done already passed the standers, like that old son of a gun actually was a hant,[8] like Simon and the other field hands said he was, and we busted out of a thicket, and sho enough there was Uncle Ike and Willy standing beside his foot in a soft patch.

"He got through us all," Uncle Ike said. "I don't know how he done it. I just had a glimpse of him. He looked big as a elephant, with a rack on his head you could cradle a yellin' calf in. He went right on down the ridge. You better get on, too; that Hog Bayou camp might not miss him."

So I freshened my holt and Mister Ernest touched Dan again. The ridge run due south;

it was clear of vines and bushes so we could go fast, into the wind, too, because it had riz now, and now the sun was up, too; though I hadn't had time to notice it, bright and strong and level through the woods, shining and sparkling like a rainbow on the frosted leaves. So we would hear the dogs again any time now as the wind got up; we could make time now, but still holding Dan back to a canter,[9] because it was either going to be quick, when he got down to the standers from that Hog Bayou camp eight miles below ourn, or a long time, in case he got by them, too. And sho enough, after a while we heard the dogs; we was walking Dan now to let him blow a while, and we heard them, the sound coming faint up the wind, not running now, but trailing because the big son of a gun had decided a good piece back, probably, to put a end to this foolishness, and picked hisself up and soupled out and put about a mile between hisself and the dogs—until he run up on them other standers from that camp below. I could almost see him stopped behind a bush, peeping out and saying, "What's this? What's this? Is this whole durn country full of folks this morning?" Then looking back over his shoulder at where old Eagle and others was hollering along after him while he decided how much time he had to decide what to do next.

Except he almost shaved it too fine. We heard the shots; it sounded like a war. Old Eagle must 'a' been looking right up his tail again and he had to bust on through the best way he could. "Pow, pow, pow, pow" and then "Pow, pow, pow, pow," like it must 'a' been three or four ganged right up on him before he had time even to swerve, and me hollering, "No! No! No! No!" because he was ourn. It was our beans and oats he et and our brake he laid in; we had been watching him every year, and it was like we had raised him, to be killed at last on our jump, in front of our dogs, by some strangers that would probably try to beat the dogs off

---

7. **roached** *v*.: Cut so that the remainder stands upright, as with an animal's tail.
8. **hant** *n*.: Ghost.

---

9. **canter** *n*.: Three-beat gait resembling, but smoother and slower than, a gallop.

◆ **Build Vocabulary**

moiling (moi′ liŋ) *v*.: Churning; swirling
switch (swich) *n*.: Slender, flexible twig or whip

Winter in Southern Louisiana, Ellsworth Woodward, Mississippi Museum of Art

▲ **Critical Viewing** How does this painting add to your appreciation of the story's bayou setting? **[Connect]**

and drag him away before we could even git a piece of the meat.

"Shut up and listen," Mister Ernest said. So I done it and we could hear the dogs; not just the others, but Eagle, too, not trailing no scent now and not baying[10] no downed meat neither, but running hot on sight long after the shooting was over. I jest had time to freshen my holt. Yes, sir, they was running on sight. Like Willy Legate would say, if Eagle jest had a drink of whisky he would ketch that deer; going on, done already gone when we broke out of the thicket and seen the fellers that had done the shooting, five or six of them, squatting and crawling around, looking at the ground and the bushes, like maybe if they looked hard enough, spots of blood would bloom out on the stalks and leaves like frogstools or hawberries, with old Eagle still in hearing and still telling them that what blood they found wasn't coming out of nothing in front of him.

"Have any luck, boys?" Mister Ernest said.

"I think I hit him," one of them said. "I know I did. We're hunting blood now."

"Well, when you find him, blow your horn and I'll come back and tote him in to camp for you," Mister Ernest said.

So we went on, going fast now because the race was almost out of hearing again, going fast, too, like not jest the buck, but the dogs, too, had took a new leash on life from all the excitement and shooting.

We was in strange country now because we never had to run this fur before, we had always killed before now; now we had come to Hog Bayou that runs into the river a good fifteen miles below our camp. It had water in it, not to mention a mess of down trees and logs and such, and Mister Ernest checked Dan again, saying, "Which way?" I could just barely hear them, off to the east a little, like the old son of a gun had give up the idea of Vicksburg or New Orleans, like he first seemed to have, and had decided to have a look at Alabama, maybe, since he was already up and moving; so I pointed and we turned up the bayou hunting for a crossing, and maybe we could 'a' found one, except that I reckon Mister Ernest decided we never had time to wait.

---

10. **baying** v.: Barking with long, deep tones.

We come to a place where the bayou had narrowed down to about twelve or fifteen feet, and Mister Ernest said, "Look out, I'm going to touch him," and done it; I didn't even have time to freshen my holt when we was already in the air, and then I seen the vine—it was a loop of grapevine nigh as big as my wrist, looping down right across the middle of the bayou—and I thought he seen it, too, and was jest waiting to grab it and fling it over our heads to go under it, and I know Dan seen it because he even ducked his head to jump under it. But Mister Ernest never seen it atall until it skun back along Dan's neck and hooked under the head of the saddle horn,[11] us flying on through the air, the loop of the vine gitting tighter and tighter until something somewhere was going to have to give. It was the saddle girth. It broke, and Dan going on and scrabbling up the other bank bare nekkid except for the bridle, and me and Mister Ernest and the saddle, Mister Ernest still setting in the saddle holding the gun, and me still holding onto Mister Ernest's belt, hanging in the air over the bayou in the tightened loop of that vine like in the drawed-back loop of a big rubber-banded slingshot, until it snapped back and shot across the bayou and flang us clear, me still holding onto Mister Ernest's belt and on the bottom now, so that when we lit I would 'a' had Mister Ernest and the saddle both on top of me if I hadn't clumb fast around the saddle and up Mister Ernest's side, so that when we landed, it was the saddle first, then Mister Ernest, and me on top, until I jumped up, and Mister Ernest still laying there with jest the white rim of his eyes showing.

◆ **Reading Strategy**
How can you break down this sentence into a series of shorter sentences?

"Mister Ernest!" I hollered, and then clumb down to the bayou and scooped my cap full of water and clumb back and throwed it in his face, and he opened his eyes and laid there on the saddle cussing me.

---

11. **saddle horn** n.: Knob at the front and top of a saddle.

◆ **Build Vocabulary**
scrabbling (skrab´ liŋ) v.: Scrambling

"God dawg it," he said, "why didn't you stay behind where you started out?"

"You was the biggest!" I said. "You would 'a' mashed me flat!"

"What do you think you done to me?" Mister Ernest said. "Next time, if you can't stay where you start out, jump clear. Don't climb on top of me no more. You hear?"

"Yes, sir," I said.

So he got up then, still cussing and holding his back, and clumb down to the water and dipped some in his hand onto his face and neck and dipped some more up and drunk it, and I drunk some, too, and clumb back and got the saddle and the gun, and we crossed the bayou on the down logs. If we could jest ketch Dan; not that he would have went them fifteen miles back to camp, because, if anything, he would have went on by hisself to try to help Eagle ketch that buck. But he was about fifty yards away, eating buck vines, so I brought him back, and we taken Mister Ernest's galluses[12] and my belt and tied the saddle back on Dan. It didn't look like much, but maybe it would hold.

"Provided you don't let me jump him through no more grapevines without hollering first," Mister Ernest said.

"Yes, sir," I said. "I'll holler first next time—provided you'll holler a little quicker when you touch him next time, too." But it was all right; we jest had to be a little easy getting up. "Now which-a-way?" I said. Because we couldn't hear nothing now, after wasting all this time. And this was new country, sho enough. It had been cut over and growed up in thickets we couldn't 'a' seen over even standing up on Dan.

But Mister Ernest never even answered. He jest turned Dan along the bank of the bayou where it was a little more open and we could move faster again, soon as Dan and us got used to that homemade cinch strop[13] and got a little confidence in it. Which jest happened to be east, or so I thought then, because I never paid no particular attention to east then because the sun—I don't know where the morning had went, but it was gone, the morning and the frost, too—was up high now, even if

my insides had told me it was past dinnertime.

And then we heard him. No, that's wrong; what we heard was shots. And that was when we realized how fur he had come, because the only camp we knowed about in that direction was the Hollyknowe camp, and Hollyknowe was exactly twenty-eight miles from Van Dorn, where me and Mister Ernest lived—jest the shots, no dogs nor nothing. If old Eagle was still behind him and the buck was still alive, he was too wore out now to even say, "Here he comes."

"Don't touch him!" I hollered. But Mister Ernest remembered that cinch strop, too, and he jest let Dan off the snaffle. And Dan heard them shots, too; picking his way through the thickets, hopping the vines and logs when he could and going under them when he couldn't. And sho enough, it was jest like before—two or three men squatting and creeping among the bushes, looking for blood that Eagle had done already told them wasn't there. But we never stopped this time, jest trotting on by with Dan hopping and dodging among the brush and vines dainty as a dancer. Then Mister Ernest swung Dan until we was going due north.

"Wait!" I hollered. "Not this way."

But Mister Ernest jest turned his face back over his shoulder. It looked tired, too, and there was a smear of mud on it where that ere grapevine had snatched him off the horse.

"Don't you know where he's heading?" he said. "He's done done his part, give everybody a fair open shot at him, and now he's going home, back to that brake in our bayou. He ought to make it exactly at dark."

And that's what he was doing. We went on. It didn't matter to hurry now. There wasn't no sound nowhere; it was that time in the early afternoon in November when don't nothing move or cry, not even birds, the peckerwoods and yellowhammers and jays, and it seemed to me like I could see all three of us—me and Mister Ernest and Dan—and Eagle, and the other dogs, and that big old buck, moving through the quiet woods in the same direction, headed for the same place, not running now but walking, that had all run the fine race the best we knowed how, and all three of us now turned like on a agreement to walk back home, not together in a bunch because we didn't want to worry or tempt one another, because what we had all three spent this morning doing was no

---

12. **galluses** *n.*: Suspenders.
13. **cinch strop** *n.*: Strap that encircles the body of an animal and is used to fasten something on its back.

playacting jest for fun, but was serious, and all three of us was still what we was—that old buck that had to run, not because he was skeered, but because running was what he done the best and was proudest at; and Eagle and the dogs that chased him, not because they hated or feared him, but because that was the thing they done the best and was proudest at; and me and Mister Ernest and Dan, that run him not because we wanted his meat, which would be too tough to eat anyhow, or his head to hang on a wall, but because now we could go back and work hard for eleven months making a crop, so we would have the right to come back here next November—all three of us going back home now, peaceful and separate, but still side by side, until next year, next time.

◆ **Reading Strategy**
Why do you think Faulkner chose to combine all of this information into one sentence?

Then we seen him for the first time. We was out of the cut-over now; we could even 'a' cantered, except that all three of us was long past that, and now you could tell where west was because the sun was already half-way down it. So we was walking, too, when we come on the dogs—the puppies and one of the old ones—played out, laying in a little wet swag, panting, jest looking up at us when we passed, but not moving when we went on. Then we come to a long open glade, you could see about half a quarter, and we seen the three other old dogs and about a hundred yards ahead of them Eagle, all walking, not making no sound; and then suddenly, at the fur end of the glade, the buck hisself getting up from where he had been resting for the dogs to come up, getting up without no hurry, big, big as a mule, tall as a mule, and turned without no hurry still, and the white underside of his tail for a second or two more before the thicket taken him.

It might 'a' been a signal, a good-bye, a farewell. Still walking, we passed the other three old dogs in the middle of the glade, laying down, too, now jest where they was when the buck vanished, and not trying to get up neither when

we passed; and still that hundred yards ahead of them, Eagle, too, not laying down, because he was still on his feet, but his legs was spraddled and his head was down; maybe jest waiting until we was out of sight of his shame, his eyes saying plain as talk when we passed, "I'm sorry, boys, but this here is all."

Mister Ernest stopped Dan. "Jump down and look at his feet," he said.

"Ain't nothing wrong with his feet," I said. "It's his wind has done give out."

"Jump down and look at his feet," Mister Ernest said.

So I done it, and while I was stooping over Eagle I could hear the pump gun go, "Snick-cluck, Snick-cluck. Snick-cluck" three times, except that I never thought nothing then. Maybe he was jest running the shells through to be sho it would work when we seen him again or maybe to make sho they was all buckshot.[14] Then I got up again, and we went on, still walking; a little west of north now, because when we seen his white flag that second or two before the thicket hid it, it was on a beeline for that notch in the bayou. And it was evening, too, now. The wind had done dropped and there was a edge to the air and the sun jest touched the tops of the trees now, except jest now and then, when it found a hole to come almost level through onto the ground. And he was taking the easiest way, too, now, going straight as he could. When we seen his foot in the soft places he was running for a while at first after his rest. But soon he was walking, too, like he knowed, too, where Eagle and the dogs was.

And then we seen him again. It was the last time—a thicket, with the sun coming through a hole onto it like a searchlight. He crashed jest once; then he was standing there broadside to us, not twenty yards away, big as a statue and red as gold in the sun, and the sun sparking on the tips of his horns—they was twelve of them—so that he looked like he had twelve lighted candles branched around his head, standing there looking at us while Mister Ernest raised the gun and aimed at his neck, and the gun went, "Click. Snick-cluck. Click,

◆ **Build Vocabulary**
swag (swag) *n.*: Suspended cluster of branches
glade (glād) *n.*: Open space surrounded by woods

---

14. **buckshot** *n.*: Large lead shot used for shooting deer and other big game.

Old Man and the Boy, John Head, Russell A. Fink Gallery

▲ **Critical Viewing** Do you think this painting effectively illustrates the story? Explain. **[Evaluate]**

Snick-cluck. Click. Snick-cluck" three times, and Mister Ernest still holding the gun aimed while the buck turned and give one long bound, the white underside of his tail like a blaze of fire, too, until the thicket and the shadows put it out; and Mister Ernest laid the gun slow and gentle back across the saddle in front of him, saying quiet and peaceful, and not much louder than jest breathing, "God dawg. God dawg."

Then he jogged me with his elbow and we got down, easy and careful because of that ere cinch strop and he reached into his vest and taken out one of the cigars. It was busted where I had fell on it, I reckon, when we hit the ground. He throwed it away and taken out the other one. It was busted, too, so he bit off a hunk of it to chew and throwed the rest away. And now the sun was gone even from the tops of the trees and there wasn't nothing left but a big red glare in the west.

"Don't worry," I said. "I ain't going to tell them you forgot to load your gun. For that matter, they don't need to know we ever seed him."

"Much oblige," Mister Ernest said. There wasn't going to be no moon tonight neither, so he taken the compass off the whang leather loop in his buttonhole and handed me the gun and set the compass on a stump and stepped back and looked at it. "Just about the way we're headed now," he said, and taken the gun from me and opened it and put one shell in the britch and taken up the compass, and I taken Dan's reins and we started, with him in front with the compass in his hand.

And after a while it was full dark; Mister Ernest would have to strike a match ever now and then to read the compass, until the stars come out good and we could pick out one to follow, because I said, "How fur do you reckon it is?" A little more than one box of matches." So we used a star when we could, only we couldn't see it all the time because the woods was too dense and we would git a little off until he would have to spend another match. And now it was good and late, and he stopped and said, "Get on the horse."

"I ain't tired," I said.

"Get on the horse," he said. "We don't want to spoil him."

Because he had been a good feller ever since I had knowed him, which was even before that day two years ago when maw went off with the Vicksburg roadhouse feller and the next day pap didn't come home neither, and on the third one Mister Ernest rid Dan up to the door of the cabin on the river he let us live in, so pap could work his piece of land and run his fish line, too, and said, "Put that gun down and come on here and climb up behind."

So I got in the saddle even if I couldn't reach the stirrups, and Mister Ernest taken the reins and I must 'a' went to sleep, because the next thing I knowed a button hole of my lumberjack was tied to the saddle horn with that ere whang cord off the compass, and it was good and late now and we wasn't fur, because Dan was already smelling water, the river. Or maybe it was the feed lot itself he smelled, because we struck the fire road not a quarter below it, and soon I could see the river, too, with the white mist laying on it soft and still as cotton. Then the lot, home; and up yonder in the dark, not no piece akchully, close enough to hear us unsaddling and shucking corn prob'ly,

◆ **Literary Focus**
How would you restate this passage in standard English?

and sholy close enough to hear Mister Ernest blowing his horn at the dark camp for Simon to come in the boat and git us, that old buck in his brake in the bayou; home, too, resting, too, after the hard run, waking hisself now and then, dreaming of dogs behind him or maybe it was the racket we was making would wake him, but not neither of them for more than jest a little while before sleeping again.

Then Mister Ernest stood on the bank blowing until Simon's lantern went bobbing down into the mist; then we clumb down to the landing and Mister Ernest blowed again now and then to guide Simon, until we seen the lantern in the mist, and then Simon and the boat; only it looked like ever time I set down and got still, I went back to sleep, because Mister Ernest was shaking me again to git out and climb the bank into the dark camp, until I felt a bed against my knees and tumbled into it.

Then it was morning, tomorrow; it was all over now until next November, next year, and we could come back. Uncle Ike and Willy and Walter and Roth and the rest of them had come in yestiddy, soon as Eagle taken the buck out of hearing and they knowed that deer was gone, to pack up and be ready to leave this morning for Yoknapatawpha, where they lived, until it would be November again and they could come back again.

So, as soon as we et breakfast, Simon run them back up the river in the big boat to where they left their cars and pickups, and now it wasn't nobody but jest me and Mister Ernest setting on the back against the kitchen wall in the sun; Mister Ernest smoking a cigar—a whole one this time that Dan hadn't had no chance to jump through a grapevine and bust. He hadn't washed his face neither where that vine had throwed him into the mud.

But that was all right, too; his face usually did have a smudge of mud or tractor grease or beard stubble on it, because he wasn't jest a planter; he was a farmer, he worked as hard as ara one of his hands and tenants—which is why I knowed from the very first that we would git along, that I wouldn't have no trouble with him and he wouldn't have no trouble with me, from that very first day when I woke up and maw had done gone off with that Vicksburg roadhouse feller without even waiting to cook breakfast, and the next morning pap was gone, too, and it was almost night the next day when I heard a horse coming up and I taken the gun that I had already throwed a shell into the britch when pap never came home last night, and stood in the door while Mister Ernest rid up and said, "Come on. Your paw ain't coming back neither."

"You mean he give me to you?" I said.

"Who cares?" He said. "Come on. I brought a lock for the door. We'll send the pickup back tomorrow for whatever you want."

So I come home with him and it was all right, it was jest fine—his wife had died about three years ago—without no women to worry us or take off in the middle of the night with a durn Vicksburg roadhouse jake without even wanting to cook breakfast. And we would go home this afternoon, too, but not jest yet; we always stayed one more day after the others left because Uncle Ike always left what grub they hadn't et, and the rest of the homemade corn whisky he drunk and that town whisky of Roth Edmondziz he called Scotch that smelled like it come out of a old bucket of roof paint; setting in the sun for one more day before we went back home to get ready to put in next year's crop of cotton and oats and beans and hay; and across the river yonder, behind the wall of trees where the big woods started, that old buck laying up today in the sun, too—resting today, too, without nobody to bother him until next November.

So at least one of us was glad it would be eleven months and two weeks before he would have to run that fur that fast again. So he was glad of the very same thing we was sorry of, and so all of a sudden I thought about how maybe planting and working and then harvesting oats and cotton and beans and hay wasn't

jest something me and Mister Ernest done three hundred and fifty-one days to fill in the time until we could come back hunting again, but it was something we had to do, and do honest and good during the three hundred and fifty-one days, to have the right to come back into the big woods and hunt for the other fourteen; and the fourteen days that old buck run in front of dogs wasn't jest something to fill his time until the three hundred and fifty-one when he didn't have to, but the running and the risking in front of guns and dogs was something he had to do for fourteen days to have the right not to be bothered for the other three hundred and fifty-one. And so the hunting and the farming wasn't two different things atall—they was jest the other side of each other.

"Yes," I said. "All we got to do now is put in that next year's crop. Then November won't be no time away atall."

"You ain't going to put in the crop next year," Mister Ernest said. "You're going to school."

So at first I didn't even believe I had heard him. "What?" I said. "Me? Go to school?"

"Yes," Mister Ernest said. "You must make something out of yourself."

"I am," I said. "I'm doing it now. I'm going to be a hunter and a farmer like you."

"No," Mister Ernest said. "That ain't enough any more. Time was when all a man had to do was just farm eleven and a half months, and hunt the other half. But not now. Now just to belong to the farming business and the hunting business ain't enough. You got to belong to the business of mankind."

"Mankind?" I said.

"Yes," Mister Ernest said. "So you're going to school. Because you got to know why. You can belong to the farming and hunting business and you can learn the difference between what's right and what's wrong, and do right. And that used to be enough—just to do right. But not now. You got to know why it's right and why it's wrong, and be able to tell the folks that never had no chance to learn it; teach them how to do what's right, not just because they know it's right, but because they know now why it's right because you just showed them, told them, taught them why. So you're going to school."

"It's because you been listening to that durn

Will Legate and Walter Ewell!" I said.

"No," Mister Ernest said.

"Yes!" I said. "No wonder you missed that buck yestiddy, taking ideas from the very fellers that let him get away, after me and you had run Dan and the dogs durn nigh clean to death! Because you never even missed him! You never forgot to load that gun! You had done already unloaded it a purpose! I heard you!"

"All right, all right," Mister Ernest said. "Which would you rather have? His bloody head and hide on the kitchen floor yonder and half his meat in a pickup truck on the way to Yoknapatawpha County, or him with his head and hide and meat still together over yonder in that brake, waiting for next November for us to run him again?"

"And git him, too," I said. "We won't even fool with no Willy Legate and Walter Ewell next time."

"Maybe," Mister Ernest said.

"Yes," I said.

"Maybe," Mister Ernest said. "The best word in our language, the best of all. That's what mankind keeps going on: Maybe. The best days of his life ain't the ones when he said 'Yes' beforehand: they're the ones when all he knew to say was 'Maybe.' He can't say 'Yes' until afterward because he not only don't know it until then, he don't want to know 'Yes' until then . . . Step in the kitchen and make me a toddy. Then we'll see about dinner."

"All right," I said. I got up. "You want some of Uncle Ike's corn or that town whisky of Roth Edmondziz?"

"Can't you say Mister Roth or Mister Edmonds?" Mister Ernest said.

"Yes, sir," I said. "Well, which do you want? Uncle Ike's corn or that ere stuff of Roth Edmondziz?"

◆ *Literature and Your Life*

Mister Ernest is the speaker's role model. Who is yours? Why?

Guide for Responding

◆ *Literature and Your Life*

Reader's Response If you had the opportunity, would you join Mister Ernest and the narrator on the yearly trip to the bayou? Explain.

Thematic Focus Does Faulkner's description make you want to visit this region of the country?

Journal Entry Think of a place that you will remember all your life the way that the boy in this story will remember the hunting camp and the bayou. In a brief journal entry, describe the setting and the effect it had on you.

☑ Check Your Comprehension

1. When does this story take place?
2. What is the relationship of the speaker to Mister Ernest?
3. When Mister Ernest fires at the deer at the end of the day, why doesn't the deer die?
4. Why won't the boy be planting next year's crop?

◆ Critical Thinking

INTERPRET

1. At the beginning of the story, why does Faulkner include a discussion about school? **[Connect]**
2. Find two examples from the story that support the conclusion that the boy trusts and feels relaxed with Mister Ernest. **[Support]**
3. According to the boy, what is the true function of work on the farm for him and Mister Ernest? **[Analyze]**
4. According to Mister Ernest, why is it better to have the deer still alive than to have killed it? **[Analyze]**

EVALUATE

5. Evaluate Faulkner's success in connecting the significance of the hunt to the significance of Mister Ernest's plans for the boy's future. **[Evaluate]**

EXTEND

6. Why are wetlands such as bayous ecologically important? **[Science Link]**

Nobel Prize Acceptance Speech

William Faulkner

Stockholm, Sweden
December 10, 1950

I feel that this award was not made to me as a man, but to my work—a life's work in the agony and sweat of the human spirit, not for glory and least of all for profit, but to create out of the materials of the human spirit something which did not exist before. So this award is only mine in trust. It will not be difficult to find a dedication for the money part of it commensurate with the purpose and significance of its origin. But I would like to do the same with the acclaim too, by using this moment as a pinnacle from which I might be listened to by the young men and women already dedicated to the same anguish and travail, among whom is already that one who will some day stand here where I am standing.

Our tragedy today is a general and universal physical fear so long sustained by now that we can even bear it. There are no longer problems of the spirit. There is only the question: When will I be blown up? Because of this, the young man or woman writing today has forgotten the problems of the human heart in conflict with itself which alone can make good writing because only that is worth writing about, worth the agony and the sweat.

He must learn them again. He must teach himself that the basest of all things is to be afraid; and, teaching himself that, forget it forever, leaving no room in his workshop for anything but the old verities and truths of the heart, the old universal truths lacking which any story is ephemeral and doomed—love and honor and pity and pride and compassion and sacrifice. Until he does so, he labors under a curse. He writes not of love but of lust, of defeats in which nobody loses anything of value, of victories without hope and, worst of all, without pity or compassion. His griefs grieve on no universal bones, leaving no scars. He writes not of the heart but of the glands.

Until he relearns these things, he will write as though he stood among and watched the end of man. I decline to accept the end of man. It is easy enough to say that man is immortal simply because he will endure: that when the last ding-dong of doom has clanged and faded from the last worthless rock hanging tideless in the last red and dying evening, that even then there will still be one more sound: that of his puny inexhaustible voice, still talking. I refuse to accept this. I believe that man will not merely endure: he will prevail. He is immortal, not because he alone among creatures has an inexhaustible voice, but because he has a soul, a spirit capable of compassion and sacrifice and endurance. The poet's, the writer's, duty is to write about these things. It is his privilege to help man endure by lifting his heart, by reminding him of the courage and honor and hope and pride and compassion and pity and sacrifice which have been the glory of his past. The poet's voice need not merely be the record of man, it can be one of the props, the pillars to help him endure and prevail.

Guide for Responding

◆ Literature and Your Life

Reader's Response Do you agree with Faulkner's definition of good literature? If not, how would you revise it?

Thematic Focus How does Faulkner's criticism of contemporary literature reflect his experience as a writer living in a specific place and time?

☑ Check Your Comprehension

1. Of what specific physical fear does Faulkner speak?
2. According to Faulkner, what is the basest of all things?
3. According to Faulkner's Nobel acceptance speech, what is "Our tragedy today"?
4. What must young writers teach themselves?

◆ Critical Thinking

INTERPRET
1. Why does Faulkner see the Nobel Prize as something he holds in trust? **[Analyze]**
2. Why does Faulkner see modern literature as ephemeral? **[Interpret]**
3. Why does he think that people will prevail over the threats that face them? **[Draw Conclusions]**
4. How can the writer help people endure? **[Draw Conclusions]**

APPLY
5. Describe a time when a piece of literature helped you overcome some obstacle. **[Relate]**

EXTEND
6. What events not long before 1950 gave rise to the fear of which Faulkner speaks? **[Social Studies Link]**

Guide for Responding (continued)

◆ Literary Focus

DIALECT

Every **dialect**—a manner of speaking that is common to a particular region or group—has a unique set of characteristics that affect word choice, grammar, and pronunciation. Faulkner's use of southern rural dialect goes a long way in helping "Race at Morning" to achieve its authentic ring. Consider the effects of the use of dialect in this sentence:

> Maybe with a big old buck like this one, that had been running the woods for what would amount to a hundred years in a deer's life, too, him and Uncle Ike would sholy manage to be at the same place at the same time this morning—provided, of course, he managed to git away from me and Mister Ernest on the jump.

1. Explain what makes this passage an example of dialect. Analyze it in terms of word choice, nonstandard grammatical constructions, pronunciations, and word order.
2. Rewrite the passage in standard English.
3. (a) Find two or three other examples of dialect in "Race at Morning." (b) Translate each example into standard English.

◆ Reading Strategy

BREAK DOWN LONG SENTENCES

Breaking down long sentences into smaller units of meaning will help you to understand them. Read this sentence from the story:

> Then Mister Ernest loaded the gun and give me the stirrup, and I got up behind him and we taken the fire road up toward the bayou, the four big dogs dragging Simon along in front with his single-barrel britch-loader slung on a piece of plow line across his back, and the puppies moiling along in ever'body's way.

1. Divide the sentence into sections, using the punctuation as a guide.
2. Identify the section of the sentence that contains its subject.
3. Rewrite these sections as separate sentences, connected by transitions.

◆ Build Vocabulary

USING THE SUFFIX -ery

The suffix -ery (-ry) means "state or quality of" or "place of." It can also mean a "kind of behavior." Use this information and the meaning of base words or roots to define each of the following words. Then write each word in a sentence.

1. creamery   3. hatchery   5. slavery
2. finery   4. snobbery   6. bravery

USING THE WORD BANK

Basing your answer on the meaning of the italicized words in the following questions, answer *yes* or *no* to each question.
1. Can you plow a *bayou*?
2. Are the typical products of a *distillery* suitable for children to consume?
3. Is a *buck* a male animal?
4. Would a *moiling* puppy be standing still?
5. Might you find a *switch* in the woods?
6. Is *scrabbling* a quick movement?
7. Is a *swag* something you'd find in the forest?
8. If you wanted to get some sun, would you head for a *glade*?

◆ Grammar and Style

CORRECT USE OF IRREGULAR VERB FORMS

The English language contains many **irregular verbs**. If you're unsure whether a verb in your writing has an irregular past tense or past participle, check a dictionary or grammar book. In writing, it's acceptable to use incorrect verb forms only when constructing dialogue in dialect.

Practice Rewrite each incorrect verb that follows in its correct irregular form. Then write a context sentence for each verb.

1. eated   4. gived   7. taked
2. rised   5. throwed 8. getted
3. goed   6. heared   9. weared

Writing Application Using dialect, write a conversation between two characters in "Race at Morning." Underline at least three irregular verbs you've used *incorrectly*.

Build Your Portfolio

Idea Bank

Writing

1. Letter of Support A judge is considering whether to make Mister Ernest the narrator's legal guardian. Write a letter to the judge explaining why Mister Ernest is suited for this role.

2. Acceptance Speech Write a brief speech accepting an honor. As Faulkner did when he received the Nobel Prize, use your speech to express your deepest beliefs and convictions.

3. Analysis of Dialect Write a short essay in which you explain how Faulkner's use of dialect contributes to the effectiveness of his story.

Speaking and Listening

4. Debate With a classmate, debate the pros and cons of hunting. Discuss the subject from the point of view of farmers, animal rights supporters, hunters, and others. **[Social Studies Link]**

5. Broadcast As a radio announcer, broadcast the hunt in "Race at Morning" as it occurs in real time. Report on the progress of all participants. **[Performing Arts Link]**

Projects

6. Pantomime Convert your classroom into a model of the landscape of "Race at Morning" by identifying parts of the room as the canebrake, the place where the grapevines hang over the bayou, and so on. Assign classmates different roles. Then act out the day without words. **[Performing Arts Link]**

7. Musical Research Find a piece of music that could serve as a score (music composed for film) for the hunt. Play it for the class, and then explain why you chose it. **[Music Link]**

Writing Mini-Lesson

Critical Review

In his Nobel Prize acceptance speech, Faulkner says that the writer's duty is to help people "endure by lifting their hearts, by reminding them of the courage and honor and hope and pride and compassion and pity and sacrifice which have been the glory of their past."

Choose a story and evaluate it in terms of how well its author fulfilled Faulkner's idea of the writer's duty. Explain why the author succeeded or failed. Use the following tip to help you.

Writing Skills Focus: Elaboration to Support an Argument

Your main argument should be that the selected story either does or does not live up to Faulkner's standard for good writing. Once you have made this statement, you need to **elaborate** on your argument by providing precise details and examples that back up your points. Look at how Faulkner develops and supports one of his key points.

Model From the Selection

Argument: Our tragedy today is a general and universal physical fear . . .

Elaboration: There is only the question: When will I be blown up?

Prewriting Choose your story. Review Faulkner's ideals and then decide whether the author succeeds or fails according to Faulkner's standards. Jot down some reasons why the author meets or doesn't meet the criteria.

Drafting Begin your review with a clear statement of your position. Then use details and passages from the story to create a convincing argument.

Revising Did you state Faulkner's standard clearly? Do all of the details in your review show how the story does or doesn't live up to this standard? Make any necessary revisions.

Guide for Interpreting

Robert Frost (1874–1963)

In becoming one of America's most loved and re-spected poets, Robert Frost displayed the same rugged persistence and determination exhibited by the rural New Englanders he depicted in his poems. Although he eventually received four Pulitzer Prizes and read at a presidential inauguration, Frost's success as a poet didn't come easily. Only after years of rejection by book and magazine publishers did he finally achieve the ac-ceptance for which he worked so hard.

Early Struggles Frost was born in San Francisco, California, but at the age of eleven moved with his family to the gritty textile city of Lawrence, Massa-chusetts. After briefly attending Dartmouth College, he left school and spent time working as a farmer, mill hand, newspaper writer, and school-teacher. During his spare time, he wrote poetry and dreamed of someday being able to support himself solely by writing.

The English Years Frost married and spent ten years farming in New Hampshire. Unable to get his poems published, he sold his farm and moved his family to England in 1912, hoping to establish himself there as a poet. He became a friend of a number of other poets, including Ezra Pound, and he succeeded in publishing two collections of poetry, *A Boy's Will* (1913) and *North of Boston* (1914).

When Frost returned to the United States in 1915, he discovered that his success in England had spread and he was on the road to fame.

Acclaim Frost went on to publish several more volumes of poetry, for which he received many awards. He also taught at Amherst, the University of Michigan, Harvard, and Dartmouth; lectured and read at dozens of other schools; and farmed in Vermont and New Hampshire. In 1960, at John F. Kennedy's invitation, he became the first poet to read his work at a presidential inauguration.

Frost's poetry was popular not only with critics and intellectuals, but also among the general public. He used traditional verse forms and conversational language to paint vivid verbal portraits of the New England landscape and lifestyle. Despite their apparent simplicity, however, his poems are filled with hidden meanings, compelling readers to delve beneath the surface to fully appreciate his work.

Like his poetry, Frost's personality also had multiple levels. In his public appearances, Frost liked to present himself as a jovial, folksy farmer who just happened to write poetry. In reality, however, Frost was a deep thinker who was described as a complicated personality by those who knew him well.

◆ Background for Understanding

CULTURE: FROST THE NEW ENGLANDER

In the minds of many, Robert Frost is insepara-ble from the New England countryside he so loved. Much of his poetry reflects not only the landscape, but the characteristic personalities of the region. Proud, hard-working, and occasionally stubborn, the New Englanders who populate Frost's poetry are drawn from his experience.

Frost spent most of his life in New Hampshire, Vermont, and Massachusetts, often living in rural communities. Despite his city roots, he was able to gain the acceptance of his country neighbors and to enter their world—a world that was usually closed to outsiders. In doing so, he gathered a wealth of material for his poetry.

The Poetry of Robert Frost

◆ *Literature and Your Life*

CONNECT YOUR EXPERIENCE

Think for a moment about how your surroundings affect you. Popular psychology holds that we are products of our environments. Do you feel and act differently when you're on a busy city street from the way you do when you're in a natural setting? How might your personality and style be different if you lived in another part of the country?

Journal Writing Write a paragraph about your favorite type of landscape—the seaside, mountains, the city, or prairie, for instance. How do you feel when you're in that environment?

THEMATIC FOCUS: FROM EVERY CORNER OF THE LAND

Had Robert Frost remained in San Francisco, his life and his poetry might well have been very different. Frost's works are shaped by, and reflective of, New England values, people, and landscapes.

◆ Literary Focus

BLANK VERSE

Many of Frost's poems do not contain rhyme, but their lines have a regular meter, or pattern of stessed and unstressed syllables. The basic unit of meter is a foot, which usually consists of one stressed syllable and one or more unstressed syllables. The most common foot in American and English poetry is the iamb, which consists of one unstressed syllable followed by a stressed syllable. A line containing five iambs is written in **iambic pentameter.** Verse consisting of unrhymed lines of iambic pentameter is called **blank verse.** Look at this example :

> When I see birches bend to left and right
>
> Across the lines of straighter darker trees,

Notice how blank verse re-creates the natural flow of speech.

◆ Reading Strategy

READING BLANK VERSE

One way to appreciate **blank verse** is to read it aloud in sentences rather than in poetic lines. Don't pause at the end of each line. Instead, follow the punctuation as if you were reading prose: pause briefly after commas and pause longer after periods.

◆ Build Vocabulary

WORD ROOTS: *-lum-*

In "Acquainted With the Night," Frost uses the word *luminary* to describe the moon. Along with several related English words, including *luminous* and *illuminate,* the word *luminary*, which means "giving off light," is based on the Latin root *-lum-*, meaning "light."

WORD BANK

Preview these words from the poems.

poise
rueful
luminary

◆ Grammar and Style

USES OF INFINITIVES

"He will not see me stopping here / To watch his woods fill up with snow." In these lines from "Stopping by Woods on a Snowy Evening," the infinitive *to watch* modifies *stopping.* Both **infinitives**— the base form of a verb preceded by *to*—and **infinitive phrases**—which consist of the infinitive plus any complements or modifiers—can act as nouns, adjectives, or adverbs. In "Birches," for example, Frost writes, "But swinging doesn't bend them down *to stay*." Here the infinitive *to stay* acts as an adverb modifying the verb *bend.*

Birches

Robert Frost

When I see birches bend to left and right
Across the lines of straighter darker trees,
I like to think some boy's been swinging them.
But swinging doesn't bend them down to stay
5   As ice storms do. Often you must have seen them
Loaded with ice a sunny winter morning
After a rain. They click upon themselves
As the breeze rises, and turn many-colored
As the stir cracks and crazes their enamel.
10   Soon the sun's warmth makes them shed crystal shells
Shattering and avalanching on the snow crust—
Such heaps of broken glass to sweep away
You'd think the inner dome of heaven had fallen.
They are dragged to the withered bracken by the load,
15   And they seem not to break; though once they are bowed
So low for long, they never right themselves:
You may see their trunks arching in the woods
Years afterwards, trailing their leaves on the ground
Like girls on hands and knees that throw their hair
20   Before them over their heads to dry in the sun.
But I was going to say when Truth broke in
With all her matter of fact about the ice storm,
I should prefer to have some boy bend them
As he went out and in to fetch the cows—
25   Some boy too far from town to learn baseball,
Whose only play was what he found himself,
Summer or winter, and could play alone.
One by one he subdued his father's trees
By riding them down over and over again
30   Until he took the stiffness out of them,
And not one but hung limp, not one was left
For him to conquer. He learned all there was
To learn about not launching out too soon
And so not carrying the tree away

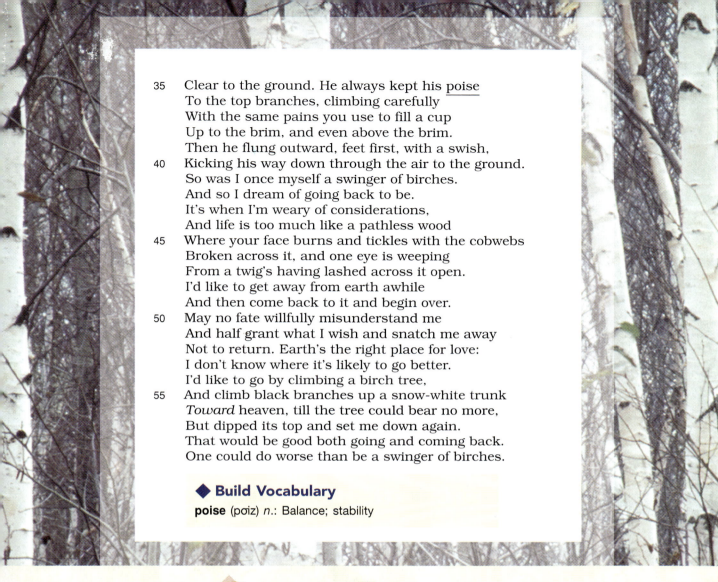

35   Clear to the ground. He always kept his <u>poise</u>
         To the top branches, climbing carefully
         With the same pains you use to fill a cup
         Up to the brim, and even above the brim.
         Then he flung outward, feet first, with a swish,
40   Kicking his way down through the air to the ground.
         So was I once myself a swinger of birches.
         And so I dream of going back to be.
         It's when I'm weary of considerations,
         And life is too much like a pathless wood
45   Where your face burns and tickles with the cobwebs
         Broken across it, and one eye is weeping
         From a twig's having lashed across it open.
         I'd like to get away from earth awhile
         And then come back to it and begin over.
50   May no fate willfully misunderstand me
         And half grant what I wish and snatch me away
         Not to return. Earth's the right place for love:
         I don't know where it's likely to go better.
         I'd like to go by climbing a birch tree,
55   And climb black branches up a snow-white trunk
         Toward heaven, till the tree could bear no more,
         But dipped its top and set me down again.
         That would be good both going and coming back.
         One could do worse than be a swinger of birches.

◆ Build Vocabulary

poise (poiz) *n.*: Balance; stability

Guide for Responding

◆ *Literature and Your Life*

Reader's Response Do you ever yearn to escape from reality for a while? Why or why not?

Thematic Response What do the speaker's activities reveal about the place where he lives?

☑ Check Your Comprehension

1. What does the speaker of "Birches" prefer to think when he sees birches "bend to left and right"?
2. When does he "dream of going back" to swing again on birches?

◆ Critical Thinking

INTERPRET

1. What is the connection between the boy in "Birches" and the poem's speaker? **[Infer]**
2. What does the activity of swinging on birches symbolize for the speaker? **[Interpret]**
3. What message does this poem convey that applies to people of all ages? **[Draw Conclusion]**

APPLY

4. What kinds of events, experiences, and feelings in his life might have caused the speaker to make the admission contained in lines 48–49? **[Speculate]**

Mending Wall

Robert Frost

Something there is that doesn't love a wall,
That sends the frozen-ground-swell under it
And spills the upper boulders in the sun,
And makes gaps even two can pass abreast.
5   The work of hunters is another thing:
I have come after them and made repair
Where they have left not one stone on a stone,
But they would have the rabbit out of hiding,
To please the yelping dogs. The gaps I mean,
10 No one has seen them made or heard them made,
But at spring mending-time we find them there.
I let my neighbor know beyond the hill;
And on a day we meet to walk the line
And set the wall between us once again.

▼ **Critical Viewing** How does this picture suggest that walls don't belong in the natural world? [Analyze]

15 We keep the wall between us as we go.
To each the boulders that have fallen to each.
And some are loaves and some so nearly balls
We have to use a spell to make them balance:
"Stay where you are until our backs are turned!"
20 We wear our fingers rough with handling them.
Oh, just another kind of outdoor game,
One on a side. It comes to little more:
There where it is we do not need the wall:
He is all pine and I am apple orchard.
25 My apple trees will never get across
And eat the cones under his pines, I tell him.
He only says, "Good fences make good neighbors."
Spring is the mischief in me, and I wonder
If I could put a notion in his head:
30 *"Why* do they make good neighbors? Isn't it
Where there are cows? But here there are no cows.
Before I built a wall I'd ask to know
What I was walling in or walling out,
And to whom I was like to give offense.
35 Something there is that doesn't love a wall,
That wants it down." I could say "Elves" to him,
But it's not elves exactly, and I'd rather
He said it for himself. I see him there,
Bringing a stone grasped firmly by the top
40 In each hand, like an old-stone savage armed.
He moves in darkness as it seems to me,
Not of woods only and the shade of trees.
He will not go behind his father's saying,
And he likes having thought of it so well
45 He says again, "Good fences make good neighbors."

Guide for Responding

◆ Literature and Your Life

Reader's Response With which character do you more closely identify—the speaker or his neighbor? Why?

Thematic Focus Is the central conflict in "Mending Wall" specifically a rural problem? Why or why not?

☑ Check Your Comprehension

1. What two causes of gaps in walls does the speaker identify?
2. Why does the speaker feel that the wall is unnecessary?
3. What is his neighbor's attitude about it?

◆ Critical Thinking

INTERPRET

1. What is the "something" that "doesn't love a wall" and why doesn't it love the wall? **[Interpret]**
2. Compare and contrast the speaker and his neighbor. **[Compare and Contrast]**
3. (a) What does the wall symbolize? (b) What is the significance of the fact that the wall breaks apart each winter? **[Interpret]**

EVALUATE

4. How valid are the neighbor's (and the speaker's) ideas about the value of walls? Explain. **[Criticize]**

"Out, Out—"

Robert Frost

The buzz saw snarled and rattled in the yard
And made dust and dropped stove-length sticks of wood,
Sweet-scented stuff when the breeze drew across it.
And from there those that lifted eyes could count
5   Five mountain ranges one behind the other
Under the sunset far into Vermont.
And the saw snarled and rattled, snarled and rattled,
As it ran light, or had to bear a load.
And nothing happened: day was all but done.
10   Call it a day, I wish they might have said
To please the boy by giving him the half hour
That a boy counts so much when saved from work.
His sister stood beside them in her apron
To tell them "Supper." At the word, the saw,
15   As if to prove saws knew what supper meant,
Leaped out at the boy's hand, or seemed to leap—
He must have given the hand. However it was,
Neither refused the meeting. But the hand!
The boy's first outcry was a <u>rueful</u> laugh,
20   As he swung toward them holding up the hand,
Half in appeal, but half as if to keep
The life from spilling. Then the boy saw all—
Since he was old enough to know, big boy
Doing a man's work, though a child at heart—

◆ **Build Vocabulary**
rueful (rōō´ fəl) *adj.*: Feeling or showing sorrow or pity

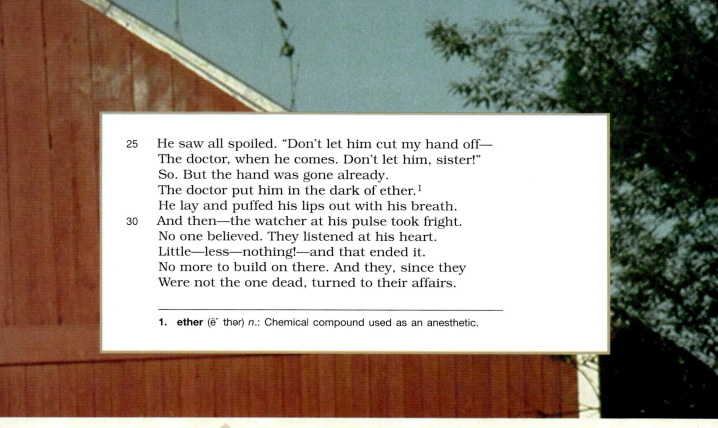

25 He saw all spoiled. "Don't let him cut my hand off—
The doctor, when he comes. Don't let him, sister!"
So. But the hand was gone already.
The doctor put him in the dark of ether.[1]
He lay and puffed his lips out with his breath.
30 And then—the watcher at his pulse took fright.
No one believed. They listened at his heart.
Little—less—nothing!—and that ended it.
No more to build on there. And they, since they
Were not the one dead, turned to their affairs.

---

1. **ether** (ē´ thər) *n.*: Chemical compound used as an anesthetic.

Guide for Responding

◆ Literature and Your Life

Reader's Response What do you find more disturbing—the boy's death or the onlookers' reaction to it? Explain.

Thematic Focus What does this poem suggest about rural life?

Group Discussion With a small group, brainstorm for a list of tragic events that might happen in a rural area. Compare these events to tragedies that might occur in an urban setting.

☑ Check Your Comprehension

1. (a) When does the accident occur?
   (b) How does it happen?
2. (a) What is the boy's very first response?
   (b) What is his second response?
3. What happens to the boy after the doctor arrives?
4. What is the family's reaction?

◆ Critical Thinking

INTERPRET

1. How does the setting contrast with the events of the poem? **[Compare and Contrast]**
2. What is ironic about the fact that the boy is cut just as his sister says the word *supper*? **[Support]**
3. What does the speaker mean by the expression "the boy saw all" in line 22? **[Interpret]**
4. The poem's title comes from a scene in Shakespeare's *Macbeth* in which Macbeth laments the premature death of his wife with these words:

   Out, out, brief candle!
   Life's but a walking shadow, a poor player,
   That struts and frets his hour upon the stage,
   And then is heard no more.

   What does this quotation reveal about the poem's theme? **[Connect]**

APPLY

5. How do you explain the family's response to the incident and to the boy's death? **[Speculate]**

Stopping by Woods on a Snowy Evening

Robert Frost

Whose woods these are I think I know.
His house is in the village though;
He will not see me stopping here
To watch his woods fill up with snow.

5　My little horse must think it queer
To stop without a farmhouse near
Between the woods and frozen lake
The darkest evening of the year.

He gives his harness bells a shake
10　To ask if there is some mistake.
The only other sound's the sweep
Of easy wind and downy flake.

The woods are lovely, dark and deep,
But I have promises to keep,
15　And miles to go before I sleep,
And miles to go before I sleep.

▲ **Critical Viewing** How does the scene of moonlit trees differ from the one the speaker describes? What do they have in common? [**Compare and Contrast**]

▶ **Critical Viewing** How does the mood of this image reflect the mood of "Acquainted With the Night"? [**Connect**]

Acquainted With the Night

Robert Frost

I have been one acquainted with the night.
I have walked out in rain—and back in rain.
I have outwalked the furthest city light.

I have looked down the saddest city lane.
5 I have passed by the watchman on his beat
And dropped my eyes, unwilling to explain.

I have stood still and stopped the sound of feet
When far away an interrupted cry
Came over houses from another street,

10 But not to call me back or say good-by;
And further still at an unearthly height
One luminary clock against the sky

Proclaimed the time was neither wrong nor right.
I have been one acquainted with the night.

◆ **Build Vocabulary**
luminary (lo͞o′ mə ner′ ē) *adj.*: Giving off light

The Gift Outright

Robert Frost

The land was ours before we were the land's.
She was our land more than a hundred years
Before we were her people. She was ours
In Massachusetts, in Virginia,
5   But we were England's, still colonials,
Possessing what we still were unpossessed by,
Possessed by what we now no more possessed.
Something we were withholding made us weak
Until we found out that it was ourselves
10   We were withholding from our land of living,
And forthwith found salvation in surrender.
Such as we were we gave ourselves outright
(The deed of gift was many deeds of war)
To the land vaguely realizing westward,
15   But still unstoried, artless, unenhanced,
Such as she was, such as she would become.

Beyond Literature

History Connection

Frost and the Inauguration of John F. Kennedy During the planning stages of John F. Kennedy's presidential inauguration, his staff approached Robert Frost with a request: Would the poet write and recite a poem for the inauguration? Frost declined to write something new for the occasion but agreed to recite "The Gift Outright." President Kennedy had a second request: Would Frost change the word "would" to "will" in the last line of the poem? The poet agreed.

Shortly before the inauguration date, Frost was struck by inspiration and, despite his earlier refusal, drafted a forty-two-line poem, "Dedication," especially for the ceremonies. The weather on January 21, 1961, Inauguration Day, was windy, clear, and sunny. As Frost stood at the presidential podium reading his new poem, the glare of the sun and the whipping wind made it almost impossible for him to see the words on the page. After struggling through the first half of "Dedication," he gave up the effort and began instead to recite "The Gift Outright" from memory. He even remembered President Kennedy's request to change the last line.

Why do you think President Kennedy might have invited Robert Frost, rather than another poet of the time, to speak at his inauguration?

Activity Use a *Readers' Guide to Periodical Literature* or the Internet to locate news articles dating from the last two presidential inaugurations. Which literary figures were invited to appear at the ceremonies? Distribute to your classmates copies of the works they recited.

Guide for Responding

◆ Literature and Your Life

Reader's Response Which of the poems on pages 810–812 made the strongest impression on you? Explain why, citing examples from the poem.

Thematic Focus In what way does land or landscape play a role in each of these poems?

Group Discussion What words would you use to describe Robert Frost's view of the natural world? What words would you use to describe his view of human society?

☑ Check Your Comprehension

1. In your own words, summarize what occurs in "Stopping by Woods on a Snowy Evening."
2. What actions does the speaker of "Acquainted With the Night" perform?
3. According to the speaker of "The Gift Outright," what did Americans do to cease being English colonials?

◆ Critical Thinking

INTERPRET

1. (a) What internal conflict does the speaker of "Stopping by Woods . . ." experience? (b) What choice does he make? **[Interpret; Infer]**
2. How does the repetition in the last two lines reinforce the meaning of "Stopping by Woods . . ."? **[Analyze]**
3. (a) In line 6 of "Acquainted With the Night," what is the speaker "unwilling to explain"? (b) What can you infer from line 10 about the speaker's hopes about the "interrupted cry"? **[Interpret; Infer]**
4. In lines 6 and 7 of "The Gift Outright," to what is the speaker referring? **[Interpret]**
5. In "The Gift Outright," to what does the speaker suggest the people surrender in order to become true Americans? **[Infer]**

EXTEND

6. How does Frost's account of America's emergence as a nation in "The Gift Outright" differ from an explanation a historian might offer? **[Social Studies Link]**

Guide for Responding (continued)

◆ Literary Focus

BLANK VERSE

Blank verse is composed of unrhymed lines of iambic pentameter. In iambic pentameter, there are five feet per line, with each foot consisting of one unstressed syllable followed by a stressed syllable. Robert Frost uses blank verse in "The Gift Outright," "Out, Out—," and "Birches."

1. Copy the first four lines of "The Gift Outright"; then mark the stressed and unstressed syllables.
2. Find two examples in "Out, Out—" where Frost deviates from blank verse.
3. Explain how Frost uses each metrical variation to emphasize an idea or an image.

◆ Grammar and Style

USES OF INFINITIVES

An **infinitive** is a verb form consisting of the base form of a verb, usually with the word *to*. It can function as a noun, adjective, or adverb. An **infinitive phrase** consists of an infinitive plus any modifiers or complements. Infinitives and infinitive phrases can be used as adjectives, adverbs, or nouns.

Practice On your paper, copy the following lines from Frost's poems. For each item, underline the infinitive or infinitive phrase and identify whether it functions as a noun, adjective, or adverb.

1. As he went out and in to fetch the cows— ...
2. And on a day we meet to walk the line ...
3. But I have promises to keep,/ And miles to go before I sleep, ...
4. Before I built a wall I'd ask to know/What I was walling in or walling out, ...
5. Such heaps of broken glass to sweep away...

Writing Application Write a few lines of verse describing an outdoor activity you recently participated in or witnessed. Use at least three infinitives or infinitive phrases.

◆ Reading Strategy

READING BLANK VERSE

Reading blank verse in sentences, rather than pausing at the end of each line, helps you to appreciate how this type of verse captures the rhythms of everyday speech. For example, reading the sixteen-line poem "The Gift Outright" as five sentences underscores Frost's use of direct and common language.

"Out, Out—" is also written largely in blank verse. Read the poem twice—first pausing at the end of each of the thirty-four poetic lines, then again, reading the poem as a series of twenty-three sentences. Describe the differences between the two readings. Which approach to reading is more effective? Why?

◆ Build Vocabulary

USING THE ROOT -lum-

Many English words are based on the Latin root -lum-, meaning "light." In your notebook, complete these sentences using the appropriate -lum- word.

    a. luminous   **b.** illuminate   **c.** illumination

1. Is that single bulb enough to __?__ the entire room?
2. The leaves of the linden tree were bathed in __?__ sunlight.
3. The students found __?__ in the wise words of the philosopher.

USING THE WORD BANK

On your paper, write the letter of the word or phrase that best completes the sentence.

1. A person with *poise* is (a) sloppy, (b) graceful, (c) wealthy.
2. A *rueful* smile might express (a) regret, (b) anger, (c) complacency.
3. The phrase "*luminary* tower" might be used to describe (a) a lighthouse, (b) a leaning tower, (c) an astronomer's lab.

Build Your Portfolio

Idea Bank

Writing

1. **Character Sketch** Using your imagination to fill in missing details, write a character sketch about the speaker in "Stopping by Woods." Who is he? Where is he coming from, and where is he headed? What are the promises he must keep?

2. **News Story** Building on the facts presented in the poem, reshape "Out, Out—" into a newspaper article. **[Media Link]**

3. **Essay** Critic Robert DiYanni commented that Frost's poetry often "'begins in delight and ends in wisdom,' offering along the way what [Frost] called 'a momentary stay against confusion.'" Write an essay in which you explain how that statement relates to "Birches."

Speaking and Listening

4. **Eulogy** Prepare a eulogy for the young boy in "Out, Out—" in which you lament his early death and pay tribute to a boy who did "a man's work." Deliver the eulogy at a "memorial service" in the classroom. **[Performing Arts Link]**

5. **Poetry Reading** Ask a librarian to help you locate recordings of Frost reciting his own poems. Select two or three poems that appeal to you, and play them for the class. Lead a discussion of the impressions created by Frost's delivery.

Projects

6. **Poster** Which line from "Mending Wall" best captures your own ideas about walls? Design a poster to illustrate this line. **[Art Link]**

7. **Travel Brochure** Create a travel brochure promoting New England tourism. Refer to travel guides or Internet sites to learn what draws visitors to the region. Include text, photos, and passages from Frost's poetry. **[Social Studies Link]**

Writing Mini-Lesson

Introduction to an Anthology

An **anthology** is a collection of literary works often focused on a specific theme (poems about nature, for example) or on a specific time period (for instance, twentieth-century short stories). Usually anthologies include an introduction that provides an overview of the content, as well as commentary on the works. Write an introduction to an anthology featuring poems by Robert Frost. Identify the key characteristics of his work, providing examples to support each of your points.

Writing Skills Focus: Transitions to Show Examples

Each time you cite a supporting example, introduce the example with a transition, such as the ones in this list.

for example	such as
along with	for instance
in other words	like

Prewriting Review the Frost poems in this group. As you read, jot down ideas about the topics, style, and themes of the works. Note the elements they have in common. Decide which characteristics you will address in your introduction; then identify supporting poems or specific lines. Finally, sketch out a table of contents that indicates which selections you will include.

Drafting Begin your introduction with a general statement about the poems, and follow by touching on a few key points related to this statement. Focus each body paragraph on one key point. Support each point with passages from the poems.

Revising Read your work for clarity and correctness. Does it reveal insights into the works and the relationships among them? Does it provide enough information to encourage readers to read the anthology? Add transitions to introduce examples where necessary.

Guide for Interpreting

James Thurber (1894–1961)

James Thurber's essays and other writings—plays, sketches, and short stories such as the well-known "The Secret Life of Walter Mitty"—generally evolved from his own experiences. In his humorous autobiographical sketches, Thurber embellishes the facts and describes events in an amusing manner. In his short stories, Thurber's characters struggle against the unpleasant realities of modern life—often with humorous consequences.

Thurber was born in Columbus, Ohio. After attending Ohio State University, he joined *The New Yorker* magazine staff in 1927. Thurber enjoyed a relationship with the magazine that lasted for years.

Thurber published many collections of his writing. For example, *The Owl in the Attic and Other Perplexities* (1931) and *The Seal in the Bedroom and Other Predicaments* (1932) contain a mixture of short stories, parodies, and cartoons. Thurber was also an able cartoonist—often creating cartoons to illustrate his writing and sometimes writing stories or essays to explain his cartoons. Thurber's humor shows a glint of unhappiness, especially in the later years when his failing vision made him increasingly bitter.

E. B. White (1899–1985)

Creating writings that capture the interest of adults as well as pieces that entertained children, E(lwyn) B(rooks) White established himself as one of the best-loved twentieth-century writers. His direct and precisely worded essays set a standard against which today's essays can be judged.

White strongly believed in individualism and simplicity, values that come through in his writing.

The relatively simple youth White has recalled with yearning took place in Mount Vernon, New York. From there, he went to study literature at Cornell University. As an undergraduate, White served as the editor of the Cornell *Daily Sun*. Later, he began a long association with *The New Yorker* magazine. His humorous, topical essays helped to establish *The New Yorker* as one of the nation's most successful general-interest magazines.

White wrote two of the most beloved children's books of all time, *Stuart Little* (1945) and *Charlotte's Web* (1952), along with many adult essays, columns, poems, and stories. In addition, his revision of William Strunk, Jr.'s classic style manual, *The Elements of Style,* has become a classic in its own right.

◆ Background for Understanding

CULTURE: HUMOR IN AMERICA

America has a strong tradition of humorous writing. Much of that humor builds on self-ridicule, with people poking fun at their own missteps and failures. Americans seem especially willing to laugh at themselves when they don't achieve everything they attempt.

Magazines have played a key role in nurturing American humor. For years, *The Saturday Evening Post* and *The New Yorker* magazine have showcased the work of cartoonists and humorous writers. Founded in 1925 as a magazine of satire, *The New Yorker* published the work of humorists Robert Benchley, S. J. Perelman, Dorothy Parker, and Frank Sullivan, in addition to James Thurber and E. B. White.

Many of today's best writers of humor reach out into other media. Garrison Keillor, for example, writes humorous essays but is most popularly known as the host of "Prairie Home Companion," a radio program that spoofs the people of the imaginary Lake Wobegon, Minnesota, much as White satirized New Yorkers.

◆ *Literature and Your Life*

CONNECT YOUR EXPERIENCE

What makes you laugh? Different people are amused by different things—movie characters slipping on banana peels, the irreverent jokes of a stand-up comedian, or the subtle wit of the humorous essay. Notice as you read these essays which parts make you laugh—or smile. How does your laughter relate to your own experiences?

Group Discussion In a small group, discuss the kind of humor you most enjoy, and why.

THEMATIC FOCUS: FROM EVERY CORNER OF THE LAND

As you read E. B. White's essay about New York City, think about what gives any place its unique character.

◆ Build Vocabulary

WORD ROOTS: -terr-

The word *subterranean* appears in "Here Is New York." Knowing that the prefix *sub-* means "under" and the root *-terr-* means "earth" will help you guess that *subterranean* means "occurring under the earth's surface."

WORD BANK

Before you read, preview this list of words from the essays.

intuitively
blaspheming
aspiration
subterranean
claustrophobia
cosmopolitan

◆ Grammar and Style

COMMAS IN SERIES

Both Thurber and White use **commas in series**—three or more parallel items linked by commas with a conjunction usually preceding the final item—to string together humorous details. Look at these examples:

White: . . . it has been hit by an airplane in a fog, struck countless times by lightning, and been jumped off of by so many unhappy people that . . .

Thurber: Bodwell was at the window in a minute, shouting, frothing a little, shaking his fist.

◆ Literary Focus

INFORMAL ESSAY

"The Night the Ghost Got In" and "Here Is New York" are both **informal essays**, brief nonfiction pieces characterized by a relaxed, conversational style and structure. Informal essays are intended to entertain. Using informal language, they address a narrow subject, and they tend to be loosely organized. They often include digressions in which the author expresses an opinion or discusses related matters.

When you read informal essays, you'll get to glimpse the writer's personality. What do these essays suggest about James Thurber and E. B. White?

◆ Reading Strategy

RECOGNIZE HYPERBOLE

These essays draw humor from **hyperbole**—lavish exaggerations of fact and outrageous overstatements. The series of bizarre events in Thurber's essays and White's litany of probable New York City disasters are good examples of how writers use hyperbole to amuse their audiences.

Watch for details that seem too absurd to be true. When Thurber describes an army of police and reporters arriving at his house, you'd be right to suspect hyperbole. Jot down a hyperbole that you find especially amusing.

The Night the Ghost Got In

James Thurber

The Night the Ghost Got In, Copyright 1933, 1961, James Thurber, From *My Life and Hard Times,* published by Harper & Row.

▲ **Critical Viewing** The humor in Thurber's drawing echoes the humor in his story. What makes this sketch humorous? **[Analyze]**

The ghost that got into our house on the night of November 17, 1915, raised such a hullabaloo of misunderstandings that I am sorry I didn't just let it keep on walking, and go to bed. Its advent caused my mother to throw a shoe through a window of the house next door and ended up with my grandfather shooting a patrolman. I am sorry, therefore, as I have said, that I ever paid any attention to the footsteps.

They began about a quarter past one o'clock in the morning, a rhythmic, quick-cadenced walking around the dining-room table. My mother was asleep in one room upstairs, my brother Herman in another; grandfather was in the attic, in the old walnut bed which, as you will remember, once fell on my father. I had just stepped out of the bathtub and was busily rubbing myself with a towel when I heard the steps. They were the steps of a man walking rapidly around the dining-room table downstairs. The light from the bathroom shone down the back steps, which dropped directly into the dining-room; I could see the faint shine of plates on the plate-rail; I couldn't see the table. The steps kept going round and round the table; at regular intervals a board creaked, when it was trod upon. I supposed at first that it was my father or my brother Roy, who had gone to Indianapolis but were expected home at any time. I suspected next that it was a burglar. It did not enter my mind until later that it was a ghost.

After the walking had gone on for perhaps three minutes, I tiptoed to Herman's room. "Psst!" I hissed, in the dark, shaking him. "Awp," he said, in the low, hopeless tone of a despondent beagle—he always half suspected that something would "get him" in the night. I told him who I was. "There's something downstairs!" I said. He got up and followed me to the head of the back staircase. We listened together. There was no sound. The steps had ceased. Herman looked at me in some alarm: I had only the bath towel around my waist. He wanted to go back to bed, but I gripped his arm. "There's something down there!" I said. Instantly the steps began again, circled the dining-room table like a man running, and started up the stairs toward us, heavily, two at a time. The light still shone palely down the stairs; we saw nothing coming; we only heard the steps. Herman rushed to his room and slammed the door. I slammed shut the door at the stairs top and held my knee against it. After a long minute, I slowly opened it again. There was nothing there. There was no sound. None of us ever heard the ghost again.

The slamming of the doors had aroused mother: she peered out of her room. "What on earth are you boys doing?" she demanded. Herman ventured out of his room. "Nothing," he said, gruffly, but he was, in color, a light green. "What was all that running around downstairs?" said mother. So she had heard the steps, too! We just looked at her. "Burglars!" she shouted intuitively. I tried to quiet her by starting lightly downstairs.

"Come on, Herman," I said.

"I'll stay with Mother," he said. "She's all excited. "

I stepped back onto the landing.

"Don't either of you go a step," said mother. "We'll call the police." Since the phone was downstairs, I didn't see how we were going to call the police—nor did I want the police—but mother made one of her quick, incomparable decisions. She flung up a window of her bedroom which faced the bedroom windows of the house of a neighbor, picked up a shoe, and whammed it through a pane of glass across the narrow space that separated the two houses. Glass tinkled into the bedroom occupied by a retired engraver named Bodwell and his wife. Bodwell had been for some years in rather a bad way and was subject to mild "attacks." Most everybody we knew or lived near had *some* kind of attacks.

It was now about two o'clock of a moonless night; clouds hung black and low. Bodwell was at the window in a minute, shouting, frothing a little, shaking his fist. "We'll sell the house and go back to Peoria," we could hear Mrs. Bodwell saying. It was some time before mother "got through" to Bodwell. "Burglars!" she shouted. "Burglars in the house!" Herman and I hadn't dared to tell her that it was not burglars but ghosts, for she was even more afraid of ghosts than of burglars. Bodwell at first thought that she meant there were burglars in his house, but finally he quieted down and called the police for us over an extension phone by his bed. After he had disappeared from the window, mother suddenly made as if to throw another shoe, not because there was further need of it, but, as she later explained, because the thrill of heaving a shoe through a window glass had enormously taken her fancy. I prevented her.

The police were on hand in a commendably short time: a Ford sedan full of them, two on motorcycles, and a patrol wagon with about eight in it and a few reporters. They began banging at our front door. Flashlights shot streaks of gleam up and down the walls, across the yard, down the walk between our house and Bodwell's. "Open up!" cried a hoarse voice. "We're men from Headquarters!" I wanted to go down and let them in, since there they were, but mother wouldn't hear of it. "You haven't a stitch on," she pointed out. "You'd catch your death." I wound the towel around me again. Finally the cops put their shoulders to our big heavy front door with its thick beveled glass and broke it in: I could hear a rending of wood and a splash of glass on the floor of the hall. Their lights played all over the living-room and crisscrossed nervously in the dining-room, stabbed into hallways, shot up the front stairs and finally up the back. They caught me standing in my towel at the top. A heavy policeman bounded up the steps. "Who are you?" he demanded. "I live here," I said. "Well, whattsa matta, ya hot?" he asked. I was, as a matter of fact, cold; I went to my room and pulled on some trousers. On my way out, a cop stuck a gun into my ribs. "Whatta you doin' here?" he demanded. "I live here," I said.

◆ **Reading Strategy**
Why is this clearly an example of exaggeration?

▲ **Critical Viewing** Thurber created this cartoon to accompany "The Night the Ghost Got In." How does the illustration add to the humorous effect of the essay? **[Assess]**

The officer in charge reported to mother. "No sign of nobody, lady," he said. "Musta got away—whatt'd he look like?" "There were two or three of them," mother said, "whooping and carrying on and slamming doors." "Funny," said the cop. "All ya windows and doors was locked on the inside tight as a tick."

Downstairs, we could hear the tromping of the other police. Police were all over the place; doors were yanked open, drawers were yanked open, windows were shot up and pulled down, furniture fell with dull thumps. A half-dozen policemen emerged out of the darkness of the front hallway upstairs. They began to ransack the floor: pulled beds away from walls, tore clothes off hooks in the closets, pulled suitcases and boxes off shelves. One of them found an old zither[1] that Roy had won in a pool tournament. "Looky here, Joe," he said, strumming it with a big paw. The cop named Joe took it and turned it over. "What is it?" he asked me. "It's an old zither our guinea pig used to sleep on," I said. It was true that a pet guinea pig we once had would never sleep anywhere except on the zither, but I should never have said so. Joe and the other cop looked at me a long time.

---

1. **zither** (zith´ ər) *n.*: Musical instrument with thirty to forty strings stretched across a flat soundboard and played with the fingers.

They put the zither back on a shelf.

"No sign o' nuthin'," said the cop who had first spoken to mother. "This guy," he explained to the others, jerking a thumb at me, "was nekked. The lady seems historical." They all nodded, but said nothing; just looked at me. In the small silence we all heard a creaking in the attic. Grandfather was turning over in bed. "What's 'at?" snapped Joe. Five or six cops sprang for the attic door before I could intervene or explain. I realized that it would be bad if they burst in on grandfather unannounced, or even announced. He was going through a phase in which he believed that General Meade's men, under steady hammering by Stonewall Jackson, were beginning to retreat and even desert.

When I got to the attic, things were pretty confused. Grandfather had evidently jumped to the conclusion that the police were deserters from Meade's army, trying to hide away in his attic. He bounded out of bed wearing a long flannel nightgown over long woolen underwear, a nightcap, and a leather jacket around his chest. The cops must have realized at once that the indignant white-haired old man belonged in the house, but they had no chance to say so. "Back, ye cowardly dogs!" roared grandfather. "Back t' the lines, ye yellow, lily-livered cattle!" With that, he fetched the officer who found the zither a flat-handed smack alongside his head that sent him sprawling. The others beat a retreat, but not fast enough; grandfather grabbed Zither's gun from its holster and let fly. The report seemed to crack the rafters; smoke filled the attic. A cop cursed and shot his hand to his shoulder. Somehow, we all finally got downstairs again and locked the door against the old gentleman. He fired once or twice more in the darkness and then went back to bed. "That was grandfather," I explained to Joe, out of breath. "He thinks you're deserters." "I'll say he does," said Joe.

The cops were reluctant to leave without getting their hands on somebody besides

◆ **Literary Focus**
What features of this passage are typical of an informal essay?

◆ **Build Vocabulary**
blaspheming (blas fēm´ iŋ) *v.*: Cursing

grandfather; the night had been distinctly a defeat for them. Furthermore, they obviously didn't like the "layout"; something looked—and I can see their viewpoint—phony. They began to poke into things again. A reporter, a thin-faced, wispy man, came up to me. I had put on one of mother's blouses, not being able to find anything else. The reporter looked at me with mingled suspicion and interest. "Just what the heck is the real lowdown here, Bud?" he asked. I decided to be frank with him. "We had ghosts," I said. He gazed at me a long time as if I were a slot machine into which he had, without results, dropped a nickel. Then he walked away. The cops followed him, the one grandfather shot holding his now-bandaged arm, cursing and blaspheming. "I'm gonna get my gun back from that old bird," said the zither-cop. "Yeh," said Joe. "You—and who else?" I told them I would bring it to the station house the next day.

"What was the matter with that one policeman?" mother asked, after they had gone. "Grandfather shot him," I said. "What for?" she demanded. I told her he was a deserter. "Of all

The Night the Ghost Got In, Copyright 1933, 1961, James Thurber, From *My Life and Hard Times*, published by Harper & Row.

▲ **Critical Viewing** Compare this illustration with Thurber's description of the police investigation. What makes each funny? **[Evaluate]**

things!" said mother. "He was such a nice-looking young man."

Grandfather was fresh as a daisy and full of jokes at breakfast next morning. We thought at first he had forgotten all about what had happened, but he hadn't. Over his third cup of coffee, he glared at Herman and me. "What was the idee of all them cops tarry-hootin' round the house last night?" he demanded. He had us there.

Guide for Responding

◆ *Literature and Your Life*

Reader's Response What did you find the most humorous point in the essay? Why?

Thematic Response Could this humorous essay have take place in a distant land—for example, Argentina or Nigeria? Explain.

☑ Check Your Comprehension

1. What event sets off the family's reactions?
2. Describe what each character in the narrator's family does on the night "the ghost" got into the house.

◆ Critical Thinking

INTERPRET

1. How does Thurber's portrayal of himself differ from his portrayal of the other characters? **[Compare and Contrast]**
2. How does lack of communication contribute to the humor of this essay? **[Support]**
3. What does the grandfather's question at breakfast reveal about him? **[Interpret]**

EXTEND

4. Explain why these characters would probably not succeed in business. **[Career Link]**

from # Here Is New York

E. B. White

New York is nothing like Paris; it is nothing like London; and it is not Spokane multiplied by sixty, or Detroit multiplied by four. It is by all odds the loftiest of cities. It even managed to reach the highest point in the sky at the lowest moment of the Depression. The Empire State Building shot 1250 feet into the air when it was madness to put out as much as six inches of new growth. (The building has a mooring mast that no dirigible[1] has ever tied to; it employs a man to flush toilets in slack times; it has been hit by an airplane in a fog, struck

---

1. **dirigible** (dir´ə jə bəl) *n.*: Large, long airship.

◄ **Critical Viewing** What objects in this photograph confirm White's attitude about New York? Explain. **[Connect]**

▲ **Critical Viewing** How does this scene compare with the New York White describes? **[Compare and Contrast]**

countless times by lightning, and been jumped off of by so many unhappy people that pedestrians instinctively quicken step when passing Fifth Avenue and Thirty-fourth Street.)

Manhattan has been compelled to expand skyward because of the absence of any other direction in which to grow. This, more than any other thing, is responsible for its physical majesty. It is to the nation what the white church spire is to the village—the visible symbol of <u>aspiration</u> and faith, the white plume saying that the way is up. The summer traveler swings in over Hell Gate Bridge and from the window of his sleeping car as it glides above the pigeon lofts and back yards of Queens looks southwest to where the morning light first strikes the steel peaks of midtown, and he sees its upward thrust unmistakable: the great walls and towers rising, the smoke rising, the heat not yet rising, the hopes and ferments of so many awakening millions rising—this vigorous spear that presses heaven hard.

It is a miracle that New York works at all. The whole thing is implausible. Every time the residents brush their teeth, millions of gallons of water must be drawn from the Catskills and the hills of Westchester. When a young man in Manhattan writes a letter to his girl in Brooklyn, the love message gets blown to her through a pneumatic[2] tube—*pfft*—just like that. The <u>subterranean</u> system of telephone cables, power lines, steam pipes, gas mains, and sewer pipes is reason enough to abandon the island to the gods and the weevils. Every time an incision is made in the

♦ **Literary Focus**
In what specific ways is White's tone typical of an informal essay?

---

2. **pneumatic** (nŏo mat´ik) *adj.*: Filled with compressed air.

♦ **Build Vocabulary**
aspiration (as´pə rā´shən) *n.*: Strong ambition
subterranean (sub´tə rā´nē ən) *adj.*: Underground

pavement, the noisy surgeons expose ganglia[3] that are tangled beyond belief. By rights New York should have destroyed itself long ago, from panic or fire or rioting or failure of some vital supply line in its circulatory system or from some deep labyrinthine short circuit. Long ago the city should have experienced an insoluble traffic snarl at some impossible bottleneck. It should have perished of hunger when food lines filed for a few days. It should have been wiped out by a plague starting in its slums or carried in by ships' rats. It should have been overwhelmed by the sea that licks at it on every side. The workers in its myriad cells should have succumbed to nerves, from the fearful pall of smoke-fog that drifts over every few days from Jersey, blotting out all light at noon and leaving the high offices suspended, men groping and depressed, and the sense of world's end. It should have been touched in the head by the August heat and gone off its rocker.

Mass hysteria is a terrible force, yet New Yorkers seem always to escape it by some tiny margin: they sit in stalled subways without claustrophobia, they extricate themselves from panic situations by some lucky wisecrack, they meet confusion and congestion with patience and grit—a sort of perpetual muddling through. Every facility is inadequate—the hospitals and schools and the playgrounds are overcrowded, the express highways are feverish, the unimproved highways and bridges are bottlenecks, there is not enough air and not enough light, and there is usually either too much heat or too little. But the city makes up for its hazards and its deficiencies by supplying its citizens with massive doses of a supplementary vitamin: the sense of belonging to something unique, cosmopolitan, mighty, and unparalleled.

To an outlander a stay in New York can be and often is a series of small embarrassments and discomforts and disappointments: not understanding the waiter, not being able to distinguish between a sucker joint and a friendly saloon, riding the wrong subway, being slapped down by a bus driver for asking an innocent question, enduring sleepless nights when the street noises fill the bedroom. Tourists make

for New York, particularly in summertime—they swarm all over the Statue of Liberty (where many a resident of the town has never set foot), they invade the Automat,[4] visit radio studios, St. Patrick's Cathedral, and they window shop. Mostly they have a pretty good time. But sometimes in New York you run across the disillusioned—a young couple who are obviously visitors, newlyweds perhaps, for whom the bright dream has vanished. The place has been too much for them; they sit languishing in a cheap restaurant over a speechless meal.

The oft-quoted thumbnail sketch of New York is, of course: "It's a wonderful place, but I'd hate to live there." I have an idea that people from villages and small towns, people accustomed to the convenience and the friendliness of neighborhood over-the-fence living, are unaware that life in New York follows the neighborhood pattern. The city is literally a composite of tens of thousands of tiny neighborhood units. There are, of course, the big districts and big units: Chelsea and Murray Hill and Gramercy (which are residential units), . . . Greenwich Village (a unit dedicated to the arts and other matters), and there is Radio City (a commercial development), Peter Cooper Village (a housing unit), the Medical Center (a sickness unit) and many other sections each of which has some distinguishing characteristic. But the curious thing about New York is that each large geographical unit is composed of countless small neighborhoods. Each neighborhood is virtually self-sufficient. Usually it is no more than two or three blocks long and a couple of blocks wide. Each area is a city within a city within a city. Thus, no matter where you live in New York, you will find within a block or two a grocery store, a barbershop, a newsstand and shoeshine shack, an ice-coal-and-wood cellar (where you write your order on a pad outside as you walk by), a dry cleaner, a laundry, a

---

4. **Automat** *n.*: Restaurant in which patrons get food from small compartments with doors opened by putting coins into slots.

---

3. **ganglia** (gaŋ′glē ə) *n.*: Mass of nerve cells serving as center of force, energy, activity.

delicatessen (beer and sandwiches delivered at any hour to your door), a flower shop, an undertaker's parlor, a movie house, a radio-repair shop, a stationer, a haberdasher,[5] a tailor, a drugstore, a garage, a tearoom, a saloon, a hardware store, a liquor store, a shoe-repair shop. Every block or two, in most residential sections of New York, is a little main street. A man starts for work in the morning and before he has gone two hundred yards he has completed half a dozen missions: bought a paper, left a pair of shoes to be soled, picked up a pack of cigarettes, . . . written a message to the unseen forces of the wood cellar, and notified the dry cleaner that a pair of trousers awaits call. Homeward-bound eight hours later, he buys a bunch of pussy willows, a Mazda bulb, a drink, a shine—all between the corner where he steps off the bus and his apartment. So complete is each neighborhood, and so strong the sense of neighborhood, that many a New Yorker spends a lifetime within the confines of an area smaller than a country village. Let him walk two blocks from his corner and he is in a

strange land and will feel uneasy till he gets back.

Storekeepers are particularly conscious of neighborhood boundary lines. A woman friend of mine moved recently from one apartment to another, a distance of three blocks. When she turned up, the day after the move, at the same grocer's that she had patronized for years, the proprietor was in ecstasy—almost in tears— at seeing her. "I was afraid," he said, "now that you've moved away I wouldn't be seeing you any- more." To him, *away* was three blocks, or about 750 feet.

I am, at the moment of writing this, living not as a neighborhood man in New York but as a transient, or vagrant, in from the country for a few days. Summertime is a good time to reex- amine New York and to receive again the gift of privacy, the jewel of loneliness. In summer the city contains (except for tourists) only die- hards and authentic characters. No casual, spotty dwellers are around, only the real arti- cle. And the town has a somewhat relaxed air, and one can lie in a loincloth, gasping and remembering things.

> ◆ **Reading Strategy**
> Is this description an example of hyper- bole? Why, or why not?

---

5. **haberdasher** *n*.: Person whose work is selling men's clothing, such as hats, shirts, neckties, and gloves.

Guide for Responding

◆ *Literature and Your Life*

Reader's Response Would you like to visit the New York City of E. B. White's description? Why or why not?

Thematic Response What are some memo- rable characteristics of New York City as E. B. White describes it?

Thumbnail Sketch E. B. White says a thumbnail sketch of New York is "It's a wonderful place, but I'd hate to live there." Write a "thumbnail sketch" of your town or city.

☑ **Check Your Comprehension**

1. List three ways in which New Yorkers escape mass hysteria, according to the essay.
2. According to E. B. White, what is New York City like in summertime?

◆ **Critical Thinking**

INTERPRET

1. How do New York City's neighborhoods com- pare to those of small towns? **[Compare and Contrast]**
2. What qualities about New York City enable it to function against all odds? **[Draw Conclusions]**
3. What general conclusion does White's essay reach about the city? **[Summarize]**

EVALUATE

4. E. B. White takes a bemused tone in this essay. Do you think he uses that tone effectively? Explain. **[Assess]**

EXTEND

5. How might someone working in the tourist in- dustry in New York City respond to E. B. White's representation of the city? **[Career Link]**

Guide for Responding (continued)

◆ Literary Focus

INFORMAL ESSAY

As **informal essays**, both "The Night the Ghost Got In" and "Here Is New York" aim to entertain. They use a conversational style, relaxed language, and narrowly defined subjects. Notice in each example how the writer's personality and opinion of the world emerge.

> **Thurber**: I decided to be frank with him. "We had ghosts," I said. He gazed at me a long time as if I were a slot machine into which he had, without results, dropped a nickel.

> **White**: Summertime is a good time to reexamine New York and to receive again the gift of privacy, the jewel of loneliness.

1. Cite an especially strong example of language that reflects the conversational style of Thurber's essay. Explain your choice.
2. What does "Here Is New York" suggest about White's attitude toward New York and the modern world it symbolizes? Support your answer.

◆ Reading Strategy

RECOGNIZE HYPERBOLE

White and Thurber use **hyperbole**—bold overstatements and extreme exaggerations—to create humor or make a point in their essays. Note this example from "Here Is New York." It tells you twice what you need to know to envision the Empire State Building—and makes you smile in the process:

> The building has a mooring mast no dirigible has ever tied to; it employs a man to flush toilets in slack times; it has been hit by an airplane in a fog, struck countless times by lightning, and been jumped off of by so many unhappy people that pedestrians instinctively quicken step when passing Fifth Avenue and Thirty-fourth Street.

1. Cite an example of hyperbole from each essay and explain why you find each amusing.
2. For what purpose do you think Thurber exaggerates the behavior of his grandfather in the essay?
3. Why is White's use of hyperbole appropriate for his subject?

◆ Build Vocabulary

USING THE WORD ROOT -terr-

Using the meaning of *-terr-* ("earth" or "land") and context clues, choose the best word for each sentence.

 a. terrain   **b.** extraterrestrial   **c.** terrarium

1. The _____?_____ was our first visitor from another planet.
2. Put some earth in a glass jar and plant some seeds to make a _____?_____.
3. Westward pioneers settled new_____?_____ .

USING THE WORD BANK

Answer *yes* or *no* to each question. Then, explain your response.

1. If Sheila has an *aspiration* to sail around the world, does she have a vague notion?
2. Must you dig a hole to reach *subterranean* pipes?
3. Could you get in trouble for *blaspheming* in class?
4. Would *claustrophobia* help an airplane pilot?
5. Would a *cosmopolitan* person enjoy Paris?
6. If you heard a very loud bang, would you *intuitively* wince?

◆ Grammar and Style

COMMAS IN SERIES

Thurber and White frequently use commas in series to string together several humorous details in a single sentence.

> **Commas in series** are placed between three or more parallel items to link them. A conjunction usually precedes the final item.

Practice Rewrite these sentences, inserting commas in their appropriate places.

1. The subterranean system of telephone cables power lines steam pipe gas mains and sewer pipes is the reason to . . .
2. Instantly the steps began again circled the dining-room table like a man running and started up the stairs toward us . . .
3. Their lights . . . crisscrossed nervously in the dining-room stabbed into hallways shot up the front stairs and finally up the back.

Build Your Portfolio

Idea Bank

Writing

1. **Humorous Tourist Guide** Using "Here Is New York" as a model, write a humorous guide to New York. Give your guide a witty title.

2. **Police Report** Suppose you're one of the police officers called to Thurber's home. Write a report describing the scene and the actions of each family member. To contrast Thurber's account, use a completely objective tone.

3. **Critical Response** E. B. White once said, "The most widely appreciated humorists are those who create characters and tell tales . . ." Write an essay responding to this statement. Cite passages from one or both essays for support.

Speaking and Listening

4. **Audition** Try out for a one-actor show about either E. B. White or James Thurber. Audition for the starring (and only) role by reading aloud excerpts from the writer's essay. Try to capture its tone in your reading. **[Performing Arts Link]**

5. **Essay Critique** With a partner, role-play Thurber and White discussing their essays in the offices of *The New Yorker*. Constructively criticize each other's essays. **[Career Link]**

Projects

6. **Historical Re-creation** Research "The Round-table," a group of very funny people associated with *The New Yorker* who gathered together on a regular basis. With classmates, take roles and stage a mock Roundtable. **[Performing Arts Link]**

7. **Set Design** Draw a graph or plan for a dramatic enactment of either essay. In your proposed set design, show movement with arrows or other graphic devices. **[Art Link]**

Writing Mini-Lesson

Toast at a Party

The essays of E. B. White and James Thurber tell humorous stories but also have subtle messages. Use the tone of their essays as a model to write a toast for a party—you might even toast White or Thurber! Grab listeners' attention quickly to engage their interest. Then use anecdotes or humor to make a point while you have "the floor."

Writing Skills Focus: Grabbing Listeners' Attention

When speaking to an audience, it's important to **grab listeners' attention**. Opening with a funny anecdote or outrageous statement can entice your audience to keep listening. See how skillfully Thurber hooks his audience and makes them eager to know what is to come:

Model From the Story

The ghost that got into our house . . . raised such a hullabaloo of misunderstanding that I am sorry I didn't just let it keep on walking. . . . Its advent caused my mother to throw a shoe through a window . . . and ended up with my grandfather shooting a patrolman.

Prewriting What are the stand-out characteristics of the person you will toast? Sort your responses by category, such as *physical appearance, world view,* or *special abilities.* Then list the person's accomplishments and the noteworthy events in his or her life.

Drafting Begin with a funny anecdote or startling comment. Review your catalogued responses to find something that will grab listeners' attention. In the body of your toast, convey the general message you want your listeners to understand.

Revising Read your toast to a friend. Notice how it flows and invite comment about its interest level. Add transitions where appropriate to make it flow more smoothly.

Guide for Interpreting

Zora Neale Hurston
(1891–1960)

When Zora Neale Hurston died in January 1960, she was buried in an unmarked grave in a segregated cemetery in Fort Pierce, Florida. There she lay, forgotten until 1973, when writer Alice Walker located and marked Hurston's grave, recording the experience in a 1975 *Ms.* magazine article. Walker's efforts restored Hurston to her rightful place in American literature, as "the dominant black woman writer" of her time and a pioneering force in the celebration of African American culture.

> **Hurston was the first writer of her day to recognize that cultural heritage was valuable in its own right.**

Her unshakable self-confidence and strong sense of personal and racial worth were fostered by a childhood in Eatonville, Florida, America's first fully incorporated African American township. One of eight children, Hurston was, by her own account, a spirited, curious child who "always wanted to go." Her mother explained this urge to wander by claiming that travel dust had been sprinkled at the door the day Zora was born.

Hurston's childhood abruptly ended, however, when her mother died. Hurston went to live with a series of friends and relatives, attending school whenever she could. By age fourteen, she was supporting herself.

Two Careers Hurston developed an interest in writing while studying at Howard University. In 1925, she moved to New York City. She soon published a story and a play, firmly establishing herself as one of the bright new talents of the Harlem Renaissance. She began attending Barnard College, where her work came to the attention of prominent anthropologist Franz Boas, who convinced Hurston to begin graduate studies in anthropology at Columbia University. With an academic grant, she began a second career as a folklorist, returning to the South to collect African American folk tales and to research customs, especially those of people from her native Florida. She published two folklore collections, *Mules and Men* (1935) and *Tell My Horse* (1938).

The Road to Obscurity Hurston achieved strong critical and popular success during the 1930's and 1940's, publishing the novels *Jonah's Gourd Vine* (1934), *Their Eyes Were Watching God* (1937), and *Moses, Man of the Mountain* (1939), along with numerous short stories, plays, and her prize-winning autobiography, *Dust Tracks on a Road* (1942). Personal scandal, however, led Hurston's career into obscurity. The 1970's saw a resurgence of interest in Hurston's work that continues to gain momentum.

◆ Background for Understanding

CULTURE: HURSTON AND THE FOLKLORE TRADITION

Folklore refers to traditional stories passed down from generation to generation by word of mouth within a particular culture or region. Most cultures, from the ancient Greeks and Romans to peoples from Eastern Europe and Latin America, have their own folk traditions. One of the world's richest and most vibrant collections of folklore is that of African Americans. The roots of African American folklore stretch back to the tales, myths, and songs that had been passed down among generations of Africans long before the first Africans were brought to America and forced into slavery. For enslaved Africans and their ancestors, folklore has served as an important means of preserving their cultural heritage, and the folk tradition has continued to grow and expand. Thanks to Zora Neale Hurston and others, this rich folk traditional is now permanently preserved in writing.

from **Dust Tracks on a Road**

◆ *Literature and Your Life*

CONNECT YOUR EXPERIENCE

Even as a child, Zora Neale Hurston was passionate about literature. What excites your interest? As you read, think about how an interest can shape your character and change your life.

Journal Writing Jot down some of your own interests—sports, hobbies, movies, travel—and trace their origins.

THEMATIC FOCUS: FROM EVERY CORNER OF THE LAND

In this excerpt from the life of an African American girl growing up in a small Florida town, character and community play important roles. What does the story reveal about the girl and her town?

◆ Literary Focus

PURPOSE IN AUTOBIOGRAPHY

All writers draw on their own experiences in their work. Autobiography, however, makes the author's life its central concern. An **autobiography** is an account of a person's life written by that person, generally in the first person. In an autobiography, the writer presents a continuous narrative of signficant events from his or her perspective. The reader sees events through the writer's eyes and comes to understand the writer's point of view.

An author's **purpose in writing an autobiography** varies. Some writers strive to justify their beliefs or sort out conflicts. Others wish to present their lives as an example for readers to follow. In her autobiography, Zora Neale Hurston strives to show that while she and other African Americans of her day suffered from racial injustice, they lived rich lives filled with laughter and had promising hopes and dreams for the future.

◆ Grammar and Style

PARALLELISM IN COORDINATE ELEMENTS

By using coordinating conjunctions—such as *and, but, or,* and *nor*—Zora Neale Hurston packs a lot of information into her sentences and creates a rhythm in her writing. Notice that she is careful to maintain **parallelism in coordinate structures** by using the same form of each grammatically equivalent element linked by coordinating conjunctions within a sentence. Look at this example:

They also *came* and *went, came* and *went.*

◆ Reading Strategy

ANALYZE HOW A WRITER ACHIEVES PURPOSE

Hurston's purpose—to share her personal experience and show the vitality of the African American community of her childhood—determines her choice of words, details, characters, and events. By linking her choices to her goals, you can analyze how she achieves her purpose. For example:

Writer's Choice

Hurston describes herself as befriending white passersby despite her family's disapproval.

Analysis

This scene shows her self-assurance and ability to feel comfortable with people of every kind. It helps the reader sense her spunk and see her outlook on life.

◆ Build Vocabulary

WORD ROOTS: *-graph-*

You have known the word *geography* since grade school, but do you know how the root *-graph-,* meaning "write," contributes to its definition? In fact, *geography* means "the study of—or writing about—the Earth."

WORD BANK

Before you read, preview this list of words from *Dust Tracks on a Road.*

foreknowledge
brazenness
caper
exalted
geography
avarice

from

Dust Tracks on a Road

Zora Neale Hurston

I used to take a seat on top of the gatepost and watch the world go by. One way to Orlando[1] ran past my house, so the carriages and cars would pass before me. The movement made me glad to see it. Often the white travelers would hail me, but more often I hailed them, and asked, "Don't you want me to go a piece of the way with you?"

They always did. I know now that I must have caused a great deal of amusement among them, but my self-assurance must have carried the point, for I was always invited to come along. I'd ride up the road for perhaps a half-mile, then walk back. I did not do this with the permission of my parents, nor with their foreknowledge. When they found out about it later, I usually got a whipping. My grandmother worried about my forward ways a great deal. She had known slavery and to her my brazenness was unthinkable.

"Git down offa dat gate-post! You li'l sow, you! Git down! Setting up dere looking dem white folks right in de face! They's gowine[2] to lynch you, yet. And don't stand in dat doorway gazing out at 'em neither. Youse too brazen to live long."[3]

Nevertheless, I kept right on gazing at them, and "going a piece of the way" whenever I could make it. The village seemed dull to me most of the time. If the village was singing a chorus, I must have missed the tune.

Perhaps a year before the old man[4] died, I came to know two other white people for myself. They were women.

It came about this way. The whites who came down from the North were often brought by their friends to visit the village school. A Negro school was something strange to them, and while they were always sympathetic and kind, curiosity must have been present, also. They came and went, came and went. Always, the room was hurriedly put in order, and we were threatened with a prompt and bloody death if we cut one caper while the visitors were present. We always sang a spiritual, led by Mr. Calhoun himself. Mrs. Calhoun always stood in the back, with a palmetto switch[5] in her hand as a squelcher. We were all little angels for the duration, because we'd better be. She would cut her eyes and give us a glare that meant trouble, then turn her face towards the visitors and beam as much as to say it was a great privilege and pleasure to teach lovely children like us. They couldn't see that palmetto hickory

---

1. **Orlando** (ôr lan´ dō): City in central Florida, about five miles from Eatonville, Hurston's hometown.
2. **gowine:** "Going."
3. **"Git down . . . live long":** Hurston's grandmother's fears reflect the belief of many people at the time that it was inappropriate for African Americans to be assertive toward whites.
4. **the old man:** White farmer who had developed a friendship with Hurston.
5. **palmetto** (pal met´ ō) **switch:** Whip made from the fan-shaped leaves of the palmetto, a type of palm tree.

The Mather School, Jonathan Green

▲ **Critical Viewing** Do you think the students in this painting enjoy going to school? On what elements of the painting do you base your decision? **[Evaluate]**

in her hand behind all those benches, but we knew where our angelic behavior was coming from.

Usually, the visitors gave warning a day ahead and we would be cautioned to put on shoes, comb our heads, and see to ears and fingernails. There was a close inspection of every one of us before we marched in that morning. Knotty heads, dirty ears and fingernails got hauled out of line, strapped and sent home to lick the calf over again.

This particular afternoon, the two young ladies just popped in. Mr. Calhoun was flustered,

◆ **Build Vocabulary**

foreknowledge (fôr′ näl′ ij) *n.*: Awareness of something before it happens or exists

brazenness (brā′ zən nis) *n.*: Shamelessness; boldness; impudence

caper (kā′ pər) *n.*: Prank

but he put on the best show he could. He dismissed the class that he was teaching up at the front of the room, then called the fifth grade in reading. That was my class.

So we took our readers and went up front. We stood up in the usual line, and opened to the lesson. It was the story of Pluto and Persephone. It was new and hard to the class in general, and Mr. Calhoun was very uncomfortable as the readers stumbled along, spelling out words with their lips, and in mumbling undertones before they exposed them experimentally to the teacher's ears.

Then it came to me. I was fifth or sixth down the line. The story was not new to me, because I had read my reader through from lid to lid, the first week that Papa had bought it for me.

That is how it was that my eyes were not in the book, working out the paragraph which I knew would be mine by counting the children ahead of me. I was observing our visitors, who held a book between them, following the lesson. They had shiny hair, mostly brownish. One had a looping gold chain around her neck. The other one was dressed all over in black and white with a pretty finger ring on her left hand. But the thing that held my eyes were their fingers. They were long and thin, and very white, except up near the tips. There they were baby pink. I had never seen such hands. It was a fascinating discovery for me. I wondered how they felt. I would have given those hands more attention, but the child before me was almost through. My turn next, so I got on my mark, bringing my eyes back to the book and made sure of my place. Some of the stories I had reread several times, and this Greco-Roman myth was one of my favorites. I was <u>exalted</u> by it, and that is the way I read my paragraph.

"Yes, Jupiter had seen her (Persephone). He had seen the maiden picking flowers in the field. He had seen the chariot of the dark monarch pause by the maiden's side. He had seen him when he seized Persephone. He had seen the black horses leap down Mount Aetna's fiery throat. Persephone was now in Pluto's dark realm and he had made her his wife."

The two women looked at each other and then back to me. Mr. Calhoun broke out with a proud smile beneath his bristly moustache, and instead of the next child taking up where I had ended, he nodded to me to go on. So I read

the story to the end, where flying Mercury, the messenger of the Gods, brought Persephone back to the sunlit earth and restored her to the arms of Dame Ceres, her mother, that the world might have springtime and summer flowers, autumn and harvest. But because she had bitten the pomegranate[6] while in Pluto's kingdom, she must return to him for three months of each year, and be his queen. Then the world had winter, until she returned to earth.

The class was dismissed, and the visitors smiled us away and went into a low-voiced conversation with Mr. Calhoun for a few minutes. They glanced my way once or twice and I began to worry. Not only was I barefooted, but my feet and legs were dusty. My hair was more uncombed than usual, and my nails were not shiny clean. Oh, I'm going to catch it now. Those ladies saw me, too. Mr. Calhoun is promising to 'tend to me. So I thought.

Then Mr. Calhoun called me. I went up thinking how awful it was to get a whipping before company. Furthermore, I heard a snicker run over the room. Hennie Clark and Stell Brazzle did it out loud, so I would be sure to hear them. The smart-aleck was going to get it. I slipped one hand behind me and switched my dress tail at them, indicating scorn.

◆ **Reading Strategy**
Analyze why Hurston includes this incident. How does it help you to step into young Zora's experience?

"Come here, Zora Neale," Mr. Calhoun cooed as I reached the desk. He put his hand on my shoulder and gave me little pats. The ladies smiled and held out those flower-looking fingers towards me. I seized the opportunity for a good look.

"Shake hands with the ladies, Zora Neale," Mr. Calhoun prompted and they took my hand one after the other and smiled. They asked if I loved school, and I lied that I did. There was *some* truth in it, because I liked <u>geography</u> and reading, and I liked to play at recess time. Whoever it was invented writing and arithmetic got no thanks from me. Neither did I like the arrangement where the teacher could sit up there with a palmetto stem and lick me

---

6. **pomegranate** (päm´ gran´ it) *n*.: Round, red-skinned fruit with many seeds.

School Bell Time, 1978 From the Profile/Part 1: The Twenties series (Mecklenburg County), Romare Bearden, Collection: Kingsborough Community College, The City University of New York; © Romare Bearden Foundation/ Licensed by VAGA, New York, NY

▲ **Critical Viewing** How does the mood of this image compare or contrast with the mood of Hurston's writing? Explain. **[Compare and Contrast]**

whenever he saw fit. I hated things I couldn't do anything about. But I knew better than to bring that up right there, so I said yes, I *loved* school.

"I can tell you do," Brown Taffeta gleamed. She patted my head, and was lucky enough not to get sandspurs in her hand. Children who roll and tumble in the grass in Florida are apt to get sandspurs in their hair. They shook hands with me again and I went back to my seat.

When school let out at three o'clock, Mr. Calhoun told me to wait. When everybody had gone, he told me I was to go to the Park House, that was the hotel in Maitland,[7] the next afternoon to call upon Mrs. Johnstone and Miss Hurd. I must tell Mama to see that I was clean and brushed from head to feet, and I must wear shoes and stockings. The ladies liked me,

he said, and I must be on my best behavior.

The next day I was let out of school an hour early, and went home to be stood up in a tub full of suds and be scrubbed and have my ears dug into. My sandy hair sported a red ribbon to match my red and white checked gingham dress, starched until it could stand alone. Mama saw to it that my shoes were on the right feet, since I was careless about left and right. Last thing, I was given a handkerchief to carry, warned again about my behavior, and sent off, with my big brother John to go as far as the hotel gate with me.

◆ **Build Vocabulary**

exalted (eg zôlt´ id) *adj.*: Filled with joy or pride; elated

geography (jē ôg´ rə fē) *n.*: The study of the surface of the earth

---

7. **Maitland** (māt´ lənd): City in Florida, close to Eatonville.

First thing, the ladies gave me strange things, like stuffed dates and preserved ginger, and encouraged me to eat all that I wanted. Then they showed me their Japanese dolls and just talked. I was then handed a copy of *Scribner's Magazine*,[8] and asked to read a place that was pointed out to me. After a paragraph or two, I was told with smiles, that that would do.

I was led out on the grounds and they took my picture under a palm tree. They handed me what was to me then a heavy cylinder done up in fancy paper, tied with a ribbon, and they told me goodbye, asking me not to open it until I got home.

My brother was waiting for me down by the lake, and we hurried home, eager to see what was in the thing. It was too heavy to be candy or anything like that. John insisted on toting it for me.

My mother made John give it back to me and let me open it. Perhaps, I shall never experience such joy again. The nearest thing to that moment was the telegram accepting my first book.

One hundred goldy-new pennies rolled out of the cylinder. Their gleam lit up the world. It was not <u>avarice</u> that moved me. It was the beauty of the thing. I stood on the mountain. Mama let me play with my pennies for a while, then put them away for me to keep.

◆ **Literary Focus**
What does Hurston want you to know about her family's values and her own?

That was only the beginning. The next day I received an Episcopal hymn-book bound in white leather with a golden cross stamped into the front cover, a copy of *The Swiss Family Robinson*, and a book of fairy tales.

I set about to commit the song words to memory. There was no music written there, just the words. But there was to my consciousness music in between them just the same. "When I Survey the Wondrous Cross" seemed the most beautiful to me, so I committed that to memory first of all. Some of them seemed dull and without life, and I pretended they were not there. If white people liked trashy singing like that, there must be something funny about them that I had not noticed before. I stuck to the pretty ones where the words marched to a

throb I could feel.

A month or so after the young ladies returned to Minnesota, they sent me a huge box packed with clothes and books. The red coat with a wide circular collar and the red tam[9] pleased me more than any of the other things. My chums pretended not to like anything that I had, but even then I knew that they were jealous. Old Smarty had gotten by them again. The clothes were not new, but they were very good. I shone like the morning sun.

But the books gave me more pleasure than the clothes. I had never been too keen on dressing up. It called for hard scrubbings with Octagon soap suds getting in my eyes, and none too gentle fingers scrubbing my neck and gouging in my ears.

In that box were *Gulliver's Travels*, *Grimm's Fairy Tales*, *Dick Whittington*, *Greek and Roman Myths*, and best of all, *Norse Tales*. Why did the Norse tales strike so deeply into my soul? I do not know, but they did. I seemed to remember seeing Thor swing his mighty short-handled hammer as he sped across the sky in rumbling thunder, lightning flashing from the tread of his steeds and the wheels of his chariot. The great and good Odin, who went down to the well of knowledge to drink, and was told that the price of a drink from that fountain was an eye. Odin drank deeply, then plucked out one eye without a murmur and handed it to the grizzly keeper, and walked away. That held majesty for me.

Of the Greeks, Hercules moved me most. I followed him eagerly on his tasks. The story of the choice of Hercules as a boy when he met Pleasure and Duty, and put his hand in that of Duty and followed her steep way to the blue hills of fame and glory, which she pointed out at the end, moved me profoundly. I resolved to be like him. The tricks and turns of the other Gods and Goddesses left me cold. There were other thin books about this and that sweet and

---

8. ***Scribner's Magazine***: Literary magazine no longer published.

9. **tam** (tam) *n*.: Cap with a wide, round, flat top and sometimes a center pompom.

◆ **Build Vocabulary**

avarice (av´ ər is) *n*.: Extreme desire for wealth; greed

gentle little girl who gave up her heart to Christ and good works. Almost always they died from it, preaching as they passed. I was utterly indifferent to their deaths. In the first place I could not conceive of death, and in the next place they never had any funerals that amounted to a hill of beans, so I didn't care how soon they rolled up their big, soulful, blue eyes and kicked the bucket. They had no meat on their bones.

But I also met Hans Andersen and Robert Louis Stevenson. They seemed to know what I wanted to hear and said it in a way that tingled me. Just a little below these friends was Rudyard Kipling in his *Jungle Books*. I loved his talking snakes as much as I did the hero.

I came to start reading the Bible through my mother. She gave me a licking one afternoon for repeating something I had overheard a neighbor telling her. She locked me in her room after the whipping, and the Bible was the only thing in there for me to read. I happened to open to the place where David[10] was doing some mighty smiting, and I got interested. David went here and he went there, and no matter where he went, he smote 'em hip and thigh. Then he sung songs to his harp awhile, and went out and smote some more. Not one time did David stop and preach about sins and other things. All David wanted to know from God was who to kill and when. He took care of the other details himself. Never a quiet moment. I liked him a lot. So I read a great deal more in the Bible, hunting for some more active people like David. Except for the beautiful language of Luke and Paul,[11] the New Testament still plays a poor second to the Old Testament for me. The Jews had a God who laid about Him when they needed Him. I could see no use waiting until Judgment Day to see a man who was just crying for a good killing, to be told to go and roast. My idea was to give him a good killing first, and then if he got roasted later on, so much the better.

---

10. **David:** In the Bible, the second king of Israel, the land of the Hebrews.

11. **Luke and Paul:** Two Christian Apostles, who wrote parts of the New Testament.

Guide for Responding

◆ *Literature and Your Life*

Reader's Response What do you think about young Zora's taste in reading? Which, if any, of the stories she read would you like to read?

Thematic Focus How does the town of Zora Neale's youth compare with the community in which you live?

☑ Check Your Comprehension

1. Why does Zora ask for rides from travelers passing by her home?
2. Who are the two white women Zora meets, and why are they at her school?
3. How does Zora command special attention from the women?
4. How does Zora respond to the gifts and attention she receives?

◆ Critical Thinking

INTERPRET

1. What do you learn from Hurston's statement "if the village was singing a chorus, I must have missed the tune"? **[Infer]**
2. (a) Why does Zora find the visitor's hands so fascinating? (b) What does her fascination suggest about her life experiences so far? **[Interpret]**
3. How can you tell that the two visitors from Minnesota made a great impression on Hurston? **[Support]**
4. What do Hurston's taste in reading reveal about her? **[Infer]**

EXTEND

5. How do you think the interests of young Zora Neale helped her succeed at the adult careers of fiction writer and folklorist? **[Career Link]**

Guide for Responding (continued)

◆ Reading Strategy

ANALYZE HOW A WRITER ACHIEVES PURPOSE

With the goal of drawing readers into her particular childhood experiences and showing the vitality of her community, Zora Neale Hurston carefully chooses words, details, characters, and events to craft her autobiography. To **analyze how the writer has achieved her purpose**, there are several issues to consider: how her details reflect her self-assurance, how the main events of the excerpt focus on her abilities, and how she uses words that capture the rural Florida setting.

1. Why does Hurston include the actual words of her grandmother in dialect?
2. How does she use small incidents and details to reveal her reputation as a school smart-aleck?
3. Why might Hurston have included her meeting with the Minnesotans in her autobiography?

◆ Build Vocabulary

USING THE WORD ROOT *-graph-*

The root *-graph-* means "write." On your paper, complete the following sentences using one of these common *-graph-* words:

a. autograph **b.** telegraph **c.** biography **d.** graphic

1. She researched Zora Neale Hurston's life and wrote a ____?____ of the artist.
2. The ____?____ enabled people to transmit messages quickly over long distances.
3. The actor was bombarded by fans seeking his ____?____.
4. A ____?____ organizer helps you visually plan your writing.

USING THE WORD BANK

On your paper, write the letter of the word or phrase that is the best synonym for the first word.

1. exalted: (a) miserable, (b) elated, (c) annoyed
2. avarice: (a) greed, (b) poverty, (c) generosity
3. foreknowledge: (a) ignorance, (b) retrospect, (c) prediction
4. caper: (a) regulation, (b) prank, (c) routine
5. brazenness: (a) shyness, (b) reserve, (c) boldness
6. geography: (a) earth study, (b) sound science, (c) acid rain

◆ Literary Focus

PURPOSE IN AUTOBIOGRAPHY

Zora Neal Hurston had a very specific **purpose in writing her autobiography**: to share her personal experiences and to portray the African American culture of her childhood.

1. (a) What impression of her childhood community does Hurston create? (b) What do you learn about the values that were important to her and to her community?
2. What does this excerpt suggest about Hurston's self-image? Explain.
3. How does Hurston convey the fact that she was comfortable in the presence of people who were not part of her African American community?

◆ Grammar and Style

PARALLELISM IN COORDINATE ELEMENTS

Parallel coordinate elements—those linked by coordinating conjunctions—may be nouns, adjectives, adverbs, clauses, or phrases. When you link grammatical elements of equal rank with a coordinate conjunction, the elements must have parallel grammatical structure.

Practice On your paper, write the following sentences. Circle the coordinate conjunction(s) and underline the parallel coordinate elements.

1. Nevertheless, I kept right on gazing at them, and "going a piece of the way" . . .
2. I did not do this with the permission of my parents, nor with their foreknowledge.
3. Then [David] sung songs to his harp awhile, and went out and smote some more.

Writing Application Rewrite the following sentences, correcting any flaws in parallelism.

1. Zora likes to watch the passing cars and reading mythology.
2. According to her grandmother, Zora shows signs of intelligence, spunk, and being brazen.
3. Zora finds something memorable or to enjoy in every book she reads.

Build Your Portfolio

 Idea Bank

Writing

1. **Autobiographical Episode** Write an autobiographical episode describing how you first developed one of your major interests. Like Hurston, turn the experience into a story.

2. **Eulogy** Suppose you had been at Hurston's funeral. What would you have said about her life? Write a eulogy, drawing on details from the excerpt and the background information.

3. **Opinion Essay** Critics felt Hurston's autobiography ignored issues of racism and inequality. Did she have a responsibility to address these topics? Can *Dust Tracks . . .* be considered effective without them? Take a stand on this issue in an essay.

Speaking and Listening

4. **Campaign Speech** Develop and deliver a speech in which young Zora persuades her classmates to elect her class president. Include details that show Zora's self-image and portray her character. **[Performing Arts Link]**

5. **Interview** Work with a partner to re-create a talk-show interview with Hurston. Prepare questions about her childhood based on the excerpt. Rehearse your questions and answers; then stage the interview for the class. **[Media Link]**

Projects

6. **Reading List** Imagine you are a librarian in young Zora's town. Investigate and recommend literature she might enjoy. Explain your choices.

7. **Folk-Tale Collection** Select three folk tales from Hurston's *Mules and Men* or from another book of folk tales. Compile them in a booklet and include a brief review of each.

 Writing Mini-Lesson

Moment of Inspiration

Hurston's encounter with the Minnesotans was a turning point in her life, leading to a greater love of reading and learning. Write a personal narrative about a moment in your life that inspired you to act or think differently. Emphasize its power by showing, rather than telling about, its impact on you.

Writing Skills Focus: Show, Don't Tell

When you **show instead of tell** how characters feel, look, and behave, readers can easily step into written experiences. For example, if you were inspired by a great athlete, you could *show* yourself planning a new fitness program rather than just recounting your feelings.

Prewriting Complete the journal activity on page 829. Which incidents that you recalled might qualify as "moments of inspiration"? Select one such incident as the focus of your narrative, and explore its impact on your life in a cause-and-effect diagram like this one:

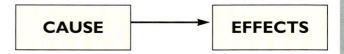

Drafting You might start your essay by showing the effects of your moment of inspiration, then flashing back to reconstruct the moment itself. Use the details in your cause-and-effect diagram to help you.

Revising Reread your narrative to make sure the connection between inspiration and reaction is clear. Have you demonstrated, rather than explained, its impact on your life?

Guide for Interpreting

Langston Hughes *(1902–1967)*

Langston Hughes emerged from the Harlem Renaissance—a cultural movement in the 1920's—as the most prolific and successful African American writer. In his poetry, he expressed pride in his heritage and voiced displeasure with the oppression he saw. Although Hughes is best known for his powerful poetry, he also wrote plays, fiction, autobiographical sketches, and movie screenplays.

Born in Missouri and raised in Kansas, Illinois, and Ohio, Hughes attended high school in Cleveland, where he contributed poetry to the school literary magazine. In 1921, he moved to New York City to attend Columbia University, but a year later he left school to work as a merchant seaman.

On his return to New York, he published his first volume of poetry, *The Weary Blues* (1926). The book attracted attention and earned him wide recognition. Hughes went on to publish several other volumes of poetry, including *The Dream Keeper* (1932), *Fields of Wonder* (1947), and *Montage of a Dream Deferred* (1951). In his poetry, he experimented with a variety of forms and techniques and often tried to re-create the rhythms of contemporary jazz.

Claude McKay *(1890–1948)*

In much of his work, Claude McKay evokes the colors and rhythms of life on his native island of Jamaica. McKay retained a lifelong attachment to Jamaica, although he also regarded Harlem as a spiritual and psychic home, even though he frequently lived elsewhere. Writing to fellow Harlem Renaissance poet Langston Hughes from abroad in 1930, McKay said, "I write of America as home [although] I am really a poet without a country."

Jamaican Roots The son of farm workers, McKay moved to Kingston, the capital of the Caribbean island, when he was fourteen. While living in Kingston, he began writing poetry. When his collection *Songs of Jamaica* (1912) won an award from the Institute of Arts and Letters, he was able to emigrate to the United States.

When McKay moved to Harlem in 1914, he opened a restaurant with a friend. The business failed, but McKay's writing continued to improve. McKay's poem "The Tropics in New York" is marked by a nostalgia for his homeland—a feeling echoed in the title of his autobiography, *A Long Way From Home* (1937).

◆ Background for Understanding

LITERATURE: THE HARLEM RENAISSANCE

During the late 1800's and early 1900's, many southern African Americans moved north, hoping to find opportunities in the northern industrial centers. With this shift in population, the New York City community of Harlem developed into the cultural center for African Americans. There, in the 1920's, a cultural movement known as the Harlem Renaissance was established. The movement encompassed music, art, and literature and included such writers as Countee Cullen, Claude McKay, Langston Hughes, Jean Toomer, Zora Neale Hurston, and Arna Bontemps. The Harlem Renaissance produced such musicians as Duke Ellington, Fats Waller, Ethel Waters, and Bessie Smith. Visual artists active at the same time include James Van Der Zee and Aaron Douglas.

Although Hughes and McKay, like many of the Harlem Renaissance writers, were not born in Harlem and lived a large part of their life somewhere else, they identified Harlem as a source of inspiration and life for African American artists. Harlem was where they felt nourished, where they felt a sense of community.

Refugee in America ◆ Ardella
The Negro Speaks of Rivers ◆ Dream Variations
◆ The Tropics in New York ◆

◆ *Literature and Your Life*

CONNECT YOUR EXPERIENCE

There are many factors that go into shaping each of our identities—the place we come from, the people who surround us, experiences that have touched our lives and those of our ancestors. Think about the things that make you who you are. Then compare them to what you learn about the places and experiences that have shaped these poets' identities.

Journal Writing Describe one place or experience that has had a great impact on you.

THEMATIC FOCUS: FROM EVERY CORNER OF THE LAND

What do these poems reveal about the shared experiences of African Americans with different backgrounds or from different regions of the country?

◆ Build Vocabulary

WORD ROOTS: *-lib-*

In "Refugee in America," Langston Hughes uses the word *liberty* with an uppercase *L*. The root *-lib-* derives from *liber,* the Latin word for "free." Other English words that contain this root include *liberal, liberate, libertarian,* and *ad-lib.*

WORD BANK

Before you read, preview this list of words from the poems.

| liberty |
| lulled |
| dusky |

◆ Grammar and Style

VERB TENSES: PAST AND PRESENT PERFECT

The **past tense** shows an action or condition that occurred at a given time in the past; it is formed without helping verbs. In contrast, the **present perfect tense** shows an action or condition that occurred at an unnamed time in the past—or one that began in the past and continues in the present. This tense is formed with the helping verb *have* or *has* placed before the past participle of the main verb. Langston Hughes uses both tenses in his poem "The Negro Speaks of Rivers":

Past: I *built* my hut near the Congo and it *lulled* me to sleep.
Present Perfect: I've *known* rivers . . .

◆ Literary Focus

SPEAKER

The **speaker** is the voice of a poem. Often the speaker is the poet. However, a speaker may also be an imaginary person, a group of people, an animal, an inanimate thing, or another type of nonhuman entity. In the poem "The Tropics in New York," for example, Claude McKay's speaker is a homesick adult who is probably the poet himself.

◆ Reading Strategy

MAKE INFERENCES ABOUT THE SPEAKER

Most often, a poem's speaker isn't revealed directly. Instead, it's left up to the reader to **make inferences**, or draw conclusions, about the speaker's identity based on the speaker's choice of words and the details included in the poem. For instance, details in the third stanza of "The Negro Speaks of Rivers" help you infer that *I* is not an individual—since a person could not have lived long enough to experience both "the Euphrates when dawns were young" and "the Mississippi when Abe Lincoln went down to New Orleans." Once you've determined the speaker's identity, you can make inferences about the speaker's attitudes, feelings, and experiences.

Refugee in America

Langston Hughes

There are words like *Freedom*
Sweet and wonderful to say.
On my heart-strings freedom sings
All day everyday.

5   There are words like *Liberty*
That almost make me cry.
If you had known what I knew
You would know why.

Ardella

Langston Hughes

I would liken you
To a night without stars
Were it not for your eyes.
I would liken you
5   To a sleep without dreams
Were it not for your songs.

▶ **Critical Viewing** Compare the
woman in this image with the subject
of the poem. [**Compare and Contrast**]

Girl in Blue Dress, 1936, Samuel Joseph Brown, Jr., Metropolitan Museum of Art

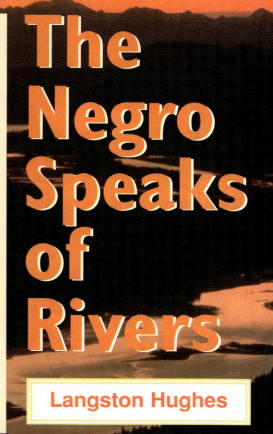

The Negro Speaks of Rivers

Langston Hughes

I've known rivers:
I've known rivers ancient as the world and older than
    the flow of human blood in human veins.

My soul has grown deep like the rivers.

I bathed in the Euphrates when dawns were young.
5 I built my hut near the Congo and it <u>lulled</u> me to sleep.
I looked upon the Nile and raised the pyramids
    above it.
I heard the singing of the Mississippi when Abe
    Lincoln went down to New Orleans, and I've seen
    its muddy bosom turn all golden in the sunset.

I've known rivers:
Ancient, <u>dusky</u> rivers.

10 My soul has grown deep like the rivers.

◆ **Build Vocabulary**

liberty (lib´ ər tē) *n.*: The condition of being free from control by others

lulled (luld) *v.*: Calmed or soothed by a gentle sound or motion

dusky (dus´ kē) *adj.*: Dim; shadowy

Guide for Responding

◆ *Literature and Your Life*

Reader's Response What associations do you have with the places Hughes describes in "The Negro Speaks of Rivers"? What places do you associate with your culture or your ancestry?

Thematic Focus In what sense is place important to the speaker in each of these poems?

List Write a list of words that describe ideas, places, people and things you associate with the word "refugee."

☑ Check Your Comprehension

1. In "Refugee in America," what is the speaker's reaction to words like "freedom"?
2. Identify four rivers the speaker names in "The Negro Speaks of Rivers."

◆ **Critical Thinking**

INTERPRET

1. (a) How does the title "Refugee in America" relate to the poem itself? (b) How would you describe the contrast between this poem's first and second stanzas? **[Interpret; Contrast]**
2. (a) Why does the subject of "Ardella" defy comparison? (b) What is the speaker's feeling toward her? **[Infer]**
3. (a) In "The Negro Speaks of River," what does the age of rivers imply about people of African ancestry? (b) How do lines 3 and 10 reflect the poem's theme? **[Interpret]**

APPLY

4. In what respects can the human race as a whole be compared with rivers? **[Support]**

Dream Variations

Girls Skipping, 1949, Hale Woodruff, Michael Rosenfeld Gallery

▲ **Critical Viewing** How does the motion of the figures in this drawing reflect the mood of the poem? **[Connect]**

Variations

Langston Hughes

To fling my arms wide
In some place of the sun,
To whirl and to dance
Till the white day is done.
5   Then rest at cool evening
Beneath a tall tree
While night comes on gently,
    Dark like me —
That is my dream!

10   To fling my arms wide
In the face of the sun,
Dance! Whirl! Whirl!
Till the quick day is done.
Rest at pale evening . . .
15   A tall, slim tree . . .
Night coming tenderly
    Black like me.

The Tropics in New York

Claude McKay

Bananas ripe and green, and ginger-root,
   Cocoa in pods and alligator pears,
And tangerines and mangoes and grape fruit,
   Fit for the highest prize at parish fairs,

5   Set in the window, bringing memories
   Of fruit-trees laden by low-singing rills,
And dewy dawns, and mystical blue skies
   In benediction over nun-like hills.

My eyes grew dim, and I could no more gaze;
10   A wave of longing through my body swept,
And, hungry for the old, familiar ways
   I turned aside and bowed my head and wept.

Guide for Responding

◆ Literature and Your Life

Reader's Response In "The Tropics in New York," the fruit in the window evokes memories of the poet's birthplace. What objects could evoke memories of your own past in you?

Thematic Focus Is the idea of home always associated with the past?

Journal Writing In "Dream Variations," the speaker describes the way he or she would express the feelings of pure joy. How would you express the same feelings?

☑ Check Your Comprehension

1. In "Dream Variations," what is the speaker's ideal experience?
2. (a) In "The Tropics in New York," what fruits are "set in the window"? (b) What memories do they stir in the speaker? (c) Why does the speaker weep?

◆ Critical Thinking

INTERPRET

1. (a) In "Dream Variations," how would you describe the speaker's daily life? (b) How do you think the speaker feels about his ethnicity? Explain. **[Infer]**
2. How does the title of "The Tropics in New York" contribute to the poem's meaning? **[Interpret]**
3. (a) In "The Tropics in New York," what impression of his homeland does the speaker convey? (b) Which words create especially vivid images? **[Infer; Analyze]**

EVALUATE

4. Do you think the speakers of these poems have a realistic impression of life? Explain. **[Assess]**

APPLY

5. Why do you think people often long for places from their past? **[Speculate]**

Guide for Responding (continued)

◆ Literary Focus

SPEAKER

Each poem has a **speaker,** or voice. The speaker can be the poet, a character, a group of people, or an inanimate or nonhuman entity.

1. How would you describe the speaker of "Refugee in America"?
2. What can you tell about the speaker of "Ardella"?
3. (a) Who is the speaker of "The Negro Speaks of Rivers"? (b) How does the title help to reveal the speaker's identity?
4. How would the effect of "Tropics in New York" be different if it were delivered by an adolescent son or daughter of the speaker?

◆ Reading Strategy

MAKE INFERENCES ABOUT THE SPEAKER

By looking closely at the details in a poem, you can **make inferences** about the speaker's attitudes, feelings, and background. For instance, you can infer from the vivid descriptions of fruits in "The Tropics in New York" that the speaker is intimately familiar with a tropical landscape like Jamaica.

1. What can you infer about the speaker of "Refugee in America" from the plain, straight-forward language in the poem?
2. What can you infer about the speaker of "The Negro Speaks of Rivers" from line 6?

◆ Build Vocabulary

USING THE WORD ROOT -lib-

Several English words contain the Latin root -lib-. Match the following words with their definitions.

1. liberty   a. improvise
2. ad-lib   b. generous
3. liberate   c. freedom
4. liberal   d. release from slavery

USING THE WORD BANK

On your paper, use the words from the word bank to complete the following sentence.

The light, _____?_____ and soft, _____?_____ the prisoner to sleep, and soon he was dreaming once again of his _____?_____.

◆ Grammar and Style

VERB TENSES: PAST AND PRESENT PERFECT

The **present perfect tense** is formed with the helping verb *have* or *has* placed before the past participle of the main verb. The **past tense** requires no helping verbs.

The **past tense** names or describes an action or condition that began and ended at a given time in the past. The **present perfect tense** names or describes an action or condition that occurred at an indefinite past time—or one that began in the past and continues into the present.

Practice Circle the verbs in the following sentences from Hughes's and McKay's poems. Label each verb as past tense or present perfect tense.

1. My soul has grown deep like the rivers.
2. I turned aside and bowed my head and wept.
3. I've known rivers ancient as the world and older than the flow of human blood in human veins.

Beyond Literature

Art Connection

Aaron Douglas and the Harlem Renaissance The Harlem Renaissance was not limited to writers alone. There were also many artists, including Aaron Douglas, who took part in the creative movement. An illustrator best known for his murals, Douglas arrived from the Midwest in the 1920's ready to take part in the artistic explosion of the Harlem Renaissance. By creating works with African themes, Douglas hoped to reunite African Americans with their African heritage. He believed that art was at the heart of life and that it could be a bridge between peoples.

Using encyclopedias and art books, locate some of Aaron Douglas's works. How did his murals contribute to the Harlem Renaissance?

Build Your Portfolio

Idea Bank

Writing

1. **Journal Entry** Langston Hughes's poems are full of rhythmic language. For several days, pay special attention to the rhythms of the speech you hear around you. For example, compare the speech of news reporters with the sound of every day talk. Write your observations in a journal.

2. **Description** Imagine that the speaker of "The Tropics in New York" returns home after twenty years. Tell the story of this visit. Would his former home live up to his memories of it?

3. **Poem** Write a poem in which vivid, memorable images lead your speaker to recall a place that evokes powerful feelings.

Speaking and Listening

4. **Speech** Deliver a political stump speech on the topic of "liberty and freedom." Refer to the themes of Hughes's poem at some point in your speech. **[Performing Arts Link; Social Studies Link]**

5. **Oral Presentation** Explore the history and culture of Jamaica, and make an oral presentation of your findings. If possible, bring in photographs, musical recordings, or objects to help capture Caribbean life. **[Social Studies Link]**

Projects

6. **Posters** Design a series of subway or bus posters to create public awareness of the cultural contributions of African Americans during the 1920's. **[Art Link; Social Studies Link]**

7. **Travel Brochure** Imagine that you are a travel agent booking vacations to Jamaica. Create a travel brochure to attract visitors to the island. **[Art Link; Social Studies Link]**

Writing Mini-Lesson

Profile of an Immigrant Group

Create a profile of an immigrant group providing factual historical information about a group's experience of immigration. Your profile can contain material on immigrants' reasons for moving from one place to another, as well as facts about their activities, interests, lifestyles, challenges, and triumphs in their new home.

Writing Skills Focus: Objective Tone

In order to write a balanced and informative profile, you will need to establish and maintain an **objective tone**—a neutral attitude toward your subject. Consider these suggestions as you write your profile:

- Avoid words that have strong positive or negative connotations.
- Use long, straightforward sentences. They often lend a more serious, objective tone than short sentences do.
- Stick to the facts and steer clear of opinions.

Prewriting Do research on an immigrant group that interests you. Take notes on the conditions in their country of origin, their reasons for leaving, the years of their emigration, and their experiences in their adopted country. Review this material, and decide on an organizational plan for your profile.

Drafting Tell the story of the group's emigration patterns and history, using facts expressed in straightforward, neutral language. When possible, include charts, maps or graphs to help readers see the patterns you are describing.

Revising Carefully review your work with an eye for any biased or unsupported ideas. Also look for places where you can add or delete details to make your paragraphs clearer and more informative.

Guide for Interpreting

Countee Cullen (1903–1946)

Unlike most other poets of his time, Countee Cullen used traditional forms and methods. However, no poet expressed the general sentiments of African Americans during the early 1900's more eloquently than Cullen.

Cullen was born in Louisville, Kentucky. He graduated from New York University and later earned a master's degree from Harvard. His first collection of poetry, *Color*, was published in 1925. This was followed by *Copper Sun* (1927), *The Ballad of the Brown Girl* (1927) and *The Black Christ* (1929). In 1932, he published *One Way to Heaven*, a satirical novel about life in Harlem. During his later years, he published two children's books, *The Lost Zoo* (1940) and *My Lives and How I Lost Them* (1942).

Arna Bontemps (1902–1973)

Arna Bontemps was one of the most scholarly figures of the Harlem Renaissance. After working as a postal worker and a teacher in several religious academies, Bontemps wrote a highly acclaimed novel, *Black Thunder* (1936), about a Virginia slave revolt. In the years that followed, he published poetry, dramas, anthologies, and children's books. He also ran the library at Fisk University in Nashville and transformed it into an important center for African American studies.

Jean Toomer (1894–1967)

Following the appearance of *Cane* (1923)—an unusual book of prose sketches, poems, stories, and a one-act play—Jean Toomer was widely considered among the most talented writers of the Harlem Renaissance. For a few years he published in leading black journals and in the Imagist journal, *The Little Review*. However, Toomer's publishing output dwindled and *Cane* fell into obscurity. As a result, Toomer was virtually forgotten as a writer. In recent years, however, *Cane* has come to be recognized as one of the greatest works of the Harlem Renaissance.

◆ Background for Understanding

LITERATURE: THE HARLEM RENAISSANCE

When Southern African Americans made the move north in the late 1800's and the early 1900's, the population shift made the New York community of Harlem a thriving cultural center. While many southerners moved north in search of industrial jobs, African American culture—art, music, and literature—experienced a huge growth.

The 1920's movement known as the Harlem Renaissance produced literature of many styles. Although the forms and techniques used by Harlem Renaissance writers varied widely, the poets, essayists, novelists, and playwrights shared a common purpose: to create art and literature that reflected the African American experience. At the same time, the Harlem Renaissance writers focused on capturing the general sentiments of the time. In doing so, they expressed their displeasure concerning their overall condition and articulated their cultural heritage.

The Harlem Renaissance helped make the general public aware of African American life. By eloquently chronicling the heritage of African Americans and expressing their pride and determination, Harlem Renaissance writers provided African Americans with a link to their cultural roots and a promise for a better future.

◆ *Literature and Your Life*

CONNECT YOUR EXPERIENCE

When you tell someone how you're feeling at a particular time, you probably make comparisons to familiar activities or events in nature. For example, if you see trouble ahead, you might say that a storm is brewing. In the same way, these poems capture the experiences of the African American people through striking images of activities and events.

Journal Writing In "Storm Ending," Jean Toomer describes a thunderstorm. Write about the types of images you associate with thunderstorms.

THEMATIC FOCUS: FROM EVERY CORNER OF THE LAND

Each of these poems emerged from a specific time and place: Harlem in the 1920's. However, the poems capture experiences shared by African Americans throughout the land.

◆ Build Vocabulary

WORD ROOTS: -cre-

Countee Cullen describes a bountiful harvest as a "golden increment." Like *increase*, *crescendo*, and *create*, the word *increment* contains the root *-cre-* which means "to grow." *Increment* means an "increase or gain." How does the root *-cre-* contribute to its meaning?

increment
countenance
beguile
stark
reaping
glean

WORD BANK

Before you read, preview this list of words from the poems.

◆ Grammar and Style

PLACEMENT OF ADJECTIVES

Ordinarily, **adjectives** precede the noun or pronoun they modify. However, for reasons of style, emphasis, or variety, writers sometimes choose to place adjectives after the words they modify. Look at these examples from "A Black Man Talks of Reaping":

Before Noun: this *stark, lean* year

After Noun: I've scattered *seed enough* to plant the land

Even in poetry, writers take care to place adjectives so that readers do not misunderstand what each word modifies.

◆ Literary Focus

METAPHOR

A **metaphor** is an implied comparison between two seemingly dissimilar things. For example, Countee Cullen compares African American life to the toil of planting.

Although metaphors are often brief, they may also be elaborate, lengthy comparisons. An **extended metaphor** is a comparison that is developed throughout the course of a poem. As you read "Storm Ending," look for the extended metaphor Toomer employs.

◆ Reading Strategy

APPLY HISTORICAL CONTEXT

Many works of literature bear a direct relation to the time and place in which they were written. For this reason, a reader must place such works in their **historical context** in order to understand and appreciate them thoroughly. For example, to fully appreciate the following poems, it is important to recognize that the writers were part of the cultural movement known as the Harlem Renaissance in the 1920's.

Read the Background for Understanding on p. 838 and p. 846. Then apply this information to your reading of these poems.

From the Dark Tower

Countee Cullen *(To Charles S. Johnson)*

▶ **Critical Viewing** What do you think is the message of this image? Do you think Countee Cullen would agree with the artist's interpretation of "aspiration"? **[Assess]**

We shall not always plant while others reap
The golden <u>increment</u> of bursting fruit,
Not always <u>countenance</u>, abject and mute,
That lesser men should hold their brothers cheap;
5 Not everlastingly while others sleep

Shall we beguile their limbs with mellow flute,
Not always bend to some more subtle brute;
We were not made eternally to weep.

The night whose sable breast relieves the stark,
10   White stars is no less lovely being dark,
And there are buds that cannot bloom at all
In light, but crumple, piteous, and fall;
So in the dark we hide the heart that bleeds,
And wait, and tend our agonizing seeds.

◆ **Build Vocabulary**

increment (in´ krə mənt) *n*.: Increase, as in a series
countenance (koun´ tə nəns) *v*.: Approve; tolerate
beguile (bē gīl´) *v*.: Charm or delight

Guide for Responding

◆ *Literature and Your Life*

Reader's Response Can you identify or empathize with the speaker of this poem? Why or why not?

Thematic Focus To which groups of people in today's America can this poem's message be applied? Explain.

Journal Writing In your journal, write a few sentences in which you explore the possible meanings of the title "From the Dark Tower."

☑ Check Your Comprehension

1. (a) According to the speaker, who is "abject and mute"? (b) Who is being tended in lines 5–6?
2. What contrast or opposition does the speaker set up in lines 9–10?

◆ Critical Thinking

INTERPRET

1. (a) Who is the "we" of the poem? (b) What distinction does the speaker draw between the circumstances of "we" and those of "others"? **[Infer; Interpret]**
2. What is the effect of Cullen's repetition of phrases using the word *not* in the first stanza? **[Analyze; Interpret]**
3. How do the ideas in the first and second stanzas differ? **[Compare and Contrast]**
4. What is the poem's theme, or central message? Support your answer. **[Draw Conclusions]**

EVALUATE

5. Do you think the waiting mentioned in the final line is an appropriate response to the conflicts described in the poem? Explain. **[Criticize]**

A Black Man Talks of Reaping

Arna Bontemps

Hoeing, Robert Gwathmey, Carnegie Institute Museum of Art, Pittsburgh, Pennsylvania, © Estate of Robert Gwathmey/Licensed by VAGA, New York, NY

▲ **Critical Viewing** What emotion does the image convey? How does it compare with the mood of the poem? **[Compare and Contrast]**

I have sown beside all waters in my day.
I planted deep, within my heart the fear
that wind or fowl would take the grain away.
I planted safe against this <u>stark</u>, lean year.

5   I scattered seed enough to plant the land
in rows from Canada to Mexico
but for my <u>reaping</u> only what the hand
can hold at once is all that I can show.

Yet what I sowed and what the orchard yields
10   my brother's sons are gathering stalk and root;
small wonder then my children <u>glean</u> in fields
they have not sown, and feed on bitter fruit.

Storm Ending

Jean Toomer

Thunder blossoms gorgeously above our heads,
Great, hollow, bell-like flowers,
Rumbling in the wind,
Stretching clappers to strike our ears . . .
5   Full-lipped flowers
Bitten by the sun
Bleeding rain
Dripping rain like golden honey—
And the sweet earth flying from the thunder.

Guide for Responding

◆ Literature and Your Life

Reader's Response What did you see as you read these poems? What did you hear?

Thematic Focus What statement do you think Bontemps is making about the experience of African Americans in the United States?

☑ Check Your Comprehension

1. In "A Black Man Talks of Reaping," why does the speaker plant "deep"?
2. (a) In "A Black Man Talks of Reaping," how much seed does the speaker scatter? (b) How much grain is he allowed to harvest? (c) Who reaps what the speaker has sown?
3. In "Storm Ending," what natural event does the poem describe?

◆ Critical Thinking

INTERPRET

1. (a) How would you describe the tone of Bontemps's poem? (b) What images or lines illustrate this tone especially vividly? **[Infer, Analyze]**
2. What does Bontemps's poem suggest about what African Americans have received in exchange for their hard work? **[Draw Conclusions]**
3. (a) In "Storm Ending," what is the speaker's attitude toward the event described? (b) How is the attitude conveyed? **[Analyze; Support]**

APPLY

4. A well-known aphorism states, "Whatsoever a man soweth, that shall he also reap." How does Bontemps's poem comment on this idea? **[Apply]**

Guide for Responding (continued)

◆ Reading Strategy

APPLY HISTORICAL CONTEXT

You can enrich your understanding of many literary works by applying their historical context to them as you read. For example, reflecting on the fact that nearly a million blacks migrated to industrial northern cities from rural areas in the South in the late 1800's and early 1900's can help you appreciate Countee Cullen's and Arna Bontemps's use of agricultural metaphors in their work.

1. How can you deepen your appreciation of "From the Dark Tower" by reflecting on the northern migration of nearly a million African Americans in the late 1800's and early 1900's?
2. How can you enrich your reading of "A Black Man Talks of Reaping" by applying historical context?
3. Does your interpretation of "Storm Ending" change when you apply historical context? Explain.

◆ Build Vocabulary

WORD ROOTS: -cre-

Many familiar words include the root -cre- meaning "to grow." Use the words that follow to complete the sentences.

a. crescendo   **b.** creation   **c.** increment

1. The salary schedule indicates the ____?____ employees receive after each year's service.
2. The symphony begins quietly but soon a ____?____ introduces the central celebratory theme.
3. The ____?____ of a new sports pavilion will bring thousands of dollars to the city.

USING THE WORD BANK

On your paper write the letter of the best synonym for each given word.

1. reap: (a) harvest, (b) sow, (c) plow
2. countenance: (a) cheer, (b) tolerate, (c) disregard
3. increment: (a) increase, (b) stability, (c) decrease
4. stark: (a) gentle, (b) steep, (c) severe
5. glean: (a) spread, (b) weigh, (c) collect
6. beguile: (a) delight, (b) annoy, (c) correspond

◆ Literary Focus

METAPHOR

A **metaphor** is an implied comparison between two dissimilar things. An **extended metaphor** develops such a comparison throughout a literary work.

1. (a) What metaphor does Countee Cullen use to evoke the struggle between African Americans and other Americans? (b) What images does he use to extend this metaphor?
2. What metaphor appears in Bontemps's poem?
3. (a) What two things are compared in the extended metaphor presented in "Storm Ending"? (b) How does Toomer establish this comparison in the first four lines? (c) How does he develop it in the lines that follow?

◆ Grammar and Style

PLACEMENT OF ADJECTIVES

Although adjectives usually precede the words they modify, adjectives can sometimes be more effective if they are placed after the modified word.

In "From the Dark Tower," for example, Cullen places the adjectives *abject* and *mute* at the end of the sentence— far from the pronoun *we* they modify.

> An **adjective** can be **placed** before or after the noun or pronoun it modifies.

> We shall . . . /
> Not always countenance, *abject* and *mute*

In this position, adjectives sometimes need to be set off with commas.

Practice On your paper, rewrite the following sentences, altering the position of the italicized adjectives. Be sure that the adjectives modify the same noun in your sentence. Make any necessary changes in wording and punctuation.

1. The *cold, merciless* wind swept through the shack and chilled the woman.
2. The ocean, *vast and cobalt,* was visible through the porthole.
3. Many *penniless but determined* refugees arrived in this country to start anew.

Build Your Portfolio

Idea Bank

Writing

1. List What was it like to live in Harlem during the 1920's among a community of artists? Ask the poets. Generate a list of questions you would ask if you had the opportunity. Then trade lists and try to answer the questions of a classmate.

2. Poem Write a poem in which you present an extended metaphor. Establish the comparison you are making early in the poem, and develop it using a variety of words and images.

3. Essay Although Cullen and Toomer were associated with the same literary movement, each had a distinct style. In an essay, compare and contrast the qualities of Cullen's sonnet and Toomer's lyric.

Speaking and Listening

4. Weather Report Take the part of a meteorologist and create a report providing a scientific explanation of a thunderstorm. In your report, use some of the words and images from Toomer's poem. **[Science Link]**

5. Advertising Campaign Design a series of radio advertisements to create awareness of the cultural contributions of the Harlem Renaissance. Focus each commercial on a writer, artist, or musician from the period. **[Media Link]**

Projects

6. Research Report Choose an artist or musician from the Harlem Renaissance period and research his or her life and accomplishments. Present your findings in a report. **[History Link; Art Link; Music Link]**

7. Painting Use watercolors to create a painting that captures a striking image from one of these poems. **[Art Link]**

Writing Mini-Lesson

Description of Weather Conditions

Jean Toomer used poetry to describe a storm. You can use the same language—strong images and precise words—to describe a storm in prose. Think about the most memorable storm you've encountered and then write a few paragraphs that convey the experience.

Writing Skills Focus: Vivid Verbs

Poetry's conciseness demands careful attention to word choice. Use vivid verbs to describe action and evoke strong, clear images and ideas. Use action verbs instead of linking verbs to make your writing more lively. For example, look at the first line of Jean Toomer's "Storm Ending":

Model From the Poem

Thunder blossoms gorgeously above our heads . . .

The line could have read, "Thunder sounds gorgeous above our heads. " However, since Toomer chose the vivid "blossoms" instead, the image of the storm is richer.

Prewriting Take a minute to imagine the storm you will describe. Consider the mood your essay will convey. It may help to personify the storm in your mind. It may be violent and dangerous, or it may be calm and reserved. Make a list of words to bring this mood across to your readers.

Drafting As you write your essay, choose precise words that communicate exactly what is happening. Include sensory details—sounds, smells, sights, textures, or tastes—that make your writing more vivid.

Revising Look for vague words to replace with more precise ones. Make sure your essay provides enough detail to bring the storm to life.

CONNECTIONS TO TODAY'S WORLD

i yearn
Ricardo Sánchez

Thematic Connection

FROM EVERY CORNER OF THE LAND

American writers in the first half of the twentieth century celebrated the nation's diversity by focusing on the environments from which they came. A writer's world may be defined by a geographic area, such as Robert Frost's New England, or by ethnic or racial connections, such as the African American identity celebrated in the Harlem Renaissance.

Historians used to describe the United States as a "melting pot" to suggest that people of different ethnic backgrounds came to the United States and blended into a single American culture. Today, many Americans argue that the "melting pot" metaphor is not accurate. They say that the United States is a multicultural society in which many distinct cultures exist side by side, retaining their individual identities. New phrases that describe the country's diversity call the United States a quilt, a rainbow, a salad bowl, or a mosaic.

In today's United States, ethnic communities nurture their own cultures and traditions while at the same time holding many distinctly American beliefs, such as freedom and equality. Just a few examples of such communities are the Chinatowns in New York and San Francisco, Arab communities in Michigan, and Scandinavian communities in the Midwest.

WRITERS CELEBRATE DIFFERENCES

Today's writers continue to explore the many ways of being an American. Hispanic Americans are growing in numbers and becoming increasingly vocal. Between 1980 and 1990, there was a 44 percent increase in the number of Hispanics living in the United States, and experts predict that by the middle of the twenty-first century, 21 percent of the U.S. population will be people of Spanish-speaking origin. Hispanic novelists, playwrights, and poets such as Ricardo Sánchez reflect on the ways in which their Hispanic roots intersect with U.S. culture to create new influences and identities.

RICARDO SÁNCHEZ (1941–1995)

Born in El Paso, Texas, and raised in a *barrio,* or Hispanic neighborhood, Ricardo Sánchez believed that his mission was to bring Mexican culture and traditions into the lives of his fellow Chicanos (Mexican Americans). He often wrote about the challenge faced by Chicanos who try to create a coherent identity from a mix of two cultures: Mexican and American.

Sánchez was an activist as well as a writer and academic: He directed a health project for migrant workers, sat on the board of an El Paso health clinic, and founded a number of organizations for Chicanos. As a lecturer, consultant, and developer of television programs as well as a poet, Sánchez worked to educate all Americans about Chicano culture.

i yearn

Ricardo Sánchez

i yearn this morning
what i've yearned
since i left

    almost a year ago . . .

5   it is hollow
this
being away
from everyday life
in the barrios[1]
10 of my homeland . . .
all those cities
like el paso, los angeles,
albuquerque,
denver, san antonio
15   (off into chicano
       infinitum[2]!);

1. **barrios** (bär´ ē ōs) *n.*: Spanish-speaking neighborhood.

2. **infinitum** (in´ fə nīt´ əm) *n.*: Latin for "that which is endless."

i yearn
to hear spanish
spoken in caló[3]—
20 that special way
chicanos[4] roll their
    tongues
to form
words
25 which dart or glide;

i yearn
for foods
that have character
and strength—the kind
30 that assail yet caress
you with the zest of life;

more than anything,
i yearn, my people,
for the warmth of you
35 greeting me with "¿qué tal,
hermano?"[5]
and the knowing that you
    mean it
when you tell me that you love
40 the fact that we exist . . .

3. **caló** (kä lō´) *n.*: Slang.
4. **chicanos** (chē kä´ nōs) *n.*: Mexican Americans, usually capitalized.

5. **¿qué tal, hermano?** (kā täl´ er mä´ nō): Spanish for "How are things, brother?"

Guide for Responding

◆ Literature and Your Life

Reader's Response The speaker describes a feeling of homesickness. What objects or experiences do you miss when you are away from home?

Thematic Focus Language and culture can bring people together or create a wall between them. What are the difficulties of a multicultural society? What are the benefits?

☑ Check Your Comprehension

1. List three things the speaker misses about his home.
2. What does the speaker miss most of all?

◆ Critical Thinking

INTERPRET
1. What is the poem's tone, or attitude? **[Interpret]**
2. What experiences make the speaker feel as he does? **[Infer]**
3. What do the cities mentioned in the poem have in common? **[Connect]**
4. What does the speaker suggest about the environment where he is currently living? **[Compare and Contrast]**

APPLY
5. What does this poem suggest about why people sometimes feel the need to be among others who share a similar background? **[Generalize]**

Thematic Connection

FROM EVERY CORNER OF THE LAND

Successive waves of immigrants have made the United States a nation of enormous diversity. Although the immigration wave of the early 1900's mostly brought new citizens from both Eastern and Western Europe, many of today's immigrants arrive from Asia and Central and South America.

Spanish-speaking immigrants live in many states; notably large numbers inhabit California, New York, New Mexico, and Florida. As of 1990, nearly four-and-a-half million Americans were born in Mexico, the country from which Ricardo Sánchez's ancestors came.

For nearly all immigrant groups, the process of becoming an American may be difficult. During this period of transition, immigrants may savor the opportunities that America offers while they simultaneously miss their country of birth and feel that their identity is threatened.

1. What does Ricardo Sánchez mean when he refers to his "homeland"?

2. What aspects of life does Sánchez particularly associate with his Chicano roots?

3. To whom is Sánchez referring when he says, "my people"?

Idea Bank

Writing

1. **Dear Ricardo** Write a letter to Ricardo Sánchez, offering him moral support and urging him to concentrate on the positive aspects of being away from home.

2. **You Yearn** Write your own poem about the things you would yearn for if you were away from home for a year. Concentrate on the distinctive features of your community that you most enjoy. **[Social Studies Link]**

3. **Literary Analysis** Analyze the way in which "i yearn" begins as a poem with a negative mood and ends in a mood of celebration. Support your points with details and passages from the poem.

Speaking and Listening

4. **Interview** Interview friends, relatives, or others in the community to learn about the ethnic or regional foods they most enjoy. Ask questions to discover what images or associations people have with these foods. Record your interviews, and share highlights with the class. **[Community Link]**

Projects

5. **Graph** Using the census or other government documents, locate statistics about the immigration of a particular group to the United States. Graph the rise and fall over a set number of years. **[Math Link; Social Studies Link]**

Writing Process Workshop

The writers of the modern era often intentionally obscured the meaning or outcome of their literary works, leaving readers to draw their own conclusions. In a statistical report, however, the writer presents numerical data, interprets them, then draws conclusions for the reader. Although the subjects of statistical reports are diverse, they share a common characteristic: They use numbers to support a thesis, or main idea. These reports often include tables, charts, and graphs, as well as written text.

The following skills, introduced in this section's Writing Mini-Lessons, will help you write a statistical report.

Writing Skills Focus

► **Use precise details,** including numerical data, to thoroughly support your thesis. (See p. 773.)

► **Define a clear and consistent purpose.** Decide on what you want your audience to learn, and focus your writing to achieve that purpose.

► **Maintain an objective tone.** Avoid argumentative, judgmental, or overly emotional language. (See p. 845.)

► **Elaborate on your main points** using a variety of methods, including charts and graphs. (See p. 801.)

MODEL FROM LITERATURE

Excerpt from "Most Immigrants Find the Dream"
by Brad Edmondson

In 1996, 9.3 percent of the U.S. population was foreign-born, according to the Census Bureau's Current Population Survey. Urban neighborhoods are crowded with Mexican, Chinese, Russian, and Filipino immigrants. ① Native-born Americans are revisiting concerns of the early 20th century. ② But there is strong evidence that today's immigrants will join the middle class just as the children of 1910 immigrants did. ③ The 1995 median income of foreign-born Americans who entered the U.S. in the 1970's ($17,400) is nearly equal to the national median for all persons with income ($17,500). Among naturalized citizens, median personal income is even higher than average ($18,500). ④

① The author names specific examples of nationalities of immigrants.

② Notice the writer's objective tone.

③ Here, the writer presents his thesis.

④ Statistics support the author's thesis.

Prewriting

Choose a Topic Begin by considering statistics associated with areas of interest to you, such as sports, politics, or music. You might also scan newspaper articles to find other possible topics. Another option is to base your report on one of the following:

> ## Topic Ideas
> - World War I
> - The World Series
> - Population trends
> - A career that interests you

Determine Your Purpose Use a K-W-L chart like the following example to define your purpose:

KNOW:	WANT to COVER:	LEARN:
a little about local charities	the giving habits of the citizens of this community	who gives money to charities in our community, and how much they give

Gather Data There are many sources for statistical data, including reference books on specific topics, such as *The Baseball Encyclopedia*. Almanacs, vertical files, and journals or magazines may also contain statistics.

Write a Thesis Statement Once you've gathered your data, look for one idea or conclusion that can be supported by the majority of the statistics you have found. Summarize this idea in a sentence in your opening paragraph.

Drafting

Cite Relevant Data Use only examples or statistics that directly relate to your thesis. Don't hesitate to return to the library for additional supporting data. Where appropriate, include charts or graphs. Introduce and explain each one you present.

Avoid Argumentative Language Don't inject your personal viewpoint; your thesis should be backed by facts and statistics. Note the differences between these examples:

▶ **Argumentative:** Only a fool could ignore the warnings about the cancer-causing effects of the sun.

▶ **Research-based:** People who want to stay healthy should protect themselves from the sun. An estimated 90 percent of skin cancers are caused by exposure to sunlight.

APPLYING LANGUAGE SKILLS: Semicolons

Use **semicolons** to join clauses that are not already joined by a conjunction or to avoid confusion when independent clauses or items in a series already contain commas.

Examples:

Cornelia was dutiful; that was the trouble with her.

Zora learned much from her mother, who taught her to save; her teachers, who taught her to read; and the young ladies, who fostered her love for reading.

Practice Rewrite the following sentences, correcting or clarifying each with semicolons:

1. Countee Cullen graduated from New York University, he later earned a master's degree from Harvard.
2. It was a challenging assignment; I had to do research, which took hours, interview the county council members, and create my own charts.

Writer's Solution Connection
Language Lab

For more practice with semicolons, see the Quotation Marks, Colons, and Semicolons lesson in the Capitalization and Punctuation unit of the Language Lab CD-ROM.

Applying LANGUAGE SKILLS: Accuracy of Charts and Graphs

Use these tips to ensure that the data in your charts and graphs are clear and accurate:

- Write labels and provide a legend for a chart or graph and its data.
- Be sure that percentages add up to 100; explain any discrepancies.
- Be consistent in labeling information (hours, minutes, seconds, and so on).
- Carefully copy the data when transferring them from one type of graph to another.

Writing Application Wherever possible, use charts and graphs to report numerical data in your statistical report. A chart conveys information that might take paragraphs to present in writing. A graph can highlight changes over a period of time. These visual aids will lend impact and clarity to your report.

Writer's Solution Connection Writing Lab

For help gathering statistical data, use the instruction in the Gathering Information section of the tutorial on Research Writing.

Revising

Review the Numbers It is easy to make typographical errors. To be sure the numbers in your report are accurate, check your statistics against your original source.

Use a Revision Checklist Use your answers to these questions, which are based on this lesson's focus points, to help you improve your statistical analysis:

- ▶ Does my introduction clearly state my purpose and present the thesis developed in the body of my report?
- ▶ Have I included enough specific examples, numerical data, and charts and graphs to support my thesis?
- ▶ Do I need to delete any examples or data that don't relate directly to my argument or thesis?
- ▶ Have I avoided argumentative, threatening, or judgmental language?

REVISION MODEL

~~Through the insensitivity of cigarette smokers, many~~ ①

~~Americans face serious health risks.~~ ① Environmental

tobacco smoke (ETS) represents a serious threat to public

② *Conditions such as aggravated asthma, impaired blood circulation, bronchitis, and pneumonia can be linked to ETS.*

health in the United States. ∧ The American Cancer Society

③ *3,000*

reports that ~~thousands of~~ people will die each year as a ∧

result of breathing the smoke of other people's cigarettes.

~~In the 1980's there were over 4.5 million cancer deaths.~~ ④

① The author deletes an argumentative and unnecessary sentence.
② Specific examples are added.
③ Numerical data is added to replace a vague reference.
④ The author deletes an irrelevant statement.

Publishing

- ▶ **Presentation** Share your report with an interested audience—your classmates or family members and friends. Add visual aids, and allow time for questions.

Real-World Reading Skills Workshop

Strategies for Success

As you read or view news and feature stories or search for numerical data on prices, you'll find that information is often presented in graph form. Graphs enable you to compare several pieces of related factual data quickly and easily. Follow these guidelines for reading graphs, and you'll see that it's easy to analyze information that's presented in a visual form.

Identify the Graph Topic Determine the content of the graph by looking at its title, captions, and labels. In what article or format does it appear? How is it explained in the accompanying text? Knowing the graph's context will help you decipher its content.

Study the Elements Begin by identifying the type of graph—bar, line, or pie.

▶ Note the labels and units of measurement on both the vertical and horizontal axes.

▶ Check for a key, and relate its data to the graph.

▶ Determine how many items are illustrated on the graph.

Read the Graph Starting at the farthest left edge of the graph, locate the first line point or bar on the graph. Trace your finger downward to the horizontal axis to determine what the bar or point represents. Then trace from the line point or top of the bar across to the vertical axis and find the corresponding unit of measurement. Repeat this process as you proceed across the line or series of bars. To quickly determine the largest and smallest values represented, locate the highest and lowest bars or points on the graph.

Apply the Strategy

You're on the planning committee for next year's senior trip from New York to a foreign country. To help determine options, you've been asked to evaluate costs using this graph from a recent travel news article.

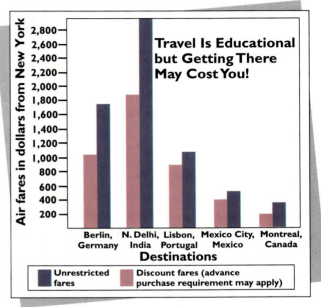

1. What is the graph's title? What are the axis headings?
2. What does the graph's key tell you?
3. Which location will be the least expensive to visit? The most expensive?
4. Which two locations can be visited for about $400? Which two for about $1,000? What are the conditions of each of these travel plans?
5. What can you conclude about the value of buying airline tickets well in advance?

✔ *Here are situations in which using these strategies for reading a graph may be useful:*

▶ Reading newspapers and magazines
▶ Conducting research
▶ Comparing sports statistics

Speaking and Listening Workshop

The news bombards you every time you turn on the television—special reports interrupt regular programming, news magazines air on a nightly basis, and some stations broadcast news twenty-four hours a day. Before taking actions or developing views, it's important to evaluate what you see on news reports.

Remember the Purpose Identify the goal of the news report. Straightforward news reports are meant to recount objective information. Other reports, called feature stories, offer in-depth exploration and description of a topic. Editorials present persuasive views. Knowing what you are viewing will help you focus your analysis.

Consider the Source Let's face it: Some journalists or news sources are better at their jobs than others. Evaluate the journalist's experience, especially with the story topic. Think about the news program—what is its reputation for accuracy and objectivity?

✔ Tips for Critically Viewing News Reports

▶ Listen carefully to the information reported.

▶ Check surprising or questionable news in other sources.

▶ Note the "experts" interviewed or quoted, and consider their qualifications to comment authoritatively on the topic.

▶ Speak with parents or other adults about any news report you find disturbing or confusing.

▶ Be aware that not every news report is objective; consider whether the journalist is sensationalizing the news or focusing on only one side of a two-sided story or issue.

▶ Develop your own views about the issues, people, and information reported in the news.

▶ View the complete report before taking any action or reaching a conclusion.

Apply the Strategies

Complete at least one of these activities to gain experience in viewing news reports critically.

1. As a class, view a daytime news report. Analyze each story, identifying its purpose and evaluating its sources.

2. Contribute to a chalkboard list of recently viewed news reports. In groups, discuss several of the reports, exploring group members' reactions to the issues and information presented. Was the report thorough, accurate, and objective?

3. View local and national news reports from several different news sources. Rate the reports, using the criteria above. Explain your final ratings in an oral presentation.

Extended Reading Opportunities

The early twentieth century is a study in contrasts—optimism and cynicism, frivolity and desperation. The literature of the period, including these suggested works, reveals the many faces of a country forever changed by war.

Suggested Titles

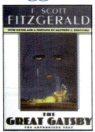

The Great Gatsby
F. Scott Fitzgerald

The Great Gatsby is the quintessential Jazz Age novel; in it, you'll find all of the glamour, decadence, and emptiness that characterized the era. This tragic tale of broken dreams and ruined lives explores self-made millionaire Jay Gatsby's quest to win the love of the wealthy, beautiful—and married—Daisy Buchanan. Fitzgerald, who lived the life portrayed in his novels, gives us an inside look at the world of the idle rich.

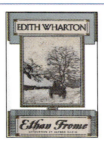

Ethan Frome
Edith Wharton

A terrible twist of events lies at the heart of this bittersweet tale of a forbidden and ill-fated love. The setting—wintry, rural New England—is a departure for author Edith Wharton, whose novels and short stories are more often set against the backdrop of society life. The painful irony that brings the plot full circle results in a story that will haunt you long after you've read the last page.

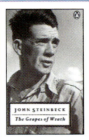

The Grapes of Wrath
John Steinbeck

This powerfully moving book recounts one family's journey from the Oklahoma Dust Bowl in search of a better life in California's "promised land." Set in the depths of the Great Depression, it is a harsh yet uplifting tale of the strength of the human spirit in the face of adversity and injustice. The novel won a Pulitzer Prize and established John Steinbeck as one of the greatest authors of his day.

Other Possibilities

The Glass Menagerie	Tennessee Williams
Winesburg, Ohio	Sherwood Anderson
The Invisible Man	Ralph Ellison
Our Town	Thornton Wilder

Telephones (detail), 1954, Colleen Browning, Butler Institute of American Art

UNIT 6

Prosperity and *Protest* *(1946–Present)*

"Sometimes I can see the future stretched out in front of me—just as plain as day. The future hanging over there at the edge of my days. Just waiting for me."

—Lorraine Hansberry

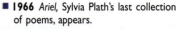

Timeline
1945 — Present

1945   **1955**   **1965**

American Events

- **1945** United States grants independence to the Philippines.
- **1946** Carson McCullers publishes *The Member of the Wedding.*
- **1949** *Death of a Salesman* by Arthur Miller is first produced.
- **1950** President Harry S. Truman sends troops to South Korea after North Korean invasion.
- **1952** Ralph Ellison publishes *Invisible Man.* ▼
- **1954** Supreme Court rules public school segregation to be unconstitutional.

- **1955** Flannery O'Connor publishes *A Good Man Is Hard to Find.* ◀
- **1959** Alaska and Hawaii admitted to the Union as the 49th and 50th states.
- **1959** Robert Lowell's *Life Studies* appears.
- **1960** John Updike publishes *Rabbit Run.*
- **1961** Joseph Heller publishes *Catch-22.*
- **1962** Environmental protection movement spurred by Rachel Carson's book *Silent Spring.*
- **1963** President John F. Kennedy assassinated in Dallas.

- **1966** *Ariel,* Sylvia Plath's last collection of poems, appears.
- **1968** Martin Luther King, Jr., civil rights leader, murdered in Memphis.

- **1969** Astronaut Neil Armstrong becomes the first person to set foot on the moon. ▲
- **1969** Joyce Carol Oates publishes *Them.*
- **1972** Last U.S. combat troops leave Vietnam; peace pact signed in 1973. ▲
- **1974** President Richard M. Nixon resigns. ▼

World Events

- **1947** India-Pakistan: India and Pakistan granted independence from Great Britain.
- **1948** Israel: United Nations establishes state of Israel.
- **1948** Germany: Soviet Union blockades Allied sectors of Berlin.
- **1950** England: Doris Lessing publishes *The Grass Is Singing.*
- **1954** England: *Lord of the Flies* by William Golding appears.

- **1955** Argentina: Jorge Luis Borges publishes *Extraordinary Tales.*
- **1957** Ghana: Ghana emerges as independent nation.
- **1957** USSR: *Doctor Zhivago* by Boris Pasternak appears.
- **1959** Cuba: Fidel Castro comes to power. ▲
- **1959** Germany: East Germany builds Berlin Wall.
- **1962** USSR: *One Day in the Life of Ivan Denisovich* by Alexander Solzhenitsyn appears.

- **1967** Israel: Israel gains territory from Arab states in Six-Day War.
- **1967** South Africa: Dr. Christiaan Barnard performs first human heart transplant.
- **1969** Northern Ireland: Long period of violence begins between Catholics and Protestants.

- **1972** China: Nixon makes historic visit to China. ◀
- **1972** Mexico: Octavio Paz publishes *The Other Mexico.*
- **1973** Middle East: Embargo on Middle East oil produces world shortages.

1975 | **1985** | **1995**

American Events

■ **1979** Militant Iranian students take more than 50 Americans hostage in Teheran.

■ **1980** Ronald Reagan elected president.

■ **1982** Vietnam Veterans Memorial dedicated in Washington, D.C. ◀

■ **1982** Alice Walker publishes *The Color Purple.*

■ **1983** Sally Ride becomes the first American woman to travel in space.

■ **1986** Compact discs (CDs) account for 10% of album sales in the United States.

■ **1986** Space shuttle *Challenger* explodes after launch from Cape Canaveral.

■ **1987** President Reagan and Soviet leader Mikhail Gorbachev sign the INF treaty, agreeing to ban short-range and medium-range nuclear missiles. ▲

■ **1988** George Bush elected president.

■ **1990** Carol Moseley Braun becomes the first African American woman elected to the Senate.

■ **1990** Congress passes the Americans With Disabilities Act, prohibiting discrimination against people with disabilities. ▶

■ **1992** Bill Clinton elected president.

■ **1993** Toni Morrison wins Nobel Prize for Literature.

■ **1993** Congress passes the North American Free Trade Agreement.

■ **1995** Amy Tan publishes her third novel, *The Kitchen God's Wife.*

■ **1996** Summer Olympic Games held in Atlanta, Georgia.

■ **1997** Frank McCourt's autobiography *Angela's Ashes* wins Pulitzer Prize.

■ **1997** Pathfinder mission and lander/rover Sojourner reach Mars; photographs of planet's landscape sent back to Earth.

■ **1997** Congress passes a law allowing the line item veto. President Clinton is the first president to exercise the power.

World Events

■ **1979** India: Mother Teresa wins Nobel Prize for Peace.

■ **1979** Vietnam: Hundreds of thousands of "boat people" flee Vietnam.

■ **1979** Trinidad: V. S. Naipaul publishes *A Bend in the River.*

■ **1979** England: Margaret Thatcher becomes British prime minister.

■ **1981** Poland: Polish trade union movement, Solidarity, suppressed.

■ **1986** USSR: Chernobyl nuclear disaster spreads radioactive cloud across Eastern Europe.

■ **1989** Eastern Europe: Berlin Wall comes down.

■ **1989** China: Pro-democracy demonstrations violently suppressed at Tiananmen Square.

■ **1991** Middle East: Unified forces led by U.S. defeat Iraq in Persian Gulf War.

■ **1992** Russia: Boris Yeltsin is elected president.

■ **1993** Middle East: Israel and the PLO sign an unprecedented peace agreement.

■ **1994** South Africa: Nelson Mandela becomes the first democratically elected president. ▲

■ **1997** China: Hong Kong returns to Chinese rule, ending 155 years of British rule. ▼

The Story of the Times

1946 – Present

Looking to the future is a natural part of the human experience. Much of the technology that has become widespread since 1945—television and computers in particular—shows us a brighter future. The new technology does make life easier and more pleasant. Paradoxically, it also introduces complexities that were unknown in earlier days.

The years from the end of World War II to the present day have been a time of change. Great strides have been made in civil rights and women's rights. Popular entertainment has changed dramatically, not just in presentation (from radio to television, from phonographs to CDs) but also in style (from big bands to rock music). These changes and others have had an effect on American literature. Their effect seems somehow less dramatic than the changes themselves, however.

Historical Background

The United States emerged from World War II as the most powerful nation on Earth. Proud of their role in the Allied victory, Americans now wanted life to return to normal. Soldiers came home, the rationing of scarce goods ended, and the nation prospered. Despite postwar jubilation, however, the dawn of the nuclear age and the ominous actions of the Soviet Union, including the establishment of dominance throughout Eastern Europe, meant that nothing would be the same again.

In 1945, the United Nations was created amid high hopes that it would prevent future wars. Nonetheless, a Cold War between the Soviet Union and the West began as soon as World War II ended. It was in Asia, however, that the first armed conflict came. In 1950, President Harry S. Truman sent American troops to help anti-Communist South Korean forces turn back a North Korean invasion.

JACKIE ROBINSON 3b of BROOKLYN DODGERS

▲ **Analyze Cause and Effect** Astonishing as it may seem today, African Americans could not play baseball in the major leagues until Jackie Robinson broke the color barrier in 1947. How might Robinson have paved the way for African Americans in other sports and other occupations?

▲ **Contrast** Automobiles like this 1958 Oldsmobile would change a great deal about the United States. The Interstate Highway Act of 1956, for example, set plans in motion for a 41,000-mile national network of roadways. What benefits do highways provide commuters that local roads do not?

From Quiet Pride to Activism Americans of the 1950's are sometimes referred to as "the Silent Generation." Many of them had lived through both the Great Depression and World War II. When peace finally arrived, they were glad to adopt a quiet, somewhat complacent attitude. They greatly admired President Dwight D. Eisenhower, one of America's wartime heroes.

Near the end of the 1950's, the Soviet Union launched *Sputnik*, the first artificial satellite to orbit the Earth. This Soviet space triumph spurred many people to call for changes in American science and education. President John F. Kennedy, elected in 1960, promised to "get the nation moving again." He had little time to do so, however, before his tragic assassination in 1963.

Kennedy's assassination was followed by an escalating and increasingly unpopular war in Vietnam. A wave of protest followed. Gone were the calm of the Eisenhower years and the high hopes of Kennedy's brief administration. In their place came idealistic but strident demands for rapid change: greater "relevance" in education, more progress on civil rights, an immediate end to the Vietnam War. It was a time of crisis and confrontations.

Real and lasting gains were made in civil rights after World War II. Segregation in the public schools was outlawed by the Supreme Court in 1954. Tragedy struck in 1968, however, when civil rights leader Martin Luther King, Jr., was assassinated in Memphis, Tennessee. Riots broke out in many cities across the nation. **A Quest for Stability** The upheavals of the 1960's brought a conservative reaction. Many Americans longed for a return to "the good old days." President Richard M. Nixon, elected in 1968, promised to end the Vietnam War and to restore order in the nation. Nixon's achievements were soon overshadowed by the Watergate affair. This scandal forced his resignation from the presidency in 1974.

Civil rights activism continued during the 1970's, and another movement attracted growing

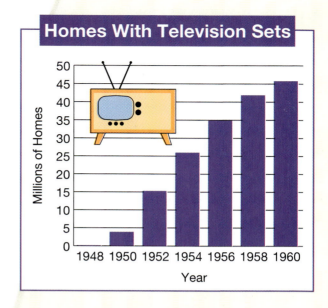

Homes With Television Sets

Bar graph: Millions of Homes (vertical axis, 0 to 50) versus Year (horizontal axis, 1948–1960)

▲ **Draw a Conclusion** Before 1950, television was a novelty. By the end of the decade, however, television sets were a common feature in American homes. What factors might have influenced the steady rise in television ownership?

▲ **Make a Connection** The Beatles—an enormously successful British rock band—took over the American music scene in 1964. They created a sensation wherever they appeared. What role does television play in creating celebrities?

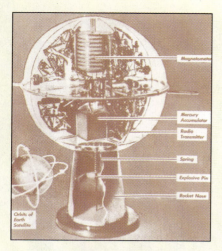

▲ **Analyze Cause and Effect**
On October 5, 1957, the Soviet Union launched the world's first artificial satellite. The satellite, called *Sputnik I*, orbited the Earth once every hour and 35 minutes. The following year, the Congress National Defense Education Act of 1958 was passed, endorsing reforms in education. Why would the Soviet Union's success lead to changes in science and math education in American schools?

▲ **Make an Inference** The American Indian Movement (AIM) was formed in 1968 to address Native American rights. One goal of Native American activists has been to force the federal government to honor treaties made in the 1800's. In this photograph, AIM leader Dennis Banks leads a protest at Mount Rushmore, South Dakota. Why were so many treaties made and then broken?

attention—the women's liberation movement. Although women had earned the right to vote in 1920, discrimination still existed. Women received lower pay than men did for the same jobs, and promotion was more difficult. Betty Friedan's *The Feminine Mystique,* published in 1963, called for change. The women's movement grew steadily through the 1970's.

After Jimmy Carter's one-term presidency, the nation sent Ronald Reagan to the White House. A former film star and governor of California, Reagan proved to be a popular and persuasive president. His reelection in 1984 was one of the biggest landslide victories in American history. In 1988, George Bush, Reagan's vice president, was elected to the presidency. Seeking reelection in 1992, Bush faced a tough fight against high unemployment, a recession, growing dissatisfaction with government, and his youthful opponent. Democrats Bill Clinton and Al Gore, the youngest ticket in American history, won the election. Despite the 1994 elections that voted many Democratic Congress members out of office, Clinton won reelection in 1996.

The Changing Scene Commercial television was still in its infancy at the end of World War II, but it was on the verge of spectacular growth. Over the next few years, television changed the leisure habits of Americans.

The postwar period was a time of explosive suburban growth, made possible by the automobile. At first, most suburban homeowners worked in the nearby city and commuted to their jobs by train, bus, or car. Then, major corporations began establishing suburban headquarters, and workers could live nearby or commute short distances from one suburb to another. Even more recently, advanced technology allows people to "telecommute"—working in home offices and staying connected by Internet, phone, and fax.

The world has changed dramatically since 1945, and it is still changing. These changes have had an impact on the literature of the time, although this impact has not always been obvious.

Literature of the Period

Variety and Promise The turbulence of contemporary times has not fostered a literary revolution of the kind that occurred in the 1920's, yet it has contributed to the development of a variety of literary movements that are often collectively referred to as Postmodernism. While many writers have been content to build on the experiments of the Modernists, others have sought to create works that stand apart from the past. Some writers have explored new literary forms and techniques, composing works from dialogue alone, creating works that blend fiction and nonfiction, and/or experimenting with the physical appearance of their work. Other writers have focused on capturing the essence of contemporary life in the content of their works, often expressing themes concerning the impersonal and commercial nature of today's world.

Authors for a New Era Although contemporary writers have produced a wide variety of impressive works, it is all but impossible to predict which writers will achieve lasting fame and which will not. Time is needed to certify greatness. Modern readers and critics have their favorites, of course. Some of them will undoubtedly become part of America's enduring literary legacy.

Every writer owes a debt to those writers who have gone before. In that sense, literature is cumulative. The earliest American literature, except for that of the Native Americans, was based on European models. Writers in the United States today can look to a rich heritage of their own. Contemporary novelists are well aware of Nathaniel Hawthorne, Mark Twain, Ernest Hemingway, and William Faulkner. Short-story writers know Edgar Allan Poe, Willa Cather, and Eudora Welty. Poets study Emily Dickinson, Walt Whitman, and Langston Hughes. Playwrights are familiar with Eugene O'Neill and Thornton Wilder.

Contemporary novelists of stature include Carson McCullers, Norman Mailer, Bernard Malamud, John Updike, Flannery O'Connor, Joyce Carol Oates, Anne Tyler, and Alice Walker. Many of these novelists have written short stories as well. Flannery O'Connor and John Updike are modern masters of the short-story form. Other writers, such as Donald Barthelme and Ann Beattie, have written novels but are better known for their short stories. Isaac Bashevis Singer, a Polish-born New Yorker who

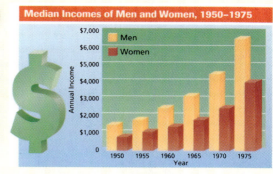

▲ **Interpret a Graph** Between 1950 and 1975, women's incomes continued to lag behind men's earnings, partly because many low-paying fields such as nursing and teaching were traditionally considered "women's work." Did the gap increase or decrease between 1950 and 1975?

▲ **Make an Inference** In May 1973, Senate committee hearings nearly a year after a break-in at Democratic party headquarters revealed that Nixon and several close advisors had been involved in trying to cover up the truth about the burglary. How would such an incident shake the public's faith in government?

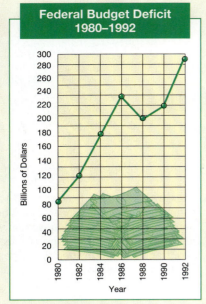

Federal Budget Deficit 1980–1992

Billions of Dollars (y-axis: 0, 20, 40, 60, 80, 100, 120, 140, 160, 180, 200, 220, 240, 260, 280, 300)

Year (x-axis: 1980, 1982, 1984, 1986, 1988, 1990, 1992)

▲ **Interpret a Graph** The rapidly growing federal budget deficit worried many Americans in the 1980's and early 1990's. (a) What was the budget deficit in 1980? (b) During which two-year period did the deficit decrease?

▲ **Draw a Conclusion** The creation of Israel in 1948 led to tension between Israel and surrounding Arab states. In 1993, Israel and the PLO stunned the world by signing a peace agreement. Here, President Clinton watches as Israeli prime minister Yitzhak Rabin shakes hands with PLO leader Yasir Arafat. Considering the Middle East's large supplies of oil as well as other factors, why do you think the United States maintains an interest in peace in the region?

wrote in Yiddish, was renowned for both his novels and his short stories. He won the Nobel Prize for Literature in 1978. John Cheever, a respected novelist, won the Pulitzer Prize for Fiction in 1979 for his collected short stories, many of which concern suburban life.

Just as realism and romanticism have tended to merge in recent literature, so, curiously, have fiction and nonfiction. Truman Capote's *In Cold Blood*, published in 1966, was billed as a "nonfiction novel." Capote, primarily a novelist and short-story writer, used fictional techniques to analyze a real and seemingly senseless crime. Later authors, such as E. L. Doctorow in his novel *Ragtime*, combined historical figures with purely fictional characters. This technique has aroused considerable controversy.

Increasing attention has been paid recently to the place of nonfiction in the literary hierarchy. The essay has always been considered an important literary form, and some outstanding essays are published every year. James Baldwin and John McPhee are accomplished essayists.

Among the many notable longer works of nonfiction are Paul Theroux's *The Great Railway Bazaar*, N. Scott Momaday's *The Names*, and Barry Lopez's *Arctic Dreams*.

Poetry Within the Tradition A number of the famous prewar poets continued to publish extensively after the war. Robert Frost, Marianne Moore, Wallace Stevens, E. E. Cummings, William Carlos Williams, and Ezra Pound all produced major collections of their works. Younger poets, starting out in the shadow of these great names, were mostly content to work within the advances made in the 1920's and 1930's. One critic observed that to a beginning poet "the reassurance of sounding like something already acclaimed" was hard to resist.

The tumultuous 1960's brought great changes in social behavior, which affected the subject matter of all literature. In poetry, as in fiction, the resulting changes were often more personal and thematic than innovative. It seems ironic that out of the turmoil of the 1960's, the finest poetry to emerge follows older patterns.

One of the most respected contemporary poets is Robert Lowell. Lowell, a great-nephew of the poet James Russell Lowell, writes poetry that is traditional in form. However, his range in theme, method, and tone is breathtaking.

Theodore Roethke, a master of poetic rhythm, was deeply influenced by his father, a strong-willed greenhouse owner in Saginaw, Michigan. The best of Roethke's poems are often referred to as his "greenhouse poems."

Two other poets of note are Elizabeth Bishop and Gwendolyn Brooks. Bishop's poems are beautifully crafted, with precise and memorable descriptions. Two of Brooks's collections, *A Street in Bronzeville* (1945) and *Annie Allen* (1949), assured her reputation.

Many fine poets are at work today. Nowhere perhaps is America's pluralism displayed more vividly than in its poets. Although it is too early to assess these poets' achievements, it seems likely that some of their works will become the classics of tomorrow.

Beyond the Horizon

One of the features of literary history is its unpredictability. No one knows what will happen next. Of this, however, we can be reasonably sure: The novel is not dead, as some were proclaiming in the 1950's and 1960's. Poetry is not dead, nor is the short story. Literature has great resilience. While it may be profoundly influenced by other media—radio, television, film—it has not been replaced by them. Indeed, for sheer technical virtuosity, there has probably never been a more impressive group of American writers at work than at the present time.

▲ **Make a Judgment** Introduced to the American public in the 1990's, the Internet has radically changed the way we live, study, and work. Why are some people finding the Internet a cause for concern?

◀ **Evaluate Technology** The ability of a single silicon chip to store and process information has dramatically reduced the size of computers. A person can carry this hand-held computer anywhere and operate it at any time with a small stylus. What are the advantages of a portable computer?

The Development of American English

THE GLOBALIZATION OF ENGLISH

by Richard Lederer

English—the linguistic wonder of the modern world—has been transported around the globe and has become the most widely spoken language in the history of humankind.

A Worldwide Language The majority of the world's books, newspapers, and magazines are written in English. Most international telephone calls are made in English. Sixty percent of the world's radio programs are beamed in English, and more than seventy percent of international mail and seventy-five percent of cable messages and telexes are written and addressed in English. It is the language in which more than eighty percent of all stored computer texts and Web sites are written.

Reverse English Planet Earth is spinning with "reverse English." The very English that through the centuries has imported so many words from so many other languages is today one of the world's most popular exports. Through its contributions to other tongues, English is beginning to repay its historical debts and establish a linguistic balance of trade.

By reverse English, we mean, for the most part, American English. If you were to read German newspapers, for example, you would recognize English words such as *scoop, holiday, paperbacks, teenagers,*

blue jeans, toasters, and *mixers,* as well as the sports terms *ref, goalkeeper, puck, body check, punch,* and *boxing.*

American words have entered Russian stores with products like *miksers, tosters, komputers,* and *antifriz,* reflecting the fact that half of all foreign language classes in the Soviet Union are courses in English. By popular Soviet request, the British Broadcasting Corporation is supplying Moscow Radio with a series of programs emphasizing the essential English vocabulary of a capitalist society. To help Soviet listeners tell a stock from a bond and a bull from a bear, the BBC-Moscow Radio broadcasts encourage familiarity with such words and phrases as *collateral, management buyouts, export guarantees, Let's talk about that over lunch,* and *Do we have a deal?*

English Is Alive and Well The English language continues to be one of the world's great growth industries, adding more than a thousand new words a year to its word store and, since World War II, garnering new speakers at an annual rate of about two percent. Over the course of a millennium and a half, it has evolved from the rude tongue of a few isolated Germanic tribes into an international medium of exchange in science, commerce, politics, diplomacy, tourism, literature, and pop culture—the closest thing we have ever had to a global language.

Activity

Identify each English word as it has been adapted by another language:
(a) *bifuteki* (Japanese)
(b) *bouledogue* (French)
(c) *beisbol* (Spanish)
(d) *pulova* (Italian)

PART **1** *Literature Confronts the Everyday*

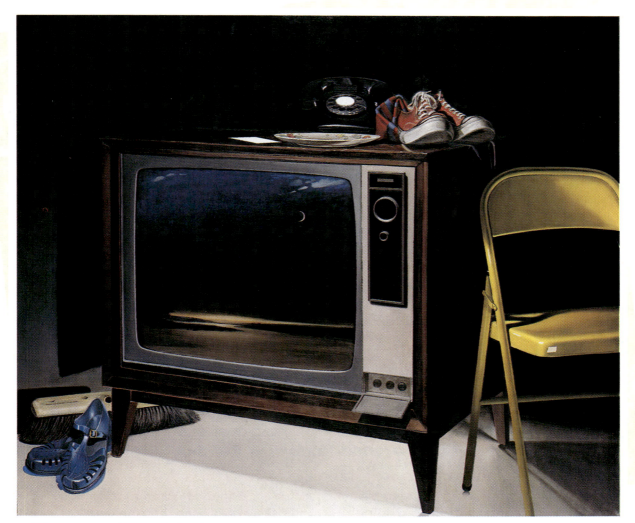

Television Moon, 1978–79, Alfred Leslie, Wichita Art Museum, Wichita, Kansas

Literature Confronts the Everyday ◆ 875

Guide for Interpreting

Flannery O'Connor
(1925–1964)

Flannery O'Connor's work reflects her intense commitment to her personal beliefs. In her exaggerated, tragic, and at times shockingly violent tales, she forces readers to confront such human faults as hypocrisy, insensitivity, self-centeredness, and prejudice.

O'Connor once said, "People are always complaining that the modern novelist has no hope and that the picture he paints of the world is unbearable. The only answer to this is that people without hope do not write novels."

"The Habit of Art" Born in Savannah, Georgia, Flannery O'Connor was raised in the small town of Milledgeville. She earned her undergraduate degree from Georgia State College for Women and then left her home state to attend the celebrated University of Iowa Writers' Workshop. In 1950, O'Connor became ill with lupus, a serious disease which restricted her independence. O'Connor moved back to the family farm outside Milledgeville, where she lived with her mother. There, she committed herself not only to her writing but to "the habit of art," an enlivened way of thinking and seeing. In 1952, she published her first novel, *Wise Blood,* the story of a violent rivalry among members of a fictional religious sect in the South. In 1955, she published a collection of stories, *A Good Man Is Hard to Find.* It was followed by a second novel, *The Violent Bear It Away* (1960), and *Everything That Rises Must Converge* (1965), a collection of short stories.

A Triumphant Spirit O'Connor lived with physical suffering and the awareness that she would probably die young. Despite her condition, she often seemed joyous, entertaining many friends at home and painting watercolors of the peacocks that she and her mother raised on the farm. In her fiction, however, she clearly feels a strong kinship with those who are outcast or suffering. Many of her characters are social outcasts or people who are physically or mentally challenged. Although she portrays these characters in an unsentimental way, there is an underlying sense of sympathy concerning their pain and suffering, which reflects both her own physical problems and her strong Catholic faith.

Background on this Story "The Life You Save May Be Your Own" is a typical O'Connor story. In its grim depiction of a group of outcasts with sharply exaggerated physical characteristics and personality traits, the story conveys a powerful moral message and captures many of the tragic realities of life in the modern world.

◆ Background for Understanding

LITERATURE: O'CONNOR AND GOTHIC LITERATURE

In England in the late 1700's, a literary style known as Gothic flourished. Gothic novels featured horror and violence, and the settings were often weird and exaggerated. In **Gothic literature,** evil is acknowledged as a real force in the world, and characters are assumed to have a dark side that lures them into violent or wicked acts.

In the twentieth century, a number of southern American writers such as Truman Capote, Carson McCullers, Tennessee Williams, William Faulkner, and Flannery O'Connor borrowed devices from Gothic literature. Their works often contain a foreboding atmosphere and doomed or grotesque characters.

Flannery O'Connor used Gothic elements to help expose the gap she saw between some people's professed religious beliefs and their morally irresponsible behavior.

The Life You Save May Be Your Own

◆ *Literature and Your Life*

CONNECT YOUR EXPERIENCE

In this story, a stranger appears at a remote farm where an elderly widow lives alone with her daughter. The woman must decide whether to trust him and whether to allow him into her home. What would you do if you were in her place? Why?

Journal Writing Discuss how you think people should react to strangers.

THEMATIC FOCUS: LITERATURE CONFRONTS THE EVERYDAY

Like many modern stories, "The Life You Save May Be Your Own" captures the everyday lives of less fortunate people. What lessons can be learned from the lives of such people?

◆ Build Vocabulary

WORD ROOTS: -sol-

O'Connor uses the word *desolate*, which has several meanings, including "forlorn." The word contains the root -sol-, meaning "alone." Knowing the meaning of this root and drawing from your prior knowledge, what are some other definitions for *desolate*?

WORD BANK

Preview this list of words from the story.

> desolate
> listed
> ominous
> ravenous
> morose
> guffawing

◆ Literary Focus

GROTESQUE CHARACTERS

A key element in gothic literature, the **grotesque character** is one who has become bizarre, usually through some kind of obsession. A grotesque character may be obsessed with an idea, a value, or an assumption. Typically, grotesque characters are one-dimensional and possess one or more exaggerated personality traits.

Many of Flannery O'Connor's characters, including those in this story, can be considered grotesque. Notice how O'Connor uses these bizarre characters to communicate a universal message.

◆ Grammar and Style

SUBJUNCTIVE MOOD

The **subjunctive mood** is any verb form indicating possibility, supposition, or desire. The verb form has two functions. One is to express a condition that is contrary to fact:

> Mr. Shiftlet talked *as if he were an ethical person.*

This sentence suggests that Mr. Shiflet may not be an ethical person. In this function, the verb form is always *were* rather than *was.*

The subjunctive mood is also used to indirectly express a demand, recommendation, suggestion, or statement of necessity:

> Mrs. Crater suggested *that Shiftlet marry her daughter.*

Here, the third-person singular verb form does not have the usual -s, -es, or -ies ending.

Reading for Success

Strategies for Reading Fiction

In a great work of fiction, every word has been chosen carefully to express a precise meaning. A plot has been structured, characters delineated, hints dropped, and themes deliberately implied to create a unique and yet believable world. By applying the following strategies, you can more fully appreciate the fictional world a writer has so carefully created.

Envision the action in your mind.

A skilled writer describes action clearly and vividly to help you picture the scenes of a story in your mind. Allow yourself to be carried away by the pictures painted by the author's words.

Identify with the characters and the situation.

If you empathize, or feel as another does, you'll be able to put yourself in a character's shoes. Imagine yourself in the story's setting and in the character's situations.

Question.

In life, you ask yourself questions about people's actions and motivations. What was he really doing? Why did she say that? Relate to a work of literature in the same way. Ask yourself why the characters behave as they do.

Predict.

When you find yourself wondering how a series of events will unfold, pause and predict what will happen. When you are trying to predict outcomes, look back, recall, and carefully weigh what you've experienced so far.

Make inferences.

Fictional characters and situations don't come neatly labeled "Villain" or "Disaster"—you have to infer information from the clues you're given. Use a character's attitudes and actions to read "between the lines."

Draw conclusions.

When you've finished reading a piece of fiction, reflect on its overall meaning. What general ideas does the writer want you to carry away?

Respond.

As you read a story, respond mentally and emotionally. A story may evoke positive responses—like laughter or recognition—or negative responses—such as disappointment or disgust with a character.

As you read "The Life You Save May Be Your Own," look at the notes along the sides. They demonstrate how to apply these strategies to your reading.

The Life You Save May Be Your Own

Flannery O'Connor

The old woman and her daughter were sitting on their porch when Mr. Shiftlet came up their road for the first time. The old woman slid to the edge of her chair and leaned forward, shading her eyes from the piercing sunset with her hand. The daughter could not see far in front of her and continued to play with her fingers. Although the old woman lived in this <u>desolate</u> spot with only her daughter and she had never seen Mr. Shiftlet before, she could tell, even from a distance, that he was a tramp and no one to be afraid of. His left coat sleeve was folded up to show there was only half an arm in it and his gaunt figure <u>listed</u> slightly to the side as if the breeze were pushing him. He had on a black town suit and a brown felt hat that was turned up in the front and down in the back and he carried a tin tool box by a handle. He came on, at an amble, up her road, his face turned toward the sun which appeared to be balancing itself on the peak of a small mountain.

The old woman didn't change her position until he was almost into her yard; then she rose with one hand fisted on her hip. The daughter, a large girl in a short blue organdy dress, saw him all at once and jumped up and began to stamp and point and make excited speechless sounds.

Mr. Shiftlet stopped just inside the yard and set his box on the ground and tipped his hat at her as if she were not in the least afflicted; then he turned toward the old woman and swung the hat all the way off. He had long black slick hair that hung flat from a part in the middle to beyond the tips of his ears on either side. His face descended in forehead for more than half its length and ended suddenly with his features just balanced over a jutting steel-trap jaw. He seemed to be a young man but he had a look of composed dissatisfaction as if he understood life thoroughly.

> This description allows you to establish a **picture in your mind**. Its effect is like that of a camera pausing on a scene before the action begins.

"Good evening," the old woman said. She was about the size of a cedar fence post and she had a man's gray hat pulled down low over her head.

The tramp stood looking at her and didn't answer. He turned his back and faced the sunset. He swung both his whole and his short arm up slowly so that they indicated an expanse of sky and his figure formed a crooked cross. The old woman watched him with her arms folded across her chest as if she were the owner of the sun, and the daughter watched, her head thrust forward and her fat helpless hands hanging at the wrists. She had long pink-gold hair and eyes as blue as a peacock's neck.

He held the pose for almost fifty seconds and then he picked up his box and came on to the porch and dropped down on the bottom step. "Lady," he said in a firm nasal voice, "I'd give a

◆ Build Vocabulary

desolate (dĕs´ə lĭt) *adj*.: Forlorn; wretched

listed (lĭst´ ĭd) *v*.: Tilted; inclined

fortune to live where I could see me a sun do that every evening."

"Does it every evening," the old woman said and sat back down. The daughter sat down too and watched him with a cautious sly look as if he were a bird that had come up very close. He leaned to one side, rooting in his pants pocket, and in a second he brought out a package of chewing gum and offered her a piece. She took it and unpeeled it and began to chew without taking her eyes off him. He offered the old woman a piece but she only raised her upper lip to indicate she had no teeth.

Mr. Shiftlet's pale sharp glance had already passed over everything in the yard—the pump near the corner of the house and the big fig tree that three or four chickens were preparing to roost in—and had moved to a shed where he saw the square rusted back of an automobile. "You ladies drive?" he asked.

"That car ain't run in fifteen year," the old woman said. "The day my husband died, it quit running."

"Nothing is like it used to be, lady," he said. "The world is almost rotten."

"That's right," the old woman said. "You from around here?"

"Name Tom T. Shiftlet," he murmured, looking at the tires.

"I'm pleased to meet you," the old woman said. "Name Lucynell Crater and daughter Lucynell Crater. What you doing around here, Mr. Shiftlet?"

He judged the car to be about a 1928 or '29 Ford. "Lady," he said, and turned and gave her his full attention, "lemme tell you something. There's one of these doctors in Atlanta that's taken a knife and cut the human heart—the human heart," he repeated, leaning forward, "out of a man's chest and held it in his hand," and he held his hand out, palm up, as if it were slightly weighted with the human heart, "and studied it like it was a day-old chicken, and lady," he said, allowing a long significant pause in which his head slid forward and his clay-colored eyes brightened, "he don't know no more about it than you or me."

"That's right," the old woman said.

"Why, if he was to take that knife and cut into every corner of it, he still wouldn't know no more than you or me. What you want to bet?"

▲ **Critical Viewing** What aspects of the story are reflected in this painting? **[Connect]**

Black Walnuts, 1945, Joseph Pollet, Oil on canvas, 30" x 40", Collection of Whitney Museum of American Art, Purchase, Gift of Gertrude Vanderbilt Whitney, by exchange

"Nothing," the old woman said wisely. "Where you come from, Mr. Shiftlet?"

He didn't answer. He reached into his pocket and brought out a sack of tobacco and a package of cigarette papers and rolled himself a cigarette, expertly with one hand, and attached it in a hanging position to his upper lip. Then he took a box of wooden matches from his pocket and struck one on his shoe. He held the burning match as if he were studying the mystery of flame while it traveled dangerously toward his skin. The daughter began to make loud noises and to point to his hand and shake her finger at him, but when the flame was just before touching him, he leaned down with his hand cupped over it as if he were going to set fire to his nose and lit the cigarette.

He flipped away the dead match and blew a stream of gray into the evening. A sly look came over his face. "Lady," he said, "nowadays, people'll do anything anyways. I can tell you my name is Tom T. Shiftlet and I come from Tarwater, Tennessee, but you never have seen me before: how you know I ain't lying? How you know my name ain't Aaron Sparks, lady, and I come from Singleberry, Georgia, or how you know it's not George Speeds and I come from Lucy, Alabama, or how you know I ain't Thompson Bright from Toolafalls, Mississippi?"

"I don't know nothing about you," the old woman muttered, irked.

"Lady," he said, "people don't care how they lie. Maybe the best I can tell you is, I'm a man; but listen lady," he said and paused and made his tone more <u>ominous</u> still, "what is a man?"

The old woman began to gum a seed. "What you carry in that tin box, Mr. Shiftlet?" she asked.

"Tools," he said, put back. "I'm a carpenter."

"Well, if you come out here to work, I'll be able to feed you and give you a place to sleep but I can't pay. I'll tell you that before you begin," she said.

There was no answer at once and no particular expression on his face. He leaned back against the two-by-four that helped support the porch roof. "Lady," he said slowly, "there's some men that some things mean more to them than money." The old woman rocked without comment and the daughter watched the trigger that moved up and down in his neck. He told the old woman then that all most

people were interested in was money, but he asked what a man was made for. He asked her if a man was made for money, or what. He asked her what she thought she was made for but she didn't answer, she only sat rocking and wondered if a one-armed man could put a new roof on her garden house. He asked a lot of questions that she didn't answer. He told her that he was twenty-eight years old and had lived a varied life. He had been a gospel singer, a foreman on the railroad, an assistant in an undertaking parlor, and he come over the radio for three months with Uncle Roy and his Red Creek Wranglers. He said he had fought and bled in the Arm Service of his country and visited every foreign land and that everywhere he had seen people that didn't care if they did a thing one way or another. He said he hadn't been raised thataway.

Identify with the characters and the situation by reflecting on a time when a person was talking to you about one thing, but you were reflecting on your own concerns.

Ask yourself: How *was* Shiftlet raised?

A fat yellow moon appeared in the branches of the fig tree as if it were going to roost there with the chickens. He said that a man had to escape to the country to see the world whole and that he wished he lived in a desolate place like this where he could see the sun go down every evening like God made it to do.

"Are you married or are you single?" the old woman asked.

There was a long silence. "Lady," he asked finally, "where would you find you an innocent woman today? I wouldn't have any of this trash I could just pick up."

The daughter was leaning very far down, hanging her head almost between her knees watching him through a triangular door she had made in her overturned hair; and she suddenly fell in a heap on the floor and began to whimper. Mr. Shiftlet straightened her out and helped her get back in the chair.

"Is she your baby girl?" he asked.

"My only," the old woman said "and she's the sweetest girl in the world. I would give her up for nothing on earth. She's smart too. She can sweep the floor, cook, wash, feed the chickens, and hoe. I wouldn't give her up for a casket of jewels."

"No," he said kindly, "don't ever let any man take her away from you."

"Any man come after her," the old woman said, "'ll have to stay around the place."

Mr. Shiftlet's eye in the darkness was focused on a part of the automobile bumper that glittered in the distance. "Lady," he said, jerking his short arm up as if he could point with it to her house and yard and pump, "there ain't a broken thing on this plantation that I couldn't fix for you, one-arm jackleg or not. I'm a man," he said with a sullen dignity, "even if I ain't a whole one. I got," he said, tapping his knuckles on the floor to emphasize the immensity of what he was going to say, "a moral intelligence!" and his face pierced out of the darkness into a shaft of doorlight and he stared at her as if he were astonished himself at this impossible truth.

The old woman was not impressed with the phrase. "I told you you could hang around and work for food," she said, "if you don't mind sleeping in that car yonder."

"Why listen, lady, " he said with a grin of delight, "the monks of old slept in their coffins!"

"They wasn't as advanced as we are," the old woman said.

The next morning he began on the roof of the garden house while Lucynell, the daughter, sat on a rock and watched him work. He had not been around a week before the change he had made in the place was apparent. He had patched the front and back steps, built a new hog pen, restored a fence, and taught Lucynell, who was completely deaf and had never said a word in her life, to say the word "bird." The big rosy-faced girl followed him everywhere, saying "Burrttddt ddbirrrttdt," and clapping her hands. The old woman watched from a distance, secretly pleased. She was <u>ravenous</u> for a son-in-law.

> Shiftlet's capable performance in his new job gives you a good basis upon which to **predict** what might happen next.

Mr. Shiftlet slept on the hard narrow back seat of the car with his feet out the side window. He had his razor and a can of water on a crate that served him as a bedside table and he put up a piece of mirror against the back glass and kept his coat neatly on a hanger that he hung over one of the windows.

In the evenings he sat on the steps and talked while the old woman and Lucynell rocked violently in their chairs on either side of him. The old woman's three mountains were black against the dark blue sky and were visited off and on by various planets and by the moon after it had left the chickens. Mr. Shiftlet pointed out that the reason he had improved this plantation was because he had taken a personal interest in it. He said he was even going to make the automobile run.

He had raised the hood and studied the mechanism and he said he could tell that the car had been built in the days when cars were really built. You take now, he said, one man puts in one bolt and another man puts in another bolt and another man puts in another bolt so that it's a man for a bolt. That's why you have to pay so much for a car: you're paying all those men. Now if you didn't have to pay but one man, you could get you a cheaper car and one that had had a personal interest taken in it, and it would be a better car. The old woman agreed with him that this was so.

Mr. Shiftlet said that the trouble with the world was that nobody cared, or stopped and took any trouble. He said he never would have been able to teach Lucynell to say a word if he hadn't cared and stopped long enough.

"Teach her to say something else," the old woman said.

"What you want her to say next?" Mr. Shiftlet asked.

The old woman's smile was broad and toothless and suggestive. "Teach her to say 'sugarpie,'" she said.

Mr. Shiftlet already knew what was on her mind.

The next day he began to tinker with the automobile and that evening he told her that if she would buy a fan belt, he would be able to make the car run.

The old woman said she would give him the money. "You see that girl yonder?" she asked, pointing to Lucynell who was sitting on the floor a foot away, watching him, her eyes blue even in the dark. "If it was ever a man wanted to take her away, I would say, 'No man on

◆ **Build Vocabulary**

ominous (äm´ ə nəs) *adj.*: Threatening; sinister
ravenous (rav´ ə nəs) *adj.*: Extremely eager

earth is going to take that sweet girl of mine away from me!' but if he was to say, 'Lady, I don't want to take her away, I want her right here,' I would say, 'Mister, I don't blame you none. I wouldn't pass up a chance to live in a permanent place and get the sweetest girl in the world myself. You ain't no fool,' I would say."

"How old is she?" Mr. Shiftlet asked casually.

"Fifteen, sixteen," the old woman said. The girl was nearly thirty but because of her innocence it was impossible to guess.

"It would be a good idea to paint it too," Mr. Shiftlet remarked. "You don't want it to rust out."

"We'll see about that later," the old woman said.

The next day he walked into town and returned with the parts he needed and a can of gasoline. Late in the afternoon, terrible noises issued from the shed and the old woman rushed out of the house, thinking Lucynell was somewhere having a fit. Lucynell was sitting on a chicken crate, stamping her feet and screaming, "Burrddtt! bddurrddtttt!" but her fuss was drowned out by the car. With a volley of blasts it emerged from the shed, moving in a fierce and stately way. Mr. Shiftlet was in the driver's seat, sitting very erect. He had an expression of serious modesty on his face as if he had just raised the dead.

That night, rocking on the porch, the old woman began her business, at once. "You want you an innocent woman, don't you?" she asked

Deep Fork Overlook, Joan Marron-LaRue

▲ **Critical Viewing** Why might an automobile be so valuable in a rural area like the one in this story? **[Draw Conclusions]**

sympathetically. "You don't want none of this trash."

"No'm, I don't," Mr. Shiftlet said.

"One that can't talk," she continued, "can't sass you back or use foul language. That's the kind for you to have. Right there," and she pointed to Lucynell sitting crosslegged in her chair, holding both feet in her hands.

"That's right," he admitted. "She wouldn't give me any trouble."

"Saturday," the old woman said, "you and her and me can drive into town and get married."

Mr. Shiftlet eased his position on the steps.

"I can't get married right now," he said. "Everything you want to do takes money and I ain't got any."

"What you need with money?" she asked.

"It takes money," he said. "Some people'll do anything anyhow these days, but the way I think, I wouldn't marry no woman that I couldn't take on a trip like she was somebody. I mean take her to a hotel and treat her. I wouldn't marry the Duchesser Windsor," he said firmly, "unless I could take her to a hotel and giver something good to eat.

"I was raised thataway and there ain't a thing I can do about it. My old mother taught me how to do."

"Lucynell don't even know what a hotel is," the old woman muttered. "Listen here, Mr. Shiftlet," she said, sliding forward in her chair, "you'd be getting a permanent house and a deep well and the most innocent girl in the world. You don't need no money. Lemme tell you something: there ain't any place in the world for a poor disabled friendless drifting man."

The ugly words settled in Mr. Shiftlet's head like a group of buzzards in the top of a tree. He didn't answer at once. He rolled himself a cigarette and lit it and then he said in an even voice, "Lady, a man is divided into two parts, body and spirit."

The old woman clamped her gums together.

"A body and a spirit," he repeated. "The body, lady, is like a house: it don't go anywhere; but the spirit, lady, is like a automobile: always on the move, always . . ."

"Listen, Mr. Shiftlet," she said, "my well never goes dry and my house is always warm in the winter and there's no mortgage on a thing about this place. You can go to the courthouse and see for yourself. And yonder under

that shed is a fine automobile." She laid the bait carefully. "You can have it painted by Saturday. I'll pay for the paint."

In the darkness, Mr. Shiftlet's smile stretched like a weary snake waking up by a fire. After a second he recalled himself and said, "I'm only saying a man's spirit means more to him than anything else. I would have to take my wife off for the weekend without no regards at all for cost. I got to follow where my spirit says to go."

"I'll give you fifteen dollars for a weekend trip," the old woman said in a crabbed voice. "That's the best I can do."

Here Shiftlet begins to change his tone with the old woman. You might **infer** that he has some scheme in mind.

"That wouldn't hardly pay for more than the gas and the hotel," he said. "It wouldn't feed her."

"Seventeen-fifty," the old woman said. "That's all I got so it isn't any use you trying to milk me. You can take a lunch."

Mr. Shiftlet was deeply hurt by the word "milk." He didn't doubt that she had more money sewed up in her mattress but he had already told her he was not interested in her money. "I'll make that do," he said and rose and walked off without treating with her further.

On Saturday the three of them drove into town in the car that the paint had barely dried on and Mr. Shiftlet and Lucynell were married in the Ordinary's office while the old woman witnessed. As they came out of the courthouse, Mr. Shiftlet began twisting his neck in his collar. He looked <u>morose</u> and bitter as if he had been insulted while someone held him. "That didn't satisfy me none," he said. "That was just something a woman in an office did, nothing but paper work and blood tests. What do they know about my blood? If they was to take my heart and cut it out," he said, "they wouldn't know a thing about me. It didn't satisfy me at all."

"It satisfied the law," the old woman said sharply.

"The law," Mr. Shiftlet said and spit. "It's the law that don't satisfy me."

He had painted the car dark green with a yellow band around it just under the windows. The three of them climbed in the front seat and the old woman said, "Don't Lucynell look pretty? Looks like a baby doll." Lucynell was dressed up in a white dress that her mother had uprooted from a trunk and there was a Panama hat on her head with a bunch of red wooden cherries on the brim. Every now and then her placid expression was changed by a sly isolated little thought like a shoot of green in the desert. "You got a prize!" the old woman said.

Mr. Shiftlet didn't even look at her. They drove back to the house to let the old woman off and pick up the lunch. When they were ready to leave, she stood staring in the window of the car, with her fingers clenched around the glass. Tears began to seep sideways out of her eyes and run along the dirty creases in her face. "I ain't ever been parted with her for two days before," she said.

Mr. Shiftlet started the motor.

"And I wouldn't let no man have her but you because I seen you would do right. Goodbye, Sugarbaby," she said, clutching at the sleeve of the white dress. Lucynell looked straight at her and didn't seem to see her there at all. Mr. Shiftlet eased the car forward so that she had to move her hands.

The early afternoon was clear and open and surrounded by pale blue sky. Although the car would go only thirty miles an hour, Mr. Shiftlet imagined a terrific climb and dip and swerve that went entirely to his head so that he forgot his morning bitterness. He had always wanted an automobile but he had never been able to afford one before. He drove very fast because he wanted to make Mobile by nightfall.

Occasionally he stopped his thoughts long enough to look at Lucynell in the seat beside him. She had eaten the lunch as soon as they were out of the yard and now she was pulling the cherries off the hat one by one and throwing them out the window. He became depressed in spite of the car. He had driven about a hundred miles when he decided that she must be hungry again and at the next small town they came to, he stopped in front of an aluminum-painted eating place called The Hot Spot and took her in and ordered her a plate of ham and grits. The ride had made her sleepy and as soon as she got up on the stool, she rested her head on the counter and shut her eyes. There was no one in The Hot Spot but Mr. Shiftlet and the boy behind the counter, a pale

youth with a greasy rag hung over his shoulder. Before he could dish up the food, she was snoring gently.

"Give it to her when she wakes up," Mr. Shiftlet said. "I'll pay for it now."

The boy bent over her and stared at the long pink-gold hair and the half-shut sleeping eyes. Then he looked up and stared at Mr. Shiftlet. "She looks like an angel of Gawd," he murmured.

"Hitchhiker," Mr. Shiftlet explained. "I can't wait. I got to make Tuscaloosa."

The boy bent over again and very carefully touched his finger to a strand of the golden hair and Mr. Shiftlet left.

He was more depressed than ever as he drove on by himself. The late afternoon had grown hot and sultry and the country had flattened out. Deep in the sky a storm was preparing very slowly and without thunder as if it meant to drain every drop of air from the earth before it broke. There were times when Mr. Shiftlet preferred not to be alone. He felt too that a man with a car had a responsibility to others and he kept his eye out for a hitchhiker. Occasionally he saw a sign that warned: "Drive carefully. The life you save may be your own."

The narrow road dropped off on either side into dry fields and here and there a shack or a filling station stood in a clearing. The sun began to set directly in front of the automobile. It was a reddening ball that through his windshield was slightly flat on the bottom and top. He saw a boy in overalls and a gray hat standing on the edge of the road and he slowed the car down and stopped in front of him. The boy didn't have his hand raised to thumb the ride, he was only standing there, but he had a small cardboard suitcase and his hat was set on his head in a way to indicate that he had left somewhere for good. "Son," Mr. Shiftlet said, "I see you want a ride."

The boy didn't say he did or he didn't but he opened the door of the car and got in, and Mr. Shiftlet started driving again. The child held the suitcase on his lap and folded his arms on top of it. He turned his head and looked out the window away from Shiftlet. Mr. Shiftlet felt

◆ Build Vocabulary

guffawing (gə fô´ iŋ) *adj.*: Laughing in a loud, coarse manner

oppressed. "Son," he said after a minute, "I got the best old mother in the world so I reckon you only got the second best."

The boy gave him a quick dark glance and then turned his face back out the window.

"It's nothing so sweet," Mr. Shiftlet continued, "as a boy's mother. She taught him his first prayers at her knee, she give him love when no other would, she told him what was right and what wasn't, and she seen that he done the right thing. Son," he said, "I never rued a day in my life like the one I rued when I left that old mother of mine."

The boy shifted in his seat but he didn't look at Mr. Shiftlet. He unfolded his arms and put one hand on the door handle.

"My mother was a angel of Gawd," Mr. Shiftlet said in a very strained voice. "He took her from heaven and giver to me and I left her." His eyes were instantly clouded over with a mist of tears. The car was barely moving.

The boy turned angrily in the seat. "You go to the devil!" he cried. "My old woman is a flea bag and yours is a stinking pole cat!" and with that he flung the door open and jumped out with his suitcase into the ditch.

Mr. Shiftlet was so shocked that for about a hundred feet he drove along slowly with the door still open. A cloud, the exact color of the boy's hat and shaped like a turnip, had descended over the sun, and another, worse looking, crouched behind the car. Mr. Shiftlet felt that the rottenness of the world was about to engulf him. He raised his arm and let it fall again to his breast. "Oh Lord!" he prayed. "Break forth and wash the slime from this earth!"

The turnip continued slowly to descend. After a few minutes there was a guffawing peal of thunder from behind and fantastic raindrops, like tin-can tops, crashed over the rear of Mr. Shiftlet's car. Very quickly he stepped on the gas and with his stump sticking out the window he raced the galloping shower into Mobile.

Guide for Responding

◆ Literature and Your Life

Reader's Response How did you react to Shiftlet's final protest, his prayer that God "Break forth and wash the slime from this earth!"?

Thematic Focus Who do you think has the most difficult time coping with the demands of everyday living: Shiftlet, the mother, or the daughter?

Journal Writing In your journal, discuss your reactions to the characters in this story and their behavior. In what ways, if any, do they remind you of people you've met?

☑ Check Your Comprehension

1. What is Mr. Shiftlet's physical disability?
2. Which of the Craters' possessions does he want?
3. (a) What arguments does the old woman use to persuade Shiftlet to marry Lucynell?
   (b) Why does Shiftlet say he cannot marry her?
   (c) What causes him to change his mind?
4. What is the outcome of the story?

◆ Critical Thinking

INTERPRET

1. Explain how Shiftlet's comment that the spirit is "always on the move" foreshadows or hints at the story's outcome. **[Analyze]**
2. Why is it ironic that at the end of the story "Mr. Shiftlet felt that the rottenness of the world was about to engulf him"? **[Analyze]**
3. Shiftlet observes that "the world is almost rotten." What does the story suggest about the cause of this condition? **[Draw Conclusions]**
4. (a) What is ironic about how Shiftlet's prayer is answered at the end? (b) What does the event suggest about those whose behavior contradicts their professed beliefs? **[Draw Conclusions]**

EVALUATE

5. Mrs. Crater decides to marry Lucynell to Shiftlet; the girl seems to have no control over her fate. Does Mrs. Crater's action have any moral justification? Explain. **[Make a Judgment]**

Guide for Responding (continued)

◆ Literary Focus

GROTESQUE CHARACTERS

All three of the main characters in O'Connor's short story are **grotesque** in some fashion. They exhibit exaggerated characteristics in both appearance and behavior. Both Shiftlet and old Mrs. Crater are driven by obsessions.

1. Find one physical description for each character that creates a grotesque effect.
2. What is Mrs. Crater's obsession?
3. Give an example of Mr. Shiftlet's obsession with the dire state of the world.
4. In what ways are the characters realistic? In what ways are they exaggerated?

◆ Reading Strategy

STRATEGIES FOR READING FICTION

By applying certain strategies, you can get more information and gain a greater understanding of a work of fiction. Review the strategies for reading fiction, and use them to answer these questions:

1. Find a description that helps you to envision the action. What images and descriptive phrases create a picture in your mind?
2. To be believable, even villainous characters exhibit some qualities—or find themselves in situations—that are sympathetic. Discuss one or two aspects of Shiftlet's character or situation that allow you occasionally to identify with him.
3. As you read this story, what questions did you ask yourself about the motivations of Shiftlet or Mrs. Crater? Did you find the answers as you read on? Explain.
4. Did your predictions about events in this story match the outcome? Explain.
5. When Shiftlet asks Mrs. Crater what word she wants him to teach Lucynell next, she says, "Teach her to say 'sugarpie.'" What inference can you draw from this reply?
6. Consider the full range of Shiftlet's behavior and actions in this story. What conclusions can you draw about him at the story's end?
7. Describe your personal response to this story. Did the story give you a new idea, or a new angle on an old idea? Explain.

◆ Build Vocabulary

USING THE WORD ROOT -sol-

Using your knowledge of the root -sol- (alone), answer the following questions.

1. Is solitaire a game played by a single person or a group of players?
2. In a soliloquy, do two actors have an exchange, or does one character address the audience?
3. Would a pilot have a co-pilot on a solo flight?
4. Would a person who loves to take walks alone enjoy the state of solitude?

USING THE WORD BANK

For each sentence, indicate whether the word in italics is used correctly. If the word is used incorrectly, write a new sentence that uses the word properly.

1. The cottage with lace curtains, flower boxes, and a fresh paint job had a desolate appearance.
2. The rickety fence listed in the strong winds.
3. With an ominous expression, the jury foreman pronounced the guilty sentence.
4. After the huge dinner, the guest was ravenous.
5. Your morose reaction tells me you love the gift.
6. He was guffawing at the comedian's antics.

◆ Grammar and Style

SUBJUNCTIVE MOOD

The use of the **subjunctive mood** in contrary-to-fact statements always requires the past-tense form were (If she were nicer, she would have more friends). In statements that recommend, demand, or suggest, be is used instead of am, is, or are (I recommend that you be well prepared for the exam).

Practice Determine whether the subjunctive mood is necessary in each example. Choose the correct form of the verb in parentheses to complete each sentence.

1. I wouldn't trust that salesman, if I (be) you.
2. He requires that everyone (pay) in cash.
3. He comes every summer and (rent) a storefront.
4. He requests that each passerby (try) a sample.
5. The sample usually (taste) better than the items he delivers later.

Build Your Portfolio

Idea Bank

Writing

1. **Missing Person Report** As a police officer, write a detailed description of Lucynell Crater to circulate in the community following her disappearance.

2. **Moral Analysis** Shiflet boasts that he has "a moral intelligence." Write an analysis in which you comment on this statement in light of his behavior.

3. **Short Story** Write a short story featuring a deceitful character, or a character who commits a deceitful act. Provide action and dialogue that let your readers draw their own conclusions.

Speaking and Listening

4. **Staged Reading** In a small group, conduct a staged reading of the story. Speaking parts should include a narrator, Shiflet, and Mrs. Crater. A fourth student can act out the part of Lucynell as the narrator describes her. **[Performing Arts Link]**

5. **Body Language Presentation** People's postures or gestures can often "speak" louder than their words. Do some research on body language and share your findings with the class.

Projects

6. **Magazine Illustration** It is 1953, and you are assigned to illustrate O'Connor's story for a popular magazine. Research illustration styles of the period, and apply what you've learned to illustrate a scene from the story. **[Art Link]**

7. **Special Education Research** In the modern world, a mentally-challenged young woman such as Lucynell would have educational opportunities. Research and report on the legislation that has led to these opportunities. **[Social Studies Link]**

Writing Mini-Lesson

Deposition

A deposition is a witness's formal, written testimony—a legal first-person recounting of events. Imagine that Shiflet has been formally accused of stealing Mrs. Crater's car and of abandoning and endangering Lucynell. As a witness to the events, write a deposition that may be used against Shiflet. Use transitions to show the causes and effects of the man's actions.

Writing Skills Focus: Transitions to Show Cause and Effect

If you were testifying about an individual's alleged criminal actions, you would use transition words carefully to show how the individual caused certain things to happen, and to demonstrate how those events had harmful effects. **Transition words that show cause and effect** include *because, as a result, consequently, if, then, as an effect, so,* and *therefore.*

Prewriting List Shiflet's statements and actions and the effects you know or imagine they had. Carefully copy quotations from the story to support your position.

Drafting Begin by explaining what Shiflet did. Establish clear transitions that show cause and effect. Include relevant quotations to back up your statements. Finally, suggest why you believe his actions were criminal or harmful.

Revising Reread your deposition to be sure that you have described Shiflet's actions in a clear and logical way. What details can you add to sharpen the picture of his criminal behavior? What transition words can you add to clarify the causes and effects of the events? Knowing that the audience for your deposition will be lawyers or law-enforcement personnel, be sure that all your information is accurate, that you have used formal language, and that your spelling and punctuation are correct.

Guide for Interpreting

Bernard Malamud (1914–1986)

"I write . . . to explain life to myself and to keep me related to men," Bernard Malamud once commented when explaining his life's work.

Childhood of Two Cultures Malamud was born in Brooklyn, New York, the son of Russian immigrants. According to his own account, Malamud's boyhood was "comparatively happy." He grew up hearing the constant mingling of Yiddish and English—an experience that contributed to his fine ear for the rhythms of spoken dialogue. A favored boyhood pastime was listening to his father recount tales of Jewish life in czarist Russia. Young Bernard soon took up this family pastime, recording stories he'd made up to tell his friends.

A Literary Range Malamud attended City College of New York and Columbia University and began publishing stories in a number of well-known magazines. Despite Malamud's strong connection to Yiddish folk tales—many stories are drawn from this oral tradition—his work depicts a broad range of settings and characters. From the gifted baseball player in *The Natural* (1952) to the handyman living in czarist Russia in the Pulitzer Prize-winning *The Fixer*

(1966), all of his characters come across to readers as real and accessible, with universal hopes and concerns.

Malamud's other novels include *The Assistant* (1957), *A New Life* (1961), *The Tenants* (1971), and *Dubin's Lives* (1979). He also wrote numerous short stories, many of which were published in *The Magic Barrel* (1958), which won the National Book Award.

Capturing Life's Lessons In much of his work, Malamud uses people who share his Jewish heritage to represent all of humanity, capturing their attempts to maintain a link to their cultural heritage while trying to cope with modern realities. While some of his characters achieve success, others experience failure.

By portraying failures as well as triumphs, he captures the essence of the human experience and creates a delicate balance between tragedy and comedy. Some of his stories amuse readers as the characters try to negotiate between fulfilling their ideals and meeting the practical demands of their lives. Other Malamud stories move readers to sadness as characters struggle courageously within tragic circumstances. "The First Seven Years" depicts a Polish immigrant's desire to see his daughter achieve a better life. His notion of that life, however, is not the same as hers.

◆ Background for Understanding

CULTURE: A GENERATION'S VALUES

Bernard Malamud's father was a grocer who, like many immigrants, worked diligently to forge a better life for his family. Similarly, the Polish immigrant father in "The First Seven Years" works hard to make his business succeed and dreams that his daughter will achieve a better life. The character's desire to see his daughter go to college or marry an educated man is typical of the hopes of parents of his generation and experience.

The 1950's, when this story takes place, were a prosperous decade in the United States. Many people were upwardly mobile; they worked hard and were virtually assured that their status in society would improve. Parents labored hard for material wealth so that their children would struggle less than they had; children took material comfort for granted and became more interested in matters of the spirit. Malamud's story explores the gap in values that sometimes occurred between children of the 1950's and their parents.

The First Seven Years

◆ *Literature and Your Life*

CONNECT YOUR EXPERIENCE

When parents or teachers push you to take college entrance exams, learn a skill, or take up an instrument, they hope to help you achieve a better life. Similarly, the father in this story pushes his daughter in a certain direction in the hope that she'll achieve happiness. However, her idea of happiness doesn't match up with his.

Journal Writing Describe the goals you have for your future and discuss any goals that adult relatives have for you.

THEMATIC FOCUS: LITERATURE CONFRONTS THE EVERYDAY

In this story, everyday choices prove important. As you read, consider which choices young people should make on their own, and which ones adult relatives might expect to make for them.

◆ Literary Focus

EPIPHANY

In a traditional short story, the plot moves toward a resolution, a point at which the conflict is resolved and the outcome of the action becomes clear. However, in an effort to capture the uncertainty of life in the modern world, many twentieth-century fiction writers have turned away from the traditional plot structure by ending their stories without a resolution. Instead, writers often construct plots that move toward an **epiphany,** a moment when a character has a flash of insight about himself or herself, another character, or life in general. In this story, the main character has an epiphany in which he suddenly sees into another character's emotions, and as a result reexamines some long-held assumptions.

◆ Grammar and Style

CORRECT USE OF *WHO* AND *WHOM*

In this story you'll find may examples of the **use of *who* and *whom*.** Notice that *who*—like he or she—is used as a subject or subject complement. *Whom*—like him or her—is used as a direct object or as an object of the preposition. Look at these examples:

direct object of respected

...could turn his thoughts from Max, the college boy ... *whom* he so much respected ...

subject

Yet he could not help but contrast the diligence of the college boy, *who* was a peddler's son, with Miriam's unconcern ...

◆ Reading Strategy

IDENTIFY WITH CHARACTERS

When you **identify with characters** in literature, you link their thoughts, actions, and situations to your own experience. Look at this example:

Story Situation

He had begged her to go, pointing out how many fathers could not afford to send their children to college, but she said she wanted to be independent.

Identifying With the Character

I can identify with the daughter in this situation. Last summer my mother wanted me to be a camp counselor, but I wanted to have a summer of freedom.

Identifying with characters will help you to understand their problems better and relate to the decisions they make.

◆ Build Vocabulary

WORD ROOTS: *-liter-*

Malamud uses the word *illiterate,* which contains the root *-liter-,* meaning "letter." Notice how the root contributes to the overall meaning of the word: "unable to read written letters."

WORD BANK

Preview this list of words from the story.

diligence
connivance
illiterate
unscrupulous
repugnant
discern

WHILE
YOU WAIT
REPAIRING
HEATING
CONTRACTOR
OLDSMOBILE
TRUCKS

The First Seven Years

Bernard Malamud

Feld, the shoemaker, was annoyed that his helper, Sobel, was so insensitive to his reverie that he wouldn't for a minute cease his fanatic pounding at the other bench. He gave him a look, but Sobel's bald head was bent over the last[1] as he worked and he didn't notice. The shoemaker shrugged and continued to peer through the partly frosted window at the nearsighted haze of falling February snow. Neither the shifting white blur outside, nor the sudden deep remembrance of the snowy Polish village where he had wasted his youth could turn his thoughts from Max the college boy, (a constant visitor in the mind since early that morning when Feld saw him trudging through the snowdrifts on his way to school) whom he so much respected because of the sacrifices he had made throughout the years—in winter or direst heat—to further his education. An old wish returned to haunt the shoemaker: that he had had a son instead of a daughter, but this blew away in

---

1. **last** *n*.: Block shaped like a person's foot, on which shoes are made or repaired.

◀ **Critical Viewing** What does this image reveal about the setting of the story? [Predict]

the snow for Feld, if anything, was a practical man. Yet he could not help but contrast the diligence of the boy, who was a peddler's son, with Miriam's unconcern for an education. True, she was always with a book in her hand, yet when the opportunity arose for a college education, she had said no she would rather find a job. He had begged her to go, pointing out how many fathers could not afford to send their children to college, but she said she wanted to be independent. As for education, what was it, she asked, but books, which Sobel, who diligently read the classics, would as usual advise her on. Her answer greatly grieved her father.

A figure emerged from the snow and the door opened. At the counter the man withdrew from a wet paper bag a pair of battered shoes for repair. Who he was the shoemaker for a moment had no idea, then his heart trembled as he realized, before he had thoroughly discerned the face, that Max himself was standing there, embarrassedly explaining what he wanted done to his old shoes. Though Feld listened eagerly, he couldn't hear a word, for the opportunity that had burst upon him was deafening.

He couldn't exactly recall when the thought had occurred to him, because it was clear he had more than once considered suggesting to the boy that he go out with Miriam. But he had not dared speak, for if Max said no, how would he face him again? Or suppose Miriam, who harped so often on independence, blew up in anger and shouted at him for his meddling? Still, the chance was too good to let by: all it meant was an introduction. They might long ago have become friends had they happened to meet somewhere, therefore was it not his duty—an obligation—to bring them together, nothing more, a harmless connivance to replace an accidental encounter in the subway, let's say, or a mutual friend's introduction in

the street? Just let him once see and talk to her and he would for sure be interested. As for Miriam, what possible harm for a working girl in an office, who met only loud-mouthed salesmen and illiterate shipping clerks, to make the acquaintance of a fine scholarly boy? Maybe he would awaken in her a desire to go to college; if not—the shoemaker's mind at last came to grips with the truth—let her marry an educated man and live a better life.

When Max finished describing what he wanted done to his shoes, Feld marked them, both with enormous holes in the soles which he pretended not to notice, with large white-chalk x's, and the rubber heels, thinned to the nails, he marked with o's, though it troubled him he might have mixed up the letters. Max inquired the price, and the shoemaker cleared his throat and asked the boy, above Sobel's insistent hammering, would he please step through the side door there into the hall. Though surprised, Max did as the shoemaker requested, and Feld went in after him. For a minute they were both silent, because Sobel had stopped banging, and it seemed they understood neither was to say anything until the noise began again. When it did, loudly, the shoemaker quickly told Max why he had asked to talk to him.

"Ever since you went to high school," he said, in the dimly-lit hallway, "I watched you in the morning go to the subway to school, and I said always to myself, this is a fine boy that he wants so much an education."

"Thanks," Max said, nervously alert. He was tall and grotesquely thin, with sharply cut features, particularly a beak-like nose. He was wearing a loose, long slushy overcoat that hung down to his ankles, looking like a rug draped over his bony shoulders, and a soggy, old brown hat, as battered as the shoes he had brought in.

"I am a business man," the shoemaker abruptly said to conceal his embarrassment, "so I will explain you right away why I talk to you. I have a girl, my daughter Miriam—she is nineteen—a very nice girl and also so pretty that everybody looks on her when she passes by in the street. She is smart, always with a book, and I thought to myself that a boy like you, an educated boy—I thought maybe you will be interested sometime to meet a girl like this." He laughed a bit when he had finished and was tempted to say more but had the good sense not to.

Max stared down like a hawk. For an uncomfortable second he was silent, then he asked, "Did you say nineteen?"

"Yes."

"Would it be all right to inquire if you have a picture of her?"

◆ **Reading Strategy**
Put yourself in Feld's place. How do you think he feels during this exchange?

"Just a minute." The shoemaker went into the store and hastily returned with a snapshot that Max held up to the light.

"She's all right," he said.

Feld waited.

"And is she sensible—not the flighty kind?"

"She is very sensible."

After another short pause, Max said it was okay with him if he met her.

"Here is my telephone," said the shoemaker, hurriedly handing him a slip of paper. "Call her up. She comes home from work six o'clock."

Max folded the paper and tucked it away into his worn leather wallet.

"About the shoes," he said. "How much did you say they will cost me?"

"Don't worry about the price."

"I just like to have an idea."

"A dollar—dollar fifty. A dollar fifty," the shoemaker said.

At once he felt bad, for he usually charged two twenty-five for this kind of job. Either he should have asked the regular price or done the work for nothing.

Later, as he entered the store, he was startled by a violent clanging and looked up to see Sobel pounding with all his might upon the naked last. It broke, the iron striking the floor and jumping with a thump against the wall, but before the enraged shoemaker could cry out, the assistant had torn his hat and coat from the hook and rushed out into the snow.

So Feld, who had looked forward to anticipating how it would go with his daughter and Max, instead had a great worry on his mind. Without his temperamental helper he was a lost man, especially since it was years now that he had carried the store alone. The shoemaker had for an age suffered from a heart condition that threat-ened collapse if he dared exert himself. Five years ago, after an attack, it had appeared as though he would have either to sacrifice his business upon the auction block and live on a pittance thereafter, or put himself at the mercy of some unscrupulous employee who would in the end probably ruin him. But just at the moment of his darkest despair, this Polish refugee, Sobel, appeared one night from the street and begged for work. He was a stocky man, poorly dressed, with a bald head that had once been blond, a severely plain face and soft blue eyes prone to tears over the sad books he read, a young man but old—no one would have guessed thirty. Though he confessed he knew nothing of shoemaking, he said he was apt and would work for a very little if Feld taught him the trade. Thinking that with, after all, a landsman,[2] he would have less to fear than from a complete stranger, Feld took him on and within six weeks the refugee rebuilt as good a shoe as he, and not long thereafter expertly ran the business for the thoroughly relieved shoemaker.

Feld could trust him with anything and did, frequently going home after an hour or two at the store, leaving all the money in the till, knowing Sobel would guard every cent of it. The amazing thing was that he demanded so little. His wants were few; in money he wasn't interested—in nothing but books, it seemed—which he one by one lent to Miriam, together with his profuse, queer written comments, manufactured during his lonely rooming house evenings, thick pads of commentary which the shoemaker peered at and twitched his shoulders over as his daughter, from her fourteenth year, read page by sanctified page, as if the word of God were inscribed on them. To protect Sobel, Feld himself had to see that he received more than he asked for. Yet his conscience bothered him for not insisting that the assistant accept a better wage than he was getting, though Feld had honestly told him he could earn a handsome salary if he worked elsewhere, or maybe opened a place of his own. But the assistant answered, somewhat ungraciously, that he was not interested in going elsewhere, and though Feld frequently asked himself what keeps him here? why does he stay? he finally answered it that the man, no

---

2. landsman *n.*: Fellow countryman.

◀ **Critical Viewing**
Which item mentioned in the story is shown in this photograph? **[Connect]**

than before, and so, for example, could no longer lie late in bed mornings because he had to get up to open the store for the new assistant, a speechless, dark man with an irritating rasp as he worked, whom he would not trust with the key as he had Sobel. Furthermore, this one, though able to do a fair repair job, knew nothing of grades of leather or prices, so Feld had to make his own purchases: and every night at closing time it was necessary to count the money in the till and lock up. However, he was not dissatisfied, for he lived much in his thoughts of Max and Miriam. The college boy had called her, and they had arranged a meeting for this coming Friday night. The shoemaker would personally have preferred Saturday, which he felt would make it a date of the first magnitude, but he learned Friday was Miriam's choice, so he said nothing. The day of the week did not matter. What mattered was the aftermath. Would they like each other and want to be friends? He sighed at all the time that would have to go by before he knew for sure. Often he was tempted to talk to Miriam about the boy, to ask whether she thought she would like his type—he had told her only that he considered Max a nice boy and had suggested he call her—but the one time he tried she snapped at him—justly—how should she know?

At last Friday came. Feld was not feeling particularly well so he stayed in bed, and Mrs. Feld thought it better to remain in the bedroom with him when Max called. Miriam received the boy, and her parents could hear their voices, his throaty one, as they talked. Just before leaving, Miriam brought Max to the bedroom door and he stood there a minute, a tall, slightly hunched figure wearing a thick, droopy suit, and apparently at ease as he greeted the shoemaker and his wife, which was surely a good sign. And Miriam, although she had

doubt because of his terrible experiences as a refugee, was afraid of the world.

After the incident with the broken last, angered by Sobel's behavior, the shoemaker decided to let him stew for a week in the rooming house, although his own strength was taxed dangerously and the business suffered. However, after several sharp nagging warnings from both his wife and daughter, he went finally in search of Sobel, as he had once before, quite recently, when over some fancied slight—Feld had merely asked him not to give Miriam so many books to read because her eyes were strained and red—the assistant had left the place in a huff, an incident which, as usual, came to nothing for he had returned after the shoemaker had talked to him, and taken his seat at the bench. But this time, after Feld had plodded through the snow to Sobel's house—he had thought of sending Miriam but the idea became repugnant to him—the burly landlady at the door informed him in a nasal voice that Sobel was not at home, and though Feld knew this was a nasty lie, for where had the refugee to go? still for some reason he was not completely sure of—it may have been the cold and his fatigue— he decided not to insist on seeing him. Instead he went home and hired a new helper.

Having settled the matter, though not entirely to his satisfaction, for he had much more to do

worked all day, looked fresh and pretty. She was a large-framed girl with a well-shaped body, and she had a fine open face and soft hair. They made, Feld thought, a first-class couple.

Miriam returned after 11:30. Her mother was already asleep, but the shoemaker got out of bed and after locating his bathrobe went into the kitchen, where Miriam, to his surprise, sat at the table, reading.

"So where did you go?" Feld asked pleasantly.

"For a walk," she said, not looking up.

"I advised him," Feld said, clearing his throat, "he shouldn't spend so much money."

"I didn't care."

The shoemaker boiled up some water for tea and sat down at the table with a cupful and a thick slice of lemon.

"So how," he sighed after a sip, "did you enjoy?"

◆ **Reading Strategy**
Looking into your own experience, why do you think Feld ends up asking Miriam about her date?

"It was all right."

He was silent. She must have sensed his disappointment, for she added, "You can't really tell much the first time."

"You will see him again?"

Turning a page, she said that Max had asked for another date.

"For when?"

"Saturday."

"So what did you say?"

"What did I say?" she asked, delaying for a moment—"I said yes."

Afterwards she inquired about Sobel, and Feld, without exactly knowing why, said the assistant had got another job. Miriam said nothing more and began to read. The shoemaker's conscience did not trouble him; he was satisfied with the Saturday date.

During the week, by placing here and there a deft question, he managed to get from Miriam some information about Max. It surprised him to learn that the boy was not studying to be either a doctor or lawyer but was taking a business course leading to a degree in accountancy. Feld was a little disappointed because he thought of accountants as bookkeepers and would have preferred "a higher profession." However, it was not long before he had

investigated the subject and discovered that Certified Public Accountants were highly respected people, so he was thoroughly content as Saturday approached. But because Saturday was a busy day, he was much in the store and therefore did not see Max when he came to call for Miriam. From his wife he learned there had been nothing especially revealing about their meeting. Max had rung the bell and Miriam had got her coat and left with him—nothing more. Feld did not probe, for his wife was not particularly observant. Instead, he waited up for Miriam with a newspaper on his lap, which he scarcely looked at so lost was he in thinking of the future. He awoke to find her in the room with him, tiredly removing her hat. Greeting her, he was suddenly inexplicably afraid to ask anything about the evening. But since she volunteered nothing he was at last forced to inquire how she had enjoyed herself. Miriam began something noncommittal but apparently changed her mind, for she said after a minute, "I was bored."

When Feld had sufficiently recovered from his anguished disappointment to ask why, she answered without hesitation, "Because he's nothing more than a materialist."

"What means this word?"

"He has no soul. He's only interested in things."

He considered her statement for a long time but then asked, "Will you see him again?"

"He didn't ask."

"Suppose he will ask you?"

"I won't see him."

He did not argue: however, as the days went by he hoped increasingly she would change her mind. He wished the boy would telephone, because he was sure there was more to him than Miriam, with her inexperienced eye, could discern. But Max didn't call. As a matter of fact he took a different route to school, no longer passing the shoemaker's store, and Feld was deeply hurt.

Then one afternoon Max came in and asked for his shoes. The shoemaker took them down

◆ **Build Vocabulary**
repugnant (ri pug′ nənt) *adj.*: Offensive; disagreeable
discern (di surn′) *v.*: To perceive or recognize; make out clearly

from the shelf where he had placed them, apart from the other pairs. He had done the work himself and the soles and heels were well built and firm. The shoes had been highly polished and somehow looked better than new. Max's Adam's apple went up once when he saw them, and his eyes had little lights in them.

"How much?" he asked, without directly looking at the shoemaker.

"Like I told you before," Feld answered sadly. "One dollar fifty cents."

Max handed him two crumpled bills and received in return a newly-minted silver half dollar.

He left. Miriam had not been mentioned. That night the shoemaker discovered that his new assistant had been all the while stealing from him, and he suffered a heart attack.

Though the attack was very mild, he lay in bed for three weeks. Miriam spoke of going for Sobel, but sick as he was Feld rose in wrath against the idea. Yet in his heart he knew there was no other way, and the first weary day back in the shop thoroughly convinced him, so that night after supper he dragged himself to Sobel's rooming house.

He toiled up the stairs, though he knew it was bad for him, and at the top knocked at the door. Sobel opened it and the shoemaker entered. The room was a small, poor one, with a single window facing the street. It contained a narrow cot, a low table and several stacks of books piled haphazardly around on the floor along the wall, which made him think how queer Sobel was, to be uneducated and read so much. He had once asked him, Sobel, why you read so much? and the assistant could not answer him. Did you ever study in a college someplace? he had asked but Sobel shook his head. He read, he said, to know. But to know what, the shoemaker demanded, and to know, why? Sobel never explained, which proved he read much because he was queer.

Feld sat down to recover his breath. The assistant was resting on his bed with his heavy back to the wall. His shirt and trousers were clean, and his stubby fingers, away from the shoemaker's bench, were strangely pallid. His face was thin and pale, as if he had been shut in this room since the day he had bolted from the store.

"So when you will come back to work?" Feld asked him.

To his surprise, Sobel burst out, "Never."

Jumping up, he strode over to the window that looked out upon the miserable street. "Why should I come back?" he cried.

"I will raise your wages."

"Who cares for your wages!"

The shoemaker, knowing he didn't care, was at a loss what else to say.

"What do you want from me, Sobel?"

"Nothing."

"I always treated you like you was my son."

Sobel vehemently denied it. "So why you look for strange boys in the street they should go out with Miriam? Why you don't think of me?"

The shoemaker's hands and feet turned freezing cold. His voice became so hoarse he couldn't speak. At last he cleared his throat and croaked, "So what has my daughter got to do with a shoemaker thirty-five years old who works for me?"

"Why do you think I worked so long for you?" Sobel cried out. "For the stingy wages I sacrificed five years of my life so you could have to eat and drink and where to sleep?"

"Then for what?" shouted the shoemaker.

"For Miriam," he blurted—"for her."

The shoemaker, after a time, managed to say, "I pay wages in cash, Sobel," and lapsed into silence. Though he was seething with excitement, his mind was coldly clear, and he had to admit to himself he had sensed all along that Sobel felt this way. He had never so much as thought it consciously, but he had felt it and was afraid.

"Miriam knows?" he muttered hoarsely.

"She knows."

"You told her?"

"No."

"Then how does she know?"

"How does she know?" Sobel said, "because she knows. She knows who I am and what is in my heart."

◆ **Literary Focus**

How can you tell Feld is having an epiphany?

Feld had a sudden insight. In some devious way, with his books and commentary, Sobel had given Miriam to understand that he loved her.

The shoemaker felt a terrible anger at him for his deceit.

"Sobel, you are crazy," he said bitterly. "She will never marry a man so old and ugly like you."

Sobel turned black with rage. He cursed the shoemaker, but then, though he trembled to hold it in, his eyes filled with tears and he broke into deep sobs. With his back to Feld, he stood at the window, fists clenched, and his shoulders shook with his choked sobbing.

Watching him, the shoemaker's anger diminished. His teeth were on edge with pity for the man, and his eyes grew moist. How strange and sad that a refugee, a grown man, bald and old with his miseries, who had by the skin of his teeth escaped Hitler's incinerators,[3] should fall in love, when he had got to America, with a girl less than half his age. Day after day, for five years he had sat at his bench, cutting and hammering away, waiting for the girl to become a woman, unable to ease his heart with speech, knowing no protest but desperation.

"Ugly I didn't mean," he said half aloud.

Then he realized that what he had called

---

3. **Hitler's incinerators:** During World War II, millions of Jews were murdered by the Nazis under the direction of German dictator Adolf Hitler (1889–1945).

ugly was not Sobel but Miriam's life if she married him. He felt for his daughter a strange and gripping sorrow, as if she were already Sobel's bride, the wife, after all, of a shoemaker, and had in her life no more than her mother had had. And all his dreams for her—why he had slaved and destroyed his heart with anxiety and labor—all these dreams of a better life were dead.

The room was quiet. Sobel was standing by the window reading, and it was curious that when he read he looked young.

"She is only nineteen," Feld said brokenly. "This is too young yet to get married. Don't ask her for two years more, till she is twenty-one, then you can talk to her."

Sobel didn't answer. Feld rose and left. He went slowly down the stairs but once outside, though it was an icy night and the crisp falling snow whitened the street, he walked with a stronger stride.

But the next morning, when the shoemaker arrived, heavy-hearted, to open the store, he saw he needn't have come, for his assistant was already seated at the last, pounding leather for his love.

Guide for Responding

◆ Literature and Your Life

Reader's Response Which ambitions for Miriam's future seem more worthy to you, Feld's or Miriam's? Explain.

Thematic Focus Explain how the everyday event of having shoes repaired becomes more than an ordinary errand in this story.

☑ Check Your Comprehension

1. (a) Why does Feld want to introduce Max to his daughter? (b) What about Max appeals to Feld?
2. How does the introduction take place?
3. How does Miriam react to her second date with Max?
4. What causes Sobel to quit his job with Feld?
5. How does Feld respond to Sobel's revelation about his feelings for Miriam?

◆ Critical Thinking

INTERPRET

1. How does Feld's belief that he wasted his youth shape his actions? **[Analyze]**
2. (a) What does education represent to Feld? (b) What does it represent to Sobel? **[Interpret]**
3. How might Feld's meddling in Miriam's life change her future? **[Speculate]**
4. In what ways are Feld and Sobel similar, despite their different goals for Miriam? **[Compare and Contrast]**

EVALUATE

5. Do you think Feld was right to interfere in Miriam's life? Explain. **[Make a Judgment]**

EXTEND

6. Discuss some pros and cons of having particular career aspirations for someone you love. **[Career Link]**

Guide for Responding (continued)

◆ Reading Strategy

IDENTIFY WITH CHARACTERS

When you **identify with characters,** you connect to their experiences, emotions, and actions by drawing links to your own life. This strategy of connecting with the story allows you to get more emotionally involved in your reading.

Choose a character from "The First Seven Years" and find as many links as possible to your own experience. Then imagine yourself in the character's situation. How would you feel? What actions might you take? Answer these questions in a short paragraph that explains the connections you discovered to your own life. You may want to use an outline like this one to organize your thoughts:

> **I. How the Character Is Like Me**
>   a.
>   b.
>
> **II. How I Might React in the Character's Situation**
>   a.
>   b.
>
> **III. Actions I Might Take if I Were the Character**
>   a.
>   b.

◆ Literary Focus

EPIPHANY

In "The First Seven Years," as in many modern stories, the action moves toward an **epiphany,** or sudden flash of insight, rather than a traditional resolution.

1. What is the epiphany that Feld experiences at the end of the story?
2. What long-held assumptions does Feld reevaluate as a result of his epiphany?
3. Speculate how this epiphany might
   (a) change Feld's way of thinking in the future.
   (b) affect Feld's attitude toward Miriam.
   (c) affect a future course of events.

◆ Build Vocabulary

USING THE WORD ROOT *-liter-*

Use your knowledge of the root *-liter-,* meaning "letter," to expand your vocabulary. Suggest a definition for each of the following words. Then check your definitions against those in a dictionary.

1. literary   2. literal   3. alliteration   4. literacy

USING THE WORD BANK

On your paper, write the Word Bank word you might find in each of these newspaper articles:

1. *Reading Rate Declines Among American Adults*
2. *Residents Complain of Dump's Disagreeable Smell*
3. *Hard-Working Teenagers Turn Vacant Lot Into Garden*
4. *Dishonorable Band of Thieves Gets Nabbed*
5. *Girl of 10 Recognizes Error in Mayor's Speech*
6. *Five Executives Caught Plotting a Takeover*

◆ Grammar and Style

CORRECT USE OF *WHO* AND *WHOM*

Using *who* and *whom* correctly helps Malamud clarify which character he's describing.

> **Correct use of *who* and *whom*** is determined by the word's function in the sentence. *Who* is used as a subject; *whom* is used as an object.

Practice On your paper, write each sentence, replacing the blank with the correct word—*who* or *whom.* Then identify the word's function in the sentence.

1. ____?____ he was the shoemaker for a moment had no idea . . .
2. So Feld, ____?____ had looked forward to anticipating how it would go with his daughter and Max . . .
3. . . .what possible harm for a working girl in an office, ____?____ met only loud-mouthed salesman . . .
4. . . .he had to get up to open the store for the new assistant . . . ____?____ he would not trust with the key . . .
5. He called Sobel ____?____ he expected would be immediately available.

Build Your Portfolio

 ## Idea Bank

Writing

1. **Diary Entry** Consider Sobel's anger and disappointment after hearing Feld's conversation with Max. Write a diary entry in which he responds to what he's heard.

2. **Matchmaker's Letter** In many times and cultures, marriages have been arranged by matchmakers. As a matchmaker, write a letter introducing Miriam to a prospective match.

3. **Literary Analysis** Considering Miriam's great interest in books, why would she turn down the opportunity to go to college? Using details from the story, write an essay answering this question.

Speaking and Listening

4. **Group Discussion** In a group, review what you know about Sobel's past. Discuss ways in which his past might have affected his personality, values, and decisions. **[Social Studies Link]**

5. **Role Play** Imagine two years have passed since the story's end. With a classmate, role-play a conversation in which Sobel reminds Feld of his earlier promise. **[Performing Arts Link]**

Projects

6. **Cultural Research** Learn about a present-day culture in which marriages are commonly arranged. In a report, describe the system and its acceptance by those within the culture.

7. **Accounting Curriculum** If Max were studying accounting today, what courses would he be taking? First, research the requirements for becoming a certified public accountant. Then describe four courses in detail. Like a true curriculum, each course should teach a different aspect of accounting. **[Career Link; Math Link]**

 ## Writing Mini-Lesson

Personality Profile

Malamud creates a believable and engaging character in Feld, the shoemaker. Suppose you are going to develop a television show based on "The First Seven Years." Write a personality profile of Feld to be used by your producers. Use this tip to help you provide a clear picture to the producer.

Writing Skills Focus: Elaboration to Give Information

When you provide information about a character or anything else, **elaborate** on each of your main ideas through the presentation of details and examples. Notice how the details in this paragraph help Malamud develop Sobel's character.

Model From the Story

Sobel opened [the door] and the shoemaker entered. The room was a small, poor one, with a single window facing the street. It contained a narrow cot, a low table and several stacks of books piled haphazardly around on the floor along the wall, which made [Max] think how queer Sobel was, to be uneducated and read so much.

Prewriting Before Feld's television character can be fully crafted, actors and producers need to know what he looks like and how he behaves. In a cluster diagram, jot down physical characteristics and personal qualities you observe in Feld.

Drafting Begin with a particularly informative detail or image of Feld. Expand your profile in layers, adding information about the shoemaker and referring to your cluster diagram as needed. Keep in mind the main impression you want to create.

Revising Have a classmate create a new cluster diagram from your profile. Compare it to your prewriting diagram to discover key information you may have omitted.

$\mathcal{G}$uide for Interpreting

John Updike (1932–)

John Updike's fiction spins the gold of insight from the straw of everyday experience. Through his depictions of ordinary situations and events, Updike explores some of the most important issues of our time and offers glimpses of the underlying significance of everyday life in contemporary America.

*Updike transfigures out-
wardly ordinary people,
places, objects, and events
with flashes of insight,
grief, and love.*

His short stories, novels, plays and poems have given shape to the lives of many Americans—children and adults, rich and poor, ordinary and gifted.

Small Town to Big City John Updike was born in Reading, Pennsylvania, and raised in the nearby town of Shillington. His father was a high-school teacher and his mother a writer. Updike thinks his experience as an only child helped to nurture his artistic temperament: "I'm sure that my capacities to fantasize and to make coherent fantasies, to have patience to sit down day after day and to whittle a fantasy out of paper, all that relates to being an only child."

Updike excelled in drawing as well as writing. In early years, he focused his hopes on a career as a cartoonist, following in the path of James Thurber. As he matured, his interest shifted toward writing, and by age eighteen, he had decided to pursue a career in writing. This aspiration may have been fostered by his mother, who had literary ambitions of her own. After graduating from Harvard, Updike studied for a year in England. When he returned to the United States, he became a staff writer for the *New Yorker* magazine, where James Thurber and E. B. White had made names for themselves earlier.

The Personal and the Global
Updike has received wide acclaim for his many novels, as well as for volumes of poetry, criticism, and short stories. His thematic concerns are broad: Four novels featuring a character called Rabbit magnify the meaning of everyday moments. Novels such as *The Coup* (1978), *Brazil* (1994), and *In the Beauty of the Lilies* (1997) use a wider lens to examine how historical and political issues have affected people across the globe. Updike is also a master of the short story form, which is ideal for capturing flashes of insight into ordinary existence. In the story "The Brown Chest," a man sifts through his deceased mother's belongings, focusing again and again on a chest filled with odds and ends that call up significant memories.

◆ Background for Understanding

CULTURE: THE BROWN CHEST AS A TIME CAPSULE

The brown chest in Updike's story is a kind of time capsule of early-twentieth century popular culture. For example, it contains auburn curls from a haircut in 1919, recalling the "bobbed" haircuts that were popular just after World War 1. The 1925 wedding dress was probably not the full-length style that brides wear today. Most likely, it was a short dress or had a short hem in the front and a long one in the back. Another item in the chest is a photograph of the main character's father as a college football player in the early 1920's. At that time, players wore little padding, and skull-hugging leather helmets provided much less protection than the large synthetic padded helmets of today.

During the period profiled by the items in the chest, there was no videotape to help future generations grasp what life was like. As a result, the items provide one of the few means of gaining insight into the times.

The Brown Chest

◆ *Literature and Your Life*

CONNECT YOUR EXPERIENCE

Whether it is a drawer stuffed with old Scout badges or valentines from the third grade, most of us have a place for keeping those things we no longer need but cannot bear to throw away. The character in this story looks through a chest that has been in his family for many years, a chest that holds a lifetime of family memories.

THEMATIC FOCUS: LITERATURE CONFRONTS THE EVERYDAY

The man in Updike's story makes many personal associations with the everyday objects in the chest. As you read, look for these associations—the unique meanings the objects have for the man.

Journal Writing Make a list of five items that you've kept from years ago. For each item, jot down your reasons for keeping it.

◆ Build Vocabulary

WORD ROOT: -sim-

You'll come across the word *assimilate* in this story. It is based on the root -*sim*-, which means "the same." To *assimilate* means to blend into or "to become the same."

WORD BANK

Before you read, preview this list of words from the selection.

> mottled
> assimilate
> unfathomable
> egregious
> proprietorial
> evanescent

◆ Grammar and Style

BEGINNING SENTENCES WITH ADVERB CLAUSES

You'll discover that Updike's sentences flow smoothly from one to another and that the ideas in the sentences are clearly connected. One of the ways in which Updike makes clear connections among sentences is by beginning many of his sentences with **adverb clauses**—subordinate clauses that modify verbs, adjectives, or adverbs. Adverb clauses begin with conjunctions like *when, where, as if, if, because, in,* and *so.* Look at this example:

If she had never done this, the room would have become haunted...

◆ Literary Focus

ATMOSPHERE

Atmosphere refers to the feeling or mood evoked in the reader by a piece of writing. In works of fiction, atmosphere arises from events and from descriptions of the setting—especially the effect the setting has on particular characters.

A storage chest full of family mementos is a key element in the setting of Updike's story. As you read, notice how this brown chest and its contents affect the atmosphere of the story over time.

◆ Reading Strategy

BREAK DOWN LONG SENTENCES

Updike tends to use long sentences filled with details. Follow these tips to **break down** these long sentences:

1. Use punctuation marks—dashes, commas, parentheses, colons, and semicolons—to help you break up the sentence into manageable sections.
2. Identify the core of the sentence—the subject and the verb that accompanies it.
3. Identify how other phrases and clauses in the sentence relate to the subject.
4. Check your understanding by restating the entire sentence or portions of the sentence in your own words.

The Brown Chest

John Updike

In the first house he lived in, it sat up on the second floor, a big wooden chest, out of the way and yet not. For in this house, the house that he inhabited as if he would never live in any other, there were popular cheerful places, where the radio played and the legs of grown-ups went back and forth, and there were haunted bad places, like the coal bin behind the furnace, and the attic with its spiders and smell of old carpet, where he would never go without a grown-up close with him, and there were places in between, that were out of the main current but were not menacing, either, just neutral, and neglected. The entire front of the house had this neglected quality, with its guest bedroom where guests hardly ever stayed; it held a gray-painted bed with silver moons on the headboard and corner posts shaped at the top like mushrooms, and a little desk by the window where his mother sometimes, but not often, wrote letters and confided sentences to her diary in her tiny backslanting hand. If she had never done this, the room would have become haunted, even though it looked out on the busy street with its telephone wires and daytime swish of cars; but the occasional scratch of her pen exerted just enough pressure to keep away the frightening shadows, the sad spirits from long ago, locked into events that couldn't change.

Outside the guest-bedroom door, the upstairs hall, having narrowly sneaked past his grandparents' bedroom's door, broadened to be almost a room, with a window all its own, and a geranium on the sill shedding brown leaves when the women of the house forgot to water it, and curtains of dotted swiss[1] he could see the telephone wires through, and a rug of braided rags shaped like the oval tracks his Lionel train[2] went around and around the Christmas tree on, and, to one side, its front feet planted on the rag rug, with just enough space left for the attic door to swing open, the chest.

It was big enough for him to lie in, but he had never dared try. It was painted brown, but in such a way that the wood grain showed through, as if paint very thinned with turpentine had been used. On the side, wavy stripes of paint had been allowed to run, making dribbles like the teeth of a big wobbly comb. The lid on its brown had patches of yellow freckles. The hinges were small and black, and there was a keyhole that had no key. All this made the chest, simple in shape as it was, strange, and ancient, and almost frightening. And when

---

1. **dotted swiss:** Sheer fabric covered in woven dots.
2. **Lionel train:** The Lionel Company is a famous manufacturer of model trains, which were a very popular hobby during Updike's youth.

he, or the grown-up with him, lifted the lid of the chest, an amazing smell rushed out—deeply sweet and musty, of mothballs and cedar, but that wasn't all of it. The smell seemed also to belong to the contents—lace tablecloths and wool blankets on top, but much more underneath. The full contents of the chest never came quite clear, perhaps because he didn't want to know. His parents' college diplomas seemed to be under the blankets, and other documents going back still farther, having to do with his grandparents, their marriage, or the marriage of someone beyond even them. There was a folded old piece of paper with drawn-on hearts and designs and words in German. His mother had once tried to explain the paper to him, but he hadn't wanted to listen. A thing so old disgusted him. And there were giant Bibles, and squat books with plush covers and a little square <u>mottled</u> mirror buried in the plush of one. These books had fat pages edged in gold, thick enough to hold, on both sides, stiff brown pictures, often oval, of dead people. He didn't like looking into these albums, even when his mother was explaining them to him. The chest went down and down, into the past, and he hated the feeling of that well of time, with its sweet deep smell of things unstirring, waiting, taking on the moldy flavor of time, not moving unless somebody touched them.

Then everything moved: the moving men came one day and everything in the house that had always been in a certain place was swiftly and casually uplifted and carried out the door. In the general upheaval the week before, he had been shocked to discover, glancing in, that at some point the chest had come to contain drawings he had done as a child, and his elementary-school report cards, and photographs—studio photographs lovingly mounted in folders of dove-gray cardboard with deckle edges[3]—of him when he was five. He was now thirteen.

The new house was smaller, with more outdoors around it. He liked it less on both

accounts. Country space frightened him, much as the coal bin and the dark triangles under the attic eaves had—spaces that didn't have enough to do with people. Fields that were plowed one day in the spring and harvested one day in the fall, woods where dead trees were allowed to topple and slowly rot without anyone noticing, brambled-around spaces where he felt nobody had ever been before he himself came upon them. Heaps and rows of overgrown stones and dumps of rusty cans and tinted bottles indicated that other people in fact had been here, people like those who had posed in their Sunday clothes in the gilded albums, but the traces they left weren't usable, the way city sidewalks and trolley-car tracks were usable. His instinct was to stay in the little thick-walled country house, and read, and eat sandwiches he made for himself of raisins and peanut butter, and wait for this phase of his life to pass. Moving from the first house, leaving it behind, had taught him that a life had phases.

The chest, on that day of moving, had been set in the new attic, which was smaller than the other, and less frightening, perhaps because gaps in the cedar-shingled roof let dabs of daylight in. When the roof was being repaired, the whole space was thrown open to the weather, and it rained in, on all the furniture there was no longer room for, except up here or in the barn. The chest was too important for the barn; it perched on the edge of the attic steps, so an unpainted back he had never seen before, of two very wide pale boards, became visible. At the ends of each board were careless splashes of the thin brown paint—stain, really—left by the chestmaker when he had covered the sides.

The chest's contents, unseen, darkened in his mind. Once in a great while his mother had to search in there for something, or to confide a treasure to its depths, and in those moments, peeking in, he was surprised at how full the

---

3. **deckle edges:** Rough edges of paper, often regarded as decorative.

◆ **Build Vocabulary**

mottled (mät´ ld) *adj.*: Blotched or streaked

Winter Bouquet, Charles Burchfield, Museum of Fine Arts, Boston

▲ **Critical Viewing** In what part of the narrator's boyhood home might this room be found—in the "popular cheerful places" or the parts of the house that he describes as "neutral and neglected"? Explain. **[Distinguish]**

chest seemed, fuller than he remembered, of dotted-swiss curtains and crocheted lap rugs and photographs in folders of soft cardboard, all smelling of camphor and cedar. There the chest perched, an inch from the attic stairwell, and there it stayed, for over forty years.

Then it moved again. His children, adults all, came from afar and joined him in the house, where their grandmother had at last died, and divided up the furniture—some for them to carry away, some for the local auctioneer to sell, and some for him, the only survivor of that first house, with its long halls and haunted places, to keep and to <u>assimilate</u> to his own house, hundreds of miles away.

Two of the three children, the two that were married, had many responsibilities and soon left; he and his younger son, without a wife and without a job, remained to empty the house and pack the U-Haul van they rented. For days they lived together, eating takeout food, poisoning mice and trapping cats, moving from crowded cellar to jammed attic like sick men changing position in bed, overwhelmed by decisions, by accumulated possessions, now and then fleeing the house to escape the oppression of the past. He found the iron scales, quite rusted by the cellar damp, whereon his grandmother used to weigh out bundles of asparagus against a set of cylindrical weights. The weights were still heavy in his hand, and left rust stains on his palm. He studied a tin basin, painted in a white-on-gray spatter-pattern that had puzzled him as a child with its apparent sloppiness, and he could see again his grandfather's paper-white feet soaking in suds that rustled as the bubbles popped one by one.

◆ **Literary Focus**
How would you describe the atmosphere in this paragraph? What details contribute to that atmosphere?

The chest, up there in the attic along with old rolled carpets and rocking chairs with broken cane seats, stacked hatboxes from the Thirties and paperback mysteries from the Forties, was too heavy to lift, loaded as it was. He and his younger son took out layers of blankets and plush-covered albums, lace tablecloths and linen napkins; they uncovered a long cardboard box labelled in his mother's handwriting "Wedding Dress 1925," and, underneath that, rumpled silk dresses that a small girl might have worn when the century was young, and patent-leather baby shoes, and a gold-plated horseshoe, and faithful notations of the last century's weather kept by his grandfather's father in limp dairies bound in red leather, and a buggy-whip. A little box labelled in his mother's handwriting "Haircut July 1919" held, wrapped in tissue paper, coils of auburn hair startlingly silky to the touch. There were stiff brown photographs of his father's college football team, his father crouching at right tackle in an unpadded helmet, and of a stageful of posing young people among whom he finally found his mother, wearing a flimsy fairy dress and looking as if she had been crying. And so on and on, until he couldn't bear it and asked his son to help him carry the chest, half unemptied, down the narrow attic stairs whose bare wooden treads had been troughed[4] by generations of use, and then down the slightly broader stairs carpeted decades ago, and out the back door to the van. It didn't fit; they had to go back to the city ten miles away to rent a bigger van. Even so, packing everything in was a struggle. At one point, exasperated and anxious to be gone, his broad-backed son, hunched in the body of the U-Haul van, picked up the chest single-handed, and inverted it, lid open, over some smaller items to save space. The old thin-painted wood gave off a sharp *crack*, a piercing quick cry of injury.

The chest came to rest in his barn. He now owned a barn, not a Pennsylvania barn with stone sides and pegged oak beams but a skimpier, New England barn, with a flat tarred roof and a long-abandoned horse stall. He found the place in the chest lid, near one of the little dark hinges, where a split had occurred, and with a few carefully driven nails repaired the damage well enough. He could not blame the boy, who was named Gordon, after his paternal grandfather, the one-time football player crouching for his picture in some sunny autumn when Harding[5] was President. On the drive north in a downpour, Gordon had driven the truck, and his father tried to read the map, and in the dim light of the cab failed, and headed him the wrong way out of Westchester County, so they wound up across the Hudson River, amid blinding headlights, on an <u>unfathomable</u>, exitless highway. After that <u>egregious</u> piece of guidance, he could not blame the boy for anything, even for failing to get a job while concentrating instead on perfecting his dart game in the fake pubs of Boston. In a way not then immediately realized,

the map-reading blunder righted the balance between them, himself and his son, as when under his grandmother's gnarled hands another stalk of asparagus would cause the tray holding the rusty cylindrical weights to rise with a soft *clunk*.

◆ **Reading Strategy**

Notice that this long sentence has two focuses: the man and his son, and the man's grandmother using a scale.

They arrived an hour late, after midnight. The unloading, including the reloading of the righted chest, all took place by flashlight, hurriedly, under the drumming sound of rain on the flat roof.

Now his barn felt haunted. He could scarcely bear to examine his inherited treasure, the chairs and cabinets and chinaware and faded best-sellers and old-fashioned bridge lamps clustered in a corner beyond the leaf-mulcher and the snow-blower and the rack of motorcycle tires left by the youngest son of the previous owner of the barn. He was the present owner. He had never imagined, as a child, owning so much. His wife saw no place in their house for even the curly-maple[6] kitchen table and the walnut corner cupboard, his mother's pride. This section of the barn became, if not as frightening as the old coal bin, a place he avoided. These pieces that his infant eyes had grazed, and that had framed his parents' lives, seemed sadly shabby now, cheap in their time, most of them, and yet devoid of antique value: useless used furniture he had lacked the courage to discard.

So he was pleased, one winter day, two years after their wayward drive north, to have Gordon call and ask if he could come look at

---

6. **curly-maple:** Maple wood with a pronounced wavy grain.

---

4. **troughed** (trôf´d) *v*.: Worn into troughs or grooves.
5. **Harding:** Warren G. Harding (1865–1923), twenty-ninth president of the United States, from 1921 to 1923.

◆ **Build Vocabulary**

assimilate (ə sim´ ə lāt´) *v*.: To absorb or incorporate

unfathomable (un fath´ əm ə bəl) *adj*.: Unable to be understood

egregious (ē grē´ jəs) *adj*.: Outstanding for undesirable qualities; remarkably bad

the furniture in the barn. He had a job, he said, or almost, and was moving into a bigger place, out from the city. He would be bringing a friend, he vaguely added. A male friend, presumably, to help him lift and load what he chose to take away.

But the friend was a female, small and exquisite, with fascinating large eyes, the whites white as china, and a way of darting back and forth like a hummingbird, her wings invisible. "Oh," she exclaimed, over this and that, explaining to Gordon in a breathy small voice how this would be useful, and that would fit right in. "Lamps!" she said. "I love lamps."

"You see, Dad," the boy explained, the words pronounced softly yet in a manner so momentous that it seemed to take all the air in the barn to give them utterance, "Morna and I are planning to get married."

"Morna"—a Celtic name, fittingly elfin. The girl was magical, there in the cold barn, emitting puffs of visible breath, moving through the clutter with quick twists of her denim-clad hips and graceful stabs of her narrow white hands. She spoke only to Gordon, as if a pane of shyness protected her from his hoary[7] father—at this late phase of his life a kind of ogre, an ancestral, <u>proprietorial</u> figure full of potency and ugliness. "Gordon, what's this?" she asked.

The boy was embarrassed, perhaps by her innocent avidity.[8] "Tell her, Dad."

"Our old guest bed." Which he used to lie diagonally across, listening to his mother's pen

▼ **Critical Viewing** How do the items in the chest tell the story of the family that owns it? **[Analyze]**

---

7. **hoary** (hôr´ē) *adj.*: Ancient; old.
8. **avidity** (ə vid´ ə tē) *n.*: Eagerness.

scratch as her diary tried to hold fast her days. Even then he knew it couldn't be done.

"We could strip off the ghastly gray, I guess," the boy conceded, frowning in the attempt to envision it and the work involved. "We *have* a bed," he reminded her.

"And this?" she went on, leaving the bed hanging in a realm of future possibility. Her headscarf had slipped back, exposing auburn hair glinting above the vapor of her breath, in <u>evanescent</u> present time.

She had paused at the chest. Her glance darted at Gordon, and then, receiving no response, at the present owner, looking him in the eyes for the first time. The ogre smiled. "Open it."

"What's in it?" she asked.
He said, "I forget, actually."

Delicately but fearlessly, she lifted the lid, and out swooped, with the same vividness that had astonished and alarmed his nostrils as a child, the sweetish deep cedary smell, undiminished, cedar and camphor and paper and cloth, the smell of family, family without end.

◆ **Build Vocabulary**

proprietorial (prō prī́ ə tôŕ ē əl) *adj.*: Like someone who owns something

evanescent (ev́ ə neś ənt) *adj.*: Tendency to fade or disappear

Guide for Responding

◆ *Literature and Your Life*

Reader's Response The brown chest clearly has had a profound effect upon the man in the story. What object or objects in your life seem to have emotional power over you, and why?

Thematic Focus Find three pieces of evidence in the story to support this statement: Everyday experiences can end up making the most powerful memories.

Partner Discussion Are you a "purger"—someone who is always throwing things away, or a "pack rat"— someone who saves every little thing? Pair up with a partner of the opposite inclination, and persuade him or her that your way is best.

☑ Check Your Comprehension

1. Describe the boy's earliest impressions of the chest and its contents.
2. What does he notice has been added to the chest when he is older?
3. (a) How much time passes in the story? (b) How do you know?
4. For whom does the man open the chest at the end of the story?

◆ **Critical Thinking**

INTERPRET
1. (a) What event "righted the balance" between the man and his son? (b) Why does that event cause the man to reevaluate his feelings toward his son? **[Analyze]**
2. How does the main character seem to feel towards Morna, and how can you tell? **[Infer]**
3. (a) Which detail about Morna connects her to the chest: her narrow white hands? her auburn hair? her large eyes? (b) Why is this detail significant? **[Support; Infer]**
4. Explain how the main character's attitude toward the chest changes from the beginning to the end of the story. **[Synthesize]**

EVALUATE
5. How well do you think Updike succeeds in showing the passing of many decades within the confines of the short story form? Explain. **[Criticize]**

EXTEND
6. The man in the story finds his mother's 1925 wedding dress. Identify two or three important social or economic events that occurred in our country in the 1920's. **[Social Studies Link]**

Guide for Responding (continued)

◆ Literary Focus

ATMOSPHERE

Through his vivid descriptions of the items in the chest and the main character's feelings about them, Updike creates a powerful **atmosphere,** or mood, in "The Brown Chest."

1. Reread each detail that follows and tell what emotion it suggests the narrator might be feeling. Identify the word or words that led you to your answer.
   (a) . . . *its guest bedroom where guests hardly ever stayed*
   (b) *studio photographs lovingly mounted in folders of dove-gray cardboard*
   (c) *faithful notations of the last century's weather kept by his grandfather's father . . .*
2. Reread the paragraph on p. 907 that begins "The chest came to rest in his barn." (a) How would you describe the atmosphere in this paragraph? (b) What details contribute to that atmosphere?
3. (a) Describe how the atmosphere changes when Morna enters the story. (b) What words signal the change? (c) Why do you think the atmosphere changes?

◆ Reading Strategy

BREAK DOWN LONG SENTENCES

To create sentence variety, writers use sentences with different lengths and structures. "The Brown Chest" includes a number of long sentences. Use the strategies presented on p. 903 to **break down** the following long sentence:

> Once in a great while his mother had to search in there for something, or to confide a treasure to its depths, and in those moments, peeking in, he was surprised at how full the chest seemed, fuller than he remembered, of dotted-swiss curtains and crocheted lap rugs and photographs in folders of soft cardboard, all smelling of camphor and cedar.

1. How does punctuation help break this sentence into meaningful sections?
2. What action or actions are being performed in this sentence?
3. Why do you think Updike used a long sentence to convey this information?

◆ Build Vocabulary

USING THE WORD ROOT -sim-

Knowing that the root -sim- means the same, complete each sentence with one of the words from the box.

similar	simultaneous	simulation

1. My arrival at the party and his departure from it were almost ____?____; I ran into him at the door.
2. Her hair style is ____?____ to mine, except hers is longer in the front.
3. The spaceflight ____?____ was so realistic that I swear I felt weightless!

USING THE WORD BANK

Write the following sentences in your notebook, replacing the italicized word or phrase in each with the appropriate word from the Word Bank.

1. The small boy found the adults' attachment to the chest *impossible to figure out.*
2. The covers of the old books were *spotted.*
3. The man had *an ownerlike* interest in the chest.
4. His joy in the smell of the chest was *likely to disappear soon,* yet powerful.
5. Try as he might, he couldn't make the chest *fit* into his everyday life two hundred miles away.
6. If the man's parents had made any *outstandingly bad* errors, there was no evidence in the chest.

◆ Grammar and Style

BEGINNING SENTENCES WITH ADVERB CLAUSES

Beginning sentences with **adverb clauses** helps to make sentences flow smoothly from one to another and to connect ideas clearly.

Practice Write a sentence that might have preceded each of the following.

1. *Because Updike is so beloved by his readers,* he receives much fan mail.
2. *Before Updike became a writer,* he dreamed of becoming a cartoonist.
3. *Although many years have passed since Updike lived in rural Pennsylvania,* he grew up there.

Writing Application Write a paragraph describing a vivid memory. Use at least three sentences containing adverb clauses.

Build Your Portfolio

Idea Bank

Writing

1. Inventory At several points, Updike lists items in the chest. Write an inventory list of important mementos you or family members keep in your house. Arrange the list by category.

2. Poem What object have you had the most feelings about over time? Write a poem in which each stanza describes your attitude toward that object at a different point in your life.

3. Analysis of a Symbol The significance of the chest for the main character in this story changes over time. Write an essay analyzing what the chest symbolizes at different points in his life.

Speaking and Listening

4. Bequest As the main character in the story, create and deliver a future bequest of the chest to your youngest son. In a brief oral explanation, share the reasons the chest is important to you, and tell why he should have it.

5. Conversation With another student, role-play a conversation between Gordon and Morna on their way home from visiting the barn. Each character should exchange impressions of the visit. **[Performing Arts Link]**

Projects

6. Fashion Report Create a feature article on women's fashions of the 1920's. Illustrate it with examples, and draw connections between fashions and the social atmosphere of the time. **[Social Studies Link; Art Link]**

7. Music Present background music for a film based on this story. Find recordings of music from each period mentioned in the story—the 1920's to the 1980's—and put them together on an audiotape for your presentation. **[Music Link]**

Writing Mini-Lesson

Guide for Collectors

Behind every great collection—whether it consists of action heroes or family mementos—is a great organizing scheme. Choose a type of item you are particularly interested in—for example, baseball cards, stamps, or coins—and create a guide for collectors. Provide clear directions on methods for assembling and organizing a superb collection.

Writing Skills Focus: Using Clear and Logical Organization

To help your readers assemble an impressive collection, give them detailed, step-by-step instructions. Use a **clear and logical organization.** Since you'll be presenting information in a series of steps, use **chronological order,** starting by detailing the first step and continuing to the last.

Prewriting Decide what your readers most need to know. Create a priority list. For a foreign stamp collection, for example, it's important to provide tips for gathering the stamps, for storing and preserving them, and for presenting them. It's less important to provide a history of stamp collecting.

Drafting Begin by providing a clear explanation of collection techniques. Organization and preservation methods should come next. Write about the organization method that best fits the type of collection. (For example, organize foreign stamps by country, then by value within each country.)

Revising Review your guide. Does it tell your readers everything they need to know to collect, organize, and preserve the items in their collection? Is the organization method the best, and is it clearly explained? If necessary, you might want to number each step or use bullets to clarify your organization for collectors. You may also want to include graphics and illustrations to make your guide more helpful.

Guide for Interpreting

Robert Lowell *(1917–1977)*

Robert Lowell was born into one of America's oldest, most prominent families. Early in his career, he used traditional poetic forms and techniques. In the late 1950's, however, Lowell began writing freer, more direct poems in what came to be called the "confessional" mode. His volume *Life Studies* (1959) launched a school of confessional poets that included Sylvia Plath, John Berryman, and Anne Sexton.

Robert Penn Warren
(1905–1989)

Among the most versatile, prolific, and distinguished writers of our time, Robert Penn Warren won the first of his three Pulitzer Prizes for *All the King's Men* (1946), a fictional study of a Southern politician (based on Louisiana Governor Huey Long). Warren's poetry collections include *Promises* (1957), and *Now and Then: Poems* (1978). Though Warren consistently used Southern settings and characters in his writing, he treated universal themes, such as the love of the land that fills the poem "Gold Glade."

Theodore Roethke *(1908–1963)*

As a child Theodore Roethke (ret´ kē) was a passionate observer of the plants that grew in his family's acres of commercial greenhouses. Through adolescence and well into adulthood, he found it difficult to relate to other people. Following the ideas of his heroes, Emerson and Thoreau, he took refuge in nature. At age thirty-three he published the first of several volumes of poetry; he grew eventually into one of the most acclaimed poets of his day. He received the Pulitzer Prize for his collection *The Waking* (1954) and the National Book Award for *The Far Field* (1964).

William Stafford *(1914–1993)*

Focusing on such subjects as the threat of nuclear war and the beauty of untamed nature, William Stafford wrote about his fear that modern technology would someday destroy the wilderness. He did not publish his first volume of verse, *West of Your City* (1960), until age forty-six, after years of working in the United States Forest Service.

◆ Background for Understanding

CULTURE: ROBERT PENN WARREN NAMED FIRST POET LAUREATE OF THE UNITED STATES

Following an English tradition that dates back to 1619, the Library of Congress named Robert Penn Warren Poet Laureate of the United States in 1985. Warren was the first poet to be elevated to this honorary position. Before 1986, the year in which Warren actually served his term, the Library of Congress had appointed only consultants in poetry (William Stafford among them).

Since then, some of America's best and brightest literary talents—including Richard Wilbur and Rita Dove—have held the title of Poet Laureate. Unlike their British counterparts, American poets laureate are under no obligation to compose poems to commemorate special occasions. Though they receive a sizable stipend and an office in the Library of Congress for the duration of the one-year term, poets laureate are free to continue writing (or not writing) as they choose.

◆ *Literature and Your Life*

CONNECT YOUR EXPERIENCE

Sometimes, when you least expect it, you make the most surprising and important discoveries about yourself, other people, and the world around you. In the following works, you will see how four poets make discoveries and find inspiration in diverse places.

Journal Writing In your journal, write about an important and unexpected discovery you've made in the past year or so. How has your new understanding affected your life?

THEMATIC FOCUS: LITERATURE CONFRONTS THE EVERYDAY

These poems address ideas drawn from the poets' everyday observations and interests—from the effect of machines on people and animals to the vitality of an artistic ancestor. How do your everyday observations compare to theirs?

◆ Build Vocabulary

RELATED WORDS: *EXHAUST*

William Stafford uses the word *exhaust* as a noun meaning "the discharge of used steam or gas from an engine." This word may also function as a verb meaning "to empty completely" or "to tire out." Other words related to *exhaust* include *exhausted, exhaustive, exhaustible, exhaustibility,* and *exhaustion.*

WORD BANK

Before you read, preview this list of words from the poems.

brooding
furtive
meditation
declivity
vestiges
exhaust

◆ Grammar and Style

SUBJECT AND VERB AGREEMENT

A **subject** and **verb** must **agree** in number, even if the verb is separated from its subject by several intervening words. Look, for example, at this passage from "The Light Comes Brighter":

>   s   v
> …the <u>caw</u> / Of restive crows <u>is</u> sharper on the ear

The singular verb *is* agrees with the singular subject *caw.* Notice that the verb does not agree with the plural noun *crows,* which is part of an intervening prepositional phrase—not the subject of the clause.

◆ Literary Focus

DICTION AND STYLE

A writer's **style** is the manner in which he or she puts ideas into words; style generally concerns *form* rather than *content.* In poetry, style is determined by a poet's use of tone, rhythm, sound devices, figurative language, symbolism, punctuation, and capitalization, as well as the length and arrangement of lines.

An important aspect of style is a poet's **diction**, or word choice. The way a poet chooses and arranges words not only reflects varying degrees of formality and abstraction, but also helps establish a unique voice.

◆ Reading Strategy

PARAPHRASE

Some poems contain passages that are especially difficult to understand because of sophisticated or unusual vocabulary, complicated sentence structure, or the ambiguities of poetic language. To improve your understanding, take a moment to **paraphrase**, or restate in your own words, any difficult passages you encounter. For example:

Roethke's Version:

> Soon field and wood will wear an April look. . .

Paraphrased Version:

> Soon spring will come.

Hawthorne

Robert Lowell

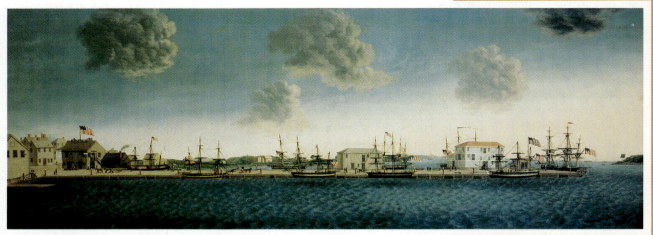

Crowninshield's Wharf, George Ropes, Peabody Museum of Salem

▲ **Critical Viewing**
What does this scene suggest about the port of Salem? How does the painting compare to Lowell's description of the town? **[Contrast]**

Follow its lazy main street lounging
from the alms house to Gallows Hill[1]
along a flat, unvaried surface
covered with wooden houses
5   aged by yellow drain
like the unhealthy hair of an old dog.
You'll walk to no purpose
in Hawthorne's Salem.

I cannot resilver the smudged plate.[2]

10   I drop to Hawthorne, the customs officer,[3]
measuring coal and mostly trying to keep warm—
to the stunted black schooner,
the dismal South-end dock,
the wharf-piles with their fungus of ice.
15   On State Street[4]
a steeple with a glowing dial-clock
measures the weary hours,
the merciless march of professional feet.

Even this shy distrustful ego
20   sometimes walked on top of the blazing roof,

---

1. Gallows Hill: Hill in Salem, Massachusetts, where nineteen people who were accused of practicing witchcraft were hanged.
2. resilver . . . plate: Early photographs were taken on a metal plate coated with silver.
3. customs officer: Nathaniel Hawthorne worked as a customs officer in Salem.
4. State Street: Street in the business district of Boston.

and felt those flashes
that char the discharged cells of the brain.

Look at the faces—
Longfellow, Lowell, Holmes and Whittier!
25   Study the grizzled silver of their beards.
Hawthorne's picture,
however, has a blond mustache
and golden General Custer[5] scalp.
He looks like a Civil War officer.
30   He shines in the firelight. His hard
survivor's smile is touched with fire.

Leave him alone for a moment or two,
and you'll see him with his head
bent down, brooding, brooding,
35   eyes fixed on some chip,
some stone, some common plant,
the commonest thing,
as if it were the clue.
The disturbed eyes rise,
40   furtive, foiled, dissatisfied
from meditation on the true
and insignificant.

---

5. **General Custer:** George Armstrong Custer (1839–1876), a general who served in the Civil War and was killed along with his troops by the Sioux at the Battle of Little Big Horn, had long blond hair.

Guide for Responding

◆ *Literature and Your Life*

Reader's Response Based on the way he is portrayed in this poem, what is your opinion of Nathaniel Hawthorne?

Thematic Focus How does the poet's focus on the "true and insignificant" aspects of daily life in Salem and Boston contribute to his portrait of Hawthorne?

Journal Writing What emotions would you expect to feel if you, like Lowell, visited the former home of a historical figure whom you admire?

✓ **Check Your Comprehension**

1. What action is detailed in the first stanza?
2. To whom does the speaker compare Hawthorne in the fifth stanza?
3. What is described in the final stanza?

◆ **Critical Thinking**

INTERPRET

1. List at least three words or images from the first stanza that contribute to the impression of Salem as a stagnant, decaying town. **[Support]**
2. What impression of professional people is created by the images in lines 15–18? **[Interpret]**
3. (a) What is the significance of the image of Hawthorne walking "on top of the blazing roof"? (b) Based on lines 23–31, how would you contrast Hawthorne with his literary contemporaries? **[Analyze; Compare and Contrast]**

APPLY

4. (a) Why do you think Lowell wrote this poem? (b) What does it reveal about the poet? **[Speculate; Apply]**

Gold Glade

Robert Penn Warren

Wandering, in autumn, the woods of boyhood,
Where cedar, black, thick, rode the ridge,
Heart aimless as rifle, boy-blankness of mood,
I came where ridge broke, and the great ledge,
5   Limestone, set the toe high as treetop by dark edge

Of a gorge, and water hid, grudging and grumbling,
And I saw, in mind's eye, foam white on
Wet stone, stone wet-black, white water tumbling,
And so went down, and with some fright on
10   Slick boulders, crossed over. The gorge-depth drew night on,

But high over high rock and leaf-lacing, sky
Showed yet bright, and declivity wooed
My foot by the quietening stream, and so I
Went on, in quiet, through the beech wood:
15   There, in gold light, where the glade gave, it stood.

The glade was geometric, circular, gold,
No brush or weed breaking that bright gold of leaf-fall.
In the center it stood, absolute and bold
Beyond any heart-hurt, or eye's grief-fall.
20   Gold-massy in air, it stood in gold light-fall,

No breathing of air, no leaf now gold-falling,
No tooth-stitch of squirrel, or any far fox bark,
No woodpecker coding, or late jay calling.
Silence: gray-shagged, the great shagbark[1]
25   Gave forth gold light. There could be no dark.

---

1. **shagbark:** Hickory tree.

◆ **Build Vocabulary**

declivity (di kliv′ ə tē) *n.*: Downward slope

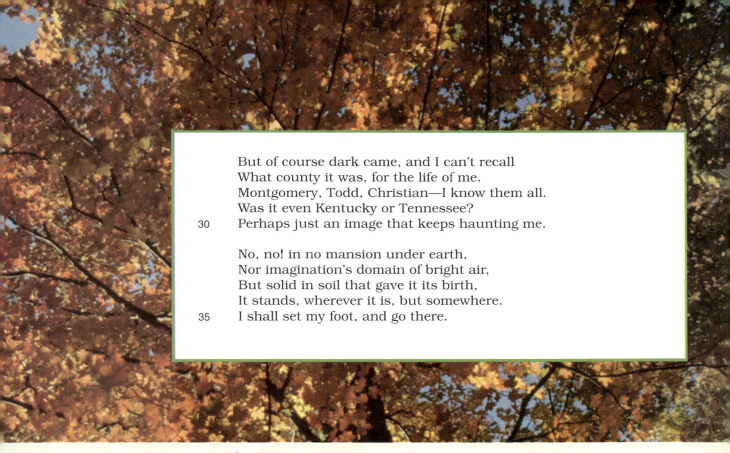

> But of course dark came, and I can't recall
> What county it was, for the life of me.
> Montgomery, Todd, Christian—I know them all.
> Was it even Kentucky or Tennessee?
> 30 Perhaps just an image that keeps haunting me.
>
> No, no! in no mansion under earth,
> Nor imagination's domain of bright air,
> But solid in soil that gave it its birth,
> It stands, wherever it is, but somewhere.
> 35 I shall set my foot, and go there.

Guide for Responding

◆ Literature and Your Life

Reader's Response What are some of your memories of autumn? How do they compare with the speaker's memories?

Thematic Focus How does the speaker compare experiences in the glade with experiences of everyday life?

Cluster Diagrams Robert Penn Warren uses the colors black, white, gold, and gray in "Gold Glade." Make four cluster diagrams containing words and images you associate with each of these colors.

☑ Check Your Comprehension

1. How does the speaker describe the glade?
2. What majestic thing does the speaker find in the center of the glade?
3. What is the speaker unable to recall about the glade?
4. What does the speaker vow to do?

◆ Critical Thinking

INTERPRET

1. At what point does the action of the poem shift from the past to the present? **[Analyze]**
2. What is the significance of the speaker's descriptions of the ledge, the gorge, and the "slick boulders" he encounters before reaching the glade? **[Interpret]**
3. (a) What does the speaker mean by the comment that the glade is "beyond any heart-hurt, or eye's grief-fall"? (b) What does he mean by the saying, "There could be no dark"? **[Interpret]**
4. (a) What does the gold glade represent to the speaker? (b) Why is he so anxious to return to the glade? **[Interpret; Infer]**

EXTEND

5. What does this poem have in common with Robert Frost's "Birches"? **[Literature Link]**

The Light Comes Brighter

Theodore Roethke

The light comes brighter from the east; the caw
Of restive crows is sharper on the ear.
A walker at the river's edge may hear
A cannon crack announce an early thaw.

5   The sun cuts deep into the heavy drift,
Though still the guarded snow is winter-sealed,
At bridgeheads buckled ice begins to shift,
The river overflows the level field.

Once more the trees assume familiar shapes,
10   As branches loose last vestiges of snow.
The water stored in narrow pools escapes
In rivulets; the cold roots stir below.

Soon field and wood will wear an April look,
The frost be gone, for green is breaking now;
15   The ovenbird[1] will match the vocal brook,
The young fruit swell upon the pear-tree bough.

And soon a branch, part of a hidden scene,
The leafy mind, that long was tightly furled,
Will turn its private substance into green,
20   And young shoots spread upon our inner world.

---

1.   **ovenbird:** Common name for any of the many
birds that build a domelike nest on the ground.

◆ **Build Vocabulary**

vestiges (ves´ tij iz) *n*.: Traces

The Adamant

Theodore Roethke

Thought does not crush to stone.
The great sledge drops in vain.
Truth never is undone;
Its shafts remain.

5   The teeth of knitted gears
Turn slowly through the night,
But the true substance bears
The hammer's weight.

Compression cannot break
10   A center so congealed;
The tool can chip no flake:
The core lies sealed.

Guide for Responding

◆ Literature and Your Life

Reader's Response Which of these poems made a stronger impression on you? Why?

Thematic Focus These poems use imagery and comparison to turn ordinary experiences into moments of discovery. How does "The Light Comes Brighter" make sense of the passage of time?

☑ Check Your Comprehension

1. What is the subject of "The Light Comes Brighter"?
2. (a) In line 4 of "The Light . . . ," what does the speaker indicate a walker might hear near a river? (b) What event does the speaker describe in the final stanza?
3. In "The Adamant," what is "the true substance"?

◆ Critical Thinking

INTERPRET

1. Identify two images or words in "The Light . . ." that suggest that the change in seasons involves action and even some violence. **[Support]**
2. What does the phrase "the leafy mind" tell you about Roethke's world view? **[Infer]**
3. An *adamant* is an extremely hard surface, such as that of a diamond. In "The Adamant," what is described as an adamant? **[Interpret]**
4. How does this imagery in "The Adamant" emphasize the indestructibility of truth? **[Analyze]**

EVALUATE

5. Does Roethke demonstrate an optimistic or a pessimistic outlook in "The Adamant"? Explain. **[Make a Judgment]**

Traveling Through

William Stafford

Traveling through the dark I found a deer
dead on the edge of the Wilson River road.
It is usually best to roll them into the canyon:
that road is narrow; to swerve might make more dead.

5　By glow of the tail-light I stumbled back of the car
and stood by the heap, a doe, a recent killing;
she had stiffened already, almost cold.
I dragged her off; she was large in the belly.

My fingers touching her side brought me the reason—
10　her side was warm; her fawn lay there waiting,
alive, still, never to be born.
Beside that mountain road I hesitated.

the Dark

The car aimed ahead its lowered parking lights;
under the hood purred the steady engine.
15 I stood in the glare of the warm <u>exhaust</u> turning red;
around our group I could hear the wilderness listen.

I thought hard for us all—my only swerving—,
then pushed her over the edge into the river.

Guide for Responding

◆ Literature and Your Life

Reader's Response How did you feel as you read this poem? What would you say to the poet if you could meet him?

Thematic Focus In an otherwise ordinary day, the speaker stumbles into a difficult dilemma. What factors does the speaker weigh in the decision?

☑ Check Your Comprehension

1. Where does the speaker find the deer?
2. What does he observe about the deer "By glow of the tail-light . . ."?
3. What does he discover when he touches the deer?
4. What does the speaker do at the end of the poem?

◆ Critical Thinking

INTERPRET

1. (a) With what details does the speaker personify his car in the fourth stanza? (b) How does the speaker's description of the car echo his discovery about the deer? **[Support; Connect]**
2. What does the speaker mean when he says, "I thought hard for all of us"? **[Interpret]**
3. What does this poem reveal about the relationship between humanity and nature in the modern world? **[Draw Conclusions]**
4. In literature, a journey is often used to symbolize life. Assuming that this applies to Stafford's poem, how might you interpret its title? **[Interpret]**

APPLY

5. If you had been traveling with the speaker, what would you have suggested that he do? **[Relate]**

Guide for Responding (continued)

◆ Literary Focus

DICTION AND STYLE

Style refers to the way in which a writer puts ideas into words. Although many writers may address the same topic, each writer's style produces a unique literary expression. Poetic style is established through the writer's use of tone, rhythm, sound devices, figurative language, symbols, punctuation and capitalization, line length and arrangement, stanza format, and **diction**—or word choice.

1. Identify and provide examples of the elements that contribute to Lowell's style in "Hawthorne."
2. What dominant characteristics of Roethke's style are revealed in these two poems?
3. (a) Which poem displays diction that is most like everyday speech? (b) Which poem displays diction that is most unlike everyday speech?

◆ Build Vocabulary

USING RELATED WORDS: *EXHAUST*

Several English words are related to the word *exhaust*. Write the following sentences on your paper, completing each with the appropriate word from the box below. Then label the part of speech of each of the four related words.

| exhaust   exhaustive   exhausted   exhaustion |

1. The ___?___ I felt was due to lack of sleep.
2. The runner had become completely ___?___ by the time she neared the finish line.
3. The truck's thick, black ___?___ obscured my vision.
4. The congressman spoke for more than twenty-three hours in an ___?___ attempt to block a vote on the proposed new legislation.

USING THE WORD BANK

On your paper, write the letter of the word in the right column that is the best synonym for the word in the left column.

1. brooding   a. slope
2. furtive   b. fumes
3. meditation   c. traces
4. declivity   d. worrying
5. vestiges   e. pensiveness
6. exhaust   f. sneaky

◆ Reading Strategy

PARAPHRASE

You can clarify difficult phrases, lines, or passages by **paraphrasing**—or restating them in your own words. In fact, you may find it useful to paraphrase every sentence of especially challenging poems. For example, you might paraphrase lines 19–22 of "Hawthorne" as *Though he was a shy and distrustful man, Hawthorne was capable of passionate feelings and extraordinary mental and artistic insights.* How would you paraphrase the following passages?

1. The glade was geometric, circular, gold, / No brush or weed breaking that bright gold of leaf-fall. / In the center it stood, absolute and bold / Beyond any heart-hurt, or eye's grief-fall.
2. The teeth of knitted gears / Turn slowly through the night, / But the true substance bears / The hammer's weight.

◆ Grammar and Style

SUBJECT AND VERB AGREEMENT

Remember in your own writing that the subject is not always the noun or pronoun that immediately precedes the verb. Sometimes you have to look closely to identify the subject—who or what is actually performing the action of the verb.

> **Subjects** and **verbs** must **agree** in number, even when they are separated by intervening words.

Practice Write the following sentences on a sheet of paper. For each sentence, underline the subject, then choose the correct form of the verb in parentheses.

1. The water stored in narrow pools (escapes/escape) in rivulets.
2. Walkers at the river's edge (hears/hear) a cannon crack.
3. The teeth of knitted gears (turns/turn) slowly through the night.
4. My fingers touching her side (reveals/reveal) the reason.
5. The leafy mind, that long was tightly furled, (turn/turns) its private substance into green.

Build Your Portfolio

 ## Idea Bank

Writing

1. **Explanation** If you were going to write a poem about one of your favorite writers, whom would you choose? Explain your choice in a paragraph.

2. **Poem** Using Warren's "Gold Glade" for inspiration, write a poem in which you use vivid imagery to re-create an important childhood experience.

3. **Critical Response** Critic Robert Boyers has commented that Roethke's best poems "permit us to embrace the principle of change as the root of stability." Write an essay in which you discuss this comment in relation to "The Light Comes Brighter" or "The Adamant."

Speaking and Listening

4. **Oral Presentation** Conduct research to learn more about Lowell and confessional poetry. In an oral report, share your findings on the confessional poets and their works. Include recitations of two or three poems.

5. **Debate** In recent years the nation's deer population has increased dramatically. Deer have even been found roaming city streets. Should special measures be taken to control the deer population? Express your opinions about the issue in a class debate. **[Social Studies Link; Science Link]**

Projects

6. **Mural** The Peabody Museum in Salem houses a fifty-panel mural, *The Chronicle of Salem*. Create another panel (based on Lowell's description of Hawthorne's Salem) for this mural. **[Art Link]**

7. **Dictionary** In "Gold Glade" Warren invents a number of compound words: boy-blankness, grief-fall, and so on. Create a "Warren dictionary" in which you define each word as it is used in the context of the poem.

 ## Writing Mini-Lesson

One Writer Reviews Another

In the book review section of many newspapers, magazines, and literary journals, you can read a writer's review of another writer's work. Often writers review works within their own genre—for instance, poets review the work of other poets, and novelists review works of fiction. Choose two poets from this section. Using one poet's work as a guide, decide what that poet might consider to be the criteria for good poetry. Then review the other poet's work using those criteria.

Writing Skills Focus: Suitable Criteria

A critical review evaluates a work of literature by discussing its positive and negative aspects. Responsible reviewers use **suitable criteria** to judge literary works. Although many of these criteria are universally accepted, some criteria reflect the reviewer's unique perspective. William Stafford's idea of what makes a good poem, for example, might be very different from Robert Lowell's. Some suitable criteria for evaluating poems include:

- skillful or inspired use of language
- effective use of poetic devices
- appropriate relationship between form and content
- compelling subject matter

Prewriting Decide on the poet from whose point of view you will speak. Review his or her poetry to determine and list the elements of writing that he values. Using these criteria, read and make notes about the poems you will review.

Drafting Establish and maintain a tone that is appropriate for a poet reviewing the work of a peer.

Revising Read the review aloud. Is your tone respectful? How thoroughly did you review the second poet's work? Did you use criteria that the first poet would have deemed especially important?

Guide for Interpreting

Anne Tyler (1941–)

As the wife of a child psychiatrist and the mother of two daughters, Anne Tyler has for years successfully juggled the demands of family life while maintaining her commitment to writing. Mondays through Thursdays she writes; Fridays she reserves for errands; weekends she devotes entirely to family matters. She works on a daybed in a starkly plain study, penning her fiction in longhand so that, as she explains it, she can hear her characters speak. During occasional bouts of insomnia, she often records her ideas in boxes of index cards.

Young Talent Born in Minneapolis, Tyler spent most of her childhood in Quaker communes in the Midwest and South. After attending high school in Raleigh, North Carolina, she went on to study Russian at Duke University when she was only sixteen. She published her first novel, *If Morning Ever Comes* (1964), at age twenty-four and since then has produced a string of novels to ever-increasing acclaim. Among them are *Dinner at the Homesick Restaurant* (1982), *The Accidental Tourist* (1985), and *Ladder of Years* (1995). Tyler has also published numerous short stories in prestigious literary magazines such as *The New Yorker*.

Serious Fiction Tyler's characters are not fictionalized versions of people from her own quiet life; they are products of a fertile imagination, drawn with her gift for fine, realistic detail. When Tyler works on a novel, she follows a pattern that entails writing out a first draft in longhand. She then reads the draft to "find out what it means." She revises the draft to enhance "the subconscious intentions" she has discovered in the work. Tyler keeps the goal of writing "serious fiction" firmly in sight.

"A serious book," Tyler explains, "is one that removes me to another life as I am reading it. It has to have layers and layers, like life does. It has to be an extremely believable lie."

"Average Waves in Unprotected Waters" displays Tyler's ability to create well-developed, realistic characters and evoke an emotional response through an unsentimental portrayal of the characters' tragic lives.

Tyler, who has remained a private person despite her fame, now lives in Baltimore, Maryland. Preferring this to living in a larger city, she has been called "the nearest thing we have to an urban southern writer."

◆ Background for Understanding

SOCIAL STUDIES: CARING FOR MENTALLY OR PHYSICALLY CHALLENGED CHILDREN

In "Average Waves in Unprotected Waters," Anne Tyler explores a mother's attempts to cope with a severely challenged child. The decision to institutionalize a child is an extremely difficult one. When this story was written in the mid-1970's, however, a single parent like the mother in "Average Waves" may have felt that she had few other options available to her. That knowledge probably offered little comfort to the parents facing such decisions. Then, as now, the cost of private care was so high that many patients wound up in state-run or charitable hospitals that were often severely underfunded. Lack of funds sometimes resulted in grim conditions, outdated equipment, and an inadequate staff.

Fortunately, today's ever-increasing array of educational, medical, and counseling programs for children with special needs makes it possible for many children who might once have been institutionalized to remain at home.

Journal Writing Explore the difficulties and emotions that parents might face in dealing with a severely challenged child.

Average Waves in Unprotected Waters

◆ *Literature and Your Life*

CONNECT YOUR EXPERIENCE

A family move, a new school, the change of seasons—these situations can present either a terrible problem to overcome or an exciting challenge to greet. Some changes present difficulties and others offer great rewards. In this story, the main character, Bet, faces a tremendous change in her life. Are you willing to make difficult changes if they are for the better?

THEMATIC FOCUS: LITERATURE CONFRONTS THE EVERYDAY

Tyler depicts the unchanging nature of Bet's character through her use of details that are ordinary as well as extraordinary. How do the everyday details enhance the emotions underlying both Bet's experiences and her resistance to change?

◆ Literary Focus

FORESHADOWING

Foreshadowing is the use of details or clues that hint at what will occur later in a plot or suggest a certain outcome. In the opening paragraphs of this story, for example, readers learn that Bet is wearing the dress "she usually saved for Sundays." This detail suggests that this day will be special or important in some way.

Foreshadowing builds suspense, because it makes the reader wonder what will happen next and what will happen at the end of the story. As you read, notice how Tyler's use of foreshadowing keeps you guessing about how the story will turn out.

◆ Grammar and Style

CORRECT USE OF ADJECTIVES AND ADVERBS

Adjectives modify nouns or pronouns; **adverbs** modify verbs, adjectives, and other adverbs. You could not, for example, use the adjective *slow* in the following sentence; the adverb *slowly* is required to modify the verb *went*.

They went down the stairs *slowly*. [not *slow*]

However, use an adjective, rather than an adverb, after a linking verb, such as a form of *be*. You must use an adjective because you are modifying the subject of the sentence, not the verb.

The collar was *askew*.   She always felt *bad*. [not *badly*]

◆ Reading Strategy

ORDER EVENTS

Most stories are written in chronological order, the order in which events happened. Sometimes, however, the writer interrupts the sequence to present a **flashback,** a scene or an event from an earlier time. As you read Tyler's story, **order events** by noting the sequence, or order, in which events actually occurred. Using an expanded version of a chain-of-events diagram like the one below, record the earliest event at the top and the latest at the bottom.

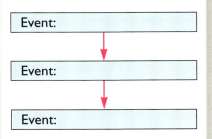

◆ Build Vocabulary

PREFIXES: *trans-*

Bet describes her son Arnold's skin as so *transparent* that "she imagined she could see the blood traveling in his veins." The prefix *trans-* means "across," "over," or "through." Something *transparent* is "clear or thin enough to be seen through."

WORD BANK

Before you read, preview this list of words from the selection.

orthopedic
transparent
stocky
staunch
viper

Average Waves in Unprotected Waters

Anne Tyler

As soon as it got light, Bet woke him and dressed him, and then she walked him over to the table and tried to make him eat a little cereal. He wouldn't, though. He could tell something was up. She pressed the edge of the spoon against his lips till she heard it click on his teeth, but he just looked off at a corner of the ceiling—a knobby child with great glassy eyes and her own fair hair. Like any other nine-year-old, he wore a striped shirt and jeans, but the shirt was too neat and the jeans too blue, unpatched and unfaded, and would stay that way till he outgrew them. And his face was elderly—pinched, strained, tired—though it should have looked as unused as his jeans. He hardly ever changed his expression.

She left him in his chair and went to make the beds. Then she raised the yellowed shade, rinsed a few spoons in the bathroom sink, picked up some bits of magazines he'd torn the night before. This was a rented room in an ancient, crumbling house, and nothing you could do to it would lighten its cluttered look. There was always that feeling of too many lives layered over other lives, like the layers of brownish wallpaper her child had peeled away in the corner by his bed.

She slipped her feet into flat-heeled loafers and absently patted the front of her dress, a worn beige knit she usually saved for Sundays. Maybe she should take it in a little; it hung from her shoulders like a sack. She felt too slight and frail, too wispy for all she had to do today. But she reached for her coat anyhow, and put it on and tied a blue kerchief under her chin. Then she went over to the table and slowly spun, modeling the coat. "See, Arnold?" she said. "We're going out."

Arnold went on looking at the ceiling, but his gaze turned wild and she knew he'd heard.

She fetched his jacket from the closet—brown corduroy, with a hood. It had set her back half a week's salary. But Arnold didn't like it; he always wanted his old one, a little red duffel coat he'd long ago outgrown. When she came toward him, he started moaning and rocking and shaking his head. She had to struggle to stuff his arms in the sleeves. Small though he was, he was strong, wiry; he was getting to be too much for her. He shook free of her hands and ran over to his bed. The jacket was on, though. It wasn't buttoned, the collar was askew, but never mind; that just made him look more real. She always felt bad at how he stood inside his clothes, separate from them, passive, unaware of all the buttons and snaps she'd fastened as carefully as she would a doll's.

She gave a last look around the room, checked to make sure the hot plate was off, and then picked up her purse and Arnold's suitcase. "Come along, Arnold," she said.

He came, dragging out every step. He looked at the suitcase suspiciously, but only because it was new. It didn't have any meaning for him. "See?" she said. "It's yours. It's Arnold's. It's going on the train with us."

But her voice was all wrong. He would pick it up, for sure. She paused in the middle of locking the door and glanced over at him fearfully. Anything could set him off nowadays. He hadn't noticed, though. He was too busy staring around the hallway, goggling at a freckled, walnut-framed mirror as if he'd never seen it before. She touched his shoulder. "Come, Arnold," she said.

They went down the stairs slowly, both of them clinging to the sticky mahogany railing. The suitcase banged against her shins. In the entrance hall, old Mrs. Puckett stood waiting outside her door—a huge, soft lady in a black crepe dress and orthopedic shoes. She was holding a plastic bag of peanutbutter cookies, Arnold's favorites. There were tears in her eyes. "Here, Arnold," she said, quavering. Maybe she felt to blame that he was going. But she'd done the best she could: babysat him all these years and only given up when he'd grown too strong and wild to manage. Bet wished Arnold would give the old lady some sign—hug her, make his little crowing noise, just take the cookies, even. But he was too excited. He raced on out the front door, and it was Bet who had to take them. "Well, thank you, Mrs. Puckett," she said. "I know he'll enjoy them later."

"Oh, no . . ." said Mrs. Puckett, and she flapped her large hands and gave up, sobbing.

They were lucky and caught a bus first thing. Arnold sat by the window. He must have thought he was going to work with her; when they passed the red-and-gold Kresge's sign, he jabbered and tried to stand up. "No, honey," she said, and took hold of his arm. He settled down then and let his hand stay curled in hers awhile. He had very small, cool fingers, and nails as smooth as thumbtack heads.

At the train station, she bought the tickets and then a pack of Wrigley's spearmint gum. Arnold stood gaping at the vaulted ceiling,

◆ **Literary Focus**
What does Mrs. Puckett's behavior hint about subsequent events?

with his head flopped back and his arms hanging limp at his sides. People stared at him. She would have liked to push their faces in. "Over here, honey," she said, and she nudged him toward the gate, straightening his collar as they walked.

He hadn't been on a train before and acted a little nervous, bouncing up and down in his seat and flipping the lid of his ashtray and craning forward to see the man ahead of them. When the train started moving, he crowed and pulled at her sleeve. "That's right, Arnold. Train. We're taking a trip," Bet said. She unwrapped a stick of chewing gum and gave it to him. He loved gum. If she didn't watch him closely, he sometimes swallowed it—which worried her a little because she'd heard it clogged your kidneys; but at least it would keep him busy. She looked down at the top of his head. Through the blond prickles of his hair, cut short for practical reasons, she could see his skull bones moving as he chewed. He was so thin-skinned, almost transparent; sometimes she imagined she could see the blood traveling in his veins.

When the train reached a steady speed, he grew calmer, and after a while he nodded over against her and let his hands sag on his knees. She watched his eyelashes slowly drooping—two colorless, fringed crescents, heavier and heavier, every now and then flying up as he tried to fight off sleep. He had never slept well, not ever, not even as a baby. Even before they'd noticed anything wrong, they'd wondered at his jittery, jerky catnaps, his tiny hands clutching tight and springing open, his strange single wail sailing out while he went right on sleeping. Avery said it gave him the chills. And after the doctor talked to them Avery wouldn't have anything to do

◆ **Build Vocabulary**

orthopedic (ôr´ thō pē´ dik) *adj.*: Correcting posture or other disorders of the skeletal system and related muscles and joints

transparent (trans per´ ənt) *adj.*: Capable of being seen through

with Arnold anymore—just walked in wide circles around the crib, looking stunned and sick. A few weeks later, he left. She wasn't surprised. She even knew how he felt, more or less. Halfway, he blamed her; halfway, he blamed himself. You can't believe a thing like this will just fall on you out of nowhere.

She'd had moments herself of picturing some kind of evil gene in her husband's ordinary, stocky body—a dark little egg like a black jelly bean, she imagined it. All his fault. But other times she was sure the gene was hers. It seemed so natural; she never could do anything as well as most people. And then other times she blamed their marriage. They'd married too young, against her parents' wishes. All she'd wanted was to get away from home. Now she couldn't remember why. What was wrong with home? She thought of her parents' humped green trailer, perched on cinder blocks near a forest of masts in Salt Spray, Maryland. At this distance (parents dead, trailer rusted to bits, even Salt Spray changed past recognition), it seemed to her that her old life had been beautifully free and spacious. She closed her eyes and saw wide gray skies. Everything had been ruled by the sea. Her father (who'd run a fishing boat for tourists) couldn't arrange his day till he'd heard the marine forecast—the wind, the tides, the small-craft warnings, the height of average waves in unprotected waters. He loved to fish, offshore and on, and he swam every chance he could get. He'd tried to teach her to bodysurf, but it hadn't worked out. There was something about the breakers: she just gritted her teeth and stood <u>staunch</u> and let them slam into her. As if standing staunch were a virtue, really. She couldn't explain it. Her father thought she was scared, but it wasn't that at all.

She'd married Avery against their wishes and been sorry ever since—sorry to move so far from home, sorrier when her parents died within a year of each other, sorriest of all when the marriage turned grim and cranky. But she never would have thought of leaving him. It was Avery who left; she would have stayed forever. In fact, she did stay on in their apartment for months after he'd gone, though the rent was far too high. It wasn't that she expected him back. She just took some comfort from enduring.

Arnold's head snapped up. He looked around him and made a gurgling sound. His chewing gum fell onto the front of his jacket. "Here, honey," she told him. She put the gum in her ashtray. "Look out the window. See the cows?"

He wouldn't look. He began bouncing in his seat, rubbing his hands together rapidly.

"Arnold? Want a cookie?"

If only she'd brought a picture book. She'd meant to and then forgot. She wondered if the train people sold magazines. If she let him get too bored, he'd go into one of his tantrums, and then she wouldn't be able to handle him. The doctor had given her pills just in case, but she was always afraid that while he was screaming he would choke on them. She looked around the car. "Arnold," she said, "see the . . . see the hat with feathers on? Isn't it pretty? See the red suitcase? See the, um . . ."

The car door opened with a rush of clattering wheels and the conductor burst in, singing "Girl of my dreams, I love you." He lurched down the aisle, plucking pink tickets from the back of each seat. Just across from Bet and Arnold, he stopped. He was looking down at a tiny black lady in a purple coat, with a fox fur piece biting its own tail around her neck. "You!" he said.

The lady stared straight ahead.

"You, I saw you. You're the one in the washroom."

A little muscle twitched in her cheek.

"You got on this train in Beulah, didn't you. Snuck in the washroom. Darted back like you thought you could put something over on me. I saw that bit of purple! Where's your ticket gone to?"

She started fumbling in a blue cloth purse. The fumbling went on and on. The conductor shifted his weight.

"Why!" she said finally. "I must've left it back in my other seat."

"What other seat?"

"Oh, the one back . . ." She waved a spidery hand.

The conductor sighed. "Lady," he said, "you owe me money."

"I do no such thing!" she said. "Viper! Monger! Hitler!"[1] Her voice screeched up all at once; she sounded like a parrot. Bet winced and felt herself flushing, as if *she* were the one. But then at her shoulder she heard a sudden, rusty clang, and she turned and saw that Arnold was laughing. He had his mouth wide open and his tongue curled, the way he did when he watched "Sesame Street." Even after the scene had worn itself out, and the lady had paid and the conductor had moved on, Arnold went on chortling and la-la-ing, and Bet looked gratefully at the little black lady, who was settling her fur piece fussily and muttering under her breath.

From the Parkinsville Railroad Station, which they seemed to be tearing down or else remodeling—she couldn't tell which—they took a taxicab to Parkins State Hospital. "Oh, I been out there many and many a time," said the driver. "Went out there just the other—"

But she couldn't stop herself; she had to tell him before she forgot. "Listen," she said, "I want you to wait for me right in the driveway. I don't want you to go on away."

"Well, fine," he said.

"Can you do that? I want you to be sitting right by the porch or the steps or whatever, right where I come out of, ready to take me back to the station. Don't just go off, and—"

"I *got* you, I got you," he said.

She sank back. She hoped he understood. Arnold wanted a peanut-butter cookie. He was reaching and whimpering. She didn't know what to do. She wanted to give him anything he asked for, anything; but he'd get it all over his face and arrive not looking his best. She couldn't stand it if they thought he was just ordinary and unattractive. She

---

1. **Hitler:** German dictator Adolf Hitler (1889–1945).

Girl Looking at Landscape, 1957, Richard Diebenkorn, oil on canvas, 59 x 60 3/8 inches, (149.9 x 153.4 cm), Gift of Mr. and Mrs. Alan H. Temple, 61.49, Collection of Whitney Museum of American Art, photograph by Geoffrey Clements, N.Y., Photograph copyright © 1997. Whitney Museum of American Art

▲ **Critical Viewing** Bet probably experienced a range of emotions after leaving the hospital. Which of her possible emotions are reflected in this painting? [Interpret]

wanted them to see how small and neat he was, how somebody cherished him. But it would be awful if he went into one of his rages. She broke off a little piece of cookie from the bag. "Here," she told him. "Don't mess, now."

He flung himself back in the corner and ate it, keeping one hand flattened across his mouth while he chewed.

The hospital looked like someone's great, pillared mansion, with square brick buildings all around it. "Here we are," the driver said.

"Thank you," she said. "Now you wait here, please. Just wait till I get—"

"*Lady*," he said. "I'll wait."

She opened the door and nudged Arnold out ahead of her. Lugging the suitcase, she started toward the steps. "Come on, Arnold," she said.

He hung back.

"Arnold?"

Maybe he wouldn't allow it, and they would go on home and never think of this again.

But he came, finally, climbing the steps in his little hobbled way. His face was clean, but there were a few cookie crumbs on his jacket. She set down the suitcase to brush them off. Then she buttoned all his buttons and smoothed his shirt collar over his jacket collar before she pushed open the door.

In the admitting office, a lady behind a wooden counter showed her what papers to sign. Secretaries were clacketing typewriters all around. Bet thought Arnold might like that, but instead he got lost in the lights—chilly, hanging ice-cube-tray lights with a little flicker to them. He gazed upward, looking astonished. Finally a flat-fronted nurse came in and touched his elbow. "Come along, Arnold. Come, Mommy. We'll show you where Arnold is staying," she said.

They walked back across the entrance hall, then up wide marble steps with hollows worn in them. Arnold clung to the banister. There was a smell Bet hated, pine-oil disinfectant, but Arnold didn't seem to notice. You never knew; sometimes smells could just put him in a state.

The nurse unlocked a double door that had chicken-wired windows. They walked through a corridor, passing several fat, ugly women in shapeless gray dresses and ankle socks. "Ha!" one of the women said, and fell giggling into the arms of a friend. The nurse said, "*Here* we are." She led them into an enormous hallway lined with little white cots. Nobody else was in it; there wasn't a sign that children lived here except for a tiny cardboard clown picture hanging on one vacant wall. "This one is your bed, Arnold," said the nurse. Bet laid the suitcase on it. It was made up so neatly, the sheets might have been painted on. A steely-gray blanket was folded across the foot. She looked over at Arnold, but he was pivoting back and forth to hear how his new sneakers squeaked on the linoleum.

"Usually," said the nurse, "we like to give new residents six months before the family visits. That way they settle in quicker, don't you see." She turned away and adjusted the clown picture, though as far as Bet could tell it was fine the way it was. Over her shoulder, the nurse said, "You can tell him goodbye now, if you like."

"Oh," Bet said. "All right." She set her hands on Arnold's shoulders. Then she laid her face against his hair, which felt warm and fuzzy. "Honey," she said. But he went on pivoting. She straightened and told the nurse, "I brought his special blanket."

"Oh, fine," said the nurse, turning toward her again. "We'll see that he gets it."

"He always likes to sleep with it; he has ever since he was little."

"All right."

"Don't wash it. He hates if you wash it."

"Yes. Say goodbye to Mommy now, Arnold."

"A lot of times he'll surprise you. I mean there's a whole lot to him. He's not just—"

"We'll take very good care of him, Mrs. Blevins, don't worry."

"Well," she said. " 'Bye, Arnold."

She left the ward with the nurse and went down the corridor. As the nurse was unlocking the doors for her, she heard a single, terrible scream, but the nurse only patted her shoulder and pushed her gently on through.

In the taxi, Bet said, "Now, I've just got fifteen minutes to get to the station. I wonder if you could hurry?"

"Sure thing," the driver said.

She folded her hands and looked straight ahead. Tears seemed to be coming down her face in sheets.

Once she'd reached the station, she went to the ticket window. "Am I in time for the twelve-thirty-two?" she asked.

"Easily," said the man. "It's twenty minutes late."

"What?"

"Got held up in Norton somehow."

"But you can't!" she said. The man looked startled. She must be a sight, all swollen-eyed and wet-cheeked. "Look," she said, in a lower voice. "I figured this on purpose. I chose the one train from Beulah that would let me catch another one back without waiting. I do not want to sit and wait in this station."

"Twenty *minutes*, lady. That's all it is."

"What am I going to do?" she asked him.

He turned back to his ledgers.

She went over to a bench and sat down. Ladders and scaffolding towered above her, and only ten or twelve passengers were dotted through the rest of the station. The place looked bombed out—nothing but a shell. "Twenty minutes!" she said aloud. "What am I going to do?"

Through the double glass doors at the far end of the station, a procession of gray-suited men arrived with briefcases. More men came behind them, dressed in work clothes, carrying folding chairs, black trunklike boxes with silver hinges, microphones, a wooden lectern, and an armload of bunting. They set the lectern down in the center of the floor, not six feet from Bet. They draped the bunting

across it—an arc of red, white, and blue. Wires were connected, floodlights were lit. A microphone screeched. One of the workmen said, "Try her, Mayor." He held the microphone out to a fat man in a suit, who cleared his throat and said, "Ladies and gentlemen, on the occasion of the expansion of this fine old railway station—"

"Sure do get an echo here," the workman said. "Keep on going."

The Mayor cleared his throat again. "If I may," he said, "I'd like to take about twenty minutes of your time, friends."

He straightened his tie. Bet blew her nose, and then she wiped her eyes and smiled. They had come just for her sake, you might think. They were putting on a sort of private play. From now on, all the world was going to be like that—just something on a stage, for her to sit back and watch.

Guide for Responding

◆ *Literature and Your Life*

Reader's Response What do you think of Bet's new outlook on life? Explain.

Thematic Focus Which details of everyday life enhance or underscore the emotions at work beneath the story's surface?

Group Discussion Do you think that Bet will be able to cope with the consequences of her choice? In a group, discuss the evidence in the story that supports your predictions.

☑ Check Your Comprehension

1. Where is Bet taking Arnold?
2. Why is she caring for Arnold without the support of her husband or family?
3. Summarize what you learned of Bet's childhood and marriage.
4. What does Bet hear just as she leaves Arnold?
5. What happens while Bet is waiting for the train home?

◆ Critical Thinking

INTERPRET

1. How does Bet's behavior when her father tried teaching her to bodysurf relate to her behavior later in life? **[Connect]**
2. Why does Bet insist that the cab driver wait for her outside the hospital? **[Infer]**
3. (a) What impression does Tyler convey in her description of the hospital? (b) What seems to be the nurse's attitude concerning Arnold's situation? **[Draw Conclusions]**
4. Explain the single, terrible scream that Mrs. Blevins hears as the nurse unlocks the doors for her. **[Interpret]**
5. What is ironic, or surprising, about the mayor's plans to speak in the train station for twenty minutes? **[Support]**
6. (a) What is the meaning of the story's final sentence? (b) How does the story's title relate to its meaning? **[Analyze]**

APPLY

7. Do you think that most people would act as Bet did if they were in her place? Why or why not? **[Generalize]**

Guide for Responding (continued)

◆ Literary Focus

FORESHADOWING

Foreshadowing is the use of hints or clues in a narrative to suggest later events. For example, in the first paragraph of the story, Tyler hints at later events when she writes that Arnold "could tell something was up."

1. Find three more examples of foreshadowing in the story. Explain each example.
2. How does Tyler's use of foreshadowing help to build suspense?
3. Why would the story be less effective if Tyler had not used foreshadowing?

◆ Build Vocabulary

USING THE PREFIX *trans-*

The prefix *trans-* means "across," "over," or "through." For each of the following words, write a sentence on your paper, explaining how the meaning of the prefix relates to the meaning of the given word.

1. translate   3. transfer
2. transatlantic 4. transportation

USING THE WORD BANK

On a separate sheet of paper, write the letter of the choice that best completes each of the following statements.

1. Something *transparent* is often made of (a) glass, (b) wool, (c) polished brass.
2. A *stocky* person looks (a) sloppy, (b) rich, (c) sturdy.
3. A *staunch* ally (a) betrays you, (b) stands by you through thick and thin, (c) abandons you at the first sign of trouble.
4. *Orthopedic* shoes are designed to (a) make you look thinner, (b) correct your posture, (c) cost less than most shoes.
5. A *viper* might (a) bite you, (b) sing to you, (c) walk up and shake your hand.

◆ Reading Strategy

ORDER EVENTS

Because Tyler's story includes a flashback that interrupts the chronological sequence of events to present an event from an earlier time, you have to pay careful attention to the **order of events** in the story.

1. State the main events and details of the story in chronological order.
2. (a) What flashback does Bet have? (b) What prompts this flashback, and what causes it to end? (c) What does it add to your understanding of the story?

◆ Grammar and Style

CORRECT USE OF ADJECTIVES AND ADVERBS

Be careful to use an adverb, never an adjective, to modify an action verb. Look at this passage from the story.

> Use an **adjective** to modify a noun or a pronoun. Use an **adverb** to modify a verb, an adjective, or another adverb.

She never could do anything as *well* as most people.

Notice how Tyler uses the adverb *well*, rather than the adjective *good*, to modify the verb *do*. Remember, however, to use an adjective, not an adverb, after a linking verb such as *be*, *am*, *is*, or *seem* if the modifier describes the subject.

Practice For each item, choose the correct modifier and write the complete sentence in your notebook. Circle the word being modified.

1. Arnold stared (suspicious, suspiciously) at the suitcase.
2. Sometimes Arnold looked (pathetic, pathetically) in his neatly buttoned clothes.
3. Arnold behaved (good, well) when he had something to entertain him.
4. His mother told him to chew his gum (careful, carefully).
5. The hospital smelled (awful, awfully).
6. After she left Arnold there, she felt very (bad, badly).

Build Your Portfolio

 ## Idea Bank

Writing

1. **New Version** Write an account of the story's events as Arnold might have perceived them.
2. **Letter** Writing as Bet, draft a letter to the director of the hospital in which you make a case for the need to institutionalize Arnold.
3. **Critical Response** Write an essay in which you use examples from the story to explore one critic's observation that Tyler "does not trivialize motives with rationalizations. She launches her imagined lives and describes their trajectories with an unpretentious sense of fate."

Speaking and Listening

4. **Conversation** With another student, role-play the conversation that might take place between Bet and Mrs. Puckett when Bet returns to her rented room after bringing Arnold to the institution. **[Performing Arts Link]**
5. **Political Speech** Imagine that the subject of the mayor's speech was the need for more funding and improved care at state-run institutions like the one in which Arnold was placed. Present the speech he might have given, using Arnold's case to support your points. **[Social Studies Link]**

Projects

6. **Fact-Finding Report** Work with a classmate to find out more about a state-run institution in your area. Would you conclude that it is well run and/or well funded? Present your facts and conclusions in a written report. **[Social Studies Link]**
7. **Medical Brochure** Find out more about autism, childhood schizophrenia, Downs syndrome, or another childhood illness or condition that can result in severe mental or emotional challenges. Present your findings in a medical brochure like the kind often found in a doctor's office. **[Health Link]**

 ## Writing Mini-Lesson

Social Worker's Report

Imagine that you are the social worker assigned to Bet and Arnold's case. Write a report explaining Arnold's condition and the events and situations that led to the decision to have him institutionalized.

Writing Skills Focus: Transitions to Show Cause and Effect

In writing about Arnold's illness and the decision to institutionalize him, you will be tracing **cause-and-effect** relationships. Words and phrases like these can help make those relationships clear:

Transitions to Show Cause and Effect

- because
- since
- as
- owing to
- as a result
- as a consequence
- consequently
- therefore
- thus
- if . . . then
- arising from
- stemming from

Prewriting Scan the story for details and incidents that indicate that Bet can no longer care for Arnold. Record each in a diagram like this one to show how it contributes to the decision to institutionalize him.

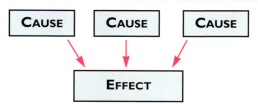

Drafting Build your report on the information you outlined in your graphic organizer. Use clear transitions like those listed above to show cause-and-effect and other relationships. Try to maintain the objective tone of an effective social worker.

Revising Read your report as though you were a supervisor reviewing the case for the first time. Are there sufficient details to support the report's general conclusions? Check that your facts are accurate, your word choice precise, and your transitions adequate to make the cause-and-effect relationships clear.

Guide for Interpreting

N. Scott Momaday
(1934–   )

A member of the Kiowa nation, N. Scott Momaday has devoted his life to preserving Native American culture. As a young boy, he often visited his grandparents, whose home was a meeting place for elderly Kiowas, whom Momaday describes as people made of "lean leather." Inspired by his boyhood experiences, Momaday devoted himself to preserving his Kiowa heritage. After receiving his doctorate from Stanford University, he wrote his first book, a novel about a young Native American torn between his roots and white society. Momaday has since published poetry, essays, anecdotes, and retellings of Kiowa legends. His works provide the reader with a deeper understanding of Native American culture, both past and present.

Naomi Shihab Nye
(1952–   )

Arab-American poet Naomi Shihab Nye spent her teenage years in Jerusalem—far from the American cities of St. Louis, Missouri, and San Antonio, Texas, where she grew up. In addition to publishing award-winning volumes of poetry, this versatile writer has also created picture books for children. Nye, whose works are built on the sturdy foundation of everyday experiences, believes that "the primary source of poetry has always been local life, random characters met on the streets, our own ancestry sifting down to us through small essential daily tasks."

Joy Harjo   (1951–   )

The influence of Joy Harjo's Native American Creek (or Muscogee) and Cherokee heritage is evident in many aspects of her life, including her writing. As a teenager, she became interested in dance and joined a troupe of Native American dancers. She attended the Institute of American Indian Arts, the University of New Mexico, and the Writers' Workshop of the University of Iowa. In addition to publishing books of poetry and prose, Harjo has also written film scripts and taught at the state universities of California, New Mexico, and Montana.

◆ Background for Understanding

LITERATURE: PERSONAL AND CULTURAL EXPRESSION IN ESSAYS

If you were asked to name a literary form that you associate with personal, creative expression, what would you say—poetry? short stories? novels? The essay might not be your immediate response; however, its flexible form may provide the best arena for personal expression.

You're probably not accustomed to thinking of essays as personal or expressive. Though they are a form of nonfiction, essays can be as moving, entertaining, and enriching as your favorite piece of fiction. Because they can explore any topic the writer chooses, there are as many types of personal essays as there are people who write them.

In personal essays (like those you are about to read), the writers approach their subjects in a rather casual and intimate way, often providing a personal insight into a general subject. In each of the three essays that follow, the writer uses a vivid memory of a particular experience or object—a journey on a horse, a special dessert, the dawning of a childhood awareness—as the springboard to an analysis of her or his identity. The essay then explores how that identity is related to the writer's ancestors, place of birth, and culture. When taken together, these essays provide new insight into the rich and varied cultures that make up our nation.

from The Names ◆ Mint Snowball
◆ Suspended ◆

◆ *Literature and Your Life*

CONNECT YOUR EXPERIENCE

Watching home videos or flipping through a family photo album may bring back some very special memories of your childhood. You may recognize the comfort of a treasured toy, react to the smile of a long-forgotten friend, or remember the warmth of special occasions. Think about childhood experiences that you remember most vividly. Do you think they have helped form your identity? Why did they have such a strong effect on you?

Journal Writing Describe a childhood memory. The act of writing about it may help you remember more details.

THEMATIC FOCUS: LITERATURE CONFRONTS THE EVERYDAY

Two of these essays deal with details and everyday experiences: the taste of a favorite dessert, the sound of music on a car radio. How do the essays lend greater meaning to seemingly ordinary experiences?

◆ Reading Strategy

RELATE TO YOUR OWN EXPERIENCES

As you start to read these essays, you may think at first you have little in common with a Kiowa youth seeking adventure on horseback, or the great-granddaughter of a Midwestern pharmacist, or a little Creek girl riding in her father's Cadillac. However, if you have ever taken a journey, yearned for the past, or experienced a mysterious inner awakening, you can find a connection between your experiences and theirs. Making such a connection will increase your understanding and enjoyment of the essay.

◆ Grammar and Style

ELLIPTICAL CLAUSES

An **elliptical clause** is one in which certain words are omitted because they are understood. In the following sentences from the essays by Momaday and Nye, the elliptical clauses are in italics. Notice that the elliptical clauses make the writing flow smoothly.

> . . . the Kiowas owned more horses . . . *than any other tribe on the Great Plains* [*owned*]." (The verb *owned* is understood rather than stated.)

> My grandfather thought [*that*] *he should have inherited it*. . . . " (The relative pronoun *that* is understood.)

◆ Literary Focus

ANECDOTES

An **anecdote** is a short account of an amusing or interesting event. People tell anecdotes all the time—mostly for entertainment. Some anecdotes can be used to make a point. For example, you might share an anecdote about a favorite gift to demonstrate the giver's thoughtfulness. A reporter writing an article might grab the reader's attention with an anecdote about an individual who suffers from an illness before providing medical data about it.

An essayist often recounts an anecdote and then draws a conclusion or makes a generalization based on the anecdote. As you read, identify the anecdotes in these essays.

◆ Build Vocabulary

PREFIXES: *con-*

The prefix *con-* (or *com-*) means "with" or "together." In "Suspended," Joy Harjo uses the word *confluence,* which means "a flowing together."

WORD BANK

Preview these words from the essays.

supple
concocted
flamboyant
elixir
permeated
replicate
revelatory
confluence

from

THE NAMES

N. Scott Momaday

I sometimes think of what it means that in their heyday—in 1830, say—the Kiowas owned more horses *per capita* than any other tribe on the Great Plains, that the Plains Indian culture, the last culture to evolve in North America, is also known as "the horse culture" and "the centaur[1] culture," that the Kiowas tell the story of a horse that died of shame after its owner committed an act of cowardice, that I am a Kiowa, that therefore there is in me, as there is in the Tartars,[2] an old, sacred notion of the horse. I believe that at some point in my racial life, this notion must needs be expressed in order that I may be true to my nature.

It happened so: I was thirteen years old, and my parents gave me a horse. It was a small nine-year-old gelding of that rare, soft color that is called strawberry roan. This my horse and I came to be, in the course of our life together, in good understanding, of one mind, a true story and history of that large landscape in which we made the one entity of whole motion, one and the same center of an intricate, pastoral composition, evanescent,[3] ever changing. And to this my horse I gave the name Pecos.

On the back of my horse I had a different view of the world. I could see more of it, how it reached away beyond all the horizons I had ever seen; and yet it was more concentrated in its appearance, too, and more accessible to my mind, my imagination. My mind loomed upon the farthest edges of the earth, where I could feel the full force of the planet whirling into space. There was nothing of the air and light that was not pure exhilaration, and nothing of time and eternity. Oh, Pecos, *un poquito mas*! Oh, my hunting horse! Bear me away, bear me away!

It was appropriate that I should make a long journey. Accordingly I set out one early morning, traveling light. Such a journey must begin in the nick of time, on the spur of the moment, and one must say to himself at the outset: Let there be wonderful things along the way; let me hold to the way and be thoughtful in my going; let this journey be made in beauty and belief.

I sang in the sunshine and heard the birds call out on either side. Bits of down from the cottonwoods drifted across the air, and butterflies fluttered in the sage. I could feel my horse under me, rocking at my legs, the bobbing of the reins to my hand; I could feel the sun on my face and the stirring of a little wind at my hair. And through the hard hooves, the slender limbs, the supple shoulders, the fluent back of my horse I felt the earth under me. Everything was under me, buoying me up; I rode across the top of the world. My mind soared; time and again I saw the fleeting shadow of my mind moving about me as it went winding upon the sun.

When the song, which was a song of riding, was finished, I had Pecos pick up the pace. Far down on the road to San Ysidro I overtook my

---

1. **centaur** (sen´ tôr) *adj.*: Pertaining to a mythical creature with the head and upper body of a man and the lower body of a horse.
2. **Tartars** (tär´ tərz) *n.*: Nomadic Turkish peoples that took part in the invasions of Eastern Europe during the Middle Ages.
3. **evanescent** (ev´ ə nes´ ənt) *adj.*: Transient; tending to fade from sight.

Passion of Paints, Bob Peters

▲ **Critical Viewing** Using the third paragraph of the essay as a guide, how do you think Momaday would describe this painting? [**Hypothesize**]

friend Pasqual Fragua. He was riding a rangy, stiff-legged black and white stallion, half wild, which horse he was breaking for the rancher Cass Goodner. The horse skittered and blew as I drew up beside him. Pecos began to prance, as he did always in the company of another horse. "Where are you going?" I asked in the Jemez language. And he replied, "I am going down the road." The stallion was hard to manage, and Pasqual had to keep his mind upon it; I saw that I had taken him by surprise. "You know," he said after a moment, "when you rode up just now I did not know who you were." We rode on for a time in silence, and our horses got used to each other, but still they wanted their heads.[4] The longer I looked at the stallion the more I admired it, and I suppose that Pasqual knew this, for he began to say good things about it: that it was a thing of good blood, that it was very strong and fast, that it felt very good to ride it. The thing was this: that the stallion was half wild, and I came to wonder about the wild half of it; I wanted to know what its wildness was worth in the riding. "Let us trade horses for a while," I said, and, well,

all right, he agreed. At first it was exciting to ride the stallion, for every once in a while it pitched and bucked and wanted to run. But it was heavy and raw-boned and full of resistance, and every step was a jolt that I could feel deep down in my bones. I saw soon enough that I had made a bad bargain, and I wanted my horse back, but I was ashamed to admit it. There came a time in the late afternoon, in the vast plain far south of San Ysidro, after thirty miles, perhaps, when I no longer knew whether it was I who was riding the stallion or the stallion who was riding me. "Well, let us go back now," said Pasqual at last. "No. I am going on; and I will have my horse back, please," I said, and he was surprised and sorry to hear it, and we said goodbye. "If you are going south or east," he said, "look out for the sun, and keep

---

4. **. . . they wanted their heads:** The horses wanted to be free of the control of the reins.

◆ **Build Vocabulary**

supple (sup´ əl) *adj*.: Able to bend and move easily and nimbly; flexible

Indian on Galloping Horse after Remington, No. 2, 1976, Fritz Scholder, Courtesy Museum of Fine Arts, Museum of New Mexico

▲ **Critical Viewing** How do Momaday's feelings about riding his horse compare with the mood of this image? **[Connect]**

your face in the shadow of your hat. *Vaya con Dios.*"[5] And I went on my way alone then, wiser and better mounted, and thereafter I held on to my horse. I saw no one for a long time, but I saw four falling stars and any number of jackrabbits, roadrunners, and coyotes, and once, across a distance, I saw a bear, small and black, lumbering in the ravine. The mountains drew close and withdrew and drew close again, and after several days I swung east.

Now and then I came upon settlements. For the most part they were dry, burnt places with Spanish names: Arroyo Seco, Las Piedras, Tres Casas. In one of these I found myself in a narrow street between high adobe walls. Just

---

5. *Vaya con Dios* (vī yə kən dē´ ōs): "Go with God" (Spanish).

ahead, on my left, was a door in the wall. As I approached the door was flung open, and a small boy came running out, rolling a hoop. This happened so suddenly that Pecos shied very sharply, and I fell to the ground, jamming the thumb of my left hand. The little boy looked very worried and said that he was sorry to have caused such an accident. I waved the matter off, as if it were nothing; but as a matter of fact my hand hurt so much that tears welled up in my eyes. And the pain lasted for many days. I have fallen many times from a horse, both before and after that, and a few times I fell from a running horse on dangerous ground, but that was the most painful of them all.

In another settlement there were some boys who were interested in racing. They had good horses, some of them, but their horses were not so good as mine, and I won easily. After that, I began to think of ways in which I might even the odds a little, might give some advantage to my competitors. Once or twice I gave them a head start, a reasonable head start of, say, five or ten yards to the hundred, but that was too simple, and I won anyway. Then it came to me that I might try this: we should all line up in the usual way, side by side, but my competitors should be mounted and I should not. When the signal was given I should then have to get up on my horse while the others were breaking away; I should have to mount my horse during the race. This idea appealed to me greatly, for it was both imaginative and difficult, not to mention dangerous; Pecos and I should have to work very closely together. The first few times we tried this I had little success, and over a course of a hundred yards I lost four races out of five. The principal problem was that Pecos simply could not hold still among the other horses. Even before they broke away he was hard to manage, and when they were set running nothing could hold him back, even for an instant. I could not get my foot in the stirrup, but I had to throw myself up across the saddle on my stomach, hold on as best I could, and twist myself into position, and all this while racing at full speed. I could ride well enough to accomplish this feat, but it was a very awkward and inefficient business. I had to find some way to use the whole energy of my horse, to get it all

938 ◆ *Prosperity and Protest (1946–Present)*

into the race. Thus far I had managed only to break his motion, to divert him from his purpose and mine. To correct this I took Pecos away and worked with him through the better part of a long afternoon on a broad reach of level ground beside an irrigation ditch. And it was hot, hard work. I began by teaching him to run straight away while I ran beside him a few steps, holding on to the saddle horn, with no pressure on the reins. Then, when we had mastered this trick, we proceeded to the next one, which was this: I placed my weight on my arms, hanging from the saddle horn, threw my feet out in front of me, struck them to the ground, and sprang up against the saddle. This I did again and again, until Pecos came to expect it and did not flinch or lose his stride. I sprang a little higher each time. It was in all a slow process of trial and error, and after two or three hours both Pecos and I were covered with bruises and soaked through with perspiration. But we had much to show for our efforts, and at last the moment came when we must put the whole performance together. I had not yet leaped into the saddle, but I was quite confident that I could now do so; only I must be sure to get high enough. We began this dress rehearsal then from a standing position. At my signal Pecos lurched and was running at once, straight away and smoothly. And at the same time I sprinted forward two steps and gathered myself up, placing my weight precisely at my wrists, throwing my feet out and together, perfectly. I brought my feet down sharply to the ground and sprang up hard, as hard as I could, bringing my legs astraddle of my horse—and everything was just right, except that I sprang too high. I vaulted all the way over my horse, clearing the saddle by a considerable margin, and came down into the irrigation ditch. It was a good trick, but it was not the one I had in mind, and I wonder what Pecos thought of it after all. Anyway, after a while I could mount my horse in this way and so well that there was no challenge in it, and I went on winning race after race.

I went on, farther and farther into the wide world. Many things happened. And in all this I knew one thing: I knew where the journey was begun, that it was itself a learning of the beginning, that the beginning was infinitely worth the learning. The journey was well undertaken, and somewhere in it I sold my horse to an old Spanish man of Vallecitos. I do not know how long Pecos lived. I had used him hard and well, and it may be that in his last days an image of me like thought shimmered in his brain.

◆ **Literary Focus**
What is the point of this anecdote?

Guide for Responding

◆ *Literature and Your Life*

Reader's Response What kind of animal seems "sacred" or special in some way to you? Why?

Journal Writing Describe an especially positive or negative relationship or encounter with an animal.

☑ Check Your Comprehension

1. What inspires Momaday's decision to take a journey?
2. List the highlights of the journey. What did young Momaday see and do in his travels?
3. In the end, how did Momaday get rid of his horse?

◆ Critical Thinking

INTERPRET

1. What motivated Momaday to temporarily trade Pecos for the horse his friend Pasqual was riding? **[Analyze]**
2. Provide one detail that supports the statement that Pecos was an extremely good horse. **[Support]**
3. Why is it significant that Momaday's first long journey was on horseback? **[Draw Conclusions]**

APPLY

4. What life lesson have you learned that was "infinitely worth the learning"? **[Connect]**

Mint Snowball

Naomi Shihab Nye

My great-grandfather on my mother's side ran a drugstore in a small town in central Illinois. He sold pills and rubbing alcohol from behind the big cash register and creamy ice cream from the soda fountain. My mother remembers the counter's long polished sweep, its shining face. She twirled on the stools. Dreamy fans. Wide summer afternoons. Clink of nickels in anybody's hand. He sold milkshakes, cherry cokes, old fashioned sandwiches. What did an old fashioned sandwich look like? Dark wooden shelves. Silver spigots on chocolate dispensers.

My great-grandfather had one specialty: a Mint Snowball which he invented. Some people drove all the way in from Decatur just to taste it. First he stirred fresh mint leaves with sugar and secret ingredients in a small pot on the stove for a very long time. He <u>concocted</u> a <u>flamboyant</u> elixir of mint. Its scent clung to his fingers even after he washed his hands. Then he shaved ice into tiny particles and served it mounted in a glass dish. <u>Permeated</u> with mint syrup. Scoops of rich vanilla ice cream to each side. My mother took a bite of minty ice and ice cream mixed together. The Mint Snowball tasted like winter. She closed her eyes to see the Swiss village my great-grandfather's parents came from.

◆ **Reading Strategy**
Are there certain foods that you associate with a particular time, place, or emotion?

Snow frosting the roofs. Glistening, dangling spokes of ice.

Before my great-grandfather died, he sold the recipe for the mint syrup to someone in town for one hundred dollars. This hurt my grandfather's feelings. My grandfather thought he should have inherited it to carry on the tradition. As far as the family knew, the person who bought the recipe never used it. At least not in public. My mother had watched my grandfather make the syrup so often she thought she could replicate it. But what did he have in those little unmarked bottles? She experimented. Once she came close. She wrote down what she did. Now she has lost the paper.

Perhaps the clue to my entire personality connects to the lost Mint Snowball. I have always felt out-of-step with my environment, disjointed in the modern world. The crisp flush of cities makes me weep. Strip centers, Poodle grooming and Take-out Thai. I am angry over lost department stores, wistful for something I have never tasted or seen.

Although I know how to do everything one needs to know—change airplanes, find my exit off the interstate, charge gas, send a fax—there is something missing. Perhaps the stoop of my great-grandfather over the pan, the slow patient swish of his spoon. The spin of my mother on the high stool with her whole life in front of her, something fine and fragrant still to happen. When I breathe a handful of mint, even pathetic sprigs from my sunbaked Texas earth, I close my eyes. Little chips of ice on the tongue, their cool slide down. Can we follow the long river of the word "refreshment" back to its spring? Is there another land for me? Can I find any lasting solace in the color green?

◆ Build Vocabulary

concocted (kən käkt′ əd) *v.*: Made by combining various ingredients

flamboyant (flam boi′ ənt) *adj.*: Too extravagant

elixir (ē liks′ ir) *n.*: Supposed remedy for all ailments

permeated (pur′ mē āt id) *adj.*: Penetrated and spread through

replicate (rep′ li kāt) *v.*: Duplicate

Guide for Responding

◆ Literature and Your Life

Reader's Response Do you feel out of step with the modern world or in tune with it? Explain your feelings.

Thematic Focus Naomi Shihab Nye is primarily a poet. What are some of the ways in which her essay transforms the everyday into a type of poetry?

Journal Writing Jot down images that come to mind when you think of your parents' or grandparents' generation.

☑ Check Your Comprehension

1. What happened to the original Mint Snowball recipe?
2. Which family member came close to duplicating the recipe?

◆ Critical Thinking

INTERPRET

1. How did the Mint Snowball remind Nye's mother of the country from which her ancestors came? **[Connect]**
2. Contrast Nye's images of the past and present. **[Compare and Contrast]**
3. (a) What is the mood of the final paragraph of this essay? (b) Which details create it? **[Analyze]**

EVALUATE

4. Does the image of the Mint Snowball successfully capture a past time? Explain. **[Evaluate]**

EXTEND

5. Relate "Mint Snowball" to another literary work that expresses the theme of yearning for a way of life that is long gone. **[Literature Link]**

SUSPENDED

Joy Harjo

Getting Down, Joseph Holston

▲ **Critical Viewing** Does this illustration of a jazz musician effectively convey Harjo's belief that jazz is "a way to speak beyond the confines of ordinary language"? Explain. **[Evaluate]**

Once I was so small that I could barely peer over the top of the backseat of the black Cadillac my father polished and tuned daily; I wanted to see everything. It was around the time I acquired language, or even before that time, when something happened that changed my relationship to the spin of the world. My concept of language, of what was possible with music was changed by this revelatory moment. It changed even the way I looked at the sun. This suspended integer of time probably escaped ordinary notice in my parents' universe, which informed most of my vision in the ordinary world. They were still omnipresent gods. We were driving somewhere in Tulsa, the northern border of the Creek Nation.[1] I don't know where we were going or where we had been, but I know the sun was boiling the asphalt, the car windows open for any breeze as I stood on tiptoes on the floorboard behind my father, a handsome god who smelled of Old Spice, whose slick black hair was always impeccably groomed, his clothes perfectly creased and ironed. The radio was on. I loved the radio, jukeboxes or any magic thing containing music even then.

◆ *Literature and Your Life*

What everyday objects were fascinating or magical to you as a small child?

I wonder now what signaled this moment, a loop of time that on first glance could be any

---

1. **Creek Nation:** Nation of Native American peoples, mainly Muscogean, formerly of Georgia and Alabama. Most now live in Oklahoma and Florida.

place in time. I became acutely aware of the line the jazz trumpeter was playing (a sound I later associated with Miles Davis). I didn't know the word jazz or trumpet, or the concepts. I don't know how to say it, with what sounds or words, but in that confluence of hot southern afternoon, in the breeze of aftershave and humidity, I followed that sound to the beginning, to the place of the birth of sound. I was suspended in whirling stars, a moon to which I'd traveled often by then. I grieved my parents' failings, my own life which I saw stretched the length of that rhapsody.

My rite of passage into the world of humanity occurred then, via jazz. The music made a startling bridge between familiar and strange lands, an appropriate vehicle, for though the music is predominantly west African in concept, with European associations, jazz was influenced by the Creek (or Muscogee) people, for we were there when jazz was born. I recognized it, that humid afternoon in my formative years, as a way to speak beyond the confines of ordinary language. I still hear it.

◆ Build Vocabulary

revelatory (rev´ ə lə tôr´ ē) *adj*.: Revealing; disclosing
confluence (kän´ flōō əns) *n*.: A flowing together

Guide for Responding

◆ *Literature and Your Life*

Reader's Response Can you recall a personal experience that was important in your life, but which is difficult for you to analyze or describe?

Thematic Focus How does Harjo's essay lend a sense of wonder and mystery to the ordinary experiences of childhood?

Group Discussion Do your memories tend to be mostly of sights, or sounds, or something else? Do scents have the power to take you back in time?

☑ Check Your Comprehension

1. During what season did Harjo's experience take place?
2. What kind of music was playing on the radio?

◆ Critical Thinking

INTERPRET

1. Roughly, what age was Harjo at the time she describes? **[Infer]**
2. How did she feel about her father? **[Analyze]**
3. What did the music teach Harjo about communication? **[Draw Conclusions]**
4. How does Harjo suggest that growing up involves sadness and disillusion? **[Deduce]**

APPLY

5. What does this essay suggest about the mysterious workings of each individual's inner world? **[Generalize]**

Guide for Responding (continued)

◆ Reading Strategy

RELATE TO YOUR OWN EXPERIENCES

For most people, it is quite natural to **relate reading to personal experiences**. By identifying similar situations, emotions, attitudes, and behaviors, readers can connect and compare a writer's ideas and experiences with their own. Completing a chart like the one below will help you to analyze the ways in which your experiences connect to those of Momaday, Nye, and Harjo.

In the first column, use short phrases to refer to elements from each essay. List at least one image or experience from each essay. In the second column, describe an experience or emotion of your own that parallels the item in the first column. In the third column, briefly analyze the relationship between the two experiences.

Writer's Experience	My Experience	How They Relate

◆ Literary Focus

ANECDOTES

Each of the three essays you have just read contains one or more **anecdotes**—brief accounts of entertaining or interesting events and experiences. N. Scott Momaday tells several stories about a horse. Naomi Shihab Nye relates how her great-grandfather sold a secret recipe. Joy Harjo recalls a very early memory of hearing jazz on the radio. Think about each writer's reasons for recounting his or her anecdote as you answer these questions.

1. How do Momaday's anecdotes relate to the theme sounded in his opening paragraph?
2. What is the significance of the lost recipe to Nye's life and personality?
3. (a) How did Harjo's experience of hearing jazz affect her at the moment? (b) How did that experience change her life?

◆ Build Vocabulary

USING THE PREFIX *con-*

Each of the words in the box contains the prefix *con-* or *com-,* meaning "with" or "together." Using at least four of the words, write a paragraph about a group of workers who have gathered to protest a new company policy. You may change the form of a word if necessary—*communication* to *communicate,* for example.

conference	congregated	conform
communication	concocted	combative

USING THE WORD BANK

On your paper, write the word bank word closest in meaning to the italicized word or phrase.

1. The smell of chocolate *filled* the kitchen.
2. Our journey ended at the *meeting place* of the rivers.
3. The diners stared at the woman's *extravagant* hat.
4. Everyone who read the report agreed it was *highly informative*.
5. Mimi *created* a delicious sauce from herbs and tomatoes.
6. A gifted seamstress could *copy* a designer dress.
7. The health food store has sold out the latest *magical remedy*.
8. The *flexible* leather saddlebags grew even softer with age.

◆ Grammar and Style

ELLIPTICAL CLAUSES

Practice Copy each sentence on your paper, then underline the elliptical clause and write the understood word(s).

> In an **elliptical clause,** one or more words are omitted because they are understood.

1. Pecos ran faster than the other horses.
2. Momaday thought the stallion was better than his own horse.
3. Nye's grandfather sold the recipe he invented.
4. Harjo recalls hearing the music in the car more vividly than she does any other early experience.

Build Your Portfolio

 Idea Bank

Writing

1. **Recipe** Write a recipe in your own words. List the precise ingredients and each step involved in preparation. Make sure that your instructions are clear, concise, and complete, and that each step is presented in the correct order.

2. **Description** In his essay, Momaday describes in great physical detail his attempts to vault his horse while it was running. Write one or two paragraphs in which you describe, in similar detail, a series of physical maneuvers that you have executed. **[Physical Education Link]**

3. **Analytical Essay** Momaday's journey on his horse, Nye's family's Mint Snowball, and Harjo's jazz song all have both a literal and a symbolic meaning. Choose one and analyze its symbolic meaning.

Speaking and Listening

4. **Evocative Music** A line of jazz gave Joy Harjo a new vision of the world. Perform or play a recording of a piece of music that does the same for you. Explain how it affected you. **[Music Link]**

5. **Retellings** Retell one anecdote from the essays in your own words, with your own style. Then have listeners compare and contrast your version with the original.

Projects

6. **Photographs and Memories** With a group of classmates, put together a class anthology consisting of personal photographs and accompanying anecdotes.

7. **Illustration** Create a two-paneled illustration for "Mint Snowball." The first panel should portray Nye's image of the past, and the other her impressions of contemporary life. **[Art Link]**

 Writing Mini-Lesson

Oral History

Have you ever heard family friends or relatives recall how their ancestors immigrated to the United States, or describe what it was like to watch live coverage of the first moon walk? Stories like these are a form of *oral history*—a spoken record of personally or historically significant events. Collect a bit of oral history and record it in writing. To make the history understandable to your readers, you will need to supply relevant background information.

Writing Skills Focus: Necessary Context

An oral history flows from the speaker's personality, experiences, and cultural background. To create a successful oral history, you must decide what **context**, or background information, is necessary in order for your readers to understand the full meaning of the experiences you present. In *The Names*, for example, Momaday explains his special connection to horses by informing his readers that the animals are sacred to his Kiowa heritage.

Model From the Selection

. . . I am a Kiowa . . .therefore there is in me, as there is in the Tartars, an old sacred notion of the horse.

Prewriting Interview an interesting person about significant events in his or her life. Take careful notes or tape record the interview. Then review your notes and select one experience which you will present. Determine what background information you will need to provide.

Drafting Draft the oral history, using the exact words of the teller. Incorporate necessary background information to provide a context for the story.

Revising Ask a friend to read your draft. Does the history have a clear beginning, middle, and end? Is it written in the "voice" of the teller? Does your friend have any questions about it that are not answered by the background information?

Guide for Interpreting

Alice Walker *(1944–   )*

Born in Eatonton, Georgia, Alice Walker was the youngest child in a family of sharecroppers.

Of her childhood, Walker writes, "It was great fun being cute. But then, one day, it ended."

Her childhood self-confidence was challenged by an accident with a BB-gun that scarred and nearly blinded her. Walker reports that she did not lift her head for six years.

When the scar tissue on her eye was removed, her self-confidence returned. Walker left high school as the valedictorian and the most popular student. She attended Spelman College in Atlanta, an elite college for African American women, and after two years she transferred to Sarah Lawrence College in Bronxville, New York. *Once* (1968), Walker's first book of poetry, was written when she was a student there.

The Movement After graduating from Sarah Lawrence, Walker moved to Mississippi to work in the civil rights movement, demonstrating with African Americans and whites alike who were fighting for equality on all fronts. During this period, Walker also taught African American studies at Jackson State University, where she was writer-in-residence.

Cultural Pride Much of Alice Walker's fiction—novels including *The Third Life of Grange Copeland* (1970), story collections including *You Can't Keep a Good Woman Down* (1981), and *In Love and Trouble* (1973)—delves into the lives of African American women. Her fiction and essays reflect a pride in her personal heritage and the heritage of her people. The title essay from *In Search of Our Mothers' Gardens* (1983), often described as the nonfiction relative of "Everyday Use," explores Walker's maternal heritage, describing the creative legacy of "ordinary" black southern women. The 1982 publication of her third novel, *The Color Purple*, transformed "an intense reputation into a national one." This novel about an indomitable woman named Celie was both a critical and a popular success. Awarded both a Pulitzer Prize and an American Book Award, it was later made into a successful motion picture.

◆ Background for Understanding

CULTURE: PRESERVING TRADITIONS THROUGH FOLK ART

In this story, the character Dee is interested in the artifacts that reveal her family's history. Today, folk art is much celebrated for its beauty, originality, and connection to a culture's history. Most "folk art," however, was originally created for utilitarian purposes. In America, European settlers, Native Americans, and enslaved Africans took pride in creating items that were attractive as well as useful.

When families moved, they brought a few treasured items with them. In each new home, objects would again be created from locally available materials and tools. Families thus accumulated a cherished collection of heirlooms.

Quilts—an important symbol in this story—are an example of American folk art; they have been made in America since colonial times. Like most folk art, they served a number of purposes—keeping people warm; recycling pieces of cloth from worn-out clothing; providing a focal point for creative, recreational, and social gatherings of women; and, perhaps most important, recording bits of family history.

Everyday Use

◆ *Literature and Your Life*

CONNECT YOUR EXPERIENCE

A cousin now living far away comes to visit your family, and you think, "She sure lives in a different world than I do!" Time and new experiences can create gaps between people—even relatives. In this story you'll see how distance and the passage of time have caused a mother and her daughter to have very different views of the world.

Journal Writing Brainstorm for a list of reasons why people leave home. Note some reasons why they return home.

THEMATIC FOCUS: LITERATURE CONFRONTS THE EVERYDAY

In this story of a reunion between a rural southern family and an urban daughter, Walker explores how everyday experiences change people. As you read, ask yourself how family members can remain close despite experiences that might divide them.

◆ Literary Focus

CHARACTER'S MOTIVATION

To know a character truly, you need to understand that **character's motivation**—the reasons for his or her thoughts, feelings, actions, or speech. Sometimes a character's motivation results from his or her values or experiences. At other times, characters are motivated by their needs or dreams.

The characters in "Everyday Use" reveal their motivations through their actions and speech. As you read, ask: Why is this character doing or saying this? What need is she trying to satisfy? What goal does she have in mind? The answers will help you piece together each character's motivation.

◆ Reading Strategy

CONTRASTING CHARACTERS

As this story opens, one sister awaits the arrival of another. You learn almost immediately that the two sisters and their experiences are quite different. By **contrasting characters,** or identifying the ways in which they differ, you can begin to uncover the major conflict in the story. As you read, use a graphic organizer like this one to note the personality characteristics and details of behavior that distinguish Dee from Maggie. Think about how their individual experiences have shaped their differences.

◆ Build Vocabulary

ROOTS: *-doc-/-doct-*

The word *doctrines* includes the word root *-doc-* or *-doct-,* meaning "teach." Notice how the root contributes to the meaning of *doctrines:* "ideas, beliefs, or rules that are taught."

WORD BANK

Preview this list of words from the story.

| furtive |
| lye |
| oppress |
| doctrines |

◆ Grammar and Style

SENTENCE FRAGMENTS

A **sentence fragment** is a group of words that is punctuated as a sentence but fails to express a complete thought because it lacks a subject, a verb, or both. Look at this example from "Everyday Use." Notice that it lacks a subject.

Never could carry a tune.

While fragments are not generally acceptable in formal writing, writers do use them to re-create the way people speak. In this story, Walker uses fragments to make it seem as if the story's first-person narrator is speaking informally to the reader.

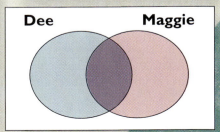

Everyday Use

Alice Walker

I will wait for her in the yard that Maggie and I made so clean and wavy yesterday afternoon. A yard like this is more comfortable than most people know. It is not just a yard. It is like an extended living room. When the hard clay is swept clean as a floor and the fine sand around the edges lined with tiny, irregular grooves, anyone can come and sit and look up into the elm tree and wait for the breezes that never come inside the house.

Maggie will be nervous until after her sister goes: she will stand hopelessly in corners, homely and ashamed of the burn scars down her arms and legs, eyeing her sister with a mixture of envy and awe. She thinks her sister has held life always in the palm of one hand, that "no" is a word the world never learned to say to her.

You've no doubt seen those TV shows where the child who has "made it" is confronted, as a surprise, by her own mother and father, tottering in weakly from backstage. (A pleasant surprise, of course: What would they do if parent and child came on the show only to curse out and insult each other?) On TV mother and child embrace and smile into each other's faces. Sometimes the mother and father weep, the child wraps them in her arms and leans across the table to tell how she would not have made it without their help. I have seen these programs.

Sometimes I dream a dream in which Dee and I are suddenly brought together on a TV program of this sort. Out of a dark and soft-seated limousine I am ushered into a bright room filled with many people. There I meet a smiling, gray, sporty man like Johnny Carson who shakes my hand and tells me what a fine girl I have. Then we are on the stage and Dee is embracing me with tears in her eyes. She pins on my dress a large orchid, even though she has told me once that she thinks orchids are tacky flowers.

In real life I am a large, big-boned woman with rough, man-working hands. In the winter I wear flannel nightgowns to bed and overalls during the day. I can kill and clean a hog as mercilessly as a man. My fat keeps me hot in zero weather. I can work outside all day, breaking ice to get water for washing; I can eat pork liver cooked over the open fire minutes after it comes steaming from the hog. One winter I knocked a bull calf straight in the brain between the eyes with a sledge hammer and had the meat hung up to chill before nightfall. But of course all of this does not show on television. I am the way my daughter would want me to be: a hundred pounds lighter, my skin like an uncooked barley pancake. My hair glistens in the hot bright lights. Johnny Carson has much to do to keep up with my quick and witty tongue.

But that is a mistake. I know even before I wake up. Who ever knew a Johnson with a quick tongue? Who can even imagine me looking a strange white man in the eye? It seems to me I have talked to them always with one foot raised in flight, with my head turned in whichever way is farthest from them. Dee, though. She would always look anyone in the eye. Hesitation was no part of her nature.

"How do I look, Mama?" Maggie says, showing just enough of her thin body enveloped in pink skirt and red blouse for me to know she's there, almost hidden by the door.

"Come out into the yard," I say.

Have you ever seen a lame animal, perhaps a dog run over by some careless person rich enough to own a car, sidle up to someone who is ignorant enough to be kind to him? That is the way my Maggie walks. She has been like this, chin on chest, eyes on ground, feet in shuffle, ever since the fire that burned the other house to the ground.

Dee is lighter than Maggie, with nicer hair and a fuller figure. She's a woman now, though sometimes I forget. How long ago was it that the other house burned? Ten, twelve years? Sometimes I can still hear the flames and feel Maggie's arms sticking to me, her hair smoking and her dress falling off her in little black papery flakes. Her eyes seemed stretched open, blazed open by the flames reflected in them. And Dee. I see her standing off under the sweet gum tree she used to dig gum out of; a look of concentration on her face as she watched the last dingy gray board of the house fall in toward the red-hot brick chimney. Why don't you do

a dance around the ashes? I'd want to ask her. She had hated the house that much.

I used to think she hated Maggie, too. But that was before we raised the money, the church and me, to send her to Augusta to school. She used to read to us without pity; forcing words, lies, other folks' habits, whole lives upon us two, sitting trapped and ignorant underneath her voice. She washed us in a river of make-believe, burned us with a lot of knowledge we didn't necessarily need to know. Pressed us to her with the serious way she read, to shove us away at just the moment, like dimwits, we seemed about to understand.

Dee wanted nice things. A yellow organdy dress to wear to her graduation from high school; black pumps to match a green suit she'd made from an old suit somebody gave me. She was determined to stare down any disaster in her efforts. Her eyelids would not flicker for minutes at a time. Often I fought off the temptation to shake her. At sixteen she had a style of her own, and knew what style was.

◆ **Reading Strategy**
Explain why Maggie might not care about "nice things" in the same way Dee does.

I never had an education myself. After second grade the school was closed down. Don't ask me why: in 1927 colored asked fewer questions than they do now. Sometimes Maggie reads to me. She stumbles along good-naturedly but can't see well. She knows she is not bright. Like good looks and money, quickness passed her by. She will marry John Thomas (who has mossy teeth in an earnest face) and then I'll be free to sit here and I guess just sing church songs to myself. Although I never was a good singer. Never could carry a tune. I was always better at a man's job. I used to love to milk till I was hooved in the side in '49. Cows are soothing and slow and don't bother you, unless you try to milk them the wrong way.

I have deliberately turned my back on the house. It is three rooms, just like the one that burned, except the roof is tin; they don't make shingle roofs any more. There are no real windows, just some holes cut in the sides, like the portholes in a ship, but not round and not square, with rawhide holding the shutters up on the outside. This house is in a pasture, too, like the other one. No doubt when Dee sees it she will want to tear it down. She wrote me once that no matter where we "choose" to live, she will manage to come see us. But she will never bring her friends. Maggie and I thought about this and Maggie asked me, "Mama, when did Dee ever *have* any friends?"

She had a few. <u>Furtive</u> boys in pink shirts hanging about on washday after school. Nervous girls who never laughed. Impressed with her they worshiped the well-turned phrase, the cute shape, the scalding humor that erupted like bubbles in <u>lye</u>. She read to them.

When she was courting Jimmy T she didn't have much time to pay to us, but turned all her faultfinding power on him. He *flew* to marry a cheap city girl from a family of ignorant flashy people. She hardly had time to recompose herself.

When she comes I will meet—but there they are!

Maggie attempts to make a dash for the house, in her shuffling way, but I stay her with my hand. "Come back here," I say. And she stops and tries to dig a well in the sand with her toe.

It is hard to see them clearly through the strong sun. But even the first glimpse of leg out of the car tells me it is Dee. Her feet were always neat-looking, as if God himself had shaped them with a certain style. From the other side of the car comes a short, stocky man. Hair is all over his head a foot long and hanging from his chin like a kinky mule tail. I hear Maggie suck in her breath. "Uhnnnh," is what it sounds like. Like when you see the wriggling end of a snake just in front of your foot on the road. "Uhnnnh."

Dee next. A dress down to the ground, in this hot weather. A dress so loud it hurts my eyes. There are yellows and oranges enough to throw back the light of the sun. I feel my whole face warming from the heat waves it throws out. Earrings gold, too, and hanging down to her shoulders. Bracelets dangling and making noises when she moves her arm up to shake the folds of the dress out of her armpits. The dress is loose and flows, and as she walks closer, I like it. I hear Maggie go "Uhnnnh" again. It is her sister's hair. It stands straight up like the wool on a sheep. It is black as night and around the edges are two long pigtails that rope about like small lizards disappearing behind her ears.

"Wa-su-zo-Tean-o!"[1] she says, coming on in that gliding way the dress makes her move. The short stocky fellow with the hair to his navel is all grinning and he follows up with "Asalamalakim,[2] my mother and sister!" He moves to hug Maggie but she falls back, right up against the back of my chair. I feel her trembling there and when I look up I see the perspiration falling off her chin.

"Don't get up," says Dee. Since I am stout it takes something of a push. You can see me trying to move a second or two before I make it. She turns, showing white heels through her sandals, and goes back to the car. Out she peeks next with a Polaroid. She stoops down quickly and lines up picture after picture of me sitting there in front of the house with Maggie cowering behind me. She never takes a shot without making sure the house is included. When a cow comes nibbling around the edge of the yard she snaps it and me and Maggie and the house. Then she puts the Polaroid in the back seat of the car, and comes up and kisses me on the forehead.

◆ **Literary Focus**
Considering that Dee is not proud of the house, what is her motivation for taking these pictures?

Meanwhile Asalamalakim is going through motions with Maggie's hand. Maggie's hand is as limp as a fish, and probably as cold, despite the sweat, and she keeps trying to pull it back. It looks like Asalamalakim wants to shake hands but wants to do it fancy. Or maybe he don't know how people

---

1. **Wa-su-zo-Tean-o** (wä sōō zō tēn′ ō): African greeting.
2. **Asalamalakim:** *Salaam aleikhim* (sə läm′ ä lī′ kēm′): Islamic greeting meaning "Peace be with you."

shake hands. Anyhow, he soon gives up on Maggie.

"Well," I say. "Dee."

"No, Mama," she says. "Not 'Dee,' Wangero Leewanika Kemanjo!"

"What happened to 'Dee'?" I wanted to know.

"She's dead," Wangero said. "I couldn't bear it any longer, being named after the people who <u>oppress</u> me."

"You know as well as me you was named after your aunt Dicie," I said. Dicie is my sister. She named Dee. We called her "Big Dee" after Dee was born.

"But who was *she* named after?" asked Wangero.

"I guess after Grandma Dee," I said.

"And who was she named after?" asked Wangero.

"Her mother," I said, and saw Wangero was getting tired. "That's about as far back as I can trace it," I said. Though, in fact, I probably could have carried it back beyond the Civil War through the branches.

"Well," said Asalamalakim, "there you are."

"Uhnnnh," I heard Maggie say.

"There I was not," I said, "before 'Dicie' cropped up in our family, so why should I try to trace it that far back?"

He just stood there grinning, looking down on me like somebody inspecting a Model A car. Every once in a while he and Wangero sent eye signals over my head.

"How do you pronounce this name?" I asked.

"You don't have to call me by it if you don't want to," said Wangero.

"Why shouldn't I?" I asked. "If that's what you want us to call you, we'll call you."

◆ Build Vocabulary

furtive (fur´ tiv) *adj*.: Sneaky

lye (lī) *n*.: Strong alkaline solution used in cleaning and making soap

oppress (ə pres´) *v*.: Keep down by cruel or unjust use of power or authority

doctrines (däk´ trinz) *n*.: Religious beliefs or principles

"I know it might sound awkward at first," said Wangero.

"I'll get used to it," I said. "Ream it out again."

Well, soon we got the name out of the way. Asalamalakim had a name twice as long and three times as hard. After I tripped over it two or three times he told me to just call him Hakim-a-barber. I wanted to ask him was he a barber, but I didn't really think he was, so I didn't ask.

"You must belong to those beef-cattle people down the road," I said. They said "Asalamalakim" when they met you, too, but they didn't shake hands. Always too busy: feeding the cattle, fixing the fences, putting up salt-lick shelters, throwing down hay. When the white folks poisoned some of the herd the men stayed up all night with rifles in their hands. I walked a mile and a half just to see the sight.

Hakim-a-barber said, "I accept some of their <u>doctrines</u>, but farming and raising cattle is not my style." (They didn't tell me, and I didn't ask, whether Wangero (Dee) had really gone and married him.)

We sat down to eat and right away he said he didn't eat collards[3] and pork was unclean. Wangero, though, went on through the chitlins[4] and corn bread, the greens and everything else. She talked a blue streak over the sweet potatoes. Everything delighted her. Even the fact that we still used the benches her daddy made for the table when we couldn't afford to buy chairs.

"Oh, Mama!" she cried. Then turned to Hakim-a-barber. "I never knew how lovely these benches are. You can feel the rump prints," she said, running her hands underneath her and along the bench. Then she gave a sigh and her hand closed over Grandma Dee's butter dish. "That's it!" she said. "I knew there was something I wanted to ask you if I could have." She jumped up from the table and went over in the corner

---

3. **collards** (käl´ ərdz) *n*.: Leaves of the collard plant, often referred to as "collard greens."

4. **chitlins** (chit´ lənz) *n*.: Chitterlings, a pork dish popular among southern African Americans.

where the churn stood, the milk in it clabber by now. She looked at the churn and looked at it.

"This churn top is what I need," she said. "Didn't Uncle Buddy whittle it out of a tree you all used to have?"

"Yes," I said.

"Uh huh," she said happily. "And I want the dasher, too."

"Uncle Buddy whittle that, too?" asked the barber.

Dee (Wangero) looked up at me.

"Aunt Dee's first husband whittled the dash, " said Maggie so low you almost couldn't hear her. "His name was Henry, but they called him Stash."

"Maggie's brain is like an elephant's," Wangero said, laughing. "I can use the churn top as a centerpiece for the alcove table," she said, sliding a plate over the churn, "and I'll think of something artistic to do with the dasher."

When she finished wrapping the dasher the handle stuck out. I took it for a moment in my hands. You didn't even have to look close to see where hands pushing the dasher up and down to make butter had left a kind of sink in the wood. In fact, there were a lot of small sinks; you could see where thumbs and fingers had sunk into the wood. It was beautiful light yellow wood, from a tree that grew in the yard where Big Dee and Stash had lived.

After dinner Dee (Wangero) went to the trunk at the foot of my bed and started rifling through it. Maggie hung back in the kitchen over the dishpan. Out came Wangero with two quilts. They had been pieced by Grandma Dee and then Big Dee and me had hung them on the quilt frames on the front porch and quilted them. One was in the Lone Star pattern. The other was Walk Around the Mountain. In both of them were scraps of dresses Grandma Dee had worn fifty and more years ago. Bits and pieces of Grandpa Jarrell's Paisley shirts. And one teeny faded blue piece, about the size of a penny matchbox, that was from Great Grandpa Ezra's uniform that he wore in the Civil War.

"Mama," Wangero said sweet as a bird. "Can I have these old quilts?"

I heard something fall in the kitchen, and a minute later the kitchen door slammed.

"Why don't you take one or two of the others?" I asked. "These old things was just done by me and Big Dee from some tops your grandma pieced before she died."

"No," said Wangero. "I don't want those. They are stitched around the borders by machine."

"That'll make them last better," I said.

"That's not the point," said Wangero. "These are all pieces of dresses Grandma used to wear. She did all this stitching by hand. Imagine!" She held the quilts securely in her arms, stroking them.

"Some of the pieces, like those lavender ones, come from old clothes her mother handed down to her," I said, moving up to touch the quilts. Dee (Wangero) moved back just enough so that I couldn't reach the quilts. They already belonged to her.

"Imagine!" she breathed again, clutching them closely to her bosom.

"The truth is," I said, "I promised to give them quilts to Maggie, for when she marries John Thomas."

She gasped like a bee had stung her.

"Maggie can't appreciate these quilts!" she said. "She'd probably be backward enough to put them to everyday use."

"I reckon she would," I said. "God knows I been saving 'em for long enough with no-body using 'em. I hope she will!" I didn't want to bring up how I had offered Dee (Wangero) a quilt when she went away to college. Then she had told me they were old-fashioned, out of style.

"But they're *priceless*!" she was saying now, furiously; for she has a temper. "Maggie would put them on the bed and in five years they'd be in rags. Less than that!"

"She can always make some more," I said. "Maggie knows how to quilt."

Dee (Wangero) looked at me with hatred. "You just will not understand. The point is these quilts, *these quilts*!"

"Well," I said, stumped. "What would *you* do with them?"

"Hang them," she said. As if that was the only thing you *could* do with quilts.

Maggie by now was standing in the door. I could almost hear the sound her feet made as they scraped over each other.

"She can have them, Mama," she said, like somebody used to never winning anything, or having anything reserved for her. "I can 'member Grandma Dee without the quilts."

I looked at her hard. She had filled her bottom lip with checkerberry snuff and it gave her face a kind of dopey, hangdog look. It was Grandma Dee and Big Dee who taught her how to quilt herself. She stood there with her scarred hands hidden in the folds of her skirt. She looked at her sister with something like fear but she wasn't mad at her. This was Maggie's portion. This was the way she knew God to work.

When I looked at her like that something hit me in the top of my head and ran down to the soles of my feet. Just like when I'm in church and the spirit of God touches me and I get happy and shout. I did something I never had done before: hugged Maggie to me, then dragged her on into the room, snatched the quilts out of Miss Wangero's hands and dumped them into Maggie's lap. Maggie just sat there on my bed with her mouth open.

"Take one or two of the others," I said to Dee.

But she turned without a word and went out to Hakim-a-barber.

"You just don't understand," she said, as Maggie and I came out to the car.

"What don't I understand?" I wanted to know.

"Your heritage," she said. And then she turned to Maggie, kissed her, and said, "You ought to try to make something of yourself, too, Maggie. It's really a new day for us. But from the way you and Mama still live you'd never know it."

She put on some sunglasses that hid everything above the tip of her nose and her chin.

Maggie smiled; maybe at the sunglasses. But a real smile, not scared. After we watched the car dust settle I asked Maggie to bring me a dip of snuff. And then the two of us sat there just enjoying, until it was time to go in the house and go to bed.

Guide for Responding

◆ Literature and Your Life

Reader's Response How did you feel about Dee's behavior on her visit home? Explain.

Thematic Focus Do you think Dee has effectively blended an awareness of her African heritage with her everyday life? Explain.

☑ Check Your Comprehension

1. (a) How was Maggie injured? (b) How did she and her sister react to that experience?
2. (a) What objects does Dee ask to have? (b) What does she intend to do with each one?
3. What is Dee's response when the narrator says that she has promised to give the quilts to Maggie?

◆ Critical Thinking

INTERPRET

1. (a) What is revealed about the narrator's relationships with her daughters early in the story? (b) How does the mother's relationship with each daughter change? **[Infer]**
2. What is ironic about Dee's professed interest in her heritage? **[Interpret]**
3. (a) What do the quilts mean to Dee? (b) What do they mean to Maggie? **[Interpret]**
4. What message does this story convey about family relationships and the meaning of a family's heritage? **[Draw Conclusions]**

APPLY

5. What does your heritage mean to you? **[Define]**

Guide for Responding (continued)

◆ Reading Strategy

CONTRASTING CHARACTERS

Although Dee and Maggie are sisters, they have very little in common, aside from their mother and their interest in the two quilts. By **contrasting characters**—analyzing the differences between them—you can better understand each character and gain insight into the story's conflict and theme.

1. How do Maggie and Dee differ (a) physically, (b) intellectually, and (c) emotionally?
2. (a) What does each sister know about her African heritage and her American heritage? (b) To what extent does each sister think it is important to incorporate knowledge of her African heritage into her daily life? Support your answers with examples from the story.
3. Contrast the relationship each daughter has with her mother.

◆ Build Vocabulary

USING THE WORD ROOTS -doc-/-doct-

Using the meaning of -doc-/-doct- ("teach") and context clues, choose the best word in the box to complete each sentence.

documents	docile
indoctrinate	documentary

1. We watched a film ____?____ that traced the history of quilt-making in the United States.
2. A ____?____ learner is one who accepts without question anything he or she is taught.
3. The political leader tried to ____?____ his followers by repeating his ideology every day.
4. Immigrants were asked to show ____?____ to prove their citizenship in other countries.

USING THE WORD BANK

On your paper, write the letter of the synonym for the first word.

1. furtive: (a) open, (b) shifty, (c) annoying
2. lye: (a) cleanser, (b) liquid, (c) explosive
3. tyrant: (a) victim, (b) politician, (c) dictator
4. doctrines: (a) beliefs, (b) papers, (c) charters

◆ Literary Focus

CHARACTER'S MOTIVATION

It is particularly important to understand the **characters' motivations**—reasons for behavior—in "Everyday Use," a story about how people change over time. For example, Walker shows you that Maggie's hesitancy results, in part, from the childhood accident that has left more than a physical scar. Analyze the characters' motivations to answer these questions:

1. What appears to motivate Dee's interest in her heritage?
2. Discuss the personality characteristics that enable Dee to return home after a long absence and immediately assume she can get the churn top, the dasher, and the quilts.
3. What does the narrator's act of snatching up the quilts from Dee reveal about her personal values?

◆ Grammar and Style

SENTENCE FRAGMENTS

In this story, Walker uses **sentence fragments** to make it seem as if the first-person narrator is speaking informally to readers.

> **Sentence fragments** are parts of sentences incorrectly punctuated as complete.

Practice On your paper, explain why each example is a sentence fragment and identify the missing part or parts of speech. Rewrite each fragment as a complete sentence.

1. Furtive boys in pink shirts hanging about on washday after school.
2. Nervous girls who never laughed.
3. Earrings gold, too, and hanging down to her shoulder.
4. Always too busy: feeding the cattle, fixing the fences, putting up salt-lick shelters, throwing down hay.

Writing Application Write a short dialogue featuring characters from "Everyday Use." Incorporate sentence fragments to capture speech and thought patterns.

Build Your Portfolio

 **Idea Bank**

Writing

1. **Journal Entry** Write a journal entry describing the events in this story from either Maggie's or Dee's point of view.

2. **Speech** In the character of either Maggie or Dee, write a speech to a local women's group about the value of cultural heritage. **[Social Studies Link]**

3. **Character Analysis** Write a character analysis of Maggie. In your analysis, respond to one critic's suggestion that Maggie is a "silent, suffering" character. Using evidence from the story, argue for or against the critic's analysis of Maggie.

Speaking and Listening

4. **Television Talk Show** With a partner, dramatize the narrator's dream of a television reunion between herself and Dee. Add dialogue of your own to extend and elaborate on the dream in the story. **[Performing Arts Link]**

5. **Debate** In two teams, take pro and con positions to argue this statement: Handicrafts that reflect a culture's heritage should be taken out of general use and displayed in museums. **[Social Studies Link]**

Projects

6. **Heritage Exhibit** As a class, gather examples or pictures of folk art from cultures represented in the class. Create an exhibit with explanatory captions. **[Social Studies Link; Art Link]**

7. **African Languages Project** The names *Wangero* and *Hakim-a-barber* come from one of the 800–1,000 languages spoken in Africa today. Gather information on one of the four major language families, and present your findings to the class, along with audiotaped examples, if possible. **[Social Studies Link]**

 Writing Mini-Lesson

Review of a Short Story

What are your reactions to Walker's story? Were the characters interesting and believable? Did the story convey a message that you feel is important? Write a critical review of the story in which you respond to these and other questions that come to mind. Explain the ways in which you think the story is and is not effective. Keep the following tip in mind as you develop your review.

Writing Skills Focus: Accuracy

Focus on **accuracy** when gathering examples or evidence to support your opinions:

- Double-check any quotations to make sure they reflect the source word for word.
- Test and prove any cause-and-effect links you discuss.
- To avoid confusion, organize evidence about individual characters on separate pieces of paper.
- Clearly distinguish your opinions, and those of any critics you quote, from facts about the story and its characters.

Prewriting Create a two-column chart in which you list some positive and negative aspects of the story. Next to each item, note relevant page numbers of appropriate examples. Review the information on your chart and try to sum up your overall opinion in a sentence or two.

Drafting Begin by stating your overall opinion of the story. Then present a series of paragraphs in which you back up your opinion by accurately citing details from the story.

Revising Replace weak modifiers (such as *poor, good, nicely*) with precise adjectives and adverbs that capture your reactions (such as *cleverly, gripping, bold, challenging*). Be sure that your facts are accurate, and that you've copied all quotations word for word.

Guide for Interpreting

Maxine Hong Kingston

(1940–)

"I was born to be a writer," Maxine Hong Kingston once told an interviewer. "In the midst of any adventure, a born writer has a desire to hurry home and put it into words."

Crossing Cultures Kingston did not begin describing her adventures in English until she was nearly ten, because at home her first language was a form of Cantonese—a Chinese dialect spoken around Canton, now Guangzhou, China. Both her parents came from a village near Canton: Her father left first for "the Golden Mountain" of America, settling in New York City. Her mother used the money he sent home to run a clinic in their native village until 1939, when she escaped war-torn China and joined her husband. Not long afterward the couple resettled in Stockton, California, where Maxine Hong was born.

Young Maxine was a shy girl who earned straight A's in school. She won a scholarship to the University of California at Berkeley, which she attended in its heyday as a center of intellectual activity and political activism in the 1960's. Kingston recalls those years fondly: "Peace on earth. Friendship. We in Berkeley thought we were going to change the world."

At Berkeley, Maxine Hong met Earll Kingston, whom she married in 1962. After graduation the couple supported themselves as teachers while pursuing success in their chosen fields—Earll in acting, Maxine in writing.

Maxine Hong Kingston shot to success with her first book, The Woman Warrior.

The Woman Warrior, a unique blend of folklore, myth, feminism and autobiography, won the National Book Critics' Circle Award in 1976. The major focus of the book is on Brave Orchid (Kingston's mother) and the "talk stories" she tells her daughter about China and the female members of their family.

Kingston also earned the National Book Critics' Circle Award for *China Men* in 1980. In 1989, she published the novel *Tripmaster Monkey.* After living in Hawaii for many years, Kingston and her husband and son returned to the mainland, settling in Oakland, California.

◆ Background for Understanding

CULTURE: *THE WOMAN WARRIOR* AND THE CHINESE AMERICAN EXPERIENCE

The Woman Warrior is an innovative autobiography that attempts to capture both the outer and inner experience of growing up in a bicultural world—part Chinese, part American—and feeling torn between the two. To accomplish her purpose, Kingston often presents the "talk stories" that she heard as a girl growing up among native Chinese speakers. The book's subtitle, *Memoirs of a Girlhood Among Ghosts,* refers to the pale ghosts of white America as well as the ghosts of the narrator's ancestors back in China.

The woman warrior of the title is one of the latter ghosts, the brave heroine of a "talk story" from China's past, with whom the narrator identifies so strongly that at one point she practically becomes her. However, the title *Woman Warrior* may have a double meaning; it may also refer to the other Chinese and Chinese American women portrayed in the book, including the narrator's mother, Brave Orchid, on whom this selection focuses. This selection comes from a section of the book called "At the Western Palace."

from The Woman Warrior

◆ Literature and Your Life

CONNECT YOUR EXPERIENCE

If you've ever felt a gap between the way you and older relatives view the world, you'll appreciate this selection. In families whose adults and children were born in different countries, this gap can be particularly pronounced. As you read, think about the many ways in which the culture you grow up in influences your general outlook.

Journal Writing Jot down a "talk story," or oral tale or anecdote, that you recall. It might be a family tale or something you heard from a neighbor.

THEMATIC FOCUS: LITERATURE CONFRONTS THE EVERYDAY

This selection captures the details of everyday American life through the eyes of a woman who is something of an outsider.

◆ Literary Focus

MEMOIRS

Most **memoirs** are first-person nonfiction narratives. Most recount historically or personally significant events in which the writer was a participant or an eyewitness. While *The Woman Warrior* is not a traditional memoir, Kingston subtitled her writing *Memoirs of a Girlhood Among Ghosts.* As you read this selection from *The Woman Warrior,* consider how it does and does not conform to the standard definition of a memoir.

◆ Reading Strategy

APPLY BACKGROUND INFORMATION

Background information can often help you fully appreciate a piece of literature. Information found in book-jacket copy, a fore-word or introduction, footnotes, or your own knowledge from prior experience can help you understand a work's central message and subtleties.

In this textbook, you can gain background information from reading the author biography and Background for Understanding sections in the Guide for Interpreting. For example, by reading the background information for this selection from *The Woman Warrior,* you'll gain a frame of reference for details in the selection that are not otherwise explained.

◆ Build Vocabulary

WORD ROOTS: -aud-

From the Latin word *audire,* which means "to hear," comes the root *-aud-,* which also conveys the idea of sound or hearing. The adverb *inaudibly* means "in a tone too low to be heard."

WORD BANK

Preview this list of words.

> hysterically
> encampment
> inaudibly
> gravity
> oblivious

◆ Grammar and Style

PUNCTUATING A QUOTATION WITHIN A QUOTATION

Use single quotation marks to enclose a **quotation within a quotation**. As with double quotation marks, place commas and periods inside the closing single quotation marks. Place colons and semi-colons outside, and place question and exclamation marks inside or outside, depending on who is speaking. Look at these examples:

"He will say, 'Abandon ship,' but my son won't hear."

"The captain will say, 'Abandon ship'; or he might say, 'Watch out for bombs.'"

"Did the captain say, 'I believe we are under attack'?" Brave Orchid asked.

from The Woman Warrior

Maxine Hong Kingston

When she was about sixty-eight years old, Brave Orchid took a day off to wait at San Francisco International Airport for the plane that was bringing her sister to the United States. She had not seen Moon Orchid for thirty years. She had begun this waiting at home, getting up a half-hour before Moon Orchid's plane took off in Hong Kong.[1] Brave Orchid would add her will power to the forces that keep an airplane up. Her head hurt with the concentration. The plane had to be light, so no matter how tired she felt, she dared not rest her spirit on a wing but continuously and gently pushed up on the plane's belly. She had already been waiting at the airport for nine hours. She was wakeful.

Next to Brave Orchid sat Moon Orchid's only daughter, who was helping her aunt wait. Brave Orchid had made two of her own children come too because they could drive, but they had been lured away by the magazine racks and the gift shops and coffee shops. Her American children could not sit for very long. They did not understand sitting; they had wandering feet. She hoped they would get back from the pay TV's or the pay toilets or wherever they were spending their money before the plane arrived. If they did not come back soon, she would go look for them. If her son thought he could hide in the men's room, he was wrong.

"Are you all right, Aunt?" asked her niece.

"No, this chair hurts me. Help me pull some chairs together so I can put my feet up."

She unbundled a blanket and spread it out to make a bed for herself. On the floor she had two shopping bags full of canned peaches, real peaches, beans wrapped in taro leaves,[2] cookies, Thermos bottles,[3] enough food for everybody, though only her niece would eat with her. Her bad boy and bad girl were probably sneaking hamburgers, wasting their money. She would scold them.

Many soldiers and sailors sat about, oddly calm, like little boys in cowboy uniforms. (She thought "cowboy" was what you would call a Boy Scout.) They should have been crying hysterically on their way to Vietnam.[4] "If I see one that looks Chinese," she thought, "I'll go over and give him some advice." She sat up suddenly; she had forgotten about her own son, who was even now in Vietnam. Carefully she split her attention, beaming half of it to the ocean, into the water to keep him afloat. He was on a ship. He was in Vietnamese waters. She was sure of it. He and the other children were lying to her. They had said he was in Japan, and then they said he was in the Philippines. But when she sent him her help, she could feel that he was on a ship in Da Nang.[5] Also she had seen the children hide the envelopes that his letters came in.

"Do you think my son is in Vietnam?" she asked her niece, who was dutifully eating.

---

2. **taro** (te′ rō) **leaves:** Leaves of an edible tuberous plant widely eaten in Asia.
3. **Thermos** (thʉr′ məs) **bottles:** Insulated containers for holding liquids and keeping them warm or cold.
4. **Vietnam:** Southeast Asian nation where, in the late 1960's when this selection takes place, the U.S. had joined the fighting known as the Vietnam War (1954–1975).
5. **Da Nang** (da naŋ): City in central Vietnam that was the site of an important U.S. military base during the Vietnam War; also spelled Danang.

---

1. **took off in Hong Kong:** After mainland China fell to the Communists in the late 1940's, many native Chinese fled first to Hong Kong (a British colony until 1997) before emigrating to the United States.

"No. Didn't your children say he was in the Philippines?"

"Have you ever seen any of his letters with Philippine stamps on them?"

"Oh, yes. Your children showed me one."

"I wouldn't put it past them to send the letters to some Filipino they know. He puts Manila[6] postmarks on them to fool me."

"Yes, I can imagine them doing that. But don't worry. Your son can take care of himself. All your children can take care of themselves."

"Not him. He's not like other people. Not normal at all. He sticks erasers in his ears, and the erasers are still attached to the pencil stubs. The captain will say, 'Abandon ship,' or 'Watch out for bombs,' and he won't hear. He doesn't listen to orders. I told him to flee to Canada,[7] but he wouldn't go."

She closed her eyes. After a short while, plane and ship under control, she looked again at the children in uniforms. Some of the blond ones looked like baby chicks, their crew cuts like the downy yellow on baby chicks. You had to feel sorry for them even though they were Army and Navy Ghosts.

Suddenly her son and daughter came running. "Come, Mother. The plane's landed early. She's here already." They hurried, folding up their mother's <u>encampment</u>. She was glad her children were not useless. They must have known what this trip to San Francisco was about then. "It's a good thing I made you come early," she said.

Brave Orchid pushed to the front of the crowd. She had to be in front. The passengers were separated from the people waiting for them by glass doors and walls. Immigration Ghosts were stamping papers. The travellers crowded along some conveyor belts to have their luggage searched. Brave Orchid did not see her sister anywhere. She stood watching for four hours. Her children left and came back. "Why don't you sit down?" they asked.

"The chairs are too far away," she said.

"Why don't you sit on the floor then?"

No, she would stand, as her sister was probably standing in a line she could not see from here. Her American children had no feelings and no memory.

To while away time, she and her niece talked about the Chinese passengers. These new immigrants had it easy. On Ellis Island[8] the people were thin after forty days at sea and had no fancy luggage.

"That one looks like her," Brave Orchid would say.

"No, that's not her."

Ellis Island had been made out of wood and iron. Here everything was new plastic, a ghost trick to lure immigrants into feeling safe and spilling their secrets. Then the Alien Office could send them right back. Otherwise, why did they lock her out, not letting her help her sister answer questions and spell her name? At Ellis Island when the ghost asked Brave Orchid what year her husband had cut off his pigtail, a Chinese who was crouching on the floor motioned her not to talk. "I don't know," she had said. If it weren't for that Chinese man, she might not be here today, or her husband either. She hoped some Chinese, a janitor or a clerk, would look out for Moon Orchid. Luggage conveyors fooled immigrants into thinking the Gold Mountain was going to be easy.

◆ **Reading Strategy**
What does the background information in the Guide for Interpreting indicate that "the Gold Mountain" is?

Brave Orchid felt her heart jump—Moon Orchid. "There she is," she shouted. But her niece saw it was not her mother at all. And it shocked her to discover the woman her aunt was pointing out. This was a young woman, younger than herself, no older than Moon Orchid the day the sisters parted. "Moon Orchid will have changed a little, of course," Brave Orchid was saying. "She will have learned to wear western clothes." The woman wore a navy blue suit with a bunch of dark cherries at the shoulder.

---

6. **Manila** (mə nil´ ə): Capital of the Philippines.

7. **flee to Canada:** During the Vietnam War era, thousands of Americans fled to Canada to escape the military draft, even though such draft dodgers were subject to prosecution upon returning to the U.S.

8. **Ellis Island:** Island in the harbor off New York City that was the chief U.S. immigration station from 1892 to 1943.

◆ **Build Vocabulary**

hysterically (hi ster´ ik lē) *adv.*: In a highly emotional or uncontrolled manner

encampment (en kamp´ mənt) *n.*: Place where a person has set up camp

"No, Aunt," said the niece. "That's not my mother."

"Perhaps not. It's been so many years. Yes, it is your mother. It must be. Let her come closer, and we can tell. Do you think she's too far away for me to tell, or is it my eyes getting bad?"

"It's too many years gone by," said the niece.

Brave Orchid turned suddenly—another Moon Orchid, this one a neat little woman with a bun. She was laughing at something the person ahead of her in line said. Moon Orchid was just like that, laughing at nothing. "I would be able to tell the difference if one of them would only come closer," Brave Orchid said with tears, which she did not wipe. Two children met the woman with the cherries, and she shook their hands. The other woman was met by a young man. They looked at each other gladly, then walked away side by side.

Up close neither one of those women looked like Moon Orchid at all. "Don't worry, Aunt," said the niece. "I'll know her."

"I'll know her too. I knew her before you did."

The niece said nothing, although she had seen her mother only five years ago. Her aunt liked having the last word.

Finally Brave Orchid's children quit wandering and drooped on a railing. Who knew what they were thinking? At last the niece called out, "I see her! I see her! Mother! Mother!" Whenever the doors parted, she shouted, probably embarrassing the American cousins, but she didn't care. She called out, "Mama! Mama!" until the crack in the sliding doors became too small to let in her voice. "Mama!" What a strange word in an adult voice. Many people turned to see what adult was calling, "Mama!" like a child. Brave Orchid saw an old, old woman jerk her head up, her little eyes blinking confusedly, a woman whose nerves leapt toward the sound anytime she heard "Mama!" Then she relaxed to her own business again. She was a tiny, tiny lady, very thin, with little fluttering hands, and her hair was in a gray knot. She was dressed in a gray wool suit; she wore

pearls around her neck and in her earlobes. Moon Orchid *would* travel with her jewels showing. Brave Orchid momentarily saw, like a larger, younger outline around this old woman, the sister she had been waiting for. The familiar dim halo faded, leaving the woman so old, so gray. So old. Brave Orchid pressed against the glass. *That* old lady? Yes, that old lady facing the ghost who stamped her papers without questioning her was her sister. Then, without noticing her family, Moon Orchid walked smiling over to the Suitcase Inspector Ghost, who took her boxes apart, pulling out puffs of tissue. From where she was, Brave Orchid could not see what her sister had chosen to carry across the ocean. She wished her sister would look her way. Brave Orchid thought that if *she* were entering a new country, she would be at the windows. Instead Moon Orchid hovered over the unwrapping, surprised at each reappearance as if she were opening presents after a birthday party.

"Mama!" Moon Orchid's daughter kept calling. Brave Orchid said to her children, "Why don't you call your aunt too? Maybe she'll hear us if all of you call out together." But her children slunk away. Maybe that shame-face they so often wore was American politeness.

"Mama!" Moon Orchid's daughter called again, and this time her mother looked right at her. She left her bundles in a heap and came running. "Hey!" the Customs Ghost yelled at her. She went back to clear up her mess, talking inaudibly to her daughter all the while. Her daughter pointed toward Brave Orchid. And at last Moon Orchid looked at her—two old women with faces like mirrors.

Their hands reached out as if to touch the other's face, then returned to their own, the fingers checking the grooves in the forehead and along the sides of the mouth. Moon Orchid, who never understood the gravity of things, started smiling and laughing, pointing at Brave Orchid. Finally Moon Orchid gathered up her stuff, strings hanging and papers loose, and met her sister at the door, where they shook hands, oblivious to blocking the way.

"You're an old woman," said Brave Orchid.

"Aiaa. *You're* an old woman."

"But you are really old. Surely, you can't say that about me. I'm not old the way you're old."

"But *you* really are old. You're one year older than I am."

"Your hair is white and your face all wrinkled."

"You're so skinny."

"You're so fat."

"Fat women are more beautiful than skinny women."

The children pulled them out of the doorway. One of Brave Orchid's children brought the car from the parking lot, and the other heaved the luggage into the trunk. They put the two old ladies and the niece in the back seat. All the way home—across the Bay Bridge,[9] over the Diablo hills,[10] across the San Joaquin River[11] to the valley, the valley moon so white at dusk—all the way home, the two sisters exclaimed every time they turned to look at each other, "Aiaa! How old!"

Brave Orchid forgot that she got sick in cars, that all vehicles but palanquins[12] made her dizzy. "You're so old," she kept saying. "How did you get so old?"

Brave Orchid had tears in her eyes. But Moon Orchid said, "You look older than I. You *are* older than I," and again she'd laugh. "You're wearing an old mask to tease me." It surprised Brave Orchid that after thirty years she could still get annoyed at her sister's silliness.

---

9. **Bay Bridge:** One of the bridges across San Francisco Bay.
10. **Diablo** (dē äb´ lō) **hills:** Hills outside San Francisco.
11. **San Joaquin** (wô kēn´) **River:** River of central California; its valley is one of the state's richest agricultural areas.
12. **palanquins** (pal´ ən kēnz´): Hand-carried covered litters once widely used to transport people in China and elsewhere in eastern Asia.

Guide for Responding

◆ Literature and Your Life

Reader's Response With which character did you identify the most? Why?

Thematic Focus The mother and children in this selection might have contrasting definitions of "everyday events." Cite an example of such an event and explain the generational difference it reveals.

☑ Check Your Comprehension

1. Identify the family members waiting for Moon Orchid at the airport, and briefly describe each one's behavior.
2. What two things does Brave Orchid try to keep safe by applying her will power?
3. What is Brave Orchid's main impression when she finally sees her sister?

◆ Critical Thinking

INTERPRET

1. What sort of person is Brave Orchid? **[Connect]**
2. What seems to be her attitude toward America and American culture? **[Infer]**
3. When the two sisters finally meet, why do they speak to each other as they do? **[Interpret]**

EVALUATE

4. Did Kingston succeed in evoking the lives of people from very different cultures? Explain. **[Assess]**

APPLY

5. What does this selection suggest about the conflicts that face immigrants and the children of immigrants in America? **[Generalize]**

$\mathscr{G}$uide for Responding (continued)

◆ Literary Focus

MEMOIRS

If you were comparing the features of this selection with those of traditional **memoirs**—nonfiction narratives similar to autobiographies—you would notice both similarities and differences.

1. Upon whose impressions does this selection focus? Cite examples to support your answer.

2. (a) From what narrative point of view is this selection told? (b) Explain the difference between the point of view of this selection and that of traditional memoirs.

3. (a) Cite two memories Brave Orchid has while waiting in the airport. (b) Explain why these memories are—or are not—features typical of the memoir form.

4. Based on this selection, would you classify *The Woman Warrior* as a standard memoir? Why or why not?

◆ Reading Strategy

APPLY BACKGROUND INFORMATION

The **background information** provided for a piece of literature can help you to understand the details and cultural and historical references in that work. Knowing a bit about a country's history, for example, enables you to understand named historic events.

The background information from the Guide for Interpreting, footnotes, or your own knowledge can help you better understand the selection. Using this background knowledge, answer these questions.

1. (a) From what province in China is Moon Orchid probably coming? (b) What evidence did you use to draw your conclusion?

2. What does the narrator mean by (a) Army and Navy Ghosts? (b) Customs Ghost?

3. (a) Where is the family probably headed in the last paragraphs? (b) How do you know?

4. Brave Orchid has packed beans wrapped in taro leaves. How does knowing what taro leaves are increase your understanding of her character?

◆ Build Vocabulary

USING THE WORD ROOT -aud-

The root *-aud-* indicates "hearing" or "sound." Explain how its meaning is connected to each of these words:

1. audiocassette   3. auditorium
2. auditory   4. audition

USING THE WORD BANK

In your notebook, write each sentence, replacing the blank with the appropriate word from the Word Bank.

1. We left our homey ____?____ and hiked up the mountain.

2. ____?____ to the time, she worked on into the night.

3. When she answered ____?____, I asked her to speak up.

4. The boy yelled ____?____ when he thought he was lost.

5. The ____?____ of the situation silenced us all.

◆ Grammar and Style

PUNCTUATING A QUOTATION WITHIN A QUOTATION

Remember to place commas and periods inside closing quotation marks, colons and semicolons outside, and question marks and exclamation points inside or outside, depending on the words to which they apply.

> Use single quotation marks to enclose a **quotation within a quotation**.

Practice Copy this paragraph about the characters in *The Woman Warrior* into your notebook, adding all the missing single quotation marks.

"My sister wrote, I am coming to America," Brave Orchid told her family. "She asked, Will you be able to pick me up? I told her, Yes, I will leave my house before your plane takes off from Hong Kong. Do you think she knows I am excited?"

Writing Application Write a second paragraph in which Brave Orchid quotes her sister. Use single quotations marks to indicate quotations within quotations. Punctuate according to the rules that apply.

Build Your Portfolio

Idea Bank

Writing

1. **Diary Entry** Write the diary entry that Moon Orchid might have written on the night of her arrival in California.

2. **Prequel** Write a scene that explains why Moon Orchid and her daughter were separated. In your prequel to the story, reveal why Moon Orchid is coming to America now or why Moon Orchid's daughter came to America earlier.

3. **Character Analysis** In an essay, analyze Brave Orchid's character. Identify three or four of her character traits, and connect these traits to her background and her behavior. Cite appropriate supporting examples from the selection.

Speaking and Listening

4. **Talk Story** As an adult, tell your grown children a "talk story"—an oral account of a dramatic event that took place when you were a child.

5. **Panel Discussion** When *The Woman Warrior* won a 1976 national award for nonfiction, many debated its qualifications. Based on what you've read, hold a panel discussion to decide whether this work fits the definition of nonfiction.

Projects

6. **Written Report** Research and report on the history of Chinese immigration to the United States. Study the arrivals of immigrants and their patterns of settlement. Create a supplementary chart of statistical information. **[Math Link]**

7. **Historical Travelogue** Suppose you were travelling to Guangzhou (then Canton), China, around the 1930's when Brave Orchid still lived there. Present an audiotaped travelogue describing what you saw. Show pictures if possible. **[Social Studies Link]**

Writing Mini-Lesson

Guide for Planning a Family Reunion

Many families hold organized reunions to bring family members living in distant places together for a visit. Such a reunion takes a lot of planning. Relatives in far-flung places must be contacted; travel routes must be suggested; a meeting place has to be chosen; menus must be planned. Create a guide in which you cover these essentials as well as any details that you think go into making a successful family reunion.

Writing Skills Focus: Explain a Procedure

In writing your guide, it's important to explain a procedure clearly.

- Use headings or spacing to make the main parts of the procedure clear. One main part might be "Compiling a Guest List"; another might be "Arranging the Picnic," and so on.
- Divide each main part of the procedure into numbered or lettered steps.
- Include diagrams or graphic aids to clarify your information. For example, you might include a checklist to help readers chart their progress.

Prewriting List the main parts of the plan in an outline or on index cards organized in separate piles.

Drafting Include an introduction that states the purpose of reunions and your reunion plan; a body that uses subheadings, numerals, and other graphic aids; and a conclusion that sums up the key points of your plan.

Revising Make sure you have included all necessary steps and details, including appropriate information on organizing *who*, *what*, *where*, *when*, *why*, and *how*. Check that all steps are presented in logical order with headings, spacing, and numerals used to make the reading easy.

Guide for Interpreting

Julia Alvarez (1950–)

"I came into English as a ten-year-old from the Dominican Republic, and I consider this radical uprooting from my culture, my native language, my country, the reason I began writing," Julia Alvarez once explained.

Writing to Ease the Pain While moving to a new country changed her world forever, Alvarez quickly found her voice as a writer.

As a young adult, Alvarez found that writing helped her deal with the pain of trying to adjust to a new culture and language.

"In high school, I fell in love with how words can make you feel complete in a way that I hadn't felt complete since leaving the island," she said.

After graduating from college, where she was awarded several poetry prizes, Alvarez earned a masters degree in creative writing at Syracuse University. She went on to join the Kentucky Arts Commission's poetry-in-the-schools program. For two years, she traveled around Kentucky teaching poetry. She then held a variety of teaching jobs before settling in Vermont as a Professor of English at Middlebury College.

New Directions Alvarez's poetry often focuses on details of daily life as well as her Caribbean heritage. She has published two volumes of poetry, *Homecomings* (1984) and *The Other Side* (1995). After *Homecomings* was published, Alvarez began to focus on a new area of writing: fiction.

"My own island background was steeped in a tradition of storytelling that I wanted to explore in prose," Alvarez explained. The move to prose proved fruitful, for Alvarez has won fame for three semi-autobiographical novels rooted in Hispanic American tradition: *How the García Girls Lost Their Accents* (1991), *In the Time of the Butterflies* (1994), and *¡Yo!* (1997).

As the story "Antojos" illustrates, Alvarez has also shown that she is a talented short-story writer. Like her novels, "Antojos" tells the story of a Dominican woman who has settled in the United States. The story captures what happens when she revisits her homeland.

◆ Background for Understanding

SOCIAL STUDIES: JULIA ALVAREZ AND DOMINICAN POLITICS

Alvarez's homeland, the Dominican Republic, takes up the eastern two thirds of Hispaniola, an island that is part of the West Indies. The western third of the island is the country of Haiti.

The Dominican Republic won independence in 1844, after a successful rebellion against Haitian rule. Since then, however, the country has suffered through several dictatorships and frequent foreign domination. One of the most ruthless dictators was Rafael Trujillo, who ruled the country from 1930 until he was assassinated in 1961.

Julia Alvarez's father was part of the underground movement against Trujillo, and it was this involvement that forced the family to flee the country. Three months after they left, three of her father's co-conspirators were killed. Alvarez's emigration experience and the political turmoil of the time have influenced much of her writing.

Antojos

◆ *Literature and Your Life*

CONNECT YOUR EXPERIENCE

In this story, the main character becomes fearful because she is unsure of the motives of two strangers. Have you ever been in a similar situation? Why are we more comfortable dealing with familiar people?

Journal Writing Think back to your first impression of someone whom you now know well. How much has your initial impression of that person changed? In what way is it the same?

THEMATIC FOCUS: LITERATURE CONFRONTS THE EVERYDAY

People are constantly confronted with conflict; we disagree with others or struggle to make decisions daily. Sometimes, an unforeseen event can put the resolution of even a small problem in doubt. The main character in "Antojos" faces such a situation.

◆ Build Vocabulary

WORDS FROM SPANISH

This story contains many words that come to English from Spanish. For example, a *machete* (mə shet´ ē) is a large, heavy knife used to cut down vegetation. The word is taken directly from Spanish (pronounced mä che´ tä). It is a form of the Spanish word *macho*, meaning "sledge hammer."

WORD BANK

Preview this list of words from the story.

> dissuade
> loath
> appease
> machetes
> collusion
> docile
> enunciated

◆ Grammar and Style

ABSOLUTE PHRASES

An **absolute phrase** usually consists of a noun or noun phrase modified by a participle or participial phrase. It has no direct grammatical connection with any single word in the sentence; instead, it stands absolutely by itself and modifies the entire clause to which it is attached. Absolute phrases can open, interrupt, or conclude sentences and are always set off with commas, as in these sentences:

A bus came lurching around the curve, *the driver saluting.*

His friend bracing him, he pumped the jack vigorously.

Sometimes the participle is omitted as understood:

His friend (being) weary, they exchanged places.

◆ Literary Focus

FLASHBACK

A **flashback** is an interruption in the chronological presentation of events in a story to present a scene or event from an earlier time. Flashbacks often provide valuable information about characters' backgrounds, personalities, and motives. When you come to a flashback in "Antojos," consider what it reveals about the main character.

◆ Reading Strategy

IDENTIFY WITH A CHARACTER

You can often understand a literary work better if you **identify with a character** who appears in the work. Think about what you and the character have in common in terms of background, personality, attitudes, motives, or behavior. For example, as you read "Antojos," think about ways in which you are like the main character, Yolanda. List similarities in a chart like this one.

	Yolanda	Me
Background		
Personality		
Attitudes		
Motives		
Behavior		

Antojos¹

Julia Alvarez

Fruit Vendor, 1951, Olga Costa, Museo de Arte Moderno, Mexico

▲ **Critical Viewing** How is the artist's portrayal of fruit similar to Yolanda's feelings about guavas? **[Compare]**

F or the first time since Yolanda had reached the hills, there was a shoulder on the left side of the narrow road. She pulled the car over out of a sense of homecoming: every other visit she had stayed with her family in the capital.

1. **Antojos** (än tō´ hōs)

Once her own engine was off, she heard the sound of another motor, approaching, a pained roar as if the engine were falling apart. She made out an undertow of men's voices. Quickly, she got back into the car, locked the door, and pulled off the shoulder, hugging her right side of the road.

—Just in time too. A bus came lurching around the curve, obscuring her view with a belching of exhaust, the driver saluting or warning with a series of blasts on his horn. It was an old army bus, the official name brushed over with paint that didn't quite match the regulation gray. The passengers saw her only at the last moment, and all up and down her side of the bus, men poked out of the windows, hooting and yelling, waving purple party flags, holding out bottles and beckoning to her. She speeded up and left them behind, the small compact climbing easily up the snakey highway, its well-oiled hum a gratifying sound after the hullabaloo of the bus.

She tried the radio again, but all she could tune to was static even here on the summit hills. She would have to wait until she got to the coast to hear news of the hunger march in the capital. Her family had been worried that trouble would break out, for the march had been scheduled on the anniversary of the failed revolution nineteen years ago today. A huge turnout was expected. She bet that bus she had just passed had been delayed by breakdowns on its way to the capital. In fact, earlier on the road when she had first set out, Yolanda had passed buses and truckloads of men, drinking and shouting slogans. It crossed her mind that her family had finally agreed to loan her a car because they knew she'd be far safer on the north coast than in the capital city where revolutions always broke out.

The hills began to plane out into a high plateau, the road widening. Left and right, roadside stands began appearing. Yolanda slowed down and kept an eye out for guavas, supposedly in season this far north. Piled high on wooden stands were fruits she hadn't seen in so many years: pinkish-yellow mangoes, and tamarind pods oozing their rich sap, and small cashew fruits strung on a rope to keep them from bruising each other. There were little brown packets of roasted cashews and bars of milk fudge wrapped in waxed paper and tied with a string, the color of which told what filling was inside the bar. Strips of meat, buzzing with flies, hung from the windows of butcher stalls. An occasional display of straw hats and baskets and hammocks told that tourists sometimes did pass by here. Looking at the stores spread before her, it was hard to believe the poverty the organizers of the march kept discussing on the radio. There seemed to be plenty here to eat—except for guavas.

In the capital, her aunts had plied her with what she most craved after so many years away. "Any little *antojo*, you must tell us!" They wanted to spoil her, so she'd stay on in her nativeland before she forgot where she had come from. "What exactly does it mean, *antojo*?" Yolanda asked. Her aunts were proven right: After so many years away, their niece was losing her Spanish.

"An *antojo*—" The aunts exchanged quizzical looks. "How to put it? An *antojo* is like a craving for something you have to eat."

A cousin blew out her cheeks. "Calories."

An *antojo*, one of the older aunts continued, was a very old Spanish word from before "your United States was thought of," she added tartly. In the countryside some *campesinos*[2] still used the word to mean possession by an island spirit demanding its due.

Her island spirit certainly was a patient soul, Yolanda joked. She hadn't had her favorite *antojo*, guavas, since her last trip seven years ago. Well, on this trip, her aunts promised, Yoyo could eat guavas to her heart's content. But when the gardener was summoned, he

---

2. *campesinos* (käm´ pe sē´ nōs): "Poor farmers; simple rural dwellers" (Spanish).

wasn't so sure. Guavas were no longer in season, at least not in the hotter lowlands of the south. Maybe up north, the chauffeur could pick her up some on his way back from some errand. Yolanda took this opportunity to inform her aunts of her plans: she could pick the guavas herself when she went up north in a few days.

—She was going up north? By herself? A woman alone on the road! "This is not the States." Her old aunts had tried to <u>dissuade</u> her. "Anything can happen." When Yolanda challenged them, "What?" they came up with boogeymen stories that made her feel as if she were talking to china dolls.[3] Haitian hougans[4] and Communist kidnappers. "And Martians?" Yolanda wanted to tease them. They had led such sheltered lives, riding from one safe place to another in their air-conditioned cars.

◆ **Literary Focus**
What does this flashback reveal about Yolanda and her aunts?

She had left the fruit stands behind her and was approaching a compound very much like her family's in the capital. The underbrush stopped abruptly at a high concrete wall, topped with broken bottle glass. Parked at the door was a chocolate brown Mercedes. Perhaps the owners had come up to their country home for the weekend to avoid the troubles in the capital?

Just beyond the estate, Yolanda came upon a small village—ALTAMIRA in rippling letters on the corrugated tin roof of the first little house. It was a little cluster of houses on either side of the road, a good place to stretch her legs before what she'd heard was a steep and slightly (her aunts had warned "very") dangerous descent to the coast. Yolanda pulled up at a cantina, the thatched roof held up by several posts. Instead of a menu, there was a yellowing, grimy poster for Palmolive soap tacked on one of the posts with a picture of a blonde woman under a spraying shower, her head thrown back in seeming ecstasy, her mouth opened in a wordless cry. ("Palmolive"? Yolanda wondered.) She felt even thirstier and grimier looking at this lathered beauty after her hot day on the road.

An old woman emerged at last from a shack behind the cabana, buttoning up a torn housedress, and followed closely by a little boy, who kept ducking behind her whenever Yolanda smiled at him. Asking him his name just drove him further into the folds of the old woman's skirt.

"You must excuse him, Doña,"[5] she apologized. "He's not used to being among people." But Yolanda knew the old woman meant, not the people in the village, but the people with money who drove through Altamira to the beaches on the coast. "Your name," the old woman repeated, as if Yolanda hadn't asked him in Spanish. The little boy mumbled at the ground. "Speak up!" the old woman scolded, but her voice betrayed pride when she spoke up for him. "This little know-nothing is Jose Duarte Sanchez y Mella Garcia."

Yolanda laughed. Not only were those a lot of names for such a little boy, but they certainly were momentous: the surnames of the three liberators of the country!

"Can I serve the Doña in any way?" the woman asked. Yolanda gave the tree line beyond the woman's shack a glance. "You think you might have some guavas around?"

The old woman's face scrunched up. "Guavas?" she murmured and thought to herself a second. "Why, they're all around, Doña. But I can't say as I've seen any."

"With your permission—" Jose Duarte had joined a group of little boys who had come out

---

3. **china dolls:** Old-fashioned, delicate dolls made of fragile high-quality porcelain or ceramic ware.
4. **Haitian hougans** (o͞o gänz´): Voodoo priests or cult leaders.

5. **Doña** (dō´ nyä): "Madam" (Spanish).

of nowhere and were milling around the car, boasting how many automobiles they had ridden in. At Yolanda's mention of guavas, he sprung forward, pointing across the road towards the summit of the western hills. "I know where there's a whole grove of them." Behind him, his little companions nodded.

"Go on, then!" His grandmother stamped her foot as if she were scatting a little animal. "Get the Doña some."

A few boys dashed across the road and disappeared up a steep path on the hillside, but before Jose could follow, Yolanda called him back. She wanted to go along too. The little boy looked towards his grandmother, unsure of what to think. The old woman shook her head. The Doña would get hot, her nice clothes would get all dirty. Jose would get the Doña as many guavas as she was wanting.

◆ Reading Strategy
Can you identify with Yolanda's feelings at this point in the story? Why or why not?

"But they taste so much better when you've picked them yourself," Yolanda's voice had an edge, for suddenly, it was as if the woman had turned into the long arm of her family, keeping her away from seeing her country on her own.

The few boys who had stayed behind with Jose had congregated around the car. Each one claimed to be guarding it for the Doña. It occurred to Yolanda that there was a way to make this a treat all the way around. "What do you say we take the car?"

"*Sí, Sí, Sí*,"[6] the boys screamed in a riot of excitement.

The old woman hushed them but agreed that was not a bad idea if the Doña insisted on going. There was a dirt road up ahead she could follow a ways and then cross over onto the road that was paved all the way to the coffee barns. The woman pointed south in the direction of the big house. Many workers took that short cut to work.

They piled into the car, half a dozen boys in the back, and Jose as co-pilot in the passenger seat beside Yolanda. They turned onto a bumpy road off the highway, which got bumpier and bumpier, and climbed up into wilder, more desolate country. Branches scraped the sides and pebbles pelted the underside of the car. Yolanda wanted to turn back, but there was no room to maneuver the car around. Finally, with a great snapping of twigs and thrashing of branches across the windshield, as if the countryside were <u>loath</u> to release them, the car burst forth onto smooth pavement and the light of day. On either side of the road were groves of guava trees. Among them, the boys who had gone ahead on foot were already pulling down branches and shaking loose a rain of guavas. The fruit was definitely in season.

For the next hour or so, Yolanda and her crew scavenged the grove, the best of the pick going into the beach basket Yolanda had gotten out of the trunk, with the exception of the ones she ate right on the spot, relishing the slightly bumpy feel of the skin in her hand, devouring the crunchy, sweet, white meat. The boys watched her, surprised by her odd hunger.

Yolanda and Jose, partners, wandered far from the path that cut through the grove. Soon they were bent double to avoid getting entangled in the thick canopy of branches overhead. Each addition to the basket caused a spill from the stash already piled high above the brim. Finally, it was a case of abandoning the treasure in order to cart some of it home. With Jose hugging the basket to himself and Yolanda parting the wayward branches in front of them, they headed back toward the car.

When they finally cleared the thicket of guava branches, the sun was low on the

---

6. *Sí, Sí, Sí* (sē): "Yes, Yes, Yes" (Spanish).

◆ Build Vocabulary

dissuade (di swād´) *v.*: Convince someone not to do something; discourage

loath (lōth) *adj.*: Reluctant

western horizon. There was no sign of the other boys. "They must have gone to round up the goats," Jose observed.

Yolanda glanced at her watch: it was past six o'clock. She'd never make the north coast by nightfall, but at least she could get off the dangerous mountain roads while it was still light. She hurried Jose back to the car, where they found a heap of guavas the other boys had left behind on the shoulder of the road. Enough guavas to appease even the greediest island spirit for life!

They packed the guavas in the trunk quickly and climbed in, but the car had not gone a foot before it lurched forward with a horrible hobble. Yolanda closed her eyes and laid her head down on the wheel, then glanced over at Jose. The way his eyes were searching the inside of the car for a clue as to what could have happened, she could tell he didn't know how to change a flat tire either.

It was no use regretting having brought the car up that bad stretch of road. The thing to do now was to act quickly. Soon the sun would set and night would fall swiftly, no lingering dusk as in the States. She explained to Jose that they had a flat tire and had to hike back to town and send for help down the road to the big house. Whoever tended to the brown Mercedes would know how to change the tire on her car.

"With your permission," Jose offered meekly. He pointed down the paved road. "This goes directly to the big house." The Doña could just wait in the car and he would be back in no time with someone from the Miranda place.

She did not like the idea of staying behind in the car, but Jose could probably go and come back much quicker without her. "All right," she said to the boy. "I'll tell you what." She pointed to her watch. It was almost six thirty. "If you're back by the time this hand is over here, I'll give you"—she held up one finger "a dollar." The boy's mouth fell open. In no time, he had shot out of his side of the car and was headed at a run toward the Miranda place. Yolanda climbed

out as well and walked down a pace, until the boy had disappeared in one of the turnings of the road.

Suddenly, the countryside was so very quiet. She looked up at the purple sky. A breeze was blowing through the grove, rustling the leaves, so they whispered like voices, something indistinct. Here and there a light flickered on the hills, a *campesino* living out his solitary life. This was what she had been missing without really knowing that she was missing it all these years. She had never felt at home in the States, never, though she knew she was lucky to have a job, so she could afford her own life and not be run by her family. But independence didn't have to be exile. She could come home, home to places like these very hills, and live here on her own terms.

Heading back to the car, Yolanda stopped. She had heard footsteps in the grove. Could Jose be back already? Branches were being thrust aside, twigs snapped. Suddenly, a short, dark man, and then a slender, light-skin man emerged from a footpath on the opposite side of the grove from the one she and Jose had scavenged. They wore ragged work clothes stained with patches of sweat; their faces were drawn and tired. Yolanda's glance fell on the machetes that hung from their belts.

The men's faces snapped awake from their stupor at the sight of her. They looked beyond her at the car. "Yours?" the darker man spoke first. It struck her, even then, as an absurd question. Who else's would it be here in the middle of nowhere?

"Is there some problem?" the darker man spoke up again. The taller one was looking her up and down with interest. They were now both in front of her on the road, blocking her escape. Both—she had looked them up and down as well—were strong and quite capable of catching her if she made a run for the Miranda's. Not that she could have moved, for her legs seemed suddenly to have been hammered into the ground beneath her. She thought of explaining

◆ *Literature and Your Life*

How do you react to situations in which you feel a threat? Do you think you would react in a different manner than Yolanda? Explain.

that she was just out for a drive before dinner at the big house, so that these men would think someone knew where she was, someone would come looking for her if they tried to carry her off. But she found she could not speak. Her tongue felt as if it'd been stuffed in her mouth like a rag to keep her quiet.

The men exchanged a look—it seemed to Yolanda of <u>collusion</u>. Then the shorter, darker one spoke up again, "Señorita,[7] are you all right?" He peered at her. The darkness of his complexion in the growing darkness of the evening made it difficult to distinguish an expression. He was no taller than Yolanda, but he gave the impression of being quite large, for he was broad and solid, like something not yet completely carved out of a piece of wood. His companion was tall and of a rich honey-brown color that matched his honey-brown eyes. Anywhere else, Yolanda would have found him extremely attractive, but here on a lonely road, with the sky growing darker by seconds, his good looks seemed dangerous, a lure to catch her off her guard.

"Can we help you?" the shorter man repeated.

The handsome one smiled knowingly. Two long, deep dimples appeared like gashes on either side of his mouth. "*Americana*," he said to the other in Spanish, pointing to the car. "She doesn't understand."

The darker man narrowed his eyes and studied Yolanda a moment. "*Americana*?" he asked her as if not quite sure what to make of her.

She had been too frightened to carry out any strategy, but now a road was opening before her. She laid her hand on her chest—she could feel her pounding heart—and nodded. Then, as if the admission itself loosened her tongue, she explained in English how it came that she was on a back road by herself, her craving for guavas, her never having learned to change a flat. The two men stared at her, uncomprehendingly, rendered <u>docile</u> by her gibberish. Strangely enough, it soothed her to hear herself speaking something they could not understand. She thought of something her teacher used to say to her when as a young immigrant girl she was learning English, "Language is power." It was her only defense now.

Yolanda made the motions of pumping. The darker man looked at the other, who had shown better luck at understanding the foreign lady. But his companion shrugged, baffled as well. "I'll show you," Yolanda waved for them to follow her. And suddenly, as if after pulling and pulling at roots, she had finally managed to yank them free of the soil they had clung to, she found she could move her own feet forward to the car.

The small group stood staring at the sagging tire a moment, the two men kicking at it as if punishing it for having failed the Señorita. They squatted by the passenger's side, conversing in low tones. Yolanda led them to the rear of the car, where the men lifted the spare out of its sunken nest—then set to work, fitting the interlocking pieces of the jack, unpacking the tools from the deeper hollows of the trunk. They laid their machetes down on the side of the road,

---

7. **Señorita** (se´ nyō rē´ tä): "Miss" (Spanish).

◆ **Build Vocabulary**

appease (ə pēz´) *v.*: Satisfy

machetes (mə shet´ ēz) *n.*: Large heavy knives with broad blades, used to clear overgrown paths or cut down vegetation

collusion (kə lōō´ zhən) *n.*: Secret agreement; conspiracy

docile (däs´ əl) *adj.*: Easy to direct or manage; obedient

out of the way. Yolanda turned on the head-lights to help them see in the growing dark-ness. Above the small group, the sky was purple with twilight.

There was a problem with the jack. It squeaked and labored, but the car would not rise. The shorter man squirmed his way under-neath and placed the mechanism deeper under the bowels of the car. There, he pumped vigor-ously, his friend bracing him by holding him down by the ankles. Slowly, the car rose until the wheel hung suspended. When the man came out from under the car, his hand was bloody where his knuckles had scraped against the pavement.

Yolanda pointed to the man's hand. She had been sure that if any blood were going to be spilled tonight, it would be hers. She offered him the towel she kept draped on her car seat to ab-sorb her perspiration. But he waved it away and sucked his knuckles to make the bleeding stop.

Once the flat had been replaced with the spare, the two men lifted the deflated tire into the trunk and put away the tools. They handed Yolanda her keys. There was still no sign of Jose and the Miranda's. Yolanda was relieved. As she had waited, watching the two men hard at work, she had begun to dread the boy's re-turn with help. The two men would realize she spoke Spanish. It was too late to admit that she had tricked them, to explain she had done so only because she thought her survival was on the line. The least she could do now was to try and repay them, handsomely, for their trouble.

"I'd like to give you something," she began reaching for the purse she'd retrieved from the trunk. The English words sounded hollow on her tongue. She rolled up a couple of American bills and offered them to the men. The shorter man held up his hand. Yolanda could see where the blood had dried dark streaks on his palm. "No, no, Señorita. *Nuestro placer.*"[8] Our pleasure.

Yolanda turned to the other man, who had struck her as more pliant than his sterner companion. "Please," she urged the bills on him. But he too looked down at the ground with the bashfulness she had observed in Jose of country people not wanting to offend. She felt the poverty of her response and stuffed the bills quickly into his pocket.

The two men picked up their machetes and raised them to their shoulders like soldiers their guns. The tall man motioned towards the big house. "*Directo, directo,*"[9] he enunciated the words carefully. Yolanda looked in the direction of his hand. In the faint light of what was left of day, she could barely make out the road ahead. It was as if the guava grove had overgrown into the road and woven its mat of branches so se-curely and tightly in all directions, she would not be able to escape.

But finally, she was off! While the two men waited a moment on the shoulder to see if the tire would hold, Yolanda drove a few yards, pok-ing her head out the window before speeding up. "*Gracias!*"[10] she called, and they waved, ap-preciatively, at the foreign lady making an effort in her native tongue. When she looked for them in her rear-view mirror, they had disap-peared into the darkness of the guava grove.

Just ahead, her lights described the figure of a small boy: Jose was walking alone, listlessly, as if he did not particularly want to get to where he was going.

Yolanda leaned over and opened the door for him. The small overhead light came on; she saw that the boy's face was streaked with tears.

"Why, what's wrong, Jose?"

The boy swallowed hard. "They would not come. They didn't believe me." He took little breaths between words to keep his tears at bay. He had lost his chance at a whole dollar. "And the guard, he said if I didn't stop telling stories, he was going to whip me."

"What did you tell him, Jose?"

---

8. *Nuestro placer* (no͞o es´ trō plä ser´): "Our pleasure" (Spanish).

9. *Directo, directo* (dē rek´ tō): "Straight, straight" (Spanish).
10. *Gracias* (grä´ sē äs): "Thank you" (Spanish).

"I told him you had broken your car and you needed help fixing it."

She should have gone along with Jose to the Miranda's. Given all the trouble in the country, they would be suspicious of a boy coming to their door at nightfall with some story about a lady on a back road with a broken car. "Don't you worry, Jose," Yolanda patted the boy. She could feel the bony shoulder through the thin fabric of his worn shirt. "You can still have your dollar. You did your part."

But the shame of being suspected of lying seemed to have obscured any immediate pleasure he might feel in her offer. Yolanda tried to distract him by asking what he would buy with his money, what he most craved, thinking that on a subsequent trip, she might bring him his little *antojo*. But Jose Duarte Sanchez y Mella said nothing, except a bashful thank you when she left him off at the cantina with his promised dollar. In the glow of the headlights, Yolanda made out the figure of the old woman in the black square of her doorway, waving good-bye. Above the picnic table on a near post, the Palmolive woman's skin shone; her head was thrown back, her mouth opened as if she were calling someone over a great distance.

◆ **Build Vocabulary**

enunciated (ē nun´ sē āt´əd) *v.*: Pronounced; stated precisely

Guide for Responding

◆ *Literature and Your Life*

Reader's Response Did this story surprise you in any way? Explain.

Thematic Focus How does a commonplace annoyance like a flat tire become an opportunity for highlighting the kindness of strangers?

Journal Entry Put yourself in Yolanda's place and write the journal entry she might have written about her adventure.

☑ Check Your Comprehension

1. What warnings do family members give Yolanda?
2. What are *antojos*?
3. (a) What deal with Yolanda prompts Jose to go with her? (b) What happens to that deal?
4. Summarize what happens after the car gets a flat tire.

◆ Critical Thinking

INTERPRET

1. (a) How is Yolanda different from her aunts? (b) How is she different from the men who change her flat tire? **[Compare and Contrast]**
2. (a) Why does Yolanda pretend she has no island background? (b) Why is she suspicious of the two men? **[Analyze]**
3. What theme do you think the story title stresses? **[Connect]**
4. What might the Palmolive poster on p. 968 and p. 973 symbolize? **[Interpret]**

EVALUATE

5. Are Yolanda's suspicions of the men warranted? Cite details to support your evaluation. **[Evaluate]**
6. Does Yolanda learn or grow in the story? Explain. **[Assess]**

Guide for Responding (continued)

◆ Reading Strategy

IDENTIFY WITH A CHARACTER

When you **identify with the story's main character**, you imagine yourself in the situation the story presents. At the same time, you consider any similarities in your backgrounds, personalities, attitudes, motives, and behavior.

1. (a) What would you identify as the chief similarities between yourself and Yolanda? (b) What are the chief differences?
2. Do you think you would have reacted as she did to the two men who came by when she had the flat tire? Explain.

◆ Build Vocabulary

USING WORDS FROM SPANISH

Machete comes to English directly from Spanish, a language in which it has the same meaning. Many other English words also come from Spanish. Use the story context to help you answer these questions about three more such words.

1. What English word used in the story probably comes from *guayaba,* the Spanish name for the same tropical fruit?
2. *Cantina,* from the Spanish for "bar" or "tavern," is related to an Italian word for "wine cellar." What other English word do you guess has a similar origin?
3. In English, a *cabana* or *cabaña* is usually a small building used as a beach house at a swimming pool or beach. Is that the word's meaning on p. 968 in the story? Explain.

USING THE WORD BANK

On a separate sheet of paper, indicate whether the following pairs of words are synonyms or antonyms.

1. dissuade, discourage
2. loath, eager
3. appease, arouse
4. machetes, knives
5. collusion, plotting
6. docile, cantankerous
7. enunciated, slurred

◆ Literary Focus

FLASHBACK

You can often obtain valuable information about characters' backgrounds, personalities, and motives from a **flashback**—a section of a literary work that interrupts the chronological presentation of events to relate an event from an earlier time. Alvarez's story contains a revealing flashback to Yolanda's time with her aunts in the capital.

1. What does the flashback reveal about the social and economic situation of Yolanda's family?
2. What does the flashback reveal about Yolanda's reasons for making the car trip up north?

◆ Grammar and Style

ABSOLUTE PHRASES

An **absolute phrase** is made up of a subject and a participle or participial phrase. It stands absolutely by itself and is not considered part of the subject or predicate. It is set off from the rest of the sentence by a comma or commas.

Practice Copy these sentences into your notebook, and underline all the absolute phrases. If a sentence contains no absolute phrase, write *none*.

1. It was an old army bus, the official name brushed over with paint that didn't quite match the regulation gray.
2. She speeded up and left them behind, the small compact climbing easily up the snakey highway.
3. Yolanda pulled up at a cantina, the thatched roof held up by several posts.
4. Yolanda and her crew scavenged the grove, the best of the pick going into the beach basket.
5. The small group stood staring at the sagging tire a moment, the two men kicking it as if punishing it.

Writing Application Write a description of an important childhood memory. Include at least three absolute phrases.

Build Your Portfolio

Idea Bank

Writing

1. Postcard Message Write the postcard message that Yolanda might have sent to a close friend back in the States. Briefly describe her adventure.

2. New Version Write a new version of this story from the point of view of one of the men who changed the flat tire for Yolanda.

3. Personal Essay Like Yolanda, have you ever encountered goodness or kindness where you expected only trouble? How was your response like—or unlike—Yolanda's? Describe your experience and what you learned from it in an essay.

Speaking and Listening

4. Multimedia Report Working with several classmates, contribute to a multimedia group report about the Dominican Republic. Choose one area to research—geography, for example, or economics. Add music and images and report your findings in a presentation to the class. **[Social Studies Link]**

5. Dialogue Role-play the conversation the two men might have held after watching Yolanda drive away, or the conversation Jose might have had with the old woman. **[Performing Arts Link]**

Projects

6. Flowchart Create a cause-and-effect flowchart illustrating how the decisions made by Yolanda and the story's other characters affect the plot. Diagram the characters' choices in each situation, and show how the action of the story stems from their decisions. **[Math Link]**

7. Set Design Use the details of the story to design sets and scenery for a dramatic version of "Antojos." Provide a detailed sketch for two different scenes. **[Art Link]**

Writing Mini-Lesson

Pointers for Travel Safety

Write a brief essay or magazine article giving pointers for travel safety. If you prefer, you can give safety tips on a particular method of travel—flying, for example, or traveling by car across unknown terrain.

Writing Skills Focus: Transitions to Show Importance

In offering your pointers for travel safety, it's probably a good idea to organize them in order of importance. You can put the most important tip first or last. No matter which order you choose, use **transitions** like these to clarify the importance of the information:

- first and foremost
- of primary importance
- more/more importantly
- more/most crucial
- less importantly
- above all
- primarily
- secondarily
- even better
- best of all
- finally
- last but not least

Prewriting Choose the area or mode of transportation you will discuss, and list your safety pointers. You may want to use note cards and devote one card to each tip. Then organize the cards in order of importance, placing the most important tip first or last.

Drafting Incorporate all your travel tips in a logical order, using transitions to make the order of importance clear. Include a catchy introduction and a brief conclusion. Avoid using a tone that might frighten your readers.

Revising Ask a friend to read your pointers and identify the most important tip. Did you succeed in conveying the order of importance to your reader? If not, revise your pointers by adding clear transitions to indicate which ideas are more, or less, important. Make sure that your word choice is precise and clear and that your sentences flow smoothly.

Guide for Interpreting

Lorna Dee Cervantes (1954–)

California native Lorna Dee Cervantes has been writing poetry since she was eight years old. A committed feminist and Hispanic rights activist, she founded her own small press in 1976 "in order to broaden not only the horizons but also the definitions of what was Chicana literature."

Cervantes published her own first book of poetry, *Emplumada,* in 1981. She also established the literary magazine *Mango* to help nurture other Hispanic American writers.

Martín Espada (1957–)

Not many lawyers pursue simultaneous careers as poets, but Martín Espada was—until 1993—an exception. Born in Brooklyn, New York, Espada was inspired to creativity by his father, a talented photographer with whom he helped produce a 1981 photo documentary called *The Puerto Rican Diaspora Documentary Project.*

A year later came Espada's own first volume of poetry, *The Immigrant Iceboy's Bolero.* He now teaches poetry at the University of Massachusetts at Amherst.

Simon Ortiz (1941–)

A native of the Acoma Pueblo in New Mexico, Simon Ortiz grew up steeped in the oral tradition of his people. Writing came naturally to him, and in 1980 he was honored at a White House "Salute to Poetry and American Poets." Ortiz has published more than a dozen books of poetry and prose. A creative-writing teacher, he also edits the literary magazine *Wanbli Ho.*

Diana Chang (1934–)

Born in New York City, Diana Chang spent most of her childhood in China. She returned to the United States following World War II and attended Barnard College in New York. In addition to writing poetry, she has written several novels, including *The Frontiers of Love* (1993). Chang's spare, introspective poetry, collected in volumes such as *What Matisse Is After* (1984), shows the influence of traditional Asian verse forms. She has also translated Asian writings into English.

Garrett Hongo (1951–)

One of the shining stars among recent Asian American poets, Garrett Hongo is a fourth-generation Japanese American who spent most of his early boyhood in Hawaii. His father, an electrical technician, figures prominently in Hongo's poems and is profiled in his book *Volcano*: *A Memoir of Hawaii* (1995). Hongo has won numerous awards including fellowships from the Thomas Watson and Guggenheim foundations. Among Hongo's other works are *Yellow Light* (1982) and *The River of Heaven* (1988).

◆ Background for Understanding

CULTURE: REFLECTING MULTICULTURAL ROOTS

The poems you are about to read reflect the cultural roots of their authors. Cervantes writes of her Chicana heritage in a familiar California setting, a barrio beside a freeway. Ortiz describes how life in New York City prompts a hunger for his southwestern Native American home. Chinese American writer Chang offers a poem whose subject (nature) and style are reminiscent of Asian verse. Garrett Hongo's poem draws on his heritage as one of many Japanese Americans in Hawaii, some of whom practice the Buddhist faith of their Japanese ancestors.

◆ *Literature and Your Life*

CONNECT YOUR EXPERIENCE

Although the citizens of the United States share national traditions, people also bring their own unique backgrounds and heritages to their community. What role does family heritage play in your life? What are the benefits of strong cultural ties? Share your experiences in a group discussion.

Journal Writing Describe an activity or tradition associated with your cultural background or heritage.

THEMATIC FOCUS: LITERATURE CONFRONTS THE EVERYDAY

As you read each of these poems, think about the role that family background or heritage plays in each speaker's everyday life.

◆ Build Vocabulary

PREFIXES: *auto-*

From the Greek word *autos* comes the prefix *auto-*, which means "self." For example, the word *automation* refers to manufacturing conducted using self-operating machinery.

WORD BANK

Preview this list of words from the poems.

> crevices
> automation
> pervade
> liturgy
> conjure
> calligraphy
> trough

◆ Grammar and Style

PARTICIPIAL PHRASES

A **participial phrase** consists of a participle—a verb acting as an adjective—and the words that modify or complete it. The entire phrase works as an adjective to modify a noun or a pronoun. A participial phrase must be placed so that it is clear what word it modifies. Usually this means placing it as close as possible to the modified noun or pronoun, as in these examples:

We made legal pads from yellow paper *stacked seven feet high.*

My hands, *smoothing the exact rectangle,* would slide along the paper.

Occupied by snow, I see that matter matters.

◆ Literary Focus

VOICE

Every person has a distinctive way of speaking. Similarly, every poet has an individual **voice.** A poet's distinctive sound is based on word choice and combinations, rhyme (or lack of it), pace, attitude, and even the pattern of vowels and consonants.

◆ Reading Strategy

SUMMARIZE

Sometimes you can understand a poem better if you briefly restate the main points in a **summary.** Consider these passages from Espada's poem and the summary that follows.

> At sixteen, I worked after high school hours / at a printing plant / that manufactured legal pads: /. . . I slipped cardboard / between the pages, / then brushed red glue / up and down the stack. . . ./ Sluggish by 9 PM, the hands / would slide along suddenly sharp paper, / and gather slits thinner than the crevices / of the skin, hidden.

Summary

At sixteen, the speaker had a routine but often painful evening job at a plant that manufactured legal pads.

Untitled (detail), Peter Malone

Freeway 280[1]

Lorna Dee Cervantes

Las casitas[2] near the gray cannery,
nestled amid wild abrazos[3] of climbing roses
and man-high red geraniums
are gone now. The freeway conceals it
5   all beneath a raised scar.

But under the fake windsounds of the open lanes,
in the abandoned lots below, new grasses sprout,
wild mustard remembers, old gardens
come back stronger than they were,
10   trees have been left standing in their yards.
Albaricoqueros, cerezos, nogales . . .[4]
Viejitas[5] come here with paper bags to gather greens.
Espinaca, verdolagas, yerbabuena . . .[6]

I scramble over the wire fence
15   that would have kept me out.
Once, I wanted out, wanted the rigid lanes
to take me to a place without sun,
without the smell of tomatoes burning
on swing shift in the greasy summer air.

20   Maybe it's here
en los campos extraños de esta ciudad[7]
where I'll find it, that part of me
mown under
like a corpse
25   or a loose seed.

---

1. **Freeway 280:** Freeway in California.
2. **Las casitas** (läs kä sē´ täs): "The little houses" (Spanish).
3. **abrazos** (ä brä´ sōs): "Hugs" (Spanish).
4. **Albaricoqueros, cerezos, nogales** (äl bär´ rē kō ker´ ōs, se rē´ sōs, nō gä´ les): "Apricot trees, cherry trees, walnut trees" (Spanish).
5. **Viejitas** (bye hē´ täs): "Old women" (Spanish).
6. **Espinaca, verdolagas, yerbabuena** (es pē nä´ kä, ber thō lä´ gäs, yer´ bä bwe´ nä): "Spinach, purslane, peppermint" (Spanish).
7. **en los campos estraños de esta ciudad** (en lōs käm´ pōs es trä´ nyōs de es´ tä syōō thath): "In the strange fields of this city" (Spanish).

◀ **Critical Viewing** What do you think this freeway scene represents for the artist? **[Interpret]**

Who Burns for the Perfection of Paper
Martín Espada

At sixteen, I worked after high school hours
at a printing plant
that manufactured legal pads:
Yellow paper
5   stacked seven feet high
and leaning
as I slipped cardboard
between the pages,
then brushed red glue
10 up and down the stack.
No gloves: fingertips required
for the perfection of paper,
smoothing the exact rectangle.
Sluggish by 9 PM, the hands
15 would slide along suddenly sharp paper,
and gather slits thinner than the crevices
of the skin, hidden.
Then the glue would sting,
hands oozing
20 till both palms burned
at the punchclock.

Ten years later, in law school,
I knew that every legal pad
was glued with the sting of hidden cuts,
25 that every open lawbook
was a pair of hands
upturned and burning.

◆ **Build Vocabulary**

crevices (krev´ is iz) *n*.: Narrow cracks or splits

Guide for Responding

◆ *Literature and Your Life*

Reader's Response Each of these poems reflects back on the speaker's childhood. With which one could you relate more strongly? Explain.

Thematic Focus Did these poems change the way you look at everyday objects such as legal pads and highways? How?

☑ Check Your Comprehension

1. What sort of neighborhood once stood on the site of "Freeway 280"?
2. In "Who Burns . . . ," cite the two ways the speaker has come to know legal pads.

◆ Critical Thinking

INTERPRET
1. (a) How is "Freeway 280" like a scar? (b) What might it represent? **[Interpret]**
2. (a) In "Freeway 280," why does the speaker liken a part of herself to a "corpse" and a "loose seed"? (b) How do lines 7–10 imply that the "loose seed" will take root? **[Infer; Connect]**
3. (a) In "Who Burns . . . ," how would you describe the printing plant job? (b) What did the speaker learn from his experience making legal pads? **[Classify; Connect]**
4. What aspects of the law student's background might the hidden cuts represent? **[Interpret]**

HUNGER IN New York City

Simon Ortiz

Hunger crawls into you
from somewhere out of your muscles
or the concrete or the land
or the wind pushing you.

5   It comes to you, asking
for food, words, wisdom, young memories
of places you ate at, drank cold spring water,
or held somebody's hand,
or home of the gentle, slow dances,
10   the songs, the strong gods, the world
you know.

That is, hunger searches you out.
It always asks you,
How are you, son? Where are you?
15   Have you eaten well?
Have you done what you as a person
of our people is supposed to do?

And the concrete of this city,
the oily wind, the blazing windows,
20   the shrieks of <u>automation</u> cannot,
truly cannot, answer for that hunger
although I have hungered,
truthfully and honestly, for them
to feed myself with.

25   So I sang to myself quietly:
I am feeding myself
with the humble presence
of all around me;
I am feeding myself
30   with your soul, my mother earth;
make me cool and humble.
Bless me.

▼ **Critical Viewing** What words would you use to describe the emotions conveyed by both the poem and the photograph? **[Interpret]**

◆ **Build Vocabulary**

automation (ôt′ ə mā′ shən) *n.*: Manufacturing conducted with partly or fully self-operating machinery

Most Satisfied by Snow

Diana Chang

Against my windows,
fog knows
what to do, too

5   Spaces <u>pervade</u>
us, as well

But occupied by snow,
I see

Matter
matters

10 I, too,
flowering

▲ **Critical Viewing** How do the trees in this photograph relate to the last two lines of the poem? **[Connect]**

◆ **Build Vocabulary**

pervade (pər vād´) v.: To spread throughout

Guide for Responding

◆ *Literature and Your Life*

Reader's Response Did the contents of either poem surprise you, given the titles? Explain.

Thematic Focus How can your everyday surroundings either emotionally nourish or starve you?

Journal Writing Chang makes an observation about herself after watching a natural event. What feelings do storms evoke in you?

☑ Check Your Comprehension

1. (a) In "Hunger in New York City," what four questions does the hunger ask? (b) What four things cannot answer for that hunger? (c) With what does the speaker feed himself in the end?
2. (a) In "Most Satisfied by Snow," what two aspects of nature does the speaker observe? (b) What does she conclude?

◆ Critical Thinking

INTERPRET

1. What kind of hunger does "Hunger in New York City" describe? **[Interpret]**
2. (a) What impressions does the speaker give of New York City and of his home? (b) Compare the two sets of impressions. **[Compare and Contrast]**
3. In "Most Satisfied by Snow," what might the speaker mean when she comments that "spaces pervade us"? **[Interpret]**
4. (a) What differences between fog and snow does this poem highlight? (b) How is this contrast embodied in humans? **[Analyze]**

APPLY

5. Chang's poem suggests that we can learn about ourselves by observing nature. Do you agree? Why or why not? **[Apply]**

WHAT FOR

Garrett Hongo

At six I lived for spells:
how a few Hawaiian words could call
up the rain, could hymn like the sea
in the long swirl of chambers
5   curling in the nautilus of a shell,[1]
how Amida's[2] ballads of the Buddhaland
in the drone of the priest's <u>liturgy</u>
could <u>conjure</u> money from the poor
and give them nothing but mantras,[3]
10   the strange syllables that healed desire.

I lived for stories about the war
my grandfather told over *hana* cards,[4]
slapping them down on the mats
with a sharp Japanese *kiai*.[5]

15   I lived for songs my grandmother sang
stirring curry into a thick stew,
weaving a <u>calligraphy</u> of Kannon's[6] love
into grass mats and straw sandals.

I lived for the red volcano dirt
20   staining my toes, the salt residue
of surf and sea wind in my hair,
the arc of a flat stone skipping
in the hollow <u>trough</u> of a wave.

---

1. **nautilus** (nôt´ əl əs) **of a shell**: Spiral of a seashell such as the chambered nautilus or paper nautilus.
2. **Amida's** (ä mēd ä): Referring to Amida, the great savior worshiped by members of the Pure Land sect of Buddhism popular in eastern Asia.
3. **mantras** (män´ trəz): Sacred words repeated in prayers, hymns, or chants.
4. *hana* (hä´ nä) **cards:** Cards with flower patterns that players try to pair up in a popular Japanese card game. *Hana* is Japanese for "flower."
5. *kiai* (kē ī´): Japanese word for the sound made by slapping down *hana* cards.
6. **Kannon's** (kä´ nənz): Referring to an enlightened savior of Japanese Buddhism who, out of infinite compassion and mercy, forgoes the heavenly state of nirvana in order to save others.

◆ **Build Vocabulary**

liturgy (lit´ ər jē) *n.*: Public religious ceremonies; religious ritual

conjure (kän´ jər) *v.*: To summon by magic or as if by magic; to call forth

calligraphy (kə lig´ rə fē) *n.*: Artistic handwriting; beautiful penmanship

trough (trôf) *n.*: Low point of a wave

I lived a child's world, waited
25 for my father to drag himself home,
dusted with blasts of sand, powdered rock,
and the strange ash of raw cement,
his deafness made worse by the clang
of pneumatic drills,[7] sore in his bones
30 from the buckings of a jackhammer.
He'd hand me a scarred lunchpail,
let me unlace the hightop G.I. boots,[8]
call him the new name I'd invented
that day in school, write it for him
35 on his newspaper. He'd rub my face
with hands that felt like gravel roads,
tell me to move, go play, and then he'd
walk to the laundry sink to scrub,
rinse the dirt of his long day
40 from a face brown and grained as koa wood.[9]

I wanted to take away the pain
in his legs, the swelling in his joints,
give him back his hearing,
clear and rare as crystal chimes,
45 the fins of glass that wrinkled
and sparked the air with their sound.

I wanted to heal the sores that work
and war had sent to him,
let him play catch in the backyard
50 with me, tossing a tennis ball
past papaya trees without the shoulders
of pain shrugging back his arms.

---

7. pneumatic (noō mat′ ik) **drills:** Air drills used
in construction.
8. hightop G.I. boots: Army boots.
9. koa (kō′ ə) **wood:** Grainy wood of the Hawaiian
acacia tree.

▲ **Critical Viewing**
How does the poet use the
image of the fragrant plumeria flower to communicate
his desire to heal his father's
pain? **[Analyze]**

I wanted to become a doctor of
    pure magic,
to string a necklace of sweet
    words
55 fragrant as pine needles and
        plumeria,[10]
fragrant as the bread my mother
    baked,
place it like a lei of cowrie shells[11]
and *pikake*[12] flowers around my
    father's neck,
and chant him a blessing,
    a sutra.[13]

---

10. **plumeria** (plōō mer´ ē ə): Tropical tree bearing flowers known for their fragrance.
11. **lei** (lā) **of cowrie** (kou´ rē) **shells:** Garland made of brightly colored seashells found in the South Pacific.
12. *pikake* (pē kä´ kā): Hawaiian word for jasmine, a fragrant flowering shrub.
13. **sutra** (sōō´ trə): One of the sacred texts or scriptures of Buddhism.

Guide for Responding

◆ *Literature and Your Life*

Reader's Response Do you think the speaker had a happy childhood? Why or why not?

Thematic Focus How effectively does the poem capture the details of the speaker's childhood days? Cite details to support your opinion.

Journal Writing What do you remember of the people who formed your world as a six-year-old child? Record your memories in a journal entry.

☑ Check Your Comprehension

1. What kinds of songs or other forms of communication does the speaker say he lived for?
2. Did the speaker live near the desert, the ocean, or the mountains? How do you know?
3. (a) Cite three details in "What For" that describe the father's condition when he returns from work. (b) What does the speaker want to do for his father?

◆ Critical Thinking

INTERPRET

1. Cite examples from the text that suggest that the speaker considers at least two members of his family as models of compassion and self-sacrifice. **[Support]**
2. (a) What sort of person is the speaker's father? (b) How does the speaker feel about him? Support your answer. **[Infer]**
3. Based on this poem, what values do you think are important to the poet? **[Draw Conclusions]**

EVALUATE

4. Evaluate the title's relationship to the content of the poem. Is the title an effective one? Explain. **[Evaluate]**

EXTEND

5. What parallels can you draw between "What For" and Espada's "Who Burns for the Perfection of Paper"? **[Literature Link]**

Guide for Responding (continued)

◆ Literary Focus

VOICE

Each one of these poets has a distinctive **voice**, or sound, which results from word choice, tone, pace, and use of sound devices.

1. What adjectives would you use to describe each poet's voice? Why?
2. Which of the five voices do you find most appealing? Why?

◆ Build Vocabulary

USING THE PREFIX *auto-*

Automation, "manufacturing conducted with self-operating machinery," contains the prefix *auto-*, which means "self." Explain how the meaning of *auto-* is conveyed in each of these words.

1. automobile
2. autopilot
3. autograph (The root -*graph*- means "writing.")

USING THE WORD BANK

Choose the letter of the word or phrase that best completes each statement. Write your answers on your paper.

1. A wave's *trough* is its (a) high point, (b) low point, (c) surf.
2. Someone trying to *conjure* a rabbit is most likely (a) a magician, (b) an animal-rights activist, (c) a French chef.
3. You'd most likely use *calligraphy* on (a) a merry-go-round, (b) a woman's hairdo, (c) a wedding invitation.
4. For information on Jewish *liturgy*, it would be best to consult (a) a prayer book, (b) an atlas, (c) a cookbook.
5. After *automation*, the plant probably had (a) more workers, (b) fewer workers, (c) the same number of workers.
6. *Crevices* in rock are likely to (a) be brightly colored, (b) be used in jewelry, (c) fill up with rainwater.
7. If bad odors *pervade*, people are likely to (a) hold their noses, (b) not notice them, (c) breathe a sigh of relief.

◆ Reading Strategy

SUMMARIZE

As you read these poems, you may have created mental **summaries** of the main points. This strategy can often help you better understand the poems you read.

1. "Freeway 280" is divided into four stanzas, or groups of lines. Write a four-sentence summary in which each sentence sums up a different stanza of the poem.
2. Write a summary of each of the following two poems: (a) "Hunger in New York City," (b) "What For."

◆ Grammar and Style

PARTICIPIAL PHRASES

In choosing where to place a participial phrase, make sure that it is clear what word it modifies.

> A **participial phrase** is a participle—a verb form that can be used as an adjective—and the words that modify or complete it.

Practice Copy the following sentences into your notebook and underline each participial phrase. Draw an arrow to the noun or pronoun it modifies.

1. Seeking an after-school job, I found one at a printing plant.
2. I worked hard, slipping cardboard between the papers.
3. Cut by the sharp edges, my hands were often stinging.
4. The glue, oozing over them, made the stinging worse.
5. I can still visualize my hands, upturned in pain.

Writing Application For each numbered item, write a sentence that uses the participial phrase provided. Be sure to place the participial phrase so that it is clear what word it modifies. If you like, you can base your sentences on "Freeway 280."

1. nestled among climbing roses
2. sitting beside the freeway
3. abandoned in the open lots
4. scrambling over a wire fence
5. burning in the greasy summer air

Build Your Portfolio

Idea Bank

Writing

1. **Letter** Choose one of the poems and turn it into a letter the speaker might write to a friend.

2. **Editorial** Write a newspaper editorial inspired by the details in one of these poems. You might focus, for example, on how to redevelop the area around Freeway 280 or how to improve the quality of life in the New York City of Ortiz's poem.

3. **Compare-and-Contrast Essay** Write an essay in which you compare and contrast two of these poems. Focus on the poems' messages and the poets' use of language.

Speaking and Listening

4. **Interview** Do you know someone whose personal or professional life reflects his or her cultural heritage? Prepare a list of questions; then interview that person about the influences in his or her life. Videotape or record the interview to share with the class. **[Social Studies Link]**

5. **Oral Interpretation** Using background music or other sound effects, give an oral reading of one of the poems. **[Performing Arts Link]**

Projects

6. **Cultural Report** Find out more about the cultural background reflected in one of the poems. For example, you might research and report on Japanese Buddhism or customs of New Mexico's Acoma Pueblo. **[Social Studies Link]**

7. **Anthology** Locate and gather Asian poetry in English translations. Create an anthology of these poems. In a brief introduction to your anthology, explain how Diana Chang's "Most Satisfied by Snow" shows the influence of Asian verse. **[Literature Link]**

Writing Mini-Lesson

Observation of a Storm

Carefully observe a rainstorm, snowstorm, or windstorm. Then write a description of it. Your description may take the form of a poem or a prose passage. Use language creatively to convey the physical and emotional effects of the storm.

Writing Skills Focus: Figurative Language

To help you capture the storm and the feelings it inspires, you will probably want to use **figurative language**—language not meant to be taken literally. Most types of figurative language compare something vague or abstract to an image that can readily be perceived by the senses.

- A **simile** compares two unlike things using *like* or *as* to show that a comparison is being made: *His hearing was as clear as crystal chimes.*
- A **metaphor** equates two unlike things without using *like* or *as*: *The freeway is a raised scar.*
- **Personification** describes something non-human as if it were human: *Hunger crawls into you, asking for food, words, wisdom.*

Prewriting Jot down details that describe the storm—perhaps using a cluster diagram to help you recall and organize them. Review your notes, writing down any comparisons they inspire.

Drafting Decide what comparison you'd like to develop in your observation. Get your ideas down on paper; you can polish your language later.

Revising Make sure that your language is vivid and your word choice is clear and precise. Did you use figurative language to bring the sights and sounds of the storm to life for the reader? If you are writing prose, check that you have used transitions to make your sentences flow logically and smoothly. Correct any grammar, spelling, and mechanical errors.

Writing Process Workshop

The process of writing a piece of nonfiction doesn't begin with setting words down on paper. Writers often spend days, weeks, or even months researching and gathering information on their topics before ever writing a word. Scholars and students use these same skills when writing a research paper—a formal paper that presents and supports a thesis statement, or main idea, with research gathered from a variety of reliable sources.

Use the following writing skills, introduced in this section's Writing Mini-Lessons, to help you write a strong, coherent research paper.

Writing Skills Focus

▶ **Use a clear organization.** Begin with an introduction that states the thesis, then develop and support the thesis in the body of the paper. Conclude with a restatement of the main points. (See p. 911.)

▶ **Elaborate** by including direct quotations from a variety of credible sources. (See p. 901.)

▶ To clearly link your ideas and details, **use transitions that show cause and effect**. (See p. 889.)

This passage from a research paper on Amy Tan demonstrates these skills.

WRITING MODEL

Though Amy Tan did not begin writing fiction until age thirty-three, she quickly established herself as a unique and powerful literary voice. ① She had wanted to write fiction from the time she won an essay contest at age eight, but was told "if you liked doing something, it wasn't worth doing." (Clark, 36) ② It was 1985 before she entered a creative writing workshop because ③ she realized that she was not satisfied with her hectic career as a business writer. Though Tan claims her first few short stories were barely understandable, she found her literary voice when she began to envision her Chinese mother as her reader. (Grieg, 89)

① The writer opens with a thesis statement that clearly establishes the paper's topic.

② Parenthetical notes indicate the source of the information.

③ The transition word "because" clearly shows the cause-and-effect relationship between Tan's dissatisfaction with her career and the decision to join the workshop.

Applying LANGUAGE SKILLS: Topic and Supporting Sentences

A **topic sentence**—which most often appears at the beginning of a paragraph—states the main idea of the paragraph. The rest of the sentences in the paragraph should support the main idea; these are called **supporting sentences**. The topic sentence in this example is underlined:

Julia Alvarez uses her Dominican heritage as inspiration for her fiction. Books like ¡Yo! detail the life of fictional characters and include details of the Hispanic American tradition.

Practice In a brief paragraph, describe one of the selections you read in this section. Include a topic sentence and a series of supporting sentences.

Writing Application Keep your paper clear and focused by building each paragraph around a topic sentence.

Writer's Solution Connection Writing Lab

For additional support on gathering information, see the instruction and activities in the tutorial on Research Writing.

Prewriting

Choose a Topic Choose a subject that you would like to study. You might browse through a newspaper or skim a history text for inspiration. Keep in mind that your topic must be narrow enough to research and present in a single paper, yet broad enough to enable you to find information in a variety of sources. If you can't come up with a topic on your own, consider one of these:

Topic Ideas

- The life and literature of N. Scott Momaday
- A local historical event
- The effects of the end of the Cold War
- The planet Mars

Gather Information To create an effective research paper, you will need a variety of quality sources. Locate at least three sources on your topic by consulting reference resources such as the *Reader's Guide to Periodical Literature*; a library card or computer catalog; vertical files; or Internet search engines that can help you locate Web sites related to your topic.

Take Notes As you research, record each item of information on an individual note card. Record all direct quotations accurately and note the source of the information. Group note cards by subtopic.

Write a Thesis Statement The thesis statement is a concise presentation of your main point. To develop yours, organize and review your notes. Decide on an idea that best synthesizes your notes, then summarize it in a single sentence. Use your thesis to develop an outline for your paper.

Drafting

Create an Introduction, Body, and Conclusion An organized paper begins with an effective introduction that includes the thesis statement. Consider opening with a dramatic quote or startling fact for greater impact. Develop your thesis in the body of the paper. Be sure the topic sentence and details of each paragraph support the thesis statement, and use transition words to clarify relationships among details and ideas. Finish with a conclusion that summarizes the main idea or findings presented in your paper.

Credit Sources Each time you use another person's exact words, present an original idea that is not your own, or report a fact available only in one source, you must credit the original source in a footnote, endnote, or parenthetical citation. Include a complete bibliography listing each of your research sources.

Revising

Review the Essay's Coherence Confirm that your introduction and conclusion agree. Then check the first and last sentence of every paragraph to be sure that each idea follows in a logical sequence. If necessary, add transitional sentences to make connections in your essay more clear.

Use a Checklist Set aside some time to step back and evaluate your work using a checklist like the following:

- ▶ Have I clearly stated my thesis in the introduction? Is the thesis supported with enough information?
- ▶ Is the paper organized, with a clear introduction, body, and conclusion? Does every paragraph have a topic sentence?
- ▶ Have I used transitions to show how the ideas in successive sentences and paragraphs are related?
- ▶ Have I used—and cited—a variety of credible sources?

REVISION MODEL

When a bill is introduced in Congress, it has already passed
① *House members introduce bills by dropping them in the hopper at the clerk's desk in the House chamber. Then,*
a number of hurdles. Subcommittees made up of members
② *When the bill has been thoroughly researched and reviewed,*
of both parties review each bill. Next, the subcommittee

reports to the full Congress with a recommendation.

① *The author adds an interesting, little known detail to maintain the reader's interest.*
② *A cause-and-effect transition and explanatory phrase help the reader link the work of the subcommittee to the process.*

Publishing

- ▶ **Multimedia Presentation** Enhance your research paper with pictures, videotape, or other appropriate media. Invite classmates or family members to see your presentation.

APPLYING LANGUAGE SKILLS: Proper Bibliographic Form

When you use **proper bibliographic form**, you present sources in a standardized format based on the type of resource. This enables readers to check the accuracy of information or learn more about the topic.

For a Book With One Author:
Welty, Eudora. *One Writer's Beginnings.* New York: Warner Books, Inc., 1984.

For a Reference Book:
"Hockey." *The World Book Encyclopedia.* 1998 ed.

For a Magazine Article:
Corliss, Richard. "The Deal That Wasn't." *Time,* June 19, 1995: 51.

Writing Application During the research phase of your work, keep a list of the sources you consult. Following the style your teacher requires, create a bibliography of your sources.

Writer's Solution Connection Writing Lab

For additional information on citing sources, consult the instruction in the Drafting section of the tutorial on Research Writing.

Real-World Reading Skills Workshop

Strategies for Success

The sole purpose of a manual is to make life easier for the reader. These informative booklets provide precise instructions or information in a clearly organized format that often features numbered or bulleted lists, diagrams, photographs, charts, or other visual aids that clarify or enhance the written material. They can make everything from using your new CD player to identifying resources in your community a whole lot easier—if you follow a few simple guidelines.

Know What You Need Identify the information you need from the manual. Do you want a complete overview of the subject? Are you doing a quick search for a particular piece of data? Focus your search to suit your goals.

Find the Facts Begin by familiarizing yourself with the manual's organization. Use these tips to help you locate information:

▶ Survey the table of contents for an overview of the topics covered in each chapter. Is there a chapter on your particular area of interest?

▶ Read the introduction or summary section for an overview of the instructions or information presented in the manual.

▶ Study the index for an alphabetical listing of detailed topics that can help you locate a specific piece of information.

▶ Scan appendixes for reference lists of key data.

▶ Refer to diagrams and maps as you use the manual.

Apply the Strategy

It's your family's first summer in a new city. Use this manual provided by your real estate agent to answer some common questions.

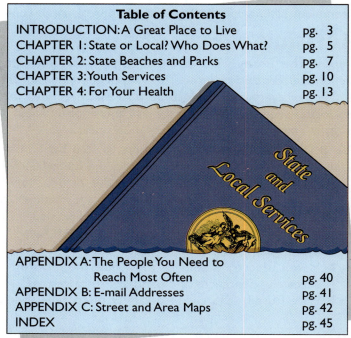

State and Local Services

1. Where would you find an overview of your new state? Where would you turn to locate information on a specific topic?

2. Can you find information in this manual about what to do for fun? Where?

3. Which chapters would help your dad learn about emergency services?

4. Where might you learn what highway to take to Hammotuquet State Park?

5. How could your mom find the name, phone number, and address for the superintendent of schools?

✔ *Here are other situations in which reading manuals is useful:*

▶ *Learning a new computer program*

▶ *Assembling or operating electronic equipment*

▶ *Gathering information on a college*

PART 2

Focus on Literary Forms:
Essay

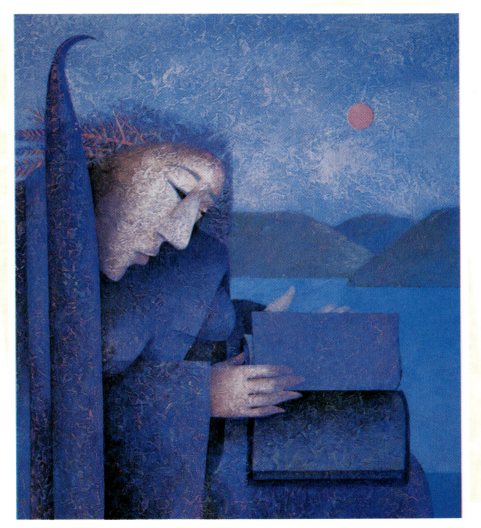

My Mother's Book of Life, Lee Lawson

Analytic, expository, satiric, or personal, the essay has been used for centuries to express ideas that range from personal reflection to national revolution. In the busy modern world, readers have embraced the essay form, which presents ideas in a limited space. From comedy to personal triumph, the essays in this section demonstrate the flexibility of the form.

Guide for Interpreting

Carson McCullers (1917–1967)

Carson McCullers, whose writing has been praised as a brilliant fusion of compassion and the grotesque, led a troubled life marked by serious health problems. She was raised in Columbus, Georgia, a town that later formed the backdrop for all her fiction. At the age of seventeen, she moved to New York and married Reeves McCullers three years later. While still in her twenties, she suffered a series of strokes, which incapacitated her for long periods. In later years, partial paralysis confined her to a wheelchair, yet she still managed to type new manuscripts. Her loneliness and suffering are reflected in her novels, which include *The Heart Is a Lonely Hunter* (1940), *The Member of the Wedding* (1946), and *Clock Without Hands* (1961).

William Safire (1929–)

When it comes to questions about the use—and misuse—of the English language, few people have more answers or observations than William Safire. A political commentator and the author of the "On Language" column of *The New York Times,* Safire is one of the world's most widely read writers on language in America today. The 1978 Pulitzer Prize winner for distinguished commentary, Safire was once a political speech writer for the White House. His books include *On Language* (1980), *What's the Good Word?* (1982), *I Stand Corrected* (1984), *Take My Word for It* (1986), *You Could Look It Up* (1988), and *Coming to Terms* (1991). He has also written two novels, *Full Disclosure* (1977) and *Freedom* (1987).

Ian Frazier (1951–)

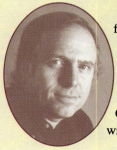

Known for humorous essays and for affectionate descriptions of rural America, Ian Frazier brings "an antic sense of fun" to whatever he writes. He was born in Cleveland, Ohio, and now lives in New York City, where he works as a staff writer for *The New Yorker* magazine. Frazier's humorous and often ironic essays are collected in a series of nonfiction books, including *Dating Your Mom* (1986), *Nobody Better, Better Than Nobody* (1987), *Great Plains* (1989), and *Family* (1994). "Coyote v. Acme" is typical of his work: a ludicrous premise packaged in serious style. As you read the essay, ask yourself what Frazier is really satirizing—the cartoon character who is his subject or the legal profession.

◆ Background for Understanding

POPULAR CULTURE: HALF A CENTURY OF CARTOONS

Ian Frazier's essay "Coyote v. Acme" is the fictional opening statement of a lawsuit by Mr. Wile E. Coyote, charging the Acme Company with the sale of defective merchandise. Do those names sound familiar? You may have a childhood memory of watching Wile E. Coyote chase the Road Runner through the desert. The Warner Brothers cartoon "Road Runner and Coyote" made its debut in 1948; half a century later, both the coyote and the elusive bird are still going strong. Perhaps fifty years from now your grandchildren will be watching Coyote's ill-fated attempts—many involving Acme products—to capture the fleet-footed bird.

◆ *Literature and Your Life*

CONNECT YOUR EXPERIENCE

Think about what is important to you. It might be enjoying friendship, overcoming loneliness, or finding your own personal identity. You may explore the ideas that mean the most to you in your journal or in letters or e-mails to close friends. Some writers use a more public form of writing—the essay—to express themes or to make a point about something that they consider important.

THEMATIC FOCUS: LITERATURE CONFRONTS THE EVERYDAY

In these essays, writers confront common elements of American culture: loneliness, language, and our legal system. As you read, consider whether you share the writers' views on their subjects.

Journal Writing Safire's essay is about words that sound like what they name, such as *buzz* and *hum*. How many of these words can you list?

◆ Reading Strategy

IDENTIFY LINE OF REASONING

When presenting an argument in an essay, a writer offers a **line of reasoning** in an attempt to convince readers of the essay's key points. As you read these essays, identify the writers' main points and note the reasons, facts, and examples each writer offers to back up the points. Also look carefully at the relationships among the pieces of evidence cited. Are the cause-and-effect relationships valid?

◆ Grammar and Style

PRONOUNS WITH APPOSITIVES

McCullers observes that "... we Americans are always seeking." Notice that the pronoun *we* is followed by the noun *Americans* and acts as the subject of the clause. When a pronoun is followed by an **appositive**—a noun that renames the pronoun—choose the correct pronoun by mentally dropping the appositive.

Subject: [*Us/We*] players had to win. **Object:** It was up to [*us/we*] players.
    [*Us/We*] ~~players~~ had to win.   It was up to *us* ~~players~~.
    We players had to win.   It was up to *us* players.

When a pronoun renames a sentence's subject, use *I, he, she, we,* or *they.* To rename an object, use *me, him, her, us,* or *them.*

◆ Literary Focus

ESSAYS

An **essay** is a short piece of nonfiction in which a writer expresses a personal view or a topic. Among the many types of essays are the analytical essay, the satirical essay, and the expository essay.

- An **analytical essay** attempts to analyze—or break down and explain the parts of—a topic.

- A **satirical essay** uses irony, ridicule, or sarcasm to comment on a topic.

- An **expository essay** provides information about or explains a topic. As you read, look for details that help you decide how you might classify each of these essays.

◆ Build Vocabulary

WORD ROOTS: *-ten-*

In "Coyote v. Acme," Frazier describes the *tensile* strength of Acme springs. The word *tensile* contains the word root *-ten-,* meaning "to stretch tightly." Tensile springs would be "stretchable."

WORD BANK

Preview this list of words from the essays.

pristine
corollary
aesthetic
maverick
contiguous
precipitate
caveat
tensile

from The Mortgaged Heart

Carson McCullers

This city, New York—consider the people in it, the eight million of us. An English friend of mine, when asked why he lived in New York City, said that he liked it here because he could be so alone. While it was my friend's desire to be alone, the aloneness of many Americans who live in cities is an involuntary and fearful thing. It has been said that loneliness is the great American malady. What is the nature of this loneliness? It would seem essentially to be a quest for identity.

To the spectator, the amateur philosopher, no motive among the complex ricochets of our desires and rejections seems stronger or more enduring than the will of the individual to claim his identity and belong. From infancy to death, the human being is obsessed by these dual motives. During our first weeks of life, the question of identity shares urgency with the need for milk. The baby reaches for his toes, then explores the bars of his crib; again and again he compares the difference between his own body and the objects around him, and in the wavering, infant eyes there comes a pristine wonder.

Consciousness of self is the first abstract problem that the human being solves. Indeed, it is this self-consciousness that removes us from lower animals. This primitive grasp of identity develops with constantly shifting emphasis through all our years. Perhaps maturity is simply the history of those mutations that reveal to the individual the relation between himself and the world in which he finds himself.

After the first establishment of identity there comes the imperative need to lose this new-found sense of separateness and to belong to something larger and more powerful than the weak, lonely self. The sense of moral isolation is intolerable to us.

In *The Member of the Wedding*[1] the lonely twelve-year-old girl, Frankie Addams, articulates this universal need: "The trouble with me is that for a long time I have just been an *I* person. All people belong to a *We* except me. Not to belong to a *We* makes you too lonesome."

Love is the bridge that leads from the *I* sense to the *We*, and there is a paradox about personal love. Love of another individual opens a new relation between the personality and the world. The lover responds in a new way to nature and may even write poetry. Love is affirmation; it motivates the *yes* responses and the sense of wider communication. Love casts out fear, and in the security of this togetherness we find contentment, courage. We no longer fear the age-old haunting questions: "Who am I?" "Why am I?" "Where am I going?"—and having cast out fear, we can be honest and charitable.

1. ***The Member of the Wedding:*** Novel and play by Carson McCullers.

◆ Build Vocabulary

pristine (pris´ tēn) *adj.*: Pure; uncorrupted

corollary (kôr´ ə ler´ ē) *n.*: Easily drawn conclusion

aesthetic (es *thet*´ ik) *adj.*: Pertaining to the study or theory of beauty and of the psychological response to it

maverick (mav´ ər ik) *n.*: Nonconformist

For fear is a primary source of evil. And when the question "Who am I?" recurs and is unanswered, then fear and frustration project a negative attitude. The bewildered soul can answer only: "Since I do not understand 'Who I am,' I only know what I am *not*." The <u>corollary</u> of this emotional incertitude is snobbism, intolerance and racial hate. The xenophobic[2] individual can only reject and destroy, as the xenophobic nation inevitably makes war.

The loneliness of Americans does not have its source in xenophobia; as a nation we are an outgoing people, reaching always for immediate contacts, further experience. But we tend to seek out things as individuals, alone. The European, secure in his family ties and rigid class loyalties, knows little of the moral loneliness that is native to us Americans. While the European artists tend to form groups or <u>aesthetic</u> schools, the American artist is the eternal <u>maverick</u>—not only from society in the way of all creative minds, but within the orbit of his own art.

Thoreau took to the woods to seek the ultimate meaning of his life. His creed was simplicity and his *modus vivendi*[3] the deliberate stripping of external life to the Spartan[4] necessities in order that his inward life could freely flourish. His objective, as he put it, was to back the world into a corner. And in that way did he discover "What a man thinks of himself, that it is which determines, or rather indicates, his fate."

On the other hand, Thomas Wolfe turned to the city, and in his wanderings around New York he continued his frenetic and lifelong search for the lost brother, the magic door. He too backed the world into a corner, and as he passed among the city's millions, returning their stares, he experienced "That silent meeting [that] is the summary of all the meetings of men's lives."

Whether in the pastoral joys of country life or in the labyrinthine city, we Americans are always seeking. We wander, question. But the answer waits in each separate heart—the answer of our own identity and the way by which we can master loneliness and feel that at last we belong.

---

2. **xenophobic** (zen′ ə fō′ bik) *adj.*: Afraid of strangers or foreigners.

3. *modus vivendi* (mō′ dəs vi ven′ dī): "Manner of living" (Latin).
4. **Spartan** (spär′ tən) *adj.*: Characteristic of the people of ancient Sparta: hardy, stoical, severe, frugal.

Guide for Responding

◆ Literature and Your Life

Reader's Response If you could meet Carson McCullers, which of the observations in this essay would you most like to discuss with her? Explain your reasons for choosing this observation.

Thematic Focus McCullers says that love "is the bridge that leads from the *I* sense to the *We*." How do the situations you encounter in everyday life support her observation?

☑ Check Your Comprehension

1. Why does McCullers's English friend like living in New York City?
2. What does McCullers believe is the biggest problem for most Americans?
3. How does she say we can find contentment and courage and get rid of our fears?

◆ Critical Thinking

INTERPRET

1. What is McCullers's opinion about the cause of loneliness in America? **[Analyze]**
2. Find evidence in the essay that McCullers thinks love helps a person find true happiness. **[Support]**
3. (a) What does McCullers mean by the terms "moral isolation" and "moral loneliness"? (b) What does she mean when she comments that love "motivates the *yes* response"? **[Interpret]**

EXTEND

4. Do you think Americans today are likely to be more or less lonely than the early settlers? Explain the societal changes that prompted your answer. **[Social Studies Link]**

Onomatopoeia

WILLIAM SAFIRE

Blam, 1962, Roy Lichtenstein

▲ **Critical Viewing** What is the connection between this illustration and the subject of the essay? **[Connect]**

The word *onomatopoeia* was used above, and it had better be spelled right or one usage dictator and six copy editors will get zapped. That word is based on the Greek for "word making"—the *poe* is the same as in *poetry*, "something made"—and is synonymous with *imitative* and *echoic*, denoting words that are made by people making sounds like the action to be described. (The *poe* in *onomatopoeia* has its own rule for pronunciation. Whenever a vowel follows *poe*, the *oe* combination is pronounced as a long *e*: *onomato-PEE-ia*. Whenever a consonant follows, as in *poetry* and *onomatopoetic*, pronounce the long *o* of Edgar Allan's name.)

Henry Peacham, in his 1577 book on grammar and rhetoric called *The Garden of Eloquence*, first used *onomatopoeia* and defined it as "when we invent, devise, fayne, and make a name intimating the sound of that it signifieth, as *hurlyburly*, for an uprore and tumultuous stirre." He also gave *flibergib* to "a gossip," from which we derive *flibbertigibbet*, and the long-lost *clapperclaw* and *kickle-kackle*.

Since Willard Espy borrowed the title of Peacham's work for his rhetorical bestiary in 1983, the author went beyond the usual examples of *buzz*, *hiss*, *bobwhite* and *babble*. He pointed out that one speculation about the origin of language was the *bow-wow theory*, holding that words originated in imitation of natural sounds of animals and thunder. (Proponents of the *pooh-pooh theory* argued that interjections like *ow!* and *oof!* started us all yakking toward language. Other theories—*arrgh!*—abound.)

Reaching for an alliterative onomatope, the poet Milton chose "melodious *murmurs*;" Edgar Allan Poe one-upped him with "the *tintinnabulation* of the bells." When carried too far, an obsession with words is called *onomatomania*; in the crunch (a word imitating the sound of an icebreaker breaking through ice) Gertrude Stein turned into an *onomatomaniac*.

What makes a word like *zap* of particular interest is that it imitates an imaginary noise—the sound of a paralyzing ray gun. Thus we can see another way that the human mind creates new words: imitating what can be heard only in the mind's ear. The coinage filled a need for an unheard sound and—*pow!*—slammed the vocabulary right in the kisser. Steadily, surely, under the watchful eye of great lexicographers and with the encouragement of columnists and writers who ache for color in verbs, the creation of Buck Rogers's creator has blasted its way into the dictionaries. The verb will live long after superpowers agree to ban ray guns; no sound thunders or crackles like an imaginary sound turned into a new word.

Took me a while to get to the point today, but that is because I did not know what the point was when I started.

"I now zap all the commercials," says the merry Ellen Goodman. "I zap to the memory of white tornadoes past. I zap headaches, arthritis, bad breath and laundry detergent. I zap diet-drink maidens and hand-lotion mavens . . . Wiping out commercials could entirely and joyfully upend the TV industry. Take the word of The Boston Zapper."

Guide for Responding

◆ Literature and Your Life

Reader's Response Had you ever noticed the connection between the onomatopoetic words Safire discusses and the sounds they describe?

Thematic Focus How might the origins of many onomatopoetic words be tied to everyday situations and events?

☑ Check Your Comprehension

1. What is onomatopoeia?
2. What is the *bow-wow theory* concerning the origin of language?
3. What does Safire find so interesting about the word *zap*?

◆ Critical Thinking

INTERPRET

1. What is the origin of the word *onomatopoeia*? **[Classify]**
2. Compare and contrast the *bow-wow* and the *pooh-pooh theories* of language. **[Compare and Contrast]**
3. Why does Safire believe that the word *zap* will "live long after superpowers agree to ban ray guns"? **[Analyze]**

EVALUATE

4. Do you think Safire's humorous style is more or less effective than a factual explanation as a way of speaking about language? Explain. **[Assess]**

COYOTE V. ACME

IAN FRAZIER

In the United States District Court,
Southwestern District,
Tempe, Arizona
Case No. B19294,
JUDGE JOAN KUJAVA, PRESIDING

WILE E. COYOTE, Plaintiff
—v.—
ACME COMPANY, Defendant

Opening Statement of Mr. Harold Schoff, attorney for Mr. Coyote: My client, Mr. Wile E. Coyote, a resident of Arizona and contiguous states, does hereby bring suit for damages against the Acme Company, manufacturer and retail distributor of assorted merchandise, incorporated in Delaware and doing business in every state, district and territory. Mr. Coyote seeks compensation for personal injuries, loss of business income, and mental suffering caused as a direct result of the actions and/or gross negligence of said company, under Title 15 of the United States Code, Chapter 47, section 2072, subsection (a), relating to product liability.

Mr. Coyote states that on eighty-five separate occasions he has purchased of the Acme Company (hereinafter, "Defendant"), through that company's mail-order department, certain products which did cause him bodily injury due to defects in manufacture or improper cautionary labeling. Sales slips made out to Mr. Coyote as proof of purchase are at present in the possession of the Court, marked Exhibit A. Such injuries sustained by Mr. Coyote have temporarily restricted his ability to make a living in his profession of predator. Mr. Coyote is self-employed and thus not eligible for Workmen's Compensation.[1]

Mr. Coyote states that on December 13th he received of Defendant via parcel post one Acme Rocket Sled. The intention of Mr. Coyote was to use the Rocket Sled to aid him in pursuit of his prey. Upon receipt of the Rocket Sled Mr. Coyote removed it from its wooden shipping crate and, sighting his prey in the distance, activated the ignition. As Mr. Coyote gripped the handlebars, the Rocket Sled accelerated with such sudden and precipitate force as to stretch Mr. Coyote's forelimbs to a length of fifty feet. Subsequently, the rest of Mr. Coyote's body shot forward with a violent jolt, causing severe strain to his back and neck and placing him unexpectedly astride the Rocket Sled. Disappearing over the horizon at such speed as to leave a diminishing jet trail along its path, the Rocket Sled soon brought Mr. Coyote abreast of his prey. At that moment the animal he was pursuing veered sharply to the right. Mr. Coyote vigorously attempted to follow this maneuver but was unable to, due to poorly designed steering on the Rocket Sled and a faulty or nonexistent braking system. Shortly thereafter, the unchecked progress of the Rocket Sled brought it and Mr. Coyote into collision with the side of a mesa.[2]

Paragraph One of the Report of Attending Physician (Exhibit B), prepared by Dr. Ernest Grosscup, M.D., D.O., details the multiple fractures, contusions, and tissue damage suffered by Mr. Coyote as a result of this collision. Repair of the injuries required a full bandage around the head (excluding the ears), a neck brace, and full or partial casts on all four legs.

Hampered by these injuries, Mr. Coyote was nevertheless obliged to support himself. With

---

1. **Workmen's Compensation:** Form of disability insurance that provides income to workers who are unable to work due to injuries sustained on the job.
2. **mesa** (mā´ sə) *n*.: Small, high plateau with steep sides.

► **Critical Viewing** Based on this illustration, how might you describe Coyote's occupational goals as a professional predator? **[Analyze]**

this in mind, he purchased of Defendant as an aid to mobility one pair of Acme Rocket Skates. When he attempted to use this product, however, he became involved in an accident remarkably similar to that which occurred with the Rocket Sled. Again, Defendant sold over the counter, without <u>caveat</u>, a product which attached powerful jet engines (in this case, two) to inadequate vehicles, with little or no provision for passenger safety. Encumbered by his heavy casts, Mr. Coyote lost control of the Rocket Skates soon after strapping them on, and collided with a roadside billboard so violently as to leave a hole in the shape of his full silhouette.

Mr. Coyote states that on occasions too numerous to list in this document he has suffered mishaps with explosives purchased of Defendant: the Acme "Little Giant" Firecracker, the Acme Self-Guided Aerial Bomb, etc. (For a full listing, see the Acme Mail Order Explosives Catalogue and attached deposition,[3] entered in evidence as Exhibit C.) Indeed, it is safe to say that not once has an explosive purchased of Defendant by Mr. Coyote performed in an expected manner. To cite just one example: At the expense of much time and personal effort, Mr. Coyote constructed around the outer rim of a butte[4] a wooden trough beginning at the top of the butte and spiraling downward around it

to some few feet above a black X painted on the desert floor. The trough was designed in such a way that a spherical explosive of the type sold by Defendant would roll easily and swiftly down to the point of detonation indicated by the X. Mr. Coyote placed a generous pile of birdseed directly on the X, and then, carrying the spherical Acme Bomb (Catalogue #78-832), climbed to the top of the butte. Mr. Coyote's prey, seeing the birdseed, approached, and Mr. Coyote proceeded to light the fuse. In an instant, the fuse burned down to the stem, causing the bomb to detonate.

In addition to reducing all Mr. Coyote's careful preparations to naught, the premature detonation of Defendant's product resulted in the following disfigurements to Mr. Coyote:

1. Severe singeing of the hair on the head, neck, and muzzle.
2. Sooty discoloration.
3. Fracture of the left ear at the stem, causing the ear to dangle in the aftershock with a cracking noise.
4. Radical widening of the eyes, due to brow and lid charring.

◆ **Build Vocabulary**

contiguous (kən tig′ yoo əs) *adj*.: Bordering; adjacent

precipitate (prē sip′ ə tit) *adj*.: Very sudden; unexpected or abrupt

caveat (kā′ vē at′) *n*.: Formal notice; warning

---

3. **deposition** (dep′ ə zish′ ən) *n*.: Legal term for the written testimony of a witness.
4. **butte** (byoot) *n*.: Steep hill standing alone in a plain.

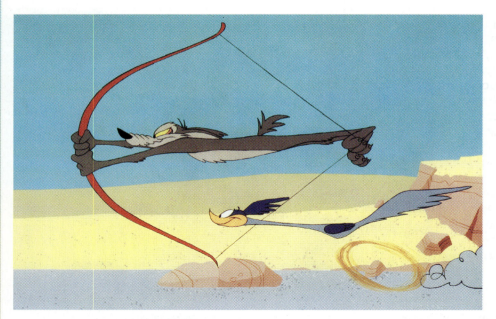

◀ **Critical Viewing**
Which word from the Word Bank might be used to describe Coyote's bow? Explain. **[Connect]**

We come now to the Acme Spring-Powered Shoes. The remains of a pair of these purchased by Mr. Coyote on June 23rd are Plaintiff's Exhibit D. Selected fragments have been shipped to the metallurgical laboratories of the University of California at Santa Barbara for analysis, but to date no explanation has been found for this product's sudden and extreme malfunction. As advertised by Defendant, this product is simplicity itself: two wood-and-metal sandals, each attached to milled-steel springs of high <u>tensile</u> strength and compressed in a tightly coiled position by a cocking device with a lanyard release. Mr. Coyote believed that this product would enable him to pounce upon his prey in the initial moments of the chase, when swift reflexes are at a premium.

To increase the shoes' thrusting still further, Mr. Coyote affixed them by their bottoms to the side of a large boulder. Adjacent to the boulder was a path which Mr. Coyote's prey was known to frequent. Mr. Coyote put his hind feet in the wood-and-metal sandals and crouched in readiness, his right forepaw holding firmly to the lanyard release. Within a short time Mr. Coyote's prey did indeed appear on the path coming toward him. Unsuspecting, the prey stopped near Mr. Coyote, well within range of the springs at full extension. Mr. Coyote gauged the distance with care and proceeded to pull the lanyard release.

At this point, Defendant's product should have thrust Mr. Coyote forward and away from the boulder. Instead, for reasons yet unknown, the Acme Spring-Powered Shoes thrust the boulder away from Mr. Coyote. As the intended prey looked on unharmed, Mr. Coyote hung suspended in air. Then the twin springs recoiled, bringing Mr. Coyote to a violent feet-first collision with the boulder, the full weight of his head and forequarters falling upon his lower extremities.

The force of this impact then caused the springs to rebound, whereupon Mr. Coyote was thrust skyward. A second recoil and collision followed. The boulder, meanwhile, which was roughly ovoid in shape, had begun to bounce down a hillside, the coiling and recoiling of the springs adding to its velocity. At each bounce, Mr. Coyote came into contact with the boulder, or the boulder came into contact with Mr. Coyote, or both came into contact with the ground. As the grade was a long one, this process continued for some time.

The sequence of collisions resulted in systemic physical damage to Mr. Coyote, viz., flattening of the cranium, sideways displacement of the tongue, reduction of length of legs and upper body, and compression of vertebrae from base of tail to head. Repetition of blows along a vertical axis produced a series of regular horizontal folds in Mr. Coyote's body tissues—a rare and painful condition which caused Mr. Coyote to expand upward and contract downward alternately as he walked, and to emit an off-key accordion-like wheezing with every step. The distracting and embarrassing nature of this symptom has been a major impediment to Mr. Coyote's pursuit of a normal social life.

As the Court is no doubt aware, Defendant has a virtual monopoly of manufacture and sale of goods required by Mr. Coyote's work. It is our contention that Defendant has used its market advantage to the detriment of the consumer of such specialized products as itching powder, giant kites, Burmese tiger traps, anvils, and two-hundred-foot-long rubber bands. Much as he has come to mistrust Defendant's products, Mr. Coyote has no other domestic source of supply to which to turn. One can only wonder what our trading partners in Western Europe and Japan would make of such a situation, where a giant company is allowed to victimize the consumer in the most reckless and wrongful manner over and over again.

Mr. Coyote respectfully requests that the Court regard these larger economic implications and assess punitive damages in the amount of seventeen million dollars. In addition, Mr. Coyote seeks actual damages (missed meals, medical expenses, days lost from professional occupation) of one million dollars; general damages (mental suffering, injury to reputation) of twenty million dollars; and attorney's fees of seven hundred and fifty thousand dollars. Total damages: thirty-eight million seven hundred and fifty thousand dollars. By awarding Mr. Coyote the full amount, this Court will censure Defendant, its directors, officers, shareholders, successors, and assigns, in the only language they understand, and reaffirm the right of the individual predator to equal protection under the law.

◆ **Build Vocabulary**

tensile (ten´ sil) *adj*.: Stretchable

Guide for Responding

◆ *Literature and Your Life*

Reader's Response As you read the attorney's statement, did you sympathize with Wile E. Coyote? Why or why not?

Thematic Focus How does this essay suggest that product liability lawsuits have become an all-too-common occurrence?

☑ Check Your Comprehension

1. Why is Coyote suing the Acme Company?
2. What pieces of evidence does the attorney submit to the court?
3. (a) Describe the way in which the Rocket Sled malfunctioned. (b) How was Wile E. Coyote injured while using the Rocket Skates?
4. (a) Where did the lawyer for Wile E. Coyote send fragments of the Spring-Powered Shoes? (b) Why?
5. What action is Wile E. Coyote seeking from the court?

◆ Critical Thinking

INTERPRET

1. What is the relationship between Wile E. Coyote and (a) Harold Schoff? (b) the Acme Company? (c) Dr. Ernest Grosscup? **[Classify]**
2. What details in this essay suggest that Wile E. Coyote is a cartoon character? **[Support]**
3. Find evidence to explain why Wile E. Coyote kept buying from Acme, even though eighty-five products did not work properly. **[Support]**

EVALUATE

4. What do you believe was Frazier's purpose in writing this essay—was he simply trying to be funny or was he making a point? Explain your answer. **[Evaluate]**

APPLY

5. If you were a member of the jury in this case, what would your recommendation be? Explain. **[Make a Judgment]**

Guide for Responding (continued)

◆ Literary Focus

ESSAYS

You have just read three very different types of essays: an **analytical essay**, in which the writer considers many aspects of a topic in an attempt to define, understand, or clarify it; a **satirical essay,** which uses irony, ridicule, or sarcasm to comment on a topic; and an **expository essay,** which explains or provides information about a topic.

1. (a) What type of essay is "The Mortgaged Heart"? (b) What aspects of loneliness does McCullers explore?
2. (a) What type of essay is "Onomatopoeia"? (b) Give an example of something that is explained in the essay.
3. How does "Coyote v. Acme" use humor to make a point about the increasing number of product liability suits?

◆ Build Vocabulary

USING THE WORD ROOT -ten-

The word root -ten- means "to stretch tightly." The words in the box each take their meaning from the root -ten-. Use at least four of the words to write a paragraph about a disastrous camping trip in which everything seems to go wrong. If you are unsure about a word, look it up in a dictionary.

tension	tense	tent	extent	tendon	intensify

USING THE WORD BANK

For each sentence, choose the word from the word bank that is suggested by the italicized word or phrase. Write the answers on your paper.

1. California and Oregon *share a common border.*
2. Redheads sunburn easily; *therefore, they must use sunscreen.*
3. Since he was usually gracious, we were all surprised by his *sudden, abrupt* exit.
4. The sign gave this *formal notice: Danger! Beware!*
5. The film director was a *nonconformist* in every way.
6. The *stretchable quality* of the rubber band was amazing.
7. The garish colors and loud music of the theater offended my *sense of appropriate decor.*
8. The newly fallen snow was *completely untouched.*

◆ Reading Strategy

IDENTIFY LINE OF REASONING

As you read these essays you **identified the line of reasoning** by asking yourself how the writer made a case for the main ideas he or she presented.

1. In "The Mortgaged Heart," how does McCullers convince the reader that (a) loneliness stems from the quest for identity and (b) love is the means of overcoming loneliness?
2. (a) Summarize the attorney's case for Mr. Coyote's compensation in "Coyote v. Acme." (b) What is the connection between Exhibits A–D and the main points of the attorney's argument?

◆ Grammar and Style

PRONOUNS WITH APPOSITIVES

When you use a pronoun preceding an appositive—a noun that renames the pronoun—you may be confused about which pronoun form to use. To choose the proper pronoun form, drop the noun or noun phrase the pronoun replaces as you say the sentence aloud.

When a pronoun acts as a subject, use *I, he, she, we,* or *they.* When a pronoun acts as an object, use *me, him, her, us,* or *them.*

Practice For each item, choose the correct form of the pronoun in parentheses, then write the completed sentence in your notebook.

1. Loneliness is common among (we, us) Americans.
2. Love can help us, you and (I, me), feel less lonely.
3. Two students, (she, her) and Carlos, were tied for the longest list of examples of onomatopoeia.
4. (We, Us) cartoon lovers all know Wile E. Coyote.

Writing Application Rewrite this paragraph using the correct form of the pronouns in parentheses.

The whole family, Mom, Dad, Grandma, Caroline, and (I, me), settled in front of the TV. The young people—Caroline and (I, me), that is—wanted to watch Road Runner cartoons. "That's not very entertaining for (we, us) adults," said Mom. I told Caroline that I hoped we, meaning (she, her) and (I, me), would never outgrow our love of cartoons.

Build Your Portfolio

Idea Bank

Writing

1. **Letter** Write a letter to Carson McCullers in which you respond to one of the ideas in her essay. Do you agree or disagree with her analysis?

2. **News Article** Write a newspaper article based on "Coyote v. Acme." You may wish to include details about the plaintiff's appearance in court and his reaction to the verdict. **[Media Link]**

3. **Analytical Essay** McCullers describes the American artist as "the eternal maverick." Use a dictionary to trace the origin of *maverick*. In an essay, explore the connection between the American origin and current usage of the word. Is being a *maverick* an "American" quality? Explain.

Speaking and Listening

4. **Opening Statement for the Defense** As the attorney defending the Acme Company, how would you respond to the arguments presented in "Coyote v. Acme"? Present your statement to the class. **[Social Studies Link]**

5. **Invented Words** Working with a partner, take turns inventing onomatopoetic words for everyday sounds. Present eight to ten new words to the class and see whether your classmates can identify the sound each word describes.

Projects

6. **Essay Collection** Look through a book of Safire's "On Language" columns. Select five or six that you find most appealing and collect them in a booklet for display in the classroom. Include an introduction explaining your choices.

7. **Cartoon Strip** Create a cartoon strip showing one of Coyote's experiences with an Acme product as described in "Coyote v. Acme." **[Art Link]**

Writing Mini-Lesson

Résumé for Wile E. Coyote

Wile E. Coyote's attorney frequently refers to his client's profession of predator. He mentions the tools his clients uses (or tries to use), and he implies that his client is quite well experienced in his field. Write a résumé that Wile E. Coyote might use to search for a job. Follow Ian Frazier's example and use your sense of humor as you compose a satirical version of a standard résumé.

Writing Skills Focus: Keeping to a Format

Successful résumés generally follow a standard format. After a name, address, and phone number, the writer divides information into clearly labeled sections. For example, you might establish these categories for Coyote's résumé:
- Objective or Goal
- Qualifications
- Work Experience
- Education
- Awards
- References

Prewriting Jot down some notes concerning the kinds of experience and training Coyote might include in his résumé. How did he prepare himself for his career? What jobs might he have had before becoming a full-fledged predator? Refer to Frazier's essay for ideas about Coyote's experience.

Drafting Begin your draft with the résumé heading described in the above format. Then use your notes to complete the résumé by organizing the appropriate qualifications under each heading.

Revising Ask a classmate to read the résumé and tell you which sections need more detail. Replace any vague verbs with more powerful, active ones. For example, change "kept inventory" to "organized and maintained inventory."

Guide for Interpreting

Sandra Cisneros (1954–)

Sandra Cisneros was born in Chicago into a large Mexican American family. Because her family was poor, Cisneros moved frequently and lived for the most part in small, cramped apartments. To cope with these conditions, she retreated into herself, spending much of her time reading fairy tales and classic literature. Cisneros attended Loyola University in Chicago and the Writer's Workshop at the University of Iowa. Her book *The House on Mango Street* (1984) was a modest success. However, her later book, *Woman Hollering Creek* (1991), won critical acclaim and earned Cisneros widespread recognition.

Rita Dove (1953–)

Now a famous poet, Rita Dove's first writing efforts—at the age of nine or ten—were comic books with female superheroines. Born in Akron, Ohio, she attended Miami University in Oxford, Ohio, and later the University of Iowa. Dove has published several volumes of poetry, including the Pulitzer Prize-winning *Thomas and Beulah* (1986). In 1993, Dove was appointed Poet Laureate of the United States. She was the first African American and the youngest person ever to hold that position. Dove has also written a play, a novel, and a collection of short stories.

Amy Tan (1952–)

When Amy Tan was thirty-five, she visited China with her mother. Until then, Tan, who was born in Oakland, California, to Chinese immigrants, had rejected her Chinese heritage. On that trip, however, she made peace with her Chinese roots. At the time, she was leaving a successful career as a business writer to become a fiction writer. When she returned to the United States, she began *The Joy Luck Club* (1989), a novel about four Chinese American women and their mothers. The book made Tan an overnight celebrity. *The Kitchen God's Wife* (1991) was even more enthusiastically received. Her third novel, *The Hundred Secret Senses,* was published in 1995.

◆ Background for Understanding

LITERATURE: THE DEVELOPMENT OF THE ESSAY

Although writers were using the form earlier, the word *essai* was not coined until 1580, when the French philosopher Montaigne published a book called *Essais.* Translated, the French word *essai* means "try," which describes the essay's original sense: an exploratory piece of writing that lacked finish. In 1597, the English philosopher Francis Bacon said that his own *Essays* were "grains of salt which will rather give an appetite than offend with satiety." Montaigne and Bacon share fame for the development of the genre.

Eventually, the essay lost its original "unfinished" sense and writers began to think of it as an elegant, well-thought-out, polished piece of writing. Today, the essay has become one of the most popular literary forms—both among writers and readers.

Essays are one of the most flexible of all literary forms. They can be as short as a few hundred words or as long as a few hundred pages. They can be formal or informal, and they can discuss a wide variety of subjects, ranging from philosophy, literature, history, and current events to personal reflections on just about anything.

◆ *Literature and Your Life*

CONNECT YOUR EXPERIENCE

Are you confident around other people, or are you often a little insecure? The writers of these essays say they were shy or insecure as girls. They retreated to the world of books, and their love of reading led them to write—and in writing, each found her voice.

Journal Writing Imagine that ten years from now you have become a writer. Consider the kind of writer you might be. Then draft a short biographical sketch highlighting your background and interests for the jacket of your first book.

THEMATIC FOCUS: LITERATURE CONFRONTS THE EVERYDAY

Each of these essays focuses on an ordinary aspect of the writer's past, turning everyday events into material for reflective thought.

◆ Reading Strategy

EVALUATE A WRITER'S MESSAGE

Most writers write essays to communicate an idea. As the reader, your job is not only to get the point, but also to decide what you think about it. When you **evaluate a writer's message,** you think about whether the writer's idea is valid and whether you agree or disagree with it. As you read each essay that follows, identify and then evaluate the writer's message.

◆ Grammar and Style

VARYING SENTENCE STRUCTURE

The right mix of sentence structures helps keep writing lively and interesting. **Simple sentences**—those consisting of one independent clause—can convey ideas concisely and directly. **Compound sentences,** which contain two or more independent clauses, and **complex sentences,** which contain an independent clause and one or more subordinate clauses, can enhance the flow of ideas. In this example from "Straw Into Gold," Cisneros follows a complex sentence with a simple one:

> To make matters worse, I had left before any of my six brothers had ventured away from home. I had broken a terrible taboo.

As you read these essays, notice how each author varies her sentences to create interesting, readable prose.

◆ Literary Focus

REFLECTIVE ESSAY

An essay is a short piece of nonfiction in which a writer expresses a personal view of a topic. In a **reflective essay,** the writer uses an informal tone to describe personal experiences or pivotal events. The essay conveys the writer's feelings about these events or experiences. The writer often considers the significance of the experience being described and arrives at a deeper understanding through this reflection.

◆ Build Vocabulary

WORD ROOTS: -*scrib*- AND -*script*-

In "Mother Tongue," Amy Tan transcribes a taped conversation. The word *transcribe* is formed from the Latin root -*scrib*-, which means "write." *Transcribe* means "write out or type out in full." Other familiar words containing -*scribe*- or -*script*- include *scribble, scripture,* and *inscribe.*

WORD BANK

Before you read, preview this list of words from the essays.

nomadic
transcribed
empirical
benign
semantic
quandary
nascent

Straw Into Gold:
The Metamorphosis of the Everyday

Sandra Cisneros

When I was living in an artists' colony in the south of France, some fellow Latin-Americans who taught at the university in Aix-en-Provence[1] invited me to share a home-cooked meal with them. I had been living abroad almost a year then on an NEA[2] grant, subsisting mainly on French bread and lentils while in France so that my money could last longer. So when the invitation to dinner arrived, I accepted without hesitation. Especially since they had promised Mexican food.

What I didn't realize when they made this invitation was that I was supposed to be involved in preparing this meal. I guess they assumed I knew how to cook Mexican food because I was Mexican. They wanted specifically tortillas, though I'd never made a tortilla in my life.

It's true I had witnessed my mother rolling the little armies of dough into perfect circles, but my mother's family is from Guanajuato,[3] *provinciales*,[4] country folk. They only know how to make flour tortillas. My father's family, on the other hand, is *chilango*,[5] from Mexico City. We ate corn tortillas but we didn't make them. Someone was sent to the corner tortilleria to buy some. I'd never seen anybody make corn tortillas. Ever.

Well, somehow my Latino hosts had gotten a hold of a packet of corn flour, and this is what they tossed my way with orders to produce tortillas. *Asi como sea.* Any ol' way, they said and went back to their cooking.

Why did I feel like the woman in the fairy tale who was locked in a room and ordered to spin straw into gold? I had the same sick feeling when I was required to write my critical essay for my MFA[6] exam—the only piece of noncreative writing necessary in order to get my graduate degree. How was I to start? There were rules involved here, unlike writing a poem or story, which I did intuitively. There was a step-by-step process needed and I had better know it. I felt as if making tortillas, or writing a critical paper for that matter, were tasks so impossible I wanted to break down into tears.

Somehow though, I managed to make those tortillas—crooked and burnt, but edible nonetheless. My hosts were absolutely ignorant when it came to Mexican food; they thought my tortillas were delicious. (I'm glad my mama wasn't there.) Thinking back and looking at that photograph documenting the three of us consuming those lopsided circles I am amazed. Just as I am amazed I could finish my MFA exam (lopsided and crooked, but finished all the same). Didn't think I could do it. But I did.

I've managed to do a lot of things in my life I didn't think I was capable of and which many others didn't think me capable of either.

---

1. **Aix-en-Provence** (eks än prō väns´): City in southeastern France.
2. **NEA:** National Endowment for the Arts.
3. **Guanajuato** (gwä´ nä hwä´ tō): State in central Mexico.
4. *provinciales* (prō bēn sē ä´ läs): "Country folk" (Spanish).
5. *chilango* (chē län´ gō): "City folk" (Spanish).

6. **MFA:** Master of Fine Arts.

▲ **Critical Viewing** This painting, titled *Biography*, challenges the viewer to piece together the experiences of a lifetime from a variety of small objects. What parallels can you draw between the picture and the essay? **[Connect]**

Biography, 1988, Marina Gutierrez, Courtesy of the artist

Especially because I am a woman, a Latina, an only daughter in a family of six men. My father would've liked to have seen me married long ago. In our culture, men and women don't leave their father's house except by way of marriage. I crossed my father's threshold with nothing carrying me but my own two feet. A woman whom no one came for and no one chased away.

To make matters worse, I had left before any of my six brothers had ventured away from home. I had broken a terrible taboo. Somehow, looking back at photos of myself as a child, I wonder if I was aware of having begun already my own quiet war.

I like to think that somehow my family, my Mexicanness, my poverty all had something to do with shaping me into a writer. I like to think my parents were preparing me all along for my life as an artist even though they didn't know it. From my father I inherited a love of wandering. He was born in Mexico City but as a young man he traveled into the U.S. vagabonding. He eventually was drafted and thus became a citizen. Some of the stories he has told about his first months in the U.S. with little or no English surface in my stories in *The House on Mango Street* as well as others I have in mind to write in the future. From him I inherited a sappy heart. (He still cries when he watches the Mexican soaps—especially if they deal with children who have forsaken their parents.)

My mother was born like me—in Chicago but of Mexican descent. It would be her tough, streetwise voice that would haunt all my stories and poems. An amazing woman who loves to draw and read books and can sing an opera. A smart cookie.

When I was a little girl we traveled to Mexico City so much I thought my grandparents' house on La Fortuna, Number 12, was home. It was the only constant in our <u>nomadic</u> ramblings from one Chicago flat to another. The house on Destiny Street, Number 12, in the colonia Tepeyac,[7] would be perhaps the only home I knew, and that nostalgia for a home would be a theme that would obsess me.

My brothers also figured greatly in my art. Especially the oldest two; I grew up in their shadows. Henry, the second oldest and my favorite, appears often in poems I have written and in stories which at times only borrow his nickname, Kiki. He played a major role in my childhood. We were bunkbed mates. We were co-conspirators. We were pals. Until my oldest brother came back from studying in Mexico and left me odd-woman-out for always.

What would my teachers say if they knew I was a writer? Who would've guessed it? I wasn't a very bright student. I didn't much like school because we moved so much and I was always new and funny-looking. In my fifth-grade report card, I have nothing but an avalanche of C's and D's, but I don't remember being that stupid. I was good at art and I read plenty of library books and Kiki laughed at all my jokes. At home I was fine, but at school I never opened my mouth except when the teacher called on me, the first time I'd speak all day.

---

7. **colonia Tepeyac** (cô lō´ nēä tä pā´ yäc): District of Mexico City.

When I think how I see myself, it would have to be at age eleven. I know I'm thirty-two on the outside, but inside I'm eleven. I'm the girl in the picture with skinny arms and a crumpled shirt and crooked hair. I didn't like school because all they saw was the outside me. School was lots of rules and sitting with your hands folded and being very afraid all the time. I liked looking out the window and thinking. I liked staring at the girl across the way writing her name over and over again in red ink. I wondered why the boy with the dirty collar in front of me didn't have a mama who took better care of him.

I think my mama and papa did the best they could to keep us warm and clean and never hungry. We had birthday and graduation parties and things like that, but there was another hunger that had to be fed. There was a hunger I didn't even have a name for. Was this when I began writing?

In 1966 we moved into a house, a real one, our first real home. This meant we didn't have to change schools and be the new kids on the block every couple of years. We could make friends and not be afraid we'd have to say good-bye to them and start all over. My brothers and the flock of boys they brought home would become important characters eventually for my stories—Louie and his cousins, Meme Ortiz and his dog with two names, one in English and one in Spanish.

My mother flourished in her own home. She took books out of the library and taught herself to garden, producing flowers so envied we had to put a lock on the gate to keep out the midnight flower thieves. My mother is still gardening to this day.

This was the period in my life, that slippery age when you are both child and woman and neither, I was to record in *The House on Mango Street*. I was still shy. I was a girl who couldn't come out of her shell.

How was I to know I would be recording and documenting the women who sat their sadness on an elbow and stared out a window? It would be the city streets of Chicago I would later record, but from a child's eyes.

I've done all kinds of things I didn't think I could do since then. I've gone to a prestigious university, studied with famous writers, and taken away an MFA degree. I've taught poetry in the schools in Illinois and Texas. I've gotten

◆ Reading Strategy
Why do you think Cisneros emphasizes the fact that her life has unfolded in ways she never expected?

an NEA grant and run away with it as far as my courage would take me. I've seen the bleached and bitter mountains of the Peloponnesus.[8] I've lived on a Greek island. I've been to Venice[9] twice. In Rapallo, I met Ilona once and forever and took her sad heart with me across the south of France and into Spain.

I've lived in Yugoslavia. I've been to the famous Nice[10] flower market behind the opera house. I've lived in a village in the pre-Alps[11] and witnessed the daily parade of promenaders.

I've moved since Europe to the strange and wonderful country of Texas, land of polaroid-blue skies and big bugs. I met a mayor with my last name. I met famous Chicana/o artists and writers and *politicos*.[12]

Texas is another chapter in my life. It brought with it the Dobie-Paisano Fellowship, a six-month residency on a 265-acre ranch. But most important Texas brought Mexico back to me.

Sitting at my favorite people-watching spot, the snaky Woolworth's counter across the street from the Alamo,[13] I can't think of anything else I'd rather be than a writer. I've traveled and lectured from Cape Cod to San Francisco, to Spain, Yugoslavia, Greece, Mexico, France, Italy, and finally today to Seguin, Texas. Along the way there is straw for the taking. With a little imagination, it can be spun into gold.

---

8. **Peloponnesus** (pel´ ə pə nē´ səs): Peninsula forming the southeastern part of the Greek mainland.
9. **Venice** (ven´ is): Seaport in northern Italy.
10. **Nice** (nēs): Seaport and resort in southeastern France.
11. **pre-Alps:** Foothills of the Alps, a mountain range in south-central Europe.

---

12. *politicos* (pō lē´ tē cōs): "Politicians" (Spanish).
13. **the Alamo** (al´ ə mō´): Mission in San Antonio, Texas, that was the scene of a famous battle between Texans and Mexican troops in 1836.

Guide for Responding

◆ *Literature and Your Life*

Reader's Response Does Cisneros seem like someone you would like to meet? Why or why not?

Thematic Focus What phase of Cisneros's life seems to have been the most important in shaping her writing? Support your answer.

Journal Writing Briefly describe a time when you did something that neither you nor others thought you were capable of doing.

☑ Check Your Comprehension

1. What experience reminded Cisneros of the woman who had to spin straw into gold?
2. What obstacles stood in the way of Cisneros's goal of becoming a writer?
3. What does Cisneros believe contributed to shaping her as a writer?

◆ Critical Thinking

INTERPRET

1. (a) What point is Cisneros trying to make through her anecdote about making tortillas? (b) How is this anecdote connected to the rest of her essay? **[Interpret; Connect]**
2. What does the essay suggest about Cisneros's imagination and eye for detail? **[Infer]**
3. What is the main point of the essay? Support your answer. **[Draw Conclusions]**

EVALUATE

4. Do you agree with Cisneros that "with a little imagination, [straw] can be spun into gold"? Explain. **[Evaluate]**

APPLY

5. How could you apply Cisneros's message to your own life? Explain. **[Apply]**

For the Love of Books

Rita Dove

When I am asked: "What made you want to be a writer?" my answer has always been: "Books." First and foremost, now, then, and always, I have been passionate about books. From the time I began to read, as a child, I loved to feel their heft in my hand and the warm spot caused by their intimate weight in my lap; I loved the crisp whisper of a page turning, the musky odor of old paper and the sharp inky whiff of new pages. Leather bindings sent me into ecstasy. I even loved to gaze at a closed book and daydream about the possibilities inside—it was like contemplating a genie's lamp. Of course, my favorite fairy tale was *A Thousand and One Nights*—imagine buying your life with stories!—and my favorite cartoons were those where animated characters popped out of books and partied while the unsuspecting humans slept. In books, I could travel anywhere, be anybody, understand worlds long past and imaginary colonies in the future. My idea of a bargain was to go to the public library, wander along the bookshelves, and emerge with a chin-high stack of books that were mine, all mine, for two weeks—free of charge!

What I remember most about long summer days is browsing the bookshelves in our solarium to see if there were any new additions. I grew up with those rows of books; I knew where each one was shelved and immediately spotted newcomers. And after months had gone by and there'd be no new books, I would think: Okay, I guess I'll try this one—and then discover that the very book I had been avoiding because of a drab cover or small print was actually a wonderful read. Louis Untermeyer's *Treasury of Best Loved Poems* had a sickeningly sweet lilac and gold cover and was forbiddingly thick, but I finally pulled it off the shelf and discovered a cornucopia of emotional and linguistic delights, from "The Ballad of Barbara Fritchie," which I adored for its sheer length and rather numbing rhymes, to Langston Hughes's dazzlingly syncopated "Dream Boogie." Then there was Shakespeare—daunting for many years because it was his entire oeuvre,[1] in matching wine-red volumes that were so thick they looked more like over-sized bouillon cubes than books, and yet it was that ponderous title—*The Complete Works of William Shakespeare*—that enticed me, because here was a lifetime's work—a lifetime!—in two compact, dense packages. I began with the long poem "The Rape of Lucrece" . . . I sampled a few sonnets, which I found beautiful but rather adult; and finally wandered into the plays—first *Romeo and Juliet*, then *Macbeth, Julius Caesar, A Midsummer Night's Dream, Twelfth Night*—enthralled by the language, by the fact that poetry was spinning the story. Of course I did not understand every single word, but I was too young to know that this was supposed to be difficult; besides, no one was waiting to test me on anything, so, free from pressure, I dove in.

At the same time, my brother, two years my senior, had become a science fiction buff, so I'd read his *Analog* and *Fantasy and Science Fiction* magazines after he was finished with them. One story particularly fascinated me: A retarded boy in a small town begins building a sculpture in his backyard, using old and discarded

---

1. **oeuvre** (ĕ´ vrə) *n.*: All the works, usually of a lifetime, of a particular writer, artist, or composer.

materials—coke bottles, scrap iron, string, and bottle caps. Everyone laughs at him, but he continues building. Then one day he disappears. And when the neighbors investigate, they discover that the sculpture has been dragged onto the back porch and that the screen door is open. Somehow the narrator of the story figures out how to switch on the sculpture: The back door frame begins to glow, and when he steps through it, he's in an alternate universe, a town the mirror image of his own—even down to the colors, with green roses and an orange sky. And he walks through this town until he comes to the main square, where there is a statue erected to—who else?—the village idiot.

I loved this story, the idea that the dreamy, mild, scatter-brained boy of one world could be the hero of another. And in a way, I identified with that village idiot because in real life I was painfully shy and awkward; the place where I felt most alive was between the pages of a book.

Although I loved books, for a long time I had no aspirations to be a writer. The possibility was beyond my imagination. I liked to write, however—and on long summer days when I ran out of reading material or my legs had fallen asleep because I had been curled up on the couch for hours on end, I made up my own stories. Most were abandoned midway. Those that I did bring to a conclusion I neither showed to others nor considered saving.

My first piece of writing I thought enough of to keep was a novel called *Chaos*, which was about robots taking over the earth. I had just entered third or fourth grade; the novel had forty-three chapters, and each chapter was twenty lines or less because I used each week's spelling list as the basis for each chapter, and there were twenty words per list. In the course of the year I wrote one installment per week, and I never knew what was going to happen next—the words led me, not the other way around.

At that time I didn't think of writing as an activity people admitted doing. I had no living role models—a "real" writer was a long-dead white male, usually with a white beard to match. Much later, when I was in eleventh grade, my English teacher, Miss Oechsner, took me to a book-signing in a downtown hotel. She didn't ask me if I'd like to go—she asked my parents instead, signed me and a classmate (who is now a professor of literature) out of school one day, and took us to meet a writer. The writer was John Ciardi, a poet who also had translated Dante's *Divine Comedy*, which I had heard of, vaguely. At that moment I realized that writers were real people and how it was possible to write down a poem or story in the intimate sphere of one's own room and then share it with the world.

Guide for Responding

◆ Literature and Your Life

Reader's Response Might you have been friends with Rita Dove if you had known her as a child? Why or why not?

Thematic Focus Why do you think reading and writing are often the favorite pastime of shy people?

Journal Writing List your five favorite activities. Is reading one of them? Explore your answer.

☑ Check Your Comprehension

1. How does Rita Dove feel about books?
2. What was the first piece of writing Dove liked well enough to keep?
3. What made Dove realize that she could be a "real" writer?

◆ Critical Thinking

INTERPRET

1. What does Dove mean when she says that gazing at a closed book was "like contemplating a genie's lamp"? **[Interpret]**
2. What influences contributed to Dove's goal of becoming a writer? **[Deduce]**
3. Do you think Dove would have gone on to become a writer if she had not attended the book signing? **[Speculate]**

EVALUATE

4. In an interview, Dove has said, "My first and really only piece of advice [to young writers] is to read, read, read." After reading this essay, do you think this is good advice? Explain. **[Criticize]**

Mother Tongue

Amy Tan

I am not a scholar of English or literature. I cannot give you much more than personal opinions on the English language and its variations in this country or others.

I am a writer. And by that definition, I am someone who has always loved language. I am fascinated by language in daily life. I spend a great deal of my time thinking about the power of language—the way it can evoke an emotion, a visual image, a complex idea, or a simple truth. Language is the tool of my trade. And I use them all—all the Englishes I grew up with.

Recently, I was made keenly aware of the different Englishes I do use. I was giving a talk to a large group of people, the same talk I had already given to half a dozen other groups. The nature of the talk was about my writing, my life, and my book, *The Joy Luck Club*. The talk was going along well enough, until I remembered one major difference that made the whole talk sound wrong. My mother was in the room. And it was perhaps the first time she had heard me give a lengthy speech, using the kind of English I have never used with her. I was saying things like, "The intersection of memory upon imagination" and "There is an aspect of my fiction that relates to thus-and-thus"—a speech filled with carefully wrought grammatical phrases, burdened, it suddenly seemed to me, with nominalized forms, past perfect

▲ **Critical Viewing** Based on this photograph of Amy Tan and her mother, what kind of a relationship do you think they now share? Explain. **[Infer]**

tenses, conditional phrases, all the forms of standard English that I had learned in school and through books, the forms of English I did not use at home with my mother.

Just last week, I was walking down the street with my mother, and I again found myself conscious of the English I was using, the English I do use with her. We were talking about the price of new and used furniture and I heard myself saying this: "Not waste money that way." My husband was with us as well, and he didn't notice any switch in my English. And then I realized why. It's because over the twenty years we've been together I've often used the same kind of English with him, and sometimes he even uses it with me. It has become our language of intimacy, a different sort of English that relates to family talk, the language I grew up with.

So you'll have some idea of what this family talk I heard sounds like, I'll quote what my mother said during a recent conversation which I videotaped and then <u>transcribed</u>. During this conversation, my mother was talking about a political gangster in Shanghai[1] who had the same last name as her family's, Du, and how the gangster in his early years wanted to be adopted by her family, which was rich by comparison. Later, the gangster became more powerful, far richer than my mother's family, and one day showed up at my mother's wedding to pay his respects. Here's what she said in part:

"Du Yusong having business like fruit stand. Like off the street kind. He is Du like Du Zong—but not Tsung-ming Island people. The local people call putong, the river east side, he belong to that side local people. That man want to ask Du Zong father take him in like become own family. Du Zong father wasn't look down on him, but didn't take seriously, until that man big like become a mafia. Now important person, very hard to inviting him. Chinese way, come only to show respect, don't stay for dinner. Respect for making big celebration, he shows up. Mean gives lots of respect. Chinese custom. Chinese social life that way. If too important won't have to stay too long. He come to my wedding. I didn't see, I heard it. I gone to boy's side, they have YMCA[2] dinner. Chinese age I was nineteen."

You should know that my mother's expressive command of English belies how much she actually understands. She reads the *Forbes*[3] report, listens to *Wall Street Week*,[4] converses daily with her stockbroker, reads all of Shirley MacLaine's[5] books with ease—all kinds of things I can't begin to understand. Yet some of my friends tell me they understand 50 percent of what my mother says. Some say they understand 80 to 90 percent. Some say they understand none of it, as if she were speaking pure Chinese. But to me, my mother's English is perfectly clear, perfectly natural. It's my mother tongue. Her language, as I hear it, is vivid, direct, full of observation and imagery. That was the language that helped shape the way I saw things, expressed things, made sense of the world.

Lately, I've been giving more thought to the kind of English my mother speaks. Like others, I have described it to people as "broken," or "fractured" English. But I wince when I say that. It has always bothered me that I can think of no way to describe it other than "broken," as if it were damaged and needed to be fixed, as if it lacked a certain wholeness and soundness. I've heard other terms used, "limited English," for example. But they seem just as bad, as if everything is limited, including people's perceptions of the limited English speaker.

I know this for a fact, because when I was growing up, my mother's "limited" English limited *my* perception of her. I was ashamed of her English. I believed that her English reflected the quality of what she had to say. That is, because she expressed them imperfectly her thoughts were imperfect. And I had plenty of empirical evidence to support me: the fact that people in department stores, at banks, and at restaurants did not take her seriously, did not give her good service, pretended not to understand her, or even acted as if they did not hear her.

◆ **Literary Focus**
What significance does Tan attach to this personal experience?

My mother has long realized the limitations of her English as well. When I was fifteen, she used to have me call people on the phone to pretend I was she. In this guise, I was forced to ask for information or even to complain and yell at people who had been rude to her. One time it was a call to her stockbroker in New York. She had cashed out her small portfolio and it just so happened we were going to go to New York the next week, our very first trip outside California. I had to get on the phone and say in an adolescent voice that was not very convincing, "This is Mrs. Tan."

And my mother was standing in the back whispering loudly, "Why he don't send me check, already two weeks late. So mad he lie to me, losing me money."

And then I said in perfect English, "Yes, I'm getting rather concerned. You had agreed to

---

1. **Shanghai** (shaŋ´ hī´): Seaport in eastern China.
2. **YMCA:** Young Men's Christian Association.
3. *Forbes:* Magazine of business and finance.
4. *Wall Street Week:* Weekly television program that reports business and investment news.
5. **Shirley MacLaine's** (mək lānz´): Shirley MacLaine is an American actress who has written several books.

◆ **Build Vocabulary**
transcribed (tran skrībd´) *v*.: Wrote or typed a copy of
empirical (em pir´ i kəl) *adj*.: Derived from observation or experiment

send the check two weeks ago, but it hasn't arrived."

Then she began to talk more loudly. "What he want, I come to New York tell him front of his boss, you cheating me?" And I was trying to calm her down, make her be quiet, while telling the stockbroker, "I can't tolerate any more excuses. If I don't receive the check immediately, I am going to have to speak to your manager when I'm in New York next week." And sure enough, the following week there we were in front of this astonished stockbroker, and I was sitting there red-faced and quiet, and my mother, the real Mrs. Tan, was shouting at his boss in her impeccable broken English.

We used a similar routine just five days ago, for a situation that was far less humorous. My mother had gone to the hospital for an appointment, to find out about a benign brain tumor a CAT scan[6] had revealed a month ago. She said she had spoken very good English, her best English, no mistakes. Still, she said, the hospital did not apologize when they said they had lost the CAT scan and she had come for nothing. She said they did not seem to have any sympathy when she told them she was anxious to know the exact diagnosis, since her husband and son had both died of brain tumors. She said they would not give her any more information until the next time and she would have to make another appointment for that. So she said she would not leave until the doctor called her daughter. She wouldn't budge. And when the doctor finally called her daughter, me, who spoke in perfect English—lo and behold—we had assurances the CAT scan would be found, promises that a conference call on Monday would be held, and apologies for any suffering my mother had gone through for a most regrettable mistake.

I think my mother's English almost had an effect on limiting my possibilities in life as well. Sociologists and linguists probably will tell you that a person's developing language skills are more influenced by peers. But I do think that the language spoken in the family, especially in immigrant families which are more insular, plays a large role in shaping the language of the child. And I believe that it affected my

results on achievement tests, IQ tests, and the SAT.[7] While my English skills were never judged as poor, compared to math, English could not be considered my strong suit. In grade school I did moderately well, getting perhaps B's, sometimes B-pluses, in English and scoring perhaps in the sixtieth or seventieth percentile on achievement tests. But those scores were not good enough to override the opinion that my true abilities lay in math and science, because in those areas I achieved A's and scored in the ninetieth percentile or higher.

This was understandable. Math is precise; there is only one correct answer. Whereas, for me at least, the answers on English tests were always a judgment call, a matter of opinion and personal experience. Those tests were constructed around items like fill-in-the-blank sentence completion, such as, "Even though Tom was _____, Mary thought he was _____." And the correct answer always seemed to be the most bland combinations of thoughts, for example, "Even though Tom was shy, Mary thought he was charming," with the grammatical structure "even though" limiting the correct answer to some sort of semantic opposites, so you wouldn't get answers like, "Even though Tom was foolish, Mary thought he was ridiculous." Well, according to my mother, there were very few limitations as to what Tom could have been and what Mary might have thought of him. So I never did well on tests like that.

The same was true with word analogies, pairs of words in which you were supposed to find some sort of logical, semantic relationship—for example, "*Sunset* is to *nightfall* as _____ is to _____." And here you would be presented with a list of four possible pairs, one of which showed the same kind of relationship: *red* is to *stoplight*, *bus* is to *arrival*, *chills* is to *fever*, *yawn* is to *boring*. Well, I could never think that way. I knew what the tests were asking, but I could not block out of my mind the images already created by the first pair, "*sunset* is to *nightfall*"—and I would see a burst of colors against a darkening sky, the moon rising, the lowering of a curtain of stars. And all the other pairs of words—red, bus, stoplight,

---

6. **CAT scan:** Method used by doctors to diagnose brain disorders.

7. **SAT:** Scholastic Aptitude Test; national college entrance exam.

▶ **Critical Viewing** Is the language on these signs in San Francisco's Chinatown district the "mother tongue" to which Tan refers? Explain. [Distinguish]

boring—just threw up a mass of confusing images, making it impossible for me to sort out something as logical as saying: "A sunset precedes nightfall" is the same as "a chill precedes a fever." The only way I would have gotten that answer right would have been to imagine an associative situation, for example, my being disobedient and staying out past sunset, catching a chill at night, which turns into feverish pneumonia as punishment, which indeed did happen to me.

I have been thinking about all this lately, about my mother's English, about achievement tests. Because lately I've been asked, as a writer, why there are not more Asian Americans represented in American literature. Why are there few Asian Americans enrolled in creative writing programs? Why do so many Chinese students go into engineering? Well, these are broad sociological questions I can't begin to answer. But I have noticed in surveys—in fact, just last week—that Asian students, as a whole, always do significantly better on math achievement tests than in English. And this makes me think that there are other Asian-American students whose English spoken in the home might also be described as "broken" or "limited." And perhaps they also have teachers who are steering them away from writing and into math and science, which is what happened to me.

Fortunately, I happen to be rebellious in nature and enjoy the challenge of disproving assumptions made about me. I became an English major my first year in college, after being enrolled as pre-med. I started writing nonfiction as a freelancer the week after I was told by my former boss that writing was my worst skill and I should hone my talents toward account management.

◆ **Build Vocabulary**

benign (bi nīn´) *adj.*: Not injurious or malignant; not cancerous

semantic (sə man´ tik) *adj.*: Pertaining to meaning in language

But it wasn't until 1985 that I finally began to write fiction. And at first I wrote using what I thought to be wittily crafted sentences, sentences that would finally prove I had mastery over the English language. Here's an example from the first draft of a story that later made its way into *The Joy Luck Club*, but without this line: "That was my mental quandary in its nascent state." A terrible line, which I can barely pronounce.

Fortunately, for reasons I won't get into today, I later decided I should envision a reader for the stories I would write. And the reader I decided upon was my mother, because these were stories about mothers. So with this reader in mind—and in fact she did read my early drafts—I began to write stories using all the Englishes I grew up with: the English I spoke to my mother, which for lack of a better term might be described as "simple"; the English she used with me, which for lack of a better term might be described as "broken"; my translation

of her Chinese, which could certainly be described as "watered down"; and what I imagined to be her translation of her Chinese if she could speak in perfect English, her internal language, and for that I sought to preserve the essence, but neither an English nor a Chinese structure. I wanted to capture what language ability tests can never reveal: her intent, her passion, her imagery, the rhythms of her speech and the nature of her thoughts.

Apart from what any critic had to say about my writing, I knew I had succeeded where it counted when my mother finished reading my book and gave me her verdict: "So easy to read."

◆ Build Vocabulary

quandary (kwän´ dä rē) *n*.: State of uncertainty; dilemma

nascent (nas´ ənt, nā´ sənt) *adj*.: Coming into existence; emerging

Guide for Responding

◆ Literature and Your Life

Reader's Response Having read this essay, what are your feelings about Tan and her mother? Explain.

Thematic Focus What effect do you think using different "Englishes" might have on Tan's fiction?

Journal Writing Consider the obstacles that might be faced by a person who has a limited understanding of the English language. Then write about the obstacle you think would be most difficult for you.

☑ Check Your Comprehension

1. When her mother was present at a speech she was giving, Amy Tan had a realization about the way each of them spoke English. What was it?
2. Summarize one experience Tan has had involving her mother's difficulty with English.
3. Why does Tan believe Asian students, including herself, generally score higher on math achievement tests than on English tests?
4. What different kinds of English does Tan use when she writes fiction?

◆ Critical Thinking

INTERPRET

1. How has her mother shaped Tan's writing? Support your answer. **[Analyze]**
2. How does the way Tan views her mother's English differ from how others view it? **[Compare and Contrast]**
3. (a) What can you infer from this essay about Amy Tan's character? (b) What can you infer about her mother's character? **[Infer]**

EVALUATE

4. Assess Tan's conclusion that successful writing is "easy to read." **[Assess]**

APPLY

5. (a) What would it be like to live in a place where a language barrier made it difficult for you to communicate with others? (b) How would you try to overcome the barrier? **[Speculate]**

EXTEND

6. What services can a government or community provide to people with a limited understanding of English? **[Community Link]**

Guide for Responding *(continued)*

◆ Reading Strategy

EVALUATE A WRITER'S MESSAGE

All of these writers use their own experiences to convey messages that readers may be able to apply to their own lives. As a reader, it's your job to **evaluate each writer's message**—to judge it critically and to decide whether you do or do not agree with it.

1. (a) What does Rita Dove believe about the power of books? (b) What evidence does she provide to support her opinion? (c) How might someone disagree with this opinion? (d) Considering your answers to the previous questions, explain whether you do or do not agree with the author's message. Support your answer.

2. (a) What does Amy Tan's essay reveal about how language differences can lead to misconceptions or stereotypes? (b) What evidence does she provide to support her opinion? (c) How might someone disagree with this opinion? (d) Considering your answers to the previous questions, explain whether you do or do not agree with the author's message. Support your answer.

◆ Literary Focus

REFLECTIVE ESSAY

A **reflective essay** explores the meaning of a writer's personal experiences or observations. Because of their informal and autobiographical nature, reflective essays generally reveal something about the writer's personality and values.

1. (a) What does Cisneros's list of accomplishments suggest about her values? (b) Does the last paragraph confirm or contradict that idea? Explain.

2. (a) What kind of child does Dove say she was? (b) How do you think Dove feels about her childhood?

3. How has Tan's attitude toward her mother changed as she has grown older? Support your answer with evidence from her essay.

◆ Build Vocabulary

USING THE WORD ROOTS -scrib- AND -script-

The roots -*scrib*- and -*script*- mean "write." Using each pair of words below, write a sentence that demonstrates the meaning of this root.

1. scribble, child   3. inscription, trophy

2. prescription, doctor   4. author, manuscript

USING THE WORD BANK

Write the following sentences in your notebook. Fill in each blank with a word from the Word Bank.

1. The wandering tribe led a ____?____ life in the desert.
2. A person who loves language and words might pursue ____?____ studies.
3. The kindly old neighbor had a ____?____ influence on the children.
4. Her ____?____ social extroversion began to reveal itself even before she could talk.
5. The archaeologist ____?____ the message that was carved on the wall of the tomb.
6. Having accepted two invitations for the same date, he found himself in a social ____?____.
7. Scientists use ____?____ evidence to prove or disprove a hypothesis.

◆ Grammar and Style

VARYING SENTENCE STRUCTURE

Writers use a variety of sentence structures to lend a rhythmic flow to their work and avoid choppiness and dull predictability. As you read these essays, you may have noticed that the writers used a variety of simple, compound, and complex sentences.

Looking at Style Compare Tan's first two paragraphs with the rest of her essay. (a) What do you notice? (b) How does choice of sentence structure affect the rhythm of her writing? (c) How does this style relate to Tan's message?

Writing Application Using a variety of sentence structures, write a paragraph in which you discuss the essay you enjoyed most and explain the reasons.

Build Your Portfolio

 **Idea Bank**

Writing

1. Letter to the Author Respond to one of these essays by writing a letter to the author. Explain what you liked, what you didn't like, and ask any questions you might have.

2. Science-Fiction Story In "For the Love of Books," Rita Dove summarizes a science-fiction story she read as a child that made a big impression on her. Write your own science-fiction story in which you are the central character.

3. Television Pilot Imagine Sandra (Cisneros), Rita (Dove), and Amy (Tan) spending the summer of 1967 together at a creative-writing camp. Using this as a premise, write a script for a television sit-com pilot. Use your imagination as well as what you know from the essays you have read. **[Media Link]**

Speaking and Listening

4. Speech What message would Cisneros, Dove, or Tan convey in a speech to aspiring young writers? Develop and deliver the speech that one of these writers might present.

5. Monologue As Tan argues, do you use more than one kind of English in your daily life? Write and deliver a monologue that utilizes all the "Englishes" in your life. **[Performing Arts Link]**

Projects

6. Icons To overcome language barriers, icons or symbols are often used in place of words in public places. Create a series of icons to represent places and people in your school. **[Art Link]**

7. Readers' Club In a group, choose another work by Cisneros, Dove, or Tan. After reading the work, discuss it—taking into account what you know about the author.

 Writing Mini-Lesson

A Treasured Memory

In each of the essays you read, the author vividly describes memories from childhood. Such remembrances are an integral part of personal and reflective essays. Think of an event or moment from your past that meant a great deal to you. Write a remembrance of it. In describing your experience, concentrate on creating a single impression that will stand out in your reader's mind.

Writing Skills Focus: Main Impression

To create a **main impression,** use language and sensory details that contribute to the impression you're developing, and avoid details that don't fit in.

Model From the Essay

From the time I began to read, as a child, I loved to feel [books's] heft in my hand and the warm spot caused by their intimate weight in my lap; I loved the crisp whisper of a page turning, the musky odor of old paper and the sharp inky whiff of new pages. . . .

Notice how Rita Dove uses precise sensory details, like "warm spot," "crisp whisper," and "sharp inky whiff." Together these details add up to a single impression: her passion for books.

Prewriting Once you have decided on the topic for your remembrance, gather descriptive details. Make lists of sensory words and images that relate to the moment or event you are going to describe.

Drafting Refer to your list of sensory details as you draft your remembrance. Include only those details that will help build the impression you're creating. Be aware that the tone of your writing also conveys your attitude toward your subject.

Revising Think about whether you've created a single strong impression. To focus your impression, consider adding or eliminating details. Check that your organization is clear and that the tone of your writing accurately reflects your feelings.

Writing Process Workshop

Job Portfolio

Essays like the ones in this section serve as a written record of where our culture has been—and perhaps as an indication of where it is going. A résumé serves a similar purpose for the individual; it is a written summary of education, qualifications, and work experience that a prospective employer can use to evaluate your suitability for a new position. A job portfolio that includes a résumé, a cover letter, and, where appropriate, job samples or references, gives an employer a quick summary of what you have to offer. The portfolio often determines whether you will progress to the next step in the job-seeking process: the interview.

Use these skills, introduced in this section's Writing Mini-Lessons, to help you develop a professional job portfolio.

Writing Skills Focus

▶ **Keep to a format** by following the conventions of business letters and résumés. (See p. 1003.)

▶ **Convey a main impression.** Highlight information that is relevant to the prospective job and downplay irrelevant details. (See p. 1018.)

▶ **Maintain accuracy** by truthfully representing job descriptions, achievements, and other details.

Look at this sample résumé.

WRITING MODEL

Excerpt from a résumé

QUALIFICATIONS
Experienced musician. Own two guitars; familiar with all major brands. ①

WORK EXPERIENCE ②
Sept. 1997–Present: Cashier
Carlyle Clothing, Riverview Mall.
  • Ring up sales and returns.
  • Keep inventory up to date.
Summer 1995–1996 ③: Library Clerk
Holmstead Branch Library.
  • Helped patrons locate resources.
  • Shelved and repaired books. ④

① The author includes information that is relevant to the music store job she is seeking.

② Each section of the résumé is clearly labeled.

③ The résumé accurately reflects the dates of employment.

④ Beyond job titles, the résumé provides details about responsibilities.

Applying Language Skills: Capitalization

Capitalize all proper nouns and adjectives; months and days of the week; and geographical names, such as the name of a street, city, state, country, or body of water.

Examples:

WORK EXPERIENCE:

May 1998–August 1998

   Computer Corner

   660 King's Highway, Grenville

EDUCATION:

June 1998–July 1998

   Oxford University, England

   Young Scholars of America study program

Practice Revise the following, correcting any errors in capitalization.

As my Résumé indicates, I was a student at Kennedy high school in dallas until last may, when I moved to Austin.

Writing Application Check that you have capitalized businesses, organizations, or schools in your job portfolio.

Writer's Solution Connection
Writing Lab

For tips on formatting business letters and résumés, review the Interactive Workplace Writing Models in the Organizing Details section of the tutorial on Practical and Technical Writing.

Prewriting

Choose a Topic Look through the help wanted ads in a newspaper. Find a job that interests you, and create either your own job portfolio or that of an "ideal candidate" for that job. You may find it helpful to learn more about the backgrounds of people who have held similar positions. You may also use any of the career openings suggested below:

Topic Ideas

- Intern at a law office
- Tour guide in Mexico
- Poet Laureate of your town or community
- President of the United States

Make Note Cards For each skill or experience you wish to include on your résumé, create an individual note card on which you record the *who*, *what*, *where*, and *when* of the experience. Here's how a note card might look:

1997–1998	Production assistant
	Mayer's Printing Co.
	Detroit, MI
Assisted with page layout and copyediting.	

Include All Relevant Abilities Don't forget to record additional qualifications or skills, such as fluency in a foreign language, computer skills, and so on.

Drafting

Follow a Clear Organization Organize your note cards to help you decide which section headings—Objective, Qualifications, Work Experience, Related Experience, Education, Awards, References, and so on—to use. Record the headings, then fill in the information from the appropriate note cards.

Use a Template Use a consistent format; for example, if you write the first section heading in bold capital letters, use the same type style for subsequent headings. Follow a standard business letter format for your cover letter. Most word-processing programs include templates for résumés and business letters. Adapt them to fit your needs.

Be Accurate Do not exaggerate your duties, skills, or other details when describing your personal job experiences. Make sure all employment dates and job titles are correct.

Revising

Use a Peer Reviewer Ask a classmate to take on the role of a potential employer. Have him or her review and critique your portfolio, paying particular attention to the following:

▶ Is the portfolio well organized and professional?

▶ Is the résumé consistent in format? Has the writer used formal business letter format for the cover letter?

▶ Does the portfolio emphasize experiences and qualifications that are relevant to the prospective job?

▶ Is information truthful and accurate?

Proofread Reread your portfolio, checking for errors in spelling, capitalization, punctuation, and formatting. Finally, review each component to be sure that any personal information is accurate and factually correct.

REVISION MODEL

① Ms. Singer:
Dear ∧Anne,∘

I am currently a junior at J.L. Mann High School

② National Championship
and the president of the ∧Debate team. I have extensive∘

③ I have enjoyed spending the last two semesters as a disc jockey
experience in radio. I am interested in a summer
for my school's dances.
internship at your radio station so that I can learn more

about the field of communications and media.

① In keeping with the format of a business letter, an informal greeting is replaced with a formal salutation.

② Inserting this detail reinforces the writer's qualifications as a skilled communicator.

③ By deleting a misleading statement and adding a more accurate one, the writer avoids exaggerating her experience.

Publishing

▶ **Send Your Portfolio Out** Submit your portfolio to several prospective employers. If your work is fictitious, ask employers in appropriate professions to review your writing.

▶ **Personal Portfolio** Keep copies of all your cover letters and résumés in a binder for future reference. Date each copy, noting any responses it may have received. Use your samples as models the next time you need to prepare a job portfolio.

APPLYING LANGUAGE SKILLS: Action Verbs

An **action verb** expresses physical or mental action and tells what the subject is doing or thinking. Wherever possible, replace the linking verbs *am, is, are, was,* and *were* with action verbs to make your résumé stronger and more effective:

Linking Verb:
I was the manager.

Action Verb:
I managed four clerks and organized the schedule.

Practice Replace each italicized phrase with an action verb, revising the sentences as necessary.

1. He *was a* stock clerk.

2. She *is* a camp counselor.

3. I *am* the director.

Writing Application Use a variety of action verbs to describe work-related responsibilities and experiences.

Writer's Solution Connection
Language Lab

For more help with action verbs, see the Writing With Nouns and Verbs lesson in the Writing Style Unit of the Language Lab CD-ROM.

Ads are everywhere—billboards, posters, television, radio, and print media. They demand: Do this! Buy this! Think this! It can be overwhelming. Which claims can you believe? Which products or services are right for you? To make those decisions, you need to learn to evaluate the advertisements you see and hear.

The Bottom Line The underlying goal of any advertisement is to persuade you to buy a product or service or to take a certain action. By employing various persuasive techniques, ads may distract you from thorough evaluation of their contents. Recognize this persuasive purpose, and resist making too quick judgments.

What Is the Message? Before responding to an ad, understand its contents. Examine statements and facts carefully.

- What does the ad want you to do, buy, or think?
- How does the ad appeal to emotions and attitudes?
- Does the product or service offer any real benefits or is its appeal based only on image or perception?
- Are the ad's statements well supported by evidence? Are any statements simply opinions?

Take the Next Step Responding to ads is very personal. Only you can decide whether an ad's statements and appeals are convincing. Evaluate carefully before taking action to pursue or reject the ad's appeal.

Apply the Strategy

You and your friends are serious music fans, but you have limited time and money to spend on buying cassettes and CDs. Evaluate this advertisement and the service it presents:

1. What is this advertisement selling?
2. What costs and benefits are presented?
3. How does the ad appeal to your feelings?
4. How does the evidence support the ad's claims?
5. List the potential hidden costs of buying through this service.
6. Based on your evaluation of this advertisement, would you buy from SoundBites? Explain.

Don't waste your money on music that doesn't move you! Don't waste your time traveling to the mall's music store!
With SoundBites you can listen to—and buy—music without ever leaving home!

For the price of a phone call, you get:

- Listings of this week's hot new releases in Jazz, New Age, Pop, or Classical
- Instant access to the latest information to help you buy smart, including:
  — artists and producers
  — brief comments by top music reviewers
  — 30-second cuts from selected songs
  — cost and local availability
- News of upcoming live performances in your area
- Direct purchase of cassettes or CDs

Maximize your music experience and budget today!

SoundBites
the direct music source
Call **GO MUSIC (466-8742)**

or visit us at
www.soundbite.com
It's the newest and easiest way to buy the music you love.

✔ *Here are other situations in which evaluating advertising is important:*
- *Deciding where to shop*
- *Deciding what brands to buy*
- *Choosing a film to see*
- *Planning a vacation or other trip*

PART **3**

Social Protest

Choke, 1964, Robert Rauschenberg, Oil and screenprint on canvas, 60" x 48", Washington University Gallery of Art, St. Louis, © Robert Rauschenberg/Licensed by VAGA, New York, NY

The freedom to speak out against policies we disagree with and to fight against injustices we see has always been one of the rights that Americans most cherish. During the 1950's, 1960's, and early 1970's, Americans passionately exercised this right, fighting for civil rights, opposing an unpopular war, and pointing out the dangers of nuclear proliferation. The literature in this section illustrates the important contributions made by writers in addressing such issues.

Guide for Interpreting

James Baldwin *(1924–1987)*

James Baldwin once told an interviewer that he "never had a childhood." Because his stepfather worked long hours as both a preacher and a factory hand, Baldwin had much of the responsibility for raising his eight siblings. The only leisure activity he was able to pursue was reading, and Baldwin read *Uncle Tom's Cabin* and *A Tale of Two Cities* "over and over again." This early passion for reading fueled his imagination, planting the seeds of inspiration for his later success as a writer.

A Harlem Childhood Baldwin was born in Harlem, New York. Even as a boy, it was clear that he had a gift for words, but his deeply religious parents disapproved of his interest in literature. They wanted him to become a preacher like his stepfather. At age fourteen, he did. He didn't give up his literary pursuits, however.

Baldwin was encouraged by African American poet Countee Cullen, who taught at his junior high school.

With Cullen's support, he wrote poetry and worked on his school's literary magazine. Inspired by the success of Richard Wright's novel *Native Son,* which proved to him that an African American could have success as a writer, Baldwin eventually decided to abandon preaching and devote his life to writing.

The Road to "Writer" For several years, Baldwin worked at odd jobs while writing and reading in his spare time. At age twenty-four, he won a fellowship that enabled him to travel to Europe and write. In 1953, he published his first novel, *Go Tell It on the Mountain*, a semi-autobiographical story about a boy preacher. The novel marked the beginning of a distinguished literary career that included the novels *Giovanni's Room* (1956), *Another Country* (1962), and *Tell Me How Long the Train's Been Gone* (1968); a play set in the American South called *Blues for Mr. Charlie* (1964); and several notable essay collections.

A Powerful Witness Baldwin once said, "One writes out of one thing only—one's own experience. Everything depends on how relentlessly one forces from this experience the last drop, sweet or bitter, it can possibly give." Baldwin's work bears powerful witness to his own experience as an African American. In his writing, he expresses the need for social justice, while delving into such universal concerns as the desire for love and the need for acceptance. His books, which dig deeply into contemporary life, are sometimes painful to read, but the pain is always tempered by hope.

Baldwin often repeated one phrase—"People can be better than they are." This simple idea is woven into everything he wrote.

◆ Background for Understanding

ART: HARLEM AS A CULTURAL CENTER

Harlem, the New York City neighborhood where James Baldwin grew up, has been a vital center of African American life and culture since southern blacks began migrating there in the 1910's. In the 1920's, it was the hub of the Harlem Renaissance, an African American literary and artistic movement. One of the leading writers of that movement was James Baldwin's teacher, Countee Cullen.

When the Depression hit in the 1930's, the largely poor population of Harlem plunged even deeper into poverty. Despite economic hardships, however, Harlem's culture—its churches, theaters, music, and dance centers—remained strong.

◆ *Literature and Your Life*

CONNECT YOUR EXPERIENCE

As you'll see, "The Rockpile" takes place in a poor urban community where people faced difficult obstacles. However, from the penthouse apartments on the wealthiest city block to the sprawling acres of land in isolated farm communities, every neighborhood has distinct advantages and unique problems.

Journal Writing How do you think communities can shape people's actions, attitudes, or values? Jot down your response.

THEMATIC FOCUS: SOCIAL PROTEST

Although Baldwin may have written this story to explore the way people interact when under pressure, he also reveals how poverty's problems can extend beyond simple finances.

◆ Build Vocabulary

PREFIXES: *mal-*

In this story, you'll find the word *malevolence*, which begins with *mal-*, a prefix meaning "bad" or "wrong." *Mal-* is a clue that *malevolence* refers to something bad. In fact, it means "ill will" or "the state of wishing evil toward others."

WORD BANK

Before you read, preview this list of words from the story.

> intriguing
> benevolent
> decorously
> latent
> engrossed
> jubilant
> arrested
> malevolence
> perdition

◆ Grammar and Style

RESTRICTIVE AND NONRESTRICTIVE ADJECTIVE CLAUSES

"The Rockpile" contains examples of **adjective clauses** — subordinate clauses used as adjectives to modify nouns or pronouns. **Restrictive adjective clauses** are necessary to complete the meaning of the noun or pronoun they modify. **Nonrestrictive adjective clauses** provide additional but not necessary information. They are set off from the rest of the sentence with commas. Here are two examples from the story:

> . . . he was afraid of the rockpile and of the boys *who played there.*
> [restrictive clause explains essential information—which *boys* he fears]

> Once a boy, *whose name was Richard*, drowned in the river.
> [nonrestrictive clause provides more information about the *boy*]

◆ Literary Focus

SETTING

Just as real people are shaped to some extent by the environments in which they live, the characters in a work of fiction are often shaped by the **setting**—the specific time and place in which the action of the story occurs. Drawn from Baldwin's childhood experiences, "The Rockpile" is set in Harlem during the 1930's. Life in that place and time was influenced by the difficult economic and social realities that people faced. In addition, Harlem's physical features at times had a direct impact on people's lives. As you read, think about how the setting affects the characters' personalities and actions.

◆ Reading Strategy

IDENTIFY CAUSE AND EFFECT

In "The Rockpile," a child's disobedience sparks a painful family confrontation. You will understand the characters better if you **identify cause-and-effect** relationships in the text. This means determining what causes the characters' behavior and noting what effects each character's words or actions have on other characters or on the situation. Identifying causes and effects can give you insight into the complicated family dynamics exposed in "The Rockpile."

The Rockpile

James Baldwin

Push to Walk, (collage 48" x 48"), Phoebe Bea

▲ **Critical Viewing** How does the setting depicted in this painting connect to Baldwin's story? **[Connect]**

A cross the street from their house, in an empty lot between two houses, stood the rockpile. It was a strange place to find a mass of natural rock jutting out of the ground; and someone, probably Aunt Florence, had once told them that the rock was there and could not be taken away because without it the subway cars underground would fly apart, killing all the people. This, touching on some natural mystery concerning the surface and the center of the earth, was far too intriguing an explanation to be challenged, and it invested the rockpile, moreover, with such mysterious importance that Roy felt it to be his right, not to say his duty, to play there.

Other boys were to be seen there each afternoon after school and all day Saturday and Sunday. They fought on the rockpile. Sure footed, dangerous, and reckless, they rushed each other and grappled on the heights, sometimes disappearing down the other side in a confusion of dust and screams and upended, flying feet. "It's a wonder they don't kill themselves," their mother said, watching sometimes from the fire escape. "You children stay away from there, you hear me?" Though she said "children" she was looking at Roy, where he sat beside John on the fire escape. "The good Lord knows," she continued, "I don't want you to come home bleeding like a hog every day the Lord sends." Roy shifted impatiently, and continued to stare at the street, as though in this gazing he might somehow acquire wings. John said nothing. He had not really been spoken to: he was afraid of the rockpile and of the boys who played there.

Each Saturday morning John and Roy sat on the fire escape and watched the forbidden street below. Sometimes their mother sat in the room behind them, sewing, or dressing their younger sister, or nursing the baby, Paul. The sun fell across them and across the fire escape with a high, <u>benevolent</u> indifference; below them, men and women, and boys and girls, sinners all, loitered; sometimes one of the church-members passed and saw them and waved. Then, for the moment that they waved <u>decorously</u> back, they were intimidated. They watched the saint, man or woman, until he or she had disappeared from sight. The passage of one of the redeemed made them consider, however vacantly, the wickedness of the street,

◆ **Literary Focus**
Note that the story begins with the setting. What is the significance of this?

their own <u>latent</u> wickedness in sitting where they sat; and made them think of their father, who came home early on Saturdays and who would soon be turning this corner and entering the dark hall below them.

But until he came to end their freedom, they sat, watching and longing above the street. At the end of the street nearest their house was the bridge which spanned the Harlem River[1] and led to a city called the Bronx; which was where Aunt Florence lived. Nevertheless, when they saw her coming, she did not come from the bridge, but from the opposite end of the street. This, weakly, to their minds, she explained by saying that she had taken the subway, not wishing to walk, and that, besides, she did not live in *that* section of the Bronx. Knowing that the Bronx was across the river, they did not believe this story ever, but, adopting toward her their father's attitude, assumed that she had just left some sinful place which she dared not name, as, for example, a movie palace.

In the summertime boys swam in the river, diving off the wooden dock, or wading in from the garbage-heavy bank. Once a boy, whose name was Richard, drowned in the river. His mother had not known where he was; she had even come to their house, to ask if he was there. Then, in the evening, at six o'clock, they had heard from the street a woman screaming and wailing; and they ran to the windows and looked out. Down the street came the woman, Richard's mother, screaming, her face raised to the sky and tears running down her face. A woman walked beside her, trying to make her quiet and trying to hold her up. Behind them walked a man, Richard's father, with Richard's body in his arms. There were two white policemen walking in the gutter, who did not seem to know what should be done. Richard's father and Richard were wet, and Richard's body lay across his father's arms like a cotton baby. The woman's screaming filled all the street; cars slowed down and the people in the cars stared; people opened their windows and looked out and came rushing out of doors to stand in the gutter, watching. Then the small procession disappeared within the house which stood beside the rockpile. Then, *"Lord, Lord, Lord!"*

◆ **Build Vocabulary**

intriguing (in trēg´ iŋ) *adj.*: Interesting or curious

benevolent (bə nev´ ə lənt) *adj.*: Kindly; charitable

decorously (dek´ ər əs lē) *adv.*: Characterized by or showing decorum and good taste

latent (lāt´ ənt) *adj.*: Present but invisible or inactive

---

1. **Harlem River:** River that separates Manhattan Island from the Bronx in New York City.

cried Elizabeth, their mother, and slammed the window down.

One Saturday, an hour before his father would be coming home, Roy was wounded on the rockpile and brought screaming upstairs. He and John had been sitting on the fire escape and their mother had gone into the kitchen to sip tea with Sister McCandless. By and by Roy became bored and sat beside John in restless silence; and John began drawing into his schoolbook a newspaper advertisement which featured a new electric locomotive. Some friends of Roy passed beneath the fire escape and called him. Roy began to fidget, yelling down to them through the bars. Then a silence fell. John looked up. Roy stood looking at him.

"I'm going downstairs," he said.

"You better stay where you is, boy. You know Mama don't want you going downstairs."

"I be right *back*. She won't even know I'm gone, less you run and tell her."

"I ain't *got* to tell her. What's going to stop her from coming in here and looking out the window?"

"She's talking," Roy said. He started into the house.

◆ **Reading Strategy**
What causes Roy to go to the rockpile?

"But Daddy's going to be home soon!"

"I be back before *that*. What you all the time got to be so *scared* for?" He was already in the house and he now turned, leaning on the windowsill, to swear impatiently, "I be back in *five* minutes."

John watched him sourly as he carefully unlocked the door and disappeared. In a moment he saw him on the sidewalk with his friends. He did not dare to go and tell his mother that Roy had left the fire escape because he had practically promised not to. He started to shout, *Remember, you said five minutes!* but one of Roy's friends was looking up at the fire escape. John looked down at his schoolbook: he became engrossed again in the problem of the locomotive.

When he looked up again he did not know how much time had passed, but now there was a gang fight on the rockpile. Dozens of boys fought each other in the harsh sun: clambering up the rocks and battling hand to hand, scuffed shoes sliding on the slippery rock; filling the bright air with curses and jubilant

cries. They filled the air, too, with flying weapons: stones, sticks, tin cans, garbage, whatever could be picked up and thrown. John watched in a kind of absent amazement—until he remembered that Roy was still downstairs, and that he was one of the boys on the rockpile. Then he was afraid; he could not see his brother among the figures in the sun; and he stood up, leaning over the fire-escape railing. Then Roy appeared from the other side of the rocks; John saw that his shirt was torn; he was laughing. He moved until he stood at the very top of the rockpile. Then, something, an empty tin can, flew out of the air and hit him on the forehead, just above the eye. Immediately, one side of Roy's face ran with blood, he fell and rolled on his face down the rocks. Then for a moment there was no movement at all, no sound, the sun, arrested, lay on the street and the sidewalk and the arrested boys. Then someone screamed or shouted; boys began to run away, down the street, toward the bridge. The figure on the ground, having caught its breath and felt its own blood, began to shout. John cried, "Mama! Mama!" and ran inside.

"Don't fret, don't fret," panted Sister McCandless as they rushed down the dark, narrow, swaying stairs, "don't fret. Ain't a boy been born don't get his knocks every now and again. *Lord*!" they hurried into the sun. A man had picked Roy up and now walked slowly toward them. One or two boys sat silent on their stoops; at either end of the street there was a group of boys watching. "He ain't hurt bad," the man said, "wouldn't be making this kind of noise if he was hurt real bad."

Elizabeth, trembling, reached out to take Roy, but Sister McCandless, bigger, calmer, took him from the man and threw him over her shoulder as

◆ **Reading Strategy**
What is the immediate effect of Roy's accident?

she once might have handled a sack of cotton. "God bless you," she said to the man, "God bless you, son." Roy was still screaming.

◆ **Build Vocabulary**

engrossed (in grōst´) *adj.*: Occupied wholly; absorbed

jubilant (jo͞o´ bəl ənt) *adj.*: Joyful and triumphant

arrested (ə rest´ id) *adj.*: Stopped

Elizabeth stood behind Sister McCandless to stare at his bloody face.

"It's just a flesh wound," the man kept saying, "just broke the skin, that's all." They were moving across the sidewalk, toward the house. John, not now afraid of the staring boys, looked toward the corner to see if his father was yet in sight.

Upstairs, they hushed Roy's crying. They bathed the blood away, to find, just above the left eyebrow, the jagged, superficial scar. "Lord, have mercy," murmured Elizabeth, "another inch and it would've been his eye." And she looked with apprehension toward the clock. "Ain't it the truth," said Sister McCandless, busy with bandages and iodine.

"When did he go downstairs?" his mother asked at last.

Sister McCandless now sat fanning herself in the easy chair, at the head of the sofa where Roy lay, bound and silent. She paused for a moment to look sharply at John. John stood near the window, holding the newspaper advertisement and the drawing he had done.

"We was sitting on the fire escape," he said. "Some boys he knew called him."

"When?"

"He said he'd be back in five minutes."

"Why didn't you tell me he was downstairs?"

He looked at his hands, clasping his notebook, and did not answer.

"Boy," said Sister McCandless, "you hear your mother a-talking to you?"

He looked at his mother. He repeated:

"He said he'd be back in five minutes."

"He said he'd be back in five minutes," said Sister McCandless with scorn, "don't look to me like that's no right answer. You's the man of the house, you supposed to look after your baby brothers and sisters—you ain't supposed to let them run off and get half-killed. But I expect," she added, rising from the chair, dropping the cardboard fan, "your Daddy'll make you tell the truth. Your Ma's way too soft with you."

He did not look at her, but at the fan where it lay in the dark red, depressed seat where she had been. The fan advertised a pomade[2] for the hair and showed a brown woman and her baby, both with glistening hair, smiling happily at each other.

"Honey," said Sister McCandless, "I got to be moving along. Maybe I drop in later tonight. I don't reckon you going to be at Tarry Service tonight?"

Tarry Service was the prayer meeting held every Saturday night at church to strengthen believers and prepare the church for the coming of the Holy Ghost on Sunday.

"I don't reckon," said Elizabeth. She stood up; she and Sister McCandless kissed each other on the cheek. "But you be sure to remember me in your prayers."

"I surely will do that." She paused, with her hand on the door knob, and looked down at Roy and laughed. "Poor little man," she said, "reckon he'll be content to sit on the fire escape *now.*"

Elizabeth laughed with her. "It sure ought to be a lesson to him. You don't reckon," she asked nervously, still smiling, "he going to keep that scar, do you?"

"Lord, no," said Sister McCandless, "ain't nothing but a scratch. I declare, Sister Grimes, you worse than a child. Another couple of weeks and you won't be able to *see* no scar. No, you go on about your housework, honey, and thank the Lord it weren't no worse." She opened the door; they heard the sound of feet on the stairs. "I expect that's the Reverend," said Sister McCandless, placidly, "I *bet* he going to raise cain."[3]

"Maybe it's Florence," Elizabeth said. "Sometimes she get here about this time." They stood in the doorway, staring, while the steps reached the landing below and began again climbing to their floor. "No," said Elizabeth then, "that ain't her walk. That's Gabriel."

"Well, I'll just go on," said Sister McCandless, "and kind of prepare his mind." She pressed Elizabeth's hand as she spoke and started into the hall, leaving the door behind her slightly ajar. Elizabeth turned slowly back into the room. Roy did not open his eyes, or move; but she knew that he was not sleeping; he wished to delay until the last possible moment any contact with his father. John put his newspaper and his notebook on the table and stood, leaning on the table, staring at her.

"It wasn't my fault," he said. "I couldn't stop him from going downstairs."

"No," she said, "you ain't got nothing to worry about. You just tell your Daddy the truth."

---

2. **pomade** (päm ād´) *n.*: Perfumed ointment.

3. **raise cain:** Slang for "cause trouble."

He looked directly at her, and she turned to the window, staring into the street. What was Sister McCandless saying? Then from her bedroom she heard Delilah's thin wail and she turned, frowning, looking toward the bedroom and toward the still open door. She knew that John was watching her. Delilah continued to wail, she thought, angrily, *Now that girl's getting too big for that*, but she feared that Delilah would awaken Paul and she hurried into the bedroom. She tried to soothe Delilah back to sleep. Then she heard the front door open and close—too loud, Delilah raised her voice, with an exasperated sigh Elizabeth picked the child up. Her child and Gabriel's, her children and Gabriel's: Roy, Delilah, Paul. Only John was nameless and a stranger, living, unalterable testimony to his mother's days in sin.

"What happened?" Gabriel demanded. He stood, enormous, in the center of the room, his black lunchbox dangling from his hand, staring at the sofa where Roy lay. John stood just before him, it seemed to her astonished vision just below him, beneath his fist, his heavy shoe. The child stared at the man in fascination and terror—when a girl down home she had seen rabbits stand so paralyzed before the barking dog. She hurried past Gabriel to the sofa, feeling the weight of Delilah in her arms like the weight of a shield, and stood over Roy, saying:

"Now, ain't a thing to get upset about, Gabriel. This boy sneaked downstairs while I had my back turned and got hisself hurt a little. He's alright now."

Roy, as though in confirmation, now opened his eyes and looked gravely at his father. Gabriel dropped his lunchbox with a clatter and knelt by the sofa.

"How you feel, son? Tell your Daddy what happened?"

Roy opened his mouth to speak and then, relapsing into panic, began to cry. His father held him by the shoulder.

"You don't want to cry. You's Daddy's little man. Tell your Daddy what happened."

"He went downstairs," said Elizabeth, "where he didn't have no business to be, and got to fighting with them bad boys playing on the rockpile. That's what happened and it's a mercy it weren't nothing worse."

He looked up at her. "Can't you let this boy answer me for hisself?"

Ignoring this, she went on, more gently: "He got cut on the forehead, but it ain't nothing to worry about."

"You call a doctor? How you know it ain't nothing to worry about?"

◆ **Reading Strategy**
Why is Gabriel so upset by Roy's injury?

"Is you got money to be throwing away on doctors? No, I ain't called no doctor. Ain't nothing wrong with my eyes that I can't tell whether he's hurt bad or not. He got a fright more'n anything else, and you ought to pray God it teaches him a lesson."

"You got a lot to say *now*," he said, "but I'll have *me* something to say in a minute. I'll be wanting to know when all this happened, what you was doing with your eyes *then*." He turned back to Roy, who had lain quietly sobbing eyes wide open and body held rigid: and who now, at his father's touch, remembered the height, the sharp, sliding rock beneath his feet, the sun, the explosion of the sun, his plunge into darkness and his salty blood; and recoiled, beginning to scream, as his father touched his forehead. "Hold still, hold still," crooned his father, shaking, "hold still. Don't cry. Daddy ain't going to hurt you, he just wants to see this bandage, see what they've done to his little man." But Roy continued to scream and would not be still and Gabriel dared not lift the bandage for fear of hurting him more. And he looked at Elizabeth in fury: "Can't you put that child down and help me with this boy? John, take your baby sister from your mother—don't look like neither of you got good sense."

John took Delilah and sat down with her in the easy chair. His mother bent over Roy, and held him still, while his father, carefully—but still Roy screamed—lifted the bandage and stared at the wound. Roy's sobs began to lessen. Gabriel readjusted the bandage. "You see," said Elizabeth, finally, "he ain't nowhere near dead."

"It sure ain't your fault that he ain't dead." He and Elizabeth considered each other for a moment in silence. "He came mightly close to losing an eye. Course, his eyes ain't as big as your'n, so I reckon you don't think it matters so much." At this her face hardened; he smiled. "Lord, have mercy," he said, "you think you ever going to learn to do right? Where was you when all this happened? Who let him go downstairs?"

"Ain't nobody let him go downstairs, he just went. He got a head just like his father, it got to be broken before it'll bow. I was in the kitchen."

"Where was Johnnie?"

"He was in here."

"Where?"

"He was on the fire escape."

"Didn't he know Roy was downstairs?"

"I reckon."

"What you mean, you reckon? He ain't got your big eyes for nothing, does he?" He looked over at John. "Boy, you see your brother go downstairs?"

"Gabriel, ain't no sense in trying to blame Johnnie. You know right well if you have trouble making Roy behave, he ain't going to listen to his brother. He don't hardly listen to me."

"How come you didn't tell your mother Roy was downstairs?"

John said nothing, staring at the blanket which covered Delilah.

"Boy, you hear me? You want me to take a strap to you?"

"No, you ain't," she said. "You ain't going to taken no strap to this boy, not today you ain't. Ain't a soul to blame for Roy's lying up there now but you—you because you done spoiled him so that he thinks he can do just anything

and get away with it. I'm here to tell you that ain't no way to raise no child. You don't pray to the Lord to help you do better than you been doing, you going to live to shed bitter tears that the Lord didn't take his soul today." And she was trembling. She moved, unseeing, toward John and took Delilah from his arms. She looked back at Gabriel, who had risen, who stood near the sofa, staring at her. And she found in his face not fury alone, which would not have surprised her; but hatred so deep as to become insupportable in its lack of personality. His eyes were struck alive, unmoving, blind with malevolence —she felt, like the pull of the earth at her feet, his longing to witness her perdition. Again, as though it might be propitiation, she moved the child in her arms. And at this his eyes changed, he looked at Elizabeth, the mother of his children, the helpmeet given by the Lord. Then her eyes clouded; she moved to leave the room; her foot struck the lunchbox lying on the floor.

"John," she said, "pick up your father's lunchbox like a good boy."

She heard, behind her, his scrambling movement as he left the easy chair, the scrape and jangle of the lunchbox as he picked it up, bending his dark head near the toe of his father's heavy shoe.

◆ **Build Vocabulary**

malevolence (mə lev´ ə ləns) *n*.: Malice; spitefulness

perdition (pər dish´ ən) *n*.: Complete and irreparable loss; ruin

---

Guide for Responding

◆ Literature and Your Life

Reader's Response Does this story call to mind any of your own childhood experiences? Explain.

Thematic Focus Do you think the author is making a statement about families, about society, or about both in this story? Explain.

Role Play With a partner, act out a conversation between Roy and John after their father and mother have left them alone.

☑ Check Your Comprehension

1. Where are the various characters when the action of the story begins?
2. What draws Roy to the rockpile?
3. What happens at the rockpile?
4. (a) Whom does Gabriel blame for Roy's injury? (b) Whom does Elizabeth blame?

Guide for Responding (continued)

◆ Critical Thinking

INTERPRET

1. What role does John serve in the family? Support your answer. **[Analyze]**
2. What evidence is there that John's relationship with Gabriel is different from that of the other children? **[Support]**
3. (a) What conclusions can you draw about Gabriel's relationship with Elizabeth? Explain. (b) Why do his feelings toward Elizabeth soften at the end of the story? **[Draw Conclusions]**

EVALUATE

4. Whom do you blame for Roy's injury? Explain. **[Make a Judgment]**

APPLY

5. What lessons can you learn from this story that you could apply to your own life? Explain. **[Apply]**

◆ Reading Strategy

IDENTIFY CAUSE AND EFFECT

When you **identify cause-and-effect** relationships in the text, you think about what causes the characters' behavior and what effects their behavior has on others.

1. (a) Why doesn't John immediately tell his mother that Roy went to the rockpile? (b) What is the effect of this decision?
2. (a) What are the causes of Elizabeth's protectiveness toward John? (b) What is the effect on Gabriel of this protectiveness?

◆ Literary Focus

SETTING

The setting of "The Rockpile"—Harlem during the 1930's—clearly plays a dominant role in the characters' lives, shaping both their attitudes and their behavior.

1. What can you infer, or conclude, about how the setting affects the way Gabriel and Elizabeth raise their children?
2. (a) What are some of the potential dangers that the setting presents? (b) What evidence is there that the rockpile symbolizes these dangers?

◆ Build Vocabulary

USING THE PREFIX mal-

Knowing that the prefix *mal-* means "bad," "wrong," or "ill," write a definition in your notebook for these words.

1. maladjusted
2. malfunction
3. malnutrition
4. malodorous

USING THE WORD BANK

Decide whether the words in each of the following pairs are synonyms or antonyms. On your paper, write S for *Synonyms* or A for *Antonyms*.

1. intriguing, boring
2. benevolent, charitable
3. decorously, tastefully
4. latent, obvious
5. engrossed, detached
6. jubilant, despondent
7. arrested, halted
8. malevolence, kindness
9. perdition, salvation

◆ Grammar and Style

RESTRICTIVE AND NONRESTRICTIVE ADJECTIVE CLAUSES

A **restrictive adjective clause** is necessary to complete the meaning of the noun or pronoun it modifies. A **nonrestrictive adjective clause**, set off by commas, provides additional but not essential information.

Practice Copy the sentences into your notebook. Underline the adjective clause(s) in each one. For each clause, identify whether it is restrictive or nonrestrictive.

1. There were two white policemen, who did not seem to know what should be done, walking in the gutter.
2. At the end of the street nearest their house was the bridge which spanned the Harlem River . . .
3. . . . made them think of their father, who came home early on Saturdays and who . . .
4. Then the small procession disappeared within the house which stood beside the rockpile.
5. He did not look at her, but at the fan where it lay in the dark red, depressed seat where she had been.

Build Your Portfolio

Idea Bank

Writing

1. **Flyer** Create a flyer announcing the start-up meeting of a block association for Roy's block. Your first goal will be to find ways to keep children from playing on the rockpile.

2. **Movie Proposal** Write a proposal for a film based on the characters in Baldwin's story. Explain the issues and events that will be explored in the film. **[Media Link]**

3. **Psychological Profile** Imagine that you are a therapist and that Roy's family has come to you for family counseling. Write a profile of each family member and summarize the issues they face as a family. Include your recommendations for resolving these issues. **[Career Link]**

Speaking and Listening

4. **Radio Play** Turn "The Rockpile" into a radio play. Divide the story into scenes and develop a script. Include a narrator and sound effects. Record your play and share it with the class.

5. **Public Service Announcement** Many communities have recreation or after-school programs to keep kids off the streets. Write and record a public service announcement for a program in Roy's neighborhood. **[Community Link]**

Projects

6. **Book Jacket** Create a cover design for a short-story collection featuring "The Rockpile." Include a photograph, fine art, or an original drawing. Explain your concept and design. **[Art Link]**

7. **Illustrated Report** Prepare an illustrated report, based on research, comparing Harlem today with Harlem in the 1930's. Share your report with the class. **[Social Studies Link]**

Writing Mini-Lesson

Roy's Journal

In "The Rockpile," Roy's actions spark a family crisis in which much is revealed about Elizabeth, Gabriel, and John. But we never really get to look inside Roy. What is his side of the story? Write a journal entry for Roy in which he reveals his inner thoughts and conflicts. Make it convincing by using the kind of thoughts and feelings that Roy might express.

Writing Skills Focus: Personal Tone

Any time you put words in a character's mouth, it's important to make the ideas sound realistic. To make Roy's journal true to Roy's character, use a **personal tone**. To do so, consider the following suggestions:

- Use informal language—the language of everyday speech. Since journals are not meant for a wide audience, they can include sentence fragments, contractions, and slang.
- Choose words that Roy would use.
- Instead of simply recording events, include Roy's reactions, thoughts, and emotions. This may mean including details that only Roy would know.

Prewriting Consider what you already know about Roy and his relationships with his family members. Reread the story to create a timeline of events. Then, for each point on the line, jot down ideas about what Roy may be thinking and feeling.

Drafting Your primary goal is to make sure that the feelings and conflicts you present make sense for this particular character. As you draft Roy's journal, refer to your notes and keep the language personal and informal.

Revising As you revise, look for opportunities to make the tone of the journal more personal. Change words that may be too formal. Then ask yourself whether your writing shows Roy's side of the story. Does it provide insight into his behavior?

Guide for Interpreting

John Hersey *(1914–1993)*

Born in China and raised there until age ten, John Hersey returned repeatedly to East Asia during his long career as a war correspondent, novelist, and essayist.

Hersey's novels and essays examined the moral implications of the major political and historical events of his day. In 1945, he won a Pulitzer Prize for his novel *A Bell for Adano,* in which an American major discovers the human dignity of the villagers who were his enemies in World War II.

During the next two years, Hersey traveled to China and Japan for *New Yorker* and *Life* magazines, gathering material for his most famous and acclaimed book, *Hiroshima* (1946), a shocking, graphic depiction of the devastation caused by the atomic bomb that was dropped on the Japanese city of Hiroshima at the end of World War II.

Randall Jarrell *(1914–1965)*

Randall Jarrell was a talented poet, literary critic, and teacher whose poetry was praised by both writers and critics. His literary essays, many of which appear in his book *Poetry and the Age* (1953), have been credited with changing the critical tastes and trends of his time.

Born in Tennessee, Jarrell graduated from Vanderbilt University and served in the U.S. Air Force during World War II. His war experiences provided him with the material for the poems in his book *Losses* (1948). Jarrell's collections *The Seven-League Crutches* (1951) and *The Lost World* (1965) focus on childhood and innocence. *The Woman at the Washington Zoo* (1960) deals with aging and loneliness.

"The Death of the Ball Turret Gunner"—a brief poem told in the first person of a soldier experiencing his last moments in a World War II bomber plane—is one of Jarrell's most famous poems.

◆ Background for Understanding

HISTORY: WORLD WAR II

World War II began in August 1939, when German forces, following the orders of the dictator Adolf Hitler, invaded Poland. In response to this unprovoked invasion, France and Great Britain declared war on Germany. Just over two years later, the United States entered the war when Japan, a German ally, launched a surprise attack on an American naval base at Pearl Harbor in Hawaii. The war continued to escalate during the early 1940's. More than two dozen nations were eventually drawn into the conflict, and tens of millions of soldiers and civilians were killed. By 1945, the tide had turned strongly in favor of the United States and its allies. In early May 1945, the German forces surrendered. Fighting continued in the Pacific, however, as the Japanese refused to surrender.

In August 1945, American President Harry Truman faced a difficult choice. The United States had just finished developing an atomic bomb capable of mass destruction. President Truman pondered whether to use this new technology in the hope of bringing a swift end to the war, knowing that it would cause thousands of deaths. The president ultimately decided that the potential losses from a prolonged war outweighed the damage that using the bomb would cause. On August 6, an atomic bomb was dropped on Hiroshima. Three days later, one was dropped on Nagasaki. These two bombs killed more than 200,000 people, and forced the Japanese to surrender. The dropping of the bombs also marked the start of a nuclear arms race that dominated the next several decades.

from Hiroshima ◆ Losses
The Death of the Ball Turret Gunner

◆ *Literature and Your Life*

CONNECT YOUR EXPERIENCE

You may have seen movies that captured heroic deeds and bloody battles from World War II. You may even have a relative who has described firsthand experiences during the war. Yet it's probably still difficult for you to imagine what it was truly like to live through the war. These pieces will give you a better sense of what it was like to be involved in the war and help provide a picture of the events that ended the war and changed the world forever.

Journal Writing Jot down what you know about World War II. Then share this information with your classmates.

THEMATIC FOCUS: SOCIAL PROTEST

These selections all express concerns relating to the cruelties of war. Why do you think war is a frequent subject of social protest?

◆ Build Vocabulary

WORD ROOTS: -vol-

In *Hiroshima*, John Hersey uses the word *volition,* which means "the act of using the will." The meaning of the word is derived largely from the root *-vol-,* meaning "to will" or "to wish." How does this root contribute to the meaning of *volunteer* and *voluntary*?

> evacuated
> volition
> rendezvous
> philanthropies
> incessant
> convivial

WORD BANK

Preview these words from the story before you read.

◆ Grammar and Style

TRANSITIONS AND TRANSITIONAL PHRASES

Hiroshima begins: "At exactly fifteen minutes past eight in the morning, on August 6, 1945, . . ." With these words, John Hersey pins down the precise moment at which the atomic bomb exploded over Hiroshima. Hersey's opening words are an excellent example of a **transitional phrase**, a group of words that shows the relationship among ideas and details in a piece of writing. A single word that functions in the same way is a **transition**. Often, as in the example from Hersey's book, transitions and transitional phrases show time relationships, but they can also show comparisons, degrees of importance, and spatial relationships.

◆ Literary Focus

IMPLIED THEME

The **theme** is the central idea that a writer hopes to convey in a work of literature. Most often a theme is **implied**, or revealed indirectly, through the writer's choice of details, portrayal of characters and events, and use of literary devices. All three of these pieces have implied themes about war.

◆ Reading Strategy

MAKE INFERENCES ABOUT THEME

When the theme of a literary work is conveyed indirectly, it's left up to the reader to **make inferences**, or draw conclusions, about the theme by looking closely at the writer's choice of details, events, characters, and literary devices. Look at this line from "Losses":

> . . . we burned,/The cities we
> had learned about in school—

From this ironic, or surprising, contrast between education and destruction, you can infer that one of the themes of the poem is the apparent senselessness of war.

As you read, jot down details that strike you as particularly important. They will probably point to an implied theme.

from

Hiroshima

John Hersey

▲ **Critical Viewing** How effectively do these remains of the sacred tree of a Hiroshima temple convey the physical and emotional devastation of the blast? Explain. **[Evaluate]**

At exactly fifteen minutes past eight in the morning, on August 6, 1945, Japanese time, at the moment when the atomic bomb flashed above Hiroshima, Miss Toshiko Sasaki, a clerk in the personnel department of the East Asia Tin Works, had just sat down at her place in the plant office and was turning her head to speak to the girl at the next desk. At that same moment, Dr. Masakazu Fujii was settling down cross-legged to read the Osaka *Asahi* on the porch of his private hospital, overhanging one of the seven deltaic rivers which divide Hiroshima; Mrs. Hatsuyo Nakamura, a tailor's widow, stood by the window of her kitchen, watching a neighbor tearing down his house because it lay in the path of an air-raid-defense fire lane . . . and the Reverend Mr. Kiyoshi Tanimoto, pastor of the Hiroshima Methodist Church, paused at the door of a rich man's house in Koi, the city's western suburb, and prepared to unload a handcart full of things he had <u>evacuated</u> from town in fear of the massive B-29 raid which everyone expected Hiroshima to suffer. A hundred thousand people were killed by the atomic bomb, and these [four] were among the survivors. They still wonder why they lived when so many others died. Each of them counts many small items of chance or <u>volition</u>—a step taken in time, a decision to go indoors, catching one streetcar instead of the next—that spared him. And now each knows that in the act of survival he lived a dozen lives and saw more death than he ever thought he would see. At the time, none of them knew anything.

◆ **Reading Strategy**
What underlying meaning can you draw from these details about the survivors?

The Reverend Mr. Tanimoto got up at five o'clock that morning. He was alone in the parsonage, because for some time his wife had been commuting with their year-old baby to spend nights with a friend in Ushida, a suburb to the north. Of all the important cities of Japan, only two, Kyoto and Hiroshima, had not been visited in strength by *B-san*, or Mr. B, as the Japanese, with a mixture of respect and unhappy familiarity, called the B-29; and Mr. Tanimoto, like all his neighbors and friends, was almost sick with anxiety. He had heard uncomfortably detailed accounts of mass raids on Kure, Iwakuni, Tokuyama, and other nearby towns; he was sure Hiroshima's turn would come soon. He had slept badly the night before, because there had been several air-raid warnings. Hiroshima had been getting such warnings almost every night for weeks, for at that time the B-29s were using Lake Biwa, northeast of Hiroshima, as a <u>rendezvous</u> point, and no matter what city the Americans planned to hit, the Superfortresses streamed in over the coast near Hiroshima. The frequency of the warning and the continued abstinence of Mr. B with respect to Hiroshima had made its citizens jittery; a rumor was going around that the Americans were saving something special for the city.

Mr. Tanimoto was a small man, quick to talk, laugh, and cry. He wore his black hair parted in the middle and rather long; the prominence of the frontal bones just above his eyebrows and the smallness of his mustache, mouth, and chin gave him a strange old-young look, boyish and yet wise, weak and yet fiery. He moved nervously and fast, but with a restraint which suggested that he is a cautious, thoughtful man. He showed, indeed, just those qualities in the uneasy days before the bomb fell. Mr. Tanimoto had been carrying all the portable things from his church, in the close-packed residential district called Nagaragawa, to a house that belonged to a rayon manufacturer in Koi, two miles from the center of town.

◆ **Build Vocabulary**
evacuated (ē vak´ yōō āt´ əd) *v*.: To have made empty; withdrawn
volition (vō lish´ ən) *n*.: Act of using the will
rendezvous (rän´dā vōō´) *n*.: Meeting place

▲ **Critical Viewing** You may have seen photographs like this one of the aftermath of the Hiroshima bombing. How does Hersey's account change the way you view such pictures? **[Relate]**

The rayon man, a Mr. Matsui, had opened his then unoccupied estate to a large number of his friends and acquaintances, so that they might evacuate whatever they wished to a safe distance from the probable target area. Mr. Tanimoto had had no difficulty in moving chairs, hymnals, Bibles, altar gear, and church records by pushcart himself, but the organ console and an upright piano required some aid. A friend of his named Matsuo had, the day before, helped him get the piano out to Koi; in return, he had promised this day to assist Mr. Matsuo in hauling out a daughter's belongings. That is why he had risen so early.

Mr. Tanimoto cooked his own breakfast. He felt awfully tired. The effort of moving the piano the day before, a sleepless night, weeks of worry and unbalanced diet, the cares of his parish—all combined to make him feel hardly adequate to the new day's work. There was another thing, too: Mr. Tanimoto had studied theology at Emory College, in Atlanta, Georgia; he had graduated in 1940; he spoke excellent English; he dressed in American clothes; he had corresponded with many American friends right up to the time the war began; and among a people obsessed with a fear of being spied upon—perhaps almost obsessed himself—he found himself growing increasingly uneasy. The police had questioned him several times, and just a few days before, he had heard that an influential acquaintance, a Mr. Tanaka, a retired officer of the Toyo Kisen Kaisha steamship line, an anti-Christian, a man famous in Hiroshima for his showy philanthropies and notorious for his personal tyrannies, had been telling people that Tanimoto should not be trusted. In compensation, to show himself publicly a good Japanese, Mr. Tanimoto had taken on the chairmanship of his local *tonarigumi*, or Neighborhood Association, and to his other duties and concerns this position had added the business of organizing air-raid defense for about twenty families.

Before six o'clock that morning, Mr. Tanimoto started for Mr. Matsuo's house. There he found that their burden was to be a *tansu*, a large Japanese cabinet, full of clothing and household goods. The two men set out. The morning was perfectly clear and so warm that the day promised to be uncomfortable. A few minutes after they started, the air-raid siren went off—a minute-long blast that warned of approaching planes but indicated to the people of Hiroshima only a slight degree of danger, since it sounded every morning at this time, when an American weather plane came over. The two men pulled and pushed the handcart through the city streets. Hiroshima was a fan-shaped city, lying mostly on the six islands formed by the seven estuarial rivers that branch out from the Ota River; its main commercial and residential districts, covering about four square miles in the center of the city, contained three-quarters of its population, which had been reduced by several evacuation programs from a wartime peak of 380,000 to about 245,000. Factories and other residential districts, or suburbs, lay compactly around the edges of the city. To the south were the docks, an airport, and the island-studded Inland Sea. A rim of mountains runs around the other three sides of the delta. Mr. Tanimoto and Mr. Matsuo took their way through the shopping center, already full of people, and across two of the rivers to the sloping streets of Koi, and up them to the outskirts and foothills. As they started up a valley away from the tight-ranked houses, the all-clear sounded. (The Japanese radar operators, detecting only three planes,

supposed that they comprised a reconnaissance.) Pushing the handcart up to the rayon man's house was tiring, and the men, after they had maneuvered their load into the driveway and to the front steps, paused to rest awhile. They stood with a wing of the house between them and the city. Like most homes in this part of Japan, the house consisted of a wooden frame and wooden walls supporting a heavy tile roof. Its front hall, packed with rolls of bedding and clothing, looked like a cool cave full of fat cushions. Opposite the house, to the right of the front door, there was a large, finicky rock garden. There was no sound of planes. The morning was still; the place was cool and pleasant.

Then a tremendous flash of light cut across the sky. Mr. Tanimoto has a distinct recollection that it travelled from east to west, from the city toward the hills. It seemed a sheet of sun. Both he and Mr. Matsuo reacted in terror—and both had time to react (for they were 3,500 yards, or two miles, from the center of the explosion). Mr. Matsuo dashed up the front steps into the house and dived among the bedrolls and buried himself there. Mr. Tanimoto took four or five steps and threw himself between two big rocks in the garden. He bellied up very hard against one of them. As his face was against the stone, he did not see what happened. He felt a sudden pressure, and then splinters and pieces of board and fragments of tile fell on him. He heard no roar. (Almost no one in Hiroshima recalls hearing any noise of the bomb. But a fisherman in his sampan on the Inland Sea near Tsuzu, the man with whom Mr. Tanimoto's mother-in-law and sister-in-law were living, saw the flash and heard a tremendous explosion; he was nearly twenty miles from Hiroshima, but the thunder was greater than when the B-29s hit Iwakuni, only five miles away.)

When he dared, Mr. Tanimoto raised his head and saw that the rayon man's house had collapsed. He thought a bomb had fallen directly on it. Such clouds of dust had risen that there was a sort of twilight around. In panic, not thinking for the moment of Mr. Matsuo under the ruins, he dashed out into the street. He noticed as he ran that the concrete wall of the estate had fallen over—toward the house rather than away from it. In the street, the first thing

◆ **Build Vocabulary**

philanthropies (fə lan´ thrə pēz) *n*.: Charitable acts or gifts

he saw was a squad of soldiers who had been burrowing into the hillside opposite, making one of the thousands of dugouts in which the Japanese apparently intended to resist invasion, hill by hill, life for life; the soldiers were coming out of the hole, where they should have been safe, and blood was running from their heads, chests, and backs. They were silent and dazed.

Under what seemed to be a local dust cloud, the day grew darker and darker.

At nearly midnight, the night before the bomb was dropped, an announcer on the city's radio station said that about two hundred B-29s were approaching southern Honshu and advised the population of Hiroshima to evacuate to their designated "safe areas." Mrs. Hatsuyo Nakamura, the tailor's widow, who lived in the section called Nobori-cho and who had long had a habit of doing as she was told, got her three children—a ten-year-old boy, Toshio, an eight-year-old girl, Yaeko, and a five-year-old girl, Myeko—out of bed and dressed them and walked with them to the military area known as the East Parade Ground, on the northeast edge of the city. There she unrolled some mats and the children lay down on them. They slept until about two, when they were awakened by the roar of the planes going over Hiroshima.

As soon as the planes had passed, Mrs. Nakamura started back with her children. They reached home a little after two-thirty and she immediately turned on the radio, which, to her distress, was just then broadcasting a fresh warning. When she looked at the children and saw how tired they were, and when she thought of the number of trips they had made in past weeks, all to no purpose, to the East Parade Ground, she decided that in spite of the instructions on the radio, she simply could not face starting out all over again. She put the children in their bedrolls on the floor, lay down herself at three o'clock, and fell asleep at once, so soundly that when planes passed over later, she did not waken to their sound.

The siren jarred her awake at about seven. She arose, dressed quickly, and hurried to the house of Mr. Nakamoto, the head of her Neighborhood Association, and asked him what she should do. He said that she should remain at home unless an urgent warning—a series of intermittent blasts of the siren—was sounded. She returned home, lit the stove in the kitchen, set some rice to cook, and sat down to read that mornings Hiroshima *Chugoku*. To her relief, the all-clear sounded at eight o'clock. She heard the children stirring, so she went and gave each of them a handful of peanuts and told them to stay in their bedrolls, because they were tired from the night's walk. She had hoped that they would go back to sleep, but the man in the house directly to the south began to make a terrible hullabaloo of hammering, wedging, ripping, and splitting. The prefectural government,[1] convinced, as everyone in Hiroshima was, that the city would be attacked soon, had begun to press with threats and warnings for the completion of wide fire lanes, which, it was hoped, might act in conjunction with the rivers to localize any fires started by an incendiary[2] raid; and the neighbor was reluctantly sacrificing his home to the city's safety. Just the day before, the prefecture had ordered all able-bodied girls from the secondary schools to spend a few days helping to clear these lanes, and they started work soon after the all-clear sounded.

Mrs. Nakamura went back to the kitchen, looked at the rice, and began watching the man next door. At first, she was annoyed with him for making so much noise, but then she was moved almost to tears by pity. Her emotion was specifically directed toward her neighbor, tearing down his home, board by board, at a time when there was so much unavoidable destruction, but undoubtedly she also felt a generalized, community pity, to say nothing of self-pity. She had not had an easy time. Her husband, Isawa, had gone into the Army just after Myeko was born, and she had heard nothing from or of him for a long time, until, on March 5, 1942, she received a seven-word telegram: "Isawa died an honorable death at Singapore." She learned later that he

♦ Literary Focus
How does Hersey's characterization of Mrs. Nakamura hint at an implied theme related to the strength of the human spirit?

---

1. **prefectural government:** Regional districts of Japan which are administered by a governor.
2. **incendiary** (in sen´ dē er´ ē) *adj.*: Designed to cause fires.

▲ **Critical Viewing** There are no people shown in this photograph—nor in many others—depicting the devastation wrought by the Hiroshima bomb. Does the lack of humanity lessen or intensify the impact of the image? Explain. [**Assess**]

had died on February 15th, the day Singapore fell, and that he had been a corporal. Isawa had been a not particularly prosperous tailor, and his only capital was a Sankoku sewing machine. After his death, when his allotments stopped coming, Mrs. Nakamura got out the machine and began to take in piecework herself, and since then had supported the children, but poorly, by sewing.

As Mrs. Nakamura stood watching her neighbor, everything flashed whiter than any white she had ever seen. She did not notice what happened to the man next door; the reflex of a mother set her in motion toward her children. She had taken a single step (the house was 1,350 yards, or three-quarters of a mile, from the center of the explosion) when something picked her up and she seemed to fly into the next room over the raised sleeping platform, pursued by parts of her house.

Timbers fell around her as she landed, and a shower of tiles pommelled her; everything became dark, for she was buried. The debris did not cover her deeply. She rose up and freed herself. She heard a child cry, "Mother, help me!" and saw her youngest—Myeko, the

five-year-old—buried up to her breast and unable to move. As Mrs. Nakamura started frantically to claw her way toward the baby, she could see or hear nothing of her other children.

In the days right before the bombing, Dr. Masakazu Fujii, being prosperous, hedonistic,[3] and at the time not too busy, had been allowing himself the luxury of sleeping until nine or nine-thirty, but fortunately he had to get up early the morning the bomb was dropped to see a house guest off on a train. He rose at six, and half an hour later walked with his friend to the station, not far away, across two of the rivers. He was back home by seven, just as the siren sounded its sustained warning. He ate breakfast and then, because the morning was already hot, undressed down to his underwear and went out on the porch to read the paper. This porch—in fact, the whole building—was curiously constructed. Dr. Fujii was the proprietor of a peculiarly Japanese institution; a private, single-doctor hospital. This building, perched beside and over the water of the Kyo River, and next to the bridge of the same name, contained thirty rooms for thirty patients and their kinfolk—for, according to Japanese custom, when a person falls sick and goes to a hospital, one or more members

---

3. hedonistic (he de nis´ tik) *adj.*: Indulgently seeking out pleasure.

of his family go and live there with him, to cook for him, bathe, massage, and read to him, and to offer <u>incessant</u> familial sympathy, without which a Japanese patient would be miserable indeed. Dr. Fujii had no beds—only straw mats—for his patients. He did, however, have all sorts of modern equipment: an X-ray machine, diathermy[4] apparatus, and a fine tiled laboratory. The structure rested two-thirds on the land, one-third on piles over the tidal waters of the Kyo. This overhang, the part of the building where Dr. Fujii lived, was queer-looking, but it was cool in summer and from the porch, which faced away from the center of the city, the prospect of the river, with pleasure boats drifting up and down it, was always refreshing. Dr. Fujii had occasionally had anxious moments when the Ota and its mouth branches rose to flood, but the piling was apparently firm enough and the house had always held.

Dr. Fujii had been relatively idle for about a month because in July, as the number of untouched cities in Japan dwindled and as Hiroshima seemed more and more inevitably a target, he began turning patients away, on the ground that in case of a fire raid he would not be able to evacuate them. Now he had only two patients left—a woman from Yano, injured in the shoulder, and a young man of twenty-five recovering from burns he had suffered when the steel factory near Hiroshima in which he worked had been hit. Dr. Fujii had six nurses to tend his patients. His wife and children were safe; his wife and one son were living outside Osaka, and another son and two daughters were in the country on Kyushu. A niece was living with him, and a maid and a manservant. He had little to do and did not mind, for he had saved some money. At fifty, he was healthy, <u>convivial</u>, and calm, and he was pleased to pass the evenings drinking whiskey with friends, always sensibly and for the sake of conversation. Before the war, he had affected brands imported from Scotland and America; now he was perfectly satisfied with the best Japanese brand, Suntory.

◆ **Reading Strategy**
What does this detail about Dr. Fujii suggest about the effects of war on people's decisions?

---

4. **diathermy** (dī´ ə thʉr´ mē) *n*: Medical treatment in which heat is produced beneath the skin to warm or destroy tissue.

Dr. Fujii sat down cross-legged in his underwear on the spotless matting of the porch, put on his glasses, and started reading the Osaka *Asahi*. He liked to read the Osaka news because his wife was there. He saw the flash. To him—faced away from the center and looking at his paper—it seemed a brilliant yellow. Startled, he began to rise to his feet. In that moment (he was 1,550 yards from the center), the hospital leaned behind his rising and, with a terrible ripping noise, toppled into the river. The Doctor, still in the act of getting to his feet, was thrown forward and around and over; he was buffeted and gripped; he lost track of everything, because things were so speeded up; he felt the water.

Dr. Fujii hardly had time to think that he was dying before he realized that he was alive, squeezed tightly by two long timbers in a V across his chest, like a morsel suspended between two huge chopsticks—held upright, so that he could not move, with his head miraculously above water and his torso and legs in it. The remains of his hospital were all around him in a mad assortment of splintered lumber and materials for the relief of pain. His left shoulder hurt terribly. His glasses were gone. . . .

Miss Toshiko Sasaki, the East Asia Tin Works clerk, . . . got up at three o'clock in the morning on the day the bomb fell. There was extra housework to do. Her eleven-month-old brother, Akio, had come down the day before with a serious stomach upset; her mother had taken him to the Tamura Pediatric Hospital and was staying there with him. Miss Sasaki, who was about twenty, had to cook breakfast for her father, a brother, a sister, and herself, and—since the hospital, because of the war, was unable to provide food—to prepare a whole day's meals for her mother and the baby, in time for her father, who worked in a factory making rubber earplugs for artillery crews, to take the food by on his way to the plant. When she had finished

◆ **Build Vocabulary**
incessant (in ses´ənt) *adj*.: Constant; continuing or repeating in a way that seems endless
convivial (kən viv´ ē əl) *adj*.: Fond of eating, drinking, and good company; sociable

and had cleaned and put away the cooking things, it was nearly seven. The family lived in Koi, and she had a forty-five-minute trip to the tin works, in the section of town called Kannonmachi. She was in charge of the personnel records in the factory. She left Koi at seven, and as soon as she reached the plant, she went with some of the other girls from the personnel department to the factory auditorium. A prominent local Navy man, a former employee, had committed suicide the day before by throwing himself under a train—a death considered honorable enough to warrant a memorial service, which was to be held at the tin works at ten o'clock that morning. In the large hall, Miss Sasaki and the others made suitable preparations for the meeting. This work took about twenty minutes.

Miss Sasaki went back to her office and sat down at her desk. She was quite far from the windows, which were off to her left, and behind her were a couple of tall bookcases containing all the books of the factory library, which the personnel department had organized. She settled herself at her desk, put some things in a drawer, and shifted papers. She thought that before she began to make entries in her lists of new employees, discharges, and departures for the Army, she would chat for a moment with the girl at her right. Just as she turned her head away from the windows, the room was filled with a blinding light. She was paralyzed by fear, fixed still in her chair for a long moment (the plant was 1,600 yards from the center).

Everything fell, and Miss Sasaki lost consciousness. The ceiling dropped suddenly and the wooden floor above collapsed in splinters and the people up there came down and the roof above them gave way; but principally and first of all, the bookcases right behind her swooped forward and the contents threw her down, with her left leg horribly twisted and breaking underneath her. There, in the tin factory, in the first moment of the atomic age, a human being was crushed by books.

Guide for Responding

◆ Literature and Your Life

Reader's Response What thoughts remain with you after reading this account of the bombing of Hiroshima?

Thematic Focus What details imply that the author does not condone, or agree with, the bombing of Japanese cities?

Journal Writing Briefly describe your reactions to the events depicted in this account.

☑ Check Your Comprehension

1. Describe the city of Hiroshima in the hours and days preceding the explosion of the atomic bomb.
2. What factors determined whether certain individuals in Hiroshima survived or perished when the bomb exploded?
3. Describe the roles of the following people in this story: Miss Toshiko Sasaki, Dr. Masakazu Fujii, and Mrs. Hatsuyo Nakamura.

◆ Critical Thinking

INTERPRET
1. Why does Hersey spend so much time describing details of the hours preceding the bomb? **[Draw Conclusions]**
2. What is the effect of Hersey's returning to the moment of the actual explosion in his account of each individual's experience? **[Interpret]**
3. Explain the effect Hersey probably intended for the ending—Miss Sasaki's being "crushed by books"—to have on the reader. **[Infer]**
4. Why do you think Hersey told this story through the experiences and perceptions of these individuals? **[Draw Conclusions]**

APPLY
5. What does this selection reveal to you about nuclear war in general? **[Generalize]**

EXTEND
6. Compare this account of war with fictional accounts of war you have read or seen in films. **[Literature Link]**

LOSSES

Randall Jarrell

It was not dying: everybody died.
It was not dying: we had died before
In the routine crashes—and our fields
Called up the papers, wrote home to our folks,
5   And the rates rose, all because of us.
We died on the wrong page of the almanac,
Scattered on mountains fifty miles away;
Diving on haystacks, fighting with a friend,
We blazed up on the lines we never saw.
10   We died like aunts or pets or foreigners.
(When we left high school nothing else had died
For us to figure we had died like.)

In our new planes, with our new crews, we bombed
The ranges by the desert or the shore,
15   Fired at towed targets, waited for our scores—
And turned into replacements and woke up
One morning, over England, operational.
It wasn't different: but if we died
It was not an accident but a mistake
20   (But an easy one for anyone to make).
We read our mail and counted up our missions—
In bombers named for girls, we burned
The cities we had learned about in school—
Till our lives wore out; our bodies lay among
25   The people we had killed and never seen.
When we lasted long enough they gave us medals;
When we died they said, "Our casualties were low."

THE DEATH OF THE BALL TURRET GUNNER

Randall Jarrell

A ball turret was a plexiglass sphere, or circular capsule, in the underside of certain World War II bombers; it held a small man and two machine guns. When the bomber was attacked by a plane below, the gunner, hunched in his little sphere, would revolve with the turret to fire his guns from an upside-down position.

From my mother's sleep I fell into the State,
And I hunched in its belly till my wet fur froze.
Six miles from earth, loosed from its dream of life,
I woke to black flak[1] and the nightmare fighters.
5   When I died they washed me out of the turret with a hose.

---

1. flak *n.*: Anti-aircraft fire.

Guide for Responding

◆ Literature and Your Life

Reader's Response Do you share the poet's attitude toward war as he expresses it in "Losses"? Why or why not?

Thematic Focus How would you describe Randall Jarrell's view of war?

☑ Check Your Comprehension

1. In "Losses," to whom do the words *we, our,* and *us* refer?
2. For what reason did the soldiers get medals in "Losses"?
3. In "The Death of the Ball Turret Gunner," what woke the speaker when he was six miles from Earth?

◆ Critical Thinking

INTERPRET

1. In "Losses," what is the impact of the various ways in which the pilots' deaths are described in the opening stanza? **[Interpret]**
2. What is the significance of the fact that the pilots never see the people they kill? **[Analyze]**
3. (a) Who is the "they" referred to in the final line? (b) What does their comment reveal about their attitude toward the pilots? **[Infer]**
4. In "The Death ...," why might the gunner view life on Earth as a "dream"? **[Speculate]**
5. What does the final line reveal about the realities of war? **[Interpret]**

APPLY

6. How well can the ideas conveyed in these two poems be applied to other wars? **[Apply]**

Guide for Responding (continued)

◆ Reading Strategy

MAKE INFERENCES ABOUT THEME

All three pieces convey important messages about war. To grasp these messages, however, you have to **make inferences,** or draw conclusions, from key lines or passages. Explain what underlying meaning you can grasp from each of these lines.

1. "... each knows that in the act of survival he lived a dozen lives ..." (*Hiroshima*)
2. "... the night before the bomb was dropped, an announcer ... advised the population ... to evacuate to their designated 'safe areas.'" (*Hiroshima*)
3. "We died like aunts or pets or foreigners." ("Losses")
4. "When we died, they said, 'Our casualties were low.'" ("Losses")

◆ Literary Focus

IMPLIED THEME

In each of these selections, the **theme** is **implied,** rather than directly stated. State the theme of each selection, using lines like those above to support your answer. Why would the selections be less effective if their themes were directly stated?

Beyond Literature

History Connection

The Manhattan Project The Manhattan Project was the American effort to create the atomic bomb. It was a top-secret undertaking that took seven years, employed over 120,000 people, and cost more than $2 billion. On July 16, 1945, the first atomic device was set off in the desert at Alamogordo, New Mexico. It left a huge crater and shattered windows 125 miles away. As he watched the blast, physicist J. Robert Oppenheimer, who had spearheaded the entire project, remembered the words of the *Bhagavad Gita*, the Hindu holy book: "Now I am become Death, the destroyer of worlds." Do you think this quote is an appropriate description of nuclear weapons? Explain.

◆ Build Vocabulary

USING THE WORD ROOT -vol-

Several English words come from the Latin root *-vol-,* meaning "to will" or "to wish." Use a dictionary to find and write the definitions of the following words in your notebook.

1. volunteer   2. benevolence   3. malevolence

USING THE WORD BANK

On your paper, write the word that best completes each sentence.

a. incessant   **c.** rendezvous   **e.** evacuated
b. convivial   **d.** volition   **f.** philanthropies

1. The birds _____?_____ their nest and never returned to it.
2. She did extra homework of her own _____?_____, not because it was expected of her.
3. Let's establish a _____?_____, so we don't miss each other.
4. Among the financier's _____?_____ was a fund to send talented young musicians to music camp.
5. The child's _____?_____ whining bothered fellow train passengers.
6. The _____?_____ friends attend parties together regularly.

◆ Grammar and Style

TRANSITIONS AND TRANSITIONAL PHRASES

John Hersey makes it easy for the reader to place events in time order through his frequent use of **transitional phrases**—groups of words that show relationships among ideas—and **transitions**—single words that function in the same way.

Practice Add transitions to this paragraph summarizing some of the events in Hersey's account.

Mr. Tanimoto cooked his own breakfast. He started for Mr. Matsuo's house. The two men set out. An air-raid siren went off. The all-clear sounded. There was no sound of planes. A tremendous flash of light cut across the sky. Both Mr. Tanimoto and Mr. Matsuo reacted in terror.

Writing Application Write a series of paragraphs summarizing your activities one day during the past week. Use transitions to link your details.

Build Your Portfolio

Idea Bank

Writing

1. **Journal** Suppose you were aboard the airplane that dropped the atomic bomb on Hiroshima. Write a journal entry that you might have written before going to sleep that night.

2. **Poem** Write a poem of three stanzas or more in which you state your feelings about war. Imply your theme through the details you choose.

3. **Essay** Write an essay in which you explain what you can infer about either Jarrell's or Hersey's attitude toward war based on what you've just read. Cite details from the literature for support.

Speaking and Listening

4. **Debate** These selections concern events and observations of World War II, once known as "the good war." Is a "good war" possible? With classmates, divide into teams to debate this question. **[Social Studies Link]**

5. **Dramatic Reading** Rehearse and present a dramatic reading of one of Jarrell's poems. If you wish, you can supplement the reading with music. **[Performing Arts Link]**

Projects

6. **Map** Prepare a world map that shows the locations of major events of World War II, including the bombings of Hiroshima and Nagasaki. **[Social Studies Link; Art Link]**

7. **Research Report** Use library or Internet resources to learn more about Hiroshima before and after August 1945. Report on your findings in a written report. If possible, include eyewitness accounts of Japanese near the bombing sites. **[Social Studies Link]**

Writing Mini-Lesson

Introduction to a Documentary on World War II

In a film documentary on World War II, still photographs, film clips, and the recollections of eye-witnesses might be tied together with commentary provided by a narrator. Write an introduction to be read by a narrator at the beginning of such a documentary. Capture the interest of viewers and help prepare them for the events to come.

Writing Skills Focus: Knowledge Level of Readers

To write an effective introduction to a documentary, consider how much your audience already knows about the topic. Reflect on the type of audience likely to watch your documentary, and think about the following points as you decide what information to include:

- An audience familiar with World War II requires fewer basic details than one not familiar with it.
- A general audience may be bored by the small details that are apt to fascinate real World War II buffs.
- For a less-knowledgeable audience, it is important to define specialized terms and provide adequate background information.

Prewriting Conduct research in the library or on the Internet to gather information for the documentary. Choose a particular event or time period on which to focus. Then decide which events you will highlight in your introduction.

Drafting Begin with a vivid introductory sentence that grabs viewers' attention. Then describe the documentary they are about to see, using a conversational style that lends itself to oral presentation.

Revising Read your introduction aloud to make sure it is interesting and informative. Ask yourself whether you have appropriately targeted the knowledge level of your expected audience.

Guide for Interpreting

Sylvia Plath *(1932–1963)*

Despite her success as a writer, Sylvia Plath lived a short, unhappy life. She received scholastic and literary awards as a youth, and—although she suffered a nervous breakdown in her junior year—she graduated with highest honors from Smith College. In 1956, Plath married poet Ted Hughes and settled in England. Her first book of verse, *The Colossus* (1960), was the only one published during her lifetime. Four more books of poetry and a novel, *The Bell Jar* (1963), were published posthumously.

Adrienne Rich *(1929–)*

Adrienne Rich's career can be divided into two distinct stages. During the early part of her career, she wrote neatly crafted traditional verse. In contrast, her later poems are written in free verse and often explore her deepest personal feelings.

Her first volume of poetry, *A Change of World* (1951), was published just after she graduated from Radcliffe College. Since abandoning traditional poetic forms for free verse in the early 1960's, she has produced several other collections of poetry. Her later books include *An Atlas of the Difficult World* (1991) and *Dark Fields of the Republic* (1995).

Gwendolyn Brooks *(1917–)*

Gwendolyn Brooks was raised in a Chicago neighborhood known as "Bronzeville"—the setting for her first book, *A Street in Bronzeville* (1945). Though her early poems focus on suffering urban blacks who feel uprooted and are unable to make a living, Brooks's own youth was quite different—her home was warm, and her family loving and supportive. Of her childhood, she recalls, "I began to put rhymes together at about seven, at which time my parents expressed most earnest confidence that I would one day be a writer." In 1950, Brooks became the first African American writer to win a Pulitzer Prize.

Robert Hayden *(1913–1980)*

As a young, politically active writer in the 1930's, Robert Hayden protested not only the condition of African Americans, but also what he saw as the nation's inadequate care of the poor. In the 1940's, he became a poet, and he began to focus his writing on a wide range of topics; he wrote about mythology, folklore, and spiritual matters, as well as historical and current events. His volumes include *Heart-Shape in the Dust* (1940) and *A Ballad of Remembrance* (1966).

◆ Background for Understanding

LITERATURE: ROBERT HAYDEN AS POET-HISTORIOGRAPHER

Though Robert Hayden's poetry spans the range of human experience, much of it reflects his passionate, lifelong interest in African American history. His first job after graduating from Detroit City College was as a researcher of local African American history with Detroit's Federal Writer's Project. Throughout his career as a professor of literature, Hayden continued to research and write about his heritage. Several of his most significant poems deal with figures from African and African American history. In "Frederick Douglass," he pays tribute to the famous African American abolitionist; "Runagate Runagate" brings the experiences of the Underground Railroad vividly to life.

Mirror ◆ In a Classroom ◆ The Explorer
Frederick Douglass ◆ Runagate Runagate

◆ Literature and Your Life

CONNECT YOUR EXPERIENCE

It's human nature to find fault with the situations, policies, and attitudes reflected in everyday life. Maybe you think we should recycle more, or you dislike society's emphasis on appearance. While you may discuss your social concerns with your family and friends or volunteer for causes you believe in, poets often use their writing as a means of expressing their views.

Journal Writing What social issues or attitudes bother you? How do you express your concern about them?

THEMATIC FOCUS: SOCIAL PROTEST

Several of these poems reflect dissatisfaction with societal values and attitudes. What aspect of society is each poet critiquing?

◆ Reading Strategy

INTERPRET

In most poems, the central message isn't directly stated. Instead, it's left up to you to **interpret** the poem's message by looking for an underlying meaning in the words and images. Because poems tend to be brief, every word is important. Consider the impressions and associations that each word calls to mind. What common thread ties together these impressions and associations? The answer to this question will lead you to the poem's message.

◆ Grammar and Style

PARALLEL STRUCTURE

Parallel structure is the expression of similar ideas in similar grammatical forms. Poets often use parallel structure for emphasis. For example, in "The Explorer," Brooks repeats the phrase *there were* twice, to emphasize her subject's failure to find peace. While parallel structure is an effective literary device, it's important to be careful to avoid faulty parallelism—the incorrect use of dissimilar grammatical structures to express similar ideas.

Faulty: We hiked, we biked, and *camping was another activity.*

Parallel: We hiked, we biked, *and we camped.*

◆ Literary Focus

THEME AND CONTEXT

Poems often contain references, images, symbols, or ideas closely connected to historical events, mythology, or the poet's own life. To understand the **theme**, or central message, of such poems it is essential to place the details in an appropriate **context**. For example, the historical context of "Runagate Runagate" is the Underground Railroad—the method by which many slaves escaped to freedom during the 1800's. Knowing this context can help a reader determine that the theme of the poem is that people are willing to take risks and make great sacrifices to gain their freedom.

◆ Build Vocabulary

WORD ROOTS: *-cep-* AND *-cept-*

The speaker of "Mirror" asserts that it has no *preconceptions,* or "ideas formed beforehand." This word is built around the root *-cep-* or *-cept-*, meaning "to take, hold, or seize."

WORD BANK

Preview these words from the poems.

| preconceptions |
| meditate |
| din |
| wily |

MIRROR
Sylvia Plath

Mirror II, George Tooker, © Addison Gallery of American Art, Phillips Academy, Andover, Massachusetts

► **Critical Viewing**
The artist titled this painting *Mirror II*. What ideas are common to both the painting and poem? What do both names say about the human condition? **[Connect; Synthesize]**

I am silver and exact. I have no <u>preconceptions</u>.
Whatever I see I swallow immediately
Just as it is, unmisted by love or dislike.
I am not cruel, only truthful—
5   The eye of a little god, four-cornered.
Most of the time I <u>meditate</u> on the opposite wall.
It is pink, with speckles. I have looked at it so long
I think it is a part of my heart. But it flickers.
Faces and darkness separate us over and over.
10   Now I am a lake. A woman bends over me,
Searching my reaches for what she really is.
Then she turns to those liars, the candles or the moon.
I see her back, and reflect it faithfully.
She rewards me with tears and an agitation of hands.
15   I am important to her. She comes and goes.
Each morning it is her face that replaces the darkness.
In me she has drowned a young girl, and in me an old woman
Rises toward her day after day, like a terrible fish.

◆ **Build Vocabulary**

preconceptions (prē´ kən sep´ shənz) *n*.: Ideas formed beforehand

meditate (med´ ə tāt´) *v*.: Think deeply; ponder

In a CLASSROOM

Adrienne Rich

Talking of poetry, hauling the books
arm-full to the table where the heads
bend or gaze upward, listening, reading aloud,
talking of consonants, elision,[1]
5 caught in the how, oblivious of why:
I look in your face, Jude,
neither frowning nor nodding,
opaque in the slant of dust-motes over the table:
a presence like a stone, if a stone were thinking
10 *What I cannot say, is me. For that I came.*

1. **elision** (ē lizh′ ən) *n.*: Omission or slurring over of a vowel or syllable; often used in poetry to preserve meter.

Guide for Responding

◆ Literature and Your Life

Reader's Response The speaker of "Mirror" maintains: "I am not cruel, only truthful—." If the truth hurts, do you think that being truthful is cruel? Explain.

Thematic Focus What is Plath saying about the way society conditions people—particularly women—to regard the natural process of aging?

Journal Writing How would life be different if there were no mirrors? Explore this idea in a journal entry.

☑ Check Your Comprehension

1. In "Mirror," what two reflecting surfaces does the speaker name?
2. Why does the woman react to the mirror "with tears and an agitation of hands"?

◆ Critical Thinking

INTERPRET

1. (a) Who is the speaker in "Mirror"? (b) How is the speaker personified? (c) How is the speaker *unlike* a person? **[Analyze; Distinguish]**
2. In what way are the candle and the moon "liars"? **[Interpret]**
3. (a) Who is the "young girl" who has drowned? (b) Who is the "old woman"? **[Infer]**
4. (a) How does the woman feel about aging? (b) How is her attitude revealed? **[Analyze; Support]**

EVALUATE

5. Would it be possible for the woman in "Mirror" to change her attitude toward aging? Why or why not? **[Assess]**

APPLY

6. Do you think that most people share the woman's attitude toward aging? Why or why not? **[Synthesize]**

THE EXPLORER
Gwendolyn Brooks

Somehow to find a still spot in the noise
Was the frayed inner want, the winding, the frayed hope
Whose tatters he kept hunting through the <u>din</u>.
A satin peace somewhere.
5   A room of <u>wily</u> hush somewhere within.

So tipping down the scrambled halls he set
Vague hands on throbbing knobs. There were behind
Only spiraling, high human voices,
The scream of nervous affairs,
10 Wee griefs,
Grand griefs. And choices.

He feared most of all the choices, that cried to be taken.

There were no bourns.[1]
There were no quiet rooms.

---

1. **bourns** (bōrnz) *n.*: Limits; boundaries

◆ **Build Vocabulary**

din (din) *n.*: Loud continuous noise or clamor
wily (wī´ lē) *adj.*: Sly; cunning

Guide for Responding

◆ *Literature and Your Life*

Reader's Response What did you see and hear as you read this poem?

Thematic Focus Are those who live in apartment buildings deprived by their environment of the opportunity to enjoy inner—and outer—peace?

Group Discussion With a small group of classmates, share your thoughts about living in a large apartment building. What do you think are the benefits of living in such an environment? What are the drawbacks?

☑ **Check Your Comprehension**

1. What is the "inner want" of the poem's speaker?
2. What is he doing to find it?

◆ **Critical Thinking**

INTERPRET

1. (a) To which sense do Brooks's images most often appeal? Give three examples to support your answer. (b) Why is it fitting for this poem to be filled with images like these? **[Analyze]**
2. The poem's title casts a symbolic light on the lines that follow. (a) What might the explorer's apartment building symbolize? (b) What might his actions and feelings symbolize? **[Interpret]**
3. What conclusion does the explorer reach in the final two lines? **[Interpret]**
4. Why might the explorer fear choices "most of all"? **[Speculate]**

APPLY

5. Why do you think people often fear having to make choices? **[Speculate]**

Frederick Douglass[1]

Robert Hayden

When it is finally ours, this freedom, this liberty, this beautiful
and terrible thing, needful to man as air,
usable as earth; when it belongs at last to all,
when it is truly instinct, brain matter, diastole, systole,[2]
5 reflex action; when it is finally won; when it is more
than the gaudy mumbo jumbo of politicians:
this man, this Douglass, this former slave, this Negro
beaten to his knees, exiled, visioning a world
where none is lonely, none hunted, alien,
10 this man, superb in love and logic, this man
shall be remembered. Oh, not with statues' rhetoric,
not with legends and poems and wreaths of bronze alone,
but with the lives grown out of his life, the lives
fleshing his dream of the beautiful, needful thing.

---

1. **Frederick Douglass:** American abolitionist (1817?–1895).
2. **diastole** (dī as' tə lē'), **systole** (sis' tə lē'): Diastole is the normal rhythmic dilation, or opening, of the heart. Systole is the normal rhythmic closing of the heart.

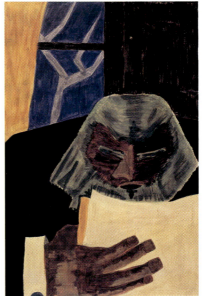

▲ **Critical Viewing** What impression of Douglass does this painting convey? **[Analyze]**

Guide for Responding

◆ *Literature and Your Life*

Reader's Response What impression do you have of Frederick Douglass after reading this poem? What kind of a person was he?

Thematic Focus What is the poet saying about the condition of African Americans in the United States at the time the poem was written?

☑ Check Your Comprehension

1. According to the speaker of "Frederick Douglass," what does not yet belong to African Americans?
2. What does the speaker say will happen when African Americans finally possess this prize?
3. In what way does the speaker say Douglass will truly be memorialized?

◆ Critical Thinking

INTERPRET

1. (a) What is paradoxical about Hayden's notion that freedom is both a beautiful and terrible thing? (b) How would you explain this characterization of freedom? **[Analyze; Interpret]**
2. What does the speaker think of the value of statues and memorials as a way of remembering a person's achievements? **[Infer]**
3. What does the speaker mean when he says that Douglass will be remembered "with the lives grown out of his life"? **[Interpret]**

APPLY

4. How do you think Frederick Douglass would respond to this poem? Explain. **[Speculate]**

Runagate Runagate[1]

Robert Hayden

I

Runs falls rises stumbles on from darkness into darkness
and the darkness thicketed with shapes of terror
and the hunters pursuing and the hounds pursuing
and the night cold and the night long and the river
5   to cross and the jack-muh-lanterns beckoning beckoning
and blackness ahead and when shall I reach that somewhere
morning and keep on going and never turn back and keep on going

        Runagate
            Runagate
                Runagate

Many thousands rise and go
10   many thousands crossing over

                O mythic North
            O star-shaped yonder Bible city[2]

Some go weeping and some rejoicing
some in coffins and some in carriages
15   some in silks and some in shackles

        Rise and go or fare you well

No more auction block for me
no more driver's lash for me

        If you see my Pompey, 30 yrs of age,
20   new breeches, plain stockings, negro shoes;
        if you see my Anna, likely young mulatto
        branded E on the right cheek, R on the left
        catch them if you can and notify subscriber.[3]
        Catch them if you can, but it won't be easy.
25   They'll dart underground when you try to catch them,
        plunge into quicksand, whirlpools, mazes,
        turn into scorpions when you try to catch them.

And before I'll be a slave
I'll be buried in my grave

30   North star and bonanza gold
        I'm bound for the freedom, freedom-bound
        and oh Susyanna don't you cry for me.

---

1. **Runagate** (run´ ə gāt): Runaway; fugitive.
2. **star-shaped yonder Bible city:** Bethlehem, a town in the free state of Pennsylvania.
3. **subscriber:** Slave holder from whom the slaves are fleeing.

Runagate

Runagate

II

Rises from their anguish and their power,

35   Harriet Tubman,[4]

woman of earth, whip-scarred,
a summoning, a shining

Mean to be free

And this was the way of it, brethren brethren,
40   way we journeyed from Can't to Can.

Moon so bright and no place to hide,
the cry up and the patterollers[5] riding,
hound dogs belling in bladed air.
And fear starts a-murbling, Never make it,
45   we'll never make it. *Hush that now,*
and she's turned upon us, leveled pistol
glinting in the moonlight:
Dead folks can't jaybird-talk, she says;
You keep on going now or die, she says.

50   Wanted   Harriet Tubman   alias The General
alias Moses   Stealer of Slaves

In league with Garrison   Alcott   Emerson
Garrett   Douglass   Thoreau   John Brown[6]

Armed and known to be Dangerous

55   Wanted   Reward   Dead or Alive

Tell me, Ezekiel, oh tell me do you see
mailed Jehovah[7] coming to deliver me?
Hoot-owl calling in the ghosted air,
five times calling to the hants[8] in the air.
60   Shadow of a face in the scary leaves,
shadow of a voice in the talking leaves:

Come ride-a my train

Oh that train, ghost-story train
through swamp and savanna
    movering movering,
over trestles of dew, through caves of
65   *the wish*
Midnight Special on a sabre track
    movering movering,
first stop Mercy and the last
    Hallelujah.

Come ride-a my train

Mean mean mean to be free.

---

4. **Harriet Tubman:** (c. 1820–1913) Escaped enslaved African American who led other slaves to safety in the North.
5. **patterollers:** Patrollers, hunting the escaped slaves.

6. **Garrison . . . John Brown:** Prominent abolitionists.
7. **Ezekiel . . . mailed Jehovah** (ē zē′ kē əl, ji hō′ və): Ezekiel was a sixth-century B.C. Hebrew prophet; Jehovah is an Old Testament name for the Judeo-Christian God.
8. **hants:** Haunts; ghosts.

Guide for Responding

◆ Literature and Your Life

Reader's Response How did your response to this poem change from stanza to stanza?

Thematic Focus What are the risks involved in the struggle for freedom?

☑ Check Your Comprehension

1. What is being described in this poem?
2. How does Harriet Tubman prevent frightened fugitives from giving themselves up?

◆ Critical Thinking

INTERPRET

1. How do lines 1–7 convey the feeling of running? **[Analyze]**
2. (a) Do you think that this poem reflects the experiences of a single speaker, or does it reflect a chorus of voices? (b) If there is more than one voice, whose voices are they? Explain your answers and support them with examples from the poem. **[Interpret; Support]**

Guide for Responding (continued)

◆ Reading Strategy

INTERPRET

To **interpret** the underlying message of most poems, it's necessary to look closely at individual words and images to find their underlying meaning. Then look for a common thread that ties together the meanings of the individual words and images.

1. (a) In "Mirror," what is the significance of the word *swallow* in line 2? (b) How does this word contribute to the message of the poem?
2. What is the significance of the medical terms Hayden uses in describing a time when freedom is "brain matter, diastole, systole, reflex action"?
3. Based on the subject of the poem, how do you interpret the meaning of lines 26–29 of "Runagate Runagate"?

◆ Grammar and Style

PARALLEL STRUCTURE

Parallel structure is the expression of similar ideas in similar grammatical forms. Be careful to avoid faulty parallelism—the incorrect use of dissimilar grammatical structures to express similar ideas.

Practice On your paper, rewrite the following sentences using correct parallel structure.

1. The woman rewards the mirror's faithful accuracy with tears, tantrums, and getting depressed.
2. High human voices are heard in one room, and from another room comes the scream of nervous affairs.
3. There is no quiet for the explorer and he's not finding any peace.
4. The runagates escaped from slavery, some in coffins, some in carriages, some in silks, and some were wearing shackles.
5. They saw the shadow of a face in the scary leaves and heard the shadow of a voice in the leaves that were talking.

Looking at Style Give at least two examples of parallel structure in the poem "Frederick Douglass." Explain how Hayden's use of parallel structure in each example reinforces key ideas.

◆ Literary Focus

THEME AND CONTEXT

Putting a poem in its historical or biographical **context** can help you reach a deeper understanding of the **theme,** or central message, of the work. For instance, in reading "Runagate Runagate," an understanding of the Underground Railroad can help you appreciate how the images in lines 37–54 contribute to the theme—the willingness of people to make sacrifices and take risks for freedom.

1. How is your understanding of "Frederick Douglass" deepened by knowing that Robert Hayden was an African American whose birth occurred a century after that of the African American abolitionist Frederick Douglass?
2. How is your understanding of the setting and theme of "The Explorer" enhanced by knowing that Gwendolyn Brooks grew up in a poor urban neighborhood?

◆ Build Vocabulary

USING THE WORD ROOTS -cep- AND -cept-

The word *preconception*—like other English words such as *deception, inception, conception, concept, reception,* and *intercept*—derives from the Latin root -cep- or -cept-, meaning "to take, hold, or seize."

Write a paragraph about a football game, using the words *concept, deceptive, reception,* and *intercept.* Refer to a dictionary if you are unsure of the meaning of a word.

USING THE WORD BANK

Write each sentence on your paper, filling in the blank with the appropriate word from the Word Bank.

1. The guru said she needed to ____?____ on the question I had posed.
2. All the jurors were required to state under oath that they had no ____?____ about the honesty of journalists.
3. The factory workers wore earplugs to protect them from the ____?____ of the machines.
4. The clever raccoon is one of the most ____?____ of animals.

Build Your Portfolio

Idea Bank

Writing

1. Letter Imagine that you are the person described in "The Explorer." In a letter to an advice columnist, outline your dilemma and ask for help in resolving it.

2. Poem or Paragraph Review "Mirror" and then rewrite it from the woman's point of view.

3. Comparison-and-Contrast Essay Write an essay in which you compare and contrast Hayden's poem about Frederick Douglass with the one written by Paul Laurence Dunbar (p. 600).

Speaking and Listening

4. Oral Interpretation "Runagate Runagate" contains vivid imagery, sound devices, and a compelling theme. Deliver a reading of the poem in which you use your voice to reinforce these elements. **[Performing Arts Link]**

5. Debate What does freedom mean to you? Do you believe that everyone in present-day America is free? With a group of classmates, stage a debate on these questions. **[Social Studies Link]**

Projects

6. Multimedia Presentation Using a mix of media—such as magazine ads, song tracks, and oral commentary—create a presentation showing our culture's emphasis on youth. **[Social Studies Link]**

7. Collage Create an illustrated profile of someone who, like Frederick Douglass, has affected the lives of many people. Use photographs, drawings, and words to capture the nature of the person's influence. **[Art Link]**

Writing Mini-Lesson

Literary Analysis

The purpose of a literary analysis is to show how various elements of a work of literature combine to convey an overall meaning or effect. Write a literary analysis of one of the poems you have just read.

Writing Skills Focus: Use of Specific Examples

A successful literary analysis contains examples and details from the work that illustrate or support the ideas presented. Review all the elements of the poetry—from form and sound devices, to figurative language, mood, and theme. Consider the following tips as you analyze a poem:

- Jot down examples of any sound devices, such as repetition, rhyme, alliteration, or onomatopoeia.
- Find examples of figurative language—language not meant to be interpreted literally—and other imagery that contribute to the poem's meaning.
- Provide several examples of how the poet's diction—or word choice—affects the tone—or the poet's or speaker's attitude toward the subject.

Prewriting Review the five poems and decide which will be the subject of your literary analysis. Read the poem you select several times and take notes on how you would describe its overall effect or meaning. Then gather examples of the poet's use of various elements to achieve this effect.

Drafting Begin your analysis with a general statement about the poem, including the points you plan to cover. Then, in the body, discuss each point in a separate paragraph, supporting each point with examples and direct quotations from the poem.

Revising Strengthen your analysis by adding support for your interpretation and replacing vague language with precise words. Double-check the accuracy of quotations and examples from the poem.

Guide for Interpreting

Colleen McElroy (1935–   )

Like a modern-day explorer, Colleen McElroy enjoys experiencing new places and has traveled widely throughout the United States and abroad. This wandering spirit is reflected in many of her poems, which are inspired by people and scenes she has discovered during her travels. McElroy's love of travel has led her to embark on ancestral searches. In her poetry, she often delves into her rich African American heritage to find connections between experiences of the past, realities of the present, and hope for the future.

After growing up in St. Louis, Missouri, McElroy graduated from Kansas State University and earned a doctorate from the University of Washington, where she is now a professor of English. A prolific writer, she has published several collections of poetry, including *The Mules Done Long Since Gone* (1973), *Music from Home: Selected Poems* (1976), and *Bone Flames* (1987). She has also published numerous short stories, as well as educational books, articles, and film scripts.

Louise Erdrich (1954–   )

Louise Erdrich, whose Chippewa ancestry has shaped her identity, was born in Little Falls, Minnesota. After receiving degrees from Dartmouth College and Johns Hopkins University, she settled in central New Hampshire and published her first volume of poems, *Jacklight* (1984). Her debut novel, *Love Medicine* (1984), is the story of three Chippewa families living on a North Dakota reservation in the early part of the twentieth century. The novel, planned and written as part of a four-novel series, enjoyed great critical and commercial success. Erdrich's reputation grew with the publication of two sequels to this book, *The Beet Queen* (1986) and *Tracks* (1988). The following year she released a second volume of poetry, *Baptism of Fire*, and in 1991 she co-wrote *The Crown of Columbus*, which offers a Native American perspective of American historical events.

Although she is principally known to the public through her fiction, Erdrich has also been praised for her poetry.

◆ Background for Understanding

SOCIAL STUDIES: ORAL HISTORY

In recent years, many Americans have grown fascinated by history gathered through interviews with individuals—especially older people—who can recall events and people of years past. Oral histories of families (containing stories, jokes, legends, and facts) are especially popular, and oral histories of communities have blossomed as well.

Oral history is as old as the study of history itself. As early as the fifth century B.C., the Greek historians Herodotus and Thucydides were relying upon the oral accounts of survivors of wars to provide a basis for their written histories. In other societies without a written language, oral information passed down from one generation to the next took the place of written historical accounts.

Oral history has been advanced by a growing interest in the lives of ordinary people from all cultures and by the commitment of anthropologists, sociologists, historians, and artists who regard oral history as a serious and vital part of all cultures.

The speaker of "For My Children" is a collector of the oral history of her people; in telling this poem, she sifts through many facts and images of the past and hands down to you those she finds most striking.

◆ *Literature and Your Life*

CONNECT YOUR EXPERIENCE

The stories we hear from relatives, family friends, and neighbors help shape our awareness of our heritage. "For My Children" vividly captures how a sense of identity is passed on from one generation to the next.

Journal Writing Make a list of images you associate with your ethnic or cultural heritage. Your list could be any combination of names of people, places, kinds of clothing, customs, or rituals.

THEMATIC FOCUS: SOCIAL PROTEST

These poems focus on Native American and African cultures. As you read, think about whether each poet is writing to celebrate, to educate, to protest—or to achieve some other purpose.

◆ Build Vocabulary

RELATED WORDS: *HERITAGE*

In "For My Children," McElroy uses the word *heritage,* which means "something handed down from ancestors." It derives from the Latin word *heres,* meaning "heir." This root also forms the basis for words such as *inherit* and *hereditary.*

> shackles
> heritage
> effigies

WORD BANK

Before you read, preview this list of words from the selections.

◆ Grammar and Style

SEQUENCE OF TENSES

By using the correct **sequence of tenses,** writers make the relationship of events in time clear. Look at these examples from "Bidwell Ghost":

Line 1: Each night she *waits* (present) by the road

Lines 4–5: It *has been* (present perfect) twenty years/since her house *surged* and *burst* (past) in the dark trees

The **present tense** in line 1 indicates habitual action. In lines 4–5, the **present perfect** indicates something that began in the past and continues to the present; the **past-tense** verbs indicate the point in the past at which the present-perfect action began.

◆ Literary Focus

LYRIC POETRY

One of the oldest and most popular verse forms, **lyric poetry** is melodic poetry that expresses the observations and feelings of a single speaker. Lyric poems were originally sung to the accompaniment of a stringed instrument called a lyre. Though no longer set to music, lyric poems still tend to be brief and melodic.

Unlike a narrative poem, which focuses on relating a story, a lyric poem focuses on producing a single, unified effect. "Bidwell Ghost," for example, focuses on the speaker's vivid impressions of a fiery tragedy that occurred twenty years before.

◆ Reading Strategy

READ IN SENTENCES

Like prose, many poems are written in sentences. They are also written in lines. However, poets don't always complete a sentence at the end of a line. A sentence may extend for several lines and then end in the middle of a line so that the poet can keep to the chosen rhythm and rhyme scheme. To understand the meaning of a poem, **read in sentences.** Notice the punctuation. Don't make a full stop at the end of a line unless there is a period, comma, colon, semicolon, or dash.

For My Children

Colleen McElroy

The Madonna and Child 1990,
Momodou Ceesay

I have stored up tales for you, my children
    My favorite children, my only children;
Of <u>shackles</u> and slaves and a bill of rights.
But skin of honey and beauty of ebony begins
5   In the land called Bilad as-Sudan,[1]
So I search for a <u>heritage</u> beyond St. Louis.

My memory floats down a long narrow hall,
    A calabash[2] of history.
Grandpa stood high in Watusi[3] shadows
10   In this land of yearly rituals for alabaster beauty;
Where <u>effigies</u> of my ancestors are captured
    In Beatle tunes,
And crowns never touch Bantu[4] heads.

My past is a slender dancer reflected briefly
15   Like a leopard in fingers of fire.
The future of Dahomey[5] is a house of 16 doors,
The totem of the Burundi[6] counts 17 warriors—
    In reverse generations.
While I cling to one stray Seminole.[7]

1. **Bilad as-Sudan** (bē lād′ äs so͞o dan′): "Land of the blacks," an Arabic expression by which Arab geographers referred to the settled African countries north of the southern edge of the Sahara.
2. **calabash** (kal′ ə bash′) n.: Dried, hollow shell of a gourd, used as a bowl or a cup.
3. **Watusi** (wä to͞o′ sē): People of east-central Africa.
4. **Bantu** (ban′ to͞o): Bantu-speaking peoples of southern Africa.
5. **Dahomey** (də hō′ mē): Old name for Benin, in west-central Africa.
6. **Burundi** (bo͝o ro͞on′ dē): Country in east-central Africa.
7. **Seminole** (sem′ ə nōl′): Native American people from Florida.

20 My thoughts grow thin in the urge to travel
        Beyond Grandma's tale
    Of why cat fur is for kitten britches;
    Past the wrought-iron rail of first stairs
        In baby white shoes,
25 To Ashanti[8] mysteries and rituals.

    Back in the narrow hallway of my childhood.
        I cradled my knees
    In limbs as smooth and long as the neck of a bud vase,
    I began this ancestral search that you children yield now
30   In profile and bust
    By common invention, in being and belonging.

    The line of your cheeks recalls Ibo[9] melodies
        As surely as oboe and flute.
    The sun dances a honey and cocoa duet on your faces.
35 I see smiles that mirror schoolboy smiles
        In the land called Bilad as-Sudan;
    I see the link between the Mississippi and the Congo.

8. Ashanti (ə shän´ tə): People of western Africa.

9. Ibo (ē´ bō´): African people of southeastern Nigeria.

◆ **Build Vocabulary**

shackles (shak´ əlz) n.: Any things that restrain a freedom or expression or action

heritage (her´ i tij´) n.: Something handed down from one's ancestors or the past

effigies (ef´ i jēz) n.: Likenesses

Guide for Responding

◆ *Literature and Your Life*

Reader's Response What is your reaction to this poem? Does it stir up thoughts about your own ancestors and cultural traditions? Why or why not?

Thematic Focus Could the poet's "ancestral search" be understood as a form of social protest? If so, how?

☑ **Check Your Comprehension**

1. Identify the cultures in which the speaker searches for evidence of her heritage.

2. Which culture mentioned in this poem is not associated with Africa?

3. To whom does the speaker address this poem?

◆ **Critical Thinking**

INTERPRET

1. What is the meaning of the word *travel* as the speaker uses it in line 20? **[Interpret]**

2. (a) What impressions of her ancestors does the speaker convey in the second and third stanzas? (b) Which images shape these impressions? **[Analyze]**

3. Describe this poem's theme. **[Interpret]**

APPLY

4. In what specific ways might educating one's children about their heritage affect the way they live today? **[Generalize]**

EXTEND

5. Identify three facts related to the heritage of a culture that is not your own—such as a friend's or neighbor's. **[Social Studies Link]**

BIDWELL GHOST
Louise Erdrich

Winter, Ozz Franca

◀ **Critical Viewing** What features of this painting are reminiscent of phrases from the poem? Explain. **[Connect]**

Each night she waits by the road
in a thin white dress
embroidered with fire.

It has been twenty years
5   since her house surged and burst in the dark trees.
Still nobody goes there.

The heat charred the branches
of the apple trees,
but nothing can kill that wood.

10 She will climb into your car
but not say where she is going
and you shouldn't ask.

Nor should you try to comb the blackened nest of hair
or press the agates of tears
15 back into her eyes.

First the orchard bowed low and complained
of the unpicked fruit,
then the branches cracked apart and fell.

The windfalls sweetened to wine
20 beneath the ruined arms and snow.
Each spring now, in the grass, buds form on the tattered wood.

The child, the child, why is she so persistent
in her need? Is it so terrible
to be alone when the cold white blossoms
25 come to life and burn?

Guide for Responding

◆ Literature and Your Life

Reader's Response What question or questions arose in your mind as you read this poem? Were they answered? Explain.

Thematic Focus In your view, how does the speaker feel about the predicament and behavior of the Bidwell ghost?

Cluster Diagram Explore your own associations by creating a cluster diagram with the word *ghost* at the center. Use the diagram as a basis for writing a ghost story.

☑ Check Your Comprehension

1. What occurred twenty years ago?
2. How does the Bidwell ghost respond to people driving along the road?
3. What happens each spring at the site in the orchard where the branches once cracked apart?

◆ Critical Thinking

INTERPRET
1. (a) How would you describe the Bidwell ghost's attitude or behavior? (b) Why might the ghost feel or behave this way? **[Interpret; Speculate]**
2. How does Erdrich suggest nature's resilience? **[Analyze]**
3. (a) Who is "the child" in the final stanza? (b) Why do you think the speaker uses this term? **[Interpret; Speculate]**

APPLY
4. Why do you think people from so many cultures are fascinated with ghosts? **[Speculate]**

EXTEND
5. How does this poem compare and contrast with stories, tales, or legends or other poems written about Native American cultures? **[Literature Link]**

Guide for Responding (continued)

◆ Literary Focus

LYRIC POETRY

Lyric poetry is melodic verse that conveys the personal observations and feelings of a single speaker and produces a single, unified effect. "For My Children" is an example of a lyric poem—a half-dozen highly musical stanzas expressing a woman's thoughts and emotions.

1. How would you describe the "observations and feelings" the speaker expresses in "Bidwell Ghost"?
2. What philosophy of life does "For My Children" convey?

◆ Reading Strategy

READ IN SENTENCES

Part of the nature of poetry is its unique form. Poets write in lines and stanzas, often breaking sentences in the process. However, sentences express complete thoughts and are critical to the poet's ability to communicate.

Reading a poem in sentences rather than in poetic lines can help you understand and appreciate the writer's ideas. For example, reading the first stanza of "For My Children" in sentences allows you to focus on the contrast between the tales of America ("shackles and slaves and a bill of rights") and those of Africa ("Skin of honey and beauty of ebony begins/In the land called Bilad as-Sudan"). Once you've become familiar with the ideas in "For My Children," you may want to read it again, pausing at line breaks to appreciate the poem's rhythms.

1. (a) By focusing on Louise Erdrich's use of punctuation, what do you notice about every stanza in "Bidwell Ghost"? (b) Why do you think Erdrich chose to punctuate this poem as she did?
2. Identify the figurative language in the last stanza of "For My Children," and explain how reading the stanza in sentences helped you to understand and appreciate this figurative language.

◆ Build Vocabulary

USING RELATED WORDS: *HERITAGE*

Several English words—such as *hereditary, inherit,* and *inheritance*—are related to the word *heritage* ("something handed down from one's ancestors or the past"). Use these four related words to complete the four sentences below.

1. His slender physique has nothing to do with lack of exercise; it's ____?____.
2. The siblings' ____?____ included their uncle's prized collection of hand tools.
3. My twin cousins are very proud of their Scandinavian ____?____.
4. Most children ____?____ some physical and emotional characteristics from both parents.

USING THE WORD BANK

On your paper, write the letter of the best synonym for each of the first words.

1. effigies: (a) representations, (b) toys, (c) machines
2. shackles: (a) imprisoned, (b) worries, (c) chains
3. heritage: (a) folk art, (b) traditions, (c) society

◆ Grammar and Style

SEQUENCE OF TENSES

Using the correct **sequence of verb tenses** allows you to show the relationship of events in time.

The **present tense** shows action that exists at the present time.

The **present-perfect tense** indicates something that began in the past and continues to the present.

The **past tense** shows action that began and ended at a given time in the past.

Practice For each of the following sentences, identify the tense of the italicized verb. Then, for each sentence, explain the relationship of events in time that the verbs express.

1. Each night she *waits* by the road where her house once stood.
2. The heat *charred* the branches of the apple trees, but nothing can kill that wood.
3. Is it so terrible to be alone when the cold white blossoms *come* to life and *burn*?
4. She *has wondered* about this all her life.

Build Your Portfolio

Idea Bank

Writing

1. **Letter** As yourself or as a fictional character, write a letter to the children of the future in which you convey something important you have learned about your heritage.

2. **Song Lyrics** Rewrite one of these poems in the form of popular song lyrics. If you like, use details of your own cultural heritage.

3. **Comparison-and-Contrast Essay** Write a short essay comparing and contrasting the two lyric poems in this section. Consider such literary elements as figurative language, rhythm, and imagery.

Speaking and Listening

4. **Legend** Share a tale or legend—one you remember from childhood or one you create— with your classmates. Use pacing and gestures to heighten the story's suspense or interest level. **[Performing Arts Link]**

5. **Oral Report** Research and deliver a short oral presentation about one of the African cultures noted in "For My Children"—Watusi, Bantu, Dahomey, Burundi, Ashanti, or Ibo. **[Social Studies Link]**

Projects

6. **Drawing/Painting** Choose a single stanza from "Bidwell Ghost" to use as the subject of a drawing or painting. **[Art Link]**

7. **Illustrated Report** Erdrich uses an image featuring embroidery, an ancient art involving stitching patterns or designs on cloth. Prepare an illustrated research report on distinctive embroideries of various Native American tribes. **[Social Studies Link; Art Link]**

Writing Mini-Lesson

Ghost Story

Stories involving ghosts are common in Gothic fiction, folk literature, legends, and oral histories. Almost all ghost stories contain an element of mystery and eeriness; some also feature a noticeable air of humor or melancholy. Write an original ghost story based on a story you heard as a child or a new idea you develop in your imagination.

Writing Skills Focus: Sensory Details

In works of imaginative writing, it is important to create a vivid impression using **sensory details**— those that tell how something looks, smells, feels, sounds, and tastes. In a single stanza of "Bidwell Ghost," for example, Louise Erdrich uses details involving touch, smell, sight, and taste:

Model From the Selection

The heat charred the branches / of the apple trees, / but nothing can kill that wood.

Prewriting Consider the storyline you will develop. Once you know the *who*, *what*, *when*, and *how*, begin to plan the eerie quality of the story. Brainstorm for sensory details using a chart like this one:

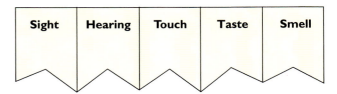

Sight	Hearing	Touch	Taste	Smell

Drafting Try to grab your audience's interest from the start. You can do this with a vivid description of the setting or by starting off with a description of an eerie event. As you develop your story, focus on building suspense.

Revising Read your story several times—both silently and aloud. How can you make it more suspenseful? What, if any, details should you add or delete? How can you sharpen your language?

Guide for Interpreting

E. L. Doctorow (1931–)

The literary work of E(dgar) L(awrence) Doctorow defies strict categorization. It is distinguished by a unique and authoritative blend of fact and fiction—sometimes called "faction," a term first coined around Doctorow's work.

Doctorow's work is known for pushing the limits of style, form, and content.

Doctorow has always been aware of the political unrest, social rootlessness, and constant motion of his time; his literary experimentation seems both to respond to and reflect an era brimming with contradiction and irony.

Rising to a Challenge As a reader for Columbia Pictures, Doctorow was dismayed at the inferior scripts he read. Certain he could make up better stories, Doctorow started writing himself. In his first novel, *Welcome to Hard Times* (1960), he focused on stretching the boundaries of western fiction by addressing serious themes not usually treated in this type of literature. He continued writing, producing novels, short stories, essays, plays, and screen adaptations that exhibit the same type of inventiveness that he showed in his first novel.

Mixing Fact and Fiction Doctorow frequently incorporates fact and fiction in his writing to create powerful dramatic effects. *The Book of Daniel* (1971) weaves factual details about Esther and Julius Rosenberg—Communists found guilty of treason and sentenced to die—into a story centering on the lives of fictional children parted from their parents amidst political scandal. Doctorow's 1975 novel, *Ragtime,* also blends fictional characters with the invented and real experiences of historical figures such as Harry Houdini and J. P. Morgan. Doctorow has won two National Book Critic Circle Awards, one for *Ragtime* and another for the 1990 novel, *Billy Bathgate.* Four of his novels have been made into major motion pictures. "The Writer in the Family" is a traditionally structured short story written from the point of view of a young writer who finds himself in a strange dilemma.

◆ Background for Understanding

CULTURE: SHI'VA

Most cultures have unique mourning rituals. For Jews, that ritual is called shi'va, meaning "seven" in Hebrew. When a parent, child, sibling, or spouse dies, the family observes shi'va for seven days.

During shi'va, mourners follow certain traditional rules. They remain at home and conduct no ordinary business. Comfortable furniture is exchanged for seating on low stools or the floor. Neither men nor women shave or cut their hair. Mourners do not wear leather footwear or don new clothes. Traditionally, friends and fellow mourners join the family in their home to express sympathy and recite prayers.

Many Jews in contemporary society observe these traditions in modified ways—perhaps shortening the length of the traditional shi'va or choosing only a few rituals to follow.

In "The Writer in the Family," the shi'va's ritual acknowledgment of death contrasts sharply with the pretense at the story's center.

The Writer in the Family

◆ *Literature and Your Life*

CONNECT YOUR EXPERIENCE

One of the most difficult aspects of life is coping with the loss of loved ones. People cope with such a loss in a variety of ways. In this story, the characters deal with the death of a loved one in a complicated way that will probably surprise you.

Journal Writing Jot down your thoughts about how people should deal with the loss of a loved one. What types of behavior might you consider unacceptable in such a situation?

THEMATIC FOCUS: SOCIAL PROTEST

Social protest in the twentieth century has involved the questioning of a wide range of rules and codes of conduct. As you read, ask yourself whether there are some rules that should never be bent or questioned.

◆ Build Vocabulary

SUFFIXES: *-itis*

A character in this story is said to have *bronchitis*. You can piece together a meaning for this word by learning that the suffix *-itis* means "disease" or "inflammation." *Bronchitis* means "inflammation of the bronchial tubes."

WORD BANK

Before you read, preview this list of words from the story.

bronchitis
cronies
barometer
anthology

◆ Grammar and Style

COMMONLY CONFUSED WORDS: *AFFECT* AND *EFFECT*

Commonly confused words are those that look or sound alike but have different meanings. In this story, for example, Doctorow uses the word *effect* in its most frequently used form—as a noun to describe the result of an action. **Affect**, which is often confused with **effect**, is a verb meaning "to influence."

My aunt called some days later and told me it was when she read this letter aloud to the old lady that the full *effect* of Jack's death came over her.

◆ Literary Focus

STATIC AND DYNAMIC CHARACTERS

Doctorow uses static and dynamic characters to create a heightened sense of contrast in his story. A **static character** is one whose attitudes and behavior remain essentially stable throughout a literary work. **Dynamic characters**, on the other hand, experience a shift or change in attitude and behavior during the course of the work. As you read "The Writer in the Family," identify each of the main characters as either static or dynamic. Consider how the contrasts between these character types add to the story's impact.

◆ Reading Strategy

JUDGE THE CHARACTERS' ACTIONS

The characters in this story bend the rules relating to a pivotal event in their lives— the death of a family member. Would you behave the same way faced with similar circumstances? When you **judge the characters' actions**, you evaluate their behavior against moral or other criteria. As you read, consider the actions of each character in light of the circumstances Doctorow describes. Are their actions morally defensible? Against what standards are you judging?

The Writer in the Family

E. L. Doctorow

*I*n 1955 my father died with his ancient mother still alive in a nursing home. The old lady was ninety and hadn't even known he was ill. Thinking the shock might kill her, my aunts told her that he had moved to Arizona for his bronchitis. To the immigrant generation of my grandmother, Arizona was the American equivalent of the Alps, it was where you went for your health. More accurately, it was where you went if you had the money. Since my father had failed in all the business enterprises of his life, this was the aspect of the news my grandmother dwelled on, that he had finally had some success. And so it came about that as we mourned him at home in our stocking feet,[1] my grandmother was bragging to her cronies about her son's new life in the dry air of the desert.

My aunts had decided on their course of action without consulting us. It meant neither my mother nor my brother nor I could visit Grandma because we were supposed to have moved west too, a family, after all. My brother Harold and I didn't mind—it was always a nightmare at the old people's home, where they all sat around staring at us while we tried to make conversation with Grandma. She looked terrible, had numbers of ailments, and her mind wandered. Not seeing her was no disappointment either for my mother, who had never gotten along with the old woman and did not visit when she could have. But what was disturbing was that my aunts had acted in the manner of that side of the family of making government on everyone's behalf, the true citizens by blood and the lesser citizens by marriage. It was exactly this attitude that had tormented my mother all her married life. She claimed Jack's family had never accepted her. She had battled them for twenty-five years as an outsider.

A few weeks after the end of our ritual mourning my Aunt Frances phoned us from her home in Larchmont. Aunt Frances was the wealthier of my father's sisters. Her husband was a lawyer, and both her sons were at Amherst.[2] She had called to say that Grandma was asking why she didn't hear from Jack. I had answered the phone. "You're the writer in the family," my aunt said. "Your father had so much faith in you. Would you mind making up something? Send it to me and I'll read it to her. She won't know the difference."

That evening, at the kitchen table, I pushed my homework aside and composed a letter. I tried to imagine my father's response to his new life. He had never been west. He had never traveled anywhere. In his generation the great journey was from the working class to the professional class. He hadn't managed that either. But he loved New York, where he had been born and lived all his life, and he was always discovering new things about it. He especially loved the old parts of the city below Canal Street, where he would find ships' chandlers or firms that wholesaled in spices and teas. He was a salesman for an appliance jobber[3] with accounts all over the city. He liked to bring home rare cheeses or exotic foreign vegetables that were sold only in certain neighborhoods. Once he brought home a barometer, another

---

1. **as we mourned . . . in our stocking feet:** Refers to the Jewish custom of not wearing leather footwear during the traditional mourning period known as shi'va.

2. **Amherst:** Amherst College in Amherst, Massachusetts.
3. **jobber:** Industry jargon for a person who buys goods in quantity from manufacturers and sells them to dealers; a wholesaler or middleman.

▶ **Critical Viewing** How might the boy in this picture use the familiar surroundings to help him concoct a believable letter? **[Connect]**

time an antique ship's telescope in a wooden case with a brass snap.

"Dear Mama," I wrote. "Arizona is beautiful. The sun shines all day and the air is warm and I feel better then I have in years. The desert is not as barren as you would expect, but filled with wildflowers and cactus plants and peculiar crooked trees that look like men holding their arms out. You can see great distances in whatever direction you turn and to the west is a range of mountains maybe fifty miles from here, but in the morning with the sun on them you can see the snow on their crests."

My aunt called some days later and told me it was when she read this letter aloud to the old lady that the full effect of Jack's death came over her. She had to excuse herself and went out in the parking lot to cry. "I wept so," she said. "I felt such terrible longing for him. You're so right, he loved to go places, he loved life, he loved everything."

*W*e began trying to organize our lives. My father had borrowed money against his insurance and there was very little left. Some commissions were still due but it didn't look as if his firm would honor them. There was

Laurence Typing, 1952, Fairfield Porter, Oil on canvas 40" x 30 1/8", The Parrish Art Museum, Southampton, New York, Gift of the Estate of Fairfield Porter

◆ **Build Vocabulary**

bronchitis (brän kīt′ is) *n.:* Inflammation of the lining of the major air passageways of the lungs

cronies (krō′ nēz) *n.:* Close companions

barometer (bə räm′ ət ər) *n.:* Instrument for measuring atmospheric pressure; used in forecasting weather or finding height above sea level

a couple of thousand dollars in a savings bank that had to be maintained there until the estate was settled. The lawyer involved was Aunt Frances' husband and he was very proper. "The estate!" my mother muttered, gesturing as if to pull out her hair. "The estate!" She applied for a job part-time in the admissions office of the hospital where my father's terminal illness had been diagnosed, and where he had spent some months until they had sent him home to die. She knew a lot of the doctors and staff and she had learned "from bitter experience," as she told them, about the hospital routine. She was hired.

I hated that hospital, it was dark and grim and full of tortured people. I thought it was masochistic[4] of my mother to seek out a job there, but did not tell her so.

We lived in an apartment on the corner of 175th Street and the Grand Concourse, one flight up. Three rooms. I shared the bedroom with my brother. It was jammed with furniture because when my father had required a hospital bed in the last weeks of his illness we had moved some of the living-room pieces into the bedroom and made over the living room for him. We had to navigate bookcases, beds, a gateleg table, bureaus, a record player and radio console, stacks of 78 albums, my brother's trombone and music stand, and so on. My mother continued to sleep on the convertible sofa in the living room that had been their bed before his illness. The two rooms were connected by a narrow hall made even narrower by bookcases along the wall. Off the hall were a small kitchen and dinette and a bathroom. There were lots of appliances in the kitchen— broiler, toaster, pressure cooker, counter-top dishwasher, blender—that my father had gotten through his job, at cost. A treasured phrase in our house: *at cost.* But most of these fixtures went unused because my mother did not care for them. Chromium devices with timers or gauges that required the reading of elaborate instructions were not for her. They were in part responsible for the awful clutter of our lives and now she wanted to get rid of them. "We're being buried," she said. "Who needs them!"

So we agreed to throw out or sell anything

---

4. **masochistic** (mas´ ə kis´ tik) *adj*.: Deriving pleasure from physical or psychological pain.

inessential. While I found boxes for the appliances and my brother tied the boxes with twine, my mother opened my father's closet and took out his clothes. He had several suits because as a salesman he needed to look his best. My mother wanted us to try on his suits to see which of them could be altered and used. My brother refused to try them on. I tried on one jacket which was too large for me. The lining inside the sleeves chilled my arms and the vaguest scent of my father's being came to me.

"This is way too big," I said.

"Don't worry," my mother said. "I had it cleaned. Would I let you wear it if I hadn't?"

It was the evening, the end of winter, and snow was coming down on the windowsill and melting as it settled. The ceiling bulb glared on a pile of my father's suits and trousers on hangers flung across the bed in the shape of a dead man. We refused to try on anything more, and my mother began to cry.

"What are you crying for?" my brother shouted. "You wanted to get rid of things, didn't you?"

A few weeks later my aunt phoned again and said she thought it would be necessary to have another letter from Jack. Grandma had fallen out of her chair and bruised herself and was very depressed.

"How long does this go on?" my mother said.

"It's not so terrible," my aunt said, "for the little time left to make things easier for her."

My mother slammed down the phone. "He can't even die when he wants to!" she cried. "Even death comes second to Mama! What are they afraid of, the shock will kill her? Nothing can kill her. She's indestructible! A stake through the heart couldn't kill her!"

When I sat down in the kitchen to write the letter I found it more difficult than the first one. "Don't watch me," I said to my brother. "It's hard enough."

"You don't have to do something just because someone wants you to," Harold said. He was two years older than me and had started at City College; but when my father became ill he had switched to night school and gotten a job in a record store.

"Dear Mama," I wrote. "I hope you're feeling well. We're all fit as a fiddle. The life here is good and the people are very friendly and informal. Nobody wears suits and ties here. Just a pair of slacks and a short-sleeved shirt. Perhaps a sweater in the evening. I have bought into a very successful radio and record business and I'm doing very well. You remember Jack's Electric, my old place on Forty-third Street? Well, now it's Jack's Arizona Electric and we have a line of television sets as well."

I sent that letter off to my Aunt Frances, and as we all knew she would, she phoned soon after. My brother held his hand over the mouthpiece. "It's Frances with her latest review," he said.

"Jonathan? You're a very talented young man. I just wanted to tell you what a blessing your letter was. Her whole face lit up when I read the part about Jack's store. That would be an excellent way to continue."

◆ **Reading Strategy**

Do you agree with the narrator's statement that the letter writing is dishonest? Why or why not?

"Well, I hope I don't have to do this anymore, Aunt Frances. It's not very honest."

Her tone changed. "Is your mother there? Let me talk to her."

"She's not here," I said.

"Tell her not to worry," my aunt said. "A poor old lady who has never wished anything but the best for her will soon die."

I did not repeat this to my mother, for whom it would have been one more in the family anthology of unforgivable remarks. But then I had to suffer it myself for the possible truth it might embody. Each side defended its position with rhetoric, but I, who wanted peace, rationalized the snubs and rebuffs each inflicted on the other, taking no stands, like my father himself.

Years ago his life had fallen into a pattern of business failures and missed opportunities. The great debate between his family on one side, and my mother Ruth on the other, was this: who was responsible for the fact that he had not lived up to anyone's expectations?

As to the prophecies, when spring came my mother's prevailed. Grandma was still alive.

One balmy Sunday my mother and brother and I took the bus to the Beth El cemetery in New Jersey to visit my father's grave. It was situated on a slight rise. We stood looking over rolling fields embedded with monuments. Here and there processions of black cars wound their way through the lanes, or clusters of people stood at open graves. My father's grave was planted with tiny shoots of evergreen but it lacked a headstone. We had chosen one and paid for it and then the stonecutters had gone on strike. Without a headstone my father did not seem to be honorably dead. He didn't seem to me properly buried.

My mother gazed at the plot beside his, reserved for her coffin. "They were always too fine for other people," she said. "Even in the old days on Stanton Street. They put on airs. Nobody was ever good enough for them. Finally Jack himself was not good enough for them. Except to get them things wholesale. Then he was good enough for them."

"Mom, please," my brother said.

"If I had known. Before I ever met him he was tied to his mama's apron strings. And Essie's apron strings were like chains, let me tell you. We had to live where we could be near them for the Sunday visits. Every Sunday, that was my life, a visit to mamaleh. Whatever she knew I wanted, a better apartment, a stick of furniture, a summer camp for the boys, she spoke against it. You know your father, every decision had to be considered and reconsidered. And nothing changed. Nothing ever changed."

She began to cry. We sat her down on a nearby bench. My brother walked off and read the names on stones. I looked at my mother, who was crying, and I went off after my brother.

"Mom's still crying," I said. "Shouldn't we do something?"

"It's all right," he said. "It's what she came here for."

"Yes," I said, and then a sob escaped from my throat. "But I feel like crying too."

My brother Harold put his arm around me. "Look at this old black stone here," he said. "The way it's carved. You can see the changing fashion in monuments—just like everything else."

◆ **Build Vocabulary**

anthology (an thäl′ ə jē) n.: Collection of poems, stories, songs, excerpts, etc.

Somewhere in this time I began dreaming of my father. Not the robust father of my childhood, the handsome man with healthy pink skin and brown eyes and a mustache and the thinning hair parted in the middle. My dead father. We were taking him home from the hospital. It was understood that he had come back from death. This was amazing and joyous. On the other hand, he was terribly mysteriously damaged, or, more accurately, spoiled and unclean. He was very yellowed and debilitated by his death, and there were no guarantees that he wouldn't soon die again. He seemed aware of this and his entire personality was changed. He was angry and impatient with all of us. We were trying to help him in some way, struggling to get him home, but something prevented us, something we had to fix, a tattered suitcase that had sprung open, some mechanical thing: he had a car but it wouldn't start; or the car was made of wood; or his clothes, which had become too large for him, had caught in the door. In one version he was all bandaged and as we tried to lift him from his wheelchair into a taxi the bandage began to unroll and catch in the spokes of the wheelchair. This seemed to be some unreasonableness on his part. My mother looked on sadly and tried to get him to cooperate.

That was the dream. I shared it with no one. Once when I woke, crying out, my brother turned on the light. He wanted to know what

I'd been dreaming but I pretended I didn't remember. The dream made me feel guilty. I felt guilty *in* the dream too because my enraged father knew we didn't want to live with him. The dream represented us taking him home, or trying to, but it was nevertheless understood by all of us that he was to live alone. He was this derelict back from death, but what we were doing was taking him to some place where he would live by himself without help from anyone until he died again.

At one point I became so fearful of this dream that I tried not to go to sleep. I tried to think of good things about my father and to remember him before his illness. He used to call me "matey." "Hello, matey," he would say when he came home from work. He always wanted us to go someplace—to the store, to the park, to a ball game. He loved to walk. When I went walking with him he would say: "Hold your shoulders back, don't slump. Hold your head up and look at the world. Walk as if you meant it!" As he strode down the street his shoulders moved from side to side, as if he was hearing some kind of cakewalk. He moved with a bounce. He was always eager to see what was around the corner.

Letters and Postcards, Reid Christman

▲ **Critical Viewing**   How would a person who might save letters and mementos like these feel about the narrator of this story? **[Infer]**

The next request for a letter coincided with a special occasion in the house. My brother Harold had met a girl he liked and had gone out with her several times. Now she was coming to our house for dinner.

We had prepared for this for days, cleaning everything in sight, giving the house a going-over, washing the dust of disuse from the glasses and good dishes. My mother came home early from work to get the dinner going. We opened the gateleg table in the living room and brought in the kitchen chairs. My mother spread the table with a laundered white cloth and put out her silver. It was the first family occasion since my father's illness.

I liked my brother's girlfriend a lot. She was a thin girl with very straight hair and she had a terrific smile. Her presence seemed to excite the air. It was amazing to have a living breathing girl in our house. She looked around and what she said was: "Oh, I've never seen so many books!" While she and my brother sat at the table my mother was in the kitchen putting the food into serving bowls and I was going from the kitchen to the living room, kidding around like a waiter, with a white cloth over my arm and a high style of service, placing the serving dish of green beans on the table with a flourish. In the kitchen my mother's eyes were sparkling. She looked at me and nodded and mimed the words: "She's adorable!"

My brother suffered himself to be waited on. He was wary of what we might say. He kept glancing at the girl—her name was Susan—to see if we met with her approval. She worked in an insurance office and was taking courses in accounting at City College. Harold was under a terrible strain but he was excited and happy too. He had bought a bottle of Concord-grape wine to go with the roast chicken. He held up his glass and proposed a toast. My mother said: "To good health and happiness," and we all drank, even I. At that moment the phone rang and I went into the bedroom to get it.

"Jonathan? This is your Aunt Frances. How is everyone?"

"Fine, thank you."

"I want to ask one last favor of you. I need a letter from Jack. Your grandma's very ill. Do you think you can?"

◆ **Reading Strategy**

Do you think the narrator is making the right choice here? Why or why not?

"Who is it?" my mother called from the living room.

"OK, Aunt Frances," I said quickly. "I have to go now, we're eating dinner." And I hung up the phone.

"It was my friend Louie," I said, sitting back down. "He didn't know the math pages to review."

The dinner was very fine. Harold and Susan washed the dishes and by the time they were done my mother and I had folded up the gateleg table and put it back against the wall and I had swept the crumbs up with the carpet sweeper. We all sat and talked and listened to records for a while and then my brother took Susan home. The evening had gone very well.

Once when my mother wasn't home my brother had pointed out something: the letters from Jack weren't really necessary. "What is this ritual?" he said, holding his palms up. "Grandma is almost totally blind, she's half deaf and crippled. Does the situation really call for a literary composition? Does it need verisimilitude? Would the old lady know the difference if she was read the phone book?"

"Then why did Aunt Frances ask me?"

"That is the question, Jonathan. Why did she? After all, she could write the letter herself—what difference would it make? And if not Frances, why not Frances' sons, the Amherst students? They should have learned by now to write."

"But they're not Jack's sons," I said.

"That's exactly the point," my brother said. "The idea is *service*. Dad used to break his back getting them things wholesale, getting them deals on things. Frances of Westchester really needed things at cost. And Aunt Molly. And Aunt Molly's husband, and Aunt Molly's ex-husband. Grandma, if she needed an errand done. He was always on the hook for something. They never thought his time was important. They never thought every favor he got was one he had to pay back. Appliances, records, watches, china, opera tickets, . . . anything. Call Jack."

"It was a matter of pride to him to be able to do things for them," I said. "To have connections."

"Yeah, I wonder why," my brother said. He looked out the window.

Then suddenly it dawned on me that I was being implicated.

"You should use your head more," my brother said.

Yet I had agreed once again to write a letter from the desert and so I did. I mailed it off to Aunt Frances. A few days later, when I came home from school, I thought

I saw her sitting in her car in front of our house. She drove a black Buick Roadmaster, a very large clean car with whitewall tires. It was Aunt Frances all right. She blew the horn when she saw me. I went over and leaned in at the window.

"Hello, Jonathan," she said. "I haven't long. Can you get in the car?"

"Mom's not home," I said. "She's working."

"I know that. I came to talk to you."

"Would you like to come upstairs?"

"I can't, I have to get back to Larchmont. Can you get in for a moment, please?"

I got in the car. My Aunt Frances was a very pretty white-haired woman, very elegant, and she wore tasteful clothes. I had always liked her and from the time I was a child she had enjoyed pointing out to everyone that I looked more like her son than Jack's. She wore white gloves and held the steering wheel and looked straight ahead as she talked, as if the car was in traffic and not sitting at the curb.

"Jonathan," she said, "there is your letter on the seat. Needless to say I didn't read it to Grandma. I'm giving it back to you and I won't ever say a word to anyone. This is just between us. I never expected cruelty from you. I never thought you were capable of doing something so deliberately cruel and perverse."

I said nothing.

◆ Literary Focus
In what ways do her comments show that Aunt Frances is a static character?

"Your mother has very bitter feelings and now I see she has poisoned you with them. She has always resented the family. She is a very strong-willed, selfish person."

"No she isn't," I said.

"I wouldn't expect you to agree. She drove poor Jack crazy with her demands. She always had the highest aspirations and he could never fulfill them to her satisfaction. When he still had his store he kept your mother's brother . . . on salary. After the war when he began to make a little money he had to buy Ruth a mink jacket because she was so desperate to have one. He had debts to pay but she wanted a mink. He was a very special person, my brother, he should have accomplished something special, but he loved your mother and devoted his life to her. And all she ever thought about was keeping up with the Joneses."

I watched the traffic going up the Grand Concourse. A bunch of kids were waiting at the bus stop at the corner. They had put their books on the ground and were horsing around.

"I'm sorry I have to descend to this," Aunt Frances said. "I don't like talking about people this way. If I have nothing good to say about someone, I'd rather not say anything. How is Harold?"

"Fine."

"Did he help you write this marvelous letter?"

"No."

After a moment she said more softly: "How are you all getting along?"

"Fine."

"I would invite you up for Passover if I thought your mother would accept."

I didn't answer.

She turned on the engine. "I'll say good-bye now, Jonathan. Take your letter. I hope you give some time to thinking about what you've done."

That evening when my mother came home from work I saw that she wasn't as pretty as my Aunt Frances. I usually thought my mother was a good-looking woman, but I saw now that she was too heavy and that her hair was undistinguished.

"Why are you looking at me?" she said.

"I'm not."

"I learned something interesting today," my mother said. "We may be eligible for a V.A. pension because of the time your father spent in the Navy."

That took me by surprise. Nobody had ever told me my father was in the Navy.

"In World War I," she said, "he went to Webb's Naval Academy on the Harlem River. He was training to be an ensign. But the war ended and he never got his commission."

After dinner the three of us went through the closets looking for my father's papers, hoping to find some proof that could be filed with the Veterans Administration. We came up with two things, a Victory medal, which my brother said everyone got for being in the service during the Great War, and an astounding sepia photograph of my father and his shipmates on the deck of a ship. They were dressed in bell-bottoms and T-shirts and armed with mops and pails, brooms and brushes.

"I never knew this," I found myself saying. "I never knew this."

"You just don't remember," my brother said.

I was able to pick out my father. He stood at the end of the row, a thin, handsome boy with a full head of hair, a mustache, and an intelligent smiling countenance. . . .

Neither the picture nor the medal was proof of anything, but my brother thought a duplicate of my father's service record had to be in Washington somewhere and that it was just a matter of learning how to go about finding it.

"The pension wouldn't amount to much," my mother said. "Twenty or thirty dollars. But it would certainly help."

I took the picture of my father and his shipmates and propped it against the lamp at my bedside. I looked into his youthful face and tried to relate it to the Father I knew. I looked at the picture a long time. Only gradually did my eye connect it to the set of Great Sea Novels in the bottom shelf of the bookcase a few feet away. My father had given that set to me: it was uniformly bound in green with gilt lettering and it included works by Melville, Conrad, Victor Hugo and Captain Marryat. And lying across the top of the books, jammed in under the sagging shelf above, was his old ship's telescope in its wooden case with the brass snap.

I thought how stupid, and imperceptive, and self-centered I had been never to have understood while he was alive what my father's dream for his life had been.

◆ **Literary Focus**
In what ways has Jonathan changed since the story's opening scene?

On the other hand, I had written in my last letter from Arizona—the one that had so angered Aunt Frances—something that might allow me, the writer in the family, to soften my judgment of myself. I will conclude by giving the letter here in its entirety.

Dear Mama,

This will be my final letter to you since I have been told by the doctors that I am dying.

I have sold my store at a very fine profit and am sending Frances a check for five thousand dollars to be deposited in your account. My present to you, Mamaleh. Let Frances show you the passbook.

As for the nature of my ailment, the doctors haven't told me what it is, but I know that I am simply dying of the wrong life. I should never have come to the desert. It wasn't the place for me.

I have asked Ruth and the boys to have my body cremated and the ashes scattered in the ocean.

Your loving son,
Jack

Guide for Responding

◆ *Literature and Your Life*

Reader's Response What did you find admirable or disappointing about the narrator?

Thematic Response: As you read this story, did you want Jonathan to keep writing the letters? Why or why not?

Group Activity As a class, develop a "yes" or "no" question to address the central dilemma of this story. Then poll friends, family, and schoolmates for their responses. Submit and total the responses as a class.

☑ **Check Your Comprehension**

1. What has happened to the narrator's father?
2. What is the narrator's grandmother told about her son's whereabouts and situation?
3. (a) What key decision is made about communicating with the grandmother? (b) Who makes this decision?
4. What does the narrator do to help his Aunt Frances with her plan?
5. What point of view does the narrator express in the final paragraphs of the story?

Guide for Responding (continued)

◆ Critical Thinking

INTERPRET

1. Why do the aunts make such a key family decision without consulting the narrator and his mother? **[Interpret]**
2. What does Aunt Frances's desire to conceal Jack's death from their mother reveal about her character? **[Analyze]**
3. (a) How does Jonathan's mother feel about deceiving Grandma? (b) What do these feelings suggest about her values? **[Infer]**
4. What do you think the narrator's dream symbolizes? **[Interpret]**
5. Why does Jonathan ultimately change his mind about writing the letters? **[Connect]**

EVALUATE

6. Do you think Doctorow's portrayal of a family in mourning is realistic? Explain. **[Criticize]**

◆ Grammar and Style

COMMONLY CONFUSED WORDS: *AFFECT* AND *EFFECT*

Affect and *effect* are commonly confused words that look or sound alike but have different meanings. If you're confused about when to use a particular word, check the meanings in a dictionary or grammar book.

Effect is usually used as a noun, meaning "the result of some action." *Affect* is a verb, meaning "to influence."

Practice On your paper, name the part of speech for each italicized word, and indicate whether the word is used correctly, explaining why or why not.

1. How did her husband's death *affect* Ruth?
2. Jack's illness had a serious *effect* on his business.
3. How was Jonathan *effected* by his family?
4. What *affect* might Arizona's climate have on bronchitis?

Writing Application Write a brief essay explaining the impact you think Jack's death had on Jonathan. Use the commonly confused words *affect* and *effect* at least once.

◆ Literary Focus

STATIC AND DYNAMIC CHARACTERS

In this story, the characters' approaches to life, decision making, and death contrast sharply. Doctorow's use of both **static characters**—who remain basically unchanged during the story—and **dynamic characters**—who undergo a shift during the story—adds to these contrasts.

1. Is Jonathan a dynamic character? Give three reasons or examples to support your answer.
2. Identify Aunt Frances as either a static or dynamic character. Support your answer.

◆ Reading Strategy

JUDGE THE CHARACTERS' ACTIONS

When you **judge the characters' actions,** you evaluate each character's behaviors and actions by weighing them according to your own standards of right and wrong.

1. Contrast Aunt Frances's and Ruth's approach to death. Which do you think is more productive?
2. Who do you think was "right" at the end of the story—Aunt Frances or Jonathan? Why?

◆ Build Vocabulary

USING THE SUFFIX -*itis*

The suffix -*itis* means "disease or inflammation." With that knowledge, define each of these words on your paper. If necessary, use a dictionary to define the root or base word indicated.

1. sinusitis (*sinus*)
3. tendonitis (*tendon*)
2. appendicitis (*appendix*)
4. tonsilitis (*tonsil*)

USING THE WORD BANK

On your paper, write the word from the Word Bank that fits best in each sentence.

1. According to the _____?_____, it will probably rain in a day or two.
2. Grandpa and his _____?_____ play golf every week.
3. My bout with _____?_____ left me coughing for days.
4. We developed an _____?_____ of short stories to share with the children.

Build Your Portfolio

 ## Idea Bank

Writing

1. Final Letter If you were in Jonathan's situation, what would you have written in Jack's final letter to Grandma? Write a final letter in your own voice.

2. Eulogy As Jonathan, write a speech you might deliver at your father's memorial service. Write about the unique value of your father's life.

3. Critical Essay E. L. Doctorow once said, "A novelist is someone who lives in other people's skins." In a critical essay, link this statement to "The Writer in the Family."

Speaking and Listening

4. Family Conference With a group, role-play the family conference at which the aunts decide to deceive their mother. Introduce Jonathan, Ruth, and Harold into the discussion to argue against this approach. **[Performing Arts Link]**

5. Debate In pairs, take turns debating the morality of Jonathan's deceptive letters. Invite questions from the audience to further the discussion. **[Social Studies Link]**

Projects

6. Costume Proposal This story takes place in the 1950's. How would the characters dress and wear their hair? Discuss, plan, and illustrate the costumes and makeup you would propose for a dramatic presentation of the story. **[Art Link]**

7. Grief Hotline Research a crisis center in your area. Collect brochures and information on how the center helps people in need. If possible, interview a counselor. Share your findings with classmates. **[Community Link]**

 ## Writing Mini-Lesson

Advice Column

Doctorow's story explores a difficult dilemma. How should Jonathan handle the situation with his Aunt Frances? Write an advice column that includes a brief letter from Jonathan describing his problem and a response from the columnist proposing certain actions. As the columnist, use elaboration to support your argument.

Writing Skills Focus: Elaboration to Support an Argument

When you write persuasively, use **elaboration to support your argument.** Use the following techniques to help you create a convincing case for your position:

- Give coherent, logical reasons for each of your points.
- Support your reasons with facts and statistics.
- If appropriate, include statements from experts.

Prewriting First, list the elements of the dilemma that Jonathan's letter will include; then decide on the advice you will give him in response. Next, identify several reasons you might use to persuade Jonathan to follow your advice. To back up your reasons, do some research to collect facts about how older people cope with news of the death of a loved one.

Drafting After drafting Jonathan's letter, begin your response with a sympathetic line about his problem and a summary statement of the action you believe he should take. Follow up with a clear and logical argument to convince him to take your advice, elaborating each point with reasons and facts.

Revising Reread your column to be sure that Jonathan's problem and the response are clearly stated. Ask yourself whether you have made a strong case that will persuade Jonathan to follow the advice. How can you strengthen your argument? What additional reasons and support can you add?

Guide for Interpreting

Yusef Komunyakaa (1947–)

"It took me fourteen years to write poems about Vietnam," said Yusef Komunyakaa (yoo´ sef kō mun yä´ kä) in 1994, shortly after winning the Pulitzer Prize for *Neon Vernacular,* the collection from which "Camouflaging the Chimera" is taken. "I had never thought about writing about it, and in a way I had been systematically writing around it."

Komunyakaa joined the army and went to Vietnam in 1965. Serving as an "information specialist," he reported from the front lines, edited a military newspaper, and earned a Bronze Star. After the war, he pursued his education, earning a B.A. and an M.A. at the University of Colorado and an M.F.A. at the University of California, Irvine. He then took a variety of teaching jobs, and in 1977 published his first collection of poetry. In 1983, he returned to his native Louisiana, working as a poet-in-the-schools in New Orleans. During this time, he let Vietnam reenter his consciousness. "And it was as if I had uncapped some hidden place in me," Komunyakaa said. "Poem after poem came spilling out."

Tim O'Brien (1946–)

No writer has more effectively captured the Vietnam War than Tim O'Brien. O'Brien has written five books that focus on the war, providing readers with vivid pictures of the fighting in the dense Vietnamese jungles and allowing them to share the fear and homesickness experienced by American soldiers during this bitter conflict.

Born in Austin, Minnesota, O'Brien was drafted a month after graduating from college and was sent to Vietnam. After coming home in 1970, he began writing essays about his experiences. His first published work, *If I Die in a Combat Zone, Box Me Up and Ship Me Home* (1973), is a memoir. Several subsequent novels include a National Book Award winner, *Going After Cacciato* (1978), and the widely praised *The Things They Carried* (1990), from which "Ambush" is taken. In this fictional memoir of Vietnam—narrated by a character named Tim O'Brien—the author artfully straddles the line between fact and fiction. O'Brien has said that he writes fiction ". . . to get at the essence of things, not merely the surface."

◆ Background for Understanding

HISTORY: THE VIETNAM WAR

In 1961, President John F. Kennedy sent 400 military advisors to aid the South Vietnamese government in its fight against communist rebels supported by North Vietnam. As the war escalated, the United States poured massive military resources into defeating the rebels, known as Vietcong, or—as you'll read in "Camouflaging the Chimera"—the VC. However, traditional military strategies were useless in dense jungle, against a guerrilla army that could blend in at will with the civilian population. American soldiers grew increasingly frustrated, fighting a tenacious but elusive enemy.

At home, the war sparked mass protests.

College students and other citizens demonstrated against what they saw as a pointless war and a useless sacrifice of lives on both sides. The United States became deeply divided between those who supported the war and those who opposed it. In 1968, the United States began peace talks, even as the war continued. The talks failed. By 1973, when the United States finally pulled out of Vietnam, more than 58,000 Americans had died and thousands more had been wounded.

Many American writers continue to produce memoirs, analyses, novels, short stories, and poems reflecting on the Vietnam War and its aftermath.

◆ Camouflaging the Chimera ◆
Ambush *from* The Things They Carried

◆ *Literature and Your Life*

CONNECT YOUR EXPERIENCE

Most soldiers who went to Vietnam were only a few years older than you are now. Can you imagine finding yourself in a jungle, far from home, where you must kill or be killed? This is the reality that faces the narrators of "Camouflaging the Chimera" and "Ambush."

THEMATIC FOCUS: SOCIAL PROTEST

Tim O'Brien was a war protester who went to Vietnam, he says, in order "not to be thought of as a coward...." Reading "Ambush" might leave you wondering: Which takes more courage—to fight a war or to refuse to fight?

Journal Writing Describe one or two examples of courageous behavior that you have admired in another person.

◆ Literary Focus

FIRST-PERSON NARRATOR

Sometimes the most compelling stories are those told in the **first person**; that is, by a narrator who—using the pronouns *I* and *we*—takes part in the action and reveals his or her thoughts and feelings about the events being described. Both selections you are about to read are narrated in the first person. As you read, think about how this point of view pulls you inside the narrator's head, making you feel as though you are actually living through the events.

◆ Grammar and Style

NOUN CLAUSES

A **noun clause** is a subordinate clause (a group of words with a subject and a verb that cannot stand by itself as a sentence) that functions as a noun. Here is an example from "Ambush":

...my daughter Kathleen asked *if I had ever killed anyone*.

In this sentence, "if I had ever killed anyone" is a noun clause functioning as the direct object of *asked*. Several common words that introduce noun clauses are *that, which, what, if, how, when, where, why, whatever, whoever,* and *whether*. Sometimes, the introductory word *that* is understood, not stated. In this example, *that* is understood before "I'd been a soldier":

...She knew *I'd been a soldier*.

◆ Reading Strategy

ENVISION THE ACTION

As you read these suspenseful pieces set during wartime in remote jungles of Southeast Asia, utilize the details the writers provide to **envision the action**—form a mental picture of what you are reading. Both pieces describe soldiers lying in wait for the enemy—a particularly suspenseful action. When Komunyakaa writes, "We painted our faces & rifles/with mud from a riverbank," picture doing what he says. Like a movie in your head, these mental images will help the works come alive.

◆ Build Vocabulary

WORDS FROM WAR

Throughout history, soldiers have spoken their own language, the language of warfare. Each war produces unique terms. World War I, for example, gave us *doughboy, over the top,* and *no man's land*. Many words of war, such as *ambush* and *ammunition*, have long since entered our everyday language. As you read these selections, notice which words are specifically military in origin.

WORD BANK

Before you read, preview this list of words from the selections.

refuge
ambush
ammunition
muzzle
gape

Camouflaging the Chimera[1]

Yusef Komunyakaa

We tied branches to our helmets.
We painted our faces & rifles
with mud from a riverbank,

blades of grass hung from the pockets
5   of our tiger suits. We wove
ourselves into the terrain,
content to be a hummingbird's target.

We hugged bamboo & leaned
against a breeze off the river,
10   slow-dragging with ghosts

from Saigon to Bangkok,
with women left in doorways
reaching in from America.
We aimed at dark-hearted songbirds.

15   In our way station of shadows
rock apes tried to blow our cover,
throwing stones at the sunset. Chameleons

crawled our spines, changing from day
to night: green to gold,
20   gold to black. But we waited
till the moon touched metal,

---

1. Chimera (kĭ mĭr´ ə): From Greek mythology, a firebreathing monster with a lion's head, a goat's body, and a serpent's tail.

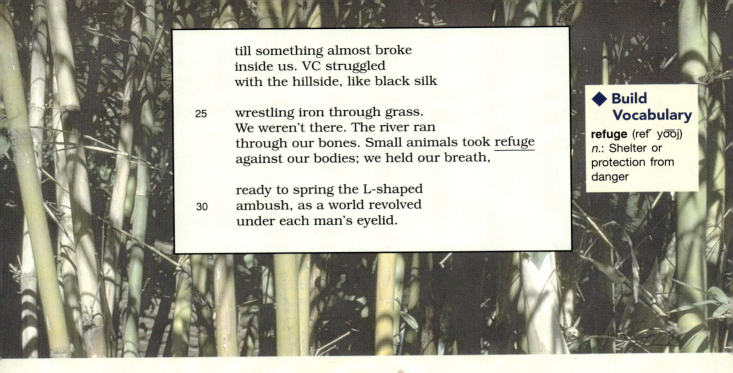

till something almost broke
inside us. VC struggled
with the hillside, like black silk

25   wrestling iron through grass.
We weren't there. The river ran
through our bones. Small animals took refuge
against our bodies; we held our breath,

ready to spring the L-shaped
30   ambush, as a world revolved
under each man's eyelid.

Beyond Literature

Architecture Connection

The Vietnam Veterans Memorial
Since its completion in 1982, millions of
people have visited the Vietnam Veterans
Memorial in Washington, D.C. Designed
by architect Maya Ying Lin, the memorial
honoring those who died in the Vietnam
War consists of two black granite walls
which slope down into the ground and
meet to form a V. Etched into the wall
are the names of more than 58,000
Americans who died in Vietnam.

Lin has said of her design, "It does not
glorify the war or make an antiwar statement. It is a place for private reckoning."
Visitors from across the nation leave
notes and small mementos at the wall.
The National Park Service collects
these items and plans to exhibit them.

Locate a photograph of the memorial.
How does its design support Lin's description of its purpose?

Guide for Responding

◆ Literature and Your Life

Reader's Response With what emotion
were you left as you finished the poem? Explain.
Thematic Focus Do the images in this poem
suggest that the speaker is opposed to the war he
is fighting? Explain.

☑ Check Your Comprehension

1. Where does this poem take place?
2. What happens in this poem?
3. Who are the VC in the seventh stanza?

◆ Critical Thinking

INTERPRET
1. What obstacles and burdens does the speaker
   face in this poem? **[Interpret]**
2. What images suggest that the speaker is
   merging with his surroundings? **[Support]**
3. What is the meaning of the title? Support
   your answer. **[Interpret]**

EVALUATE
4. Komunyakaa has said: "I like connecting the
   abstract to the concrete." Has he succeeded
   in this poem? Explain. **[Assess]**

AMBUSH
from The Things They Carried

Tim O'Brien

When she was nine, my daughter Kathleen asked if I had ever killed anyone. She knew about the war; she knew I'd been a soldier. "You keep writing these war stories," she said, "so I guess you must've killed somebody." It was a difficult moment, but I did what seemed right, which was to say, "Of course not," and then to take her onto my lap and hold her for a while. Someday, I hope, she'll ask again. But here I want to pretend she's a grown-up. I want to tell her exactly what happened, or what I remember happening, and then I want to say to her that as a little girl she was absolutely right. This is why I keep writing war stories:

He was a short, slender young man of about twenty. I was afraid of him—afraid of something—and as he passed me on the trail I threw a grenade that exploded at his feet and killed him.

Or to go back:

Shortly after midnight we moved into the ambush site outside My Khe. The whole platoon was there, spread out in the dense brush along the trail, and for five hours nothing at all happened. We were working in two-man teams—one man on guard while the other slept, switching off every two hours—and I remember it was still dark when Kiowa shook me awake for the final watch. The night was foggy and hot. For the first few moments I felt lost, not sure about directions, groping for my helmet and weapon. I reached out and found three grenades and lined them up in front of me; the pins had already been straightened for quick throwing.

And then for maybe half an hour I kneeled there and waited. Very gradually, in tiny slivers, dawn began to break through the fog, and from my position in the brush I could see ten or fifteen meters up the trail. The mosquitoes were fierce. I remember slapping at them, wondering if I should wake up Kiowa and ask for some repellent, then thinking it was a bad idea, then looking up and seeing the young man come out of the fog. He wore black clothing and rubber sandals and a gray ammunition belt. His shoulders were slightly stooped, his head cocked to the side as if listening for something. He seemed at ease. He carried his weapon in one hand, muzzle down, moving without any hurry up the center of the trail. There was no sound at all—none that I can remember. In a way, it seemed, he was part of the morning fog, or my own imagination, but there was also the reality of what was happening in my stomach. I had already pulled the pin on a grenade. I had come up to a crouch. It was entirely automatic. I did not hate the young man; I did not see him as the enemy; I did not ponder issues of morality or politics or military duty. I crouched and kept my head low. I tried to swallow whatever was rising from my stomach, which tasted like lemonade, something fruity and sour. I was terrified. There were no thoughts about killing. The grenade was to make him go away—just evaporate—and I leaned back and felt my mind go empty and then felt it fill up again. I had already thrown the grenade before telling myself to throw it. The brush was thick and I had to lob it high, not aiming, and I remember the grenade seeming to freeze above me for an instant, as if a camera had clicked, and I remember ducking down and holding my breath and seeing little wisps of fog rise from the earth. The grenade bounced once and rolled across the trail. I did not hear it, but there must've been a sound, because the young man dropped his weapon and began to run, just two or three quick steps, then he hesitated, swiveling to his right, and he glanced down at the grenade and tried to cover his head but never did. It occurred to me then that he was about to die. I wanted to warn him. The grenade made a popping noise—not soft but not loud either—not what I'd expected—and there was a puff of dust and smoke—a small white puff—and the young man seemed to jerk upward as if pulled by invisible wires. He fell on his back. His rubber sandals had been blown off. There was no wind. He lay at the center of the trail, his right leg bent beneath him, his one eye shut, his other eye a huge star-shaped hole.

It was not a matter of live or die. There was no real peril. Almost certainly the young man would have passed by. And it will always be that way.

Later, I remember, Kiowa tried to tell me that the man would've died anyway. He told me that it was a good kill, that I was a soldier and this was a war, that I should shape up and stop staring and ask myself what the dead man would've done if things were reversed.

None of it mattered. The words seemed far too complicated. All I could do was gape at the fact of the young man's body.

Even now I haven't finished sorting it out. Sometimes I forgive myself, other times I don't. In the ordinary hours of life I try not to dwell on it, but now and then, when I'm reading a newspaper or just sitting alone in a room, I'll look up and see the young man coming out of the morning fog. I'll watch him walk toward me, his shoulders slightly stooped, his head cocked to the side, and he'll pass within a few yards of me and suddenly smile at some secret thought and then continue up the trail to where it bends back into the fog.

◆ Build Vocabulary

ambush (am′ boosh′) *n.*: Lying in wait to attack by surprise

ammunition (am′ yoo nish′ ən) *n.*: Anything hurled by a weapon or exploded as a weapon; for example, bullets, shot, shells, etc.

muzzle (muz′ əl) *n.*: Front end of a barrel of a gun; the snout of an animal

gape (gāp) *v.*: Stare, open-mouthed

Guide for Responding

◆ *Literature and Your Life*

Reader's Response If you had been the narrator, would you have told your nine-year-old this story? Explain.

Thematic Focus Is this a war story or an anti-war story? Explain.

☑ Check Your Comprehension

1. Why does the narrator throw the grenade?
2. What is the narrator's reaction to what he has done?
3. How did Kiowa respond to the narrator's reaction to the killing?

◆ Critical Thinking

INTERPRET

1. What does the narrator mean when he says "And it will always be that way"? **[Interpret]**
2. (a) Why does the narrator have the fantasy he describes at the end of the story? (b) What effect does this fantasy have on the story? **[Infer]**

EVALUATE

3. Kiowa uses the expression "a good kill." Is there such a thing? Explain. **[Make a Judgment]**

EXTEND

4. Both of these selections look at Vietnam through a soldier's eyes. Compare and contrast the thoughts, feelings, and perceptions of the narrators of the two selections. **[Literature Link]**

Guide for Responding (continued)

◆ Literary Focus

FIRST-PERSON NARRATOR

Both "Ambush" and "Camouflaging the Chimera" are told by a first-person narrator who participates in the action and reveals inner thoughts, feelings, and perceptions. Writers often use the first person when they want to show the narrator's personal responses or to focus on the narrator's personality or viewpoint.

1. Komunyakaa has said, "I believe the reader or listener should be able to enter the poem as a participant." In what specific ways does his use of the first person in "Camouflaging the Chimera" help make that happen?
2. (a) Why do you think that Komunyakaa uses "we" instead of "I" in "Camouflaging the Chimera"? (b) What is the impact of this choice?
3. Do you think O'Brien's use of the first person makes you more sympathetic to his protagonist? Why or why not?

◆ Reading Strategy

ENVISION THE ACTION

When you use your imagination and your experience, along with the details that a writer provides, to **envision the action** of a literary work, you can picture the events in your mind—almost as if you're watching a movie.

1. Which action segments from these selections were easiest for you to picture in your mind as you read? Why?
2. What specific images especially helped you to envision the action? Why?
3. How does envisioning images such as "We hugged bamboo & leaned/against a breeze off the river" help you understand and appreciate "Camouflaging the Chimera"?
4. Explain how your ability to envision the action in the following passage from "Ambush" draws you into Tim O'Brien's world.

> Very gradually, in tiny slivers, dawn began to break through the fog, and from my position in the brush I could see ten or fifteen meters up the trail.

◆ Build Vocabulary

USING WORDS FROM WAR

In these selections, you encountered terms of warfare and words drawn from military jargon. Write a paragraph about a military practice maneuver using these words: ammunition, ambush, platoon, grenade.

USING THE WORD BANK

In your notebook, write a sentence responding to each of the following specific instructions. Include one word from the Word Bank in each sentence.

a. refuge	**c.** ambush	**e.** muzzle
b. gape	**d.** ammunition	

1. Tell what you would do if you were caught outside in a thunderstorm.
2. Tell how a sergeant might instruct recruits to hold a gun when standing at ease.
3. Describe your reaction when your best friend reveals that she's really from Mars.
4. Explain your strategy for capturing the leader of a rival team at camp.
5. Make a rule that would prevent children from injuring themselves with guns in the home.

◆ Grammar and Style

NOUN CLAUSES

When identifying a **noun clause**, remember that the word *that* is often implied, and not stated.

Practice Write each sentence in your notebook, and underline the noun clause.

> A **noun clause** is a subordinate clause that functions as a noun.

1. This is why I keep writing war stories.
2. . . . but there was also the reality of what was happening in my stomach.
3. I tried to swallow whatever was rising from my stomach . . .
4. Later, I remember, Kiowa tried to tell me that the man would've died anyway.
5. . . . she said, "so I guess you must've killed somebody."

Build Your Portfolio

Idea Bank

Writing

1. **Letter to an Author** Writer a letter to either O'Brien or Komunyakaa, sharing your reactions to his work and asking any questions you have about his experiences during the war.

2. **Newspaper Article** Retell the events from "Ambush" in the form of a brief news article. Make sure to answer the questions *who, what, when, where, why,* and *how.* **[Social Studies Link]**

3. **Literary Analysis** Write an essay in which you analyze the message about war that one of the two selections conveys. Support your points with details and passages from the work.

Speaking and Listening

4. **Interview** Interview a Vietnam War veteran about his or her wartime experiences. Ask questions about the events that stand out in his or her memory and about the lessons that he or she feels can be learned from the war. Tape-record the interview, and share highlights with the class. **[Social Studies Link]**

5. **Choral Reading** With a group of classmates, perform a choral reading of Komunyakaa's poem. Practice reading the poem in unison before performing for the class. **[Performing Arts Link]**

Projects

6. **Dance** "Camouflaging the Chimera" is filled with images of body movement. Create a dance, with or without music, that captures the events of the poem. **[Performing Arts Link]**

7. **Multimedia Presentation** Create a multimedia presentation about the Vietnam War and the controversy surrounding it during the 1960's. Use newspaper and magazine articles, photographs, political cartoons, television news reports, and protest songs. **[Media Link]**

Writing Mini-Lesson

Suspenseful Personal Account

Both Tim O'Brien and Yusef Komunyakaa turned suspenseful personal experiences into gripping and moving pieces of literature. Follow their examples by writing a personal account about a suspenseful experience that you've had. For example, you might focus on a time when you were caught in a natural disaster, such as an earthquake or a hurricane.

Writing Skills Focus: Suspense

As you develop your account, create suspense by providing details that create a mood of uncertainty and make readers want to find out what's going to happen next. Notice the details that Tim O'Brien uses to create suspense in this passage:

Model From the Selection

. . . I remember it was still dark when Kiowa shook me awake for the final watch. The night was foggy and hot. For the first few moments I felt lost, not sure about directions, groping for my helmet and weapons. I reached out and found three grenades and lined them up in front of me; the pins had already been straightened for quick throwing. And then for maybe half an hour I kneeled there and waited.

The details of the setting create an ominous atmosphere, and the narrator's descriptions of his preparations make you feel that something dramatic is going to happen.

Prewriting After you decide on your topic, jot down the key details of the event. Then arrange them in the order in which they happened.

Drafting Begin by grabbing the reader's interest—for example, by jumping right into the action or describing the tremendous impact that the experience had on you. As you continue writing, create suspense by including details that create a mood of uncertainty and by withholding key details.

Revising As you revise, look for ways in which you can make your account more suspenseful.

Guide for Interpreting

Arthur Miller (1915–   )

On October 20, 1995, the stars were out at a theater called Town Hall in New York City. The occasion was the eightieth birthday of playwright Arthur Miller, and dozens of celebrities from the world of literature and the theater had come together to honor one of their own.

A living legend of the American theater, Miller has chronicled the dilemma of common people pitted against powerful and unyielding social forces.

A native New Yorker, Miller has known bad times as well as good. During the Depression, his family lost its money and was forced to move from Manhattan to more modest living quarters in Brooklyn. Miller had to drop out of high school to take a job as a shipping clerk in a warehouse—an experience that he later dramatized in *A Memory of Two Mondays* (1955). Despite his inability to finish high school, he persuaded the University of Michigan to accept him as a student and used his savings from the warehouse job to finance his first year of studies.

Promising Playwright Miller first began writing drama while still in college. Though he held a variety of jobs after graduation, he continued to write. In 1947, his play *All My Sons* opened on Broadway to immediate acclaim, establishing Miller as a bright new talent. Two years later, he won international fame and a Pulitzer Prize for *Death of a Salesman* (1949), which critics hailed as a modern American tragedy.

His next play, *The Crucible* (1953), was less warmly received, for it used the Salem witchcraft trials of 1692 as a means of attacking the anti-communist "witch hunts" in Congress. Miller believed that the hysteria surrounding the witchcraft trials paralleled the contemporary political climate of McCarthyism—Senator Joseph McCarthy's obsessive quest to uncover Communist party infiltration of American institutions.

In the introduction to his *Collected Plays* (1957), Miller described his perceptions of the atmosphere during the McCarthy era and the way in which those perceptions influenced the writing of *The Crucible*: "It was as though the whole country had been born anew, without a memory even of certain elemental decencies which a year or two earlier no one would have imagined could be altered, let alone forgotten. Astounded, I watched men pass me by without a nod whom I had known rather well for years; and again, the astonishment was produced by my knowledge, which I could not give up, that the terror in these people was being knowingly planned and consciously engineered, and yet that all they knew was terror. That so interior and subjective an emotion could have been so manifestly created from without was a marvel to me. It underlies every word in *The Crucible.*"

In the Shadows of McCarthyism During the two years following the publication and production of *The Crucible*, Miller was investigated for possible associations with the Communist party. In 1956, he was called to testify before the House Committee on Un-American Activities. Although he never became a member of the Communist party, Miller, like so many of his contemporaries, had advocated principles of social justice and equality among the classes. He had become disillusioned, however, by the reality of communism as practiced in the Soviet Union. At the hearings, he testified about his own experiences, but he refused to discuss his colleagues and associates. He was found guilty of contempt (a sentence later overturned) for his refusal.

In 1956, the spotlight was focused on Miller's personal life when he married glamorous film star Marilyn Monroe. Though he did little writing during their five-year marriage, he did pen a screenplay of a film, *The Misfits* (1961), in which Monroe starred. After their divorce, Miller went on to write other noteworthy plays, including *The Price* (1968) and *The Last Yankee* (1991).

The Crucible

◆ Background for Understanding

HISTORY: THE SALEM WITCHCRAFT TRIALS

In 1692, the British colony of Massachusetts was swept by a witchcraft hysteria that resulted in the execution of twenty people and the jailing of at least 150 others. The incident was not isolated: It is estimated that between one million and nine million Europeans were executed as witches in the sixteenth and seventeenth centuries. Many of these individuals were merely practicing folk customs that had survived in Europe since pre-Christian times. In addition, in an era when religion and politics were closely allied, witch hunts were often politically motivated. England's James I, for example, wrote a treatise on witchcraft and sometimes accused his enemies of practicing the black arts. It was a cry that resonated well in a superstitious populace.

For the New England colonies, however, the witchcraft episode was unusual, though perhaps inevitable. The colonists endured harsh conditions and punishing hardship in their lives. Finding themselves at the mercy of forces beyond their control—bitter weather, sickness and death, devastating fires, drought, and insect infestations that killed their crops—many colonists attributed their misfortunes to the Devil. They were fearful (some would say paranoid) people, and their Puritan faith stressed the biblical teaching that witches were real and dangerous.

In the small parish of Salem Village, many were

The Trial of "Two Witches" at Salem, Massachusetts, in 1662, Howard Pyle

quick to blame witchcraft when the minister's daughter and several other girls were afflicted by seizures and lapses into unconsciousness, especially after it was learned that the girls had been dabbling in fortune-telling with the minister's slave Tituba. (They were not dancing in the woods, as they were in the play.) At first, only Tituba and two elderly women were named as witches, but then the hunt spread, until some of the colony's most prominent citizens stood accused. Many historians have seen a pattern of social and economic animosity behind the accusations, but most feel that mass hysteria was also a strong contributing factor.

When *The Crucible* was first published, Arthur Miller added a note about the play's historical accuracy: "This play is not history in the sense in which the word is used by the academic historian. Dramatic purposes have sometimes required many characters to be fused into one; the number of girls involved in the 'crying-out' has been reduced; Abigail's age has been raised; while there were several judges of almost equal authority, I have symbolized them in Hathorne and Danforth. However, I believe that the reader will discover here the essential nature of one of the strangest and most awful chapters in human history. The fate of each character is exactly that of his historical model, and there is no one in the drama who did not play a similar—and in some cases exactly the same—role in history."

Guide for Interpreting, Act I

◆ Literature and Your Life

CONNECT YOUR EXPERIENCE

If you have ever observed a rumor spread through your school or helped to spread one yourself, you know how easy it is to be swept along with a crowd, believing blindly rather than using your judgment.

Journal Writing Briefly describe an incident from a film or your own life in which a false rumor was accepted by many as the truth. What were the consequences?

THEMATIC FOCUS: SOCIAL PROTEST

As you read Act I of *The Crucible*, think about what Miller is saying about the weaknesses and faults of people past and present.

◆ Reading Strategy

QUESTION THE CHARACTERS' MOTIVES

"A man can smile and smile and be a villain," William Shakespeare once observed. And indeed, like people in real life, characters in plays are not always what they seem. Often we must **question their motives**, or reasons, for behaving in a certain way. Ambition, fear, greed, guilt, jealousy, love, loyalty, revenge—these are just some of the driving forces behind human behavior. As you read Act I of *The Crucible,* ask yourself the following questions about each character:

- What motivates the character to speak or act in this way?
- Does the character hide his or her true motives? If so, how?
- Might the character be unaware of his or her true motives?

◆ Grammar and Style

PRONOUN CASE IN INCOMPLETE CONSTRUCTIONS

In written and, especially, in spoken English, some sentences use **incomplete constructions**, omitting words that are understood. In such cases, it may be hard to determine whether to use a subject or an object pronoun. The best way to decide is to mentally complete the incomplete construction. You can then tell whether the pronoun should be a subject such as *I, he, she, we,* or *they* or an object such as *me, him, her, us,* or *them.* In the following examples, the words that mentally complete each sentence are in brackets.

subject
They want slaves, not such as *I* [am].

object
They want slaves more than [they want] *me.*

◆ Literary Focus

DRAMA: DIALOGUE AND STAGE DIRECTIONS

Drama consists of **dialogue,** or the words characters speak, and **stage directions,** or the instructions the playwright gives actors, the director, and technicians involved in putting on the play. Dialogue not only moves the plot along, but also reveals the characters' personalities and backgrounds to the audience. Stage directions usually indicate where a scene takes place, what it should look like, and how the characters should move and speak. Stage directions may also convey valuable background information. As you read Act I of *The Crucible,* look for information in both the stage directions and dialogue.

◆ Build Vocabulary

WORD ROOTS: *-grat-*

From *gratus,* Latin for "pleasing," comes the root *-grat-*, which means "pleasing" or "agreeable." An *ingratiating* attitude, for example, is one designed to please others.

WORD BANK

Before you read, preview this list of words from Act I.

predilection
ingratiating
dissembling
calumny
inculcation
propitiation
licentious

The Crucible[1]

Arthur Miller

CHARACTERS

Reverend Parris	Mercy Lewis	Francis Nurse
Betty Parris	Mary Warren	Ezekiel Cheever
Tituba	John Proctor	Marshal Herrick
Abigail Williams	Rebecca Nurse	Judge Hathorne
Susanna Walcott	Giles Corey	Deputy Governor Danforth
Mrs. Ann Putnam	Reverend John Hale	Sarah Good
Thomas Putnam	Elizabeth Proctor	Hopkins

ACT I

(An Overture)

A small upper bedroom in the home of REVEREND SAMUEL PARRIS, *Salem, Massachusetts, in the spring of the year 1692.*

There is a narrow window at the left. Through its leaded panes the morning sunlight streams. A candle still burns near the bed, which is at the right. A chest, a chair, and a small table are the other furnishings. At the back a door opens on the landing of the stairway to the ground floor. The room gives off an air of clean spareness. The roof rafters are exposed, and the wood colors are raw and unmellowed.

---

1. **crucible** (krōō′ sə bəl) *n.*: Heat-resistant container in which metals are melted or fused at very high temperatures; thus, a severe trial or test.

As the curtain rises, REVEREND PARRIS *is discovered kneeling beside the bed, evidently in prayer. His daughter,* BETTY PARRIS, *aged ten, is lying on the bed, inert.*

At the time of these events Parris was in his middle forties. In history he cut a villainous path, and there is very little good to be said for him. He believed he was being persecuted wherever he went, despite his best efforts to win people and God to his side. In meeting, he felt insulted if someone rose to shut the door without first asking his permission. He was a widower with no interest in children, or talent with them. He regarded them as young adults, and until this strange crisis he, like the rest of Salem, never conceived that the children were anything but thankful for being permitted to walk straight, eyes slightly lowered, arms at the sides, and mouths shut until bidden to speak.

His house stood in the "town"—but we today would hardly call it a village. The meeting house was nearby, and from this point outward—toward the bay or inland—there were a few small-windowed, dark houses snuggling against the raw Massachusetts winter. Salem had been established hardly forty years before. To the European world the whole province was a barbaric frontier inhabited by a sect of fanatics who, nevertheless, were shipping out products of slowly increasing quantity and value.

No one can really know what their lives were like. They had no novelists—and would not have permitted anyone to read a novel if one were handy. Their creed forbade anything resembling a theater or "vain enjoyment." They did not celebrate Christmas, and a holiday from work meant only that they must concentrate even more upon prayer.

Which is not to say that nothing broke into this strict and somber way of life. When a new farmhouse was built, friends assembled to "raise the roof," and there would be special foods cooked and probably some potent cider passed around. There was a good supply of ne'er-do-wells in Salem, who dallied at the shovelboard[2] in Bridget Bishop's tavern. Probably more than the creed, hard work kept the morals of the place from spoiling, for the people were forced to fight the land like heroes for every grain of corn, and no man had very much time for fooling around.

That there were some jokers, however, is indicated by the practice of appointing a two-man patrol whose duty was to "walk forth in the time of God's worship to take notice of such as either lie about the meeting house, without attending to the word and ordinances, or that lie at home or in the fields without giving good account thereof, and to take the names of such persons, and to present them to the magistrates, whereby they may be accordingly proceeded against." This predilection for minding other people's business was time-honored among the people of Salem, and it undoubtedly created many of the suspicions which were to feed the coming madness. It was also, in my opinion, one of the things that a John Proctor would rebel against, for the time of the armed camp had almost passed, and since the country was reasonably—although not wholly—safe, the old disciplines were beginning to rankle. But, as in all such matters, the issue was not clear-cut, for danger was still a possibility, and in unity still lay the best promise of safety.

The edge of the wilderness was close by. The American continent stretched endlessly west, and it was full of mystery for them. It stood, dark and threatening, over their shoulders night and day, for out of it Indian tribes marauded from time to time, and Reverend Parris had parishioners who had lost relatives to these heathen.

The parochial snobbery of these people was partly responsible for their failure to convert the Indians. Probably they also preferred to take land from heathens rather than from fellow Christians. At any rate, very few Indians were converted, and the Salem folk believed that the virgin forest was the Devil's last preserve, his home base and the citadel of his final stand. To the best of their knowledge the American forest was the last place on earth that was not paying homage to God.

For these reasons, among others, they carried about an air of innate resistance, even of persecution. Their fathers had, of course, been persecuted in England. So now they and their church found it necessary to deny any other sect its freedom, lest their New Jerusalem[3] be defiled and corrupted by wrong ways and deceitful ideas.

They believed, in short, that they held in their steady hands the candle that would light the world. We have inherited this belief, and it has helped and hurt us. It helped them with the discipline it gave them. They were a dedicated folk, by and large, and they had to be to survive the life they had chosen or been born into in this country.

The proof of their belief's value to them may be taken from the opposite character of the

---

2. **shovelboard:** Game in which a coin or other disk is driven with the hand along a highly polished board, floor, or table marked with transverse lines.

---

3. **New Jerusalem:** In the Bible, the holy city of heaven.

first Jamestown settlement, farther south, in Virginia. The Englishmen who landed there were motivated mainly by a hunt for profit. They had thought to pick off the wealth of the new country and then return rich to England. They were a band of individualists, and a much more ingratiating group than the Massachusetts men. But Virginia destroyed them. Massachusetts tried to kill off the Puritans, but they combined; they set up a communal society which, in the beginning, was little more than an armed camp with an autocratic and very devoted leadership. It was, however, an autocracy by consent, for they were united from top to bottom by a commonly held ideology whose perpetuation was the reason and justification for all their sufferings. So their self-denial, their purposefulness, their suspicion of all vain pursuits, their hard-handed justice, were altogether perfect instruments for the conquest of this space so antagonistic to man.

But the people of Salem in 1692 were not quite the dedicated folk that arrived on the *Mayflower*. A vast differentiation had taken place, and in their own time a revolution had

The Execution of the Reverend Stephen Burroughs for Witchcraft at Salem, Massachusetts, in 1692, 19th-Century Engraving

EXECUTION OF REV. STEPHEN BURROUGHS.

▲ **Critical Viewing** This nineteenth-century engraving shows the hanging of the Reverend Stephen Borroughs during the Salem witchcraft trials. What does it suggest about the condemned man's state of mind? **[Infer]**

unseated the royal government and substituted a junta[4] which was at this moment in power. The times, to their eyes, must have been out of joint, and to the common folk must have seemed as insoluble and complicated as do ours today. It is not hard to see how easily many could have been led to believe that the time of confusion had been brought upon them by deep and darkling forces. No hint of such speculation appears on the court record, but social disorder in any age breeds such mystical suspicions, and when, as in Salem, wonders are brought forth from below the social surface, it is too much to expect people to hold back very long from laying on the victims with all the force of their frustrations.

The Salem tragedy, which is about to begin in these pages, developed from a paradox. It is a paradox in whose grip we still live, and there is no prospect yet that we will discover its resolution. Simply, it was this: for good purposes, even high purposes, the people of Salem developed a theocracy, a combine of state and religious power whose function was to keep the community together, and to prevent any kind of disunity that might open it to destruction by material or ideological enemies. It was forged for a necessary purpose and accomplished that purpose. But all organization is and must be grounded on the idea of exclusion and prohibition, just as two objects cannot occupy the same space. Evidently the

◆ Build Vocabulary

predilection (pred′ əl ek′ shən) *n.*: Preexisting liking; preference

ingratiating (in grā′ shē āt iŋ) *adj.*: Having a quality that brings oneself into favor; charming or flattering

---

4. **junta** (hoon′ tə) *n.*: Assembly or council.

time came in New England when the repressions of order were heavier than seemed warranted by the dangers against which the order was organized. The witch-hunt was a perverse manifestation of the panic which set in among all classes when the balance began to turn toward greater individual freedom.

When one rises above the individual villainy displayed, one can only pity them all, just as we shall be pitied someday. It is still impossible for man to organize his social life without repressions, and the balance has yet to be struck between order and freedom.

The witch-hunt was not, however, a mere repression. It was also, and as importantly, a long overdue opportunity for everyone so inclined to express publicly his guilt and sins, under the cover of accusations against the victims. It suddenly became possible—and patriotic and holy—for a man to say that Martha Corey had come into his bedroom at night, and that, while his wife was sleeping at his side, Martha laid herself down on his chest and "nearly suffocated him." Of course it was her spirit only, but his satisfaction at confessing himself was no lighter than if it had been Martha herself. One could not ordinarily speak such things in public.

Long-held hatreds of neighbors could now be openly expressed, and vengeance taken, despite the Bible's charitable injunctions. Landlust which had been expressed before by constant bickering over boundaries and deeds, could now be elevated to the arena of morality; one could cry witch against one's neighbor and feel perfectly justified in the bargain. Old scores could be settled on a plane of heavenly combat between Lucifer[5] and the Lord; suspicions and the envy of the miserable toward the happy could and did burst out in the general revenge.

REVEREND PARRIS *is praying now, and, though we cannot hear his words, a sense of his confusion hangs about him. He mumbles, then seems about to weep; then he weeps, then prays again; but his daughter does not stir on the bed.*

The door opens, and his Negro slave enters. TITUBA *is in her forties.* PARRIS *brought her with him from Barbados, where he spent some years*

as a merchant before entering the ministry. She enters as one does who can no longer bear to be barred from the sight of her beloved, but she is also very frightened because her slave sense has warned her that, as always, trouble in this house eventually lands on her back.*

◆ **Reading Strategy**
What do you learn here about Tituba's motives?

TITUBA, *already taking a step backward:* My Betty be hearty soon?

PARRIS: Out of here!

TITUBA, *backing to the door:* My Betty not goin' die . . .

PARRIS, *scrambling to his feet in a fury:* Out of my sight! *She is gone.* Out of my— *He is overcome with sobs. He clamps his teeth against them and closes the door and leans against it, exhausted.* Oh, my God! God help me! *Quaking with fear, mumbling to himself through his sobs, he goes to the bed and gently takes* BETTY's *hand.* Betty. Child. Dear child. Will you wake, will you open up your eyes! Betty, little one . . .

He is bending to kneel again when his niece, ABIGAIL WILLIAMS, *seventeen, enters—a strikingly beautiful girl, an orphan, with an endless capacity for dissembling. Now she is all worry and apprehension and propriety.*

ABIGAIL: Uncle? *He looks to her.* Susanna Walcott's here from Doctor Griggs.

PARRIS: Oh? Let her come, let her come.

ABIGAIL, *leaning out the door to call to Susanna, who is down the hall a few steps:* Come in, Susanna.

SUSANNA WALCOTT, *a little younger than* ABIGAIL, *a nervous, hurried girl, enters.*

PARRIS, *eagerly:* What does the doctor say, child?

SUSANNA, *craning around* PARRIS *to get a look at* BETTY: He bid me come and tell you, reverend sir, that he cannot discover no medicine for it in his books.

PARRIS: Then he must search on.

SUSANNA: Aye, sir, he have been searchin' his

---

5. **Lucifer** (lōō sə fər): The Devil.

books since he left you, sir. But he bid me tell you, that you might look to unnatural things for the cause of it.

PARRIS, *his eyes going wide:* No—no. There be no unnatural cause here. Tell him I have sent for Reverend Hale of Beverly, and Mr. Hale will surely confirm that. Let him look to medicine and put out all thought of unnatural causes here. There be none.

SUSANNA: Aye, sir. He bid me tell you. *She turns to go.*

ABIGAIL: Speak nothin' of it in the village, Susanna.

PARRIS: Go directly home and speak nothing of unnatural causes.

SUSANNA: Aye, sir. I pray for her. *She goes out.*

ABIGAIL: Uncle, the rumor of witchcraft is all about; I think you'd best go down and deny it yourself. The parlor's packed with people, sir. I'll sit with her.

PARRIS, *pressed, turns on her:* And what shall I say to them? That my daughter and my niece I discovered dancing like heathen in the forest?

ABIGAIL: Uncle, we did dance; let you tell them I confessed it—and I'll be whipped if I must be. But they're speakin' of witchcraft. Betty's not witched.

PARRIS: Abigail, I cannot go before the congregation when I know you have not opened with me. What did you do with her in the forest?

ABIGAIL: We did dance, uncle, and when you leaped out of the bush so suddenly, Betty was frightened and then she fainted. And there's the whole of it.

PARRIS: Child. Sit you down.

ABIGAIL, *quavering, as she sits:* I would never hurt Betty. I love her dearly.

PARRIS: Now look you, child, your punishment will come in its time. But if you trafficked with

spirits in the forest I must know it now, for surely my enemies will, and they will ruin me with it.

ABIGAIL: But we never conjured spirits.

PARRIS: Then why can she not move herself since midnight? This child is desperate! *Abigail lowers her eyes.* It must come out—my enemies will bring it out. Let me know what you done there. Abigail, do you understand that I have many enemies?

ABIGAIL: I have heard of it, uncle.

PARRIS: There is a faction that is sworn to drive me from my pulpit. Do you understand that?

ABIGAIL: I think so, sir.

PARRIS: Now then, in the midst of such disruption, my own household is discovered to be the very center of some obscene practice. Abominations are done in the forest—

ABIGAIL: It were sport, uncle!

PARRIS, *pointing at* BETTY: You call this sport? *She lowers her eyes. He pleads:* Abigail, if you know something that may help the doctor, for God's sake tell it to me. *She is silent.* I saw Tituba waving her arms over the fire when I came on you. Why was she doing that? And I heard a screeching and gibberish coming from her mouth. She were swaying like a dumb beast over that fire!

ABIGAIL: She always sings her Barbados songs, and we dance.

PARRIS: I cannot blink what I saw, Abigail, for my enemies will not blink it. I saw a dress lying on the grass.

ABIGAIL, *innocently:* A dress?

PARRIS—*it is very hard to say:* Aye, a dress. And I thought I saw—someone naked running through the trees!

ABIGAIL, *in terror:* No one was naked! You mistake yourself, uncle!

PARRIS, *with anger:* I saw it! *He moves from her. Then, resolved:* Now tell me true, Abigail. And I pray you feel the weight of truth upon you, for now my ministry's at stake, my ministry and

---

◆ **Build Vocabulary**

dissembling (di sem´ bliŋ) *n.:* Disguising one's real nature or motives; pretense

perhaps your cousin's life. Whatever abomination you have done, give me all of it now, for I dare not be taken unaware when I go before them down there.

ABIGAIL: There is nothin' more. I swear it, uncle.

PARRIS, *studies her, then nods, half convinced:* Abigail, I have fought here three long years to bend these stiff-necked people to me, and now, just now when some good respect is rising for me in the parish, you compromise my very character. I have given you a home, child, I have put clothes upon your back—now give me upright answer. Your name in the town—it is entirely white, is it not?

ABIGAIL, *with an edge of resentment:* Why, I am sure it is, sir. There be no blush about my name.

PARRIS, *to the point:* Abigail, is there any other cause than you have told me, for your being discharged from Goody[6] Proctor's service? I have heard it said, and I tell you as I heard it, that she comes so rarely to the church this year for she will not sit so close to something soiled. What signified that remark?

ABIGAIL: She hates me, uncle, she must, for I would not be her slave. It's a bitter woman, a lying, cold, sniveling woman, and I will not work for such a woman!

PARRIS: She may be. And yet it has troubled me that you are now seven month out of their house, and in all this time no other family has ever called for your service.

ABIGAIL: They want slaves, not such as I. Let them send to Barbados for that. I will not black my face for any of them! *With ill-concealed resentment at him:* Do you begrudge my bed, uncle?

PARRIS: No—no.

ABIGAIL, *in a temper:* My name is good in the village! I will not have it said my name is soiled! Goody Proctor is a gossiping liar!

Enter MRS. ANN PUTNAM. *She is a twisted soul of forty-five, a death-ridden woman, haunted by dreams.*

---

6. **Goody:** Title used for a married woman; short for *Goodwife.*

PARRIS, *as soon as the door begins to open:* No—no, I cannot have anyone. *He sees her, and a certain deference springs into him, although his worry remains.* Why, Goody Putnam, come in.

MRS. PUTNAM, *full of breath, shiny-eyed:* It is a marvel. It is surely a stroke of hell upon you.

PARRIS: No, Goody Putnam, it is—

MRS. PUTNAM, *glancing at* BETTY: How high did she fly, how high?

PARRIS: No, no, she never flew—

MRS. PUTNAM, *very pleased with it:* Why, it's sure she did. Mr. Collins saw her goin' over Ingersoll's barn, and come down light as bird, he says!

PARRIS: Now, look you, Goody Putnam, she never—*Enter* THOMAS PUTNAM, *a well-to-do, hard-handed landowner, near fifty.* Oh, good morning, Mr. Putnam.

PUTNAM: It is a providence the thing is out now! It is a providence. *He goes directly to the bed.*

PARRIS: What's out, sir, what's—?

MRS. PUTNAM *goes to the bed.*

PUTNAM, *looking down at* BETTY: Why, *her* eyes is closed! Look you, Ann.

MRS. PUTNAM: Why, that's strange. *To* PARRIS: Ours is open.

PARRIS, *shocked:* Your Ruth is sick?

MRS. PUTNAM, *with vicious certainty:* I'd not call it sick; the Devil's touch is heavier than sick. It's death, y'know, it's death drivin' into them, forked and hoofed.

PARRIS: Oh, pray not! Why, how does Ruth ail?

MRS. PUTNAM: She ails as she must—she never waked this morning, but her eyes open and she walks, and hears naught, sees naught, and cannot eat. Her soul is taken, surely.

PARRIS *is struck.*

PUTNAM, *as though for further details:* They say you've sent for Reverend Hale of Beverly?

PARRIS *with dwindling conviction now:* A precaution only. He has much experience in all demonic arts, and I—

MRS. PUTNAM: He has indeed; and found a witch in Beverly last year, and let you remember that.

PARRIS: Now, Goody Ann, they only thought that were a witch, and I am certain there be no element of witchcraft here.

PUTNAM: No witchcraft! Now look you, Mr. Parris—

PARRIS: Thomas, Thomas, I pray you, leap not to witchcraft. I know that you—you least of all, Thomas, would ever wish so disastrous a charge laid upon me. We cannot leap to witchcraft. They will howl me out of Salem for such corruption in my house.

A word about Thomas Putnam. He was a man with many grievances, at least one of which appears justified. Some time before, his wife's brother-in-law, James Bayley, had been turned down as minister at Salem. Bayley had all the qualifications, and a two-thirds vote into the bargain, but a faction stopped his acceptance, for reasons that are not clear.

Thomas Putnam was the eldest son of the richest man in the village. He had fought the Indians at Narragansett, and was deeply interested in parish affairs. He undoubtedly felt it poor payment that the village should so blatantly disregard his candidate for one of its more important offices, especially since he regarded himself as the intellectual superior of most of the people around him.

◆ **Reading Strategy**
What does Miller tell you about Putnam's motives?

His vindictive nature was demonstrated long before the witchcraft began. Another former Salem minister, George Burroughs, had had to borrow money to pay for his wife's funeral, and, since the parish was remiss in his salary, he was soon bankrupt. Thomas and his brother John had Burroughs jailed for debts the man did not owe. The incident is important only in that Burroughs succeeded in becoming minister where Bayley, Thomas Putnam's brother-in-law, had been rejected; the motif of resentment is clear here. Thomas Putnam felt that his own name and the honor of his family had been smirched by the village, and he meant to right matters however he could.

Another reason to believe him a deeply embittered man was his attempt to break his father's will, which left a disproportionate amount to a stepbrother. As with every other public cause in which he tried to force his way, he failed in this.

So it is not surprising to find that so many accusations against people are in the handwriting of Thomas Putnam, or that his name is so often found as a witness corroborating the supernatural testimony, or that his daughter led the crying-out at the most opportune junctures of the trials, especially when—But we'll speak of that when we come to it.

PUTNAM—*at the moment he is intent upon getting* PARRIS, *for whom he has only contempt, to move toward the abyss:*[7] Mr. Parris, I have taken your part in all contention here, and I would continue; but I cannot if you hold back in this. There are hurtful, vengeful spirits layin' hands on these children.

PARRIS: But, Thomas, you cannot—

PUTNAM: Ann! Tell Mr. Parris what you have done.

MRS. PUTNAM: Reverend Parris, I have laid seven babies unbaptized in the earth. Believe me, sir, you never saw more hearty babies born. And yet, each would wither in my arms the very night of their birth. I have spoke nothin', but my heart has clamored intimations. And now, this year, my Ruth, my only—I see her turning strange. A secret child she has become this year, and shrivels like a sucking mouth were pullin' on her life too. And so I thought to send her to your Tituba—

PARRIS: To Tituba! What may Tituba—?

MRS. PUTNAM: Tituba knows how to speak to the dead, Mr. Parris.

PARRIS: Goody Ann, it is a formidable sin to conjure up the dead!

MRS. PUTNAM: I take it on my soul, but who else may surely tell us what person murdered my babies?

PARRIS, *horrified:* Woman!

---

7. **abyss** (ə bis´) *n.:* Deep crack in the Earth.

MRS. PUTNAM: They were murdered, Mr. Parris! And mark this proof! Mark it! Last night my Ruth were ever so close to their little spirits; I know it, sir. For how else is she struck dumb now except some power of darkness would stop her mouth? It is a marvelous sign, Mr. Parris!

PUTNAM: Don't you understand it, sir? There is a murdering witch among us, bound to keep herself in the dark. PARRIS *turns to* BETTY, *a frantic terror rising in him.* Let your names make of it what they will, you cannot blink it more.

PARRIS, *to* ABIGAIL: Then you were conjuring spirits last night.

ABIGAIL, *whispering:* Not I, sir—Tituba and Ruth.

PARRIS *turns now, with new fear, and goes to* BETTY, *looks down at her, and then, gazing off:* Oh, Abigail, what proper payment for my charity! Now I am undone.

PUTNAM: You are not undone! Let you take hold here. Wait for no one to charge you—declare it yourself. You have discovered witchcraft—

PARRIS: In my house? In my house, Thomas? They will topple me with this! They will make of it a—

Enter MERCY LEWIS, *the Putnams' servant, a fat, sly, merciless girl of eighteen.*

MERCY: Your pardons. I only thought to see how Betty is.

PUTNAM: Why aren't you home? Who's with Ruth?

MERCY: Her grandma come. She's improved a little, I think—she give a powerful sneeze before.

MRS. PUTNAM: Ah, there's a sign of life!

MERCY: I'd fear no more, Goody Putnam. It were a grand sneeze; another like it will shake her wits together, I'm sure. *She goes to the bed to look.*

PARRIS: Will you leave me now, Thomas? I would pray a while alone.

ABIGAIL: Uncle, you've prayed since midnight. Why do you not go down and—

PARRIS: No—no. *To* PUTNAM: I have no answer for that crowd. I'll wait till Mr. Hale arrives. *To get*

MRS. PUTNAM *to leave:* If you will, Goody Ann . . .

PUTNAM: Now look you, sir. Let you strike out against the Devil, and the village will bless you for it! Come down, speak to them—pray with them. They're thirsting for your word, Mister! Surely you'll pray with them.

PARRIS, *swayed:* I'll lead them in a psalm, but let you say nothing of witchcraft yet. I will not discuss it. The cause is yet unknown. I have had enough contention since I came; I want no more.

MRS. PUTNAM: Mercy, you go home to Ruth, d'y'hear?

MERCY: Aye, mum.

MRS. PUTNAM *goes out.*

PARRIS, *to* ABIGAIL: If she starts for the window, cry for me at once.

ABIGAIL: I will, uncle.

PARRIS, *to* PUTNAM: There is a terrible power in her arms today. *He goes out with* PUTNAM.

ABIGAIL, *with hushed trepidation:* How is Ruth sick?

MERCY: It's weirdish, I know not—she seems to walk like a dead one since last night.

ABIGAIL, *turns at once and goes to* BETTY, *and now, with fear in her voice:* Betty? BETTY *doesn't move. She shakes her.* Now stop this! Betty! Sit up now!

BETTY *doesn't stir.* MERCY *comes over.*

MERCY: Have you tried beatin' her? I gave Ruth a good one and it waked her for a minute. Here, let me have her.

ABIGAIL, *holding* MERCY *back:* No, he'll be comin' up. Listen, now; if they be questioning us, tell them we danced—I told him as much already.

MERCY: Aye. And what more?

ABIGAIL: He knows Tituba conjured Ruth's sisters to come out of the grave.

MERCY: And what more?

ABIGAIL: He saw you naked.

MERCY: *clapping her hands together with a frightened laugh:* Oh, Jesus!

Enter MARY WARREN, *breathless. She is seventeen, a subservient, naive, lonely girl.*

MARY WARREN: What'll we do? The village is out! I just come from the farm; the whole country's talkin' witchcraft! They'll be callin' us witches, Abby!

MERCY, *pointing and looking at* MARY WARREN: She means to tell, I know it.

MARY WARREN: Abby, we've got to tell. Witchery's a hangin' error, a hangin' like they done in Boston two year ago! We must tell the truth, Abby! You'll only be whipped for dancin', and the other things!

ABIGAIL: Oh, *we'll* be whipped!

MARY WARREN: I never done none of it, Abby. I only looked!

MERCY, *moving menacingly toward* MARY: Oh, you're a great one for lookin', aren't you, Mary Warren? What a grand peeping courage you have!

BETTY, *on the bed, whimpers.* ABIGAIL *turns to her at once.*

ABIGAIL: Betty? *She goes to* BETTY. Now, Betty, dear, wake up now. It's Abigail. *She sits* BETTY *up and furiously shakes her.* I'll beat you, Betty! BETTY *whimpers.* My, you seem improving. I talked to your papa and I told him everything. So there's nothing to—

BETTY, *darts off the bed, frightened of* ABIGAIL, *and flattens herself against the wall:* I want my mama!

ABIGAIL, *with alarm, as she cautiously approaches* BETTY: What ails you, Betty? Your mama's dead and buried.

BETTY: I'll fly to Mama. Let me fly! *She raises her arms as though to fly, and streaks for the window, gets one leg out.*

ABIGAIL, *pulling her away from the window:* I told him everything; he knows now, he knows everything we—

BETTY: You drank blood, Abby! You didn't tell him that!

ABIGAIL: Betty, you never say that again! You will never—

▲ **Critical Viewing** You'll find movie stills from the 1996 film version of *The Crucible* throughout the text. As you come across each photograph, identify the character(s) or scene it portrays.

BETTY: You did, you did! You drank a charm to kill John Proctor's wife! You drank a charm to kill Goody Proctor!

ABIGAIL, *smashes her across the face:* Shut it! Now shut it!

BETTY: *collapsing on the bed:* Mama, Mama! *She dissolves into sobs.*

ABIGAIL: Now look you. All of you. We danced. And Tituba conjured Ruth Putnam's dead sisters. And that is all. And mark this. Let either of you breathe a word, or the edge of a word, about the other things, and I will come to you in the black of some terrible night and I will bring a pointy reckoning that will shudder you. And you know I can do it; I saw Indians smash my dear parents' heads on the pillow next to mine, and I have seen some reddish work done at night, and I can make you wish you had never seen the sun go down! *She goes to* BETTY *and roughly sits her up.* Now, you—sit up and stop this!

But BETTY *collapses in her hands and lies inert on the bed.*

MARY WARREN, *with hysterical fright:* What's got her? ABIGAIL *stares in fright at* BETTY. Abby, she's going to die! It's a sin to conjure, and we—

ABIGAIL, *starting for* MARY: I say shut it, Mary Warren!

Enter JOHN PROCTOR. *On seeing him.* MARY WARREN *leaps in fright.*

Proctor was a farmer in his middle thirties. He need not have been a partisan of any faction in the town, but there is evidence to suggest that he had a sharp and biting way with hypocrites. He was the kind of man—powerful of body, even-tempered, and not easily led—who cannot refuse support to partisans without drawing their deepest resentment. In Proctor's presence a fool felt his foolishness instantly—and a Proctor is always marked for <u>calumny</u> therefore.

But as we shall see, the steady manner he displays does not spring from an untroubled soul. He is a sinner, a sinner not only against the moral fashion of the time, but against his own vision of decent conduct. These people had no ritual for the washing away of sins. It is another trait we inherited from them, and it has helped to discipline us as well as to breed hypocrisy among us. Proctor, respected and even feared in Salem, has come to regard himself as a kind of fraud. But no hint of this has yet appeared on the surface, and as he enters from the crowded parlor below it is a man in his prime we see, with a quiet confidence and an unexpressed, hidden force. Mary Warren, his servant, can barely speak for embarrassment and fear.

MARY WARREN: Oh! I'm just going home, Mr. Proctor.

PROCTOR: Be you foolish, Mary Warren? Be you deaf? I forbid you leave the house, did I not? Why shall I pay you? I am looking for you more often than my cows!

MARY WARREN: I only come to see the great doings in the world.

PROCTOR: I'll show you a great doin' on your arse one of these days. Now get you home; my wife is waitin' with your work! *Trying to retain a shred of dignity, she goes slowly out.*

MERCY LEWIS, *both afraid of him and strangely titillated:* I'd best be off. I have my Ruth to watch. Good morning, Mr. Proctor.

MERCY *sidles out. Since* PROCTOR's *entrance,* ABIGAIL *has stood as though on tiptoe, absorbing his presence, wide-eyed. He glances at her then goes to* BETTY *on the bed.*

ABIGAIL: Gad. I'd almost forgot how strong you are, John Proctor!

PROCTOR, *looking at* ABIGAIL *now, the faintest suggestion of a knowing smile on his face:* What's this mischief here?

ABIGAIL, *with a nervous laugh:* Oh, she's only gone silly somehow.

PROCTOR: The road past my house is a pilgrimage to Salem all morning. The town's mumbling witchcraft.

ABIGAIL: Oh, posh! *Winningly she comes a little closer, with a confidential, wicked air.* We were dancin' in the woods last night, and my uncle leaped in on us. She took fright, is all.

PROCTOR, *his smile widening:* Ah, you're wicked yet, aren't y'! *A trill of expectant laughter escapes her, and she dares come closer, feverishly looking into his eyes.* You'll be clapped in the stocks before you're twenty.

> ◆ **Literary Focus**
> How do the stage directions help you interpret Abigail's behavior?

He takes a step to go, and she springs into his path.

ABIGAIL: Give me a word, John. A soft word. *Her concentrated desire destroys his smile.*

PROCTOR: No, no, Abby. That's done with.

ABIGAIL, *tauntingly:* You come five mile to see a silly girl fly? I know you better.

PROCTOR, *setting her firmly out of his path:* I come to see what mischief your uncle's brewin' now. *With final emphasis:* Put it out of mind, Abby.

◆ **Build Vocabulary**

calumny (kal´ əm nē) *n.:* False accusation; slander

ABIGAIL, *grasping his hand before he can release her:* John—I am waitin' for you every night.

PROCTOR: Abby, I never give you hope to wait for me.

ABIGAIL, *now beginning to anger—she can't believe it:* I have something better than hope, I think!

PROCTOR: Abby, you'll put it out of mind. I'll not be comin' for you more.

ABIGAIL: You're surely sportin' with me.

PROCTOR: You know me better.

ABIGAIL: I know how you clutched my back behind your house and sweated like a stallion whenever I come near! Or did I dream that? It's she put me out, you cannot pretend it were you. I saw your face when she put me out, and you loved me then and you do now!

PROCTOR: Abby, that's a wild thing to say—

ABIGAIL: A wild thing may say wild things. But not so wild, I think. I have seen you since she put me out; I have seen you nights.

PROCTOR: I have hardly stepped off my farm this seven-month.

ABIGAIL: I have a sense for heat, John, and yours has drawn me to my window, and I have seen you looking up, burning in your loneliness. Do you tell me you've never looked up at my window?

PROCTOR: I may have looked up.

ABIGAIL, *now softening:* And you must. You are no wintry man. I know you, John. I *know* you. *She is weeping.* I cannot sleep for dreamin'; I cannot dream but I wake and walk about the house as though I'd find you comin' through some door. *She clutches him desperately.*

PROCTOR, *gently pressing her from him, with great sympathy but firmly:* Child—

ABIGAIL, *with a flash of anger:* How do you call me child!

PROCTOR: Abby, I may think of you softly from time to time. But I will cut off my hand before I'll ever reach for you again. Wipe it out of mind. We never touched, Abby.

ABIGAIL: Aye, but we did.

PROCTOR: Aye, but we did not.

ABIGAIL, *with a bitter anger:* Oh, I marvel how such a strong man may let such a sickly wife be—

PROCTOR, *angered—at himself as well:* You'll speak nothin' of Elizabeth!

ABIGAIL: She is blackening my name in the village! She is telling lies about me! She is a cold, sniveling woman, and you bend to her! Let her turn you like a—

PROCTOR, *shaking her:* Do you look for whippin'?

A psalm is heard being sung below.

ABIGAIL, *in tears:* I look for John Proctor that took me from my sleep and put knowledge in my heart! I never knew what pretense Salem was, I never knew the lying lessons I was taught by all these Christian women and their covenanted men! And now you bid me tear the light out of my eyes? I will not, I cannot! You loved me, John Proctor, and whatever sin it is, you love me yet! *He turns abruptly to go out. She rushes to him.* John, pity me, pity me!

The words "going up to Jesus" are heard in the psalm, and BETTY *claps her ears suddenly and whines loudly.*

ABIGAIL: Betty? *She hurries to* BETTY, *who is now sitting up and screaming.* PROCTOR *goes to* BETTY *as* ABIGAIL *is trying to pull her hands down, calling "Betty!"*

PROCTOR, *growing unnerved:* What's she doing? Girl, what ails you? Stop that wailing!

The singing has stopped in the midst of this, and now PARRIS *rushes in.*

PARRIS: What happened? What are you doing to her? Betty! *He rushes to the bed, crying, "Betty, Betty!"* MRS. PUTNAM *enters, feverish with curiosity, and with her* PUTNAM *and* MERCY LEWIS. PARRIS, *at the bed, keeps lightly slapping* BETTY's *face, while she moans and tries to get up.*

ABIGAIL: She heard you singin' and suddenly she's up and screamin'.

MRS. PUTNAM: The psalm! The psalm! She cannot bear to hear the Lord's name!

PARRIS: No, God forbid. Mercy, run to the

doctor! Tell him what's happened here! MERCY LEWIS *rushes out.*

MRS. PUTNAM: Mark it for a sign, mark it!

REBECCA NURSE, *seventy-two, enters. She is white-haired, leaning upon her walking-stick.*

PUTNAM, *pointing at the whimpering* BETTY: That is a notorious sign of witchcraft afoot, Goody Nurse, a prodigious sign!

MRS. PUTNAM: My mother told me that! When they cannot bear to hear the name of—

PARRIS, *trembling:* Rebecca, Rebecca, go to her, we're lost. She suddenly cannot bear to hear the Lord's—

GILES COREY, *eighty-three, enters. He is knotted with muscle, canny, inquisitive, and still powerful.*

REBECCA: There is hard sickness here, Giles Corey, so please to keep the quiet.

GILES: I've not said a word. No one here can testify I've said a word. Is she going to fly again? I hear she flies.

PUTNAM: Man, be quiet now!

Everything is quiet. REBECCA *walks across the room to the bed. Gentleness exudes from her.* BETTY *is quietly whimpering, eyes shut.* REBECCA *simply stands over the child, who gradually quiets.*

And while they are so absorbed, we may put a word in for Rebecca. Rebecca was the wife of Francis Nurse, who, from all accounts, was one of those men for whom both sides of the argument had to have respect. He was called upon to arbitrate disputes as though he were an unofficial judge, and Rebecca also enjoyed the high opinion most people had for him. By the time of the delusion, they had three hundred acres, and their children were settled in separate homesteads within the same estate. However, Francis had originally rented the land, and one theory has it that, as he gradually paid for it and raised his social status, there were those who resented his rise.

Another suggestion to explain the systematic campaign against Rebecca, and inferentially against Francis, is the land war he fought with

his neighbors, one of whom was a Putnam. This squabble grew to the proportions of a battle in the woods between partisans of both sides, and it is said to have lasted for two days. As for Rebecca herself, the general opinion of her character was so high that to explain how anyone dared cry her out for a witch—and more, how adults could bring themselves to lay hands on her—we must look to the fields and boundaries of that time.

As we have seen, Thomas Putnam's man for the Salem ministry was Bayley. The Nurse clan had been in the faction that prevented Bayley's taking office. In addition, certain families allied to the Nurses by blood or friendship, and whose farms were contiguous with the Nurse farm or close to it, combined to break away from the Salem town authority and set up Topsfield, a new and independent entity whose existence was resented by old Salemites.

That the guiding hand behind the outcry was Putnam's is indicated by the fact that, as soon as it began, this Topsfield-Nurse faction absented themselves from church in protest and disbelief. It was Edward and Jonathan Putnam who signed the first complaint against Rebecca; and Thomas Putnam's little daughter was the one who fell into a fit at the hearing and pointed to Rebecca as her attacker. To top it all, Mrs. Putnam—who is now staring at the bewitched child on the bed—soon accused Rebecca's spirit of "tempting her to iniquity," a charge that had more truth in it than Mrs. Putnam could know.

MRS. PUTNAM, *astonished:* What have you done?

REBECCA, *in thought, now leaves the bedside and sits.*

PARRIS, *wondrous and relieved:* What do you make of it, Rebecca?

PUTNAM, *eagerly:* Goody Nurse, will you go to my Ruth and see if you can wake her?

REBECCA, *sitting:* I think she'll wake in time. Pray calm yourselves. I have eleven children, and I am twenty-six times a grandma, and I have seen them all through their silly seasons, and when it come on them they will run the Devil bowlegged keeping up with their mischief. I think she'll wake when she tires of it. A child's spirit is like a child, you can never catch it by running after it; you must stand still, and, for

love, it will soon itself come back.

PROCTOR: Aye, that's the truth of it, Rebecca.

MRS. PUTNAM: This is no silly season, Rebecca. My Ruth is bewildered, Rebecca; she cannot eat.

REBECCA: Perhaps she is not hungered yet. *To* PARRIS: I hope you are not decided to go in search of loose spirits, Mr. Parris. I've heard promise of that outside.

PARRIS: A wide opinion's running in the parish that the Devil may be among us, and I would satisfy them that they are wrong.

PROCTOR: Then let you come out and call them wrong. Did you consult the wardens before you called this minister to look for devils?

PARRIS: He is not coming to look for devils!

PROCTOR: Then what's he coming for?

PUTNAM: There be children dyin' in the village, Mister!

PROCTOR: I seen none dyin'. This society will not be a bag to swing around your head, Mr. Putnam. *To* PARRIS: Did you call a meeting before you—?

PUTNAM: I am sick of meetings; cannot the man turn his head without he have a meeting?

PROCTOR: He may turn his head, but not to Hell!

REBECCA: Pray, John, be calm. *Pause. He defers to her.* Mr. Parris, I think you'd best send Reverend Hale back as soon as he come. This will set us all to arguin' again in the society, and we thought to have peace this year. I think we ought rely on the doctor now, and good prayer.

MRS. PUTNAM: Rebecca, the doctor's baffled!

REBECCA: If so he is, then let us go to God for the cause of it. There is prodigious danger in the seeking of loose spirits. I fear it, I fear it. Let us rather blame ourselves and—

PUTNAM: How may we blame ourselves? I am one of nine sons; the Putnam seed have peopled this province. And yet I have but one child left of eight—and now she shrivels!

REBECCA: I cannot fathom that.

MRS. PUTNAM, *with a growing edge of sarcasm:* But I must! You think it God's work you should never lose a child, nor grandchild either, and I bury all but one? There are wheels within wheels in this village, and fires within fires!

PUTNAM, *to* PARRIS: When Reverend Hale comes, you will proceed to look for signs of witchcraft here.

PROCTOR, *to* PUTNAM: You cannot command Mr. Parris. We vote by name in this society, not by acreage.

PUTNAM: I never heard you worried so on this society, Mr. Proctor. I do not think I saw you at Sabbath meeting since snow flew.

PROCTOR: I have trouble enough without I come five mile to hear him preach only hellfire and bloody damnation. Take it to heart, Mr. Parris. There are many others who stay away from church these days because you hardly ever mention God any more.

PARRIS, *now aroused:* Why, that's a drastic charge!

REBECCA: It's somewhat true; there are many that quail to bring their children—

PARRIS: I do not preach for children, Rebecca. It is not the children who are unmindful of their obligations toward this ministry.

REBECCA: Are there really those unmindful?

PARRIS: I should say the better half of Salem village—

PUTNAM: And more than that!

PARRIS: Where is my wood? My contract provides I be supplied with all my firewood. I am waiting since November for a stick, and even in November I had to show my frostbitten hands like some London beggar!

GILES: You are allowed six pound a year to buy your wood, Mr. Parris.

PARRIS: I regard that six pound as part of my salary. I am paid little enough without I spend six pound on firewood.

PROCTOR: Sixty, plus six for firewood—

PARRIS: The salary is sixty-six pound, Mr. Proctor! I am not some preaching farmer with a book under my arm; I am a graduate of Harvard College.

GILES: Aye, and well instructed in arithmetic!

PARRIS: Mr. Corey, you will look far for a man of my kind at sixty pound a year! I am not used to this poverty; I left a thrifty business in the Barbados to serve the Lord. I do not fathom it, why am I persecuted here? I cannot offer one proposition but there be a howling riot of argument. I have often wondered if the Devil be in it somewhere; I cannot understand you people otherwise.

PROCTOR: Mr. Parris, you are the first minister ever did demand the deed to this house—

PARRIS: Man! Don't a minister deserve a house to live in?

PROCTOR: To live in, yes. But to ask ownership is like you shall own the meeting house itself; the last meeting I were at you spoke so long on deeds and mortgages I thought it were an auction.

PARRIS: I want a mark of confidence, is all! I am your third preacher in seven years. I do not wish to be put out like the cat whenever some majority feels the whim. You people seem not to comprehend that a minister is the Lord's man in the parish; a minister is not to be so lightly crossed and contradicted—

PUTNAM: Aye!

PARRIS: There is either obedience or the church will burn like Hell is burning!

PROCTOR: Can you speak one minute without we land in Hell again? I am sick of Hell!

PARRIS: It is not for you to say what is good for you to hear!

PROCTOR: I may speak my heart, I think!

PARRIS, *in a fury:* What, are we Quakers?[8] We are not Quakers here yet, Mr. Proctor. And you may tell that to your followers!

PROCTOR: My followers!

PARRIS—*now he's out with it:* There is a party in this church. I am not blind; there is a faction and a party.

PROCTOR: Against you?

PUTNAM: Against him and all authority!

PROCTOR: Why, then I must find it and join it.

There is shock among the others.

REBECCA: He does not mean that.

PUTNAM: He confessed it now!

PROCTOR: I mean it solemnly, Rebecca; I like not the smell of this "authority."

REBECCA: No, you cannot break charity with your minister. You are another kind, John. Clasp his hand, make your peace.

---

8. **Quakers:** Members of the Society of Friends, a Christian religious sect that was founded in the mid-17th century and has no formal creed, rites, or priesthood. Unlike the Quakers, the Puritans had a rigid code of conduct and were expected to heed the words of their ministers.

PROCTOR: I have a crop to sow and lumber to drag home. *He goes angrily to the door and turns to* COREY *with a smile.* What say you, GILES, let's find the party. He says there's a party.

GILES: I've changed my opinion of this man, John. Mr. Parris, I beg your pardon. I never thought you had so much iron in you.

PARRIS, *surprised*: Why, thank you, Giles!

GILES: It suggests to the mind what the trouble be among us all these years. *To all:* Think on it. Wherefore is everybody suing everybody else? Think on it now, it's a deep thing, and dark as a pit. I have been six time in court this year—

PROCTOR, *familiarly, with warmth, although he knows he is approaching the edge of Giles' tolerance with this:* Is it the Devil's fault that a man cannot say you good morning without you clap him for defamation? You're old, Giles, and you're not hearin' so well as you did.

GILES—*he cannot be crossed:* John Proctor, I have only last month collected four pound damages for you publicly sayin' I burned the roof off your house, and I—

PROCTOR, *laughing:* I never said no such thing, but I've paid you for it, so I hope I can call you deaf without charge. Now come along, Giles, and help me drag my lumber home.

PUTNAM: A moment, Mr. Proctor. What lumber is that you're draggin', if I may ask you?

PROCTOR: My lumber. From out my forest by the riverside.

PUTNAM: Why, we are surely gone wild this year. What anarchy is this? That tract is in my bounds, it's in my bounds, Mr. Proctor.

PROCTOR: In your bounds! *Indicating* REBECCA: I bought that tract from Goody Nurse's husband five months ago.

PUTNAM: He had no right to sell it. It stands clear in my grandfather's will that all the land between the river and—

PROCTOR: Your grandfather had a habit of willing land that never belonged to him, if I may say it plain.

GILES: That's God's truth; he nearly willed away my north pasture but he knew I'd break his fingers before he'd set his name to it. Let's get your lumber home, John. I feel a sudden will to work coming on.

PUTNAM: You load one oak of mine and you'll fight to drag it home!

GILES: Aye, and we'll win too, Putnam—this fool and I. Come on! *He turns to* PROCTOR *and starts out.*

PUTNAM: I'll have my men on you, Corey! I'll clap a writ on you!

Enter REVEREND JOHN HALE *of Beverly.*

Mr. Hale is nearing forty, a tight-skinned, eager-eyed intellectual. This is a beloved errand for him; on being called here to ascertain witchcraft he felt the pride of the specialist whose unique knowledge has at last been publicly called for. Like almost all men of learning, he spent a good deal of time pondering the invisible world, especially since he had himself encountered a witch in his parish not long before. That woman, however, turned into a mere pest under his searching scrutiny, and the child she had allegedly been afflicting recovered her normal behavior after Hale had given her his kindness and a few days of rest in his own house. However, that experience never raised a doubt in his mind as to the reality of the underworld or the existence of Lucifer's many-faced lieutenants. And his belief is not to his discredit. Better minds than Hale's were— and still are—convinced that there is a society of spirits beyond our ken. One cannot help noting that one of his lines has never yet raised a laugh in any audience that has seen this play; it is his assurance that "We cannot look to superstition in this. The Devil is precise." Evidently we are not quite certain even now whether diabolism is holy and not to be scoffed at. And it is no accident that we should be so bemused.

Like Reverend Hale and the others on this stage, we conceive the Devil as a necessary part of a respectable view of cosmology. Ours is a divided empire in which certain ideas and emotions and actions are of God, and their opposites are of Lucifer. It is as impossible for most men to conceive of a morality without sin as of an earth without "sky." Since 1692 a great but superficial change has wiped out God's beard and the Devil's horns, but the world is still gripped between two diametrically opposed absolutes. The concept of unity, in which positive and negative are attributes of the same force, in which good and evil are relative, ever-changing, and always joined to the same phenomenon—such a concept is still reserved to the physical sciences and to the few who have grasped the history of ideas. When it is recalled that until the Christian era the underworld was never regarded as a hostile area, that all gods were useful and essentially friendly to man despite occasional lapses; when we see the steady and methodical <u>inculcation</u> into humanity of the idea of man's worthlessness—until redeemed—the necessity of the Devil may become evident as a weapon, a weapon designed and used time and time again in every age to whip men into a surrender to a particular church or church-state.

Our difficulty in believing the—for want of a better word—political inspiration of the Devil is due in great part to the fact that he is called up and damned not only by our social antagonists but by our own side, whatever it may be. The Catholic Church, through its Inquisition,[9] is famous for cultivating Lucifer as the arch-fiend, but the Church's enemies relied no less upon the Old Boy to keep the human mind enthralled. Luther[10] was himself accused of alliance with Hell, and he in turn accused his enemies. To complicate matters further, he believed that he had had contact with the Devil and had argued theology with him. I am not surprised at this, for at my own university a professor of history—a Lutheran,[11] by the way—used to assemble his graduate students, draw the shades, and commune in the classroom with Erasmus.[12] He was never, to my knowledge, officially scoffed at for this, the reason being that the university officials, like most of us, are the children of a history which still sucks at the Devil's teats. At this writing, only England has held back before the temptations of contemporary diabolism. In the countries of the Communist ideology, all resistance of any import is linked to the totally malign capitalist succubi,[13] and in America any man who is not reactionary in his views is open to the charge of alliance with the Red hell. Political opposition, thereby, is given an inhumane overlay which then justifies the abrogation[14] of all normally applied customs of civilized intercourse. A political policy is equated with moral right, and opposition to it with diabolical malevolence. Once such an equation is effectively made, society becomes a congerie[15] of plots and counterplots, and the main role of government changes from that of the arbiter to that of the scourge of God.

The results of this process are no different now from what they ever were, except sometimes in the degree of cruelty inflicted, and not always even in that department. Normally, the actions and deeds of a man were all that society felt comfortable in judging. The secret intent of an action was left to the ministers, priests, and rabbis to deal with. When diabolism rises, however, actions are the least important manifests of the true nature of a man. The Devil, as Reverend Hale said, is a wily one, and until an hour before he fell, even God thought him beautiful in Heaven.

The analogy, however, seems to falter when one considers that, while there were no witches then, there are Communists and capitalists now, and in each camp there is certain proof that spies of each side are at work undermining the other. But this is a snobbish objection and not at all warranted by the facts. I have no doubt that people *were* communing with, and even worshiping, the Devil in Salem, and if the

---

9. **Inquisition:** General tribunal established in the 13th century for the discovery and suppression of beliefs and opinions opposed to the orthodox doctrines of the Church.
10. **Luther:** Martin Luther (1483–1546), German theologian who led the Protestant Reformation.
11. **Lutheran:** Member of the Protestant denomination founded by Martin Luther.

12. **Erasmus:** Desiderius Erasmus (1466?–1536), Dutch humanist, scholar, and theologian.
13. **succubi** (suk′ yoo bī): Female demons thought to lie on sleeping men.
14. **abrogation** (ab′ rō gā′ shən): Abolishment.
15. **congerie** (kän′ jə rē′): Heap; pile.

whole truth could be known in this case, as it is in others, we should discover a regular and conventionalized <u>propitiation</u> of the dark spirit. One certain evidence of this is the confession of Tituba, the slave of Reverend Parris, and another is the behavior of the children who were known to have indulged in sorceries with her.

There are accounts of similar *klatches*[16] in Europe, where the daughters of the towns would assemble at night and, sometimes with fetishes,[17] sometimes with a selected young man, give themselves to love, with some bastardly results. The Church, sharp-eyed as it must be when gods long dead are brought to life, condemned these orgies as witchcraft and interpreted them, rightly, as a resurgence of the Dionysiac[18] forces it had crushed long before. Sex, sin, and the Devil were early linked, and so they continued to be in Salem, and are today. From all accounts there are no more puritanical mores in the world than those enforced by the Communists in Russia, where women's fashions, for instance, are as prudent and all-covering as any American Baptist would desire. The divorce laws lay a tremendous responsibility on the father for the care of his children. Even the laxity of divorce regulations in the early years of the revolution was undoubtedly a revulsion from the nineteenth-century Victorian[19] immobility of marriage and the consequent hypocrisy that developed from it. If for no other reasons, a state so powerful, so jealous of the uniformity of its citizens, cannot long tolerate the atomization of the family. And yet, in American eyes at least, there remains the conviction that the Russian attitude toward women is lascivious. It is the Devil working again, just as he is working within the Slav who is shocked at the very idea of a woman's disrobing herself in a burlesque show. Our opposites are always robed in sexual sin,

and it is from this unconscious conviction that demonology gains both its attractive sensuality and its capacity to infuriate and frighten.

Coming into Salem now, Reverend Hale conceives of himself much as a young doctor on his first call. His painfully acquired armory of symptoms, catchwords, and diagnostic procedures are now to be put to use at last. The road from Beverly is unusually busy this morning, and he has passed a hundred rumors that make him smile at the ignorance of the yeomanry in this most precise science. He feels himself allied with the best minds of Europe— kings, philosophers, scientists, and ecclesiasts of all churches. His goal is light, goodness and its preservation, and he knows the exaltation of the blessed whose intelligence, sharpened by minute examinations of enormous tracts, is finally called upon to face what may be a bloody fight with the Fiend himself.

He appears loaded down with half a dozen heavy books.

HALE: Pray you, someone take these!

PARRIS, *delighted:* Mr. Hale! Oh! it's good to see you again! *Taking some books:* My, they're heavy!

HALE, *setting down his books:* They must be; they are weighted with authority.

PARRIS, *a little scared:* Well, you do come prepared!

HALE: We shall need hard study if it comes to tracking down the Old Boy. *Noticing* REBECCA: You cannot be Rebecca Nurse?

REBECCA: I am, sir. Do you know me?

HALE: It's strange how I knew you, but I suppose you look as such a good soul should. We have all heard of your great charities in Beverly.

---

16. *klatches* (klächz): Informal gatherings.
17. **fetishes** (fet´ ish iz): Objects believed to have magical power.
18. **Dionysiac** (dī´ ə nish´ ē ak): Characteristic of Dionysus, Greek god of wine and revelry; thus, wild, frenzied, sensuous.
19. **Victorian:** Characteristic of the time when Victoria was queen of England (1837–1901), an era associated with respectability, prudery, and hypocrisy.

◆ **Build Vocabulary**

inculcation (in´ kul kā´ shən) *n.*: Teaching by repetition and insistent urging

propitiation (prə pish´ ē ā´ shən) *n.*: Action designed to soothe or satisfy a person, a cause, etc.; conciliation

PARRIS: Do you know this gentleman? Mr. Thomas Putnam. And his good wife Ann.

HALE: Putnam! I had not expected such distinguished company, sir.

PUTNAM, *pleased:* It does seem to help us today, Mr. Hale. We look to you to come to our house and save our child.

HALE: Your child ails too?

MRS. PUTNAM: Her soul, her soul seems flown away. She sleeps and yet she walks . . .

PUTNAM: She cannot eat.

HALE: Cannot eat! *Thinks on it. Then, to* PROCTOR *and* GILES COREY: Do you men have afflicted children?

PARRIS: No, no, these are farmers. John Proctor—

GILES COREY: He don't believe in witches.

PROCTOR, *to* HALE: I never spoke on witches one way or the other. Will you come, Giles?

GILES: No—no, John, I think not. I have some few queer questions of my own to ask this fellow.

PROCTOR: I've heard you to be a sensible man, Mr. Hale. I hope you'll leave some of it in Salem.

PROCTOR *goes.* HALE *stands embarrassed for an instant.*

PARRIS, *quickly:* Will you look at my daughter, sir? *Leads* HALE *to the bed.* She has tried to leap out the window; we discovered her this morning on the highroad, waving her arms as though she'd fly.

HALE, *narrowing his eyes:* Tries to fly.

PUTNAM: She cannot bear to hear the Lord's name, Mr. Hale; that's a sure sign of witchcraft afloat.

HALE, *holding up his hands:* No, no. Now let me instruct you. We cannot look to superstition in this. The Devil is precise; the marks of his presence are definite as stone, and I must tell you all that I shall not proceed unless you are prepared to believe me if I should find no bruise of hell upon her.

PARRIS: It is agreed, sir—it is agreed—we will abide by your judgment.

HALE: Good then. *He goes to the bed, looks down at* BETTY. *To* PARRIS: Now, sir, what were your first warning of this strangeness?

PARRIS: Why, sir—I discovered her—*indicating* ABIGAIL—and my niece and ten or twelve of the other girls, dancing in the forest last night.

HALE, *surprised:* You permit dancing?

PARRIS: No, no, it were secret—

MRS. PUTNAM, *unable to wait:* Mr. Parris's slave has knowledge of conjurin', sir.

PARRIS, *to* MRS. PUTNAM: We cannot be sure of that, Goody Ann—

MRS. PUTNAM, *frightened, very softly:* I know it, sir. I sent my child—she should learn from Tituba who murdered her sisters.

REBECCA, *horrified:* Goody Ann! You sent a child to conjure up the dead?

MRS. PUTNAM: Let God blame me, not you, not you, Rebecca! I'll not have you judging me any more! *To* HALE: Is it a natural work to lose seven children before they live a day?

PARRIS: Sssh!

REBECCA, *with great pain, turns her face away. There is a pause.*

HALE: Seven dead in childbirth.

MRS. PUTNAM, *softly:* Aye. *Her voice breaks; she looks up at him. Silence.* HALE *is impressed.* PARRIS *looks to him. He goes to his books, opens one, turns pages, then reads. All wait, avidly.*

PARRIS, *hushed:* What book is that?

MRS. PUTNAM: What's there, sir?

HALE, *with a tasty love of intellectual pursuit:* Here is all the invisible world, caught, defined, and calculated. In these books the Devil stands stripped of all his brute disguises. Here are all your familiar spirits—your incubi[20] and succubi, your witches that go by land, by air, and by sea;

---

20. **incubi** (in´ kyoo bī): Spirits or demons thought to lie on sleeping women.

your wizards of the night and of the day. Have no fear now—we shall find him out if he has come among us, and I mean to crush him utterly if he has shown his face! *He starts for the bed.*

REBECCA: Will it hurt the child, sir?

HALE: I cannot tell, If she is truly in the Devil's grip we may have to rip and tear to get her free.

REBECCA: I think I'll go, then. I am too old for this. *She rises.*

PARRIS, *striving for conviction:* Why, Rebecca, we may open up the boil of all our troubles today!

REBECCA: Let us hope for that. I go to God for you, sir.

PARRIS, *with trepidation—and resentment:* I hope you do not mean to go to Satan here! *Slight pause.*

REBECCA: I wish I knew. *She goes out; they feel resentful of her note of moral superiority.*

PUTNAM, *abruptly:* Come, Mr. Hale, let's get on. Sit you here.

GILES: Mr. Hale, I have always wanted to ask a learned man—what signifies the readin' of strange books?

HALE: What books?

GILES: I cannot tell; she hides them.

HALE: Who does this?

GILES: Martha, my wife. I have waked at night many a time and found her in a corner, readin' of a book. Now what do you make of that?

HALE: Why, that's not necessarily—

GILES: It discomfits me! Last night—mark this—I tried and tried and could not say my prayers. And then she close her book and walks out of the house, and suddenly—mark this—I could pray again!

Old Giles must be spoken for, if only because his fate was to be so remarkable and so different from that of all the others. He was in his early eighties at this time, and was the most comical hero in the history. No man has ever been blamed for so much. If a cow was missed, the first thought was to look for her around Corey's house; a fire blazing up at night brought suspicion of arson to his door. He didn't give a hoot for public opinion, and only in his last years—after he had married Martha—did he bother much with the church. That she stopped his prayer is very probable, but he forgot to say that he'd only recently learned any prayers and it didn't take much to make him stumble over them. He was a crank and a nuisance, but withal a deeply innocent and brave man. In court, once, he was asked if it were true that he had been frightened by the strange behavior of a hog and had then said he knew it to be the Devil in an animal's shape. "What frighted you?" he was asked. He forgot everything but the word "frighted," and instantly replied, "I do not know that I ever spoke that word in my life."

HALE: Ah! The stoppage of prayer—that is strange. I'll speak further on that with you.

GILES: I'm not sayin' she's touched the Devil, now, but I'd admire to know what books she reads and why she hides them. She'll not answer me, y' see.

HALE: Aye, we'll discuss it. *To all:* Now mark me, if the Devil is in her you will witness some frightful wonders in this room, so please to keep your wits about you. Mr. Putnam, stand close in case she flies. Now, Betty, dear, will you sit up? PUTNAM *comes in closer, ready-handed.* HALE *sits* BETTY *up, but she hangs limp in his hands.* Hmmm. *He observes her carefully. The others watch breathlessly.* Can you hear me? I am John Hale, minister of Beverly. I have come to help you, dear. Do you remember my two little girls in Beverly? *She does not stir in his hands.*

PARRIS, *in fright:* How can it be the Devil? Why would he choose my house to strike? We have all manner of <u>licentious</u> people in the village!

HALE: What victory would the Devil have to win a soul already bad? It is the best the Devil

---

◆ Build Vocabulary

licentious (lī sen´ shəs) *adj.*: Lacking moral restraint; disregarding accepted rules, especially in moral conduct

wants, and who is better than the minister?

GILES: That's deep, Mr. Parris, deep, deep!

PARRIS, *with resolution now:* Betty! Answer Mr. Hale! Betty!

HALE: Does someone afflict you, child? It need not be a woman, mind you, or a man. Perhaps some bird invisible to others comes to you— perhaps a pig, a mouse, or any beast at all. Is there some figure bids you fly? *The child remains limp in his hands. In silence he lays her back on the pillow. Now, holding out his hands toward her, he intones:* In nomine Domini Sabaoth sui filiique ite ad infernos.[21] *She does not stir. He turns to* ABIGAIL, *his eyes narrowing.* Abigail, what sort of dancing were you doing with her in the forest?

ABIGAIL: Why—common dancing is all.

PARRIS: I think I ought to say that I—I saw a kettle in the grass where they were dancing.

ABIGAIL: That were only soup.

HALE: What sort of soup were in this kettle, Abigail?

ABIGAIL: Why, it were beans—and lentils, I think, and—

HALE: Mr. Parris, you did not notice, did you,

---

21. **In nomine Domini Sabaoth sui filiique ite ad infernos** (in nō′mē nā dō′ mē nē sab′ ā äth sōō′ ē fē′ lēē kwā ē′ tā äd in fur′ nōs): "In the name of the lord of hosts and his son, get thee to the lower world" (Latin).

---

any living thing in the kettle? A mouse, perhaps, a spider, a frog—?

PARRIS, *fearfully:* I—do believe there were some movement—in the soup.

ABIGAIL: That jumped in, we never put it in!

HALE, *quickly:* What jumped in?

ABIGAIL: Why, a very little frog jumped—

PARRIS: A frog, Abby!

HALE, *grasping* ABIGAIL: Abigail, it may be your cousin is dying. Did you call the Devil last night?

ABIGAIL: I never called him! Tituba, Tituba . . .

PARRIS, *blanched:* She called the Devil?

HALE: I should like to speak with Tituba.

PARRIS: Goody Ann, will you bring her up? MRS. PUTNAM *exits.*

HALE: How did she call him?

ABIGAIL: I know not—she spoke Barbados.

HALE: Did you feel any strangeness when she called him? A sudden cold wind, perhaps? A trembling below the ground?

ABIGAIL: I didn't see no Devil! *Shaking* BETTY: Betty, wake up. Betty! Betty!

HALE: You cannot evade me, Abigail. Did your cousin drink any of the brew in that kettle?

ABIGAIL: She never drank it!

HALE: Did you drink it?

ABIGAIL: No, sir!

HALE: Did Tituba ask you to drink it?

ABIGAIL: She tried, but I refused.

HALE: Why are you concealing? Have you sold yourself to Lucifer?

ABIGAIL: I never sold myself! I'm a good girl! I'm a proper girl!

MRS. PUTNAM *enters with* TITUBA, *and instantly* ABIGAIL *points at* TITUBA.

ABIGAIL: She made me do it! She made Betty do it!

TITUBA, *shocked and angry:* Abby!

ABIGAIL: She makes me drink blood!

PARRIS: Blood!!

MRS. PUTNAM: My baby's blood?

TITUBA: No, no, chicken blood. I give she chicken blood!

HALE: Woman, have you enlisted these children for the Devil?

TITUBA: No, no, sir, I don't truck with no Devil!

HALE: Why can she not wake? Are you silencing this child?

TITUBA: I love me Betty!

HALE: You have sent your spirit out upon this child, have you not? Are you gathering souls for the Devil?

ABIGAIL: She sends her spirit on me in church; she makes me laugh at prayer!

PARRIS: She have often laughed at prayer!

ABIGAIL: She comes to me every night to go and drink blood!

TITUBA: You beg *me* to conjure! She beg *me* make charm—

ABIGAIL: Don't lie! *To* HALE: She comes to me while I sleep; she's always making me dream corruptions!

TITUBA: Why you say that, Abby?

ABIGAIL: Sometimes I wake and find myself standing in the open doorway and not a stitch on my body! I always hear her laughing in my sleep. I hear her singing her Barbados songs and tempting me with—

TITUBA: Mister Reverend, I never—

HALE, *resolved now:* Tituba, I want you to wake this child.

TITUBA: I have no power on this child, sir.

HALE: You most certainly do, and you will free her from it now! When did you compact with the Devil?

TITUBA: I don't compact with no Devil!

PARRIS: You will confess yourself or I will take you out and whip you to your death, Tituba!

PUTNAM: This woman must be hanged! She must be taken and hanged!

TITUBA, *terrified, falls to her knees:* No, no, don't hang Tituba! I tell him I don't desire to work for him, sir.

PARRIS: The Devil?

HALE: Then you saw him! TITUBA *weeps.* Now Tituba, I know that when we bind ourselves to Hell it is very hard to break with it. We are going to help you tear yourself free—

> ◆ **Reading Strategy**
> What does this dialogue reveal about Tituba's motives for suddenly admitting that she has trafficked with the Devil?

TITUBA, *frightened by the coming process:* Mister Reverend, I do believe somebody else be witchin' these children.

HALE: Who?

TITUBA: I don't know, sir, but the Devil got him numerous witches.

HALE: Does he! *It is a clue.* Tituba, look into my eyes. Come, look into me. *She raises her eyes to his fearfully.* You would be a good Christian woman, would you not, Tituba?

TITUBA: Aye, sir, a good Christian woman.

HALE: And you love these little children?

TITUBA: Oh, yes, sir, I don't desire to hurt little children.

HALE: And you love God, Tituba?

TITUBA: I love God with all my bein'.

HALE: Now, in God's holy name—

TITUBA: Bless Him. Bless Him. *She is rocking on her knees, sobbing in terror.*

HALE: And to His glory—

TITUBA: Eternal glory. Bless Him—bless God . . .

HALE: Open yourself, Tituba—open yourself and let God's holy light shine on you.

TITUBA: Oh, bless the Lord.

HALE: When the Devil come to you does he ever come—with another person? *She stares up into his face.* Perhaps another person in the village? Someone you know.

PARRIS: Who came with him?

PUTNAM: Sarah Good? Did you ever see Sarah Good with him? Or Osburn?

PARRIS: Was it man or woman came with him?

TITUBA: Man or woman. Was—was woman.

PARRIS: What woman? A woman, you said. What woman?

TITUBA: It was black dark, and I—

PARRIS: You could see him, why could you not see her?

TITUBA: Well, they was always talking; they was always runnin' round and carryin' on—

PARRIS: You mean out of Salem? Salem witches?

TITUBA: I believe so, yes, sir.

Now HALE *takes her hand. She is surprised.*

HALE: Tituba. You must have no fear to tell us who they are, do you understand? We will protect you. The Devil can never overcome a minister. You know that, do you not?

TITUBA, *kisses* HALE's *hand:* Aye, sir, oh, I do.

HALE: You have confessed yourself to witchcraft, and that speaks a wish to come to Heaven's side. And we will bless you, Tituba.

TITUBA, *deeply relieved:* Oh, God bless you, Mr. Hale!

HALE, *with rising exaltation:* You are God's instrument put in our hands to discover the Devil's agent among us. You are selected, Tituba, you are chosen to help us cleanse our village. So speak utterly, Tituba, turn your back on him and face God—face God, Tituba, and God will protect you.

TITUBA, *joining with him:* Oh, God, protect Tituba!

HALE, *kindly:* Who came to you with the Devil? Two? Three? Four? How many?

Tituba pants, and begins rocking back and forth again, staring ahead.

TITUBA: There was four. There was four.

PARRIS, *pressing in on her:* Who? Who? Their names, their names!

TITUBA, *suddenly bursting out:* Oh, how many times he bid me kill you, Mr. Parris!

PARRIS: Kill me!

TITUBA, *in a fury:* He say Mr. Parris must be kill! Mr. Parris no goodly man, Mr. Parris mean man and no gentle man, and he bid me rise out of my bed and cut your throat! *They gasp.* But I tell him "No! I don't hate that man. I don't want kill that man." But he say, "You work for me, Tituba, and I make you free! I give you pretty dress to wear, and put you way high up in the air, and you gone fly back to Barbados!" And I say, "You lie, Devil, you lie!" And then he come one stormy night to me, and he say, "Look! I have *white* people belong to me." And I look— and there was Goody Good.

PARRIS: Sarah Good!

TITUBA, *rocking and weeping:* Aye, sir, and Goody Osburn.

MRS. PUTNAM: I knew it! Goody Osburn were midwife to me three times. I begged you, Thomas, did I not? I begged him not to call Osburn because I feared her. My babies always shriveled in her hands!

HALE: Take courage, you must give us all their names. How can you bear to see this child suffering? Look at her, Tituba. *He is indicating* BETTY *on the bed.* Look at her God-given innocence; her soul is so tender; we must protect her, Tituba; the Devil is out and preying on her like a beast upon the flesh of the pure lamb. God will bless you for your help.

ABIGAIL *rises, staring as though inspired, and cries out.*

ABIGAIL: I want to open myself! *They turn to her, startled. She is enraptured, as though in a pearly light.* I want the light of God, I want the sweet love of Jesus! I danced for the Devil; I saw him; I wrote in his book; I go back to Jesus; I kiss His hand. I saw Sarah Good with the Devil! I saw Goody Osburn with the Devil! I saw Bridget Bishop with the Devil!

As she is speaking, BETTY *is rising from the bed, a fever in her eyes, and picks up the chant.*

BETTY, *staring too:* I saw George Jacobs with the Devil! I saw Goody Howe with the Devil!

PARRIS: She speaks! *He rushes to embrace* BETTY. She speaks!

HALE: Glory to God! It is broken, they are free!

BETTY, *calling out hysterically and with great relief:* I saw Martha Bellows with the Devil!

ABIGAIL: I saw Goody Sibber with the Devil! *It is rising to a great glee.*

PUTNAM: The marshal, I'll call the marshal!

PARRIS *is shouting a prayer of thanksgiving.*

BETTY: I saw Alice Barrow with the Devil!

The curtain begins to fall.

HALE, *as* PUTNAM *goes out:* Let the marshal bring irons!

ABIGAIL: I saw Goody Hawkins with the Devil!

BETTY: I saw Goody Bibber with the Devil!

ABIGAIL: I saw Goody Booth with the Devil!

On their ecstatic cries—

THE CURTAIN FALLS

Guide for Responding

◆ Literature and Your Life

Reader's Response Were you surprised when the accusations multiplied? Explain.

Thematic Focus: What aspects of society does Miller seem to be criticizing through the characters of Reverend Parris and the Putnams?

Group Discussion Discuss the types of situations that could cause a contemporary American town to become afflicted by a general hysteria.

☑ Check Your Comprehension

1. (a) What is Betty's condition as the play opens? (b) What were she and her cousin Abigail doing the night before?
2. Summarize Abigail's prior relationship with the Proctors.
3. (a) Who is Reverend Hale? (b) Why is he contacted?

◆ Critical Thinking

INTERPRET

1. What seems to be the main motivation for Reverend Parris's concern about Abigail and Betty's behavior in the forest? **[Infer]**
2. (a) When Reverend Parris leaves the room, Abigail, Mercy, Mary, and Betty talk in private. What does their discussion reveal? (b) How does this scene hint at events that will occur later in the play? **[Interpret; Speculate]**
3. (a) How does Betty's reaction to the psalm support the assertion that there is "witchcraft afoot"? (b) What other incidents do the various characters use to support this assertion? **[Infer]**
4. What evidence is there that sharp divisions exist among the people of Salem Village? **[Support]**

APPLY

5. (a) Name two others you think will be accused. (b) Who will accuse them? Why? **[Speculate]**

Guide for Responding, *Act I* (continued)

◆ Literary Focus

DRAMA: DIALOGUE AND STAGE DIRECTIONS

Drama consists of **dialogue** that the characters speak and **stage directions** that the playwright gives to the actors, director, and others reading or staging the play. Though the extent of stage directions varies from playwright to playwright, Miller's inclusion of such lengthy background information is unusual.

1. (a) What does the dialogue reveal about Abby's personality and motives? (b) In the stage directions, what does Miller state directly about her personality?
2. (a) Why do you think Miller includes such extensive background information about Salem and its inhabitants? (b) To whom do you think this information is addressed?

◆ Reading Strategy

QUESTION THE CHARACTERS' MOTIVES

To improve your ability to interpret and analyze the characters in a drama, you should **question the characters' motives**, or consider the reasons they behave as they do. Identify what each of the following character's comments and actions reveal about his or her motivations.

1. Reverend Parris
2. Mary Warren
3. Abigail Williams
4. Tituba

◆ Grammar and Style

PRONOUN CASE IN INCOMPLETE CONSTRUCTIONS

In an **incomplete construction**—a sentence where understood words are omitted—you may be uncertain about which form of a pronoun to use. Mentally complete the construction by inserting the missing words to help you decide

Practice Indicate which pronoun would best complete each sentence.

1. Proctor is a sinner, but others are more sinful than (he, him).
2. Proctor has some lingering affection for Abigail but cares more for his wife than (she, her).
3. Betty lies, but Abigail is craftier than (she, her).
4. "Blame others more than (I, me)," Tituba says.

◆ Build Vocabulary

USING THE WORD ROOT -grat-

The root *-grat-* means "pleasing" or "agreeable." Explain how *-grat-* relates to the meaning of each of these words. Use a dictionary, if necessary.

1. gratify
2. ingrate
3. congratulate

USING THE WORD BANK

Write these sentences in your notebook, completing each with the appropriate word bank word.

1. Gossip and _____?_____ can destroy a person's reputation.
2. Months of _____?_____ helped me master Latin.
3. A born actor, he hid his true nature by _____?_____.
4. His _____?_____ behavior was the town scandal.
5. To soothe their gods, they made sacrifices as an act of _____?_____.
6. Her _____?_____ manner pleased the most demanding customers.
7. With my _____?_____ for historical settings, it was predictable that I would enjoy *The Crucible.*

Idea Bank

Writing

1. **Medical Chart** Imagine that you are Betty's doctor. Write her medical chart for the day she takes ill. Describe her condition and its possible cause. **[Science Link]**

2. **News Account** Write an account of the events in Salem as they might be described in a Boston newspaper of the day. **[Media Link]**

Speaking and Listening

3. **Oral Presentation** Working in a small group, research and report on the belief in witches in seventeenth-century Europe. Present your findings to the class in an oral report. **[Social Studies Link]**

4. **Dramatization** Working in a small group, choose a scene from Act I to rehearse and perform for classmates. **[Performing Arts Link]**

Guide for Interpreting, Act II

◆ Review and Anticipate

As Act I draws to a close, Salem is in the grip of mounting hysteria. What had begun as concern over the strange behavior of Betty, the minister's daughter—a reaction that may have stemmed from guilty feelings about her activities in the woods the night before—had by the act's end swelled to a mass hysteria in which accusations of witchcraft were being made and accepted against a growing number of Salem's citizens.

Which characters do you think will most readily believe the accusations of witchcraft? Who do you think will be accused next? Record your predictions about the characters from Act I in a chart like the one below. Then read Act II to see whether your predictions are correct.

Character	Prediction	Is Prediction Correct?

◆ Build Vocabulary

SUFFIXES: -logy

The suffix -logy means "the science, theory, or study of." Combining it with the Greek root -theo-, which means "god," you get theology, "the study of religion or a particular religious philosophy."

WORD BANK

Preview this list of words from Act II.

> pallor
> ameliorate
> avidly
> base
> deference
> theology
> quail
> gingerly
> abomination
> blasphemy

◆ Grammar and Style

COMMAS AFTER INTRODUCTORY WORDS

Use a comma to set off a mild interjection or another interrupter that introduces a sentence. Look at these examples from Act II:

> Oh, you're not done then.
> Aye, the farm is seeded.
> No, she walked into the house this afternoon.
> Why, she's weepin'!

◆ Literary Focus

ALLUSION

An **allusion** is a brief reference within a work to something outside the work, such as another literary work, a well-known person, a place, or a historical event. The Crucible, not surprisingly, makes many allusions to the Bible. For example, Act I mentions the New Jerusalem, a term for the holy city of heaven. Look for other biblical allusions as you read Act II.

◆ Reading Strategy

READ DRAMA

When you view a play, action and staging elements such as sets, lighting, and costumes work with the dialogue to advance the play's plot and develop the characters. When you **read a play**, instead of watching the action and staging, you read stage directions. Because stage directions often interrupt the dialogue, the experience of reading a play is usually not as smooth as that of reading a novel or story. The stage directions, however, can provide crucial information. In this passage from Act II of The Crucible, for example, you might think Elizabeth's words are cheerful and happy if you did not read the two words of stage directions in italics.

> ELIZABETH—it is hard to say: I know it, John.

ACT II

The common room of PROCTOR's *house, eight days later.*

◆ **Reading Strategy**
What important information do you learn here about when Act II takes place in relation to Act I?

At the right is a door opening on the fields outside. A fireplace is at the left, and behind it a stairway leading upstairs. It is the low, dark, and rather long living room of the time. As the curtain rises, the room is empty. From above, ELIZABETH *is heard softly singing to the children. Presently the door opens and* JOHN PROCTOR *enters, carrying his gun. He glances about the room as he comes toward the fireplace, then halts for an instant as he hears her singing. He continues on to the fireplace, leans the gun against the wall as he swings a pot out of the fire and smells it. Then he lifts out the ladle and tastes. He is not quite pleased. He reaches to a cupboard, takes a pinch of salt, and drops it into the pot. As he is tasting again, her footsteps are heard on the stair. He swings the pot into the fireplace and goes to a basin and washes his hands and face.* ELIZABETH *enters.*

ELIZABETH: What keeps you so late? It's almost dark.

PROCTOR: I were planting far out to the forest edge.

ELIZABETH: Oh, you're done then.

PROCTOR: Aye, the farm is seeded. The boys asleep?

ELIZABETH: They will be soon. *And she goes to the fireplace, proceeds to ladle up stew in a dish.*

PROCTOR: Pray now for a fair summer.

ELIZABETH: Aye.

PROCTOR: Are you well today?

ELIZABETH: I am. *She brings the plate to the table, and, indicating the food:* It is a rabbit.

PROCTOR, *going to the table:* Oh, is it! In Jonathan's trap?

ELIZABETH: No, she walked into the house this afternoon; I found her sittin' in the corner like she come to visit.

PROCTOR: Oh, that's a good sign walkin' in.

ELIZABETH: Pray God. It hurt my heart to strip her, poor rabbit. *She sits and watches him taste it.*

PROCTOR: It's well seasoned.

ELIZABETH, *blushing with pleasure:* I took great care. She's tender?

PROCTOR: Aye. *He eats. She watches him.* I think we'll see green fields soon. It's warm as blood beneath the clods.

ELIZABETH: That's well.

PROCTOR *eats, then looks up.*

PROCTOR: If the crop is good I'll buy George Jacob's heifer. How would that please you?

ELIZABETH: Aye, it would.

PROCTOR, *with a grin:* I mean to please you, Elizabeth.

ELIZABETH—*it is hard to say:* I know it, John.

He gets up, goes to her, kisses her. She receives it. With a certain disappointment, he returns to the table.

PROCTOR, *as gently as he can:* Cider?

ELIZABETH, *with a sense of reprimanding herself for having forgot:* Aye! *She gets up and goes and pours a glass for him. He now arches his back.*

PROCTOR: This farm's a continent when you go foot by foot droppin' seeds in it.

ELIZABETH, *coming with the cider:* It must be.

PROCTOR, *drinks a long draught, then, putting the glass down:* You ought to bring some flowers in the house.

ELIZABETH: Oh! I forgot! I will tomorrow.

PROCTOR: It's winter in here yet. On Sunday let you come with me, and we'll walk the farm together; I never see such a load of flowers on the earth. *With good feeling he goes and looks up at* *the sky through the open doorway.* Lilacs have a purple smell. Lilac is the smell of nightfall, I think. Massachusetts is a beauty in the spring!

ELIZABETH: Aye, it is.

There is a pause. She is watching him from the table as he stands there absorbing the night. It is as though she would speak but cannot. Instead, now, she takes up his plate and glass and fork and goes with them to the basin. Her back is turned to him. He turns to her and watches her. A sense of their separation rises.

PROCTOR: I think you're sad again. Are you?

ELIZABETH—*she doesn't want friction, and yet she must:* You come so late I thought you'd gone to Salem this afternoon.

PROCTOR: Why? I have no business in Salem.

ELIZABETH: You did speak of going, earlier this week.

PROCTOR—*he knows what she means:* I thought better of it since.

ELIZABETH: Mary Warren's there today.

PROCTOR: Why'd you let her? You heard me forbid her go to Salem any more!

ELIZABETH: I couldn't stop her.

PROCTOR, *holding back a full condemnation of her:* It is a fault, it is a fault, Elizabeth—you're the mistress here, not Mary Warren.

ELIZABETH: She frightened all my strength away.

PROCTOR: How may that mouse frighten you, Elizabeth? You—

ELIZABETH: It is a mouse no more. I forbid her go, and she raises up her chin like the daughter of a prince and says to me, "I must go to Salem, Goody Proctor; I am an official of the court!"

PROCTOR: Court! What court?

ELIZABETH: Aye, it is a proper court they have now. They've sent four judges out of Boston, she says, weighty magistrates of the General Court, and at the head sits the Deputy Governor of the Province.

PROCTOR, *astonished:* Why, she's mad.

ELIZABETH: I would to God she were. There be fourteen people in the jail now, she says. PROCTOR *simply looks at her, unable to grasp it.* And they'll be tried, and the court have power to hang them too, she says.

PROCTOR, *scoffing but without conviction:* Ah, they'd never hang—

ELIZABETH: The Deputy Governor promise hangin' if they'll not confess, John. The town's gone wild, I think. She speak of Abigail, and I thought she were a saint, to hear her. Abigail brings the other girls into the court, and where she walks the crowd will part like the sea for Israel.[1] And folks are brought before them, and if they scream and howl and fall to the floor—the person's clapped in the jail for bewitchin' them.

> **◆ Literary Focus**
> What does the allusion to Moses parting the Red Sea suggest about Abby?

PROCTOR, *wide-eyed:* Oh, it is a black mischief.

ELIZABETH: I think you must go to Salem, John. *He turns to her.* I think so. You must tell them it is a fraud.

PROCTOR, *thinking beyond this:* Aye, it is, it is surely.

ELIZABETH: Let you go to Ezekiel Cheever—he knows you well. And tell him what she said to you last week in her uncle's house. She said it had naught to do with witchcraft, did she not?

PROCTOR, *in thought:* Aye, she did, she did. *Now, a pause.*

ELIZABETH, *quietly, fearing to anger him by prodding:* God forbid you keep that from the court, John. I think they must be told.

PROCTOR, *quietly, struggling with his thought:* Aye, they must, they must. It is a wonder they do believe her.

ELIZABETH: I would go to Salem now, John—let you go tonight.

PROCTOR: I'll think on it.

---

1. **part like . . . Israel:** In the Bible, God commanded Moses, the leader of the Jews, to part the Red Sea to enable the Jews to escape from the Egyptians into Canaan.

ELIZABETH, *with her courage now:* You cannot keep it, John.

PROCTOR, *angering:* I know I cannot keep it. I say I will think on it!

ELIZABETH, *hurt, and very coldly:* Good, then, let you think on it. *She stands and starts to walk out of the room.*

PROCTOR: I am only wondering how I may prove what she told me, Elizabeth. If the girl's a saint now, I think it is not easy to prove she's fraud, and the town gone so silly. She told it to me in a room alone—I have no proof for it.

ELIZABETH: You were alone with her?

PROCTOR, *stubbornly:* For a moment alone, aye.

ELIZABETH: Why, then, it is not as you told me.

PROCTOR, *his anger rising:* For a moment, I say. The others come in soon after.

ELIZABETH, *quietly—she has suddenly lost all faith in him:* Do as you wish, then. *She starts to turn.*

PROCTOR: Woman. *She turns to him.* I'll not have your suspicion any more.

ELIZABETH, *a little loftily:* I have no—

PROCTOR: I'll not have it!

ELIZABETH: Then let you not earn it.

PROCTOR, *with a violent undertone:* You doubt me yet?

ELIZABETH, *with a smile, to keep her dignity:* John, if it were not Abigail that you must go to hurt, would you falter now? I think not.

PROCTOR: Now look you—

ELIZABETH: I see what I see, John.

PROCTOR, *with solemn warning:* You will not judge me more, Elizabeth. I have good reason to think before I charge fraud on Abigail, and I will think on it. Let you look to your own improvement before you go to judge your husband any more. I have forgot Abigail, and—

ELIZABETH: And I.

PROCTOR: Spare me! You forget nothin' and forgive nothin'. Learn charity, woman. I have gone tiptoe in this house all seven month since she is gone. I have not moved from there to there without I think to please you, and still an everlasting funeral marches round your heart. I cannot speak but I am doubted, every moment judged for lies, as though I come into a court when I come into this house!

ELIZABETH: John, you are not open with me. You saw her with a crowd, you said. Now you—

PROCTOR: I'll plead my honesty no more, Elizabeth.

ELIZABETH—*now she would justify herself:* John, I am only—

PROCTOR: No more! I should have roared you down when first you told me your suspicion. But I wilted, and, like a Christian, I confessed. Confessed! Some dream I had must have mistaken you for God that day. But you're not, you're not, and let you remember it! Let you look sometimes for the goodness in me, and judge me not.

ELIZABETH: I do not judge you. The magistrate sits in your heart that judges you. I never thought you but a good man, John—*with a smile*—only somewhat bewildered.

PROCTOR, *laughing bitterly:* Oh, Elizabeth, your justice would freeze beer! *He turns suddenly toward a sound outside. He starts for the door as* MARY WARREN *enters. As soon as he sees her, he goes directly to her and grabs her by the cloak, furious.* How do you go to Salem when I forbid it? Do you mock me? *Shaking her.* I'll whip you if you dare leave this house again!

Strangely, she doesn't resist him, but hangs limply by his grip.

MARY WARREN: I am sick, I am sick, Mr. Proctor. Pray, pray, hurt me not. *Her strangeness throws him off, and her evident pallor and weakness. He frees her.* My insides are all shuddery; I am in the proceedings all day, sir.

♦ **Reading Strategy**
What do the stage directions here clarify?

PROCTOR, *with draining anger—his curiosity is draining it:* And what of these proceedings here? When will you proceed to keep this house, as you are paid nine pound a year to do—and my wife not wholly well?

As though to compensate, MARY WARREN *goes to* ELIZABETH *with a small rag doll.*

MARY WARREN: I made a gift for you today, Goody Proctor. I had to sit long hours in a chair, and passed the time with sewing.

ELIZABETH, *perplexed, looking at the doll:* Why,

thank you, it's a fair poppet.[2]

MARY WARREN, *with a trembling, decayed voice:* We must all love each other now, Goody Proctor.

ELIZABETH, *amazed at her strangeness:* Aye, indeed we must.

MARY WARREN, *glancing at the room:* I'll get up early in the morning and clean the house. I must sleep now. *She turns and starts off.*

PROCTOR: Mary. *She halts.* Is it true? There be fourteen women arrested?

MARY WARREN: No, sir. There be thirty-nine now— *She suddenly breaks off and sobs and sits down, exhausted.*

ELIZABETH: Why, she's weepin'! What ails you, child?

MARY WARREN: Goody Osburn—will hang!

There is a shocked pause, while she sobs.

PROCTOR: Hang! *He calls into her face.* Hang, y'say?

MARY WARREN, *through her weeping:* Aye.

PROCTOR: The Deputy Governor will permit it?

MARY WARREN: He sentenced her. He must. *To ameliorate it:* But not Sarah Good. For Sarah Good confessed, y'see.

PROCTOR: Confessed! To what?

MARY WARREN: That she—*in horror at the memory*—she sometimes made a compact with Lucifer, and wrote her name in his black book—with her blood—and bound herself to torment Christians till God's thrown down—and we all must worship Hell forevermore.

Pause.

PROCTOR: But—surely you know what a jabberer she is. Did you tell them that?

---

2. **poppet:** Doll.

♦ **Build Vocabulary**
pallor (pal´ ər) *n.:* Paleness
ameliorate (ə mēl´ yə rāt) *v.:* Make better

MARY WARREN: Mr. Proctor, in open court she near to choked us all to death.

PROCTOR: How, choked you?

MARY WARREN: She sent her spirit out.

ELIZABETH: Oh, Mary, Mary, surely you—

MARY WARREN, *with an indignant edge:* She tried to kill me many times, Goody Proctor!

ELIZABETH: Why, I never heard you mention that before.

MARY WARREN: I never knew it before. I never knew anything before. When she come into the court I say to myself, I must not accuse this woman, for she sleep in ditches, and so very old and poor. But then—then she sit there, denying and denying, and I feel a misty coldness climbin' up my back, and the skin on my skull begin to creep, and I feel a clamp around my neck and I cannot breathe air; and then— *entranced*—I hear a voice, a screamin' voice, and it were my voice—and all at once I remembered everything she done to me!

PROCTOR: Why? What did she do to you?

MARY WARREN, *like one awakened to a marvelous secret insight:* So many time, Mr. Proctor, she come to this very door, beggin' bread and a cup of cider—and mark this: whenever I turned her away empty, she *mumbled*.

ELIZABETH: Mumbled! She may mumble if she's hungry.

MARY WARREN: But *what* does she mumble? You must remember, Goody Proctor. Last month—a Monday, I think—she walked away, and I thought my guts would burst for two days after. Do you remember it?

ELIZABETH: Why—I do, I think, but—

MARY WARREN: And so I told that to Judge Hathorne, and he asks her so. "Goody Osburn," says he, "what curse do you mumble that this girl must fall sick after turning you away?" And then she replies—*mimicking an old crone*—"Why, your excellence, no curse at all. I only say my commandments; I hope I may say my commandments," says she!

ELIZABETH: And that's an upright answer.

MARY WARREN: Aye, but then Judge Hathorne say, "Recite for us your commandments!"—*leaning avidly toward them*—and of all the ten she could not say a single one. She never knew no commandments, and they had her in a flat lie!

PROCTOR: And so condemned her?

MARY WARREN, *now a little strained, seeing his stubborn doubt:* Why, they must when she condemned herself.

PROCTOR: But the proof, the proof!

MARY WARREN, *with greater impatience with him:* I told you the proof. It's hard proof, hard as rock, the judges said.

PROCTOR, *pauses an instant, then:* You will not go to court again, Mary Warren.

MARY WARREN: I must tell you, sir, I will be gone every day now. I am amazed you do not see what weighty work we do.

PROCTOR: What work you do! It's strange work for a Christian girl to hang old women!

MARY WARREN: But, Mr. Proctor, they will not hang them if they confess. Sarah Good will only sit in jail some time—*recalling*—and here's a wonder for you; think on this. Goody Good is pregnant!

ELIZABETH: Pregnant! Are they mad? The woman's near to sixty!

MARY WARREN: They had Doctor Griggs examine her, and she's full to the brim. And smokin' a pipe all these years, and no husband either! But she's safe, thank God, for they'll not hurt the innocent child. But be that not a marvel? You must see it, sir, it's God's work we do. So I'll be gone every day for some time. I'm—I am an official of the court, they say, and I—*She has been edging toward offstage.*

PROCTOR: I'll official you! *He strides to the mantel, takes down the whip hanging there.*

MARY WARREN, *terrified, but coming erect, striving for her authority:* I'll not stand whipping any more!

ELIZABETH, *hurriedly, as* PROCTOR *approaches:* Mary, promise you'll stay at home—

MARY WARREN, *backing from him, but keeping her erect posture, striving, striving for her way:* The Devil's loose in Salem, Mr. Proctor; we must discover where he's hiding!

PROCTOR: I'll whip the Devil out of you! *With whip raised he reaches out for her, and she streaks away and yells.*

MARY WARREN, *pointing at* ELIZABETH: I saved her life today!

Silence. His whip comes down.

ELIZABETH, *softly:* I am accused?

MARY WARREN, *quaking:* Somewhat mentioned. But I said I never see no sign you ever sent your spirit out to hurt no one, and seeing I do live so closely with you, they dismissed it.

ELIZABETH: Who accused me?

MARY WARREN: I am bound by law, I cannot tell it. *To* PROCTOR: I only hope you'll not be so sarcastical no more. Four judges and the King's deputy sat to dinner with us but an hour ago. I—I would have you speak civilly to me, from this out.

PROCTOR, *in horror, muttering in disgust at her:* Go to bed.

MARY WARREN, *with a stamp of her foot:* I'll not be ordered to bed no more, Mr. Proctor! I am eighteen and a woman, however single!

PROCTOR: Do you wish to sit up? Then sit up.

MARY WARREN: I wish to go to bed!

PROCTOR, *in anger:* Good night, then!

MARY WARREN: Good night. *Dissatisfied, uncertain of herself, she goes out. Wide-eyed, both* PROCTOR *and* ELIZABETH *stand staring.*

ELIZABETH, *quietly:* Oh, the noose, the noose is up!

PROCTOR: There'll be no noose.

◆ **Build Vocabulary**

avidly (av´ id lē) *adv.*: Eagerly; intently

ELIZABETH: She wants me dead. I knew all week it would come to this!

PROCTOR, *without conviction:* They dismissed it. You heard her say—

ELIZABETH: And what of tomorrow? She will cry me out until they take me!

PROCTOR: Sit you down.

ELIZABETH: She wants me dead, John, you know it!

PROCTOR: I say sit down! *She sits, trembling. He speaks quickly, trying to keep his wits.* Now we must be wise, Elizabeth.

ELIZABETH, *with sarcasm, and a sense of being lost:* Oh, indeed, indeed!

PROCTOR: Fear nothing. I'll find Ezekiel Cheever. I'll tell him she said it were all sport.

ELIZABETH: John, with so many in the jail, more than Cheever's help is needed now, I think. Would you favor me with this? Go to Abigail.

PROCTOR, *his soul hardening as he senses . . .:* What have I to say to Abigail?

ELIZABETH, *delicately:* John—grant me this. You have a faulty understanding of young girls. There is a promise made in any bed—

PROCTOR, *striving against his anger:* What promise!

ELIZABETH: Spoke or silent, a promise is surely made. And she may dote on it now—I am sure she does—and thinks to kill me, then to take my place.

PROCTOR's *anger is rising; he cannot speak.*

ELIZABETH: It is her dearest hope, John, I know it. There be a thousand names; why does she call mine? There be a certain danger in calling such a name—I am no Goody Good that sleeps in ditches, nor Osburn, drunk and half-witted. She'd dare not call out such a farmer's wife but there be monstrous profit in it. She thinks to take my place, John.

PROCTOR: She cannot think it! *He knows it is true.*

ELIZABETH, *"reasonably":* John, have you ever shown her somewhat of contempt? She cannot pass you in the church but you will blush—

PROCTOR: I may blush for my sin.

ELIZABETH: I think she sees another meaning in that blush.

PROCTOR: And what see you? What see you, Elizabeth?

ELIZABETH, *"conceding":* I think you be somewhat ashamed, for I am there, and she so close.

PROCTOR: When will you know me, woman? Were I stone I would have cracked for shame this seven month!

ELIZABETH: Then go and tell her she's a whore. Whatever promise she may sense—break it, John, break it.

PROCTOR, *between his teeth:* Good, then. I'll go. *He starts for his rifle.*

ELIZABETH, *trembling, fearfully:* Oh, how unwillingly!

PROCTOR, *turning on her, rifle in hand:* I will curse her hotter than the oldest cinder in hell. But pray, begrudge me not my anger!

ELIZABETH: Your anger! I only ask you—

PROCTOR: Woman, am I so base? Do you truly think me base?

ELIZABETH: I never called you base.

PROCTOR: Then how do you charge me with such a promise? The promise that a stallion gives a mare I gave that girl!

ELIZABETH: Then why do you anger with me when I bid you break it?

PROCTOR: Because it speaks deceit, and I am honest! But I'll plead no more! I see now your spirit twists around the single error of my life, and I will never tear it free!

ELIZABETH, *crying out:* You'll tear it free—when you come to know that I will be your only wife, or no wife at all! She has an arrow in you yet, John Proctor, and you know it well!

Quite suddenly, as though from the air, a figure appears in the doorway. They start slightly. It is

MR. HALE. *He is different now—drawn a little, and there is a quality of deference, even of guilt, about his manner now.*

HALE: Good evening.

PROCTOR, *still in his shock:* Why, Mr. Hale! Good evening to you, sir. Come in, come in.

HALE, *to Elizabeth:* I hope I do not startle you.

ELIZABETH: No, no, it's only that I heard no horse—

HALE: You are Goodwife Proctor.

PROCTOR: Aye; Elizabeth.

HALE, *nods, then:* I hope you're not off to bed yet.

PROCTOR, *setting down his gun:* No, no. HALE *comes further into the room. And* PROCTOR, *to explain his nervousness:* We are not used to visitors after dark, but you're welcome here. Will you sit you down, sir?

HALE: I will. *He sits.* Let you sit, Goodwife Proctor.

She does, never letting him out of her sight. There is a pause as HALE *looks about the room.*

PROCTOR, *to break the silence:* Will you drink cider, Mr. Hale?

HALE: No, it rebels my stomach; I have some further traveling yet tonight. Sit you down, sir. PROCTOR *sits.* I will not keep you long, but I have some business with you.

PROCTOR: Business of the court?

HALE: No—no, I come of my own, without the court's authority. Hear me. *He wets his lips.* I know not if you are aware, but your wife's name is—mentioned in the court.

PROCTOR: We know it, sir. Our Mary Warren told us. We are entirely amazed.

HALE: I am a stranger here, as you know. And in my ignorance I find it hard to draw a clear opinion of them that come accused before the court. And so this afternoon, and now tonight, I go from house to house—I come now from Rebecca Nurse's house and—

ELIZABETH, *shocked:* Rebecca's charged!

HALE: God forbid such a one be charged. She is, however—mentioned somewhat.

ELIZABETH, *with an attempt at a laugh:* You will never believe, I hope, that Rebecca trafficked with the Devil.

HALE: Woman, it is possible.

PROCTOR, *taken aback:* Surely you cannot think so.

HALE: This is a strange time, Mister. No man may longer doubt the powers of the dark are gathered in monstrous attack upon this village. There is too much evidence now to deny it. You will agree, sir?

PROCTOR, *evading:* I—have no knowledge in that line. But it's hard to think so pious a woman be secretly a Devil's bitch after seventy year of such good prayer.

HALE: Aye. But the Devil is a wily one, you cannot deny it. However, she is far from accused, and I know she will not be. *Pause.* I thought, sir, to put some questions as to the Christian character of this house, if you'll permit me.

PROCTOR, *coldly, resentful:* Why, we—have no fear of questions, sir.

HALE: Good, then. *He makes himself more comfortable.* In the book of record that Mr. Parris keeps, I note that you are rarely in the church on Sabbath Day.

PROCTOR: No, sir, you are mistaken.

HALE: Twenty-six time in seventeen month, sir. I must call that rare. Will you tell me why you are so absent?

PROCTOR: Mr. Hale, I never knew I must account to that man for I come to church or stay at home. My wife were sick this winter.

HALE: So I am told. But you, Mister, why could you not come alone?

◆ **Build Vocabulary**

base (bās) *adj.:* Low; contemptible

deference (def´ ər əns) *n.:* Courteous regard or respect

theology (thē äl´ ə jē) *n.:* Religious philosophy or teachings; the study of religion

PROCTOR: I surely did come when I could, and when I could not I prayed in this house.

HALE: Mr. Proctor, your house is not a church; your theology must tell you that.

PROCTOR: It does, sir, it does; and it tells me that a minister may pray to God without he have golden candlesticks upon the altar.

HALE: What golden candlesticks?

PROCTOR: Since we built the church there were pewter candlesticks upon the altar; Francis Nurse made them y'know, and a sweeter hand never touched the metal. But Parris came, and for twenty week he preach nothin' but golden candlesticks until he had them. I labor the earth from dawn of day to blink of night, and I tell you true when I look to heaven and see my money glaring at his elbows—it hurt my prayer, sir, it hurt my prayer. I think, sometimes, the man dreams cathedrals, not clapboard meetin' houses.

HALE, *thinks, then:* And yet, Mister, a Christian on Sabbath Day must be in church. *Pause.* Tell me—you have three children?

PROCTOR: Aye. Boys.

HALE: How comes it that only two are baptized?

PROCTOR, *starts to speak, then stops, then, as though unable to restrain this:* I like it not that Mr. Parris should lay his hand upon my baby. I see no light of God in that man. I'll not conceal it.

HALE: I must say it, Mr. Proctor; that is not for you to decide. The man's ordained, therefore the light of God is in him.

PROCTOR, *flushed with resentment but trying to smile:* What's your suspicion, Mr. Hale?

HALE: No, no, I have no—

PROCTOR: I nailed the roof upon the church, I hung the door—

HALE: Oh, did you! That's a good sign, then.

PROCTOR: It may be I have been too quick to bring the man to book, but you cannot think we ever desired the destruction of religion. I think that's in your mind, is it not?

HALE, *not altogether giving way:* I—have—there is a softness in your record, sir, a softness.

ELIZABETH: I think, maybe, we have been too hard with Mr. Parris. I think so. But sure we never loved the Devil here.

HALE, *nods, deliberating this. Then, with the voice of one administering a secret test:* Do you know your Commandments, Elizabeth?

ELIZABETH, *without hesitation, even eagerly:* I surely do. There be no mark of blame upon my life, Mr. Hale. I am a covenanted Christian woman.

HALE: And you, Mister?

PROCTOR, *a trifle unsteadily:* I—am sure I do, sir.

HALE, *glances at her open face, then at* JOHN, *then:* Let you repeat them, if you will.

PROCTOR: The Commandments.

HALE: Aye.

PROCTOR, *looking off, beginning to sweat:* Thou shalt not kill.

HALE: Aye.

PROCTOR, *counting on his fingers:* Thou shalt not steal. Thou shalt not covet thy neighbor's goods, nor make unto thee any graven image. Thou shalt not take the name of the Lord in vain; thou shalt have no other gods before me. *With some hesitation:* Thou shalt remember the Sabbath Day and keep it holy. *Pause. Then:* Thou shalt honor thy father and mother. Thou shalt not bear false witness. *He is stuck. He counts back on his fingers, knowing one is missing.* Thou shalt not make unto thee any graven image.

HALE: You have said that twice, sir.

PROCTOR, *lost:* Aye. *He is flailing for it.*

ELIZABETH, *delicately:* Adultery, John.

PROCTOR, *as though a secret arrow had pained his heart:* Aye. *Trying to grin it away—to* HALE: You see, sir, between the two of us we do know them all. HALE *only looks at* PROCTOR, *deep in his attempt to define this man.* PROCTOR *grows more uneasy.* I think it be a small fault.

HALE: Theology, sir, is a fortress; no crack in a fortress may be accounted small. *He rises; he seems worried now. He paces a little, in deep thought.*

PROCTOR: There be no love for Satan in this house, Mister.

HALE: I pray it, I pray it dearly. *He looks to both of them, an attempt at a smile on his face, but his misgivings are clear.* Well, then—I'll bid you good night.

ELIZABETH, *unable to restrain herself:* Mr. Hale. *He turns.* I do think you are suspecting me somewhat? Are you not?

HALE, *obviously disturbed—and evasive:* Goody Proctor, I do not judge you. My duty is to add what I may to the godly wisdom of the court. I pray you both good health and good fortune. *To* JOHN: Good night, sir. *He starts out.*

ELIZABETH, *with a note of desperation:* I think you must tell him, John.

HALE: What's that?

ELIZABETH, *restraining a call:* Will you tell him?

Slight pause. HALE *looks questioningly at* JOHN.

PROCTOR, *with difficulty:* I—I have no witness and cannot prove it, except my word be taken. But I know the children's sickness had naught to do with witchcraft.

HALE, *stopped, struck:* Naught to do—?

PROCTOR: Mr. Parris discovered them sportin' in the woods. They were startled and took sick.

Pause.

HALE: Who told you this?

PROCTOR, *hesitates, then:* Abigail Williams.

HALE: Abigail.

PROCTOR: Aye.

HALE, *his eyes wide:* Abigail Williams told you it had naught to do with witchcraft!

PROCTOR: She told me the day you came, sir.

HALE, *suspiciously:* Why—why did you keep this?

PROCTOR: I never knew until tonight that the world is gone daft with this nonsense.

HALE: Nonsense! Mister, I have myself examined Tituba, Sarah Good, and numerous others that have confessed to dealing with the Devil. They have *confessed* it.

PROCTOR: And why not, if they must hang for denyin' it? There are them that will swear to anything before they'll hang; have you never thought of that?

HALE: I have. I—I have indeed. *It is his own suspicion, but he resists it. He glances at* ELIZABETH, *then at* JOHN. And you—would you testify to this in court?

PROCTOR: I—had not reckoned with goin' into court. But if I must I will.

HALE: Do you falter here?

PROCTOR: I falter nothing, but I may wonder if my story will be credited in such a court. I do wonder on it, when such a steady-minded minister as you will suspicion such a woman that never lied, and cannot, and the world knows she cannot! I may falter somewhat, Mister; I am no fool.

HALE, *quietly—it has impressed him:* Proctor, let you open with me now, for I have a rumor that troubles me. It's said you hold no belief that there may even be witches in the world. Is that true, sir?

PROCTOR—*he knows this is critical, and is striving against his disgust with* HALE *and with himself for even answering:* I know not what I have said, I may have said it. I have wondered if there be witches in the world—although I cannot believe they come among us now.

HALE: Then you do not believe—

PROCTOR: I have no knowledge of it; the Bible speaks of witches, and I will not deny them.

HALE: And you, woman?

ELIZABETH: I—I cannot believe it.

HALE, *shocked:* You cannot!

PROCTOR: Elizabeth, you bewilder him!

ELIZABETH, *to* HALE: I cannot think the Devil may own a woman's soul, Mr. Hale, when she keeps an upright way, as I have. I am a good woman, I know it; and if you believe I may do only good

work in the world, and yet be secretly bound to Satan, then I must tell you, sir, I do not believe it.

HALE: But, woman, you do believe there are witches in—

ELIZABETH: If you think that I am one, then I say there are none.

HALE: You surely do not fly against the Gospel, the Gospel—

PROCTOR: She believe in the Gospel, every word!

ELIZABETH: Question Abigail Williams about the Gospel, not myself!

HALE *stares at her.*

PROCTOR: She do not mean to doubt the Gospel, sir, you cannot think it. This be a Christian house, sir, a Christian house.

HALE: God keep you both; let the third child be quickly baptized, and go you without fail each Sunday to Sabbath prayer; and keep a solemn, quiet way among you. I think—

GILES COREY *appears in doorway.*

GILES: John!

PROCTOR: Giles! What's the matter?

GILES: They take my wife.

FRANCIS NURSE *enters.*

GILES: And his Rebecca!

PROCTOR, *to* FRANCIS: Rebecca's in the *jail!*

FRANCIS: Aye, Cheever come and take her in his wagon. We've only now come from the jail, and they'll not even let us in to see them.

ELIZABETH: They've surely gone wild now, Mr. Hale!

FRANCIS, *going to* HALE: Reverend Hale! Can you not speak to the Deputy Governor? I'm sure he mistakes these people—

HALE: Pray calm yourself, Mr. Nurse.

FRANCIS: My wife is the very brick and mortar of the church, Mr. Hale—*indicating* GILES—and Martha Corey, there cannot be a woman closer yet to God than Martha.

HALE: How is Rebecca charged, Mr. Nurse?

FRANCIS, *with a mocking, half-hearted laugh:* For murder, she's charged! *Mockingly quoting the warrant:* "For the marvelous and supernatural murder of Goody Putnam's babies." What am I to do, Mr. Hale?

HALE, *turns from* FRANCIS, *deeply troubled, then:* Believe me, Mr. Nurse, if Rebecca Nurse be tainted, then nothing's left to stop the whole green world from burning. Let you rest upon the justice of the court; the court will send her home. I know it.

FRANCIS: You cannot mean she will be tried in court!

HALE, *pleading:* Nurse, though our hearts break, we cannot flinch; these are new times, sir. There is a misty plot afoot so subtle we should be criminal to cling to old respects and ancient friendships. I have seen too many frightful proofs in court—the Devil is alive in Salem, and we dare not quail to follow wherever the accusing finger points!

PROCTOR, *angered:* How may such a woman murder children?

HALE, *in great pain:* Man, remember, until an hour before the Devil fell, God thought him beautiful in Heaven.

GILES: I never said my wife were a witch, Mr. Hale; I only said she were reading books!

HALE: Mr. Corey, exactly what complaint were made on your wife?

GILES: That bloody mongrel Walcott charge her. Y'see, he buy a pig of my wife four or five years ago, and the pig died soon after. So he come dancin' in for his money back. So my Martha, she says to him, "Walcott, if you haven't the wit to feed a pig properly, you'll not live to own many," she says. Now he goes to court and claims that from that day to this he cannot keep a pig alive for more than four weeks because my Martha bewitch them with her books!

Enter EZEKIEL CHEEVER. *A shocked silence.*

CHEEVER: Good evening to you, Proctor.

PROCTOR: Why, Mr. Cheever. Good evening.

CHEEVER: Good evening, all. Good evening, Mr. Hale.

PROCTOR: I hope you come not on business of the court.

CHEEVER: I do, Proctor, aye. I am clerk of the court now, y'know.

Enter MARSHAL HERRICK, *a man in his early thirties, who is somewhat shamefaced at the moment.*

GILES: It's a pity, Ezekiel, that an honest tailor might have gone to Heaven must burn in Hell. You'll burn for this, do you know it?

CHEEVER: You know yourself I must do as I'm told. You surely know that, Giles. And I'd as lief[3] you'd not be sending me to Hell. I like not the sound of it, I tell you; I like not the sound of it. *He fears* PROCTOR, *but starts to reach inside his coat.* Now believe me, Proctor, how heavy be the law, all its tonnage I do carry on my back tonight. *He takes out a warrant.* I have a warrant for your wife.

PROCTOR, *to* HALE: You said she were not charged!

HALE: I know nothin' of it. *To* CHEEVER: When were she charged?

CHEEVER: I am given sixteen warrant tonight, sir, and she is one.

PROCTOR: Who charged her?

CHEEVER: Why, Abigail Williams charge her.

PROCTOR: On what proof, what proof?

CHEEVER, *looking about the room:* Mr. Proctor, I have little time. The court bid me search your house, but I like not to search a house. So will you hand me any poppets that your wife may keep here?

PROCTOR: Poppets?

◆ Build Vocabulary

quail (kwāl) *v.:* Cringe from; pull back in fear

---

3. **as lief** (as lēf) *adv.:* Rather.

ELIZABETH: I never kept no poppets, not since I were a girl.

CHEEVER, *embarrassed, glancing toward the mantel where sits* MARY WARREN'*s poppet:* I spy a poppet, Goody Proctor.

ELIZABETH: Oh! *Going for it:* Why, this is Mary's.

CHEEVER, *shyly:* Would you please to give it to me?

ELIZABETH, *handing it to him, asks* HALE: Has the court discovered a text in poppets now?

CHEEVER, *carefully holding the poppet:* Do you keep any others in this house?

PROCTOR: No, nor this one either till tonight. What signifies a poppet?

CHEEVER: Why, a poppet—*he gingerly turns the poppet over*—a poppet may signify—Now, woman, will you please to come with me?

PROCTOR: She will not! *To* ELIZABETH: Fetch Mary here.

CHEEVER, *ineptly reaching toward* ELIZABETH: No, no, I am forbid to leave her from my sight.

PROCTOR, *pushing his arm away:* You'll leave her out of sight and out of mind, Mister. Fetch Mary, Elizabeth. ELIZABETH *goes upstairs.*

HALE: What signifies a poppet, Mr. Cheever?

CHEEVER, *turning the poppet over in his hands:* Why, they say it may signify that she—*he has lifted the poppet's skirt, and his eyes widen in astonished fear.* Why, this, this—

◆ **Reading Strategy**
What is the tone of this scene?

PROCTOR, *reaching for the poppet:* What's there?

CHEEVER: Why—*He draws out a long needle from the poppet*—it is a needle! Herrick, Herrick, it is a needle!

HERRICK *comes toward him.*

PROCTOR, *angrily, bewildered:* And what signifies a needle!

CHEEVER, *his hands shaking:* Why, this go hard with her, Proctor, this—I had my doubts, Proctor, I had my doubts, but here's calamity. *To* HALE, *showing the needle:* You see it, sir, it is a needle!

HALE: Why? What meanin' has it?

CHEEVER, *wide-eyed, trembling:* The girl, the Williams girl, Abigail Williams, sir. She sat to dinner in Reverend Parris's house tonight, and without word nor warnin' she falls to the floor. Like a struck beast, he says, and screamed a scream that a bull would weep to hear. And he goes to save her, and, stuck two inches in the flesh of her belly, he draw a needle out. And demandin' of her how she come to be so stabbed, she—*to* PROCTOR *now*—testify it were your wife's familiar spirit pushed it in.

PROCTOR: Why, she done it herself! *To* HALE: I hope you're not takin' this for proof, Mister!

HALE, *struck by the proof, is silent.*

CHEEVER: 'Tis hard proof! *To* HALE: I find here a poppet Goody Proctor keeps. I have found it, sir. And in the belly of the poppet a needle's stuck. I tell you true, Proctor, I never warranted to see such proof of Hell, and I bid you obstruct me not, for I—

Enter ELIZABETH *with* MARY WARREN. PROCTOR, *seeing* MARY WARREN, *draws her by the arm to* HALE.

PROCTOR: Here now! Mary, how did this poppet come into my house?

MARY WARREN, *frightened for herself, her voice very small:* What poppet's that, sir?

PROCTOR, *impatiently, points at the doll in* CHEEVER'*s hand:* This poppet, this poppet.

MARY WARREN, *evasively, looking at it:* Why, I—I think it is mine.

PROCTOR: It is your poppet, is it not?

MARY WARREN, *not understanding the direction of this:* It—is, sir.

PROCTOR: And how did it come into this house?

MARY WARREN, *glancing about at the avid faces:* Why—I made it in the court, sir, and—give it to Goody Proctor tonight.

PROCTOR, *to* HALE: Now, sir—do you have it?

◆ **Build Vocabulary**

gingerly (jin´ jər lē) *adv.*: With delicate care; cautiously

HALE: Mary Warren, a needle have been found inside this poppet.

MARY WARREN, *bewildered:* Why, I meant no harm by it, sir.

PROCTOR, *quickly:* You stuck that needle in yourself?

MARY WARREN: I—I believe I did, sir, I—

PROCTOR, *to* HALE: What say you now?

HALE, *watching* MARY WARREN *closely:* Child, you are certain this be your natural memory? May it be, perhaps that someone conjures you even now to say this?

MARY WARREN: Conjures me? Why, no, sir, I am entirely myself, I think. Let you ask Susanna Walcott—she saw me sewin' it in court. *Or better still:* Ask Abby, Abby sat beside me when I made it.

PROCTOR, *to* HALE, *of* CHEEVER: Bid him begone. Your mind is surely settled now. Bid him out, Mr. Hale.

ELIZABETH: What signifies a needle?

HALE: Mary—you charge a cold and cruel murder on Abigail.

MARY WARREN: Murder! I charge no—

HALE: Abigail were stabbed tonight; a needle were found stuck into her belly—

ELIZABETH: And she charges me?

HALE: Aye.

ELIZABETH, *her breath knocked out:* Why—! The girl is murder! She must be ripped out of the world!

CHEEVER, *pointing at* ELIZABETH: You've heard that, sir! Ripped out of the world! Herrick, you heard it!

PROCTOR, *suddenly snatching the warrant out of* CHEEVER's *hands:* Out with you.

CHEEVER: Proctor, you dare not touch the warrant.

PROCTOR, *ripping the warrant:* Out with you!

CHEEVER: You've ripped the Deputy Governor's warrant, man!

PROCTOR: Damn the Deputy Governor! Out of my house!

HALE: Now, Proctor, Proctor!

PROCTOR: Get y'gone with them! You are a broken minister.

HALE: Proctor, if she is innocent, the court—

PROCTOR: If *she* is innocent! Why do you never wonder if Parris be innocent, or Abigail? Is the accuser always holy now? Were they born this morning as clean as God's fingers? I'll tell you what's walking Salem—vengeance is walking Salem. We are what we always were in Salem, but now the little crazy children are jangling the keys of the kingdom, and common vengeance writes the law! This warrant's vengeance! I'll not give my wife to vengeance!

ELIZABETH: I'll go, John—

PROCTOR: You will not go!

HERRICK: I have nine men outside. You cannot keep her. The law binds me, John, I cannot budge.

PROCTOR, *to* HALE, *ready to break him:* Will you see her taken?

HALE: Proctor, the court is just—

PROCTOR: Pontius Pilate![4] God will not let you wash your hands of this!

ELIZABETH: John—I think I must go with them. *He cannot bear to look at her.* Mary, there is bread enough for the morning; you will bake, in the afternoon. Help Mr. Proctor as you were his daughter—you owe me that, and much more. *She is fighting her weeping. To* PROCTOR: When the children wake, speak nothing of witchcraft—it will frighten them. *She cannot go on.*

PROCTOR: I will bring you home. I will bring you soon.

ELIZABETH: Oh, John, bring me soon!

PROCTOR: I will fall like an ocean on that court! Fear nothing, Elizabeth.

---

4. **Pontius** (pän´ shəs) **Pilate** (pī´lət): Roman leader who condemned Jesus to be crucified.

ELIZABETH, *with great fear:* I will fear nothing. *She looks about the room, as though to fix it in her mind.* Tell the children I have gone to visit someone sick.

She walks out the door, HERRICK *and* CHEEVER *behind her. For a moment,* PROCTOR *watches from the doorway. The clank of chain is heard.*

PROCTOR: Herrick! Herrick, don't chain her! *He rushes out the door. From outside:* Damn you, man, you will not chain her! Off with them! I'll not have it! I will not have her chained!

There are other men's voices against his. HALE, *in a fever of guilt and uncertainty, turns from the door to avoid the sight:* MARY WARREN *bursts into tears and sits weeping.* GILES COREY *calls to* HALE.

GILES: And yet silent, minister? It is fraud, you know it is fraud! What keeps you, man?

PROCTOR *is half braced, half pushed into the room by two deputies and* HERRICK.

PROCTOR: I'll pay you, Herrick, I will surely pay you!

HERRICK, *panting:* In God's name, John, I cannot help myself. I must chain them all. Now let you keep inside this house till I am gone! *He goes out with his deputies.*

PROCTOR *stands there, gulping air. Horses and a wagon creaking are heard.*

HALE, *in great uncertainty:* Mr. Proctor—

PROCTOR: Out of my sight!

HALE: Charity, Proctor, charity. What I have heard in her favor, I will not fear to testify in court. God help me, I cannot judge her guilty or innocent—I know not. Only this consider: the world goes mad, and it profit nothing you should lay the cause to the vengeance of a little girl.

PROCTOR: You are a coward! Though you be ordained in God's own tears, you are a coward now!

HALE: Proctor, I cannot think God be provoked so grandly by such a petty cause. The jails are packed—our greatest judges sit in Salem now—and hangin's promised. Man, we must look to cause proportionate. Were there murder done, perhaps, and never brought to light? <u>Abomination</u>? Some secret <u>blasphemy</u> that stinks to Heaven? Think on cause, man, and let you help me to discover it. For there's your way, believe it, there is your only way, when such confusion strikes upon the world. *He goes to* GILES *and* FRANCIS. Let you counsel among yourselves; think on your village and what may have drawn from heaven such thundering wrath upon you all. I shall pray God open up our eyes.

HALE *goes out.*

FRANCIS, *struck by* HALE'S *mood:* I never heard no murder done in Salem.

PROCTOR—*he has been reached by* HALE'S *words:* Leave me, Francis, leave me.

GILES, *shaken:* John—tell me, are we lost?

PROCTOR: Go home now, Giles. We'll speak on it tomorrow.

GILES: Let you think on it. We'll come early, eh?

PROCTOR: Aye. Go now, Giles.

GILES: Good night, then.

GILES COREY *goes out. After a moment:*

MARY WARREN, *in a fearful squeak of a voice:* Mr. Proctor, very likely they'll let her come home once they're given proper evidence.

PROCTOR: You're coming to the court with me, Mary. You will tell it in the court.

MARY WARREN: I cannot charge murder on Abigail.

◆ **Build Vocabulary**

abomination (ə bäm′ ə nā′ shən) *n.*: Something that causes great horror or disgust

blasphemy (blas′ fə mē) *n.*: Sinful act or remark

PROCTOR, *moving menacingly toward her:* You will tell the court how that poppet come here and who stuck the needle in.

MARY WARREN: She'll kill me for sayin' that! PROCTOR *continues toward her.* Abby'll charge lechery[5] on you, Mr. Proctor!

PROCTOR, *halting:* She's told you!

MARY WARREN: I have known it, sir. She'll ruin you with it, I know she will.

PROCTOR, *hesitating, and with deep hatred of himself:* Good. Then her saintliness is done with. MARY *backs from him.* We will slide together into our pit; you will tell the court what you know.

MARY WARREN, *in terror:* I cannot, they'll turn on me—

PROCTOR *strides and catches her, and she is*

repeating, "I cannot, I cannot!"

PROCTOR: My wife will never die for me! I will bring your guts into your mouth but that goodness will not die for me!

MARY WARREN, *struggling to escape him:* I cannot do it. I cannot!

PROCTOR, *grasping her by the throat as though he would strangle her:* Make your peace with it! Now Hell and Heaven grapple on our backs, and all our pretense is ripped away—make your peace! *He throws her to the floor, where she sobs, "I cannot, I cannot . . ."* And now, half to himself, staring, and turning to the open door: Peace. It is a providence, and no great change; we are only what we always were, but naked now. *He walks as though toward a great horror, facing the open sky.* Aye, naked! And the wind, God's icy wind, will blow!

And she is over and over again sobbing, "I cannot, I cannot, I cannot."

---

5. **lechery** (lech´ ər ē) *n.*: Lust; adultery—a charge almost as serious as witchcraft in this Puritan community.

Guide for Responding

◆ *Literature and Your Life*

Reader's Response Which character do you find the most intriguing? Why?

Thematic Response What criticisms of society does this act make?

Journal Activity Write the report that Reverend Hale might have written following his visit to the Proctors.

☑ Check Your Comprehension

1. What evidence is used to support Abigail Williams's assertion that Elizabeth Proctor is guilty of witchcraft?
2. What does Sarah Good do to save herself from hanging?

◆ Critical Thinking

INTERPRET

1. At one point, John Proctor identifies revenge as the true evil that is afflicting Salem Village. What evidence is there to support Proctor's assertion? **[Interpret]**
2. (a) What is ironic about John Proctor's comment that the witchcraft trials are "a black mischief"? (b) Why is it ironic that Rebecca Nurse is charged with witchcraft? (c) What is ironic about the fact that Ezekiel Cheever is the one who arrests Elizabeth Proctor? **[Analyze]**

EXTEND

3. How are legal principles and evidence-gathering procedures different in America today? **[Social Studies Link]**

Guide for Responding, Act II (continued)

◆ Literary Focus

ALLUSION

An **allusion** is a brief reference within a work, to something outside the work, such as another literary work, a well-known person, a place, or a historical event. *The Crucible* contains many allusions to the Bible and to Christianity.

1. Early in Act II, Elizabeth Proctor comments that when Abigail walks into the court, the crowd parts "like the sea for Israel." What does this biblical allusion to Moses and the parting of the Red Sea suggest about how the crowd views Abigail?
2. (a) With the allusion to Pontius Pilate on p. 1127, what does John Proctor imply about Reverend Hale? (b) What does he imply about the witchcraft proceedings in Salem?

◆ Build Vocabulary

USING THE SUFFIX *-logy*

The suffix *-logy* means "the science, theory, or study of." For each item below, write a word that combines the root with the suffix *-logy*, and then explain the new word's meaning.

1. *astro-*, "star"
2. *bio-*, "life"
3. *geo-*, "earth"
4. *phono-*, "sound"

USING THE WORD BANK

Indicate whether each statement is *true* or *false*.

1. Lying and stealing are examples of *base* behaviors.
2. Someone who steps *gingerly* really pounds the pavement.
3. Someone who watches sports *avidly* probably knows very little about them.
4. Well-behaved youngsters show *deference* to their elders.
5. For the Puritans, witchcraft was an *abomination*.
6. A fearful animal may *quail* at the sight of a whip.
7. A minister is always pleased to hear *blasphemy*.
8. A *pallor* usually comes over the face of a blushing person.
9. The Puritans encouraged community members to question their *theology*.
10. People who *ameliorate* a situation are likely to win praise.

◆ Reading Strategy

READ DRAMA

As you read Act II, you paid attention to the stage directions as well as to the dialogue in order to understand the play's plot, characters, and themes.

1. Cite two examples of dialogue in which a character's attitudes would have been unclear to you if you had not read the stage directions. Explain.
2. In addition to characters' attitudes, what other significant information did the stage directions in Act II reveal to you?

◆ Grammar and Style

COMMAS AFTER INTRODUCTORY WORDS

Use a comma to set off an introductory word from the rest of the sentence in which it appears.

Practice Copy the following sentences into your notebook, and add commas to set off introductory words. If a sentence is correct as is, write *correct*.

1. Hey did you ever see *The Crucible*?
2. Yes I saw a local theater group's production.
3. Well which characters did you find the most sympathetic?
4. Perhaps it is a fine play but I found all the characters unpleasant.
5. Perhaps but the problem could have been with the performance you saw.

Idea Bank

Writing

1. **Wanted Poster** Imagine that one of the accused witches has disappeared. Describe her and her crimes in a wanted poster. **[Art Link]**

2. **Additional Scene** Write a scene showing Rebecca Nurse's arrest. Make the style of your scene consistent with that of the rest of the play.

Speaking and Listening

3. **Pantomime** Working in a small group, use gestures—not words—to act out the incident in which Abigail finds the needle in her stomach. **[Performing Arts Link]**

Guide for Interpreting, Act III

◆ Review and Anticipate

Act II ends as Elizabeth Proctor is accused of witchcraft and carted off to jail at the connivance of Abigail Williams. John Proctor demands that Mary Warren tell the court the truth; Mary, though aware of Abigail's ploys, is terrified of exposing her. Do you think John will convince Mary to overcome her fears and testify against Abby? If she does, how will the judges receive her testimony? Read Act III to see what happens in the Salem courtroom.

◆ Reading Strategy

CATEGORIZE CHARACTERS BY ROLE

As you read a play, you'll often find it helpful to **categorize the characters** in some way. For example, one way you can classify characters in *The Crucible* is by their roles in the community:

Property owners and other community leaders
Reverend Parris, Thomas and Ann Putnam, John and Elizabeth Proctor, Francis and Rebecca Nurse, Giles Corey, Ezekiel Cheever, Marshal Herrick, Judge Hathorne
Servants, outcasts, and minors
Betty Parris, Tituba, Abigail Williams, Susanna Walcott, Mercy Lewis, Mary Warren, Sarah Good, Hopkins
Outsiders
Reverend John Hale, Deputy Governor Danforth

As you read Act III, think of other useful categories into which you might organize the characters.

◆ Grammar and Style

SUBJECT AND VERB AGREEMENT IN INVERTED SENTENCES

A **verb** must **agree** in number with its **subject,** regardless of the word order of subject and verb. In most sentences, the subject precedes the verb, but in an **inverted sentence** the verb comes first. Notice how the verb agrees in number with the subject of the following inverted sentences.

Singular: There *is* a prodigious *fear* in this country.

Plural: Now there *are* no *spirits* attacking her.

◆ Literary Focus

DRAMATIC AND VERBAL IRONY

Have you ever watched a horror film and wanted to yell, "Don't go in there, dummy!" as a character went to investigate noises? If so, you've experienced the riveting effects of dramatic irony. Irony arises when things are not what they seem. In **dramatic irony,** there is a contradiction between what a character thinks and what the audience knows to be true. In **verbal irony,** a character says one thing but means something quite different. For example, if John Proctor said, "Abigail is a sweet and innocent maiden," he would be using verbal irony. Look for both forms of irony in Act III.

◆ Build Vocabulary

LEGAL TERMS

The Crucible has several court scenes and contains a number of **legal terms.** *Deposition* is a term for the written testimony of a witness. A deposition, a legal document made under oath but not in open court, is used during a trial.

WORD BANK

Preview this list of words.

contentious
deposition
imperceptible
deferentially
anonymity
prodigious
effrontery
confounded
incredulously
blanched

ACT III

The vestry room of the Salem meeting house, now serving as the anteroom of the General Court.

As the curtain rises, the room is empty, but for sunlight pouring through two high windows in the back wall. The room is solemn, even forbidding. Heavy beams jut out, boards of random widths make up the walls. At the right are two doors leading into the meeting house proper, where the court is being held. At the left another door leads outside.

There is a plain bench at the left, and another at the right. In the center a rather long meeting table, with stools and a considerable armchair snugged up to it.

Through the partitioning wall at the right we hear a prosecutor's voice, JUDGE HATHORNE'S, *asking a question; then a woman's voice,* MARTHA COREY'S, *replying.*

HATHORNE'S VOICE: Now, Martha Corey, there is abundant evidence in our hands to show that you have given yourself to the reading of fortunes. Do you deny it?

MARTHA COREY'S VOICE: I am innocent to a witch. I know not what a witch is.

HATHORNE'S VOICE: How do you know, then, that you are not a witch?

MARTHA COREY'S VOICE: If I were, I would know it.

HATHORNE'S VOICE: Why do you hurt these children?

MARTHA COREY'S VOICE: I do not hurt them. I scorn it!

GILES'S VOICE, *roaring:* I have evidence for the court!

Voices of townspeople rise in excitement.

DANFORTH'S VOICE: You will keep your seat!

GILES' VOICE: Thomas Putnam is reaching out for land!

DANFORTH'S VOICE: Remove that man, Marshal!

GILES' VOICE: You're hearing lies, lies!

A roaring goes up from the people.

HATHORNE'S VOICE: Arrest him, excellency!

GILES' VOICE: I have evidence. Why will you not hear my evidence?

The door opens and GILES *is half carried into the vestry room by* HERRICK.

GILES: Hands off, damn you, let me go!

HERRICK: Giles, Giles!

GILES: Out of my way, Herrick! I bring evidence—

HERRICK: You cannot go in there, Giles; it's a court!

Enter HALE *from the court.*

HALE: Pray be calm a moment.

GILES: You, Mr. Hale, go in there and demand I speak.

HALE: A moment, sir, a moment.

GILES: They'll be hangin' my wife!

JUDGE HATHORNE *enters. He is in his sixties, a bitter, remorseless Salem judge.*

HATHORNE: How do you dare come roarin' into this court! Are you gone daft, Corey?

GILES: You're not a Boston judge, Hathorne. You'll not call me daft!

Enter DEPUTY GOVERNOR DANFORTH *and, behind him,* EZEKIEL CHEEVER *and* PARRIS. *On his appearance, silence falls.* DANFORTH *is a grave man in his sixties, of some humor and sophistication that does not, however, interfere with an exact loyalty to his position and his cause. He comes down to* GILES, *who awaits his wrath.*

DANFORTH, *looking directly at* GILES: Who is this man?

PARRIS: Giles Corey, sir, and a more <u>contentious</u>—

GILES, *to* PARRIS: I am asked the question, and I am old enough to answer it! *To* DANFORTH, *who* *impresses him and to whom he smiles through his strain:* My name is Corey, sir, Giles Corey. I have six hundred acres, and timber in addition. It is my wife you be condemning now. *He indicates the courtroom.*

DANFORTH: And how do you imagine to help her cause with such contemptuous riot? Now be gone. Your old age alone keeps you out of jail for this.

GILES, *beginning to plead:* They be tellin' lies about my wife, sir, I—

DANFORTH: Do you take it upon yourself to determine what this court shall believe and what it shall set aside?

GILES: Your Excellency, we mean no disrespect for—

DANFORTH: Disrespect indeed! It is disruption, Mister. This is the highest court of the supreme government of this province, do you know it?

GILES, *beginning to weep:* Your Excellency, I only said she were readin' books, sir, and they come and take her out of my house for—

DANFORTH, *mystified:* Books! What books?

GILES, *through helpless sobs:* It is my third wife, sir; I never had no wife that be so taken with books, and I thought to find the cause of it, d'y'see, but it were no witch I blamed her for. *He is openly weeping.* I have broke charity with the woman, I have broke charity with her. *He covers his face, ashamed.* DANFORTH *is respectfully silent.*

HALE: Excellency, he claims hard evidence for his wife's defense. I think that in all justice you must—

DANFORTH: Then let him submit his evidence in proper affidavit.[1] You are certainly aware of our procedure here, Mr. Hale. *To* HERRICK: Clear this room.

---

1. **affidavit** (af´ ə dā´ vit) *n.:* Written statement made under oath.

◆ **Build Vocabulary**

contentious (kən ten´ shəs) *adj.:* Argumentative

HERRICK: Come now, Giles. *He gently pushes* COREY *out.*

FRANCIS: We are desperate, sir; we come here three days now and cannot be heard.

DANFORTH: Who is this man?

FRANCIS: Francis Nurse, Your Excellency.

HALE: His wife's Rebecca that were condemned this morning.

DANFORTH: Indeed! I am amazed to find you in such uproar. I have only good report of your character, Mr. Nurse.

HERRICK: I think they must both be arrested in contempt, sir.

DANFORTH, *to* FRANCIS: Let you write your plea, and in due time I will—

FRANCIS: Excellency, we have proof for your eyes; God forbid you shut them to it. The girls, sir, the girls are frauds.

DANFORTH: What's that?

FRANCIS: We have proof of it, sir. They are all deceiving you.

DANFORTH *is shocked, but studying* FRANCIS.

HATHORNE: This is contempt, sir, contempt!

DANFORTH: Peace, Judge Hathorne. Do you know who I am, Mr. Nurse?

FRANCIS: I surely do, sir, and I think you must be a wise judge to be what you are.

DANFORTH: And do you know that near to four hundred are in the jails from Marblehead to Lynn, and upon my signature?

FRANCIS: I—

DANFORTH: And seventy-two condemned to hang by that signature?

FRANCIS: Excellency, I never thought to say it to such a weighty judge, but you are deceived.

Enter GILES COREY *from left. All turn to see as he beckons in* MARY WARREN *with* PROCTOR. MARY *is keeping her eyes to the ground;* PROCTOR *has her elbow as though she were near collapse.*

PARRIS, *on seeing her, in shock:* Mary Warren!

He goes directly to bend close to her face. What are you about here?

PROCTOR, *pressing* PARRIS *away from her with a gentle but firm motion of protectiveness:* She would speak with the Deputy Governor.

DANFORTH, *shocked by this, turns to* HERRICK: Did you not tell me Mary Warren were sick in bed?

HERRICK: She were, Your Honor. When I go to fetch her to the court last week, she said she were sick.

GILES: She has been strivin' with her soul all week, Your Honor; she comes now to tell the truth of this to you.

DANFORTH: Who is this?

PROCTOR: John Proctor, sir. Elizabeth Proctor is my wife.

PARRIS: Beware this man, Your Excellency, this man is mischief.

HALE, *excitedly:* I think you must hear the girl, sir, she—

DANFORTH, *who has become very interested in* MARY WARREN *and only raises a hand toward* HALE: Peace. What would you tell us, Mary Warren?

PROCTOR *looks at her, but she cannot speak.*

PROCTOR: She never saw no spirits, sir.

DANFORTH, *with great alarm and surprise, to* MARY: Never saw no spirits!

GILES, *eagerly:* Never.

PROCTOR, *reaching into his jacket:* She has signed a <u>deposition</u>, sir—

DANFORTH, *instantly:* No, no, I accept no depositions. *He is rapidly calculating this; he turns from her to* PROCTOR. Tell me, Mr. Proctor, have you given out this story in the village?

PROCTOR: We have not.

PARRIS: They've come to overthrow the court, sir! This man is—

DANFORTH: I pray you, Mr. Parris. Do you know, Mr. Proctor that the entire contention of the state in these trials is that the voice of Heaven is speaking through the children?

PROCTOR: I know that, sir.

DANFORTH, *thinks, staring at* PROCTOR, *then turns to* MARY WARREN: And you, Mary Warren, how come you to cry out people for sending their spirits, against you?

MARY WARREN: It were pretense, sir.

DANFORTH: I cannot hear you.

PROCTOR: It were pretense, she says.

DANFORTH: Ah? And the other girls? Susanna Walcott, and—the others? They are also pretending?

MARY WARREN: Aye, sir.

DANFORTH, *wide-eyed:* Indeed. *Pause. He is baffled by this. He turns to study* PROCTOR's *face.*

PARRIS, *in a sweat:* Excellency, you surely cannot think to let so vile a lie be spread in open court.

DANFORTH: Indeed not, but it strike hard upon me that she will dare come here with such a tale. Now, Mr. Proctor, before I decide whether I shall hear you or not, it is my duty to tell you this. We burn a hot fire here; it melts down all concealment.

> **◆ Reading Strategy**
> Would you classify either Parris or Danforth as a villain? Why or why not?

PROCTOR: I know that, sir.

DANFORTH: Let me continue. I understand well, a husband's tenderness may drive him to extravagance in defense of a wife. Are you certain in your conscience, Mister, that your evidence is the truth?

PROCTOR: It is. And you will surely know it.

DANFORTH: And you thought to declare this revelation in the open court before the public?

PROCTOR: I thought I would, aye—with your permission.

DANFORTH, *his eyes narrowing:* Now, sir, what is your purpose in so doing?

PROCTOR: Why, I—I would free my wife, sir.

DANFORTH: There lurks nowhere in your heart, nor hidden in your spirit, any desire to undermine this court?

PROCTOR, *with the faintest faltering:* Why, no, sir.

CHEEVER, *clears his throat, awakening:* I—Your Excellency.

DANFORTH: Mr. Cheever.

CHEEVER: I think it be my duty, sir—*Kindly, to* PROCTOR: You'll not deny it, John. *To* DANFORTH: When we come to take his wife, he damned the court and ripped your warrant.

PARRIS: Now you have it!

DANFORTH: He did that, Mr. Hale?

HALE, *takes a breath:* Aye, he did.

PROCTOR: It were a temper, sir. I knew not what I did.

DANFORTH, *studying him:* Mr. Proctor.

PROCTOR: Aye, sir.

DANFORTH, *straight into his eyes:* Have you ever seen the Devil?

PROCTOR: No, sir.

DANFORTH: You are in all respects a Gospel Christian?

PROCTOR: I am, sir.

PARRIS: Such a Christian that will not come to church but once in a month!

DANFORTH, *restrained—he is curious:* Not come to church?

PROCTOR: I—I have no love for Mr. Parris. It is no secret. But God I surely love.

CHEEVER: He plow on Sunday, sir.

DANFORTH: Plow on Sunday!

CHEEVER, *apologetically:* I think it be evidence, John. I am an official of the court, I cannot keep it.

PROCTOR: I—I have once or twice plowed on Sunday. I have three children, sir, and until last year my land give little.

◆ **Build Vocabulary**

deposition (dep´ ə zish´ ən) *n.:* The testimony of a witness made under oath but not in open court

GILES: You'll find other Christians that do plow on Sunday if the truth be known.

HALE: Your Honor, I cannot think you may judge the man on such evidence.

DANFORTH: I judge nothing. *Pause. He keeps watching* PROCTOR, *who tries to meet his gaze.* I tell you straight, Mister—I have seen marvels in this court. I have seen people choked before my eyes by spirits; I have seen them stuck by pins and slashed by daggers. I have until this moment not the slightest reason to suspect that the children may be deceiving me. Do you understand my meaning?

PROCTOR: Excellency, does it not strike upon you that so many of these women have lived so long with such upright reputation, and—

PARRIS: Do you read the Gospel, Mr. Proctor?

PROCTOR: I read the Gospel.

PARRIS: I think not, or you should surely know that Cain were an upright man, and yet he did kill Abel.[2]

PROCTOR: Aye, God tells us that. *To* DANFORTH: But who tells us Rebecca Nurse murdered seven babies by sending out her spirit on them? It is the children only, and this one will swear she lied to you.

DANFORTH *considers, then beckons* HATHORNE *to him.* HATHORNE *leans in, and he speaks in his ear.* HATHORNE *nods.*

HERRICK: Aye, she's the one.

DANFORTH: Mr. Proctor, this morning, your wife send me a claim in which she states that she is pregnant now.

PROCTOR: My wife pregnant!

DANFORTH: There be no sign of it—we have examined her body.

PROCTOR: But if she say she is pregnant, then she must be! That woman will never lie, Mr. Danforth.

DANFORTH: She will not?

---

2. **Cain . . . Abel:** In the Bible Cain, the oldest son of Adam and Eve, killed his brother, Abel.

PROCTOR: Never, sir, never.

DANFORTH: We have thought it too convenient to be credited. However, if I should tell you now that I will let her be kept another month; and if she begin to show her natural signs, you shall have her living yet another year until she is delivered—what say you to that? JOHN PROCTOR *is struck silent.* Come now. You say your only purpose is to save your wife. Good, then, she is saved at least this year, and a year is long. What say you, sir? It is done now. *In conflict,* PROCTOR *glances at* FRANCIS *and* GILES. Will you drop this charge?

PROCTOR: I—I think I cannot.

DANFORTH, *now an almost* <u>imperceptible</u> *hardness in his voice:* Then your <u>purpose</u> is somewhat larger.

PARRIS: He's come to overthrow this court, Your Honor!

PROCTOR: These are my friends. Their wives are also accused—

DANFORTH, *with a sudden briskness of manner:* I judge you not, sir. I am ready to hear your evidence.

PROCTOR: I come not to hurt the court; I only—

DANFORTH, *cutting him off:* Marshal, go into the court and bid Judge Stoughton and Judge Sewall declare recess for one hour. And let them go to the tavern, if they will. All witnesses and prisoners are to be kept in the building.

HERRICK: Aye, sir. *Very* <u>deferentially</u>: If I may say it, sir. I know this <u>man all my</u> life. It is a good man, sir.

DANFORTH—*it is the reflection on himself he resents:* I am sure of it, Marshal. HERRICK *nods, then goes out.* Now, what deposition do you have for us, Mr. Proctor? And I beg you be clear, open as the sky, and honest.

PROCTOR, *as he takes out several papers:* I am no lawyer, so I'll—

DANFORTH: The pure in heart need no lawyers. Proceed as you will.

PROCTOR, *handing* DANFORTH *a paper:* Will you read this first, sir? It's a sort of testament. The people signing it declare their good opinion of Rebecca, and my wife, and Martha Corey.
DANFORTH *looks down at the paper.*

PARRIS, *to enlist* DANFORTH'S *sarcasm:* Their good opinion! *But* DANFORTH *goes on reading, and* PROCTOR *is heartened.*

PROCTOR: These are all landholding farmers, members of the church. *Delicately, trying to point out a paragraph:* If you'll notice, sir—they've known the women many years and never saw no sign they had dealings with the Devil.

PARRIS *nervously moves over and reads over* DANFORTH'S *shoulder.*

DANFORTH, *glancing down a long list:* How many names are here?

FRANCIS: Ninety-one, Your Excellency.

PARRIS, *sweating:* These people should be summoned. DANFORTH *looks up at him questioningly.* For questioning.

FRANCIS. *trembling with anger:* Mr. Danforth, I gave them all my word no harm would come to them for signing this.

PARRIS: This is a clear attack upon the court!

HALE, *to* PARRIS, *trying to contain himself:* Is every defense an attack upon the court? Can no one—?

PARRIS: All innocent and Christian people are happy for the courts in Salem! These people are gloomy for it. *To* DANFORTH *directly:* And I think you will want to know, from each and every one of them, what discontents them with you!

HERRICK: I think they ought to be examined, sir.

DANFORTH: It is not necessarily an attack, I think. Yet—

FRANCIS: These are all covenanted Christians, sir.

DANFORTH: Then I am sure they may have nothing to fear. *Hands* CHEEVER *the paper.* Mr. Cheever, have warrants drawn for all of these—arrest for examination. *To* PROCTOR: Now, Mister, what other information do you have for us?

◆ **Literary Focus**
What makes this an example of verbal irony?

FRANCIS *is still standing, horrified.* You may sit, Mr. Nurse.

FRANCIS: I have brought trouble on these people: I have—

DANFORTH: No, old man, you have not hurt these people if they are of good conscience. But you must understand, sir, that a person is either with this court or he must be counted against it, there be no road between. This is a sharp time, now, a precise time—we live no longer in the dusky afternoon when evil mixed itself with good and befuddled the world. Now, by God's grace, the shining sun is up, and them that fear not light will surely praise it. I hope you will be one of those. MARY WARREN *suddenly sobs.* She's not hearty, I see.

PROCTOR: No, she's not, sir. *To* MARY, *bending to her, holding her hand, quietly:* Now remember what the angel Raphael said to the boy Tobias.[3] Remember it.

MARY WARREN, *hardly audible:* Aye.

PROCTOR: "Do that which is good, and no harm shall come to thee."

MARY WARREN: Aye.

DANFORTH: Come, man, we wait you.

MARSHAL HERRICK *returns, and takes his post at the door.*

GILES: John, my deposition, give him mine.

PROCTOR: Aye. *He hands* DANFORTH *another paper.* This is Mr. Corey's deposition.

DANFORTH: Oh? *He looks down at it.* Now

---

3. **Raphael. . . Tobias:** In the Bible, Tobias is guided by the archangel Raphael to save two people who have prayed for their deaths. One of the two is Tobias's father, Tobit, who has prayed for his death because he has lost his sight; the other is Sara, a woman who is afflicted by a demon and has killed her seven husbands on their wedding day. With Raphael's assistance, Tobias exorcises the devil from Sara and cures his father of blindness.

HATHORNE *comes behind him and reads with him.*

HATHORNE, *suspiciously:* What lawyer drew this, Corey?

GILES: You know I never hired a lawyer in my life, Hathorne.

DANFORTH, *finishing the reading:* It is very well phrased. My compliments. Mr. Parris, if Mr. Putnam is in the court, will you bring him in? HATHORNE *takes the deposition, and walks to the window with it.* PARRIS *goes into the court.* You have no legal training, Mr. Corey?

GILES, *very pleased:* I have the best, sir—I am thirty-three time in court in my life. And always plaintiff, too.

DANFORTH: Oh, then you're much put-upon.

GILES: I am never put-upon; I know my rights, sir, and I will have them. You know, your father tried a case of mine—might be thirty-five year ago, I think.

DANFORTH: Indeed.

GILES: He never spoke to you of it?

DANFORTH: No, I cannot recall it.

GILES: That's strange, he gave me nine pound damages. He were a fair judge, your father. Y'see, I had a white mare that time, and this fellow come to borrow the mare—*Enter* PARRIS *with* THOMAS PUTNAM. *When he sees* PUTNAM, GILES' *ease goes; he is hard.* Aye, there he is.

DANFORTH: Mr. Putnam, I have here an accusation by Mr. Corey against you. He states that you coldly prompted your daughter to cry witchery upon George Jacobs that is now in jail.

PUTNAM: It is a lie.

DANFORTH, *turning to* GILES: Mr. Putnam states your charge is a lie. What say you to that?

GILES, *furious, his fists clenched:* A fart on Thomas Putnam, that is what I say to that!

DANFORTH: What proof do you submit for your charge, sir?

GILES: My proof is there! *Pointing to the paper.* If

Jacobs hangs for a witch he forfeit up his property—that's law! And there is none but Putnam with the coin to buy so great a piece. This man is killing his neighbors for their land!

DANFORTH: But proof, sir, proof.

GILES, *pointing at his deposition:* The proof is there! I have it from an honest man who heard Putnam say it! The day his daughter cried out on Jacobs, he said she'd given him a fair gift of land.

HATHORNE: And the name of this man?

GILES, *taken aback:* What name?

HATHORNE: The man that give you this information.

GILES, *hesitates, then:* Why, I—I cannot give you his name.

HATHORNE: And why not?

GILES, *hesitates, then bursts out:* You know well why not! He'll lay in jail if I give his name!

HATHORNE: This is contempt of the court, Mr. Danforth!

DANFORTH, *to avoid that:* You will surely tell us the name.

GILES: I will not give you no name. I mentioned my wife's name once and I'll burn in hell long enough for that. I stand mute.

DANFORTH: In that case, I have no choice but to arrest you for contempt of this court, do you know that?

GILES: This is a hearing; you cannot clap me for contempt of a hearing.

DANFORTH: Oh, it is a proper lawyer! Do you wish me to declare the court in full session here? Or will you give me good reply?

GILES, *faltering:* I cannot give you no name, sir, I cannot.

DANFORTH: You are a foolish old man. Mr. Cheever, begin the record. The court is now in session. I ask you, Mr. Corey—

PROCTOR, *breaking in:* Your Honor—he has the story in confidence, sir, and he—

PARRIS: The Devil lives on such confidences! *To* DANFORTH: Without confidences there could be no conspiracy, Your Honor!

HATHORNE: I think it must be broken, sir.

DANFORTH, *to* GILES: Old man, if your informant tells the truth let him come here openly like a decent man. But if he hide in anonymity I must know why. Now sir, the government and central church demand of you the name of him who reported Mr. Thomas Putnam a common murderer.

HALE: Excellency—

DANFORTH: Mr. Hale.

HALE: We cannot blink it more. There is a prodigious fear of this court in the country—

DANFORTH: Then there is a prodigious guilt in the country. Are you afraid to be questioned here?

HALE: I may only fear the Lord, sir, but there is fear in the country nevertheless.

DANFORTH, *angered now:* Reproach me not with the fear in the country; there is fear in the country because there is a moving plot to topple Christ in the country!

HALE: But it does not follow that everyone accused is part of it.

DANFORTH: No uncorrupted man may fear this court, Mr. Hale! None! *To* GILES: You are under arrest in contempt of this court. Now sit you down and take counsel with yourself, or you will be set in the jail until you decide to answer all questions.

GILES COREY *makes a rush for* PUTNAM. PROCTOR *lunges and holds him.*

PROCTOR: No, Giles!

GILES, *over* PROCTOR'S *shoulder at* PUTNAM: I'll cut your throat, Putnam, I'll kill you yet!

PROCTOR, *forcing him into a chair:* Peace, Giles, peace. *Releasing him.* We'll prove ourselves. Now we will. *He starts to turn to* DANFORTH.

GILES: Say nothin' more, John. *Pointing at* DANFORTH: He's only playin' you! He means to hang us all!

MARY WARREN *bursts into sobs.*

DANFORTH: This is a court of law, Mister. I'll have no <u>effrontery</u> here!

PROCTOR: Forgive him, sir, for his old age. Peace, Giles, we'll prove it all now. *He lifts up* MARY's *chin.* You cannot weep, Mary. Remember the angel, what he say to the boy. Hold to it, now; there is your rock. MARY *quiets. He takes out a paper, and turns to* DANFORTH. This is Mary War-

◆ **Build Vocabulary**

anonymity (an′ ə nim′ ə tē) *n.*: The condition of being unknown or unacknowledged

prodigious (prə dij′ əs) *adj.*: Of great size, power, or extent

effrontery (e frun′ tər ē) *n.*: Shameless boldness

ren's deposition. I—I would ask you remember, sir, while you read it, that until two week ago she were no different than the other children are today. *He is speaking reasonably, restraining all his fears, his anger, his anxiety.* You saw her scream, she howled, she swore familiar spirits choked her; she even testified that Satan, in the form of women now in jail, tried to win her soul away, and then when she refused—

DANFORTH: We know all this.

PROCTOR: Aye, sir. She swears now that she never saw Satan; nor any spirit, vague or clear, that Satan may have sent to hurt her. And she declares her friends are lying now.

PROCTOR *starts to hand* DANFORTH *the deposition, and* HALE *comes up to* DANFORTH *in a trembling state.*

HALE: Excellency, a moment. I think this goes to the heart of the matter.

DANFORTH, *with deep misgivings:* It surely does.

HALE: I cannot say he is an honest man; I know him little. But in all justice, sir, a claim so weighty cannot be argued by a farmer. In God's name, sir, stop here; send him home and let him come again with a lawyer—

DANFORTH, *patiently:* Now look you, Mr. Hale—

HALE: Excellency, I have signed seventy-two death warrants; I am a minister of the Lord, and I dare not take a life without there be a proof so immaculate no slightest qualm of conscience may doubt it.

DANFORTH: Mr. Hale, you surely do not doubt my justice.

HALE: I have this morning signed away the soul of Rebecca Nurse, Your Honor. I'll not conceal it, my hand shakes yet as with a wound! I pray you, sir, *this* argument let lawyers present to you.

DANFORTH: Mr. Hale, believe me; for a man of such terrible learning you are most bewildered—I hope you will forgive me. I have been thirty-two year at the bar, sir, and I should be <u>confounded</u> were I called upon to defend these people. Let you consider, now—*To* PROCTOR *and the others:* And I bid you all do likewise. In an ordinary crime, how does one defend the accused? One calls up witnesses to prove his innocence. But witchcraft is *ipso facto*,[4] on its face and by its nature, an invisible crime, is it not? Therefore, who may possibly be witness to it? The witch and the victim. None other. Now we cannot hope the witch will accuse herself; granted? Therefore, we must rely upon her victims—and they do testify, the children certainly do testify. As for the witches, none will deny that we are most eager for all their confessions. Therefore, what is left for a lawyer to bring out? I think I have made my point. Have I not?

> **◆ Reading Strategy**
> Based on this speech, how would you classify Danforth?

HALE: But this child claims the girls are not truthful, and if they are not—

DANFORTH: That is precisely what I am about to consider, sir. What more may you ask of me? Unless you doubt my probity?[5]

HALE, *defeated:* I surely do not, sir. Let you consider it, then.

DANFORTH: And let you put your heart to rest. Her deposition, Mr. Proctor.

PROCTOR *hands it to him.* HATHORNE *rises, goes beside* DANFORTH, *and starts reading.* PARRIS *comes to his other side.* DANFORTH *looks at* JOHN PROCTOR, *then proceeds to read.* HALE *gets up, finds position near the judge, reads too.* PROCTOR *glances at* GILES. FRANCIS *prays silently, hands pressed together.* CHEEVER *waits placidly, the sublime official, dutiful.* MARY WARREN *sobs once.* JOHN PROCTOR *touches her hand reassuringly. Presently* DANFORTH *lifts his eyes, stands up, takes out a kerchief and blows his nose. The others stand aside as he moves in thought toward the window.*

PARRIS, *hardly able to contain his anger and fear:* I should like to question—

DANFORTH—*his first real outburst, in which his contempt for* PARRIS *is clear:* Mr. Parris, I bid you be silent! *He stands in silence, looking out the window. Now, having established that he will set the gait:* Mr. Cheever, will you go into the court and bring the children here? CHEEVER *gets up and goes out upstage.* DANFORTH *now turns to* MARY. Mary Warren, how came you to this turnabout? Has Mr. Proctor threatened you for this deposition?

MARY WARREN: No, sir.

DANFORTH: Has he ever threatened you?

MARY WARREN, *weaker:* No, sir.

DANFORTH, *sensing a weakening:* Has he threatened you?

MARY WARREN: No, sir.

DANFORTH: Then you tell me that you sat in my court, callously lying, when you knew that people would hang by your evidence? *She does not answer.* Answer me!

---

4. ***ipso facto*** (ip′ sō fak′ tō): "By that very fact"; "therefore" (Latin).

5. **probity** (prō′ bə tē) *n.:* Complete honesty: integrity.

MARY WARREN, *almost inaudibly:* I did, sir.

DANFORTH: How were you instructed in your life? Do you not know that God damns all liars? *She cannot speak.* Or is it now that you lie?

MARY WARREN: No, sir—I am with God now.

DANFORTH: You are with God now.

MARY WARREN: Aye, sir.

DANFORTH, *containing himself:* I will tell you this—you are either lying now, or you were lying in the court, and in either case you have committed perjury and you will go to jail for it. You cannot lightly say you lied, Mary. Do you know that?

MARY WARREN: I cannot lie no more. I am with God, I am with God.

But she breaks into sobs at the thought of it, and the right door opens, and enter SUSANNA WALCOTT, MERCY LEWIS, BETTY PARRIS, *and finally* ABIGAIL. CHEEVER *comes to* DANFORTH.

CHEEVER: Ruth Putnam's not in the court, sir, nor the other children.

DANFORTH: These will be sufficient. Sit you down, children. *Silently they sit.* Your friend, Mary Warren, has given us a deposition. In which she swears that she never saw familiar spirits, apparitions, nor any manifest of the Devil. She claims as well that none of you have seen these things either. *Slight pause.* Now, children, this is a court of law. The law, based upon the Bible, and the Bible, writ by Almighty God, forbid the practice of witchcraft, and describe death as the penalty thereof. But likewise, children, the law and Bible damn all bearers of false witness. *Slight pause.* Now then. It does not escape me that this deposition may be devised to blind us; it may well be that Mary Warren has been conquered by Satan, who sends her here to distract our sacred purpose. If so, her neck will break for it. But if she speak true, I bid you now drop your guile and confess your pretense, for a quick confession will go easier with you. *Pause.* Abigail Williams, rise. ABIGAIL *slowly rises.* Is there any truth in this?

ABIGAIL: No, sir.

DANFORTH, *thinks, glances at* MARY *then back to* ABIGAIL: Children, a very augur bit[6] will now be turned into your souls until your honesty is proved. Will either of you change your positions now, or do you force me to hard questioning?

ABIGAIL: I have naught to change, sir. She lies.

DANFORTH, *to* MARY: You would still go on with this?

MARY WARREN, *faintly:* Aye, sir.

DANFORTH, *turning to* ABIGAIL: A poppet were discovered in Mr. Proctor's house, stabbed by a needle. Mary Warren claims that you sat beside her in the court when she made it, and that you saw her make it and witnessed how she herself stuck the needle into it for safe-keeping. What say you to that?

ABIGAIL, *with a slight note of indignation:* It is a lie, sir.

DANFORTH, *after a slight pause:* While you worked for Mr. Proctor, did you see poppets in that house?

ABIGAIL: Goody Proctor always kept poppets.

PROCTOR: Your Honor, my wife never kept no poppets. Mary Warren confesses it was her poppet.

CHEEVER: Your Excellency.

DANFORTH: Mr. Cheever.

CHEEVER: When I spoke with Goody Proctor in that house, she said she never kept no poppets. But she said she did keep poppets when she were a girl.

PROCTOR: She has not been a girl these fifteen years, Your Honor.

HATHORNE: But a poppet will keep fifteen years, will it not?

♦ **Build Vocabulary**

confounded (kən found′ id) *v.:* Confused; dismayed

6. **augur bit:** Sharp point of an augur, a tool used for boring holes.

PROCTOR: It will keep if it is kept, but Mary War-ren swears she never saw no poppets in my house, nor anyone else.

PARRIS: Why could there not have been poppets hid where no one ever saw them?

PROCTOR, *furious:* There might also be a dragon with five legs in my house, but no one has ever seen it.

PARRIS: We are here, Your Honor, precisely to discover what no one has ever seen.

PROCTOR: I do, sir. I believe she means to murder.

DANFORTH, *pointing at* ABIGAIL, *incredulously:* This child would murder your wife?

PROCTOR: It is not a child. Now hear me, sir. In the sight of the congregation she were twice this year put out of this meetin' house for laughter during prayer.

DANFORTH, *shocked, turning to* ABIGAIL: What's this? Laughter during—!

PARRIS: Excellency, she were under Tituba's power at that time, but she is solemn now.

GILES: Aye, now she is solemn and goes to hang people!

DANFORTH: Quiet, man.

HATHORNE: Surely it have no bearing on the question, sir. He charges contemplation of murder.

DANFORTH: Aye. *He studies* ABIGAIL *for a moment, then:* Continue, Mr. Proctor.

PROCTOR: Mary. Now tell the Governor how you danced in the woods.

PARRIS, *instantly:* Excellency, since I come to Salem this man is blackening my name. He—

DANFORTH: In a moment, sir. *To* MARY WARREN, *sternly, and surprised.* What is this dancing?

MARY WARREN: I—*She glances at* ABIGAIL, *who is staring down at her remorselessly. Then, appealing to* PROCTOR: Mr. Proctor—

PROCTOR, *taking it right up:* Abigail leads the girls to the woods, Your Honor, and they have danced there naked—

PARRIS: Your Honor, this—

PROCTOR: Mr. Danforth, what profit this girl to turn herself about? What may Mary Warren gain but hard questioning and worse?

DANFORTH: You are charging Abigail Williams with a marvelous cool plot to murder, do you understand that?

◆ **Build Vocabulary**

incredulously (in krej′ ōō ləs lē) *adv.*: Skeptically

PROCTOR, *at once:* Mr. Parris discovered them himself in the dead of night! There's the "child" she is!

DANFORTH—*it is growing into a nightmare, and he turns, astonished, to* PARRIS: Mr. Parris—

PARRIS: I can only say, sir, that I never found any of them naked, and this man is—

DANFORTH: But you discovered them dancing in the woods? *Eyes on* PARRIS, *he points at* ABIGAIL. Abigail?

HALE: Excellency, when I first arrived from Beverly, Mr. Parris told me that.

DANFORTH: Do you deny it, Mr. Parris?

PARRIS: I do not, sir, but I never saw any of them naked.

DANFORTH: But she have *danced?*

PARRIS, *unwillingly:* Aye, sir.

DANFORTH, *as though with new eyes, looks at* ABIGAIL.

HATHORNE: Excellency, will you permit me? *He points at* MARY WARREN.

DANFORTH, *with great worry:* Pray, proceed.

HATHORNE: You say you never saw no spirits, Mary, were never threatened or afflicted by any manifest of the Devil or the Devil's agents.

MARY WARREN, *very faintly:* No, sir.

HATHORNE, *with a gleam of victory:* And yet, when people accused of witchery confronted you in court, you would faint, saying their spirits came out of their bodies and choked you—

MARY WARREN: That were pretense, sir.

DANFORTH: I cannot hear you.

MARY WARREN: Pretense, sir.

PARRIS: But you did turn cold, did you not? I myself picked you up many times, and your skin were icy. Mr. Danforth, you—

DANFORTH: I saw that many times.

PROCTOR: She only pretended to faint, Your Excellency. They're all marvelous pretenders.

HATHORNE: Then can she pretend to faint now?

PROCTOR: Now?

PARRIS: Why not? Now there are no spirits attacking her, for none in this room is accused of witchcraft. So let her turn herself cold now, let her pretend she is attacked now, let her faint. *He turns to* MARY WARREN. Faint!

MARY WARREN: Faint?

PARRIS: Aye, faint. Prove to us how you pretended in the court so many times.

MARY WARREN, *looking to* PROCTOR: I—cannot faint now, sir.

PROCTOR, *alarmed, quietly:* Can you not pretend it?

MARY WARREN: I—*She looks about as though searching for the passion to faint.* I—have no *sense* of it now, I—

DANFORTH: Why? What is lacking now?

MARY WARREN: I—cannot tell, sir, I—

DANFORTH: Might it be that here we have no afflicting spirit loose, but in the court there were some?

MARY WARREN: I never saw no spirits.

PARRIS: Then see no spirits now, and prove to us that you can faint by your own will, as you claim.

MARY WARREN, *stares, searching for the emotion of it, and then shakes her head:* I— cannot do it.

PARRIS: Then you will confess, will you not? It were attacking spirits made you faint!

MARY WARREN: No, sir, I—

PARRIS: Your Excellency, this is a trick to blind the court!

MARY WARREN: It's not a trick! *She stands.* I—I used to faint because I—I thought I saw spirits.

DANFORTH: *Thought* you saw them!

MARY WARREN: But I did not, Your Honor.

HATHORNE: How could you think you saw them unless you saw them?

MARY WARREN: I—I cannot tell how, but I did. I—I heard the other girls screaming, and you,

Your Honor, you seemed to believe them, and I—It were only sport in the beginning, sir, but then the whole world cried spirits, spirits, and I—I promise you, Mr. Danforth, I only thought I saw them but I did not.

DANFORTH *peers at her.*

PARRIS, *smiling, but nervous because* DANFORTH *seems to be struck by* MARY WARREN'S *story:* Surely Your Excellency is not taken by this simple lie.

DANFORTH, *turning worriedly to* ABIGAIL: Abigail. I bid you now search your heart and tell me this—and beware of it, child, to God every soul is precious and His vengeance is terrible on them that take life without cause. Is it possible, child, that the spirits you have seen are illusion only, some deception that may cross your mind when—

ABIGAIL: Why, this—this—is a base question, sir.

DANFORTH: Child, I would have you consider it—

ABIGAIL: I have been hurt, Mr. Danforth; I have seen my blood runnin' out! I have been near to murdered every day because I done my duty pointing out the Devil's people—and this is my reward? To be mistrusted, denied, questioned like a—

DANFORTH, *weakening:* Child, I do not mistrust you—

ABIGAIL, *in an open threat:* Let you beware, Mr. Danforth. Think you to be so mighty that the power of Hell may not turn *your* wits? Beware of it! There is—*Suddenly, from an accusatory attitude, her face turns, looking into the air above—it is truly frightened.*

DANFORTH, *apprehensively:* What is it, child?

ABIGAIL, *looking about in the air, clasping her arms about her as though cold:* I—I know not. A wind, a cold wind, has come. *Her eyes fall on* MARY WARREN.

MARY WARREN, *terrified, pleading:* Abby!

MERCY LEWIS, *shivering:* Your Honor, I freeze!

PROCTOR: They're pretending!

HATHORNE, *touching* ABIGAIL'S *hand:* She is cold, Your Honor, touch her!

MERCY LEWIS, *through chattering teeth:* Mary, do you send this shadow on me?

MARY WARREN: Lord, save me!

SUSANNA WALCOTT: I freeze, I freeze!

ABIGAIL, *shivering, visibly:* It is a wind, a wind!

MARY WARREN: Abby, don't do that!

DANFORTH, *himself engaged and entered by* ABIGAIL: Mary Warren, do you witch her? I say to you, do you send your spirit out?

With a hysterical cry MARY WARREN *starts to run.* PROCTOR *catches her.*

MARY WARREN, *almost collapsing:* Let me go, Mr. Proctor, I cannot, I cannot—

ABIGAIL, *crying to Heaven:* Oh, Heavenly Father, take away this shadow!

Without warning or hesitation, PROCTOR *leaps at* ABIGAIL *and, grabbing her by the hair, pulls her to her feet. She screams in pain.* DANFORTH, *astonished, cries,* "What are you about?" *and* HATHORNE *and* PARRIS *call,* "Take your hands off her!" *and out of it all comes* PROCTOR'S *roaring voice.*

PROCTOR: How do you call Heaven! Whore! Whore!

HERRICK *breaks* PROCTOR *from her.*

HERRICK: John!

DANFORTH: Man! Man, what do you—

PROCTOR, *breathless and in agony:* It is a whore!

DANFORTH, *dumfounded:* You charge—?

ABIGAIL: Mr. Danforth, he is lying!

PROCTOR: Mark her! Now she'll suck a scream to stab me with, but—

DANFORTH: You will prove this! This will not pass!

PROCTOR, *trembling, his life collapsing about him:* I have known her, sir. I have known her.

DANFORTH: You—you are a lecher?

FRANCIS, *horrified:* John, you cannot say such a—

PROCTOR: Oh, Francis, I wish you had some evil in you that you might know me! *To* DANFORTH: A man will not cast away his good name. You surely know that.

DANFORTH, *dumfounded:* In—in what time? In what place?

PROCTOR, *his voice about to break, and his shame great:* In the proper place—where my beasts are bedded. On the last night of my joy, some eight months past. She used to serve me in my house, sir. *He has to clamp his jaw to keep from weeping.* A man may think God sleeps, but God sees everything. I know it now. I beg you, sir, I beg you—see her what she is. My wife, my dear good wife, took this girl soon after, sir, and put her out on the highroad. And being what she is, a lump of vanity, sir—*He is being overcome.* Excellency, forgive me, forgive me. *Angrily against himself, he turns away from the* GOVERNOR *for a moment. Then, as though to cry out is his only means of speech left:* She thinks to dance with me on my wife's grave! And well she might, for I thought of her softly. God help me, I lusted, and there *is* a promise in such sweat. But it is a whore's vengeance, and you must see it; I set myself entirely in your hands. I know you must see it now.

DANFORTH, *blanched, in horror, turning to* ABIGAIL: You deny every scrap and tittle of this?

ABIGAIL: If I must answer that, I will leave and I will not come back again!

DANFORTH *seems unsteady.*

PROCTOR: I have made a bell of my honor! I have rung the doom of my good name—you will believe me, Mr. Danforth! My wife is innocent, except she knew a whore when she saw one!

ABIGAIL, *stepping up to* DANFORTH: What look do you give me? DANFORTH *cannot speak.* I'll not have such looks! *She turns and starts for the door.*

DANFORTH: You will remain where you are! HERRICK *steps into her path. She comes up short, fire in her eyes.* Mr. Parris, go into the court and bring Goodwife Proctor out.

PARRIS, *objecting:* Your Honor, this is all a—

DANFORTH, *sharply to* PARRIS: Bring her out! And tell her not one word of what's been spoken here. And let you knock before you enter. PARRIS *goes out.* Now we shall touch the bottom of this swamp. *To* PROCTOR: Your wife, you say, is an honest woman.

PROCTOR: In her life, sir, she have never lied. There are them that cannot sing, and them that cannot weep—my wife cannot lie. I have paid much to learn it, sir.

DANFORTH: And when she put this girl out of your house, she put her out for a harlot?

PROCTOR: Aye, sir.

DANFORTH: And knew her for a harlot?

PROCTOR: Aye, sir, she knew her for a harlot.

DANFORTH: Good then. *To* ABIGAIL: And if she tell me, child, it were for harlotry, may God spread His mercy on you! *There is a knock. He calls to the door.* Hold! *To* ABIGAIL: Turn your back. Turn your back. *To* PROCTOR: Do likewise. *Both turn their backs—*ABIGAIL *with indignant slowness.* Now let neither of you turn to face Goody Proctor. No one in this room is to speak one word, or raise a gesture aye or nay. *He turns toward the door, calls:* Enter! *The door opens.* ELIZABETH *enters with* PARRIS. PARRIS *leaves her. She stands alone, her eyes looking for* PROCTOR. Mr. Cheever, report this testimony in all exactness. Are you ready?

CHEEVER: Ready, sir.

DANFORTH: Come here, woman. ELIZABETH *comes to him, glancing at* PROCTOR'S *back.* Look at me only, not at your husband. In my eyes only.

ELIZABETH, *faintly:* Good, sir.

DANFORTH: We are given to understand that at one time you dismissed your servant, Abigail Williams.

ELIZABETH: That is true, sir.

DANFORTH: For what cause did you dismiss her? *Slight pause. Then* ELIZABETH *tries to glance at*

◆ **Build Vocabulary**

blanched (blancht) *adj.:* Paled; whitened

PROCTOR. You will look in my eyes only and not at your husband. The answer is in your memory and you need no help to give it to me. Why did you dismiss Abigail Williams?

ELIZABETH, *not knowing what to say, sensing a situation, wetting her lips to stall for time:* She—dissatisfied me. *Pause.* And my husband.

DANFORTH: In what way dissatisfied you?

ELIZABETH: She were—*She glances at* PROCTOR *for a cue.*

DANFORTH: Woman, look at me? ELIZABETH *does.* Were she slovenly? Lazy? What disturbance did she cause?

ELIZABETH: Your Honor, I—in that time I were sick. And I—My husband is a good and righteous man. He is never drunk as some are, nor wastin' his time at the shovelboard, but always at his work. But in my sickness—you see, sir, I were a long time sick after my last baby, and I thought I saw my husband somewhat turning from me. And this girl—*She turns to* ABIGAIL.

DANFORTH: Look at me.

ELIZABETH: Aye, sir. Abigail Williams—*She breaks off.*

DANFORTH: What of Abigail Williams?

ELIZABETH: I came to think he fancied her. And so one night I lost my wits, I think, and put her out on the highroad.

DANFORTH: Your husband—did he indeed turn from you?

ELIZABETH, *in agony:* My husband—is a goodly man, sir.

DANFORTH: Then he did not turn from you.

ELIZABETH, *starting to glance at* PROCTOR: He—

DANFORTH, *reaches out and holds her face, then:* Look at me! To your own knowledge, has John Proctor ever committed the crime of lechery? *In a crisis of indecision she cannot speak.* Answer my question! Is your husband a lecher!

ELIZABETH, *faintly:* No, sir.

DANFORTH: Remove her, Marshal.

PROCTOR: Elizabeth, tell the truth!

DANFORTH: She has spoken. Remove her!

PROCTOR, *crying out:* Elizabeth, I have confessed it!

ELIZABETH: Oh, God! *The door closes behind her.*

PROCTOR: She only thought to save my name!

HALE: Excellency, it is a natural lie to tell; I beg you, stop now before another is condemned! I may shut my conscience to it no more—private vengeance is working through this testimony! From the beginning this man has struck me true. By my oath to Heaven, I believe him now, and I pray you call back his wife before we—

DANFORTH: She spoke nothing of lechery, and this man has lied!

HALE: I believe him! *Pointing at* ABIGAIL: This girl has always struck me false! She has—

ABIGAIL, *with a weird, wild, chilling cry, screams up to the ceiling.*

ABIGAIL: You will not! Begone! Begone, I say!

DANFORTH: What is it, child? *But* ABIGAIL, *pointing with fear, is now raising up her frightened eyes, her awed face, toward the ceiling—the girls are doing the same—and now* HATHORNE, HALE, PUT-NAM, CHEEVER, HERRICK, *and* DANFORTH *do the same.* What's there? *He lowers his eyes from the ceiling, and now he is frightened; there is real tension in his voice.* Child! *She is transfixed—with all the girls, she is whimpering, open-mouthed, agape at the ceiling.* Girls! Why do you—?

MERCY LEWIS, *pointing:* It's on the beam! Behind the rafter!

DANFORTH, *looking up:* Where!

ABIGAIL: Why—? *She gulps.* Why do you come, yellow bird?

PROCTOR: Where's a bird? I see no bird!

ABIGAIL, *to the ceiling:* My face? My face?

PROCTOR: Mr. Hale—

DANFORTH: Be quiet!

PROCTOR, *to* HALE: Do you see a bird?

DANFORTH: Be quiet!!

> **◆ Literary Focus**
> What does the audience know that Danforth does not know?

ABIGAIL, *to the ceiling, in a genuine conversation with the "bird," as though trying to talk it out of attacking her:* But God made my face; you cannot want to tear my face. Envy is a deadly sin, Mary.

MARY WARREN, *on her feet with a spring, and horrified, pleading:* Abby!

ABIGAIL, *unperturbed, continuing to the "bird":* Oh, Mary, this is a black art to change your shape. No, I cannot, I cannot stop my mouth; it's God's work I do.

MARY WARREN: Abby, I'm *here!*

PROCTOR, *frantically:* They're pretending, Mr. Danforth!

ABIGAIL—*now she takes a backward step, as though in fear the bird will swoop down momentarily:* Oh, please, Mary! Don't come down.

SUSANNA WALCOTT: Her claws, she's stretching her claws!

PROCTOR: Lies, lies.

ABIGAIL, *backing further, eyes still fixed above:* Mary, please don't hurt me!

MARY WARREN, *to* DANFORTH: I'm not hurting her!

DANFORTH, *to* MARY WARREN: Why does she see this vision?

MARY WARREN: She sees nothin'!

ABIGAIL, *now staring full front as though hypnotized, and mimicking the exact tone of* MARY WARREN'S *cry:* She sees nothin'!

MARY WARREN, *pleading:* Abby, you mustn't!

ABIGAIL AND ALL THE GIRLS, *all transfixed:* Abby, you mustn't!

MARY WARREN, *to all the girls:* I'm here, I'm here!

GIRLS: I'm here, I'm here!

DANFORTH, *horrified:* Mary Warren! Draw back your spirit out of them!

MARY WARREN: Mr. Danforth!

GIRLS, *cutting her off:* Mr. Danforth!

DANFORTH: Have you compacted with the Devil? Have you?

MARY WARREN: Never, never!

GIRLS: Never, never!

DANFORTH, *growing hysterical:* Why can they only repeat you?

PROCTOR: Give me a whip—I'll stop it!

MARY WARREN: They're sporting. They—!

GIRLS: They're sporting!

MARY WARREN, *turning on them all hysterically and stamping her feet:* Abby, stop it!

GIRLS, *stamping their feet:* Abby, stop it!

MARY WARREN: Stop it!

GIRLS: Stop it!

MARY WARREN, *screaming it out at the top of her lungs, and raising her fists:* Stop it!!

GIRLS, *raising their fists:* Stop it!!

MARY WARREN, *utterly confounded, and becoming overwhelmed by* ABIGAIL'S—*and the girls'—utter conviction, starts to whimper, hands half raised, powerless, and all the girls begin whimpering exactly as she does.*

DANFORTH: A little while ago you were afflicted. Now it seems you afflict others; where did you find this power?

MARY WARREN, *staring at* ABIGAIL: I—have no power.

GIRLS: I have no power.

PROCTOR: They're gulling[7] you, Mister!

DANFORTH: Why did you turn about this past two weeks? You have seen the Devil, have you not?

HALE, *indicating* ABIGAIL *and the* GIRLS: You cannot believe them!

MARY WARREN: I—

PROCTOR, *sensing her weakening:* Mary, God damns all liars!

DANFORTH, *pounding it into her:* You have seen the Devil, you have made compact with Lucifer, have you not?

PROCTOR: God damns liars, Mary!

---

7. **gulling:** Fooling.

MARY *utters something unintelligible, staring at* ABIGAIL, *who keeps watching the "bird" above.*

DANFORTH: I cannot hear you. What do you say? MARY *utters again unintelligibly.* You will confess yourself or you will hang! *He turns her roughly to face him.* Do you know who I am? I say you will hang if you do not open with me!

PROCTOR: Mary, remember the angel Raphael— do that which is good and—

ABIGAIL, *pointing upward:* The wings! Her wings are spreading! Mary, please, don't, don't—!

HALE: I see nothing, Your Honor!

DANFORTH: Do you confess this power! *He is an inch from her face.* Speak!

ABIGAIL: She's going to come down! She's walking the beam!

DANFORTH: Will you speak!

MARY WARREN, *staring in horror:* I cannot!

GIRLS: I cannot!

PARRIS: Cast the Devil out! Look him in the face! Trample him! We'll save you, Mary, only stand fast against him and—

ABIGAIL, *looking up:* Look out! She's coming down!

She and all the girls run to one wall, shielding their eyes. And now, as though cornered, they let out a gigantic scream, and MARY, *as though infected, opens her mouth and screams with them. Gradually* ABIGAIL *and the girls leave off, until only* MARY *is left there, staring up at the "bird," screaming madly. All watch her, horrified by this evident fit.* PROCTOR *strides to her.*

PROCTOR: Mary, tell the Governor what they— *He has hardly got a word out, when, seeing him coming for her, she rushes out of his reach, screaming in horror.*

MARY WARREN: Don't touch me—don't touch me! *At which the girls halt at the door.*

PROCTOR, *astonished:* Mary!

MARY WARREN, *pointing at* PROCTOR: You're the Devil's man!

He is stopped in his tracks.

PARRIS: Praise God!

GIRLS: Praise God!

PROCTOR, *numbed:* Mary, how— ?

MARY WARREN: I'll not hang with you! I love God, I love God.

DANFORTH, *to* MARY: He bid you do the Devil's work?

MARY WARREN, *hysterically, indicating* PROCTOR: He come at me by night and every day to sign, to sign, to—

DANFORTH: Sign what?

PARRIS: The Devil's book? He come with a book?

MARY WARREN, *hysterically, pointing at* PROCTOR, *fearful of him:* My name, he want my name. "I'll murder you," he says, "if my wife hangs! We must go and overthrow the court," he says!

DANFORTH's *head jerks toward* PROCTOR, *shock and horror in his face.*

PROCTOR, *turning, appealing to* HALE: Mr. Hale!

MARY WARREN, *her sobs beginning:* He wake me every night, his eyes were like coals and his fingers claw my neck, and I sign, I sign . . .

HALE: Excellency, this child's gone wild!

PROCTOR, *as* DANFORTH's *wide eyes pour on him:* Mary, Mary!

MARY WARREN, *screaming at him:* No, I love God; I go your way no more. I love God, I bless God. *Sobbing, she rushes to* ABIGAIL. Abby, Abby, I'll never hurt you more! *They all watch, as* ABIGAIL, *out of her infinite charity, reaches out and draws the sobbing* MARY *to her, and then looks up to* DANFORTH.

◆ **Literary Focus**
Which two words in these stage directions are an example of verbal irony?

DANFORTH, *to* PROCTOR: What are you? PROCTOR *is beyond speech in his anger.* You are combined with anti-Christ,[8] are you not? I have seen your power; you will not deny it! What say you, Mister?

HALE: Excellency—

---

8. **anti-Christ:** In the Bible, the great antagonist of Christ expected to spread universal evil.

DANFORTH: I will have nothing from you, Mr. Hale! *To* PROCTOR: Will you confess yourself befouled with Hell, or do you keep that black allegiance yet? What say you?

PROCTOR, *his mind wild, breathless:* I say—I say—God is dead!

PARRIS: Hear it, hear it!

PROCTOR, *laughs insanely, then:* A fire, a fire is burning! I hear the boot of Lucifer, I see his filthy face! And it is my face, and yours, Danforth! For them that quail to bring men out of ignorance, as I have quailed, and as you quail now when you know in all your black hearts that this be fraud—God damns our kind especially, and we will burn, we will burn together.

DANFORTH: Marshal! Take him and Corey with him to the jail!

HALE, *staring across to the door:* I denounce these proceedings!

PROCTOR: You are pulling Heaven down and raising up a whore!

HALE: I denounce these proceedings, I quit this court! *He slams the door to the outside behind him.*

DANFORTH, *calling to him in a fury:* Mr. Hale! Mr. Hale!

> **◆ Reading Strategy**
> If you were classifying characters as static (unchanging) and dynamic (changing or growing), in which category would you place Reverend Hale? Why?

Guide for Responding

◆ Literature and Your Life

Reader's Response What incident in Act III provoked the strongest emotional response in you? Why?

Thematic Focus What dangers of the legal system does Act III point out?

Class Debate Hold an informal debate on this issue: Who bears more guilt for the fate of those hanged in the Salem witch trials—the young girls who accused innocent people or the judges and magistrates who sentenced them to death?

☑ Check Your Comprehension

1. Which three depositions are presented to the court?
2. Cory charges that Putnam is "killing his neighbors for their land." What does Danforth demand as proof?
3. Summarize the events leading to John Proctor's arrest.
4. After rejoining the other girls in their hysterical behavior, what accusation does Mary make about Proctor?
5. What does Reverend Hale denounce at the end of Act III?

◆ Critical Thinking

INTERPRET

1. How do the judges effectively discourage anyone from defending the good character or innocence of a person accused of witchcraft? Support your answer with an incident or quotation from the play. **[Analyze; Support]**
2. What does Proctor's decision to confess his involvement with Abigail reveal about his character? **[Infer]**
3. (a) Why does Elizabeth Proctor lie when questioned by Danforth? (b) What are the consequences of her lie? **[Analyze]**
4. Why does Mary Warren change her testimony and turn on John Proctor? **[Analyze]**

EVALUATE

5. Do you find Hale sympathetic? Why or why not? **[Evaluate]**

APPLY

6. Imagine that Elizabeth Proctor had told Danforth the truth. How might the outcome of the witchcraft hysteria have been different? **[Modify]**

EXTEND

7. Which qualities of a good judge do you think are lacking in Hathorne and Danforth? **[Career Link]**

Guide for Responding, *Act III* (continued)

◆ Reading Strategy

CATEGORIZE CHARACTERS BY ROLE

As you've seen, the characters in the play can be classified into different categories according to their roles.

1. Organize a chart to categorize the characters in the play. You may categorize according to their attitudes toward the witchcraft trials or their roles in the trials: accuser and accused, or judge and other officials, for example.
2. What other categories, if any, do you think would be useful for classifying the characters? Explain.

◆ Literary Focus

DRAMATIC AND VERBAL IRONY

Irony arises when there is a discrepancy between the way things seem and the way they really are. In **dramatic irony,** there is a contrast between what a character thinks is true and what the audience knows. In **verbal irony,** words that seem to say one thing actually mean something quite different.

1. Find two examples of verbal irony in the dialogue in Act III. Explain what each speaker really means.
2. Consider the dramatic irony that occurs when Elizabeth testifies about her husband's behavior. (a) What does she not know that the audience knows? (b) Why is the effect of her testimony so ironic?

◆ Grammar and Style

SUBJECT AND VERB AGREEMENT IN INVERTED SENTENCES

In an **inverted sentence**, the common subject-verb order of a sentence is reversed. Even in an inverted sentence, a **verb** should **agree** in number with its **subject.**

Practice In your notebook, complete each sentence by choosing the correct form of the verb in parentheses and underlining the subject.

1. There (is, are) a courtroom scene in Act III of *The Crucible.*
2. In the courtroom (sits, sit) many townspeople.
3. Hearing the case (is, are) Danforth and Hathorne.
4. Here (is, are) Abigail and her cohorts.

◆ Build Vocabulary

LEGAL TERMS

The Crucible contains many terms from the specialized vocabulary of trials and the law. Determine the meaning of each of these words from the context in which it appears in Act III, and then use it in a sentence about a modern trial.

1. prosecutor
2. witness
3. contempt
4. perjury

USING THE WORD BANK

For each item, indicate whether the paired words are synonyms or antonyms. Write your answers on a separate sheet of paper.

1. contentious, combative
2. deposition, testimony
3. imperceptible, obvious
4. deferentially, politely
5. anonymity, notoriety
6. prodigious, minuscule
7. effrontery, timidity
8. confounded, puzzled
9. incredulously, disbelievingly
10. blanched, darkened

Idea Bank

Writing

1. **Character Sketch** Write a character sketch of Mary Warren in which you describe her personality, including her strengths and weaknesses. Is she essentially good, bad, or just weak?

2. **Letter to the Editor** By the end of Act III, Reverend Hale has openly denounced the court he once supported. As Hale, write a letter to the editor of the *Salem Voice* in which you explain why you now oppose the court's actions.

Speaking and Listening

3. **Soliloquy** Show how Elizabeth Proctor might react when she learns the effects of her lie. Present her private thoughts in a soliloquy—a monologue she delivers while she is alone on stage.

Guide for Interpreting, Act IV

◆ Review and Anticipate

"Is every defense an attack upon the court?" Hale asks in Act III; and Danforth observes, "A person is either with this court or he must be counted against it." Such remarks stress how little people like John Proctor and Giles Corey can do against the mounting injustices in Salem. Instead, their efforts backfire, and their own names join the list of those accused. What do you think the final outcome will be? Who will survive, and who will perish? Read the final act to see if your predictions are correct.

◆ Reading Strategy

APPLY THEMES TO CONTEMPORARY EVENTS

The Crucible was written during the McCarthy era of the 1950's, when fear of Communism swept America. The fears were understandable—eastern Europe and China had recently fallen to Communism—but they were also exploited for political ends. In Congress, a Republican senator named Joseph McCarthy leapt into the limelight when he charged that the State Department had been infiltrated by more than two hundred Communists. Leading a Senate investigation, McCarthy often charged that those who opposed his hearings were themselves Communists and began investigating them. The parallels between the Salem events, as Miller depicts them, and ongoing events in Congress at the time Miller wrote the play are clear. As you read Act IV, think about what **themes**, or messages, Miller was conveying that specifically **related to current events** of the time.

◆ Grammar and Style

COMMONLY CONFUSED WORDS: *RAISE* AND *RISE*

Be careful not to confuse the verbs *raise* and *rise*. *Raise*, meaning "to lift up," always has a direct object, a noun or pronoun that receives the action of the verb. In contrast *rise*, meaning "to go up or get up," never has a direct object.

She *raises* the flask. [*flask* is direct object]
You'll never *rise* off the ground. [no direct object]

Forms of *raise*	*raise* or *raises, raising, raised,* (have) *raised*
Forms of *rise*	*rise* or *rises, rising, rose,* (have) *risen*

◆ Literary Focus

THEME

A **theme** is a central idea or insight into life that a writer tries to convey in a work of literature. Like most longer works, *The Crucible* has several themes. One theme is that fear and suspicion are infectious and can swell into a mass hysteria that destroys public order and rationality. As you read Act IV, consider how this theme is conveyed through the comments and actions of the characters. In addition, look for other themes, such as the idea that people can commit evil deeds in the name of good.

◆ Build Vocabulary

WORDS FROM MYTHS: *TANTALIZE*

In Greek mythology, the gods punished King Tantalus for his crimes. They placed him in a pool of water that shrank away whenever he tried to drink it. Fruit hanging above him receded whenever he tried to reach it. From this myth comes the word *tantalize*, which means "to entice with something that cannot be reached or achieved; to tease only to frustrate."

WORD BANK

Preview this list of words from Act IV.

agape
conciliatory
beguile
floundering
retaliation
adamant
cleave
sibilance
tantalized
purged

ACT IV

A cell in Salem jail, that fall.

At the back is a high barred window; near it, a great, heavy door. Along the walls are two benches.

The place is in darkness but for the moonlight seeping through the bars. It appears empty. Presently footsteps are heard coming down a corridor beyond the wall, keys rattle, and the door swings open. MARSHAL HERRICK *enters with a lantern.*

He is nearly drunk, and heavy-footed. He goes to a bench and nudges a bundle of rags lying on it.

HERRICK: Sarah, wake up! Sarah Good! *He then crosses to the other benches.*

SARAH GOOD, *rising in her rags:* Oh, Majesty! Comin', comin'! Tituba, he's here, His Majesty's come!

HERRICK: Go to the north cell; this place is wanted now. *He hangs his lantern on the wall.* TITUBA *sits up.*

TITUBA: That don't look to me like His Majesty; look to me like the marshal.

HERRICK, *taking out a flask:* Get along with you now, clear this place. *He drinks, and* SARAH GOOD *comes and peers up into his face.*

SARAH GOOD: Oh, is it you, Marshal! I thought sure you be the devil comin' for us. Could I have a sip of cider for me goin'-away?

HERRICK, *handing her the flask:* And where are you off to, Sarah?

TITUBA, *as* SARAH *drinks:* We goin' to Barbados, soon the Devil gits here with the feathers and the wings.

HERRICK: Oh? A happy voyage to you.

SARAH GOOD: A pair of bluebirds wingin' southerly, the two of us! Oh, it be a grand transformation, Marshal! *She raises the flask to drink again.*

HERRICK, *taking the flask from her lips:* You'd best give me that or you'll never rise off the ground. Come along now.

TITUBA: I'll speak to him for you, if you desires to come along, Marshal.

HERRICK: I'd not refuse it, Tituba; it's the proper morning to fly into Hell.

TITUBA: Oh, it be no Hell in Barbados. Devil, him be pleasure man in Barbados, him be singin' and dancin' in Barbados. It's you folks—you riles him up 'round here; it be too cold 'round here for that Old Boy. He freeze his soul in Massachusetts, but in Barbados he just as sweet and—*A bellowing cow is heard, and* TITUBA *leaps up and calls to the window:* Aye, sir! That's him, Sarah!

SARAH GOOD: I'm here, Majesty! *They hurriedly pick up their rags as* HOPKINS, *a guard, enters.*

HOPKINS: The Deputy Governor's arrived.

HERRICK, *grabbing* TITUBA: Come along, come along.

TITUBA, *resisting him:* No, he comin' for me. I goin' home!

HERRICK, *pulling her to the door:* That's not Satan, just a poor old cow with a hatful of milk. Come along now, out with you!

TITUBA, *calling to the window:* Take me home, Devil! Take me home!

SARAH GOOD, *following the shouting* TITUBA *out:* Tell him I'm goin', Tituba! Now you tell him Sarah Good is goin' too!

In the corridor outside TITUBA *calls on—"Take me home, Devil: Devil take me home!" and* HOPKINS' *voice orders her to move on.* HERRICK *returns and begins to push old rags and straw into a corner. Hearing footsteps, he turns, and enter* DANFORTH *and* JUDGE HATHORNE. *They are in greatcoats and wear hats against the bitter cold. They are followed in by* CHEEVER, *who carries a dispatch case and a flat wooden box containing his writing materials.*

HERRICK: Good morning, Excellency.

DANFORTH: Where is Mr. Parris?

HERRICK: I'll fetch him. *He starts for the door.*

DANFORTH: Marshal. HERRICK *stops.* When did Reverend Hale arrive?

HERRICK: It were toward midnight, I think.

DANFORTH, *suspiciously:* What is he about here?

HERRICK: He goes among them that will hang, sir. And he prays with them. He sits with Goody Nurse now. And Mr. Parris with him.

DANFORTH: Indeed. That man have no authority to enter here, Marshal. Why have you let him in?

HERRICK: Why, Mr. Parris command me, sir. I cannot deny him.

DANFORTH: Are you drunk, Marshal?

HERRICK: No, sir; it is a bitter night, and I have no fire here.

DANFORTH, *containing his anger:* Fetch Mr. Parris.

HERRICK: Aye, sir.

DANFORTH: There is a prodigious stench in this place.

HERRICK: I have only now cleared the people out for you.

DANFORTH: Beware hard drink, Marshal.

HERRICK: Aye, sir. *He waits an instant for further orders. But* DANFORTH, *in dissatisfaction, turns his back on him, and* HERRICK *goes out. There is a pause.* DANFORTH *stands in thought.*

HATHORNE: Let you question Hale, Excellency; I should not be surprised he have been preaching in Andover lately.

DANFORTH: We'll come to that; speak nothing of Andover. Parris prays with him. That's strange. *He blows on his hands, moves toward the window, and looks out.*

HATHORNE: Excellency, I wonder if it be wise to let Mr. Parris so continuously with the prisoners. DANFORTH *turns to him, interested.* I think, sometimes, the man has a mad look these days.

DANFORTH: Mad?

HATHORNE: I met him yesterday coming out of his house, and I bid him good morning—and he wept and went his way. I think it is not well the village sees him so unsteady.

DANFORTH: Perhaps he have some sorrow.

CHEEVER, *stamping his feet against the cold:* I think it be the cows, sir.

DANFORTH: Cows?

CHEEVER: There be so many cows wanderin' the highroads, now their masters are in the jails, and much disagreement who they will belong to now. I know Mr. Parris be arguin' with farmers all yesterday—there is great contention, sir, about the cows. Contention make him weep, sir; it were always a man that weep for contention. *He turns, as do* HATHORNE *and* DANFORTH

◆ **Reading Strategy**
What warning may the details about changes in Salem convey about the growing anti-Communist fear and suspicion in Miller's own time?

hearing someone coming up the corridor. DANFORTH *raises his head as* PARRIS *enters. He is gaunt, frightened, and sweating in his greatcoat.*

PARRIS, *to* DANFORTH, *instantly:* Oh, good morning, sir, thank you for coming. I beg your pardon wakin' you so early. Good morning, Judge Hathorne.

DANFORTH: Reverend Hale have no right to enter this—

PARRIS: Excellency, a moment. *He hurries back and shuts the door.*

HATHORNE: Do you leave him alone with the prisoners?

DANFORTH: What's his business here?

PARRIS, *prayerfully holding up his hands:* Excellency, hear me. It is a providence. Reverend Hale has returned to bring Rebecca Nurse to God.

DANFORTH, *surprised:* He bids her confess?

PARRIS, *sitting:* Hear me. Rebecca have not given me a word this three month since she came. Now she sits with him, and her sister and Martha Corey and two or three others, and he pleads with them, confess their crimes and save their lives.

DANFORTH: Why—this is indeed a providence. And they soften, they soften?

PARRIS: Not yet, not yet. But I thought to summon you, sir, that we might think on whether it be not wise, to—*He dares not say it.* I had thought to put a question, sir, and I hope you will not—

DANFORTH: Mr. Parris, be plain, what troubles you?

PARRIS: There is news, sir, that the court—the court must reckon with. My niece, sir, my niece—I believe she has vanished.

DANFORTH: Vanished!

PARRIS: I had thought to advise you of it earlier in the week, but—

DANFORTH: Why? How long is she gone?

PARRIS: This be the third night. You see, sir, she told me she would stay a night with Mercy Lewis. And next day, when she does not return, I send to Mr. Lewis to inquire. Mercy told him she would sleep in *my* house for a night.

DANFORTH: They are both gone?!

PARRIS, *in fear of him:* They are, sir.

DANFORTH, *alarmed:* I will send a party for them. Where may they be?

PARRIS: Excellency, I think they be aboard a ship. DANFORTH *stands agape.* My daughter tells me how she heard them speaking of ships last week, and tonight I discover my—my strongbox is broke into. *He presses his fingers against his eyes to keep back tears.*

HATHORNE, *astonished:* She have robbed you?

PARRIS: Thirty-one pound is gone. I am penniless. *He covers his face and sobs.*

DANFORTH: Mr. Parris, you are a brainless man! *He walks in thought, deeply worried.*

PARRIS: Excellency, it profit nothing you should blame me. I cannot think they would run off except they fear to keep in Salem any more. *He is pleading.* Mark it, sir, Abigail had close knowledge of the town, and since the news of Andover[1] has broken here—

DANFORTH: Andover is remedied. The court returns there on Friday, and will resume examinations.

PARRIS: I am sure of it, sir. But the rumor here speaks rebellion in Andover, and it—

DANFORTH: There is no rebellion in Andover!

PARRIS: I tell you what is said here, sir. Andover

---

1. **news of Andover:** During the height of the terror in Salem Village, a similar hysteria broke out in the nearby town of Andover. There, many respected people were accused of practicing witchcraft and confessed to escape death. However, in Andover people soon began questioning the reality of the situation and the hysteria quickly subsided.

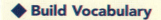

◆ **Build Vocabulary**
agape (ə gāp´) *adj.:* Wide open

have thrown out the court, they say, and will have no part of witchcraft. There be a faction here, feeding on that news, and I tell you true, sir, I fear there will be riot here.

HATHORNE: Riot! Why at every execution I have seen naught but high satisfaction in the town.

PARRIS: Judge Hathorne—it were another sort that hanged till now. Rebecca Nurse is no Bridget that lived three year with Bishop before she married him. John Proctor is not Isaac Ward that drank his family to ruin. *To* DANFORTH: I would to God it were not so, Excellency, but these people have great weight yet in the town. Let Rebecca stand upon the gibbet[2] and send up some righteous prayer, and I fear she'll wake a vengeance on you.

---

2. **gibbet** (jib´ it) *n.:* Gallows.

HATHORNE: Excellency, she is condemned a witch. The court have—

DANFORTH, *in deep concern, raising a hand to* HATHORNE: Pray you. *To* PARRIS: How do you propose, then?

PARRIS: Excellency, I would postpone these hangin's for a time.

DANFORTH: There will be no postponement.

PARRIS: Now Mr. Hale's returned, there is hope, I think—for if he bring even one of these to God, that confession surely damns the others in the public eye, and none may doubt more that they are all linked to Hell. This way, unconfessed and claiming innocence, doubts are multiplied, many honest people will weep for them, and our good purpose is lost in their tears.

DANFORTH, *after thinking a moment, then going to* CHEEVER: Give me the list.

CHEEVER *opens the dispatch case, searches.*

PARRIS: It cannot be forgot, sir, that when I summoned the congregation for John Proctor's excommunication there were hardly thirty people come to hear it. That speak a discontent, I think, and—

DANFORTH, *studying the list:* There will be no postponement.

PARRIS: Excellency—

DANFORTH: Now, sir—which of these in your opinion may be brought to God? I will myself strive with him till dawn. *He hands the list to* PARRIS, *who merely glances at it.*

PARRIS: There is not sufficient time till dawn.

DANFORTH: I shall do my utmost. Which of them do you have hope for?

PARRIS, *not even glancing at the list now, and in a quavering voice, quietly:* Excellency—a dagger—*He chokes up.*

DANFORTH: What do you say?

PARRIS: Tonight, when I open my door to leave my house—a dagger clattered to the ground. *Silence.* DANFORTH *absorbs this. Now* PARRIS *cries out:* You cannot hang this sort. There is danger for me. I dare not step outside at night!

REVEREND HALE *enters. They look at him for an instant in silence. He is steeped in sorrow, exhausted, and more direct than he ever was.*

DANFORTH: Accept my congratulations, Reverend Hale; we are gladdened to see you returned to your good work.

HALE, *coming to* DANFORTH *now:* You must pardon them. They will not budge.

HERRICK *enters, waits.*

DANFORTH, *conciliatory:* You misunderstand, sir; I cannot pardon these when twelve are already hanged for the same crime. It is not just.

PARRIS, *with failing heart:* Rebecca will not confess?

HALE: The sun will rise in a few minutes. Excellency, I must have more time.

DANFORTH: Now hear me, and beguile yourselves no more. I will not receive a single plea for pardon or postponement. Them that will not confess will hang. Twelve are already executed; the names of these seven are given out, and the village expects to see them die this morning. Postponement now speaks a floundering on my part; reprieve or pardon must cast doubt upon the guilt of them that died till now. While I speak God's law, I will not crack its voice with whimpering. If retaliation is your fear, know this—I should hang ten thousand that dared to rise against the law, and an ocean of salt tears could not melt the resolution of the statutes. Now draw yourselves up like men and help me, as you are bound by Heaven to do. Have you spoken with them all, Mr. Hale?

> ◆ **Literary Focus**
> What theme about authority or hypocrisy do you think Danforth's attitude here may convey?

HALE: All but Proctor. He is in the dungeon.

DANFORTH, *to* HERRICK: What's Proctor's way now?

HERRICK: He sits like some great bird; you'd not know he lived except he will take food from time to time.

DANFORTH, *after thinking a moment:* His wife—his wife must be well on with child now.

HERRICK: She is, sir.

DANFORTH: What think you, Mr. Parris? You have closer knowledge of this man; might her presence soften him?

PARRIS: It is possible, sir. He have not laid eyes on her these three months. I should summon her.

DANFORTH, *to* HERRICK: Is he yet adamant? Has he struck at you again?

HERRICK: He cannot, sir, he is chained to the wall now.

DANFORTH, *after thinking on it:* Fetch Goody Proctor to me. Then let you bring him up.

HERRICK: Aye, sir. HERRICK *goes. There is silence.*

HALE: Excellency, if you postpone a week and publish to the town that you are striving for their confessions, that speak mercy on your part, not faltering.

DANFORTH: Mr. Hale, as God have not empowered me like Joshua to stop this sun from rising,[3] so I cannot withhold from them the perfection of their punishment.

HALE, *harder now:* If you think God wills you to raise rebellion, Mr. Danforth, you are mistaken!

DANFORTH, *instantly:* You have heard rebellion spoken in the town?

HALE: Excellency, there are orphans wandering from house to house; abandoned cattle bellow on the highroads, the stink of rotting crops hangs everywhere, and no man knows when the harlots' cry will end his life—and you wonder yet if rebellion's spoke? Better you should marvel how they do not burn your province!

DANFORTH: Mr. Hale, have you preached in Andover this month?

HALE: Thank God they have no need of me in Andover.

DANFORTH: You baffle me, sir. Why have you returned here?

HALE: Why, it is all simple. I come to do the Devil's work. I come to counsel Christians they should belie themselves. *His sarcasm collapses.* There is blood on my head! Can you not see the blood on my head!!

---

3. **Joshua . . . rising:** In the Bible, Joshua, leader of the Jews after the death of Moses, asks God to make the sun and the moon stand still during a battle, and his request is granted.

◆ **Build Vocabulary**

conciliatory (kən sil′ ē ə tôr′ ə) *adj.:* Tending to soothe the anger of

beguile (bē gīl′) *v.:* Trick; delude

floundering (floun′ dər in) *n.:* Awkward struggling

retaliation (ri tal′ ē ā′ shən) *n.:* Act of returning an injury or wrong

adamant (ad′ ə mənt) *adj.:* Firm; unyielding

cleave (clēv) *v.:* Adhere; cling

PARRIS: Hush! *For he has heard footsteps. They all face the door.* HERRICK *enters with* ELIZABETH. *Her wrists are linked by heavy chain, which* HERRICK *now removes. Her clothes are dirty; her face is pale and gaunt.* HERRICK *goes out.*

DANFORTH, *very politely:* Goody Proctor. *She is silent.* I hope you are hearty?

ELIZABETH, *as a warning reminder:* I am yet six months before my time.

DANFORTH: Pray be at your ease, we come not for your life. We—*uncertain how to plead, for he is not accustomed to it.* Mr. Hale, will you speak with the woman?

HALE: Goody Proctor, your husband is marked to hang this morning

Pause.

ELIZABETH, *quietly:* I have heard it.

HALE: You know, do you not, that I have no connection with the court? *She seems to doubt it.* I come of my own, Goody Proctor. I would save your husband's life, for if he is taken I count myself his murderer. Do you understand me?

ELIZABETH: What do you want of me?

HALE: Goody Proctor, I have gone this three month like our Lord into the wilderness. I have sought a Christian way, for damnation's doubled on a minister who counsels men to lie.

HATHORNE: It is no lie, you cannot speak of lies.

HALE: It is a lie! They are innocent!

DANFORTH: I'll hear no more of that!

HALE, *continuing to* ELIZABETH: Let you not mistake your duty as I mistook my own. I came into this village like a bridegroom to his beloved, bearing gifts of high religion; the very crowns of holy law I brought, and what I touched with my bright confidence, it died; and where I turned the eye of my great faith, blood flowed up. Beware, Goody Proctor—<u>cleave</u> to no faith when faith brings blood. It is mistaken law that leads you to sacrifice. Life, woman, life is God's most precious gift; no principle, however glorious, may justify the taking of it. I beg you, woman, prevail upon your husband to

◆ **Literary Focus**
What theme or themes does Reverend Hale state in this speech?

confess. Let him give his lie. Quail not before God's judgment in this, for it may well be God damns a liar less than he that throws his life away for pride. Will you plead with him? I cannot think he will listen to another.

ELIZABETH, *quietly:* I think that be the Devil's argument.

HALE, *with a climactic desperation:* Woman, before the laws of God we are as swine! We cannot read His will!

ELIZABETH: I cannot dispute with you, sir; I lack learning for it.

DANFORTH, *going to her:* Goody Proctor, you are not summoned here for disputation. Be there no wifely tenderness within you? He will die with the sunrise. Your husband. Do you understand it? *She only looks at him.* What say you? Will you contend with him? *She is silent.* Are you stone? I tell you true, woman, had I no other proof of your unnatural life, your dry eyes now would be sufficient evidence that you delivered up your soul to Hell! A very ape would weep at such calamity! Have the devil dried up any tear of pity in you? *She is silent.* Take her out. It profit nothing she should speak to him!

ELIZABETH, *quietly:* Let me speak with him, Excellency.

PARRIS, *with hope:* You'll strive with him? *She hesitates.*

DANFORTH: Will you plead for his confession or will you not?

ELIZABETH: I promise nothing. Let me speak with him.

A sound—the <u>sibilance</u> of dragging feet on stone. They turn. A pause. HERRICK *enters with* JOHN PROCTOR. *His wrists are chained. He is another man, bearded, filthy, his eyes misty as though webs had overgrown them. He halts inside the doorway, his eyes caught by the sight of* ELIZABETH. *The emotion flowing between them prevents anyone from speaking for an instant. Now* HALE, *visibly affected, goes to* DANFORTH *and speaks quietly.*

HALE: Pray, leave them Excellency.

DANFORTH, *pressing* HALE *impatiently aside:* Mr. Proctor, you have been notified, have you not? PROCTOR *is silent, staring at* ELIZABETH. I see light in the sky, Mister; let you counsel with your wife, and may God help you turn your back on Hell. PROCTOR *is silent, staring at* ELIZABETH.

HALE, *quietly:* Excellency, let—

DANFORTH *brushes past* HALE *and walks out.* HALE *follows.* CHEEVER *stands and follows,* HATHORNE *behind.* HERRICK *goes.* PARRIS, *from a safe distance, offers:*

PARRIS: If you desire a cup of cider, Mr. Proctor, I am sure I—PROCTOR *turns an icy stare at him, and he breaks off.* PARRIS *raises his palms toward* PROCTOR. God lead you now. PARRIS *goes out.*

Alone, PROCTOR *walks to her, halts. It is as though they stood in a spinning world. It is beyond sorrow, above it. He reaches out his hand as though toward an embodiment not quite real, and as he touches her, a strange soft sound, half laughter, half amazement, comes from his throat. He pats her hand. She covers his hand with hers. And then, weak, he sits. Then she sits, facing him.*

PROCTOR: The child?

ELIZABETH: It grows.

PROCTOR: There is no word of the boys?

ELIZABETH: They're well. Rebecca's Samuel keeps them.

◆ Build Vocabulary

sibilance (sib´ əl əns) *n.:* Hissing sound

PROCTOR: You have not seen them?

ELIZABETH: I have not. *She catches a weakening in herself and downs it.*

PROCTOR: You are a—marvel, Elizabeth.

ELIZABETH: You—have been tortured?

PROCTOR: Aye. *Pause. She will not let herself be drowned in the sea that threatens her.* They come for my life now.

ELIZABETH: I know it.

Pause.

PROCTOR: None—have yet confessed?

ELIZABETH: There be many confessed.

PROCTOR: Who are they?

ELIZABETH: There be a hundred or more, they say. Goody Ballard is one; Isaiah Goodkind is one. There be many.

PROCTOR: Rebecca?

ELIZABETH: Not Rebecca. She is one foot in Heaven now; naught may hurt her more.

PROCTOR: And Giles?

ELIZABETH: You have not heard of it?

PROCTOR: I hear nothin', where I am kept.

ELIZABETH: Giles is dead.

He looks at her incredulously.

PROCTOR: When were he hanged?

ELIZABETH, *quietly, factually:* He were not hanged. He would not answer aye or nay to his indictment; for if he denied the charge they'd hang him surely, and auction out his property. So he stand mute, and died Christian under the law. And so his sons will have his farm. It is the law, for he could not be condemned a wizard without he answer the indictment, aye or nay.

PROCTOR: Then how does he die?

ELIZABETH, *gently:* They press him, John.

PROCTOR: Press?

ELIZABETH: Great stones they lay upon his chest until he plead aye or nay. *With a tender smile for the old man:* They say he give them but two words. "More weight," he says. And died.

PROCTOR, *numbed—a thread to weave into his agony:* "More weight."

ELIZABETH: Aye. It were a fearsome man, Giles Corey.

Pause.

PROCTOR, *with great force of will, but not quite looking at her:* I have been thinking I would confess to them, Elizabeth. *She shows nothing.* What say you? If I give them that?

ELIZABETH: I cannot judge you, John.

Pause.

PROCTOR, *simply—a pure question:* What would you have me do?

ELIZABETH: As you will, I would have it. *Slight pause:* I want you living, John. That's sure.

PROCTOR, *pauses, then with a flailing of hope:* Giles' wife? Have she confessed?

ELIZABETH: She will not.

Pause.

PROCTOR: It is a pretense, Elizabeth.

ELIZABETH: What is?

PROCTOR: I cannot mount the gibbet like a saint. It is a fraud. I am not that man. *She is silent.* My honesty is broke, Elizabeth; I am no good man. Nothing's spoiled by giving them this lie that were not rotten long before.

ELIZABETH: And yet you've not confessed till now. That speak goodness in you.

PROCTOR: Spite only keeps me silent. It is hard to give a lie to dogs. *Pause, for the first time he turns directly to her.* I would have your forgiveness, Elizabeth.

ELIZABETH: It is not for me to give, John, I am—

PROCTOR: I'd have you see some honesty in it. Let them that never lied die now to keep their souls. It is pretense for me, a vanity that will not blind God nor keep my children out of the wind. *Pause.* What say you?

ELIZABETH, *upon a heaving sob that always threatens:* John, it come to naught that I should forgive you, if you'll not forgive yourself. *Now he turns away a little, in great agony.* It is not my soul, John, it is yours. *He stands, as though in physical pain, slowly rising to his feet with a great immortal longing to find his answer. It is difficult to say, and she is on the verge of tears.* Only be sure of this, for I know it now: Whatever you will do, it is a good man does it. *He turns his doubting, searching gaze upon her.* I have read my heart this three month, John. *Pause.* I have sins of my own to count. It needs a cold wife to prompt lechery.

PROCTOR, *in great pain:* Enough, enough—

ELIZABETH, *now pouring out her heart:* Better you should know me!

PROCTOR: I will not hear it! I know you!

ELIZABETH: You take my sins upon you, John—

PROCTOR, *in agony:* No, I take my own, my own!

ELIZABETH: John, I counted myself so plain, so poorly made, no honest love could come to me! Suspicion kissed you when I did; I never knew how I should say my love. It were a cold house I kept! *In fright, she swerves, as* HATHORNE *enters.*

HATHORNE: What say you Proctor? The sun is soon up.

PROCTOR, *his chest heaving, stares, turns to* ELIZABETH. *She comes to him as though to plead, her voice quaking.*

ELIZABETH: Do what you will. But let none be your judge. There be no higher judge under Heaven than Proctor is! Forgive me, forgive me, John—I never knew such goodness in the world! *She covers her face, weeping.*

PROCTOR *turns from her to* HATHORNE; *he is off the earth, his voice hollow.*

PROCTOR: I want my life.

HATHORNE *electrified, surprised:* You'll confess yourself?

PROCTOR: I will have my life.

HATHORNE, *with a mystical tone:* God be praised! It is a providence! *He rushes out the door, and his voice is heard calling down the corridor:* He will confess! Proctor will confess!

PROCTOR, *with a cry, as he strides to the door:* Why do you cry it? *In great pain he turns back to her.* It is evil, is it not? It is evil.

ELIZABETH, *in terror, weeping:* I cannot judge you, John, I cannot!

PROCTOR: Then who will judge me? *Suddenly clasping his hands:* God in Heaven, what is John Proctor, what is John Proctor? *He moves as an animal, and a fury is riding in him, a* <u>tantalized</u> *search.* I think it is honest, I think so; I am no saint. *As though she had denied this he calls angrily at her:* Let Rebecca go like a saint; for me it is fraud!

Voices are heard in the hall, speaking together in suppressed excitement.

ELIZABETH: I am not your judge, I cannot be. *As though giving him release:* Do as you will, do as you will!

PROCTOR: Would you give them such a lie? Say it. Would you ever give them this? *She cannot answer.* You would not; if tongs of fire were singeing you you would not! It is evil. Good, then—it is evil, and I do it!

HATHORNE *enters with* **DANFORTH,** *and, with them,* **CHEEVER, PARRIS,** *and* **HALE.** *It is a businesslike, rapid entrance, as though the ice had been broken.*

DANFORTH, *with great relief and gratitude:* Praise to God, man, praise to God; you shall be blessed in Heaven for this. **CHEEVER** *has hurried to the bench with pen, ink, and paper.* **PROCTOR** *watches him.* Now then, let us have it. Are you ready, Mr. Cheever?

PROCTOR, *with a cold, cold horror at their efficiency:* Why must it be written?

DANFORTH: Why, for the good instruction of the village, Mister; this we shall post upon the church door! *To* **PARRIS,** *urgently:* Where is the marshal?

PARRIS, *runs to the door and calls down the*

corridor: Marshal! Hurry!

DANFORTH: Now, then, Mister, will you speak slowly, and directly to the point, for Mr. Cheever's sake. *He is on record now, and is really dictating to* **CHEEVER,** *who writes.* Mr. Proctor, have you seen the Devil in your life? **PROCTOR**'s *jaws lock.* Come, man, there is light in the sky; the town waits at the scaffold; I would give out this news. Did you see the Devil?

PROCTOR: I did.

PARRIS: Praise God!

DANFORTH: And when he come to you, what were his demand?

PROCTOR *is silent.* **DANFORTH** *helps.* Did he bid you to do his work upon the earth?

PROCTOR: He did.

DANFORTH: And you bound yourself to his service? **DANFORTH** *turns, as* **REBECCA NURSE** *enters, with* **HERRICK** *helping to support her. She is barely able to walk.* Come in, come in, woman!

REBECCA, *brightening as she sees* **PROCTOR:** Ah, John! You are well, then, eh?

PROCTOR *turns his face to the wall.*

DANFORTH: Courage, man, courage—let her witness your good example that she may come to God herself. Now hear it, Goody Nurse! Say on, Mr. Proctor. Did you bind yourself to the Devil's service?

REBECCA, *astonished:* Why, John!

PROCTOR, *through his teeth, his face turned from* **REBECCA:** I did.

DANFORTH: Now, woman, you surely see it profit nothin' to keep this conspiracy any further. Will you confess yourself with him?

REBECCA: Oh, John—God send his mercy on you!

DANFORTH: I say, will you confess yourself, Goody Nurse?

REBECCA: Why, it is a lie, it is a lie; how may I damn myself? I cannot, I cannot.

◆ **Build Vocabulary**

tantalized (tan´ tə līzd) *adj.:* Tormented; frustrated

DANFORTH: Mr. Proctor. When the Devil came to you did you see Rebecca Nurse in his company? PROCTOR *is silent.* Come, man, take courage—did you ever see her with the Devil?

PROCTOR, *almost inaudibly:* No.

DANFORTH, *now sensing trouble, glances at* JOHN *and goes to the table, and picks up a sheet—the list of condemned.*

DANFORTH: Did you ever see her sister, Mary Easty, with the Devil?

PROCTOR: No, I did not.

DANFORTH, *his eyes narrow on* PROCTOR: Did you ever see Martha Corey with the Devil?

PROCTOR: I did not.

DANFORTH, *realizing, slowly putting the sheet down:* Did you ever see anyone with the Devil?

PROCTOR: I did not.

DANFORTH: Proctor, you mistake me. I am not empowered to trade your life for a lie. You have most certainly seen some person with the Devil. PROCTOR *is silent.* Mr. Proctor, a score of people have already testified they saw this woman with the Devil.

PROCTOR: Then it is proved. Why must I say it?

DANFORTH: Why "must" you say it! Why, you should rejoice to say it if your soul is truly purged of any love for Hell!

PROCTOR: They think to go like saints. I like not to spoil their names.

◆ **Build Vocabulary**

purged (pŭrjd) *v.*: Cleansed; purified

DANFORTH, *inquiring, incredulous:* Mr. Proctor, do you think they go like saints?

PROCTOR, *evading:* This woman never thought she done the Devil's work.

DANFORTH: Look you, sir. I think you mistake your duty here. It matter nothing what she thought—she is convicted of the unnatural murder of children, and you for sending your spirit out upon Mary Warren. Your soul alone is the issue here, Mister, and you will prove its whiteness or you cannot live in a Christian country. Will you tell me now what persons conspired with you in the Devil's company? PROCTOR *is silent.* To your knowledge was Rebecca Nurse ever—

PROCTOR: I speak my own sins; I cannot judge another. *Crying out, with hatred:* I have no tongue for it.

HALE, *quickly to* DANFORTH: Excellency, it is enough he confess himself. Let him sign it, let him sign it.

PARRIS, *feverishly:* It is a great service, sir. It is a weighty name; it will strike the village that Proctor confess. I beg you, let him sign it. The sun is up, Excellency!

DANFORTH, *considers; then with dissatisfaction:* Come, then, sign your testimony. *To* CHEEVER: Give it to him. CHEEVER *goes to* PROCTOR, *the confession and a pen in hand.* PROCTOR *does not look at it.* Come, man, sign it.

PROCTOR, *after glancing at the confession:* You have all witnessed it—it is enough.

DANFORTH: You will not sign it?

PROCTOR: You have all witnessed it; what more is needed?

DANFORTH: Do you sport with me? You will sign your name or it is no confession, Mister! *His breast heaving with agonized breathing,* PROCTOR *now lays the paper down and signs his name.*

PARRIS: Praise be to the Lord!

◆ **Reading Strategy**
How might Proctor's insistence on not incriminating others relate to the McCarthy hearings of the 1950's?

PROCTOR *has just finished signing when* DAN-FORTH *reaches for the paper. But* PROCTOR *snatches it up, and now a wild terror is rising in him, and a boundless anger.*

DANFORTH, *perplexed, but politely extending his hand:* If you please, sir.

PROCTOR: No.

DANFORTH, *as though* PROCTOR *did not understand:* Mr. Proctor, I must have—

PROCTOR: No, no. I have signed it. You have seen me. It is done! You have no need for this.

PARRIS: Proctor, the village must have proof that—

PROCTOR: Damn the village! I confess to God, and God has seen my name on this! It is enough!

DANFORTH: No, sir, it is—

PROCTOR: You came to save my soul, did you not? Here! I have confessed myself; it is enough!

DANFORTH: You have not con—

PROCTOR: I have confessed myself! Is there no good penitence but it be public? God does not need my name nailed upon the church! God sees my name; God knows how black my sins are! It is enough!

DANFORTH: Mr. Proctor—

PROCTOR: You will not use me! I am no Sarah Good or Tituba, I am John Proctor! You will not use me! It is no part of salvation that you should use me!

DANFORTH: I do not wish to—

PROCTOR: I have three children—how may I teach them to walk like men in the world, and I sold my friends?

DANFORTH: You have not sold your friends—

PROCTOR: Beguile me not! I blacken all of them when this is nailed to the church the very day they hang for silence!

DANFORTH: Mr. Proctor, I must have good and legal proof that you—

PROCTOR: You are the high court, your word is good enough! Tell them I confessed myself; say Proctor broke his knees and wept like a woman; say what you will, but my name cannot—

DANFORTH, *with suspicion:* It is the same, is it not? If I report it or you sign to it?

PROCTOR—*he knows it is insane:* No, it is not the same! What others say and what I sign to is not the same!

DANFORTH: Why? Do you mean to deny this confession when you are free?

PROCTOR: I mean to deny nothing!

DANFORTH: Then explain to me, Mr. Proctor, why you will not let—

PROCTOR, *with a cry of his whole soul:* Because it is my name! Because I cannot have another in my life! Because I lie and sign myself to lies! Because I am not worth the dust on the feet of them that hang! How may I live without my name? I have given you my soul; leave me my name!

DANFORTH, *pointing at the confession in* PROCTOR's *hand:* Is that document a lie? If it is a lie I will not accept it! What say you? I will not deal in lies, Mister! PROCTOR *is motionless.* You will give me your honest confession in my hand, or I cannot keep you from the rope. PROCTOR *does not reply.* What way do you go, Mister?

His breast heaving, his eyes staring, PROCTOR *tears the paper and crumples it, and he is weeping in fury, but erect.*

DANFORTH: Marshal!

PARRIS, *hysterically, as though the tearing paper were his life:* Proctor, Proctor!

HALE: Man, you will hang! You cannot!

PROCTOR, *his eyes full of tears:* I can. And there's your first marvel, that I can. You have made your magic now, for now I do think I see some shred of goodness in John Proctor. Not enough to weave a banner with, but white enough to keep it from such dogs. ELIZABETH, *in a burst of terror, rushes to him and weeps against his hand.* Give them no tear! Tears pleasure them! Show honor now, show a stony heart and sink them with it! *He has lifted her, and kisses her now with great passion.*

REBECCA: Let you fear nothing! Another judgment waits us all!

DANFORTH: Hang them high over the town! Who weeps for these, weeps for corruption! *He sweeps out past them.* HERRICK *starts to lead* REBECCA, *who almost collapses, but* PROCTOR *catches her, and she glances up at him apologetically.*

REBECCA: I've had no breakfast.

HERRICK: Come, man.

HERRICK *escorts them out,* HATHORNE *and* CHEEVER *behind them.* ELIZABETH *stands staring at the empty doorway.*

PARRIS, *in deadly fear, to* ELIZABETH: Go to him, Goody Proctor! There is yet time!

From outside a drumroll strikes the air. PARRIS *is startled.* ELIZABETH *jerks about toward the window.*

PARRIS: Go to him! *He rushes out the door, as though to hold back his fate.* Proctor! Proctor!

Again, a short burst of drums.

HALE: Woman, plead with him! *He starts to rush out the door, and then goes back to her.* Woman! It is pride, it is vanity. *She avoids his eyes, and moves to the window. He drops to his knees.* Be his helper!—What profit him to bleed? Shall the dust praise him? Shall the worms declare his truth? Go to him, take his shame away!

ELIZABETH, *supporting herself against collapse, grips the bars of the window, and with a cry:* He have his goodness now. God forbid I take it from him!

The final drumroll crashes, then heightens violently. HALE *weeps in frantic prayer, and the new sun is pouring in upon her face, and the drums rattle like bones in the morning air.*

Guide for Responding

◆ Literature and Your Life

Reader's Response How did you react to the ending of the play? Would you recommend this play to a friend? Why or why not?

Thematic Focus What does the ending of the play suggest about the value of integrity and holding fast to principles? How might that idea relate to the McCarthy era?

Journal Writing Write an epitaph for John Proctor or Rebecca Nurse.

☑ Check Your Comprehension

1. (a) What worries Parris when he meets with Danforth at the beginning of Act IV? (b) What does he propose to Danforth?
2. Summarize Hale's argument favoring Proctor's confession.
3. Why does Danforth arrange a meeting between John and Elizabeth Proctor?
4. What does Proctor have "no tongue for"?

◆ Critical Thinking

INTERPRET

1. (a) What might have motivated Abigail to leave Salem? (b) How does Parris exhibit his self-centeredness when he relates the news of Abigail's disappearence to Hathorne and Danforth? **[Infer]**
2. What motivates Reverend Hale to seek confessions from the condemned prisoners? **[Infer]**
3. Why is Elizabeth unable to offer her husband advice on whether to confess? **[Interpret]**
4. (a) Why does Proctor confess? (b) Why does he retract his confession? **[Analyze]**
5. Why does Elizabeth say her husband has "his goodness" as he is about to be hanged? **[Interpret]**

EVALUATE

6. Do you think John Proctor made the right decision? Why or why not? **[Evaluate]**

EXTEND

7. Could a tragedy like the Salem witchcraft trials occur today? Explain. **[Social Studies Link]**

Guide for Responding, *Act IV* (continued)

◆ Reading Strategy

APPLY THEMES TO CONTEMPORARY EVENTS

As Arthur Miller himself mentions often in the background sections within *The Crucible*, there are several parallels between the witchcraft hysteria of 1692 and the events that occurred during the McCarthy era of the 1950's.

1. Based on the play's details, what criticisms might Miller be making about the way McCarthy's Senate committee dealt with those it questioned and those who criticized it?

2. What does the play suggest about the motives behind political "witch hunts" like Senator Joseph McCarthy's?

◆ Grammar and Style

COMMONLY CONFUSED WORDS: *RAISE* AND *RISE*

To *raise* means "to lift up"; it takes a direct object. To *rise* means "to go up or get up"; it does not take a direct object. Study the forms of the two verbs on the chart below.

Verb	Present	Present Participle	Past	Past Participle
raise	raise, raises	raising	raised	(have) raised
rise	rise, rises	rising	rose	(have) risen

Practice Complete each sentence with the correct form of *rise* or *raise* in the tense indicated in parentheses.

1. All (past) when the judge entered.
2. They were (present participle) the flag outside the courthouse.
3. In 1692, cries of witchcraft (past) a ruckus in Salem.
4. Spirits were reported to have (past participle) to the courtroom ceiling.
5. Citizens in a nearby town had (past participle) a rebellion.

◆ Literary Focus

THEME

A **theme** is a central idea or insight about life conveyed in a work of literature. Longer works like *The Crucible* often express many themes.

1. Use evidence from the play to show how Miller conveys the following themes in *The Crucible*: (a) Fear and suspicion are infectious and can produce a mass hysteria that destroys public order and rationality. (b) It is more noble to die with integrity than to live with compromised principles that harm others.

2. State and support another theme that you feel the play expresses.

◆ Build Vocabulary

USING WORDS FROM MYTHS: *TANTALIZE*

Tantalize, from the myth about King Tantalus, is just one of several English words that come from Greek and Roman mythology. Review the three mythological figures below. Then, for each, write a sentence using the word in parentheses.

1. *Ceres*: The goddess of the harvest (cereal)
2. *Titan*: A race of giants with brute strength (titanic)
3. *Narcissus*: A boy punished by the gods for vanity (narcissistic)

USING THE WORD BANK

In your notebook, write the letter of the word that is most nearly the same in meaning as the first word.

1. agape: (a) dark, (b) open, (c) shocking
2. conciliatory: (a) soothing, (b) rude, (c) vengeful
3. beguile: (a) plead, (b) fool, (c) straighten
4. floundering: (a) groping, (b) jogging, (c) smelling
5. retaliation: (a) narration, (b) restatement, (c) revenge
6. adamant: (a) calm, (b) first, (c) stubborn
7. cleave: (a) depart, (b) grow, (c) stick
8. sibilance: (a) hissing, (b) humming, (c) screaming
9. tantalized: (a) freed, (b) tempted, (c) danced
10. purged: (a) soothed, (b) washed, (c) filled

Build Your Portfolio

 Idea Bank

Writing

1. **Casting Profiles** As a casting director for this play, describe two or three of the main characters and the requirements for playing each.

2. **Literary Analysis** How is the play's title appropriate to its themes and content? Answer in a brief essay that begins with a definition of *crucible*.

3. **Critical Response** Some have claimed that *The Crucible*'s characters are only "mouthpieces" for Miller's ideas. In an essay, support or refute critic Walter Kerr, who said, "For Salem, and the people . . . in it, are really only conveniences to Mr. Miller, props to his theme. He does not make them interesting in and of themselves, and you wind up analyzing them . . . rather than losing yourself in any rounded, deeply rewarding personalities."

Speaking and Listening

4. **Mock Trial** Stage a mock trial to determine whether Danforth and Hathorne are guilty of murder for their roles in the Salem witch trials. Appoint a prosecutor, a defense attorney, defendants, witnesses, and a jury. **[Social Studies Link]**

5. **Group Discussion** Research the McCarthy era of the 1950's. Present your findings; then lead a group discussion about the accuracy of Miller's views of that era. **[Social Studies Link]**

Projects

6. **Compare-and-Contrast Chart** Working with a partner, research the facts of the Salem witchcraft trials. Then present a compare-and-contrast chart on differences between the trials and events in this play. Give possible reasons Miller had for making those changes. **[Social Studies Link]**

7. **Memorial** Design a memorial commemorating those killed in the Salem witch trials. **[Art Link]**

 Writing Mini-Lesson

Defend a Character's Actions

Did John Proctor do the right thing in the end? What did you think of Reverend Hale's decisions, or Elizabeth Proctor's, or Judge Danforth's? Write an essay in which you defend a character's actions or final decision in the play. Like a good trial lawyer, you need not agree with your "client's" actions—just present the best defense possible.

Writing Skills Focus: Pro-and-Con Argument

To defend a character as effectively as possible, you need to anticipate and refute the attacks or criticisms that others may make. Your defense should include the following elements:

- **"Cons"**—reasons against your argument. In this case, list the reasons some people may find the character's actions or decisions to be wrong.

- **"Pros"**—reasons supporting your argument. In this case, list the reasons you find the character's actions or decisions to be right.

- **Refutation** Provide reasons that show the "pros" outweigh the "cons."

Prewriting Skim the play to decide which character's actions you will defend. Record possible "pros" and "cons" in a two-column chart. You might discuss the character with others to come up with as complete a list of "pros" and "cons" as possible.

Drafting Begin by presenting the "cons," then move on to the "pros." Use forceful, persuasive language to explain why the "pros" outweigh the "cons."

Revising Make sure you have effectively refuted the "cons" and included enough "pros" to support your argument. Is your word choice clear and precise? Do your sentences flow logically and smoothly?

Writing Process Workshop

From the authors and signers of the Declaration of Independence to the creators of the social protest literature of recent decades, writers have tried, with reason or emotional appeal, to persuade readers to accept a wide range of ideas. Arthur Miller's play, for example, protests McCarthyism. A position paper presents one side of a controversial issue and tries to persuade its audience to take that side. The intended audience often has some power to shape policy on the issue.

These writing tips, introduced in this section's Writing Mini-Lessons, will help you write your position paper:

Writing Skills Focus

▶ **Consider the knowledge level of readers.** Use language and details that they can understand. (See p. 1047.)

▶ **Elaborate** by providing both logical reasons and emotional appeals to support your argument. (See p. 1077.)

▶ **Use specific examples** to back up your position. (See p. 1057.)

This introduction to a position paper demonstrates many of these skills:

① The author begins by stating her position.

② Clear, jargon-free language is appropriate for the average voter to understand.

③ The writer's personal experience supports her thesis.

WRITING MODEL

A higher minimum wage destroys jobs by making it unprofitable to hire young, inexperienced job seekers. ① Its impact will be felt by the people with the fewest skills and the most to learn. I know because I'm proof. ②

I was a single mother when I started at Cousins Submarine shop in 1981. My first job was as a part-time cashier earning $2.90 per hour, less than I wanted, but more than I deserved. Within months, I had gotten a raise and moved up to making sandwiches. . . . Today, I supervise eight Cousins shops in Milwaukee and oversee nearly 300 employees. ③

Prewriting

Choose a Topic Read the editorial page of a newspaper. Choose an issue from the paper that interests you or that evokes a strong personal response—either positive or negative. You may also take a position on one of the topics listed below.

> ### Topic Ideas
> - U.S. military intervention in foreign conflicts
> - The use of dialect in literature
> - Term limits for U.S. Congress members
> - Required seat belts on school buses

Gather Facts and Examples Use current, credible resources to gather specific facts, examples, and evidence to support your position and persuade others to adopt it. You may run across information that disputes your position. Your ability to understand and refute the opposition can only strengthen your paper.

Drafting

Use Appropriate Vocabulary and Style Keep your readers in mind as you write. You will most likely be writing for a general audience, so remember to define any technical terms or jargon. At the same time, avoid "talking down" to your audience.

Avoid Faulty Logic In order to persuade your readers to adopt your position on an issue, you must present adequate supporting evidence. Avoid building your argument on faulty logic and unreasonable appeals, which a discerning audience will soon see through. Some tactics to avoid include the following:

▶ **Overgeneralization:** a statement that is too broad for the evidence that backs it up; for example: Modern poets have abandoned all traditional literary forms.

▶ **Circular reasoning:** an attempt to support a point by merely restating it in other words; for example: Sylvia Plath is a famous poet because many people know her work.

▶ **Either/or argument:** a statement that offers only two extremes, when there are other possibilities; for example: Either we lead the military peacekeeping effort or we risk a return to the foreign policy of isolationism.

▶ **Bandwagon appeal:** a statement that urges acceptance of an idea or action simply because "everyone" believes it or is doing it; for example: Anyone who is anybody has read the works of Arthur Miller.

APPLYING LANGUAGE SKILLS:
Varying Sentence Length

Add interest to your writing and prevent it from becoming monotonous by **varying your sentence lengths.** Notice the varying lengths of these sentences from *The Rockpile*:

John took Delilah and sat down with her in the easy chair. His mother bent over Roy, and held him still, while his father, carefully—but still Roy screamed—lifted the bandage and stared at the wound. Roy's sobs began to lessen.

Practice Revise the following paragraph by varying the sentence lengths.

Puerto Rico is not a state. It is a protectorate. It is also an island. Puerto Rico lies off the east coast of the United States. Soon, its citizens will vote. They will vote on the issue of statehood.

Writing Application Combine shorter sentences with conjunctions and appropriate punctuation to create longer, more complex, sentences.

Writer's Solution Connection
Writing Lab

For help gathering forceful language, use the Persuasive Words Word Bin in the Revising and Editing section of the tutorial on Persuasion.

Use Persuasive Words Emphasize your main points with positive persuasive language—words such as *superior, intelligent, wise, brilliant*—to make your ideas seem more appealing. Use negative persuasive language—terms such as *implausible, misguided, unreasonable*—to convey criticism of opposing views.

Revising

Add Necessary Information Reread your position paper to be sure it explains the issue completely. Where necessary, add background or explanatory information

Read Out Loud Ask a classmate to read your paper out loud while you listen. Use the following revision checklist, based on this lesson's Writing Skills Focus, to guide your listening:

▶ How can I revise my choice of words or details to better suit my audience?

▶ Have I presented enough facts, quotations, reasons, or other evidence to support my opinion? How can I strengthen this evidence?

▶ What logical reasons have I used to make my point? Have I avoided faulty logic? What opposing arguments have I considered or should I consider to make my viewpoint seem more reasonable?

REVISION MODEL

You are about to consider cutting funds spent to support

① As you take up the issue of PBS, consider the far-reaching ramifications of canceling funding.

Public Television. Everyone knows that the children's

② Current research indicates that high-school students who regularly

programming makes children snarter.

watched Sesame Street as preschoolers routinely scored higher than peers who were not exposed to such programming.

① The author substitutes a more sophisticated sentence that is appropriate for the background and knowledge level of the intended audience.

② The author eliminates faulty logic; in this case, a bandwagon appeal. A verifiable fact adds credibility to the author's argument.

Publishing

▶ **Letter** Send your position paper to the editor of your local newspaper or to an elected official who may have power to impact the issue addressed in your paper.

Real-World Reading Skills Workshop

Strategies for Success

When you spend your hard-earned money on something—a video game, a new television, or even a car—you want the best product for the price. Consumer reports offer comparative information and evaluations of products and services. These reports contain data about price and features, opinions based on the tester's experience. They also provide comparisons among competitors. It pays to invest time in reading consumer reports to learn about your options before you make a purchase.

> ### Wisdom on Wheels: The 1999 Quark
> ### Building on a Positive Experience
> by Carol Inipriati
>
> I believe that the best meals begin with quality ingredients. With that in mind, the 1999 Quark seems a promising bet. It begins with the same basic ingredients as its sucessful predecessor, the Spectrum, then adds some fun new features. The XL model comes with a standard sun-roof, power windows, and sport wheels. With basics like front-wheel drive, driver's side air bag, a 2.5-liter 4-cylinder engine, and solid 22/30 mpg mileage rating, Quark guarantees safety and economy—with more excitement. Panto Motors is known for quality production and professional service, making the Quark worth a test drive as a practical—but never dull—mid-price ($14,900 base price) vehicle.
> Here's a look at how the Quark stacks up against the competition:
>
> | CONSUMER REPORT CARD ON MIDPRICE SEDANS | | | |
> |---|---|---|---|
> | | Quark | Frontier | Zoom |
> | Price | A | B | B+ |
> | Mileage | B | C | A- |
> | Safety Features | A- | A | B |
> | Standard Features | A | C | B |
> | Handling | A- | B | B+ |
> | Design | A | B+ | C |

Define Your Search Develop criteria for your product review. What are you prepared to spend? Do you have any brand loyalty? What features matter most to you? Determining your priorities will help you focus your consumer report reading.

Check for Relevance If you are reading a report on an individual brand or product, begin by determining whether the item meets your criteria. Does the product being reviewed have the necessary features? Is it within your price range? Scan titles, charts, and captions for data to verify the match.

Read the Report Read the writer's conclusion about the product and then evaluate the evidence that supports it. Before making a final decision, compare your findings with reports on alternative products. Consumer reports or reviews of a single product often include comparative information—often presented in a chart—on competitors in the same price or product category.

Apply the Strategy

Your dream is to buy your own car. For now, the closest you'll get is helping your parents choose their new vehicle. They want a car that costs under $16,000, has a proven track record, good gas mileage, dual air bags, and front-wheel drive.

1. Does the report at left fall within your defined price criteria?
2. Does the Quark have all the features your parents seek? Explain.
3. In what categories does the Quark outperform the competition?
4. Which car would you prefer if your primary concern were price? Safety?
5. How does the writer view the Quark? What evidence does she cite to support her opinion?
6. Based on this writer's views, would you recommend the Quark to your parents?

> ✔ **Here are other situations in which reading consumer reports is helpful:**
> ▶ Purchasing computer software
> ▶ Purchasing a new camera or CD player
> ▶ Choosing a test-preparation course

Meetings can either produce highly energized brainstorming sessions or disintegrate into undirected chat that wastes everyone's time. When you take the trouble to gather busy people into one room, make sure that you use their time efficiently and productively. Use these strategies to help you.

Set an Action Plan Before starting the meeting, identify precisely what you want to get from this discussion. For example, if your meeting involves planning a newsletter, you might clarify the steps needed to complete it or assign the different tasks required for getting the job done.

Use Chalkboards to Record Ideas To be sure everyone agrees with decisions the group is making, appoint a note taker. If possible, use a chalkboard or large paper, and keep a running list of ideas and plans. Follow up with written notes after the meeting.

Leave Time for New Concerns Add a few minutes at the end of a meeting to air any problems, questions, or concerns. Allowing five minutes while the group is still together may save much more time later.

Tips for Conducting a Meeting

✔ *These strategies can help you conduct a successful meeting:*
- ▶ Take the time to plan ahead and organize your ideas for the meeting.
- ▶ Develop and distribute an agenda, along with any handouts, at least one day before the meeting.
- ▶ Locate any display tools you may need.
- ▶ Sit or stand where everyone can see and hear you.
- ▶ Appoint a note taker to record meeting discussion.
- ▶ Clarify your expected time frame. For example, allot 15 minutes for each main agenda item.

Apply the Strategies

In a group, choose a current school issue or one of the situations that follow. Plan a meeting—working alone or in teams—to develop an agenda, handouts, and a time frame. Then role-play the meeting with the full class.

- ▶ The annual spring dance is coming up. Committees are needed for overall planning, food and drinks, music, decorations, and safety/security.
- ▶ Each fall, new student officers are added to your school's conflict-resolution team. Explain the program to the incoming officers.
- ▶ It's your turn to plan the monthly meeting of the cheerleading, science, or other special-interest club.
- ▶ You see major problems in your community, state, or in the nation. Organize a social-action group to address one of these problems.

Extended Reading Opportunities

As American lifestyles have changed, so has the nation's literature, becoming increasingly complex and diverse since World War II. Consider these possibilities as you explore the best that modern literature has to offer.

Suggested Titles

The Kitchen God's Wife
Amy Tan

As a young woman, Amy Tan rejected her Chinese heritage; as a mature writer, she celebrates it in her fiction. *The Kitchen God's Wife,* the follow-up to Tan's first blockbuster novel, *The Joy Luck Club,* recounts the fascinating yet tragic life story of a Chinese American widow. Told in the elderly woman's own distinctive voice, the eventful tale is rich in both history and heartache; it has earned the praise of critics and devoted readers alike.

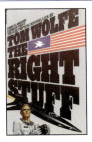

The Right Stuff
Tom Wolfe

By the 1960's, the only frontier left to explore was outer space. The pioneers of old were replaced by high-tech astronauts, and America held its collective breath as the men of the Mercury space program broke from the confines of Earth to orbit the moon. If you're excited by the prospect of facing the unknown, of going where no one has gone before, you'll enjoy this gripping and satirical account of the first manned space mission.

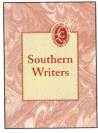

Southern Writers

From William Faulkner and Thomas Wolfe to Flannery O'Connor, Eudora Welty, and Alice Walker, many of America's greatest writers have come from the South. This collection features some of the best short works by many of the region's most famous traditional and contemporary authors. Their words paint a vivid picture of the language, landscapes, and personalities of southern life.

Other Possibilities

Death of a Salesman	Arthur Miller
Cold Sassy Tree	Olive Ann Burns
I Know Why the Caged Bird Sings	Maya Angelou
The Road Ahead	Bill Gates

Access Guide to Vocabulary

KEY TO PRONUNCIATION SYMBOLS USED

Symbol	Key Words	Symbol	Key Words
a	asp, fat, parrot	b	bed, fable, dub
ā	ape, date, play	d	dip, beadle, had
ä	ah, car, father	f	fall, after, off
e	elf, ten, berry	g	get, haggle, dog
ē	even, meet, money	h	he, head, hotel
i	is, hit, mirror	j	joy, agile, badge
ī	ice, bite, high	k	kill, tackle, bake
ō	open, tone, go	l	let, yellow, ball
ô	all, horn, law	m	met, camel, trim
o͞o	ooze, tool, crew	n	not, flannel, ton
o͝o	look, pull, moor	p	put, apple, tap
yo͞o	use, cute, few	r	red, port, dear
yoo	united, cure, globule	s	sell, castle, pass
oi	oil, point, toy	t	top, cattle, hat
ou	out, crowd, plow	v	vat, hovel, have
u	up, cut, color	w	will, always, swear
ur	urn, fur, deter	y	yet, onion, yard
ə	a in ago	z	zebra, dazzle, haze
	e in agent	ch	chin, catcher, arch
	i in sanity	sh	she, cushion, dash
	o in comply	th	thin, nothing, truth
	u in focus	th	then, father, lathe
ər	perhaps, murder	zh	azure, leisure
		ŋ	ring, anger, drink

abeyance, 409

ablutions, 27

abomination, 1128

abundance, 17

abyss, 387

acquiesce, 142

adamant, 1159

admonitory, 761

adversary, 178

aesthetic, 994

affliction, 17

agape, 1156

aggregation, 444

aggrieved, 579

agues, 195

alacrity, 381

alliance, 178

ambush, 1083

ameliorate, 1117

ammunition, 1083

anarchy, 483

anathema, 536

anomalous, 300

anonymity, 1139

antagonism, 761

anthology, 1071

apparition, 661

appease, 971

appellation, 298

apprised, 472

arduous, 131, 169

arrested, 1028

artifice, 106

aspiration, 823

assimilate, 907

asylum, 199

audaciously, 497

automation, 980

autonomous, 55

avarice, 44, 131, 240, 834

aversion, 367

avidly, 1119

avuncular, 354

barometer, 1069

base, 1121

bastions, 368

bayou, 787

beguile, 849, 1159

bellicose, 536

benevolent, 459, 1027

benign, 1015

bivouac, 251

blanched, 1146

blaspheming, 820

blasphemy, 1128

blithe, 364

brazenness, 831

bronchitis, 1069

brooding, 915

brutal, 771

buck, 787

cacophony, 206

calligraphy, 982

calumny, 1098

caper, 831

capitulate, 497

caveat, 999

celestial, 151

chaos, 367

circumspection, 231

claustrophobia, 824

cleave, 1159

collusion, 971

commiseration, 765

compunctions, 231

conceits, 67

conciliatory, 1159

concocted, 941

confederate, 29

conflagration, 561

confluence, 943

confounded, 1141

congealed, 204

congenial, 459

conjectural, 557

conjectured, 525

conjure, 982

connate, 364

connivance, 894

consanguinity, 142

consecrate, 480

conspicuous, 277

consternation, 461

contentious, 1133

contiguous, 999

contingent, 231

contrition, 763

convivial, 1042

copious, 44

cornice, 397

corollary, 994

cosmopolitan, 824

countenance, 849

covertly, 349

craven, 310

crevices, 979

cronies, 1069

crux, 204

cunning, 771

declivity, 916

decorously, 1027

deference, 469, 1121

deferentially, 1137

defiance, 573

degenerate, 608

deliberation, 29

demarcation, 279

deposition, 1135

depravity, 459

deprecated, 481

depredations, 548

derivative, 715

desolate, 879

despotic, 199

despotism, 173

dictum, 470

digress, 649

dilapidated, 375

diligence, 894

din, 1052

discern, 482, 897

disdainfully, 446

dispatched, 38

disposition, 29, 132

dissembling, 1093

dissuade, 969

distillery, 787

divines, 367

docile, 971

doctrines, 951

dogma, 657

dolorous, 101

dominion, 711

dusky, 841

dyspepsia, 781

efface, 253

effaced, 471

effigies, 1061

effrontery, 1139

effuse, 411

egregious, 907

elixir, 941

elusive, 594

embankment, 689

emigrants, 547

eminence, 523

empirical, 1013

encampment, 959

engrossed, 1028

entreated, 35

enunciated, 973

epitaph, 609

equanimity, 536

equivocal, 298

eradicate, 178

etiquette, 469

evacuated, 1037

evanescent, 909

evitable, 377

exalted, 833

excavated, 279

exhaust, 921

expatriated, 536

expedient, 381

expended, 53

exquisite, 15

extort, 243

extricate, 195

fallowness, 670

fasting, 189

feigned, 35

felicity, 134

filigree, 386

finite, 400

flagrant, 158

flamboyant, 941

floundering, 1159

foppery, 134

foreboding, 497

foreknowledge, 831

forestall, 594

fortuitous, 672

frippery, 781

furtive, 915, 951

galvanic, 354

gape, 1083

garrulous, 525

genial, 349, 546

geography, 833

gingerly, 1126

glade, 447, 793

glean, 850

gloaming, 265

grave, 741

gravity, 960

gregarious, 349

guffawing, 886

guile, 601

hallow, 480

heirs, 177

heritage, 1061

hovel, 387

hysterically, 959

illiterate, 894

immersed, 106

impelled, 158

imperceptible, 1137

imperially, 607

imperious, 470

impertinent, 323

impious, 145

importunate, 298

importunities, 594

imprecations, 497

improvident, 44

inappeasable, 231

inaudibly, 960

incessant, 1042

incredulously, 1143

increment, 849

inculcation, 1105

indecorous, 321

indications, 17

ineffable, 101, 475

inert, 617

infallibility, 173

infidel, 145

infinity, 400

ingratiating, 1091

iniquity, 321

insatiable, 710

inscrutable, 335, 444

insidious, 170, 647

insurgents, 481

interminable, 525

intriguing, 1027

intuitively, 819

invalided, 734

invective, 178

invoke, 178

jettisoned, 80

jocularity, 619

jubilant, 1028

labyrinth, 279

latent, 1027

liberty, 841

licentious, 1107

limber, 741

listed, 879

literalists, 715

liturgy, 982

loath, 72, 969

loathsome, 44

lulled, 841

luminary, 811

lye, 951

machetes, 971

magnanimity, 142, 379

malaise, 106

maledictions, 337

malevolence, 1031

malevolent, 80

malice, 482

malign, 475

malingered, 106

malingers, 650

manifest, 173

manifold, 91

manuscript, 763

maverick, 944

meditate, 1050

meditation, 915

meticulous, 650

moiling, 789

mollified, 69

monotonous, 525

monotony, 158

morose, 885

mortality, 35

motives, 157

mottled, 905

multifarious, 281

multitudinous, 281

mundane, 676

munificent, 298

muzzle, 1083

myriad, 601

nomadic, 1008

nonplused, 549

obeisance, 310

obliterated, 80

oblivious, 960

obstinacy, 323

obstinate, 497, 745

obtuse, 650

ominous, 267, 883

omnipotent, 99

oppress, 951

oppressed, 399, 453

ornery, 526

orthopedic, 927

oscillation, 471

ostentation, 243
ostentatious, 321
pacify, 47
palisades, 67
pall, 575
pallor, 1117
palpable, 713
paranoia, 487
parsimony, 243
patriarch, 268
pensive, 151, 261
penury, 199
perdition, 1031
peremptorily, 563
perfidy, 142
peril, 72
permeated, 941
persevere, 91
pertinaciously, 342
pervade, 981
pervading, 547
pestilential, 44
philanthropies, 1039
piety, 781
pilfer, 67
pittance, 231
placid, 152
poignant, 679
poise, 805
polemics, 231
posterity, 173, 381
precipitate, 444, 999
preconceptions, 1050
predilection, 1091
prelude, 618
preposterous, 672
prescient, 340
pristine, 994
privations, 231
prodigious, 523, 1139

profundity, 158
profusion, 548
propitiation, 1105
propitious, 151
proprietorial, 909
protruded, 27, 689
psychology, 697
pugilistic, 681
purged, 1165
purported, 105
quail, 1125
querulous, 268, 540
radiant, 368
ravenous, 883
reaping, 850
recompense, 74, 91
recumbent, 536
redolence, 53
redolent, 462
redress, 142, 483
refluent, 151
refuge, 1081
refulgent, 151
reiterate, 231
rendezvous, 1037
replicate, 941
repose, 608
repression, 594
repugnant, 897
retaliation, 1159
retrospective, 761
revelatory, 943
reverential, 615
rudiments, 231
rueful, 808
sagacious, 321
salient, 600
sallow, 705
salutary, 173
scepter, 152

scintillating, 158
scourge, 482
scrabbling, 791
semantic, 1015
semi-somnambulant, 616
sentience, 303
sepulcher, 261
serenity, 498
shackles, 1061
sibilance, 1161
sinuous, 675
slovenly, 711
smite, 453
somnolent, 681
specious, 298
squander, 189
stark, 600, 850
statistics, 697
staunch, 929
stocky, 929
stringency, 459
subjugation, 170
sublime, 251, 279, 377
subsisted, 37
subsistence, 199
subterranean, 823
suffice, 710
suffrage, 367
sullen, 705
summarily, 470
sundry, 72
superfluous, 377
superseding, 231
supple, 937
surmised, 397
swag, 793
switch, 789
tantalized, 1163
tempest, 600
tempo, 703

tensile, 1001
terra firma, 547
theology, 1121
timorous, 705
trajectory, 80
transcribed, 1013
transient, 521
transparent, 927
traversed, 37
tremulous, 323
tremulously, 616
trough, 982
tumultuous, 368
tumultuously, 594
tyranny, 178
unalienable, 140
unanimity, 173
unfathomable, 907
unscrupulous, 894
untoward, 106
unwonted, 557
usurers, 243
usurpations, 140
vagary, 321
venerable, 261, 321
vestiges, 918
vigilance, 132
vigilant, 170
viper, 929
visage, 705
vitality, 158
vituperative, 539
vociferation, 539
volition, 1037
voluminous, 657
waggery, 323
wanton, 771
wily, 1052

LITERARY TERMS HANDBOOK

ALLEGORY An *allegory* is a story or tale with two or more levels of meaning—a literal level and one or more symbolic levels. The events, setting, and characters in an allegory are symbols for ideas or qualities. Many of Nathaniel Hawthorne's short stories, such as "The Minister's Black Veil," on page 318, are allegories.

ALLITERATION *Alliteration* is the repetition of consonant sounds at the beginning of words or accented syllables. Sara Teasdale uses alliteration in the second stanza of her poem "Understanding":

> But you I never understood,
> Your spirit's secret hides like gold
> Sunk in a Spanish galleon
> Ages ago in water cold.

Poets and other writers use alliteration to link and to emphasize ideas as well as to create pleasing, musical sounds.

ALLUSION An *allusion* is a reference to a well-known person, place, event, literary work, or work of art. Writers often make allusions to stories from the Bible, to Greek and Roman myths, to plays by Shakespeare, to political and historical events, and to other materials with which they can expect their readers to be familiar. In "The Love Song of J. Alfred Prufrock," on page 647, T. S. Eliot alludes to, among other things, Dante's *Inferno*, Italian artist Michelangelo, Shakespeare's *Hamlet*, and to several incidents and people from the Bible. By using allusions, writers can bring to mind complex ideas simply and easily.

ALMANAC An *almanac* is a magazine or book, published monthly, seasonally, or yearly, that contains weather forecasts, tide tables, important dates, lists of upcoming events, statistics, and other information of use or interest to readers. The selection on page 188 is from *Poor Richard's Almanack* by Benjamin Franklin. Franklin's almanac is famous for its humorous and wise sayings.

ANECDOTE An *anecdote* is a brief story about an interesting, amusing, or strange event. An anecdote is told to entertain or to make a point. In the excerpt from *Life on the Mississippi*, on page 520, Mark Twain tells several anecdotes about his experiences on the Mississippi River.

ANTAGONIST An *antagonist* is a character or force in conflict with a main character, or protagonist. In Jack London's "To Build a Fire," on page 556, the antagonist is neither a person nor an animal but is rather the extreme cold of the Yukon. Not all stories contain antagonists. However, in many stories the conflict between the antagonist and the protagonist is the basis for the plot.

See Conflict, Plot, and Protagonist.

APHORISM An *aphorism* is a general truth or observation about life, usually stated concisely and pointedly. Often witty and wise, aphorisms appear in many kinds of works. An essay writer may have an aphoristic style, making many such statements. Ralph Waldo Emerson was famous for his aphoristic style. His essay entitled "Fate" contains the following aphorisms:

> The book of Nature is the book of Fate.
> Men are what their mothers made them.
> Nature is what you may do.
> So far as a man thinks, he is free.
> A man's fortunes are the fruit of his character.

Used in an essay, an aphorism can be a memorable way to sum up or to reinforce a point or an argument.

APOSTROPHE An *apostrophe* is a figure of speech in which a speaker directly addresses an absent person or a personified quality, object, or idea. Phillis Wheatley uses apostrophe in this line from "To the University of Cambridge, in New England":

> Students, to you 'tis given to scan the heights

Apostrophe is often used in poetry and in speeches to add emotional intensity.

See Figurative Language.

ASSONANCE *Assonance* is the repetition of vowel sounds in conjunction with dissimilar consonant sounds. Emily Dickinson uses assonance in the line "The mountain at a given distance." The *i* sound is repeated in the words *given* and *distance*, in the context of the dissimilar consonant sounds *g–v* and *d–s*.

ATMOSPHERE See Mood.

AUTOBIOGRAPHY An *autobiography* is a form of nonfiction in which a person tells his or her own life story. Notable examples of autobiographies include those by Benjamin Franklin and Frederick Douglass. *Memoirs*, a first-person account of personally or historically significant events in which the writer was a participant or an eyewitness, are a form of autobiographical writing.

See Biography and Journal.

BALLAD A *ballad* is a songlike poem that tells a story, often one dealing with adventure and romance. Most ballads have the following characteristics:

1. Simple language
2. Four- or six-line stanzas
3. Rhyme
4. A regular meter

A *folk ballad* is one that originated in the oral tradition and was passed by word of mouth from generation to generation. Examples of folk ballads include "Yankee Doodle," "Casey Jones," and "John Henry." A *literary ballad* is one written by a specific person in imitation of the folk ballad. Henry Wadsworth Longfellow's "The Wreck of the Hesperus" is an example of a literary ballad.

BIOGRAPHY A *biography* is a form of nonfiction in which a writer tells the life story of another person. Carl Sandburg's *Abe Lincoln Grows Up* is a famous biography of President Lincoln.

See Autobiography.

BLANK VERSE *Blank verse* is poetry written in unrhymed iambic pentameter. An iamb is a poetic foot consisting of one weak stress followed by one strong stress. A pentameter line is a line of five poetic feet. Robert Frost's "Birches," on page 804, is written in blank verse.

CHARACTER A character is a person or an animal that takes part in the action of a literary work. The following are some terms used to describe various types of characters:

The *main character* in a literary work is the one on whom the work focuses. *Major characters* in a literary work include the main character and any other characters who play significant roles. A *minor character* is one who does not play a significant role. A *round character* is one who is complex and multi-faceted, like a real person. A *flat character* is one who is one-dimensional. A *dynamic character* is one who changes in the course of a work. A *static character* is one who does not change in the course of a work.

See Characterization and Motivation.

CHARACTERIZATION *Characterization* is the act of creating and developing a character. There are two primary methods of characterization: direct and indirect. In *direct characterization,* a writer simply states a character's traits, as when F. Scott Fitzgerald writes of the main character in his story "Winter Dreams," on page 670, "He wanted not association with glittering things and glittering people—he wanted the glittering things themselves." In *indirect characterization,* character is revealed by one of the following means:

1. By the words, thoughts, or actions of the character
2. By descriptions of the character's appearance or background
3. By what other characters say about the character
4. By the ways in which other characters react toward the character

See Character.

CINQUAIN *See Stanza.*

CLASSICISM *Classicism* is an approach to literature and the other arts that stresses reason, balance, clarity, ideal beauty, and orderly form in imitation of the arts of ancient Greece and Rome. Classicism is often contrasted with *Romanticism,* which stresses imagination, emotion, and individualism. Classicism also differs from *Realism,* which stresses the actual rather than the ideal.

See Realism and Romanticism.

CLIMAX The *climax* is the high point of interest or suspense in a literary work. For example, Jack London's "To Build a Fire," on page 556, reaches its climax when the man realizes that he is going to freeze to death. The climax generally appears near the end of a story, play, or narrative poem.

See Plot.

CONFLICT A *conflict* is a struggle between opposing forces. Sometimes this struggle is internal, or within a character, as in Bernard Malamud's "The First Seven Years," on page 892. At other times this struggle is external, or between a character and an outside force, as in Jack London's "To Build a Fire," on page 556. Conflict is one of the primary elements of narrative literature because most plots develop from conflicts.

See Antagonist, Plot, and Protagonist.

CONNOTATION A *connotation* is an association that a word calls to mind in addition to the dictionary meaning of the word. Many words that are similar in their dictionary meanings, or denotations, are quite different in their connotations. Consider, for example, Jose Garcia Villa's line, "Be beautiful, noble, like the antique ant." This line would have a very different effect if it were "Be pretty, classy, like the old ant." Poets and other writers choose their words carefully so that the connotations of those words will be appropriate.

See Denotation.

CONSONANCE *Consonance* is the repetition of similar final consonant sounds at the ends of words or accented syllables. Emily Dickinson uses consonance in the following lines:

> But if he ask where you are hid
> Until to-morrow,—happy letter!
> Gesture, coquette, and shake your head!

COUPLET *See Stanza.*

CRISIS In the plot of a narrative, the *crisis* is the turning point for the protagonist—the point at which the protagonist's situation or understanding changes dramatically. In Bernard Malamud's "The First Seven Years," on page 892, the crisis comes when Feld recognizes that Sobel loves Miriam.

DENOTATION The *denotation* of a word is its objective meaning, independent of other associations that the word brings to mind.

See Connotation.

DENOUEMENT *See Plot.*

DESCRIPTION A *description* is a portrayal, in words, of something that can be perceived by the senses. Writers create descriptions by using images, as John Wesley Powell does in the following passage from "The Most Sublime Spectacle on Earth," his description of the Grand Canyon, on page 278:

> When the clouds play in the canyon, as they often do in the rainy season, another set of effects is produced. Clouds creep out of canyons and wind into other canyons. The heavens seem to be alive, not moving as move the heavens over a plain, in one direction with the wind, but following the multiplied courses of these gorges.

Description is one of the major forms of discourse and appears quite often in literary works of all genres.

See Image.

DEVELOPMENT *See Plot.*

DIALECT A *dialect* is the form of a language spoken by people in a particular region or group. Every dialect differs from every other dialect in the details of its vocabulary, grammar, and pronunciation. Writers often use dialect to make their characters seem realistic and

to create local color. See, for example, Mark Twain's "The Notorious Jumping Frog of Calaveras County," on page 525.

See Local Color.

DIALOGUE A *dialogue* is a conversation between characters. Writers use dialogue to reveal character, to present events, to add variety to narratives, and to arouse their readers' interest.

See Drama.

DICTION *Diction* is a writer's or speaker's word choice. Diction is part of a writer's style and may be described as formal or informal, plain or ornate, common or technical, abstract or concrete. In the selection from *The Mortgaged Heart*, on page 994, Carson McCullers uses formal diction suitable to her essay's serious purpose.

See Style.

DRAMA A *drama* is a story written to be performed by actors. The playwright supplies dialogue for the characters to speak as well as stage directions that give information about costumes, lighting, scenery, properties, the setting, and the characters' movements and ways of speaking. The audience accepts as believable the many dramatic conventions that are used, such as soliloquies, asides, poetic language, or the passage of time between acts or scenes. An *act* is a major division in a drama. A *scene* is a minor division.

See Genre.

DRAMATIC MONOLOGUE A *dramatic monologue* is a poem or speech in which an imaginary character speaks to a silent listener. T. S. Eliot's "The Love Song of J. Alfred Prufrock," on page 647, is a dramatic monologue.

See Dramatic Poem and Monologue.

DRAMATIC POEM A *dramatic poem* is one that makes use of the conventions of drama. Such poems may be monologues or dialogues or may present the speech of many characters. Robert Frost's "The Death of the Hired Man" is a famous example of a dramatic poem.

See Dramatic Monologue.

DYNAMIC CHARACTER *See Character.*

EPIGRAM An *epigram* is a brief, pointed statement, in prose or in verse, often characterized by use of some rhetorical device or figure of speech. Benjamin Franklin was famous for his epigrams, which include "Fools make feasts, and wise men eat them," and "A plowman on his legs is higher than a gentleman on his knees."

EPIPHANY An *epiphany* is a sudden revelation or flash of insight. The shoemaker in Bernard Malamud's "The First Seven Years," on page 892, experiences an epiphany when he suddenly and thoroughly comprehends that the actions of his apprentice, Sobel, are motivated by his hidden love for Miriam.

ESSAY An *essay* is a short nonfiction work about a particular subject. Essays can be classified as *formal* or *informal*, *personal* or *impersonal*. They can also be classified according to purpose, such as *analytical* (see the excerpt from *The Mortgaged Heart* on page 994), *satirical* (see "Coyote v. Acme" on p. 998), or *reflective* (see Amy Tan's "Mother Tongue" on page 1012). Modes of discourse, such as *expository, descriptive, persuasive,* or *narrative,* are other means of classifying essays.

See Satire, Exposition, Description, Persuasion, and Narration.

EXPOSITION *Exposition* is writing or speech that explains, informs, or presents information. The main techniques of expository writing include analysis, classification, comparison and contrast, definition, and exemplification, or illustration. An essay may be primarily expository, as is William Safire's "Onomatopoeia" on page 996, or it may use exposition to support another purpose, such as persuasion or argumentation, as in Ian Frazier's satirical essay "Coyote v. Acme" on page 998.

In a story or play, the exposition is that part of the plot that introduces the characters, the setting, and the basic situation.

See Plot.

FALLING ACTION See Plot.

FICTION *Fiction* is prose writing that tells about imaginary characters and events. Short stories and novels are works of fiction.

See Genre, Narrative, Nonfiction, and Prose.

FIGURATIVE LANGUAGE *Figurative language* is writing or speech not meant to be taken literally. Writers use figurative language to express ideas in vivid and imaginative ways. For example, Emily Dickinson begins one poem with the following description of snow:

> It sifts from leaden sieves,
> It powders all the wood

By describing the snow as if it were flour, Dickinson renders a precise and compelling picture of it.

See Figure of Speech.

FIGURE OF SPEECH A *figure of speech* is an expression or a word used imaginatively rather than literally. Many types of figures of speech are used by writers in English, including apostrophe, hyperbole, irony, metaphor, oxymoron, paradox, personification, and simile.

See Figurative Language. See *also the entries for individual figures of speech.*

FLASHBACK A *flashback* is a section of a literary work that interrupts the chronological presentation of events to relate an event from an earlier time. A writer may present a flashback as a character's memory or recollection, as part of an account or story told by a character, as a dream or a daydream, or simply by having the narrator switch to a time in the past. A flashback occurs in Part II of "An Occurrence at Owl Creek Bridge" on page 468, as the narrator recounts events that took place before those in the story's opening. Writers often use flashbacks as a dramatic way of providing background information.

FLAT CHARACTER See Character.

FOIL A *foil* is a character who provides a contrast to another character. In F. Scott Fitzgerald's "Winter Dreams," on page 670, Irene Scheerer is a foil for the tantalizing Judy Jones.

FOLK LITERATURE *Folk literature* is the body of stories, legends, myths, ballads, songs, riddles, sayings, and other works arising out of the oral traditions of peoples around the globe. The folk literature traditions of the United States, including those of Native Americans and of the American pioneers, are especially rich.

FOOT See Meter.

FORESHADOWING *Foreshadowing* is the use, in a literary work, of clues that suggest events that have yet to occur.

FREE VERSE *Free verse* is poetry that lacks a regular rhythmical pattern, or meter. A writer of free verse is at liberty to use any rhythms that are appropriate to what he or she is saying. Free verse has been widely used by twentieth-century poets such as Leslie Marmon Silko, who begins "Where Mountain Lion Lay Down With Deer" with these lines:

> I climb the black rock mountain
> stepping from day to day
> silently.

See Meter.

GENRE A *genre* is a division, or type, of literature. Literature is commonly divided into three major genres: poetry, prose, and drama. Each major genre can in turn be divided into smaller genres. Poetry can be divided into lyric, concrete, dramatic, narrative, and epic poetry. Prose can be divided into fiction (novels and short stories) and nonfiction (biography, autobiography, letters, essays, and reports). Drama can be divided into serious drama, tragedy, comic drama, melodrama, and farce.

See Drama, Poetry, and Prose.

GOTHIC *Gothic* refers to the use of primitive, medieval, wild, or mysterious elements in literature. Gothic elements offended eighteenth-century classical writers but appealed to the Romantic writers who followed them. Gothic novels feature places like mysterious and gloomy castles, where horrifying, supernatural events take place. Their influence on Edgar Allan Poe is evident in "The Fall of the House of Usher," on page 297.

GROTESQUE *Grotesque* refers to the use of bizarre, absurd, or fantastic elements in literature. The grotesque is generally characterized by distortions or striking incongruities. *Grotesque characters*, like those in Flannery O'Connor's "The Life You Save May Be Your Own," on page 879, are characters who have become ludicrous or bizarre through their obsession with an idea or value, or as a result of an emotional problem.

HARLEM RENAISSANCE The *Harlem Renaissance*, which occurred during the 1920's, was a time of African American artistic creativity centered in Harlem, in New York City. Writers of the Harlem Renaissance include Countee Cullen, Claude McKay, Jean Toomer, Langston Hughes, and Arna Bontemps.

HYPERBOLE A *hyperbole* is a deliberate exaggeration or overstatement. In Mark Twain's "The Notorious Jumping Frog of Calaveras County," on page 525, the claim that Jim Smiley would follow a bug as far as Mexico to win a bet is a hyperbole. As this example shows, hyperboles are often used for comic effect.

IAMBIC PENTAMETER *Iambic pentameter* is a line of poetry with five iambic feet, each containing one unstressed syllable followed by one stressed syllable (˘ ´). Iambic pentameter may be rhymed or unrhymed. Unrhymed iambic pentameter is called blank verse. These concluding lines from Anne Bradstreet's "The Author to Her Book" are in iambic pentameter:

> And for thy Mother, she alas is poor,
>
> Which caused her thus to send thee out
>
> of door.

See Blank Verse and Meter.

IDYLL An *idyll* is a poem or part of a poem that describes and idealizes country life. John Greenleaf Whittier's "Snowbound," on page 266, is an idyll.

IMAGE An *image* is a word or phrase that appeals to one or more of the five senses—sight, hearing, touch, taste, or smell.

See Imagery.

IMAGERY *Imagery* is the descriptive or figurative language used in literature to create word pictures for the reader. These pictures, or images, are created by details of sight, sound, taste, touch, smell, or movement. The following stanza, from Kuangchi C. Chang's "Garden of My Childhood," shows how a poet can use imagery to appeal to several senses:

> I ran past the old maple by the terraced hall
> And the singing crickets under the latticed wall,
>
> And I kept on running down the walk
> Paved with pebbles of memory big and small
> Without turning to look until I was out of
>   the gate
> Through which there be no return at all.

IMAGISM *Imagism* was a literary movement that flourished between 1912 and 1927. Led by Ezra Pound and Amy Lowell, the Imagist poets rejected nineteenth-century poetic forms and language. Instead, they wrote short poems that used ordinary language and free verse to create sharp, exact, concentrated pictures. "Oread," by H. D., illustrates how the Imagists concentrated on describing a scene or object without making abstract comments:

> Whirl up, sea—
> whirl your pointed pines,
> splash your great pines
> on our rocks,
> hurl your green over us,
> cover us with your pools of fir.

IRONY *Irony* is a contrast between what is stated and what is meant, or between what is expected to happen and what actually happens. In *verbal irony*, a word or a phrase is used to suggest the opposite of its usual meaning. In *dramatic irony*, there is a contradiction between what a character thinks and what the reader or audience knows to be true. In *irony of situation*, an event occurs that directly contradicts the expectations of the characters, of the reader, or of the audience.

JOURNAL A *journal* is a daily autobiographical account of events and personal reactions. For example, Mary Chesnut's journal, on page 496, records events during the Civil War.

LEGEND A *legend* is a traditional story. Usually a legend deals with a particular person—a hero, a saint, or a national leader. Often legends reflect a people's cultural values. American legends include those of the early Native Americans and those about folk heroes such as Davy Crockett and Daniel Boone.

See Myth.

LETTER A *letter* is a written message or communication addressed to a reader or readers that is generally sent by mail. Letters may be *private* or *public*, depending on their intended audience. Robert E. Lee's "Letter to His Son," on page 482, is an example of a *private* or *personal letter* because it was intended only for the writer's son, to whom it was addressed. A *public letter*, also called a *literary letter* or *epistle*, is a work of literature written in the form of a personal letter, but created for publication. Michel-Guillaume Jean de Crèvecoeur's "Letters From an American Farmer," excerpted on page 197, are public letters.

LOCAL COLOR *Local color* is the use in a literary work of characters and details unique to a particular geographic area. Local color can be created by the use of dialect and by descriptions of customs, clothing, manners, attitudes, scenery, and landscape. Local-color stories were especially popular after the Civil War, bringing readers the West of Bret Harte, the Mississippi River of Mark Twain, and the New England of Sarah Orne Jewett.

See Realism and Regionalism.

LYRIC POEM A *lyric poem* is a melodic poem that expresses the observations and feelings of a single speaker. Unlike a narrative poem, a lyric focuses on producing a single, unified effect. Types of lyrics include the elegy, the ode, and the sonnet. Among contemporary American poets, the lyric is the most common poetic form.

MAIN CHARACTER See Character.

METAPHOR A *metaphor* is a figure of speech in which one thing is spoken of as though it were something else. The identification suggests a comparison between the two things that are identified, as in "death is a long sleep" or "the sleeping dead."

A *mixed metaphor* occurs when two metaphors are jumbled together. For example, thorns and rain are illogically mixed in "the thorns of life rained down on him." A *dead metaphor* is one that has been overused and has become a common expression, such as "the arm of the chair" or "nightfall." Metaphors are used to make writing, especially poetry, more vivid, imaginative, and meaningful.

METER The *meter* of a poem is its rhythmical pattern. This pattern is determined by the number and types of stresses, or beats, in each line. To describe the meter of a poem, you must scan its lines. *Scanning* involves marking the stressed and unstressed syllables, as follows:

> Soon as the sun forsook the eastern main
>
> The pealing thunder shook the heav'nly plain;
>
> —Phillis Wheatley, "An Hymn to the Evening"

As the example shows, each strong stress is marked with a slanted line (´) and each weak stress with a horseshoe symbol (˘). The weak and strong stresses are then divided by vertical lines (|) into groups called *feet*. The following types of feet are common in poetry written in English:

1. *Iamb*: a foot with one unstressed syllable followed by one stressed syllable, as in the word "around"
2. *Trochee*: a foot with one stressed syllable followed by one unstressed syllable, as in the word "broken"
3. *Anapest*: a foot with two unstressed syllables followed by one stressed syllable, as in the phrase "in a flash"
4. *Dactyl*: a foot with one stressed syllable followed by two unstressed syllables, as in the word "argument"
5. *Spondee*: a foot with two stressed syllables, as in the word "airship"
6. *Pyrrhic*: a foot with two unstressed syllables, as in the last foot of the word "imag|ining"

Lines of poetry are often described as *iambic, trochaic, anapestic*, or *dactylic*.

Lines are also described in terms of the number of feet that occur in them, as follows:

1. *Monometer*: verse written in one-foot lines

> Evil
>
> Begets
>
> Evil
>
> —Anonymous

2. *Dimeter:* verse written in two-foot lines

    Thĭs ĭs | thĕ tíme
  ŏf thĕ trăg|ĭc mán
       —Elizabeth Bishop, "Visits to St.
         Elizabeth's"

3. *Trimeter:* verse written in three-foot lines:

  Óvĕr | thĕ wín|tĕr glácĭĕrs
   Ĭ sée | thĕ súm|mĕr glów,
  Ănd thróugh | thĕ wíld-|pĭled snówdrift
    Thĕ wárm | rósebŭds | bĕlów.
      —Ralph Waldo Emerson, "Beyond
        Winter"

4. *Tetrameter:* verse written in four-foot lines:

  Thĕ sún | thăt bríef | Dĕcém|bĕr dáy
  Rŏse chéer|lĕss óv|ĕr hílls | ŏf gráy
      —John Greenleaf Whittier,
        "Snowbound"

5. *Pentameter:* verse written in five-foot lines:

  Ĭ doúbt | nŏt Gód | ĭs góod, | wĕll-méan|ĭng,
    kínd,
  Ănd díd | Hĕ stóop | tŏ quíb|blĕ cóuld | tĕll
    whý
  Thĕ lít|tlĕ búr|ĭed móle | cŏntín|ŭes blínd
      —Countee Cullen, "Yet Do I Marvel"

A complete description of the meter of a line tells both how many feet there are in the line and what kind of foot is most common. Thus the lines from Countee Cullen's poem would be described as *iambic pentameter. Blank verse* is poetry written in unrhymed *iambic pentameter.* Poetry that does not have a regular meter is called *free verse.*

MONOLOGUE
A *monologue* is a speech delivered entirely by one person or character.

See Dramatic Monologue.

MOOD
Mood, or atmosphere, is the feeling created in the reader by a literary work or passage. Elements that can influence the mood of a work include its setting, tone, and events.

See Setting and Tone.

MOTIVATION
A *motivation* is a reason that explains a character's thoughts, feelings, actions, or speech. Characters are motivated by their values and by their wants, desires, dreams, wishes, and needs. Sometimes the reasons for a character's actions are stated directly, as in Willa Cather's "A Wagner Matinée," on page 614, when Clark explains his reception of his aunt by saying, "I owed to this woman most of the good that ever came my way in my boyhood." At other times, the writer will just suggest a character's motivation.

MYTH
A *myth* is a fictional tale that explains the actions of gods or heroes or the causes of natural phenomena. Myths that explain the origins of earthly life, as do the Onondaga, Najavo, and Modoc myths in this text, are known as origin myths. Other myths express the central values of the people who created them.

NARRATION
Narration is writing that tells a story. The act of telling a story is also called *narration.* The *narrative,* or story, is told by a storyteller called the *narrator.* A story is usually told chronologically, in the order in which events take place in time, though it may include flashbacks and foreshadowing. Narratives may be true, as are the events recorded in Mary Chesnut's journal, on page 496, or fictional, as are the events in Flannery O'Connor's "The Life You Save May Be Your Own," on page 879. Narration is one of the forms of discourse and is used in novels, short stories, plays, narrative poems, anecdotes, autobiographies, biographies, and reports.

See Narrative Poem and Narrator.

NARRATIVE
A *narrative* is a story told in fiction, nonfiction, poetry, or drama. Narratives are often classified by their content or purpose. An *exploration narrative* is a firsthand account of an explorer's travels in a new land. Alvar Núñez Cabeza de Vaca's account of his exploration of the wilderness that is now Texas, "A Journey Through Texas," appears on page 34. "The Interesting Narrative of the Life of Olaudah Equiano," on page 44, is an example of a *slave narrative,* an autobiographical account of the experiences of an enslaved person. A *historical narrative* is a narrative account of significant historical events, such as John Smith's *The General History of Virginia,* on page 66, or William Bradford's *Of Plymouth Plantation,* on page 71.

See Narration.

NARRATIVE POEM
A *narrative poem* tells a story in verse. Three traditional types of narrative verse are *ballads,* songlike poems that tell stories; *epics,* long poems about the deeds of gods or heroes; and *metrical romances,* poems that tell tales of love and chivalry. Examples of American narrative poems include Stephen Vincent Benét's *John Brown's Body* and the ballad "John Henry."

See Ballad.

NARRATOR A *narrator* is a speaker or character who tells a story. A story or novel may be narrated by a main character, by a minor character, or by someone uninvolved in the story. The narrator may speak in the first person, as in John Updike's "The Brown Chest," on page 904, or in the third person, as in Anne Tyler's "Average Waves in Unprotected Waters" on page 926. In addition, the narrator may have an omniscient or a limited point of view. The *omniscient narrator* is all-knowing, while the *limited narrator* knows only what one character does. Because the writer's choice of narrator helps determine the point of view, this decision affects what version of a story is told and how readers will react to it.

See Point of View.

NATURALISM *Naturalism* was a literary movement among novelists at the end of the nineteenth century and during the early decades of the twentieth century. The Naturalists tended to view people as hapless victims of immutable natural laws. Early exponents of Naturalism included Stephen Crane, Jack London, and Theodore Dreiser.

See Realism.

NONFICTION *Nonfiction* is prose writing that presents and explains ideas or that tells about real people, places, objects, or events. Essays, biographies, autobiographies, journals, and reports are all examples of nonfiction.

See Fiction and Genre.

NOVEL A *novel* is a long work of fiction. A novel often has a complicated plot, many major and minor characters, a significant theme, and several varied settings. Novels can be classified in many ways, based on the historical periods in which they are written, on the subjects and themes that they treat, on the techniques that are used in them, and on the literary movements that inspired them. Classic nineteenth-century novels include Herman Melville's *Moby-Dick*, an excerpt of which appears on page 332, and Nathaniel Hawthorne's *The Scarlet Letter*, an extended reading suggestion. Well-known twentieth-century novels include F. Scott Fitzgerald's *The Great Gatsby* and Edith Wharton's *Ethan Frome*, both of which are recommended selections for extended reading. A *novella* is not as long as a novel but is longer than a short story. Ernest Hemingway's *The Old Man and the Sea* is a novella.

ODE An *ode* is a long, formal lyric poem with a serious theme that may have a traditional stanza structure. An ode may be written for a private occasion or for a public ceremony. Odes often honor people, commemorate events, respond to natural scenes, or consider serious human problems.

See Lyric Poem.

OMNISCIENT NARRATOR See Narrator and Point of View.

ONOMATOPOEIA *Onomatopoeia* is the use of words that imitate sounds. Examples of such words are *buzz, hiss, murmur*, and *rustle*. Isabella Stewart Gardner uses onomatopoeia in "Summer Remembered":

> Sounds sum and summon the remembering
> of summers.
> The humming of the sun
> The mumbling in the honey-suckle vine
> The whirring in the clovered grass
> The pizzicato plinkle of ice in an auburn uncle's
> amber glass.

ORAL TRADITION *Oral tradition* is the passing of songs, stories, and poems from generation to generation by word of mouth. The oral tradition in America has preserved Native American myths and legends, spirituals, folk ballads, and other stories or songs originally heard and memorized rather than written down.

See Ballad, Folk Literature, Legend, Myth, and Spiritual.

ORATORY *Oratory* is public speaking that is formal, persuasive, and emotionally appealing. Patrick Henry's "Speech in the Virginia Convention," on page 168, is an example of oratory.

OXYMORON An *oxymoron* is a figure of speech that combines two opposing or contradictory ideas. An oxymoron, such as "freezing fire" or the often used "conspicuous by his absence," suggests a paradox in just a few words.

See Figurative Language and Paradox.

PARADOX A *paradox* is a statement that seems to be contradictory but that actually presents a truth. Marianne Moore uses paradox in "Nevertheless" when she says, "Victory won't come/to me unless I go/to it." Because a paradox is surprising or even shocking, it draws the reader's attention to what is being said.

See Figurative Language and Oxymoron.

PARALLELISM *Parallelism* is the repetition of a grammatical structure. Robert Hayden concludes his poem "Astronauts" with these questions in parallel form:

> What do we want of these men?
> What do we want of ourselves?

Parallelism is used in poetry and in other writing to emphasize and to link related ideas.

PARODY A *parody* is a humorous imitation of a literary work, one that exaggerates or distorts the characteristic features of the original. American author Donald Barthelme was noted for his parodic style, which he used to point out absurd aspects of modern life.

PERSONIFICATION *Personification* is a figure of speech in which a nonhuman subject is given human characteristics. In "April Rain Song," Langston Hughes personifies the rain:

> Let the rain kiss you.
> Let the rain sing you a lullaby.

Effective personification of things or ideas makes them seem vital and alive, as if they were human.

See Figurative Language.

PERSUASION *Persuasion* is writing or speech that attempts to convince a reader to think or act in a particular way. During the Revolutionary War period, leaders such as Patrick Henry, Thomas Paine, and Thomas Jefferson used persuasion in their political arguments. Persuasion is also used in advertising, in editorials, in sermons, and in political speeches.

PLAIN STYLE *Plain style* is a type of writing in which uncomplicated sentences and ordinary words are used to make simple, direct statements. This style was favored by those Puritans who rejected ornate style because they wanted to express themselves clearly and directly, in accordance with the austerity of their religious beliefs. In the twentieth century, Ernest Hemingway was a master of plain style.

See Style.

PLOT *Plot* is the sequence of events in a literary work. In most novels, dramas, short stories, and narrative poems, the plot involves both characters and a central conflict. The plot usually begins with an *exposition* that introduces the setting, the characters, and the basic situation. This is followed by the *inciting incident*, which introduces the central conflict. The conflict then increases during the *development* until it reaches a high point of interest or suspense, the *climax*. The climax is followed by the end, or *resolution*, of the central conflict. Any events that occur after the resolution make up the *denouement*. The events that lead up to the climax comprise the *rising action*. The events that follow the climax comprise the *falling action*.

See Conflict.

POETRY *Poetry* is one of the three major types of literature. In poetry, form and content are closely connected, like the two faces of a single coin. Poems are often divided into lines and stanzas and often employ regular rhythmical patterns, or meters. Most poems make use of highly concise, musical, and emotionally charged language. Many also make use of imagery, figurative language, and special devices such as rhyme.

See Genre.

POINT OF VIEW *Point of view* is the perspective, or vantage point, from which a story is told. Three commonly used points of view are first person, omniscient third person, and limited third person.

In the *first-person point of view*, the narrator is a character in the story and refers to himself or herself with the first-person pronoun *I*. "The Fall of the House of Usher," on page 297, is told by a first-person narrator.

The two kinds of third-person point of view, limited and omniscient, are called "third person" because the narrator uses third-person pronouns such as *he* and *she* to refer to the characters. There is no "I" telling the story.

In stories told from the *omniscient third-person point of view*, the narrator knows and tells about what each character feels and thinks. "The Devil and Tom Walker," on page 236, is written from the omniscient third-person point of view.

In stories told from the *limited third-person point of view*, the narrator relates the inner thoughts and feelings of only one character, and everything is viewed from this character's perspective. "An Occurrence at Owl Creek Bridge," on page 468, is written from the limited third-person point of view.

See Narrator.

PROSE *Prose* is the ordinary form of written language. Most writing that is not poetry, drama, or song is considered prose. Prose is one of the major genres of literature and occurs in two forms: fiction and nonfiction.

See Fiction, Genre, and Nonfiction.

PROTAGONIST The *protagonist* is the main character in a literary work. In "The Jilting of Granny Weatherall," on page 776, the protagonist is the dying grandmother.

See Antagonist.

QUATRAIN *See* Stanza.

REALISM *Realism* is the presentation in art of the details of actual life. Realism was also a literary movement that began during the nineteenth century and stressed the actual as opposed to the imagined or the fanciful. The Realists tried to write truthfully and objectively about ordinary characters in ordinary situations. They reacted against Romanticism, rejecting heroic, adventurous, unusual, or unfamiliar subjects. The Realists, in turn, were followed by the Naturalists, who traced the effects of heredity and environment on people helpless to change their situations. American realism grew from the work of local-color writers such as Bret Harte and Sarah Orne Jewett and is evident in the writings of major figures such as Mark Twain and Henry James.

See Local Color, Naturalism, and Romanticism.

REFRAIN A *refrain* is a repeated line or group of lines in a poem or song. Most refrains end stanzas, as does "And the tide rises, the tide falls," the refrain in Henry Wadsworth Longfellow's poem on page 252; or "Coming for to carry me home," the refrain in "Swing Low, Sweet Chariot," on page 452. Although some refrains are nonsense lines, many increase suspense or emphasize character and theme.

REGIONALISM *Regionalism* in literature is the tendency among certain authors to write about specific geographical areas. Regional writers, like Willa Cather and William Faulkner, present the distinct culture of an area, including its speech, customs, beliefs, and history. Local-color writing may be considered a type of Regionalism, but Regionalists, like the southern writers of the 1920's, usually go beyond mere presentation of cultural idiosyncrasies and attempt, instead, a sophisticated sociological or anthropological treatment of the culture of a region.

See Local Color and Setting.

RESOLUTION *See* Plot.

RHYME *Rhyme* is the repetition of sounds at the ends of words. Rhyming words have identical vowel sounds in their final accented syllables. The consonants before the vowels may be different, but any consonants occurring after these vowels are the same, as in *frog* and *bog* or *willow* and *pillow*. *End rhyme* occurs when rhyming words are repeated at the ends of lines. *Internal rhyme* occurs when rhyming words fall within a line. *Approximate*, or *slant*, *rhyme* occurs when the rhyming sounds are similar, but not exact, as in *prove* and *glove*.

See Rhyme Scheme.

RHYME SCHEME A *rhyme scheme* is a regular pattern of rhyming words in a poem. To describe a rhyme scheme, one uses a letter of the alphabet to represent each rhyming sound in a poem or stanza. Consider how letters are used to represent the rhymes in the following example:

> With innocent wide penguin eyes, three   a
> large fledgling mocking-birds below   b
> the pussywillow tree,   a
> stand in a row.   b
> —Marianne Moore, "Bird-Witted"

The rhyme scheme of this section of Moore's poem is *abab*.

See Rhyme.

RHYTHM *Rhythm* is the pattern of beats, or stresses, in spoken or written language. Prose and free verse are written in the irregular rhythmical patterns of everyday speech. Consider, for example, the rhythmical pattern in the following free verse lines by Gwendolyn Brooks:

> Life for my child is simple, and is good.
> He knows his wish. Yes, but that is not all.
> Because I know mine too.

Traditional poetry often follows a regular rhythmical pattern, as in the following lines by America's first great female poet, Anne Bradstreet:

> In critic's hands beware thou dost not come,
> And take thy way where yet thou art not
> known
> —"The Author to Her Book"

See Meter.

RISING ACTION *See* Plot.

ROMANTICISM *Romanticism* was a literary and artistic movement of the nineteenth century that arose in reaction against eighteenth-century Neoclassicism and placed a premium on fancy, imagination, emotion, nature, individuality, and exotica. Romantic elements can be found in the works of American writers as diverse as Cooper, Poe, Thoreau, Emerson, Dickinson, Hawthorne, and Melville. Romanticism is particularly evident in the works of the New England Transcendentalists.

See Classicism and Transcendentalism.

ROUND CHARACTER See Character.

SATIRE *Satire* is writing that ridicules or criticizes individuals, ideas, institutions, social conventions, or other works of art or literature. The writer of a satire, or satirist, may use a tolerant, sympathetic tone or an angry, bitter tone. Some satire is written in prose and some in poetry. Examples of satire in this text include W. H. Auden's "The Unknown Citizen," on page 696, and Ian Frazier's "Coyote v. Acme," on page 998.

SCANSION *Scansion* is the process of analyzing a poem's metrical pattern. When a poem is scanned, its stressed and unstressed syllables are marked to show what poetic feet are used and how many feet appear in each line. The last two lines of Edna St. Vincent Millay's "I Shall Go Back Again to the Bleak Shore" may be scanned as follows:

> Bŭt Í | shăll fínd | thĕ súl|lĕn rocks | and skíes
> Ŭnchángĕd | from whắt | thĕy wére | whĕn Í | wăs young.

See Meter.

SENSORY LANGUAGE *Sensory language* is writing or speech that appeals to one or more of the five senses.

See Image.

SETTING The *setting* of a literary work is the time and place of the action. A setting may serve any of a number of functions. It may provide a background for the action. It may be a crucial element in the plot or central conflict. It may also create a certain emotional atmosphere, or mood. The setting of Ernest Hemingway's "In Another Country," on page 731, is Milan, Italy, during World War I. The story centers on the hospital in which the protagonist receives physical therapy for a war injury. The setting provides a backdrop for the action and is central to the plot.

SHORT STORY A *short story* is a brief work of fiction. The short story resembles the novel but generally has a simpler plot and setting. In addition, the short story tends to reveal character at a crucial moment rather than develop it through many incidents. For example, Thomas Wolfe's "The Far and the Near," on

page 702, concentrates on what happens to the engineer when he visits the people who waved to him every day.

See Fiction and Genre.

SIMILE A *simile* is a figure of speech that makes a direct comparison between two subjects using either like or as. Here are two examples of similes:

> The trees looked like pitch forks against the sullen sky.
> Her hair was as red as a robin's breast.

See Figurative Language.

SLANT RHYME See Rhyme.

SONNET A *sonnet* is a fourteen-line lyric poem focused on a single theme. Sonnets have many variations but are usually written in iambic pentameter, following one of two traditional patterns: the *Petrarchan,* or *Italian, sonnet,* which is divided into two parts, the eight-line octave and the six-line sestet; and the *Shakespearean,* or *English, sonnet,* which consists of three quatrains and a concluding couplet.

See Lyric Poem.

SPEAKER The *speaker* is the voice of a poem. Although the speaker is often the poet, the speaker may also be a fictional character or even an inanimate object or another type of nonhuman entity. Interpreting a poem often depends upon recognizing who the speaker is, whom the speaker is addressing, and what the speaker's attitude, or tone, is.

See Point of View.

SPIRITUAL A *spiritual* is a type of African American folk song dating from the period of slavery and Reconstruction. A typical spiritual deals both with religious freedom and, on an allegorical level, with political and economic freedom. For example, in some spirituals the biblical river Jordan was used as a symbol for the Ohio River, which separated slave states from free states, and the biblical promised land, Canaan, was used as a symbol for the free northern United States. Most spirituals contained biblical allusions and made use of repetition, parallelism, and rhyme. Spirituals had a profound influence on the development of both poetry and song in the United States. See "Swing Low, Sweet Chariot," on page 452, and "Go Down, Moses," on page 453.

STAGE DIRECTIONS See Drama.

STANZA A *stanza* is a group of lines in a poem that are considered to be a unit. Many poems are divided into stanzas that are separated by spaces. Stanzas often function just like paragraphs in prose. Each stanza states and develops a single main idea.

Stanzas are commonly named according to the number of lines found in them, as follows:

1. *Couplet*: a two-line stanza
2. *Tercet*: a three-line stanza
3. *Quatrain*: a four-line stanza
4. *Cinquain*: a five-line stanza
5. *Sestet*: a six-line stanza
6. *Heptastich*: a seven-line stanza
7. *Octave*: an eight-line stanza

STATIC CHARACTER See Character.

STREAM OF CONSCIOUSNESS *Stream of consciousness* is a narrative technique that presents thoughts as if they were coming directly from a character's mind. Instead of being arranged in chronological order, the events of the story are presented from the character's point of view, mixed in with the character's feelings and memories just as they might spontaneously occur in the mind of a real person. Katherine Anne Porter uses this technique in "The Jilting of Granny Weatherall," on page 776, to capture Granny's dying thoughts and feelings. Ambrose Bierce also uses the stream-of-consciousness technique in his short story "An Occurrence at Owl Creek Bridge," which appears on page 468. Stream-of-consciousness writing reveals a character's complex psychology and presents it in realistic detail.

See Point of View.

STYLE A writer's *style* is his or her typical way of writing. Style includes word choice, tone, degree of formality, figurative language, rhythm, grammatical structure, sentence length, organization—in short, every feature of a writer's use of language. Ernest Hemingway, for example, is noted for a simple prose style that contrasts with Thomas Paine's aphoristic style and with N. Scott Momaday's reflective style.

See Diction and Plain Style.

SUSPENSE *Suspense* is a feeling of growing uncertainty about the outcome of events in a literary work. Writers create suspense by raising questions in the minds of their readers. Because readers are curious or concerned, they keep reading to find out what will happen next. Suspense builds until the climax of the plot, at which point the suspense reaches its peak.

Thereafter, the suspense is generally resolved.

See Climax and Plot.

SYMBOL A *symbol* is anything that stands for or represents something else. A *conventional symbol* is one that is widely known and accepted, such as a voyage symbolizing life or a skull symbolizing death. A *personal symbol* is one developed for a particular work by a particular author. Examples in this text include Hawthorne's black veil and Melville's white whale.

SYMBOLISM *Symbolism* was a literary movement during the nineteenth century that influenced many poets, including the Imagists and T. S. Eliot. Symbolists turned away from everyday realistic details, trying instead to express emotions by using a pattern of symbols.

See Imagism and Realism.

THEME A *theme* is a central message or insight into life revealed by a literary work. An essay's theme is often directly stated in its thesis statement. In most works of fiction, the theme is only indirectly stated: a story, poem, or play most often has an *implied theme*. For example, in "A Worn Path," on page 740, Eudora Welty does not directly say that Phoenix Jackson's difficult journey shows the power of love, but readers learn this indirectly by the end of the story.

TONE The *tone* of a literary work is the writer's attitude toward his or her subject, characters, or audience. A writer's tone may be formal or informal, friendly or distant, personal or pompous. For example, William Faulkner's tone in his "Nobel Prize Acceptance Speech," on page 798, is earnest and serious, whereas James Thurber's tone in "The Night the Ghost Got In," on page 818, is humorous and ironic.

See Mood.

TRANSCENDENTALISM *Transcendentalism* was an American literary and philosophical movement of the nineteenth century. The Transcendentalists, who were based in New England, believed that intuition and the individual conscience "transcend" experience and thus are better guides to truth than are the senses and logical reason. Influenced by Romanticism, the Transcendentalists respected the individual spirit and the natural world, believing that divinity was present everywhere, in nature and in each person. The Transcendentalists included Ralph Waldo Emerson, Henry David Thoreau, Bronson Alcott, W. H. Channing, Margaret Fuller, and Elizabeth Peabody.

See Romanticism.

WRITING HANDBOOK

THE WRITING PROCESS

A polished piece of writing can seem to have been effortlessly created, but most good writing is the result of a process of writing, rethinking, and rewriting. The process can be roughly divided into stages: prewriting, drafting, revising, editing, proofreading, and publishing.

It's important to remember that the writing process is one that moves backward as well as forward. Even while you are moving forward in the creation of your composition, you may still return to a previous stage—to rethink or rewrite.

Following are stages of the writing process, with key points to address during each stage.

Prewriting

In this stage, you plan out the work to be done. You prepare to write by exploring ideas, gathering information, and working out an organization plan. Following are the key steps to take at this stage.

Step 1: Analyze the writing situation. Start by clarifying your assignment, so that you know exactly what you are supposed to do.

- *Focus your topic.* If necessary, narrow the topic—the subject you are writing about—so that you can write about it fully in the space you have.
- *Know your purpose.* What is your goal for this paper? What do you want to accomplish? Your purpose will determine what you include in the paper.
- *Know your audience.* Who will read your paper influences what you say and how you say it.

Step 2: Gather ideas and information. You can do this in a number of ways:

- *Brainstorm.* When you brainstorm, either alone or with others, you come up with possible ideas to use in your paper. Not all of your brainstormed ideas will be useful or suitable. You'll need to evaluate them later.
- *Consult other people about your subject.* Speaking informally with others may suggest an idea or approach you did not see at first.
- *Make a list of questions about your topic.* When your list is complete, find the answers to your questions.

- *Do research.* Your topic may require information that you don't have, so you will need to go to other sources to find information. There are numerous ways to find information on a topic. See the Research Handbook on p. 1206 for suggestions.

The ideas and information you gather will become the content of your paper. Not all of the information you gather will be needed. As you develop and revise your paper, you will make further decisions about what to include and what to leave out.

Step 3: Organize. First, make a rough plan for the way you want to present your information. Sort your ideas and notes; decide what goes with what and which points are the most important. You can make an outline to show the order of ideas, or you can use some other organizing plan that works for you.

There are many ways in which you can organize and develop your material. Use a method that works for your topic. Following are common methods of organizing information in the development of a paper.

- *Chronological Order* In this method, events are presented in the order in which they occurred. This organization works best for presenting narrative material or explaining in a "how to."
- *Spatial Order* In spatial order, details are presented as seen in space, for example, from left to right or from foreground to background. This order is good for descriptive writing.
- *Order of Importance* This order helps readers see the relative importance of ideas. You present ideas from most to least important or from least to most important.
- *Main Idea and Details* This logical organization works well to support an idea or opinion.

Drafting

When you draft, you put down your ideas on paper in rough form. Working from your prewriting notes and your outline or plan, you develop and present your ideas in sentences and paragraphs.

Don't worry about getting everything perfect at the drafting stage. Concentrate on getting your ideas down.

Draft in a way that works for you. Some writers

work best by writing a quick draft—putting down all their ideas without stopping to evaluate them. Other writers prefer to develop each paragraph carefully and thoughtfully, making sure each main idea is supported by details.

As you are developing a draft, keep in mind your purpose and your audience. These determine what you say and how you say it.

Don't be afraid to change your original plans during drafting. Some of the best ideas are those that were not planned at the beginning. Write as many drafts as you like. You can draft over and over until you're happy with the results.

Most papers, regardless of the topic, are developed with an introduction, a body, and a conclusion. Here are tips for developing these parts:

Introduction In the introduction to a paper, you want to engage your readers' attention and let them know the purpose of your paper. You may use the following strategies in your introduction:

- State your main idea.
- Take a stand.
- Use an anecdote.
- Quote someone.
- Startle your readers.

Body of the paper In the body of your paper, you present your information and make your points. Your **organization** is an important factor in leading readers through your ideas. Your elaboration on your main ideas is also important. **Elaboration** is the development of ideas to make your written work precise and complete. You can use the following kinds of details to elaborate your main ideas:

- Facts and statistics
- Anecdotes
- Sensory details
- Examples
- Explanation and definition
- Quotations

Conclusion The ending of your paper is the final impression you leave with your readers. Your conclusion should give readers the sense that you have pulled everything together. Following are some effective ways to end your paper:

- Summarize and restate.
- Ask a question.
- State an opinion.
- Tell an anecdote.
- Call for action.

Revising

Once you have a draft, you can look at it critically or have others review it. This is the time to make changes—on many levels. Revising is the process of reworking what you have written to make it as good as it can be. You may change some details so that your ideas flow smoothly and are clearly supported. You may discover that some details don't work and you'll need to discard them. Two strategies may help you start the revising process:

1. Read your work aloud. This is an excellent way to catch any ideas or details that have been left out and to notice errors in logic.
2. Ask someone else to read your work. Choose someone who can point out its strengths as well as suggest how to improve it.

How do you know what to look for and what to change? Here is a checklist of major writing issues. If the answer to any of these questions is no, then that is an area that needs revision.

1. Does the writing achieve your purpose?
2. Does the paper have unity? That is, does it have a single focus, with all details and information contributing to that focus?
3. Is the arrangement of information clear and logical?
4. Have you elaborated enough to give your audience adequate information?

Editing

When you edit, you look more closely at the language you have used to ensure that the way you express your ideas is the most effective.

- Replace dull language with vivid, precise words.
- Cut or change redundant expressions (unnecessary repetition).
- Cut empty words and phrases, those that do not add anything to the writing.
- Check passive voice. Usually active voice is more effective.
- Replace wordy expressions with shorter, more precise ones.

Proofreading

After you finish your final draft, you must proofread it, either on your own or with the help of a partner.

It's useful to have handy both a dictionary and a usage handbook to help you check for correctness. Here are the tasks in proofreading:

- Correct errors in grammar and usage.
- Correct errors in punctuation and capitalization.
- Correct errors in spelling.

Publishing

Now your paper is ready to be shared by others.

THE MODES OF WRITING

Description

Description is writing that creates a vivid picture, draws readers into a scene, and makes readers feel as if they are meeting a character or experiencing an event firsthand. A description may stand on its own or be part of a longer work, such as a short story.

When you write a description, bring it to life with sensory details, which tell how your subject looks, smells, sounds, tastes, or feels. You'll want to choose your details carefully so that you create a single main impression of your subject. Avoid language and details that don't contribute to this main impression. Keep these guidelines in mind whenever you are assigned one of the following types of description:

Observation In an observation, you describe an event that you have witnessed firsthand, often over an extended period of time. You may focus on an aspect of daily life or on a scientific phenomenon, such as a storm or an eclipse.

Remembrance When you write a remembrance, you use vivid descriptive details to bring to life memorable people, places, or events from your past.

Reflective Essay A reflective essay is more than just a description of personal experiences or pivotal events from your life; it also describes your thoughts and feelings about the significance of those events.

Character Profile In a character profile, you capture a person's appearance and personality traits and reveal information about his or her life. Your subject may be a real person or a fictional character.

Travel Brochure Present details about culture, architecture, food, and scenery to describe a vacation destination in a way that appeals to potential visitors.

Narration

Whenever writers tell any type of story, they are using **narration**. While there are many kinds of narration, most narratives share certain elements—characters, a setting, a sequence of events (or plot, in fiction), and, often, a theme. You might be asked to write one of these types of narration:

Personal Narrative A personal narrative is a true story about a memorable experience or period in your life. In a personal narrative, your feelings about events shape the way you tell the story—even the way you describe people and places.

Myth, Legend, or Folk Tale When you write a myth, legend, or folk tale, you are setting down in writing a story—often fantastic—that has been handed down orally over the years.

Firsthand Biography A firsthand biography tells about the life (or a period in the life) of a person whom you know personally. Use your close relationship with the person to help you include personal insights not found in biographies based solely on research.

Short Story Short stories are short fictional, or made-up, narratives in which a main character faces a conflict that is resolved by the end of the story. In planning a short story, you focus on developing the plot, the setting, and the characters. You must also decide on a point of view: Will your story be told by a character who participates in the action or by someone who describes the action as an outside observer?

Exposition

Exposition is writing that informs or explains. The information you include in expository writing is factual or (when you're expressing an opinion) based on fact.

Your expository writing should reflect a well-thought-out organization—one that includes a clear introduction, body, and conclusion and is appropriate for the type of exposition you are writing. Here are some types of exposition you may be asked to write:

Cause-and-Effect Essay In a cause-and-effect essay, you consider the reasons something did happen or might happen. You may examine several causes of a single effect or several effects of a single cause.

Comparison-and-Contrast Essay When you write a comparison-and-contrast essay, you consider the similarities and differences between two or more subjects. You may organize your essay point by point—discussing each aspect of your subject in turn—or subject by subject—discussing all the qualities of one subject first, then the qualities of the next subject.

Problem-and-Solution Essay In a problem-and-solution essay, you identify a conflict or problem and offer a resolution. Begin by clearly stating the problem, then present a reasoned path to a solution.

Consumer Report A consumer report presents up-to-date information and relevant statistical data about one or more products in a given category.

Because readers use consumer reports to help them make purchasing decisions, you might also rate the product or products you profile and discuss the advantages or disadvantages of each.

Summary To write a summary or synopsis of an event or a literary work, you include only the details that your readers will need in order to understand the key features of the event or the literary work. Omit any personal opinions; include only factual details.

Persuasion

Persuasion is writing or speaking that attempts to convince people to agree with a position or take a desired action. When used effectively, persuasive writing has the power to change people's lives. As a reader and a writer, you will find yourself engaged in many forms of persuasion. Here are a few of them:

Persuasive Essay In writing a persuasive essay, you build an argument, supporting your opinions with a variety of evidence: facts, statistics, examples, statements from experts. You also anticipate and develop counter-arguments to opposing opinions.

Advertisement Advertisements are probably the most common type of persuasion. When you write an advertisement, you present information in an appealing way to make the product or service seem desirable.

Position Paper In a position paper, you try to persuade readers to accept your views on a controversial issue. Most often, your audience will consist of people who have some power to shape policy related to the issue. As they are in other types of persuasion, your views in a position paper should be supported with evidence.

Persuasive Speech A persuasive speech is a piece of persuasion that you present orally instead of in writing. As a persuasive speaker, you use a variety of techniques, such as repetition of key points, to capture your audience's interest and to add force to your argument.

Editorial An editorial expresses an opinion or position on a current issue or concern. When you write an editorial, you state and then defend your opinion with logical reasons, facts, examples, and other details.

Research Writing

Writers often use outside research to gather information and explore subjects of interest. The product of that research is called **research writing.** In connection with your reading, you may occasionally be assigned one of the following types of research writing:

Research Paper A research paper uses information gathered from a variety of outside sources to explore a topic. In your research paper, you will usually include an introduction, in which your thesis, or main point, is stated; a body, in which you present support for the thesis; and a conclusion that summarizes, or restates, your main points. You should credit the sources of information, using footnotes or other types of citation, and include a bibliography, or general list of sources, at the end.

Multimedia Presentation In preparing a multimedia presentation, you will gather and organize information in a variety of media, or means of communication. You may use written materials, slides, videos, audio cassettes, sound effects, art, photographs, models, charts, and diagrams.

Annotated Bibliography An annotated bibliography is a list of materials about a certain topic. For each entry, you must provide source information (title, author, date of publication, and so on), as well as a summary of the material that includes your personal review or comments about it.

Statistical Report A statistical report uses numbers to support a thesis, or main idea. Before drafting your report, you must first interpret and draw conclusions from the numerical data you've gathered. Then present and support your findings in the report.

Creative Writing

Creative writing blends imagination, ideas, and emotions, and allows you to present your own unique view of the world. Poems, plays, short stories, dramas, and even some cartoons are examples of creative writing. Many are found in this anthology; use them as an inspiration to produce your own creative works, such as the following:

Poem In a poem, you use sensory images, figurative language, and sound devices to communicate ideas, tell a story, describe feelings, or create a mood. Using exact and highly charged language will help you convey meaning and create vivid images for your readers.

Drama When you write a drama or a dramatic scene, you are writing a story that is intended to be performed. Since a drama consists largely of the words and actions of the characters, be sure to write dialogue that clearly shows the characters' personalities, thoughts, and emotions, as well as stage directions that convey your ideas about sets, props, sound effects, and the speaking style and movements of the characters.

Monologue A monologue is a speech delivered by a single character. You may create a monologue within the context of a longer drama or as a work to be read or performed in its own right.

Video Script A video script or screenplay is a drama written for television, film, or video production. In addition to dialogue and stage directions, you must also include detailed stage and camera directions in your video script. These instructions indicate the specific actions or effects necessary to telling the story clearly.

Imitation of an Author's Style In this type of creative writing, you take the recognizable elements of an author's style and use them to create your own piece of writing. You may write your imitation in a true attempt to replicate a writer's style or in the spirit of a humorous parody.

Response to Literature

In a **response to literature,** you express your thoughts and feelings about a work and often, in so doing, gain a better understanding of what the work is all about. Your response to literature can take many forms—oral or written, formal or informal. During the course of your reading, you may be asked to respond to a work of literature in one of these forms:

Retelling of a Literary Work When you retell a literary work, you restate the work in your own words. The subtle changes or emphases you bring to the retelling reveal your response to the work—what you particularly liked or what you wanted to change about the original piece of literature. You might also choose to adapt the work for another medium or literary genre.

Critical Review In a critical review of a literary work, you discuss various elements in the work and offer opinions about them. You may also give a summary of the work and a recommendation to readers.

Comparative Analysis of Two Literary Works A comparative analysis shows the similarities and differences between several elements—such as characters and plot—of two literary works. You might compare the works on a point-by-point basis or analyze one work before moving on to the next. Use quotations and specific details from the works to support your points.

Response to a Short Story In your response to a short story, you present your reactions to elements of the story—such as the setting, a particular character, or a plot twist—that made a strong impression on you.

Include supporting quotations from the story, as well as a brief summary and personal evaluation of the work.

Literary Analysis In a literary analysis, you take a critical look at various important elements in the work. You then attempt to explain how the author has used those elements and how they work together to convey the author's message.

Practical and Technical Writing

Practical writing is fact-based writing that people do in the workplace or in their day-to-day lives. Business letters, memos, school forms, and job applications are examples of practical writing. **Technical writing,** which is also based on facts, explains procedures, provides instructions, or presents specialized information. You encounter technical writing every time you read a manual or a set of instructions.

In the following descriptions, you'll find tips for tackling several types of practical and technical writing.

Résumé A résumé is a written summary of your education background, work experience, and job qualifications presented in a concise format.

Cover and Follow-up Letters Accompany a résumé with a cover letter in which you introduce yourself and briefly explain your qualifications for the position. It's also a good idea to send a brief thank-you letter to follow up an interview. Use proper business letter format for both types of correspondence.

Proposal When you wish to present a new idea for consideration, describe your suggested plan of action in a proposal. While your proposal can take many different forms—from a simple business letter or memo to a formal plan—it should include specific information about the benefits of the proposed action. It should also provide relevant background information that a reader considering the proposal might need, such as costs or materials required to implement the plan.

Test Essay Good organization is key to writing an effective essay under test conditions. Adhering to an organizational plan will help you create a coherent essay, even under tight time restrictions. Your introduction should include a thesis statement—a one-sentence summary of your response to the test essay question. Make sure that each paragraph in the body of the essay supports this main idea, and conclude with a restatement of the thesis and a summary of the main points in the body.

GRAMMAR AND MECHANICS HANDBOOK

Summary of Grammar

Nouns A **noun** names a person, place, or thing. A **common noun** names any one of a class of people, places, or things. A **proper noun** names a specific person, place, or thing.

Common Nouns	Proper Nouns
essayist	William Safire, Carson McCullers
city	Boston, New Orleans

Pronouns A **pronoun** is a word that stands for a noun or for words that take the place of a noun. A **personal pronoun** refers to (1) the person speaking, (2) the person spoken to, or (3) the person, place, or thing spoken about.

	Singular	Plural
First Person	I, me, my, mine	we, us, our, ours
Second Person	you, your, yours	you, your, yours
Third Person	he, him, his, she, her, hers, it, its	they, them, their, theirs

A **reflexive pronoun** ends in *-self* or *-selves* and adds information to a sentence by pointing back to a noun or pronoun near the beginning of the sentence.

> . . . They click upon *themselves*
> as the breeze rises . . .
> —*Frost, p. 804*

An **intensive pronoun** ends in *-self* or *-selves* and simply adds emphasis to a noun or pronoun in the same sentence.

> The United States *themselves* are essentially the greatest poem.
> —*Whitman, p. 406*

A **demonstrative pronoun** directs attention to a specific person, place, or thing.

> *this* hat   *these* coats   *that* frame

A **relative pronoun** begins a subordinate clause and connects it to another idea in the sentence.

> The brave men, living and dead, *who* struggled here, have consecrated it . . .
> —*Lincoln, p. 480*

> I made a little book, in *which* I allotted a page for each of the virtues.
> —*Franklin, p. 132*

An **indefinite pronoun** refers to a noun or pronoun that is not specifically named.

> *Few* could refrain from twisting their heads toward the door; *many* stood upright and turned directly about; . . .
> —*Hawthorne, p. 319*

Verbs A **verb** is a word or group of words that expresses time while showing an action, a condition, or the fact that something exists.

An **action verb** is a verb that tells what action someone or something is performing.

> The sun that brief December day
> *Rose* cheerless over hills of gray, . . .
> —*Whittier, p. 267*

A **linking verb** is a verb that connects its subject with a word generally found near the end of the sentence. All linking verbs are intransitive.

> Her name *was* Phoenix Jackson.
> —*Welty, p. 740*

A **helping verb** is a verb that can be added to another verb to make a single verb phrase.

> Sir, we *have* done everything that could be done to avert the storm which is now coming on.
> —*Henry, p. 170*

Adjectives An **adjective** is a word used to describe a noun or pronoun or to give a noun or pronoun a more specific meaning. Adjectives answer these questions:

What kind?	*green* leaf, *tall* chimney
Which one?	*this* clock, *those* pictures
How many?	*six* days, *several* concerts
How much?	*more* effort, *enough* applause
Whose?	*Kennedy's* address, *my* name

The articles *the, a,* and *an* are adjectives. *An* is used before a word beginning with a vowel sound.

A noun or pronoun may sometimes be used as an adjective.

Adverbs An **adverb** is a word that modifies a verb, an adjective, or another adverb. Adverbs answer the questions *where? when? in what way? to what extent?*

> She came *yesterday*. (modifies verb *came*)
> Please sit *here*. (modifies verb *sit*)
> We departed *immediately*. (modifies verb *departed*)
> They were *completely* unaware. (modifies adjective *unaware*)
> It rained *rather* often. (modifies adverb *often*)

Prepositions A **preposition** is a word that relates a noun or pronoun that appears with it to another word in the sentence. Prepositions are almost always followed by nouns or pronouns.

aboard the train	*among* us	*below* our plane
into view	*toward* them	*until* dark

Conjunctions A **conjunction** is a word used to connects other words or groups of words.

A **coordinating conjunction** connects similar kinds or groups of words.

dogs *and* cats   friendly *but* dignified

Correlative conjunctions are used in pairs to connect similar words or groups of words.

both Prem *and* Sanjay   *neither* she *nor* I

A **subordinating conjunction** connects two complete ideas by placing one idea below the other in rank or importance.

> *Even before they'd noticed anything wrong,* they'd wondered at his jittery, jerky catnaps . . .
> —Tyler, p. 927

A **conjunctive adverb** is an adverb used as a conjunction to connect complete ideas.

> Flannery O'Connor portrayed social outcasts in an unsentimental way; *nevertheless,* her underlying sympathy for their suffering is evident.

Interjections An **interjection** is a word that expresses feeling or emotion and functions independently of a sentence.

Oh, woe is me!

Subject and Verb Agreement To make a subject and verb agree, make sure that both are *singular* or both are *plural.*

> All of it, all that the *land is* and *evokes,* its actual meaning as well as its metaphorical reverberation, *was* and *is* understood differently.
> —"Arctic Dreams,"
> Barry Lopez

Phrases A **phrase** is a group of words, without a subject and verb, that functions in a sentence as one part of speech.

A **prepositional phrase** is a group of words that includes a preposition and a noun or pronoun.

beyond the horizon	inside the corral
in front of the store	throughout his life

An **adjective phrase** is a prepositional phrase that modifies a noun or pronoun by telling what kind or which one.

> And the concrete *of this city*
> the oily wind, the blazing windows,

the shrieks *of automation* cannot,
truly cannot answer for that hunger . . .
> —Ortiz, p. 980

An **adverb phrase** is a prepositional phrase that modifies a verb, an adjective, or an adverb by pointing out where, when, in what manner, or to what extent.

> *During the intermission before the second half of the concert,* I questioned my aunt and found that the "Prize Song" was not new to her.
> —Cather, p. 618

An **appositive phrase** is a noun or pronoun with modifiers, placed next to a noun or pronoun to add information and details.

> I drop to Hawthorne, *the customs officer,* measuring coal and mostly trying to keep warm— . . .
> —Lowell, p. 914

A **participial phrase** is a participle that is modified by an adjective or adverb phrase or that has a complement. The entire phrase acts as an adjective.

> Two or three men, *conversing earnestly together,* ceased as he approached, . . .
> —Harte, p. 534

A **nominative absolute** is a noun or pronoun followed by a participle or participial phrase that functions independently of the rest of the sentence.

> *The preparations being complete,* the two private soldiers stepped aside and each drew away the plank upon which he had been standing.
> —Bierce, p. 469

An **infinitive phrase** is an infinitive with modifiers, complements, or a subject, all acting together as a single part of speech.

> . . . some set *to mow,* others *to bind thatch,* some *to build houses,* others *to thatch them* . . .
> —Smith, p. 68

Clauses A **clause** is a group of words with its own subject and verb.

An **independent clause** can stand by itself as a complete sentence. A **subordinate clause** cannot stand by itself as a complete sentence; it can only be part of a sentence.

An **adjective clause** is a subordinate clause that modifies a noun or pronoun by telling what kind or which one.

> In compliance with the request of a friend of mine, *who wrote me from the East,* I called on good-natured, garrulous old Simon Wheeler . . .
> —Twain, p. 525

A **subordinate adverb clause** modifies a verb, adjective, adverb, or verbal by telling *where, when, in what way, to what extent, under what condition,* or *why.*

> Whenever Richard Cory went down town,
> We people on the pavement looked at him.
> —*Robinson, p. 607*

A **noun clause** is a subordinate clause that acts as a noun.

> As I knew, or thought I knew, *what was right and wrong,* I did not see why I might not always do one and avoid the other.
> —*Franklin, p. 131*

Summary of Capitalization and Punctuation

CAPITALIZATION

Capitalize the first word in sentences, interjections, and incomplete questions. Also capitalize the first word in a quotation if the quotation is a complete sentence.

> And then I said in perfect English, "Yes, I'm getting rather concerned."
> —*Tan, p. 1013*

Capitalize all proper nouns and adjectives.

> T. S. Eliot　Mississippi River　Harvard University
> Turkish　November　Puerto Rican

Capitalize a person's title when it is followed by the person's name or when it is used in direct address.

> Rev. Leonidas W. Smiley　General Robert E. Lee

Capitalize titles showing family relationships when they refer to a specific person, unless they are preceded by a possessive noun or pronoun.

> Granny Weatherall　　my grandfather Mammedaty

Capitalize the first word and all other key words in the titles of books, periodicals, poems, stories, plays, paintings, and other works of art.

> *The Crucible*　　"Anecdote of the Jar"

Capitalize the first word and all nouns in letter salutations and the first word in letter closings.

> Dear Henry:　　Yours truly,

PUNCTUATION

End Marks Use a **period** to end a declarative sentence, a mild imperative sentence, an indirect question, and most abbreviations.

> The early afternoon was clear and open and surrounded by pale blue sky.
> —*O'Connor, p. 886*
> Pile the bodies high at Austerlitz and Waterloo.
> —*Sandburg, p. 771*

> Ask yourselves how this gracious reception of our petition comports with those warlike preparations which cover our waters and darken our land.
> —*Henry, p. 170*

Use a **question mark** to end an interrogative sentence, an incomplete question, or a statement that is intended as a question.

> Was it even Kentucky or Tennessee?
> —*Warren, p. 917*

Use an **exclamation mark** after an exclamatory sentence, a forceful imperative sentence, or an interjection expressing strong emotion.

> We wear the mask!
> —*Dunbar, p. 601*
> "Don't let him, sister!"
> —*Frost, p. 809*

Commas Use a comma before the conjunction to separate two independent clauses in a compound sentence.

> From my mother's sleep I fell into the State,
> And I hunched in its belly till my wet fur froze.
> —*Jarrell, p. 1045*

Use commas to separate three or more words, phrases, or clauses in a series.

> I spun, I wove, I kept the house, I nursed the sick, . . .
> —*Masters, p. 608*

Use commas to separate adjectives of equal rank. Do not use commas to separate adjectives that must stay in a specific order.

> She carried a thin, small cane made from an umbrella . . .
> —*Welty, p. 740*
> Feathery drifts of snow, shaken from the long pine boughs, flew like white-winged birds, and settled about them as they slept.
> —*Harte, p. 541*

Use a comma after an introductory word, phrase, or clause.

> Finding Tom so squeamish on this point, he did not insist upon it, . . .
> —*Irving, p. 242*

Use commas to set off parenthetical and nonessential expressions.

> My poor aunt's figure, however, would have presented astonishing difficulties to any dressmaker.
> —*Cather, p. 615*

Use commas with places, dates, and titles.

Boston, Massachusetts   November 17, 1915
Dr. Martin Luther King, Jr.

Use commas after items in addresses, after the salutation in a personal letter, after the closing in all letters, and in numbers of more than three digits.

Linden Lane, Princeton, N.J.   Dear Marian,
Affectionately yours,   6,778

Use a comma to indicate words left out of an elliptical sentence and to set off a direct quotation.

In T. S. Eliot's poetry, allusions are perhaps the most prominent device; in Ezra Pound's, images.
"Well, Granny," he said, "you must be a hundred years old, and scared of nothing."

—Welty, p. 743

Semicolons Use a semicolon to join independent clauses that are not already joined by a conjunction.

The old woman didn't change her position until he was almost into her yard; then she rose with one hand fisted on her hip.

—O'Connor, p. 879

Use semicolons to avoid confusion when independent clauses or items in a series already contain commas.

Before these events, the day was glorious with expectancy; after them, the day was a dead and empty thing.

—Twain, p. 521

Colons Use a colon before a list of items following an independent clause.

Great literature provides us with many things: entertainment, enrichment, and inspiration.

Use a colon to introduce a formal or lengthy quotation.

In *The Member of the Wedding* the lonely twelve-year-old girl, Frankie Addams, articulates this universal need: "The trouble with me is that for a long time I have just been an *I* person."

—McCullers, p. 994

Quotation Marks A **direct quotation** represents a person's exact speech and is enclosed in quotation marks.

"Good," he said. "You will be able to play football again better than ever."

—Hemingway, p. 731

An **indirect quotation** reports only the general meaning of what a person said and does not require quotation marks.

One day I had said that Italian seemed such an easy language to me that I could not take a great interest in it, . . .

—Hemingway, p. 733

Always place a comma or a period inside the final quotation mark.

"Well, Missy, excuse me," Doctor Harry patted her cheek.

—Porter, p. 776

Place a question mark or an exclamation mark inside the final quotation mark if the end mark is part of the quotation; if it is not part of the quotation, place it outside the final quotation mark.

"Cornelia! Cornelia!" No footsteps, but a sudden hand on her cheek. "Bless you, where have you been?"

—Porter, p. 777

Use single quotation marks for a quotation within a quotation.

"'All right,' I say, 'I can't afford to pay
Any fixed wages, though I wish I could.'
'Someone else can.' 'Then someone else will
have to.'"

—"The Death of the Hired Man," Robert Frost

Underline the titles of long written works, movies, television and radio shows, lengthy works of music, paintings, and sculptures.

The Great Gatsby   Mary Poppins   Aida

Use quotation marks around the titles of short written works, episodes in a series, songs, and titles of works mentioned as parts of collections.

"Winter Dreams"   "Go Down, Moses"

Dashes Use dashes to indicate an abrupt change of thought, a dramatic interrupting idea, or a summary statement.

She'd had moments herself of picturing some kind of evil gene in her husband's ordinary, stocky body—a dark little egg like a black jelly bean, she imagined it.

—Tyler, p. 928

Use dashes to set off a nonessential appositive or modifier when it is long, when it is already punctuated, or when you want to be dramatic.

. . . for some reason he was not completely sure of—it may have been the cold and his fatigue—he decided not to insist on seeing him.

—Malamud, p. 896

Hyphens Use a hyphen with certain numbers, after certain prefixes, with two or more words used as one word, with a compound modifier coming before a noun, and within a word when a combination of letters might otherwise be confusing.

> fifty-four daughter-in-law
> up-to-date report

Apostrophes Add an apostrophe and -s to show the possessive case of most singular nouns.

> Taylor's poetry a poet's career

Add an apostrophe to show the possessive case of plural nouns ending in -s and -es.

> the boys' ambition the Cruzes' house

Add an apostrophe and -s to show the possessive case of plural nouns that do not end in -s or -es.

> the men's suits the deer's antlers

Use an apostrophe in a contraction to indicate the position of the missing letter or letters.

> "You look like a saint, Doctor Harry, and I vow that's as near as you'll ever come to it."
> —Porter, p. 780

GLOSSARY OF COMMON USAGE

adapt, adopt

Adapt is a verb meaning "to change." *Adopt* is a verb meaning "to take as one's own."

> Washington Irving *adapted* many characters and situations from folk tales for his short stories.
> Ezra Pound's followers *adopted* a spare, almost lean style in their verse.

advice, advise

Advice is a noun meaning "an opinion." *Advise* is a verb meaning "to give an opinion."

> The man in Jack London's "To Build a Fire" ignores the *advice* of the old-timer from Sulphur Creek.
> How might Lucinda Matlock *advise* the younger generation of today's world?

affect, effect

Affect is almost always a verb meaning "to influence." *Effect* is usually a noun meaning "result." *Effect* can also be a verb meaning "to bring about" or "to cause."

> An understanding of T. S. Eliot's multiple allusions can *affect* one's appreciation of his poetry.
> In Willa Cather's story, the Wagner concert has a profound *effect* on the emotions of Clark's Aunt Georgiana.
> The aim of persuasive writing is often to *effect* a change in the attitudes of the audience.

among, between

Among is usually used with three or more items. *Between* is generally used with only two items.

> *Among* the writers of the Harlem Renaissance, Langston Hughes stands out for his mastery of many literary genres.
> At the end of Robert Frost's "Mending Wall," the speaker reports a conversation *between* himself and his neighbor.

as, because, like, as to

The word *as* has several meanings and can function as several parts of speech. To avoid confusion, use *because* rather than *as* when you want to indicate cause and effect.

> *Because* Jonathan Edwards firmly believed that his listeners' souls were in danger, he desperately wanted them to repent.

Do not use the preposition *like* to introduce a clause that requires the conjunction *as*.

> The Puritans reacted to music and dancing *as* one might expect: They considered that such entertainments were dangerous occasions of sin.

The use of *as to* for *about* is awkward and should be avoided.

> Captain Ahab's bitter vehemence *about* the white whale must seem puzzling to the crew.

bad, badly

Use the predicate adjective *bad* after linking verbs such as *feel, look,* and *seem.* Use *badly* whenever an adverb is required.

> Although Granny Weatherall looks *bad*, she is not at all happy to see Doctor Harry at the beginning of Katherine Anne Porter's story.
> Elizabeth is *badly* shaken when Mr. Hooper refuses to remove the black veil.

because of, due to

Use *due to* if it can logically replace the phrase *caused by.* In introductory phrases, however, *because of* is better usage than *due to.*

> Peyton Farquhar's failure to recognize the trap of the Federal scout may be *due to* his eagerness to aid the Confederate cause.
> *Because of* Edgar Lee Masters's ability to sketch small-town characters accurately and accessibly, *Spoon River Anthology* became extremely popular.

being as, being that

Avoid using the expressions *being as* and *being that.* Use *because* or *since* instead.

Because Walt Whitman believed that new styles were needed in American poetry, he consciously broke with traditional forms and experimented with free verse.

Since Mr. Shiftlet is more interested in the car than in young Lucynell, it is hardly surprising that he abandons her at the roadside diner in Flannery O'Connor's "The Life You Save May Be Your Own."

beside, besides

Beside is a preposition meaning "at the side of" or "close to." Do not confuse *beside* with *besides*, which means "in addition to." *Besides* can be a preposition or an adverb.

When Clark sits *beside* his Aunt Georgiana at the concert, he tries to imagine her emotions as she hears the music.

Besides Mr. Oakhurst, which other characters are run out of town at the beginning of Bret Harte's "The Outcasts of Poker Flat"?

Thomas Jefferson was the third president of the United States; he was a gifted architect and inventor, *besides*.

can, may

The verb *can* generally refers to the ability to do something. The verb *may* generally refers to permission to do something.

One of Ralph Waldo Emerson's major themes is that human beings *can* acquire from nature a sense of their own potential and autonomy.

Robert Frost's poetry *may* appear to be simple, but it is rich with hidden meaning.

different from, different than

The preferred usage is *different from*.

In her powerful exploration of women's consciousness, Kate Chopin was *different from* the vast majority of her contemporaries.

due to the fact that

Replace this awkward expression with *because* or *since*.

Because Dexter Green cherishes his memories of the glamourous Judy Jones, it is not surprising that he is saddened by the knowledge that her youth and beauty have faded.

farther, further

Use *farther* when you refer to distance. Use *further* when you mean "to a greater degree."

The *farther* Phoenix Jackson travels in Eudora Welty's story "A Worn Path," the more her determination to reach her goal grows.

In his speech Patrick Henry urges his countrymen to trust the British no *further*.

fewer, less

Use *fewer* for things that can be counted. Use *less* for amounts or quantities that cannot be counted.

William Carlos Williams's poem "The Red Wheelbarrow" uses *fewer* words than most other poems I've read.

The train engineer felt *less* anticipation with each step that drew him nearer to the house by the railroad tracks.

good, well

Use the predicate adjective *good* after linking verbs such as *feel, look, smell, taste,* and *seem.* Use *well* whenever you need an adverb.

At the end of F. Scott Fitzgerald's "Winter Dreams," Devon implies to Dexter that Judy Jones does not look as *good* as she used to.

Anne Tyler writes especially *well* about ordinary people and family relationships.

hopefully

You should not loosely attach this adverb to a sentence, as in "Hopefully, the rain will stop by noon." Rewrite the sentence so that *hopefully* modifies a specific verb. Other possible ways of revising such sentences include using the adjective *hopeful* or a phrase such as *everyone hopes that*.

In his Nobel Prize acceptance speech, William Faulkner wrote *hopefully* about mankind's ability to endure and prevail.

Mai was *hopeful* that she could locate some more biographical information about Jean Toomer at her local library.

Everyone hopes that Diane will win the oral interpretation contest with her rendition of Robert Frost's "Out, Out—."

its, it's

Do not confuse the possessive pronoun *its* with the contraction *it's,* standing for "it is" or "it has."

Perhaps the most memorable line in Emerson's poem "The Rhodora" is "Beauty is *its* own excuse for being."

Wallace Stevens's "Anecdote of the Jar" suggests that *it's* impossible to mediate completely between the wilderness and the world of civilization.

kind of, sort of

In formal writing you should not use these colloquial expressions. Instead, use a word such as *rather* or *somewhat*.

Robert Lowell's train of thought in "Hawthorne" is *rather* difficult to follow.

In describing the events that launched the Civil War, Mary Chesnut is accurate, but *somewhat* emotional.

lay, lie

Do not confuse these verbs. *Lay* is a transitive verb meaning "to set or put something down." Its principal parts are *lay, laying, laid, laid. Lie* is an intransitive verb meaning "to recline." Its principal parts are *lie, lying, lay, lain.*

Stream-of-consciousness narration *lays* a special responsibility on the reader to piece together the events in a story or narrative poem.

The speaker of Emily Dickinson's "I heard a Fly buzz—when I died—" *lies* in a silent room as her life slips away.

many, much

Use *many* to refer to a specific quantity. Use *much* for an indefinite amount or for an abstract concept.

Many of William Faulkner's novels deal with the themes of pride, guilt, and the search for identity.

Much of Mark Twain's fiction was influenced by his boyhood along the Mississippi.

may be, maybe

Be careful not to confuse the verb phrase *may be* with the adverb *maybe* (meaning "perhaps").

In some of Emily Dickinson's poems, the speaker *may be* the poet herself; in others, the speaker is clearly a different persona.

The most memorable, and *maybe* the most ineffectual, character in T. S. Eliot's poetry is J. Alfred Prufrock.

plurals that do not end in *-s*

The plurals of certain nouns from Greek and Latin are formed as they were in their original language. Words such as *criteria, media,* and *phenomena* are plural and should not be treated as if they are singular (*criterion, medium, phenomenon*).

In "Ars Poetica," Archibald MacLeish seems to deny that meaning is the most important *criterion* for the evaluation of poetry.

The *phenomena* discussed by the "learn'd astronomer" in Whitman's poem may have included planetary orbits and the influence of the moon on the tides.

raise, rise

Raise is a transitive verb that usually takes a direct object. *Rise* is intransitive and never takes a direct object.

Suspense *raises* readers' expectations and moti-

vates them to continue reading a story to see how the plot will be resolved.

Some of Flannery O'Connor's best short stories can be found in her collection entitled *Everything That Rises Must Converge.*

set, sit

Do not confuse these verbs. *Set* is a transitive verb meaning "to put (something) in a certain place." Its principal parts are *set, setting, set, set. Sit* is an intransitive verb meaning "to be seated." Its principal parts are *sit, sitting, sat, sat.*

Phillis Wheatley's poem is so complimentary to Washington that it seems to *set* him on a pedestal.

As Mrs. Mallard *sits* upstairs alone, she suddenly realizes that the death of her husband has freed her to live for herself.

that, which, who

Use the relative pronoun *that* to refer to things or people. Use *which* only for things, and *who* only for people.

The modern poet *that* Lee liked best was Sylvia Plath.

The Romantic movement, *which* emphasized inner feelings and emotions, took place during the early 1800's.

The poet *who* was the first to read his work at a presidential inauguration was Robert Frost.

unique

Because *unique* means "one of a kind," you should not use it carelessly instead of the words "interesting" or "unusual." Avoid such illogical expressions as "most unique," "very unique," and "extremely unique."

Some critics have argued that its themes and style make Herman Melville's *Moby-Dick* unique in the history of the American novel.

who, whom

In formal writing, remember to use *who* only as a subject in clauses and sentences and *whom* only as an object.

Walt Whitman, *who* grieved profoundly at Lincoln's assassination, rendered his tribute to the slain president in a long elegy entitled "When Lilacs Last in the Dooryard Bloom'd."

F. Scott Fitzgerald, *whom* many have heralded as the voice of the Jazz Age, wrote the American literary classic *The Great Gatsby.*

Speaking and Listening Handbook

Language is both spoken and written. The literature in this book is written, which is one form of communication, but most of your communication is probably oral. Oral communication involves both speaking and listening. Having strong speaking and listening skills benefits you both in your school life and your life outside of school.

Many of the assignments accompanying the literature in this textbook involve speaking and listening. This handbook identifies some of the terminology related to speaking and listening, both the oral communication you experience every day and the assignments you may do in conjunction with the literature in this book.

Oral Communication

You use many different kinds of oral communication each day. When you communicate with your friends, when you communicate with your teachers or your parents, when you interact with a cashier in a store, you are communicating orally. In addition to ordinary, everyday conversation, oral communication includes class discussions, speeches, interviews, presentations, and debates. When you communicate face to face, you usually use more than your voice to get your message across. If you communicate by telephone, however, you must rely solely on your verbal skills.

The following terms will give you a better understanding of the many elements that are a part of oral communication.

ARTICULATION is the process of forming sounds into words; it is the way in which the tongue, teeth, lower jaw, and soft palate are used to produce speech sounds.

BODY LANGUAGE refers to the use of facial expressions, eye contact, gestures, posture, and movement to communicate a feeling or idea.

CONNOTATION is the set of associations a word calls to mind. The connotations of the words you choose influence the message you send. For example, most people respond more favorably to being described as "slim" rather than as "skinny." The connotation of *slim* is more appealing than that of *skinny*.

EYE CONTACT is direct visual contact with another person's eyes.

FEEDBACK is the set of verbal and nonverbal reactions that indicate to a speaker that a message has been received and understood.

GESTURES are the movements made with arms, hands, face, and fingers to communicate.

INFLECTION refers to the rise and fall in the pitch of the voice in speaking; it is also called **intonation.**

LISTENING is understanding and interpreting sound in a meaningful way. You listen differently for different purposes.

Listening for key information: For example, when a teacher gives an assignment, or when someone gives you directions to a place, you listen for key information.

Listening for main points: In a classroom exchange of ideas or information, or while watching a television documentary, you listen for main points.

Listening critically: When you evaluate a performance, song, or a persuasive or political speech, you listen critically, questioning and judging the speaker's message.

NONVERBAL COMMUNICATION is communication without the use of words. People communicate nonverbally through gestures, facial expressions, postures, and body movements. Sign language is an entire language based on nonverbal communication.

PROJECTION is speaking in such a way that the voice carries clearly to an audience. It's important to project your voice when speaking in a large space like a classroom or an auditorium.

VOCAL DELIVERY is the way in which you present a message. Your vocal delivery involves all of the following elements:

    Volume: the loudness or quietness of your voice
    Pitch: the high or low quality of your voice
    Rate: the speed at which you speak; also called *pace*
    Stress: the amount of emphasis placed on different syllables in a word or on different words in a sentence

All of these elements individually, and the way in which they are combined, contribute to the meaning of a spoken message.

Speaking and Listening Situations

The following are some of the many types of situations in which you apply your speaking and listening skills.

AUDIENCE Your audience in any situation refers to the person or people to whom you direct your message. An audience can be a group of people sitting in a classroom or auditorium observing a performance, or it may be just one person to whom you address a question or a comment. When preparing for any speaking situation, it's useful to analyze your audience, learning what you can about their background, interests, and attitudes so that you can tailor your message to them.

DEBATE A debate is a formal public-speaking situation in which participants prepare and present arguments on opposing sides of a question, stated as a **proposition**. The proposition must be controversial: It must concern an issue that may be solved in two different, valid ways.

The two sides in a debate are the *affirmative* (pro) and the *negative* (con). The affirmative side argues in favor of the proposition, while the negative side argues against it. The affirmative side begins the debate, since it is seeking a change in belief or policy. The opposing sides take turns presenting their arguments, and each side has an opportunity for *rebuttal*, in which they may challenge or question the other side's argument.

GROUP DISCUSSION results when three or more people meet to solve a common problem, arrive at a decision, or answer a question of mutual interest. Group discussion is one of the most widely used forms of interpersonal communication in modern society. **Meetings** are a kind of organized group discussion for a specific purpose.

INTERVIEW An interview is a form of interaction in which one person, the interviewer, asks questions of another person, the interviewee. Interviews may take place for many purposes: to obtain information, to discover a person's suitability for a job or a college, or to inform the public of a notable person's opinions.

ORAL INTERPRETATION is the reading or speaking of a piece of literature aloud for an audience. Oral interpretation involves giving expression to the ideas, meaning, or even the structure of a piece of literature. The speaker interprets the piece through his or her vocal delivery. **Storytelling**, in which a speaker reads or tells a story expressively, is a form of oral interpretation.

PANEL DISCUSSION is a group discussion on a topic of interest common to all members of a panel and to a listening audience. A panel is usually composed of four to six experts on a particular topic who are brought together to share information and opinions.

PANTOMIME is a form of nonverbal communication in which an idea or a story is communicated completely through the use of gesture, body language, and facial expressions, without any words at all.

PARLIAMENTARY PROCEDURE refers to the set of rules used to conduct a meeting in an orderly manner. Rules make discussions more efficient and protect the rights of individuals attending the meeting.

All of the business conducted according to parliamentary procedure is handled through motions. *Motions* are proposals for action. For example, besides main motions that set forth the items of business that will be considered, a motion can be made to *adjourn*—or end the meeting—or to *amend,* or alter the wording of a motion.

These are the main principles of parliamentary procedure:

1. Only one item of business may be considered at a time.
2. Everyone has a right to express an opinion, and each opinion is treated as valuable.
3. Every member of the group has the right to vote, and each vote is counted as equal.
4. The group always follows the decision of the majority.

READERS THEATRE is a dramatic reading of a piece of literature. Participants take parts from a story or play and read aloud in expressive voices. Sets and costumes are not part of the performance; participants remain seated as they deliver their lines.

ROLE PLAY To role-play is to take the role of a person or character and act out a situation, speaking, acting, and responding in the manner of the character.

SPEECH A speech is an address given to an audience. A speech may be **impromptu**—delivered on the spur of the moment with no preparation—or formally prepared and delivered for a specific occasion.

- *Purposes*: The most common purposes of speeches are to persuade (e.g., political speeches), to entertain, to explain, and to inform.

- *Occasions*: Different occasions call for different types of speeches. Speeches given on these occasions could be persuasive, entertaining, or informative, as appropriate. The following are common occasions for speeches.

  Introduction: Introducing a speaker or presenter at a meeting or assembly

  Presentation: Giving an award or acknowledging the contributions of someone

  Acceptance: Accepting an award or tribute

  Keynote: An inspirational address given at a large meeting or convention

  Commencement: A celebration and honoring of the graduates of a school or university

RESEARCH HANDBOOK

Many of the assignments and activities in this literature book require you to find out more about your topic. Whenever you need ideas, details, or information, you must conduct research. You can find information by using library resources and computer resources, as well as by interviewing experts in a field.

Before you begin, create a research plan that lists the questions you want answered about your topic. Then decide which sources will best provide answers to those questions. When gathering information, it is important to use a variety of sources and not to rely on one main source of information. It is also important to document where you find different pieces of information you use so that you can cite those sources in your work.

The suggestions that follow can help you locate your sources.

Library Resources

Libraries contain many sources of information in both print and electronic form. You'll save time if you plan your research before actually going to the library. Make a list of the information you think you will need, and for each item list possible sources for the information. Here are some sources to consider:

NONFICTION BOOKS An excellent starting point for researching your topic, nonfiction books can provide either broad coverage or specific details, depending on the book. To find appropriate nonfiction books, use the library catalog, which may be in card files or in electronic form on computers. In either case, you can search by author, title, or subject; in a computer catalog, you can also search by key word. When you find the listing for a book you want, print it out or copy down the title, author, and call number. The call number, which also appears on the book's spine, will help you locate the book in the library.

NEWSPAPERS AND MAGAZINES Books are often not the best places for finding up-to-the-minute information. Instead, you might try newspapers and magazines. To find information about an event that occurred on a specific date, go directly to newspapers and magazines for that date. To find articles on a particular topic, use indexes like the *Readers' Guide to Periodical Literature*, which lists magazine articles under subject

headings. For each article that you want, jot down the title, author (if given), page number or numbers, and the name and date of the magazine in which the article appears. If your library does not have the magazine you need, either as a separate issue or on microfilm, you may still be able to obtain photocopies of the article through an interlibrary loan.

REFERENCE WORKS The following important reference materials can also help you with your research.

- *General encyclopedias* have articles on thousands of topics and are a good starting point for your research, although they shouldn't be used as primary sources.
- *Specialized encyclopedias* contain articles in particular subject areas, such as science, music, or art.
- *Biographical dictionaries and indexes* contain brief articles on people and often suggest where to find more information.
- *Almanacs* provide statistics and data on current events and act as a calendar for the upcoming year.
- *Atlases,* or books of maps, usually include geographical facts and may also include information like population and weather statistics.
- *Indexes and bibliographies,* such as the *Readers' Guide to Periodical Literature*, tell you in what publications you can find specific information, articles, or shorter works (such as poems or essays).
- *Vertical files* (drawers in file cabinets) hold pamphlets, booklets, and government publications that often provide current information.

Computer Research

The Internet Use the Internet to get up-to-the-minute information on virtually any topic. The Internet provides access to a multitude of resource-rich sources such as news media, museums, colleges and universities, and government institutions. There are a number of indexes and directories organized by subject to help you locate information on the Internet, including Yahoo!, the World Wide Web Virtual Library, the Kids Web, and the Webcrawler. These indexes and directories will help you find direct links to information related to your topic.

Internet Sources and Addresses

- *Yahoo! Directory* allows you to do word searches or link directly to your topic by clicking on such subjects as the arts, computers, entertainment, or government.
  http://www.yahoo.com

- *World Wide Web Virtual Library* is a comprehensive and easy-to-use subject catalog that provides direct links to academic subjects in alphabetical order.
  http://celtic.stanford.edu/vlib/Overview.html

- *Kids Web* supplies links to reference materials, such as dictionaries, *Bartlett's Familiar Quotations,* a thesaurus, and a world fact book.
  http://www.npac.syr.edu/textbook/kidsweb/

- *Webcrawler* helps you to find links to information about your topic that are available on the Internet when you type in a concise term or key word.
  http://www.webcrawler.com

CD-ROM References

Other sources that you can access using a computer are available on CD-ROM. The Wilson Disk, Newsquest, the *Readers' Guide to Periodical Literature,* and many other useful indexes are available on CD-ROM, as are encyclopedias, almanacs, atlases, and other reference works. Check your library to see which are available.

Interviews as Research Sources

People who are experts in their field or who have experience or knowledge relevant to your topic are excellent sources for your research. If such people are available to you, the way to obtain information from them is through an interview. Follow these guidelines to make your interview successful and productive:

- Make an appointment at a time convenient to the person you want to interview, and arrange to meet in a place where he or she will feel comfortable talking freely.

- If necessary, do research in advance to help you prepare the questions you will ask.

- Before the interview, list the questions you will ask, wording them so that they encourage specific answers. Avoid questions that can be answered simply with *yes* or *no.*

- Make an audiotape or videotape of the interview if possible. If not, write down the answers as accurately as you can.

- Include the date of the interview at the top of your notes or on the tape.

- Follow up with a thank-you note or phone call to the person you interviewed.

Sources for a Multimedia Presentation

When preparing a multimedia presentation, keep in mind that you'll need to use some of your research findings to illustrate or support your main ideas when you actually give the presentation. Do research to find media support, such as visuals, CDs, and so on—in addition to those media you might create yourself. Here are some media that may be useful as both sources and illustrations:

- Musical recordings on audio cassette or compact disk (CD) (often available at libraries)
- Videos that you prepare yourself
- Fine art reproductions (often available at libraries and museums)
- Photographs that you or others have taken
- Computer presentations using slide shows, graphics, and so on
- Video or audio cassette recordings of interviews that you conduct.

Crediting Sources

Whatever form you use to present your research results, remember to credit your sources for any ideas you use that are not common knowledge and are not your own. In addition, be sure that you acknowledge passages or distinctive phrases that come from a source. In written work, credit others' ideas or words with footnotes, endnotes, or parenthetical notes.

Failure to credit sources properly is **plagiarism,** the presenting of someone else's words or ideas as your own. Plagiarism is a form of stealing. Words and ideas may not seem as tangible as physical property, but they are forms of intellectual property. As you know from your own experience, it takes hard work to formulate a new idea or to find just the right phrase to describe something. Acknowledge this work.

INDEX OF AUTHORS AND TITLES

INDEX OF SKILLS

LITERARY TERMS

WRITING SKILLS

SPEAKING AND LISTENING

PROJECTS

LIFE AND WORK SKILLS

BACKGROUND

Culture

History

Literature

Media

Philosophy

Popular culture

Social Studies

INDEX OF FINE ART

O'Connor. "Everyday Use" from *In Love & Trouble: Stories of Black Women*, copyright © 1973 by Alice Walker. Reprinted by permission of Harcourt Brace & Company.

Joy Harjo
"Suspended" by Joy Harjo from *In Short: A Collection of Brief Creative Nonfiction*, edited by Judith Kitchen and Mary Paumier Jones. Copyright © 1996. Reprinted by permission of the author.

HarperCollins Publishers, Inc.
"The Boys' Ambition" from *Life on the Mississippi* by Mark Twain. "The Notorious Jumping Frog of Calaveras County" from *Sketches New and Old* by Mark Twain. Excerpt from *Pilgrim at Tinker Creek* by Annie Dillard. Copyright © 1974 by Annie Dillard. "Bidwell Ghost" from *Baptism of Desire* by Louise Erdrich. Copyright © 1990 by Louise Erdrich. From *Dust Tracks on a Road* by Zora Neale Hurston. Copyright 1942 by Zora Neale Hurston. Copyright renewed 1970 by John C. Hurston. "Here Is New York" from *Essays by E. B. White* by E. B. White. Copyright 1949 by E. B. White. Copyright renewed 1977 by E. B. White. All rights reserved. Reprinted by permission of HarperCollins Publishers, Inc.

HarperCollins Publishers, Inc., and Faber and Faber Ltd.
"Mirror" from *Crossing the Water* by Sylvia Plath. Copyright © 1963 by Ted Hughes. Originally appeared in *The New Yorker*. Reprinted by permission of HarperCollins Publishers, Inc., and Faber and Faber Ltd.

Harvard University Press
"I heard a Fly buzz—when I died" (#465), "There's a certain Slant of light" (#258), "My life closed twice before its close—" (#1732), "The soul selects her own Society—" (#303), "Because I could not stop for Death—" (#712), and "There is a solitude of space" (#1695) reprinted by permission of the publishers and the Trustees of Amherst College from *The Poems of Emily Dickinson*, Thomas H. Johnson, ed., Cambridge, Mass.: The Belknap Press of Harvard University Press, Copyright © 1951, 1955, 1979, 1983 by The President and Fellows of Harvard College.

Hill and Wang, a division of Farrar, Straus & Giroux, Inc.
Excerpts from "Sinners in the Hands of an Angry God" from *Jonathan Edwards: Representative Selections* edited by Clarence H. Faust and Thomas H. Johnson. Copyright © 1935, 1962 by Hill and Wang, Inc. Reprinted by permission of Hill and Wang, a division of Farrar, Straus & Giroux, Inc.

Henry Holt and Company, Inc.
"The Gift Outright," "Acquainted With the Night," and "Stopping by Woods on a Snowy Evening" from *The Poetry of Robert Frost*, edited by Edward Connery Lathem. Copyright 1942, 1951, © 1956 by Robert Frost. Copyright © 1970 by Lesley Frost Ballantine, copyright 1923, 1928, © 1969 by Henry Holt and Company, Inc. Reprinted by permission of Henry Holt & Company, Inc. "Birches," "Out, Out—," and "Mending Wall" from *The Poetry of Robert Frost* edited by Edward Connery Lathem. Copyright 1944, © 1958 by Robert Frost, © 1967

by Lesley Frost Ballantine, copyright 1916, 1930, 1939, © 1969 by Henry Holt and Company, Inc.

Houghton Mifflin Company
From "The Navajo Origin Legend" in *Navajo Legends*, collected and translated by Washington Matthews. "A Noiseless Patient Spider" and "When I Heard the Learn'd Astronomer" from *Complete Poetry and Selected Prose of Walt Whitman*, edited by J. E. Miller, Jr. From *The Mortgaged Heart* by Carson McCullers. Copyright 1940, 1941, 1942, 1945, 1948, 1949, 1953, © 1956, 1959, 1963, 1971 by Floria V. Lasky, Executrix of the Estate of Carson McCullers. "Ars Poetica" from *New and Collected Poems 1917–1982* by Archibald MacLeish. Copyright © 1985 by the Estate of Archibald MacLeish. Reprinted by permission of Houghton Mifflin Company. All rights reserved.

International Creative Management, Inc.
"Ambush" from *The Things They Carried* by Tim O'Brien. Copyright © 1990 by Tim O'Brien. Reprinted by permission of International Creative Management, Inc.

Joelsongs
"Allentown" by Billy Joel. Copyright © 1981 Joelsongs. All rights reserved. Used by permission of Joelsongs.

Johnson Publishing Company, Inc.
From *My Bondage and My Freedom* by Frederick Douglass. Copyright 1970. Used by permission.

Alfred A. Knopf, Inc.
From *The Woman Warrior* by Maxine Hong Kingston. Copyright © 1975, 1976 by Maxine Hong Kingston. "The Brown Chest" from *The Afterlife and Other Stories* by John Updike. Copyright © 1994 by John Updike. "Dream Variations," "Ardella," and "Refugee in America" from *Collected Poems* by Langston Hughes. Copyright © 1994 by the Estate of Langston Hughes. "A Noiseless Flash" from *Hiroshima* by John Hersey. Copyright 1946 and renewed 1974 by John Hersey. Originally appeared in *The New Yorker*. "Anecdote of the Jar" from *Collected Poems* by Wallace Stevens. Copyright 1923 and renewed 1951 by Wallace Stevens. "Of Modern Poetry" from *Collected Poems* by Wallace Stevens. Copyright 1942 by Wallace Stevens and renewed 1970 by Holly Stevens. "The Negro Speaks of Rivers" and "I, Too" from *Selected Poems* by Langston Hughes. Copyright 1926 by Alfred A. Knopf, Inc., and renewed 1954 by Langston Hughes. From *Of Plymouth Plantation* by William Bradford, edited by Samuel Eliot Morison. Copyright 1952 by Samuel Eliot Morison and renewed 1980 by Emily M. Beck. Reprinted by permission of Alfred A. Knopf, Inc.

Latin American Literary Review Press
"Freeway 280" by Lorna Dee Cervantes. Reprinted by permission of the publisher, *Latin American Literary Review*, Volume 15, No. 10, 1977, Pittsburgh, Pa.

Hal Leonard Corporation
"Hammer and a Nail" words and music by Emily Saliers. Copyright © 1990 EMI Virgin Songs, Inc. and Godhap Music. All rights controlled and administered by EMI Virgin Songs, Inc. All rights reserved. International copyright secured. Used by permission.

Liveright Publishing Corporation
"Runagate Runagate" copyright © 1966 by Robert Hayden, from *Collected Poems of Robert Hayden* by Frederick Glaysher, editor. "Frederick Douglass," copyright © 1966 by Robert Hayden, from *Angle of Ascent: New and Selected Poems* by Robert Hayden. "anyone lived in a pretty how town," copyright 1940, © 1968, 1991 by the Trustees for the E. E. Cummings Trust, "old age sticks," copyright © 1958, 1986, 1991 by the Trustees for the E. E. Cummings Trust, from *Complete Poems: 1904–1962* by E. E. Cummings. Edited by George J. Firmage. "Storm Ending" from *Cane* by Jean Toomer. Copyright 1923 by Boni & Liveright, renewed 1951 by Jean Toomer. Reprinted by permission of Liveright Publishing Corporation.

Ellen C. Masters
"Lucinda Matlock" from *Spoon River Anthology* by Edgar Lee Masters, published by Macmillan Publishing Company.

Archives of Claude McKay
"The Tropics in New York" from *The Poems of Claude McKay* by Claude McKay, Harcourt Brace, publisher, copyright © 1981. Reprinted by permission of the Archives of Claude McKay, Carl Cowl, administrator.

N. Scott Momaday
From *The Names: A Memoir by N. Scott Momaday,* published by Harper & Row Publishers, Inc., Copyright © 1976 by N. Scott Momaday. Reprinted by permission of the author.

New Directions Publishing Corporation
"Heat" (Heat, Part II of Garden) and "Pear Tree" by H. D., *Collected Poems, 1912–1944.* Copyright © 1982 by the Estate of Hilda Doolittle. "In a Station of the Metro" and "The River-Merchant's Wife: A Letter" by Ezra Pound, from *Personae.* Copyright 1926 by Ezra Pound. "The Great Figure," "The Red Wheelbarrow" and "This Is Just to Say" by William Carlos Williams, from *Collected Poems Volume 1: 1909–1939.* Copyright 1938 by New Directions Publishing Corporation. Excerpts from "A Few Don'ts by an Imagist" (A Retrospect) from *Literary Essays of Ezra Pound.* Copyright © 1935 by Ezra Pound. Reprinted by permission.

The New York Times
"Onomatopoeia" by William Safire from *You Could Look It Up.* Copyright © 1988 by The Cobbett Corporation. Originally appeared in *The New York Times.* Reprinted by permission.

W. W. Norton & Company, Inc.
From "Civil Disobedience," reprinted from *Walden and Civil Disobedience* by Henry David Thoreau, edited by Owen Thomas. Copyright ©1966 by W. W. Norton & Company, Inc. "Who Burns for the Perfection of Paper" from *City of Coughing and Dead Radiators* by Martin Espada. Copyright © 1993 by Martin Espada. Reprinted by permission of W. W. Norton & Company, Inc.

W. W. Norton & Company, Inc., and Adrienne Rich
"In a Classroom" from *Time's Power: Poems 1985–1988* by Adrienne Rich. Copyright ©1989 by Adrienne Rich. All rights reserved. Used by permission of W. W. Norton & Company, Inc., and the author.

Naomi Shihab Nye
"Mint Snowball" by Naomi Shihab Nye. Reprinted by permission of the author.

Harold Ober Associates, Inc.
"The Corn Planting" from *Sherwood Anderson Short Stories*, edited by Maxwell Geismar. © 1962 by Eleanor Anderson. "A Black Man Talks of Reaping" by Arna Bontemps. Copyright © 1963 by Arna Bontemps. Reprinted by permission of Harold Ober Associates Incorporated.

Simon J. Ortiz
"Hunger in New York City" from *Going for the Rain: Poems* by Simon J. Ortiz. Published by Harper & Row. Reprinted by permission of Simon J. Ortiz.

Grace Paley c/o Elaine Markson Literary Agency, Inc.
"Anxiety" from *Later the Same Day* by Grace Paley, Farrar, Straus and Giroux, 1985. Copyright © 1985 by Grace Paley. All rights reserved. Reprinted by permission of the author, c/o Elaine Markson Literary Agency, Inc.

Princeton University Press
From *Walden: The Writings of Henry D. Thoreau,* edited by J. Lyndon Shanley. Copyright © 1971 Princeton University Press. Reprinted by permission of Princeton University Press.

Random House, Inc.
"The Nobel Prize Acceptance Speech" by William Faulkner, © 1950 The Nobel Foundation. "The Unknown Citizen" from *W. H. Auden: Collected Poems* by W. H. Auden, edited by Edward Mendelson. Copyright 1940 and renewed 1968 by W. H. Auden. "The Writer in the Family" from *Lives of the Poets* by E. L. Doctorow. Copyright © 1984 by E. L. Doctorow. "Cats" from *Living Out Loud* by Anna Quindlen. Copyright © 1987 by Anna Quindlen. "Race at Morning" from *Big Woods* by William Faulkner. Copyright © 1955 by The Curtis Publishing Company. "Gold Glade" from *Selected Poems 1923–1975* by Robert Penn Warren. Copyright © 1957 by Robert Penn Warren. Reprinted by permission of Random House, Inc.

Russell & Volkening as agents for the author
"Average Waves in Unprotected Waters" by Anne Tyler. Copyright © 1977 by Anne Tyler. Originally published by *The New Yorker.* Reprinted by permission of Russell & Volkening as agents for the author.

Estate of Ricardo Sánchez
"i yearn" by Ricardo Sánchez. Copyright © 1975 by Ricardo Sánchez. Reprinted by permission of the Estate of Ricardo Sánchez.

Scribner, A Division of Simon & Schuster, Inc.
"In Another Country" is reprinted with permission of Scribner, a Division of Simon & Schuster, from *Men Without Women* by Ernest Hemingway. Copyright 1927 by Charles Scribner's Sons. Copyright renewed 1955 by Ernest Hemingway. F. Scott Fitzgerald, "Winter Dreams" by F. Scott Fitzgerald from *All The Sad Young Men.* Copyright 1922 by Frances Scott Fitzgerald

Lanahan; copyright renewed 1950. "Gulf War Journal" is reprinted with the permission of Scribner, a Division of Simon & Schuster, from *A Woman at War: Storming Kuwait With the U. S. Marines* by Molly Moore. Copyright © 1993 by Molly Moore. "Luke Havergal" from *Collected Poems* by Edwin Arlington Robinson, published by Charles Scribner's Sons. "Richard Cory" from *The Children of the Night* by Edwin Arlington Robinson, published by Charles Scribner's Sons. "The Far and the Near" is reprinted with the permission of Scribner, a Division of Simon & Schuster, from *Death to Morning* by Thomas Wolfe. Copyright 1935 by International Magazine Company; copyright renewed © 1963 by Paul Gitlin.

Signet Classic, an imprint of Dutton Signet, a division of Penguin Books USA Inc.
"Richard Bone" from *Spoon River Anthology* by Edgar Lee Masters, published by Penguin USA.

Simon & Schuster, Inc.
From *Lonesome Dove* by Larry McMurtry, is reprinted with the permission of Simon & Schuster. Copyright © 1985 by Larry McMurtry. "Poetry" by Marianne Moore is reprinted with the permission of Simon & Schuster from *Collected Poems of Marianne Moore.* Copyright 1935 by Marianne Moore; copyright renewed © 1963 by Marianne Moore and T. S. Eliot.

Estate of William Stafford
"Traveling Through the Dark" from *Stories That Could Be True: New and Collected Poems* by William Stafford. Copyright © 1960 by William Stafford. Reprinted by permission of the Estate of William Stafford.

Estate of Donald E. Stanford
"Huswifery" is reprinted from *The Poems of Edward Taylor* edited by Donald E. Stanford, copyright © 1960 Donald E. Stanford.

Sterling Lord Literistic, Inc.
"The Crisis, Number 1," excerpts from "The Crisis, Number 1" by Thomas Paine, published in *Citizen Tom Paine*, edited by Howard Fast. Copyright © 1945 by Howard Fast. Reprinted by permission of Sterling Lord Literistic, Inc.

Syracuse University Press
From "The Iroquois Constitution" from Arthur C. Parker, "The Constitution of the Five Nations" in *Parker on the Iroquois*, edited with an introduction by William N. Fenton, Syracuse, N.Y., Syracuse University Press, 1968. By permission of the publisher.

Terry Teachout
Excerpt from "The Case of the Missing Laugh Track" by Terry Teachout, published in *Civilization*, Aug/Sept 1997.

Rosemary A. Thurber
"The Night the Ghost Got In" copyright 1933, © 1961 by James Thurber. From *My Life and Hard Times*, published by Harper & Row. Reprinted by permission.

Time Life Syndication
"Iron Bird" by Steve Wulf from *Time Magazine*, September 11, 1995. Copyright ©1995 Time Inc. Reprinted by permission.

The University of Nebraska Press
Reprinted from *The Journals of the Lewis and Clark Expedition, July 28–November 1, 1805* (volume 5), edited by Gary Moulton by permission of the University of Nebraska Press. Copyright 1988 by the University of Nebraska Press.

The University of North Carolina Press
"To His Excellency, General Washington" and lines from "An Hymn to the Evening" from *The Poems of Phillis Wheatley,* edited by Julian D. Mason, Jr. Copyright © 1966, 1989 by The University of North Carolina Press. Used by permission of the publisher.

University of Texas Press and the author
"El Corrido de Gregorio Cortez" from *With His Pistol in His Hand: A Border Ballad and Its Hero* by Americo Paredes, Copyright © 1958, renewed 1986. By permission of the author and the University of Texas Press.

University Press of New England
Garrett Kaoru Hongo, "What For" from *Yellow Light,* © 1982 by Garrett Kaoru Hongo, Wesleyan University Press, by permission of University Press of New England. Colleen McElroy, "For My Children" from *What Madness Brought Me Here,* © 1990 by Colleen McElroy, Wesleyan University Press, by permission of University Press of New England. Yusef Komunyakaa, "Camouflaging the Chimera" from *Neon Vernacular,* © 1993 originally published in *Dien Cai Dau,* © 1988 by Yusef Komunyakaa, Wesleyan University Press, by permission of University Press of New England.

Viking Penguin, a division of Penguin Books USA, Inc.
The Crucible by Arthur Miller. Copyright 1952, 1953, 1954, renewed © 1980, 1981, 1982 by Arthur Miller. "The Turtle" from *The Grapes of Wrath* by John Steinbeck. Copyright 1939, renewed © 1967 by John Steinbeck. Used by permission of Viking Penguin, a division of Penguin Books USA Inc.

Albert Whitman & Co.
"Pecos Bill Becomes a Coyote" from *Pecos Bill The Greatest Cowboy of All Time* by James Cloyd Bowman. Copyright © 1937, 1964 by Albert Whitman & Company. Reprinted by permission of the publisher. All rights reserved.

Darryl Babe Wilson
"Diamond Island: Alcatraz" by Darryl Babe Wilson. Copyright © 1991 by Darryl Babe Wilson. Reprinted by permission of the author.

Writers House, Inc.
"Why We Can't Wait," from "Letter From Birmingham Jail" by Martin Luther King, Jr., Copyright 1963 by Martin Luther King, Jr., copyright renewed 1991 by Coretta Scott King. Reprinted by arrangement with The Heirs to the Estate of Martin Luther King, Jr., c/o Writers House, Inc. as agent for the proprietor.

Note: Every effort has been made to locate the copyright owner of material reprinted in this book. Omissions brought to our attention will be corrected in subsequent editions.

NASA; **357:** Ken Karp Photography; **361:** *Early Morning at Cold Spring*, 1850, oil on canvas, 60" x 48", Asher B. Durand, Collection of the Montclair Art Museum, Montclair, New Jersey; **362:** *Ralph Waldo Emerson* (detail), Frederick Gutekunst/National Portrait Gallery, Smithsonian Institution, Washington, D.C./Art Resource, NY; **365:** *Sunset*, 1856, Frederick E. Church, Oil on canvas, 24" x 36", Collection of Munson-Williams-Proctor Institute Museum of Art, Utica, New York, Proctor Collection; **368:** (background) Frank Whitney/The Image Bank; **369:** Leonard Harris/Stock, Boston; **372:** The Granger Collection, New York; **374–375:** Owen Franken/PNI; **380:** The Granger Collection, New York; **384:** (background) NASA; (center) © Spencer Jarnagan; (bottom) Epic Records; **385** (top) & (bottom) & **387:** Corel Professional Photos CD-ROM™; **388:** NASA; **389:** Corel Professional Photos CD-ROM™; **393:** *Walden Pond Revisited*, 1942, N.C. Wyeth, tempera, possibly mixed with other media on panel, 42" x 48" Collection of the Brandywine River Museum, Bequest of Miss Carolyn Wyeth; **394:** The Granger Collection, New York; **396:** *Room With a Balcony*, Adolph von Menzel, Staatliche Museen Preubischer Kulturbesitz, Nationgalerie, Berlin; **399:** Corel Professional Photos CD-ROM™; **400:** Frederic Edwin Church, American, 1826–1900. *Twilight in the Wilderness*, 1860s. Oil on canvas, 101.6 x 162.6 cm. © The Cleveland Museum of Art, 1997, Mr. and Mrs. William H. Marlett Fund, 1965.233; **401:** Darrel Gulin/Tony Stone Images; **404:** The Granger Collection, New York; **408:** Culver Pictures, Inc.; **412–413:** *The Reaper*, c.1881, Louis C. Tiffany, oil on canvas, National Academy of Design, New York City; **414–415:** *The Lawrence Tree*, 1929, Georgia O'Keeffe, Wadsworth Atheneum, Hartford, The Ella Gallup Sumner and Mary Catlin Sumner Collection, © 1997 The Georgia O'Keeffe Foundation/Artists Rights Society (ARS), New York; **418:** (background) NASA; (tr) *Langston Hughes* (detail), c. 1925, Winold Reiss, The National Portrait Gallery, Smithsonian Institution, Washington, D.C./Art Resource, New York; (br) Photo by M&A Productions; **419:** *Nobody Around Here Calls Me Citizen*, 1943, Robert Gwathmey, oil on canvas, H. 14¼" x W. 17", Collection Frederick R. Weisman Art Museum at the University of Minnesota, Minneapolis, Bequest of Hudson Walker from the Ione and Hudson Walker Collection. © Estate of Robert Gwathmey/Licensed by VAGA, New York, NY; **420:** *Mandolin*, Rosa Ibarra, Courtesy of the artist; **421:** NASA; **422:** Ken Karp Photography; **426:** Bob Daemmrich/Stock, Boston; **427:** (left) Full Unabridged cover from "Great Short Works of Herman Melville" by Herman Melville. Selection reprinted by permission of HarperCollins Publishers; (center) Reprinted by permission of Barnes & Noble, Inc. Photograph provided by Superstock, Inc.; **428–429:** *Detail of Battle of Cedar Creek* (partial study for larger painting), Julian Scott, Historical Society of Plainfield, New Jersey. Photograph by John Lei/Omni Photo-Communications; **429:** (left) *Portrait of Abraham Lincoln*, William Willard, National Portrait Gallery, Smithsonian Institution, Washington, D.C./Art Resource, NY; (right) The Granger Collection, New York; **430:** (tc) Chicago Historical Society; (1855) & (1859 Darwin) & (1859

John Brown) & (1865) & (1876) & (1877) The Granger Collection, New York; (1864) National Portrait Gallery, Smithsonian Institution/Art Resource, NY; **431:** (1881) Corbis-Bettmann; (1886) & (1888) & (1903) & (1908) The Granger Collection, New York; (1905) *Albert Einstein*, Tomassetti/Superstock; **432:** (top) New York Public Library/Rare Book Division; (bottom) Courtesy of the Library of Congress; **433:** (tl) & (tr) Courtesy of the Library of Congress; (bottom) Corbis-Bettmann; **434:** (top) Courtesy of the Library of Congress; (bottom) Nebraska State Historical Society; **436:** (bottom) North Wind Picture Archives; **437:** (tc) Chicago Historical Society; **438:** (top) *Sampler* (detail), 1797 by Mary Wiggin. 18x 21 1/2." Philadelphia Museum of Art, Whitman Sampler Collection/Given by Pet, Incorporated; (center) *Samuel Langhorne Clemens (Mark Twain)* (detail), 1935, Frank Edwin Larson, National Portrait Gallery, Smithsonian Institution, Washington, D.C./Art Resource, New York; **439:** *Fight for the Standard*, oil on canvas, H 26¾ inches, W 21½ inches, Wadsworth Atheneum, Hartford. The Ella Gallup Sumner and Mary Catlin Sumner Collection Fund; **440:** (top) UPI/Corbis-Bettmann; (rc) Museum of the Confederacy, Richmond, Virginia, Photography by Katherine Wetzel; (bottom) The Granger Collection, New York; **443:** Courtesy of the Library of Congress; **444:** Courtesy National Archives; **446:** *Young Soldier: Separate Study of a Soldier Giving Water to a Wounded Companion*, 1861 (detail), Winslow Homer, Oil, gouache, black crayon on canvas, 36x17.5 cm., United States, 1836–1910, Cooper-Hewitt, National Museum of Design, Smithsonian Institution, Gift of Charles Savage Homer, Jr., 1912-12-110, Photo by Ken Pelka, Courtesy of Art Resource, New York; **450:** Sophia Smith Collection, Smith College; **452:** Courtesy of the Library of Congress; **456:** *Frederick Douglass* (detail), c.1844, Attributed to Elisha Hammond, The National Portrait Gallery, Smithsonian Institution, Washington, D.C./Art Resource, New York; **458:** *The Chimney Corner*, 1863, Eastman Johnson, oil on cardboard, 15½ x 13 in., Munson-Williams-Proctor Institute Museum of Art, Utica, New York; Gift of Edmund G. Munson, Jr.; **460:** *A Home on the Mississippi*, 1871, Currier & Ives, The Museum of the City of New York, Harry T. Peters Collection; **466:** Corbis-Bettmann; **468:** Superstock; **469:** The Kobal Collection; **473:** © David Muench 1994; **478:** (left) *Portrait of Abraham Lincoln* (detail), William Willard, National Portrait Gallery, Smithsonian Institution, Washington, D.C./Art Resource, New York; (right) *Robert E. Lee* (detail), 1864–1865, Edward Caledon Bruce, The National Portrait Gallery, Smithsonian Institution, Washington, D.C./Art Resource, New York; **480:** *Abraham Lincoln's Address at the Dedication of the Gettysburg National Cemetery, 19 November 1863*, lithograph, 1905, The Granger Collection, New York; **486:** (background) NASA; (bl) © 1969 Dennis Brack/Black Star; (right) AP/Wide World Photos; **488:** (background) NASA; **489:** *Robert E. Lee*, 1864–1865, Edward Caledon Bruce, The National Portrait Gallery, Smithsonian Institution, Washington, D.C./Art Resource, New York; **493:** *Newspapers in the Trenches '64*, William Ludwell Sheppard, Museum of the Confederacy, Richmond, Virginia, Photography by Katherine Wetzel; **494:** **498:** Courtesy of the Library of Congress; **501 &

502:** The Granger Collection, New York; **506:** (background) NASA; (bl) Sygma; (br) The Washington Post; **507:** D. Hudson/Sygma; **508:** Chip Hires/Liaison International; **510:** Sygma; **512:** (background) NASA; **513:** Courtesy of the Library of Congress; **517:** *The Old Stage Coach of the Plains*, 1901, Frederic Remington, oil on canvas, Amon Carter Museum, Forth Worth; **518:** *Samuel Langhorne Clemens (Mark Twain)* (detail), 1935, Frank Edwin Larson, National Portrait Gallery, Smithsonian Institution, Washington, D.C./Art Resource, New York; **520–521:** *Paddle Steamboat Mississippi*, Shelburne Museum, Shelburne, Vermont, Photo by Ken Burris; **522:** *Plantations on the Mississippi River - from Natchez to New Orleans 1858* (Norman Chart), Historic New Orleans Collection, accession no. 1947.11-v; **525:** *Mark Twain (Samuel L. Clemens) Riding the Celebrated Jumping Frog*, an English caricature, 1872, Frederic Waddy, The Granger Collection, New York; **527 & 532:** The Granger Collection, New York; **534–535:** *Edge of Town*, Charles Burchfield, The Nelson-Atkins Museum of Art, Kansas City, Missouri, (Gift of Friends of Art) 41–52; **540:** Esbin/Anderson/Omni-Photo Communications, Inc.; **544:** *Chief Joseph* (detail), 1878, Cyrenius Hall, National Portrait Gallery, Smithsonian Institution, Washington, D.C./Art Resource, New York; **546 & 549:** Kansas State Historical Society; **551:** National Museum of American History, Smithsonian Institution; **554:** Corbis-Bettmann; **558:** Wayne Lynch/DRK Photo; **562:** Annie Griffiths/DRK Photo; **568:** Courtesy of the Museum of Texas Tech University; **571:** The Granger Collection, New York; **572:** Index Stock Photography, Inc.; **574:** *Headin' Up the Range*, Edward Borein, oil on canvas, 30 by 20 inches, Signed Lower Right: Edward Borein, Photo courtesy of the Gerald Peters Gallery, Santa Fe, New Mexico; **578:** (background) NASA; (br) AP/Wide World Photos; **580–581:** *Open Range*, 1942, Maynard Dixon, oil on canvas, 34½" x 39", Museum of Western Art, Denver. #36.79. Bernard O. Milmoe, Photographer; **584:** (background) NASA; **585:** © Pete Winkle/Stock South/PNI; **589:** *Channel to the Mills*, 1913, Edwin M. Dawes, oil on canvas, 51 x 39½ in. Minneapolis Institute of Arts, anonymous gift; **590:** The Granger Collection, New York; **592–593:** *Afternoon in Piedmont*, c. 1911, Xavier Martínez, Collection of The Oakland Museum of California, Gift of Dr. William S. Porter; **598:** The Granger Collection, New York; **600:** Stock Montage, Inc.; **604:** (left) *Edwin Arlington Robinson* (detail), 1933, Thomas Richard Hood, National Portrait Gallery, Smithsonian Institution, Washington, D.C./Art Resource, New York; (right) *Edgar Lee Masters* (detail), 1946, Francis J. Quirk, National Portrait Gallery, Smithsonian Institution, Washington, D.C./Art Resource, New York; **606:** Horst Oesterwinter/International Stock Photography, Ltd.; **607:** *The Thinker (Portrait of Louis N. Kenton, 1900)*, Thomas Eakins, The Metropolitan Museum of Art, Kennedy Fund, 1917, Copyright © 1967, 1984 by The Metropolitan Museum of Art; **608:** *Barn Dance*, 1950, Grandma Moses, © 1989, Grandma Moses Properties Co., New York; **609:** Joel Greenstein/Omni-Photo Communications, Inc.; **612:** Corbis-Bettmann; **614:** *From Arkansas*, George Schreiber, Sheldon Swope Art Museum, Terre Haute, Indiana; **616:** The Granger Collection,

Watercolor on paper, H. 30½ in., W. 21½ in., The Metropolitan Museum of Art, Gift of the Pennsylvania W.P.A., 1943, (43.46.13), Photograph ©1991 The Metropolitan Museum of Art; **841:** Corel Professional Photos CD-ROM™; **842:** *Girls Skipping*, 1949, Hale Woodruff, oil on canvas, 24" x 32", Private Collection. Courtesy of Michael Rosenfeld Gallery, New York; **843:** Michael Skott/The Image Bank; **846:** (top) *Countee Cullen* (detail), c.1925, Winold Reiss, The National Portrait Gallery, Smithsonian Institution, Washington, D.C./Art Resource, New York; (center) UPI/Corbis-Bettmann; (bottom) *Jean Toomer* (detail), c.1925, Winold Reiss, Gift of Laurence A. Fleischman and Howard Garfinkle with a matching grant from the National Endowment of the Arts, National Portrait Gallery, Smithsonian Institution, Washington, D.C./Art Resource, New York; **848:** *Aspiration*, Aaron Douglas, ©1936 The Estate of Thurlow E. Tibbs, Jr.; **850:** *Hoeing*, 1943, Robert Gwathmey, Oil on canvas, 40 by 60¼ (101.6 by 153), Carnegie Institute Museum of Art, Pittsburgh, Pennsylvania, Patrons Art Fund, 44.3. Photograph by Richard Stoner, © Estate of Robert Gwathmey/Licensed by VAGA, New York, NY; **851:** Corel Professional Photos CD-ROM™; **854:** (background) NASA; (bottom) Rikard Sergei Sanchez/Arte Publico Press; **855 & 856:** Huipil (blouse) from the Tarascans of Michoacan. Embroidered cotton. Museo de Indumentaria Mexicana, Mexico City, D.F. Mexico. Schalkwijk/Art Resource, NY; **857:** NASA; **858:** © Laima Druskis/Stock, Boston/PNI; **862:** C. Blankenhorn/PNI; **863:** (left) Jacket cover of THE GREAT GATSBY by F. Scott Fitzgerald (Scribner Paperback Fiction edition, 1995). Reprinted with the permission of Scribner, a Divison of Simon & Schuster.; (center) Reprinted with the permission of Scribner Paperback Fiction, a division of Simon & Schuster, from *Ethan Frome* by Edith Wharton. Cover illustration *The Cart, Snow-Covered Road at Honfleur, 1867* by Claude Monet, Musée d'Orsay, Paris, France. Photograph by Erich Lessing/Art Resource, NY; (right) Cover from *The Grapes of Wrath* by John Steinbeck. Published by the Penguin Group, a division of Penguin Books USA Inc.; **864–865:** *Telephones*, (detail), 1954, Colleen Browning, oil on plywood, 14" x 32.5" (33.56 x 82.55 cm), Signed, lower right. Butler Institute of American Art. Museum purchase, 1955; **866:** (1952) Nancy Crampton; (1955) Leviton-Atlanta/Black Star; (1959) St. George Andrew/ Magnum Photos, Inc.; (1969) The Granger Collection, New York; (1972 China) UPI/Corbis-Bettmann; (1972 Vietnam) Peter Garfield/Folio, Inc.; (1974) Alex Webb/Magnum Photos; **867:** (1982) © 1985 Peter Marlow/ Magnum Photos, Inc.; (1987) © Larry Downing/Woodfin Camp & Associates; (1990 Carol Moseley Braun) National Organization of Women; (1990 Handicapped) ©The Stock Market/Wes Thompson; (1994) © Tomas Muscionico/Contact Press Images; (1997) © Dan Groshong/Sygma; **868:** (top) The Granger Collection, New York; (bottom) Wright/National Motor Museum; **869:** (bottom) UPI/Corbis-Bettmann; **870:** (top) AP/Wide World Photos; (bottom) Rick Smolan/Against All Odds; **871:** (bottom) Sven Simon; **872:** (bottom) © Les Stone/Sygma; **873:** (top) © Mark Bolster/International Stock Photogra-

phy, Ltd.; (bottom) Courtesy of Apple Computer, Inc.; **874:** (top) *Sampler* (detail), 1797 by Mary Wiggin. 18x 21 1/2." Philadelphia Museum of Art, Whitman Sampler Collection/Given by Pet, Incorporated.; (center) Christopher Morris/Black Star/PNI; **875:** *Television Moon*, 1978–79, Alfred Leslie, oil on canvas, Wichita Art Museum, gift of Virginia and George Ablah; **876:** Flannery O'Connor Collection, Ina Dillard Russel Library, Georgia College; **880–881:** *Black Walnuts*, 1945, Joseph Pollet, Oil on canvas 30" x 40", Collection of Whitney Museum of American Art, Purchase, Gift of Gertrude Vanderbilt Whitney, by exchange; **884:** *Deep Fork Overlook*, Joan Marron-LaRue; **890:** Nancy Crampton; **892–893:** Culver Pictures, Inc.; **896:** © The Stock Market/Shiki; **902:** Thomas Victor; **904:** Corel Professional Photos CD-ROM™; **906:** *Winter Bouquet*, 1933, Charles Burchfield, Watercolor and gouache over graphite on paper, Sight: 35⅜ x 16¾ in. (91 x 69 cm) Ellen Gardner Fund, Courtesy, Museum of Fine Arts, Boston; **908:** © The Stock Market/Dick Frank Studios; **912:** (tl) Rollie McKenna; (tr) AP/Wide World Photos; (bl) *Robert Penn Warren* (detail), 1935, Conrad A. Albrizio, The National Portrait Gallery, Smithsonian Institution, Washington, D.C./Art Resource, New York; (br) Kit Stafford; **914:** *Crowninshield's Wharf, Around the Wharf are the Vessels America, Fame, Prudent, and Belisaurius*, George Ropes, Peabody Museum of Salem, Photo by Mark Sexton; **916–917 & 918:** Corel Professional Photos CD-ROM™; **920–921:** Tim Lynch/Stock, Boston; **924:** Diana Walker; **929:** *Girl Looking at Landscape*, 1957, Richard Diebenkorn, oil on canvas, 59 x 60⅜ inches, (149.9 x 153.4 cm), Gift of Mr. and Mrs. Alan H. Temple, 61.49, Collection of Whitney Museum of American Art, photograph by Geoffrey Clements, N.Y., Photograph copyright © 1997: Whitney Museum of American Art; **934:** (top) Thomas Victor; (center) Photo by Michael Nye; (bottom) Photo by Paul Abdoo; **937:** *Passion of Paints*, ©1997 Bob Peters, Exclusively represented by Applejack Licensing International; **938:** *Indian on Galloping Horse after Remington, No. 2, 1976*, Fritz Scholder, color lithograph, 30 x 22¼ in. Gift of Mr. and Mrs. Ben Q.Adams, 1979, Courtesy Museum of Fine Arts, Museum of New Mexico, Santa Fe NM; **940–941:** Culver Pictures, Inc.; **942:** *Getting Down*, Joseph Holston, 14" x 14", Holston Originals; **946:** Thomas Victor; **956:** © Anthony Barboza/Life Magazine; **964:** Prentice Hall; **966:** *Fruit Vendor*, 1951, Olga Costa, Museo de Arte Moderno, Mexico, ©Olga Costa - SOMAAP, Mexico, 1999; **976:** (lc) Shelley Rotner/Omni-Photo Communications, Inc.; (tl) Georgia McInnis/Courtesy of Arte Publico Press; (bl) Marlene Fostor; (tr) Rollie McKenna; **978:** *Untitled*, Peter Malone, Chen/Art Resource, NY; **979:** Colllins/Monkmeyer; **980:** Mitchell Funk/The Image Bank; **981:** Corel Professional Photos CD-ROM™; **982, 983, 984:** © John Lemker/Animals Animals; **987:** Ken Karp Photography; **991:** *My Mother's Book of Life*, 1987, Lee Lawson, acrylic on panel, 34 x 30 in., Photo courtesy of Pomegranate Artbooks; **992:** (top) The Granger Collection, New York; (center) AP/Wide World Photos; (bottom) © 1996 Sigrid Estrada; **996:** *Blam*, 1962, © Roy Lichtenstein, oil on canvas, 68 x 80 in.; **999 & 1000:** Warner

Bros./Photofest; **1004:** (top) AP/Wide World Photos; (center) Robert Severi/Liaison International; (bottom) Robert Foothorap; **1007:** *Biography*, 1988, Marina Gutierrez, Courtesy of the artist; **1012:** Jim McHugh; **1015:** Gary Gay/The Image Bank; **1019:** Bob Daemmrich / Stock, Boston; **1023:** *Choke*, 1964, Robert Rauschenberg, Oil and screenprint on canvas, 60" x 48", Washington University Gallery of Art, St. Louis, Gift of Mr. and Mrs. Richard K. Weil, 1972; **1024:** Thomas Victor; **1026:** *Push to Walk*, collage 48" x 48", Phoebe Beasley; **1034:** (left) AP/Wide World Photos; (right) Rollie McKenna; **1036–1038:** FPG International Corp.; **1041:** Courtesy National Archives; **1044–1045:** Stock Montage, Inc.; **1048:** (tl) AP/Wide World Photos; (tr) UPI/Corbis-Bettmann; (bl) Thomas Victor; (br) Pach/Corbis-Bettmann; **1050:** *Mirror II*, George Tooker, (1920–1938), Egg tempera on gesso panel, 20 x 20 in., 1968.4, Gift of R. H. Donnelley Erdman (PA 1956), Addison Gallery of American Art, Phillips Academy, Andover, Massachusetts. All Rights Reserved.; **1053:** *Part II, The Free Man, No. 30, The Frederick Douglass Series*, Jacob Lawrence, Hampton University Museum, Hampton, Virginia; **1058:** (left) Nihad Becirovic; (right) Thomas Victor; **1060:** *The Madonna And Child*, 1990, Momodou Ceesay, Dialogue Systems, Inc.; **1062:** *Winter*, Franca Ozz, Oil, 24" x 18", Edition of 999 s/n, Courtesy of The Hadley Companies; **1066:** Andrea Renault/Globe Photos; **1069:** *Laurence Typing*, 1952, Fairfield Porter, oil on canvas 40 x 30⅛ inches, The Parrish Art Museum, Southampton, New York, Gift of the Estate of Fairfield Porter; **1072:** *Letters and Postcards*, Reid Christman, 24" x 18" (61 cm x 45.7 cm), Fredrix linen canvas; **1078:** (left) Photo by Mandy Sayer; (right) AP/Wide World Photos; **1080–1081:** (background) Brian Parker/Tom Stack & Associates; **1080:** (bl) Corel Professional Photos CD-ROM™; **1082:** P.J. Griffiths/Magnum Photos, Inc.; **1086:** AP/Wide World Photos; **1087:** *The Trial of Two Witches at Salem, Massachusetts, in 1662*, Howard Pyle, The Granger Collection, New York; **1091:** *The Execution of the Reverend Stephen Burroughs for Witchcraft at Salem Massachusetts, in 1692*, 19th century engraving, The Granger Collection, New York; **1097, 1101, 1108, 1116, 1124, 1139, 1142–1143, 1147, 1154, 1157, 1160, 1164–1165:** Photofest; **1170:** John Neubauer/PhotoEdit; **1174:** M. K. Denny/PhotoEdit; **1175:** (left) Reprinted by permission of G.P. Putnam's Sons from *The Kitchen God's Wife* by Amy Tan. Copyright © 1991 by Amy Tan. (center) *From The Right Stuff* (Jacket cover) by Tom Wolfe. Copyright ©1979 by Tom Wolfe. Used by permission of Bantam Books, a division of Bantam Doubleday Dell Publishing Group, Inc.

Illustration Credits:
86, 113, 184, 211, 292, 360, 392, 425, 435, 437, 492, 516, 588, 627, 629, 642, 645, 726, 756, 861, 947, 990, 1022, 1173: Ernest Albanese. 12, 32, 42, 62, 274, 964: Ortelius Design.